Lecture Notes in Artificial Intelligence 13551

Subseries of Lecture Notes in Computer Science

Series Editors

Randy Goebel
University of Alberta, Edmonton, Canada
Wolfgang Wahlster
DFKI, Berlin, Germany
Zhi-Hua Zhou
Nanjing University, Nanjing, China

Founding Editor

Jörg Siekmann
DFKI and Saarland University, Saarbrücken, Germany

More information about this subseries at https://link.springer.com/bookseries/1244

Wei Lu · Shujian Huang ·
Yu Hong · Xiabing Zhou (Eds.)

Natural Language Processing and Chinese Computing

11th CCF International Conference, NLPCC 2022
Guilin, China, September 24–25, 2022
Proceedings, Part I

Springer

Editors
Wei Lu (ID)
Singapore University of Technology
and Design
Singapore, Singapore

Yu Hong
Soochow University
Suzhou, China

Shujian Huang
Nanjing University
Nanjing, China

Xiabing Zhou
Soochow University
Suzhou, China

ISSN 0302-9743   ISSN 1611-3349 (electronic)
Lecture Notes in Artificial Intelligence
ISBN 978-3-031-17119-2   ISBN 978-3-031-17120-8 (eBook)
https://doi.org/10.1007/978-3-031-17120-8

LNCS Sublibrary: SL7 – Artificial Intelligence

This Springer imprint is published by the registered company Springer Nature Switzerland AG
The registered company address is: Gewerbestrasse 11, 6330 Cham, Switzerland

Preface

Welcome to NLPCC 2022, the eleventh CCF International Conference on Natural Language Processing and Chinese Computing. Following the success of previous conferences held in Beijing (2012), Chongqing (2013), Shenzhen (2014), Nanchang (2015), Kunming (2016), Dalian (2017), Hohhot (2018), Dunhuang (2019), Zhengzhou (2020), and Qingdao (2021), this year's NLPCC was held in Guilin. As a premier international conference on natural language processing and Chinese computing, organized by CCF-NLP (the Technical Committee of Natural Language Processing, China Computer Federation, formerly known as the Technical Committee of Chinese Information, China Computer Federation), NLPCC serves as an important forum for researchers and practitioners from academia, industry, and government to share their ideas, research results, and experiences, and to promote their research and technical innovations.

The fields of natural language processing (NLP) and Chinese computing (CC) have boomed in recent years. Following NLPCC's tradition, we welcomed submissions in 10 areas for the main conference: Fundamentals of NLP; Machine Translation and Multilinguality; Machine Learning for NLP; Information Extraction and Knowledge Graphs; Summarization and Generation; Question Answering; Dialogue Systems; Social Media and Sentiment Analysis; NLP Applications and Text Mining; and Multimodality and Explainability. This year, despite the non-negligible influence of COVID-19, we still received 327 valid submissions to the main conference by the submission deadline.

After a thorough reviewing process, including meta reviewing, out of the 327 submissions (some of which were desk-rejected due to policy violations), 83 papers were finally accepted as regular papers to appear in the main conference, resulting in an acceptance rate of 25.4%. Each paper was reviewed in a double-blind manner by at least 3 members of the Program Committee, with the help of additional reviewers. In total, 73 of the accepted papers were written in English and 10 in Chinese. Among them, 62 submissions were presented as oral papers and 21 as poster papers at the conference. Six papers were nominated by our area chairs for the best paper award. An independent best paper award committee was formed to select the best papers from the shortlist. This proceedings includes only the accepted English papers; the Chinese papers will appear in the ACTA Scientiarum Naturalium Universitatis Pekinensis. In addition to the main proceedings, three papers were accepted to the Student workshop and 21 papers were accepted to the Evaluation workshop.

We were honored to have four internationally renowned keynote speakers, Jason Eisner (Johns Hopkins University), Ray Mooney (University of Texas at Austin), Alexander Rush (Cornell University), and Luke Zettlemoyer (University of Washington), sharing their findings on recent research progress and achievements in natural language processing.

We would like to thank all the people who contributed to NLPCC 2022. First of all, we would like to thank our 20 area chairs for their hard work recruiting reviewers, monitoring the review and discussion processes, and carefully rating and recommending submissions. We would like to thank all 330 reviewers for their time and efforts to review the submissions. We are also grateful for the help and support from the general chairs, Bonnie Webber and Ya Zhou, and from the organization committee chairs, Guimin Huang and Xiaojun Wan. Special thanks go to Yu Hong and Xiabing Zhou, the publication chairs. We greatly appreciate all your help!

Finally, we would like to thank all the authors who submitted their work to NLPCC 2022, and thank our sponsors for their contributions to the conference. Without your support, we could not have such a strong conference program.

We were happy to see you at NLPCC 2022 in Guilin and hope you enjoyed the conference!

August 2022

Wei Lu
Shujian Huang

Organization

NLPCC 2022 was organized by the China Computer Federation (CCF) and hosted by Guilin University of Electronic Technology. Publishers comprise Lecture Notes on Artificial Intelligence (LNAI), Springer, and ACTA Scientiarum Naturalium Universitatis Pekinensis.

Organization Committee

General Chairs

Bonnie Webber	University of Edinburgh, UK
Ya Zhou	Guilin University of Electronic Technology, China

Program Committee Chairs

Wei Lu	Singapore University of Technology and Design, Singapore
Shujian Huang	Nanjing University, China

Student Workshop Chairs

Zhongqing Wang	Soochow University, China
Piji Li	Nanjing University of Aeronautics and Astronautics, China

Evaluation Chairs

Yunbo Cao	Tencent, China
Youzheng Wu	JD AI Research, China

Tutorial Chairs

Hai Zhao	Shanghai Jiao Tong University, China
Yang Feng	Institute of Computing Technology, Chinese Academy of Sciences, China

Publication Chairs

Yu Hong	Soochow University, China
Xiabing Zhou	Soochow University, China

Journal Coordinator

Yunfang Wu   Peking University, China

Conference Handbook Chair

Jun Li   Guilin University of Electronic Technology, China

Sponsorship Chairs

Haofen Wang   Tongji University, China
Ruifeng Xu   Harbin Institute of Technology, Shenzhen, China
Guoyong Cai   Guilin University of Electronic Technology, China

Publicity Chairs

Jianxing Yu   Sun Yat-sen University, China
Siyou Liu   Macao Polytechnic University, China

Organization Committee Chairs

Guimin Huang   Guilin University of Electronic Technology, China
Xiaojun Wan   Peking University, China

Area Chairs

Fundamentals of NLP

Nanyun Peng   University of California, Los Angeles, USA
Zhenghua Li   Soochow University, China

Machine Translation and Multilinguality

Lei Li   University of California, Santa Barbara, USA
Jiajun Zhang   Chinese Academy of Sciences, China

Machine Learning for NLP

Zhiting Hu   University of California, San Diego, USA
Piji Li   Nanjing University of Aeronautics and Astronautics,
                                       China

Dialogue Systems

Lili Mou   University of Alberta, Canada
Weinan Zhang   Harbin Institute of Technology, China

Question Answering

Rui Zhang	Pennsylvania State University, USA
Nan Yang	Microsoft Research Asia, China

Summarization and Generation

Chenghua Lin	University of Sheffield, UK
Deyi Xiong	Tianjin University, China

Information Extraction and Knowledge Graph

Ruihong Huang	Texas A&M University, USA
Kang Liu	Chinese Academy of Sciences, China

Social Media and Sentiment Analysis

Anh Tuan Luu	Nanyang Technological University, Singapore
Rui Xia	Nanjing University of Science and Technology, China

NLP Applications and Text Mining

Jey Han Lau	University of Melbourne, China
Lemao Liu	Tencent, China

Multimodality and Explainability

Lizi Liao	Singapore Management University, Singapore
Mingxuan Wang	ByteDance

Treasurers

Yajing Zhang	Soochow University, China
Xueying Zhang	Peking University, China

Webmaster

Hui Liu	Peking University, China

Program Committee

Bo An	Institute of Ethnology and Anthropology, Chinese Academy of Social Sciences, China
Xiang Ao	Institute of Computing Technology, Chinese Academy of Sciences, China
Guirong Bai	Institute of Automation, Chinese Academy of Sciences, China
Yu Bao	ByteDance AI Lab, China
Qiming Bao	University of Auckland, New Zealand
Junwei Bao	JD AI Research, China
Xiangrui Cai	Nankai University, China

Yi Cai	South China University of Technology, China
Yuan Cao	Google Brain, USA
Yixin Cao	Singapore Management University, Singapore
Pengfei Cao	Institute of Automation, Chinese Academy of Sciences, China
Jun Cao	ByteDance AI Lab, China
Zhangming Chan	Alibaba Group, China
Shuaichen Chang	Ohio State University, USA
Xiuying Chen	Peking University, China
Yufeng Chen	Beijing Jiaotong University, China
Xinchi Chen	Amazon AWS, USA
Kehai Chen	Harbin Institute of Technology, China
Bo Chen	Institute of Software, Chinese Academy of Sciences, China
Yubo Chen	Institute of Automation, Chinese Academy of Sciences, China
Yi Chen	Harbin Institute of Technology, Shenzhen, China
Shuang Chen	Harbin Institute of Technology, China
Wei Chen	Fudan University, China
Hanjie Chen	University of Virginia, USA
Pei Chen	Texas A&M University, USA
Yulong Chen	Zhejiang University and Westlake University, China
Jiangjie Chen	Fudan University, China
Chen Chen	Nankai University, China
Liang Chen	Peking University, China
Guanyi Chen	Utrecht University, The Netherlands
Shanbo Cheng	ByteDance AI Lab, Singapore
Chenhui Chu	Kyoto University, Japan
Yiming Cui	Joint Laboratory of HIT and iFLYTEK Research, China
Cunli Mao	Kunming University of Science and Technology, China
Xiang Deng	Ohio State University, USA
Chenchen Ding	NICT, Japan
Qianqian Dong	ByteDance AI Lab, China
Ziyi Dou	University of California, Los Angeles, USA
Longxu Dou	Harbin Institute of Technology, China
Rotem Dror	University of Pennsylvania, USA
Xinya Du	University of Illinois Urbana-Champaign, USA
Jinhua Du	Huawei, UK
Chaoqun Duan	Harbin Institute of Technology, China
Junwen Duan	Central South University, China
Xiangyu Duan	Soochow University, China
Alex Fabbri	Salesforce AI Research, USA
Zhihao Fan	Fudan University, China
Biaoyan Fang	University of Melbourne, Australia
Zhiyuan Fang	Amazon, USA

Xiachong Feng   Harbin Institute of Technology, China
Jiazhan Feng   Peking University, China
Yansong Feng   Peking University, China
Shi Feng   Northeastern University, China
Yang Feng   Institute of Computing Technology, Chinese Academy
                          of Sciences, China
Mauajama Firdaus   University of Alberta, Canada
Lea Frermann   Melbourne University, Australia
Qiankun Fu   Zhejiang University, China
Xingyu Fu   University of Pennsylvania, USA
Guohong Fu   Soochow University, China
Jun Gao   Harbin Institute of Technology, Shenzhen, China
Shen Gao   Peking University, China
Ruiying Geng   Alibaba Group, China
Yu Gu   Ohio State University, USA
Jiachen Gu   University of Science and Technology of China, China
Yi Guan   Harbin Institute of Technology, China
Tao Gui   Fudan University, China
Shaoru Guo   Institute of Automation, Chinese Academy of Sciences,
                          China
Jiale Han   Beijing University of Posts and Telecommunications,
                          China
Lifeng Han   University of Manchester, UK
Xudong Han   University of Melbourne, Australia
Tianyong Hao   South China Normal University, China
Yongchang Hao   University of Alberta, Canada
Hongkun Hao   Shanghai Jiao Tong University, China
Ziwei He   Shanghai Jiao Tong University, China
Ruifang He   Tianjin University, China
Yanqing He   Institute of Scientific and Technical Information of
                          China, China
Ihung Hsu   University of Southern California, USA
Jingwen Hu   Harbin Institute of Technology, China
Minghao Hu   Information Research Center of Military Science,
                          China
Chenyang Huang   University of Alberta, Canada
Ruihong Huang   Texas A&M University, USA
Jiangping Huang   Chongqing University of Posts and
                          Telecommunications, China
Qingbao Huang   Guangxi University and South China University of
                          Technology, China
Fei Huang   Tsinghua University, China
Changzhen Ji   Harbin Institute of Technology, China
Tong Jia   Northeastern University, China
Hao Jia   Soochow University, China

Zhongtao Jiang	Institute of Automation, Chinese Academy of Sciences, China
Xuhui Jiang	Institute of Computing Technology, Chinese Academy of Sciences, China
Jingchi Jiang	Harbin Institute of Technology, China
Yong Jiang	Alibaba DAMO Academy, China
Wenbin Jiang	Baidu Inc., China
Yiping Jin	FreeDa Language Space, Spain
Peng Jin	Leshan Normal University, China
Zhu Junguo	Kunming University of Science and Technology, China
Fajri Koto	University of Melbourne, Australia
Tuan Lai	University of Illinois Urbana-Champaign, USA
Yuxuan Lai	Peking University, China
Yuanyuan Lei	Texas A&M University, USA
Miao Li	University of Melbourne, Australia
Irene Li	Yale University, USA
Mingzhe Li	Peking University, China
Fei Li	Wuhan University, China
Fenghuan Li	Guangdong University of Technology, China
Mingda Li	Harbin Institute of Technology, China
Jiajun Li	University of Chinese Academy of Sciences and Institute of Computing Technology, Chinese Academy of Sciences, China
Zhenghua Li	Soochow University, China
Maoxi Li	Jiangxi Normal University, China
Jing Li	Hong Kong Polytechnic University, China
Mingda Li	University of California, Los Angeles, USA
Jiaqi Li	Harbin Institute of Technology, China
Yanran Li	Hong Kong Polytechnic University, China
Shasha Li	National University of Defense Technology, China
Lishuang Li	Dalian University of Technology, China
Yanyang Li	Chinese University of Hong Kong, China
Qintong Li	University of Hong Kong, China
Bin Li	Nanjing Normal University, China
Xinyi Li	National University of Defense Technology, China
Zuchao Li	Shanghai Jiao Tong University, China
Hongzheng Li	Beijing Institute of Technology, China
Zheng Li	Stockton University, USA
Xin Li	Alibaba Group, China
Haonan Li	University of Melbourne, Australia
Zhixu Li	Fudan University, China
Yucheng Li	University of Surrey, UK
Chenliang Li	Wuhan University, China
Dongfang Li	Harbin Institute of Technology, Shenzhen, China
Zujie Liang	Sun Yat-sen University, China
Lizi Liao	Singapore Management University, Singapore

Ying Lin	Apple, USA
Yuchen Liu	National Laboratory of Pattern Recognition, CASIA, China
Kang Liu	Institute of Automation, Chinese Academy of Sciences, China
Xiao Liu	Microsoft Research Asia, China
Pengyuan Liu	Beijing Language and Culture University, China
Xuebo Liu	Harbin Institute of Technology, Shenzhen, China
Qian Liu	Beihang University, China
Yongbin Liu	University of South China, China
Qingbin Liu	Tencent, China
Chunhua Liu	University of Melbourne, Australia
Chuang Liu	Tianjin University, China
Yan Liu	Tianjin University, China
Xianggen Liu	Sichuan University, China
Yuanxing Liu	Harbin Institute of Technology, China
Jian Liu	Beijing Jiaotong University, China
Zhicheng Liu	ByteDance, China
Lemao Liu	Tencent AI Lab, China
Qun Liu	Chongqing University of Posts and Telecommunications, China
Shujie Liu	Microsoft Research Asia, China
Puyuan Liu	University of Alberta, Canada
Yaojie Lu	Institute of Software, Chinese Academy of Sciences, China
Xin Lu	Harbin Institute of Technology, China
Hengtong Lu	Beijing University of Posts and Telecommunications, China
Yinglong Ma	North China Electric Power University, China
Longxuan Ma	Harbin Institute of Technology, China
Mingyu Derek Ma	University of California, Los Angeles, USA
Xuezhe Ma	University of Southern California, USA
Yunshan Ma	National University of Singapore, Singapore
Zhao Meng	ETH Zurich, Switzerland
Tao Mingxu	Peking University, China
Xiangyang Mou	Meta, USA
Yulia Otmakhova	University of Melbourne, Australia
Jiaxin Pei	University of Michigan, USA
Xutan Peng	University of Sheffield, UK
Jianzhong Qi	University of Melbourne, Australia
Jun Qi	Georgia Institute of Technology, USA
Xian Qian	ByteDance AI Lab, USA
Lihua Qian	ByteDance, China
Tao Qian	Hubei University of Science and Technology, China
Yanxia Qin	National University of Singapore, Singapore
Libo Qin	Harbin Institute of Technology, China

Liang Qiu	Amazon Alexa AI, USA
Yuqi Ren	Tianjin University, China
Shuo Ren	Microsoft Research Asia, China
Yubin Ruan	Harbin Institute of Technology, China
Lei Sha	University of Oxford, UK
Wei Shao	City University of Hong Kong, China
Lingfeng Shen	Johns Hopkins University, USA
Haoran Shi	Amazon Inc., USA
Xing Shi	ByteDance Inc., China
Lei Shu	Google Research, USA
Jyotika Singh	Placemakr, USA
Linfeng Song	Tencent AI Lab, USA
Kaiqiang Song	Tencent AI Lab, USA
Zhenqiao Song	ByteDance AI Lab, China
Haoyu Song	Harbin Institute of Technology, China
Jinsong Su	Xiamen University, China
Dianbo Sui	Institute of Automation, Chinese Academy of Sciences, China
Kai Sun	Cornell University, USA
Zewei Sun	ByteDance, China
Chengjie Sun	Harbin Institute of Technology, China
Simon Suster	University of Melbourne, Australia
Zhixing Tan	Tsinghua University, China
Minghuan Tan	Singapore Management University, Singapore
Ping Tan	Universiti Malaysia Sarawak, Malaysia
Yun Tang	Facebook, USA
Buzhou Tang	Harbin Institute of Technology, Shenzhen, China
Duyu Tang	Tencent, China
Jialong Tang	Institute of Software, Chinese Academy of Sciences, China
Xunzhu Tang	University of Luxembourg, Luxembourg
Zhiyang Teng	Westlake University, China
Lin Tian	RMIT University, Australia
Thinh Hung Truong	University of Melbourne, Australia
Zhaopeng Tu	Tencent AI Lab, China
Gisela Vallejo	University of Melbourne, Australia
Lijie Wang	Baidu, China
Le Wang	Chinese Academy of Military Science, China
Tao Wang	King's College London, UK
Xing Wang	Tencent, China
Shaolei Wang	Harbin Institute of Technology, China
Yunli Wang	Beihang University, China
Wei Wang	Shenzhen International Graduate School, Tsinghua University, China
Ruize Wang	Fudan University, China
Hongling Wang	Soochow University, China

Danqing Wang	Bytedance AI Lab, China
Liang Wang	Microsoft Research Asia, China
Yuxuan Wang	Zhejiang Lab, China
Lingzhi Wang	Chinese University of Hong Kong, China
Siyuan Wang	Fudan University, China
Zijian Wang	AWS AI Labs, USA
Jun Wang	University of Melbourne, Australia
Sijia Wang	Virginia Tech, USA
Bo Wang	Tianjin University, China
Yaqiang Wang	Chengdu University of Information Technology, China
Yufei Wang	Macquaire University, Australia
Hongwei Wang	Tencent AI Lab, USA
Qingyun Wang	University of Illinois Urbana-Champaign, USA
Tao Wang	ByteDance AI Lab, China
Zhen Wang	Ohio State University, USA
Jiaqiang Wang	ByteDance, China
Xuesong Wang	Harbin Institute of Technology, China
Xuepeng Wang	Tencent AI Lab, China
Xiao Wang	Fudan University, China
Wei Wei	Huazhong University of Science and Technology, China
Yang Wei	Bytedance AI Lab, China
Haoyang Wen	Carnegie Mellon University, USA
Yuqiao Wen	University of Alberta, Canada
Sixing Wu	Peking University, China
Yuxia Wu	Xi'an Jiaotong University, China
Shun Wu	Institute of Automation, Chinese Academy of Sciences, China
Liwei Wu	Bytedance AI Lab, China
Lijun Wu	Microsoft Research, China
Changxing Wu	East China Jiaotong University, China
Qingrong Xia	Soochow University, China
Congying Xia	Salesforce Research, USA
Yang Xiang	Peng Cheng Laboratory, China
Tong Xiao	Northeastern University, China
Ruiyu Xiao	Harbin Institute of Technology, China
Jun Xie	Alibaba DAMO Academy, China
Yuqiang Xie	Institute of Information Engineering, Chinese Academy of Sciences, China
Xin Xin	Beijing Institute of Technology, China
Kang Xu	Nanjing University of Posts and Telecommunications, China
Yan Xu	Hong Kong University of Science and Technology, China
Wenda Xu	University of California, Santa Barbara, USA
Xiao Xu	Harbin Institute of Technology, China

Zhixing Xu	Nanjing Normal University, China
Jinan Xu	Beijing Jiaotong University, China
Peng Xu	Google, Canada
Ying Xu	Oracle Australia, Australia
Jiahao Xu	Nanyang Technological University, Singapore
Yiheng Xu	Microsoft Research Asia, China
Wang Xu	Harbin Institute of Technology, China
Lingyong Yan	Baidu Inc., China
Yuanmeng Yan	Beijing University of Posts and Telecommunications, China
Hang Yang	Institute of Automation, Chinese Academy of Sciences, China
Ziqing Yang	iFLYTEK Research, China
Liner Yang	Beijing Language and Culture University, China
Shiquan Yang	University of Melbourne, Australia
Ziqing Yang	Peking University, China
Muyun Yang	Harbin Institute of Technology, China
Jun Yang	MarcPoint, China
Qiang Yang	KAUST, Saudi Arabia
Baosong Yang	Alibaba DAMO Academy, China
Songlin Yang	ShanghaiTech University, China
Zhiwei Yang	Jilin University, China
Liang Yang	Dalian University of Technology, China
Haoran Yang	Chinese University of Hong Kong, China
Wenlin Yao	Tencent AI Lab, USA
Jianmin Yao	Soochow University, China
Rong Ye	ByteDance AI Lab, China
Tiezheng Yu	Hong Kong University of Science and Technology, China
Dong Yu	Beijing Language and Culture University, China
Junjie Yu	Soochow University, China
Zhe Yu	Sun Yat-sen University, China
Heng Yu	Alibaba, China
Pengfei Yu	University of Illinois Urbana-Champaign, USA
Guoxin Yu	Institute of Computing Technology, Chinese Academy of Sciences, China
Chunyuan Yuan	Institute of Information Engineering, Chinese Academy of Sciences, China
Xiang Yue	Ohio State University, USA
Xiangrong Zeng	Kuaishou, China
Qi Zeng	University of Illinois Urbana-Champaign, USA
Daojian Zeng	Hunan Normal University, China
Shuang (Sophie) Zhai	University of Oklahoma, USA
Weidong Zhan	Peking University, China
Wenxuan Zhang	Alibaba DAMO Academy, Singapore
Zhirui Zhang	Tencent AI Lab, China

Zhihao Zhang	Beihang University, China
Shuaicheng Zhang	Virginia Polytechnic Institute and State University, USA
Peng Zhang	Tianjin University, China
Xiuzhen Zhang	RMIT University, Australia
Xingxing Zhang	Microsoft Research Asia, China
Dakun Zhang	SYSTRAN, France
Yuanzhe Zhang	Institute of Automation, Chinese Academy of Sciences, China
Zhuosheng Zhang	Shanghai Jiao Tong University, China
Biao Zhang	University of Edinburgh, UK
Yazhou Zhang	Zhengzhou University of Light Industry, China
Tongtao Zhang	Siemens Corporate Technology, USA
Kaiyan Zhang	Harbin Institute of Technology, China
Mengjie Zhao	LMU Munich, Germany
Zhenjie Zhao	Nanjing University of Information Science and Technology, China
Xiang Zhao	National University of Defense Technology, China
Jun Zhao	Fudan University, China
Yufan Zhao	Microsoft, China
Zhedong Zheng	National University of Singapore, Singapore
Wanjun Zhong	Sun Yat-sen University, China
Bo Zhou	Institute of Automation, Chinese Academy of Sciences, China
Guangyou Zhou	Central China Normal University, China
Wenxuan Zhou	University of Southern California, USA
Chunting Zhou	Meta AI, USA
Wangchunshu Zhou	Beihang Univeristy, China
Xin Zhou	Fudan University, China
Peng Zhou	Kuaishou, China
Junnan Zhu	Institute of Automation, Chinese Academy of Sciences, China
Qingfu Zhu	Harbin Institute of Technology, China
Tong Zhu	Soochow University, China
Rongxin Zhu	University of Melbourne, Australia
Yaoming Zhu	ByteDance AI lab, China
Jie Zhu	Soochow University, China
Conghui Zhu	Harbin Institute of Technology, China
Muhua Zhu	Meituan Group, China
Zhou Qian	ByteDance AI Lab, China

Organizers

Organized by the China Computer Federation, China

Hosted by the Guilin University of Electronic Technology

In Cooperation with Lecture Notes in Computer Science, Springer

ACTA Scientiarum Naturalium Universitatis Pekinensis

Sponsoring Organizations

Diamond Sponsor

Alibaba

Platinum Sponsors

Huawei

Tencent AI Lab

Baidu

GTCOM

ByteDance

Gold Sponsors

LeYan

WoFeng

Xiaomi

Vivo

Contents – Part I

Information Extraction and Knowledge Graph (Oral)

Summarization and Generation (Oral)

Question Answering (Oral)

Dialogue Systems (Oral)

Social Media and Sentiment Analysis (Oral)

NLP Applications and Text Mining (Oral)

Multimodality and Explainability (Oral)

Fundamentals of NLP (Poster)

Information Extraction and Knowledge Graph (Poster)

Summarization and Generation (Poster)

Question Answering (Poster)

Contents – Part II

Student Workshop (Poster)

Evaluation Workshop (Poster)

Fundamentals of NLP (Oral)

Exploiting Word Semantics to Enrich Character Representations of Chinese Pre-trained Models

Wenbiao Li[1,2], Rui Sun[1,2], and Yunfang Wu[1,3(✉)]

[1] MOE Key Laboratory of Computational Linguistics, Peking University,
Beijing, China
{2001210322,sunrui0720}@stu.pku.edu.cn
[2] School of Software and Microelectronics, Peking University, Beijing, China
[3] School of Computer Science, Peking University, Beijing, China
wuyf@pku.edu.cn

Abstract. Most of the Chinese pre-trained models adopt characters as basic units for downstream tasks. However, these models ignore the information carried by words and thus lead to the loss of some important semantics. In this paper, we propose a new method to exploit word structure and integrate lexical semantics into character representations of pre-trained models. Specifically, we project a word's embedding into its internal characters' embeddings according to the similarity weight. To strengthen the word boundary information, we mix the representations of the internal characters within a word. After that, we apply a word-to-character alignment attention mechanism to emphasize important characters by masking unimportant ones. Moreover, in order to reduce the error propagation caused by word segmentation, we present an ensemble approach to combine segmentation results given by different tokenizers. The experimental results show that our approach achieves superior performance over the basic pre-trained models BERT, BERT-wwm and ERNIE on different Chinese NLP tasks: sentiment classification, sentence pair matching, natural language inference and machine reading comprehension. We make further analysis to prove the effectiveness of each component of our model.

Keywords: Word semantics · Character representation · Pre-trained models

1 Introduction

Pre-trained language models (PLMs) such as BERT [3], RoBERTa [10] and XLNet [20] have shown great power on a variety of natural language processing (NLP) tasks, such as natural language understanding, text classification and automatic question answering. In addition to English, pre-trained models also prove their effectiveness on Chinese NLP tasks [2,19].

ⓒ The Author(s), under exclusive license to Springer Nature Switzerland AG 2022
W. Lu et al. (Eds.): NLPCC 2022, LNAI 13551, pp. 3–15, 2022.
https://doi.org/10.1007/978-3-031-17120-8_1

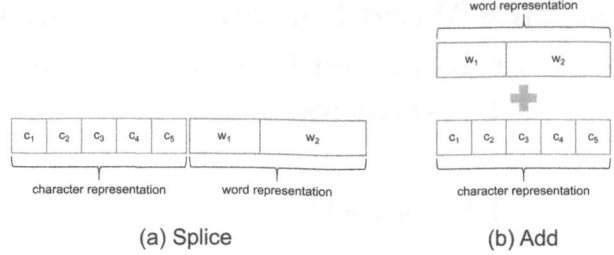

Fig. 1. Two ways to integrate word information to character representation.

Pre-trained models were originally designed for English, where spaces are considered as natural delimiters between words. But in Chinese, since there is no explicit word boundary, it is intuitive to utilize characters directly to build pre-trained models, such as BERT for Chinese [3], BERT-wwm [2] and ERNIE [19]. In Chinese, words instead of characters are the basic semantic units that have specific meanings and can behave independently [22] to build a sentence. The meaning of a single Chinese character is always ambiguous. For example, "足" has four meanings specified in the Chinese dictionary: foot, attain, satisfy and enough. Therefore, One single character can not express the meaning precisely. In contrast, the Chinese word which is constructed by combining several characters can accurately express semantic meaning. For example, if the character "足" is combined with the character "不(no)", we get the Chinese word "不足(insufficient)". If the character "足" is combined with the character "球(ball)", we get the Chinese word "足球(soccer)". Therefore, to understand Chinese text, the knowledge of words can greatly avoid ambiguity caused by single characters.

Previous ways to integrate word information into the pre-trained model can be categorized into two ways, as shown in Fig. 1. The first way (shown as 1(a)) is to splice character information and word information, and merge them through the self-attention mechanism [6,7,14]. This type of method increases the length of the input sequence, and because the self-attention mechanism is position-insensitive, the model needs to be specified with the positional relation between characters and their corresponding words. The other way (shown as 1(b)) is to add word information into their internal characters' information, which can either use one encoder to operate [8], or use two encoders to encode characters and words separately [4]. Previous work tends to integrate multiple words' information into a character representation, which might introduce redundant information and bring noises. Our work is in line with Method (b), but we design a more comprehensive strategy to exploit word semantics and enrich character representation.

In this paper, we propose a new method, Hidden Representation Mix and Fusion (HRMF), exploiting word semantics to enrich character representations of Chinese pre-trained models in the fine-tuning stage. Firstly, the importance of each character in a word is calculated based on the cosine similarity between the character's representation and its paired word's representation. Then we integrate the word embedding into the representation of each internal character according to the importance weight. After that, we apply a mixing mechanism to enable characters within a word exchange information with each other to further enhance the character representation. In addition, we apply a multi-head attention and a masked multi-head attention which masks the unimportant characters, and the final representation is obtained by fusing the representations given by the two attention mechanisms, which is then applied in downstream tasks. Moreover, in order to minimize the impact of word segmentation errors, we adopt a multi-tokenizer voting mechanism to obtain the final word segmentation result.

We conduct extensive experiments on several NLP tasks, including sentiment classification, sentence pair matching, natural language inference and machine reading comprehension. Experimental results show that our proposed method consistently improves the performance of BERT, BERT-wwm and ERNIE on different NLP tasks, and the ablation study shows that each component of our model yields improvement over the basic pre-trained models. Our code are made available at https://github.com/liwb1219/HRMF.

To sum, the contributions of this paper are as follows:

- We define the character's importance in a word, which enables our model to lay particular emphasis on important characters in a word.
- We apply a mixing mechanism to facilitate information exchange between characters, which further enriches our character representation.
- We present a masked multi-head attention mechanism to discard the semantics of unimportant characters in a word, which provides a supplement to the original sentence representation.
- Our proposed method outperforms the main-stream Chinese pre-trained models on a variety of NLP tasks.

2   Related Work

To exploit word information and help the model extract a enhanced representation of Chinese characters, the related work can be roughly divided into traditional methods and transformer-based methods.

In traditional methods, Su et al. [18] propose a word-lattice based Recurrent Neural Network (RNN) encoder for NMT, which generalizes the standard RNN to a word lattice topology. Zhang et al. [21] propose a word-lattice based LSTM network to integrate latent word information into the character-based LSTM-CRF model, which uses gated cells to dynamically route information from different paths to each character. Ma et al. [13] propose a simple but effective method for incorporating lexicon information into the character representations, which requires only a subtle adjustment of the character representation layer to introduce the lexicon information.

As for the transformer-based pre-trained method, there are two main approaches: Splice and Add, as illustrated in Fig. 1.

Splice. Pre-trained models are mostly constructed through the multi-head self-attention mechanism, which is not sensitive to location, the location information needs to be clearly specified in the model. Xue et al. [14] propose PLTE, which models all the characters and matched lexical words in parallel with batch processing. Lai et al. [6] propose a novel pre-training paradigm for Chinese-Lattice-BERT, which explicitly incorporates word representations along with characters, thus can model a sentence in a multi-granularity manner. Li et al. [7] propose FLAT: Flat-LAttice Transformer for Chinese NER, which converts the lattice structure into a flat structure consisting of spans. Each span corresponds to a character or latent word and its position in the original lattice.

Add. The Splice method not only increases the complexity of sequence modeling, but also needs to be specified with the positional relation between characters and words. The Add method is relatively flexible, where the word information can be added to it's corresponding character representation based on word boundary. The model can use one encoder or two. By using one encoder, the encoder can be used to simultaneously encode character information and word information. As for two encoders, they can be used to encode character information and word information separately. Diao et al. [4] propose ZEN, a BERT-based Chinese text encoder enhanced by N-gram representations. They use one encoder to encode character and the other encoder to encode N-gram, and combine the two lines of information at each layer of the model. Liu et al. [8] propose Lexicon Enhanced BERT (LEBERT) to integrate lexicon information between Transformer layers of BERT directly, where a lexicon adapter is designed to dynamically extract the most relevant matched words for each character using a char-to-word bilinear attention mechanism, and then is applied between adjacent layers.

3   Multiple Word Segmentation Aggregation

In the experiment, we use three tokenizers to vote, namely PKUSEG [12], LAC [5] and snownlp[1]. With the segmentation results given by the tokenizers, we select the final segmentation result following two rules, the majority rule and the granularity rule. Firstly, with the beginning character c_s, we extract the segmented word starts with c_s from the segmentation results of different tokenizers. We get $\{T_{c_s}^A, T_{c_s}^B, T_{c_s}^C\}$, which means the set of segmented words from different tokenizers starting with c_s. Then, following the majority rule, we select the one appears the most in $\{T_{c_s}^A, T_{c_s}^B, T_{c_s}^C\}$ as the first part of the segmentation result. If there are two words having the same time of occurrence, we choose the one with larger granularity. After determining the first segmented word T_{c_s}, we set the character after T_{c_s} as the next beginning character and repeat this process until we get the final segmentation result. For a clear understanding, Fig. 2 shows an example.

---

[1] https://github.com/isnowfy/snownlp.

Fig. 2. Example of voting segmentation plan. Firstly, with the character "重" as the beginning character, "重庆" appears twice, and "重庆人" appears once. Following the majority rule, we choose "重庆" as the first part of the segmentation result. Then, we choose "人" as the beginning character. "人和" appears once, and "人和中学" appears once, which has the same time of occurrence. Following the granularity rule, the word with larger granularity is preferred, so we choose "人和中学". Finally, the word segmentation result is "重庆/人和中学".

4 Projecting Word Semantics to Character Representation

The overall structure of our model is shown in Fig. 3. We employ the pre-trained model BERT and its updated variants (BERT-wwm, ERNIE) to obtain the original character representation, and a parallel multi-head attention module is applied to facilitate the fusion of character representation and word semantics.

4.1 Integrating Word Embedding to Character Representation

At present, the mainstream Chinese pre-trained models usually use character-level features. In order to make use of lexical semantics, we integrate word knowledge into character representation. Specifically, we first calculate the cosine similarity between the character and its corresponding word. And then, we assign the word information to its internal characters based on the similarity score.

The input text is denoted as $\mathbf{S} = (c_1, c_2, ..., c_n)$, and the hidden layer representation after BERT encoding is expressed as $\mathbf{H} = \mathrm{BERT}(\mathbf{S}) = (h_1, h_2, ..., h_n)$. The t-th word in the text is $w_t = (c_i, ..., c_j)$. We first obtain word embedding by:

$$x_t = e^w(w_t) \tag{1}$$

where e^w is a pre-trained word embedding lookup table [17].

We use two linear layers to transform dimensions and learn the difference between two different sets of vector spaces.

$$v_t = (\tanh(x_t \mathbf{W}_1 + \mathbf{b}_1))\mathbf{W}_2 + \mathbf{b}_2 \tag{2}$$

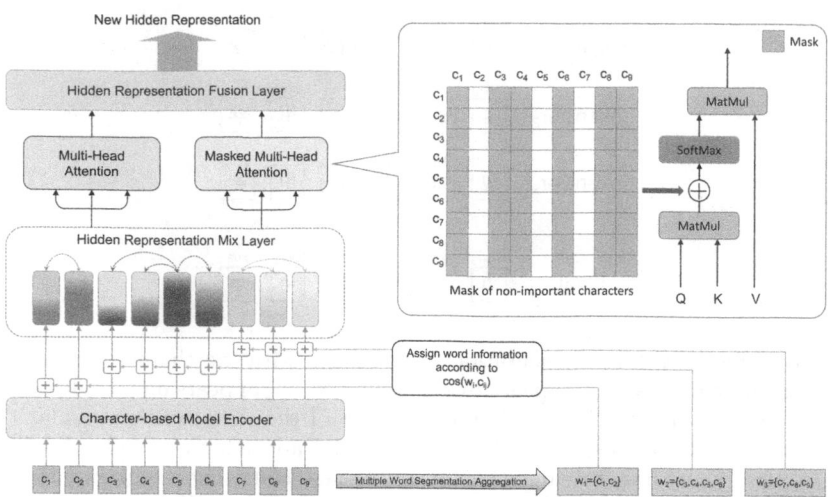

Fig. 3. The architecture of our proposed model. The color shades of squares in the hidden representation mix layer indicate the importance weights of different characters. The masked multi-head attention means that unimportant characters are masked when calculating the attention score. (Color figure online)

where $\mathbf{W}_1 \in \mathbb{R}^{d_w \times d_h}$, $\mathbf{W}_2 \in \mathbb{R}^{d_h \times d_h}$, $\mathbf{b}_1$ and $\mathbf{b}_2$ are scaler bias. d_w and d_h denote the dimension of word embedding and the hidden size of BERT respectively.

To measure the semantic weight of each character within a word, we compute the cosine similarity:

$$\text{score}_k = \cos(h_k, v_t), k = i, ..., j \tag{3}$$

where score_k represents the cosine similarity between the word and its k-th character.

We integrate word information into character embeddings based on the similarity score:

$$h_k^w = h_k + \frac{\text{score}_k}{\sum\limits_{m=i}^{j} \text{score}_m} v_t, k = i, ..., j \tag{4}$$

where h_k^w denotes the updated hidden representation of character k.

4.2   Mixing Character Representations Within a Word

In order to enrich the representations of characters, we mix the embeddings of characters within a word, that is, we let the characters in one word exchange information with each other. First, we define the key character as the one that has the highest similarity score with the corresponding word:

$$p = \text{argmax}(\text{score}_k), k = i, ..., j \tag{5}$$

where p denotes the index of the key character in a word.

Accordingly, the key character collect information from all other characters, and at the same time, the key character also passes its own information to all other characters.

Specifically, for single-character words, they keep the original representations. For two-character words, we let the key character passes a small amount of information to the non-important character, and the non-important character gives a small amount of information to the key character. For multi-character words (larger than or equal to three), we let the key character passes a small amount of information to all non-important characters, and all non-important characters give a small amount of information to the key character, while there is no information exchange among non-important characters.

We set a parameter λ as the retention ratio of the key character information. We introduce a non-linear function to degrade its reduction rate. The hidden representation of characters in non-single-character words is calculated as follows:

$$
\widetilde{h_k^w} =
\begin{cases}
f(\lambda)h_k^w + g(\lambda) \sum\limits_{\substack{i \leq m \leq j \\ m \neq p}} h_m^w, & k = p \\[2em]
g(\lambda)h_p^w + (1 - g(\lambda))h_k^w, & k \neq p
\end{cases}
\tag{6}
$$

$$
f(\lambda) = e^{\lambda - 1} \tag{7}
$$

$$
g(\lambda) = \frac{1 - f(\lambda)}{j - i} \tag{8}
$$

where $\widetilde{h_k^w}$ is the mixed hidden representation of character k.

Therefore, the new sequence is represented as:

$$
\widetilde{\mathbf{H}} = (\widetilde{h_1^w}, \widetilde{h_2^w}, ..., \widetilde{h_n^w}) \tag{9}
$$

4.3   Fusing New Character Embedding to Sentence Representation

We apply the self-attention mechanism on the mixed hidden representation obtained in the previous step to get a new hidden representation $\mathbf{H}^1$:

$$
\mathbf{H}^1 = \text{softmax}(\frac{(Q\mathbf{W}_q^1)(K\mathbf{W}_k^1)}{\sqrt{d_h}})(V\mathbf{W}_v^1) \tag{10}
$$

where Q, K and V are all equal to the collective representation $\widetilde{\mathbf{H}}$ obtained in the previous step. $\mathbf{W}_q^1$, $\mathbf{W}_k^1$, $\mathbf{W}_v^1$ are trainable parameter matrices.

Taking into account that the non-important characters' information has been integrated into the key character's representation, when calculating the attention score, those non-important characters can be masked. In this way, a new hidden representation $\mathbf{H}^2$ is obtained by a masked self-attention:

$$\mathbf{H}^2 = \text{softmax}(\frac{(Q\mathbf{W}_q^2)(K\mathbf{W}_k^2)}{\sqrt{d_h}} + mask)(V\mathbf{W}_v^2) \tag{11}$$

$$mask_{ij} = \begin{cases} 0, j \in \mathbf{\Omega} \\ \\ -inf, j \notin \mathbf{\Omega} \end{cases} \tag{12}$$

where $\mathbf{W}_q^2$, $\mathbf{W}_k^2$, $\mathbf{W}_v^2$ are trainable parameter matrices, $mask \in \mathbb{R}^{n \times n}$, $\mathbf{\Omega}$ is the set of subscripts corresponding to important words.

The final representation is obtained by fusing two sorts of embeddings:

$$\hat{\mathbf{H}} = \mu\mathbf{H}^1 + (1 - \mu)\mathbf{H}^2 \tag{13}$$

where $\hat{\mathbf{H}}$ is the final hidden representation, which will be applied to downstream tasks.

5 Experimental Setup

5.1 Tasks and Datasets

In order to prove the effectiveness of our proposed method, we conduct experiments on the following four public datasets with several NLP tasks. For data statistics of these datasets, please refer to Table 1.

Sentiment Classification (SC): ChnSentiCorp[2] is a Chinese sentiment analysis data set, containing online shopping reviews of hotels, laptops and books.

Sentence Pair Matching (SPM): LCQMC [9] is a large Chinese question matching corpus, aiming to identify whether two sentences have the same meaning.

Natural Language Inference (NLI): XNLI [1] is a cross-lingual natural language inference corpus, which is a crowdsourced collection of multilingual corpora. We only use the Chinese part.

Machine Reading Comprehension (MRC): DRCD [16] is a span-extraction MRC dataset written in Traditional Chinese.

5.2 Baseline Models

We adopt the pre-trained models BERT [3], BERT-wwm [2] and ERNIE [19] as our base architectures.

---

[2] https://github.com/pengming617/bert_classification.

Table 1. Hyper-parameter settings and data statistics in different tasks. Blr* represents the initial learning rate of BERT/BERT-wwm model for the AdamW optimizer.

Dataset	Task	MaxLen	Batch	Epoch	Blr*	ERNIE lr*	Train	Dev	Test	Domain
ChnSentiCorp	SC	256	64	4	3e−5	3e−5	9.6 K	1.2 K	1.2 K	Various
LCQMC	SPM	128	64	3	2e−5	3e−5	239 K	8.8 K	12.5 K	Zhidao
XNLI	NLI	128	64	2	3e−5	5e−5	393 K	2.5 K	5 K	Various
DRCD	MRC	512	16	2	3e−5	5e−5	27 K	3.5 K	3.5 K	Wikipedia

5.3   Training Details

In order to ensure the fairness and robustness of the experiment, for the same dataset and encoder, we use the same parameters, such as maximum length, warm-up ratio, initial learning rate, optimizer, etc. We repeated each experiment five times and reported the average score.

We do experiments using the Pytorch [15] framework, and all the baseline weight files were converted to the Pytorch version. At training time, we fix the pretrained word embeddings, using the AdamW optimizer [11], the weight decay is 0.02, and the warm-up ratio is 0.1. The proportion of the key character information retention λ is set to 0.9. The fusion coefficient μ is set to 0.5. For detailed hyper-parameter settings, please see Table 1.

6   Results and Analysis

6.1   Overall Results

Table 2 shows the experimental results on four public data sets with different NLP tasks, which demonstrates that our method obtains an obvious improvement compared with the baseline pre-trained models.

Table 2. Experimental results on four datasets. The classification tasks (SC, SPM, NLI) adopt *Accuracy* as the evaluation metric, and the machine reading comprehension task adopts *EM* and *F*1 as evaluation metrics.

Task	SC	SPM	NLI	MRC	avg.	
Dataset	ChnSentiCorp	LCQMC	XNLI	DRCD[EM/F1]	cls	all
BERT	94.72	86.61	77.85	85.48/91.36	86.39	87.20
+HRMF	95.48	87.24	78.44	86.32/91.76	87.05	87.85
BERT-wwm	94.82	86.67	78.02	85.79/91.66	86.50	87.39
+HRMF	95.36	86.96	78.21	86.55/92.11	86.84	87.84
ERNIE	95.32	87.26	78.26	87.78/93.20	86.95	88.36
+HRMF	**96.12**	**88.29**	**78.87**	**88.59/93.70**	**87.76**	**89.11**

Specifically, in the classification task, our method yields the most obvious improvement in sentiment analysis, with an improvement of 0.76 over BERT, 0.54 over BERT-wwm and 0.80 over ERNIE. We believe that this is because the emotional polarity of a sentence is more sensitive to word semantics. In other words, the emotional tendency of a sentence is likely to be determined by some of the words. Similarly, in sentence meaning matching and natural language inference, our method also achieves an average improvement of 0.65 and 0.46 compared with three baseline models. As for the task of machine reading comprehension, our method significantly improves the EM index with an average improvement of 0.80, which shows that after incorporating word knowledge, the model judges the boundary of answers more accurately. The baseline models already achieve a relatively high F1 score, and our method still obtains an average improvement of 0.45 on F1.

6.2   Ablation Study

In order to verify the effectiveness of our method, we strip off different parts of the model to conduct experiments, as shown in Table 3.

Table 3. Ablation study of different components. As shown in Fig. 2, $HRMF$ is the complete model of this paper. $-HRML$ is to remove the hidden representation of mix layer; $-MMHA$ means to remove the masked multi-head attention module.

Task	SC	SPM	NLI	MRC
Dataset	ChnSentiCorp	LCQMC	XNLI	DRCD[EM / F1]
BERT	94.72	86.61	77.85	85.48/91.36
BERT+HRMF	95.48	87.24	78.44	86.32/91.76
BERT+HRMF-HRML	95.30	86.92	78.18	86.00/91.73
BERT+HRMF-MMHA	95.40	87.14	78.16	86.09/91.77

After stripping off the hidden representation mix layer, the model has an obvious drop in the performance. It decreases by 0.18, 0.32, 0.26, 0.32 respectively on the four data sets. The performance of the model declines the most compared with other stripped off models on three data sets, which shows that mixing the representation of the characters within a word greatly enhances the representation of the original character representation. Besides, after stripping off the masked multi-head attention module, the model also gets a drop in the performance, which demonstrates that downstream tasks benefit from the additional representation of masked multi-head attention module that masks unimportant characters.

Case	Task	Dataset	Example	BERT predict	BERT+HRMF predict	True label
1	SC	ChnSentiCorp	酒店有点偏，（没有地铁站），19：30后就没有shuttle bus了。大堂很小，也没有什么设施。不过，房间很好，也有海景。(The hotel is a bit biased (there is no subway station), and there is no shuttle bus after 19:30. The lobby is small and has few facilities. However, the room was nice and had a sea view.)	negative	positive	positive
2	SPM	LCQMC	S_1: 孕妇吃核桃对胎儿有什么好处（What are the benefits of pregnant women eating walnuts for the fetus） S_2: 我刚怀孕4周吃核桃对宝宝有什么好处（I'm just 4 weeks pregnant what are the benefits of eating walnuts for the baby）	no	yes	yes
3	NLI	XNLI	S_1: 他是我的祖父，他不是一个好人。（He was my grandfather and he was not a good man.） S_2: 我爷爷是个混蛋。（My grandpa was an asshole.）	neutral	entailment	entailment

Fig. 4. Some examples of classification tasks.

6.3 Case Study

To better demonstrate our model's improvement on the understanding of semantics, we conduct case studies on several specific instances, as shown in Fig. 4 for classification tasks.

Compared with BERT, our proposed model obtains better performance on several tasks. On the Sentiment Classification (SC) task, our model has a better understanding on the sentences that have a emotional semantic transition. For example, in Case 1, the sentences' emotional tendencies change from negative to positive through the word "不过(However) ", which is accurately understood by our model. On the Sentence Pair Matching (SPM) task, our proposed model shows a better understanding on the relation between sentences' semantic information. For example, our model can accurately understand that "胎儿(fetus) " has the same meaning from "宝宝(baby) " in Case 2. On the Natural Language Inference (NLI) task, our model can accurately identify the relation between semantic information and make correct inference. For example, in case 3, our model recognizes that "不是一个好人(not a good man) " has the same meaning with "是个混蛋(an asshole) ". One possible reason that our model outperforms BERT is that our model integrates word semantic information.

7 Conclusion

In this paper, we propose a method HRMF to improve charater-based Chinese pre-trained models by integrating lexical semantics into character representations. We enrich the representations by mixing the intra-word characters' embeddings, and add a masked multi-head attention module by masking unimportant characters to provide a supplement to the original sentence representation. We conduct extensive experiments on four different NLP tasks. Based on the main-stream Chinese pre-trained models BERT, BERT-wwm, and ERNIE, our proposed method achieves obvious improvements, which proves its effectiveness and universality. In future work, we will combine more knowledge with Chinese characteristics to further improve Chinese pre-trained models for downstream tasks.

Acknowledgement. This work is supported by the National Hi-Tech RD Program of China (2020AAA0106600), the National Natural Science Foundation of China (62076008) and the KeyProject of Natural Science Foundation of China (61936012).

References

1. Conneau, A., et al.: XNLI: evaluating cross-lingual sentence representations. In EMNLP, pp. 2475–2485 (2018)
2. Cui, Y., et al.: Pre-training with whole word masking for Chinese BERT. arXiv preprint arXiv:1906.08101 (2019)
3. Devlin, J., Chang, M.W., Lee, K., Toutanova, K.: BERT: pre-training of deep bidirectional transformers for language understanding. In NAACL, pp. 4171–4186 (2019)
4. Diao, S., Bai, J., Song, Y., Zhang, T., Wang, Y.: ZEN: pre-training Chinese text encoder enhanced by n-gram representations. In EMNLP, pp. 4729–4740 (2019)
5. Jiao, Z., Sun, S., Sun, K.: Chinese lexical analysis with deep BI-GRU-CRF network. arXiv preprint arXiv:1807.01882 (2018)
6. Lai, Y., Liu, Y., Feng, Y., Huang, S., Zhao, D.: Lattice-BERT: leveraging multi-granularity representations in Chinese pre-trained language models. In NAACL, pp. 1716–1731 (2021)
7. Li, X., Yan, H., Qiu, X., Huang, X.: Flat: Chinese NER using flat-lattice transformer. In ACL, (2020)
8. Liu, W., Fu, X., Zhang, Y., Xiao, W.: Lexicon enhanced Chinese sequence labelling using BERT adapter. In ACL, pp. 5847–5858 (2021)
9. Liu, X., Chen, Q., Deng, C., Zeng, H., Chen, J., Li, D., Tang, B.: Lcqmc: A large-scale chinese question matching corpus. In COLING, pp. 1952–1962 (2018)
10. Liu, Y., et al.: RoBERTa: a robustly optimized BERT pretraining approach. arXiv preprint arXiv:1907.11692 (2019)
11. Loshchilov, I., Hutter, F.: Fixing weight decay regularization in adam (2018)
12. Luo, R., Xu, J., Zhang, Y., Ren, X., Sun, X.: Pkuseg: A toolkit for multi-domain chinese word segmentation. CoRR abs/1906.11455 (2019)
13. Ma, R., Peng, M., Zhang, Q., Huang, X.: Simplify the usage of lexicon in Chinese NER. In ACL, pp. 5951–5960 (2019)
14. Mengge, X., Yu, B., Liu, T., Zhang, Y., Meng, E., Wang, B.: Porous lattice transformer encoder for Chinese NER. In COLING, pp. 3831–3841 (2020)
15. Paszke, A., et al.: PyTorch: an imperative style, high-performance deep learning library. In NeurIPS, pp. 8026–8037 (2019)
16. Shao, C.C., Liu, T., Lai, Y., Tseng, Y., Tsai, S.: DRCD: a Chinese machine reading comprehension dataset. arXiv preprint arXiv:1806.00920 (2018)
17. Song, Y., Shi, S., Li, J., Zhang, H.: Directional skip-gram: explicitly distinguishing left and right context for word embeddings. In NAACL, pp. 175–180 (2018)
18. Su, J., Tan, Z., Xiong, D., Ji, R., Shi, X., Liu, Y.: Lattice-based recurrent neural network encoders for neural machine translation. In AAAI, pp. 3302–3308 (2017)

19. Sun, Y., et al.: Ernie: enhanced representation through knowledge integration. arXiv preprint arXiv:1904.09223 (2019)
20. Yang, Z., Dai, Z., Yang, Y., Carbonell, J., Salakhutdinov, R.R., Le, Q.V.: XLNET: generalized autoregressive pretraining for language understanding. In NeurIPS, pp. 5754–5764 (2019)
21. Zhang, Y., Yang, J.: Chinese NER using lattice LSTM. In ACL, pp. 1554–1564 (2018)
22. Zhu, D.: Lexical notes on Chinese grammar (in Chinese). The Commercial Press (1982)

PGBERT: Phonology and Glyph Enhanced Pre-training for Chinese Spelling Correction

Lujia Bao[1]([envelope]), XiaoShuai Chen[2], Junwen Ren[3], Yujia Liu[2], and Chao Qi[2]

[1] Beijing University of Posts and Telecommunications, Beijing, China
baolj@bupt.edu.cn
[2] Tencent, Beijing, China
{sheltonchen,ruoruoliu,chaoqi}@tencent.com
[3] Beijing Institute of Technology, Beijing, China
3220190720@bit.edu.cn

Abstract. Chinese Spelling Correction (CSC) is a challenging task that requires the ability to model the language and capture the implicit pattern of spelling error generation. In this paper, we propose PGBERT as Phonology and Glyph Enhanced Pre-training for CSC. For phonology, PGBERT uses Bi-GRU to encode single Chinese character's Pinyin sequence as phonology embedding. For glyph, we introduce Ideographic Description Sequence (IDS) to decompose Chinese character into binary tree of basic strokes, and then an encoder based on gated units is utilized to encode the glyph tree structure recursively. At each layer of original model, PGBERT extends extra channels for phonology and glyph encoding respectively, then performs a multi-channel fusion function and a residual connection to yield an output for each channel. Empirical analysis shows PGBERT is a powerful method for CSC and achieves state-of-the-art performance on widely-used benchmarks.

Keywords: Chinese spelling correction · Ideographic description sequence · Pre-train language model

1 Introduction

As Chinese is one of the most widely-used languages in the world, it is inevitable to make mistakes when communicating in Chinese. Hence, it is crucial to correct spelling errors in Chinese. According to the research results of [18], Chinese spelling errors can be roughly divided into two types: homophones, accounting for 83%; and homoglyphs, accounting for 48%. So the effectual use of phonology and glyph features is necessary for high-quality CSC model. Table 1 illustrates two types of Chinese spelling errors, the misspelled character "完(wán)" and the correct one "玩(wán)" share the same pronunciation, while "愁" and "秋" are visually similar.

CSC is a complex and challenging task in the NLP field, because Pinyin and glyphs are not the sole factors causing Chinese spelling errors—in fact,

© The Author(s), under exclusive license to Springer Nature Switzerland AG 2022
W. Lu et al. (Eds.): NLPCC 2022, LNAI 13551, pp. 16–28, 2022.
https://doi.org/10.1007/978-3-031-17120-8_2

Table 1. Examples of homoglyph and homophone. The top row is the misspelled sentence, and the bottom row is the correct sentence. Erroneous/correct characters are marked in red/green and their Pinyin are given in parentheses. Their English translations are in the last column.

Type	CSC example	
homoglyph	愁(chóu)天很舒服。	Worry day is comfortable。
	秋(qiū)天很舒服。	Autumn day is comfortable。
homophone	我们今天去哪里完(wán)?	Where shall we finish today ?
	我们今天去哪里玩(wán)?	Where shall we play today?

context can be significant as well. There have been numerous efforts in the academic community and industry to improve the performance of CSC. Previous CSC methods were mainly based on language model [3,14,18,20,32] or sequence annotation model [6,15,27]. These methods did not take phonology and glyph into account, resulting in unsatisfactory correction performance.

Recent researchers have begun to focus on Chinese character's homophones and homoglyphs. [13] calculates the characters similarity by phonology and glyph. The glyph similarity is calculated by the Levenshtein Edit Distance of preorder traversal path of Ideographic Description Sequence (IDS[1]), which is viewed as a binary tree structure. However, it does not embedding phonology and glyph representation into low-dimensional vector spaces, rendering the DNN language model unaware of explicit phonology or glyph information. [4] models the phonology and glyph by a Graph Convolution Network (GCN) [17] respectively to get the similar relationship between characters. But the similar relationship is only used as the target of prediction, without taking phonology and glyph as input features directly. [19] disintegrates the Chinese character glyph into stroke sequences and the Pinyin into letter sequences, and then represent them through Gated Recurrent Unit (GRU) [5] respectively. Then, the phonology, glyph and semantic representations are superimposed as the BERT model's input features. This direct superposition leads to a loss of phonology and glyph information. As we can see, glyph is the manifestation of characters in two-dimensional space, but the stroke sequence will compress them into one-dimensional space, which will lose the spatial information of glyph.

Therefore, we propose PGBERT: Phonology and Glyph Enhanced Pre-training for Chinese spelling correction. We refer to the IDS method to disintegrate Chinese character into a binary tree structure, and then carry out recursive calculation on the IDS tree to get glyph representation, with the intention that our modeling of glyph is more sufficient than stroke sequences. We also split Chinese pronunciation to letter sequences, then use GRU to embed them. After obtaining the representation of phonology and glyph, instead of directly superimpose them onto the character representations, we further enhance the phonology and glyph feature representation capabilities through multi-channel interaction.

We conduct experiments on the widely used SIGHAN [24,28,33] benchmark datasets, and compare PGBERT with other baseline models. The experimental

---

[1] https://github.com/cjkvi/cjkvi-ids.

results show that PGBERT remarkably outperforms the latest baseline models, including FASPell [13], SpellGCN [4], PLOME [19], and ReaLiSe [30].

A summary of our contributions is listed below:

- For Chinese character representation, we propose a gated unit to recursively model the IDS tree, which can intuitively preserve the two-dimensional spatial features of Chinese character, and improve the model's ability to capture the similarity signal of Chinese character.
- We build a multi-channel interaction and integration method of Chinese character, phonology and glyph, in which phonology and glyph are treated as a separate channel rather than directly superimposed with character representation to enhance the capacity for expression.
- The effect of our method is verified on multiple Chinese spelling correction datasets, indicating that PGBERT does have stronger capabilities for phonology and glyph representation, and consequently presents a more favorable result on CSC tasks.

2   Related Work

In a variety of Chinese natural language processing tasks, such as information retrieval [10,21], and essay scoring [2], CSC tends to be considered as the first step in preprocessing to the above-mentioned downstream tasks. In the light of this statement, CSC can be regarded as an essential capacity in the field of natural language processing in Chinese.

The early implementations of CSC, such as [9,16,24,29], are primarily realized in three sequential stages: error detection, candidate generation and candidate verification. The first stage detects and locates existent errors in the text. If any error is captured, the second stage will construct correction candidates for the erroneous portion. Generally, the correction candidates are created by looking up a confusion set. Next, the third stage measures the fluency of the corrected sentences by perplexity metric on a given language model. However, the above-mentioned procedure fails to take sufficient contextual information into account. Moreover, the three stages are separately organized, and a lack of support to each other leads to an unremarkable performance.

Subsequently, a number of end-to-end CSC methods were proposed. [26] was based on the sequence tagging model, which enhanced the use of the context features. Simultaneously, [11,27] improved CSC performance using an end-to-end generation model. Later, with the successful application of BERT [8] in NLP (e.g., [22,31]), BERT has gradually become the preferred model for solving CSC problems. [13] proposed the Denoising Autoencoder(DAE) and Decoder framework with BERT. [34] constructed an additional detection module to produce the masking vector to assist the BERT-based correction module in making decisions. Nonetheless, these methods did not directly model Chinese characters glyph and pronunciation, so they cannot fully adapt to the CSC scenario.

Since then, some research work began to integrate Chinese glyph and pronunciation features with BERT model. [4] adopted a GCN [17] to represent Chinese glyph and pronunciations, and combined GCN with BERT. But it did not apply

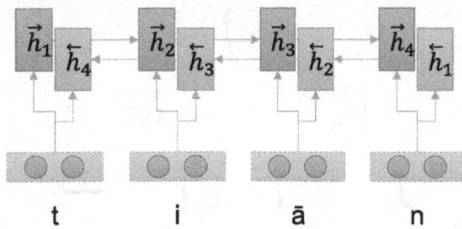

Fig. 1. An overview of Pinyin encoding module. Taking Chinese character 天 (sky) as an example, its phonetic transcription is "tiān", a sequence of letters. We send each letter's one-hot vector into embedding layer to obtain its embedding, and then encode the sequence of letter with Bi-GRU.

these basic features as input for BERT. [19] split glyph into sequences of strokes and pronunciation into sequences of letters, then embedded them separately through the GRU [5]. Additionally, they designed an additional task—prediction of pronunciation, improving efficiency of CSC to a certain extent. However, it was still suboptimal, because it under-represented the similarity of glyph, due to a loss of spatial information in the process of constructing stroke sequences. More seriously, superimposing glyph and phonology embedding directly onto the character embedding resulted in a loss of information. In our work, we decompose Chinese characters into IDS trees, and encode the glyph information by calculating representation of IDS tree node recursively using a gated unit based tree encoder. For further optimization, we propose a multi-channel interaction model to minimize the information loss during fusion process.

3   Our Approach

3.1   Problem and Motivation

CSC is aimed at detecting erroneously spelled Chinese characters and replacing them with correct ones. Formally, the model takes a sequence of n characters $X = \{x_1, x_2, \ldots, x_n\}$ as input, and outputs correct character y_i at each position of input.

Most Chinese characters with spelling errors resemble correct ones in terms of both phonology and glyph. The current state-of-the-art model uses stroke sequences to express the structure of Chinese character, which can, to some extent, lead to information loss in spatial structures of characters. Moreover, in an effort to fuse phonology and glyph characteristics, the majority of prior researches tends to superpose their embeddings onto the character embedding, which would lead to an additional loss of information. These aforementioned challenges drive us to design a more powerful CSC model.

3.2   Model

Phonology Embedding. As depicted in Fig. 1, Pinyin, used as Chinese phonetic notation, is a sequence of Romanian letters. In this paper, we use pypinyin,

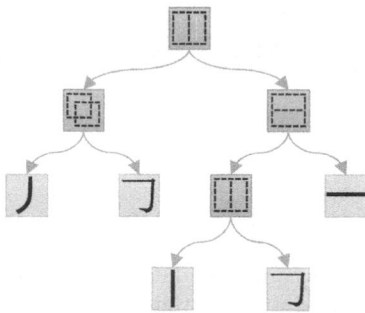

Fig. 2. An example showing how Chinese character 加 (add) is decomposed into IDS tree. The IDC node in first layer indicates that 加 is a left-right structure, in which the left part is 力, and the right part is 口. Recursively, its left child in second layer suggests that 力 is a stack structure composed of two basic strokes (yellow nodes). (Color figure online)

an open-source Pinyin notation package, to obtain Pinyin sequences. Next, we feed the Pinyin letter embedding sequence of each character into Bi-GRU separately and obtain the Pinyin embedding by concatenating the last hidden states from two directions. Formally, given a character c and its Pinyin letter embedding sequence $(e^p_{l^c_1}, e^p_{l^c_2}, \ldots, e^p_{l^c_i})$ where $e^p_{l^c_i} \in R^{d_l}$ is the embedding of i-th Pinyin letter in Pinyin sequence l^c of character c, the phonology representation $h^p_c = W^p[\overrightarrow{h}_{|l^c|}, \overleftarrow{h}_1]$, where:

$$\overrightarrow{h}_i = GRU(\overrightarrow{h}_{i-1}, e^p_{l^c_i}) \tag{1}$$

$$\overleftarrow{h}_i = GRU(\overleftarrow{h}_{i+1}, e^p_{l^c_i}) \tag{2}$$

Here $W^p \in R^{d_m \times 2d_m}$ is trainable parameter and we set the hidden size of GRU to d_m.

Glyph Embedding. Inspired by FASPell [13], we use IDS to decompose a Chinese character into a binary tree consisting of basic stroke characters and Ideographic Description Characters (IDC).

As illustrated in Fig. 2, strokes are basic elements that constitute a Chinese character. Each IDC node represents an approach to combine two Chinese character components into a new Chinese character Component. For each Chinese character, IDS defines a way to disassemble it into a binary tree: leaf nodes are basic strokes, non-leaf nodes represent the Chinese character component obtained by combining its child nodes, and the root node represents the structure of the whole character. Inspired by Tree-LSTM [23], we design a tree encoder to recursively encode each node of IDS tree and use the root node representation to embed the glyph information of Chinese characters. The over structure of the IDS-Tree encoder is illustrated in Fig. 3. Formally, for any character $c \in C$, its

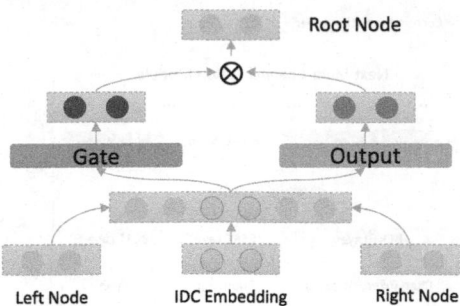

Fig. 3. IDS tree encoder.

glyph representation $h_c^g = W_{out}^{glyph} F_{glyph}(Root\,(c))$, where $W_{out}^{glyph} \in R^{d_m \times d_g}$ is trainable parameter, and $Root()$ is a function returns the root node of given character:

$$F_{glyph}(n) = \begin{cases} e_n^g, & \text{if } type(n) \in S^{stroke} \\ Comb(T), & \text{if } type(n) \in S^{IDC} \end{cases} \tag{3}$$

$$T = [e_n^g, F_{glyph}(Left(n)), F_{glyph}(Right(n))] \tag{4}$$

$$Comb\,(X) = G\,(X) \odot I(X) \tag{5}$$

$$G\,(X) = \sigma(W_G^{glyph} X) \tag{6}$$

$$I\,(X) = \tanh(W_I^{glyph} X) \tag{7}$$

Here S^{stroke} is set of all basic strokes, and $S^{IDC} = IDC \cup [PAD]$ where $[PAD]$ is special token for non-Chinese characters. $type(n)$ is the stroke or IDC type of the tree node n and the $e_n^g \in R^{d_g}$ is the embedding of $type(n)$. $Left()$ and $Right()$ denote functions returning left and right child nodes. $\odot$ is Hadamard product and $[,]$ is vector concatenation. σ and $tanh$ are sigmoid and tanh activation functions, d_g is the embedding size of glyph, W_G^{glyph}, $W_I^{glyph} \in R^{d_g \times 3d_g}$ are trainable parameters.

Multi-channel Fusion. As depicted in Fig. 4, the orange channel on the left is a vanilla character channel taking character ID embedding, position embedding, and segment embedding as input. In order to better preserve and integrate the phonology and glyph features, we do not directly integrate phonology and glyph embeddings with the character embedding in the embedding layer. Instead, in each encoder layer, we feed the multi-channel features from previous layer into independent encoder modules. Then the obtained output is concatenated and fed into fusion module. Finally, residual connections are performed to produce the final outputs. The output feature dimension of the fusion layer is consistent with that of the character channel. Formally, we denote character, phonology, glyph channels by c, p, g respectively and we use * to refer any one of them:

$$\bar{H}_i^* = Layer_i^*((H_{i-1}^*)) \tag{8}$$

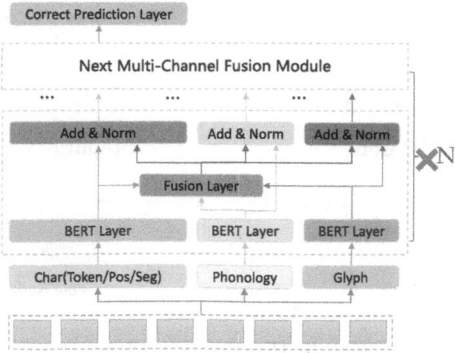

Fig. 4. Multi-channel fusion.

$$G_i^f = FFN_i^f([\bar{H}_i^c, \bar{H}_i^p, \bar{H}_i^g])) \tag{9}$$

$$G_i^* = FC_i^*(G_i^f) \tag{10}$$

$$H_i^* = Norm^*(\bar{H}_i^* + G_i^*) \tag{11}$$

Here, H_i^* are the outputs of the channels in i-th layer, $Layer_i^*$ are standard BERT encoder modules consisting of self-attention [25] and FFN. FFN^f denotes one feed-forward layer network with $GELU$ [12] as its activation function. $Norm$ is the layer normalization [1]. FC_i^* are fully connected layers, and the output dimensions of FC_i^c, FC_i^p, FC_i^g are set to d_c, d_m, d_m respectively.

Loss and Prediction. Like other CSC works, we use the output of the last layer of the character channel to predict the correct token. Formally, given the character channel output h^c and corresponding token target labels l, loss function is:

$$loss_i = CrossEntropy(CPL(H^c[i]), l_i) \tag{12}$$

A batch loss is the mean of loss calculated on all the tokens in the batch including misspelled and correct ones:

$$loss_t = \frac{1}{n} \sum_{i=1}^{n} CrossEntropy(CPL(H^c[i]), l_i) \tag{13}$$

where $H^c[i]$ is the i-th token's hidden state in the batch, l_i is the corresponding label. CPL stands for Correct Prediction Layer and n is the total number of tokens.

4   Experiment

In this section, we describe the pre-training and fine-tuning stages of PGBERT in detail, and show the results compared with baseline and SOTA models in many widely used public datasets.

4.1   Pre-training

Dataset. We use wiki2019zh[2] as the pre-training corpus. We remove sentences longer than 100 (after tokenization) or containing large proportion of non-Chinese characters, and 9.3 million sentences are obtained.

CSC Pre-training. Like most of the CSC work, we use confusion set to build a large CSC dataset on aforementioned 9.3 million sentences collected from wiki2019zh. We randomly replace 15% of tokens in sentences with other tokens, of which 60% are homophonous characters, 15% have similar glyphs, 25% are random Chinese characters. The character channel's weights are initialized with RoBERTa-wwm-ext [7], while the rest modules including glyph/phonology embedding layers are randomly initialized.

4.2   Fine Tuning

Training Data. To make comparisons more comprehensive, we follow and collect 10K sentences from SIGHAN [24,28,32] and 27K automatically generated sentences [26] as training data. SIGHAN13/14/15 are small datasets, the data in SIGHAN13 originated from the essays written by native Chinese speakers [28], while SIGHAN14/15 focuses on the essays written by learners of Chinese as a foreign language [24]. Different from SIGHAN dataset, [26] constructs constructing CSC corpus with automatically generated spelling errors induced by OCR and ASR-based methods

Evaluation Data. Following [4], we adopt the test data of SIGHAN15 [24] consisting of 1,100 testing passages. Half of these passages are correct, while the other half contain at least one spelling error. We only keep erroneous sentences for evaluation.

Metrics. We evaluate the sentence [24] and character level [4] performance on the SIGHAN13/14/15 test datasets, and both sentence and character level metrics include precision(P), recall(R), and F1(F) on detection and correction level. As explained in [4,30], SIGHAN13 contains many erroneously annotated cases, where "的", "地", "得" are perplexedly used. To tackle the problem, [4,19] purpose further fine-tuning on SIGHAN13 train dataset, while [30] argues that doing so could cause performance decline. For consistent comparison, on character level, we finetune the model on SIGHAN13 train dataset for extra epochs, while on sentence level, we adopt [30]'s practice where "的", "地", "得" are removed from model's prediction and metrics are calculated from remnants.

4.3   Parameter Setting

We train the model using AdamW optimizer. We set d_m, the dimension of glyph and phonology channels, to 128, and the dimension of character channel to 768. In the CSC pre-training stage, we set the max length of the input sequence to 100,

---

[2] https://github.com/suzhoushr/nlp_chinese_corpus.

batch size to 432 and initial learning rate to 5e–5 and train the model for 218k step. In fine turning stage, we set the max length of the input sequence to 100, batch size to 128 and initial learning rate to 5e–5 and train the model for 44k step.

4.4   Baseline Models

FASPell [13] employs BERT as DAE and designs a decoder incorporating visual and phonological information.

Soft-Masked BERT [34] proposes a end-to-end model consisting of a error detection module and a error correction module. Its results on SIGHAN15 sentence level are available only.

SpellGCN [4] designs a GCN based component to introduce phonological and visual similarity knowledge into language models.

PLOME [19] introduces stroke order and Pinyin sequence for phonics and shape embedding calculation and designs a pronunciation prediction task.

ReaLiSe [30] designs three independent single modality encoder and fuses the representation from different modalities with gate mechanism.

PGBERT w/o IDS replaces IDS tree in PGBERT with stroke sequence.

PGBERT w/o MF removes the multi-channel structure and concatenate the glyph, phonology embeddings with character embedding in embedding layer.

4.5   Main Results

Table 2. Experimental results of different methods on SIGHAN13/14/15. The symbol "*" means sentence level metrics are evaluated as described in Sect. 4.2. "A" in sentence level denotes accuracy with which the model correctly detects or corrects all tokens in single sentence.

| | Character-Level(with error)(%) | | | | | | Setence-Level(whole set)(%) | | | | | | | |
| | Detection | | | Correction | | | Detection | | | | Correction | | | |
SIGHAN13	D-P	D-R	D-F	C-P	C-R	C-F	D-A	D-P	D-R	D-F	C-A	C-P	C-R	C-F
FASPell [13]	(–)	(–)	(–)	(–)	(–)	(–)	63.1	76.2	63.2	69.1	60.5	73.1	60.5	66.2
SpellGCN [4]	82.6	88.9	85.7	98.4	88.4	93.1	(–)	80.1	74.4	77.2	(–)	78.3	72.7	75.4
PLOME [19]	**85.0**	89.3	87.1	**98.7**	89.1	93.7	(–)	(–)	(–)	(–)	(–)	(–)	(–)	(–)
*ReaLiSe** [30]	(–)	(–)	(–)	(–)	(–)	(–)	82.7	**88.6**	82.5	**85.4**	81.4	**87.2**	81.2	**84.1**
*PGBERT**	84.7	**91.1**	**87.8**	98.4	**89.7**	**93.8**	**83.1**	86.6	**82.8**	84.7	**81.7**	85.1	**81.4**	83.2
SIGHAN14	D-P	D-R	D-F	C-P	C-R	C-F	D-A	D-P	D-R	D-F	C-A	C-P	C-R	C-F
FASPell [13]	(–)	(–)	(–)	(–)	(–)	(–)	70.0	61.0	53.5	57.0	69.3	59.4	52.0	55.4
SpellGCN [4]	83.6	78.6	81.0	97.2	76.4	85.5	(–)	65.1	69.5	67.2	(–)	63.1	67.2	65.3
PLOME [19]	88.5	79.8	83.9	**98.8**	78.8	87.7	(–)	(–)	(–)	(–)	(–)	(–)	(–)	(–)
ReaLiSe [30]	(–)	(–)	(–)	(–)	(–)	(–)	78.4	**67.8**	71.5	**69.6**	77.7	**66.3**	70.0	68.1
PGBERT	**90.7**	81.2	**85.7**	98.7	**80.2**	**88.5**	**78.6**	67.1	**71.9**	69.5	**78.1**	66.1	**70.8**	**68.3**
SIGHAN15	D-P	D-R	D-F	C-P	C-R	C-F	D-A	D-P	D-R	D-F	C-A	C-P	C-R	C-F
FASPell [13]	(–)	(–)	(–)	(–)	(–)	(–)	74.2	67.6	60.0	63.5	73.7	66.6	59.1	62.6
Soft-Masked BERT [34]	(–)	(–)	(–)	(–)	(–)	(–)	80.9	73.7	73.2	73.5	77.4	66.7	66.2	66.4
SpellGCN [4]	88.9	**87.7**	88.3	95.7	83.9	89.4	(–)	74.8	80.7	77.7	(–)	72.1	77.7	75.9
PLOME [19]	94.5	87.4	90.8	**97.2**	84.3	90.3	85.0	77.4	81.5	79.4	83.7	75.3	79.3	77.2
ReaLiSe [30]	(–)	(–)	(–)	(–)	(–)	(–)	84.7	77.3	81.3	79.3	84.0	75.9	79.9	77.8
PGBERT	**95.2**	87.5	**91.2**	**97.2**	**85.1**	**90.8**	**85.5**	**78.1**	**82.8**	**80.4**	**84.4**	76.0	**80.6**	**78.2**

For consistent comparison, we test the character level metrics, which follows the definition in [4], on subsets of test data only containing wrong sentences. We also compare the performance on sentence level metric on the complete test set, which is defined in [24]. Table 2 lists the experimental results on SIGHAN test data. Compared with current SOTA model, our model acquires better or comparable result on both character and sentence level. In terms of sentence level, our model outperforms SpellGCN [4] by up to 2.7% (D-F) and 3.0% (C-F) on SIGHAN13/14/15 [24,28,33] test data; our model exceeds PLOME [19] on SIGHAN15 with a margin of 1.0% on both sentence and character level F1-score; compared with ReaLiSe [30], PGBERT persistently holds a lead on detection/correction accuracy score, and acquires significant better results on SIGHAN15. In the level of characters, PGBERT leads PLOME [19] by up to 0.6%/1.8%/0.4% (D-F) and 0.1%/0.8%/0.5% (C-F) on SIGHAN13/14/15.

4.6 Ablation Experiments

In order to verify the improvement brought by tree structure encoder and multi-channel fusion, we conduct ablation experiments. "PGBERT w/o MF" means PGBERT without Multi-channel Fusion where we simply concatenate glyph and phonology embeddings with token embeddings in the embedding layer, and remove the glyph and phonology channels and fusion modules. "PGBERT w/o IDS" means PGBERT without IDS, where we replace the IDS tree encoder module with stroke sequence encoder adopted in PLOME [19]. RoBERTa [7] is to directly adopt RoBERTa-wwm-ext model. We adopt identical training patterns and parameter settings to train the three models and choose the best checkpoint. Then we test models performance on SIGHAN14 dataset and the detailed results are shown in Table 3: PGBERT outperforms PGBERT w/o MF, PGBERT w/o IDS and RoBERTa on all metrics, where the sentence level D-A is boosted by up to 1.5%/1.2%/1.2%, and sentence-level C-A is boosted by up to 1.5%/1.4%/1.7%. It's worth noting that PGBERT has significantly higher character level C-R/D-R than PGBERT w/o MF, suggesting that multi-channel fusion module can better preserve glyph and phonology information and therefore provide the model with stronger indication. PGBERT also outperforms PGBERT w/o IDS on all metrics, from which we can conclude that IDS tree encoder is a better approach to represent glyph of Chinese characters. We notice that w/o MF actually has relatively poor performance comparing with RoBERTa on character level metrics. We conclude that the simple concatenation in embedding layer introduces too much noise (randomly initialized weights) which cannot be alleviated during CSC pretraining stage.

Table 3. Experimental results of PGBERT w/o IDS and PGBERT w/o MF on SIGHAN14

	Sentence-Leveln (whole set)(%)								Character-Level (only error)(%)					
	D-A	D-P	D-R	D-F	C-A	C-P	C-R	C-F	D-P	D-R	D-F	C-P	C-R	C-F
PGBERT	**78.6**	**67.1**	**71.9**	**69.5**	**78.1**	**66.1**	**70.8**	**68.3**	**90.7**	**81.2**	**85.7**	98.7	**80.2**	**88.5**
w/o MF	77.1	65.9	68.8	67.4	76.6	64.8	67.7	66.2	89.2	77.0	82.7	**98.8**	76.1	86.0
w/o IDS	77.4	65.0	70.8	67.8	76.7	63.8	69.4	66.5	90.7	79.8	84.9	98.2	78.3	87.2
RoBERTa	77.4	66.4	69.8	68.0	76.4	64.4	67.7	66.0	90.5	79.0	84.3	97.7	77.2	86.2

5   Conclusions

We propose PGBERT, a phonology and glyph Enhanced Pre-training model for CSC. It leverages the phonology and glyph information of Chinese characters to enhance the model's ability of capaturing context information and disambiguating homophones in Chinese. For phonology, PGBERT uses Bi-GRU to encode Pinyin sequence. For glyph, it uses IDS to decompose Chinese characters into a IDS tree, and then encodes the IDS tree recursively by the tree encoder. Parallel with the original BERT layers, extra channels for phonology and glyph are added respectively. The output of each channel is yielded by multi-channel fusion, rendering character, phonology and glyph features to interact with each other while reducing the information loss in the fusion process. The empirical analysis shows that PGBERT achieves a new state-of-the-art performance.

References

1. Ba, J.L., Kiros, J.R., Hinton, G.E.: Layer normalization. arXiv preprint arXiv:1607.06450 (2016)
2. Burstein, J., Chodorow, M.: Automated essay scoring for nonnative English speakers. In: Computer Mediated Language Assessment And Evaluation in Natural Language Processing (1999)
3. Chang, C.H.: A new approach for automatic Chinese spelling correction. In: Proceedings of Natural Language Processing Pacific Rim Symposium, vol. 95, pp. 278–283. Citeseer (1995)
4. Cheng, X., et al.: SpellGCN: incorporating phonological and visual similarities into language models for Chinese spelling check. arXiv preprint arXiv:2004.14166 (2020)
5. Cho, K., et al.: Learning phrase representations using RNN encoder-decoder for statistical machine translation. arXiv preprint arXiv:1406.1078 (2014)
6. Chollampatt, S., Taghipour, K., Ng, H.T.: Neural network translation models for grammatical error correction. arXiv preprint arXiv:1606.00189 (2016)
7. Cui, Y., Che, W., Liu, T., Qin, B., Yang, Z., Wang, S., Hu, G.: Pre-training with whole word masking for chinese bert (2019)
8. Devlin, J., Chang, M.W., Lee, K., Toutanova, K.: BERT: pre-training of deep bidirectional transformers for language understanding. arXiv preprint arXiv:1810.04805 (2018)

9. Fung, G., Debosschere, M., Wang, D., Li, B., Zhu, J., Wong, K.F.: Nlptea 2017 shared task-Chinese spelling check. In: Proceedings of the 4th Workshop on Natural Language Processing Techniques for Educational Applications (NLPTEA 2017), pp. 29–34 (2017)
10. Gao, J., Quirk, C., et al.: A large scale ranker-based system for search query spelling correction. In: COLING '10: Proceedings of the 23rd International Conference on Computational Linguistics (2010)
11. Ge, T., Wei, F., Zhou, M.: Fluency boost learning and inference for neural grammatical error correction. In: Proceedings of the 56th Annual Meeting of the Association for Computational Linguistics (Volume 1: Long Papers), pp. 1055–1065 (2018)
12. Hendrycks, D., Gimpel, K.: Gaussian error linear units (GELUS). arXiv preprint arXiv:1606.08415 (2016)
13. Hong, Y., Yu, X., He, N., Liu, N., Liu, J.: FASPell: a fast, adaptable, simple, powerful Chinese spell checker based on DAE-decoder paradigm. In: Proceedings of the 5th Workshop on Noisy User-Generated Text (W-NUT 2019), pp. 160–169 (2019)
14. Huang, C., Pan, H., Ming, Z., Zhang, L.: Automatic detecting/correcting errors in Chinese text by an approximate word-matching algorithm. In: ACL 2000: Proceedings of the 38th Annual Meeting on Association for Computational Linguistic (2000)
15. Ji, J., Wang, Q., Toutanova, K., Gong, Y., Truong, S., Gao, J.: A nested attention neural hybrid model for grammatical error correction. arXiv preprint arXiv:1707.02026 (2017)
16. Jia, Z., Wang, P., Zhao, H.: Graph model for Chinese spell checking. In: Proceedings of the Seventh SIGHAN Workshop on Chinese Language Processing, pp. 88–92 (2013)
17. Kipf, T.N., Welling, M.: Semi-supervised classification with graph convolutional networks. arXiv preprint arXiv:1609.02907 (2016)
18. Liu, C.L., Lai, M.H., Chuang, Y.H., Lee, C.Y.: Visually and phonologically similar characters in incorrect simplified chinese words. In: Coling 2010: Posters. pp. 739–747 (2010)
19. Liu, S., Yang, T., Yue, T., Zhang, F., Wang, D.: PLOME: pre-training with misspelled knowledge for Chinese spelling correction. In: Proceedings of the 59th Annual Meeting of the Association for Computational Linguistics and the 11th International Joint Conference on Natural Language Processing (Volume 1: Long Papers). pp. 2991–3000 (2021)
20. Liu, X., Cheng, K., Luo, Y., Duh, K., Matsumoto, Y.: A hybrid Chinese spelling correction using language model and statistical machine translation with reranking. In: Proceedings of the Seventh SIGHAN Workshop on Chinese Language Processing, pp. 54–58 (2013)
21. Martins, Bruno, Silva, Mário. J..: Spelling correction for search engine queries. In: Vicedo, José Luis., Martínez-Barco, Patricio, Muñoz, Rafael, Saiz Noeda, Maximiliano (eds.) EsTAL 2004. LNCS (LNAI), vol. 3230, pp. 372–383. Springer, Heidelberg (2004). https://doi.org/10.1007/978-3-540-30228-5_33
22. Reimers, N., Gurevych, I.: Sentence-BERT: sentence embeddings using Siamese BERT-networks. arXiv preprint arXiv:1908.10084 (2019)
23. Tai, K.S., Socher, R., Manning, C.D.: Improved semantic representations from tree-structured long short-term memory networks. In: Proceedings of the 53rd Annual Meeting of the Association for Computational Linguistics and the 7th International Joint Conference on Natural Language Processing (Volume 1: Long Papers) (2015)

24. Tseng, Y.H., Lee, L.H., Chang, L.P., Chen, H.H.: Introduction to SIGHAN 2015 bake-off for Chinese spelling check. In: Proceedings of the Eighth SIGHAN Workshop on Chinese Language Processing, pp. 32–37 (2015)
25. Vaswani, A., et al.: Attention is all you need. In: Advances in Neural Information Processing Systems, pp. 5998–6008 (2017)
26. Wang, D., Song, Y., Li, J., Han, J., Zhang, H.: A hybrid approach to automatic corpus generation for Chinese spelling check. In: Proceedings of the 2018 Conference on Empirical Methods in Natural Language Processing, pp. 2517–2527 (2018)
27. Wang, D., Tay, Y., Zhong, L.: Confusionset-guided pointer networks for Chinese spelling check. In: Proceedings of the 57th Annual Meeting of the Association for Computational Linguistics, pp. 5780–5785 (2019)
28. Wu, S.H., Liu, C.L., Lee, L.H.: Chinese spelling check evaluation at SIGHAN bake-off 2013. In: Proceedings of the Seventh SIGHAN Workshop on Chinese Language Processing, pp. 35–42 (2013)
29. Xin, Y., Zhao, H., Wang, Y., Jia, Z.: An improved graph model for Chinese spell checking. In: Proceedings of the Third CIPS-SIGHAN Joint Conference on Chinese Language Processing. pp. 157–166 (2014)
30. Xu, H.D., Li, Z., Zhou, Q., Li, C., Mao, X.L.: Read, listen, and see: Leveraging multimodal information helps Chinese spell checking. In: Findings of the Association for Computational Linguistics: ACL-IJCNLP 2021 (2021)
31. Yang, W., et al.: End-to-end open-domain question answering with BERTserini. arXiv preprint arXiv:1902.01718 (2019)
32. Yu, J., Li, Z.: Chinese spelling error detection and correction based on language model, pronunciation, and shape. In: Proceedings of the Third CIPS-SIGHAN Joint Conference on Chinese Language Processing, pp. 220–223 (2014)
33. Yu, L.C., Lee, L.H., Tseng, Y.H., Chen, H.H.: Overview of SIGHAN 2014 bake-off for Chinese spelling check. In: Proceedings of the Third CIPS-SIGHAN Joint Conference on Chinese Language Processing, pp. 126–132 (2014)
34. Zhang, S., Huang, H., Liu, J., Li, H.: Spelling error correction with soft-masked BERT. In: Proceedings of the 58th Annual Meeting of the Association for Computational Linguistics, pp. 882–890 (2020)

MCER: A Multi-domain Dataset
for Sentence-Level Chinese Ellipsis Resolution

Jialu Qi[1,2,1,2], Yanqiu Shao[1,2,1,2], Wei Li[1(✉)], and Zizhuo Shen[1,2]

[1] School of Information Science, Beijing Language and Culture University, Beijing 100083,
China
liweitj47@blcu.edu.cn

[2] Chinese National Language Resources Monitoring and Research Center (CNLR) Print Media
Language Branch, Beijing 100083, China

Abstract. Ellipsis is a cross-linguistic phenomenon which can be commonly seen
in Chinese. Although eliding some of the elements in the sentence that could be
understood from the context makes no difference for human beings, it is a great
challenge for machine in the procedure of natural language understanding. In
order to promote ellipsis-related researches in Chinese language, we propose an
application-oriented definition of ellipsis specifically for researches in the realm
of Chinese natural language processing. At the same time, we build and release
a multi-domain dataset for sentence-level Chinese ellipsis resolution following
the new definition we propose. In addition, we define a new task: sentence-level
Chinese ellipsis resolution, and model it with two subprocedures: 1) Elliptic position detection; 2) Ellipsis resolution. We propose several baseline methods based
on pre-trained language models, as they have obtained state-of-the-art results on
related tasks. Besides, it is also worth noticing that, to our knowledge, this is the
first study that apply the extractive method for question answering to Chinese ellipsis resolution. The results of the experiments show that it is possible for machine
to understand ellipsis within our new definition.

Keywords: Definition of ellipsis · Elliptic position detection · Ellipsis resolution

1 Introduction

Ellipsis is a common linguistic phenomenon eliding some of the elements in the sentence
that could be understood from the context. Due to its ubiquity, it is one of the main
causes of the errors in machine reading comprehension, machine translation and many
other tasks of natural language processing, which makes the phenomena of ellipsis a
non-negligible problem.

In fact, in the realm of Chinese natural language processing (Chinese NLP for short),
zero anaphora resolution (the same as zero-pronoun resolution [3]), the kind of resolution specifically pays attention to the empty grammatical slots in a sentence which stand
for a previously mentioned referent [18], is the only ellipsis-related research attempting
to moderate the influence brought by ellipsis. However, ellipsis is a much broader phenomenon than zero anaphora [8]. Generally, ellipsis can be classified into three broad

categories: **syntactic ellipsis**, **semantic ellipsis** and **pragmatic ellipsis**. Each of the categories contains various kinds of ellipsis phenomena, and zero anaphora could merely be a single part of syntactic ellipsis. There are a lot more ellipsis phenomena which are agreed to be the ones that could be restored from the context, and the restoration could undoubtedly help understanding the text [2].

It is necessary to clarify the definition of ellipsis for further researches in the realm of Chinese NLP. However, there is no definition of ellipsis that is universally acknowledged by modern linguistics, since researchers draw different conclusions based on different perspectives and emphases. Therefore, in order to promote ellipsis-related researches in Chinese NLP, we study subsistent ellipsis-related theoretical researches both in Chinese and English, and propose an application-oriented definition of ellipsis specifically for researches in Chinese NLP in consideration of the controversial problems and the error-prone parts.

For the lack of corpus, and to validate the effectiveness of our new definition, we annotate the elliptic position and restore the elided elements for 3489 sentences from 5 different domains, which are news, novels, plays, textbooks and product reviews, since sentences from different domains have different characteristics. And we introduce a new dataset, MCER, for further researches.

In addition, we define a new task: sentence-level Chinese ellipsis resolution. To resolve the ellipses in a sentence, at first, we have to find the exact position where omission occurs, thus we model the whole ellipsis resolution process with two subprocedures: 1) Elliptic position detection, which is for machine to detect the positions where ellipses occur; 2) Ellipsis resolution, which is for machine to restore the elided elements with the elliptic position of each sentence given as known information. We model subprocedure-1 as a sequence labeling task, and use BERT and RoBERTa as our baseline models, which have achieved state-of-the-art performance in various tasks. We use BART and BERT-QA as our baseline models for subprocedure-2, and model subprocedure-2 from two different aspects: for BART, we fine-tune it to perform ellipsis resolution in a classical text generation way; as for BERT-QA, we borrow the idea from QA methods, that is, to consider ellipsis resolution as a question answering task, and extract the "answers" from the context [9].

In summary, the contributions of our work are as follows: 1) We propose an application-oriented definition of ellipsis for Chinese NLP. 2) Following the new definition, we build and release a dataset, MCER, for further researches focusing on Chinese ellipsis resolution, which contains 3489 sentences from 5 different domains; 3) We define a new task: sentence-level Chinese ellipsis resolution, and model it with two subprocedures. We propose several baseline methods for each subprocedure, in which we borrow the idea from QA methods to perform subprocedure-2 [9]. To our knowledge, this is the first study that apply QA methods to Chinese ellipsis resolution. The results of the experiments show that it is possible for machine to understand ellipsis within our new definition.

2 Definition of Ellipsis

To further research ellipsis in the realm of Chinese NLP, it is necessary to clarify the definition of ellipsis first. However, there is no definition of ellipsis that is universally acknowledged by modern linguistics, since researchers draw different conclusions based on different perspectives and emphases. Therefore, we study subsistent theoretical researches of ellipsis, and propose an application-oriented definition of ellipsis for Chinese NLP in consideration of the controversial problems and the error-prone parts.

2.1 Ellipsis for Chinese NLP

We define ellipsis that we research in the realm of Chinese NLP to be the kind of ellipsis caused by linguistic context where the nonexpression should have occupied a place in the syntactic structure of the sentence or played a semantic role in the sentence. To further explain the definition, we give the main parts of the definition as follows:

1) The restored elements can be found in the context.
2) The meaning of the sentence cannot be changed after the restoration.
3) The elided elements can be validly restored, that is, after the restoration, if the sentence becomes invalid, we do not consider it as ellipsis for Chinese NLP.
4) The results of the restoration must have a complete syntactic structure, while the missing of the semantic roles are allowed.

Different from the previous works [1, 2], we restore ellipses to the maximum extent as long as we can find an exact referent for them in the sentence. Also, we eliminate the ones, the restoration of which will affect the objectivity and reasonability of the annotation process. Besides, we emphasize the integrity of the syntactic structure in the results of the restoration process, and, at the same time, we do not pursue the integrity of the semantic structure, but restore semantic roles as much as possible.

2.2 Explanations

In this section, we will give detailed explanations of our definition from different aspects.

Context. Ellipsis can be classified based on different types of contexts which cause it: ellipsis caused by linguistic context, ellipsis caused by situational context and ellipsis caused by sociocultural context. However, the latter two kinds of ellipsis both need extra knowledge from the scenario or even the social situation. For example:

(1) 中国从前的监狱，墙上大抵画着一只虎头，所以叫做"虎头牢"，狱门就建筑在

虎口里，这是说，∅一进去，∅是很难再出来的。[20]

There is usually a picture of tiger's head drew on the wall of Chinese prisons in the old days, so people called it "Tiger's head prison", where the gate was built in the tiger's mouth. It means that, as long as ∅ get into it, it is hard ∅ to make it out.

Chinese speakers would know, both of the nonexpressions could be restored as "犯人" ("offender"), but we cannot find the exact word from the sentence, and there are a lot more words that could also be the correct results of the restoration, such as "罪犯" ("criminal").

To guarantee the objectivity of further annotation, we narrow our scope down to ellipsis caused by linguistic context, which means we can find the exact restored elements in the sentence, which makes the restoration objective and well-founded.

Validity. As for the third item of the main parts of our definition: "the elided elements can be validly restored", for example, "你叫他进屋" ("You tell him come in", i.e., "You tell him to come in"), "他" ("him") is the object of "叫" ("tell"), and at the same time, "他" ("him") is also the subject of "进" ("come in"). Another "他" ("he" or "him") should be restored before or after the original one, and the result should be "你叫他他进屋" ("You tell him he come in"), which will not be said by Chinese speakers. Thus, we do not consider it as ellipsis for Chinese NLP.

The Three Aspects. Linguistics usually discuss ellipsis from 3 aspects [4, 7]: syntactic, semantic and pragmatic.

Syntactic ellipsis is defined to be the nonexpression of a word or phrase that should have occupied a place in the syntactic structure of a sentence [8]. Zero anaphora and zero cataphora are both part of syntactic ellipsis.

Zero anaphora is a kind of linguistic phenomenon paying attention to the empty grammatical slots in a sentence standing for a previously mentioned referent [18]. Zero anaphora is categorized as syntactic ellipsis, since a grammatical slot must have occupied a place in the syntactic structure of a sentence. In this situation, the nonexpression usually plays a role as subjects or objects [19]. For example:

(1) 今年六月，他流着眼泪拆了房子，∅随即在原地弄了个货柜屋。

In June of this year, he tearfully demolished the house and then ∅ built a container house on the spot.

The only difference between zero anaphora and zero cataphora is that, the elements that the nonexpression refers to in zero anaphora should be mentioned before the omission occurs, while it should be mentioned in the following part of the sentence in zero cataphora. The following sentence is an example for zero cataphora:

(2) 玛丽：∅不累，我每天都跑步。

Mary: ∅ Not tired, I jog every day.

In addition, it is important to know that, any form of the empty grammatical slots or nonexpressions standing for a mentioned referent in the context could be categorized as zero anaphora or zero cataphora. It means that, not only the ellipsis of a pronoun, but also ellipsis of noun phrases (3), verb phrases (4) or any other linguistic units that should have occupied a place in the syntactic structure of a sentence could be categorized as zero anaphora or zero cataphora.

(3) 中端产品不仅在价格上具有性价比，而且∅在主要功能上也丝毫不逊色于那些高端产品。

The mid-range products are not only cost-effective in terms of price, ∅ but also in no way inferior to those high-end products in terms of main functions.

(4) 张三会弹钢琴，李四也会∅。

Zhang San can play the piano, so can Li Si ∅.

Semantic ellipsis is defined to be the nonexpression of the elements that are not signaled by syntactic gap [8].

In this situation, the ellipsis will not be perceived by checking the syntactic structure of a sentence, while the nonexpression should have played a semantic role in the sentence. To explain the definition of semantic ellipsis, we give the following scenarios as examples: first, it is commonly seen in attribute-center structure, for instance, "的做工" ("the workmanship of") is elided in the following sentence:

(1) 诺基亚机子的做工比国产机∅好太多了。

The workmanship of the Nokia machine is much better than ∅ domestic machine.

Besides, people tend to elide the pattern "比…" ("than…") if it was referred in the former part of the sentence, which also conveys important information. For instance, "比手机" ("than phones") is elided in the following sentence:

(2) 平板电脑比手机好用，平板电脑∅更大。

Tablets are better than phones, tablets have larger screens ∅.

To complete the information to the maximum extent and guarantee the objectivity of the annotation process at the same time, we restore all the semantic ellipsis who has an exact referent in the linguistic context, but the integrity of the semantic roles is not obligatory.

Pragmatic ellipsis overlaps both syntactic ellipsis and semantic ellipsis, it refers to the kind of nonexpression caused by the context [4], while the context could be a sentence, a dialogue, a paragraph, or a whole passage. For example:

(1) -你吃饭了吗？(Have you eaten yet?)

   -没有。(No.)

In this work, all the ellipsis phenomenon we focus on are ellipses caused by linguistic context, which enables us to determine an exact referent in the context. To some extent, all the ellipsis phenomena within our definition could be categorized as pragmatic ellipsis. However, it is necessary to declare that, since we specifically pay attention to sentence-level ellipsis resolution in our dataset, the context specifically refers to the current sentence.

3 Dataset

For the lack of dataset in the field of Chinese ellipsis resolution, we build and release a new dataset, MCER, for further ellipsis-related researches. We will present our data annotation process in Sect. 3.1, and show the results of dataset analysis in Sect. 3.2, and then explain the format of our dataset in Sect. 3.3. Finally, following the new definition, we develop several considerations in the procedure of dataset constructing, which we will enumerate and explain in Sect. 3.4.

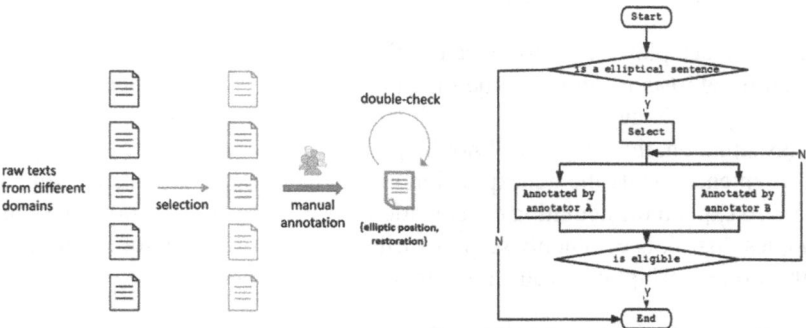

Fig. 1. The left part of the figure shows the overall data annotation procedure of the dataset. The right part shows the flow chart of the annotation procedure.

3.1 Annotation

The overall annotation procedure of the dataset is done in the following order, which is visually shown in Fig. 1 (left). And the flow chart of the annotation procedure is also shown in Fig. 1 (right).

Selection. Our dataset contains 3489 sentences from 5 different domains, including news, novels, plays, textbooks and product reviews. The reason why we select sentences from these domains are as follows: First, texts in these domains contain both formal expressions (news and textbooks) and informal expressions (novels, plays and product reviews). Second, sentences from these domains involve most of the common linguistic phenomena. Besides, they are able to cover all kinds of ellipsis phenomena within our definition.

After determining the sources of our data, we then select the sentences which are qualified to be further annotated, that is, select the sentences which are fluent, without confusion in expression, and most importantly, show at least one ellipsis phenomenon, which meets the requirements of our definition.

Manual Annotation. In practice, our manual annotation step could be further separated into two sub-steps: 1) Trial Annotation; 2) Formal Annotation.

In the procedure of trial annotation, we first evaluate the clarity of our definition, that is to see if the annotators can understand our definition correctly. If more than half of the annotators cannot understand any one of the items, we modify our definition, other than explain it to the annotators. We will repeat this test, until most of the annotators can understand it and annotate correctly following the definition, which guarantees the definition can be sustainably used in future annotation. Besides, we develop several considerations for rare scenarios led by the problems annotators encountered, which will be enumerated and explained in Sect. 3.4.

In the procedure of formal annotation, annotators annotate the restored elements at the exact position where ellipsis phenomena occur, and mark the restoration with special punctuation. We will explain the format in detail in Sect. 3.3. To improve the accuracy of annotation, annotators are divided into groups, and each group consists of two annotators. Annotators in the same group are given the same part of the data, so that we could detect annotation error much more efficiently by comparing the results, which will be done in the double-check procedure.

Double-check. This is the last step of the whole annotation procedure, which is to double-check if all the ellipsis phenomena were pointed out and restored correctly. If not, the corresponding group of annotators will have to annotate each of the questionable sentences repeatedly until all the problems of the specific sentence are settled. In this step, the annotators will exchange their results between two groups, and become the inspectors of the other group.

3.2 Dataset Analysis

The sentences we annotated are from 5 different domains, including news, novels, plays, textbooks and product reviews. The number of the sentences from each of the domains is shown in Table 1.

Table 1. The proportion of the 5 domains in MCER dataset.

News	Novels	Plays	Textbooks	Product reviews	Total
1773	471	232	579	434	3489

Table 2 shows the average sentence length of each domain. The overall average sentence length of our dataset is 49.57. Sentences from news are generally longer than sentences from other domains.

Table 2. The average sentence length of each domain.

News	Novels	Plays	Textbooks	Product reviews	Overall
70.82	24.15	15.32	31.69	32.45	49.57

Table 3 shows the average length of the restored elements of each domain. The average length of the restored elements from product reviews is the longest.

Table 3. The average length of restored elements in respect of domains.

News	Novels	Plays	Textbooks	Product reviews	Overall
3.46	2.02	1.42	2.40	4.16	3.28

3.3 Annotation Format

There are two different formats of files in total after annotation. One is txt-format files containing the original sentence and the restored elements, and the other is json-format files containing information like elliptic position, restored elements, sequence labels for elliptic position detection, etc., which is the final form of the dataset that could be used in Chinese NLP tasks.

Annotators are required to annotate in txt-format files, and annotate the restored elements at the exact position where omission occurs, so that we could get the elliptic position automatically. Each restored elements should be surrounded by punctuation "【】", for example:

(1) 平板电脑比手机好用，平板电脑【比手机】更大。Tablets are better than phones, tablets have larger screens 【than phones】.

It is necessary to explain that, the label corresponding to each token indicates whether it is an elliptic position. Label "O" indicates that it is a position where the original token should be kept, and label "I" indicates that elements should be restored before the corresponding token. In the above example, "更" is marked with "I" and all other tokens are marked with "O".

3.4 Considerations

Coreference Resolution. While annotating the sentences, we find that, in some of the scenarios, there are more than one option for the restoration. For example:

暑假他父亲归途阻塞，∅到天津改乘轮船，∅辗转回家，假期已过了一半。

During the summer vacation, his father was blocked on his way home, ∅ went to Tianjin to take a ferry, and then ∅ went back home. The vacation was halfway over.

In this sentence, the nonexpressions could be restored as "他" ("he") or "他父亲" ("his father"). In this situation, we require annotators to restore it as complete as possible. In other word, we add a coreference resolution step to our annotating process.

Multiple Restoration. In some of the scenarios, sentences need to be restored for more than one time to get a more complete result. For example, in this sentence:

你在YLT论坛里说你以前在澳大利亚开过现代，【现代的发动机】比不过通用的霍顿的发动机。

You said in the YLT forum that you had driven a Hyundai in Australia before, and 【the engine of Hyundai】 was no match for the engine of GM Holden.

If we want to get the final restored elements as "现代的发动机" ("the engine of Hyundai"), we have to restore "现代" ("Hyundai") from the former part of the sentence and restore "的发动机" ("the engine of") from the following sentence, which requires us to restore twice. It is impracticable to notate this kind of restoration, thus we do not restore a sentence for the second time.

Ellipsis of "的". The omission of "的" occurs frequently in attribute-center structure. However, in most of the times, we cannot determine an exact referent for it in the context. Therefore, when we restore ellipsis related to attribute-center structure, we require the restoration of "的" to be consistent with the referent. For example:

(1) 爱里社的配置的确比捷达【的配置】好呀。

The configuration of Elysee is indeed better than 【the configuration of】 Jetta.

(2) 现在的JD质量比刚出来时的原装JD【质量】差远了。

The current JD quality is far worse than the original JD 【quality】 when it first came out.

In the first sentence, there is a "的" in the former attribute-center structure, so we restore the element with "的" during the restoration process. On the contrary, we fill this elliptic position with the element "质量" ("quality"), without a "的" being restored, which follows the principle of consistency.

4   Experiments

In this work, we model the whole ellipsis resolution process with 2 subprocedures: 1) Elliptic position detection; 2) Ellipsis Resolution. We will introduce the subprocedures and our baseline methods for each of the subprocedures in Sect. 4.1, then we will briefly explain our evaluation metrics in Sect. 4.2, and finally we will analyze the results of the experiment in Sect. 4.3.

4.1   Baseline Methods

Elliptic Position Detection. We model this subprocedure as a sequence labeling task. In this procedure, we mark the elliptic position where the restored elements should be inserted with "I" and mark the positions where the original token should be kept with "O". Our baseline methods for this subprocedure are based on two PLMs: BERT and RoBERTa.

BERT. BERT is one of the most popular models for a lot of natural language processing tasks. Besides, it has obtained state-of-the-art results on Chinese sequence labeling tasks [5, 6]. Therefore, we choose BERT to be our first baseline model. We fine-tuned bert-base-chinese model and trained it with our train dataset, which contains 2443 sentences, for 10 epochs.

RoBERTa. RoBERTa is another PLM who has a similar backbone to BERT but is regarded as a robust version of BERT, which outperforms BERT in many tasks and datasets. Hence, we choose RoBERTa to be the second baseline model. Similar to BERT, we fine-tuned chinese-roberta-wwm-ext, and trained it with our train dataset for 10 epochs.

> **Context**: 为了帮家里种菸叶、香蕉，钟沐卿一直留在家乡美浓教书，七十三岁的他现在每天仍在田里工作。
> (In order to help the family grow tobacco leaves and bananas, Zhong Muqing has stayed in his hometown Meinong to teach. At the age of 73, he still works in the fields every day.)
>
> **Question**: 为了帮家里种菸叶、香蕉
> (In order to help the family grow tobacco leaves and bananas)
>
> **Answer**: 钟沐卿 (Zhong Muqing)

Fig. 2. An example for the triple < context, question, answer > of QA format. We make the sub-sentence where ellipsis occurs the "question", and find the elided elements within the context and make it the "answer". In this sentence, it is obvious to see that "钟沐卿" was elided before the word "为了", so "为了要帮忙家里种菸叶，香蕉" was made the "question", and "钟沐卿" was the answer.

Ellipsis Resolution. We see this subprocedure from two different aspects. First, we regard this task as a classical text generation process and choose BART to be our baseline model. From the other aspect, we borrow the idea from QA framework [9], which is to resolve the elided elements in an extractive way, and we use BERT-QA as our baseline model for this method.

BART. Although BERT has obtained state-of-the-art results on many NLP tasks, we must admit that, BERT is not the best model for text generation. Therefore, researchers presented BART [11], which could be regarded as a PLM generalizing BERT and GPT by using bidirectional encoder and left-to-right decoder at the same time. BART outperforms many PLMs on text generation tasks, so we choose BART to be our baseline model to perform the generation process.

At first, we prepare our test dataset by filling the elliptic position with special token [MASK] in our test dataset, and then fine-tune the Chinese version BART, which is also called CPT [12], and trained it with our train dataset for 10 epochs.

BERT-QA. We first convert our dataset into QA format, which consists of < context, question, answer > triples. We present an example of the reconstructuring in Fig. 2. The final form of the dataset in json-format files is similar to the form of SQuAD [10]. We fine-tuned bert-base-chinese to perform the extracting process, and trained it with the QA-format train dataset for 10 epochs.

4.2 Evaluation Metrics

Elliptic Position Detection. We regard this subprocedure as token-level binary classification. However, there are more samples which were labeled "O" than samples which were labeled "I", which makes the overall "Accuracy" metric no longer representative. Thus, we primarily pay attention to metrics of Precision, Recall and F1-score in this task, which will only be calculated on label "I".

Ellipsis Resolution. In this subprocedure, we use the metric ROUGE [13] to evaluate our baseline methods. ROUGE is an abbreviation of Recall-Oriented Understudy for Gisting Evaluation, which evaluate the results by counting the overlapping units. We use ROUGE-1, ROUGE-2 and ROUGE-L to evaluate the performance of our baseline methods. Besides, we use "Exact Match Score" to indicate the proportion of the samples that have been predicted precisely, that is, the predicted results are completely consistent with the annotated results.

4.3 Results

Elliptic Position Detection. Table 4 shows the results of the two baseline methods. We can see from the result that, after training the PLMs with our dataset, it is possible for them to understand ellipsis within our new definition. In this task, the performance of RoBERTa is slightly better than BERT. Relatively speaking, this is a simple task, but there is still room for us to further improve it.

Table 4. The results of subprocedure-1: elliptic position detection.

	Precision	Recall	F1-score
BERT	0.8113	0.8414	0.8261
RoBERTa	0.8156	0.8553	0.8350

Ellipsis Resolution. Table 5 shows the results of the two baseline methods and the performance of BART without fine-tune. It is obvious that the QA method outperform the classical generation method to a large extent.

Table 5. The results of subprocedure-2: Ellipsis Resolution.

	ROUGE-1	ROUGE-2	ROUGE-L	Exact Match Score
BART without fine-tune	0.1078	0.0199	0.1078	0.1075
BART	0.1392	0.0360	0.1392	0.1210
BERT-QA	0.8052	0.5751	0.8049	0.6817

By analyzing some of the cases from the validation dataset, which is shown in Fig. 3, we believe the reason why it is difficult for BART to predict correctly is that, Chinese

Text: 在六家长大的文化工作者陈板说，高铁带来的不是都市化，[MASK]而是将传统客家文化「连根拔除」。

(Chen Ban, a cultural worker who grew up in six schools, said what the high-speed rail brings about is not urbanization, [MASK] but eradication of traditional Hakka culture.)

Generated: 反

Label: 高铁带来的 (what the high-speed rail brings about)

Fig. 3. A case from the results BART generated. "Text" is the input, "Generated" is the output of BART model for special token [MASK], and "Label" indicates the correct restored elements.

BART (CPT) was trained with a large amount of Chinese corpus which contains a lot of ellipsis phenomena. That makes the model tends to generate sentences with ellipsis phenomena, which is idiomatic. However, the restored elements generated by BART is less meaningful for information completion than the annotated results we give in the dataset. In addition, by comparing the results generated by BART with and without training, we can see that our training process did improve the performance, but it is hard to change this generating pattern by training the model with dataset of few samples for a few epochs.

Table 6. The results of the pipelines.

	ROUGE-1	ROUGE-2	ROUGE-L	Exact Match Score
BERT + BART without fine-tune	0.0840	0.0165	0.0840	0.0785
BERT + BART	0.1148	0.0240	0.1148	0.1108
BERT + BERT-QA	0.6896	0.4824	0.6895	0.6041
RoBERTa + BART without fine-tune	0.0932	0.0214	0.0932	0.0892
RoBERTa + BART	0.1215	0.0263	0.1215	0.1154
RoBERTa + BERT-QA	**0.6955**	**0.4921**	**0.6955**	**0.6076**

Pipeline. We combine the two subprocedures and perform the whole ellipsis resolution procedure in a pipeline. Table 6 shows the results of each combination. As expected, the combination of RoBERTa and BERT-QA obtained the best performance, as each of the two methods has obtained the best performance in the corresponding subprocedure. Subprocedure-2 is much tougher than subprocedure-1, and the performance of subprocedure-2 has a greater impact on the final performance of the pipeline, which is to be further improved.

5 Conclusion

In this paper, we argued that ellipsis is an important linguistic phenomenon which is worth further researching in the realm of Chinese NLP. To promote ellipsis-related researches, we proposed an application-oriented definition of ellipsis for Chinese NLP, so that we can reduce influence of ellipsis to the maximum extent in a more reasonable and practicable way. Also, for the lack of corpus and to evaluate the effectiveness of the new definition, we built and released a multi-domain dataset, MCER, for further researches focusing on Chinese ellipsis resolution. In addition, we modeled the whole ellipsis resolution process with two subprocedures, in which we borrowed the idea from QA framework and applied it to Chinese ellipsis resolution for the first time.

In the future, we will continue expanding the size of our dataset, and at the same time, explore new methods to promote the performance of sentence-level Chinese ellipsis resolution. Besides, we will evaluate if the whole ellipsis resolution procedure could further improve the performance of downstream tasks, such as machine reading comprehension and dependency parsing. Our dataset, MCER, is publicly available at https://github.com/NLPInBLCU/MCER.

Acknowledgements. This research project is supported by the National Natural Science Foundation of China (61872402), the Humanities and Social Science Project of the Ministry of Education (17YJAZH068), Science Foundation of Beijing Language and Culture University (supported by "the Fundamental Research Funds for the Central Universities") (22YJ080002, 18ZDJ03), the Fundamental Research Funds for the Central Universities, and the Research Funds of Beijing Language and Culture University (22YCX158).

References

1. Ren, X., et al.: Building an ellipsis-aware chinese dependency treebank for web text. In: Proceedings of the 12th International Conference on Language Resources and Evaluation (2018)
2. Liu, Y., et al.: Ellipsis in Chinese AMR corpus.In: Proceedings of the First International Workshop on Designing Meaning Representations, pp. 92–99 (2019)
3. Yuru, J., Yuyao, Z., Teng, M., et al.: A survey of Chinese Zero anaphora resolution. J. Chin. Inf. Process. 34(3), 1–12 (2020)
4. Wang, S.: Study of ellipsis. studies of the Chinese Language (6), 409–415 (1985)
5. Liu, W., et al.: Lexicon enhanced Chinese sequence labeling using BERT adapter. In: Proceedings of the 59th Annual Meeting of the Association for Computational Linguistics and the 11th International Joint Conference on Natural Language Processing (vol. 1: Long Papers) (2021)
6. Yang, H.: BERT Meets Chinese Word Segmentation. arXiv preprint arXiv: 1909.09292 (2019)
7. Merchant J.: Three types of ellipsis. Context-Depend. Perspect. Relat. **6**, 141–192 (2010)
8. McShane, M.J.: A Theory of Ellipsis. Oxford University Press on Demand (2005)
9. Aralikatte, R., Lamm, M., Hardt, D., et al.: Ellipsis resolution as question answering: An evaluation. arXiv preprint arXiv:1908.11141 (2019)
10. Rajpurkar, P., Zhang, J., Lopyrev, K., Liang, P.: Squad: 100,000+ questions for machine comprehension of text. arXiv preprint arXiv:1606.05250 (2016)
11. Lewis, M., et al.: BART: denoising sequence-to-sequence pre-training for natural language generation, translation, and comprehension. In: Proceedings of the 58th Annual Meeting of the Association for Computational Linguistics (2020)
12. Shao, Y., et al.: CPT: A Pre-Trained Unbalanced Transformer for Both Chinese Language Understanding and Generation. arXiv preprint arXiv:2109.05729 (2021)

13. Lin, C.-Y.: Rouge: A package for automatic evaluation of summaries. Text summarization branches out. In: Text summarization branches out, pp. 74–81 (2004)
14. Chao, Y.R.: A Grammar of spoken Chinese. ERIC (1965)
15. Zhou,K.G., et al.: Corpus construction for Chinese zero anaphora from discourse perspective. J. Softw. **32**(12), 3782–3801 (2021)
16. Duan, D.: The baseline/elaboration organization for the constructional meaning of Chinese Ellipsis Structures. Modern Chin. 464–475 (2022)
17. Shen, S.: Chinese zero-pronoun resolution based on pretrained language model. Inf. Commun. 41–43 (2020)
18. Chen, P.: Discourse Analysis of Chinese zero-form anaphora. Stud. Chin. Lang. **5**(3), 363–378 (1987)
19. Hou, M., Sun, J.J., et al.: Zero anaphora in Chinese and how to process it in Chinese-English MT. J. Chin. Inf. Process. 14–20 (2005)
20. Zheng.: A study on the nature and norm of elliptical sentences. Appl. Linguist. (1998)

Two-Layer Context-Enhanced Representation for Better Chinese Discourse Parsing

Qiang Zhu[1,2], Kedong Wang[1,2], and Fang Kong[1,2(✉)]

[1] Institute of Artificial Intelligence, Soochow University, Suzhou, China
{qzhu,kdwang1011}@stu.suda.edu.cn
[2] School of Computer Science and Technology, Soochow University, Suzhou, China
kongfang@suda.edu.cn

Abstract. As a fundamental task of Natural Language Processing (NLP), discourse parsing has attracted more and more attention in the past decade. Previous studies mainly focus on tree construction, while for the EDU representation, most researchers just conduct a simple flat word-level representation. Structural information within EDU and relationships between EDUs, especially between non-adjacent EDUs, are largely ignored. In this paper, we propose a two-layer enhanced representation approach to better model the context of EDUs. For the bottom layer (i.e., intra-EDU), we use Graph Convolutional Network (GCN) to continuously update the representation of words according to existing dependency paths from the root to the leaves. For the upper layer (i.e., inter-EDU), we use Star-Transformer to connect non-adjacent EDUs by the delay node and thus incorporate global information. Experimental results on the CDTB corpus show that the proposed two-layer context-enhanced representation can contribute much to Chinese discourse parsing in neural architecture.

Keywords: Discourse parsing · GCN · Star-transformer

1 Introduction

Discourse parsing, one of the fundamental document-level natural language processing tasks, refers to representing each document with a hierarchical discourse tree(DT). It is beneficial for text understanding and provides structural information for down-stream tasks, such as text categorization [18], summarization [5] and so on.

Rhetorical Structure Theory(RST) [14] is the main linguistic theory in the field of Discourse Rhetorical Structure(DRS) parsing. As illustrated in Fig. 1, the Elementary Discourse Units(EDUs), which is leaf nodes in the DT, are recursively combined until to form a constituent tree, where the internal nodes represent the nuclearity and rhetorical relations between its child nodes. The

© The Author(s), under exclusive license to Springer Nature Switzerland AG 2022
W. Lu et al. (Eds.): NLPCC 2022, LNAI 13551, pp. 43–54, 2022.
https://doi.org/10.1007/978-3-031-17120-8_4

nuclearity relations include *nucleus*(N) and *satellite*(S), in which the *nucleus* plays a leading role in semantic representation in comparison with the *satellite*.

With the release of Chinese Connective-driven Discourse Treebank(CDTB) [12], many researches have been conducted. Related work mainly focuses on two aspects, i.e., EDU segmentation, correctly splitting one text into multiple EDUs, and DT construction, parsing a given text into a DT using gold EDUs.

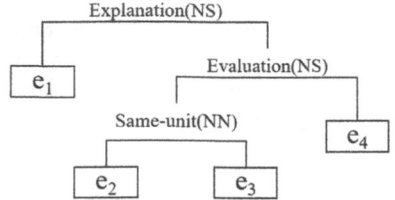

[e₁:湖北省建始县建成中国南方最大的日本落叶松人工林速生丰产林基地。/Jianshi County, Hubei Province, built the largest Japanese larch plantation fast-growing and high-yield forest base in southern China.]
[e2:目前，建始已拥有日本落叶松基地一万多公顷，/At present, Jianshi already owns more than 10,000 hectares of Japanese larch base,]
[e3:活立木蓄积量达到了三十万立方米。/and the stock of standing timber has reached 300,000 cubic meters.]
[e4:专家们认为，建始县在海拔一千二百米至二千多米区间内人工栽培日本落叶松的成功，为中国建设工业用材林基地提供了有益的经验。/Experts believe that the success of the artificial cultivation of Japanese larch in the range of 1,200 meters to more than 2,000 meters in Jianshi County has provided useful experience for China's construction of an industrial timber forest base.]

Fig. 1. An example of Chinese Discourse Rhetorical Tree.

In this paper, using the transition-based bottom-up framework as the backbone model, we mainly focus on the impact of more effective context representation on DT construction. In particular, we propose a two-layer enhanced context representation approach. The bottom layer combines word-level dependency relations within EDUs, while the upper layer models EDU-level star topology relations more globally. Our main contributions in this work are summarized below:

- **Intra-EDU encoder with GCN:** In the word-level EDU encoder, we employ an additional Graph Convolutional Network(GCN) layer, following the RNN-based word-level context encoder, to incorporate the dependency structure information in the sentence.
- **Inter-EDU encoder based on Star-Transformer** [3]: Due to the preferential combination of adjacent EDUs in DRS parsing, we utilize Star-Transformer to encode each EDU with directly connected adjacent EDUs, and further update global information through the indirectly connected relay node.

2   Related Work

Previous studies on discourse parsing mainly focus on English and can be generally classified into three categories, i.e., probabilistic CKY-like approaches [2, 4, 7], transition-based approaches [17, 19] and top-down architectures [8, 13, 21].

Probabilistic CKY-like approaches normally exploit various kinds of lexical, syntactic and semantic features to compute the probability of the relation between EDUs, fill in the probabilistic table with relational probability scores between adjacent EDUs and then merge the two with highest probability score into larger EDU spans. In this way, the final constructed parsing tree is globally optimal but the score calculating operation is time-consuming. A great number of methods have been proposed to compute the probability scores, among which deep learning models achieve great success, such as recursive deep model [10] and attention-based hierarchical neural network [11].

By contrary, transition-based approaches deal with EDUs sequentially and orderly make SHIFT/REDUCE decisions in a greedy strategy to determine whether to merge the current two EDUs or not [17, 19]. Obviously, the greedy decision-making measure is locally optimal but temporal and spatial efficiency is greatly improved compared with CKY-like approaches. Until recently, top-down architectures for discourse parsing are proposed. [13] proposed a top-down sentence-level discourse parser based on Pointer Networks which operates in linear time. [8] compared the effectiveness of explicitly dividing the process into multiple levels with implicitly embedding boundary features (sentence and paragraph boundaries) for text-level discourse parsing. [21] casted discourse parsing as a recursive split point ranking task and constructed text-level DTs in a top-down fashion.

In comparison with English, previous studies on Chinese discourse parsing are much less. Representative work includes [6, 9, 16]. Kong and Zhou [9] propose a Chinese discourse parser with multiple components in a pipeline architecture. In particular, their parser adopts a greedy bottom-up approach to generate the discourse parse trees. Jia et al. [6] propose a transition-based discourse parser in a two-step fashion with different feature representations to characterize intra- and inter- sentential discourse structures. Sun et al. [16] propose a complete transition-based Chinese discourse structure generation framework to build up bare tree structure along with nuclearity classification but didn't label internal discourse relations.

In this paper, our Chinese discourse parser employs the traditional shift-reduce method as the basic framework, but pays more attention to the representation of EDU-related context. Specifically, we propose a two-layer enhanced context representation combining both intra- and inter- EDU contexts. Experiment results show our enhanced representation is far more effective for upper-level discourse parsing.

3 Model

In this section, we firstly give a brief introduction of the basic principles of the traditional transition-based bottom-up approach, which is employed as our baseline system. Then we introduce the complete model in detail, which consists of two parts, i.e., the two-layer enhanced context encoder and the SPINN decoder.

3.1 Basic Principles of Transition-Based Approach

A shift-reduce discourse parser, which contains an auxiliary stack and queue. Initially, the queue stores all encoded EDUs in left-to-right order, while the stack is empty. The stack is designed to hold partially generated subtrees and the queue is employed to store unprocessed EDUs, until the queue is empty and the stack contains only one element which represents the whole text. At each time step, it can execute one of the transition actions as defined below:

- SHIFT: Pop the top element of the queue and push it onto the stack.
- REDUCE-Nuc-Rel: Pop the top two elements of the stack, form a subtree and push it onto the stack again. In this action, *Nuc* and *Rel* denote the nuclearity and rhetorical relations for the subtree respectively.

3.2 Bottom Layer of Enhanced Context Representation: Intra-EDU Encoder with GCN

For a given document $D = \{s_1, s_2, \dots, s_n\}$, consisting of n sentences. For ith sentence s_i, it contains one or several EDUs, where $E = \{w_1, w_2, ..., w_m\}$, m means the number of words in the current EDU.

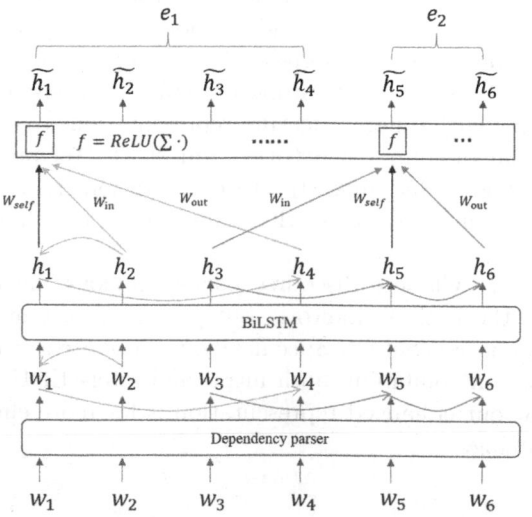

Fig. 2. Intra-EDU encoder with GCN.

In this phase, we first process a series of sentences and obtain the dependency structure through the syntax parser. As illustrated in Fig. 2, for a given sentence which consists of two EDUs, we concatenate each word and the POS embedding as inputs to the bi-directional LSTM network, to obtain the contextual representation for each word based on the flat text as Eq. 1. After encoding each word by the RNN-based encoder, we get the sequence of encoded words $W = \{h_1, h_2, ..., h_m\}$, which is further fed into a GCN-based encoder for EDU-level contextual representation based on dependency structure information.

For the GCN-based encoder layer, the sentence first goes through the syntactic parser to get the dependency graph structure $G = (V, E)$, where V represents all word nodes and E indicates the dependency relationship. As shown in Eq. 2, h_i^k represents the output of the i-th token in the k-th layer GCN network, where $c(v_i)$ returns the node connected to v_i and $l_{(v_i, vj)}$ denotes the type of edge between these two nodes. We refer to the previous practice, which only considers the direction of the edge in the dependency structure and ignores the type of relationship, noting them as IN and OUT respectively. In addition, we add $SELF$ edge that points to itself for each word. Finally, we obtain all word representations that incorporate structural information, and for words belonging to different EDUs we average the token vectors as Fig. 2.

$$h_1, h_2, ..., h_m = BiLSTM(w_1, w_2, ..., w_m) \tag{1}$$

$$h_i^k = ReLU(\sum_{v_j \in c(v_i)} (W_{l(v_i, v_j)} h_j^{k-1} + b_{l(v_i, v_j)})) \tag{2}$$

3.3 Upper Layer of Enhanced Context Representation: Inter-EDU Encoder with Star-Transformer

After obtaining the feature representation $E = \{e_1, e_2, ..., e_m\}$ with intra-EDU encoder, we utilize the Star-Transformer as the EDU-level context encoder. For the DRS parsing task, EDUs are preferentially combined with adjacent EDUs to form subtrees, so it is of great significance to take the influence of adjacent nodes into account while looking at the overall document.

Star-Transformer Encoder. Star-Transformer applies a topological structure with a relay node and n satellite nodes. As shown in Fig. 3, compared to the fully-connected Transformer, Star-Transformer eliminates redundant connections instead of a relay node, which is able to incorporate global information that is beneficial to the tree structure construction based on non-adjacent nodes. The state of j-th satellite node represents the feature of the j-th EDU in the document, each satellite node is initially a vector from the previous GCN-based encoding layer, and the relay node is initialized to the average of all tokens.

At each time step, it follows a cyclic updating method, the complete update process is shown in Eq. 3–Eq. 4, in which status update of satellite nodes based on its neighbor nodes, containing three nodes from the previous round e_{t-1}^{i-1}, e_{t-1}^i

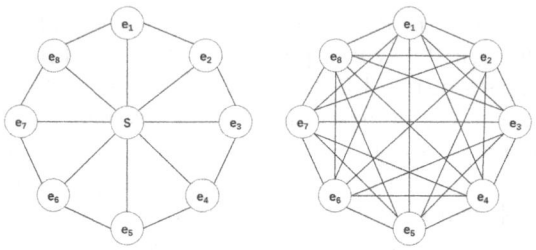

Fig. 3. Star-Transformer(left) and Transformer(right).

and e_{t-1}^{i+1}, the current processing node e_i and the relay node s^{t-1} from previous round.

$$C_i^t = \left[e_{t-1}^{i-1}; e_{t-1}^i; e_{t-1}^{i+1}; e^i; s^{t-1}\right] \tag{3}$$

$$e_i^t = MulAtt(e_i^{t-1}, C_i^t, C_i^t) \tag{4}$$

Relay node is updated by all satellite nodes and its status in previous round, we present the update process in Eq. 5

$$s^t = MulAtt(s^{t-1}, [s^{t-1}; E^t], [s^{t-1}; E^t]) \tag{5}$$

3.4   SPINN-Based Decoder

In the shift-reduce parsing framework, we convert the DRS parsing task into transition action prediction task. During the training phase, we represent the state of each step based on SPINN [1] (Stack-augmented Parser-Interpreter Neural Network), which contains the auxiliary stack, queue and the tracking LSTM. At each time step, we take the top two elements of the stack together with the first element of the queue and concatenate these three vectors as the current input. Then we get the calculation results in the tracking LSTM as input in MLPs to predict the next transition action as Eq. 6–Eq. 8, in which; denotes the concatenate operation, and p_{t+1} is the predicted probability of the next transition action, we take the one with the highest probability for the next time step.

$$h_t^{tracking} = LSTM(s_{-2}; s_{-1}; q_1) \tag{6}$$

$$h_t^{mlp} = Relu(W_{mlp}h_t^{tracking} + b_{mlp}) \tag{7}$$

$$p_{t+1} = softmax(h_t^{mlp}) \tag{8}$$

3.5   Training Loss

For a discourse tree containing n EDUs can be constructed with $2n-1$ transition actions, Eq. 9 defines the Cross-Entropy loss function we used in the training phase. Additionally, we employ L2-norm to prevent over-fitting and adopt the Adam for the optimization of learnable parameters in the model.

$$L = \frac{1}{2n-1} \sum_{t=0,\ldots,2n-2} -logp_{t+1}^{o(ct)} + \lambda \left\| \Theta \right\|_2 s \qquad (9)$$

4   Experiments

In order to compare with previous work fairly and mainly focus on the impact of our two-layer enhanced context representation approach, we firstly discuss the results using the same static word embedding as Sun et al. [16]. Then, considering the outstanding performance of the pre-trained language model in various natural language processing tasks, we also adopt the BERT-based dynamic word embedding model for further comparison.

4.1   Experimental Settings

Dataset. Following previous studies, we conduct our experiments on the Chinese CDTB corpus [12]. The Chinese CDTB corpus is annotated under the guidance of the English RST-DT and the PDTB corpus, containing 500 newswire articles in total. Different from the English RST-DT corpus where the whole document is labeled as rhetorical tree structure, the Chinese CDTB corpus is annotated in paragraphs, called Connective-driven Discourse Tree(CDT). Then a total of 2336 valid paragraph trees are included, which further divided into 2002 CDTs for training, 105 CDTs for validation and 229 CDTs for testing respectively.

Evaluation Metrics. To better demonstrate the effectiveness of the proposed scheme in this work, we adopt the strict macro averaged F_1[1] as previous studies [16,20], including the bare tree structure denoted as *Span*, tree structure labeled with nuclearity denoted as *Nuc*, tree structure labeled with 16 fine-grained rhetorical relations denoted as *Rel*, and tree structure labeled with both nuclearity and rhetorical relations denoted as *Full* respectively.

---

[1] Sun and Kong [16] proposed the strict macro averaged F_1 for Chinese discourse parsing, in which they first calculate the F_1 value for each CDT and then average the F_1 values for all CDTs. Meanwhile, the correct determination of each internal node is more strict, not only the left and right boundaries are correctly recognized but also the split point for its childs is correct.

Hyper Parameters. For static word representation, we utilize 300D vectors provided by [15] (Qiu-W2V), and we use LTP parser[2] for word segmentation and dependency structure, while the POS embedding is randomly initialized and optimized during the training process. We further adopt BERT as dynamic contexual embedding for comparison experiments. Table 1 shows all hyper-parameters in this work, and all experiments are conducted based on Pytorch 0.4.1 by GeForce RTX 2080ti GPU.

Table 1. Hyper-parameters

Parameter	Value	Parameter	Value
Epoch	20	Intra-EDU encoder	256
Batch size	32	Star-Transformer	512
Learning rate	1e−3	Tracking LSTM	256
Learning rate of BERT	1e−5	Dropout	0.33

4.2 Overall Experimental Results

In this work, we conduct all experiments on the CDTB corpus, and use the same evaluation metrics for fair comparison, from the results shown in Table 2, we can draw the following conclusions:

Table 2. Experimental results on CDTB(F_1)

Model	Span	Nuc	Rel	Full
Baseline(Qiu-W2V)	83.2	54.4	48.9	46.1
+GCN	83.5	54.8	49.8	47.0
+Transformer	84.2	55.3	49.2	46.5
+Star-Transformer	84.0	56.3	49.6	47.6
+GCN&Star-Transformer	**85.3**	**60.1**	**54.8**	**50.5**
Baseline(Bert)	84.1	60.1	53.6	49.3
+Star-Transformer	**86.0**	**61.9**	**54.3**	**51.2**

- As shown in the first row of Table 2, we first show the detailed performance of our duplicated shift-reduce parser. After the release of the CDTB corpus, Sun et al. [16] conducted the first experiment in transition-based system

---

[2] http://www.ltp-cloud.com/.

for Chinese discourse parsing, however, they only focus on structure generation and nuclearity determination, ignoring the relation classification. We duplicate their work and report all the metrics. In this paper, all subsequent experiments are conducted based on this baseline.

- After incorporating structural information with GCN to enhance intra-EDU representation, can effectively improve the performance of DRS parsing in all the metrics in comparison with our baseline. This indicates that enhanced EDU representation can improve the performance of discourse parsing. But the overall improvement is limited, we further explore the effect of inter-EDU encoder.
- We first employ Transformer as EDU-level encoder, which is a powerful global contextual information extractor and widely used in many natural language processing tasks. Taking the fully-connected Transformer improves the tree structure by 1%, but it doesn't work too well in relation classification, even drops by 0.6% in *Rel* and 0.5% in *Full* respectively in comparison with the GCN-based enhancement method.
- When Star-Transformer is adopted as inter-EDU encoder, compared with baseline, achieving 0.8%, 1.9%, 0.7% and 1.5% improvement in the above metrics respectively. Compared to the model in second row, an additional 0.5% improvement in structure is achieved with Star-Transformer as EDU-level context encoder. However, there was a 0.2% drop in rhetorical relation classification. In the Chinese CDTB corpus, including 16 fine-grained rthetorical relations, due to data sparsity problem, EDU-enhanced methods incorporating internal information are more effective for local relationship classification, while the tree structure generation is based on the entire document and can be further improved with a well-designed inter-EDU encoder.
- Moreover, to clarify the effectiveness of the two-layer enhanced context representation, we combine the two encoders simultaneously, the performance on all the evaluation metrics is further improved.

In the past few years, BERT has achieved state-of-the-art performance in many tasks, which is pre-trained based on large-scale corpus, providing dynamic word embeddings. Since BERT-BASE-CHINESE is based on character granularity, the GCN model based on word segmentation cannot be incorporated in this experiment, as shown in the bottom two lines of Table 2, compared with the previous benchmark model, significant improvement is achieved after adopting dynamic word embedding. However, the improvement on *Span* is limited by the lack of inter-EDU encoder. The last row of experimental results in Table 2 also verifies the effectiveness of Star-Transformer adopted in this work.

4.3   Compared with Other Parsing Framework

The comparison results with the top-down parsing framework are shown in Table 3, where we borrow the updated results with the strict macro evaluation metrics from [20]. In comparison with the top-down parsing approach, previous

Table 3. Performance comparison with the top-down parsing framework (The sign * means the duplicated bottom-up model from [16], and † denotes the updated top-down results we borrow from [20])

Model	Span	Nuc	Rel	Full
Bottom-up*	83.2	54.4	48.9	46.1
Top-down†	84.0	59.0	54.2	47.8
Ours(Qiu-W2V)	**85.3**	**60.1**	**54.8**	**50.5**

transition-based model has poor performance on all the evaluation metrics due to local decision-making.

After adding the two-layer enhanced context encoder, it can effectively solve the problems in the original bottom-up model. Furthermore, our final parser achieves comparable performance in *Rel* and much better results on the other three indicators. In the bottom-up parsing framework, experimental results suggest that:

- Intra-EDU representation enhancement methods incorporating structural information with GCN can effectively improve the accuracy of relation classification.
- Strong encoders that incorporate rich contextual information between EDUs are significant for global structure resolution, such as Transformer and Star-Transfomer. However, in the DRS parsing task, due to the nature of combining EDU with adjacent nodes, using Star-Transformer as an inter-EDU encoder allows us to pay more attention to neighboring EDUs while focusing on the overall structure information through the relay node.

Experimental results on the CDTB corpus show that, in comparison with baseline system, our proposed approach can better represent context and thus improve the performance of DT construction. Specifically, the bottom layer combining word-level dependency relations within EDUs can improve the performance of nuclearity and rthetorical relation labeling, while the upper layer combining EDU-level star topology relations can improve the DT construction.

5 Conclusion

In this paper, we propose a two-layer enhanced context representation approach, i.e., a GCN-based intra-EDU encoder incorporating dependency structure, and a Star-transformer based inter-EDU encoder. Experiments on the Chinese CDTB corpus show that our proposed approach can improve the performance of Chinese discourse parsing. In the future work, we will focus on data augmentation methods to extend the limited data, and joint learning methods for better representation.

Acknowledgements. The authors would like to thank the anonymous reviewers for the helpful comments. This work was supported by Projects 61876118 under the National Natural Science Foundation of China, the National Key R&D Program of China under Grant No. 2020AAA0108600 and the Priority Academic Program Development of Jiangsu Higher Education Institutions.

References

1. Bowman, S.R., Gauthier, J., Rastogi, A., Gupta, R., Manning, C.D., Potts, C.: A fast unified model for parsing and sentence understanding. In: Proceedings of the 54th Annual Meeting of the Association for Computational Linguistics, ACL 2016, 7–12 August, 2016, Berlin, Germany, Volume 1: Long Papers. The Association for Computer Linguistics (2016). https://doi.org/10.18653/v1/p16-1139

2. Feng, V.W., Hirst, G.: A linear-time bottom-up discourse parser with constraints and post-editing. In: Proceedings of the 52nd Annual Meeting of the Association for Computational Linguistics, ACL 2014, 22–27 June 2014, Baltimore, MD, USA, Volume 1: Long Papers, pp. 511–521. The Association for Computer Linguistics (2014). https://doi.org/10.3115/v1/p14-1048

3. Guo, Q., Qiu, X., Liu, P., Shao, Y., Xue, X., Zhang, Z.: Star-transformer. In: Burstein, J., Doran, C., Solorio, T. (eds.) Proceedings of the 2019 Conference of the North American Chapter of the Association for Computational Linguistics: Human Language Technologies, NAACL-HLT 2019, Minneapolis, MN, USA, 2–7 June 2019, Volume 1 (Long and Short Papers), pp. 1315–1325. Association for Computational Linguistics (2019). https://doi.org/10.18653/v1/n19-1133

4. Hernault, H., Prendinger, H., duVerle, D.A., Ishizuka, M.: HILDA: a discourse parser using support vector machine classification. Dialogue Discourse **1**(3), 1–33 (2010). http://dad.uni-bielefeld.de/index.php/dad/article/view/591

5. Ji, Y., Smith, N.A.: Neural discourse structure for text categorization. In: Barzilay, R., Kan, M. (eds.) Proceedings of the 55th Annual Meeting of the Association for Computational Linguistics, ACL 2017, Vancouver, Canada, 30 July–4 August, Volume 1: Long Papers, pp. 996–1005. Association for Computational Linguistics (2017). https://doi.org/10.18653/v1/P17-1092

6. Jia, Y., Feng, Y., Yuan, Y., Chao, L., Shi, C., Zhao, D.: Improved discourse parsing with two-step neural transition-based model. ACM Trans. Asian Low-Resource Lang. Inf. Process. **17**(2), 1–21 (2018)

7. Joty, S., Carenini, G., Ng, R., Mehdad, Y.: Combining intra-and multi-sentential rhetorical parsing for document-level discourse analysis. In: Proceedings of the 51st Annual Meeting of the Association for Computational Linguistics (Volume 1: Long Papers), pp. 486–496 (2013)

8. Kobayashi, N., Hirao, T., Kamigaito, H., Okumura, M., Nagata, M.: Top-down RST parsing utilizing granularity levels in documents. In: Proceedings of the AAAI Conference on Artificial Intelligence, vol. 34(05), 8099–8106, April 2020

9. Kong, F., Zhou, G.: A CDT-styled end-to-end Chinese discourse parser. ACM Trans. Asian Low-Resour. Lang. Inf. Process. **16**(4), 26:1–26:17, July 2017. https://doi.org/10.1145/3099557

10. Li, J., Li, R., Hovy, E.: Recursive deep models for discourse parsing. In: Proceedings of EMNLP 2014, pp. 2061–2069 (2014)

11. Li, Q., Li, T., Chang, B.: Discourse parsing with attention-based hierarchical neural networks. In: Proceedings of EMNLP 2016, pp. 362–371 (2016)

12. Li, Y., Feng, W., Jing, S., Fang, K., Zhou, G.: Building Chinese discourse corpus with connective-driven dependency tree structure. In: Conference on Empirical Methods in Natural Language Processing (2014)
13. Lin, X., Joty, S.R., Jwalapuram, P., Bari, S.: A unified linear-time framework for sentence-level discourse parsing. CoRR abs/1905.05682 (2019). http://arxiv.org/abs/1905.05682
14. Mann, W.C., Thompson, S.A.: Rhetorical structure theory: toward a functional theory of text organization. Text **8**(3), 243–281 (1988)
15. Qiu, Y., Li, H., Li, S., Jiang, Y., Hu, R., Yang, L.: Revisiting correlations between intrinsic and extrinsic evaluations of word embeddings. In: Sun, M., Liu, T., Wang, X., Liu, Z., Liu, Y. (eds.) Chinese Computational Linguistics and Natural Language Processing Based on Naturally Annotated Big Data - 17th China National Conference, CCL 2018, and 6th International Symposium, NLP-NABD 2018, Changsha, China, 19–21 October 2018, Proceedings. Lecture Notes in Computer Science, vol. 11221, pp. 209–221. Springer (2018). https://doi.org/10.1007/978-3-030-01716-3_18
16. Sun, C., Kong, F.: A transition-based framework for Chinese discourse structure parsing. J. Chin. Inf. Process. **32**(12), 26–34 (2018)
17. Wang, Y., Li, S., Wang, H.: A two-stage parsing method for text-level discourse analysis. In: Barzilay, R., Kan, M. (eds.) Proceedings of the 55th Annual Meeting of the Association for Computational Linguistics, ACL 2017, Vancouver, Canada, 30 July–4 August, Volume 2: Short Papers, pp. 184–188. Association for Computational Linguistics (2017). https://doi.org/10.18653/v1/P17-2029
18. Xu, J., Gan, Z., Cheng, Y., Liu, J.: Discourse-aware neural extractive text summarization. In: Jurafsky, D., Chai, J., Schluter, N., Tetreault, J.R. (eds.) Proceedings of the 58th Annual Meeting of the Association for Computational Linguistics, ACL 2020, Online, 5–10 July 2020, pp. 5021–5031. Association for Computational Linguistics (2020). https://doi.org/10.18653/v1/2020.acl-main.451
19. Yu, N., Zhang, M., Fu, G.: Transition-based neural RST parsing with implicit syntax features. In: Bender, E.M., Derczynski, L., Isabelle, P. (eds.) Proceedings of the 27th International Conference on Computational Linguistics, COLING 2018, 20–26 August 2018, Santa Fe, New Mexico, USA, pp. 559–570. Association for Computational Linguistics (2018). https://aclanthology.org/C18-1047/
20. Zhang, L., Kong, F., Zhou, G.: Adversarial learning for discourse rhetorical structure parsing. In: Zong, C., Xia, F., Li, W., Navigli, R. (eds.) Proceedings of the 59th Annual Meeting of the Association for Computational Linguistics and the 11th International Joint Conference on Natural Language Processing, ACL/IJCNLP 2021, (Volume 1: Long Papers), Virtual Event, 1–6 August 2021, pp. 3946–3957. Association for Computational Linguistics (2021). https://doi.org/10.18653/v1/2021.acl-long.305
21. Zhang, L., Xing, Y., Kong, F., Li, P., Zhou, G.: A top-down neural architecture towards text-level parsing of discourse rhetorical structure. In: Jurafsky, D., Chai, J., Schluter, N., Tetreault, J.R. (eds.) Proceedings of the 58th Annual Meeting of the Association for Computational Linguistics, ACL 2020, Online, 5–10 July 2020, pp. 6386–6395. Association for Computational Linguistics (2020). https://doi.org/10.18653/v1/2020.acl-main.569

How Effective and Robust is Sentence-Level Data Augmentation for Named Entity Recognition?

Runmin Jiang[1,2], Xin Zhang[3], Jiyue Jiang[4], Wei Li[1(✉)], and Yuhao Wang[1,2(✉)]

[1] School of Information and Engineering, Nanchang University, Jiangxi, China
rmjiang@email.ncu.edu.cn, {liwei.cs,wangyuhao}@ncu.edu.cn
[2] Industrial Institute of Artificial Intelligence, Nanchang University, Jiangxi, China
[3] College of Computer and Cyber Security, Fujian Normal University, Fujian, China
[4] Department of Computer Science, The University of Hong Kong, Hong Kong SAR, China
jiangjy@connect.hku.hk

Abstract. Data augmentation is a simple but effective way to improve the effectiveness and the robustness of pre-trained models. However, they are difficult to adapt to token-level tasks such as named entity recognition (NER) because of the different semantic granularity and more fine-grained labels. Inspired by some mixup augmentations in computer vision, we proposed three sentence-level data augmentations including CMix, CombiMix, TextMosaic, and adapted them to the NER task. Through empirical experiments on three authoritative datasets (OntoNotes4, CoNLL-03, OntoNotes5), we found that these methods will improve the effectiveness of the models if controlling the number of augmented samples. Strikingly, the results show our approaches can greatly improve the robustness of the pre-trained model even over strong baselines and token-level data augmentations. We achieved state-of-the-art (SOTA) in the robustness evaluation of the CCIR CUP 2021. The code is available at https://github.com/jrmjrm01/SenDA4 NER-NLPCC2022.

Keywords: Sentence-level data augmentation · Named entity recognition · Effectiveness · Robustness

1 Introduction

As a classic research topic, Named Entity Recognition (NER) is commonly adopted in the field of Natural Language Processing (NLP) [1]. It is known to all that the high performance of the NER task depends on the size and quality of the effective and robust pre-trained model [2]. At the same time, NER models have seen significant improvement in their performance with the recent advances of pre-trained language models [3], yet obtaining massive and diverse labeled data is often expensive and time-consuming [4]. Even if a large annotated corpus has already been obtained beforehand, it will inevitably have rare entities that do not appear enough to train the model to recognize them accurately in the text [5]. Therefore, the data augmentation method for NER is crucially significant [6].

W. Lu et al. (Eds.): NLPCC 2022, LNAI 13551, pp. 55–66, 2022.
https://doi.org/10.1007/978-3-031-17120-8_5

Previous work has studied lot of data augmentations for sentence-level tasks such as text classification.[4, 7–9, 21] However, because of the different semantic granularity and more fine-grained labels, they are difficult to adapt to tasks for token-level classification such as named entity recognition. Besides, the big models are often brittle to adversarial examples because of the overfitting, resulting in bad robustness for the NER tasks. [10] Dai & Adel [11] implemented research that mainly paid their attention to the simple data augmentation methods and adapted them to NER, but lack of research on data augmetation at the sentence level. Some studies have explored the impact of mixup augmentation on robustness evaluation, but lack of more variant methods and its impact on effectiveness for pre-trained model [10, 12].

To facilitate research in this direction, inspired by the Cutmix [13], Augmix [14], and Mosaic [15] augmentation methods in computer vision, we proposed three sentence-level data augmentation methods for named entity recognition including CMix, CombiMix, TextMosaic. We conducted empirical experiments on three authoritative datasets comparing our proposed method with a strong baseline (no data augmentations) and mentioned replacement (MR) which is one of the representative token-level data augmentations [11]. We find that the data augmentation methods may not necessarily improve the effectiveness of the models. However, our proposed methods are always better than the token-level method both in effectiveness and robustness. If controlling the number of augmented samples, these methods will enhance the performance of the pre-trained models. The results also show that our approaches can greatly improve the robustness of the pre-trained model even over strong baselines, and we achieved SOTA in the robustness evaluation of the CCIR CUP 2021. We release our code at https://github.com/jrm jrm01/SenDA4NER-NLPCC2022.

2   Methodology

2.1   CMix

The core idea of CMix method is that we need to randomly select a group of data from the replacement sentence source and randomly replace any group of data from the target sentence source. Before using the CMix method, there are two sentence sources, one is the target sentence source, and the other is the replacement sentence source. When randomly cutting the data from the replacement sentence source, the data from the replacement sentence source is replaced with the data from the target sentence source in a random mixing ratio of 0% to 50%, and so on for each target sentence source. However, at most 50% of the data in the target sentence source will be randomly replaced with the data in the replacement sentence source.

Algorithm1 CMix
1:**Input:** The original texts and tags
2: **function** Cmix(sentences, tags):
3:     **for** pair = 0 to pair < len(sentences) by pair++ **do**
4:         choose the reasonable data and range randomly
5:         calculate the values new_sent and new_tag for this round of replacement
6:     **end for**
7:     extend sentences and tags to the end of empty lists new_sents and new_tags
8:     mess up pair of new_sents and new_tags randomly
9: **return** new_sents, new_tags
10: **end function**
11: **Output:** The scrambled pairs of new_sents and new_tags values

2.2 CombiMix

The core idea of CombiMix method is to perform different data argument methods on samples and fuse them so as to achieve the effect of data argument. This approach also requires two sentence sources, the target sentence source and the replacement sentence source. CombiMix mainly applies to two data argument methods [11], mention replacement (MR) and label-wise Token replacement (LwTR). MR uses the binomial distribution to decide whether to replace the mentions of the target sentence source. If replacement is required, the mentions in the replacement sentence source are used to replace the mentions of the target sentence source and required to be of the same label. LwTR uses binomial distribution to determine whether each word of the target sentence source is replaced or not. If replacement is needed, a word with the same label in the replacement sentence source is randomly selected for replacement and the original label sequence remains unchanged. Finally, we fuse the data set processed by MR, and the data set processed by LwTR and the original data set form the final data set of CombiMix.

Algorithm2 CombiMix
1: **Input:** The original texts, tags and tag_scheme; ratios MR_ratio and LwTR_ratio
2: **function** CombiMix(sentences, tags, tagScheme, MR_ratio, LwTR_ratio):
3:     convert tags from sequences to spans
4:     **while** sp_id < len(sentences) **do**
5:         replace the entity, text, tag according to MR_ratio
6:         extend cur_sent and cur_tag to the end of new_sents and new_tags
7:     **end while**
8:     **for** pair = 0 to pair < len(sentences) by pair++ **do**
9:         choose texts and tags randomly according to LwTR_ratio
10:         extend lwtr_sent and lwtr_tag to the end of lwtr_sents and lwtr_tags
11:     **end for**
12:     extend new_sents, lwtr_sents, texts to the end of mix_sents
13:     extend new_tags. lwtr_tags, tags to the end of mix_tags
14:     **return** function Combimix
15: **end function**
16: **Output:** The function itself and the augment data of the CombiMix method

2.3 TextMosaic

In this section, the method of TextMosaic will be introduced in detail. This method consists of three approaches including *span sampling*, *random sampling* and *over-sampling* respectively, which can use sentence-level contexts and help train a more effective and robust NER model.

Span Sampling. It is kind of method to allow training data to be sampled across one or more sentences to obtain richer training accuracy, as illustrated in Fig. 1. By randomly selecting head and sampling length, the truncated parts of one or more sentences are obtained to form a new sentence. Generally speaking, there will be a logical association between the upper and lower sentences, especially the end of the upper sentence and the beginning of the next sentence.

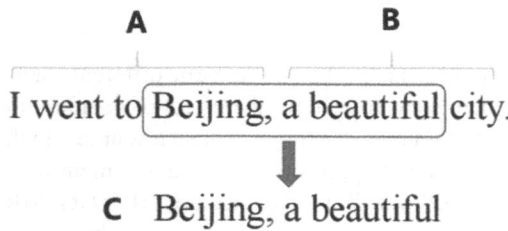

Fig. 1. The schematic diagram of span sampling. For example, sentence B is the next sentence of A, we might sample the word sequence C from the two sentences.

Random Sampling. The method refers to randomly extracting two or more data fragments from the original data and recombining them into new sentences for training, as shown in Fig. 2. By randomly sampling some fragments in different sentences, new sentences can be recombined for training. Due to certain entities can be accurately identified under common sense without much attention to contexts, thus, by superimposing multiple fragments, the diversity of textual information can be enhanced significantly. In addition, it should be noted that when randomly intercepting fragments, the interception position is generally three to five tokens before the start tag of an entity.

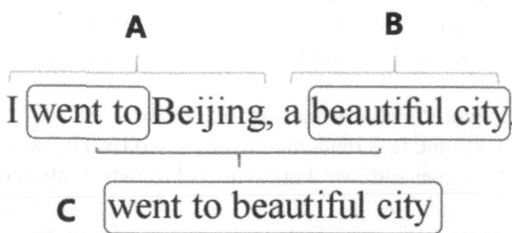

Fig. 2. The schematic diagram of random sampling. In above, the trained word sequence was sampled with two or several word sequence pieces. For example, the word sequence of C was sampled from the two sentences of A and B.

Over-Sampling. To solve the problem of uneven distribution of data labels, as shown in Fig. 3. We use the sliding window to amplify the data, which can be regarded as the process of sieving. The sliding window sampling is performed on the original context according to the specific steps. On the one hand, the position encoding of BERT is obtained by learning, so that the texts sampled by the sliding window do not overlap because of different positions. On the other hand, the specific step is obtained by sliding window sampling, which reduces the operational steps of filling and optimizes the training process of the model.

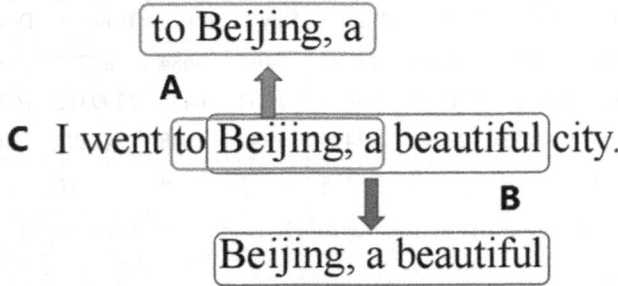

Fig. 3. The schematic diagram of over-sampling. For example, the word sequence A was sampled from the total sentence C, and with one step shifted, the word sequence B was sampled from the total sequence above.

3 Experiment

This section first introduces three authoritative NER datasets and their post-attack dataset by TextFlint [16] in Sect. 3.1, and then shows the experimental setup in Sect. 3.2. We present main results of the effectiveness evaluation in Sect. 3.3 and further explore how the augmented sample size influences the effectiveness of these methods in Sect. 3.4. The results show our method greatly improves the robustness of the pre-trained model even over strong baselines in Sect. 3.5. What's more, we participated in a NER Robustness Competition hosted by TexfFlint, where our approach achieved state-of-the-art (SOTA) in CCIR Cup2021 in Sect. 3.6.

3.1 Datasets

In order to evaluate the effectiveness of our proposed approaches, we conduct experiments on three authoritative and popular NER datasets across two languages, including the OntoNotes4.0 Chinese dataset [17], OntoNotes5.0 English dataset [18], and CoNLL-03 English dataset [19]. We show descriptive statistics of these datasets in Table 1.

In order to evaluate the effectiveness of our proposed approaches, we conduct experiments on the above datasets that were attacked by TextFlint [16]. This includes many diverse methods of attack such as universal text transformation, adversarial attack, sub-population and their combinations. We combined the datasets of OntoNotes5.0 and CoNLL-03 mentioned above after being attacked by 20 different attack methods[1,2], and evaluate the robustness of our proposed methodology. The OntoNotes4.0 dataset after being attacked by TextFlint as a benchmark competition for the CCIR CUP 2021[3].

Table 1. The statistics of the adopted datasets.

	OntoNotes4			CoNLL-03			OntoNotes5		
	Train	Dev	Test	Train	Dev	Test	Train	Dev	Test
Sentence	15723	4300	4345	14897	3466	3684	82727	10507	10393
Tokens	491903	200505	208066	203621	51362	46435	1299312	163104	169579
Mentions	41203	20573	22918	23499	5942	5648	41203	20023	22918
Entity Types	4	4	4	4	4	4	18	18	18

3.2 Experimental Setup

Baseline. Named entity recognition can be modeled as a sequence-label task. The state-of-the-art sequence models consist of distributed representations for input, context encoder, and tag decoder [20]. We adopt the BERT model [3] as the backbone model for pre-training and decoded by linear layers, then fine-tuned on the NER dataset, as shown in Fig. 4. For the BERT embedding, we used the following Huggingface-pretrained BERT models: "bert-base-chinese"[4] for the Chinese dataset and "bert-base-uncased"[5] for the English dataset. In the baseline, we do not use any data augmentation methods and set the same hyperparameters and pipeline for the following experiment.

Token-level Augmentation. Current token-level data augmentations dedicated to named entity recognition are label-wise token replacement (LwTR), mention replacement(MR), and synonym replacement(SR). [11] We choose one of the *representative* token-level methods that is *MR* and compare three sentence-level data augmentations with it.

Training. To improve the convergence and robustness of the model, we use a bag of tricks [21] and select the optimal hyper-parameters as shown in Table 2. The gradient accumulation method can achieve a similar effect to a large batch size when the algorithm is limited. Therefore, the learning rate warm-up method is utilized to speed up the

---

[1] https://www.textflint.com/.
[2] https://github.com/CuteyThyme/Robustness_experiments.
[3] https://www.datafountain.cn/competitions/510/datasets.
[4] https://huggingface.co/bert-base-chinese.
[5] https://huggingface.co/bert-base-uncased.

convergence speed. In addition, using the encapsulated optimizer AdamW [22], each parameter can be given an independent learning rate, and the past gradient history can be taken into consideration as well. To alleviate the over-fitting problem, label smoothing and limiting the non-linear parameters are conducted to solve the dilemma of over-fitting. The method of multi-model ensemble stacking uses 3-fold cross-validation.

Table 2. The hyper-parameters of the experiment

Hyperparameter	Value
Learning rate	0.00024
Weight decay	5e–3
Batch size	8
Gradient accumulation	8(step)
Warmup	5(epoch)

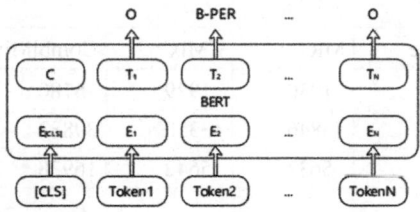

Fig. 4. The training model. BERT(backbone) + NER(head)

Metric. We adopted *span-based Micro F1* to measure the effectiveness and robustness except for CCIR Cup. The CCIR Cup used *span-based Macro F1* to evaluate the robustness.

3.3 Results of Effectiveness Evaluation

Table 3 shows the overall results of effectiveness evaluation on CoNLL-03, OntoNotes4, and OntoNotes5 datasets. However, we would also like to report a negative result, which does not apply to all datasets, such as OntoNotes4 and CoNLL-03, where the performance is reduced (except CMix) using data augmentation methods. However, at the same time, compared to MR, our proposed methods mostly outperform results, demonstrating that the sentence-level data augmentation methods are also relatively effective.

Table 3. Results of effectiveness evaluation

Dataset	Baseline	MR	CMix	CombiMix	TextMosaic
CoNLL-03	89.51	88.64	88.87	87.64	**89.07**
OntoNotes5	51.21	65.81	**67.21**	**66.18**	58.78
OntoNotes4	78.48	78.24	**78.78**	77.61	77.49

3.4 Study of the Sample Size After Data Augmentation

We counted the number of samples after data augmentation for the three training sets as shown in Table 4. MR and Cmix were twice as large as baseline, and CombiMix increased the number of samples three times as large as Cmix. The sample size for the TextMosaic(set sample length = 64) was the largest on OntoNotes4 and OntoNotes5.

Table 4. In OntoNotes4, CoNLL-03 and OntoNotes5 datasets, the data sample size after processing by five data argument methods

Datasets	Baseline	MR	CMix	CombiMix	TextMosaic
OntoNotes4	965	1930	1929	5780	7679
CoNLL-03	6893	13846	13350	39883	3175
OntoNotes5	2836	5632	5642	16938	20295

To further explore the effect of the number of samples and their distribution characteristics on the model performance after data enhancement, we take OntoNotes4 as an example and balance all samples to the same value with the following strategy.

- Baseline: Duplicate original samples three times to 3860 samples
- MR: Duplicate original samples one times to 3860 samples
- CMix: Duplicate original samples one times to 3860 samples
- CombiMix: Shuffle original samples and randomly select 3860 samples
- TextMosaic: Shuffle original samples and randomly select 3860 samples

Table 5 shows the change in F1 score before and after balancing the number of samples. We found that duplicate samples could also be used as a means of data enhancement. Although the number of duplicate samples did not change the characteristics of the data distribution, Baseline, CMix also improved by 1% compared to the previous one. In our analysis, it is possible that the data augmentation carries a large amount of irregular semantic information and noise, reducing the performance of the model. And thus the performance of the model is reduced, although it may be able to improve the robustness of the model.

Table 5. Compare the F1 score of the five data argument methods with the current F1 score before and after balancing the number of samples

	Baseline	MR	CMix	CombiMix	TextMosaic
No balanced F1	78.48	78.24	78.78	77.61	77.49
Balanced F1	79.22↑	78.24–	**79.35↑**	78.07↑	**79.37↑**

3.5 Results of Robustness Evaluation

The two datasets contain twenty transformations, such as word changes, back translations, contraction, extended sentences by irrelevant sentences, keyboard error and so on, as illustrated in Fig. 5 and Fig. 6. Table 6 shows overall results of robustness evaluation on CoNLL-03, and OntoNotes5 datasets that were attacked by TextFlint. On the one hand, the F1 of the model for both datasets dipped 7%–17% approximately. On the other hand, these methods can improve the robustness of the model, with both CombiMix and TextMosaic being higher than baseline and MR on CoNLL-03. On OntoNotes 5, all three sentence-level data augmentations show significant improvements over MR and Baseline, with the best results method CMix was 17% higher than strong baseline.

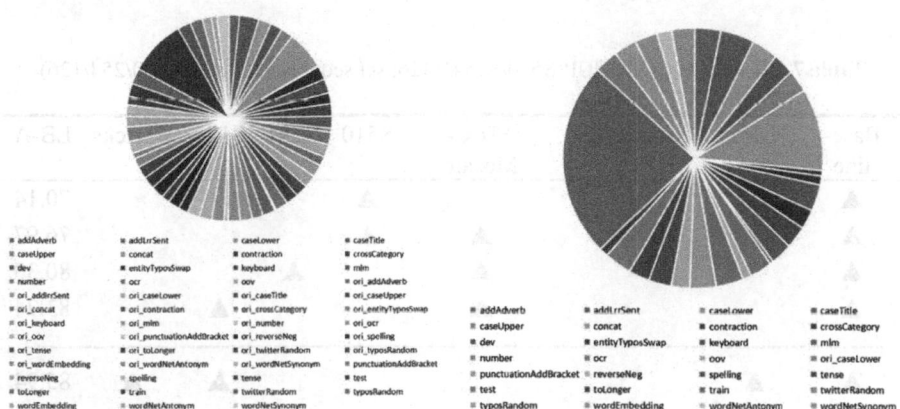

Fig. 5. CoNLL-03 data size distribution after attack by TextFlint

Fig. 6. OntoNotes5 data size distribution after attack by TextFlint

Table 6. Comparison of F1 score of five methods on robustness evaluation

Dataset	Baseline	MR	CMix	CombiMix	TextMosaic
CoNLL-03	83.28	82.73↓	82.74	**83.29↑**	**85.55↑**
OntoNotes5	43.38	52.96	**60.62↑**	56.61↑	54.12↑

3.6 Results of CCIR Cup

We participated in a robustness evaluation competition hosted by TextFlint in CCIR Cup 2021[6]. The validation sets and test sets used for the evaluation were generated by TextFlint after performing eleven forms of changes on OntoNotes4. The evaluation was divided into two phases, with LeaderBoard A (LB-A) focusing on contextual changes and LeaderBoard B(LB-B) combining more forms of contextual changes and entity changes. We test three proposed sentence-level augmentations and reported main results in Table 7. We achieved *first place* in both phases. In LB-A we got the highest F1 score with **85.99** which is 7.96 higher than the second place(F1 = 78.03), and in LB-B we got an F1 score to **76.54** which is 2.53 higher than second place(F1 = 74.01).

Different from the experiment setup, we use data augmentation methods before pre-training and semi-supervised learning in combination with out-of-domain dataset [23]. In our analysis, using generic data augmentation as a noise agent for the consistent training method may be a good choice.

Furthermore, we tested the length of the predicted sequence in model inference and found that the effect is best when the sequence length is 126. In our analysis, when the condition of the sequence length is too long, the long-distance dependence learning effect of the transformer is not good, resulting in poor model performance; Conversely, when the sequence length is too short, it is difficult to learn the semantic information of the entity context, resulting in poor NER performance.

Table 7. Results of CCIR CUP(S510/S254/S126: set sequence length = 510/254/126)

Base-line	+CMix	+CombiMix	+Text-Mosaic	S510	S254	S126	+Tricks	LB-A
▲				▲				70.14
▲			▲	▲				76.97
▲			▲		▲			80.30
▲			▲			▲		83.74
▲	▲					▲	▲	85.94
▲		▲				▲	▲	85.95
▲			▲			▲	▲	85.99

4 Conclusion

This research proposes three different strategies for sentence-level data augmentation for named entity recognition, which is a token-level task. Through experiments on three authoritative datasets, we find that the data augmentation methods may not necessarily

---

[6] https://ccir2021.dlufl.edu.cn/ccirContest/index.html.

improve the effectiveness of the models but controlling the number of augmented samples will enhances the performance of the pre-trained models to fit the feature distribution of the input contextual embeddings. The results also show that our approach can greatly improve the robustness of the pre-trained model even over strong baselines, and we achieved state-of-the-art (SOTA) in the CCIR CUP 2021.

Acknowledgement. This work was supported by the National Key Research and Development Project under Grant 2018YFB1404303, and 03 special project and 5G project of Jiangxi Province of China (Grant No.20203ABC03W08), and the National Natural Science Foundation of China under Grant 62061030 and 62106094, and the Natural Science Foundation of Zhejiang Province of China (Grant No.LQ20D010001). We would like to thank Xiangyu Shi for his contribution to the comparison experiment, and Professor Xipeng Qiu, Professor Xiangyang Xue, Professor Dongfeng Jia and Dr. Hang Yan for their guidance on this paper. Thanks to the reviewers for their hard work to help us improve the quality of this paper.

References

1. Li, J., Sun, A., Jianglei H., Li, C.: A survey on deep learning for named entity recognition. IEEE Trans. Knowl. Data Eng. **34**(1), 50-70 (2020a)
2. Wang, Y., et al.: Application of pre-training models in named entity recognition. In: 2020 12th International Conference on Intelligent Human-Machine Systems and Cybernetics (IHMSC), vol. 1. IEEE (2020)
3. Devlin, J., Chang, M.W., Lee, K., Toutanova, K.: BERT: pre-training of deep bidirectional transformers for language understanding. In: NAACL, pp. 4171–4186, Minneapolis, Minnesota (2019)
4. Wei, J, Zou, K. Eda: Easy data augmentation techniques for boosting performance on text classification tasks. arXiv preprint arXiv:1901.11196 (2019)
5. Fritzler, A., Logacheva, V., Kretov, M.: Few-shot classification in named entity recognition task. In: Proceedings of the 34th ACM/SIGAPP Symposium on Applied Computing, pp. 993-1000 (2019)
6. Feng, S.Y., Gangal, V., Wei, J., et al.: A survey of data augmentation approaches for nlp. arXiv preprint arXiv:2105.03075 (2021)
7. Karimi, A., et al.: AEDA: an easier data augmentation technique for text classification. In: EMNLP (2021)
8. Yoon, S., Kim, G., Park, K.: SSMix: Saliency-Based Span Mixup for Text Classification. ArXiv, abs/2106.08062 (2021)
9. Sun, L., et al.: Mixup-transformer: dynamic data augmentation for NLP tasks. Coling (2020)
10. Lin, B., Yuchen, J., et al.: RockNER: A simple method to create adversarial examples for evaluating the robustness of named entity recognition models. In: EMNLP (2021)
11. Dai, X., Adel, H.: An analysis of simple data augmentation for named entity recognition. ArXiv abs/2010.11683 (2020)
12. Si, C., et al.: Better robustness by more coverage: adversarial and mixup data augmentation for robust finetuning. In: Findings of the Association for Computational Linguistics: ACL-IJCNLP 2021, pp. 1569-1576 (2021)
13. Yun, S., Han, D., Oh, S.J., et al.: Cutmix: Regularization strategy to train strong classifiers with localizable features. In: Proceedings of the IEEE/CVF International Conference on Computer Vision, pp. 6023–6032 (2019)

14. Hendrycks, D., Mu, N., Cubuk, E.D., et al.: Augmix: A simple data processing method to improve robustness and uncertainty. arXiv preprint arXiv:1912.02781 (2019)
15. Bochkovskiy, A., Wang, C.Y., Liao, H.Y.M.: Yolov4: Optimal speed and accuracy of object detection. arXiv preprint arXiv:2004.10934 (2020)
16. Gui, T., et al.: TextFlint: unified multilingual robustness evaluation toolkit for natural language processing. ArXiv abs/2103.11441 (2021)
17. Weischedel, R., et al.: Ontonotes release 4.0. LDC2011T03, Philadelphia, Penn Linguist. Data Consortium (2011)
18. Pradhan, S.: Towards robust linguistic analysis using ontonotes. In Proceedings of the Seventeenth Conference on Computational Natural Language Learning, CoNLL 2013, Sofia, Bulgaria, 8–9 August 2013, pp. 143–152. ACL (2013)
19. Erik, F., Sang, T.K., De Meulder, F.: Introduction to the CoNLL-2003 shared task: language-independent named entity recognition. In Proceedings of the Seventh Conference on Natural Language Learning at HLT-NAACL 2003, pp. 142–147 (2003)
20. Li, J., Sun, A., Han, J., et al.: A survey on deep learning for named entity recognition. IEEE Trans. Knowl. Data Eng. **34**(1), 50–70 (2020)
21. Sun, C., Qiu, X., Xu, Y., Huang, X.: How to fine-tune bert for text classification? In: Sun, M., Huang, X., Ji, H., Liu, Z., Liu, Y. (eds.) CCL 2019. LNCS (LNAI), vol. 11856, pp. 194–206. Springer, Cham (2019). https://doi.org/10.1007/978-3-030-32381-3_16
22. Kingma, D.P., Ba, J.: Adam: A method for stochastic optimization. arXiv preprint arXiv:1412.6980 (2014)
23. Longpre, S. et al.: How Effective is Task-Agnostic Data Augmentation for Pretrained Transformers? Findings(2020)

Machine Translation
and Multilinguality (Oral)

Random Concatenation: A Simple Data Augmentation Method for Neural Machine Translation

Nini Xiao, Huaao Zhang, Chang Jin, and Xiangyu Duan[✉]

School of Computer Science and Technology, Soochow University, Suzhou, China
{nnxiaonnxiao,hazhang,cjin}@stu.suda.edu.cn, xiangyuduan@suda.edu.cn

Abstract. Neural machine translation system heavily depends on large-scale parallel corpus, which is not available for some low-resource languages, resulting in poor translation quality. To alleviate such data hungry problem, we present a high quality data augmentation method which merely utilize the given parallel corpus. Specifically, we propose to augment the low-resource parallel corpus with a language-mixed bitext, which is simply built by concatenating two sentences in different languages. Furthermore, our approach which only takes advantage of parallel corpus is supplementary to existing data manipulation strategies, i.e. back-translation, self-training and knowledge distillation. Experiments on several low-resource datasets show that our approach achieves significant improvement over a strong baseline, despite its simplicity.

Keywords: Neural machine translation · Data augmentation · Low-resource language translation

1 Introduction

While neural machine translation (NMT) [1, 26, 27] has achieved impressive performance on high-resource data conditions, becoming dominant in the field, it has been noticed that these models often lag behind conventional machine translation systems, such as statistical machine translation (SMT) [2, 3, 15] in the low-resource scene. Building strong and robust neural machine translation systems needs a large amount of high-quality parallel corpora, which is typically not available for most language pairs. Therefore, improving NMT's utilization of costly parallel data is meaningful for the applications of NMT in various scenarios, especially on the condition of data scarcity.

At present, the main solution to this problem is to either manually annotate more data or perform semi-supervised data augmentation. Since manual annotation of data is time-consuming, data augmentation for low-resource language pairs is a more viable approach. One successful method is back-translation

This work was supported by Project Funded by the Priority Academic Program Development of Jiangsu Higher Education Institutions.

(BT) [22,23], a method that back translates sentences from target monolingual data and augments the bitext with the resulting pseudo-parallel data. Another typical method is self-training (ST) [12,21], which utilizes the source side monolingual data. Though either BT or ST simply utilizes source side or target side monolingual data, the NMT model can not fully capture or utilize bidirectional knowledge. There are enormous potential of parallel corpus to be explored [29].

In this paper, we introduce a simple but efficient data augmentation approach to consistently improve NMT performance given the limited parallel data merely, which we called Random Concatenation (Randcat). We augment the training data by concatenating a target language sentence with a source language sentence at random and adding them to the original corpus. The proposed method is illustrated in Fig. 1. On the one hand, the idea is to utilize the information of both the source-target and target-source knowledge simultaneously, while modeling the bidirectional semantic information and performing bidirectional fusion training. On the other hand, our method that introduces pseudo long sentences is beneficial for the quality of long sentences, which is also a major weakness of NMT [15].

Experimental results show that our method consistently outperforms several representative baselines on four language pairs, demonstrating the superiority of Randcat for utilizing bilingual data. In addition, Randcat that without any change of model structure or cost of human labor throughout the whole process, can be treated as a basic data augmentation procedure that complement the existing data manipulation strategies and pre-training models [8,18,25] conveniently. In summary, the main contributions of this paper are as follows:

– We propose an extremely simple data augmentation method that makes full use of limited parallel data, involving randomly concatenate sentences in different languages to create language-mix sentences, which provides a more resource-efficient paradigm exhibited in the case of scarce data.
– We show that the translation quality can be further improved by combining Randcat with existing data manipulation strategies, i.e. back-translation, self-training and knowledge distillation.
– Experiments on four widely used low-resource language pairs (English-German, English-French, English-Romanian and English-Turkish) confirm that our approach can achieve significant improvements in both directions over strong NMT baseline systems.

2   Related Works

Improving NMT's performance of low-resource languages is still a major challenge for NMT [15]. Many existing methods focus on leveraging the resource of unlabeled monolingual data, mainly semi-supervised methods such as back-translation [22,23], self-training [12,21], and unsupervised machine translation [4,17]. The prerequisite of these approaches is a well-performed baseline model

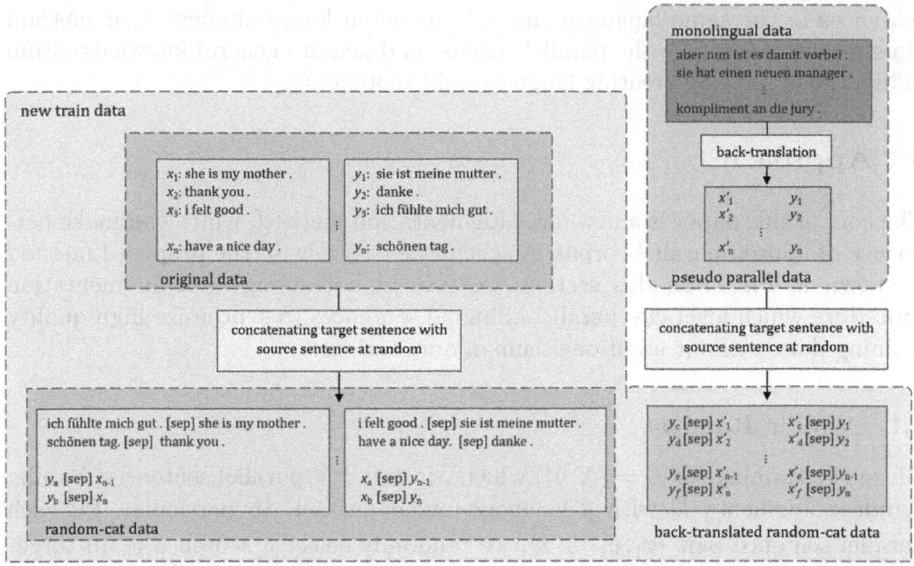

Fig. 1. Proposed method: Augmentation of data by combining the back-translation and random concatenation of two sentences in different languages. Each of a, b, c, d, e, f represents an integer between 1 and n, which is generated at random.

based on the parallel data or auxiliary tasks, and also requires several complicated preprocessing steps. Meanwhile, some scholars also point out that the parallel data of related languages is also valuable. For instance, Cheng et al. [5] and Chen et al. [4] use the annotation data of related high-resource languages as a pivot to bridge language pairs, to realize the training of low-resource language pair translation models.

A line of works has been proposed to fully exploit the parallel and monolingual data, but these approaches only use one-direction mapping of parallel data to build the single-direction translation mapping information. Some studies have confirmed that capturing bidirectional translation knowledge in NMT is useful to improve translation performance [19,28], which are motivated by some recent studies, e.g. dual learning [11] and symmetric training [6]. They usually use an amount of parallel data to pre-train source→target and target→source NMT systems, and then add monolingual data to the systems by translating a sentence from the monolingual corpus. However, their approaches rely on external resources (e.g. word alignment or monolingual data) or complicated model modifications, which limit the applicability of the method to a broader range of languages and model structures. Additionally, Ding et al. [9] propose a pre-training strategy to achieve bidirectional learning by mixing the source and the target corpus and training the model in stages.

Our proposed approach is further related to Kondo et al. [16], who generates long sentences by concatenating two sentences. However, they concatenate sentences in the same language and only focus on long sentences. Our method aims to better leverage the parallel corpus, and acquire general knowledge from bidirectional data by creating language-mix sentences.

3   Approach

The core of this paper is a new data augmentation method, which can make better use of limited parallel corpus. A schematic overview of the proposed method is shown in Fig. 1. In this section, we present a training data augmentation procedure which leverages parallel bilingual sentences to synthesize high-quality training data without additional human annotations.

3.1   Vanilla Randcat

Given the training set $D = (X, Y)$ which consist of N parallel sentences, Vanilla Randcat augments D with a language-mixed dataset. In particular, for each parallel sentence pair $(x_i, y_i) \in \overrightarrow{D}$, we randomly select a sentence y_k in target language at first, then append x_i to build a new source text "$y_k[\text{sep}]x_i$", where "[sep]" is a special token to mark the boundary between y_k and x_i. Similarly, we build a new target text "$x_k[\text{sep}]y_i$" correspondingly. In the end, a new bitext corpus is built: $\overrightarrow{D_{cat}} = \left\{ (y_k[\text{sep}]x_i, x_k[\text{sep}]y_i) \right\}_{i=1}^{N}$, where k can be any number in $[1, N]$. The $\overrightarrow{D_{cat}}$ corpus is then mixed with the bilingual parallel corpus $\overrightarrow{D}$ and no distinction is made between the two corpora. Finally, we train our NMT system from scratch with a single encoder and decoder using the mixed data. We are able to use the same encoder for both the original parallel and the language-mix sentences created by our method, because we use byte-pair encoding(BPE) [24] to represent the source and target words in the same vocabulary.

Three advantages of this method are 1) the source and target language data could enrich the semantic information for each other, without extra bitext. 2) this method increases the number of long sentences. 3) only slight modification for data preprocessing and no changes for the model architecture.

3.2   Randcat with Back-Translation

To further strengthen this method, we propose to combine it with the back-translation method [23], which better improves the utilization of monolingual data. We first train two baseline translation systems $M_{x \to y}, M_{y \to x}$ with given parallel corpus $\overrightarrow{D}(X, Y), \overleftarrow{D}(Y, X)$, and then back-translate the target-side of the monolingual corpus X_{mono}, Y_{mono} separately to create pseudo data as additional dataset, which is denoted as $D_{Y \to X}^{pseudo} = \left\{ (\widetilde{y}_s, x_s) \right\}_{s=1}^{S}$ and $D_{X \to Y}^{pseudo} = \left\{ (\widetilde{x}_t, y_t) \right\}_{t=1}^{T}$. After that, we apply our Randcat approach to the pseudo-parallel corpus, and obtain language-mix corpus $\overrightarrow{BT_{cat}}$ and $\overleftarrow{BT_{cat}}$. The final step is done by combining the original parallel D, original random-cat D_{cat} and back-translated random-cat corpus BT_{cat}, and use the three corpora to train the NMT

Algorithm 1. Data Augmentation when combining the back-translation and Randcat

Input: parallel corpus $D = (X, Y) = \{(x_i, y_i)\}_{i=1}^{N}$, monolingual corpus $X_{mono} = \{x_s\}_{s=1}^{S}$, $Y_{mono} = \{y_t\}_{t=1}^{T}$

Output: optimal trained NMT systems $M = (M_{x \to y}, M_{y \to x})$

1: **function** TRAIN(M, D)
2:    Train two baseline translation models $M_{x \to y}, M_{y \to x}$ using $\overrightarrow{D} = (X, Y)$, $\overleftarrow{D} = (Y, X)$ ▷ until the model convergence
3:    **return** M
4: **end function**
5: **function** RANDCAT WITH BT(M, D, X_{mono}, Y_{mono})
6:    generate translation $\widetilde{x}_s$, $\widetilde{y}_s$ by $M_{y \to x}$, $M_{x \to y}$ respectively
7:    build pseudo sentence pairs $D_{X \to Y}^{pseudo} = \{(\widetilde{x}_t, y_t)\}_{t=1}^{T}$ and $D_{Y \to X}^{pseudo} = \{(\widetilde{y}_s, x_s)\}_{s=1}^{S}$
8:    apply Randcat on $\overrightarrow{D}$ and $D_{X \to Y}^{pseudo}$ to create augmented training data: $\overrightarrow{D_{cat}}$ and $\overrightarrow{BT_{cat}}$
9:    train $M_{x \to y}$ using $\overrightarrow{D} \cup \overrightarrow{D_{cat}} \cup \overrightarrow{BT_{cat}}$ ▷ until the model convergence
10:    apply Randcat on $\overleftarrow{D}$ and $D_{Y \to X}^{pseudo}$ to create augmented training data: $\overleftarrow{D_{cat}}$ and $\overleftarrow{BT_{cat}}$
11:    train $M_{y \to x}$ using $\overleftarrow{D} \cup \overleftarrow{D_{cat}} \cup \overleftarrow{BT_{cat}}$ ▷ until the model convergence
12:    **return** $M_{x \to y}, M_{y \to x}$
13: **end function**

system like the normal. For clarity, we summarize the whole training algorithm in Algorithm 1 when combining back-translation with our method.

4 Experiment

4.1 Experimental Setup

Data and Preprocessing. Main experiments in Table 1 are conducted on four popular low-resource machine translation datasets: IWSLT14 German-English (DE-EN)[1], IWSLT15 English-French (EN-FR), WMT16 English-Romanian (EN-RO)[2], and WMT18 English-Turkish (EN-TR). The data sizes can be found in Table 1, ranging from 160K to 600K. For IWSLT14 DE↔EN, following Edunov et al. [10]'s pre-processing, combining multiple test sets IWSLT14.TED.dev2010, dev2012,tst2010, tst1011, tst2012 for testing. For IWSLT15 EN↔FR, we use IWSLT15.TED.tst2013 as test set. For WMT EN↔RO, we use newstest2016 as test set. For EN↔TR, we use newstest2017 as test set. The monolingual data used for back translation is randomly sampled from publicly available News Crawl provided by WMT. And the ratio of parallel to back-translated is 1:1 for all direction (a simple and effective ratio for better reproducibility). In addition, we specially prepared two very low-resource

---

[1] http://workshop2014.iwslt.org/.
[2] http://www.statmt.org/wmt16/.

and distant language pairs in Table 2, IWSLT15 Thai-English (TH-EN) and WMT21 Chvash-Russian (CHV-RU)[3], containing 80K and 700K training examples respectively.

All the data are tokenized and segmented into subword symbols using BPE [24] to restrict the size of the vocabulary. Moreover, the BPE model is learned on parallel data only (not on monolingual data). For all of experiments, we use joint vocabulary and share source and target embedding layer.

Settings. We adopt the Transformer model implemented with Pytorch in the $fairseq.py$[4] toolkit. All language pairs are trained on $transformer\_base$ except DE↔EN. The model configuration for DE↔EN is $transformer\_iwslt\_de\_en$. The model is optimized by Adam with a learning rate of 5e−4, $\beta_1 = 0.9$, $\beta_2 = 0.98$. We use $warm\_up = 4000$ to start training with initial learning rate of 1e−9. For regularization, we set dropout as 0.3 and label smoothing as 0.1. We decode using beam search on a single model with a beam size of 5. Our approach does not require any modification on architecture, therefore, the same setup is used repeatedly for all experiments.

Models. To investigate the effectiveness of the proposed method and compare with other related work. Here, we briefly introduce seven models involved and the data used in their training.

- **baseline:** The standard Transformer is trained with only original parallel data.
- **Self-Training (ST):** Following He et al. [12]'s work, we generate pseudo sentence pairs by self-training.
- **Back-Translation (BT):** Following Sennrich et al. [23]'s work, we generate pseudo parallel corpus by back-translation.
- **Bidirectional Training (BiT):** We followed Ding et al. [9]'s work to train a bidirectional translation model. By the way, in order to make a fair comparison, we do not reproduce the training techniques in the paper, but only use the data augmentation strategy.
- **Sentcat:** We reproduce Kondo et al. [16]'s work: augmenting data by randomly concatenating two sentences in the same language.
- **Randcat$_{vanilla}$:** Randomly concatenating original target sentences with source sentences to create language-mix corpus.
- **Randcat$_{BT}$:** Randomly concatenating monolingual target sentences with pseudo source sentences to create language-mix corpus.

4.2   Translation Performance

We use tokenized BLEU [20] as the evaluation metric for all languages. For final evaluation, we generate translations with a beam of size 5 and with no length penalty.

---

[3] https://www.statmt.org/wmt21/unsup_and_very_low_res.html.
[4] https://github.com/pytorch/fairseq.

Table 1. Translation Performance in BLEU on eight translation directions. Note that the total number of sentences in these methods is almost equal except "baseline" and "baseline + Randcat$_{vanilla+BT}$".

Models	IWSLT 14		IWSLT 15		WMT 16		WMT 18	
	160K		210K		600K		200K	
	DE→EN	EN→DE	FR→EN	EN→FR	EN→RO	RO→EN	EN→TR	TR→EN
baseline	34.34	28.14	42.70	43.4	34.40	33.32	17.00	18.07
+ BiT	34.54	28.74	43.11	43.61	34.39	33.73	17.43	18.81
+ Sentcat	34.82	28.64	43.28	43.84	34.81	33.76	17.54	18.51
+ Randcat$_{vanilla}$	**35.09**	**29.10**	**43.81**	**44.10**	**34.96**	**34.00**	**17.65**	**19.46**
+ ST	34.95	29.09	42.94	43.73	35.22	34.25	18.20	19.41
+ BT	35.59	29.16	42.76	44.04	37.26	36.54	18.10	21.04
+ Randcat$_{BT}$	36.24	29.39	43.57	44.50	37.34	36.92	20.58	21.37
+ Randcat$_{vanilla+BT}$	**36.43**	**29.88**	**44.02**	**45.18**	**37.74**	**37.18**	**21.20**	**21.47**

Main Experiments. The BLEU scores for each language pair and different systems are shown in Table 1. First of all, we observe statistically significant improvements that the standard transformer gets a $0.56 \sim 1.39$ BLEU improvement with Randcat only. This suggests that our method can help improve NMT in cases where only a moderate amount of parallel data is available. Secondly, our method Randcat$_{vanilla}$ performs better than Sentcat and BiT. These results prove that those language-mix sentences can make better use of parallel textual knowledge.

In addition, the overall score of "baseline + Randcat$_{BT}$" is higher than that of "baseline + BT", making the Randcat-equipped BT more effective compared to vanilla BT. The last lines show the results of the "baseline + Randcat$_{vanilla+BT}$" gets a $1.32 \sim 4.2$ BLEU improvement over the baseline NMT, and also achieves averaged $+1.08$ BLEU improvement over the "baselines + BT". Hence, it is really important to use both monolingual and bilingual effectively for improving translation quality, and our proposed method can be a powerful method for using data efficiently.

Results on Distant Language Pairs. To dispel the doubt that Randcat could merely be applied on languages within the same language family, e.g. English and German, we report the results of Randcat on distant language pairs, which belong to different language families. Table 2 lists the results, Randcat achieves averaged $+0.94$ BLEU improvement over the baselines, demonstrating the effectiveness and universality of our method across language pairs.

4.3 Analysis

Performance of Long Sentences. A desired effect of our method is to increase the number of long sentences in the training corpus, thus alleviating the poor translation quality caused by the lack of long sentences, especially in the low source scenarios. To examine the impact of augmenting the training data by creating long sentences, we analyze the translation results of the test set on

Table 2. Performance on very low-resource and distant language pairs, including TH-EN and CHV-RU. "Δ" shows the improvement of BLEU score.

Models	IWSLT 15		WMT 21		Δ
	TH→EN	EN→TH	CHV→RU	RU→CHV	avg
baseline	19.67	14.91	20.76	18.56	/
+Randcat	21.12	15.56	21.50	19.49	+0.94

EN→DE. Figure 2 depicts the breakdown in the difference between BLEU scores of the proposed method "baseline + Randcat$_{vanilla}$" and the "baseline" according to the length of each sentence. We observe that the output of the proposed method improved under almost all length conditions. In particular, the score of the sentence lengths of longer than 40 is significantly improved, which demonstrates that Randcat is more effective for long sentence translation. And according to Fig. 3, it also shows that the sentence output by "baseline" is shorter than expected. Conversely, the model trained by our method tends to generate longer sentences, which reduces the missing information.

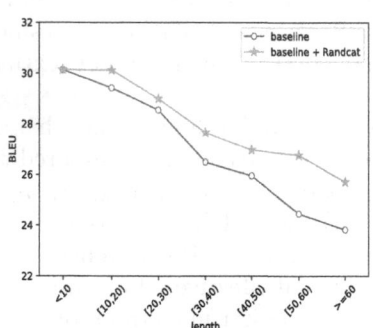
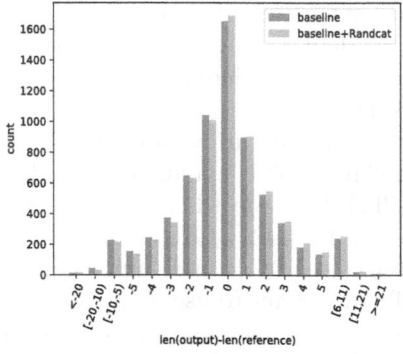

Fig. 2. BLEU scores for each sentence length breakdown on EN→DE.

Fig. 3. Length difference between the system translated sentences and references on EN→DE.

Learn Bilingual Knowledge Better. The intuition of our method is that two language data can mutually enrich the contextualized information, thus helping models master the bilingual knowledge to better facilitate translation. We assess how well our method learns bilingual information by the results of word alignment for it has the potential to induce better attention matrices.

To make the result clear, we visualize the attention matrix of a sentence as shown in Fig. 4. We compare the alignments result in the last layer for it has the greatest influence on encoding and decoding. As shown in Fig. 4(a), the target sentence word of the benchmark model pays divergent attention to the source sentence word, and it is hard to select critical information for generating the current word, which leads to poor translation. However, Fig. 4(b) presents that the model pays more attention to correct information and improves alignment quality. In a words, our method allows model to learn better attention matrices and enhance the coordination of bidirectional corpus, thereby improving translation performance.

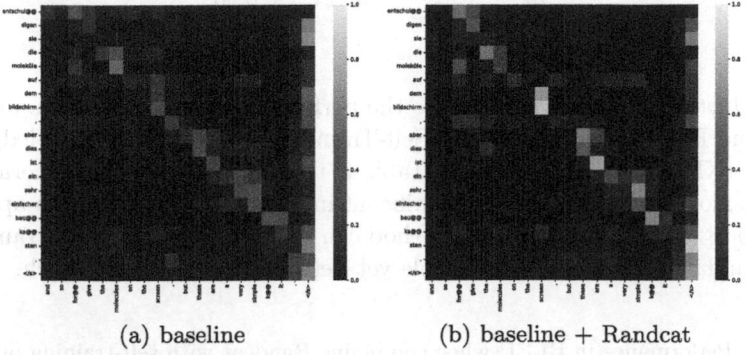

(a) baseline   (b) baseline + Randcat

Fig. 4. An example of attention matrix diagram in the last layers.

4.4 Additional Experiments

In this section, we describe a number of additional experiments to explore the potential of proposed approach. We first conduct experiment on sample setting to figure out the influence. Then we combine Randcat with several representative related work to verify the effectiveness and universality of our method. Unless otherwise stated, all results are reported on the IWSLT14 DE→EN.

Effect of Sampling Times. In Sect. 3, we introduce the proposed basic methods, which augments data by performing Randcat once. We naturally consider whether executing Randcat for many times can further improve the performance.

The BLEU results for these experiments are shown in Table 3. We can observe that the improvements are consistent due to the fact that multiple random sampling concatenation can enrich the diversity of the corpus. Meanwhile, we also see that the benefits are not in linear growth, possibly because that the approach is simply augments on training data without introducing other new information.

Complementary to Data Manipulation Approach. We take several experiments further to verify the broad applicability of our method, which can complement existing approach. We list two other typical data manipulation approaches,

Table 3. Performance in BLEU when performing Randcat with different times. Sampling 1 time is the basic method introduced and used before.

Sampling times	BLEU	Δ
0 (baseline)	34.34	/
1 (Randcat)	35.09	+ 0.75
5	35.26	+ 0.92
10	35.54	+ 1.20
20	35.24	+ 0.90

and conduct experiments to compare the performance between vanilla augmentation and Randcat augmentation: Self-Training (ST) [12] and Knowledge Distillation (KD) [13,14]. As seen in Table 4, the augmented data generated by Randcat model can yield further significant improvements over vanilla approach counterpart. This shows that our method can effectively improve the translation quality and can be viewed as a simple yet better supplement approach.

Table 4. Performance in BLEU when combining Randcat with self-training or knowledge distillation. "$ST_{vanilla}$" and "$KD_{vanilla}$" means pseudo data is generated by baseline model . "$ST_{Randcat}$" and "$KD_{Randcat}$" means pseudo data is generated by Randcat model.

Models	BLEU	Δ
baseline	34.34	/
+ $ST_{vanilla}$	34.95	+ 0.61
+ $ST_{Randcat}$	35.75	+ 1.41
+ $KD_{vanilla}$	35.67	+ 1.33
+ $KD_{Randcat}$	36.44	+ 2.10

Complementary to Pre-training Model. In recent years, pre-training is a powerful method to utilize enormous unlabeled data to improve the performance of NMT, especially for smaller parallel corpora [7]. Hence, we take a trial to investigate whether Randcat could further supplement the pre-training model. We treat pre-trained mBART [18] as our testbed, whose benefits have been sufficiently validated, and fine-tune the model with different training data prepared from the original data respectively. The results are reported in Table 5.

Experimental results show that Randcat is nicely complementary to mBART. It is surprising that though applied to such a powerful pre-training model, our proposed approach of creating language-mix sentences to augment training data is still beneficial. This shows the extensive practicability of our method again.

Table 5. Performance in BLEU when using mBART. " $+$ " means fine-tune mBART with different training corpus.

Models	BLEU	Δ
mBART	37.06	/
+ Randcat$_{vanilla}$	37.32	+ 0.26
+ Randcat$_{vanilla+BT}$	38.36	+ 1.30

5 Conclusions

In this paper, we have proposed a data augmentation method for improving low-resource NMT, which makes better use of the limited bilingual corpus. We show that this approach can greatly improve the translation quality of long sentences and help master bidirectional text knowledge. The experimental results on several pairs of low-resource translation tasks confirm that our approach is straightforward but useful. In addition, our method could be used in combination with existing data manipulation strategies and supplement the pre-training model as well, achieving significant improvement over strong baseline, which is beneficial for the common case where a large amount of monolingual data is available with insufficient parallel data. In the future, we would like to develop a data augmentation method that works well in multilingual machine translation.

References

1. Bahdanau, D., Cho, K., Bengio, Y.: Neural machine translation by jointly learning to align and translate. In: ICLR, vol. abs/1409.0473 (2015)
2. Brown, P.F., et al.: A statistical approach to machine translation. Comput. Linguist. **16**(2), 79–85 (1990)
3. Brown, P.F., Della Pietra, S.A., Della Pietra, V.J., Mercer, R.L.: The mathematics of statistical machine translation: Parameter estimation. Comput. Linguist. **19**(2), 263–311 (1993)
4. Chen, Y., Liu, Y., Li, V.O.: Zero-resource neural machine translation with multi-agent communication game. In: AAAI, pp. 5086–5093 (2018)
5. Cheng, Y., Liu, Y., Yang, Q., Sun, M., Xu, W.: Neural machine translation with pivot languages. arXiv preprint arXiv:1611.04928 (2016)
6. Cohn, T., Hoang, C.D.V., Vymolova, E., Yao, K., Dyer, C., Haffari, G.: Incorporating structural alignment biases into an attentional neural translation model. In: NAACL-HLT, pp. 876–885 (2016)
7. Conneau, A., Lample, G.: Cross-lingual language model pretraining. In: NeurIPS, pp. 7059–706 (2019)
8. Devlin, J., Chang, M.W., Lee, K., Toutanova, K.: Bert: pre-training of deep bidirectional transformers for language understanding. In: NAACL-HLT, pp. 4171–4186 (2019)
9. Ding, L., Wu, D., Tao, D.: Improving neural machine translation by bidirectional training. In: EMNLP, pp. 3278–3284 (2021)

10. Edunov, S., Ott, M., Auli, M., Grangier, D., Ranzato, M.: Classical structured prediction losses for sequence to sequence learning. In: NAACL-HLT, pp. 355–364 (2018)
11. He, D., Xia, Y., Qin, T., Wang, L., Yu, N., Liu, T.Y., Ma, W.Y.: Dual learning for machine translation. In: NeurIPS. vol. 29, pp. 820–828 (2016)
12. He, J., Gu, J., Shen, J., Ranzato, M.: Revisiting self-training for neural sequence generation. In: ICLR (2020)
13. Hinton, G.E., Vinyals, O., Dean, J.: Distilling the knowledge in a neural network. CoRR abs/1503.02531 (2015)
14. Kim, Y., Rush, A.M.: Sequence-level knowledge distillation. In: EMNLP, pp. 1317–1327 (2016)
15. Koehn, P., Knowles, R.: Six challenges for neural machine translation. In: NMT@ACL, pp. 28–39 (2017)
16. Kondo, S., Hotate, K., Hirasawa, T., Kaneko, M., Komachi, M.: Sentence concatenation approach to data augmentation for neural machine translation. In: NAACL-HLT (Student Research Workshop), pp. 143–149 (2021)
17. Lample, G., Conneau, A., Denoyer, L., Ranzato, M.: Unsupervised machine translation using monolingual corpora only. In: ICLR (2018)
18. Liu, Y., Gu, J., Goyal, N., Li, X., Edunov, S., Ghazvininejad, M., Lewis, M., Zettlemoyer, L.: Multilingual denoising pre-training for neural machine translation. Trans. Assoc. Comput. Linguist. **8**, 726–742 (2020)
19. Nguyen, X.P., Joty, S.R., Wu, K., Aw, A.T.: Data diversification: a simple strategy for neural machine translation. In: NeurIPS (2020)
20. Papineni, K., Roukos, S., Ward, T., Zhu, W.J.: Bleu: a method for automatic evaluation of machine translation. In: ACL, pp. 311–318 (2002)
21. Scudder, H.: Probability of error of some adaptive pattern-recognition machines. IEEE Trans. Inf. Theory **11**(3), 363–371 (1965)
22. Sennrich, R., Haddow, B., Birch, A.: Edinburgh neural machine translation systems for wmt 16. In: WMT, pp. 371–376 (2016)
23. Sennrich, R., Haddow, B., Birch, A.: Improving neural machine translation models with monolingual data. In: ACL (2016)
24. Sennrich, R., Haddow, B., Birch, A.: Neural machine translation of rare words with subword units. In: ACL (2016)
25. Song, K., Tan, X., Qin, T., Lu, J., Liu, T.Y.: Mass: Masked sequence to sequence pre-training for language generation. In: ICML, pp. 5926–5936 (2019)
26. Sutskever, I., Vinyals, O., Le, Q.V.: Sequence to sequence learning with neural networks. In: NeurIPS, pp. 3104–3112 (2014)
27. Vaswani, A., et al.: Attention is all you need. In: NeurIPS, pp. 5998–6008 (2017)
28. Yamada, T., Matsunaga, H., Ogata, T.: Paired recurrent autoencoders for bidirectional translation between robot actions and linguistic descriptions. IEEE Robot. Autom. Lett. **3**(4), 3441–3448 (2018)
29. Zhang, H., Qiu, S., Wu, S.: Dual knowledge distillation for bidirectional neural machine translation. In: IJCNN, pp. 1–7 (2021)

Contrastive Learning for Robust Neural Machine Translation with ASR Errors

Dongyang Hu and Junhui Li[⊠]

School of Computer Science and Technology, Soochow University, Suzhou, China
20205227106@stu.suda.edu.cn, lijunhui@suda.edu.cn

Abstract. Neural machine translation (NMT) models have recently achieved excellent performance when translating non-noised sentences. Unfortunately, they are also very brittle and easily falter when fed with noisy sentences, i.e., from automatic speech recognition (ASR) output. Due to the lack of Chinese-to-English translation test set with natural Chinese-side ASR output, related studies artificially add noise into Chinese sentences to evaluation translation performance. In this paper we eliminate such strong limitation and manually construct natural ASR output on popular Chinese-to-English NIST translation test dataset, *NISTasr* which consists of 680 documents with 7,688 sentences. To train an NMT model being robust to ASR output, we take contrastive learning framework to close the gap among representations of original input and its perturbed counterpart. Experimental results on NIST Chinese-to-English translation show that our approach significantly improves the translation performance of ASR output while having negligible effect on the translation performance of non-noised sentences. It also shows that the translation performance gap is quite big (e.g., 44.28 in BLEU v.s. 35.20) when translating non-noised sentences and sentences of ASR output.

Keywords: Neural machine translation · Automatic speech recognition · Contrastive learning

1 Introduction

Neural machine translation (NMT) models trained on large-scale non-noised parallel corpora can achieve good performance in translating non-noised text [1, 26]. Despite the great success, some perturbations in the text can cause considerable degradation of translation quality [2], especially if these perturbations are from automatic speech recognition (ASR). As shown in Table 1, when we replace a source word "涮" with its similar pronunciation word "帅",the generated translation has been completely changed and becomes an abnormal sentence. This kind of fragility to perturbations not only lowers translation quality but also inhibits NMT application in realistic scenarios [14, 20, 28]. In this paper, our

W. Lu et al. (Eds.): NLPCC 2022, LNAI 13551, pp. 81–91, 2022.
https://doi.org/10.1007/978-3-031-17120-8_7

goal is to evaluate to what extend the translation performance drops when the input sentences move from non-noised to noised ones of ASR output, and thus to alleviate the performance drop.

Table 1. An example of non-robustness issue in neural machine translation. Replacing a Chinese word with its similar pronunciation word (e.g., "涮" → "帅") leads to significant changes in English translation.

Input	比尔·盖茨愚人节遭涮。
Output	bill gates are duped .
Input	比尔盖茨愚人节遭帅。
Output	bill gates was handsome .

There have been several attempts to boost the robustness of NMT models in the scenarios where the input sentences are non-noised, or noised. On the one hand, considering two non-noised input sentences with subtle changes may have significant erroneous changes in translation, Cheng et al., (2018) [6], for example, make both the encoder and decoder in NMT models robust against input perturbations by enabling them to behave similarly for the original input and its perturbed counterpart. On the other hand, due to the recent public availability of parallel corpora of with naturally occurring noisy inputs and translations (e.g., MTMT [15]), many studies try to augment training dataset by artificially corrupting input sentences into noisy ones. However, as of yet there are no publicly available bilingual parallel corpora with both naturally occurring noisy inputs and their corresponding correct inputs, thus previous studies could not tell to what extend the translation performance would drop when we feed the NMT models with noised sentences, rather than non-noised ones.

In order to answer above question, in this paper we focus on ASR noisy and construct natural ASR output on Chinese-side input sentences of a Chinese-English parallel test dataset. To train an NMT model being robust to ASR output, then we automatically convert source-side sentences in NMT training dataset from non-noised version to noised version by mimicking typical types of ASR errors. We take this kind of corrupted input as positive instances in contrastive learning, and our key insight is to close the representation gap between original input and its perturbed counterpart as much as possible. Experimental results on NIST Chinese-to-English translation show that our approach significantly improves the translation performance of ASR output while has negligible effect on the translation performance of non-noised sentences. It also shows that the translation performance gap is quite big (e.g., 44.28 in BLEU v.s. 35.20) when translate non-noised sentences and sentences of ASR output, leaving a room for further improvement.

2 Related Work

2.1 Robust Neural Machine Translation

Szegedy et al., (2014) [23] demonstrate that neural networks is very vulnerable to noisy input. This fragility has been show to NMT models [2], and both natural and synthetic noise can greatly degrade translation performance [9]. Thus improving the robustness of NMT models has received wide attention. Many studies focus on augmenting the training dataset to improve the robustness [12]. Peitz et al., (2012) [19] and Tsvetkov et al., (2014) [25] try to induce noise by considering the realistic ASR outputs as the source corpora used for NMT model training. Though the problem of ASR errors could be alleviated by the promising end-to-end speech translation models [13], but the rare training data in forms of speech paired with text translations is barely able to train a data-hungry NMT system with high quality. Recently Sperber et al., (2017) [22] adapt the NMT model to ASR outputs, where they bring about synthetic noise inputs during training process and only achieve marginal improvements on noise inputs but degrades the translation quality on clean test data.

Cheng et al., [4–6] utilize adversarial learning to improve the robustness of NMT models. They propose two approaches to construct perturbed data and train both the encoder and decoder robust to input perturbations by enabling them to behave similarly for the original input and its perturbed counterpart. Similarly Ebrahimi et al., (2018) [7] focus on augmenting the training data to improve robustness, especially with adversarial examples.

2.2 Contrastive Learning

Contrastive learning has become a rising domain and achieved gorgeous success in various computer vision tasks [3,16,24,29]. Researchers in the NLP domain have also explored contrastive Learning for sentence representation. Wu et al., (2020) [27] employed multiple sentence-level augmentation strategies to learn a noise-invariant sentence representation. Fang et al., (2020) [8] applies back-translation to create augmentations of original sentences. Pan et al., (2021) [17] makes uses of contrastive learning for multilingual NMT to close the gap among representations of different languages.

Table 2. Two examples of original Chinese sentences in NIST02 and their ASR output.

Original	印尼重申反对外国军队进驻。
ASR Output	印尼重新反对外国军队进驻。
Original	分析人士认为,不管此次审判的结果如何,这一事件可能会削弱丹戎当选印尼总统的希望。
ASR Output	分析人士认为,不管此次审判的结果如何,这些事件可能会削弱,但荣当选印尼总统的希望。

Table 3. Statistics on NISTasr dataset.

	NIST02	NIST03	NIST04	NIST05	NIST06	NIST08	Avg.
#Documents	95	100	170	100	100	115	113
#Sentences	878	919	1788	1082	1664	1357	1281
WER (%)	11.24	16.80	12.25	13.20	12.88	13.63	13.19

Table 4. Edit distances between NIST and NISTasr dataset.

	NIST02	NIST03	NIST04	NIST05	NIST06	NIST08
Insertions	661	853	868	797	930	674
Deletions	997	1875	2967	1627	2502	2216
Substitutions	2736	4297	6248	4372	4813	4161
Edit distances	4394	7007	10083	6796	8245	7051

3   NISTasr Test Dataset

While related studies have proposed relevant datasets to evaluate the effect of ASR error on machine translation where English is the source language [28] [20], to our best knowledge we are not aware of any such Chinese-to-English translation dataset. To this end, we use popular NIST Chinese-to-English test dataset, i.e., NIST MT 02 ∼ 08 and construct natural ASR output for Chinese sentences. Specifically, we first let a Chinese-native speaker read Chinese sentences and record the reading into audio files. Then, the audio files are fed into a ASR toolkit[1] to generate ASR output. For simplicity, we refer the ASR output of NIST test dataset as NISTasr. Table 2 shows two examples of Chinese original sentences in NIST02 and their ASR outputs. In the first example, 申 /shen is mistakenly recognized as 新 /xin while in the second example, person name 丹戎 /dan_rong is recognized as their homophone characters 但 /dan and 荣 /rong.

To evaluate the ASR performance, we calculate character-wise word error rate (WER)[2] on NISTasr. As shown in Table 3, the averaged WER of the 6 NIST test sets is 13.19%, ranged from 11.24% to 16.80%. Table 4 shows edit distances between NIST and NISTasr dataset, in which substitutions account for the most.

4   Our Approach

4.1   Overview

The goal of our work is to apply contrastive learning framework to make the NMT model be more robust to ASR noise. Our key idea is to expose the model to various valid and incorrect input sentences by maintaining the consistency of behaviors for the source sequence $\mathbf{x}^{(i)} = \left(x_1^{(i)}, \cdots, x_{|\mathbf{x}^{(i)}|}^{(i)} \right)$ with length $|\mathbf{x}^{(i)}|$ and

---

[1] https://www.iflyrec.com/html/addMachineOrder.html.
[2] https://github.com/belambert/asr-evaluation.

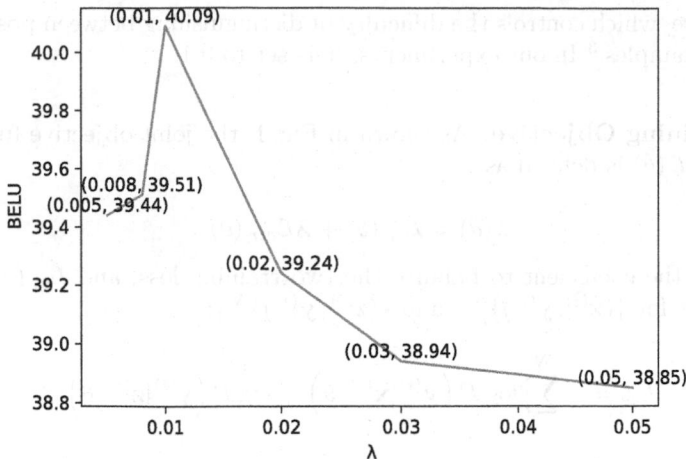

Fig. 1. The architecture of NMT with contrastive learning.

its perturbed counterpart $\mathbf{z}^{(i)} = \left(z_1^{(i)}, \cdots, z_{|\mathbf{z}^{(i)}|}^{(i)} \right)$ with length $|\mathbf{z}^{(i)}|$ when generating the target sequence $\mathbf{y}^{(i)} = \left(y_1^{(i)}, \cdots, y_{|\mathbf{y}^{(i)}|}^{(i)} \right)$ with length $|\mathbf{y}^{(i)}|$. Following the contrastive learning framework of [3], we train the model to better learn the representations of $\mathbf{x}^{(i)}$ by contrasting the positive pairs with the negative pairs. Specifically, we view $\mathbf{x}^{(i)}$ and $\mathbf{z}^{(i)}$ as a positive pair and select the negative pairs from the same training batch.

Figure 1 illustrates the architecture of our approach. Given a batch $\mathcal{S}$ with N input pairs $\{(\mathbf{x}^{(i)}, \mathbf{y}^{(i)})\}_{i=1}^N$, we first obtain input triples $\{(\mathbf{x}^{(i)}, \mathbf{z}^{(i)}, \mathbf{y}^{(i)})\}_{i=1}^N$ by perturbing source sentence $\mathbf{x}^{(i)}$ into $\mathbf{z}^{(i)}$ (see Sect. 4.2 for more details). Then we encode the source sentences and their perturbed ones into their corresponding hidden states. Based on the hidden states, we maximize the similarity between the positive pairs while minimizing the similarity between the negative pairs. The objective of contrastive learning is to minimize the following loss $\mathcal{L}_{ctr}$ as,

$$\mathcal{L}_{ctr}(\theta) = -\sum_i^N \log \frac{\exp\left(sim\left(e_\mathbf{x}^{(i)}, e_\mathbf{z}^{(i)} \right) / \tau \right)}{\sum_{j=1}^N \exp\left(sim\left(e_\mathbf{x}^{(i)}, e_\mathbf{x}^{(j)} \right) / \tau \right)}, \tag{1}$$

$$e_\mathbf{x}^{(i)} = avg\_pooling\left(h_\mathbf{x}^{(i)} \right), \tag{2}$$

$$e_\mathbf{z}^{(i)} = avg\_pooling\left(h_\mathbf{z}^{(i)} \right), \tag{3}$$

where $h_\mathbf{x}^{(i)} \in \mathbb{R}^{|\mathbf{x}^{(i)}| \times d}$ and $h_\mathbf{z}^{(i)} \in \mathbb{R}^{|\mathbf{z}^{(i)}| \times d}$ are encoder hidden states for input sequence $\mathbf{x}^{(i)}$, and $\mathbf{z}^{(i)}$, respectively, and d is the size of hidden states. τ is the temperature, which controls the difficulty of distinguishing between positive and negative examples.[3] In our experiments, it is set to 0.1.

Joint Training Objective. As shown in Fig. 1, the joint objective function of our model $\mathcal{L}(\theta)$ is defined as:

$$\mathcal{L}(\theta) = \mathcal{L}_{ce}(\theta) + \lambda \mathcal{L}_{ctr}(\theta), \tag{4}$$

where λ is the coefficient to balance the two training loss, and $L_{ce}(\theta)$ is cross entropy loss for $\{(\mathbf{x}^{(i)}, \mathbf{y}^{(i)})\}_{i=1}^{N}$ and $\{(\mathbf{z}^{(i)}, \mathbf{y}^{(i)})\}_{i=1}^{N}$:

$$L_{ce} = -\sum_{i=1}^{N} \log P\left(\mathbf{y}^{(i)} | \mathbf{x}^{(i)}, \theta\right) + \log P\left(\mathbf{y}^{(i)} | \mathbf{z}^{(i)}, \theta\right). \tag{5}$$

Note that in Eq. 5, we also augment training instances with $\left(\mathbf{z}^{(i)}, \mathbf{y}^{(i)}\right)$ pairs, as expecting the model could also generate correct translation even given noised input.

Next, we will describe how to construct perturbed inputs while mimicking ASR errors.

4.2   Constructing Perturbed Inputs

Considering the lack of efficient way to manually construct ASR output on the source-side of the training dataset, an alternative way is to automatically convert input sentences from non-noised version to noised version by mimicking typical types of ASR errors, mainly including substitution, deletion and insertion. Specifically, with respective to substitution, a word/character could be substituted by another word with same or similar pronunciation.

Given a source-side Chinese sentence $\mathbf{x} = \left(x_1, \cdots, x_{|\mathbf{x}|}\right)$ with $|\mathbf{x}|$ words, we convert it into a noised version $\mathbf{z}$ by introducing the following two types of noise:[4]

1. **Homophone (Homo.)** Homophone is a common substitution error type in ASR output which refers to different characters with the same pronunciation (e.g. 议 → 亦). We randomly choose some characters in $\mathbf{x}$ and replace these characters with their random homophone. The probability for each word x_i to be selected is 15%.
2. **Deletion (Dele.)** When the speaker reads a text with a low voice, an ASR toolkit may ignore some characters due to the weak acoustical signals. Therefore, we randomly delete some characters from $\mathbf{x}$. The probability for each word to be deleted is 10%.

---

[3] Higher temperature increases the difficulty to distinguish positive sample from negative ones.

[4] Our manual analysis on ASR errors show that insertion of error type is infrequent. Therefore, we do not randomly insert words when generating noised version of a sentence.

5   Experimentation

In this section we evaluate our approach on NIST Chinese-to-English translation benchmark.

5.1   Experimental Settings

Data Settings. The training data consists of about 1.25M sentence pairs from LDC corpora with 27.9M Chinese words and 34.5M English words respectively.[5] We use NIST 06 as the validation set and NIST 02, 03, 04, 05, and 08 as test sets. For Chinese sentences, we split them character by character. For English sentences, we perform lowercase and then split words into subword units by byte pair encoding (BPE) with 20K operations [21].

Model Settings. We use OpenNMT [11] as the implementation of the Transformer seq2seq model.[6] Following the standard Transformer base model [26], we use 6 layers in both encoder and decoder, 512 model dimensions, 2048 hidden dimensions in feed-forward network, and 8 attention heads. For optimization we use Adam with $\beta 1 = 0.9$, $\beta 2 = 0.998$ and $\epsilon = 10^{-9}$ [10]. In all experiments, we train the models for 250K steps and save a checkpoint at every 5K step intervals on a single GTX 2080Ti with initial learning rate 0.5 and batch size 4096. In inferring, we set the beam size to 5 and length penalty $\alpha = 0.6$. In the joint objective Eq. 4, we set $\lambda = 0.01$.

Evaluation. For evaluation, we report case-insensitive BLEU [18] as calculated by the multi-bleu.perl script for all the experiments.

Baselines. We compare our approach to two baselines: 1) *Transformer*, which is trained on the original training set, i.e., $\{(\mathbf{x}^{(i)}, \mathbf{y}^{(i)})\}_{i=1}^{\mathcal{N}}$ with $\mathcal{N}$ training instances; and 2) *+DA*, which augments the training set with the perturbed inputs, thus is trained on both $\{(\mathbf{x}^{(i)}, \mathbf{y}^{(i)})\}_{i=1}^{\mathcal{N}}$ and $\{(\mathbf{z}^{(i)}, \mathbf{y}^{(i)})\}_{i=1}^{\mathcal{N}}$ with $2\mathcal{N}$ training instances.

5.2   Experimental Results

Once the NMT models are trained, we feed into them with both non-noised sentences and noised sentences of ASR output. Table 5 shows the results on Chinese-English translation. First, it shows that translation performance decreases sharply (i.e., from 44.28 to 35.20 in averaged BLEU) for *Transformer* baseline when replacing the non-noised inputs with ASR ones. Second, it also shows that our approach achieves the best performance on NISTasr, with improvement of 3.18 and 1.8 averaged BLEU over the two baselines. Finally, our approach even has slight improvement on NIST test set with improvement of 0.49 averaged BLEU over *Transformer* baseline.

---

[5] The corpora include LDC 2002E18, LDC2003E07, LDC2003E14, Hansards portion of LDC2004T07, LDC2004T08 and LDC2005T06.

[6] https://github.com/OpenNMT/OpenNMT-py.

Table 5. Translation performance (BLEU) on NIST test sets. *Non-noised* and *ASR* indicate that we feed the trained NMT models with non-noised sentences and ASR outputs, respectively.

Model	Input	Val.	Test						
		NIST06	NIST02	NIST03	NIST04	NIST05	NIST08	Avg.
Transformer	Non-noised	45.03	47.18	45.85	47.28	45.66	35.41	44.28
	ASR	36.32	39.49	36.24	37.71	35.66	26.92	35.20
+DA	Non-noised	44.56	47.49	45.08	46.89	45.67	35.02	44.17
	ASR	37.40	41.21	37.45	39.29	37.59	27.37	36.58
Ours	Non-noised	46.04	47.67	46.12	47.32	46.53	36.19.66	44.77
	ASR	**40.09**	**42.18**	**38.54**	**41.30**	**40.13**	**29.78**	**38.38**

Table 6. Ablation study of noise type when constructing perturbed inputs.

Model	Input	Val.	Test					
		NIST06	NIST02	NIST03	NIST04	NIST05	NIST08	Avg.
Our	ASR	40.09	42.18	38.54	41.30	40.13	29.78	38.38
-Homo	ASR	37.85	40.16	36.45	38.70	37.21	27.70	36.04
-Dele	ASR	38.47	41.46	38.06	40.65	38.41	29.32	37.58

5.3 Ablation Analysis

Table 6 shows the ablation study when different types of noise are used in constructing perturbed inputs. It shows that both types of noise are helpful to improve the translation performance of ASR output while *Homo* contributes more than *Dele*. When only taking the advantage of *Dele*, our model outperforms the baseline Transformer by improving the translation performance from averaged 35.20 in BLEU to 36.04. Meanwhile, *Homo* is more effective to improve the translation performance of ASR output (i.e., from 35.20 to 37.58 in averaged BLEU).

5.4 Effect on Hyper-Parameter λ

We tune the hyper-parameter λ mentioned in Eq. 4 on the validation set. Fig 2 shows the effect of λ on translation performance of the validation dataset. It shows that our NMT model achieves the best performance when λ is set as 0.01.

5.5 Case Study

In Table 7, we give two concrete examples to illustrate the advantage of our robust NMT model when translating sentences of ASR output. In the first example, the original word "摇头丸" is mistakenly recognized as "腰痛丸" which does not have a concrete meaning. Here since "摇头丸" and "腰痛丸" share similar pronunciation, and generally Chinese speakers have no trouble in understanding this noised sentence. The baseline NMT model choose to ignore "腰痛"

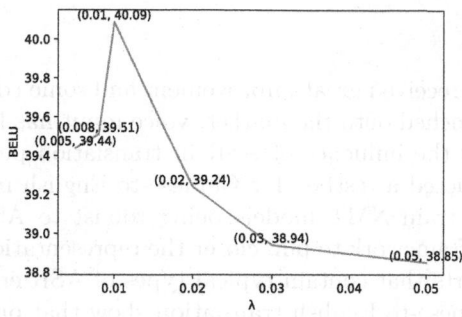

Fig. 2. Performance on nist06asr varies to different λ in Eq. 4

by translating "腰痛丸" into *pills*. By contrast, our NMT model is robust to this ASR error by correctly translating "腰痛丸" into *ecstasy pills*.

In the second example, "受审" is mistakenly recognized as "show 审" in ASR output. Not surprisingly, the baseline NMT model fails to translate such code-switched segment by translating it into *mr shihow*. Meanwhile, our NMT model is robust to this code-switched segment by ignoring *show* and translating "审" into *for trial*.

Table 7. Case study on translations of sentences from ASR output.

Example 1	
Non-noised	香港警方称,在过去的一年中,共发现数宗香港人利用互联网采取用信用卡付款方式,购买摇头丸等毒品案件。
ASR	香港警方称,在过去的一年中,共发现数宗香港人利用互联网采取用信用卡付款的方式购买**腰痛丸**等毒品案件。
Ref	According to the hong kong police, in the past year, they had several cases of hong kongers using the internet to purchase such **drugs as ecstasy** with credit cards.
Baseline	The hong kong police claimed that in the past year, a number of hong kong people were found using the internet to buy **pills** and other drug - related cases.
Our approach	The hong kong police said that in the past year, several cases of hong kong people using the internet to pay credit cards to purchase **ecstasy** and other drugs were detected.
Example 2	
Non-noised	印尼国会议长出庭受审。
ASR	印尼国会议长出庭**show** 审。
Ref	Indonesian parliament speaker stands **trial** .
Baseline	The president of the indonesian parliament, **mr shihow** .
Our approach	Indonesian parliament speaker will appear in court **for trial**

6   Conclusion

As ASR has recently received great improvement and some commercial products have successfully launched onto the market, voice input has become popular. In this paper, we study the influence of ASR in translation performance. To this end, we have constructed a testbed for Chinese-to-English machine translation of ASR dataset. To train NMT models being robust to ASR errors, we take contrastive learning framework to pull closer the representation of inputs and its perturbed counterparts that contain typical types of ASR errors. Experimental results on NIST Chinese-to-English translation show that our approach significantly improves the translation performance of ASR output while has negligible effect on the translation performance of non-noised sentence.

Acknowledgments. The authors would like to thank the anonymous reviewers for their constructive feedback. This work was supported by the National Natural Science Foundation of China (Grant No. 61876120).

References

1. Bahdanau, D., Cho, K., Bengio, Y.: Neural machine translation by jointly learning to align and translate. In: Proceedings of International Conference on Learning Representations, vol. abs/1409.0473 (2015)
2. Belinkov, Y., Bisk, Y.: Synthetic and natural noise both break neural machine translation. In: Proceedings of International Conference on Learning Representations (2018)
3. Chen, T., Kornblith, S., Norouzi, M., Hinton, G.: A simple framework for contrastive learning of visual representations. In: Proceedings of International Conference on Machine Learning, pp. 1597–1607 (2020)
4. Cheng, Y., Jiang, L., Macherey, W.: Robust neural machine translation with doubly adversarial inputs. In: Proceedings of Association for Computational Linguistics, pp. 4324–4333 (2019)
5. Cheng, Y., Jiang, L., Macherey, W., Eisenstein, J.: AdvAug: robust adversarial augmentation for neural machine translation. In: Proceedings of Association for Computational Linguistics. pp. 5961–5970 (2020)
6. Cheng, Y., Tu, Z., Meng, F., Zhai, J., Liu, Y.: Towards robust neural machine translation. In: Proceedings of Association for Computational Linguistics, pp. 1756–1766 (2018)
7. Ebrahimi, J., Lowd, D., Dou, D.: On adversarial examples for character-level neural machine translation. In: Proceedings of International Conference on Computational Linguistics, pp. 653–663 (2018)
8. Fang, H., Wang, S., Zhou, M., Ding, J., Xie, P.: CERT: contrastive self-supervised learning for language understanding. arXiv preprint arXiv:2005.12766 (2020)
9. Khayrallah, H., Koehn, P.: On the impact of various types of noise on neural machine translation. In: Proceedings of Workshop on Neural Machine Translation and Generation, pp. 74–83 (2018)
10. Kingma, D.P., Ba, J.: Adam: a method for stochastic optimization. In: Proceedings of International Conference on Learning Representations (2015)

11. Klein, G., Kim, Y., Deng, Y., Senellart, J., Rush, A.M.: OpenNMT: open-source toolkit for neural machine translation. In: Proceedings of Association for Computational Linguistics, pp. 67–72 (2017)
12. Li, Z., Specia, L.: Improving neural machine translation robustness via data augmentation: beyond back-translation. In: Proceedings of Workshop on Noisy User-generated Text, pp. 328–336 (2019)
13. Liu, Y., et al.: Synchronous speech recognition and speech-to-text translation with interactive decoding. In: Proceedings of the AAAI Conference on Artificial Intelligence, pp. 8417–8424 (2020)
14. Martucci, G., Cettolo, M., Negri, M., Turchi, M.: Lexical Modeling of ASR errors for robust speech translation. In: Proceedings of Interspeech (2021)
15. Michel, P., Neubig, G.: MTNT: a testbed for machine translation of noisy text. In: Proceedings of Empirical Methods in Natural Language Processing, pp. 543–553 (2018)
16. Misra, I., van der Maaten, L.: Self-supervised learning of pretext-invariant representations. In: Proceedings of CVPR (2020)
17. Pan, X., Wang, M., Wu, L., Li, L.: Contrastive learning for many-to-many multilingual neural machine translation. In: Proceedings of Association for Computational Linguistics, pp. 244–258 (2021)
18. Papineni, K., Roukos, S., Ward, T., Zhu, W.J.: BLEU: a method for automatic evaluation of machine translation. In: Proceedings of Association for Computational Linguistics, pp. 311–318 (2002)
19. Peitz, S., Wiesler, S., Nußbaum-Thom, M., Ney, H.: Spoken language translation using automatically transcribed text in training. In: Proceedings of International Workshop on Spoken Language Translation, pp. 276–283 (2012)
20. Qin, W., Li, X., Sun, Y., Xiong, D., Cui, J., Wang, B.: Modeling homophone noise for robust neural machine translation. In: IEEE International Conference on Acoustics, Speech and Signal Processing. pp. 7533–7537 (2021)
21. Sennrich, R., Haddow, B., Birch, A.: Neural machine translation of rare words with subword units. In: Proceedings of Association for Computational Linguistics, pp. 1715–1725 (2016)
22. Sperber, M., Neubig, G., Niehues, J., Waibel, A.: Neural lattice-to-sequence models for uncertain inputs. In: Proceedings of Empirical Methods in Natural Language Processing, pp. 1380–1389 (2017)
23. Szegedy, C., et al.: Intriguing properties of neural networks. In: Proceedings of International Conference on Learning Representations (2014)
24. Tian, Y., Krishnan, D., Isola, P.: Contrastive multiview coding. In: Proceedings of European Conference on Computer Vision, pp. 776–794 (2020)
25. Tsvetkov, Y., Metze, F., Dyer, C.: Augmenting translation models with simulated acoustic confusions for improved spoken language translation. In: Proceedings of European Association for Computational Linguistics, pp. 616–625 (2014)
26. Vaswani, A., et al.: Attention is all you need. In: Advances in Neural Information Processing Systems, pp. 5998–6008 (2017)
27. Wu, Z., Wang, S., Gu, J., Khabsa, M., Sun, F., Ma, H.: Clear: contrastive learning for sentence representation. arXiv preprint arXiv:2012.15466 (2020)
28. Xue, H., Feng, Y., Gu, S., Chen, W.: Robust neural machine translation with ASR errors. In: Proceedings of Workshop on Automatic Simultaneous Translation, pp. 15–23 (2020)
29. Zhuang, C., Zhai, A.L., Yamins, D.: Local aggregation for unsupervised learning of visual embeddings. In: Proceedings of International Conference on Computer Vision, pp. 6002–6012 (2019)

An Enhanced New Word Identification Approach Using Bilingual Alignment

Ziyan Yang[1] ⓘ, Huaping Zhang[1]([✉]) ⓘ, Jianyun Shang[1] ⓘ,
and Silamu Wushour[2] ⓘ

[1] Beijing Institute of Technology, Beijing 100081, China
{3120210997,Kevinzhang,shangjia}@bit.edu.cn
[2] Xinjiang University, Xinjiang 830046, China
wushour@xju.edu.cn

Abstract. Traditional new word detection focused on finding the positional distribution of new words on Chinese text, but rarely on other languages. It was also difficult to obtain semantic information or translations of these new words. This paper proposed NEWBA, an enhanced new word identification algorithm by using bilingual corpus alignment. It indicated that NEWBA performs better than the traditional unsupervised method. In addition, it can obtain bilingual word pairs, which was able to provide us with translations beyond detection. NEWBA can expand the scope of traditional new word detection and therefore obtain more valuable information from bilingual aligned corpora.

Keywords: New word detection · Bilingual corpus alignment · Multilingual

1 Introduction

New word detection is to find word boundaries by using statistics of candidate strings in an unannotated corpus [1]. Traditional unsupervised new word detection tended to focus mainly on Chinese texts [2]. Besides, those methods only obtained positional distribution of new words and were lacking on understanding or translations of the words [3].

Words detected in monolingual corpora may be one-sided, while different expressions of synonyms in bilingual corpora may contain more linguistic knowledge [4]. Chinese words may have many English expressions and vice versa. For example, "study" and "learn" are both defined as "学习 (study)" in Chinese. On the other hand, "study" has many different meanings in Chinese, such as "学习 (study)", "研究 (research)", "功课 (homework)" and "学业 (study)". This phenomenon inspired us to acquire cross-language knowledge from bilingual corpora. Many research institutions were devoted to the construction of bilingual corpora and used these corpora to conduct extensive research [5] such as machine translation. This paper proposed NEWBA, an enhanced new word identification algorithm: it was used to mine linguistic knowledge on bilingual

W. Lu et al. (Eds.): NLPCC 2022, LNAI 13551, pp. 92–104, 2022.
https://doi.org/10.1007/978-3-031-17120-8_8

corpora, which is different from previous researches that only focus on a single language. It should be noted that NEWBA does not require any dictionary knowledge; it worked at the word-unit level, and can therefore be used in some low-resource languages.

Word alignment over parallel corpus had a wide variety of applications, however, to our knowledge, this paper was the first one to attempt applying bilingual corpus alignment to new word detection. These bilingual corpora were easy to obtain because they were originally used for machine translation tasks and did not require additional manual annotation. In this paper, we defined three submodels: the first Multi-New model is the basis of the second model NEWBA-P and the third model NEWBA-E. The Multi-New model can detect new words in multilingual corpora and improve the recall by using the word list iterative generation method. NEWBA-P model and NEWBA-E model both can obtain bilingual word pairs to achieve translation knowledge. In addition, the NEWBA-P model was equivalent to refining the results of new word detection, which can improve the precision of the result. The NEWBA-E model used the new word list of another language to expand its own word list, which can improve the recall of the result.

In summary, NEWBA has the following contributions:

- It can work on multilingual corpora to obtain new words.
- It can obtain a refined or expanded word list from bilingual corpora.
- It can obtain bilingual word pairs to achieve translation knowledge of the new words.

2   Related Work

New word detection and recognition had caught the attention of some researchers and had achieved remarkable results in the Chinese language. The different approaches at different stages of new word detection are as follows:

In the stage of new word candidate generation, we can calculate various statistics for words [6]. Contextual Entropy (CE) can be used as the external feature of candidate words [1], and pointwise mutual information (PMI) can be used as the internal word-formation probability of candidate words [7]. Multi-word pointwise mutual information (mPMI) had a good effect on the calculation of multi-word phrases, which can detect longer words from text [8]. Overlapping score (OV score) was used to calculate features for edge substrings and adjacent strings [9]. The threshold value of OV score can be set to filter word results, but it was essentially the same as threshold screening of various statistics. In order to reduce the computational complexity, we took CE and mPMI as the statistics of candidate words and explored the optimal thresholds of CE and mPMI.

In the stage of noise pruning, WEBM used a noise pruning strategy based on word embedding [10]. But this method was based on frequent n-gram string mining: it generated a large number of junk word strings, resulting in low precision and ignorance of the context knowledge. MWEC was an improved version of WEBM [11], which used multi-semantic word vectors to solve the polysemy problem of Chinese words. It was also possible to construct word sets with weak ability of word-generation based on word embedding for noise pruning [12], but this method was likely to filter out correct words.

In addition, the presegmentation of the original corpus was affected by the performance of the word tokenizer [13,14]; we worked on word unit-level without any dictionary knowledge. To ensure the generalization ability of the model, NEWBA was different only in the morphological segmentation part for different languages.

In previous researches, new word detection and recognition were two separate tasks [15]. It was a good idea to use known words to label new ones [16]. An automatic labeling algorithm can be constructed by calculating the context similarity between known and new words, but this approach was less accurate because two words with a high contextual similarity do not imply that they would necessarily mean the same. Other researches were carried out by training annotated corpus. We believe that new word recognition should be an unsupervised process like new word detection, therefore supervised approach is not the main focus of this paper.

In summary, methods proposed in previous papers rarely explored understanding of new words. In addition, these methods may achieve good performance for a single language like Chinese, but they have not been practiced on multilingual corpora. We believe that there is a lot of valuable information in the bilingual alignment corpus, but an enhanced algorithm is still lacking to acquire translation knowledge from them. In this paper, we proposed an enhanced new word identification approach based on bilingual corpus alignment, it was also the first one to attempt applying word alignment to new word detection.

3   Methodology

3.1   Architecture

In this section, we present NEWBA, an enhanced new word identification approach based on bilingual corpus alignment.

As Fig. 1 illustrates, NEWBA was divided into two parts. The process described on the left path is the Multi-New model, a multilingual new word detection algorithm. We divided two language texts into word units using different morphological segmentation methods, and then expanded word units one by one to generate candidate words. We performed feature calculation, which included mPMI and CE, for each candidate word. We set reasonable thresholds for mPMI and CE, and a new word list was obtained after the candidate word set was filtered by the thresholds. We used the word list iterative generation method to re-input the new word list as a known dictionary into the morphological segmentation program to generate new words in a loop. The diamond component in the figure indicates whether the loop should be terminated, in this case, it is that no more new words are being produced. Specific model settings are described in Sect. 3.2.

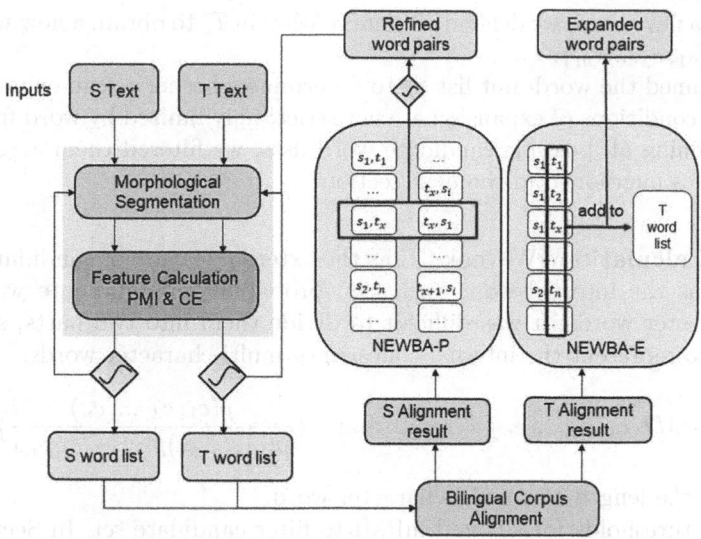

Fig. 1. NEWBA: The enhanced bilingual new words identification algorithm.

The process described on the right path is enhanced bilingual identification algorithm. We implemented two sub-models: NEWBA-P model and NEWBA-E model. We used the bilingual alignment program to obtain word unit alignment results of bilingual parallel corpus. The input of the NEWBA-P model is two word lists and the outputs are bilingual word pairs and their confidence scores obtained in each loop; the loop terminates under the condition that no new bilingual word pairs are being generated. The input of the NEWBA-E model is the final word list of the two languages in the left algorithm and the outputs are bilingual word pairs after expansion and their confidence scores. Specific model settings are described in Sect. 3.3.

3.2 Multi-new Model

Candidate Words Generation. We generated sequences of word units for multilingual language texts. In order to avoid dependence of new word detection results on the performance of word segmentation program, we conducted word-unit level new word detection. To acquire results of longer words, we expanded word units one by one to generate candidate words, which we call **extend generation method**.

We divided the monolingual text T_s into a sequence of word units $C = \{c_1, c_2, ...c_{num}\}$, where num is the total number of word units in T_s. We removed the duplicate word units in C and get a new word-unit list $C_s = \{c_1, c_2, ...c_n\}$. For each c_i in C_s, its position index in T_s is $R_i = \{r_1, r_2, ...r_f\}$, where f is the frequency of c_i in T_s. Since the combination of word units and punctuation cannot be a new word, we deleted all punctuation in T_s to obtain a new word-unit list $S_s = \{s_1, s_2, ...s_m\}$.

We scanned the word-unit list S_s to determine whether s_i can expand to the right. The conditions of expansion are not strict; only limited by word frequency. After obtaining all possible candidate word lists, we filtered them according to the statistics mentioned in the next section.

Feature Calculation. We took CE as the external feature of candidate words, and PMI as the internal word formation probability of candidate words. For multi-character words, it was difficult to divide them into two parts, so mPMI was used to represent the internal cohesion of multi-character words.

$$mPMI(c_1, c_2, ..., c_n) = \log_2 \min_{1 \leq i \leq n-1} \left\{ \frac{p(c_1, c_2, ..., c_n)}{p(c_1, ..., c_i)p(c_{i+1}, ..., c_n)} \right\} \tag{1}$$

where n is the length of a multi-character word.

We set thresholds for CE and mPMI to filter candidate set. In Sect. 4.2, we will be exploring thresholds for optimal performance.

Word List Iterative Generation Method. The first new word detection process of monolingual text T_s was at character-level, and in its subsequent new word detection process, we adopted the word list iterative generation method to add new words into the dictionary of word segmentation program. After word segmentation of the original text T_s was done, we repeated the new word detection process to generate new words in a loop. This process was being repeated until no new words are generated.

3.3   Bilingual Identification Algorithm

We looked for new words in T_s and T_t and obtained two new word lists W_s and W_t. Although T_s and T_t were bilingual parallel corpora, they were different in size due to the different word-formation characteristics of each language, and the new words obtained are not completely corresponding.

We splitted the bilingual text T_s and T_t line by line, and used an aligner [17] to get word units alignment results. The aligner produced outputs in the $i - j$ format. A pair $i - j$ indicated that the i_{th} word unit (zero-indexed) of the source sentence was aligned to the j_{th} word unit of the target sentence. An example of parallel sentence alignment in Chinese and Japanese is shown in Fig. 2.

The word unit alignment results and alignment scores of bilingual text T_s and T_t are as follows:

$$result_{align} = \{[source_i, target_i, score_i]\}_{i=1}^m \tag{2}$$

where m is the number of lines in the original text, $Source_i$ is the word unit index of the source language, $target_i$ is the word unit index of the target language, and $score_i$ is the alignment score.

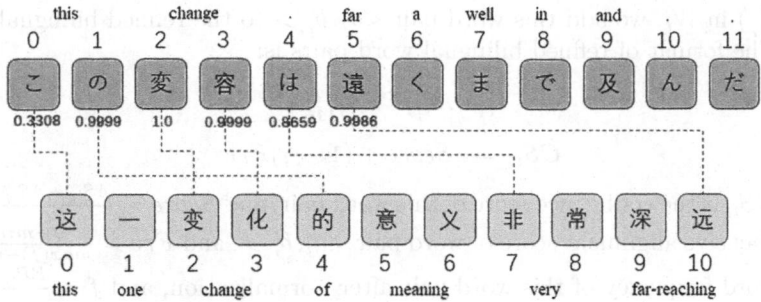

Fig. 2. Examples of Chinese and Japanese parallel sentence alignment. The numbers on the dotted line are aligned scores, which were obtained by the bilingual aligner [17]. This sentence in English means: The implications of this change are profound.

For the new word lists $W_s = \{a_1, a_2, ...a_{num_1}\}$ from $T_s = \{l_{a_1}, l_{a_2}, ...l_{a_m}\}$, where num_1 is the total number of words in W_s. For word unit a_i in W_s, scan each line in T_s and find index $index_{a_i}$ for all positions of a_i in T_s, and we can get the index of a_i in T_t and its alignment score as follows:

$$align_{a_i} = \{[a_i, b'_{i_j}, P_{i_j}]\}_{j=1}^{k} \tag{3}$$

$$P_{i_x} = \frac{\sum_{j=0}^{len} p_j}{len} \tag{4}$$

where len is the length of $a_i = \{c_1, c_2, ...c_{len}\}$, p_j is the alignment score of c_j, and p is the alignment probability score. We set the alignment score threshold $P_{threshold}$ and filtered out all alignment results that are less than this value.

We noticed that a_i may correspond to the same b'_{i_x} many times, because the word $<a_i, b'i_1>$ may appear in different la_x of T_s. For this reason, we removed the duplicate values and obtained the new alignment result of a_i:

$$align_{a_i} = \{[a_i, b'_{i_j}, AS_{i_j}, FP_{i_j}]\}_{j=1}^{k} \tag{5}$$

where $AS_{i_x} = \frac{\sum_{j=0}^{F_{i_x}} P_{i_j}}{F_{i_x}}$ is the alignment score of the word pair $<a_i, b'_{i_x}>$, $FP_{i_x} = \frac{F_{i_x}}{\sum_{u=0}^{k} F_{i_u}}$ is the probability that the word pair $<a_i, b'_{i_x}>$ occur, F_{i_x} is the frequency of the word pair $<a_i, b'_{i_x}>$, $\sum_{u=0}^{k} F_{i_u}$ is the total frequency of a_i in T_s, and $\sum_{x=0}^{k} FP_{i_x} = 1$.

NEWBA-P Model. Two sets of alignment results can be obtained from new words list W_s and W_t, that is, the alignment result $<a_i, b'_{i_k}, AS_{i_k}, FP_{i_k}>$ of a_i and the alignment result $<b_i, a'_{i_l}, AS_{i_l}, FP_{i_l}>$ of b_i. Some parts of a_{i_x} and a'_{i_x} were the same, and parts of bi_x and $b'i_x$ were also the same. This means that the b'_{i_x} corresponding to a_i in W_s also appeared in W_t. The NEWBA-P method is saying that, if $a'_{i_k} = a_i$ exists in the alignment result $<b_i, a'i_k, ASi_k, FP_{i_k}>$ of

$b_{i_x}(= b'_{i_x})$ in W_t, we add this word pair $<a_i, b'_{i_x}>$ to the refined bilingual word pairs. The format of refined bilingual word pairs is:

$$\{[a_i, b''_{i_j}, CS_{i_j}]\}_{j=1}^q \tag{6}$$

$$CS_{i_x} = \gamma Score + (1 - \gamma)Fre \tag{7}$$

where CS_{i_x} is the confidence score of this word pair, and $Score = \frac{AS_{i_k} + AS_{i_l}}{2}$ is the comprehensive alignment score of word pair $<a_i, b'_{i_x}>$, and $Fre = \frac{f - min(f)}{max(f) - min(f)}$ is the word frequency of this word pair after normalization, and $f = \frac{FP_{i_k} + FP_{i_l}}{2}$ is the average frequency of the two words. The higher the Fre and the $Score$, the higher the confidence of this word pair. Based on experimental results and experience, γ was set to 0.8.

We combined the NEWBA-P model with Multi-New model to generate the refined bilingual word pairs.

NEWBA-E Model. In some languages such as English, the amount of new words generated after detection of new words is very small; this is related to the language characteristics of English itself. But its parallel corpus, such as Chinese texts, may produce a large number of new words. This phenomenon gave us an idea of NEWBA-E method: we can use W_s generated by T_s to expand W_t of text T_t with only a few new words. The alignment result of a_i in T_t is shown in Eq. 8. We treated all b'_{i_x} as expandable to W_t:

$$\{[a_i, b'_{i_j}, AS_{i_j}, FP_{i_j}]\}_{j=1}^k \tag{8}$$

The format of expanded bilingual word pairs is shown in Eq. 9:

$$\{[a_i, b'_{i_j}, CS_{i_j}]\}_{j=1}^k \tag{9}$$

$$CS_{i_x} = \gamma Score + (1 - \gamma)Fre \tag{10}$$

where $Score = AS_{i_x}$ is the comprehensive alignment score of word pair $<a_i, b'_{i_x}>$, and $Fre = \frac{f - min(f)}{max(f) - min(f)}$ is the word frequency of this word pair after normalization, in which $f = FP_{i_x}$. The higher the Fre and the $Score$, the higher the confidence of this word pair.

The input of the NEWBA-E model was the complete new words list of T_s obtained through Multi-New model, and the output of this model was the expanded bilingual word pairs.

4   Experiment

4.1   Datasets

We conducted experiments on parallel datasets of news-commentary corpus released for the WMT series of shared tasks [18]. We used two bilingual parallel corpora, Chinese-Japanese corpus and Chinese-English corpus of the news-commentary v14 parallel dataset.

Table 1. The n-gram words statistical results of each corpus. Zh-Ja is the Chinese-Japanese parallel corpus, and Zh-En is the Chinese-English parallel corpus.

Language	# of n-gram words	# of new words
Zh-Ja (Chinese)	4210	1656
Zh-Ja (Japanese)	6069	1266
Zh-En (Chinese)	5134	1949
Zh-En (English)	5059	2040

4.2 Results of Multi-new Model

For different languages, we only needed to adopt different morpheme segmentation methods. Chinese and Japanese have no natural delimiters, so we treated each character as a word unit (each word as a word unit for English).

It is important to determine how to obtain ground truth for detecting new words from a real-world dataset. To obtain reliable evaluation indicators, we segmented the original text by word units and counted the frequency of n-gram based on word units. We perform additional artificial judgment on extra long words. We got an n-gram list, and most results of it were meaningless. Take the Japanese text for example, we asked two Japanese majors to tag these n-grams, and they were asked to decide whether an n-gram was a grammatical word. Table 1 is the n-gram words' statistical results of each corpus. The data here was filtered by repeated values and word frequency.

In order to explore the impact of CE and $mPMI$'s thresholds on the results, we first conducted experiments on Chinese text from a parallel Chinese-Japanese corpus. We set 5 different thresholds for CE and $mPMI$ for a total of 5×5 group experiments. The F1 values of the experiments performed on this dataset are shown in Fig. 3.

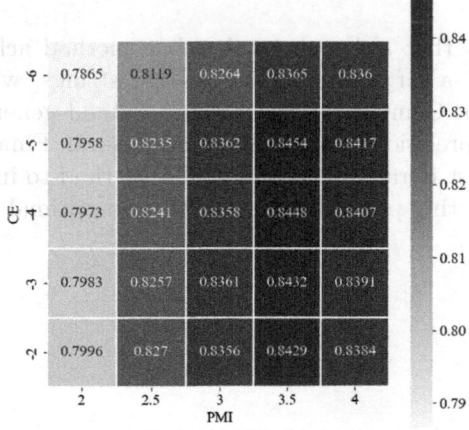

Fig. 3. F1 values of the experiments performed on Chinese text from parallel Chinese-Japanese corpus.

The results in Fig. 3 show that when CE threshold was set to -5 and mPMI threshold was set to 3.5, the optimal $F1$ value can be obtained in the experiment. Therefore, we set the thresholds of CE and mPMI to -5 and 3.5 in subsequent experiments. The results in Fig. 3 also show that under the same CE threshold, different mPMI thresholds had a great impact on $F1$. However, when the mPMI threshold has been kept the same, the threshold setting of CE had little influence on the result.

Table 2 shows the results of Multi-New method on two parallel datasets. The baseline model adopted n-gram candidate words generation method; we calculated CE and mPMI for the candidate words and removed the candidate words that were less than the mPMI or CE threshold to get the final result. In the extend generation method, we used the right-extending candidate words generation method. In the Multi-New method, we adopted the word list iterative generation (IG) method to discover more new words.

Table 2. Multilingual new word detection results.

Method	Language	Precision	Recall	F1-value
Baseline	Zh-Ja (Chinese)	56.37%	90.03%	69.33%
Extend generation	Zh-Ja (Chinese)	94.15%	61.29%	74.25%
Multi-new (Extend generation+IG)	Zh-Ja (Chinese)	86.29%	82.86%	**84.54%**
Baseline	Zh-Ja (Japanese)	33.42%	86.41%	48.20%
Extend generation	Zh-Ja (Japanese)	68.68%	47.28%	56.01%
Multi-new (Extend generation+IG)	Zh-Ja (Japanese)	65.20%	53.49%	**58.76%**
Baseline	Zh-En (Chinese)	57.46%	89.77%	70.07%
Extend generation	Zh-En (Chinese)	91.53%	56.59%	69.94%
Multi-new (Extend generation+IG)	Zh-En (Chinese)	86.19%	79.05%	**82.47%**
Baseline	Zh-En (English)	33.44%	15.24%	20.94%
Extend generation	Zh-En (English)	49.91%	13.80%	21.63%
Multi-new (Extend generation+IG)	Zh-En (English)	48.29%	15.24%	**23.17%**

The results show that although the baseline method achieves high performance, it generated a large number of garbage strings, which resulted in a decrease in precision. Compared with baseline, extend generation method significantly improved precision, but with a reduced recall. Finally, the Multi-New method used word list iterative generation (IG) method to improve recall without significantly affecting precision and obtained an optimal F1 value.

The rules mentioned above were all demonstrated by the experimental results acquired from the three different language corpora. However, differences can be seen in various language corpora's evaluation indicator values. We obtained better results in both Chinese datasets, while the results in other languages are relatively low, which is related to the characteristics of language word-formation and the manual annotation of the corpus. Nevertheless, effectiveness of the Multi-New method can be proven through these experimental results.

The results of the comparative experiments are presented in Table 3. As shown in Table 3, mPMI and CE methods performed better than the pruning strategy based on word embedding [10]. When the pruning strategy was added to the baseline model, the F1-value decreased, suggesting that the pruning strategy mistakenly deleted some correct words. The TopWORDS method was based on the EM algorithm to generate the word list [19], which had the highest recall, but the precision was not as good as extend generation method and the Multi-New model. The results in the Table 3 also showed that extend generation method can reduce noise words and has higher precision than the n-gram method. The multi-new model used the word list iterative generation method, which had a higher recall and achieved the best performance.

Table 3. The comparative results of different methods on Chinese text from parallel Chinese-Japanese corpus.

Method	Precision	Recall	F1-value
n-gram+Prune strategy	41.76%	91.60%	57.37%
n-gram+CE+mPMI	56.37%	90.03%	69.33%
n-gram+CE+mPMI+Prune strategy	56.78%	84.11%	67.80%
Extend generation	94.15%	61.29%	74.25%
Extend generation+IG (Multi-new)	86.29%	82.86%	**84.54%**
TopWORDS	67.24%	95.89%	79.05%

4.3   Results of NEWBA-P Model and NEWBA-E Model

Since the methods of bilingual alignment are not the focus of this paper, we used the third-party multilingual alignment tool Awesome-align to carry out the experiment of bilingual word identification.

Table 4. The examples of bilingual word pairs obtained from two parallel corpora on NEWBA-P model. CS is the confidence score of the word pair.

Zh-Ja	CS	Zh-En	CS
经济- 経済 (Economic)	0.8906	央行-Central banks	0.9988
经验- 経験 (Experience)	0.8033	不仅-Not only	0.8999
答案- 答え (Answer)	0.8031	即使-Even if	0.8998
事实- 事実 (Truth)	0.8015	毕竟-After all	0.8989
正确- 適切 (Correct)	0.7999	由此-The resulting	0.8759
贫困- 貧困 (Poverty)	0.7594	如今-Now that	0.7776
资产价格- 資産価格 (Asset price)	0.7135	即便-Even if	0.7345
方面- 方で (Aspect)	0.7644	他们-It was	0.6966
贫困- 貧しい (Poverty)	0.6200	第二-The second	0.5850
工人- 労働者 (Worker)	0.5898	问题-The question	0.4314

Table 5 shows the results of two NEWBA sub-models in two parallel corpora. Chinese and Japanese are two similar East Asian languages. The NEWBA-P model achieved good results in the Chinese-Japanese parallel corpus. A total of 1048 bilingual word pairs were obtained in the NEWBA-P model. However, the NEWBA-P model only got 11 valid bilingual word pairs in the Chinese-English parallel corpus, which resulted in a very low recall. The reason is that the alignment results of a great number of new words generated in Chinese were single English words. In contrast, the list of new words generated in English only included phrases composed of two or more words. Table 4 is examples of bilingual

Table 5. Experimental results of NEWBA-P model and NEWBA-E model.

Method	Language	Precision	Recall	F1-value
Multi-new	Zh-Ja (Chinese)	86.29%	82.86%	84.54%
NEWBA-P	Zh-Ja (Chinese)	97.52%	40.43%	57.16%
NEWBA-E	Zh-Ja (Chinese)	44.64%	85.81%	58.73%
Multi-new	Zh-Ja (Japanese)	65.20%	53.49%	58.76%
NEWBA-P	Zh-Ja (Japanese)	91.77%	39.65%	55.37%
NEWBA-E	Zh-Ja (Japanese)	25.22%	63.28%	36.07%
Multi-new	Zh-En (Chinese)	86.19%	79.05%	82.47%
NEWBA-P	Zh-En (Chinese)	100.0%	0.51%	1.03%
NEWBA-E	Zh-En (Chinese)	73.85%	79.10%	76.39%
Multi-new	Zh-En (English)	48.29%	15.24%	23.17%
NEWBA-P	Zh-En (English)	60.00%	0.29%	0.58%
NEWBA-E	Zh-En (English)	9.27%	21.22%	12.91%

word pairs obtained on NEWBA-P model. As expected, one word may correspond to several different words in another language. This phenomenon indicates that the bilingual corpus contains linguistic knowledge of different expressions of synonyms.

As the data in Table 2 shows, the Multi-New model worked best on the Chinese corpus, which was able to find more new words with better quality. By using the NEWBA-E model, we can utilize the results of the Chinese corpus to expand the number of new words in other languages to improve its recall. Table 5 shows that the expansion effect of Chinese to Japanese and Chinese to English is significant, on the contrary, the expansion effect of Japanese to Chinese and English to Chinese is negligible.

It should be noted that 2953 extra single-word results were generated in the NEWBA-E experiment conducted on the Chinese-English corpus, which was of course not included in the results shown in Table 5. Instead, examples of these results are shown in Table 6. We think that this phenomenon reveals the character of word units in Chinese and English.

Table 6. The examples of single-word results produced in Chinese to English NEWBA-E experiment.

国家-countries	经济-economic	因为-because	增长-growth	国际-international	危机-crisis
0.9482	0.9343	0.8994	0.8986	0.8453	0.8402

5 Conclusions

The experimental results on two bilingual parallel corpora of 3 languages revealed that the performance of NEWBA was superior to the results from the traditional unsupervised methods. NEWBA was able to obtain results beyond detection, namely bilingual word pairs, which can give us translation knowledge of words. Future research will explore new languages and introduce more benchmarked methods into comparative experiments.

Acknowledgments. This work is partly supported by the Beijing Natural Science Foundation (No. 4212026 and No. 4202069) and the Fundamental Strengthening Program Technology Field Fund (No. 2021-JCJQ-JJ-0059).

References

1. Huang, J.H., Powers, D.: Chinese word segmentation based on contextual entropy. In: Proceedings of the 17th Pacific Asia Conference on Language, Information and Computation, pp. 152–158 (2003)
2. Zhang, H.P., Shang, J.Y.: Social media-oriented open domain new word detection. J. Chin. Inf. Process. **3**, 115–121 (2017)
3. Chen, K.J., Ma, W.Y.: Unknown word extraction for Chinese documents. In: COLING 2002: The 19th International Conference on Computational Linguistics (2002)

4. Montariol, S., Allauzen, A.: Measure and evaluation of semantic divergence across two languages. In: ACL 2021 (Volume 1: Long Papers), pp. 1247–1258 (2021)
5. Chang, B.: Chinese-English parallel corpus construction and its application. In: Proceedings of The 18th Pacific Asia Conference on Language, Information and Computation, pp. 283–290 (2004)
6. Chengke, Y., Junlan, Z.: New word identification algorithm in natural language processing. In: 2020 2nd International Conference on Machine Learning, Big Data and Business Intelligence (MLBDBI), pp. 199–203. IEEE (2020)
7. Chen, F., Liu, Y.Q.: Open domain new word detection using condition random field method. J. Softw. **24**(5), 1051–1060 (2013)
8. Wang, X.: An improved neologism synthesis algorithm based on multi-word mutual information and adjacency entropy. Mod. Comput. **4**, 7–11 (2018)
9. Ye, Y., Wu, Q.: Unknown Chinese word extraction based on variety of overlapping strings. Inf. Process. Manag. **49**(2), 497–512 (2013)
10. Qian, Y., Du, Y.: Detecting new Chinese words from massive domain texts with word embedding. J. Inf. Sci. **45**(2), 196–211 (2019)
11. Le, Z., Jidong, L.: Discovering Chinese new words based on multi-sense word embedding. Data Anal. Knowl. Discov. **6**(1), 113–121 (2022)
12. Zhang, J., Huang, K.: Unsupervised new word extraction from Chinese social media data. J. Chin. Inf. Process. (2018)
13. Huang, X.J., Peng, F.C.: Applying machine learning to text segmentation for information retrieval. Inf. Retrieval **6**(3), 333–362 (2003)
14. Sproat, R., Emerson, T.: The first international Chinese word segmentation bake-off. In: Proceedings of the Second SIGHAN Workshop on Chinese Language Processing, pp. 133–143 (2003)
15. Sun, Z., Deng, Z.H.: Unsupervised neural word segmentation for Chinese via segmental language modeling. arXiv preprint arXiv:1810.03167 (2018)
16. Liang, Y., Yin, P., Yiu, S.M.: New word detection and tagging on Chinese Twitter stream. In: Madria, S., Hara, T. (eds.) DaWaK 2015. LNCS, vol. 9263, pp. 310–321. Springer, Cham (2015). https://doi.org/10.1007/978-3-319-22729-0_24
17. Dou, Z.Y., Neubig, G.: Word alignment by fine-tuning embeddings on parallel corpora. arXiv preprint arXiv:2101.08231 (2021)
18. Barrault, L., et al.: Findings of the 2019 conference on machine translation. In: Proceedings of WMT (2019)
19. Deng, K., Bol, P.K.: On the unsupervised analysis of domain-specific Chinese texts. Proc. Natl. Acad. Sci. **113**(22), 6154–6159 (2016)

Machine Learning for NLP (Oral)

Multi-task Learning with Auxiliary Cross-attention Transformer for Low-Resource Multi-dialect Speech Recognition

Zhengjia Dan[1] , Yue Zhao[1](✉) , Xiaojun Bi[1], Licheng Wu[1] , and Qiang Ji[2]

[1] School of Information Engineering, Minzu University of China, Beijing 100080, China
zhaoyueso@muc.edu.cn
[2] Department of Electrical, Computer, and Systems Engineering, Rensselaer Polytechnic Institute, Troy, NY 12180-3590, USA

Abstract. In this paper, we apply multi-task learning to perform low-resource multi-dialect speech recognition, and propose a method combining Transformer and soft parameter sharing multi-task learning. Our model has two task streams: the primary task stream that recognizes speech and the auxiliary task stream identifies the dialect. The auxiliary task stream provides the dialect identification information to the auxiliary cross-attention of the primary task stream, so that the primary task stream has dialect discrimination. Experimental results on the task of Tibetan multi-dialect speech recognition show that our model outperforms the single-dialect model and hard parameter sharing based multi-dialect model, by reducing the average syllable error rate (ASER) by 30.22% and 3.89%, respectively.

Keywords: Speech recognition · Tibetan multi-dialect · Multi-task learning · Transformer · Auxiliary cross-attention

1 Introduction

Multi-dialect speech recognition has received extensive attention in the field of speech recognition in recent years. It is more challenging than general speech recognition tasks because the various dialects of a language have more similarities in phoneme sets, word pronunciation, prosodic features and grammar. Moreover, some dialects of minority language lack the linguistic research and a large amount of labeled data. For example, Tibetan is one of the minority languages in China. It is divided into three major dialects in China, including Ü-Tsang, Kham and Amdo dialects. These dialects are pronounced very differently in different regions, but the written characters and grammar are identical. At present, the main research on Tibetan speech recognition focus on Ü-Tsang and Amdo dialects [1–5]. There is a serious lack of research work on linguistics, speech recognition, and corpus establishment for Kham dialect.

Multi-dialect speech recognition models can be constructed by fine-tuning [6] or adding dialect information [7]/I-vector [8] to speech features. However, in order to obtain a multi-dialect model that is comparable to a single-dialect model, sufficient corpus is required. In contrast, multi-task learning (MTL) seems to be less corpus-demanding, as MTL is often applied to speech recognition in low-resource languages to improve model performance [9–13]. Therefore, for a low-resource language such as Tibetan, it seems to be a better choice to build a MTL based multi-dialect speech recognition model.

Multi-task learning (MTL) is introduced into speech recognition to exploit small target datasets to train acoustic models of deep neural network for low-resource domains [9–13]. There are two main categories of multi-task deep learning architectures: one is done with hard parameter sharing and the other is soft parameter sharing of hidden layers [14]. Hard parameter sharing of MTL is the most widely used approach, which learns a shared representation from primary task and auxiliary tasks, and reduces the risk of overfitting on original task. In contrast, to learn both task-specific features and shared features between tasks, the soft parameter sharing architectures presented in the works [15, 16] use cross-stitch units or task-specific attention networks to learn features at layers shared with the other task. At present, multi-dialect or multi-language speech recognition commonly uses a hard parameter sharing of MTL. The work of [17] used this multi-task framework to carry out joint training of multiple low resource languages, and explored the universal phoneme set as a secondary task to improve the effect of phoneme models of various languages. The work of [18] adopted Wavenet-CTC to conduct a Tibetan multi-dialect speech recognition model with hard parameter sharing MTL using dialect/speaker recognition as an auxiliary task. The experiments show that the model performance can be effectively improved when dialect recognition is an auxiliary task.

In the work of [19], the ViLBERT is presented for learning task-agnostic joint representations of image content and natural language. The ViLBERT can interact with the two-stream inputs via the co-attention transformer to learn the joint representation between two modalities. Inspired by ViLBERT, in this work, we propose an auxiliary cross-attention transformer with soft parameter sharing MTL to capture the weighted features from dialect ID recognition task to help low-resource multi-dialect speech recognition task. The experimental results show that our method has significant improvement against the hard parameter sharing multi-task learning for low-resource Tibetan dialect speech recognition.

2 Related Work

The traditional multi-dialect recognition methods usually define a set of general phoneme set, use the data of dialects for joint training, and then apply to data of interested dialects for tuning of the model parameters [20–24]. They require a dialect-specific pronunciation and language model (PM and LM), which is trained independently from the multi-dialect acoustic model (AM). Therefore, if the AM predicts incorrectly, errors are propagated to the PM and LM. To solve this problem, researchers have discussed the use of end-to-end technology to build a single network multi-dialect recognition model [25–27]. The end-to-end models fold the AM, PM and LM into a single network, making them attractive to explore for multi-dialect speech recognition. Building a multi-dialect end-to-end model does not need to use a lot of language knowledge to build dialect-specific pronunciation dictionary and language models. It is hence very suitable to construct a speech recognition model for the dialects with poor linguistic knowledge. In the existing works, the attention mechanism is introduced into end-to-end model with hard parameter sharing [25–27] for improving the accuracy of decoder.

In order to further improve the recognition rate of the model, the existing multi-dialect speech recognition methods also used other tasks as auxiliary task, such as dialect-ID recognition [27], speaker recognition [28] and other tasks. Although these models differ in details, most of them adopt the hard parameter sharing to capture the common feature among different tasks. It is unclear how the auxiliary task contributes its information to help the primary tasks.

In this work, we propose an auxiliary cross-attention Transformer for soft parameter sharing MTL to demonstrate how weighted information from the dialect-ID recognition task can help multi-dialect speech recognition task. Several auxiliary cross-attention blocks are introduced between two transformer streams to compute the weights of the encoder outputs from dialect-ID task and to provide their output for the decoder of the multi-dialect transformer.

3   Method

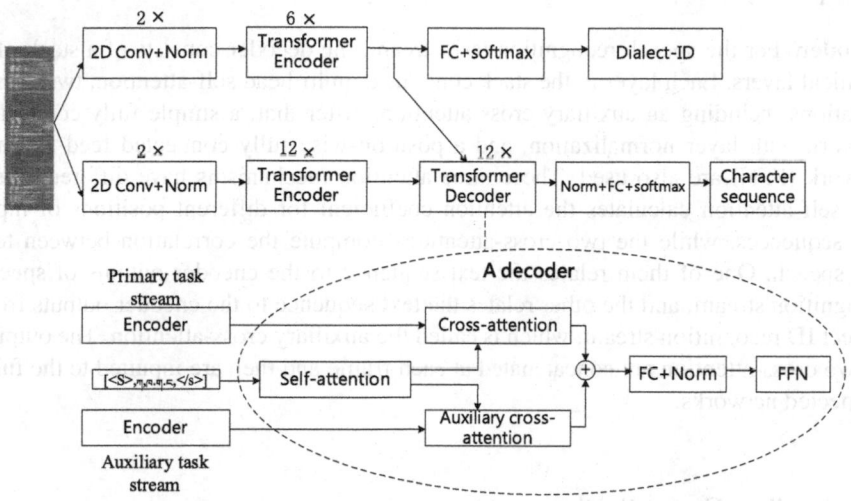

Fig. 1. The structure of auxiliary cross-attention transformer.

This section introduces our MTL with auxiliary cross-attention Transformer model, which is based on Speech-Transformer [29]. The framework of our model is shown in Fig. 1.

The MTL framework for multi-dialect speech recognition has two streams, where the upper stream belongs to the dialect ID recognition task, and the lower stream belongs to the speech recognition task. The primary task stream can be divided into three parts: convolutional blocks, Transformer encoders, and Transformer decoders. The auxiliary task stream is similar to the primary task stream, but it replaces the Transformer decoders with fully connected network (FC) and soft-max layer. Moreover, to make the Transformer decoder take into account the dialect identification information to predict character sequence, auxiliary cross-attention is added to the decoder of the primary task stream to provide the weighted dialect information. The details of the two streams and auxiliary cross-attention will be described as follows.

3.1 Two Task Streams

Convolutional Block. Similar to Speech-transformer, both task streams firstly use two convolutional layers to extract high-dimensional features of speech, and batch normalization is performed after each convolutional layer.

Encoder. The encoder of primary task stream consists of a stack of 12 identical layers. Each layer has two sub-layers. The first sub-layer is a multi-head self-attention mechanism, and the second one is a position-wise fully connected network. A residual connection is used after each of the two sublayers. This is then followed by a layer normalization, which can normalize the same feature field, so that the model has better robustness. The encoder internal structure of the auxiliary task stream is exactly the same as the primary task stream, but there are only 6 layers of encoders.

Decoder. For the speech recognition task stream, the decoder consists of a stack of 6 identical layers. Each layer in the stack contains a multi-head self-attention, two cross-attentions including an auxiliary cross-attention. After that, a simple fully connected network with layer normalization, and a position-wise fully connected feed-forward network (FFN) are also used. These three attention mechanisms have different aims. The self-attention calculates the attention coefficient for different positions of input text sequences, while the two cross-attentions compute the correlation between text and speech. One of them relates the text sequence to the encoder outputs of speech recognition stream, and the other relates the text sequence to the encoder outputs from dialect ID recognition stream, which is called the auxiliary cross-attention. The outputs of two cross-attention are concatenated at each frame and then are inputted to the fully connected networks.

3.2 Auxiliary Cross-attention

The input of auxiliary cross-attention consists of the output of self-attention layer (Output$_{self-attn}$), and the output of the encoder from the dialect recognition task (Output$_{auxiliary-encoder}$). As shown in Fig. 2, to calculate auxiliary cross-attention, the first step needs to create three vectors of Q, K, and V, respectively. These vectors are created via multiplying the two kinds of outputs by three weight matrices W^Q, W^K and W^V learned during the training process. As shown in Formulas (1)–(3), Output$_{auxiliary-encoder}$ is used to create K and V, which represents the dialect information, and Q is created by Output$_{self-attn}$, which represents the text information.

$$Q = Output_{self-attn} \cdot W^Q \tag{1}$$

$$K = Output_{auxiliary-encoder} \cdot W^K \tag{2}$$

$$V = Output_{auxiliary-encoder} \cdot W^V \tag{3}$$

After Q, K and V, we obtain the weights on V via Formula (4). The output of auxiliary cross-attention is referred to as ACA(Q, K,V).

$$ACA(Q, K, V) = softmax(\frac{Q \cdot K^T}{\sqrt{d_k}}) \cdot V \tag{4}$$

where d_k is the dimension of Q and K. The scalar $\sqrt{d_k}$ is used to prevent softmax function from generating very small gradients. The auxiliary cross-attention is performed in multi-head attention mechanism mode.

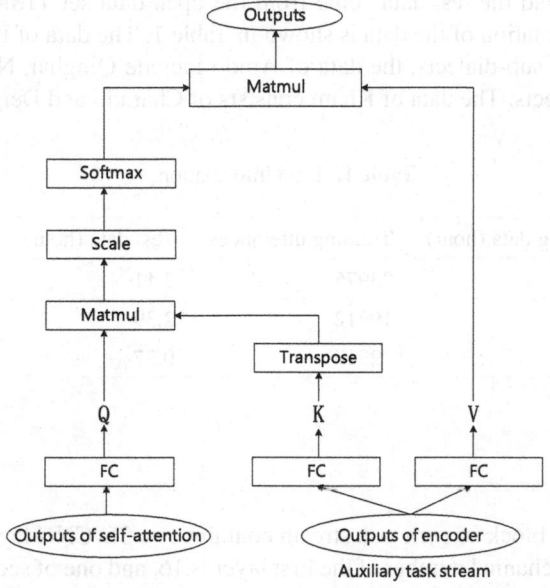

Fig. 2. One head of auxiliary cross-attention.

4 Experiment

4.1 Data

In the experiments, we evaluate our method using speech data from three Tibetan dialects for multi-dialect speech recognition. These three Tibetan dialects are pronounced quite differently. In the Ü-Tsang and Kham dialects, there are some tones that distinguish the meanings of words. However, the Amdo dialect has no tone and its compound consonants

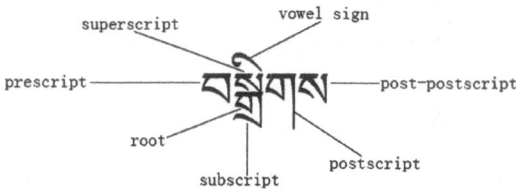

Fig. 3. The structure of a Tibetan syllable.

and vowels are pronounced clearly. Tibetan words are unified for Tibetan dialects, which are written in 34 Tibetan letters from left to right, but there is a vertical superposition in a single syllable, forming a two-dimensional planar syllable as shown in Fig. 3.

In this work, Tibetan syllable is used as recognition unit, so the error rate calculation method used is the syllable error rate (SER). The embedding vector dimension of a syllable is 256, and the speech feature adopts the 40-dimensional Fbank feature. Both the training data and the test data come from the open data set TIBMD@MUC [30]. The detailed information of the data is shown in Table 1. The data of Ü-Tsang contains Lhasa and Rikaze sub-dialects, the data of Amdo include Qinghai, Ngawa and Xiahe Post-oral sub-dialects. The data of Kham consists of Chamdo and Derge sub-dialects.

Table 1. Data information.

	Training data (hour)	Training utterances	Test data (hour)	Test utterances
Ü-Tsang	27.63	23975	3.11	2663
Amdo	21.33	19712	2.39	2190
Kham	3.24	2919	0.37	324

4.2 Settings

The convolutional block of each task stream contains two 2D CNN layers with stride 2, kernel size 3. The channel number of the first layer is 16, and one of second layer is 128.

The encoder in primary task Transformer is a stack of 12 layers, however it is 6 layers for dialect-ID recognition task stream. Each layer has 4 attention heads, and each head is a self-attention with 64 dimensions. The output of each attention head is concatenated and multiplied with a weighted matrix. Then a two-layer fully connected neural network with an activation function of "LU" is used for nonlinear mapping. The node number is 2044 and 256 in these two layers respectively.

The configuration of self-attention, cross-attention and auxiliary cross-attention have 4 heads and 64 dimensions in decoders of the primary task stream.

Cross-entropy is used as the loss function for both tasks. Let $L_{primary}$ be the loss of the primary task and $L_{auxiliary}$ be the loss of the auxiliary task, then the two streams are jointly trained by Formula (5), where λ is the multi-task learning hyper-parameter.

$$L_{sum} = \lambda \cdot L_{primary} + (1 - \lambda) \cdot L_{auxiliary} \tag{5}$$

The auxiliary cross-attention Transformer is trained with 80 epochs, and batch size is 10. Adam optimizer with gradient clipping is used for optimization [31], and its learning rate is 0.001. The label smoothing technology [32] is used during training, and the smoothing parameter $\alpha = 0.1$. Decoding process uses a beam search algorithm with 5 beam-widths.

4.3 Experimental Results

We evaluate the proposed MTL with auxiliary cross-attention Transformer against single-dialect Transformer and the multi-dialect Transformer. Moreover, we also compare the auxiliary cross-attention Transformer with hard parameter sharing MTL based Transformer. Finally, the proposed model is further optimized by reducing the number of auxiliary cross-attention layer through the analysis on the coefficients of auxiliary cross-attention in each decoder layer.

Single-dialect Transformer, Multi-dialect Transformer and Auxiliary Cross-attention Transformer for Multi-dialects. The single-dialect Transformer and the multi-dialect Transformer are trained on the same structure with dialect-specific data and a mixed data from multiple dialects, respectively. According to the work of [26], in multi-dialect Transformer, dialect ID using one-hot vector is concatenated with Fbank feature for the input of convolutional block, with which the model is referred to as "One-hot + Multi-dialect Transformer"; dialect-ID using embedding vector is added with Fbank feature for the input of convolutional block, with which the model is referred to as "Embedding + Multi-dialect Transformer"; the "Text-ID + Multi-dialect Transformer" model was trained with dialect identity tokens in the end of target sequence of each utterance. For auxiliary cross-attention Transformer, it is trained under $\lambda = 0.9$, $\lambda = 0.8$ and $\lambda = 0.7$ respectively. We choose the best results with $\lambda = 0.9$ to compare with other models. Table 2 is the experimental result.

Table 2. The experimental results of auxiliary cross-attention transformer and baseline models.

Model	SER (%)		
	Ü-Tsang	Amdo	Kham
Single-dialect transformer	14	9.08	111.13
Multi-dialect transformer	8.22	5.66	41.36
One-hot + Multi-dialect transformer [26]	8.37	6.13	34.99
Embedding + Multi-dialect transformer [26]	10.28	7.31	43.17
Text-ID + Multi-dialect transformer [26]	8.65	5.64	35.54
Auxiliary cross-attention transformer	**6.11**	**4.3**	**33.14**

In Table 2, it shows that auxiliary cross-attention Transformer has an overwhelming advantage over other models for all dialects. The SER of auxiliary cross-attention Transformer on the Ü-Tsang dialect is 6.11%, which is a drop of 2.11% compared with

8.22% of the "Multi-dialect Transformer" model. The SER of Amdo dialect is 4.3%, which is reduced by 1.34% against the "Text-ID + Multi-dialect Transformer" model. For limited-data Kham dialect, the SER is 33.14%, which is significantly reduced by 77.99% relatively to single-dialect model, and by 1.85% relatively against the "One-hot + Multi-dialect Transformer" model. For three dialects, the average SER of auxiliary cross-attention Transformer is reduced by 30.22% relatively compared with "Single-dialect Transformer".

Auxiliary Cross-attention Transformer VS Hard Parameter Sharing Transformer.
To further evaluate the advantage of MTL with auxiliary cross-attention Transformer, we compare our method with the other MTL architecture – the hard parameter sharing multi-task learning (Hard-MTL). In addition, considering the influence of multi-task learning parameter λ, experiments were also performed with different λ values.

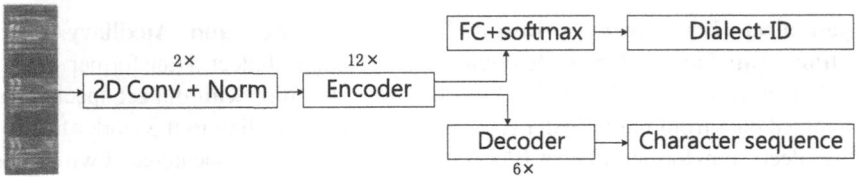

Fig. 4. The structure of hard parameter sharing Transformer.

Hard parameter sharing Transformer is applied by sharing the convolutional blocks and encoders between two tasks, while keeping task-specific top layers, as shown in Fig. 4. Except that there is no auxiliary cross-attention in the decoder, the configuration of the other modules is the same as the auxiliary cross-attention Transformer.

Table 3 shows the experimental results of the two architectures with different λ values. "Hard-MTL Transformer" represents the MTL Transformer based on hard parameter sharing. The experimental results reveals that both models have the lowest SERs

Table 3. The experimental results of auxiliary cross-attention transformer and Hard-MTL transformer.

Model	λ	SER (%)			Dialect recognition accuracy (%)		
		Ü-Tsang	Amdo	Kham	Ü-Tsang	Amdo	Kham
Auxiliary cross-attention transformer	0.9	**6.11**	**4.3**	33.14	99.71	99.85	**98.13**
	0.8	6.68	4.48	**33.09**	**99.85**	**99.95**	96.63
	0.7	8.17	4.49	38.87	99.75	99.49	97.75
Hard-MTL transformer	0.9	8.3	5.34	38.07	99.12	99.69	98.13
	0.8	9.49	6.63	43.72	98.97	98.57	97.38
	0.7	10.89	7.19	42.29	99.36	99.13	97.38

when λ is 0.9, but auxiliary cross-attention Transformer performs better than Hard-MTL Transformer on both tasks.

Auxiliary Cross-attention Weights Visualization. The auxiliary cross-attention Transformer has 6 auxiliary cross-attentions in the decoder of primary task, which provide the different weighted features of dialect ID information to the corresponding layer in primary task. We use a heat-map to visualize the weights of auxiliary cross-attention between the feature frames of the encoder in dialect ID stream and the text features. We find that for all three dialects the auxiliary cross-attention only at the 5-th layer performs good alignment between speech and text. Figure 5 shows the weight visualization of the 4 attention heads in 6 layers.

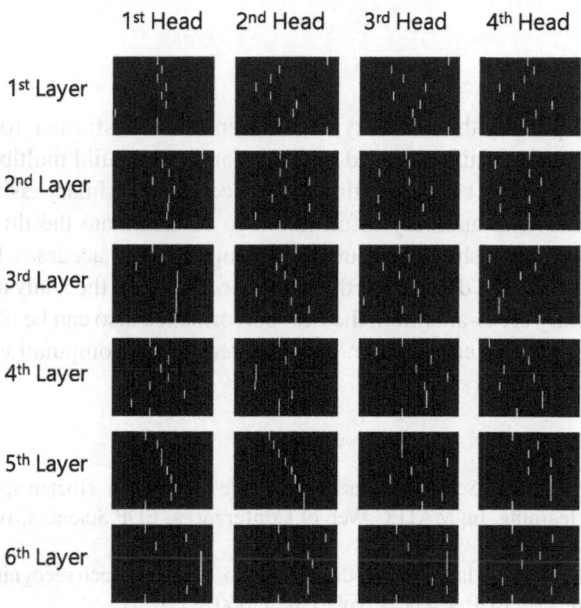

Fig. 5. Auxiliary cross-attention weight visualization.

The y-axis of the heat map is the Tibetan character sequence, and the x-axis is the speech feature frames. The white line shows the frame position of the greatest weight for each Tibetan character. Furtherly, we designed to use the auxiliary cross-attention only at the 5-th layer, and the other layers discard the auxiliary cross-attention. The experimental results are shown in Table 4 for the Transformer with 5-th auxiliary cross-attention layer represented as "Auxiliary cross-attention Transformer (5)".

Although the model of "Auxiliary cross-attention Transformer (5)" has only one layer of auxiliary cross-attention, it is competitive to the auxiliary cross-attention Transformer with 6 layers of auxiliary cross-attention. Its average SER has 0.11% lower than latter when λ is 0.9. It means that the "Auxiliary cross-attention Transformer (5)" model uses only a small amount of parameters to obtain the same recognition ability.

Table 4. The experimental results of MTL Transformer with 5-th auxiliary cross-attention layer.

Model	λ	SER (%)		
		Ü-Tsang	Amdo	Kham
Auxiliary cross-attention Transformer	0.9	6.11	4.3	33.14
	0.8	6.68	4.48	**33.09**
	0.7	8.17	4.49	38.87
Auxiliary cross-attention Transformer(5)	0.9	**5.42**	**3.3**	35.16
	0.8	6.76	4.35	34.19
	0.7	9.60	7.34	42.29

5 Conclusions

In this paper, we present the auxiliary cross-attention Transformer for low-resource multi-dialect speech recognition. Based on Transformer we build multiple task streams and introduce the auxiliary cross-attention in the decoder of primary task stream, which aims to provide the vital auxiliary information to discriminate the difference among dialects. The experiments show that our model improves the accuracy for all dialects, especially for low-resource dialect. Furthermore, according to the analysis of the weight matrix from auxiliary cross-attention, the best performance also can be obtained by only using an auxiliary cross-attention layer. This can reduce the computation cost.

References

1. Gong, B., Cai, R., et al.: Selection of acoustic modeling unit for Tibetan speech recognition based on deep learning. In: MATEC Web of Conferences, EDP Sciences, vol. 336, p. 06014 (2021)
2. Suan, T., Cai, R., et al.: A language model for Amdo Tibetan speech recognition. In: MATEC Web of Conferences, EDP Sciences, vol. 336, p. 06016 (2021)
3. Yang, X., Wang, W., et al.: Simple data augmented transformer end-to-end Tibetan speech recognition. In: 2020 IEEE 3rd International Conference on Information Communication and Signal Processing (ICICSP), pp. 148–152 (2020)
4. Gong, C., Li, G., et al.: Research on tibetan speech recognition speech dictionary and acoustic model algorithm. In: Journal of Physics: Conference Series, vol. 1570, p. 012003 (2020)
5. Wang, W., Chen, Z., et al.: Long short-term memory for tibetan speech recognition. In 2020 IEEE 4th, Information Technology, Networking, Electronic and Automation Control Conference (ITNEC), vol. 1, pp. 1059–1063 (2020)
6. Huang, Y., Yu, D., Liu, C., et al.: Multi-accent deep neural network acoustic model with accent-specific top layer using the KLD-regularized model adaptation. In 15th Annual Conference of the International Speech Communication Association (2014)
7. Jain, A., Upreti, M., Jyothi, P: Improved accented speech recognition using accent embeddings and multi-task learning. In: Proceedings of Interspeech. ISCA, pp. 2454–2458 (2018)
8. Chen, M., Yang, Z., Liang, J., et al.: Improving deep neural networks based multi-accent mandarin speech recognition using i-vectors and accent specific top layer. In: Proceedings Interspeech. ISCA (2015)

9. Siohan, O., Rybach, D.: Multitask learning and system combination for automatic speech recognition. In: IEEE Workshop on Automatic Speech Recognition and Understanding, AZ, USA: Scottsdale, pp. 589–595 (2015)
10. Qian, Y., Yin, M., You, Y., et al.: Multi-task joint-learning of deep neural networks for robust speech recognition. In: IEEE Workshop on Automatic Speech Recognition and Understanding, pp. 310–316 (2015)
11. Thanda, A., Venkatesan, S.M.: Multi-task Learning of Deep Neural Networks for Audio Visual Automatic Speech Recognition. arXiv:1701.02477 [cs] (2017)
12. Krishna, K., Toshniwal, S., Livescu, K.: Hierarchical Multitask Learning for CTC-based Speech Recognition. arXiv:1807.06234v2 (2018)
13. Meyer, J.: Multi-Task and Transfer Learning in Low-Resource Speech Recognition. PhD Thesis, University of Arizona (2019)
14. Ruder, S.: An Overview of Multi-Task Learning in Deep Neural Networks. arXiv:1706.050 98v1 [cs] (2017)
15. Misra, I., Shrivastava, A., Gupta, A., et al.: Cross-stitch networks for multi-task learning. In: IEEE Conference on Computer Vision and Pattern Recognition (CVPR 2016), Las Vegas, NV, USA, pp. 3994–4003 (2016)
16. Ruder, S., Bingel, J., Augenstein, I., et al.: Sluice Networks: Learning What to Share between Loosely Related Tasks. arXiv:1705.08142v1 (2017)
17. Chen, D., Mak, B.K.W.: Multitask Learning of Deep Neural Networks for Low-Resource Speech Recognition, pp. 1172–1183. IEEE/ACM Transactions on Audio, Speech and Language Processing (2015)
18. Zhao, Y., Yue, J., et al.: End-to-end-based tibetan multitask speech recognition. IEEE Access 7, 162519–162529 (2019)
19. Lu, J., Batra, D., Parikh, D., et al.: ViLBERT: Pretraining Task-Agnostic Visiolinguistic Representations for Vision-and-Language Tasks. arXiv:1908.02265 [cs] (2019)
20. Vu, N.T., Imseng, D., Povey, D., et al.: Multilingual deep neural network based acoustic modeling for rapid language adaptation. In: Proceedings of 2014 IEEE International Conference on Acoustics, Speech and Signal Processing (ICASSP2014), Florence, Italy, pp. 7639–764 (2014)
21. Thomas, S., Ganapathy, S., Hermansky, H: Cross-lingual and multi-stream posterior features for low resource LVCSR systems. In: Proceedings of Eleventh Annual Conference of the International Speech Communication Association (INTERSPEECH 2010), Makuhari, Chiba, Japan, pp. 877–880 (2010)
22. Heigold, G., Vanhoucke, V., Senior, A., et al.: Multilingual acoustic models using distributed deep neural networks. In: Proceedings of 2013 IEEE International Conference on Acoustics, Speech and Signal Processing (ICASSP2013), Vancouver, BC, Canada, pp. 8619–8623 (2013)
23. Rao, K., Sak:, H.: Multi-accent speech recognition with hierarchical grapheme based models. In: Proceedings of 2017 IEEE International Conference on Acoustics, Speech and Signal Processing (ICASSP 2017), New Orleans, LA, USA, pp. 4815–4819 (2017)
24. Byrne, W., Beyerlein, P., Huerta, J.M., et al.: Towards language independent acoustic modeling. In: Proceedings of 2000 IEEE International Conference on Acoustics, Speech, and Signal Processing (ICASSP 2000), Hilton Hotel and Convention Center, Istanbul, Turkey, pp.1029–1032, (2000)
25. Toshniwal, S., Sainath, T.N., Weiss, R.J., et al.: Multilingual speech recognition with a single end-to-end model. In: 2018 IEEE International Conference on Acoustics, Speech and Signal Processing, Calgary, AB, Canada, pp. 4904–4908 (2018)
26. Shetty, V.M., Sagaya, M., Mary, N.J.: Improving the performance of transformer based low resource speech recognition for Indian languages. In: ICASSP 2020 - 2020 IEEE International Conference on Acoustics, Speech and Signal Processing (ICASSP), pp. 8279–8283 (2020)

27. Li, B., Sainath, T.N., et al.: Multi-dialect speech recognition with a single sequence-to-sequence model. In: 2018 IEEE International Conference on Acoustics, Speech and Signal Processing, Calgary, AB, Canada, pp. 4749–4753 (2018)

28. Tang, Z., Li, L., Wang, D., et al.: Collaborative joint training with multitask recurrent model for speech and speaker recognition. IEEE/ACM Trans. Audio Speech Lang. Process. **25**(3), 493–504 (2017)

29. Dong, L., Xu, S., Xu, B.: Speech-transformer: a no-recurrence sequence-to-sequence model for speech recognition. In: 2018 IEEE International Conference on Acoustics, Speech and Signal Processing (ICASSP), pp. 5884–5888 (2018)

30. Open Speech and Language Resource. Available online: http://www.openslr.org/124/. Accessed 3 April 2022

31. Kingma, D.P., Ba, J.: Adam: A method for stochastic optimization. arXiv preprint: 1412.6980 (2014)

32. Szegedy, C., Vanhoucke, V., Ioffe, S., et al.: Rethinking the inception architecture for computer vision. In: Proceedings of the IEEE Conference on Computer Vision and Pattern Recognition, pp. 2818–2826 (2016)

Regularized Contrastive Learning
of Semantic Search

Mingxi Tan(✉), Alexis Rolland, and Andong Tian

Ubisoft La Forge, Ubisoft, China
{ming-xi.tan,alexis.rolland,an-dong.tian}@ubisoft.com

Abstract. Semantic search is an important task which objective is to find the relevant index from a database for query. It requires a retrieval model that can properly learn the semantics of sentences. Transformer-based models are widely used as retrieval models due to their excellent ability to learn semantic representations. in the meantime, many regularization methods suitable for them have also been proposed. In this paper, we propose a new regularization method: Regularized Contrastive Learning, which can help transformer-based models to learn a better representation of sentences. It firstly augments several different semantic representations for every sentence, then take them into the contrastive objective as regulators. These contrastive regulators can overcome overfitting issues and alleviate the anisotropic problem. We firstly evaluate our approach on 7 semantic search benchmarks with the outperforming pre-trained model SRoBERTA. The results show that our method is more effective for learning a superior sentence representation. Then we evaluate our approach on 2 challenging FAQ datasets, Cough and Faqir, which have long query and index. The results of our experiments demonstrate that our method outperforms baseline methods.

Keywords: Contrastive · Regularization · Semantic

1 Introduction

On a semantic search task, we generally have a dataset which consists of tuples of sentences <Query, Index>. The objective of the task is to find the best indices for each input query on the dataset. First, we need to calculate the embeddings of the input queries and the candidate index, then we compute their cosine similarity scores, and finally rank the candidate answers based on these scores. Therefore, superior embeddings are crucial to the task.

Recently, transformer-based models are widely used to perform this kind of task due to their powerful semantic representation capabilities. They use contextual information to create embeddings that are sensitive to the surrounding context [1]. However, learning a better sentence embedding is still a challenging task. Many regularization methods suitable for Transformers have been proposed such as attention dropout and DropHead [2]. They all can reduce overfitting and improve performance. In this work, we introduce a new regularization

© The Author(s), under exclusive license to Springer Nature Switzerland AG 2022
W. Lu et al. (Eds.): NLPCC 2022, LNAI 13551, pp. 119–130, 2022.
https://doi.org/10.1007/978-3-031-17120-8_10

method: Regularized Contrastive Learning (RCL), which augments the number of semantically similar embeddings of each sentence and uses them to construct contrastive regulators for learning better sentences semantics.

RCL mainly contains 2 steps as shown in Fig. 1. In the first step, we train several models by adding an entropy term to the contrastive objective, denoted as entropy model (Fig. 1a). Each of the entropy model can generate a semantically similar embedding for each sentence (Fig. 1b). The role of this step is to augmente the data. Different from the other widely used methods such as sentence cropping, word replacement and word deletion, which require extra effort to ensure the altered sentences have similar semantics to the original sentences, we do not directly augment the number of sentences but the number of embeddings. Unlike LAMBADA (language-model-based data augmentation) [3] which augments the number of embeddings based on GPT-2 according to specific class, our method augments the number of semantically similar embeddings. The second step is to take the embeddings of tuples <Query, Index> in the dataset and their generated embeddings into contrastive objective to fine-tune the final model (Fig. 1c). where $< Q_i, Ind_i >$ represents a query and index sentence tuple, $Emb_k\_Q_i$ represents the embedding of query i computed by entropy model k, $Emb_k\_Ind_i$ represents the embedding of index i computed by entropy model k. ϕ is the weight of entropy term.

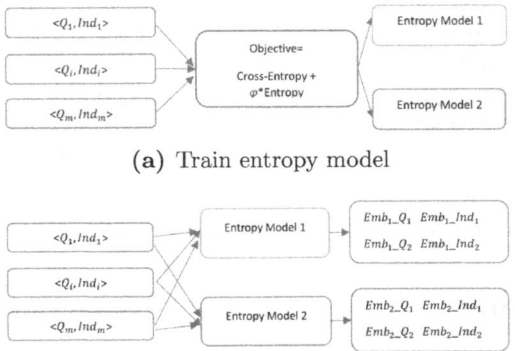

(a) Train entropy model

(b) Generate semantically similar embedding of each sentence through entropy model

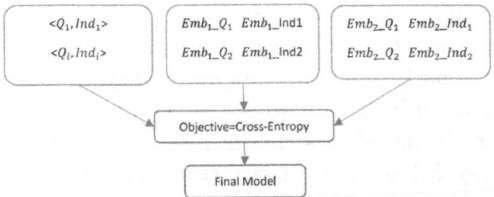

(c) Take the embeddings of tuples in the database and their corresponding augmented embeddings into the contrastive objective to train the final model

Fig. 1. Regularized contrastive learning.

We evaluate our approach on seven semantic search benchmarks and two challenging information retrieval tasks. Information retrieval (IR) task is the direct application of semantic search. Using a FAQ dataset, which consists of several tuples <Question, Answer>, our objective is to find the best answers for each input question on the given dataset. The results of our experiments show that our method is effective of learning superior sentences embeddings compared to other regularization methods such as attention dropout and DropHead. The main contributions of this paper are summarized as follows:

1. A Regularized Contrastive Learning method that augments the number of sentence embeddings and takes them into the contrastive objective as regulator.
2. Experiments results on 7 standard semantic textual similarity tasks demonstrate our method is efficient for semantic comprehension.
3. Experiments results on 2 IR tasks show that our method can improve the performance of IR models.

2   Related Work

Semantic search tasks require models with excellent semantic understanding, which is different from translation and text-classification tasks. They use the contrastive objective [6–8], shown in Eq. 1, because the corresponding dataset directly provides semantically similar tuples of <Query, Index>.

$$loss_{\{q_i, ind_i\}} = -\log \left(\frac{\exp(\cos(q_i, ind_i))}{\sum\limits_{j=1}^{M} (\exp(\cos(q_i, ind_j)))} \right), \tag{1}$$

where q_i is the embedding of $query_i$, ind_i is the embedding of $index_i$, $\cos(q_i, ind_i)$ is the cosine similarity $\frac{q_i^T ind_i}{\|q_i\|\|ind_i\|}$ and M is the number of tuples.

This objective helps the model to learn the semantic representations by pulling the embeddings of the same tuple as close as possible and pushing the embeddings of different tuples as far as possible [10].

Additionally, the contrastive objective is well aligned with alignment and uniformity proposed by [11], who uses them to measure the quality of semantic representations. The alignment calculates the distance of semantically similar tuples. Meanwhile, the uniformity measures how well the semantic representations are uniformly distributed. Equation 1 can guarantee that the distance of semantically similar tuples is close, and the distribution of semantically dissimilar tuples is scattered on the hypersphere [7].

Regularization methods can effectively improve the performance of neural networks [9]. Since Transformer-based models have demonstrated the outstanding performance in the learning of semantic representation of sentences [4,5], the traditional simple and effective regularization method Dropout has also been implemented in it. Attention dropout regularizes the attention weights in Transformers to prevent different contextual feature vectors from adapting to each other. DropHead drops the entire attention head in a certain proportion during training to prevent the multi-head attention model from being dominated by a small number of attention heads [2]. They have shown their effectiveness in translation and text-classification tasks. In this paper, we apply them in semantic search tasks and compare their results with our method.

3   Regularized Contrastive Learning

3.1   Task Description

We begin by formally defining the task of semantic search. Suppose there are M tuples in the dataset: $< Query_1, index_1 >, < Query_2, Index_2 >, \cdots, < Query_M, Index_M >$, the task is then to find the top N best indexes according to the query.

In semantic search tasks, we generally encode queries and indexes into sentence representations, and then calculate their cosine similarity scores for comparison or ranking [12]. The wildly used objective is contrastive objective such as cross-entropy shown in Eq. 1.

We use a pre-trained language model as the retrieval model because of its strong capability to learn semantic representations [4]. Our method can improve the capability of learning semantic representations from 2 aspects: data augmentation and regulators built with augmented data.

3.2   Data Augmentation

Popular methods to augment textual data usually consist in cropping sentences according to some proportions, replacing some words by synonyms or removing some words. With all these methods, it is difficult to guarantee whether the edited sentence is semantically similar to the original sentence. Our method does not directly augment the number of sentences but rather focus on augmenting the number of semantic representations of sentence: the embeddings.

We first train several entropy models based on Eq. 2.

$$J_i = -\log\left(\frac{\exp(\cos(q_i, ind_i))}{\sum\limits_{j=1}^{M}(\exp(\cos(q_i, ind_j)))}\right) - \phi * \sum_{j=1}^{M}\left(score_{train_{ij}} * \log(score_{train_{ij}})\right) \qquad (2)$$

where $i \neq j$, $score_{train_{ij}} = \frac{\exp(\cos(q_i, ind_j))}{\sum\limits_{k=1}^{M}(\exp(\cos(q_i, ind_k)))}$ is the semantic similarity score of the trainable embeddings, q_i is the semantic embedding of $query_i$, ind_j is the semantic embedding of $index_j$, ϕ is the weight.

Equation 2 has 2 terms. The first term is the cross-entropy of Eq. 1 on the given dataset. This term assumes that $query_i$ is only semantically similar to $index_i$ of the same tuple, and indiscriminately assumes that it is not semantically similar to all $index_j$ of other tuples. Datasets usually do not have information about the exact relationship between the $query_i$ and the $index_j$ of other tuples. The second term is the entropy, which can change the semantic similarity between $query_i$ and all $index_j$ of other tuples. Different ϕ determines how much the entropy term changes the similarity between $query_i$ and $index_j$ computed by the cross-entropy term. For example, if we choose a $\phi > 0$, when we minimize the Eq. 2, we will minimize the entropy term, which means we enhance the certainty of semantic similarity of the tuple of <query, index>, and a $\phi < 0$ will make the semantic similarity of tuples of <query, index> much more uncertain. We can train several entropy models with different ϕ and then use each of them to generate different semantically similar embeddings for every sentence, ultimately increasing the number of sentences semantic representations.

3.3 Contrastive Regulator

Once we have augmented the embeddings for every sentence through several entropy models, we take them into a new contrastive objective as regulators shown in Eq. 3 below.

$$
J_i = -\log\left(\frac{\exp(\cos(q_i,ind_j))}{\sum\limits_{k=1}^{M}(\exp(\cos(q_i,ind_k)))}\right) - \sum_{n=1}^{N}\log\left(\underbrace{\frac{\exp(\cos(q_i,Au_{q_i}^n))}{\sum\limits_{k=1}^{M}(\exp(\cos(q_i,Au_{q_k}^n)))}}_{Regulator}\right) - \sum_{n=1}^{N}\log\left(\underbrace{\frac{\exp(\cos(ind_i,Au_{ind_j}^n))}{\sum\limits_{k=1}^{M}(\exp(\cos(ind_i,Au_{ind_k}^n)))}}_{Regulator}\right)
$$

(3)

where $Au_{q_i}^n$ is the augmented semantic similar embedding of $query_i$ from entropy model n, $Au_{ind_i}^n$ is the augmented semantic similar embedding of $index_i$ from entropy model n, N is the number of entropy models.

3.4 Anisotropy Problem

According to [11], when the number of pairs from different tuples approaches infinity, the asymptotics of Eq. 3 can be derived as

$$
-E_{(q_i,ind_i)\sim\pi_{pos}}\left[\mathbf{q_i}^\top\mathbf{ind_i}\right] + E_{q_i\sim\pi_{data}}\left[\log E_{ind_j\sim\pi_{data}}\left[e^{\mathbf{q_i}^\top\mathbf{ind_j}}\right]\right] +
$$

$$
\sum_{n=1}^{N}\left(-E_{(q_i,Au_{q_i}^n)\sim\pi_{pos}^q}\left[\mathbf{q_i}^\top\mathbf{Au_{q_i}^n}\right] + E_{q_i\sim\pi_{data}^q}\left[\log E_{Au_{q_j}^n\sim\pi_{data}^q}\left[e^{\mathbf{q_i}^\top\mathbf{Au_{q_j}^n}}\right]\right]\right) +
$$

$$
\sum_{n=1}^{N}\left(-E_{(ind_i,Au_{ind_i}^n)\sim\pi_{pos}^{ind}}\left[\mathbf{ind_i}^\top\mathbf{Au_{ind_i}^n}\right] + E_{ind_i\sim\pi_{data}^{ind}}\left[\log E_{Au_{ind_j}^n\sim\pi_{data}^{ind}}\left[e^{\mathbf{ind_i}^\top\mathbf{Au_{ind_j}^n}}\right]\right]\right)
$$

$$
= -E_{(q_i,ind_i)\sim\pi_{pos}}\left[\mathbf{q_i}^\top\mathbf{ind_i}\right] - \sum_{n=1}^{N}E_{(q_i,Au_{q_i}^n)\sim\pi_{pos}^q}\left[\mathbf{q_i}^\top\mathbf{Au_{q_i}^n}\right] - \sum_{n=1}^{N}E_{(ind_i,Au_{ind_i}^n)\sim\pi_{pos}^{ind}}\left[\mathbf{ind_i}^\top\mathbf{Au_{ind_i}^n}\right] +
$$

$$
E_{q_i\sim\pi_{data}}\left[\log E_{ind_j\sim\pi_{data}}\left[e^{\mathbf{q_i}^\top\mathbf{ind_j}}\right]\right] + \sum_{n=1}^{N}E_{q_i\sim\pi_{data}^q}\left[\log E_{Au_{q_j}^n\sim\pi_{data}^q}\left[e^{\mathbf{q_i}^\top\mathbf{Au_{q_j}^n}}\right]\right] +
$$

$$
\sum_{n=1}^{N}E_{ind_i\sim\pi_{data}^{ind}}\left[\log E_{Au_{ind_j}^n\sim\pi_{data}^{ind}}\left[e^{\mathbf{ind_i}^\top\mathbf{Au_{ind_j}^n}}\right]\right]
$$

(4)

where π_{pos},π_{pos}^q and π_{pos}^{ind} are uniform distributions of pairs of sentences from the same tuple, π_{data},π_{data}^q and π_{data}^{ind} are uniform distribution of dataset,

$$\mathbf{q_i^\top ind_i} = \frac{q_i^\top ind_i}{\|q_i\|\|ind_i\|}, \mathbf{q_i^\top Au_{q_i}^n} = \frac{q_i^\top Au_{q_i}^n}{\|q_i\|\|Au_{q_i}^n\|} \text{ and } \mathbf{ind_i^\top Au_{ind_i}^n} = \frac{ind_i^\top Au_{ind_i}^n}{\|ind_i\|\|Au_{ind_i}^n\|}.$$

The first three terms of Eq. 4 make the sentences from the same tuples have similar semantics, while the last three terms make the sentences from the different tuples have dissimilar semantics and can be derived with Jensen's inequality as

$$E_{q_i\sim\pi_{data}}\left[\log E_{ind_j\sim\pi_{data}}\left[e^{\mathbf{q_i^\top ind_j}}\right]\right] + \sum_{n=1}^{N} E_{q_i\sim\pi_{data}^q}\left[\log E_{Au_{q_j}^n\sim\pi_{data}^q}\left[e^{\mathbf{q_i^\top Au_{q_j}^n}}\right]\right] +$$

$$\sum_{n=1}^{N} E_{ind_i\sim\pi_{data}^{ind}}\left[\log E_{Au_{ind_j}^n\sim\pi_{data}^{ind}}\left[e^{\mathbf{ind_i^\top Au_{ind_j}^n}}\right]\right]$$

$$= \frac{1}{m}\sum_{i=1}^{m}\log\left(\frac{1}{m}\sum_{j=1}^{m}e^{\mathbf{q_i^\top ind_j}}\right) + \sum_{n=1}^{N}\frac{1}{m}\sum_{i=1}^{m}\log\left(\frac{1}{m}\sum_{j=1}^{m}e^{\mathbf{q_i^\top Au_{q_j}^n}}\right) + \sum_{n=1}^{N}\frac{1}{m}\sum_{i=1}^{m}\log\left(\frac{1}{m}\sum_{j=1}^{m}e^{\mathbf{q_i^\top Au_{ind_j}^n}}\right)$$

$$(5)$$

$$\geq \frac{1}{m^2}\sum_{i=1}^{m}\sum_{j=1}^{m}\mathbf{q_i^\top ind_j} + \sum_{n=1}^{N}\frac{1}{m^2}\sum_{i=1}^{m}\sum_{j=1}^{m}\mathbf{q_i^\top Au_{qj}^n} + \sum_{n=1}^{N}\frac{1}{m^2}\sum_{i=1}^{m}\sum_{j=1}^{m}\mathbf{ind_i^\top Au_{indj}^n} \quad (6)$$

where m is a finit number of samples.

According to [13,14], only a few elements of a language model's learned embedding have large values, thus causing anisotropy problem. When we minimize Eq. 5, we are actually minimizing the upper bound of Eq. 6, which leads to minimizing $\mathbf{q^\top ind}, \mathbf{q^\top Au_q}$ and $\mathbf{ind^\top Au_{ind}}$. Since they are all almost positive according to [7], their minimization reduces the large value of the embedding, which flattens the embedding and alleviates the anisotropy problem.

4   Experiments

We first evaluate the ability of our method to learn sentence representations by conducting experiments on 7 semantic textual similarity (STS) tasks following the work of [15] and then on 2 challenging FAQ datasets: COUGH[1] and FAQIR[2]. In the following sections, we first introduce the details of the datasets in Sect. 4.1, then the experiments settings in Sect. 4.2, and finally the results of our experiments in Sect. 4.3.

4.1   Datasets

The 7 semantic textual similarity tasks are: STS 2012–2016 tasks [16–20], the STS benchmark [21] and the SICK-Relatedness dataset [22]. For each pair of sentences, these datasets provide a semantic similarity score from 0 to 5. We adopt the Spearman's rank correlation between the cosine similarity and use the entailment pairs as positive instances, and the contradiction pairs as the hard negative instances.

FAQIR contains 4133 FAQ-pairs for training and test. Most of their answers are very long, which poses a challenge to the retrieval model.

---

[1] https://github.com/sunlab-osu/covid-faq.
[2] https://takelab.fer.hr/data/faqir/.

4.2 Training Details

We start from the checkpoint of pre-trained model of $SRoBERTA_{base}$. Then we separately fine-tune the entropy models and the final model with different contrastive objectives. The main process is shown in the algorithm 1. For the semantic texture similarity tasks, we train the model on both MNLI and SNLI datasets and calculate the Spearman correlation on the development dataset of STS for evaluation. For the FAQ retrieval task, we evaluate the model by calculating the accuracy of TOP1, TOP3, TOP5 and MAP [24] with 5-fold method. More training details can be found in Appendix A.

Algorithm 1. Regularized Contrastive Learning Workflow

1: **Fine-tune the entropy model**
2: **for** $\phi = -value1, -value2, \ldots, +value1, +value2, \ldots$ **do**
3:    Fine-tune the entropy model with the Eq.2 as the objective, denoted as $Model_{entorpy}$
4:    Calculate semantically similar embeddings of each query and index through $Model_{entropy}$, denoted as $Au_{q_i}^n$ and $Au_{ind_i}^n$
5: **end for**
6: **Fine-tune the final contrastive learning model**
7: Fine-tune the final model, with the Eq.3 as the objective, denoted as $Model_{RCL}$

4.3 Results

In Table 1, we present the results of adopting DropAttention and DropHead on 7 semantic textual similarity tasks.

In Table 3, we present the results of comparing the method of Attention Dropout, DropHead and RCL on 7 semantic textual similarity tasks.

In Table 2, we present the results of $SRoberta_{base}$, and the results of the implementation of DropHead, Attention Dropout and RCL on COUGH and FAQIR, which show that RCL has a better performance on all the metrics of TOP1, TOP3, TOP5 and MAP.

4.4 Ablation Study

We investigate the impact of the number of regulators. All the reported results in this section are the average of Spearman's correlation on the 7 text semantic similarity tasks.

We use different ϕ to train several different entropy models with Eq. 2 as the objective. Each entropy model can generate one semantically similar embedding for every sentence by which we can construct 2 regulators with Eq. 3. If we train more entropy models, we will have more different semantically similar embeddings for every sentence. Consequently, the model can learn the embeddings from more regulators using Eq. 3 as the objective. The Table 4 shows how the number of regulators affect the accuracy of the model.

Table 1. Test set results (Spearman's correlation) of compared models on text semantic similarity task. In each of the tables, the results in the first row are the results of $SRoberta_{base}$ model. The results in the other rows are the results of adopting different ratio of Attention Dropout and DropHead methods on $SRoberta_{base}$ model. The results are reported as the average of 5 random runs. "_" and "*" means the statistically significance improvement with $p < 0.1$ and $p < 0.05$. These results show the Attention Dropout with $p = 0.1$ improves the performance. However, DropHead method does not improve the performance.

Model	sts12	sts13	sts14	sts15	sts16	stsb	sickr	Average
$SRoberta_{base}$	74.46%	84.80%	79.98%	85.24%	81.89%	84.84%	77.85%	81.29%
Attention dropout ($p = 0.1$)	74.53%	85.08%	80.24%	85.60%	*82.64%	85.43%	77.88%	81.63%
Attention dropout ($p = 0.2$)	73.10%	84.49%	79.38%	85.32%	81.99%	84.88%	78.81%	81.14%
Attention dropout ($p = 0.3$)	73.61%	84.79%	79.44%	85.45%	81.77%	84.81%	78.07%	81.13%

(a) Results of Attention Dropout method

Model	sts12	sts13	sts14	sts15	sts16	stsb	sickr	Average
$SRoberta_{base}$	74.46%	84.80%	79.98%	85.24%	81.89%	84.84%	77.85%	81.29%
DropHead ($p = 0.1$)	73.71%	85.04%	79.56%	85.36%	82.10%	85.00%	77.73%	81.21%
DropHead ($p = 0.2$)	74.02%	84.73%	79.58%	85.43%	81.89%	84.89%	77.86%	81.20%
DropHead ($p = 0.3$)	74.18%	84.30%	79.20%	85.18%	82.02%	84.81%	78.21%	81.13%

(b) Results of DropHead method

Table 2. Test set results (accuracy) of compared models on FAQIR and COUGH. In each of the 2 tables, the results in the first row are the results of $SRoberta_{base}$. The results in the second row are the best results of the implementation of DropHead method. The results in the third row are the best results of the implementation of Attention Dropout method. The last row are the results of RCL. These results are reported as the average of 5 random runs. "_" and "*" means the statistically significance improvement with $p < 0.1$ and $p < 0.05$.

Model	Acc_top1	Acc_top3	Acc_top5	MAP
$SRoberta_{base}$	20.74%	32.94%	39.38%	29.90%
DropHead ($p = 0.1$)	20.62%	33.22%	39.88%	29.94%
Attention dropout ($p = 0.1$)	21.42%	34.33%	41.05%	31.00%
RCL(ours) (p=0.3)	*22.01%	*35.05%	41.42%	*31.65%

(a)Results on FAQIR

Model	Acc_top1	Acc_top3	Acc_top5	MAP
$SRoberta_{base}$	5.95%	12.62%	17.67%	12.72%
DropHead ($p = 0.1$)	5.96%	12.73%	17.75%	12.90%
Attention dropout ($p = 0.1$)	6.14%	13.05%	17.95%	13.05%
RCL(ours)	*6.35%	13.31%	*18.49%	*13.41%

(b) Results on COUGH

Table 3. Test set results (Spearman's correlation) of compared models on 7 text semantic similarity tasks. The results in the first row are the results of $SRoberta_{base}$. The results in the second row are the best results of DropHead method. The results in the third row are the best results of Attention Dropout method. The results in the last row are the results of RCL. These results are reported as the average of 5 random runs. "*" means the statistically significance improvement with $p < 0.05$. These results show RCL improves the performance of 6 out of 7 text semantic similarity tasks.

Model	sts12	sts13	sts14	sts15	sts16	stsb	sickr	Average
$SRoberta_{base}$	74.46%	84.80%	79.98%	85.24%	81.89%	84.84%	77.85%	81.29%
DropHead (p = 0.1)	73.71%	85.04%	79.56%	85.36%	82.10%	85.00%	77.73%	81.21%
Attention dropout (p = 0.1)	74.53%	85.08%	80.24%	85.60%	*82.64%	85.43%	77.88%	81.63%
RCL(ours)	*76.15%	*85.84%	*80.89%	*86.58%	*83.36%	84.85%	*79.14%	82.40%

Table 4. Impact of number of regulators. "*" means the statistically significance improvement with $p < 0.05$ compared to the model precedent.

	Number of regulator: 0 (No ϕ)	Number of regulator: 2 ($\phi = 0.01$)	Number of regulator: 4 ($\phi = 0.01$, 0.02)	Number of regulator: 6 ($\phi = 0.01$, 0.02, 0.03)	Number of regulator: 8 ($\phi = 0.01$, 0.02, 0.03, 0.04)	Number of regulator: 10 ($\phi = 0.01$, 0.02, 0.03, 0.04, 0.05)
Average (Spearman Correlation)	81.29%	*81.47%	*81.98%	*82.29%	*82.40%	82.42%

Table 5. Test set results (Spearman's correlation) of compared models on 7 text semantic similarity tasks. The results from the first row to the third row are the results of entropy models. The results in the last row are the results of our method. These results are reported as the average of 5 random runs. "*" means the statistically significance improvement with $p < 0.05$. These results show RCL has better performance than all the entropy models.

Model	sts12	sts13	sts14	sts15	sts16	stsb	sickr	Average
$Model_{entropy}$ ($\phi = 0.01$)	75.97%	83.49%	78.66%	84.55%	82.35%	83.49%	78.13%	80.95%
$Model_{entropy}$ ($\phi = 0.02$)	74.31%	82.77%	78.90%	84.35%	81.55%	83.49%	76.13%	80.22%
$Model_{entropy}$ ($\phi = 0.03$)	73.30%	83.18%	79.37%	84.28%	81.09%	83.55%	75.47%	80.03%
$Model_{entropy}$ ($\phi = 0.04$)	73.31%	82.98%	79.27%	84.13%	81.21%	83.26%	74.93%	79.87%
RCL(ours)	*76.15%	*85.84%	*80.89%	*86.58%	*83.36%	84.85%	*79.14%	82.40%

From Table 4, we can see that 8 regulators (4 entropy models) can significantly improve the performance of our model. However, if we continue to increase the number of regulators, for instance up to 10 regulators, we the performance stops improving.

In Table 5, we present the results of our RCL method and the results of all the entropy models used to build the regulators. The results show that none of the entropy models is better than RCL model. But the regulators built from these entropy models help to enrich the expressive capability of learned embeddings and then alleviate the anisotropic problem.

5   Conclusion

In this work we explore a new regularization method for Transformer-based models: Regularized Contrastive Learning. Our method adopts the contrastive objective and semantically similar representation of sentences to build regulators, which help to overcome overfitting and alleviate the anisotropy problem of sentences embeddings. The results of our experiments on 7 semantic textual similarity tasks and on 2 challenging FAQ datasets demonstrate that our method outperforms widely used regularization methods, and prove that our method is more effective in learning a superior embedding of a sentence.

A   APPENDIX

A.1   A Training Details

The Base model is $SRoberta_{base}$ [8]. We download their weights from Sentence-Transformers. $SRoberta_{base}$ is trained on MNLI and SNLI by using the entailment pairs as positive instances and the contradiction pairs as hard negative instances.

For STS Tasks. We carry out the grid search of batch size $\in[32,64]$ and $\phi \in$ $[[0.01], [0.01, 0.02], [0.01, 0.02, 0.03], [0.01, 0.02, 0.03, 0.04], [0.01, 0.02, 0.03, 0.04,$ $0.05]]$. We firstly fine-tune $SRoberta_{base}$ with different ϕ on MNLI and SNLI with Eq. 2, by using the entailment pairs as positive instances and the contradiction pairs as hard negative instances. The purpose of this step is to train several entropy models who can generate different semantic similar embedding for every sentence. Since the pre-trained model has already trained on these datasets, the training process will converge quickly. We use the early stopping method to quickly stop the training process if the loss doesn't decrease within 3 steps. Then we continue to fine-tune the pre-trained $SRoberta_{base}$, by taking the augmented embeddings and the positive instances and entailment instances of MNLI and SNLI into the contrastive objectives with the Eq. 3. We train this model for 1 epoch, evaluate it every 10% of samples on the development set of STS-B by Spearman-Correlation. When the batch size is 64 and $\phi = [0.01, 0.0, 0.03, 0.04]$, our model achieves the best accuracy.

For FAQ Datasets. We implement RCL on the same pre-trained model as above. And apply the same grid-search as above for batch size and ϕ. We firstly fine-tune an initial model based on the pre-trained $SRoberta_{base}$ for several epochs with Eq. 1 and save the model who has the highest MAP value on the development dataset. Based on this initial model, we continue to fine-tune the entropy model with different ϕ with Eq. 2. Finally, we fine-tune the final retrieval model based on the pre-trained $SRoberta_{base}$ with the augmented embeddings for several epochs, saving the model who has the highest MAP value on the development dataset. When batch size is 64 and $\phi = [0.01, 0.02, 0.03, 0.04]$, the retrieval model achieves the best accuracy.

References

1. Arora, S., Liang, Y., Ma, T.: A simple but tough-to-beat baseline for sentence embeddings. In: 5th International Conference on Learning Representations, ICLR, Conference Track Proceedings. OpenReview.net, Toulon, France (2017)
2. Zhou, W., Ge, T., Wei, F., Zhou, M., Xu, k.: Scheduled DropHead: a regularization method for transformer models. In: Findings of the Association for Computational Linguistics: EMNLP, pp. 1971–1980. Association for Computational Linguistics, Online (2020)
3. Anaby-Tavor, A., et al.: Not enough data? deep learning to the rescue! In: The Thirty-Fourth AAAI Conference on Artificial Intelligence, AAAI, pp. 7383–7390 (2020)
4. Liu, Y., et al.: Roberta: a robustly optimized BERT pretraining approach. In: arXiv:1907.11692 (2019)
5. Song, K., Tan, X., Qin, T., Lu, J., Liu, T-Y.: MPNet: masked and permuted pre-training for language understanding. In: arXiv:2004.09297v2 (2020)
6. Su, J., Cao, J., Liu, W., Ou, Y.: Whitening sentence representations for better semantics and faster retrieval. In: arXiv:2103.15316 (2021)
7. Gao, T., Yao, X., Chen, D.: SimCSE: simple contrastive learning of sentence embeddings. In: Proceedings of the 2021 Conference on Empirical Methods in Natural Language Processing, EMNLP, pp. 6849–6910 (2021)
8. Reimers, N., Gurevych, I.: SentenceBERT: Sentence embeddings using Siamese BERTnetworks. In: Empirical Methods in Natural Language Processing, EMNLP, pp. 3980–3990 (2019)
9. Srivastava, N., Hinton, G., Krizhevsky, A., Sutskever, I., Salakhutdinov, R.: Dropout: a simple way to prevent neural networks from overfitting. J. Mach. Learn. Res. 15(56), 1929–1958 (2014)
10. Hadsell, R., Chopra, S., LeCun, Y.: Dimensionality reduction by learning an invariant mapping. In: IEEE/CVF Conference on Computer Vision and Pattern Recognition, CVPR, vol. 2, pp. 1735–1742. IEEE, New York, NY, USA (2006)
11. Wang, T., Isola, P.: Understanding contrastive representation learning through alignment and uniformity on the hypersphere. In: International Conference on Machine Learning, ICML, pp. 9929–9939 (2020)
12. Rahutomo, F., Kitasuka, T., Aritsugi, M.: Semantic cosine similarity. In: The 7th International Student Conference on Advanced Science and Technology, ICAST, vol. 4 (2012)
13. Ethayarajh, K.: How contextual are contextualized word representations? comparing the geometry of BERT, ELMo, and GPT-2 embeddings. In: Proceedings of the 2019 Conference on Empirical Methods in Natural Language Processing and the 9th International Joint Conference on Natural Language Processing, EMNLP-IJCNLP, pp. 55–65. Association for Computational Linguistics, Hong Kong, China (2019)
14. Li, B., Zhou, H., He, J., Wang, M., Yang, Y., Li, L.: On the sentence embeddings from pre-trained language models. In: Empirical Methods in Natural Language Processing, EMNLP, pp. 9119–9130 (2020)
15. Conneau, A., Kiela, D., Schwenk, H., Barrault, L., Bordes, A.: Supervised learning of universal sentence representations from natural language inference data. In: Empirical Methods in Natural Language Processing, EMNLP, pp. 670–680 (2017)

16. Agirre, E., Cer, D., Diab, M., Gonzalez-Agirre, A.: SemEval-2012 task 6: a pilot on semantic textual similarity. In: *SEM 2012: The First Joint Conference on Lexical and Computational Semantics, SemEval, vol. 1: Proceedings of the Main Conference and the Shared Task, vol. 2: Proceedings of the Sixth International Workshop on Semantic Evaluation, pp. 385–393. Association for Computational Linguistics, Montreal, Canada (2012)
17. Agirre, E., Cer, D., Diab, M., Gonzalez-Agirre, A., Guo, W.: *SEM 2013 shared task: semantic textual similarity. In: Second Joint Conference on Lexical and Computational Semantics (*SEM), vol. 1: Proceedings of the Main Conference and the Shared Task: Semantic Textual Similarity, pp. 32–43. Association for Computational Linguistics, Atlanta, Georgia, USA (2013)
18. Agirre, E., et al.: SemEval-2014 task 10: multilingual semantic textual similarity. In: Proceedings of the 8th International Workshop on Semantic Evaluation (SemEval 2014), pp. 81–91. Association for Computational Linguistics, Dublin, Ireland (2014)
19. Agirre, E.,et al.: SemEval-2015 task 2: semantic textual similarity, English, Spanish and pilot on interpretability. In: Proceedings of the 8th International Workshop on Semantic Evaluation (SemEval 2015), pp. 252–263. Association for Computational Linguistics, Denver, Colorado, USA (2015)
20. Agirre, E., et al.: SemEval-2016 task 1: semantic textual similarity, monolingual and cross-lingual evaluation. In: Proceedings of the 10th International Workshop on Semantic Evaluation (SemEval-2016), pp. 497–511. Association for Computational Linguistics, San Diego, California, USA (2016)
21. Cer, D., Diab, M., Agirre, E., Lopez-Gazpio, I., Specia, L.: SemEval-2017 task 1: semantic textual similarity multilingual and crosslingual focused evaluation. In: Proceedings of the 11th International Workshop on Semantic Evaluation, SemEval, pp. 1–14. Association for Computational Linguistics, Vancouver, Canada (2017)
22. Marelli, M., Menini, S., Baroni, M., Bentivogli, L., Bernardi, R., Zamparelli, R.: A SICK cure for the evaluation of compositional distributional semantic models. In: Proceedings of the Ninth International Conference on Language Resources and Evaluation, LREC2014, pp. 216–223. European Language Resources Association (ELRA), Reykjavik, Iceland (2014)
23. Zhang, X., Sun, H., Yue, X., Jesrani, E., Lin, S., Sun, H.: COUGH: a Challenge dataset and models for COVID-19 FAQ retrieval. In: arXiv:2010.12800v1 (2020)
24. Karan, M., Snajder, J.: Paraphrase-focused learning to rank for domain-specific frequently asked questions retrieval. Expert Syst. Appl. 91, 418–433 (2018)
25. Merikoski, J.K.: On the trace and the sum of elements of a matrix. Linear Algebra Appl. 60, 216–223. https://doi.org/10.1016/0024-3795(84)90078-8 (2014)

Kformer: Knowledge Injection in Transformer Feed-Forward Layers

Yunzhi Yao[1], Shaohan Huang[2], Li Dong[2], Furu Wei[2], Huajun Chen[1], and Ningyu Zhang[1(✉)]

[1] Zhejiang University, Hangzhou, China
{yyztodd,huajunsir,zhangningyu}@zju.edu.cn
[2] Microsoft Research, Beijing, China
{shaohanh,donglixp,fuwei}@microsoft.com

Abstract. Recent days have witnessed a diverse set of knowledge injection models for pre-trained language models (PTMs); however, most previous studies neglect the PTMs' own ability with quantities of implicit knowledge stored in parameters. A recent study [2] has observed knowledge neurons in the Feed Forward Network (FFN), which are responsible for expressing factual knowledge. In this work, we propose a simple model, Kformer, which takes advantage of the knowledge stored in PTMs and external knowledge via knowledge injection in Transformer FFN layers. Empirically results on two knowledge-intensive tasks, commonsense reasoning (i.e., SocialIQA) and medical question answering (i.e., MedQA-USMLE), demonstrate that Kformer can yield better performance than other knowledge injection technologies such as concatenation or attention-based injection. We think the proposed simple model and empirical findings may be helpful for the community to develop more powerful knowledge injection methods[1] (Code available in https://github.com/zjunlp/Kformer).

Keywords: Transformer · Feed Forward Network · Knowledge injection

1 Introduction

Pre-trained language models based on Transformer [17] such as BERT [3] and UniLM [4], show significant performance on many Natural Language Processing (NLP) tasks. However, recent studies have revealed that the performance of the knowledge-driven downstream task (for example, commonsense reasoning) is dependent on external knowledge; thus, the direct finetuning of pre-trained LMs yields suboptimal results.

To address this issue, several works have attempted to integrate external knowledge into pre-trained LMs, which has shed light on promising directions for knowledge-driven tasks. On the one hand, several approaches [9,12,21]

Y. Yao—Contribution during internship at Microsoft Research.

W. Lu et al. (Eds.): NLPCC 2022, LNAI 13551, pp. 131–143, 2022.
https://doi.org/10.1007/978-3-031-17120-8_11

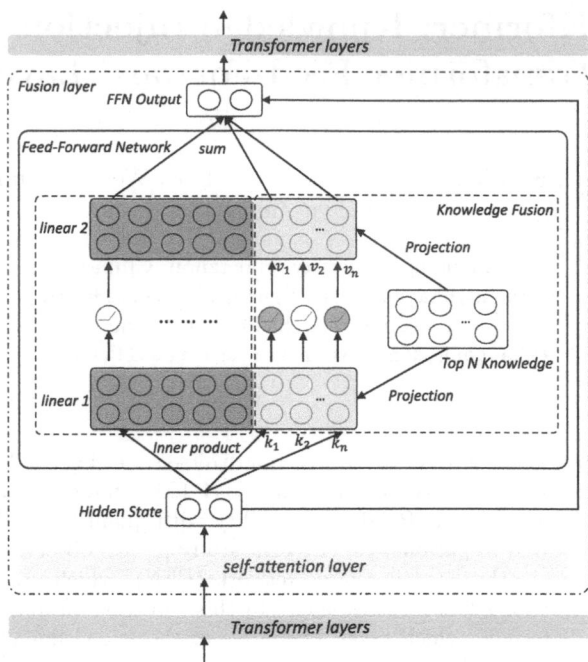

Fig. 1. An illustration of KFormer for knowledge injection. Input vectors are multiplied by each knowledge vector. The final output of the feed-forward network is the sum of the original linear layers' output and the knowledge fusion's output.

try to fuse knowledge via concatenating the input sequence with external retrieved information (e.g., Wikipedia, knowledge fact). On the other hand, other approaches [1, 18, 20, 22] obtain the representation of input and external knowledge separately and leverage interaction operations such as attention mechanism for knowledge fusion. However, most previous studies neglect the PTMs' own ability with quantities of implicit knowledge in parameters since a wealth of human knowledge is already captured by PTMs and stored in the form of "modeledge" [6].

Recently, Dai [2] has observed knowledge neurons in the Feed Forward Network (FFN), which are responsible for expressing factual knowledge, which motivates us to investigate whether it is beneficial to inject external knowledge into the language model through FFN.

In this work, we try to take advantage of the **knowledge stored in PTMs and external knowledge** and propose a general knowledge fusion model named Kformer that injects knowledge in Transformer FFN layers.

As shown in Fig. 1, Kformer is a simple and pluggable model which can adapt to different knowledge types. Specifically, we convert the knowledge into dense embedding vectors through a knowledge encoder and inject the knowledge into the Feed Forward Network of Transformer. We evaluate Kformer over several public benchmark datasets, including SocialIQA and MedQA. Experimental results show that Kformer can achieve absolute improvements in these tasks. We further discover that it is complimentary for the PLMs to have more useful knowledge by knowledge injection through FFN.

In summary, we make the following contributions to this paper:

- We present a simple-yet-effective knowledge injection model Kformer to infuse the external knowledge into PLMs via Feed Forward Network.
- Experimental results show the proposed approach can obtain better performance and yield better interpretability.

2 Knowledge Neurons in the FFN

We first introduce some background of FFN and knowledge neurons. Each layer in the Transformer contains a multi-head self-attention and a feed-forward network (FFN). Primarily, the FFN consists of two Linear Networks. Suppose the final attention output of a Transformer layer is $\mathbf{x} \in \mathbb{R}^d$, the compute of the Feed Forward Network can be formulated as (bias terms are omitted):

$$
\text{FFN}(\mathbf{x}) = f\left(\mathbf{x} \cdot K^\top\right) \cdot V \\
K, V \in \mathbb{R}^{d_m \times d}
\tag{1}
$$

Here K, V is the parameter matrices of the two Linear Networks. The input $\mathbf{x}$ are first multiplied by K to produce the coefficients, which are then activated by f and used to compute the weighted sum of V as the feed-forward layer's output. Previous work [5] observes that FFN emulates neural memory and can be viewed as unnormalized Key-Value Memories. More recently, Dai [2] present preliminary studies on how factual knowledge is stored in pre-trained Transformers by introducing the concept of **knowledge neurons**. Note that the hidden state is fed into the first linear layer and activates knowledge neurons; then, the second linear layer integrates the corresponding memory vectors.

> **Motivating.** *Knowledge neurons in the FFN module are responsible for expressing factual knowledge; thus, it is intuitive to infuse knowledge by directly modifying the corresponding parameters in FFN, which can take advantage of the knowledge stored in PTMs and external knowledge.*

3 Kformer: Knowledge Injection in FFN

Kformer contains three main components: firstly, for each question, we retrieve the top N potential knowledge from knowledge bases (Sect. 3.1). Then, we obtain the knowledge representation via Knowledge Embedding (Sect. 3.2). In the end, we fuse the retrieved N knowledge into the pre-trained model via the feed-forward layer in Transformer (Sect. 3.3).

3.1 Knowledge Retrieval

We first extract external knowledge for injection. Here, we build a hybrid retrieval system to retrieve external knowledge. Note that the retrieval process is not the main focus of this paper, and Kformer can be applied to different types of retrieval scenarios. Specifically, we utilize an off-the-shelf sparse searcher based on Apache Lucene, Elasticsearch, using an inverted index lookup followed by BM25 [14] ranking. We select sentences with top M scores from the results returned by the search engine as knowledge candidates. Since the IR system focuses primarily on lexical and semantic matching, we then conduct a simple dense retrieval on the M candidates. We obtain the dense representation of each knowledge via knowledge embedding (Sect. 3.2) and compute the input sentence representation by the average token embeddings. Then we calculate the score of each knowledge candidate by conducting an inner product on the input embedding and the knowledge embedding. We choose knowledge candidates with the top N scores as the knowledge evidence for knowledge injection (Sect. 3.3).

3.2 Knowledge Embedding

We view each knowledge candidate as a text sequence and leverage an Embedding layer to represent the knowledge. Each knowledge k is firstly tokenized as l tokens. Those tokens then would be embedded as $k_1, k_2, ..., k_l$ by the Knowledge Embedding. We initialize the knowledge embedding matrix as the same embedding matrix (first layer of the PTM) in the input sequence and update the Knowledge Embedding Layer simultaneously during training. The external knowledge is then represented as the average of these tokens' embedding:

$$\text{Embed}(k) = Avg(k_1, k_2, .., k_l) \tag{2}$$

3.3 Knowledge Injection

As shown in Fig. 1, Kformer injects knowledge in the Transformer FFN layer with the knowledge embedding. The feed-forward network in each Transformer layer consists of two linear transformations with a GeLU activation function. Suppose the final attention output of the layer l is H^l, formally we have the output of the two linear layers as:

$$FFN(H^l) = f(H^l \cdot K^l) \cdot V^l \tag{3}$$

$K, V \in \mathbb{R}^{d_m \times d}$ are parameter matrices of the first and second linear layers and f represents the non-linearity function. d_m refers to the intermediate size of Transformer and d is the hidden size. Suppose we acquire the top N knowledge documents $\mathbf{k} \in \mathbb{R}^{d_n \times d}$ after retrieval (Sect. 3.1). Through Knowledge Embedding, we can obtain each knowledge as $\mathbf{k_1, k_2, ..., k_N} \in \mathbb{R}^d$. To inject the knowledge into the specific layer l, we need to map the knowledge to the corresponding vector space. Here, for each layer l, we use two different linear layers to project the knowledge (Pr in the equation). W_k^l and W_v^l represents the weights of the two linear layers($W_k^l, W_v^l \in \mathbb{R}^{d \times d}$). The two matrices W_k^l and W_v^l are initialized randomly and will be updated during fine-tuning.

$$\phi_k^l = \text{Pr}_k \mathbf{k} = W_k^l \cdot \mathbf{k} \tag{4}$$
$$\phi_v^l = \text{Pr}_v \mathbf{k} = W_v^l \cdot \mathbf{k} \tag{5}$$

After projection, we inject ϕ_k^l and ϕ_v^l into the corresponding $\boldsymbol{K}^l$ and $\boldsymbol{V}^l$. We expand the FFN by concatenating the projected knowledge to the end of the Linear layer and obtain the expanded $\boldsymbol{K}_E^l, \boldsymbol{V}_E^l \in \mathbb{R}^{(d_m + d_n) \times d}$. Hence, after injection, the computation of FFN can be described as:

$$\begin{aligned} FFN(H^l) &= f(H^l \cdot \boldsymbol{K}_E^l) \cdot \boldsymbol{V}_E^l \\ &= f(H^l \cdot [\phi_k^l : \boldsymbol{K}^l]) \cdot [\phi_v^l : \boldsymbol{V}^l] \end{aligned} \tag{6}$$

The model activates knowledge related to the input sequence and infuses knowledge with the query through the knowledge fusion component. Next, the collected information will be processed and aggregated by the following transformer layer. We simply inject the knowledge into the top 3 layers of the model and we analyze the impact of injection layers in Sect. 5.2.

Table 1. Overall statistics of the two datasets. 'Know len.' means the length of knowledge text we extract from the knowledge Graph and TextBook. The question len. of the Social IQA dataset contains the length of the context.

Metric	Social IQA	MedQA-USMLE
# of options per question	3	4
Avg. option len.	6.12	3.5
Avg. question len.	20.16	116.6
Avg./Max. know len.	8.63/37	55/1234
# of questions		
Train	33,410	10,178
Dev	1,954	1,272
Test	2,224	12,723

4   Experiments

We do experiments on two multiple-choice tasks (Social IQA and MedQA-USMLE) to explore Kformer's performance on downstream tasks. We choose triples in the knowledge graph and documents in textbooks to examine the influence of different knowledge types.

4.1 Dataset

Social IQA [16] is a commonsense QA task that is partially derived from an external knowledge source ATOMIC [15]. We use triples in ATOMIC as our knowledge candidates. For each triple, we paraphrase it into a language sequence according to the relation template in ATOMIC. MedQA [8] is an OpenQA task in the biomedical domain, where questions are from medical board exams in the US, Mainland China, and Taiwan. We use the English dataset USMLE in our experiment. We adopt the textbooks provided by [8] as the knowledge base.

4.2 Experiment Setting

We summarize the statistics of each dataset in Table 1, and we use accuracy as the evaluation metric for the two datasets. Compared with SocialIQA, the lengths of the knowledge texts we used in MedQA is longer.

We detail the training procedures and hyperparameters for each of the datasets. We use RoBERTa as the backbone of Kformer and implement our method using Facebook's tool fairseq [13]. We utilize Pytorch to conduct experiments with one NVIDIA RTX 3090 GPU. All optimizations are performed with the AdamW optimizer with a warmup of learning rate over the first 150 steps, then polynomial decay over the remainder of the training. Gradients were clipped if their norm exceeded 1.0, and weight decay on all non-bias parameters was set to 1e−2. We mainly compare Kformer with the following injecting methods:

Table 2. Results of the Social IQA task. We compare our model with other models using ATOMIC as the knowledge source. The results marked with [†] are retrieved from the leaderboard of the dataset.

	Methods	Dev Acc	Test Acc
Base model	RoBERTa	72.26	69.26
	RoBERTa+MCQueen[†]	-	67.22
	RoBERTa+ATT	72.10	-
	Kformer	72.82	71.10
Large Model	RoBERTa	78.86	77.12
	RoBERTa+MCQueen[†]	**79.53**	78.00
	RoBERTa+ATT	78.54	-
	Kformer	79.27	**78.68**

[†] https://leaderboard.allenai.org/socialiqa/submissions/public.

Concat: This way is to simply concatenate the retrieved knowledge with the question as to the input of the model. All the retrieved knowledge is joined together to make a single knowledge text K. The sequence of tokens [CLS] K [SEP] Q [SEP] A (Q is the question, A is the answer choice) is then passed to the model to get the final prediction. We denote this method as RoBERTa+Concat in the following part.

Table 3. Results of the MedQA-USMLE task.

Method	Dev Acc	Test Acc
IR-ES	28.70	26.00
MAX-OUT	28.90	28.60
RoBERTa	31.28	27.41
RoBERTa+Concat	31.76	29.77
RoBERTa+ATT	31.70	27.37
Kformer	**33.02**	**30.01**

Attention: Multi-head self-attention plays a role of message passing between tokens [7]. Input tokens interact with each other and determine what they should pay more attention to. We conduct experiments on injecting the knowledge into the self-attention module, the fusion is calculated as follows:

$$\text{Attention}^l = \text{softmax}\left(\frac{Q^l\left[\phi_k^l; K^l\right]^T}{\sqrt{d}}\right)\left[\phi_v^l; V^l\right] \tag{7}$$

The knowledge is concatenated at the K and V parts in self-attention. During inference, the query will communicate with the injected knowledge. We denote this method as RoBERTa+ATT in the following part.

4.3 Experiments Results

We list the result of the Social IQA in Table 2. RoBERTa+MCQueen [12] explored different ways to infuse knowledge into the language model, including concat, parallel-max, simple sum and weighted sum. All four methods put the knowledge into the model at the input part. We can observe from the table

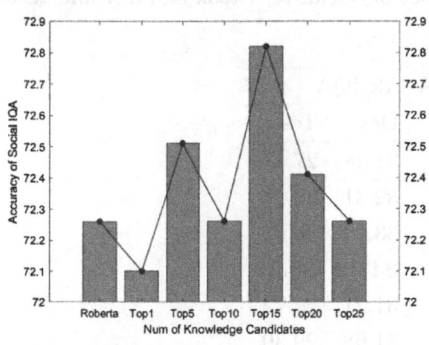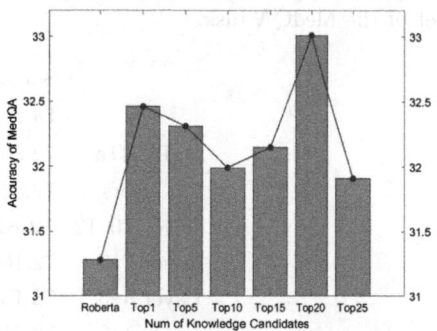

Fig. 2. Results of the model with different top N (1, 5, 10, 15, 20, 25) retrieved knowledge candidates.

that adding the knowledge into the feed-forward layer can help the model learn the external knowledge, leading to 0.41 gain in the valid set and 1.56 gain in the test set for the large model. As compared to other methods of incorporating information into the model, our model has a distinct benefit. On the test set, our model outperforms the RoBERTa+MCQueen by 0.68.

5   Analysis

For the MedQA, we list the results in Table 3. IR-ES adopts an off-the-shelf retrieval system based on ElasticSearch. For each question q and each answer a_i, we get the score for the top N retrieved sentences and the option with the highest score is selected. We use the code provided by [8][1] to get the result. We compared our model with the concatenate method.

From the Table, we notice that Kformer is still competitive for knowledge with a long sequence length. The model adding knowledge via the feed-forward layer outperforms the model concatenating the information into the input by 1.3 in the valid set and 0.3 in the test set. The average length of each knowledge text is 55 in the Textbook materials. When concatenating knowledge at the input, we may only focus on about ten potential pieces of evidence, while in our model, we can focus on much more evidence via injecting knowledge via FFN.

Meanwhile, we can find that on both two tasks, Kformer outperforms RoBERTa+ATT, indicating that injecting knowledge in FFN is better than injecting in attention.

5.1   Impact of Top N Knowledge

In this section, we examine the impact of the number of knowledge candidates retrieved in the knowledge retrieval part. We adjust the number of knowledge candidates and list the results in Fig. 2.

Table 4. Results of the model with different knowledge infusion layer. We compute every three layers of Kformer and use the dev set of Social IQA task and dev and test set of the MedQA task.

	Social IQA	MedQA	
	Dev	Dev	Test
RoBERTa	72.26	31.28	27.41
All layers	72.56	32.31	28.27
Layer 10–12	**72.82**	33.02	30.01
Layer 7–9	72.10	**34.04**	**30.32**
Layer 4–6	72.15	31.21	27.72
Layer 1–3	72.51	31.68	29.30

---

[1] https://github.com/jind11/MedQA.

As shown in the Figure, the extracted information has both positive and negative effects on the model. If we retrieve less information, the model will be unable to solve the problem due to the lack of sufficient evidence. For the MedQA task, when retrieving the top 20 documents, Kformer performs best, better than retrieving the top 5, 10, and 15 documents. For the Social IQA dataset, retrieving the top 15 sentences achieves the best result. However, if we retrieve too much information for the question, the model will suffer from knowledge noise and make incorrect predictions. In the Figure, the performance of Social IQA decreases when retrieving information more than the top 15 sentences. The same pattern can be seen in the MedQA task; when retrieving more than the top 20 documents, the model's performance drops too.

5.2 Impact of Layers

In Kformer, the layer where we incorporate external knowledge is a critical hyperparameter since different levels in Transformer may catch different information. [5] demonstrates that higher layer's feed-forward network learns more semantic knowledge. Meanwhile, [19] shows that component closer to the model's input and output are more important than component in other layers. Here, we insert the knowledge at different levels in Transformer to see where it is the most beneficial. We conduct experiments on every three layers of the base model as the knowledge fusion layers. We also try to import knowledge to all of the Transformer layers. We list the results of various knowledge infusion layers in Table 4.

On both tasks, the model that integrates evidence through the top three layers or the bottom three layers benefits from external knowledge, whereas applying knowledge into the model's 4–6 layers degrades its performance. It confirms [19]'s finding that components closer to the model's input and output are more critical. Meanwhile, top layers typically outperform bottom ones, implying a higher layer's feed-forward network has gained more semantic information. On the two tasks, layer 7–9 displays a different pattern. In the Social IQA task, the model that incorporates information via layers 7–9 performs the worst and degrades the model's performance, whereas in the MedQA task, adding knowledge via layers 7 to 9 performs the best. Finally, if we infuse knowledge into all layers, the model still has gained, but the result is lower than the top three layers' result, which could be owing to the detrimental effect of the intermediate layers.

According to these results, we discover that adding the knowledge into the top 3 layers' feed-forward layers usually performs well, which supports the findings of previous work. The top three layers perform best on the Social IQA task, with a score of 72.82 (+0.56 Acc) and also achieve good results on the MedQA task (33.03 in dev and 30.01 in test). The influence of the intermediate layers, on the other hand, is not that consistent and requires more research in the future.

5.3 Interpretability

To study how adding the knowledge into the feed-forward layer helps our model learn from external knowledge, we select one case in which RoBERTa predicts wrong, and Kformer predicts right from the Social IQA task. According to [2], here we use the output of the activation function to see what knowledge the model activates and uses.

As shown in Fig. 3, the question is, "Quinn was unhappy in the marriage and promptly filed for a divorce. What does he want to do next?" and the answer is 'separate from his wife.' RoBERTa chose the wrong answer, 'get himself a lawyer,' and Kformer chose the right one. Some knowledge we retrieved is useful to help the model, such as "PersonX files for a divorce. As a result, PersonX wants to find a new place to live." "PersonX files for divorce. As a result, PersonX wants to move on with their life.". According to the retrieved knowledge, we know that Quinn would leave his ex-wife and start a new life after his divorce while finding the lawyer is the work he needed to do before.

We can find the model mainly focuses on the 1, 7, 11, 12, and 14th knowledge it retrieved before. We list the corresponding knowledge on the right side of the Figure. As can be seen from the Figure, although the knowledge did not explicitly mention separating from wife, other information like "acclimated to a new life" and "find a new place to live" indicates the separation between the two people. The model reason over the knowledge to answer the question correctly.

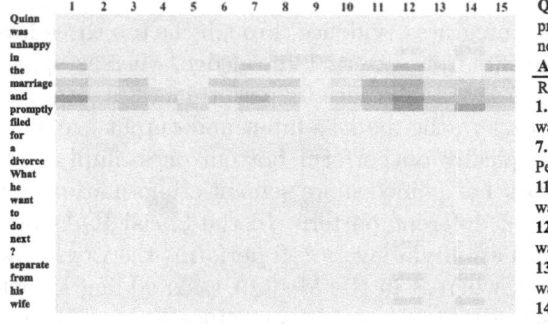

Fig. 3. One case in the Social IQA task. The question is "Quinn was unhappy in the marriage and promptly filed for a divorce. What does he want to do next?" and the answer is 'separate from his wife.' The matrix on the left is the activation function's output. The matrix's size is (seq_length × # of knowledge). Each row of the matrix represents each token in the sequence, and each column corresponds to one knowledge text we retrieved. In this experiment, we choose the top 15. On the right, we list the knowledge with higher activation output.

6   Related Work

Knowledge Fusion. External knowledge can be categorized as structured knowledge and non-structured knowledge. Most works choose to use the structured knowledge such as triples or paths extracted from the knowledge graph [11,18]. Besides, since the structured knowledge is often limited to some specific domains, some works also try to extract related contexts from open-domain corpora, such as Wikipedia. They use information retrieval or other text-matching technologies [11,21] to extract knowledge. Our method is not limited to the type of knowledge. We conduct our experiments on both structured knowledge and non-structured knowledge.

Knowledge Fusion in Pre-trained Models. In terms of explicitly fusing knowledge into pre-trained models, one way is to integrate the question text and the knowledge texts as the model's input and then send it into the pre-trained model to obtain the final results. K-BERT [10] build a sentence tree using the questions and triples in the knowledge graph and convert it into an embedding representation and a visible matrix before sending it to the encoder. [21] just concatenate the knowledge into the input and directly send it to the encoder. Due to the limitation of sequence length, these methods cannot concatenate much knowledge into their models. Another way [1,20,22] is to obtain the context representation (c) using the pre-tained model and the knowledge representation (k) through a knowledge based model. Then it projects the knowledge to the pre-trained model's hidden representation space and interacts k and c via an attention network. The results are predicted based on the concatenation of c and k by an inference model.

To obtain the knowledge representation, [18] computes the knowledge embedding using a Relational Network to aggregate the retrieved paths while [1] encodes the knowledge by retrofitting the pre-trained word embedding. These two ways may run into the Knowledge Noise problem, which occurs when too much knowledge is incorporated into a statement, causing it to lose its intended meaning. In our paper, inspired by previous work [2,5] on the feed-forward layers, we propose a novel way to filter and incorporate external knowledge through the feed-forward layers in Transformer.

7   Conclusion and Future Work

In this paper, we investigate the feed-forward layer in Transformer and discover that infusing external knowledge into the language model through the feed-forward layer can benefit the performance. We propose a simple-yet-effective knowledge injection model, Kformer, which is pluggable to any pre-trained language models and adaptable to different knowledge sources. We conduct our experiments on two multi-choice tasks (Social IQA and Med-USMLE), and Kformer achieves absolute improvements on the two tasks.

In the future, we would integrate our fusion method during pre-training to get better knowledge representation and explore more downstream tasks to improve the generalization ability of Kformer. Besides, it is also interesting to investigate the fundamental mechanism of knowledge storage in pre-trained language models and develop efficient models for knowledge-intensive tasks.

Acknowledgements. We want to express gratitude to the anonymous reviewers for their hard work and kind comments. This work is funded by NSFC U19B2027/91846204, National Key R&D Program of China (Funding No. SQ2018YFC000004), Zhejiang Provincial Natural Science Foundation of China (No. LGG22F030011), Ningbo Natural Science Foundation (2021J190), and Yongjiang Talent Introduction Programme (2021A-156-G).

References

1. Chang, T.Y., Liu, Y., Gopalakrishnan, K., Hedayatnia, B., Zhou, P., Hakkani-Tur, D.: Incorporating commonsense knowledge graph in pretrained models for social commonsense tasks. In: Proceedings of DeeLIO: The First Workshop on Knowledge Extraction and Integration for Deep Learning Architectures (2020)
2. Dai, D., Dong, L., Hao, Y., Sui, Z., Wei, F.: Knowledge neurons in pretrained transformers. In: Proceedings of ACL (2022)
3. Devlin, J., Chang, M.W., Lee, K., Toutanova, K.: BERT: pre-training of deep bidirectional transformers for language understanding. In: Proceedings of NAACL (2019)
4. Dong, L., et al.: Unified language model pre-training for natural language understanding and generation. In: Proceedings of NeurIPS (2019)
5. Geva, M., Schuster, R., Berant, J., Levy, O.: Transformer feed-forward layers are key-value memories. In: Proceedings of EMNLP (2021)
6. Han, X., et al.: Pre-trained models: past, present and future. AI Open **2**, 225–250 (2021)
7. Hao, Y., Dong, L., Wei, F., Xu, K.: Self-attention attribution: interpreting information interactions inside transformer. In: Proceedings of AAAI (2021)
8. Jin, D., Pan, E., Oufattole, N., Weng, W.H., Fang, H., Szolovits, P.: What disease does this patient have? A large-scale open domain question answering dataset from medical exams. arXiv preprint arXiv:2009.13081 (2020)
9. Lewis, P., et al.: Retrieval-augmented generation for knowledge-intensive NLP tasks. Adv. Neural. Inf. Process. Syst. **33**, 9459–9474 (2020)
10. Liu, W., et al.: K-BERT: enabling language representation with knowledge graph. In: Proceedings of AAAI (2020)
11. Lv, S., et al.: Graph-based reasoning over heterogeneous external knowledge for commonsense question answering. In: Proceedings of AAAI (2020)
12. Mitra, A., Banerjee, P., Pal, K.K., Mishra, S., Baral, C.: How additional knowledge can improve natural language commonsense question answering. arXiv Computation and Language (2020)
13. Ott, M., et al.: fairseq: A fast, extensible toolkit for sequence modeling. In: Proceedings of NAACL: Demonstrations (2019)
14. Robertson, S., Zaragoza, H.: The Probabilistic Relevance Framework: BM25 and Beyond. Now Publishers Inc., Norwell (2009)
15. Sap, M., et al.: Atomic: an atlas of machine commonsense for if-then reasoning. In: Proceedings of AAAI (2019)

16. Sap, M., Rashkin, H., Chen, D., Le Bras, R., Choi, Y.: Social IQa: commonsense reasoning about social interactions. In: Proceedings of EMNLP (2019)
17. Vaswani, A., et al.: Attention is all you need. In: Proceedings of NeurIPS (2017)
18. Wang, P., Peng, N., Ilievski, F., Szekely, P., Ren, X.: Connecting the dots: a knowledgeable path generator for commonsense question answering. In: Findings of EMNLP (2020)
19. Wang, W., Tu, Z.: Rethinking the value of transformer components. In: Proceedings of COLING (2020)
20. Wang, X., et al.: Improving natural language inference using external knowledge in the science questions domain. In: Proceedings of AAAI (2019)
21. Xu, Y., Zhu, C., Xu, R., Liu, Y., Zeng, M., Huang, X.: Fusing context into knowledge graph for commonsense reasoning. arXiv preprint arXiv:2012.04808 (2020)
22. Zhang, N., et al.: Drop redundant, shrink irrelevant: selective knowledge injection for language pretraining. In: In Proceedings of IJCAI (2021)

Doge Tickets: Uncovering Domain-General Language Models by Playing Lottery Tickets

Yi Yang[1], Chen Zhang[1], Benyou Wang[2], and Dawei Song[1](✉)

[1] Beijing Institute of Technology, Beijing, China
{yang.yi,czhang,dwsong}@bit.edu.cn
[2] The Chinese University of Hong Kong, Shenzhen, China

Abstract. Over-parameterized pre-trained language models (LMs), have shown an appealing expressive power due to their small learning bias. However, the huge learning capacity of LMs can also lead to large learning variance. In a pilot study, we find that, when faced with multiple domains, a critical portion of parameters behave unexpectedly in a domain-specific manner while others behave in a domain-general one. Motivated by this phenomenon, we for the first time posit that domain-general parameters can underpin a domain-general LM that can be derived from the original LM. To uncover the domain-general LM, we propose to identify *domain-general* parameters by playing lottery *tickets* (dubbed *doge tickets*). In order to intervene the lottery, we propose a *domain-general score*, which depicts how domain-invariant a parameter is by associating it with the variance. Comprehensive experiments are conducted on the AMAZON, MNLI, and ONTONOTES datasets. The results show that the *doge tickets* obtains an improved out-of-domain generalization in comparison with a range of competitive baselines. Analysis results further hint the existence of domain-general parameters and the performance consistency of *doge tickets*.

Keywords: Pre-trained language model · Domain generalization · Lottery tickets hypothesis

1 Introduction

It is witnessed that more and more models become increasingly over-parameterized, typically pre-trained language models (LMs). With the tremendous amounts of parameters, these models have shown an appealing expressive power [5,14,25,28]. While such LMs are enabled with small learning bias, they suffer from the limitation of large learning variance [20], especially when faced with multiple domains.

To show the consequence of such learning variance, we performed a pilot study on how different parameters of BERT behave over multiple domains (e.g., Digital Music, All Beauty, and Gift Cards). We find that a large portion

W. Lu et al. (Eds.): NLPCC 2022, LNAI 13551, pp. 144–156, 2022.
https://doi.org/10.1007/978-3-031-17120-8_12

of parameters are domain-specific, while others are domain-general. Figure 1 shows an illustrative example. Certain neurons corresponding to domain-specific parameters may be particularly activated by some domains but not so active in others. The domain-inconsistency can potentially lead to a deteriorated out-of-domain generalization capability, concerning how well a LM performs universally on any domains [20, 30]. In contrast, the neurons corresponding to domain-general parameters are similarly activated across different domains.

Motivated by the phenomenon, we for the first time posit that, a domain-general LM that is underpinned by domain-general parameters as illustrated in Fig. 1, can be derived from the original LM, and that the domain-general LM would facilitate a better out-of-domain generalization. Specifically, inspired by lottery ticket hypothesis stating that a pruned model is capable of performing as expressive as the original model, we propose to identify *do*main-*ge*neral parameters by playing lottery *tickets* (dubbed *doge tickets*) [6] under the guidance of a domain-general score. The domain-general score describes how domain-invariant a parameter is, rather than how expressive as depicted by the commonly used expressive score [18]. Driven by variance reduction [20], the domain-general score associates with the invariance of a parameter by looking at not only the mean but also the variance of its expressive scores across different domains.

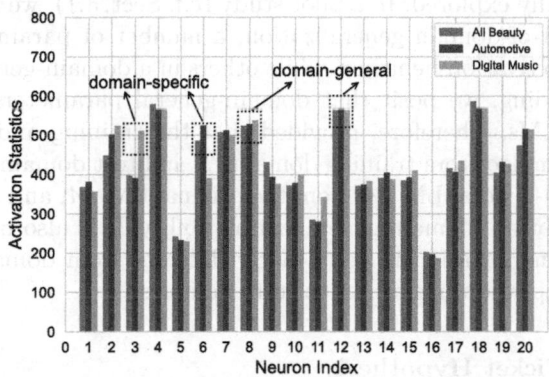

Fig. 1. A pilot study on how sampled neurons (for [CLS] token) corresponding to the last FFN block of the fine-tuned BERT [5] can be activated by training domains sampled from AMAZON [21] via activation statistics [2]. Considering that GELU [10] activation is used, we view neurons with values larger than minus two as activated. A parameter is said to be specific to a domain or a group of domains if its associated neurons are particularly activated by input from these domains, while not so active in other domains. A parameter is said to be general to domains if its associated neurons are similarly activated by input across different domains. Both domain-specific and domain-general manners are observed.

Comprehensive experiments are conducted on three datasets: the AMAZON [21], MNLI [29], and ONTONOTES [23] dataset. The results show that the proposed *doge tickets* owns a competitive out-of-domain generalization compared with an array of state-of-the-art baselines. In-depth analyses are further carried out to double-check whether the domain-specific manner holds de facto and inspect whether the *doge tickets* performs consistently. The results hint the existence of domain-general parameters and the performance consistency of *doge tickets*.

2   Background

2.1   Out-of-domain Generalization

Pre-trained LMs [5,14,25] have achieved a compelling performance on downstream tasks where the training and test examples are identically distributed [28], thanks to the smaller learning bias brought by over-parameterization. Further exploration has also been carried out on whether LMs can have a good out-of-domain generalization [11], where the training and test examples are distinguished from each other in terms of distributions. However, the performance gain is somewhat limited or even degraded, due to the large learning variance brought by over-parameterization. Therefore, there is a large room for a better out-of-domain generalization of LMs [30].

However, the issue with the large learning variance of pre-trained LMs is yet to be systematically explored. In a pilot study (c.f. Sect. 3.1), we find that under the setting of out-of-domain generalization, a number of parameters exhibit a domain-specific activation behavior, while others in a domain-general one. Motivated by this finding, we posit that domain-general parameters can underpin domain-general LMs. Therefore, provided that the training and test examples are separately sampled from training domains $\mathcal{D}$ and test domains $\mathcal{D}'$, we aim to uncover a domain-general LM $\mathcal{M}'$ from the original LM $\mathcal{M}$, and $\mathcal{M}'$ is expected to have a better out-of-domain generalization ability. It is also noteworthy that out-of-domain generalization is significantly different from domain adaptation, since domain adaptation has access to test examples.

2.2   Lottery Ticket Hypothesis

The lottery ticket hypothesis (LTH) states that a pruned model is capable of performing as good as the original over-parameterized model [6]. LTH can be applied to LMs in various ways [3,4,13,18] yet indicating a similar conclusion that *lottery tickets can win*. Previous work discovers *winning tickets* in LMs via either unstructured [4,6,26] or structured pruning techniques [4,18,24]. Unstructured pruning methods [8,16,22] concentrate on pruning parameters at neuron level. In contrast, structured pruning methods [9,12,17] prune parameters at module level. In particular, [13] investigates the transition behavior of *winning tickets* in LMs through shifting the sparsity levels, and has shown some slight performance gain with appropriate tickets (termed *super tickets*) at a small sparsity level. Inspired by LTH, we propose to identify the domain-general parameters by playing lottery tickets (dubbed *doge tickets*) under the guidance of a newly proposed domain-general score (c.f. Sect. 3.2).

2.3 Transformer Architecture

BERT [5] consists of a stack of transformer encoder layers [27]. Each of these layers contains two blocks: a multi-head self-attention block (MHA) and a feed-forward network block (FFN), with a residual connection and a normalization layer around each. In the following description, we omit the details of residual connections, normalization layers and bias terms for brevity. Assuming there are n independent heads in each MHA block and the i-th head is parameterized by $\mathbf{W}_Q^{(i)}$, $\mathbf{W}_K^{(i)}$, and $\mathbf{W}_V^{(i)} \in \mathbb{R}^{d \times d_h}$, then the output from the MHA block, which is sum of the intermediate outputs of all parallel heads, can be depicted as:

$$\mathbf{Z} = \mathrm{MHA}(\mathbf{X}) = \sum_{i=1}^{n} \mathbf{H}^{(i)}(\mathbf{X})\mathbf{W}_O^{(i)} = \sum_{i=1}^{n} \mathrm{Att}(\mathbf{X}\mathbf{W}_Q^{(i)}, \mathbf{X}\mathbf{W}_K^{(i)}, \mathbf{X}\mathbf{W}_V^{(i)})\mathbf{W}_O^{(i)}$$

where $\mathbf{X} \in \mathbb{R}^{l \times d}$ represents d-dimensional vectors that stand for l sequential input token representations and $\mathbf{W}_O^{(i)} \in \mathbb{R}^{d_h \times d}$ is the output linear layer for the i-th head. Likewise, we denote the output of the FFN block, which is composed of two linear layers with proper activation in-between as:

$$\mathbf{X}' = \mathrm{FFN}(\mathbf{Z}) = \mathbf{W}_2 \mathrm{GELU}(\mathbf{W}_1\mathbf{Z})$$

where $\mathbf{W}_1 \in \mathbb{R}^{d \times d_i}$ and $\mathbf{W}_2 \in \mathbb{R}^{d_i \times d}$ correspond to the two layers. Our work exactly targets at improving out-of-domain generalization through uncovering a domain-general BERT from the original BERT by playing lottery tickets.

3 Identifying Doge Tickets

3.1 Uncovering Domain-general LM

LMs are perceived to bring large learning variance due to over-parameterization. Accordingly, we suspect that the variance to some extent showcases itself within

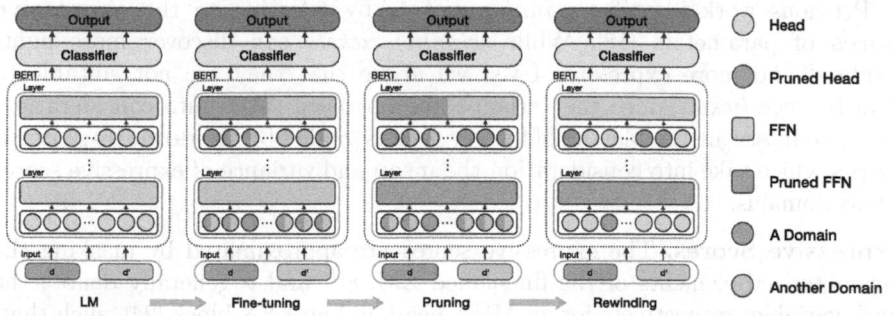

Fig. 2. *first fine-tuning, then pruning, finally rewinding* paradigm when playing lottery tickets. It is found that parameters can behave in either a domain-specific or domain-general manner after fine-tuning.

the LMs. Under the setting of out-of-domain generalization, we conduct a pilot study to examine how neurons activation [2] can vary from a domain to another, as in Fig. 1. In the study, the activation statistics towards three training domains of a sampled neuron (for [CLS] token) from each FFN block are attained by 1) feeding the examples sampled from these domains into the fined-tuned BERT; and 2) counting the accumulated times of activation. Recapping the results in Fig. 1, we can find that quite a few neurons, or parameters without loss of generality, unexpectedly behave in a domain-specific manner, which may well cause the unsatisfying out-of-domain generalization performance. Yet, other parameters may behave in a domain-general manner.

Motivated by the phenomenon, we hypothesize that domain-general parameters may essentially underpin a domain-general BERT that can be derived from the original BERT. This makes it possible to uncover a domain-general BERT by simply identifying domain-general parameters. Witnessing the success of LTH that states a well-performing pruned model can be uncovered by playing lottery tickets [6], we seek an effective solution customized for the domain-general BERT from intervening lottery tickets (dubbed *doge tickets*).

3.2   Playing Lottery Tickets

The identification of tickets typically follows a *first fine-tuning, then pruning, finally rewinding* paradigm [6]. Following recent advances [13,18,24], we would like to apply structured pruning to a LM to identify *doge tickets* by pruning MHA heads and FFN blocks. The most basic reason sits in that unstructured pruning requires maintaining a global pool of scores for all parameters, leading to a predominant memory overhead. Although we have only discovered domain-specific manner at neuron level in Sect. 3.1, we believe the same can apply at module level.The procedure is illustrated in Fig. 2, including the following steps: 1) fine-tuning: train the LM on a specific task; 2) pruning: prune parameters of the LM to a target sparsity under the guidance of the domain-general scores computed with the trained LM; 3) rewinding: set the pruned LM to the initial point of fine-tuning and train it on the task again.

Previous work identifies *winning tickets* by referring to the **expressive scores** of parameters [18]. While *winning tickets* can discover more light-weighted and more expressive LMs, we argue that they are not suitable to identify *doge tickets* since the variance has not been taken into consideration. Thus, we intervene the playing of lottery tickets guided by the **domain-general scores** which take into consideration the mean and variance of expressive scores across domains.

Expressive Scores. The expressive scores are approximated by masking the parameterized elements of the fine-tuned LM. $\xi^{(i)}$ and ν generally denote the mask variables respectively for an MHA head and an FFN block [24], such that:

$$^{\circ}\text{MHA}(\mathbf{X}) = \sum_{i=1}^{n} \xi^{(i)} \mathbf{H}^{(i)}(\mathbf{X}) \mathbf{W}_O^{(i)}, {}^{\circ}\text{FFN}(\mathbf{Z}) = \nu \mathbf{W}_2 \text{GELU}(\mathbf{W}_1 \mathbf{Z})$$

where we initialize the mask variables $\xi^{(i)} = 1$ and $\nu = 1$ for the corresponding MHA head and FFN block to preserve the original LM. Then the expected absolute gradient over all training data for the MHA head and FFN block gives the expressive scores:

$$\mathbb{I}_{\text{MHA}}^{(i)} = \mathbb{E}_{(x,y)\sim\mathcal{D}} \left| \frac{\partial \mathcal{L}(x,y)}{\partial \xi^{(i)}} \right|, \mathbb{I}_{\text{FFN}} = \mathbb{E}_{(x,y)\sim\mathcal{D}} \left| \frac{\partial \mathcal{L}(x,y)}{\partial \nu} \right|$$

where (x, y) is a data point and $\mathcal{L}$ is the loss function. $\mathbb{E}$ represents expectation. The absolute value of gradient for a mask indicates how large the impact of masking the corresponding element is, thus implying how expressive an element is. Intuitively, a less expressive element should be pruned preferentially.

Domain-general Scores. After obtaining expressive scores in all domains, the domain-general scores take the mean and further the variance of expressive scores across domains. The domain-general scores can be formulated as:

$$\mathbb{I}_{\text{MHA}}^{(i)\prime} = \mathbb{E}_{d\sim\mathcal{D}}\mathbb{E}_{(x,y)\sim d} \left| \frac{\partial \mathcal{L}(x,y)}{\partial \xi^{(i)}} \right| - \lambda\mathbb{V}_{d\sim\mathcal{D}}\mathbb{E}_{(x,y)\sim d} \left| \frac{\partial \mathcal{L}(x,y)}{\partial \xi^{(i)}} \right|,$$

$$\mathbb{I}_{\text{FFN}}' = \mathbb{E}_{d\sim\mathcal{D}}\mathbb{E}_{(x,y)\sim d} \left| \frac{\partial \mathcal{L}(x,y)}{\partial \nu} \right| - \lambda\mathbb{V}_{d\sim\mathcal{D}}\mathbb{E}_{(x,y)\sim d} \left| \frac{\partial \mathcal{L}(x,y)}{\partial \nu} \right|$$

where (x, y) is a data point from the domain d. The domain-general score measures the balance between the mean and variance of expressive scores across domains. λ is adopted to quantify the trade-off.

As suggested by [19], we normalize the expressive scores of MHA heads with ℓ_2 norm. We gradually increase sparsity level by pruning the elements with lowest domain-general scores, therefore producing LMs with different sparsity levels. Rewinding is applied to these LMs by setting the remaining parameters' values to what they were in the early stage of fine-tuning [7] (i.e., the initialization point for fine-tuning). We expect the LM with remaining parameters can achieve better out-of-domain generalization, thus regarding them as *doge tickets*.

Table 1. Statistics of datasets. **#train.**, **#dev.**, and **#test** indicate average number of training, development, and test examples per domain.

Dataset	$\mathcal{D}$	#train.	#dev.	$\mathcal{D}'$	#test
AMAZONA	{All Beauty, Automotive, Digital Music, Gift Cards}	5,400	600	{Industrial and Scientific, Movies, Software}	6,000
AMAZONB	{All Beauty, Industrial and Scientific, Movies, Software}			{Automotive, Digital Music, Gift Cards}	
AMAZONC	{Digital Music, Gift Cards, Movies, Software}			{All Beauty, Automotive, Industrial and Scientific}	
MNLI	{Fiction, Government, Slate, Telephone, Travel}	78,540	1,963	{Face to Face, Letters, Nine, Oup, Verbatim}	1,966
ONTONOTES	{Broadcast Conversation, Broadcast News, Magazine, Newswire}	16,111	2,488	{Telephone Conversation, Web Data}	1,837

4　Experiments

4.1　Datasets

We conduct our experiments on the AMAZON sentiment classification dataset [21], the MNLI language inference dataset [29] and the ONTONOTES named entity recognition dataset [23]. They are described as follows:

- AMAZON originally contains reviews from a variety of product categories. We randomly select 7 product categories as domains and sample 6,000 reviews from each domain. Since each review is associated with a score ranging from 1 to 5 stars, we derive a 3-way sentiment labels from the score by viewing a score larger than 3 as positive, a score smaller than 3 as negative, and a score of 3 as neutral. Then we randomly select 4 out of 7 domains as training set ($\mathcal{D}$) and the rest 3 as test set ($\mathcal{D}'$). In this way, we can construct an out-of-domain dataset and repeat for three times, resulting in a total of 3 out-of-domain datasets, denoted as AMAZONA, AMAZONB, and AMAZONC respectively.
- MNLI covers a range of genres of spoken and written sentence pairs with textual entailment information. We strictly follow its original data split and use the mismatched (i.e., different genres from those in the training set) development set of the dataset as out-of-domain test set, giving us 5 training domains and 5 test domains.
- ONTONOTES consists of annotated named entities types from 6 genres. We randomly choose 4 domains as training set and the rest 2 as test set.

Table 1 present the detailed information and statistics of the datasets.

4.2　Models and Implementation

We directly fine-tune the pre-trained BERT [5] (in fact, BERT-base) without pruning to obtain a solid baseline for out-of-domain generalization measure, and further carry out comparisons among the following models:

- BERT w/ invariant risk minimization (IRM) applies a domain-invariant classifier [1] to the BERT, as a strong baseline for out-of-domain generalization.
- BERT w/ *random tickets* rewinds on a set of *random tickets* randomly sampled from the structured modules (MHA heads and FFN blocks).
- BERT w/ *winning tickets* rewinds on a set of *winning tickets* chosen according to the expressive scores over training data. We identify the tickets through pruning the BERT to an expected sparsity.
- BERT w/ *doge tickets* rewinds on a set of *doge tickets* chosen according to the domain-general scores over training data, which is akin to the procedure of BERT w/ *winning tickets*.

We use AdamW [15] as the optimizer in our experiments. The learning rate is searched within $\{1, 2, 3, 5\} \times 10^{-5}$ and the batch size is searched within $\{16, 32\}$. Both training and rewinding last no longer than 10 epochs, with an early-stopping. For out-of-domain generalization, models are learned from training domains and evaluated on ever unseen test domains. The averaged Accuracy and the average F1-score over test domains are adopted as evaluation metrics during our experiments.

4.3 Main Comparison

Table 2 shows the main comparison results on all datasets. As we can see, BERT w/ *doge tickets* certainly generalizes better than BERT. Specifically, the improvements over BERT brought by *doge tickets* are 1.9% on AMAZONA, 1.2% on AMAZONB, 2.6% on AMAZONC, 0.2% on MNLI and 1.3% on ONTONOTES. Further, compared to the competitive out-of-domain generalization baseline, BERT w/ IRM, our model BERT w/ *doge tickets* also achieves a performance improvement, which illustrates that domain-specific parameters would better be pruned instead of regularized. Finally, BERT w/ *doge tickets* gains 0.5% on average over that with *winning tickets*, implying that domain variance should be considered as a significant part when playing the lotteries. Surprisingly, BERT w/ *random tickets* can be competitive with BERT w/ *winning tickets*, suggesting the sub-optimality of using *winning tickets* for out-of-domain generalization. Meanwhile, we notice that *doge tickets* favors a comparably smaller sparsity. This observation can be seen as an evidence that, with the variance, we should cautiously prune parameters. We also provide results for `BERT-large` in Table 3, which show that *doge tickets* can be applied to larger LMs and achieve a performance gain.

Table 2. Main comparison results in percentage. The best results on datasets are **boldfaced**. Average Score is the average metric over used datasets. Average Sparsity is the average sparsity to achieve best out-of-domain generalization among all sparsity levels over used datasets.

Model	Datasets					Average Score	Average Sparsity
	AMAZONA	AMAZONB	AMAZONC	MNLI	ONTONOTES		
	Acc	Acc	Acc	Acc	F1		
BERT	69.8	72.6	69.6	84.8	57.2	70.8	0.0%
w/ IRM	70.4	72.5	70.7	84.3	56.3	70.8	0.0%
w/ *random tickets*	71.4	73.3	70.1	84.6	57.9	71.5	12.8%
w/ *winning tickets*	70.9	73.7	71.3	84.8	57.9	71.7	17.5%
w/ *doge tickets*	**71.7**	**73.8**	**72.2**	**85.0**	**58.5**	**72.2**	15.0%

Table 3. Extended comparison results in percent. Larger LMs are used.

Model	Datasets
	AMAZONA
	Acc
BERT-large	73.1
w/ IRM	73.5
w/ *winning tickets*	74.0
w/ *doge tickets*	**74.3**

Table 4. Results in percentage on MNLI with different training domain numbers. Δ means generalization margin.

Model	Datasets		
	MNLI-5	MNLI-4	MNLI-3
	Acc	Acc	Acc
BERT	84.8	84.2	83.0
w/ *winning tickets*	84.8	84.3	83.3
w/ *doge tickets*	85.0	84.5	83.6
Δ	0.2	0.3	0.6

5   Analysis

5.1   Sensitivity to Learning Variance

To investigate the effect of learning variance for out-of-domain generalization, Fig. 3 shows the results from different settings, {0, 10, 50, 100}, of the variance coefficient λ on AMAZONA. The results suggest that it is necessary to take into account the variance when quantifying domain-general scores. The model performance first increases till a certain λ and then decreases, hinting that we can count the variance as much as possible on the same sparsity level to increase model generalization.

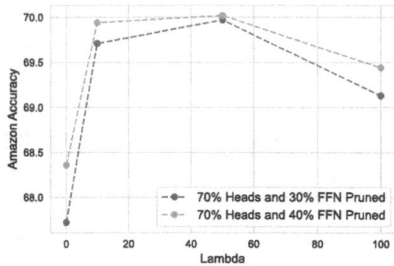

Fig. 3. *doge tickets* on AMAZONA under various λ values with two sparsity levels.

5.2   Impact of the Number of Training Domains

One may well note that the performance improvement of *doge tickets* is not significant on MNLI. We conjecture this is subject to the number of training domains. To explore whether training domain number matters, we conduct experiments by randomly selecting domains from the original 5 in MNLI (MNLI-5) as training domains, denoted as MNLI-4 and MNLI-3. As shown in Table 4, we observe that BERT w/ *doge tickets* discovers a larger generalization margin, when fewer (i.e., 4 and 3) training domains are used. That is, when using a smaller number of training domains, the impact of domain-specific (or domain-general) parameters on generalization results becomes more significant. According to the existing literature and intuition [11], more training domains can help LMs to extrapolate to unseen domains to some extent, thereby achieving a better out-of-domain generalization than the use of less training domains.

5.3   Existence of Domain-specific Manner

While we have found that a critical portion of parameters behave in a domain-specific manner through our pilot observation over intermediate activation distributions within the LM, we would like to verify the finding via intuitively visualizing expressive scores of parameters across domains. We use AMAZONA and show the expressive scores of elements across different domains in Fig. 4.

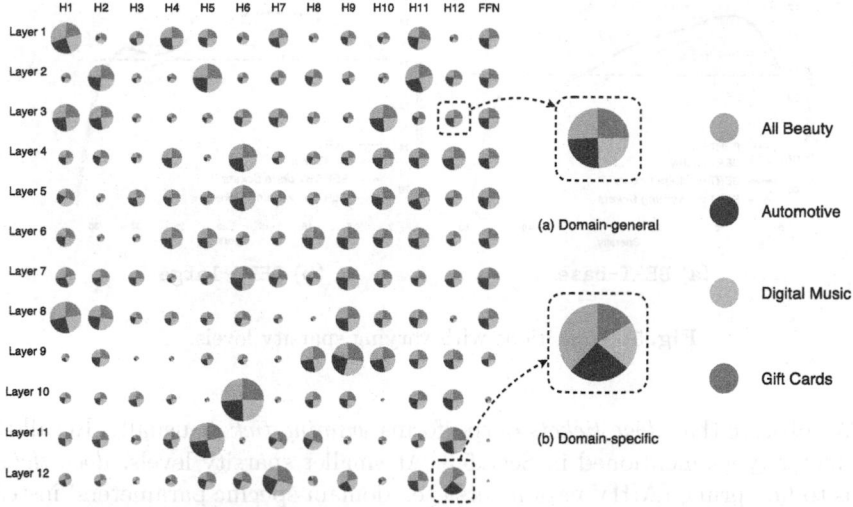

Fig. 4. Illustration of expressive scores across domains. Each pie represents a parameterized element (either an MHA head or FFN block). The mean and variance is measured by the radius of a pie and the proportion of each color in a pie respectively. We use 4 distinguished colors to represent domains, whose details are shown in legend.

Based on the mean and variance of expressive scores across domains, the parameters can be divided into 4 types: (1) high mean with high variance (HMHV); (2) high mean with low variance (HMLV); (3) low mean with high variance (LMHV); and (4) low mean with low variance (LMLV). It is obvious that there exists quite a number of elements with small radius, showing they play a less important role in the LM. This kind of parameters are exactly LMHV and LMLV parameters. If we merely consider this, *winning tickets* seems already a promising choice. However, more importantly, some elements are indeed behave unexpectedly in a domain-specific manner if we look at the proportions of different colors within pies, i.e., LMHV and HMHV parameters, suggesting the need of considering variance as in *doge tickets*.

To highlight, LMLV and HMLV elements are actually applicable across different domains, such as Fig. 4 (a). On the other hand, LMHV and HMHV ones are dedicated to a domain or two, for example "All Beauty" domain as Fig. 4 (b) shows. So *doge tickets* chooses to prune LMHV parameters in the first place yet HMLV in the last, leading to domain-general LMs.

5.4   Consistency with Varying Sparsity Levels

We prune the parameters under 25 sparsity levels for BERT. While both *doge tickets* and *winning tickets* can be identified at any sparsity levels, the evaluation results of them present transitions when we vary the sparsity levels continuously. We display the transitions of both BERT-base and BERT-large on AMAZONA in Fig. 5 to see whether *doge tickets* performs consistently better.

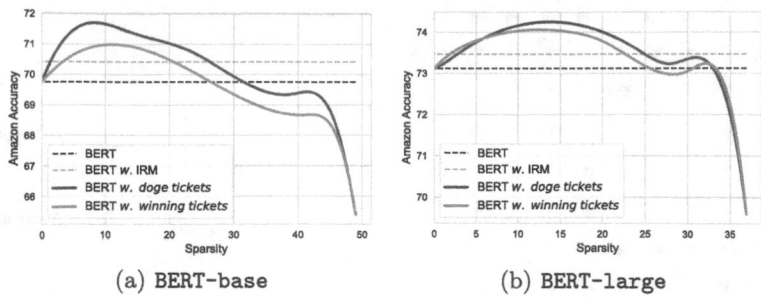

(a) BERT-base   (b) BERT-large

Fig. 5. Transitions with varying sparsity levels.

We observe that *doge tickets* outperforms *winning tickets* usually. Recall the parameter types mentioned in Sect. 5.3. At smaller sparsity levels, *doge tickets* tends to first prune LMHV parameters (i.e., domain-specific parameters) instead of LMLV and LMHV parameters which are first considered by *winning tickets*. *doge tickets* shall preserve more domain-general parameters than winning tickets for a better out-of-domain generalization. On the other end, at larger sparsity levels, *winning tickets* and *doge tickets* start to prune expressive parameters. It occurs that HMLV parameters (i.e., domain-general parameters) will be pruned earlier than HMHV for *winning tickets*. Contrarily, *doge tickets* will certainly prune HMLV parameters later whenever possible. Hence, compared to *winning tickets*, *doge tickets* consistently makes LMs packed with invariant parameters at all sparsity levels to maintain a good out-of-domain generalization.

6   Conclusions

In this paper, we address the issue of learning variance of over-parameterized LMs, which we find through a pilot study can lead a critical portion of parameters to behave unexpectedly in a domain-specific manner. Neurons corresponding to these domain-specific parameters are particularly activated for some domains, yet not so active in others. Consequently, LMs are more likely to suffer from a low out-of-domain generalization, as it requires LMs to perform universally well on different domains.

Motivated by this observation, we posit that the other parameters are domain-general, essentially underpinning a domain-general LM that can appropriately derived from the original LM. To uncover the domain-general LM, we have proposed to identify domain-general parameters by playing lottery tickets under the vision of our proposed domain-general score (*doge tickets*). By taking into consideration both the mean and variance of parameter expressiveness, *doge tickets* shows advantages over previous *winning tickets* on the out-of-domain datasets. Further analyses verify the existence of domain-general parameters and performance consistency of *doge tickets*. We have empirically shown pruning can improve out-of-domain generalization of LMs at large. In the future, we plan to examine the maximum potential of pruning by applying it under 1) unsupervised and 2) multi-task scenarios.

Acknowledgements. This research was supported in part by Natural Science Foundation of Beijing (grant number: 4222036) and Huawei Technologies (grant number: TC20201228005).

References

1. Arjovsky, M., Bottou, L., Gulrajani, I., Lopez-Paz, D.: Invariant risk minimization. arXiv:1907.02893 (2019)
2. Bengio, Y.: Deep learning of representations: looking forward. In: Dediu, A.-H., Martín-Vide, C., Mitkov, R., Truthe, B. (eds.) SLSP 2013. LNCS (LNAI), vol. 7978, pp. 1–37. Springer, Heidelberg (2013). https://doi.org/10.1007/978-3-642-39593-2_1
3. Brix, C., Bahar, P., Ney, H.: Successfully applying the stabilized lottery ticket hypothesis to the transformer architecture. In: ACL, pp. 3909–3915 (2020)
4. Chen, T., et al.: The lottery ticket hypothesis for pre-trained BERT networks. In: NeurIPS (2020)
5. Devlin, J., Chang, M., Lee, K., Toutanova, K.: BERT: pre-training of deep bidirectional transformers for language understanding. In: NAACL, pp. 4171–4186 (2019)
6. Frankle, J., Carbin, M.: The lottery ticket hypothesis: finding sparse, trainable neural networks. In: ICLR (2019)
7. Frankle, J., Dziugaite, G.K., Roy, D.M., Carbin, M.: Linear mode connectivity and the lottery ticket hypothesis. In: ICML. Proceedings of Machine Learning Research, vol. 119, pp. 3259–3269 (2020)
8. Han, S., Pool, J., Tran, J., Dally, W.J.: Learning both weights and connections for efficient neural network. In: NeurIPS, pp. 1135–1143 (2015)
9. He, Y., Zhang, X., Sun, J.: Channel pruning for accelerating very deep neural networks. In: ICCV, pp. 1398–1406 (2017)
10. Hendrycks, D., Gimpel, K.: Bridging nonlinearities and stochastic regularizers with gaussian error linear units. arXiv:1606.08415 (2016)
11. Hendrycks, D., Liu, X., Wallace, E., Dziedzic, A., Krishnan, R., Song, D.: Pre-trained transformers improve out-of-distribution robustness. In: ACL, pp. 2744–2751 (2020)
12. Li, H., Kadav, A., Durdanovic, I., Samet, H., Graf, H.P.: Pruning filters for efficient convnets. In: ICLR (2017)
13. Liang, C., et al.: Super tickets in pre-trained language models: from model compression to improving generalization. In: ACL, pp. 6524–6538 (2021)
14. Liu, Y., et al.: Roberta: a robustly optimized BERT pretraining approach. arXiv:1907.11692 (2019)
15. Loshchilov, I., Hutter, F.: Decoupled weight decay regularization. In: ICLR (2019)
16. Louizos, C., Welling, M., Kingma, D.P.: Learning sparse neural networks through L0 regularization. In: ICLR (2018)
17. Luo, J., Wu, J., Lin, W.: Thinet: A filter level pruning method for deep neural network compression. In: ICCV, pp. 5068–5076 (2017)
18. Michel, P., Levy, O., Neubig, G.: Are sixteen heads really better than one? In: NeurIPS, pp. 14014–14024 (2019)

19. Molchanov, P., Tyree, S., Karras, T., Aila, T., Kautz, J.: Pruning convolutional neural networks for resource efficient inference. In: ICLR (2017)
20. Namkoong, H., Duchi, J.C.: Variance-based regularization with convex objectives. In: NeurIPS, pp. 2971–2980 (2017)
21. Ni, J., Li, J., McAuley, J.J.: Justifying recommendations using distantly-labeled reviews and fine-grained aspects. In: EMNLP, pp. 188–197 (2019)
22. Park, J., Li, S.R., Wen, W., Tang, P.T.P., Li, H., Chen, Y., Dubey, P.: Faster CNNs with direct sparse convolutions and guided pruning. In: ICLR (2017)
23. Pradhan, S., et al.: Towards robust linguistic analysis using ontonotes. In: Hockenmaier, J., Riedel, S. (eds.) CoNLL, pp. 143–152 (2013)
24. Prasanna, S., Rogers, A., Rumshisky, A.: When BERT plays the lottery, all tickets are winning. In: EMNLP, pp. 3208–3229 (2020)
25. Raffel, C., et al.: Exploring the limits of transfer learning with a unified text-to-text transformer. J. Mach. Learn. Res. **21**, 140:1-140:67 (2020)
26. Renda, A., Frankle, J., Carbin, M.: Comparing rewinding and fine-tuning in neural network pruning. In: ICLR (2020)
27. Vaswani, A., et al.: Attention is all you need. In: NeurIPS, pp. 5998–6008 (2017)
28. Wang, A., Singh, A., Michael, J., Hill, F., Levy, O., Bowman, S.R.: GLUE: a multi-task benchmark and analysis platform for natural language understanding. In: ICLR (2019)
29. Williams, A., Nangia, N., Bowman, S.R.: A broad-coverage challenge corpus for sentence understanding through inference. In: NAACL, pp. 1112–1122 (2018)
30. Ye, H., Xie, C., Cai, T., Li, R., Li, Z., Wang, L.: Towards a theoretical framework of out-of-distribution generalization. arXiv:2106.04496 (2021)

Information Extraction and Knowledge Graph (Oral)

BART-Reader: Predicting Relations Between Entities via Reading Their Document-Level Context Information

Hang Yan[1,2], Yu Sun[1,2], Junqi Dai[1,2], Xiangkun Hu[3], Qipeng Guo[3], Xipeng Qiu[1,2(✉)], and Xuanjing Huang[1,2]

[1] Shanghai Key Laboratory of Intelligent Information Processing, Fudan University, Shanghai, China
{hyan19,jqdai19,xpqiu,xjhuang}@fudan.edu.cn, yusun21@m.fudan.edu.cn
[2] School of Computer Science, Fudan University, Shanghai, China
[3] Amazon AWS AI, Shanghai, China
{xiangkhu,gqipeng}@amazon.com

Abstract. Document-level relation extraction (Doc-RE) aims to classify relations between entities spread over multiple sentences. When one entity is paired with separate entities, the importance of its mentions varies, which means the entity representation should be different. However, most of the previous RE models failed to make the relation classification entity-pair aware effectively. To that end, we propose a novel adaptation to simultaneously utilize the encoder and decoder of the sequence-to-sequence (Seq2Seq) pre-trained model BART in a non-generative manner to tackle the Doc-RE task. The encoder encodes the document to get the entity-aware contextualized mention representation. The decoder uses a non-causal self-attention mechanism and masked cross-attention to model the interactions between the entity pair under consideration explicitly. By doing so, we can fully take advantage of the pre-trained model in the encoder and decoder sides. And experiments in three Doc-RE datasets show that our model can not only take more advantage of BART, but surpass various BERT and RoBERTa based models.

Keywords: Document-level relation extraction · Encoder-decoder

1 Introduction

Relation Extraction (RE) is a fundamental task of Information Extraction (IE). Previous work mainly focused on the sentence-level RE, where the relation between two entities in one sentence is concerned [15,21]. However, for document-level RE (Doc-RE), one entity usually has several entity mentions in a document, and the clues about the relations between entities may spread over several sentences.

The **Portland Golf Club** is a private golf club in the northwest **United States**, in suburban Portland, Oregon. The **golf club** is located in the unincorporated Raleigh Hills area of eastern Washington County, southwest of downtown Portland and east of Beaverton. **PGC** was established in the winter of **1914**, ... The **U.S.** team defeated Great Britain 11 to 1 in wet conditions in early November.
Entity e_1: {Portland Golf Club, golf club, PGC}   Entity e_2: {United States, U.S.}   Entity e_3: {1914}
Relation Fact #1: ({Portland Golf Club, golf club, PGC} , *country*, {United States, U.S.})   Relation Fact #2: ({Portland Golf Club, golf club, PGC} , *inception*, {1914})

Fig. 1. An example document from the DocRED dataset with partial entities colored. Entities in this dataset are represented by their mentions (annotated by the dataset), and these mentions may spread over several sentences. For different relation facts, the importance of mentions varies. With the same entity colored in blue, when judging the relation between e_1 and e_2, the mention "Portland Golf Club" is useful. While the mention "PGC" is useful to recognize the Relation Fact #2. (Color figure online)

Recently, Yao et al. [19] proposed a large-scale human-annotated Doc-RE dataset, DocRED. An example of this dataset is presented in Fig. 1. Some previous works first encoded the document, then used a pooling method to get a global entity representation from its mention hidden states, and paired the entity representations to conduct the relation classification [4,17]. Moreover, other graph-based methods usually constructed a graph based on a parser, the sentence relations or the entity mention coreferences, etc., then used the graph neural network (GNN) to propagate through the graph to get the entity representation [18,22,23]. After achieving the entity representation, they combined the entity representations and some entity-pair aware features to conduct relation classifications. However, these entity-pair aware features depended on entity distances or weighted pooling of the entity path in the graph.

In this paper, instead of using simple features or graph-based path pooling, we explicitly get entity-pair aware representations, which means the entity should get different contextualized representations when paired with separate entities. We propose a new model which first encodes the document to get the contextualized mention representation, and then for each entity pair, the model alternates interaction between the entity pair with reading corresponding contextualized mention representations. We can use the widely adopted Transformer encoder and decoder [14] to implement this model. Since each entity has several mentions, we add entity nodes in the encoder input to make mentions aware of its other coreferences, and each entity node represents one entity. We modify the encoder self-attention map to force the entity nodes to only attend to other entity nodes and their corresponding mentions tokens and vice versa. On the decoder side, we enumerate entity pairs in the document and put them sequentially, and each entity can only attend to its paired entity on the decoder side (through the decoder self-attention) and to its corresponding mentions and entity node on the encoder side (through the decoder cross-attention). In this architecture, the model only needs to encode the document once to get all entity-pair aware representations.

Although Doc-RE is a natural language understanding (NLU) task, the model structure we proposed is similar to the generative encoder-decoder model [5,14]. Therefore, we can use the pre-trained Seq2Seq model BART [5] to initialize this model, thus we named this model as **BART-Reader**. Experiments reveal that our model outperforms various BERT and RoBERTa based models.

In summary, our main contribution is as follows:

- We formulate the Doc-RE as an entity pair representation learning problem. Unlike previous models, we explicitly capture the entity-pair aware information via deep cross-attention rather than simple pooling or shallow entity path pooling in the graph.
- With the novel design of masked attention, we can utilize BART, a pre-trained Seq2Seq model, to tackle a NLU task. Moreover, the design of adding entity nodes on encoder and using flexibility of position embedding on decoder, make the model more suitable for Doc-RE task.
- The model is based on standard Transformer blocks and is simple to implement. And experiments in three Doc-RE datasets show that this adaptation of BART can not only surpass the recommended usage of BART [5], but outperform various BERT and RoBERTa based models.

2   Task Formulation

Given a document $D = [s_1, ..., s_N]$ with N sentences, where the i-th sentence $s_i = [w_{i1}, ..., w_{iL}]$ contains L words. The document D can also be represented as a sequence of N' words like $X = [w_1, ..., w_{N'}]$. Among the document, there exist M entities $\mathscr{E} = \{e_i\}_{i=1}^{M}$. Each entity can be represented as $e_i = \{m_j\}_{j=1}$, where m_j is a span of words belongs to the j-th mention of the i-th entity. The target of this task is to find all relations between entity pairs, namely to find $\{e_i, e_j, r_{ij} | e_i, e_j \in \mathscr{E}, r_{ij} \in \mathcal{R}\}$, where $\mathcal{R}$ is the set of predefined relation types.

3   BART-Reader

In this part, we will show the usage of Transformer blocks in our model. Firstly, we introduce how to achieve entity-aware contextualized document representations with entity nodes. Then we show how to use the cross-attention mechanism to get entity-pair representations. And through a novel design of attention masks and position ids, we can calculate multiple entity pairs concurrently. Lastly, we present the relation classification module and loss function.

3.1   Entity-aware Document Context Representation

This part introduces how to use the Transformer encoder to interact between entities and document context to get entity-aware representations. Unlike

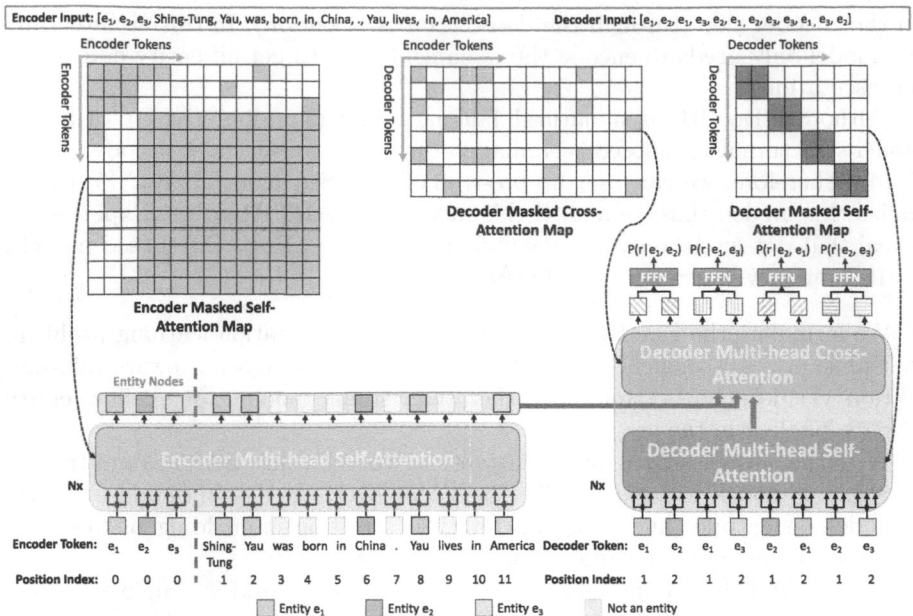

Fig. 2. A Transformer encoder-decoder model for the Doc-RE. Colored squares in the attention maps are tokens needed to be attended to. Instead of making the decoder generate the tokens, we send the entity pair sequence to it and take the hidden states of these entities to do the relation classification.

previous work, which usually used entity coreference embeddings [22,23] or inserted special tags [24,26] to indicate entity-mention information, we propose using the entity nodes to achieve this goal. Specifically, we first prepend M entity nodes to the input sequence, making the input sequence as $X' = [e_1, ..., e_M, w_1, ..., w_{N'}]$. Here, we use the entity type to represent entity nodes in X'. The token embeddings of these entity types are initialized by the word surface of the entity type names. Since we want the entity nodes to be order-agnostic, the position ids correspond to X' is $P_e = [0, ..., 0, 1, ..., N']$, there are M 0s before the 1. Besides, instead of using a dense attention map, we make the following modifications in the self-attention map $\mathbf{M} \in \mathbb{R}^{(M+N') \times (M+N')}$

$$
\mathbf{M}[i,j] =
\begin{cases}
1 & \text{if } 1 \le i,j \le M \quad \text{or} \quad M < i,j \\
1 & \text{if } 1 \le i \le M \ \& \ j-M \in \mathbf{I}_{\mathbf{e_i}} \\
1 & \text{if } 1 \le j \le M \ \& \ i-M \in \mathbf{I}_{\mathbf{e_j}} \\
0 & \text{otherwise}
\end{cases}
\tag{1}
$$

where $\mathbf{I}_{\mathbf{e_i}}$ are the indexes of tokens that belong to the entity e_i. The four cases with value 1 in Eq. 1 mean: (1) attentions between entity nodes; (2) attentions between tokens; (3) the entity node can attend to its mention tokens; (4) the mention token can attend to its entity node. An example of this attention map is presented in Fig. 2, named as "Encoder Masked Self-Attention Map".

Then we use the encoder to encode this sequence

$$\mathbf{H}^e = \text{Encoder}(X', P_e, \mathbf{M}) \tag{2}$$

where $\mathbf{H}^e \in \mathbb{R}^{N' \times d}$.

3.2   Entity-Pair Representation

As discussed before, when the entity is in distinct pairs, the importance of its mentions varies. Therefore, the model needs to read from different contextualized mention representations in various pairs. To that end, we first use the self-attention to interact within the entity pairs, then for each entity, we use the cross-attention mechanism to select proper mentions to attend to softly. The internal interaction and reading processes repeat several times to help the model choose thoroughly appropriate mentions. For the Transformer decoder to distinguish between head and tail entities, we use position id 1 and 2 for them, respectively. We use $Z = [e_1, e_2]$ to represent the decoder input.

To help the model to find its corresponding contextualized mention representations on the encoder side, we change the cross-attention map $\mathbf{C} \in \mathbb{R}^{|Z| \times (M+N')}$ as follows

$$\mathbf{C}[i, j] = \begin{cases} 1 & \text{if } 1 \leq j \leq M \ \& \ Z[i] = X'[j] \\ 1 & \text{if } M < j \& j - M \in \mathbf{I}_{Z[i]} \\ 0 & \text{otherwise} \end{cases} \tag{3}$$

where $\mathbf{I}_{Z[i]}$ are source token indexes belong to the entity $Z[i]$. With the cross-attention map $\mathbf{C}$, the entities on the decoder side can only attend to their corresponding entity node and mention tokens.

A Parallel Implementation For All Pairs. Instead of getting entity pair representations one by one, we propose a novel way to get them concurrently by properly manipulating the attention mask and position ids. Specifically, we enumerate all entity pairs and put them in a sequence $Z = [e_1, e_2, e_1, e_3, ..., e_2, e_1, ...e_M, e_1, ..., e_M, e_{M-1}]$. Since there are $M * (M-1)$ pairs, the length of this sequence is $|Z| = 2M * (M-1)$. The position ids of Z is $P_d = [1, 2, 1, 2, ..., 1, 2]$, by alternating the decoding position ids with 1 and 2, the decoder can distinguish the head and tail entities and be entity pair order-agnostic. The self-attention of the decoder $\mathbf{S} \in \mathbb{R}^{|Z| \times |Z|}$ is as follows

$$\mathbf{S}[i, j] = \begin{cases} 1 & \text{if } i = j \\ 1 & \text{if } |i - j| = 1 \ \&\& \ \max(i, j)\%2 = 0 \\ 0 & \text{otherwise} \end{cases} \tag{4}$$

With the decoder self-attention map $\mathbf{S}$, the entity can only attend to its paired entity. This attention pattern is very different from the causal mask used to train a generative Seq2Seq model. Therefore, we name this kind of attention as "NonCausalSelfAttn.", an example of this attention map is depicted in the "Decoder Masked Self-Attention Map" of Fig. 2. Besides, one example of the decoder cross-attention map in this parallel implementation can be found in Fig. 2, named as the "Decoder Masked Cross-Attention Map".

Then we use the decoder to encode Z as follows

$$\mathbf{H}^d = \text{Decoder}(\mathbf{H}^e, Z, P_d, \mathbf{S}, \mathbf{C}) \tag{5}$$

where $\mathbf{H}^d \in \mathbb{R}^{|Z| \times d}$.

3.3 Relation Prediction

For each pair of entities, we achieve the relation probability distribution with the following equation

$$P(r|e_{2i-1}, e_{2i}) = \text{FFNN}([\mathbf{H}^d[2i-1]; \mathbf{H}^d[2i]]), \tag{6}$$

$$\text{FFNN}(x) = \text{Sigmoid}(W_b \max(W_a x, 0)) \tag{7}$$

where $i \in [1, M * (M-1)]$ and $P(r|e_{2i-1}, e_{2i}) \in \mathbb{R}^{|\mathcal{R}|}$. $W_a \in \mathbb{R}^{2d \times d}, W_b \in \mathbb{R}^{d \times |R|}$ are randomly initialized parameters. $[\cdot ; \cdot]$ means concatenation in the last dimension.

Although the encoder and decoder are not the same as the generative encoder-decoder models, the differences are mainly on the attention maps and we do not change the shape of weights of the Transformer block. Therefore, we can still use the weights from the pre-trained encoder-decoder BART [5] to initialize our model, the overall structure of BART-Reader can be seen in Fig. 2.

3.4 Loss Function

Since multiple relations may exist between entities, we use the binary cross-entropy to train our model,

$$\mathcal{L} = -\sum_{\mathcal{D} \in \mathcal{S}} \sum_{i \neq j} \sum_{r_k \in \mathcal{R}} [\mathbb{I}(r_k = 1) \log P(r_k|\mathbf{e}_i, \mathbf{e}_j) + \mathbb{I}(r_k = 0) \log(1 - P(r_k|\mathbf{e}_i, \mathbf{e}_j))]$$

where S denotes the whole corpus, and $\mathbb{I}(\cdot)$ refers to the indication function.

4   Experiments

4.1   Dataset

We evaluate our model on three widely used Doc-RE datasets,

- **DocRED** [19] is originated from Wikipedia and Wikidata, and annotated by human. Models need to determine relations between any two entities in the document. The test performance needs online evaluation[1]. It consists of 97 relation types and 7 entity types, with 5,053 documents in total.

---

[1] https://competitions.codalab.org/competitions/20717.

- **CDR** [6] is in the biomedical domain. The task is to predict whether there exist relations between given Chemical and Disease concept. It consists of 1,500 documents.
- **GDA** [16] is a large-scale biomedical Doc-RE dataset with 30,192 documents, which needs to predict whether there exist relations between given Gene and Disease concept. Following previous work [1,23], we split the training set into an 80/20 split as training and validation.

4.2   Experiment Settings

We initialize BART-Reader with pretrained Encoder-Decoder model BART, including BART-base and BART-large. For DocRED, instead of using all possible entity pairs during training, we use all entity pairs with at least one relation and randomly sample some negative entity pairs. We also use the slanted triangle learning rate warmup to stabilize the training process, and the warmup steps are 10% of the total optimization steps. We train our model with the AdamW optimizer [9]. Models with the best development set performance during training are used to evaluate the test set. Performance is averaged from three runs. Inspired by the BART-based question answering model [5], we introduce two BART baseline models, "Enc-BART" and "EncDec-BART", the first model uses the encoder of BART model to be as encoder, and the second model uses the BART encoder and decoder simultaneously. The relation classification module of these two models is similar to previous pooling-based models [19,20]. Experiments are conducted on NVIDIA GTX 3090.

4.3   Main Results

Since the significant impact of pre-trained models on performance, we only compare our BART-Reader model with previous methods using BERT [3], RoBERTa [8] or CorefBERT [20]. RE-CorefBERT [20], ATLOP [26] and SSAN [17] first encoded the documents and then used pooling methods to aggregate representations from mentions, then paired entity representations to conduct the relation classification. LSR [10], SIRE [22], HeterGSAN [18] and GAIN [23] methods tried to use the graph neural network to help models conduct reasoning between entity pairs. The DocuNet [24] viewed the relation classification as an image semantic segmentation problem that exploited the interaction between entity pairs.

The performance comparison in DocRED between "Enc-BART$_{base/large}$" and "EncDec-BART$_{base/large}$" in Table 1 implies that the usage of BART decoder can gain better performance. And with proper adaptation, the performance of BART can be significantly enhanced, as the "BART-Reader$_{base/large}$" rows show near 2% F1 improvement compared with the "EncDec-BART$_{base/large}$" models. Besides, our BART-Reader$_{base}$ outperforms all previous base-version-based models. And as the lower block of Table 1 shows, the performance of BART-Reader$_{large}$ model is similar to the BERT$_{large}$- or RoBERTa$_{large}$-based models. The better performance of RoBERTa$_{large}$ may

Table 1. Performance comparison between our model and previous work in DocRED. The upper block uses base version pre-trained models, and the lower block uses large version pre-trained models. In both cases, our BART-Reader model can significantly improve the performance of BART-based models.

Model	Dev		Test	
	Ign F1	F1	Ign F1	F1
RE-CorefBERT$_{base}$ [20]	55.32	57.51	54.54	56.96
LSR-BERT$_{base}$ [10]	52.43	59.00	56.97	59.05
GAIN-BERT$_{base}$ [23]	59.14	61.22	59.00	61.24
ATLOP-BERT$_{base}$ [26]	59.22±0.15	61.09±0.16	59.31	61.30
SIRE-BERT$_{base}$ [22]	59.82	61.6	60.18	62.05
SSAN-RoBERTa$_{base}$ [17]	58.83	60.89	57.71	59.94
HeterGSAN-BERT$_{base}$ [18]	58.13	60.18	57.12	59.45
DocuNet-BERT$_{base}$ [24]	59.86±0.13	61.83±0.19	**59.93**	61.86
Enc-BART$_{base}$	56.56±0.33	58.67±0.35	–	–
EncDec-BART$_{base}$	57.25±0.25	59.51±0.13	–	–
BART-Reader$_{base}$(Ours)	**59.72±0.15**	**61.90±0.20**	59.87	**62.28**
RE-CorefBERT$_{large}$ [20]	56.73	58.88	56.48	58.70
RE-CorefRoBERTa$_{large}$ [20]	57.84	59.93	57.68	59.91
GAIN-BERT$_{large}$ [23]	60.87	63.09	60.31	62.76
ATLOP-RoBERTa$_{large}$ [26]	61.32±0.14	63.18±0.19	61.39	63.40
SSAN-RoBERTa$_{large}$ [17]	60.25	62.08	59.47	61.42
DocuNet-RoBERTa$_{large}$ [24]	**62.23±0.12**	**64.12±0.14**	**62.39**	**64.55**
Enc-BART$_{large}$	58.51±0.17	60.62±0.20	–	–
EncDec-BART$_{large}$	59.66±0.16	61.76±0.11	–	–
BART-Reader$_{large}$(Ours)	61.38±0.17	63.50±0.14	61.34	63.54

caused by that it has 12 more encoder layers than the BART$_{large}$ model which may be important for mentions to thoroughly interact with each other.

We also use the BART-Reader in the CDR and GDA datasets, and the results are presented in Table 2. Our proposed BART-Reader$_{base}$ not only outperforms our BART-based baseline models but surpasses previous BERT-based models. We ignore results that used SciBERT [17,22,24,26], since the domain further train can concretely increase the in-domian performance [13].

4.4   Ablation Study

In this paper, we propose three main modifications to a standard Seq2Seq Transformer model: (1) entity nodes; (2) masked decoder self-attention; (3) masked decoder cross-attention. We want to test whether these changes are useful for this task. These three modifications are named as "EntityNode", "NonCausal-SelfAttn" and "MaskedCrossAttn" in Table 3, respectively. From this table, it is clear that all three modifications are useful in the DocRED dataset. And among them, the masked cross attention is vital to the performance of this model. This is as expected since the decoder needs the masked cross-attention to distinguish between different entity pairs.

4.5   Cross-attention Attends on Proper Mentions

In this part, we want to study the behavior of the cross-attention. Firstly, we compare the cross-attention patterns between entity pairs with and without relations. Secondly, we want to study whether the cross-attention mechanism can find the proper mentions to attend to when there exist relations between entity pairs. All experiments in this part are conducted on the development set of the DocRED dataset.

Table 2. Results on the test set of the CDR and GDA dataset.

	CDR	GDA
EOG [1]	63.6	81.5
LSR-BERT$_{base}$ [10]	64.8	82.2
DHG-BERT$_{base}$ [25]	65.9	83.1
SSAN-BERT$_{base}$ [17]	64.7	81.6
Enc-BART$_{base}$	72.36	80.16
EncDec-BART$_{base}$	73.22	81.31
BART-Reader$_{base}$(Ours)	**75.96**	**83.7**

Table 3. Ablation study on the development set of DocRED. Each of the three modifications contributes to the performance of our proposed model.

Model	Ign F1	F1
BART-Reader$_{base}$	**59.92**	**62.01**
-EntityNode	58.74	60.96
-NonCausalSelfAttn	59.21	61.32
-MaskedCrossAttn	20.09	20.46

To show the cross-attention patterns of entity pairs with and without relations, we define a "MentionScore" metric, which means the percentage of entities in decoder input that assign the largest attention score to mentions instead of entity nodes. We study the "MentionScore" of entity pairs without relations (In total, 385,272) and with relations (In total, 11518). It is clear from Fig. 3a that with no interaction between entities (at layer 1), the entity tends to attend on the entity nodes instead of corresponding mentions in evidence sentences. However, with the interaction between entities, entity pairs that have relations will gradually focus on the mentions, while entity pairs that have no relations will mostly attend to the entity nodes at last. The results show that our model will try to find the relevant mentions if relations exist between entities.

Since we have shown that the cross-attention will attend to mentions if the entity pairs have relations, we want to study whether the cross-attention can find

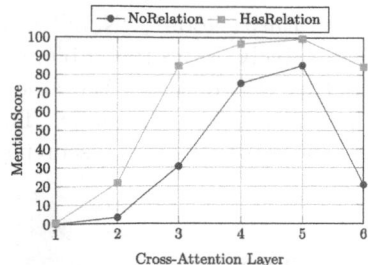 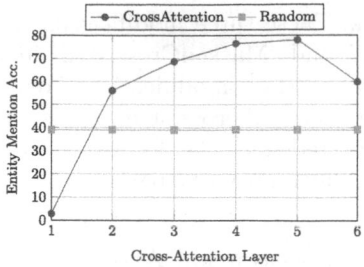

(a) MentionScore in different layers. "NoRelation" means entity pairs without relations, "HasRelation" means entity pairs have at least one relation.

(b) Entity mention accuracy in different layers. The "Random" line means randomly choose a mention of an entity.

Fig. 3. Two plots imply the pattern of the cross-attention layers. If the entity pair has no relation, it will tend to attend to the entity nodes. If an entity pair has relations, the cross-attention tends to put more weight on relevant mentions with the increment of layers. The abnormal trend in the last layer may be caused by that the model tends to make the decision boundary more smooth.

the proper mention based on evidence sentences[2] even without direct mention supervision. Suppose an entity has several entity mentions, but only one of these mentions appears in the evidence sentences of a relation fact. In that case, we deem that the model should attend to this entity mention to extract this fact (There are 4848 such mentions). And the cross-attention of this entity should assign the largest attention score to this mention (to any token of this mention) when predicting this fact[3]. Figure 3b shows the accuracy for finding such entity mentions in different layers. With the increase of layer, the cross-attention can find the mention more accurately, implying the need to use deeper decoder layers.

5   Related Work

Previous researches on relation extraction mainly focus on predicting relations between two entities within a single sentence. Various methods [15,21] have been explored to tackle this problem effectively. However, since many real-world relationships can only be extracted across multiple sentences, the sentence-level RE model faces an inevitable restriction in practice. Besides, Doc-RE datasets, such as CDR, GDA and DocRED [6,16,19], have been proposed in recent years, contributing to Doc-RE research.

Some graph-based studies [10,18,23] proposed to pay more attention to intersentence or focus on constructing more effective graph structures. Besides, other common Doc-RE models [17,26] directly applied pre-trained language models

---

[2] The DocRED corpus provides each fact with evidence sentences which indicate the sentences used to infer this fact.

[3] We first average the attention scores along the head dimension.

without using extra graph structure since pre-trained language models might learn dependency structures implicitly and automatically. In addition to the above, Zhang et al. [24] firstly regarded Doc-RE as a semantic segmentation problem in computer vision.

Most previous models mentioned above only considered single entity global representation. However, an entity may appear in multiple relation triples, Dai [2] noticed this issue but heavily relied on intricate graph structure. Zeng [22] and Xu [18] further utilized path mechanism, which just extracted quite shallow entity-pair aware representations. In this study, we propose to get entity-pair aware representations explicitly by using an encoder-decoder architecture based on the widely-used Transformer block [14]. Therefore, we can leverage the pre-trained BART with an encoder and decoder [5]. This adaptation can achieve entity-pair aware representations and avoid high computational complexity compared with the pairwise models.

The encoder-decoder framework has been extensively studied in NLP fields and is widely used in the Seq2Seq formulation [7,11]. The success of pre-training models [8,12] has attracted several attempts to pre-train an encoder-decoder model [5]. Although the pre-trained encoder-decoder model has been extensively used in downstream tasks [7,11], these methods usually utilized them in a generative way, which is similar to their pre-training tasks. While in this paper, we exploit to use the transformer-based [14] pre-trained BART in a very different way, which can shed light to exploit more diverse usage of encoder-decoder pre-trained models.

6 Conclusion

We introduced an encoder-decoder model to get the entity-pair aware representations for the Doc-RE task. The encoder first encodes the document with entity nodes to get the contextualized mention representations, and then the decoder uses the self-attention to interact within the entity pair and the cross-attention to read relevant information from the contextualized encoder outputs. With proper attention masking strategies, we can use the standard Transformer encoder and decoder to implement this model. Therefore, we can use the pre-trained BART model with an encoder and decoder to initialize it. And experiments from three Doc-RE datasets show that this BART initialized model can take more advantage of BART and surpass various graph-enhanced Doc-RE models. This good performance also sheds some light on the diverse usage of the BART model in the natural language understanding (NLU) tasks.

(https://github.com/fastnlp/fastNLP. FastNLP is a natural language processing python package.) (https://github.com/fastnlp/fitlog. Fitlog is an experiment tracking package.)

Acknowledgements. We would like to thank the anonymous reviewers for their insightful comments. We also thank the developers of fastNLP and fitlog. This work was supported by the National Key Research and Development Program of China (No. 2020AAA0108702) and National Natural Science Foundation of China (No. 62022027).

References

1. Christopoulou, F., Miwa, M., Ananiadou, S.: Connecting the dots: document-level neural relation extraction with edge-oriented graphs. In: EMNLP-IJCNLP (2019)
2. Dai, D., Ren, J., Zeng, S., Chang, B., Sui, Z.: Coarse-to-fine entity representations for document-level relation extraction. CoRR abs/2012.02507 (2020)
3. Devlin, J., Chang, M., Lee, K., Toutanova, K.: BERT: pre-training of deep bidirectional transformers for language understanding. In: NAACL-HLT (2019)
4. Huang, Q., Zhu, S., Feng, Y., Ye, Y., Lai, Y., Zhao, D.: Three sentences are all you need: local path enhanced document relation extraction. In: ACL/IJCNLP (2021)
5. Lewis, M., et al.: BART: denoising sequence-to-sequence pre-training for natural language generation, translation, and comprehension. In: ACL (2020)
6. Li, J., et al.: Biocreative V CDR task corpus: a resource for chemical disease relation extraction. Database J. Biol, Databases Curation (2016)
7. Li, S., Ji, H., Han, J.: Document-level event argument extraction by conditional generation. CoRR abs/2104.05919 (2021). https://arxiv.org/abs/2104.05919
8. Liu, Y., et al.: Roberta: a robustly optimized BERT pretraining approach. CoRR abs/1907.11692 (2019). http://arxiv.org/abs/1907.11692
9. Loshchilov, I., Hutter, F.: Decoupled weight decay regularization. In: ICLR (2019)
10. Nan, G., Guo, Z., Sekulic, I., Lu, W.: Reasoning with latent structure refinement for document-level relation extraction. In: ACL (2020)
11. Paolini, G., et al.: Structured prediction as translation between augmented natural languages. In: ICLR (2021)
12. Qiu, X., Sun, T., Xu, Y., Shao, Y., Dai, N., Huang, X.: Pre-trained models for natural language processing: a survey. CoRR abs/2003.08271 (2020)
13. Sun, C., Qiu, X., Xu, Y., Huang, X.: How to fine-tune BERT for text classification? In: CCL (2019)
14. Vaswani, A., et al.: Attention is all you need. In: Proceedings of NeuIPS (2017)
15. Wu, T., Li, X., et al.: Curriculum-meta learning for order-robust continual relation extraction. In: Proceedings of AAAI (2021)
16. Wu, Y., Luo, R., Leung, H.C.M., Ting, H., Lam, T.W.: RENET: a deep learning approach for extracting gene-disease associations from literature. In: RECOMB (2019)
17. Xu, B., Wang, Q., Lyu, Y., Zhu, Y., Mao, Z.: Entity structure within and throughout: Modeling mention dependencies for document-level relation extraction. In: Proceedings of AAAI (2021)
18. Xu, W., Chen, K., Zhao, T.: Document-level relation extraction with reconstruction. In: Proceedings of AAAI (2021)
19. Yao, Y., et al.: Docred: a large-scale document-level relation extraction dataset. In: ACL (2019)
20. Ye, D., Lin, Y., Du, J., Liu, Z., Sun, M., Liu, Z.: Coreferential reasoning learning for language representation. arXiv:2004.06870 (2020)
21. Ye, H., et al.: Contrastive triple extraction with generative transformer. In: Proceedings of AAAI (2021)
22. Zeng, S., Wu, Y., Chang, B.: SIRE: separate intra- and inter-sentential reasoning for document-level relation extraction. In: Findings of ACL/IJCNLP (2021)
23. Zeng, S., Xu, R., Chang, B., Li, L.: Double graph based reasoning for document-level relation extraction. In: EMNLP 2020 (2020)
24. Zhang, N., et al.: Document-level relation extraction as semantic segmentation. In: IJCAI (2021)

25. Zhang, Z., et al.: Document-level relation extraction with dual-tier heterogeneous graph. In: Proceedings of COLING (2020)
26. Zhou, W., Huang, K., Ma, T., Huang, J.: Document-level relation extraction with adaptive thresholding and localized context pooling. In: Proceedings of AAAI (2021)

DuEE-Fin: A Large-Scale Dataset for Document-Level Event Extraction

Cuiyun Han[✉], Jinchuan Zhang, Xinyu Li, Guojin Xu, Weihua Peng,
and Zengfeng Zeng

Baidu Inc., Beijing, China
{hancuiyun,zhangjinchuan,lixinyu13,xuguojin,
pengweihua,zengzengfeng}@baidu.com

Abstract. To tackle the data scarcity problem of document-level event extraction, we come up with a large-scale benchmark, DuEE-Fin, which consists of 15,000+ events categorized into 13 event types, and 81,000+ event arguments mapped in 92 argument roles. We constructed DuEE-Fin from real-world Chinese financial news, which allows one document to contain several events, multiple arguments to share the same argument role and one argument to play different roles in different events. Therefore, it presents some considerable challenges in document-level event extraction task such as multi-event recognition and multi-value argument identification, that are referred to as key issues for document-level event extraction task. Along with DuEE-Fin, we also hosted an open competition, which has attracted 1,690 teams and achieved exciting results. We performed experiments on DuEE-Fin with most popular document-level event extraction systems. However, results showed that even some SOTA models performed poorly with our data. Facing these challenges, we found it necessary to propose more effective methods.

Keywords: Document-level event extraction · Dataset · DuEE-Fin

1 Introduction

Event Extraction is a subtask of Information Extraction, which aims to extract structured events from unstructured text under a pre-defined schema, where each event would at least be composed of its event type and corresponding arguments. Event Extraction plays a vital role in a variety of downstream applications, such as Knowledge Base Construction [9], Misinformation Detection [3] and News Understanding [6]. Furthermore, the capability of identifying events from text could enable our research transit to Event-centric Natural Language Processing [1], where we can focus more on "what is actually happening", not just focus on "what the text says".

In the past decades, plenty of datasets have been proposed to promote the development of event extraction. Most of them are sentence-level based, in which a short paragraph mostly describes only one event at a time, and arguments of an

W. Lu et al. (Eds.): NLPCC 2022, LNAI 13551, pp. 172–183, 2022.
https://doi.org/10.1007/978-3-031-17120-8_14

event are usually restricted to a limited scope. Benefit from the leverage of Pre-trained Language Models (PLM), various methods have made great progress in sentence-level event extraction [10,11,13]. However, most text in real application scenarios appears in the form of long documents, such as financial announcements, medical reports and news articles. Simply applying models trained on sentence-level datasets to these documents will probably lead to incomplete and uninformative extraction results [7]. Nevertheless, the lack of supervised training data has prohibited the development of document-level event extraction (DEE).

For SEE task, ACE05 is the most frequently used multi-lingual dataset, which contains English, Chinese, Arabic. DuEE [8] is a large scale Chinese dataset for event extraction task at sentence level. ACE05 and DuEE have a wide scope of event types in their schema. Neither of them has contain for where their corpus came from. For DEE task, there are also some influential proposed datasets. Grishman and Sundheim [4] formalized DEE as a role filling task and proposed MUC-4 dataset, which contains approximately 1700 English news articles, 4 event types and 5 argument roles. Since these argument roles were shared by all event types, they are lack of type-oriented refinement. RAMS [2] is also an English dataset for DEE task, which is presented for finding explicit arguments for each role of an event as *argument linking*, but it limited the scope of the arguments in a 5-sentence window, which circumvented some main challenges of DEE, such as long-input and multi-event problems. To enlarge the scale of DEE dataset, Zheng et al. [16] utilized event knowledge bases to conduct distant supervision based (DS-based) event labeling and finally got a dataset consisting of 32040 entries, while the supervision offered by fixed KBs lack of diversity, so there are only 5 event types in their ChFinAnn.

To this end, we propose a novel large-scale DEE benchmark labeled by human, DuEE-Fin, which has the following characteristics: 1) Large-scale, We have labeled 11,645 non-repetitive financial documents and 11,699 entries in total, including 15,850 events and 81,632 event arguments. 2) Diversity, our data covers 13 event types and 92 argument roles, which has a more diverse coverage than most of previous DEE benchmarks. 3) Challenging, 29.2% of documents contain multiple events, and 16.8% of events consist of multi-value arguments, even the performance of SOTA models is still far from satisfactory. You are welcomed to join the open competition and download our dataset at *AIStudio*[1].

2   Preliminary

2.1   Concepts

Event Schema. A pre-defined ontology, which describes how event annotations are designed, including what types of events are there, and what argument roles should be filled for each specific event type.

---

[1] https://aistudio.baidu.com/aistudio/competition/detail/46/0/task-definition.

Event Trigger. An event trigger refers to a verb or a phrase that is most likely to indicate the occurrence of a certain type of event. For example, *attack* could be a trigger word for event type *Conflict.Attack*.

Event Argument. An entity or phrase that constitutes an attribute of an event.

Argument Role. A role played by an argument in a concrete event.

Event Mention or Event Record. An occurrence or an entry of a specific event type, including trigger words and corresponding arguments.

2.2   Task Definition

Given a document D, which consists of a sequence of words $\{w_1, w_2, \ldots, w_{|D|}\}$, there are usually three subtasks of document-level event extraction.

Trigger Detection: identifying the trigger words of all possible events in D, which can be regarded as a sequence labeling problem. Note that, each event should contain exactly one trigger.

Event Type Classification: classifying the document D into pre-defined event types, usually modeled as a multi-label classification task as there are likely to be different types of events in one document.

Argument Extraction: including identifying all the arguments that appear in the whole document and classifying them into pre-defined argument roles, which can also be seen as a sequence labeling problem.

Table 1. An example annotated document in DuEE-Fin.

Document	Annotated result
Title: 波奇宠物: 拟募资8000万美元月底上市Text: 宠物电商企业波奇宠物（股票代码为：“BQ”）日前更新招股书，发行700万股，发行区间为10到12美元，准备在美国纽交所上市。波奇宠物此次募资规模为7000万美元到8400万美元。一旦波奇宠物在美国上市，将成为国内宠物电商第一股。2014年波奇宠物曾宣布完成2500万美元B轮融资，投资方包括高盛。2016年，波奇宠物宣布完成C轮融资，总金额1.02亿美元全额到账，招银国际领投，原有投资者高盛等及管理层均跟投。…	{trigger: 融资, event_type: 企业融资, arguments: [{role: 事件时间, argument: 2014年}, {role: 被投资方, argument: 波奇宠物}, {role: 融资金额, argument: 2500万美元}, {role: 融资轮次, argument: B}, {role: 投资方, argument: 高盛}]}
	{trigger: 上市, event_type: 公司上市, arguments: [{role: 上市公司, argument: 波奇宠物}, {role: 发行价格, argument: 10到12美元}, {role: 募资金额, argument: 7000万美元到8400万美元}, {role: 披露时间, argument: 日前}, {role: 环节, argument: ”筹备上市”}, {role: 证券代码, argument: BQ}]}
	{trigger: 融资, event_type: 企业融资, arguments: [{role: 被投资方, argument: 波奇宠物}, {role: 融资轮次, argument: C}, {role: 融资金额, argument: 1.02亿美元}, {role: 投资方, argument: 招银国际}, {role: 领投方, argument: 招银国际}, {role: 投资方, argument: 高盛}, {role: 事件时间, argument: 2016年}, {role: 投资方, argument: 管理层}]}

2.3 Challenges of DEE

Difficulty in Modeling the Long-input Document
Similar to many document-level NLP tasks, DEE also meets the challenge of long-input documents. Generally, a large proportion of documents have a length of more than one thousand characters, exceeding the maximum input length limit of many pre-trained models (PLMs), such as 512 in BERT. Thus, it's common to see arguments scattering in a long distance. Simply truncating a fixed-length text from the original document will lead to the missing of many arguments. While sliding window method will lead to the conflicts of results from different windows. Previous studies have explored inputting documents at sentence granularity [14–16], which can not leverage the strong ability of PLMs to model the whole context, and requires extra modules to establish relations among sentences and arguments.

Multi-event Recognition Problem
As Table 1 shows, one document would report more than one event at a time, solely regarding argument extraction as a sequence labeling problem will result in a dilemma that models can not figure out which argument belongs to which event, especially for those events with the same event type. For example, the first and the third event in Table 1 share the same event type *financing*. Therefore, it is a challenge for DEE models to group all arguments into separate events.

Complex Argument Identification Problem
In our dataset, we propose a new challenge called *complex argument problem*, that shows its complexity in the following three aspects. Firstly, one argument could play the same or different roles in separate events, as we could see in the given example, argument *Boqii Holding Ltd.* (波奇宠物) played the role of *Financier* in two financing events and played the role of *company to be listed* in the listing event. Secondly, one argument could play the different roles in one event, for example, *CMB International Capital Corporation Ltd.* (招银国际) played the role of both *investor* and *lead investor* in the third event shown in Table 1. Thirdly, multiple arguments could play the same role in one event, as it is more significant in our dataset, we would like to give it a name as **multi-value argument problem** for latter analysis. As shown in Table 1, for the role of *investor*, there are three arguments under it in the third event of the example. Most previous dataset do not present such complexity between roles and arguments, for example, ChFinAnn simply annotated them as two different events when there were two arguments play the same role in one event, which broke the completeness of a whole event. And the complex argument identification problem leads the DEE task more challenging as the model has to deal with the above three sub-problems simultaneously.

3 Dataset Construction

The dataset was constructed with mainly three steps: event schema construction, candidate documents collection and annotation. A detailed introduction will be presented in this section.

3.1   Event Schema Construction

For DEE task, we usually extract all structured events according to the given
event schema. The quality of the schema would directly reflect the performance of
DEE models. In order to focus on the event extraction ability of specialized fields,
we selected documents in the financial field as the object of this annotation. We
investigated the real business needs of enterprises to ensure that our data has
both research value and application value. And we adhered to following principles
while designing the schema:

- Each event type in the schema must be clear and definite, and there should
  not be overlap between two different event types. Event types that describe
  similar events will be merged, for example, investment and financing.
- All of the arguments should be named entity, time expression or value, thus
  our schema will not include any non-entity roles such as *cause* and *effect*.

Table 2. Schema examples in DuEE-Fin.

Event type	Argument roles
质押	质押方,质权方,质押物,质押股票/股份数量,质押物占持股比,质押物占总股比, 质押物所属公司, 披露时间, 事件时间
Equity Pledge	Pledgor, Pledgee, Pledged property, Number of Pledged Shares, Proportion of pledged property in shareholding, Proportion of pledge in total shares, To whom the pledge belongs, Publish time, Event time
企业融资	被投资方,投资方,领投方,融资金额, 融资轮次, 披露时间, 事件时间
Financing	Financier,Investors,Lead investor,Financing amount, Financing rounds, Publish time,Event time
公司上市	上市公司,证券代码,**环节**,发行价格, 募资金额, 披露时间, 事件时间,市值
Company Listing	Listed company,Securities code,**Listing step**,Issue price, Sum of funds raised, Publish time,Event time,Market value
中标	中标公司,招标方,中标金额,披露时间, 中标时间, 中标标的
Bidding	Winner,Bid inviter,Price,Publish time,Bid-winning time, Bidding target

Finally, with statistical results and expert experience, we got the event
schema with 13 event types and 92 individual argument roles. Examples could
be seen in Table 2. Note that a special role, *Listing step*, exists in the event type
of *Company listing*, which is defined as an enumerable role and is given exactly
4 standard arguments, which includes *preparation for listing, formal listing, suspension of listing, terminating of listing*. Actually, we could define four separate

event types instead, but we found that it would result in a heave repetition of roles between them. Moreover, it's common to see some roles are nature to be combined with enumerable arguments, such as *Gender, Country, etc.*. Thus, we would like to group them in this way and make it an interesting research point for upcoming DEE models.

3.2 Candidate Data Collection

We collected documents of financial announcements, judgements and news articles within one year, conducted a coarse-grained classification based on some heuristic rules, and we got 100,000 documents under defined event types in total for further filtering. To ensure the quality of the dataset, we then conducted a pre-annotation step to tell if each document under its classified event type meets the definition for that type, and only took documents really tell events under their classified types as our target documents. For those documents do not meet their classified types, we would conduct a further review to select documents do not belong to any target type as our negative samples. Finally, we got 11,699 documents to train, development and test. In order to avoid overfitting, a small amount of negative examples is included in training and development, and 55,881 negative examples are added to the test set.

3.3 Annotation Process

Pilot Annotation. In this stage, we selected dozens of documents from each event type for experts to annotate, forming a small-scale standard dataset, and we would adjust our event schema according to the feedback from this process and define the annotation rules for arguments under each role. Then we trained our annotators with the standard dataset until they were qualified to start annotation. Consistent with situations from real world, we allow one document to include multiple events, several arguments to share the same role in one event and one argument to play the same or different roles in separate events. During the process of annotation, we found that it's difficult to tell how many events are there exactly in the document. And we deal this problem with the help of triggers, for example, document in Table 1 shows the third event with just one trigger *financing* (融资) to denote what happened in 2016 and thus, we took the investment from different companies as one single event and took multiple companies to play the same role *investor* in the event.

Formal Annotation We divided the labeling process into several rounds. In each round we would construct a small-scale standard dataset and also invite experts to annotate, then insert them into the whole candidate data. We would use the standard dataset to evaluate the performance of annotators during their labeling. If their performance was lower than the preset threshold, the annotated data in this round would be re-labeled again to ensure the annotation quality.

4 Data Analysis

4.1 Overall Statics

We have labeled 11,645 non-repetitive financial documents and 11,699 entries in total, including 15,850 events and 81,632 event arguments. The average length of all documents is 499 characters, and the longest is more than 3,000. Also, on average, each document contains 1.4 events and 6.9 arguments. We divided DuEE-Fin into train, development and test set and Table 3 gives the statistical results of all three sub sets. Where we refer MER as a ratio of documents containing multiple events and MAER as the ratio of events containing more than one argument for one role.

Table 3. Dataset statistics about the number of documents, events, arguments, MER and MAER for the train (Train), development (Dev) and test (Test) set. And we also offer a whole view of all documents.

	Train	Dev	Test	Total
Documents	7015	1171	3513	11699
Events	7015	1171	3513	11699
Arguments	48,891	7,915	24,826	81,632
MER	29.1%	27.8%	30.0%	29.2%
MAER	16.7%	16.2%	17.2%	16.8%

Table 4. Distribution of all event types in DuEE-Fin.

EventType	Ratio	EventType	Ratio	EventType	Ratio
股份回购 Equity Repurchase	13.9%	亏损 Enterprise Loss	11.1%	质押 Equity Pledge	10.7%
企业收购 Enterprise Acquisition	10.1%	中标 Bidding	9.7%	股东减持 Stock Reduction	9.3%
高管变动 Senior Manager Changes	9.3%	解除质押 Cancellation of Pledge	7.5%	企业融资 Financing	5.6%
公司上市 Company Listing	5.3%	股东增持 Equity Overweight	3.5%	企业破产 Go Bankruptcy	2.4%
被约谈 Be Grilled	1.6%				

4.2 Event Types and Argument Roles

DuEE-Fin covers a total of 13 event types and 92 argument roles related to financial activities, such as *Equity Pledge* and *Equity Repurchase*. Table 4 shows the distribution of all event types, in which *Equity Repurchase* accounts for the largest proportion (25.3%). And each event type has 7 argument roles to be filled in average.

4.3   Comparison with Existing Benchmarks

As Table 5 shows, we can find that our dataset has the most event and argument entries, the richest argument types and the highest multi-event rate (MER) of all human-annotated datasets, which exactly makes our dataset more in line with real applications.

Table 5. Comparison with existing benchmarks: Ann. tells if the dataset is manually annotated, Y denotes for yes and N denotes for no; SEE is short for sentence-level event extraction; DEE is short for document-level event extraction; Entries mans the number of documents; Entries means the number of sentences for SEE task and the number of documents for DEE task; ETs means the number of event types; Args means the number of arguments; For ACE05, we only pay attention on the Chinese part and took sentences as its entries.

Dataset	Ann.	Type	Entries	ETs	Events	Roles	Args	MER	MAER
ACE05	Y	SEE	7914	33	3333	35	6,198	9.2%	15.7%
DuEE	Y	SEE	16,956	65	19,640	121	41,520	14.4%	7.5%
MUC-4	Y	DEE	1,700	4	1,514	5	2,641	18.9%	27.8%
RAMS	Y	DEE	9,124	139	8,823	65	21,237	0.0%	6.4%
ChFinAnn	N	DEE	32,040	5	47,824	35	289,871	29.0%	0.0%
DuEE-Fin	Y	DEE	11,699	13	15,850	92	81,632	29.2%	16.8%

Multi-event Challenges
As we mentioned in Sect. 2.3, the main challenge of DEE lies in multi-event recognition in a long document, especially events within the same event type. In DuEE-Fin, the proportion of passages which contain multiple events totaled 29.2%, and a small portion of documents contain as many as 10 events, which brings considerable challenges to the event extraction models.

Complex Argument Indentification
There is a new challenge that called *complex argument problem* in our dataset, as we mentioned in Sect. 2.3. Among three aspects we mentioned above for this challenge, the third one is the most common to see in our dataset and we use MAER to measure it. For example, there are usually more than one investor or company in an investment event, and we avoided simply annotating them as several different events as ChFinAnn did, to maintain the completeness of a whole event. Although MUC-4 presents a higher MAER, it mostly comes from its limited number of event types and roles.

Besides, we also labeled trigger words to support subtasks like event detection, which is missed in the DS-based ChFinAnn.

5   Experiment

5.1   Baseline

To evaluate the performance of some SOTA models on our benchmark, we selected several competitive models as baselines.

BERT-span. Following recent research, we used BERT as an encoder and a multi-layer point network to recognize argument spans (i.e. start and end) at passage or chunk-level. During this process, roles were flatten using their event types, which means the start/end position label for each argument span is updated to a form of *event type - role*. Finally, we simply grouped arguments within the same event type as a whole event.

OneIE [10]. OneIE is one of SOTA models in SEE, which explicitly models cross-subtask and cross-instance inter-dependencies by identifying entity mentions and triggers as nodes and searching for the globally optimal graph with a beam decoder.

Doc2EDAG [16]. It utilizes Transformer [12] to encode sentences and conduct argument recognition, followed by a new Transformer serving as the document and argument encoder. To solve the multi-event problem, Doc2EDAG predefines a decoding order of roles for each event type, and expands them sequentially. Then, an entity-based directed acyclic graph (EDAG) is formed, in which each path from the root node to a leaf node represents a single event.

GIT [14]. GIT constructs a heterogeneous graph of sentences and arguments based on some heuristic rules. The encoded sentences and arguments can be used as initial node features and updated by GCN [5]. During decoding, based on EDAG, GIT introduces a novel *Tracker* module to track the extracted event records to ease the difficulty of extracting correlated events.

PTPCG [17]. PTPCG recognizes all event types and arguments at sentence level, and decodes the event list with a pruned complete graph. It selects the most distinguish role for each event type and takes arguments under those roles as *pruned trigger* to assist the decoding process.

5.2   Evaluation Metric

We evaluate the performance of DEE as Doc2EDAG [16] did, by directly comparing the predicted event table with the ground-truth. Specifically, for each predicted record in a document, we find the most similar ground-truth record to get a detailed matching score. For two matched events, they have to share the same event type and their matching score is determined by the number of arguments that are exactly matched. We count the number of all matched arguments and give the result of precision, recall and F1 score for evaluation.

5.3 Results

We directly adopted results on Doc2EDAG and GIT from PTPCG for convenience, and it is worth noting that both of Doc2EDAG and GIT use vanilla Transformers as their backbone and results presented here did not use PLMs for efficiency. As shown in Table 6, even SOTA models of SEE, OneIE, still underperformed on DuEE-Fin and got a slightly lower score than the simple baseline BERT-span, mainly due to the lack of modules to handle the multi-event issue. Although Doc2EDAG, GIT and PTPCG showed competitive performance on ChFinAnn, they still could not achieve a better performance than BERT-span on DuEE-Fin. There could be two main reasons for this. First of all, their BiLSTM encoders are not as strong as PLMs used in BERT-span and further more, they split the documents into sentences to decrease parameters. Secondly, the decoding strategy of Doc2EDAG and GIT will lead to incomplete extraction results while handling the events with multi-value arguments. BERT-span outperforms other models for the recall score, since it identifies different events in a document by their event types, and naturally supports the extraction of multiple arguments for each role. Although BERT-span achieved the best performance among compared methods, it still does not totally deal with DEE task on DuEE-Fin as it could not tell apart two events with the same event type in one document, as the example we could see from Table 1, and it does not support giving the standard result for enumerable arguments. Thus, it is necessary to propose new methods to deal with challenges in our dataset.

Table 6. Performance on DuEE-Fin, the BERT version used in all above models is bert-base.

Model	Dev			Test		
	P	R	F1	P	R	F1
BERT-span	68.3	62.8	65.5	64.5	60.8	62.6
OneIE	75.5	53.5	62.6	75.2	52.3	61.7
Doc2EDAG	70.8	55.3	62.1	66.7	50.0	57.2
GIT	72.4	58.4	64.7	68.2	43.4	53.1
PTPCG	71.0	61.7	66.0	66.7	54.6	60.0

6 Conclusion

In this article, we released a challenging benchmark DuEE-Fin to improve the data scarcity problem of DEE and offered some experimental results on it. We also gave our insights on the actual main challenges of DEE task and hope to provide a direction for following researchers to deal with the key issues of this task. Moreover, for now, most works handle with event extraction task within documents and few works concentrate on cross document event understanding tasks let alone cross document event extraction task, which we refer to as a more realistic problem.

References

1. Chen, M., et al.: Event-centric natural language processing. In: Proceedings of the 59th Annual Meeting of the Association for Computational Linguistics and the 11th International Joint Conference on Natural Language Processing: Tutorial Abstracts. pp. 6–14. Association for Computational Linguistics, Online (Aug 2021). https://doi.org/10.18653/v1/2021.acl-tutorials.2, https://aclanthology.org/2021.acl-tutorials.2

2. Ebner, S., Xia, P., Culkin, R., Rawlins, K., Van Durme, B.: Multi-sentence argument linking. In: Proceedings of the 58th Annual Meeting of the Association for Computational Linguistics. pp. 8057–8077. Association for Computational Linguistics, Online (2020). https://doi.org/10.18653/v1/2020.acl-main.718, https://www.aclweb.org/anthology/2020.acl-main.718

3. Fung, Y., et al.: InfoSurgeon: cross-media fine-grained information consistency checking for fake news detection. In: Proceedings of the 59th Annual Meeting of the Association for Computational Linguistics and the 11th International Joint Conference on Natural Language Processing (Volume 1: Long Papers). pp. 1683–1698. Association for Computational Linguistics, Online (2021). https://doi.org/10.18653/v1/2021.acl-long.133, https://aclanthology.org/2021.acl-long.133

4. Grishman, R., Sundheim, B.: Message understanding conference- 6: a brief history. In: COLING 1996 Volume 1: The 16th International Conference on Computational Linguistics (1996). https://aclanthology.org/C96-1079

5. Kipf, T.N., Welling, M.: Semi-supervised classification with graph convolutional networks. CoRR abs/1609.02907 (2016). http://arxiv.org/abs/1609.02907

6. Li, M., et al.: GAIA: A fine-grained multimedia knowledge extraction system. In: Proceedings of the 58th Annual Meeting of the Association for Computational Linguistics: System Demonstrations. pp. 77–86. Association for Computational Linguistics, Online (2020). https://doi.org/10.18653/v1/2020.acl-demos.11, https://www.aclweb.org/anthology/2020.acl-demos.11

7. Li, S., Ji, H., Han, J.: Document-level event argument extraction by conditional generation. In: Proceedings of the 2021 Conference of the North American Chapter of the Association for Computational Linguistics: Human Language Technologies. pp. 894–908. Association for Computational Linguistics, Online (2021). https://doi.org/10.18653/v1/2021.naacl-main.69, https://www.aclweb.org/anthology/2021.naacl-main.69

8. Li, X., Li, F., Pan, L., Chen, Y., Peng, W., Wang, Q., Lyu, Y., Zhu, Y.: Duee: a large-scale dataset for Chinese event extraction in real-world scenarios. In: Zhu, X., Zhang, M., Hong, Y., He, R. (eds.) Natural Language Processing and Chinese Computing, pp. 534–545. Springer International Publishing, Cham (2020). https://doi.org/10.1007/978-3-319-73618-1.10.1007/978-3-319-73618-1

9. Li, Z., Ding, X., Liu, T.: Constructing narrative event evolutionary graph for script event prediction. In: Proceedings of the Twenty-Seventh International Joint Conference on Artificial Intelligence. pp. 4201–4207. International Joint Conferences on Artificial Intelligence Organization, Stockholm, Sweden (Jul 2018). https://doi.org/10.24963/ijcai.2018/584, https://www.ijcai.org/proceedings/2018/584

10. Lin, Y., Ji, H., Huang, F., Wu, L.: A joint neural model for information extraction with global features. In: Proceedings of the 58th Annual Meeting of the Association for Computational Linguistics. pp. 7999–8009. Association for Computational Linguistics, Online (Jul 2020). https://doi.org/10.18653/v1/2020.acl-main.713, https://aclanthology.org/2020.acl-main.713

11. Liu, J., Chen, Y., Liu, K., Bi, W., Liu, X.: Event extraction as machine reading comprehension. In: Proceedings of the 2020 Conference on Empirical Methods in Natural Language Processing (EMNLP). pp. 1641–1651. Association for Computational Linguistics, Online (Nov 2020). https://doi.org/10.18653/v1/2020.emnlp-main.128, https://aclanthology.org/2020.emnlp-main.128
12. Vaswani, A., et al.: Attention is all you need. In: Proceedings of the 31st International Conference on Neural Information Processing Systems. vol. 30, pp. 5998–6008 (2017)
13. Wadden, D., Wennberg, U., Luan, Y., Hajishirzi, H.: Entity, relation, and event extraction with contextualized span representations. In: Proceedings of the 2019 Conference on Empirical Methods in Natural Language Processing and the 9th International Joint Conference on Natural Language Processing (EMNLP-IJCNLP). pp. 5784–5789. Association for Computational Linguistics, Hong Kong, China (Nov 2019). https://doi.org/10.18653/v1/D19-1585, https://aclanthology.org/D19-1585
14. Xu, R., Liu, T., Li, L., Chang, B.: Document-level event extraction via heterogeneous graph-based interaction model with a tracker. In: Proceedings of the 59th Annual Meeting of the Association for Computational Linguistics and the 11th International Joint Conference on Natural Language Processing (Volume 1: Long Papers). pp. 3533–3546. Association for Computational Linguistics, Online (2021). https://doi.org/10.18653/v1/2021.acl-long.274, https://aclanthology.org/2021.acl-long.274
15. Yang, H., Chen, Y., Liu, K., Xiao, Y., Zhao, J.: DCFEE: a document-level chinese financial event extraction system based on automatically labeled training data. In: Proceedings of ACL 2018, System Demonstrations. pp. 50–55. Association for Computational Linguistics, Melbourne, Australia (2018). https://doi.org/10.18653/v1/P18-4009, http://aclweb.org/anthology/P18-4009
16. Zheng, S., Cao, W., Xu, W., Bian, J.: Doc2EDAG: an end-to-end document-level framework for chinese financial event extraction. In: Proceedings of the 2019 Conference on Empirical Methods in Natural Language Processing and the 9th International Joint Conference on Natural Language Processing (EMNLP-IJCNLP). pp. 337–346. Association for Computational Linguistics, Hong Kong, China (2019). https://doi.org/10.18653/v1/D19-1032, https://www.aclweb.org/anthology/D19-1032
17. Zhu, T., et al.: Efficient document-level event extraction via pseudo-trigger-aware pruned complete graph (2021)

Temporal Relation Extraction on Time Anchoring and Negative Denoising

Liang Wang, Peifeng Li[⊠], and Qiaoming Zhu

School of Computer Science and Technology, Soochow University, Jiangsu, China
docy@vip.qq.com, {pfli,qmzhu}@suda.edu.cn

Abstract. Identifying temporal relationship between events is crucial to text understanding. Recent work on temporal relation extraction only focuses on single Event-Event (E-E) relations, ignoring the other Event-DCT (E-D) and Event-Timex (E-T) relations and suffering from imbalanced annotation. Moreover, few previous work can directly learn time intervals of events, a critical temporal clue, because the intervals are rarely occur in real-world texts. In this paper, we propose a novel Time interval Anchoring Model TAM for temporal relation extraction. Specially, we first propose a multi-task learning framework to joint three tasks, i.e., E-E, E-D and E-T, and then we design a novel anchor loss to determine the time intervals of events (i.e., the start and the end time-points). Moreover, we introduce a negative denoising mechanism to effectively reduce ambiguousness for the whole model. Experimental results on three datasets prove that our TAM significantly outperforms the SOTA baselines.

Keywords: Temporal relation extraction · Multi-task learning · Time anchoring · Negative denoising

1 Introduction

As an important component of natural language understanding, temporal relation extraction (TRE) focuses on arranging the events and time expressions (timexes) in chronological order. Currently, TRE is often regarded as a classification problem which assigns a specific relation (e.g., *Before* and *After*) to a mention pair. Take the two sentences "Dow **jumps** over 900 points...Powell **rules out** larger rate hike." as examples, TRE should identify the *After* relation between the event mention "jumps" and "rules out". In NLP community, TRE can benefit many downstream NLP tasks, e.g., question answering [1] and schema induction [2].

Recent neural network methods on TRE achieve significant progress thanks to the pre-trained language models. To discover the document-level temporal clues, previous work usually exploits the syntactic and rhetorical structure within sentences [3], or adds global constraints considering the symmetry and transitivity of temporal relationships [4], or puts external knowledge into classifier [5]. Another clue is to re-define the events and their temporal relations, like designing new annotation systems on subsets of existing corpus [6, 7]. However, their disadvantages are still obvious as follows. Firstly, their

W. Lu et al. (Eds.): NLPCC 2022, LNAI 13551, pp. 184–196, 2022.
https://doi.org/10.1007/978-3-031-17120-8_15

models only focus on event-centered TRE, in which timex and Document Creation Time (DCT) are neglected in most previous work. Secondly, the models are often harmed by the high proportion of negative samples.

In a standard annotation system, events temporal relations are determined by the corresponding time intervals, i.e., the start and the end time-points of events. Unfortunately, few previous work can directly learn such a critical temporal clue due to the time intervals of events are rarely occur in the real-world texts. Recently, Wen and Ji [8] propose a joint model with a stack-propagation framework to connect relative event time prediction and temporal relation extraction, which is intuitive and achieves fair success. However, since only start time-points are involved, their method fails to cope with interval-determined relations (e.g., *include*). Furthermore, without supervised data of time values, they essentially regard the predicted event time as another feature of the TRE task. Lastly, it's inefficient when there are a large number of *vague* (unknown relation) samples because there are no constraints for those negative samples in their model.

In this paper, we propose a novel **T**ime interval **A**nchoring **M**odel **TAM** for general temporal relation extraction. Because the ground-truth time intervals of events are rarely annotated in the corpus, we find out that the annotated timexes and DCT are important clues as they have clear time intervals. To address the first issue, we propose a multi-task learning framework to joint three tasks, i.e., Event-Event (E-E), Event-DCT (E-D) and Event-Timex (E-T). Moreover, we design a negative denoising mechanism that utilizes smooth learning curves to schedule the learning scheme on those *vague* samples during the training process, which is able to effectively reduce ambiguousness for the whole model. To address the second issue, we design a novel anchor loss to determine the start and the end time-points of events, which is effective for identifying their temporal relations. Specially, we train four scoring functions to indicate the time intervals of input mention pairs, and utilize an anchored loss to softly constrain the intervals within their related temporal relations. The experimental results on both the sentence-level and discourse-level datasets prove that our TAM significantly outperforms the SOTA baselines.

2 Related Work

Early work on temporal relation extraction [10–14] took efforts on manually designed rules and various linguistic features, such as part-of-speech (POS) tagging, syntactic and clause-ordering information, etc. Recent work focused on neural networks showed remarkable progress on temporal relation extraction. Liu et al. [15] proposed a discourse-level graph, which consists of graph mask pre-training and prediction. Mathur et al. [3] integrated syntactic information, temporal order, and rhetorical structure into GCN (Graph Convolutional Networks) to provide rich contextual and temporal-aware information. Another clue is to incorporate massive external knowledge and training resources, such as jointly learning of temporal and subevent relations [16], injecting temporal knowledge into pre-trained language models [17], and using of distantly-supervised examples [5] or complementary datasets [18].

Recently, the global relational dependency (e.g., transitivity and symmetry) among the events is proven to be efficient on neural network method, e.g., utilizing probabilistic soft logic rules [19], projecting traditional event embeddings of Euclidean space into hyperbolic space [20], and constraining the predicted event time with minimal conflicts within the temporal graph [8]. Different from the above work, our model focuses on learning the start-end points of real-world mentions.

Besides, Cheng et al. [9] provided a unified neural architecture that jointly learns three kinds of TLINKs, i.e. E-E, E-T and E-D, which benefits from the resource-shared training procedure over different kinds of mention pairs. As the ground-truth time intervals of events are rarely mentioned explicitly, we continue this thread to take advantage of timex and DCT for event time anchoring.

3   TAM: Time Anchoring Model for TRE

Figure 1 illustrates an overview of our TAM framework. TAM mainly consists of four modules: 1) Mention Embedding (ME) module that encodes the labeled document by RoBERTa; 2) Multi-Task Learning (MTL) module that coordinates E-E, E-T and E-D examples together into the same training process; 3) Interval Anchoring (IA) module that outputs the start-end points of each mention; 4) Negative Denoising (ND) module that schedules the negative samples across the training process.

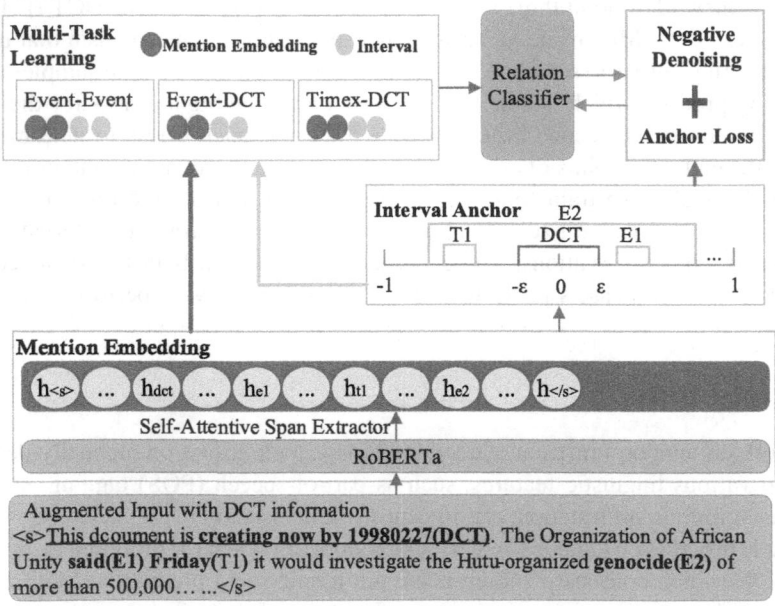

Fig. 1. An overview of the TAM framework.

3.1   Mention Embedding Module

Due to the different expression forms and the different amounts of tokens, it is a challenge to identify those E-T and E-D relations directly. Moreover, DCT does not explicitly occur in the document, making it hard to represent its semantics for temporal relation extraction. However, DCT is an anchor to connect those event mentions or timexes in a document-level temporal ordering graph. To address this issue, we propose a sentence-style DCT representation, which uses a generated sentence to express the token-level DCT as follows: "This document is creating now by {DCT}.", where DCT is a date like <20220507>. We insert this sentence at the head of the document to enrich the document-level semantics. Besides, all annotated event mentions and timexes in the document are tagged with the label "Ti" and "Ei", respectively, where "i" indicates the serial number of event mentions and timexes.

Let the document be $D = [w_1, w_2, \ldots, w_k, \ldots w_n]$, where w_k denotes the k-th token, n is the total number of tokens. Since RoBERTa is better than BERT in previous work [17] on TRE, we use RoBERTa as our encoder. Hence, We encode D by RoBERTa to obtain the mention embeddings $H = [h_{ei}, \ldots h_{tj}, \ldots, h_{DCT}, \ldots]$, where h_{ei}, h_{tj}, h_{DCT} denote the embeddings of the i-th event mention, the j-th timex and DCT. For mentions consist of multiple tokens (e.g., timex), we apply a self-attention mechanism over their sub-token embeddings to obtain their final embeddings following [21].

3.2 Multi-task Learning Module

Inspired by Cheng et al. [9], we integrate multiple types of TLINKs into a unified neural architecture to enhance event time anchor. In this manner, the problem of event mentions owning no practical time interval can be relieved, where event mentions are able to learn ground-truth time intervals of DCT and time expressions.

However, Cheng et al. [9] just simply utilized a learnable vector to represent DCT, as DCT does not explicitly occur in the documents. To address this issue, we augment the input documents by inserting a sentence-style DCT at the head of each document. In this way, our TAM can learn both the absolute value (i.e., date) and the relative time (e.g., "yesterday") of DCT. Hence, we conduct the multi-task learning by the accumulated Cross-Entropy loss as follows.

$$\mathcal{L}_{CE}(\text{tsk}) = - \sum_{(o_i, o_j)} \log P(r_{(o_i, o_j)} | o_i, o_j) \tag{1}$$

$$\mathcal{L}_1 = \mathcal{L}_{CE}(\text{EE}) + \mathcal{L}_{CE}(\text{ET}) + \mathcal{L}_{CE}(\text{ED}) \tag{2}$$

where $tsk \in \{EE, ET, ED\}$ refers to one of the E-E, E-T and E-D tasks, and (o_i, o_j) is a mention pair belongs to tsk.

3.3 Interval Anchoring Module

The purpose of IA is to train four scoring functions that output the relative start-end points of the given mention pairs. Formally, for an E-E or E-T pair (o_1, o_2) and its embedding (h_1, h_2), the scoring functions are as follows.

$$t_{1-start} = \tanh(\mathbf{W}_1 \cdot h_1 + \mathbf{b}_1) \tag{3}$$

$$t_{1-end} = \tanh(\mathbf{W}_2 \cdot h_1 + \mathbf{b}_2) \tag{4}$$

$$t_{2-start} = \tanh(\mathbf{W}_3 \cdot h_2 + \mathbf{b}_3) \tag{5}$$

$$t_{2-end} = \tanh(\mathbf{W}_4 \cdot h_2 + \mathbf{b}_4) \tag{6}$$

where $\mathbf{W_k}$ and $\mathbf{b_k}$ ($k \in \{1, 2, 3, 4\}$) are the weights and bias in the Feed Forward Network (FFN) layer, and $t_{i-start}, t_{i-end} \in (-1, 1)$, ($i \in \{1, 2\}$). Then we obtain the pair representation $c_{(1,2)}$ of (o_1, o_2) for relation classifier via combining their original embeddings and time intervals as follows.

$$c_{(1,2)} = [h_1; h_2; t_{1-start}; t_{1-end}; t_{2-start}; t_{2-end}] \tag{7}$$

Table 1 shows the constraints for mention pair's intervals based on the definition of five temporal relations in TimeBank-Dense [22]. To train those scoring functions, we design a soft **Anchor Loss** that constrains the pairwise intervals as follows.

$$\mathcal{D}(t_1, t_2) = \max(0, 1 - (t_2 - t_1)) \tag{8}$$

$$\mathcal{L}_2 = I(o_1, \text{Before}, o_2) \cdot \mathcal{D}(t_{1-end}, t_{2-start})$$
$$+ I(o_1, \textit{After}, o_2) \cdot \mathcal{D}(t_{2-end}, t_{1-start})$$
$$+ I(o_1, \textit{Include}, o_2) \cdot (\mathcal{D}(t_{1-start}, t_{2-start}) + \mathcal{D}(t_{2-end}, t_{1-end}))$$
$$+ I(o_1, \textit{IsIncluded}, o_2) \cdot (\mathcal{D}(t_{2-start}, t_{1-start}) + \mathcal{D}(t_{1-end}, t_{2-end})) +$$

$$I(o_1, \textit{Simultaneous}, o_2) \cdot (|t_{1-start} - t_{2-start}| + |t_{1-end} - t_{2-end}|) \tag{9}$$

where $I(o_1, r, o_2)$ is an indicator function (1: if the relation between o_1 and o_2 is r; otherwise, 0), and $\mathcal{D}(t_1, t_2)$ measures the distance between the time pair (t_1, t_2) as our training objective. In detail, $\mathcal{D}(t_1, t_2)$ decreases as the value of $(t_2 - t_1)$ increases. For example, if o_1 before o_2, according to Table 1, then we hope that the value of $t_{2-start} - t_{1-end}$ be as large as possible so that the system obtains less Anchor Loss $\mathcal{L}_2$, and vice versa.

Table 1. Constraints for mention pair's intervals, where $t_{i-start}$, t_{i-end} denotes the scoring functions' output of event e_i.

Relation	Interval
Before	$t_{1-end} < t_{2-start}$
After	$t_{1-start} < t_{2-end}$
Include	$t_{1-start} < t_{2-start} \wedge t_{1-end} > t_{2-end}$
Is Include	$t_{1-start} > t_{2-start} \wedge t_{1-end} < t_{2-end}$
Simultaneous	$t_{1-start} = t_{2-start} \wedge t_{1-end} = t_{2-end}$
Vague	Others

Since anchor Loss only constrains the relatively large-small relationship within mention intervals, the model is still confused about their absolute values. In Subsect. 3.2, MTL synchronously learns three kinds of TLINKs, which can make events directly refer to the practical intervals of timex and DCT with Anchor Loss. However, how to legitimately map timexes into the timeline space of $(-1, 1)$ is still a challenge, because most timexes are not well normed or even ambiguous (e.g., "recently", "a few years ago") in real-world documents. To address this issue, we ensure that DCT can be a perfect anchor. In detail, since DCT is equal to the time span of a day, namely "today", by contrast with past and future, we manually set the time interval of DCT as $(-\varepsilon, \varepsilon)$, where $\varepsilon \in (-1, 1)$ is a hyper-parameter. Therefore, our whole system can anchor "past", "today", and "future" to $(-1, \varepsilon)$, $(-\varepsilon, \varepsilon)$, and $(\varepsilon, 1)$, respectively.

3.4 Negative Denoising Module

Although our MTL module and IA module propose a reasonable approach for mention time anchoring, our TAM still suffers from the imbalanced sample distribution (e.g., the *vague* pairs account for 46% in TimeBank-Dense), since the IA module has no constraints on negative samples.

To address this issue, we propose an intuitive denoising mechanism to handle the negative examples. Empirically, if we decrease the weight of *vague* instances in Cross-Entropy loss function, then the classifier should focus on the positive ones. Hence, we propose four weight decreasing methods to deal with negative samples that shown in Fig. 2 as follows.

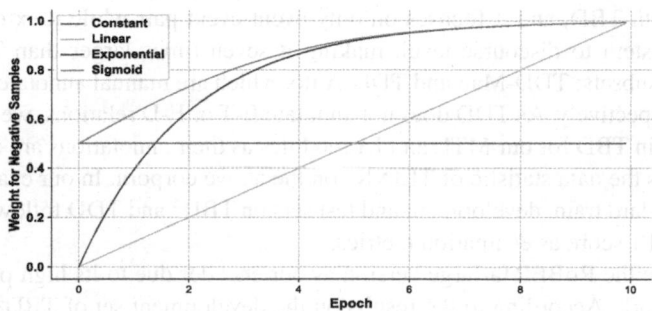

Fig. 2. Learning curves for negative samples.

- **Constant:** We set a constant weight value c ($0 < c < 1$) for negative samples.
- **Linear:** The weight value c linearly increases with the training process pushes on.
- **Exponential:** The weight value c smoothly increases from 0 to 1 ($c^{exp}(t) = 1 - e^{-\alpha t}$, where t indicates training epoch, and α is a hyper-parameter that measures the curvature, similarly hereinafter).
- **Sigmoid:** The weight value c smoothly increases from 0.5 to 1 ($c^{sig}(t) = \frac{1}{1+e^{-\alpha t}}$). The Sigmoid curve learns positive and negative samples simultaneously, while the

Exponential curve only pays attention to the positive ones at the beginning of the training process.

We obtain the decreased weight value of the vague samples c for specific training stage. Let the class weight matrix be $W_l = [1, \ldots c, \ldots 1]$, where the position for c stands for *vague* relation. Therefore, the combined loss function of our TAM system is as follows.

$$\mathcal{L} = p \cdot W_l \cdot \mathcal{L}_1 + (1 - p) \cdot \mathcal{L}_2 \qquad (10)$$

where p is a trade-off parameter.

4 Experimentation

In this section, we first introduce the datasets and experimental settings, and then report the results and analyze the effectiveness of TAM on different aspects.

4.1 Datasets and Experimental Settings

We evaluate our TAM architecture on two widely used datasets TimeBank-Dense (TBD) [22] and TDDiscourse (TDD) [7]. TBD is an extended version of TimeBank [23] and it applies a dense annotation scheme within adjacent sentences. TBD contains four kinds of TLINKs, i.e. E-E, E-T, E-D, T-D[1], and six temporal relationships, i.e. *Before, After, Include, Is Included, Simultaneous* and *Vague*. TDD shares the same document and event annotation with TBD, and it focuses on only event-event pair while it extends TBD's annotation system to discourse-level, making it seven times larger than TBD. TDD contains two subsets: TDD-Man and TDD-Auto, which are manual annotated and auto-generated, respectively. As TDD does not annotate E-T or E-D relations, we include the E-D samples in TBD for our MTL and IA modules as their annotations are compatible. Table 2 shows the data statistic of TLINKs on the above corpora. In our evaluation, we split[2] the standard train, development and test sets on TBD[3] and TDD following [3] and report micro-F1 score as estimation metrics.

We choose the RoBERTa-large version as our encoder due to its high performance in previous work. According to the results on the development set of TBD, we choose Sigmoid curve for the ND module, and the values of hyper-parameters ε and p are 0.1 and 0.5, respectively. The number of total training epoch is set to 10. All the results are averaged by three random seeds.

---

[1] T-D samples only account for 2%, we do not distinguish it with E-D for simplicity.

[2] http://www.usna.edu/Users/cs/nchamber/caevo/..

[3] We regard vague as no-link following previous work.

Table 2. Data statistic on TBD and TDD.

Dataset	E-E	E-T	E-D
TBD	6088	2001	1737
TDD-Man	6150	–	1221[a]
TDD-Auto	38302	–	1221

[a]516 vague samples in TBD are excluded as TDD contains no vague relation.

4.2 Results

To verify the effectiveness of our TAM model, we conduct six strong baselines for comparison as follows.

- **Pairwise**: It conducts a pairwise classification on the original RoBERTa [24] embeddings of mention pairs. For the E-D, we also augment the input document as described in Subsect. 3.2.
- **DP-RNN** [25]: It takes the Shortest Dependency Path (SDP) as a critical event feature and only feeds the single SDP branch of event for the E-D task.
- **GCL** [26]: It incorporates global context information with a unified architecture for three TLINKs (i.e., E-E, E-T and E-D).
- **SEC** [9]: It dynamically introduces centric-event representations to a multi-task learning framework for three TLINKs.
- **UCGraph** [15]: It introduces graph representation learning and uncertainty modeling to enhance discourse-level TRE.
- **TIMERS** [3]: It merges syntactic, temporal, and rhetorical information into GCN to improve the E-E task.

Table 3 (left part) shows the results on TBD and we can find that our TAM achieves significant improvement on all three tasks. Compared with the SOTA model TIMERS on E-E, our TAM improves the F1-score by 1.9. Compared with the SOTA model SEC on E-T and E-D, our TAM significantly improves the F1-score by 10.4 and 15.7, respectively. Even our simplified model Pairwise also achieves the comparable performance on all three tasks. These results indicate that our model can take advantage of the effective DCT representation via pre-trained language model and provide more reliable anchored intervals for the main E-E task. Besides, the three tasks can complement each other under our unified multi-task learning framework.

Table 3. F1 scores of three tasks on TBD and TDD datasets.

Model	TimeBank-dense			TDD-man	TDD-auto
	E-E	E-T	E-D	E-E	E-E
Pairwise	62.4	51.5	76.3	44.8	75.7
DP-RNN	52.9	47.1	54.6	24.3	51.8
GCL	57.0	48.7	48.9	–	–
SEC	65.0	55.8	65.9	–	–
UCGraph	59.1	–	–	43.4	61.2
TIMERS	67.8	–	–	45.5	71.1
TAM	**69.7**	**66.2**	**81.6**	**51.1**	**79.2**

We also evaluate TAM on the other two discourse-level datasets TDD-Man and TDD-Auto, and the results are shown in Table 3 (right part). TAM also achieves the top performance with the improvements of 5.6 and 3.5 (F1-score), in comparison with the SOTA TIMERS and Pairwise on TDD-man and TDD-auto, respectively. These results further ensure the effectiveness of TAM on discourse-level datasets.

4.3 Ablation Study

To evaluate the effectiveness of our main modules IA, MTL and ND in TAM, we conduct the experiments on TBD with the following TAM variants: 1) *w/o* **IA**, in which we remove the IA module; 2) *w/o* **MTL**, in which each task is separately trained; 3) *w/o* **ND**, in which the system utilizes the ordinary Cross-Entropy loss and the module ND is removed.

Table 4 shows the results of TAM and its variants on TBD and TDD. For TBD, we can find that all of our proposed modules contribute to TAM. When the IA module is excluded, the F1 scores of the tasks E-E, E-T and E-D decrease by 3.5, 3.8 and 1.3, respectively, indicating that the neural network can benefit from direct relation-definition features. As for the MTL module, it can provide more training resources and referential interval anchors for events, which contributes 2.9, 10.6 and 0.7 performance gains for E-E, E-T and E-D, respectively. Specially, the E-T task relies heavily on our MTL module. Moreover, the ND module is more important to all three tasks as it causes the most performance degradation (i.e., 5.2, 6.0 and 3.2). To some extent, the data imbalance problem can be relieved by our negative denoising method.

The right part of Table 4 shows the results of TAM and its variants on TDD-Man and TDD-Auto. In discourse-level TRE case, TAM still achieves success from two aspects, i.e., IA and MTL. It is worth mentioning that we do not apply ND to the evaluation on TDD because it does not contain negative samples.

Due to the difficulty of TDD-Man, single IA module (i.e., *w/o* MTL) only contributes 1.4 of enhancement in comparison with Pairwise. The reason can be the ambiguous and contradictory predictions of event pairs. While the MTL module provides a gain of 2.7, proving that indirect temporal clues (like transitivity within E-E and E-D samples) can effectively help identify those ambiguous E-E cases. As for TDD-Auto, the system

Table 4. Ablative results (F1-score) on TBD and TDD datasets.

	TimeBank-Dense			TDD-Man	TDD-Auto
Model	E-E	E-T	E-D	E-E	E-E
Pairwise	62.4	51.5	76.3	44.8	75.7
TAM	69.7	66.2	81.6	51.1	79.2
w/o IA	66.2	62.4	80.3	47.5	78.1
w/o MTL	66.8	55.6	80.9	46.2	77.9
w/o ND	64.5	60.2	78.4	–	–

obtains comparable gains (2.4 and 2.2) from the IA and MTL modules in comparison with Pairwise.

4.4 Effects of Learning Curves

In Subsect. 0, we introduce four negative weight decreasing curves and we apply them to our ND module. The results are shown in Table 5, and Fig. 3 shows the gain curve of performance across training process on the development set of TBD.

If we simply adjust the weight value from 1.0 to 0.4, our model using Constant can improve the F1-score by 3.0, 3.4 and 1.4 for three tasks. In this case the classifier can learn fewer negative samples throughout the whole training process. Both of Linear and Exponential curves force the model to learn the positive pairs at the initial stage, and then the vague samples gradually are involved while the model already fits well on the positive ones. The main advantage of Exponential curve is that its smoothness can better adapt the fine-tuning pace of RoBERTa. Sigmoid curve achieves a balance between Constant and Exponential curves, as it makes the model synchronously study all samples (paying less attention to the *vague* ones) at first, then smoothly increase the weight of the negative ones.

Table 5. F1 scores of four negative weight decreasing methods.

Curve	E-E	E-T	E-D
Constant ($c = 1.0$)	64.5	60.2	78.4
Constant ($c = 0.4$)	67.5	63.6	79.8
Linear	68.4	62.5	79.3
Exponential	68.9	65.4	80.6
Sigmoid (proposed)	69.7	66.2	81.6

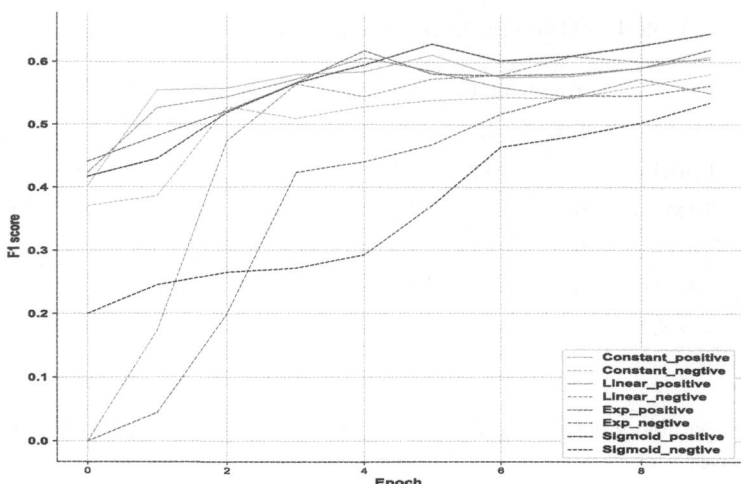

Fig. 3. F1 scores of positive and negative samples over four curves on TBD development set.

4.5 Case Study and Error Analysis

Table 6 shows the results of the confused matrix of the E-E pairs on TBD. While our TAM could well distinguish within the positive samples (not including *Vague*), the majority of errors (90%) are caused by the negative samples. In detail, the vague errors come from two aspects: 1) the model incorrectly predicts the positive samples as vague ones; 2) the vague samples are predicted as positive ones. Two corresponding examples are as follows.

Table 6. Confused matrix of E-E pairs. Notations: **B**efore, **A**fter, **I**nclude, **I**s **I**ncluded, **S**imultaneous, **V**ague; Vague Error (%) denotes the error percentage that the positive samples incorrectly recognized as negative samples, and whose counterpart is Positive Error (%).

	B	A	I	II	S	V	Vague error (%)	Positive error (%)
B	347	3	6	1	0	102	91.1%	8.9%
A	4	258	2	8	0	47	74.6%	25.4%
I	8	1	28	0	0	24	72.7%	27.3%
II	4	1	0	21	0	28	84.8%	15.2%
S	4	3	0	0	0	17	70.8%	29.2%
V	108	43	84	53	0	454	–	–

E1 (Before): More planes **headed** (e1, [−0.16, 0.09]) from the united states and senior officials say Iraq's president Saddam Hussein can expect punishing air strikes to continue if he doesn't **stop** (e2, [−0.23, −0.05]) building biological weapons.

E2 (Vague): One of the scenarios widely **advanced** (e1, [−0.36, −0.22]) before the visit is that through the Pope, Cuba, still **led** (e2, [−0.83, 0.76]) by Castro.

In example E1, due to the negative word "doesn't", TAM fails to recognize the reasonable intervals of "stop", which should be a future event, causing a false negative error. In example E2, TAM learns that "led" owns a wider time duration than "advanced", and labels the pair as *Is Included*, in this case, TAM is confused by the ambiguous annotation.

5 Conclusion

In this paper, we propose a novel time anchoring method TAM that involves multi-task learning and negative denoising approaches. Experimental results on three datasets prove the success of our proposal on both the sentence-level and discourse-level datasets. Furthermore, we find out that our main modules are complementary in the ablation study. In future work, we will focus on the end-to-end temporal relation extraction with joint event and timex interval anchoring.

References

1. Ning, Q., Wu, H., Han, R., et al.: TORQUE: a reading comprehension dataset of temporal ordering questions. In: Proceedings of EMNLP 2020, pp. 1158–1172 (2020)
2. Lin, S., Chambers, N., Durrett, G.: Conditional generation of temporally-ordered event sequences. In: Proceedings of ACL 2021, pp. 7142–7157 (2021)
3. Mathur, P., Jain, R., Dernoncourt, F., et al.: TIMERS: document-level temporal relation extraction. In: Proceedings of ACL 2021, pp. 524–533 (2021)
4. Ning, Q., Feng, Z., Roth, D.: A structured learning approach to temporal relation extraction. In: Proceedings of EMNLP 2017, pp. 1027–1037 (2017)
5. Zhao, X., Lin, S., Durrett, G.: Effective distant supervision for temporal relation extraction. In: Proceedings of EACL 2021, pp. 195–203 (2021)
6. Ning, Q., Wu, H., Roth, D.: A multi-axis annotation scheme for event temporal relations. In: Proceedings of ACL 2018, pp. 1318–1328 (2018)
7. Naik, A., Breitfeller, L., Rose, C.: TDDiscourse: a dataset for discourse-level temporal ordering of events. In: Proceedings of the 20th Annual SIGdial Meeting on Discourse and Dialogue, pp. 239–249 (2019)
8. Wen, H., Ji, H.: Utilizing relative event time to enhance event-event temporal relation extraction. In: Proceedings of EMNLP 2021, pp. 10431–10437 (2021)
9. Cheng, F., Asahara, M., Kobayashi, I., Kurohashi, S.: Dynamically updating event representations for temporal relation classification with multi-category learning. In: Findings of EMNLP 2020, pp. 1352–1357 (2020)
10. Lapata, M., Lascarides, A.: Learning sentence internal temporal relations. J. AI Res. **27**, 85–117 (2006)
11. Chambers, N., Jurafsky, D.: Jointly combining implicit constraints improves temporal ordering. In: Proceedings of EMNLP 2008, pp. 698–706 (2008)
12. Do, Q., Lu, W., Roth, D.: Joint inference for event timeline construction. In: Proceedings of EMNLP 2012, pp. 677–687 (2012)
13. D'Souza, J., Ng, V.: Classifying temporal relations with rich linguistic knowledge. In: Proceedings of NAACL 2013, pp. 918–927 (2013)
14. Chambers, N., Cassidy, T., McDowell, B., Bethard, S.: Dense event ordering with a multi-pass architecture. TACL **2**, 273–284 (2014)

15. Liu, J., Xu, J., Chen, Y., et al.: Discourse-level event temporal ordering with uncertainty-guided graph completion. In: Proceedings of IJCAI 2021, pp. 3871–3877 (2021)
16. Wang, H., Chen, M., Zhang, H., et al.: Joint constrained learning for event-event relation extraction. In: Proceedings of EMNLP 2020, pp. 696–706 (2020)
17. Han, R., Ren, X., Peng, N.: ECONET: effective continual pre-training of language models for event temporal reasoning. In: Proceedings of EMNLP 2021, pp. 5367–5380 (2021)
18. Ballesteros, M., Anubhai, R., Wang, S., et al.: Severing the edge between before and after: neural architectures for temporal ordering of events. In: Proceedings of the EMNLP 2020, pp. 5412–5417 (2020)
19. Zhou, Y., Yan, Y., Han, R., et al.: Clinical temporal relation extraction with probabilistic soft logic regularization and global inference. In: Proceedings of AAAI 2021, pp. 14647–14655 (2021)
20. Tan, X., Pergola, G., He, Y.: Extracting event temporal relations via hyperbolic geometry. In: Proceedings of EMNLP 2021, pp. 8065–8077 (2021)
21. Lee, K., He, L., Lewis, M., et al.: End-to-end neural coreference resolution. In: Proceedings of EMNLP 2017, pp. 188–197 (2017)
22. Cassidy, T., McDowell, B., Chambers, N., Bethard, S.: An annotation framework for dense event ordering. In: Proceedings of ACL 2014, pp. 501–506 (2014)
23. Pustejovsky, J., Hanks, P., Sauri, R., et al.: The TIMEBANK corpus. Corpus linguistics, pp. 647–656 (2003)
24. Liu, Y., Ott, M., Goyal, N., et al.: Roberta: A robustly optimized BERT pretraining approach. ArXiv: 1907.11692 (2019)
25. Cheng, F., Miyao, Y.: Classifying temporal relations by bidirectional LSTM over dependency paths. In: Proceedings of ACL 2017, pp. 1–6 (2017)
26. Meng, Y., Rumshisky, A.: Context-aware neural model for temporal information extraction. In: Proceedings of ACL 2018, pp. 527–536 (2018)

Label Semantic Extension for Chinese Event Extraction

Zuohua Chen⬡, Guohua Wu, Qiuhua Wang, Zhen Zhang, Qisen Xi⬡,
Yizhi Ren, and Lifeng Yuan(✉)

School of Cyberspace, Hangzhou Dianzi University, Hangzhou 310018, China
{chenzuohua,wugh,wangqiuhua,zhangzhen,xiqs,renyz,yuanlifeng}@hdu.edu.cn

Abstract. Event extraction (EE) is an essential yet challenging information extraction task, which aims at extracting event structures from unstructured text. Recent work on Chinese event extraction has achieved state-of-the-art performance by modeling events using the pre-trained model. However, the event type information has not been well utilized in existing event extraction methods. To address the issue, we propose the label semantic extension, which selects extension words according to the semantics of event type labels and adds them to the input sequence. Moreover, we propose $p - n$ ETF values to measure the relationship between words and event types. Experiments on the ACE 2005 corpus show that our proposed method can significantly improve the performance of event extraction.

Keywords: Event extraction · Pre-trained model

1 Introduction

Event extraction (EE) is a challenging task in natural language processing. In this paper, we focus on the Chinese event extraction proposed by the automatic content extraction (ACE) program [1]. There are two primary subtasks of the ACE corpus, namely trigger extraction (identifying and classifying event triggers) and argument extraction (identifying arguments and labeling their roles).

In Chinese event extraction, current state-of-the-art approaches usually rely on the powerful semantic representation capabilities of the pre-trained model. JMCEE [2] adopts the bidirectional encoder representation from the transformer (BERT [3]) as the encoder to obtain the feature representation, which achieves better performance than typical neural networks (CNNs, RNNs, etc.). Despite pre-trained based approaches performing well on the publicly available Chinese benchmark dataset (ACE 2005), they only capture the internal patterns of the input text and ignore fine-grained information. Some approaches based on the pre-trained model employ three different fine-grained information in English event extraction, including entity, syntactic structure, and document-level information. However, such methods usually require well-designed encoders, which are poorly interpretable.

W. Lu et al. (Eds.): NLPCC 2022, LNAI 13551, pp. 197–208, 2022.
https://doi.org/10.1007/978-3-031-17120-8_16

Several studies have started to use event type as additional feature information to improve model performance in recent years. There are two strategies for incorporating event type information into the model, i.e., continuous methods and discrete methods. Continuous methods such as CasEE [4] represent event types as hidden layer vectors and use a cascaded decoding strategy to model the relationship between event types, trigger words, and arguments. Inspired by prefix prompt learning, discrete methods such as GDAP [5] combine event type labels and raw sentences into the input of a pre-trained model. Although CasEE [4] and GDAP [5] noticed the value of event type information, they did not further analyze the reasons for improvement after adding event type information. We note that trigger words and event type labels have semantic connections at different granularities and perspectives. For example, consider the following Chinese sentence:

S1: 恐怖分子**袭击**了正在执勤的警察。

Terrorists **attacked** police officers on duty.

S2: 军方使用精确制导炸弹对城市外围的军事设施发动**打击**。

The military used precision-guided bombs to **strike** military installations on the outskirts of the city.

The "Conflict" event is contained in S1 and S2, and the trigger word "袭击" in S1 and the trigger word "打击" in S2 are semantically related to the event type label "Conflict". Thus, Take trigger extracting on the following sentences for example:

S3: 军人政权在去年10 月发生的不流血**政变**中被推翻。

The military regime was overthrown in a bloodless **coup** last October.

The semantic connection between the word "coup" and the event type label "Conflict" can be used as the basis for judging trigger words.

In this paper, we propose the label semantic extension to strengthen the semantic connection between trigger words and event type labels, choosing multiple words instead of event type labels to establish semantic connections with trigger words. These words are called label semantic extension words. Furthermore, we propose LSE-CEE, a **L**abel **S**emantic **E**xtension based **C**hinese **E**vent **E**xtraction framework, which utilizes event type information to enhance event extraction. We incorporate extension words into the pre-trained model. Same as prefix prompt learning, the input to the pre-trained model was constructed as "$[CLS]<ExtensionWords>[SEP]<Sentence>[SEP]$". Then, the model learned hidden semantic relations between trigger words and extension words using the powerful self-attention mechanism of the pre-trained model. We use the conditional random field (CRF) linear layer [6] as the output layer.

The contributions of this paper are as follows:

(1) We propose LSE-CEE, a novel joint learning framework with label semantic extension, which employs additional event type information to enhance the performance of event extraction.

(2) We propose the p-nETF value to measure the relevance of words to event types. Thus, high-quality label semantic extension words could be found by the p-nETF value.

(3) The experiments on the public event extraction benchmark (ACE 2005) reveal that LSE-CEE achieves significant improvements over existing competitive methods.

2   Related Work

Event extraction is a long-standing information extraction task that has attracted considerable attention. Researchers mainly focus on how to learn the semantic representation of events from original sentences. Early approaches rely on manually-crafted features, such as lexical, syntactic, and kernel-based features. With the development of deep learning, methods based on neural network structure have become mainstream. DMCNN [7] proposed a Dynamic Multi-pooling Convolutional Neural Network, which first used the CNN network for event extraction. Nguyen et al. [8] introduced Recurrent Neural Networks (RNNs) to learn richer representations from contexts.

With the success of BERT, pre-trained models have also been used for EE. Yang et al. [9] employ BERT architectures for feature learning and achieved a huge improvement compared to methods using traditional neural networks. JMCEE [2] adopted the bidirectional encoder representation from the transformer as the encoder to obtain the feature representation, and achieved state-of-the-art performance in Chinese event extraction. Since the event structure is intuitively complex, some researchers employ additional fine-grained information, including entity [10,11], syntactic structure [12,13], and document-level information [14,15], to boost semantic representation learning in the neural models.

Compared with event extraction methods on English corpus, Chinese event extraction is mainly concerned with the absence of natural word delimiters and word-trigger mismatch problem [17]. Since Chinese has no natural delimiters, segmentation is the first step in Chinese NLP tasks, but this may lead to propagation errors. Some works [18,19] designed exquisite methods to eliminate the above problems. However, these methods also inevitably have errors. At present, Chinese event extraction based on pre-trained models usually adopts the character-level paradigm instead of the word-level paradigm.

3   Methodology

This section describes a novel framework, LSE-CEE. As shown in Fig. 1, it divides event extraction into three stages: event type detection, label semantic extension, and event extraction. In the first stage, we use a multi-label classifier to identify event types in sentences. Then, we select the corresponding label semantic extension words according to the identified event type and construct the input of the event extraction model with the raw text. In the last stage, the above constructed text is used for joint event extraction.

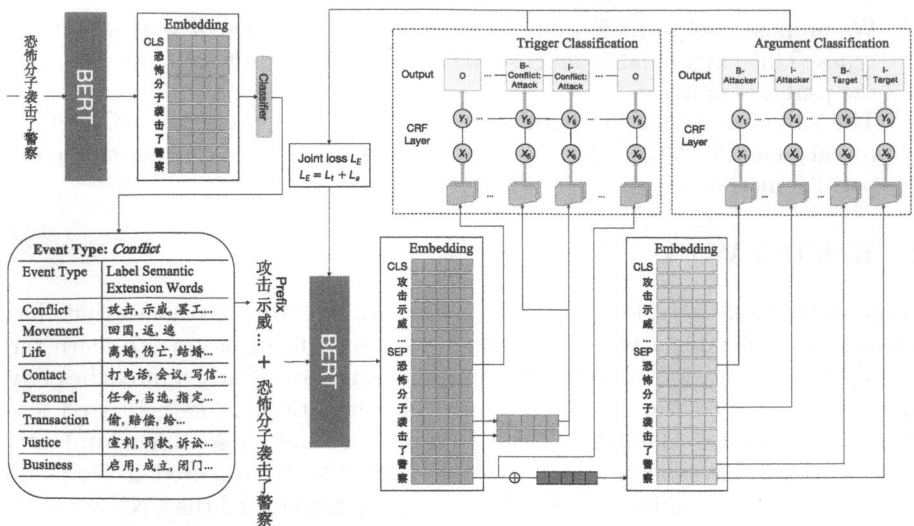

Fig. 1. The overview of LSE-CEE. For examples of label semantic extension words, please see the lower left corner of figure.

3.1 Event Type Detection

In event type detection, we formalize it as a multi-label text classification problem. Let $X = x_0, \ldots, x_n$ be an input sentence with n as the number of characters and x_i as the ith character. The goal of event type detection is to identify the event types $e_t, t \in 1, 2, \ldots, N$, where N is the number of event types. We use a multi-label classifier to identify event types.

The input follows the BERT [3], i.e., the sum of three types of embeddings, including WordPiece embedding, Position embedding, and Segment embedding. The event type is predicted by the classifier and we minimize the loss through the cross-entropy function:

$$\widehat{e_t} = \text{sigmoid}(W\beta(X) + b), \tag{1}$$

$$\mathcal{L} = -\sum_t^N [e_t \log(\widehat{e_t}) + (1 - e_t)\log(1 - \widehat{e_t})], \tag{2}$$

where W and b are weights and bias, N is the number of event types, and β is the BERT embedding.

3.2 Label Semantic Extension

This subsection describes how to obtain label semantic extension words and use extension words to establish semantic associations with trigger words. First, we need to select vocabulary from the external knowledge base (KB) as candidate vocabulary for extension words. Then, we filter and denoise the candidate extension words. The obtained extension words are used to construct the input of the pre-trained model with the raw text to establish the semantic connection between the extension words and trigger words. The construction and refinement of label semantic extension are shown in Fig. 2.

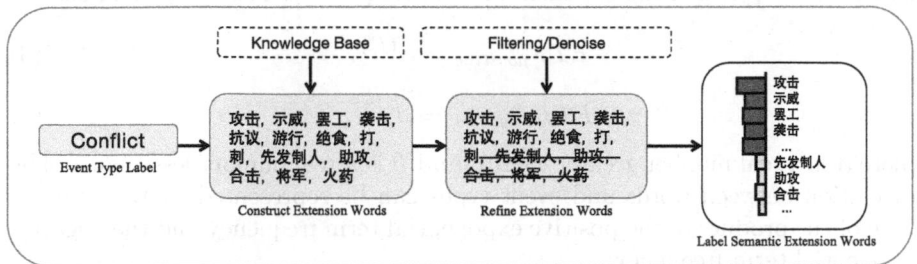

Fig. 2. The construct and refine processes of label semantic extension words. Taking event type label "Conflict" for instance.

Select Extension Words. We choose the external KB HowNet [20] as the source of extension words. Unlike semantic dictionaries such as WordNet, HowNet does not take concepts as the smallest unit but tries to describe concepts with sememes. A set of sememes can describe the semantics of a word, e.g., the sememe set of "袭击" : "{attack| 攻打, military| 军, sudden| 骤然}". For each event type, we choose some sememes for selecting candidate extension words from HowNet, which come from event type labels and common trigger words.

Filtering and Denoise. Although we have got comprehensive extension words, the collected vocabulary can be very noisy. There are two main issues for candidate extension words. First of all, some of the words recommended by KB have not appeared in the ACE 2005 corpus, and these words cannot establish a semantic connection with trigger words and should be removed. Therefore, we counted the occurrences of the candidate extension words in the corpus and filtered out the words with zero occurrences. The second problem is weakly related words. After filtering, the number of words is still far beyond the maximum input length that the pre-trained model can accept, and most of the words have little relevance to the event type. Inspired by TFIDF [21], we propose the p-nETF value to measure the relevance of words to event types. We assume that when a word appears many times in sentences set of a particular event type, but rarely appears in sentences set of other event types, and it means that the word has a strong correlation with the event type.

Like many information retrieval theories, we consider term frequency (TF) as an important attribute of natural language terms, that is, the number of times a term occurs in the sample set. We use the properties of exponential functions to represent the relationship between term frequency and event type. Formally, let N_{e_t} denote the set of sentences annotated as event type e_t, and N_{e_o} denote the set of sentences annotated as other event types e_o. $tf_{e_t}^w$ is the term frequency of the word w in the sentence set N_{e_t}, and $tf_{e_o}^w$ is the term frequency in the sentence set N_{e_o}, then the exponential term frequency (ETF) is defined as:

$$ETF_{positive} = \alpha^{tf_{e_t}^w}, \tag{3}$$

$$ETF_{negative} = \beta^{tf_{e_o}^w}, \tag{4}$$

where α is a real number greater than 1, and β is a real number less than 1. The correlation between words and event types can be represented by the p-nETF value of the product of the positive exponential term frequency and the negative exponential term frequency:

$$\text{p-nETF} = ETF_{positive} * ETF_{negative}. \tag{5}$$

We use the p-nETF value to denoise the candidate words. For each event type, the candidate words w_{e_t} with p-nETF value greater than the threshold λ are selected as the label semantic extension words.

Warp. After the classifier identifies the event type, we reconstruct the sentence using the corresponding label semantic extension words. Similar to prompt learning, we do not directly feed the raw sentences into the pre-trained model but wrap the raw sentences using the following natural language templates:

$$[CLS]<Extension\ Words>[SEP]<Sentence>[SEP].$$

For example, the raw sentence "恐怖分析袭击了警察" was first identified by the event type classifier as the "Conflict" event. Then select the extension words corresponding to the "Conflict" event to wrap the original sentence:

$$[CLS]\ 攻击示威 ... [SEP]\ 恐怖分子袭击了警察\ [SEP],$$

where token $[CLS]$ and $[SEP]$ are placed at the start and end of the sentence. It is worth noting that there are cases where a sentence contains multiple event types. So the prefix may contain extension words for multiple event types.

3.3   Event Extraction

In this paper, we propose a joint extraction model to jointly extract trigger words and arguments using a multi-task learning approach. The model input is the text processed by label semantic extension.

Trigger Extractor. Trigger extractor targets to predict whether a token triggers an event and identify its spans and classify them into a specific event type. Since Chinese has no delimiter, we formalize trigger extraction as a character-level classification task to eliminate the error caused by word segmentation.

Let $X = x_0, \ldots, x_n$ be a raw sentence with n as the number of characters and x_i as the ith character. And the label semantic extension words $W = w_0, \ldots, w_m$ with m as the number of characters. We adopt BERT as the encoder to learn the hidden representations:

$$h_{[CLS]}, h_0^w, \ldots, h_m^w, h_{[SEP]}, h_0^x, h_1^x, \ldots, h_n^x, h_{[SEP]},$$

where h_i^x is the hidden state of ith input token and h_j^w is the hidden state of jth token of extension words. Then, the hidden representations will be the input of the CRF linear layer.

In sequence labeling problems, softmax classifiers are usually used to output label sequences in the prediction stage. However, the softmax classifier does not consider the dependencies between labels, while the CRF uses a log-linear model to represent the joint probability of the entire feature sequence.

Follow Lafferty et al. [6],CRF defines P to be the matrix of scores output by the BERT. P is of size $n \times l$, where l is the number of trigger labels follow BIO sequence labeling rule. $P_{i,j}$ corresponds to the score of the jth label of the ith word in raw sentence. For a trigger label sequence of predictions $t = t_0, t_1, \ldots, t_n$, its score is calculated according to:

$$S(X, t) = \sum_{i=0}^{n} A_{t_i, t_{i+1}} + \sum_{i=1}^{n} P_{i, t_i}, \qquad (6)$$

where A is a matrix of transition scores such that $A_{i,j}$ represents the score of a transition from the label i to label j.

The probability of predicting trigger label sequence can be obtained by using softmax over all possible label sequence:

$$p(t|X) = \frac{e^{S(X,t)}}{\sum_{\tilde{t} \in t_X} e^{S(X,\tilde{t})}}, \qquad (7)$$

where t_X denotes all possible trigger label sequences for raw sentence X.

Argument Extractor. Once the triggers and their event type have been identified, the argument extractor needs to identify the arguments spans and classify them into corresponding argument roles. Note that when no trigger words are identified in the sentence, we simply skip the following operation for argument extraction.

To better learn the inter-dependencies among the trigger and argument, we integrate the predicted trigger word into the input. The argument extractor uses the same hidden layer representation as the trigger extractor, like trigger extraction. We pick the embedding vectors of start character h_s^x and end character h_e^x

of one predicted trigger words and then generate the representation of trigger words h^t by averaging these vectors:

$$h^t = \frac{\sum_{i=s}^{e} h_i^x}{e - s + 1},\tag{8}$$

where s is the start index of raw sentence and e is the end index. When obtained representation of each trigger word, We can formalize the input as:

$$h_{[CLS]}, h_0^w, \ldots, h_m^w, h_{[SEP]}, h_0^x, h_1^x, \ldots, h_n^x, h_{[SEP]}, h_0^t, \ldots, h_k^t, h_{[SEP]},$$

where h_i^x is the hidden state of ith input token, h_j^w is the hidden state of jth token of extension words and h_k^t is the hidden state of kth triggers. In argument extraction, we use the same CRF linear layer as trigger extraction.

Joint Training. We train the joint model using L_t and L_a as the loss function for trigger word prediction, which denotes the sum of negative log-likelihood of output probabilities, shown as follows:

$$L_t = -\sum_{s \in S} \log\left(P\left(t_s | s\right)\right),\tag{9}$$

$$L_a = -\sum_{s \in S} \log\left(P\left(a_s | s\right)\right),\tag{10}$$

where s denotes a sentence of train set S. t_s and t_a denotes prediction sequence of trigger and argument. The final loss function is $L_E = L_t + L_a$. We minimize the final loss function to optimize the parameters of the model.

4 Experiments

4.1 Dataset and Experiment Setup

We evaluate the LSE-CEE framework on the ACE 2005 Chinese corpus. The corpus contains 633 Chinese documents. For fair comparisons, we follow the same setup as previous work [17]. We randomly select 505/64/64 documents for the train/dev/test set. We also follow the criteria of the previous work [17] to evaluate models by micro-averaged precision (P), recall (R), and F1 score (F1).

The following criteria are used to evaluate the correctness of the event extraction:

- A trigger is correctly prediction if its event type and offsets exactly match a reference trigger.
- An argument is correctly prediction if its event type, offsets and role exactly match the reference argument.

We use HuggingFace's model (bert-base-chinese) as the encoder, which consists of 12 layers, 768 hidden units, and 12 attention heads. The optimizer is Adam. We set the batch size to 16, the learning rate to 2e−5, and the dropout rate to 0.5. We run all experiments using PyTorch on NVIDIA RTX3090 GPU.

4.2 Main Result

We compare our method with following state-of-the-art methods on Chinese event extraction: **DMCNN** [7] adopts dynamic multi-pooling CNN to extract sentence-level features automatically; **Rich-C** [22] a joint-learning, knowledge-rich approach including character-based features and discourse consistency features; **C-BiLSTM** [23] designs a convolutional Bi-LSTM model for character-level event extraction; **NPNs** [16] capture both structural and semantic information from characters and words; **L-HGAT** [19] use semantic information provided by event labels to address word-trigger mismatch problem; **JMCEE** [2] jointly performs predictions for event triggers and arguments based on shared feature representations.

Table 1. The overall performance on Chinese event extraction. Bold denotes the best results.

Metric	Trigger identification			Trigger classification			Argument identification			Argument classification		
	P	R	F1	P	R	F1	P	R	F1	P	R	F1
DMCNN	66.6	63.6	65.1	61.6	58.8	60.2	-	-	-	-	-	-
Rich-C	62.2	71.9	66.7	58.9	68.1	63.2	43.6	**57.3**	49.5	39.2	**51.6**	44.6
C-BiLSTM	65.6	66.7	66.1	60.0	60.9	60.4	53.0	52.2	52.6	47.3	46.6	46.9
NPNs	75.9	61.2	67.8	73.8	59.6	65.9	-	-	-	-	-	-
L-HGAT	72.0	70.3	71.4	69.4	68.3	68.8	-	-	-	-	-	-
JMCEE	**84.3**	80.4	82.3	76.4	71.7	74.0	66.3	45.2	53.7	53.7	46.7	50.0
LSE-CEE(*Ours*)	81.7	**83.9**	**82.8**	**80.2**	**82.4**	**81.3**	**66.8**	45.7	**54.3**	**61.5**	44.4	**51.5**

Table 1 lists the result of Chinese event extraction on ACE 2005. The table reveals that:

(1) In trigger extraction, our model has a significant performance improvement. Compared with typical neural-based methods, LSE-CEE improves at least 11.4% and 12.5% in F1 scores on trigger word recognition and classification. Compared with the same BERT-based model, its performance on trigger word classification is significantly improved, with a 7.3% increase in F1 value.

(2) In argument extraction, the improvement of our model is not obvious. Compared with the BERT-based model, its F1 scores on argument identification and classification are only improved by 0.6% and 1.5%. This may be due to the propagation error of the model in the stage of identifying the event type. It is worth noting that Rich-C used 10-fold cross-validation experiments, so the recall is obviously better than other models.

The most interesting aspect of the experimental results is that the trigger extraction improves significantly, while the argument extraction does not. This phenomenon may come from the similarity of trigger words and expansion words, the latter being provided as examples to help the model identify the correct trigger word. But due to the complex structure of event arguments, the improvement of argument extraction is not obvious.

4.3   Ablation Study

We additionally conducted three ablation studies, with results exhibited in Table 2. To begin with, we downgrade our proposed framework by omitting the label semantic extension step. We find a precision drop for variants, which proves that extension words are the main reason for the performance improvement.

The accuracy of event type detection directly affects the performance of event extraction, but the micro-F1 of our event type classifier is only 80.3%. To further demonstrate how errors in event type detection affect model performance, we provide the golden event type of the sentence during the warping step. It is not surprising that the performance of the tested model rises in all aspects. Lastly, to further demonstrate how the quality of extension words affects model performance. We randomly choose some words as extension words. This change will mislead the model to predict the wrong trigger word. As expected, the F1 scores of the model immediately dropped by about 5%.

Table 2. Result of ablation study, where TI, TC, AI, AC denote trigger identification, trigger classification, argument identification and argument classification. F1 scores are reported for each evaluation metric.

Variants	TI (%)	TC (%)	AI (%)	AC (%)
LSE-CEE	82.8	81.3	54.3	51.5
- w/o extension words	80.6	78.1	54.0	50.3
- golden event types	85.0	83.5	56.5	54.7
- random extension words	81.9	79.5	48.0	46.5

4.4   Effect of Threshold λ

In LSE-CEE, we use p-nETF values on the development set to select extension words. Specifically, we choose words with p-nETF values greater than the threshold λ. The choice of threshold λ directly affects the model's performance.

In order to study the effect of threshold λ on the model, we extracted seven groups of extension words at threshold $\lambda = 16, 32, 64, 128, 256, 512, 1024$ respectively. We use these seven sets of label semantic extension words on the LSE-CEE with golden event type to make predictions on the validation set. Figure 3 shows the result of the threshold setting. It can be found that when the threshold is set to 128, the model achieves the best performance in both trigger and argument extraction.

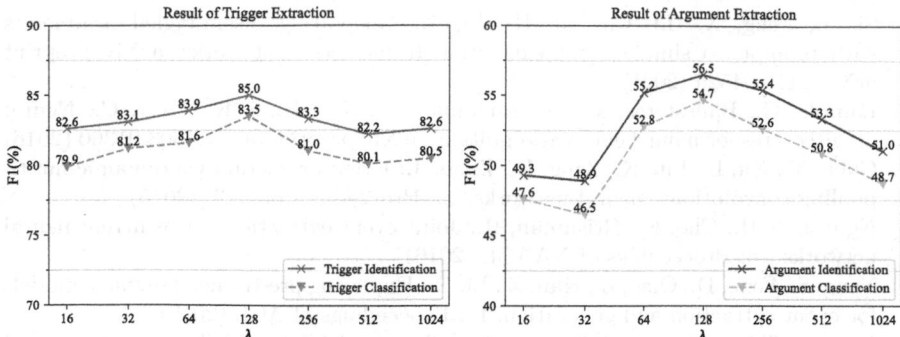

Fig. 3. Result of thresholds settings for event extraction, when α set to 2 and β set to 0.5.

5   Conclusions

This paper proposes a joint learning framework with label semantic extension to exploit event type information, LSE-CEE. Previous work usually uses the information of event type labels directly, which cannot establish an robust semantic connection with trigger words. LSE-CEE extends event type labels with an external knowledge base, enhancing semantic associations. Experiments on the public benchmark demonstrate that our work outperforms previous competitive methods. Our future work will tackle the error problem on the label semantic extension and applied to general event extraction, such as document-level Chinese event extraction.

Acknowledgment. This research is supported by "Pioneer" and "Leading Goose" R&D Program of Zhejiang (Grant No. 2022C03174), Fundamental Research Funds for the Provincial Universities of Zhejiang (NO. GK229909299001-023) and A Project Supported by Scientific Research Fund of Zhejiang Provincial Education Department (NO. Y202147115).

References

1. Doddington, G.R., Mitchell, A., Przybocki, M.A., Ramshaw, L.A., Strassel, S.M., Weischedel, R.M.: The automatic content extraction (ACE) program-tasks, data, and evaluation. In: Proceedings of LREC (2004)
2. Xu, N., Xie, H., Zhao, D.: A novel joint framework for multiple Chinese events extraction. In: Proceedings of CCL (2020)
3. Devlin, J., Chang, M.W., Lee, K., Toutanova, K.: Bert: pre-training of deep bidirectional transformers for language understanding. arXiv preprint arXiv:1810.04805 (2018)
4. Sheng, J., et al.: Casee: a joint learning framework with cascade decoding for overlapping event extraction. arXiv preprint arXiv:2107.01583 (2021)

5. Si, J., Peng, X., Li, C., Xu, H., Li, J.: Generating disentangled arguments with prompts: a simple event extraction framework that works. arXiv preprint arXiv:2110.04525 (2021)
6. Lample, G., Ballesteros, M., Subramanian, S., Kawakami, K., Dyer, C.: Neural architectures for named entity recognition. arXiv preprint arXiv:1603.01360 (2016)
7. Chen, Y., Xu, L., Liu, K., Zeng, D., Zhao, J.: Event extraction via dynamic multi-pooling convolutional neural networks. In: Proceedings of ACL (2015)
8. Nguyen, T.H., Cho, K., Grishman, R.: Joint event extraction via recurrent neural networks. In: Proceedings of NAACL (2016)
9. Yang, S., Feng, D., Qiao, L., Kan, Z., Li, D.: Exploring pre-trained language models for event extraction and generation. In: Proceedings of ACL (2019)
10. Nguyen, T.M., Nguyen, T.H.: One for all: neural joint modeling of entities and events. In: Proceedings of AAAI (2019)
11. Wadden, D., Wennberg, U., Luan, Y., Hajishirzi, H.: Entity, relation, and event extraction with contextualized span representations. arXiv preprint arXiv:1909.03546 (2019)
12. Liu, X., Luo, Z., Huang, H.: Jointly multiple events extraction via attention-based graph information aggregation. arXiv preprint arXiv:1809.09078 (2018)
13. Sha, L., Qian, F., Chang, B., Sui, Z.: Jointly extracting event triggers and arguments by dependency-bridge RNN and tensor-based argument interaction. In: Proceedings of AAAI (2018)
14. Zhao, Y., Jin, X., Wang, Y., Cheng, X.: Document embedding enhanced event detection with hierarchical and supervised attention. In: Proceedings of ACL (2018)
15. Liu, S., Cheng, R., Yu, X., Cheng, X.: Exploiting contextual information via dynamic memory network for event detection. arXiv preprint arXiv:1810.03449 (2018)
16. Lin, H., Lu, Y., Han, X., Sun, L.: Nugget proposal networks for Chinese event detection. arXiv preprint arXiv:1805.00249 (2018)
17. Chen, Z., Ji, H.: Language specific issue and feature exploration in Chinese event extraction. In: Proceedings of NAACL (2009)
18. Ding, N., Li, Z., Liu, Z., Zheng, H., Lin, Z.: Event detection with trigger-aware lattice neural network. In: Proceedings of EMNLP (2019)
19. Cui, S., Yu, B., Cong, X., Liu, T., Li, Q., Shi, J.: Label enhanced event detection with heterogeneous graph attention networks. arXiv preprint arXiv:2012.01878 (2020)
20. Dong, Z., Dong, Q.: HowNet-a hybrid language and knowledge resource. In: International Conference on Natural Language Processing and Knowledge Engineering, Proceedings (2003)
21. Salton, G., Yu, C.T.: On the construction of effective vocabularies for information retrieval. ACM SIGPLAN Not. (1973)
22. Chen, C., Ng, V.: Joint modeling for Chinese event extraction with rich linguistic features. In: Proceedings of COLING (2012)
23. Zeng, Y., Yang, H., Feng, Y., Wang, Z., Zhao, D.: A convolution BILSTM neural network model for Chinese event extraction. In: Natural Language Understanding and Intelligent Applications (2016)

QuatSE: Spherical Linear Interpolation of Quaternion for Knowledge Graph Embeddings

Jiang Li[1,2,3], Xiangdong Su[1,2,3(✉)], Xinlan Ma[1,2,3], and Guanglai Gao[1,2,3]

[1] College of Computer Science, Inner Mongolia University, Hohhot, China
[2] National and Local Joint Engineering Research Center of Intelligent Information Processing Technology for Mongolian, Hohhot, China
[3] Inner Mongolia Key Laboratory of Mongolian Information Processing Technology, Hohhot, China
cssxd@imu.edu.cn

Abstract. Knowledge graph embedding aims to learn representations of entities and relations in a knowledge graph. Recently, QuatE has introduced the graph embeddings into the quaternion space. However, there are still challenges in dealing with complex patterns, including 1-N, N-1, and multiple-relations between two entities. Since the learned entity embeddings tend to overlap with each other in the first two cases, and the learned relation embeddings tend to overlap with each other in the last case. To deal with these issues, we propose QuatSE, a novel knowledge embedding model that adjusts graph embeddings via spherical linear interpolation (Slerp) of entities and relations. For a triple (head entity, relation, tail entity), QuatSE calculates Slerp between each entity and its relation, and adds the normalized interpolation to the corresponding entity. The operation avoids the problem of embedding overlap and ensures the information of original entity is not missed. We further compare the effect of interpolation using different normalization strategies (L_1 or L_2) for Slerp. Several experiments suggest that QuatSE works well in 1-N, N-1 and multiple-relations pattern. QuatSE outperforms the existing quaternion-based models.

Keywords: Knowledge graph embedding · Spherical linear interpolation · Quaternion

1 Introduction

Knowledge graphs (KGs) are multi-relation graphs of fact triples, which are extracted from documents and databases and represented as (h, r, t). Since KGs possess a distinct advantage in their ability to learn structural representations, they are often used for downstream tasks. However, real-world KGs are usually incomplete. As such, calculating KGs and predicting missing links between entities have received much attention in recent years.

© The Author(s), under exclusive license to Springer Nature Switzerland AG 2022
W. Lu et al. (Eds.): NLPCC 2022, LNAI 13551, pp. 209–220, 2022.
https://doi.org/10.1007/978-3-031-17120-8_17

Learning knowledge graph embeddings in the low-dimensional real-valued space is an effective solution. ComplEx [21] improves it recently, which learns graphs embeddings in complex-valued space. To further have a higher degree of freedom in the embedding representations and richer interaction capabilities, QuatE [26] extends graph embeddings from the complex plane to quaternion hypercomplex space. The quaternion performs expressive rotation in four dimensions and has a higher degree of rotational freedom than complex space.

However, QuatE and its variants have problems distinguishing semantic information about tail entities in 1-N, head entities in N-1, and relations in multiple-relations pattern using the score function of QuatE and its variants. Specifically, 1-N represents triples composed of the same head entities, the same relations, and different tail entities. N-1 represents triples are made up of the different head entities, the same relations, and the same tail entities. Multiple-relations pattern represents triples consisting of the same head entities, different relations, and the same tail entities. As a result of the overlapping graph embeddings of QuatE and its variants, when learning from 1-N, N-1, and multiple-relations pattern, the problem would arise. Overlapping embeddings have the negative effect of lowering link prediction accuracy. Further details are presented in Sect. 3.3.

To address these issues, we propose QuatSE that uses spherical linear interpolation to distinguish head entities, tail entities and relations in a KG. QuatSE first computes spherical linear interpolation between each entity and its relation, and then adds the normalized interpolation to the corresponding entities. QuatSE normalizes the spherical linear interpolation values before adding them to the embeddings of the head and the tail entities. The operation enables QuatSE to adjust the embeddings adaptively within the constraints. Additionally, it can avoid the loss of original information and avoid the problem of embedding overlap. Several experiments indicate that QuatSE works well for 1-N, N-1, and multiple-relation pattern. Our contribution is summarized as follows:

- We introduce spherical linear interpolation in knowledge graph embedding and propose QuatSE, which can avoid the problem of embedding overlap in learning knowledge graph embeddings and increase the performance of link prediction.
- We demonstrate the effectiveness of QuatSE through extensive experiments on benchmark link prediction datasets. Notably, the proposed model significantly outperforms existing quaternion-based methods in MRR and Hits@1.
- We further analyze the effect of interpolation using different normalization strategies (L_1 or L_2) on the performance of link prediction.

2   Related Work

Knowledge graph embedding has recently become a hot research topic and numerous approaches have been proposed. These approaches fall into three categories: (i) translation models, (ii) real-valued space models, (iii) complex-valued space models.

Translation Models. The translation models describe a relation as the translation between a head entity and a tail entity. The score function is defined as the distance between $h + r$ and t subject to a L_1 or L_2 norm constraint. Although TransE has made great progress in knowledge graph embedding, it still faces challenges in dealing with complex relations such as 1-N, N-1 and N-N. After that, TransH [23], TransR [11], TransD [9] and TransA [24] all use different projection strategies to improve TransE. TranSparse [10] overcomes heterogeneity and imbalance by applying two versions of the model: TranSparse(share) and TranSparse(separate). TransMS [25] performs multi-directional semantic transfer with non-linear functions and linear deviation vectors.

Real-Valued Space Models. A common feature of real-valued space models learn the representations of knowledge graphs in real-valued space. For instance, ConvE [4] and ConvKB [14] use convolutional neural network to learn the entity and relation embeddings. InteractE [22] improves ConvE by adding entity-relation interactions. HypER [1] uses the hyper networks to generate one-dimensional relation-specific convolutional filters for multi-task knowledge sharing.

Complex-valued Space Models. Complex-valued space models represent entities and relations in complex-valued space. ComplEx [21] firstly introduces complex-valued space into knowledge graph embedding. The RotatE [19] defines each relation as a rotation from the source entity to the target entity in complex vector space. QuatE [26] learns graph embeddings in quaternion space and uses Hamiltonian Products to obtain the potential interdependence between entities and relations. After that, QuatRE [15] adds two relation matrics in the head and the tail embedding space, respectively. QuatDE [6] introduces a mapping matrix of entities and relations, respectively. DualE [3] maps entities and relations to the dual quaternion space to learn their representations.

3 Proposed Model

Given a knowledge graph (KG) is usually described as $\mathcal{G} = (\mathcal{E}, \mathcal{R}, \mathcal{T})$. $\mathcal{E}$ and $\mathcal{R}$ denote the set of entities and relations, respectively. $\mathcal{T}$ denotes the set of triples (h, r, t). h, r and t denote head entity, relation and tail entity, respectively. The real-valued space and the quaternion space are defined as $\mathbb{R}$ and $\mathbb{H}$, respectively. The following two subsections discuss in detail the quaternion background and the proposed QuatSE.

3.1 Quaternion Background

The quaternion is a system of hypercomplex numbers introduced by William Rowan Hamilton in 1843. It avoids the problem of cardinal locks in the Eulerian representation of angles. A quaternion is defined as $q = a + b\mathbf{i} + c\mathbf{j} + d\mathbf{k}$, which is composed of real numbers and three imaginary units $\mathbf{i}$, $\mathbf{j}$, $\mathbf{k}$, where $a, b, c, d \in \mathbb{R}$. In addition, $\mathbf{i}^2 = \mathbf{j}^2 = \mathbf{k}^2 = \mathbf{ijk} = -1$. We define $q_1 = a_1 + b_1\mathbf{i} + c_1\mathbf{j} + d_1\mathbf{k}$, $q_2 = a_2 + b_2\mathbf{i} + c_2\mathbf{j} + d_2\mathbf{k}$. The following are some widely used operations of quaternion algebra:

- **Inner Product**

$$q_1 \cdot q_2 = \langle a_1, a_2 \rangle + \langle b_1, b_2 \rangle + \langle c_1, c_2 \rangle + \langle d_1, d_2 \rangle \tag{1}$$

- **Norm**

  The normalized quaternion q is expressed as:

$$q^\triangleleft = \frac{a + b\mathbf{i} + c\mathbf{j} + d\mathbf{k}}{\sqrt{a^2 + b^2 + c^2 + d^2}} \tag{2}$$

- **Hamilton Product**

$$q_1 \otimes q_2 = (a_1 a_2 - b_1 b_2 - c_1 c_2 - d_1 d_2) + (a_1 b_2 + b_1 a_2 + c_1 d_2 - d_1 c_2)\mathbf{i} \\ + (a_1 c_2 - b_1 d_2 + c_1 a_2 + d_1 b_2)\mathbf{j} + (a_1 d_2 + b_1 c_2 - c_1 b_2 + d_1 a_2)\mathbf{k} \tag{3}$$

3.2   QuatSE

In this section, we provide a detailed description of QuatSE. QuatSE adaptively adjusts graph embeddings via spherical linear interpolation (Slerp) in graph embedding learning to avoid the problem of entities and relations embedding overlap in 1-N, N-1 and multiple-relations pattern. Figure 1 illustrates QuatSE's details in calculating head entity and relation.

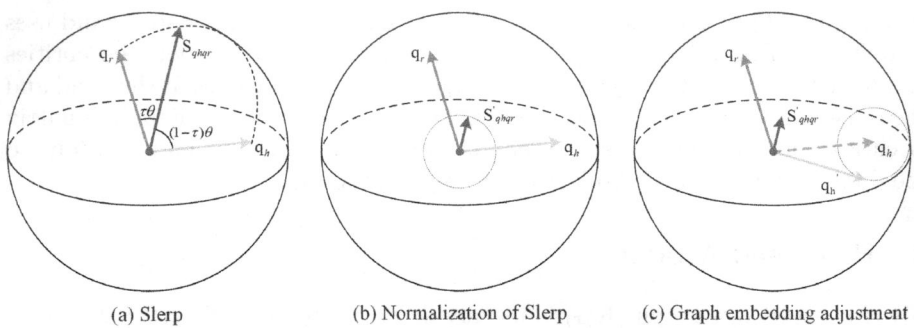

| (a) Slerp | (b) Normalization of Slerp | (c) Graph embedding adjustment |

Fig. 1. Overview of QuatSE in calculating head entity and relation. The spherical linear interpolation (Slerp) in the proposed QuatSE. $\mathcal{S}_{qhqr} = Slerp(q_h, q_r, \tau)$, $\mathcal{S}'_{qhqr} = Slerp(q_h, q_r, \tau)_{norm}$, $\tau\theta$ is an angle between q_r and $\mathcal{S}_{qhqr}$, $(1-\tau)\theta$ is an angle between $\mathcal{S}_{qhqr}$ and q_h, $q'_h = q_h + \mathcal{S}'_{qhqr}$.

Knowledge Graph Embedding Initialization. Concretely, h, r and t are head entity, relation and tail entity of each triple (h, r, t). h, t and r are represented by $q_h = a_h + b_h\mathbf{i} + c_h\mathbf{j} + d_h\mathbf{k}$, $q_t = a_t + b_t\mathbf{i} + c_t\mathbf{j} + d_t\mathbf{k}$ and $q_r = a_r + b_r\mathbf{i} + c_r\mathbf{j} + d_r\mathbf{k}$, respectively. In this paper, we adopt the initialization algorithm in [26]. The embeddings of entity and relation are initialized as follows:

$$\omega_{\mathbf{r}} = \varphi \cos(\theta), \omega_{\mathbf{i}} = \varphi q_{imgi}^{\triangleleft} \sin(\theta), \omega_{\mathbf{j}} = \varphi q_{imgj}^{\triangleleft} \sin(\theta), \omega_{\mathbf{k}} = \varphi q_{imgk}^{\triangleleft} \sin(\theta) \quad (4)$$

The angle θ is generated randomly in the interval $[-\pi, \pi]$. The imaginary quaternion q_{img} is generated via the uniform distribution in the interval $[0, 1]$. The normalization of the imaginary unit is $q_{img}^{\triangleleft}$. φ is a random number generated by He algorithm [8] in the interval $[-\frac{1}{\sqrt{2k}}, \frac{1}{\sqrt{2k}}]$.

Quaternion Spherical Linear Interpolation. Since general linear interpolation is computing along a straight line, there is a problem of non-uniform changes in vector angular velocity. Therefore, we introduce spherical linear interpolation (Slerp) [17] to obtain a smooth interpolation of entities and relations in the quaternion embedding space. Compared with the traditional linear interpolation (Lerp), Slerp can be used to smooth the rotation difference between two quaternion embeddings and avoid the problem of information loss between entities and relations. In Fig. 1, (a) shows the Slerp between q_h and q_r. Unlike general linear interpolation, Slerp interpolates along an arc on the sphere surface rather than along a line. Hence, Slerp can smooth the difference between two representing rotations. We calculate the spherical linear interpolation between head entities and relations in the quaternion space, as follows:

$$Slerp(q_h, q_r, \tau) = \frac{\sin[(1 - \tau)\theta]q_h + \sin \tau\theta q_r}{\sin \theta} \quad (5)$$

We compute the spherical linear interpolation between tail entities and relations $Slerp(q_t, q_r, \tau)$ similarly. Graph embedding adjustment is to differentiate entities in 1-N, N-1 and multiple-relations patterns. Thus, we normalize (L_1 or L_2 norms) the $Slerp(q_h, q_r, \tau)$ and $Slerp(q_t, q_r, \tau)$, and add them to their corresponding entities, as

$$q_h' = q_h + Slerp(q_h, q_r, \tau)_{norm}, q_t' = q_t + Slerp(q_t, q_r, \tau)_{norm} \quad (6)$$

Normalization of spherical linear interpolation ensures that the embedding adjustment resides within a constraint range and increases the differences of graph embeddings.

Graph Embedding Updating. Following QuatE [26], the score function of QuatSE is represented as:

$$f_r(h, t) = q_h' \otimes q_r^{\triangleleft} \cdot q_t' \quad (7)$$

We update the graph embeddings according to the loss function of QuatSE as

$$\mathcal{L} = \sum_{(h,r,t)\in\{\mathcal{G}\cup\mathcal{G}^-\}} log(1 + exp(-\phi_{(h,r,t)}f_r(h, t))) + \lambda\|\omega\|, \quad (8)$$

where $\phi_{(h,r,t)}$ is

$$\phi_{(h,r,t)} = \begin{cases} 1, \text{ for } (h,r,t) \in \mathcal{G} \\ -1, \text{ for } (h,r,t) \in \mathcal{G}^- \end{cases} \tag{9}$$

where $\mathcal{G}$ and $\mathcal{G}^-$ are the sets of valid and invalid triples respectively. We use L_2 norm with regularization for ω.

3.3 Theoretical Analysis

This section analyzes the advantages of our model as opposed to QuatE in dealing with complex triple patterns. Let $Slerp(a,b,\tau) = \mathcal{S}_{ab}$, $Slerp(a,b,\tau)_{norm} = \mathcal{S}'_{ab}$.

1-N QuatE: The score function of QuatE is $f_r(h,t) = q_h \otimes q_r^\triangleleft \cdot q_t$. The model learns the representations of entity and relation in a KG, and $f_r(h,t)$ converges to the Max-Score eventually. If $(h,r,t_1) \in \mathcal{T}$ and $(h,r,t_2) \in \mathcal{T}$, we have

$$f_r(h,t_1) = f_r(h,t_2) \Rightarrow q_h \otimes q_r^\triangleleft \cdot q_{t1} = q_h \otimes q_r^\triangleleft \cdot q_{t2} \Rightarrow q_{t1} = q_{t2} \tag{10}$$

Hence, learning from 1-N with QuatE leads to unexpected graph embeddings result in $q_{t1} = q_{t2}$, which raises the problem of embedding overlap in tail entities.

QuatSE: For cases like 1-N, following the score function of QuatSE, we have

$$f_r(h,t_1) = f_r(h,t_2) \Rightarrow$$
$$[q_h + \mathcal{S}'_{q_h q_r}] \otimes q_r^\triangleleft \cdot [q_{t1} + \mathcal{S}'_{(q_{t1} q_r)}] = [q_h + \mathcal{S}'_{q_h q_r}] \otimes q_r^\triangleleft \cdot [q_{t2} + \mathcal{S}'_{q_{t2} q_r}] \tag{11}$$

Without affecting the conclusion, we set τ to 0.5 for simplicity, and obtain $\mathcal{S}'_{ab} = \alpha \frac{a+b}{2} \sec(\frac{\theta}{2})$, where $\theta \in [0,\pi]$. According to Eq. 11, we have

$$q_{t1} + \alpha \frac{q_{t1} + q_r}{2} \sec(\frac{\theta_1}{2}) = q_{t2} + \alpha \frac{q_{t2} + q_r}{2} \sec(\frac{\theta_2}{2}) \tag{12}$$

For the training samples (h,r,t_1) and (h,r,t_2), there are infinite solutions for Eq. 12. One special solution is $q_{t1} = q_{t2} = q_r$. Since q_r, q_{t1} and q_{t2} are randomly initialized and updated according to the loss function, it is almost impossible that $q_{t1} = q_{t2}$ in the process of embedding learning. Specifically, $q_{t1} = q_{t2}$ is a sufficient conditions that are not necessary for Eq. 12. Thus, QuatSE can avoid the problem of embedding overlap when learning knowledge graph embeddings in 1-N.

N-1 QuatE: If $(h_1,r,t) \in \mathcal{T}$ and $(h_2,r,t) \in \mathcal{T}$, we have

$$f_r(h_1,t) = f_r(h_2,t) \Rightarrow q_{h1} \otimes q_r^\triangleleft \cdot q_t = q_{h2} \otimes q_r^\triangleleft \cdot q_t \Rightarrow q_{h1} = q_{h2} \tag{13}$$

Learning the pattern like N-1 with QuatE leads to unexpected graph embeddings result in $q_{h1} = q_{h2}$, which causes the problem of enbedding overlap in head entities.

QuatSE: According to our score function, we have

$$f_r(h_1, t) = f_r(h_2, t) \Rightarrow q_{h1} + \mathcal{S}'_{(q_{h1}q_r)} = q_{h2} + \mathcal{S}'_{(q_{h2}q_r)} \tag{14}$$

Like 1-N, we obtain $q_{h1} \neq q_{h2}$ in most cases. Thus, QuatSE can avoid the problem of embedding overlap $q_{h1} = q_{h2}$, and improves the link prediction in N-1.

Multiple Relations QuatE: If $(h, r_1, t) \in \mathcal{T}$ and $(h, r_2, t) \in \mathcal{T}$, we have

$$f_{r1}(h, t) = f_{r2}(h, t) \Rightarrow q_h \otimes q_{r1}^{\triangleleft} \cdot q_t = q_h \otimes q_{r2}^{\triangleleft} \cdot q_t \Rightarrow q_{r1} = q_{r2} \tag{15}$$

This indicates that QuatE would cause the problem of relation embeddings overlap $q_{r1} = q_{r2}$ when it learns from the triples with multiple-relations. **QuatSE:** In QuatSE, when learning from the samples $(h, r_1, t) \in \mathcal{T}$ and $(h, r_2, t) \in \mathcal{T}$, we have

$$f_{r1}(h, t) = f_{r2}(h, t) \Rightarrow$$
$$(q_h + \mathcal{S}'_{q_h q_{r1}}) \otimes q_{r1}^{\triangleleft} \cdot (q_t + \mathcal{S}'_{q_t q_{r1}}) = (q_h + \mathcal{S}'_{q_h q_{r2}}) \otimes q_{r2}^{\triangleleft} \cdot (q_t + \mathcal{S}'_{q_t q_{r2}}) \tag{16}$$

By using inverse matrix multiplication, we have

$$(q_h + \mathcal{S}'_{q_t q_{r2}})^{-1}(q_h + \mathcal{S}'_{q_h q_{r1}}) \otimes q_{r1}^{\triangleleft} \cdot (q_t + \mathcal{S}'_{q_t q_{r1}})(q_t + \mathcal{S}'_{q_t q_{r2}})^{-1} = q_{r2}^{\triangleleft} \tag{17}$$

For the training samples $(h, r1, t)$ and $(h, r2, t)$, there are infinite solutions for Eq. 17. $q_{r1} = q_{r2}$ is a special solution, which a sufficient but not necessary condition. Since q_h, q_t, q_{r1} and q_{r2} are randomly initialized and updated according to the loss function, it is often the case that $q_{r1} \neq q_{r2}$ in the process of embedding learning. Concretely, $q_{r1} = q_{r2}$ is a sufficient conditions that are not necessary for Eq. 17. QuatSE can avoid the problem of embedding overlap via Slerp in learning multiple-relations pattern.

4 Experiment

4.1 Datasets

In the experiment, we evaluate the proposed QuatSE for link prediction on the benchmark datasets, including WN18RR [4], FB15k-237 [20], FB15K [2] and YAGO3-10 [18]. We summarize the detailed information of these datasets in Table 1. FB15K is a subset of the Freebase knowledge base, while FB15k-237 removes the inverse relations from FB15K. WN18RR extracts from WordNet [13] and removes the inverse relations. YAGO3-10 is a subset of YAGO3.

Table 1. Statistics of the datasets in the experiment.

Dataset	$|\mathcal{E}|$	$|\mathcal{R}|$	Train	Valid	Test
WN18RR	40,943	11	86,835	3034	3,134
FB15K-237	14,541	237	272,115	17,535	20,466
FB15K	14,951	1,345	483,142	50,000	59,071
YAGO3-10	123,182	37	1,079,040	5,000	5,000

4.2   Evaluation Protocol

In the experiment, we choose mean inverse rank (MRR) and Hits@n as evaluation metrics. MRR is the average inverse rank for correct entities. Hits@n means the proportion of correct entities in the top n entities, we choose $n = 1, 10$. Higher MRR and H@N values indicate better performance.

4.3   Implementation Details

We initialize the hyperparameters of experiments are as follows: learning rate $\alpha \in \{0.02, 0.05, 0.1\}$, embedding dimension $k \in \{100, 200, 300, 400\}$, regularization rate $\lambda \in \{0.01, 0.05, 0.1, 0.2, 0.3\}$, number of negatives per training sample $ns \in \{1, 5, 10\}$. τ in $Slerp(p, q, \tau)$ are set to 0.5. In the appendix, Table 4 provides the best hyperparameters. We use Adagrad [5] to optimize the graph embeddings. Additionally, we compare different methods of normalization for the datasets, including L_1 and L_2 norms.

4.4   Baselines

In our experiments, we compare QuatSE with the following baselines, which are categorized as:

- **Non-Quaternion Space:** These models embed graph entities and relations in non-quaternion space, including TransE [2], ComplEx [21], R-GCN+ [16], ConvE [4], RotatE [19] and InteractE [22].
- **Quaternion Space:** These models represent graph entities and relations in quaternion space, including QuatE [26], QuatRE [15], QuatDE [6], DualE [3] and DualQuatE [7].

5   Results and Analysis

5.1   Main Results

The results are shown in Table 2. QuatSE obtains the highest Hits@1 and MRR on WN18RR, FB15K-237, FB15K and YAGO3-10. Besides, QuatSE achieves the best Hits@10 on FB15K-237 and YAGO3-10. On other datasets, QuatSE is the second best in Hits@10. Compared with QuatE on FB15K, the proposed QuatSE gains a significant improvement of 6.7 in Hits@1 (which represents an improvement of approximately 9.4%). The MRR is improved by 0.039 (representing an improvement of approximately 4.9%). Besides, QuatSE obtains more relative gains of 6.3%, 4.5% in Hits@1 and MRR than QuatE on FB15K-237.

We employ different strategies of normalization for interpolation. Experimental results suggest that $L_1 L_1$ norms are a better approach for normalizing Slerp on WN18RR and FB15K-237. Using $L_1 L_2$ norms can achieve better performance on FB15K and YAGO3-10. FB15K and YAGO3-10 infer inverse patterns. WN18RR and FB15K-237 remove the inverse relations from WN18 [2] and FB15K. As a consequence, if inverse relations exist in the datasets, it is preferable to avoid embedding overlap by using $L_1 L_2$ norms for S_{qhqr} and S_{qtqr}, respectively.

Table 2. Link prediction results on WN18RR, FB15K-237, FB15K and YAGO3-10. QuatSE$_{L_1/L_1}$, QuatSE$_{L_1/L_2}$, QuatSE$_{L_2/L_1}$ and QuatSE$_{L_2/L_2}$ use different normalization strategies for $Slerp(h, r)$ and $Slerp(t, r)$ respectively. Best results are in bold and second best results are underlined. H@n: Hits@n.

	WN18RR			FB15K-237			FB15K			YAGO3-10		
	MRR	H@10	H@1	MRR	H@10	H@1	MRR	H@10	H@1	MRR	H@10	H@1
TransE(2013)	0.266	50.1	-	0.294	46.5	-	0.463	74.9	29.7	-	-	-
DistMult(2015)	0.430	49.0	39.0	0.241	41.9	15.5	0.798	89.3	-	0.340	54.0	24.0
ComplEx(2016)	0.440	51.0	41.0	0.247	42.8	15.8	0.692	84.0	59.9	0.360	55.0	26.0
ConvE(2018)	0.430	52.0	40.0	0.325	50.1	23.7	0.657	83.1	55.8	0.440	62.0	35.0
RotatE(2019)	0.470	56.5	42.2	0.297	48.0	20.5	0.699	87.2	58.5	0.495	67.0	40.2
QuatE(2019)	0.488	58.2	43.8	0.348	55.0	24.8	0.782	**90.0**	71.1	-	-	-
InteractE(2020)	0.463	52.8	43.0	0.354	53.5	26.3	-	-	-	0.541	68.7	46.2
QuatRE(2020)	<u>0.493</u>	**59.2**	43.9	0.367	56.3	26.9	0.808	89.6	75.1	-	-	-
QuatDE(2021)	0.489	58.6	43.8	0.365	56.3	26.8	-	-	-	-	-	-
DualE(2021)	0.492	58.4	<u>44.4</u>	0.365	55.9	26.8	0.813	89.6	76.6	-	-	-
DualQuatE(2021)	0.470	58.2	41.5	0.342	53.5	24.5	0.754	88.4	66.4	0.534	69.5	44.5
QuatSE$_{L_1/L_1}$	**0.496**	<u>58.7</u>	**44.8**	**0.370**	**56.7**	**27.3**	0.812	89.5	75.8	0.547	<u>70.3</u>	46.2
QuatSE$_{L_1/L_2}$	0.491	57.9	<u>44.4</u>	<u>0.369</u>	<u>56.5</u>	<u>27.1</u>	**0.821**	<u>89.7</u>	**77.8**	0.550	70.4	<u>46.4</u>
QuatSE$_{L_2/L_1}$	0.488	57.6	44.0	0.368	56.4	<u>27.1</u>	0.818	89.4	77.2	0.548	70.2	46.3
QuatSE$_{L_2/L_2}$	0.487	57.4	44.1	0.368	56.4	<u>27.1</u>	<u>0.819</u>	89.3	<u>77.4</u>	**0.550**	<u>70.3</u>	**46.7**

5.2   1-N, N-1 and Multiple-Relations Pattern

This section analyzes the performance of the proposed QuatSE on complex patterns, including 1-N, N-1 and multiple-relations pattern. Following TransE [2], we classify the relations based on the average number of tails per head and the average number of heads per tail into 1-N and N-1. Multiple-relations pattern indicates that triples consist of the same head entities, different relations, and the same tail entities.

In Table 3, QuatSE yields a significant performance in MRR, Hits@10 and Hits@1 than QuatE and its variants on both FB15K-237 and FB15K for modeling complex patterns. This is because spherical linear interpolation in QuatSE can avoid the embedding overlap in graph embedding learning and improve the performance of link prediction.

In order to demonstrate the advantages of QuatSE in dealing with the complex patterns. We utilize t-SNE [12] to visualize the graph embeddings learned by QuatE and QuatSE on FB15-237 for 1-N, N-1 and multiple-relations pattern. In Fig. 2, (a) and (d) show the entity embeddings related to the four specified relations in N-1. Besides, (b) and (e) are visualisations of the entity embeddings in N-1. Compared with QuatE, QuatSE increases the differences of the entity embeddings. Meanwhile, QuatSE makes the distribution of the entity embeddings of the same relation more dispersed and avoids the problem of embedding overlap between different entities. (c) and (f) show the relation embeddings learned by QuatE and QuatSE in multiple-relations pattern on FB15K-237. Compared with the relation embeddings learned by QuatE, the relation embeddings learned by QuatSE tend to be more scattered. This indicates that QuatSE can avoid the problem of relation embedding overlap.

Table 3. Link prediction results by relation category on the test data of FB15K-237 and FB15K for QuatE, QuatRE, QuatDE and QuatSE. Head: predicting h given (r, t), Tail: predicting t given (h, r), H@n: Hits@n, MR: multiple-relations pattern.

			QuatE			QuatRE			QuatDE			QuatSE		
			MRR	H@10	H@1	MRR	H@10	H@1	MRR	H@10	H@1	MRR	H@10	H@1
FB15K-237	Head	1-N	0.425	66.0	35.5	0.459	65.9	35.2	0.456	67.1	35.2	**0.460**	**67.3**	**35.8**
		N-1	0.268	36.5	21.3	0.288	39.4	22.7	0.292	40.6	23.2	**0.296**	**40.9**	**23.4**
		MR	0.193	32.5	11.1	0.229	**40.1**	13.8	0.228	38.8	13.9	**0.230**	40.1	**14.0**
	Tail	1-N	0.149	24.2	9.9	0.161	27.1	10.5	0.163	27.2	10.9	**0.167**	**26.7**	**11.2**
		N-1	0.761	87.8	69.5	0.777	88.7	71.2	0.777	88.7	77.1	**0.781**	**88.9**	**71.8**
		MR	0.409	55.8	33.4	0.434	57.9	35.9	0.433	56.2	35.7	**0.437**	**58.1**	**36.0**
FB15K	Head	1-N	0.938	97.1	91.2	0.941	96.4	91.9	0.933	97.0	90.5	**0.942**	**97.3**	**92.0**
		N-1	0.588	67.1	54.0	0.598	67.0	55.5	0.577	66.8	52.7	**0.606**	**68.0**	**56.4**
		MR	0.579	78.5	47.3	0.595	78.5	47.2	0.593	78.9	47.1	**0.611**	**79.3**	**49.7**
	Tail	1-N	0.644	72.3	59.3	0.663	72.6	62.5	0.633	71.5	58.0	**0.674**	**73.2**	**63.8**
		N-1	0.912	95.9	87.8	0.912	96.1	87.0	0.907	95.3	87.0	**0.912**	**96.3**	**88.0**
		MR	0.801	94.1	70.6	0.798	95.0	69.8	0.787	94.5	68.4	**0.807**	**95.2**	**71.3**

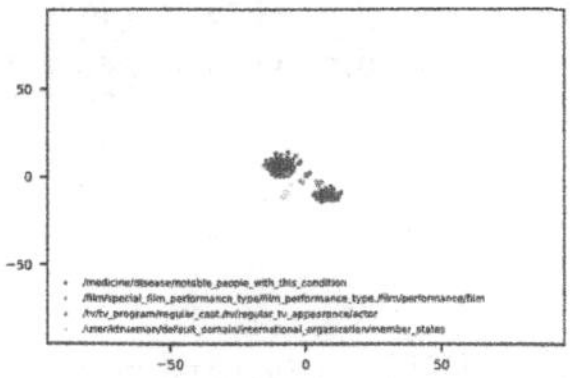

(a) QuatE$_{(1-N)}$ 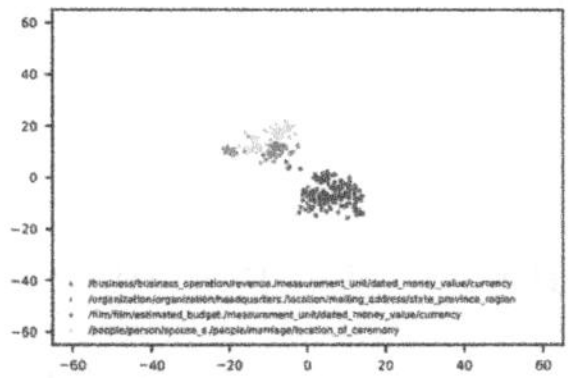   (b) QuatE$_{(N-1)}$ 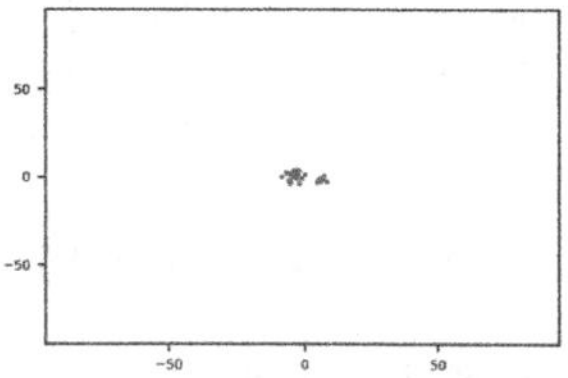   (c) QuatE$_{(MR)}$

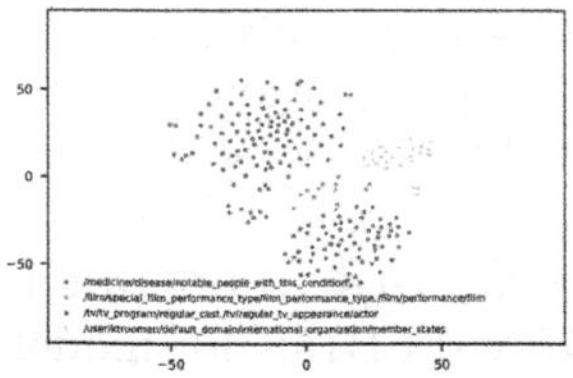

(d) QuatSE$_{(1-N)}$ 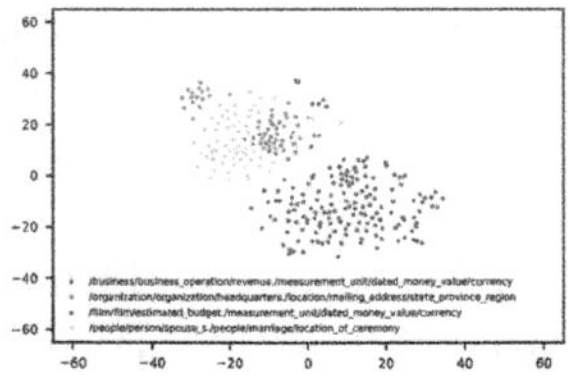   (e) QuatSE$_{(N-1)}$ 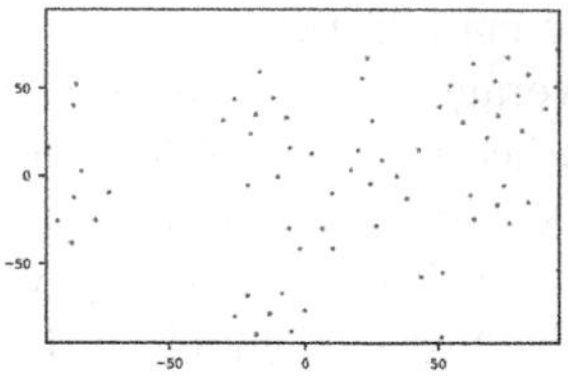   (f) QuatSE$_{(MR)}$

Fig. 2. Visualisations of the graph embeddings on the FB15K-237 test set. (a) and (d) are visualisations of the entity embeddings in 1-N. (b) and (e) are visualisations of the entity embeddings in N-1. (c) and (f) are visualisations of the 100 relation embeddings in multiple-relations pattern. MR: multiple-relations pattern.

6   Conclusion

This paper proposes an effective model which uses spherical linear interpolation to solve the problem of embedding overlap in graph embedding learning. QuatSE computes the spherical linear interpolation between each entity and its relation, and adds the normalized interpolation to the corresponding entities in embedding learning. We also theoretically analyze the effectiveness of QuatSE in dealing with complex triple patterns. Experimental results indicate that QuatSE achieves a consistent improvement for knowledge graph complementation task on benchmark databases. The experimental results suggest that QuatSE can avoid the problem of embedding overlap in learning 1-N, N-1 and multiple-relations pattern.

Acknowledgement. This work was funded by National Natural Science Foundation of China (Grant No. 61762069), Key Technology Research Program of Inner Mongolia Autonomous Region (Grant No. 2021GG0165), Key R&D and Achievement Transformation Program of Inner Mongolia Autonomous Region (Grant No. 2022YFHH0077), Big Data Lab of Inner Mongolia Discipline Inspection and Supervision Committee (Grant No. 21500-5206043).

References

1. Balažević, I., Allen, C., Hospedales, T.M.: Hypernetwork knowledge graph embeddings. In: Tetko, I.V., Kůrková, V., Karpov, P., Theis, F. (eds.) ICANN 2019. LNCS, vol. 11731, pp. 553–565. Springer, Cham (2019). https://doi.org/10.1007/978-3-030-30493-5_52

2. Bordes, A., Usunier, N., Garcia-Duran, A., Weston, J., Yakhnenko, O.: Translating embeddings for modeling multi-relational data. Advances in neural information processing systems 26 (2013)

3. Cao, Z., Xu, Q., Yang, Z., Cao, X., Huang, Q.: Dual quaternion knowledge graph embeddings. In: Proceedings of the AAAI Conference on Artificial Intelligence, vol. 35, pp. 6894–6902 (2021)

4. Dettmers, T., Minervini, P., Stenetorp, P., Riedel, S.: Convolutional 2d knowledge graph embeddings. In: Thirty-Second AAAI Conference on Artificial Intelligence (2018)

5. Duchi, J., Hazan, E., Singer, Y.: Adaptive subgradient methods for online learning and stochastic optimization. J. Mach. Learn. Res. **12**(7) (2011)

6. Gao, H., Yang, K., Yang, Y., Zakari, R.Y., Owusu, J.W., Qin, K.: Quatde: dynamic quaternion embedding for knowledge graph completion. arXiv preprint arXiv:2105.09002 (2021)

7. Gao, L., Zhu, H., Zhuo, H.H., Xu, J.: Dual quaternion embeddings for link prediction. Appl. Sci. **11**(12) (2021). https://doi.org/10.3390/app11125572

8. He, K., Zhang, X., Ren, S., Sun, J.: Delving deep into rectifiers: surpassing human-level performance on imagenet classification. In: Proceedings of the IEEE International Conference on Computer Vision, pp. 1026–1034 (2015)

9. Ji, G., He, S., Xu, L., Liu, K., Zhao, J.: Knowledge graph embedding via dynamic mapping matrix. In: Proceedings of the 53rd Annual Meeting of the Association for Computational Linguistics and the 7th International Joint Conference on Natural Language Processing (Volume 1: Long Papers). pp. 687–696 (2015)

10. Ji, G., Liu, K., He, S., Zhao, J.: Knowledge graph completion with adaptive sparse transfer matrix. In: Thirtieth AAAI Conference on Artificial Intelligence (2016)

11. Lin, Y., Liu, Z., Sun, M., Liu, Y., Zhu, X.: Learning entity and relation embeddings for knowledge graph completion. In: Twenty-ninth AAAI Conference on Artificial Intelligence (2015)

12. Van der Maaten, L., Hinton, G.: Visualizing data using t-sne. J. Mach. Learn. Res. **9**(11) (2008)

13. Miller, G.A.: Wordnet: a lexical database for English. Commun. ACM **38**(11), 39–41 (1995)
14. Nguyen, D.Q., Nguyen, T.D., Nguyen, D.Q., Phung, D.: A novel embedding model for knowledge base completion based on convolutional neural network. arXiv preprint arXiv:1712.02121 (2017)
15. Nguyen, D.Q., Vu, T., Nguyen, T.D., Phung, D.: Quatre: Relation-aware quaternions for knowledge graph embeddings. arXiv preprint arXiv:2009.12517 (2020)
16. Schlichtkrull, M., Kipf, T.N., Bloem, P., van den Berg, R., Titov, I., Welling, M.: Modeling relational data with graph convolutional networks. In: Gangemi, A., Navigli, R., Vidal, M.-E., Hitzler, P., Troncy, R., Hollink, L., Tordai, A., Alam, M. (eds.) ESWC 2018. LNCS, vol. 10843, pp. 593–607. Springer, Cham (2018). https://doi.org/10.1007/978-3-319-93417-4_38
17. Shoemake, K.: Animating rotation with quaternion curves. In: Proceedings of the 12th Annual Conference on Computer Graphics and Interactive Techniques, pp. 245–254 (1985)
18. Suchanek, F.M., Kasneci, G., Weikum, G.: Yago: a core of semantic knowledge. In: Proceedings of the 16th International Conference on World Wide Web, pp. 697–706 (2007)
19. Sun, Z., Deng, Z.H., Nie, J.Y., Tang, J.: Rotate: Knowledge graph embedding by relational rotation in complex space. arXiv preprint arXiv:1902.10197 (2019)
20. Toutanova, K., Chen, D.: Observed versus latent features for knowledge base and text inference. In: Proceedings of the 3rd Workshop on Continuous Vector Space Models and Their Compositionality, pp. 57–66 (2015)
21. Trouillon, T., Welbl, J., Riedel, S., Gaussier, É., Bouchard, G.: Complex embeddings for simple link prediction. In: International Conference on Machine Learning, pp. 2071–2080. PMLR (2016)
22. Vashishth, S., Sanyal, S., Nitin, V., Agrawal, N., Talukdar, P.: Interacte: Improving convolution-based knowledge graph embeddings by increasing feature interactions. In: Proceedings of the AAAI Conference on Artificial Intelligence, vol. 34, pp. 3009–3016 (2020)
23. Wang, Z., Zhang, J., Feng, J., Chen, Z.: Knowledge graph embedding by translating on hyperplanes. In: Proceedings of the AAAI Conference on Artificial Intelligence, vol. 28 (2014)
24. Xiao, H., Huang, M., Hao, Y., Zhu, X.: Transa: An adaptive approach for knowledge graph embedding. arXiv preprint arXiv:1509.05490 (2015)
25. Yang, S., Tian, J., Zhang, H., Yan, J., He, H., Jin, Y.: Transms: knowledge graph embedding for complex relations by multidirectional semantics. In: IJCAI, pp. 1935–1942 (2019)
26. Zhang, S., Tay, Y., Yao, L., Liu, Q.: Quaternion knowledge graph embeddings. Advances in neural information processing systems 32 (2019)

Entity Difference Modeling Based Entity Linking for Question Answering over Knowledge Graphs

Meiling Wang, Min Li, Kewei Sun, and Zhirong Hou[✉]

ICBC Technology Co Ltd., Beijing, China
{wangml,lim02,sunkw,houzr}@tech.icbc.com.cn

Abstract. Entity linking plays a vital role in Question Answering over Knowledge Graphs (KGQA), and the representation of entities is a fundamental component of entity linking for user questions. In order to alleviate the problem of entity descriptions that unrelated texts obfuscate similar entities, we present a new entity linking framework, which refines the encodings of entity descriptions based on entity difference modeling, so that entity linking's ability to distinguish among similar entities is improved. The entity differences are modeled in a two-stage approach: the initial differences are first computed among similar entity candidates by comparing their descriptions, and then interactions between the initial differences and questions are performed to extract key differences, which identify critical information for entity linking. On the basis of the key differences, subsequent entity description encodings are refined, and entity linking is then performed using the refined entity representations. Experimental results on end-to-end benchmark datasets demonstrate that our approach achieves state-of-the-art precision, recall and F1-score.

Keywords: Question answering over knowledge graphs · Entity linking · Mention detection · Entity disambiguation · Entity difference

1 Introduction

Question Answering systems over Knowledge Graphs (KGQA), which answer users' natural language questions with facts in Knowledge Graph (KG), allows users to obtain reliable information from KGs [5]. In order to obtain answers and build robust KGQA, Entity Linking for KGQA (ELQA), which links user questions with corresponding entities in KGs, is the first step [10]. ELQA typically involves two basic tasks: mention detection and entity disambiguation [7,12]. Mention detection extracts mention spans in the questions, and entity disambiguation maps these mentions to their correct entities. Taking the question "who played bilbo in lord of the rings?" in Table 1 as an example, the mention detection task tries to identify "lord of the rings" as a mention, and the entity disambiguation task attempts to link it to the appropriate WikiData entity.

© The Author(s), under exclusive license to Springer Nature Switzerland AG 2022
W. Lu et al. (Eds.): NLPCC 2022, LNAI 13551, pp. 221–233, 2022.
https://doi.org/10.1007/978-3-031-17120-8_18

Table 1. Results for linking an example question to entities using introductory texts. Entity introductory texts in parentheses are from Wikipedia articles.

Question	who played bilbo in lord of the rings?
GOLD result	lord of the rings→ "The Lord of the Rings (1978)" (The Lord of the Rings (1978) is a 1978 animated high fantasy film directed by Ralph Bakshi. It is an adaptation of J. R. R. Tolkien's high fantasy epic "The Lord of the Rings".)
PRED result	lord of the rings→ "The Lord of the Rings" (The Lord of the Rings is an epic high-fantasy novel by English author and scholar J. R. R. Tolkien.)

In ELQA, the major challenge lies in the fact that most real-world user questions are usually short texts and the scarce context can result in mention misidentification and linkage error [10,11], especially for similar entity candidates. For example, for entity candidate "The Lord of the Rings (1978)" and "The Lord of the Rings", it can be difficult to determine which one is linked to the mention "lord of the rings" in question "who played bilbo in lord of the rings?" based on the limited information of entity titles and question context. Numerous researchers have studied utilizing additional texts and knowledge graph context to enrich entity representations and tackle the challenge. In detail, descriptive texts, such as introductory texts of Wikipedia articles, are used to enrich descriptive knowledge [1,7,15], while knowledge graph context such as entities, relations and attributes are employed to enhance contextual knowledge [1,12]. Between the two approaches, encodings of entity descriptions are more accessible, but entity descriptions may contain many texts unrelated to user questions, which add noise to the distinguishing among similar entity candidates. As shown in Table 1, the word "Lord of the Rings" and "film" in the introductory text of "The Lord of the Rings (1978)" are the key clues for correct linking, but the other texts such as "high fantasy" and "J. R. R. Tolkien" are of little importance and cause obfuscation with "The Lord of the Rings". The problem can be alleviated by introducing entity difference information. The intuition is that humans generally distinguish similar entity candidates by comparing their descriptions and matching them with the user question to get critical information, and then make the decision for entity linking. For the above example, with the word "film", which appears exclusively in the description text of "The Lord of the Rings (1978)" and most related with the question context, human can determine that the mention "lord of the rings" is linked to the film entity but not the novel entity. Entity linking can be improved by introducing difference features among entity descriptions without adding additional data.

Based on the above idea, we propose an entity difference modeling based framework to improve the effectiveness of entity linking in distinguishing among similar entity candidates. We focus on the modeling of entity differences and its utilization to highlight critical information for entity linking and refine the encodings of entity descriptions. In detail, we retrieve similar entity candidates by matching encodings of entity descriptions, and the initial differences among the similar entity candidates are computed by comparing their descriptions. Furthermore, the initial differences are interacted with user question to extract key differences, which identify critical information for entity linking. With the key differences, the encodings of entity descriptions are refined to generate entity representations. Specifically, we respectively design lexical level and context-level difference computing and utilization approaches, and study their effects on entity linking. With the refined entity representations, mention detection and entity disambiguation are obtained by applying joint training to achieve their mutual enhancement. We conduct experimental evaluations on the end-to-end ELQA benchmark datasets WebQSP$_{EL}$ and GraphQ$_{EL}$ [7]. Results of model comparison demonstrate that our approach achieves state-of-the-art ELQA precision, recall and F1-score. In addition, results of ablation study and case study demonstrate the effectiveness of our design on entity difference modeling and utilization.

The contributions of this paper are threefold.

(1) We introduce entity difference to improve the ability of entity linking to distinguish among similar entity candidates. In our knowledge, this is the first work that introduces entity difference explicitly to solve ELQA.
(2) We propose a framework for entity difference modeling and its utilization to entity representation refinement, and the framework guarantees the applicability of entity difference in practice.
(3) We present the lexical level and context-level strategies for entity difference modeling, which improve ELQA effectively.

2 Related Work

We discuss related studies on entity linking in the context of KGQA, including aspects of entity representation and model architecture.

2.1 Entity Representation

Researchers have studied the solutions of utilizing descriptive texts and knowledge graph context to extend the basic representations of entity labels and titles. For the utilization of entity descriptions such as introductory texts from Wikipedia articles, Banerjee et al. [1] employ fastText embeddings of Wikidata descriptions, and Wu et al. [15] and Li et al. [7] apply BERT model [3] to encode Wikipedia descriptions. For the utilization of knowledge graph context such as entities, relations and attributes, Sorokin and Gurevych [12] train knowledge graph embeddings with TransE algorithm [2] and apply the embeddings of entities and relations that are connected to entity candidates. Banerjee et al. [1] employ pre-computed and pre-indexed embeddings learned with TransE algorithm over Wikidata.

Compared with knowledge graph context, encodings of entity descriptions are more accessible but may contain much unrelated information about question understanding. In this paper, we solve the problem by modeling the differences among entity descriptions.

2.2 Model Architecture

Existing approaches for ELQA are designed with pipeline architectures or joint architectures. In the approaches with pipeline architectures, mention detection and entity disambiguation are performed sequentially, where mention detection is mainly tackled by enumerating token n-grams and matching with certain dictionaries [4,8,9], and entity disambiguation is typically regarded as a ranking problem and solved by matching between mentions and entity candidates [15]. The deficiency of pipeline architectures lies in errors caused by mention detection will propagate to entity disambiguation without possibility of recovery.

Joint architectures are applied to alleviate the error propagation problems. Sorokin and Gurevych [12] propose a jointly optimized architecture using variable context granularity network, Banerjee et al. [1] propose an end-to-end model applying pointer network [14], and Li et al. [7] employ a bi-encoder based end-to-end model. In this paper, we follow the joint architecture of [7] to achieve mutual enhancement between mention detection and entity disambiguation.

3   Framework

Given a user question $q = (x_1, \cdots, x_{N_q})$ containing N_q tokens and the set of entity candidates $\mathcal{E} = \{e_i\}$, where e_i has a descriptive text $d(e_i)$, the goal of the ELQA task is to output a list of tuples, $(e, [start, end])$, whereby $e \in \mathcal{E}$ is the entity corresponding to the mention span from $start$-th to end-th token in q. Taking entity "The Lord of the Rings (1978)" as an example, its description is an introductory text from Wikipedia articles, as shown in Table 1.

Aiming to solve the ELQA task, our entity difference modeling based framework contains four modules as shown in Fig. 1. We employ a bi-encoder architecture based on BERT model for *Question Encoder* module and *Entity Encoder* module. *Question Encoder* module derives initial token-level encodings for user questions. For each entity candidate, *Entity Encoder* module generates its representation by encoding descriptive text off-line, retrieving similar entities off-line and refining description encoding based on the differences extracted among similar entities. Particularly, entity differences are initially computed by comparing the descriptions of similar entity candidates, and then key differences are extracted by the interaction with user question. We implement the difference computing and utilization with lexical level and context-level strategies. Base on the representations of user questions and entity candidates, *Mention Detection* module computes the likelihood scores of mention spans, and *Entity Disambiguation* module computes the likelihood distribution over all the entity candidates conditioned on mentions, and they are trained with joint optimization to achieve mutual enhancement.

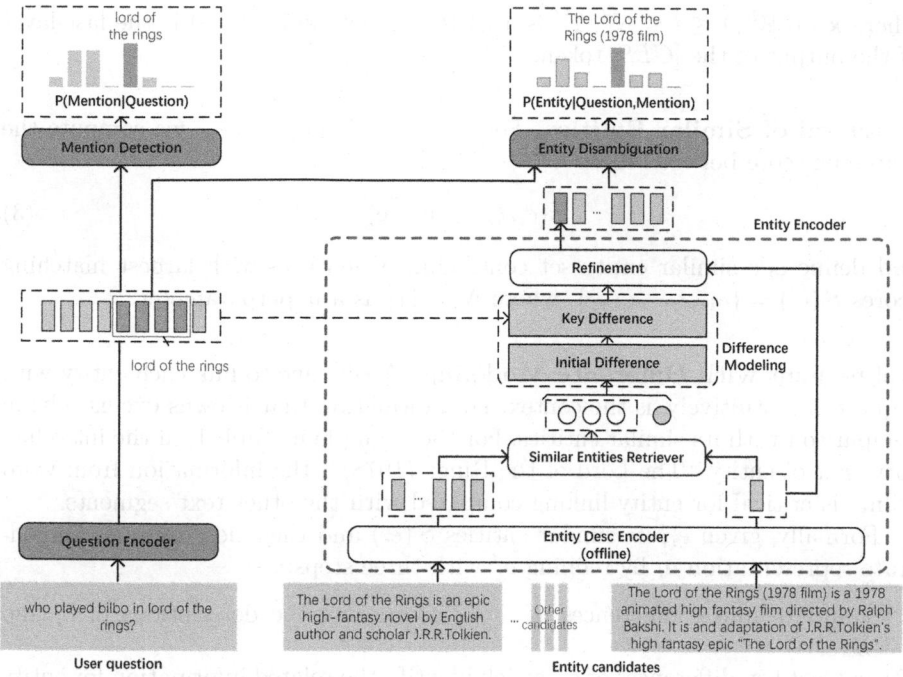

Fig. 1. Architecture of entity difference modeling based framework.

3.1   Question Encoder

For the user question $q = (x_1, \cdots, x_{N_q})$, we apply an encoder T^q to encode the context of q into token-level encodings $\mathbf{q} = (\mathbf{x}_1, \cdots, \mathbf{x}_{N_q})$,

$$(\mathbf{x}_1, \cdots, \mathbf{x}_{N_q}) = T^q(x_1, \cdots, x_{N_q}) \tag{1}$$

where $\mathbf{x}_j \in \mathbb{R}^h, 1 \le j \le N_q$ and T^q is a BERT model.

3.2   Entity Encoder

For each entity $e_i \in \mathcal{E}$, which has a descriptive text $d(e_i)$, we firstly encode $d(e_i)$ into vector $\mathbf{e}_i^d \in \mathbb{R}^h$, then retrieve its similar entities $S(e_i)$ by matching between vectors of entity descriptions, further encode differences between e_i and $S(e_i)$, and finally refine $\mathbf{e}_i^d$ as $\mathbf{e}_i \in \mathbb{R}^h$ with the difference encoding.

Encoding of Entity Descriptions. For e_i and its descriptive text $d(e_i) = (x_{i1}, \cdots, x_{iN_i^d})$ containing N_i^d tokens, we firstly apply an encoder T^d to encode $d(e_i)$ into sequence of vectors $(\mathbf{x}_{i1}, \cdots, \mathbf{x}_{iN_i^d})$, and then generate a context vector $\mathbf{e}_i^d \in \mathbb{R}^h$ with a reduction function $red^d(\cdot)$:

$$\mathbf{e}_i^d = red^d\left(T^d\left(x_{i1}, \cdots, x_{iN_i^d}\right)\right) \tag{2}$$

where $\mathbf{x}_{it} \in \mathbb{R}^h, 1 \leq t \leq N_i^d$, T^d is a BERT model, and $red^d(\cdot)$ is the last layer of the output of the $[CLS]$ token.

Retrieval of Similar Entities. For $\forall e_i, e_k \in \mathcal{E}$ and $e_i \neq e_k$, we compute the matching score between them:

$$s(e_i, e_k) = \mathbf{e}_i^d \cdot \mathbf{e}_k^d \tag{3}$$

and define e_i's similar entity set containing N_s entities with largest matching scores $S(e_i) = \{e_{i1}, \cdots, e_{iN_s}\}$, where $N_s \in \mathbb{N}_+$ is a hyperparameter.

Refinement with Difference Modeling. A key clue to link each entity with a question, intuitively, is the contextual information that it owns exclusively, in comparison with its similar entities. For the example in Table 1, in the introductory text of entity "The Lord of the Rings (1978)", the information from word "film" is critical for entity linking compared with the other text segments.

Formally, given e_i, its similar entities $S(e_i)$ and their descriptions, we generate representation $\mathbf{e}_i$ by refining $\mathbf{e}_i^d$ with three steps:

(1) compute initial differences of e_i by comparing the descriptions of e_i and $S(e_i)$;
(2) extract key differences of e_i, which identify the related information for entity linking to q, by interacting between the initial differences and q;
(3) refine $\mathbf{e}_i^d$ to $\mathbf{e}_i$ with the key differences.

We respectively explain the process at *lexical level* and *context-level*.

Lexical Level Modeling. Firstly, we compute the initial differences by subtraction on token sequences:

$$U(e_i) = (x_{i1}, \cdots, x_{iN_u}) = d(e_i) - (d(e_{i1}) \cup \cdots \cup d(e_{iN_s})) \tag{4}$$

where $U(e_i)$ contains at most N_u tokens by truncating if necessary, and $N_u \in \mathbb{N}_+$ is a hyperparameter. Then we concatenate q and $U(e_i)$, input them into the BERT encoder T^q to perform interaction and encoding, and get the vectors $(\mathbf{x}_{i1}, \cdots, \mathbf{x}_{iN_u})$ for $U(e_i)$. The key differences is computed as:

$$\mathbf{e}_i^u = \frac{1}{N_u} \sum_{t=1}^{N_u} \mathbf{x}_t \tag{5}$$

Finally, we compute the refined representation $\mathbf{e}_i$ of e_i:

$$\mathbf{e}_i = \mathbf{e}_i^d + \alpha \mathbf{e}_i^u \tag{6}$$

where α is a scaling factor and $0 \leq \alpha \leq 1$.

Context-Level Modeling. Firstly, given token-level encodings $\mathbf{q} = (\mathbf{x}_1, \cdots, \mathbf{x}_{N_q})$ of q, we obtain a sentence representation $\mathbf{q}^c$ with a reduction function $red^q(\cdot)$:

$$\mathbf{q}^c = red^q(\mathbf{x}_1, \cdots, \mathbf{x}_{N_q}) \tag{7}$$

where we choose $red^q(\cdot)$ as the average over all the vectors to catch more comprehensive information.

Then we compute the initial differences by subtraction between context vectors, i.e., $(\mathbf{e}_i^d - \mathbf{e}_{i1}^d), \cdots, (\mathbf{e}_i^d - \mathbf{e}_{iN_s}^d)$, and extract the key differences by weighted average of initial differences,

$$\mathbf{e}_i^u = \frac{1}{N_s} \sum_{t=1}^{N_s} w_{it}(\mathbf{e}_i^d - \mathbf{e}_{it}^d) \tag{8}$$

where related weights are computed with the attention to $\mathbf{q}^c$:

$$(w_{i1}, \ldots, w_{iN_s}) = \text{softmax} \left(\mathbf{q}^c \cdot (\mathbf{e}_i^d - \mathbf{e}_{i1}^d), \ldots, \mathbf{q}^c \cdot (\mathbf{e}_i^d - \mathbf{e}_{iN_s}^d) \right) \tag{9}$$

Finally, we obtain the refined representation $\mathbf{e}_i$ of e_i:

$$\mathbf{e}_i = \frac{N_s - 1}{N_s}\mathbf{e}_i^d + \mathbf{e}_i^u = \mathbf{e}_i^d - \frac{1}{N_s} \sum_{t=1}^{N_s} w_{it}\mathbf{e}_{it}^d \tag{10}$$

3.3 Mention Detection and Entity Disambiguation

Base on the entity representations for $\mathcal{E}$ and the question representation $(\mathbf{x}_1, \cdots, \mathbf{x}_{N_q})$ for $q = (x_1, \cdots, x_{N_q})$, we draw on the ideas of ELQ model [7] to implement mention detection and entity disambiguation, and jointly train them to achieve mutual enhancement. We briefly explain the process as follows.

For mention detection, we first compute scores for each token x_j in q being the start(s_l), the end(s_r) and part(s_p) of a mention, and then compute the likelihood score of each span $[start, end]$ being an entity mention in q up to length L.

$$s_l(j) = \mathbf{W}_l^T \mathbf{x}_j, \quad s_r(j) = \mathbf{W}_r^T \mathbf{x}_j, \quad s_p(j) = \mathbf{W}_p^T \mathbf{x}_j \tag{11}$$

$$p([start, end]) = \sigma \left(s_l(start) + s_r(end) + \sum_{t=start}^{end} s_p(t) \right) \tag{12}$$

where $\mathbf{W}_l, \mathbf{W}_r, \mathbf{W}_p \in \mathbb{R}^h$, $1 \leq start \leq end \leq \min(start + L - 1, N_q)$.

For entity disambiguation, we first compute the representation for mention span $[start, end]$ by averaging $\mathbf{x}_{start}, \cdots, \mathbf{x}_{end}$, and then compute the matching score $s(e, [start, end])$ between the mention and each entity $e \in \mathcal{E}$ by vector dot-product, and finally compute the likelihood distribution over all the entities in $\mathcal{E}$ conditioned on the mention:

$$p(e \mid [start, end]) = \frac{\exp(s(e, [start, end]))}{\sum_{e' \in \mathcal{E}} \exp(s(e', [start, end]))} \tag{13}$$

For joint training of mention detection and entity disambiguation, we optimize the loss:

$$\mathcal{L} = -\frac{1}{N_{mc}} \sum_{\substack{1 \leq start \leq end \leq \\ \min(start+L-1, N_q)}} (y_{[start,end]} \log(p([start, end]) \cdot p(e_g \mid [start, end]))$$

$$+ (1 - y_{[start,end]}) \log(1 - p([start, end]))) \tag{14}$$

Table 2. Dataset statistics of WebQSP$_{EL}$ and GraphQ$_{EL}$. #**Q** and #**E** indicate the number of questions and entity mentions, respectively.

Data	Train		Test	
	#Q	#E	#Q	#E
WebQSP$_{EL}$	2974	3242	1603	1806
GraphQ$_{EL}$	2089	2253	2075	2229

whereby $y_{[start,end]}$ is the label for mention span, and $y_{[start,end]} = 1$ if $[start, end]$ is a gold mention and 0 otherwise. e_g is the gold entity corresponding to mention span $[start, end]$. N_{mc} is the total number of mention candidates and its value is selected in the same manner as ELQ model.

4   Experiments

We conduct experiments on the end-to-end ELQA benchmark datasets WebQSP$_{EL}$ and GraphQ$_{EL}$ [7] to evaluate our approach. WebQSP$_{EL}$ and GraphQ$_{EL}$ are derived from publicly available QA datasets WebQSP [16] and GraphQuestions [13], where WebQSP was collected from web search logs and GraphQuestions was created from manual paraphrases for automatically generated questions. Table 2 shows the statistics of WebQSP$_{EL}$ and GraphQ$_{EL}$.

We evaluate the performance of ELQA approaches using precision, recall and F1-score of entity linking. Following the definitions of Li et al. [7], a ELQA prediction is correct only if the groundtruth entity is identified and the predicted mention span overlaps with the groundtruth span.

4.1   Model Comparison

Baselines. The compared baselines for our approach are listed below.

(1) TAGME [4] is a lightweight and on-the-fly entity linking system popular for many downstream QA tasks.
(2) VCG [12] is a jointly optimized neural architecture for ELQA. It derives entity embeddings using entity labels and knowledge graph context.
(3) BLINK [15] is an entity disambiguation model with pre-specified mention boundaries. It derives entity embeddings using descriptive texts.
(4) ELQ [7] is the current state-of-the-art model on WebQSP$_{EL}$ and GraphQ$_{EL}$. It encodes entity descriptions and questions with a BERT-based bi-encoder.

Experimental Settings. We employ BERT$_{Large}$[1] as the basic model for bi-encoder, and reuse encodings of entity descriptions released by [7]. We evaluate our framework on WebQSP$_{EL}$ and GraphQ$_{EL}$ test data under two settings.

---

[1] Model available at https://huggingface.co/bert-large-uncased/tree/main.

Table 3. Results of model comparison on test data. Highest scores per setting are underlined. Model* denotes application of our approach without training. For baselines, we follow the results reported in [7].

Setting	Model	WebQSP$_{EL}$			GraphQ$_{EL}$(zero-shot)		
		Prec	Recall	F1	Prec	Recall	F1
Wikipedia	TAGME	53.1	27.3	36.1	49.6	36.5	42.0
	BLINK	82.2	79.4	80.8	65.3	61.2	63.2
	ELQ	86.1	81.8	83.9	69.8	69.8	69.8
	DIF$^*_{lex}$	86.1	82.0	84.0	69.7	<u>70.0</u>	69.9
	DIF$^*_{ctx}$	<u>86.4</u>	<u>82.1</u>	<u>84.2</u>	<u>70.1</u>	69.9	<u>70.0</u>
WebQSP$_{EL}$	VCG	82.4	68.3	74.7	54.1	30.6	39.0
	ELQ	90.0	85.0	87.4	60.1	57.2	58.6
	DIF$_{lex}$	91.3	85.7	88.4	69.4	57.8	63.1
	DIF$_{ctx}$	<u>92.1</u>	<u>85.8</u>	<u>88.8</u>	<u>69.7</u>	<u>58.1</u>	<u>63.4</u>

(1) Wikipedia setting. We first evaluate our framework on test data without training. In detail, we implement our framework based on the inference process of Wikipedia-trained ELQ model[2] and compare with Wikipedia-trained baselines. We refer to the evaluation results of lexical level modeling and context-level modeling as DIF$^*_{lex}$ and DIF$^*_{ctx}$ respectively.

(2) WebQSP$_{EL}$ setting. We implement our framework, train it on WebQSP$_{EL}$, and predict on test data. We refer to the evaluation results of lexical level modeling and context-level modeling as DIF$_{lex}$ and DIF$_{ctx}$ respectively.

For both training and prediction, mention detection considers all the candidate spans up to length $L = 10$. 10 closest entity candidates for each mention span are retrieved by FAISS index [6] using encodings of entity descriptions, and then they are re-ranked using the refined encodings of entities. 4 most similar entities are retrieved for difference modeling, i.e., $N_s = 4$. For lexical level modeling, initial differences contain at most 9 tokens, i.e., $N_u = 9$, and scaling factor α is set as 0.01 for entity encoding refinement.

Experimental Results. Table 3 displays the evaluation results of our approach and baseline models.

We find that:

– Among all the models evaluated under Wikipedia setting, DIF$^*_{lex}$ increases recall and F1-score, and DIF$^*_{ctx}$ achieves the best precision and F1-score. The results demonstrate that improvement can be obtained by directly applying entity difference without training.

---

[2] Code, data and model available at https://github.com/facebookresearch/BLINK/tree/master/elq.

Table 4. Results of ablation study on test data.

Setting	Model	WebQSP$_{EL}$			GraphQ$_{EL}$(zero-shot)		
		Prec	Recall	F1	Prec	Recall	F1
WebQSP$_{EL}$	DIF$_{ctx}$	92.1	85.8	88.8	69.7	58.1	63.4
	w/o Ita	91.0	85.8	88.3	68.5	55.8	61.5

- Among all the models trained on WebQSP$_{EL}$, DIF$_{ctx}$ performs the best in precision, recall and F1-score on both test data. DIF$_{lex}$ is closer to DIF$_{ctx}$ than baselines. When compared with baselines, DIF$_{ctx}$ and DIF$_{lex}$ obtain greater improvement in precision than in recall and F1-score. The results demonstrate that entity difference modeling effectively improves entity linking, and benefits precision in particular.

The possible reason for better performance of context-level strategy than lexical level strategy is that it can extract more comprehensive difference information. In sum, DIF$_{ctx}$ achieves state-of-the-art precision, recall and F1-score.

4.2 Ablation Study

We evaluate whether and how the interaction between initial differences and questions in the stage of key difference extraction contributes to DIF$_{ctx}$. The experiment ablates the below component:

- w/o Ita, where the interaction is removed, that is attention is not performed in the stage of key differences extraction, and all the initial differences have equal importance weights towards the current user question.

Table 4 displays the evaluation results on WebQSP$_{EL}$ and GraphQ$_{EL}$ under the WebQSP$_{EL}$ setting in Sect. 4.1. More decline in precision and recall is observed respectively on WebQSP$_{EL}$ and GraphQ$_{EL}$, and the possible reason is that the two datasets have different complexity. The results demonstrate the necessity to perform the interaction between initial differences and questions for DIF$_{ctx}$.

4.3 Case Study

Table 5 displays three typical test cases for comparing DIF$_{lex}$, DIF$_{ctx}$ and ELQ.

- Case 1 shows that DIF$_{lex}$ and DIF$_{ctx}$ link mention "glen johnson" to entity "Glen Johnson" correctly by highlighting the information of "played predominantly as a right back", but ELQ cannot.
- Case 2 shows that ELQ misses mention "holy temple", but DIF$_{lex}$ and DIF$_{ctx}$ detect and link it to entity "Temple in Jerusalem" correctly with the key clues about religion getting from "Mosque".

Table 5. Examples for case study. Red represents incorrect entity linking.

1	Question	What position does glen johnson play?
	ELQ	glen johnson-> "Glen Johnson (Canadian soccer)"
	DIF_{lex}&DIF_{ctx}	glen johnson-> "Glen Johnson"
	Descriptive texts	"Glen Johnson": Glen McLeod Cooper Johnson is an English for-mer professional footballer who played predominantly as a right back. "Glen Johnson (Canadian soccer)": Glen Johnson is a former Canadian international soccer player.
2	Question	What kind of beliefs do the holy temple have in its religion?
	ELQ	[]
	DIF_{lex}&DIF_{ctx}	holy temple-> "Temple in Jerusalem"
	Descriptive texts	"Temple in Jerusalem": The Temple in Jerusalem was any of a series of structures which were located on the Temple Mount in the Old City of Jerusalem, the current site of the Dome of the Rock and Al-Aqsa Mosque. "Temple": A temple is a building reserved for spiritual rituals and activities such as prayer and sacrifice.
3	Question	List programming languages originating from microsoft.
	ELQ&DIF_{lex}	microsoft-> "Microsoft", list programming languages-> "List (abstract data type)"
	DIF_{ctx}	microsoft-> "Microsoft"
	Descriptive texts	"Microsoft": Microsoft Corporation is an American multinational technology company with headquarters in Redmond, Washington. "List (abstract data type)": In computer science, a list is an abst-ract data type that represents a finite number of ordered values.

- Case 3 shows that DIF_{lex} and ELQ misidentify mention "list programming languages", but DIF_{ctx} corrects the error by interacting with question more comprehensively.

The three examples demonstrate that our approaches effectively correct errors with entity difference modeling, and the context-level approach is more effective for solving mention misidentification.

5 Conclusion

In this paper, we propose an entity difference modeling based framework to improve entity linking. To alleviate the deficiency of description-based entity representations in entity linking to similar entity candidates, we design the strategies of entity difference modeling and its utilization to refine entity representations. With experimental evaluations, we demonstrate that our approach outperforms previous state-of-the-art models on precision, recall and F1-score.

In addition to its application to KBQA, our approach could be extended to broader domains of short texts including tweet and search queries, which indicates a novel insight into short text context. We plan to study strategies to improve zero-shot entity linking for short texts in the future.

References

1. Banerjee, D., Chaudhuri, D., Dubey, M., Lehmann, J.: PNEL: pointer network based end-to-end entity linking over knowledge graphs. In: Pan, J.Z., Tamma, V., d'Amato, C., Janowicz, K., Fu, B., Polleres, A., Seneviratne, O., Kagal, L. (eds.) ISWC 2020. LNCS, vol. 12506, pp. 21–38. Springer, Cham (2020). https://doi.org/10.1007/978-3-030-62419-4_2
2. Bordes, A., Usunier, N., Garcia-Durán, A., Weston, J., Yakhnenko, O.: Translating embeddings for modeling multi-relational data. In: 26th International Conference on Neural Information Processing Systems, pp. 2787–2795 (2013)
3. Devlin, J., Chang, M.W., Lee, K., Toutanova, K.: BERT: pre-training of deep bidirectional transformers for language understanding. In: 2019 Conference of the North American Chapter of the Association for Computational Linguistics: Human Language Technologies, pp. 4171–4186 (2019)
4. Ferragina, P., Scaiella, U.: Fast and accurate annotation of short texts with wikipedia pages. IEEE Softw. 29(1), 70–75 (2011)
5. Gu, Y., et al.: Beyond IID: three levels of generalization for question answering on knowledge bases. In: Web Conference 2021, pp. 3477–3488 (2021)
6. Johnson, J., Douze, M., Jégou, H.: Billion-scale similarity search with GPUs. IEEE Transactions on Big Data (2019)
7. Li, B.Z., Min, S., Iyer, S., Mehdad, Y., Yih, W.T.: Efficient one-pass end-to-end entity linking for questions. In: 2020 Conference on Empirical Methods in Natural Language Processing, pp. 6433–6441 (2020)
8. Sakor, A., et al.: Old is gold: linguistic driven approach for entity and relation linking of short text. In: 2019 Conference of the North American Chapter of the Association for Computational Linguistics: Human Language Technologies, pp. 2336–2346 (2019)
9. Sakor, A., Singh, K., Patel, A., Vidal, M.E.: Falcon 2.0: an entity and relation linking tool over wikidata. In: 29th ACM International Conference on Information & Knowledge Management, pp. 3141–3148 (2020)
10. Singh, K., Lytra, I., Radhakrishna, A.S., Shekarpour, S., Vidal, M.E., Lehmann, J.: No one is perfect: analysing the performance of question answering components over the dbpedia knowledge graph. J. Web Semant. 65, 100594 (2020)
11. Singh, K., et al.: Why reinvent the wheel: let's build question answering systems together. In: 2018 World Wide Web Conference, pp. 1247–1256 (2018)
12. Sorokin, D., Gurevych, I.: Mixing context granularities for improved entity linking on question answering data across entity categories. In: 7th Joint Conference on Lexical and Computational Semantics, pp. 65–75 (2018)
13. Su, Y., et al.: On generating characteristic-rich question sets for QA evaluation. In: 2016 Conference on Empirical Methods in Natural Language Processing, pp. 562–572 (2016)
14. Vinyals, O., Fortunato, M., Jaitly, N.: Pointer networks. Adv. Neural Info. Proc. Syst. 28, 2692–2700 (2015)

15. Wu, L., Petroni, F., Josifoski, M., Riedel, S., Zettlemoyer, L.: Scalable zero-shot entity linking with dense entity retrieval. In: 2020 Conference on Empirical Methods in Natural Language Processing, pp. 6397–6407 (2020)
16. Yih, W.T., Richardson, M., Meek, C., Chang, M.W., Suh, J.: The value of semantic parse labeling for knowledge base question answering. In: 54th Annual Meeting of the Association for Computational Linguistics, pp. 201–206 (2016)

BG-EFRL: Chinese Named Entity Recognition Method and Application Based on Enhanced Feature Representation

XianKun Zhang and SiYuan Peng$^{(\boxtimes)}$

Tianjin University of Science and Technology, Tianjin, China
`psy18986483462@mail.tust.edu.cn`

Abstract. Named Entity Recognition (NER) aims to mine meaningful entity information (eg, organization, place, person, etc.) in text. Due to the high dependence of Chinese NER on Chinese Word Segmentation (CWS), the negative impact of word segmentation errors in current models has to be bridged, but these models only focus on adjacent words and the words themselves. To this end, we propose a method that combines sentence context and text global relationship modeling (BG-EFRL), based on Transformer Encoder (BERT) and Graph Convolutional Network (GCN), with the help of the former self-attention weights to generate assist features to dynamically strengthen contextual representation. Experiments show that BG-EFRL is competitive on two real datasets, Weibo and Resume, and apply it to the food safety domain.

Keywords: Named entity recognition · Contextual features · Assist feature

1 Introduction

Named Entity Recognition (NER) [1] is a roally basic task in Natural Language Processing (NLP), and it is an important basic tool for many NLP tasks such as information extraction [2], question answering systems [3], and syntactic analysis [4], etc.

In recent years, with the continuous development of deep learning technology, many key problems in this field have also achieved corresponding breakthroughs. Lattice [5] generated an LSTM Chinese NER model similar to the "lattice" structure by pre-encoding the input characters and subwords. Compared with the character-based model, the model considers word order information, which is different from the word-based model. In contrast, this model is not affected by CWS [6]. The CAN-NER model [7] utilizes a convolutional neural network (CNN) with a local self-attention layer and a gated neural unit (GRU) with a global attention layer to capture adjacent character and sentence context information, thereby solving the problem of Segmentation errors and dictionary overflow (OOV) problems due to word-level embeddings and dictionary features.

However, the above model avoids the negative impact of Chinese word segmentation, it relies on a large amount of well-structured and labeled data for training, which makes the model often limited to training in the face of high-speed production, diverse

W. Lu et al. (Eds.): NLPCC 2022, LNAI 13551, pp. 234–245, 2022.
https://doi.org/10.1007/978-3-031-17120-8_19

expressions, and a large amount of hoarded entity information. Data type, which also leads to the poor generalization ability of the above model. Therefore, it cannot really be applied effectively.

Therefore, many studies start with models in recent. KARL [8] utilizes knowledge bases known in the domain to model tasks to extract latent entity information residing in them to generate features for feature-augmented group representations Context triples. However, the above method also has certain limitations, because the words of the language may be ambiguous, especially the Chinese words, it does not consider any semantic information about the entities, which may have the opposite effect to the expected results. WSRL [9] proposed the idea of using CWS and NER tasks for joint training to generate features. However, the model only pays attention to the commonalities of the two, and does not distinguish and prevent the differences of each task, which will bring noise to both tasks at the same time. For example, given the sentence in Fig. 1, for the word "甜蜜素", both give correct results, while for the more complex word "甘草仁面", CWS gives incorrect results, and NER expects More fine-grained recognition effects.

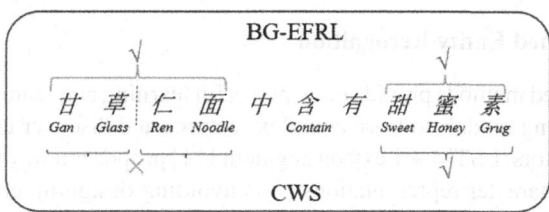

Fig. 1. An example in our dataset, in a sentence, √ indicates correct segmentation and × indicates incorrect segmentation. Both CWS and NER can correctly segment "甜蜜素", but for the more complex "甘草仁面", CWS gives wrong results.

In response to the above problems, inspired by BERT4GCN [10], this paper proposes a reinforcement representation learning network BG-EFRL that combines BERT [16] and GCN [27, 28] for Chinese named entity recognition. Specifically, BG-EFRL relies on the unique structural information of the graph neural network, that is, it can cross-aggregate the global information (sentences), vertex information (words), and edge information (relationships between words) of the graph to dynamically generate assist features used to enhance contextual representation, such as syntactic and grammatical information, compensate for the negative impact of word segmentation. Figure 2 shows the information transfer process of the dependency graph. It is worth noting that it not only uses GCN to enhance contextual features, but also dynamically initializes the graph structure of GCN with the help of BERT's self-attention mechanism, making it more suitable for Chinese NER tasks.

Our contributions are summarized as follows:

- We propose a new Chinese NER model BG-EFRL.
- For the first time, the GCN model is used in the Chinese NER task to mine the global information of the text to enhance the task.

– The effectiveness, practicability, and generalization of the model are demonstrated on two public datasets and one food dataset.

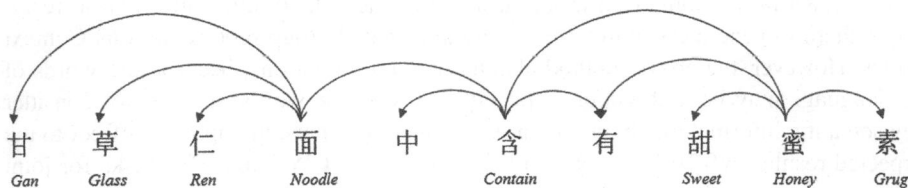

Fig. 2. An example sentence along with its dependency graph. GCNs propagate the information of anode to its nearest neighbors.

2   Related Work

2.1   Chinese Named Entity Recognition

Deep learning-based methods provide more powerful learning and feature representation capabilities, enabling models to learn complex features and discover useful representations and latent factors. LSTM + Lexicon augment [11] proposes a way to integrate word dictionaries into character representations, thus avoiding designing complex sequence modeling architectures. SLK-NER [12] presents new insights into second-order dictionary knowledge of each character in a sentence to provide more lexical information, including semantic and word boundary features. AESINER [13] leverages different types of syntactic information through attention ensemble to enhance Chinese NER tasks comprehensively and selectively. All the above models enhance the NER task from different perspectives, howerer, ignore the mining of meaningful global information.

In order to solve the above problems, this paper proposes a method that considers both word context information, syntactic and grammatical information, so as to obtain a more accurate word embedding representation for sequence labeling.

2.2   Embedding Representation

A key factor contributing to the success of NER is how we capture meaningful contextual features from the raw data through word representations, in addition we introduce assist features to reinforce the contextual features.

- **Word embeddings.** It is the cornerstone of all NLP downstream tasks and aims to embed a high-dimensional space of the number of all words into a continuous vector space of much lower dimensionality, assigning each word a specific vector representation. The main word embedding techniques are onehot, Word2vec [14], etc.

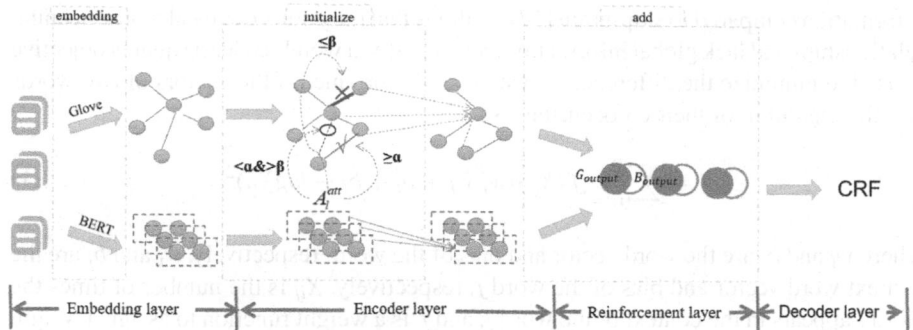

Fig. 3. Overall architecture of the model BG-EFRL

- **Contextual embeddings.** It is complementary to word vector representation because relying only on word embeddings without considering the contextual meaning of words, i.e. the contextual meaning around words, cannot satisfy the NER task. For example, "杜鹃" in two sentences "山上到处是盛开的杜鹃" and "树林里传来了杜鹃的叫声" will be given the exact same vector representation if the contextual meaning of the word is not considered, which may confuse our model and reduce its accuracy. The main contextual embedding techniques are ELMo [15], BERT [16, 26], etc.

- **Graph embeddings.** It is complement word contextual representations and can be used to capture meaningful semantic and syntactic information and disambiguate ambiguous words or sentences. For example, the Chinese combinational ambiguity includes "他将来我校讲学" and "从马上跳下来", and the Chinese intersection ambiguity includes "甘草仁面中含有甜蜜素" and "研究生命的起源". Without considering the syntactic and grammatical information of the words, it is difficult for the model to accurately identify such subtle differences. The main graph embedding techniques are skip-gram [17], Glove [18, 25] and so on.

The combination of contextual embedding and graph embedding successfully explores and exploits the contextual relevance and ambiguity of words, thus surpassing other Chinese NER tasks.

3   NER Model

This section will introduce the proposed model BG-EFRL in detail. The overall framework of the model is shown in Fig. 3, which consists of three parts: the embedding layer, the feature extraction layer and the conditional random field layer.

3.1   Embedding Representation

For one of the inputs of the encoding layer, we use the BERT embedding [26] with better contextual embedding to generate the input of the BERT layer. As another input, we use the Glove [18, 25] model based on bisection loss, which incorporates global information compared to skip-gram [17] methods that only consider local word-meaning relationships and lack global information. Specifically, a weighted least squares objective is used to minimize the difference between the dot product of the vectors of two words and the logarithm of their co-occurrences:

$$J = \sum_{i,j=1}^{V} f(X_{ij})(w_i^T \tilde{w}_j + b_i + \tilde{b}_j - logX_{ij})^2 \tag{1}$$

where w_i and b_i are the word vector and bias of the word, respectively. $\tilde{w}_j$ and $\tilde{b}_j$ are the context word vector and bias of the word j, respectively. X_{ij} is the number of times the word i appears in the context of the word j, and f is a weight function to assign a weight limit to low-frequency words and high-frequency words:

$$f(x) = \begin{cases} (x/x_{\max})^\alpha & x < x_{\max} \\ 1 & otherwise \end{cases} \tag{2}$$

where x_{max} is fixed at 100 and α is fixed at 3/4.

3.2 Initialize the Graph Structure

Since the self-attention mechanism of the pretrained BERT encoder captures long-distance dependencies between words, we directly use the self-attention weights to dynamically initialize the graph structure. Specifically, we first obtain the self-attention weight tensor $A^{att} = [W_4^{att}, W_8^{att}]$, where each $W_i^{att} \in R^{h \times n \times n}$ represents the self-attention weight tensor of the i-th layer encoder of BERT, h represents the number of attention heads, and then computes A^{att} average:

$$\overline{A}_l^{att} = \frac{1}{h} \sum_{i=1}^{h} A_{l,i}^{att} \tag{3}$$

where A_l^{att} represents the l element of A^{att}, $l \in \{1,2\}$. Finally, we remove or add directed edges between words if the averaged attention weight is greater or less than some threshold. Therefore, the graph structure of the l-th layer of the GCN after initialization can be expressed as:

$$A_{l,i,j}^{init} = \begin{cases} 1 & \alpha \leq \overline{A}_{l,i,j}^{att} \\ A_{i,j} & \beta < \overline{A}_{l,i,j}^{att} < \alpha \\ 0 & \overline{A}_{l,i,j}^{att} \leq \beta \end{cases} \tag{4}$$

3.3 Encoders

BERT Encoder. BERT [16] is a pre-trained language model based on bidirectional Transformer, which, unlike traditional neural networks, provides the best choice for extracting contextual features of each word. Its inputs are represented as [CLS] sentences [SEP], and through bidirectional context learning, it avoids the shortcomings of self-encoding language models and exhibits excellent performance in language tasks involving long contexts. We exploit the permutation language modeling objective and bidirectional self-attention architecture, combined with the relative position encoding scheme and the Transformer's fragment recursion mechanism, to obtain contextual features from the sequence:

$$Attention(Q, K, V) = softmax(\frac{QK^T}{\sqrt{d_k}})V$$

$$MultiHead(Q, K, V) = Concat(head_1, head_2, \dots, head_h)W^o$$

$$head_i = Attention\left(QW_i^Q, KW_i^K, VW_i^V\right)$$ (5)

where Q, K, V are the input word vector matrix; d_k is the input dimension; BERT adopts the multi-head mode, projects Q, K, V through h linear transformations, and finally splices different $head_i$ together as context features for output.

GCN Encoder. GCN [19] uses two layers of convolution to input the feature matrix X and the initialized adjacency matrix A into the graph convolution layer to capture assist features. Specifically, given a specific graph-based neural network model $f(X, A)$, GCN follows the layer-by-layer propagation rule:

$$H^{(l+1)} = \sigma(\tilde{D}^{-\frac{1}{2}}\tilde{A}\tilde{D}^{-\frac{1}{2}}H^{(l)}W^{(l)})$$ (6)

where D is the degree matrix, f is a neural network similar to a differentiable function, $\tilde{A} = A + I_N$ is the adjacency matrix of the undirected graph G with self-connections added, I_N is the identity matrix of N nodes, and $\tilde{D}_i = \sum_j \tilde{A}_{ij}$, $W^{(l)}$ is Neural network layer specific training weight matrix. σ is the activation function, H is the activation matrix of the l-th layer, $H^{(0)} = X$. After computing the normalized adjacency matrix $\tilde{D}^{-\frac{1}{2}}\tilde{A}\tilde{D}^{-\frac{1}{2}}$ during preprocessing, the GCN forward model can be expressed as:

$$Z = f(X, A) = softmax(\tilde{A}\sigma(\tilde{A}XW^0)W^1)$$ (7)

where W^0 and W^1 are the weight matrix from the input to the hidden layer and the weight matrix from the hidden layer to the output, respectively. The gradient descent algorithm is used for training, and the weights before input to the linear layer with activation function are output as assist features.

3.4 Feature Enhancer

After the context features and assist features obtained through BERT and GCN, since more node information needs to be preserved during graph embedding, the output feature length after graph convolution will be longer than that of BERT embedding. Therefore, we perform dimensionality reduction on the output features of the graph embedding. In order to prevent the loss of node information caused by dimensionality reduction, we use Laplacian Eigenmaps [20] (Laplacian feature maps) for dimensionality reduction. Laplacian feature map is a graph-based dimensionality reduction algorithm, which can ensure that points that are related to each other (points connected in the graph) are as close as possible in the space after dimensionality reduction, so that after dimensionality reduction the original data structure can still be maintained. Finally, we fuse the output features of the BERT embedding with the output features of the GCN embedding after dimensionality reduction. The specific formula is as follows:

$$add(B_{output}, G_{output}) \tag{8}$$

where $add(\cdot)$ is the feature fusion operation, B_{output} is the output feature of BERT, and G_{output} is the output feature of GCN.

3.5 Decoder

The essence of using CRF [21] for final prediction is to decode the output of the coding layer (BERT + GCN), calculate the label score corresponding to the named entity, get the probability of the label sequence and find the sequence with the highest probability.

The tag score consists of two parts, the emission score and the transfer score, which are denoted as E and T respectively. The former is mainly determined by the coding layer, and the latter is mainly determined by the CRF:

$$score(x) = \sum_{i=1}^{n} E_i + \sum_{i=1}^{n+1} T_i \tag{9}$$

where x represents the entire input sequence, E_i the emission fraction at the ith time step, and T_i the transition fraction at the i-th time step.

4 Experiments

4.1 Datasets and Metrics

We conduct Chinese NER tasks on two real datasets, Weibo and Resume, and the experimental results demonstrate the effectiveness of BG-EFRL. At the same time, in order to verify the generalization and practicability of our model, we use web crawler technology to continuously collect media news and food safety-related corpora published by food cases from the public Chinese food safety website and the People's Daily website, and manually annotate 4 Various entity types (food names, additive names, place names, and generic entities) were used to construct the FoodPubDatas dataset. Table 1 gives the statistical details of the three datasets.

To evaluate the performance of the BG-EFRL method, we use precision, recall, and F1-value as metrics (Fig. 4).

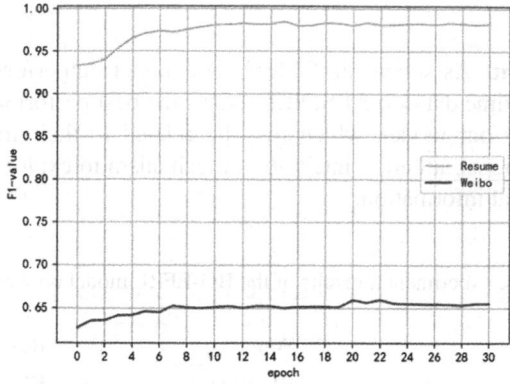

Fig. 4. Baseline experiments of BG-EFRL on weibo and resume datasets

4.2 Implementation Details

We implemented our model using PyCharm, TensorFlow, Pytorch. Specifically, we use BERT embeddings and Glove embeddings to pre-train 768-dimensional and 256-dimensional word vectors, respectively, to initialize the corresponding word embedding vectors. $Encoder_{BERT}$ uses a basic pretrained BERT model, and $Encoder_{GCN}$ uses $Encoder_{BERT}$ for initialization. The batch size for all models is set to 16. All models are optimized by the Adam optimizer. The learning rate of all models is set to 5e-5. Since the GCN model needs to be initialized with the BERT model, for BG-EFRL, BERT is trained first, and then both GCN and BERT are trained. We run all models 4 times and report the average results on the test dataset.

Table 1. Dataset statistics details.

Datasets	Train	Dev	Test	Entity type
Weibo	1.9K	0.4k	0.4K	4
Resume	13.4K	1.5k	1.6k	8
FoodPubDatas	48K	8k	8k	4

4.3 Comparison Methods

We compare our method with several classes of methods proposed for Chinese NER tasks, including i) two original models, BiLSTM [22] is a sequence labeling model including BiLSTM layers and CRF layers, BERT [16] is a Pre-trained models with deep bidirectional transformers. ii) Two models that complement word segmentation errors, Lattice [5], CAN-NER Model [6], iii) Other models with better performance, TENER [23], FLAT [24], LSTM + Lexicon augment [11], SLK-NER [12], AESINER [13].

4.4   Results

Baseline Experiment. As shown in Table 2, our model outperforms other arbitrary baselines on the Resume dataset, AESINER shows the best performance on the Weibo dataset, followed by our model, which may be related to their improving NER by introducing an additional attention integration mechanism to exploit different types of syntactic-grammatical information.

Table 2. Baseline experimental results of the BG-EFRL model on weibo and resume

Model	Weibo	Resume
	F1-value	F1-value
BiLSTM	56.6	93.5
BERT	**62.5**	**95.0**
Lattice	58.8	94.4
CAN-NER Model	**59.3**	**94.9**
TENER	58.2	95.0
FLAT	60.3	95.4
LSTM + Lexicon augment	61.2	95.5
SLK-NER	64.0	95.8
AESINER	**69.7**	**96.6**
BG-EFRL	**65.4**	**96.7**

Table 3. Ablation experiment results of BG-EFRL model on FoodPubDatas.

Model	Precision	Recall	F1-value
BG-EFRL	**94.32**	**92.32**	**93.31**
BG-EFRL-no-BERT	90.24	84.83	86.12
BG-EFRL-no-GCN	92.56	88.04	90.24

Ablation Experiment. As shown in Table 3, to verify the effectiveness of adding assist features to the BG-EFRL model, we conduct intuitive ablation experiments on the Food-PubDatas dataset, including using only the BERT encoder, only the GCN encoder, and combining the two combined. Figure 5 details the performance of the model, the latter performs the best, only the GCN encoder is the worst, that is because the graph embedding considers the relationship between nodes more than the features of the nodes themselves.

5 Conclusion

In this paper, we propose a new Chinese named entity recognition model, and demonstrate the effectiveness of the model on two widely used datasets, Weibo and Resume, and the generalization ability and practicality of the model on the FoodPubDatas dataset. In future work, we will further optimize the model and apply it to the field of food safety in the form of a question answering system.

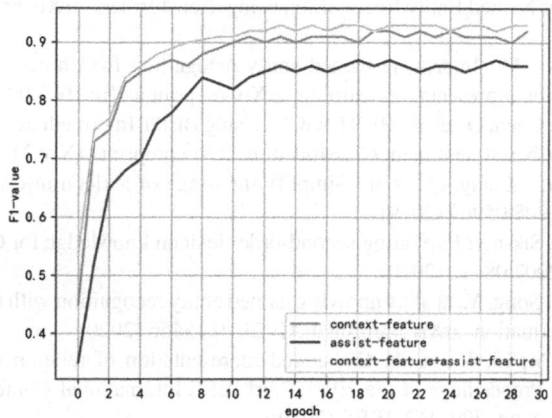

Fig. 5. Ablation experiments of BG-EFRL on the FoodPubDatas datasets

Acknowledgement. The research results of this paper have been supported by Tianjin Higher Education Undergraduate Teaching Quality and Teaching Reform Research Program (Reform and Practice of First-Class Software Engineering Based on UGE Model in the Background of Engineering Education Professional Accreditation, B201005706), Tianjin Natural Science Foundation (Multi-layer social network mass event monitoring and simulation research, 19JCYBJC15300) and Tianjin Science and Technology Program Project (Nutrition and Health Key Technology and Intelligent Manufacturing, 21ZYQCSY00050). We also thank the reviewers for their insightful comments.

References

1. Li, J., Sun, A., Han, J., et al.: A survey on deep learning for named entity recognition. IEEE Trans. Knowl. Data Eng. **34**(1), 50–70 (2020)
2. Zhou, P., Shi, W., Tian, J., et al.: Attention-based bidirectional long short-term memory networks for relation classification. In: Proceedings of the 54th Annual Meeting of the Association for Computational Linguistics, vol. 2, 207–212 (2016)
3. Phan, T., Do, P.: Building a Vietnamese question answering system based on knowledge graph and distributed CNN. Neural Comput. Appl. **33**(21), 14887–14907 (2021)
4. Xu, D., Li, J., Zhu, M., et al.: Improving AMR parsing with sequence-to-sequence pre-training. arXiv preprint arXiv:2010.01771 (2020)

5. Zhang, Y., Yang, J.: Chinese NER using lattice LSTM. arXiv preprint arXiv:1805.02023 (2018)
6. Qiu, X., Qian, P., Yin, L., Wu, S., Huang, X.: Overview of the NLPCC 2015 shared task: Chinese word segmentation and POS tagging for micro-blog texts. In: Li, J., Ji, H., Zhao, D., Feng, Y. (eds.) NLPCC 2015. LNCS (LNAI), vol. 9362, pp. 541–549. Springer, Cham (2015). https://doi.org/10.1007/978-3-319-25207-0_50
7. Zhu, Y., Wang, G., Karlsson, B.F.. CAN-NER: Convolutional attention network for Chinese named entity recognition. arXiv preprint arXiv:1904.02141 (2019)
8. Chawla, A., Mulay, N., Bishnoi, V., et al.: KARL-Trans-NER: Knowledge Aware Representation Learning for Named Entity Recognition using Transformers. arXiv preprint arXiv:2111.15436 (2021)
9. Peng, N., Dredze, M.: Improving named entity recognition for Chinese social media with word segmentation representation learning. arXiv preprint arXiv:1603.00786 (2016)
10. Xiao, Z., Wu, J., Chen, Q., et al.: BERT4GCN: Using BERT Intermediate Layers to Augment GCN for Aspect-based Sentiment Classification. arXiv preprint arXiv:2110.00171 (2021)
11. Ma, R., Peng, M., Zhang, Q., et al.: Simplify the usage of lexicon in Chinese NER. arXiv preprint arXiv:1908.05969 (2019)
12. Hu, D., Wei, L.: Slk-ner: Exploiting second-order lexicon knowledge for Chinese ner. arXiv preprint arXiv:2007.08416 (2020)
13. Nie, Y., Tian, Y., Song, Y., et al.: Improving named entity recognition with attentive ensemble of syntactic information. arXiv preprint arXiv:2010.15466 (2020)
14. Wang, X., Du, Y., Li, X., et al.: Embedded representation of relation words with visual supervision. In: Proceedings of the 2019 Third IEEE International Conference on Robotic Computing (IRC), pp. 409–412. IEEE (2019)
15. Sarzynska-Wawer, J., Wawer, A., Pawlak, A., et al.: Detecting formal thought disorder by deep contextualized word representations. Psychiatry Res. **304**, 114135 (2021)
16. Devlin, J., Chang, M.W., Lee, K., et al.: Bert: Pre-training of deep bidirectional transformers for language understanding. arXiv preprint arXiv:1810.04805 (2018)
17. Bartunov, S., Kondrashkin, D., Osokin, A., et al.: Breaking sticks and ambiguities with adaptive skip-gram. In: Proceedings of the Artificial Intelligence and Statistics, PMLR, pp. 130–138 (2016)
18. Pennington, J., Socher, R., Manning, C.D.: Glove: global vectors for word representation. In: Proceedings of the 2014 Conference on Empirical Methods in Natural Language Processing (EMNLP), pp. 1532–1543 (2014)
19. Hanh, T.T.H., Doucet, A., Sidere, N., Moreno, J.G., Pollak, S.: Named entity recognition architecture combining contextual and global features. In: Ke, H.-R., Lee, C.S., Sugiyama, K. (eds.) ICADL 2021. LNCS, vol. 13133, pp. 264–276. Springer, Cham (2021). https://doi.org/10.1007/978-3-030-91669-5_21
20. Belkin, M., Niyogi, P.: Laplacian eigenmaps and spectral techniques for embedding and clustering. Advances in Neural Information Processing Systems **14** (2001)
21. Sutton, C., McCallum, A.: An introduction to conditional random fields. Foundations and Trends® in Machine Learning **4**(4), 267–373 (2012)
22. Huang, Z., Xu, W., Yu, K.: Bidirectional LSTM-CRF models for sequence tagging. arXiv preprint arXiv:1508.01991 (2015)
23. Yan, H., Deng, B., Li, X., et al.: TENER: adapting transformer encoder for named entity recognition. arXiv preprint arXiv:1911.04474 (2019)
24. Li, X., Yan, H., Qiu, X., et al.: FLAT: Chinese NER using flat-lattice transformer. arXiv preprint arXiv:2004.11795 (2020)
25. Brochier, R., Guille, A., Velcin, J.: Global vectors for node representations. In: Proceedings of The World Wide Web Conference, pp. 2587–2593 (2019)

26. Straková, J., Straka, M., Hajič, J.: Neural architectures for nested NER through linearization. arXiv preprint arXiv:1908.06926 (2019)
27. Wang, K., Shen, W., Yang, Y., et al.: Relational graph attention network for aspect-based sentiment analysis. arXiv preprint arXiv:2004.12362 (2020)
28. Zhang, C., Li, Q., Song, D.: Aspect-based sentiment classification with aspect-specific graph convolutional networks. arXiv preprint arXiv:1909.03477 (2019)

TEMPLATE: TempRel Classification Model Trained with Embedded Temporal Relation Knowledge

Tiesen Sun and Lishuang Li[✉]

School of Computer Science and Technology, Dalian University of Technology,
Dalian, China
lils@dlut.edu.cn

Abstract. In recent years, the mainstream Temporal Relation (TempRel) classification methods may not take advantage of the large amount of semantic information contained in golden TempRel labels, which is lost by the traditional discrete one-hot labels. To solve this problem, we propose a new approach that can make full use of golden TempRel label information and make the model perform better. Firstly we build a TempRel Classification (TC) model, which consists of a RoBERTa and a Classifier. Secondly, we establish fine-grained templates to automatically generate sentences to enrich golden TempRel label information and build an Enhanced Data-set. Thirdly we use the Enhanced Data-set to train the Knowledge Encoder, which has the same structure as the TC model, and get embedded knowledge. Finally, we get a TC model Trained with EMbedded temPoral reLATion knowldgE (TEMPLATE) using our designed Cosine balanced MSE loss function. Extensive experimental results show that our approach achieves new state-of-the-art results on TB-Dense and MATRES and outperforms the TC model trained with only traditional cross entropy loss function with up to $5.51\%F_1$ on TB-Dense and $2.02\%F_1$ on MATRES.

Keywords: Temporal relation classification · Label embedding

1 Introduction

Articles such as news usually describe a series of events with different start and end times. These events seem to be narrated discretely, but in fact there are certain connections. The most important type of event connection is the Temporal Relation (TempRel). It represents the sequence of events, which connects the development and evolution of the events in the article. If we can accurately extract the TempRel of events in the article, it will help many downstream tasks such as tracking biomedical histories [1], generating stories [5], forecasting social events [8], and reading comprehension [12]. Therefore, the TempRel classification has always been an important natural language processing task.

© The Author(s), under exclusive license to Springer Nature Switzerland AG 2022
W. Lu et al. (Eds.): NLPCC 2022, LNAI 13551, pp. 246–258, 2022.
https://doi.org/10.1007/978-3-031-17120-8_20

The TempRel classification task is to determine the right TempRel of the event pair, given the candidate relationship set, two events, and their context. All recent works of the community follow the classification view: classifying the embedded representation, which is encoded by the context and events. Naturally, the training goal is how to encode the context and events into a better embedding space in which the different relations are distinguished well. All state-of-the-art TempRel classification methods use pre-trained language models to encode event representations, concatenate them, and then feed them into a classifier.

On the TempRel classification task, we can see that all state-of-the-art methods [7, 10, 11, 14, 15, 18] represent a golden TempRel label as a one-hot vector in training their classification models. However, the one-hot vector cannot adequately reflect the relation between the instances and labels, which makes the model learn the commonality/similarity of instances with the same label. This commonality is not entirely equivalent to the semantics of labels. This way results in arbitrary prediction and poor model generalization, especially for confused instances. In brief, the discrete values which represent TempRel categories lose much semantic information.

To cope with the loss of semantic information in labels, we manually construct templates to convert labels into additional sentences and design TEMPLATE method to make the baseline model learn from these additional sentences. We encode additional sentences and instance contexts into embedded knowledge. The difference between the context-based event representation and the embedded knowledge comes from the semantic information of golden label. Thus, we propose using an additional loss function to reduce the difference, which can make the baseline model learn semantic information of golden label from embedded knowledge. To our knowledge, we are the first to propose leveraging additional loss functions to learn embedded knowledge in classification tasks. In our work, we build a TempRel Classification (TC) model as our baseline model, which consists of a RoBERTa [9] and a Classifier.

The main contributions of this paper can be summarized as follows:

1. We design templates to enrich the TempRel label semantic information and encode it as embedded knowledge, and propose to leverage an additional loss function to make the TC model learn from the embedded knowledge.
2. In order to make our approach achieve better performance, we further design fine-grained templates in Sect. 4.1 and Cosine balanced MSE loss function in Sect. 4.3 as an additional loss function.
3. We demonstrate the effectiveness of our approach on TB-Dense and MATRES data-sets. Our approach outperforms the current best models with up to $2.27\%F_1$ on TB-Dense and $0.27\%F_1$ on MATRES and outperforms the TC model trained with traditional cross entropy loss function with up to $5.51\%F_1$ on TB-Dense and $2.02\%F_1$ on MATRES.

2   Related Work

The TempRel classification task has always been a popular research topic among NLP community. Before the emergence of pre-trained language models, researchers mainly used LSTM or BI-LSTM to encode sentence sequences and design additional techniques, such as encoding dependent sequences between the event nodes [3], taking global contexts and Common Sense Knowledge into account [11], and using Structured Support Vector Machine for global Maximum posterior inference [6].

After the birth of pre-trained language models, researchers focus on using them to encode event representations and propose many new methods based on them. Wang et al. [15] develop a Joint Constrained Learning (JCL) method. It conducts joint training on both temporal and hierarchical relation extraction based on RoBERTa and Bi-LSTMs. Meanwhile, it uses logical constraints and common sense knowledge. Zhou et al. [20] propose CTRL-PG method, which leverages the Probabilistic Soft Logic rules to model the temporal dependencies as a regularization term to jointly learn a relation classification model. Han et al. [7] design an ECONET system, which uses a continual pre-trained strategy with mask prediction and contrastive loss to further train the pre-trained language model with a large-scale TempRel corpus. It makes pre-trained language models focus on the event time relationship in the sentence. Additionally, ECONET performs better than the existing general language models under a low-resource setting through adequate experiments. Zhang et al. [18] propose a TGT network which utilize a syntactic graph which can explicitly find the connection between two events. Tan et al. [14] claim that the embeddings in the Euclidean space cannot capture richer asymmetric temporal relations. Therefore they embed events into hyperbolic spaces. They propose Poincaré Event Embeddings which leverages hyperbolic embeddings to directly infer event relations through a simple classifier and HGRU which embeds events into hyperbolic spaces, uses an end-to-end architecture composed of hyperbolic neural units, and introduces common sense knowledge. Wen et al. [16] propose a joint model (TCJM) for event-event temporal relation classification and an auxiliary task, relative event time prediction, which predicts the event time as real numbers.

All of the above methods use the one-hot vector and lose the semantic information of the golden label. To take advantage of the missing semantic information, we design templates that convert labels into additional sentences and make the TC model learn from them. In other classification tasks, Cohen et al. [4] and Yin et al. [17] have explored using templates and learn from them by reformulating the classification task as a pivot task (question answering or textual entailment). They transform a multi-classification task into multiple binary classification tasks, which are more computationally expensive. The underlying idea is to determine which of the label-related additional sentences is most similar to the instance. Unlike their methods, our TEMPLATE methods only build one golden label-related additional sentence for each instance. Our underlying idea is to convert golden label semantic information into embedded knowledge, and make the TC model learn from embedded knowledge directly by additional loss functions. Another difference is our TEMPLATE method only uses templates and converts label semantic information in the training stage, which we do not have to do anymore in applying or testing the trained model.

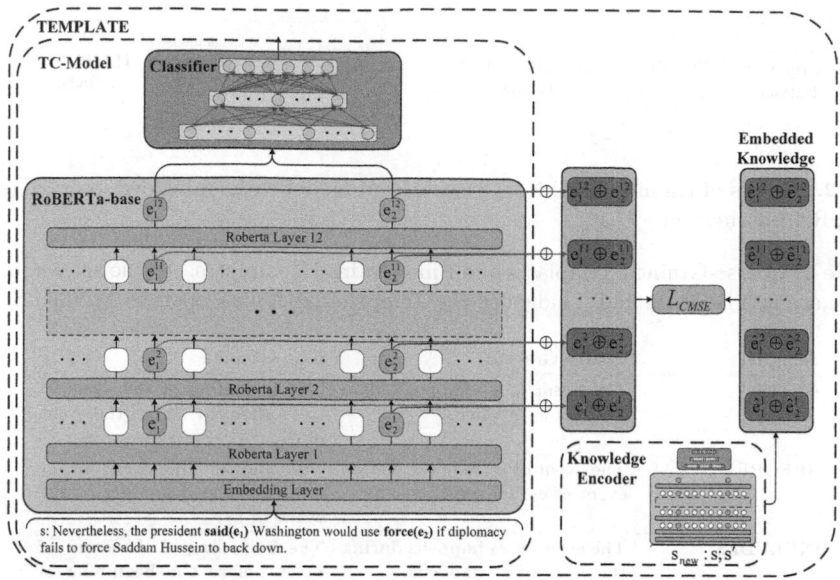

Fig. 1. Overview of our TEMPLATE.

3 Our Baseline Model

Our TempRel Classification (TC) model (i.e., baseline model), represented in Fig. 1, is comprised of a pre-trained language model and a classifier which consists of two fully connected layers and a tanh activation function between them. We use RoBERTa [9], which has been proven to be more effective than BERT in TempRel classification task by works [14,19] for domain transfer, as our pre-trained language model.

For a given example (s, e_1, e_2, r), s is a span of document, which may be a single sentence or two sentences. e_1 and e_2 are events and each of them is represented as a span of s. r is a golden TempRel label from the label set.

We first tokenize s and get a sequence $X_{[0,n)}$ of n tokens i.e. $\{x_0, x_1, \cdots, x_{n-1}\}$. Then we feed the sequence $X_{[0,n)}$ into RoBERTa and get the event contextual representations e_1^{12} and e_2^{12} corresponding to e_1 and e_2 respectively. If the number of tokens of an event is larger than one, we use the mean value of the hidden states of all the tokens of the event as the event contextual representation. Next, we combine e_1^{12} and e_2^{12} into a classification vector $c = e_1^{12} \oplus e_2^{12}$ where $\oplus$ is used to denote concatenation. Finally we feed c into the classifier followed by a soft-max function to get a distribution over the TempRel labels.

4 TEMPLATE Approach

Figure 2 shows the overall process of our approach. Firstly, we use templates to enrich the TempRel label information. We get an additional sentence set

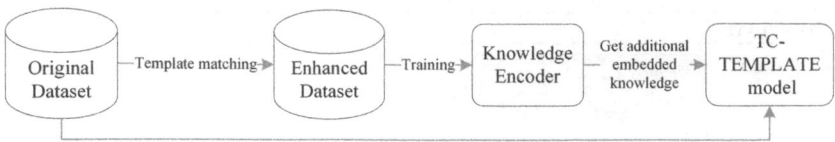

Fig. 2. Process of training TempRel Classification model with embedded knowledge of TempRel information

Table 1. Coarse-Grained Templates and Fine-Grained Templates. All the six TempRel labels are in TB-Dense and * indicates the TempRel label also exists in MATRES.

TempRel	Coarse-Grained	Fine-Grained
AFTER*	The event of e_1 happens after event of e_2 happens.	The beginning of the event of e_1 is after the end of the event of e_2.
BEFORE*	The event of e_1 happens before event of e_2 happens.	The end of the event of e_1 is before the beginning of the event of e_2.
INCLUDES	The event of e_2 happens during the event of e_1 happens.	The beginning of the event of e_1 is before the beginning of the event of e_2 and the end of event of e_1 is after the end of the event of e_2.
IS_INCLUDED	The event of e_1 happens during the event of e_2 happens.	The beginning of the event of e_1 is after the beginning of the event of e_2 and the end of event of e_1 is before the end of the event of e_2.
VAGUE*	The temporal relation between the event of e_1 and the event of e_2 is vague.	The temporal relation between the event of e_1 and the event of e_2 is vague.
SIMULTANEOUS*	The event of e_1 and the event of e_2 happens simultaneously.	The event of e_1 and the event of e_2 have the same beginning and end time.

$S_{additional}$ through matching golden TempRel labels and event pairs in Dataset. Then we connect each sentence s in the original sentence set S and sentence s' in $S_{additional}$ to get a new sentence set S_{new}, which forms Enhanced Dataset together with original labels and event pairs. Secondly, we train Knowledge Encoder, which has the same structure as the TC model in Sect. 3, with the Enhanced Data-set, then feed all sentences in S_{new} into the Knowledge Encoder to get all event pair representations of all intermediate layers in RoBERTa as additional embedded knowledge. Finally, we use the Original Data-set and additional embedded knowledge to train the TC model. We name our TC model Trained with EMbedded temPoral reLATion knowledgE as TC-TEMPLATE model. Below are the details of all the components of our approach.

4.1   Build Templates

To take full advantage of TempRel label information, we aim to create effective templates that automatically convert each golden TempRel label into a temporal information-enriched sentence s' to enrich golden TempRel label information. We argue that the time span of events (i.e., the duration of the events) guides TempRel classification. So we design fine-grained templates. We use the start and end times of events and the TempRel between different events to describe the TempRel of the event pair in a more subtle level. As a comparison, we design coarse-grained templates. We directly use the golden TempRel label and the event pair to describe the TempRel of the event pair. We show both the coarse-grained templates and the fine-grained templates in Table 1.

4.2   Embedded Knowledge of TempRel Information

Having obtained suitable templates, we next convert the TempRel label information enriched by the templates into embedded knowledge which is more convenient for the TC model to learn.

For each record (s, e_1, e_2, r) in data-set, we use r to match the templates and get s' by filling events into the corresponding positions in the template, then concatenate s and s' to get a new sentence $s_{new} = s; s'$, finally get a new record (s_{new}, e_1, e_2, r). We combine all new records into a new data-set i.e. Enhanced Data-set. We use the Enhanced Data-set to train a TC model as Knowledge Encoder, then use it to extract the embedded knowledge $k = \{\hat{e}_1^1 \oplus \hat{e}_2^1, \hat{e}_1^2 \oplus \hat{e}_2^2, \cdots, \hat{e}_1^{12} \oplus \hat{e}_2^{12}\}$ of TempRel information of each record. $\hat{e}_i^j$ is the hidden state corresponding to the event i from the j-th RoBERTa Layer, and $\hat{\ }$ is used to denote the hidden state from Knowledge Encoder. Additionally, in the process of training Knowledge Encoder, we add a dropout layer between the RoBERTa and the Classifier, in order to make the embedded knowledge k contain more useful temporal information.

4.3   Train the Model with Embedded Knowledge of TempRel Information

Having obtained the embedded knowledge $\{\hat{e}_1^j \oplus \hat{e}_2^j\}_{j=1}^{12}$, we make the all intermediate layers event pair representations $\{e_1^j \oplus e_2^j\}_{j=1}^{12}$ in TC model learn from it. e_i^j is the hidden state corresponding to the event i from the j-th RoBERTa Layer. The difference between the event pair representations and the embedded knowledge comes from the semantic information of the golden label. Therefore, using L_{MSE} in Eq. (1) to reduce the difference can make the TC model learn semantic information of golden label in embedded knowledge,

$$L_{MSE} = \sum_{j=1}^{12} \sum_{k=1}^{N} \left(\frac{1}{12 \times 2d} \cdot \left\| \frac{e_1^j \oplus e_2^j}{\left\| e_1^j \oplus e_2^j \right\|_2} - \frac{\hat{e}_1^j \oplus \hat{e}_2^j}{\left\| \hat{e}_1^j \oplus \hat{e}_2^j \right\|_2} \right\|_2^2 \right)_k \quad (1)$$

where N is the number of training samples, d is the hidden state dimension of RoBERTa.

Table 2. Data statistics for TB-Dense and MATRES

Corpora		Train	Dev	Test
TB-Dense	Documents	22	5	9
	Tempral	4032	629	1427
MATRES	Documents	204	51	20
	Tempral	10097	2643	837

Furthermore, we argue that the event representations of different intermediate layers are the event features under different perspectives. They have different importances to the learning process of the TC model. However, L_{mse} treats them as equally important. The difference between the event representation and the embedded knowledge comes from the semantic information of the golden label. So we argue that the farther the embedded knowledge of $\hat{e}_1^j \oplus \hat{e}_2^j$ is from the embedding of $e_1^j \oplus e_2^j$, the more knowledge is contained in $\hat{e}_1^j \oplus \hat{e}_2^j$ for a given layer j. Thus we propose a new method to automatically assign different weights $w_j \in \{\ w_1, w_2, \cdots, w_{12}\ \}$ to each layer MSE loss. We design w_j as:

$$w_j = \frac{1 - \sum_{k=1}^N \frac{1}{N} \cos(\hat{e}_1^j \oplus \hat{e}_2^j, e_1^j \oplus e_2^j)_k}{\sum_{t=1}^{12}(1 - \sum_{k=1}^N \frac{1}{N} \cos(\hat{e}_1^t \oplus \hat{e}_2^t, e_1^t \oplus e_2^t)_k)} \tag{2}$$

We use the cosine values of event representations and embedded knowledge in different intermediate layers to weight their importances. Then we get a new Cosine balanced MSE (C-MSE) loss L_{CMSE}:

$$L_{CMSE} = \sum_{j=1}^{12} \sum_{k=1}^N \left(\frac{w_j}{2d} \cdot \left\| \frac{e_1^j \oplus e_2^j}{\left\| e_1^j \oplus e_2^j \right\|_2} - \frac{\hat{e}_1^j \oplus \hat{e}_2^j}{\left\| \hat{e}_1^j \oplus \hat{e}_2^j \right\|_2} \right\|_2^2 \right)_k \tag{3}$$

Combined with the cross entropy loss and the C-MSE loss, the final loss function can be formulated as:

$$L_{finall} = \alpha L_{CE} + \beta L_{CMSE} \tag{4}$$

where α and β are hyper-parameters which weight the importances of discrete TempRel label information and additional enriched embedded knowledge of TempRel label semantic information.

5   Experiments and Results

In this section, we perform experiments on TB-Dense and MATERS and prove our TEMPLATE performs better than previous state-of-the-art methods. Details on the data-sets, experimental setup, and experimental results are provided in the following subsections.

5.1   Data-set

TB-Dense [2] is a densely annotated data-set for TempRel extraction, with 10 times as many relations per document as the TimeBank. It contains 6 types of relations: AFTER, BEFORE, INCLUDE, IS INCLUDED, VAGUE, SIMULTA-NEOUS. We use the same train (22 documents), dev (5 documents) and test (9 documents) splits as previous studies [7,18].

MATERS [13] contains 275 news documents from TimeBank (TB), AQUAINT (AQ), and Platinum (PT). It was annotated by a novel multi-axis annotation scheme with only 4 types of temporal relations: BEFORE, AFTER, EQUAL[1] and VAGUE. We follow the official split (i.e., TB+AQ (255 documents) as the train data-set and PT (20 documents) as the test data-set). As for the dev data-set, we use the same split strategy as previous studies [11,14]. We randomly select 51 documents (20% of the official training data) as the development data-set.

We briefly summarize the data statistics for TB-Dense and MATRES in Table 2.

5.2   Experimental Setup

In the process of training Knowledge Encoder, we set the drop probability of the dropout layer between the RoBERTa and the Classifier to 0.5, in order to make the embedded knowledge contain more useful temporal information. We use grid search strategy to select best hyper-parameters, and select learning rate of Classifier $\in \{$1e-3, 5e-4$\}$, learning rate of RoBERTa $\in \{$1e-5, 5e-6, 1e-6$\}$, $\alpha \in [0.7: 1.2]$, $\beta \in [700: 1200]$ and batch size $\in \{16, 24\}$. Since there are so many hyper-parameters to select for our approach, thus we first fix $\alpha = 1$ and $\beta = 1000$, to search the best batch size and learning rates of Classifier and RoBERTa, then we fix them to search best α and β. As for the dimension of the hidden states between two fully connected layers in the Classifier, we set it to 36.

5.3   Main Results

As shown in Table 3, we compare our approach with other state-of-the-art methods in recent years on TB-Dense and MATRES. We report the best F_1 value for each model. The results of compared methods are directly taken from the cited papers. And the compared methods have been introduced in Sect. 2.

We observe that our TC model achieves 63.56%F_1 on TB-Dense and 79.95%F_1 on MATRES. And, our TC-TEMPLATE$_{CMSE}$ outperforms previous state-of-the-art models on TempRel classification with up to 2.27%F_1 on TB-Dense and 0.27%F_1 on MATRES. These experimental results prove the effectiveness of encoding enriched golden TempRel label information and learning the embedded knowledge through C-MSE loss. There are two possible reasons for the effectiveness. One is that TEMPLATE not only takes advantage of the

---

[1] We consider EQUAL to be the same as SIMULTANEOUS.

Table 3. Comparison of various approaches on TempRel classification on TB-Dense and MATRES. Bold denotes the best performing model. TC denotes TempRel Classification model trained with only cross entropy loss. TC-TEMPLATE$_{CMse}$ denotes TempRel Classification model trained with additional embedded knowledge of fine-grained templates and C-MSE loss. F_1-score (%)

Model		TB-Dense	MATRES
JCL(2020) [15]	RoBERTa base	-	78.8
ECONET(2021) [7]	RoBERTa Large	66.8	79.3
TGT(2021) [18]	BERT Large	66.7	80.3
Poincaré Event Embeddings(2021) [14]	RoBERTa base	-	78.9
HGRU+knowledge(2021) [14]	RoBERTa base	-	80.5
TCJM(2021) [16]	RoBERTa base	-	81.7
TC (ours)	RoBERTa base	63.56	79.95
TC-TEMPLATE$_{CMSE}$ (ours)	RoBERTa base	**69.07**	**81.97**

large amount of semantic information contained in the golden TempRel label, which is lost by the traditional discrete one-hot labels, but also uses templates to enrich semantic information further. The other reason is that our C-MSE loss function can make the TempRel Classification model learn from embedded knowledge better. The difference between the event representations and the embedded knowledge comes from the semantic information of the golden label. The C-MSE loss function forces the event pair representations of intermediate layers in the TC model to near well-separated embedded knowledge containing golden label semantic information. In this process, the TC model forces itself to extract more useful information related to TempRel from sentences that do not contain any golden TempRel label.

Different from JCL and HGRU, which use external commonsense knowledge to enrich the information contained in event representations, TEMPLATE enables the model to better mine the information contained in original sentences. Compared to ECONET and TGT, which use a larger pre-trained language model, or TGT and HGRU, which use networks with complex structures followed RoBERTa base or BERT Large, our approach enables a smaller and simpler model which only contains a RoBERTa base and two fully connected layers to achieve the state-of-the-art performance.

5.4 Ablation Study and Qualitative Analysis

We observe that, compared with the TC model, the TC-TEMPLATE$_{CMSE}$ model performs better. It confirms the effectiveness of our embedded knowledge learning approach, which results in improvements of $5.51\% F_1$ and $2.02\% F_1$ on TB-Dense and MATRES respectively. We do the following ablation experiments to study further the effects of our proposed C-MSE loss function and fine-grained templates. We also qualitatively analyze embedded knowledge.

Embedding Knowledge Learning by C-MSE vs MSE. In order to determine whether our proposed Cosine balanced MSE loss has a positive effect, we conduct a comparative experiment and record the experimental results, which are shown in Table 4. We compare the TC-TEMPLATE using C-MSE loss and the TC-TEMPLATE using MSE loss on TB-Dense and MATRES respectively. We can see that the TC model with C-MSE achieves $1.2\%F_1$ and $0.46\%F_1$ performance improvement over the TC model with simple MSE respectively. It demonstrates the benefit of using the cosine values of the intermediate layer event pair representation $e_1^j \oplus e_2^j$ and the target embedded knowledge $\hat{e}_1^j \oplus \hat{e}_2^j$ to balance the MSE losses of different intermediate layers in TempRel Classification model. Our TEMPLATE calculates the MSE for each layer, and the changes in event representations in front layers affect event representations in back layers. There are two reasons for these improvements. One is that C-MSE loss assigns different weights according to the importance of different layers and avoids potential adverse effects for the current layer. The other is that C-MSE loss enables more critical layers to dominate the learning process.

Table 4. Results of TC-TEMPLATE with fine-grained templates models using C-MSE loss and MSE loss on TB-Dense and MATRES. F_1-score (%)

Model	TB-Dense	MATRES
TC-TEMPLATE$_{CMSE}$	69.07	81.97
TC-TEMPLATE$_{MSE}$	67.87	81.51
TC	63.56	79.95

Table 5. Results of TC-TEMPLATE with C-MSE loss models using fine-grained templates and coarse-grained templates on TB-Dense and MATRES. F_1-score (%)

Model	TB-Dense	MATRES
TC-TEMPLATE$_{fine}$	69.07	81.97
TC-TEMPLATE$_{coarse}$	67.72	81.27
TC	63.56	79.95

Fine-grained templates vs Coarse-grained templates. In order to study the impact of different granularity templates on model performance, we also compare F_1 values of TC-TEMPLATE models with different granularity templates and C-MSE loss function on TB-Dense and MATRES and report the results in Table 5. We can see that the TC-TEMPLATE using fine-grained templates performs better than the TC-TEMPLATE using coarse-grained templates and has $1.35\%F_1$ and $0.70\%F_1$ improvements on TB-Dense and MATRES respectively. These improvements are not just because fine-grained templates describe TempRel more precisely than coarse-grained templates. It is also because fine-grained templates use the start and end times of the events to describe the TempRel,

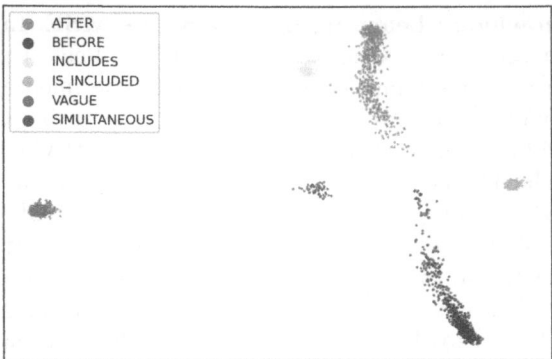

Fig. 3. The distribution of embedded knowledge of last layer in the case of TB-Dense.

making fine-grained templates closer to the annotation rules and actual basis for judgment than coarse-grained templates. Through the embedded knowledge learning process, the knowledge of fine-grained templates provides more information, reduces the difficulty of learning, and enables the model to learn the TempRel of events better heuristically.

Qualitative Analysis. In our learning process, TEMPLATE makes intermediate layer event representations of the TC model to move close to target embedded knowledge. For a positive gain, we want to get well-separated embedded knowledge. In order to verify the quality of our embedded knowledge, we reduce its dimension through PCA and represent it in Fig. 3. On the one hand, we can see that there are 6 clusters of embeddings that are well-differentiated even in two dimensions. Our method maps instances with the same category to a relatively dense region. These well demonstrate that our embedded knowledge has a strong alignment. On the other hand, we also can see that the 5 clusters, which represent temporal categories in Fig. 3 right, are farther from the VAGUE cluster than each other. It means that our embedded knowledge retains as much category information as possible. The farther away different clusters are, the more category information and differences are retained. Moreover, different instances with the same category distribute evenly within the dense region, which means that our embedded knowledge retains as much instance information as possible. Furthermore, the more evenly distributed they are, the more information they retain. These well demonstrate that our embedded knowledge has a strong uniformity.

6 Conclusion

In recent years, the mainstream TempRel classification neural networks focus on using discrete values to represent temporal relation categories and only using a cross entropy loss function to train the model. However, it loses too much semantic information contained in golden labels. So we propose TEMPLATE, which trains the TC model with C-MSE loss and embedded knowledge from fine-grained templates and golden TempRel labels. Extensive experimental results on TBDense and MATRES data-sets show that our approach makes the TC model gain a considerable improvement, and TC-TEMPLATECMSE performs better than all previous state-of-the-art methods on TempRel classification tasks.

Acknowledgments. This work is supported by grant from the National Natural Science Foundation of China (No. 62076048), the Science and Technology Innovation Foundation of Dalian (2020JJ26GX035).

References

1. Bethard, S., Savova, G., Palmer, M., Pustejovsky, J.: SemEval-2017 task 12: clinical tempeval. In: Proceedings of the 11th International Workshop on Semantic Evaluation (SemEval-2017), pp. 565–572 (2017)
2. Cassidy, T., McDowell, B., Chambers, N., Bethard, S.: An annotation framework for dense event ordering. In: ACL (Volume 2: Short Papers), pp. 501–506 (2014)
3. Cheng, F., Miyao, Y.: Classifying temporal relations by bidirectional LSTM over dependency paths. In: ACL (Volume 2: Short Papers), pp. 1–6 (2017)
4. Cohen, A.D., Rosenman, S., Goldberg, Y.: Relation classification as two-way span-prediction. arXiv preprint arXiv:2010.04829 (2020)
5. Goldfarb-Tarrant, S., Chakrabarty, T., Weischedel, R., Peng, N.: Content planning for neural story generation with aristotelian rescoring. In: EMNLP, pp. 4319–4338 (2020)
6. Han, R., Hsu, I.H., Yang, M., Galstyan, A., Weischedel, R., Peng, N.: Deep structured neural network for event temporal relation extraction. In: CoNLL, pp. 666–106 (2019)
7. Han, R., Ren, X., Peng, N.: ECONET: effective continual pretraining of language models for event temporal reasoning. In: EMNLP, pp. 5367–5380 (2021)
8. Jin, W., et al.: Forecastqa: a question answering challenge for event forecasting with temporal text data, pp. 4636–4650 (2021)
9. Liu, Y., et al.: Roberta: a robustly optimized bert pretraining approach. arXiv preprint arXiv:1907.11692 (2019)
10. Ma, M.D., et al.: Eventplus: a temporal event understanding pipeline. arXiv preprint arXiv:2101.04922 (2021)
11. Ning, Q., Subramanian, S., Roth, D.: An improved neural baseline for temporal relation extraction. In: EMNLP-IJCNLP, pp. 6203–6209 (2019)
12. Ning, Q., Wu, H., Han, R., Peng, N., Gardner, M., Roth, D.: TORQUE: a reading comprehension dataset of temporal ordering questions. In: EMNLP, pp. 1158–1172 (2020)
13. Ning, Q., Wu, H., Roth, D.: A multi-axis annotation scheme for event temporal relations. In: ACL (Volume 1: Long Papers), pp. 1318–1328 (2018)
14. Tan, X., Pergola, G., He, Y.: Extracting event temporal relations via hyperbolic geometry. In: EMNLP, pp. 8065–8077 (2021)
15. Wang, H., Chen, M., Zhang, H., Roth, D.: Joint constrained learning for event-event relation extraction. In: EMNLP, pp. 696–706 (2020)
16. Wen, H., Ji, H.: Utilizing relative event time to enhance event-event temporal relation extraction. In: EMNLP, pp. 10431–10437 (2021)

17. Yin, W., Hay, J., Roth, D.: Benchmarking zero-shot text classification: datasets, evaluation and entailment approach. In: EMNLP-IJCNLP, pp. 3914–3923 (2019)
18. Zhang, S., Huang, L., Ning, Q.: Extracting temporal event relation with syntactic-guided temporal graph transformer. arXiv preprint arXiv:2104.09570 (2021)
19. Zhao, X., Lin, S.T., Durrett, G.: Effective distant supervision for temporal relation extraction. In: Proceedings of the Second Workshop on Domain Adaptation for NLP, pp. 195–203 (2021)
20. Zhou, Y., et al.: Clinical temporal relation extraction with probabilistic soft logic regularization and global inference. In: AAAI. vol. 35, pp. 14647–14655 (2021)

Dual Interactive Attention Network for Joint Entity and Relation Extraction

Lishuang Li[✉], Zehao Wang[✉], Xueyang Qin, and Hongbin Lu

Dalian University of Technology, Dalian, China
lils@dlut.edu.cn, dutzehao@mail.dlut.edu.cn

Abstract. The joint entity and relation extraction method establishes a bond between tasks, surpassing sequential extraction based on the pipeline method. Many joint works focus on learning a unified representation for both tasks to explore the correlations between Named Entity Recognition (NER) and Relation Extraction (RE). However, they suffer from the feature confusion that features extracted from one task may conflict with those from the other. To address this issue, we propose a novel Dual Interactive Attention Network to learn independent representations and meanwhile guarantee bidirectional and fine-grained interaction between NER and RE. Specifically, we propose a Fine-grained Attention Cross-Unit to model interaction at the token level, which fully explores the correlation between entity and relation. To obtain task-specific representation, we introduce a novel attention mechanism that can capture the correlations among multiple sequences from the specific task and performs better than the traditional self-attention network. We conduct extensive experiments on five standard benchmarks (ACE04, ACE05, ADE, CoNLL04, SciERC) and achieve state-of-the-art performance, demonstrating the effectiveness of our approach in joint entity and relation extraction.

Keywords: Joint entity and relation extraction · Dual network · Fine-grained attention cross-unit · External attention

1 Introduction

Named Entity Recognition (NER) and Relation Extraction (RE) are two fundamental tasks of information extraction in Natural Language Processing (NLP). Existing entity and relation extraction methods either adopt pipeline methods or joint methods. Traditional pipeline methods ignore the intimate correlation between entity and relation, and they suffer from the error propagation that the errors generated by the NER stage are propagated to the RE stage. To resolve the drawbacks of pipeline method, the joint method performs two tasks simultaneously and has become the mainstream approach.

A typical way among existing joint approaches is to encode NER and RE into a unified label space to learn a unified representation for both tasks

W. Lu et al. (Eds.): NLPCC 2022, LNAI 13551, pp. 259–271, 2022.
https://doi.org/10.1007/978-3-031-17120-8_21

[10,14,15,18]. It fills entity and relation labels into one table and then decodes them simultaneously by an elaborate decoding algorithm. In this manner, NER and RE are performed by the same model, enabling implicitly useful interaction between two tasks. However, using a single representation for entity and relation may lead to the feature confusion problem as the features extracted for one task may coincide or conflict with those for the other, thus confusing the learning model. We argue that it can be beneficial to learn two types of representation for NER and RE separately, rather than learning a single representation.

When the objective is to learn such two types of representations, it is essential to model the feature interaction between two tasks. Some methods [1,9,16,17] achieve interaction by sharing the same parameters. They typically use two parallel networks for NER and RE, in which two tasks perform interaction by sharing the input feature and encode their specific representations respectively. However, these methods merely perform limited interaction, failing to fully explore the potential correlations between NER and RE. This limited interaction is instantiated in two aspects: the incomplete feature interaction and unidirectional information transmission. Firstly, some potentially valuable information may be lost when performing feature interaction in previous work such as [9,16]. These methods merely extract the features of entity pair or subject entity as the input of RE task, which ignores the entity context information and the global feature of NER task. Secondly, it is recognized that the entity information is helpful in predicting relation. However, there are fewer works to explore the contribution of relation information on predicting entity and previous works only model the single-direction (NER to RE) information interaction. Consequently, the valuable relevant features between two tasks are far from being excavated.

Therefore, in order to conquer these issues, we propose a novel Dual Interactive Attention Network (DIANet) for joint entity and relation extraction. Specifically, in our model, we encode respective representations for both NER and RE tasks and propose a novel Fine-grained Attention Cross-Unit (FACU) to perform feature interaction properly. The FACU generates new representations for both NER and RE. It allows the two task representations of the same token to be recombined with different weights into a new fused token representation. For the fused feature of a specific task (NER or RE), FACU can dynamically learn an appropriate fusion proportion of two tasks according to the importance of each word to the current task. Given a sentence, the fusion proportion of each word can be different, so the model can adaptively learn to enhance the useful features from the two tasks. For instance, since the entity information is vital for extracting relation, thus when generating the fused representation for RE, the FACU can enhance the weight of the entity features from the NER task and meanwhile enable all other tokens to interact with the NER features in an appropriate proportion. As both tasks can interact with each other and perform feature interaction between every token of the two tasks, our FACU can achieve bidirectional information interaction and has no feature loss problem. After feature interaction, we apply the attention network for each task to learn task-specific representation. We first propose to introduce the external attention mechanism [6] into the NLP task, which is devised for the Computer Vision to capture discriminative features. Compared with the traditional self-attention network which learns representation in one single sample, the external attention network can capture potential correlations between different samples. Our experiments demonstrate that the external attention benefits learning task-specific representation, and its performance is better than traditional attention networks.

The contributions of our work are summarized below:

- We propose a novel Dual Interactive Attention Network (DIANet) for joint entity and relation extraction. Our model achieves state-of-the-art performance on five standard benchmarks (ACE04, ACE05, ADE, CoNLL04, and SciERC) including general, medical, and scientific domains, which demonstrates the effectiveness of our approach.
- We propose a Fine-grained Attention Cross-Unit (FACU) that can achieve bidirectional and fine-grained task information interaction. Through FACU, each token's feature from one task can adaptively fuse with the corresponding feature from the other task, fully exploring the correlations between tasks.
- We first propose to introduce the External Attention (EA) mechanism into learning task-specific representation and demonstrate its effectiveness compared with the traditional attention network.

2   Related Work

In recent years, increasing joint entity and relation extraction approaches have been proposed and proved to be more efficient than pipeline-based methods like [19] which suffer from the error propagation and ignore the correlations between NER and RE. The core idea of the joint methods is to model the task interaction and find useful information from the association between tasks.

Some methods typically cast NER and RE to a unified label space and learn a unified representation trained on a single model to achieve interaction implicitly. The early method encodes both entities and relations into one sequence like [18], but it can not resolve overlapping relations. Recently, the table filling method has become a popular decoding paradigm as the two-dimensional tables can well handle nested entities and overlapping relations. Therefore, many works have been proposed based on the table filling method such as [10,14,15]. The goal of these methods is to design an efficient decoding algorithm for extracting both entities and relations. However, since the information about entity and relation could sometimes be contradictory, such approaches using a single model are unable to alleviate the conflicting information, thus confusing the learning model.

Other methods typically learn separate representations for the two tasks and specify the way of task interaction artificially. Therefore, how to effectively model the task interaction is significant. Some previous works achieve interaction by extracting the entity information to help predict the relation, such as [1, 9,16], but they lack bidirectional interaction. Although later approaches [13,

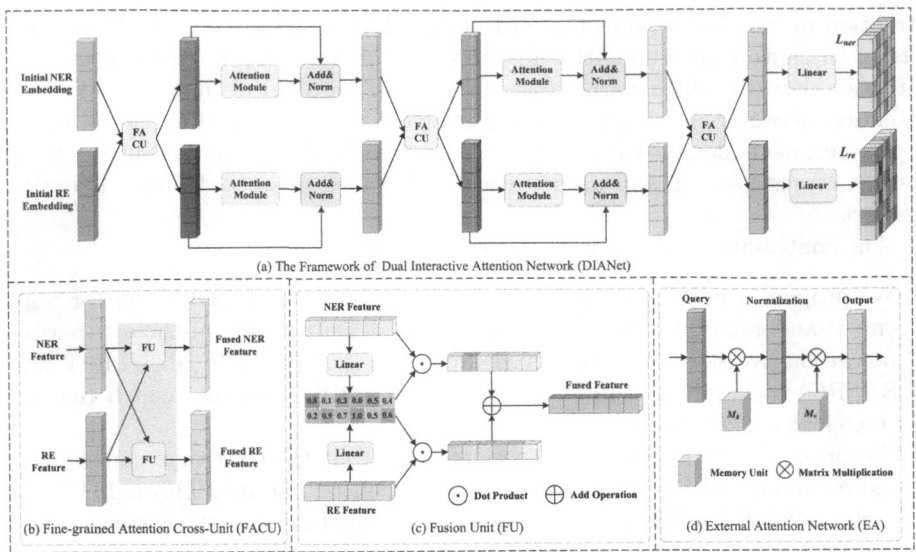

Fig. 1. (a) Overview of DIANet. The framework is a multi-layer dual network composed of two independent and identical networks used to learn representations for NER and RE respectively. The two tasks achieve task interaction by the Fine-Grained Attention Cross-Unit (FACU). (b) The design of the Fine-grained Attention Cross-Unit (FACU), which generates the fused features by respective Fusion Unit (FU). (c) The process of obtaining fused feature in the Fusion Unit. (d) The process of the External Attention.

17] have modeled two-way interaction, they may suffer from losing potentially valuable features in the process of information transmission since the improper interaction.

3   Model

The main architecture of our model is illustrated in Fig. 1a. We adopt a multi-layer dual network for NER and RE to perform interaction and learn representations. Firstly, we initialize the input embedding for NER and RE respectively. Then we enable two features to have interacted through the Fine-grained Attention Cross-Unit. After that, the fused features of each task are fed into the attention network to obtain task-specific representations. Through multi-layer task interaction, we classify the features of the two tasks based on the table filling method and calculate the loss.

3.1   Initialize Embeddings for Two Tasks

Given an input sentence $S = \{w_1, w_2, ..., w_n\}$, we use pre-trained language models (PLM) to obtain contextual representation h_i for each word w_i,

$$H_{plm} = PLM(S) = \{h_1, h_2, ..., h_n\}, \tag{1}$$

where n represents the length of the sentence. Considering the difference between NER and RE tasks, it is reasonable to initialize differentiated representations for two tasks. We use a Feed Forward Network with Dropout for each task to differentiate the initial features of entity and relation, shown as follows,

$$H_e = Dropout(W_e H_{plm} + b_e), \tag{2}$$
$$H_r = Dropout(W_r H_{plm} + b_r), \tag{3}$$

where W_e, b_e and W_r, b_r are independent trainable parameters. H_e and H_r serve as the initial representations of NER and RE tasks.

3.2   Fine-Grained Attention Cross-Unit

The joint model benefits from exploiting the correlation between entity and relation. Thus we propose a Fine-grained Attention Cross-Unit (FACU) to enable the features of the two tasks to have fully interacted. Specifically, as shown in Fig. 1b, the FACU consists of two Fusion Units (FU) in which each FU (illustrated in Fig. 1c) is designed to generate a fused feature for a certain task. Given the representations h_e^i, h_r^i respectively from NER and RE of the token i, we use a linear network to compute the attention score with *softmax* normalization, as expressed as Eq. (4). Then we do a dot product between the attention scores and the input representations, and sum the weighted representation up to obtain the fused feature for one task, processed as Eq. (5),

$$(\alpha_{\triangle,e}^i, \alpha_{\triangle,r}^i) = softmax([W_{FU} \cdot h_e^i + b_{FU}; W_{FU} \cdot h_r^i + b_{FU}]), \tag{4}$$
$$h_{\triangle}^{*i} = \alpha_{\triangle,e}^i \cdot h_e^i + \alpha_{\triangle,r}^i \cdot h_r^i, \tag{5}$$

where $\triangle$ indicates a certain task (NER or RE), $\alpha_{\triangle,x}^i$ represents the proportion of feature h_x^i in the fused feature $h_{\triangle}^i$, $[;]$ represents the concatenate operation, W_{FU}, b_{FU} is the trainable parameters of the FU. Both tasks have their own independent FU, which is trained to learn an optimal combination of h_e^i and h_r^i according to the specific task. The feature fusion of token i for two tasks can be calculated as follows,

$$\begin{bmatrix} h_e^{*i} \\ h_r^{*i} \end{bmatrix} = \begin{pmatrix} \alpha_{e,e}^i & \alpha_{e,r}^i \\ \alpha_{r,e}^i & \alpha_{r,r}^i \end{pmatrix} \begin{bmatrix} h_e^i \\ h_r^i \end{bmatrix}. \tag{6}$$

Our FACU can achieve fine-grained inter-task feature interaction that each token's feature from one task can dynamically fuse with the corresponding token from the other task. Since all token representations of both tasks are involved in feature fusion, each token can exploit the valuable information from the other task by setting up a higher or lower attention weight of the corresponding feature. We illustrate and analyze the result of attention weights of the two tasks learned by FACU in Sect. 6.2.

3.3 The External Attention Mechanism

The attention mechanism has been proved effective and successful in most information extraction tasks, among which the self-attention [12] is the most representative. Self-attention works by updating the representation at each position by aggregating features from all other locations in one single sequence. However, this method ignores potential correlations with other sequences. Therefore, we introduce a novel attention mechanism namely external attention [6] to exploit incorporating correlations between different samples, which contributes to learning a better representation of the specific task.

The process of the external attention network is shown in Fig. 1d. Firstly, we use a linear transformation on each output $H_\triangle^*$ from the FACU and then obtain the query vector Q, as shown in Eq. (7). Secondly, as Eq. (8), a trainable parameter M_k which is independent of the input query is used to compute the attention score A with $softmax$ normalization. Subsequently, we apply $L1Normalization$ to prevent the damage of original meaning of A when only using one $softmax$ normalization. Finally, we use another learnable external memory unit M_v multiplied by attention scores A to get final output $H_\triangle^{head_i}$, as expressed in Eq. (9). The calculation process is as follows,

$$Q = W_q H_\triangle^* + b_q, \tag{7}$$

$$A = L_1 Norm(Softmax(M_k Q)), \tag{8}$$

$$H_\triangle^{head_i} = A M_v. \tag{9}$$

In Transformer [12], self-attention is computed many times to learn different aspects of attentions for the same input, improving the capability of single head attention. Therefore, we incorporate the similar multi-head mechanism into external attention. Different from multi-head attention in Transformer, each head of external attention shares the same memory unit M_k and M_v, formulated as follows,

$$H_\triangle^{head_i} = ExternalAttention(H_\triangle^*, M_k, M_v), \tag{10}$$

$$H_\triangle^{multihead} = [H_\triangle^{head_1}; H_\triangle^{head_2}; ...; H_\triangle^{head_k}] \cdot W_o, \tag{11}$$

$$H_\triangle^{out} = LayerNorm(H_\triangle^{multihead} + H_\triangle^*), \tag{12}$$

where $H_\triangle^*$ is the input feature, k is the number of heads, and W_o is a linear transformation matrix making the dimensions of input and output consistent. M_k and M_v are the shared memory units. To prevent the degradation problem that accuracy gets saturated and then degrades rapidly with the layer number increasing, we adopt a residual network with Layer Normalization at the end of the attention module, processing as Eq. (12).

3.4 Classification by Table Filling Method

We adopt a table filling method to perform classification for both tasks. For NER classification, the objective is to identify and categorize all entity spans in a given sentence. We concatenate token-level entity features h_i^e and h_j^e as Eq. (13), and feed it into a fully-connected layer with ELU activation to get entity span representation $h_{i,j}^e$. With the span representation, we can predict whether the span is an entity with type $\varepsilon \in \mathcal{E}$ by feeding it into a linear layer with *sigmoid* activation. We adopt the binary cross-entropy loss for NER to compute the loss function, the calculation is as follows,

$$h_{i,j}^e = ELU(W_{fc}^e \cdot [h_i^e; h_j^e] + b_{fc}^e), \tag{13}$$

$$e_{i,j}^k = sigmoid(W_{cl}^e \cdot h_{i,j}^e + b_{cl}^e), \tag{14}$$

$$\mathcal{L}_{ner} = \Sigma_{i,j\in(1,n),\varepsilon\in\mathcal{E}} BCELoss(e_{i,j}^\varepsilon \bar{e}_{i,j}^\varepsilon), \tag{15}$$

where $\bar{e}_{i,j}^\varepsilon$ denotes the ground truth label of the corresponding entity span. Symmetrical to the computation of NER, RE aims to identify all triples in sentence. Since entity span prediction is already covered in NER classification, we only predict the start token of each entity in RE classification. Similar to NER, we concatenate relation features h_i^r and h_j^r, obtaining $h_{i,j}^r$, $r_{i,j}^\tau$ ($\tau \in \mathcal{T}$) as Eq. (16) and Eq. (17) and computing the loss function in the same way, the calculation is as follows,

$$h_{i,j}^r = ELU(W_{fc}^r \cdot [h_i^r; h_j^r] + b_{fc}^r), \tag{16}$$

$$r_{i,j}^\tau = sigmoid(W_{cl}^r \cdot h_{i,j}^r + b_{cl}^r). \tag{17}$$

$$\mathcal{L}_{re} = \Sigma_{i,j\in(1,n),\tau\subset\mathcal{T}} BCELoss(r_{i,j}^\tau, \bar{r}_{i,j}^\tau), \tag{18}$$

where $\bar{r}_{i,j}^\tau$ denotes the ground truth label relation. Since predicting the relation depends on the extracted entities, there is a priority order between the two tasks. Therefore, we introduce an equilibrium factor β to allow the convergence rate of the RE task to be slightly slower than that of NER. We multiply $\mathcal{L}_{re}$ by β and optimize two objectives as $\mathcal{L}_{ner} + \beta \cdot \mathcal{L}_{re}$, where the higher β the slower the convergence of RE. Our experiments show that β significantly affects the performance of the two tasks, and we carefully fine-tune this hyper-parameter and analyze it in Sect. 6.4.

4   Experiments

4.1   Datasets and Evaluation

We conduct experiments on five datasets, namely ACE04 [4], ACE05 [3], ADE [7], CoNLL04 [11] and SciERC [8]. ACE04 and ACE05 corpora are collected from news articles and online forums. ADE is constructed from medical reports that describe the adverse effects arising from drug use. CoNLL04 is composed of sentences from news articles. SciERC corpus collects scientific abstracts from AI conference proceedings.

For evaluation, we adopt strict evaluation criterion. For NER task, an entity is predicted as correct only if its type and boundaries strictly match those of a gold entity. For RE task, a triple prediction is considered correct only if the

Table 1. The comparison with current methods. $\triangle$ and $\blacktriangle$ denotes the use of micro-F1 and macro-F1 score. $\clubsuit$ means that the model leverages cross-sentence context information. $\mathrm{ALB_{large}}$ indicates ALBERT-xxlarge-v1.

Dataset	Method	PLM	Entity			Relation		
			P	R	F1	P	R	F1
ACE04$^\triangle$	Table-Sequence(2020) [13]	$\mathrm{ALB_{large}}$	-	-	88.6	-	-	59.6
	PURE(2021) [19]	$\mathrm{ALB_{large}}$	-	-	88.8	-	-	60.2
	PFN(2021) [17]	$\mathrm{ALB_{large}}$	-	-	89.3	-	-	62.5
	UNIRE(2021)$^\clubsuit$ [14]	$\mathrm{ALB_{large}}$	88.9	90.0	89.5	67.3	59.3	63.0
	DIANet(Ours)	$\mathrm{ALB_{large}}$	**89.5**	**90.0**	**89.8**	**70.1**	**59.5**	**64.3**
ACE05$^\triangle$	Table-Sequence(2020) [13]	$\mathrm{ALB_{large}}$	-	-	89.5	-	-	64.3
	PURE(2021) [19]	$\mathrm{ALB_{large}}$	-	-	89.7	-	-	65.5
	UNIRE(2021)$^\clubsuit$ [14]	$\mathrm{ALB_{large}}$	89.9	**90.5**	90.2	72.3	60.7	66.0
	PFN(2021) [17]	$\mathrm{ALB_{large}}$	-	-	89.5	-	-	66.8
	DIANet(Ours)	$\mathrm{ALB_{large}}$	**90.1**	90.0	91.1	72.1	64.8	**68.3**
ADE$^\blacktriangle$	SpERT(2019) [5]	$\mathrm{BERT_{base}}$	89.0	89.6	89.3	78.1	80.4	79.2
	Table-Sequence(2020) [13]	$\mathrm{ALB_{large}}$	-	-	89.7	-	-	80.1
	PFN(2021) [17]	$\mathrm{ALB_{large}}$	-	-	**91.3**	-	-	83.2
	DIANet(Ours)	$\mathrm{ALB_{large}}$	**89.8**	**92.4**	91.1	**80.8**	**86.0**	**83.3**
CoNLL04$^\triangle$	SpERT(2019) [5]	$\mathrm{BERT_{base}}$	88.3	89.6	88.9	73.0	**70.0**	71.5
	Table-Sequence(2020) [13]	$\mathrm{ALB_{large}}$	-	-	90.1	-	-	73.6
	REBEL(2021) [2]	$\mathrm{ALB_{large}}$	-	-	-	-	-	75.4
	DIANet(Ours)	$\mathrm{ALB_{large}}$	**90.4**	**90.1**	**90.3**	**84.3**	69.9	**76.4**
SciERC$^\triangle$	PURE(2021) [19]	SciBERT	-	-	66.6	-	-	35.6
	PFN(2021) [17]	SciBERT	-	-	66.8	-	-	38.4
	UNIRE(2021)$^\clubsuit$ [14]	SciBERT	65.8	**71.1**	68.4	37.3	36.6	36.9
	DIANet(Ours)	SciBERT	**67.8**	69.2	**68.5**	**44.4**	**37.7**	**40.8**

pair of entities and its relation type are strictly matched with those in gold triple. Following previous works, we adopt Marco-F1 score in ADE dataset and Micro-F1 score in other datasets.

4.2   Implementation Details

We tune all hyper-parameters based on the averaged results on ACE05 development set and keep the same settings for others. Due to the limitation of graphic memory, we set the number of attention head to 1 for the ACE05 and ACE04, and 8 for the others. We use the Adam optimizer with initial learning rate 2e–5 with a learning rate decay strategy. We set $\beta = 1.5$ and the batch size to 4 and train our model with a maximum of 200 epochs. All experiments are performed on a NVIDIA GeForce RTX 3090 GPU with 24 GB graphic memory.

4.3   Results

We compare our model with currently advanced methods as shown in Table 1. In general, our model achieves the best performance on all five datasets. Compared with the best pipeline model PURE [19], our model achieves significant improvements in both entity and relation performance, i.e., an improved F1-score of +1.0, +0.4, and +1.9 for entity as well as +4.1, +2.8, and +5.2 for relation, on ACE04, ACE05, and SciERC respectively. It should be noted that since our model does not leverage cross-sentence information, the results of PURE [19] are reported in single-sentence setting for fair comparison. Compared with the joint model UNIRE [14] which learns unified representation, our model achieves remarkable advance on relation by +1.3, +2.3, and +3.9, on ACE04, ACE05, and SciERC respectively. For the performance of entity, we make slight improvement by +0.3 and +0.1 respectively on ACE04 and SciERC, but get weaker performance by 0.1 on ACE05. We argue that UNIRE [14] benefits from the cross-sentence context information and thus helps predicts entity. Compared with the joint model PFN [17] which learns respective representations, our model also improves the F1 score of entity and relation by +0.5 and +1.8 respectively on ACE04, +0.6 and +1.5 on ACE05, -0.2 and + 0.1 on ADE, +1.7 and + 2.4 on SciERC dataset. In CoNLL04 dataset, our model surpass the REBEL [2] by +1.0 in relation. Overall, our model achieves remarkable improvements on various domain benchmarks.

Table 2. Ablation study on ACE05.

Model	Ent	Rel+
-baseline	**88.6**	**64.9**
-w/o FACU	88.3	63.8
-w/o EA	87.9	63.9
-w/o FACU&EA	87.7	63.3

Table 3. Performance on the depth.

Depth	Ent	Rel+
$\mathcal{D} = 1$	89.4	64.6
$\mathcal{D} = 2$	90.0	67.5
$\mathcal{D} = 3$	**90.1**	**68.3**
$\mathcal{D} = 4$	87.4	55.1

5   Ablation Study

In this section, we analyze the effects of our proposed components with different settings on the ACE05 test set based on $BERT_{base}$ for efficiency. As shown in Table 2, while removing the Fine-grained Attention Cross-Unit, it harms entity and relation performance with 0.3 and 1.1 decline respectively. It demonstrates that our FACU can exploit the correlations between NER and RE to benefit both tasks. When excluding the external attention network, the performance decreased by 0.7 in entity and 1.0 in relation. In this setting, although the two tasks can perform interaction, there is no part for each task to learn its specific representation, which confirms that it is essential to set up an independent learning network for each task. When we remove both FACU and attention module, the performance drops more sharply by 0.9 in entity and 1.6 in relation. Consequently, the result of the ablative experiment verifies the effectiveness of our proposed components.

6   Analysis

6.1   Performance Against the Network Depth

As shown in Fig. 1a, we adopt a multi-layer architecture in which each layer consists of a Fine-grained Attention Cross-unit and separate attention modules (or classification modules). In this section, we explore the impact of network depth $\mathcal{D}$ on the performance of the model on ACE05 test set based on ALB$_{large}$. In Table 3, with enlarging the depth $\mathcal{D}$, the performance gets better and achieves the best when $\mathcal{D} = 3$. We argue that more parameters can enhance modeling capability and each layer can obtain various aspects of features. However, when $\mathcal{D} > 3$, the performance begins to decrease. We argue that excessive parameters of the model increase the risk of over-fitting, which limits the performance.

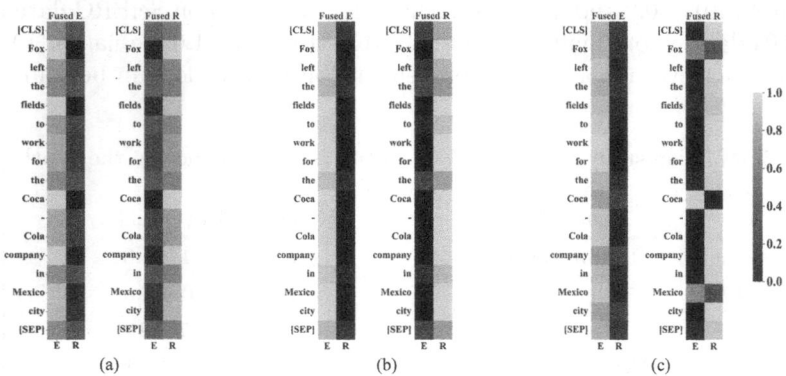

Fig. 2. The fused proportion between tasks of each word in the new fused feature.

6.2   Effects of Fine-grained Attention Cross-Unit

In this section, we detail the interaction process of the FACU by a specific example. For input sentence, "Fox left the fields to work for the Coca-Cola company in Mexico city.", it has three golden entities, "Fox", "Coca-Cola company", "Mexico city" and two golden relations "EMP-ORG" between "Fox" and "Coca-Cola company", "GPE-AFF" between "Coca-Cola company" and "Mexico city".

As shown in Fig. 2 which includes three sub-figures 2a, 2b, and 2c, each sub-figure indicates the attention weights of one FACU. The left and right figures in the sub-figure represent the combination proportion between the two tasks of every token's feature in the new fused features of NER and RE respectively. In Fig. 2a, in the FACU at the first layer, the entity information is captured by both two tasks. In Fig. 2b, the second FACU performs less interaction. We argue that in this stage, each task has learned its specific representation by the respective attention module. To alleviate the confusion between these two representations, this FACU largely retains such two different features and reduces the interaction.

Table 4. Comparison between SA and EA.

head	SA		EA	
	Ent	Rel+	Ent	Rel+
8	87.9	63.8	**88.3**	**64.4**
4	88.5	63.9	**88.5**	**64.2**
2	87.9	63.4	**88.4**	**64.3**
1	88.5	63.8	**88.6**	**64.9**

Table 5. Performance of different β.

Value	Ent	Rel+
$\beta = 1$	88.1	63.8
$\beta = 1.5$	**88.6**	**64.9**
$\beta = 2$	88.0	64.7
$\beta = 2.5$	87.9	63.3
$\beta = 3$	88.2	63.9

In Fig. 2c, it is evident that the start token's features of entities (Fox, Coca, Mexico) in the NER task are largely fused to the correspondings in the RE task. And since the "Coca" token appears in both triples, it should be more important than the other two tokens, and our FACU also notices this special token by setting the proportion of this token's feature from NER higher. Meanwhile, at the entity edge of NER fused representation like "Coca" and "company", they also incorporate features from RE tasks at a relatively higher proportion than other positions. Consequently, it can be confirmed that our FACU adaptively learns to interact valuable features in a bidirectional and fine-grained way, fully exploiting the correlations between NER and RE.

6.3 Effects of the External Attention

In this section, we compare the External Attention (EA) with the traditional Self-Attention (SA) network. We conduct a set of comparative experiments with different numbers of attention heads on ACE05 test set based on $BERT_{base}$. As shown in Table 4, the performance of using external attention is generally better than traditional self-attention, and it increases relation by 0.6, 0.3, 0.9, 1,1 when h =8, 4, 2, 1 respectively. We argue that the external attention exploits the correlation between multiple samples and thus benefits learning task-specific representation. As far as we know, we are the first to introduce the external attention to the Information Extraction domain and verify its effectiveness, inspiring future generations in the choice of attention network.

6.4 Effects of the Equilibrium Factor β

In the training stage, we introduce an equilibrium factor β to balance the convergence rate of the two tasks. We argue that the RE task depends on the NER task. Therefore, we make the convergence of RE slightly slower than that of NER by multiplying β by the loss function of RE $\mathcal{L}_{re}$ to increase the $\mathcal{L}_{re}$. Table 5 shows the results of different β. When the $\beta = 1.5$, both tasks achieve the best performance. When the $\beta = 1$, the NER and RE have the same convergence rate. However, the relation can not be correctly predicted without extracting the entity first, thus limiting performance. When the β becomes too large, the convergence difficulty of RE will increase, and the model will excessively focus on the RE task, resulting in its performance degradation.

7 Conclusion

In this paper, we encode task-specific representations for NER and RE respectively with our proposed Dual Interactive Attention Network (DIANet) for joint entity and relation extraction. We present a Fine-grained Attention Cross-Unit to perform feature interaction and explore the correlation between tasks in a fine-grained way. And we novelly introduce the external attention network into information extraction to learn representation for the first time and achieve superior performance than traditional attention network. Extensive experimental results on five standard benchmarks show that our approach improves remarkably against previous works and confirm the effectiveness of our approach.

Acknowledgments. This work is supported by grant from the National Natural Science Foundation of China (No. 62076048), the Science and Technology Innovation Foundation of Dalian (2020JJ26GX035).

References

1. Bekoulis, G., Deleu, J., Demeester, T., Develder, C.: Joint entity recognition and relation extraction as a multi-head selection problem. Expert Syst. Appl. **114**, 34–45 (2018)
2. Cabot, P.L.H., Navigli, R.: Rebel: relation extraction by end-to-end language generation. In: Proceedings of the EMNLP 2021, pp. 2370–2381 (2021)
3. Walker, C., Strassel, S., Medero, J., Maeda, K.: ACE 2005 multilingual training corpus. J. Biomed. Inf. **45**(5), 57–45 (2005)
4. Doddington, G.R., Mitchell, A., Przybocki, M.A., Ramshaw, L.A., Strassel, S.M., Weischedel, R.M.: The automatic content extraction (ACE) program-tasks, data, and evaluation. In: LREC, vol. 2, pp. 837–840 (2004)
5. Eberts, M., Ulges, A.: Span-based joint entity and relation extraction with transformer pre-training. In: ECAI 2020, pp. 2006–2013 (2019)
6. Guo, M.H., Liu, Z.N., Mu, T.J., Hu, S.M.: Beyond self-attention: external attention using two linear layers for visual tasks. arXiv preprint arXiv:2105.02358
7. Gurulingappa, H., Rajput, A.M., Roberts, A., Fluck, J., Hofmann-Apitius, M., Toldo, L.: Development of a benchmark corpus to support the automatic extraction of drug-related adverse effects from medical case reports. J. Biomed. Inf. **45**(5), 885–892 (2012)
8. Luan, Y., He, L., Ostendorf, M., Hajishirzi, H.: Multi-task identification of entities, relations, and coreference for scientific knowledge graph construction. In: Proceedings of the EMNLP, pp. 3219–3232 (2018)
9. Miwa, M., Bansal, M.: End-to-end relation extraction using LSTMs on sequences and tree structures. In: Proceedings of the ACL, pp. 1105–1116 (2016)
10. Ren, F., et al.: A novel global feature-oriented relational triple extraction model based on table filling. In: Proceedings of the EMNLP, pp. 2646–2656 (2021)

11. Roth, D., Yih, W.: A linear programming formulation for global inference in natural language tasks. In: Proceedings of the HLT-NAACL, pp. 1–8 (2004)
12. Vaswani, A., et al.: Attention is all you need. In: Proceedings of the NIPS, pp. 5998–6008 (2017)
13. Wang, J., Lu, W.: Two are better than one: joint entity and relation extraction with table-sequence encoders. In: Proceedings of the EMNLP, pp. 1706–1721 (2020)
14. Wang, Y., Sun, C., Wu, Y., Zhou, H., Li, L., Yan, J.: UniRE: a unified label space for entity relation extraction. In: Proceedings of the ACL, pp. 220–231 (2021)
15. Wang, Y., Yu, B., Zhang, Y., Liu, T., Zhu, H., Sun, L.: TPLinker: single-stage joint extraction of entities and relations through token pair linking. In: Proceedings of the COLING, pp. 1572–1582 (2020)
16. Wei, Z., Su, J., Wang, Y., Tian, Y.: A novel cascade binary tagging framework for relational triple extraction. In: Proceedings of the ACL, pp. 1476–1488 (2020)
17. Yan, Z., Zhang, C., Fu, J., Zhang, Q., Wei, Z.: A partition filter network for joint entity and relation extraction. In: Proceedings of the EMNLP, pp. 185–197 (2021)
18. Zheng, S., Wang, F., Bao, H., Hao, Y., Zhou, P., Xu, B.: Joint extraction of entities and relations based on a novel tagging scheme. In: Proceedings of the ACL, pp. 1227–1236 (2017)
19. Zhong, Z., Chen, D.: A frustratingly easy approach for entity and relation extraction. In: Proceedings of the NAACL, pp. 50–61 (2021)

Adversarial Transfer Learning for Named Entity Recognition Based on Multi-Head Attention Mechanism and Feature Fusion

Dandan Zhao[1,2], Pan Zhang[2], Jiana Meng[2(✉)], and Yue Wu[2]

[1] Dalian University of Technology, Dalian 116024, Liaoning, China
[2] Dalian Minzu University, Dalian 116600, Liaoning, China
mengjn@dlnu.edu.cn

Abstract. Named entity recognition (NER) is an important task of natural language processing. In most scenarios, there are not sufficient annotated data for NER. The existing methods can only solve the problem of a certain type of the lack of labeled data. To tackle this problem, we present a unified model named Multi-head-attention-Feature-fusion-Adversarial-Transfer-NER (MFAT-NER) to solve the cross-task, cross-lingual and cross-domain NER tasks. The proposed model has the advantages of obtaining better feature representations by word-level and character-level feature fusion and of learning relevant information in different representational subspaces of a sentence by multi-head attention mechanism that can obtain more semantic interaction information. To make the proposed model more generalization, the MFAT-NER model exploits the shared BiLSTM component for extracting the shared feature representations and introduces the adversarial transfer learning method. For the cross-lingual NER, cross-domain NER and cross-task NER, the experimental results show that the proposed unified method outperforms other state-of-the-art methods.

Keywords: Named entity recognition · Feature fusion · Multi-head attention mechanism · Adversarial transfer learning · Deep learning

1 Introduction

NER is to recognize the predefined types of entities from natural language text, such as location, person and organization. In recent years, deep neural network (DNN) has gradually become the focus of NER research [1, 2]. However, deep learning methods rely on sufficient annotated data with the same data distribution between the source and target data. Semi-supervised and unsupervised learning can alleviate the need for the annotated data, but the performance of the trained models is not as good as it could be. Transfer learning makes use of data from the relevant domain, thus reducing the need for annotated data for the target domain training task. It has gradually been used to solve the problem of lack of annotated data [3].

© The Author(s), under exclusive license to Springer Nature Switzerland AG 2022
W. Lu et al. (Eds.): NLPCC 2022, LNAI 13551, pp. 272–284, 2022.
https://doi.org/10.1007/978-3-031-17120-8_22

Previous works have shown the transfer learning approaches for solving NER tasks, which mainly include the data-based transfer learning, model-based transfer learning and adversarial transfer-based transfer learning. NER's data-based transfer learning approaches achieve good performance on the cross-lingual NER, but these models require large-scale, high-quality annotated data and alignment information, which are limited to cross-lingual transfer. NER's model-based transfer learning approaches achieve the transfer of source domain knowledge by sharing the model parameters and feature representations between languages or domains, but these approaches do not take into account the differences between resources, which leads to the poor generalization of the NER model. Most of NER's adversarial transfer learning approaches are used to solve NER problems in specific task, specific language, and specific domain, where specific task is only for NER task, specific language is only for English and specific domain is only for universal domain.

In most cases, there is insufficient annotated data for NER. Furthermore, existing NER methods are not transferable and general for specific tasks, specific languages, and specific domains. In the NER task, because there is no boundary between words in the Chinese text, the Chinese NER task is difficult. The English text has a large amount of labeled data, but for small languages, there are fewer labeled data resources. In addition, the NER model is used in the effect is very good in one domain, but it drops sharply in another domain, so the domain adaptability of the NER model still needs to be improved.

To tackle the above issues, we design a unified NER framework based on adversarial transfer learning, named MFAT-NER model, to solve cross-task, cross-lingual and cross-domain NER tasks. For cross-task NER, we perform transfer learning on the Chinese word segmentation (CWS) task and Chinese NER task, and use the information which is helpful for entity boundary detection in the word segmentation task to improve the effect of the entity recognition task. For cross-lingual NER, we perform transfer learning on English, Spanish and Dutch. For cross-domain NER, we perform transfer learning in the news domain and twitter comments domain. It effectively solves the problem of named entity recognition in specific domains and low-resource, small-language languages. The main contributions of our model are as follows.

(1) To obtain the feature representations, the proposed model concatenates the dynamic feature representations of words learned by ELMo [4] and the character-based feature representations of words learned by CNN.

(2) To obtain more semantic interaction information, the proposed model adds a multi-head attention mechanism, which can learn the relevant information in different representations subspace.

(3) To make the feature representations more compatible, the proposed model employs a shared BiLSTM component for extracting the shared feature representations and introduces the adversarial transfer learning method into the shared BiLSTM output layer.

2 Related Works

2.1 Named Entity Recognition

NER is usually defined as a sequence labeling task, and early studies applied handcrafted rules, dictionaries, and traditional machine learning models. With the development of deep learning, the research focus has turned to Deep Neural Networks. However, traditional and deep named entity recognition methods rely heavily on a large number of labeled training data with the same distribution, resulting in poor model portability. The introduction of transfer learning in named entity recognition solves this problem very well. To address the lack of hand-crafted annotations in the target language. Ni et al. [5] proposed two weakly supervised cross-linguistic NER labeling methods and representation projection methods, as well as two co-decoding schemes, which effectively improve the recognition accuracy of NER. Due to the emergence of possible new entity types in the target domain, and to address the problem of relabeling the data and retraining the model, Chen et al. [6] added new neurons to the output layer of the target model and transferred some parameters of the source model.

2.2 Adversarial Transfer Learning

NER's adversarial transfer learning is an adversarial technique inspired by the GAN networks. Cao et al. [7] first introduced the adversarial transfer learning to the NER task and proposed a Chinese NER adversarial transfer learning model with a self-attention mechanism. They exploited the rich word boundary information of the CWS task to improve the performance of NER model. In addition, a self-attention mechanism is added to the BiLSTM output layer to explicitly capture the long distance dependency between two characters. Zhu et al. [8] investigated a convolutional attention network called CAN for Chinese NER, which can capture the key information from adjacent characters and sentence contexts. Zhou et al. [9] proposed a dual adversarial transfer network, which introduces the adversarial learning on the deep transfer unit to solve the problem of the training data imbalance.

3 MFAT-NER Model

In order to tackle the cross-task, cross-lingual and cross-domain NER tasks on a unified model, we propose a unified transfer learning framework based on multi-head attention mechanism and feature fusion, named MFAT-NER model. The overall architecture of the MFAT-NER model is illustrated in Fig. 1. It mainly consists of five components, embedding layer, encoder layer, attention layer, adversarial transfer layer and decoder layer.

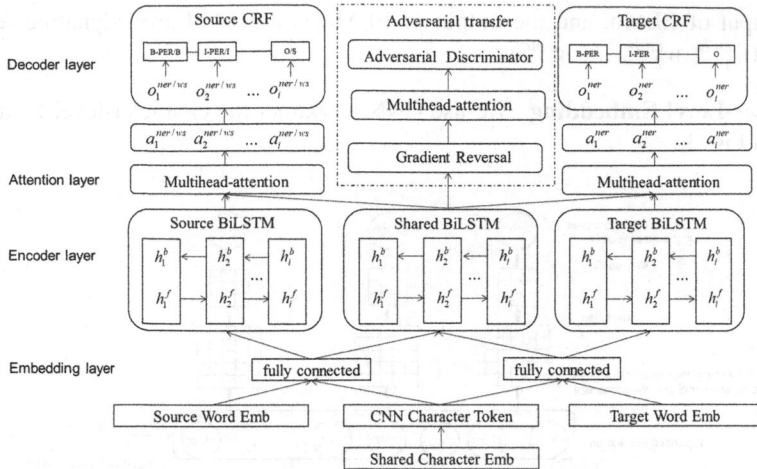

Fig. 1. Overall architecture of the MFAT-NER model

3.1 Embedded Layer

Character-level features can improve sequence labeling performance due to its ability to capture morphological and semantic information. We use the character-level CNN to capture the character-level feature representations. ELMo can obtain dynamic word-level embedding according to context, which can alleviate the polysemy problem. To capture the word-level feature representation which contains more information, we concatenate the dynamic feature representations of words learned by ELMo and the character-based feature representations of words learned by CNN.

Word-Level Embedding. We use ELMo to extract the word-level features as show in Fig. 2. Assume the input sentence is $X = (x_1, x_2, ...x_i)$, where i is the length of this sentence. Firstly, the input sequence is preprocessed into the pre-trained word-level vectors $w_i = (w_1, w_2, ..., w_i)$, and then the pre-trained word-level vectors are used

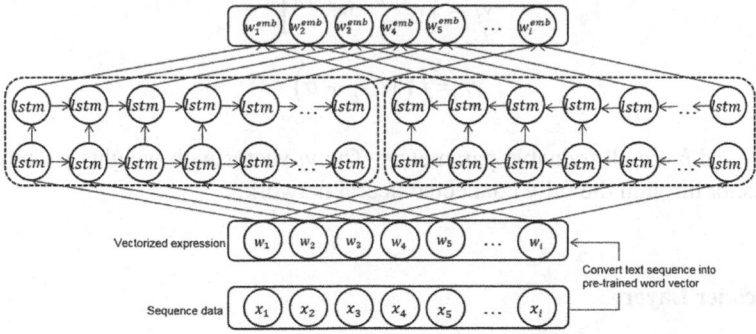

Fig. 2. Word-level dynamic features of words extracted by ELMo

as the input of ELMo, and the output of ELMo is the word-level dynamic features $w_i^{emb} = (w_1^{emb}, w_2^{emb}, ..., w_i^{emb})$.

Character-Level Embedding. We use CNN to extract the character-level features as shown in Fig. 3.

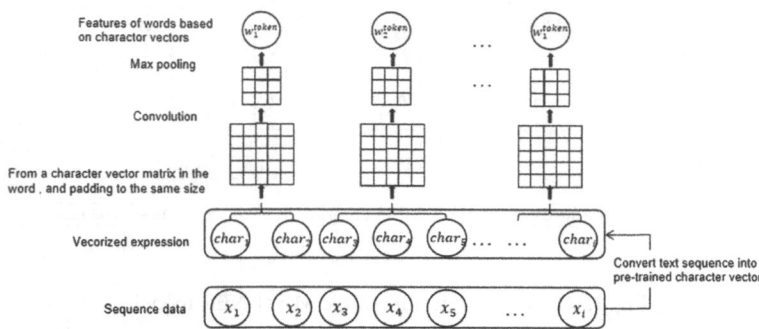

Fig. 3. Character-based feature of words extracted by CNN

The input sequence is preprocessed into the pre-trained character-level vectors $char_i$, and the pre-trained character-level embedding is used as the input of CNN. First, each character in the word is mapped to a character-level vector and these character-level vectors form an embedding matrix. Then, important features of adjacent inputs on the embedding matrix are captured using filters of different sizes. We use three filter widths to capture different features. Finally, a single feature is extracted from all feature maps by the max pooling. The final output features are $w_i^{token} = (w_1^{token}, w_2^{token}, ..., w_i^{token})$.

Integrating Word-Level and Character-Level Features. To integrate word-level and character-level features, we feed the output of the embedding layer into a fully connected neural network. The advantage of this approach is that the model can generate word vectors with more information, which is expressed by the following equations.

$$v_i' = \left[w_i^{emb}, w_i^{token} \right] \tag{1}$$

$$v_i = f\left(W_i v_i' + b \right) \tag{2}$$

where W_i and b are all trainable parameters. The v_i vector with weights is obtained v_i' by the vector through the fully connected neural network.

3.2   Encoder Layer

Traditional RNN can effectively exploit the structural information of sentences, but it suffers from problems such as gradient explosion and gradient disappearance. BiLSTM is an improved RNN model that introduces a gating mechanism to effectively utilize contextual information.

To consider the differences on the word-level features between different data, the source BiLSTM and the target BiLSTM extract the features of the source and target data, respectively. $h^{source} = \{h_1^{so}, h_2^{so}, \ldots, h_i^{so}\}$ is the output of source BiLSTM and $h^{target} = \{h_1^{ta}, h_1^{ta}, \ldots, h_i^{ta}\}$ is the output of target BiLSTM. The shared BiLSTM extracts the features that can be shared. $h^{shared} = \{h_1^{sh}, h_2^{sh}, \ldots, h_i^{sh}\}$ is the output of shared BiLSTM. The shared BiLSTM is used as an example, and the specific calculation is as follows.

$$h^{f-sh} = lstm\left(h_{i-1}^{f-sh}, v_i\right) \tag{3}$$

$$h^{b-sh} = lstm\left(h_{i-1}^{b-sh}, v_i\right) \tag{4}$$

$$h^{sh} = h_i^{f-sh} \oplus h_i^{b-sh} \tag{5}$$

3.3 Attention Layer

The important information of the text is selectively focused by the attention mechanism, so the output of the source BiLSTM and target BiLSTM is fed into the attention layer. The advantage of this approach is that the model can capture important information from different representation subspaces. Assume the input sentence is $h^{source} = \{h_1^{so}, h_2^{so}, \ldots, h_i^{so}\}$. The word vector matrix h^{source} is linearly transformed and is cut into three matrices Q, K and V with the same dimensions.

$$q_i = W_q \cdot h_i^{so} + b_q \tag{6}$$

$$k_i = W_k \cdot h_i^{so} + b_k \tag{7}$$

$$v_i = W_v \cdot h_i^{so} + b_v \tag{8}$$

$$Attention(Q, K, V) = softmax\left(\frac{QK^T}{\sqrt{d}}\right)V \tag{9}$$

Then, the attention value of each subspace is calculated in parallel. Finally, the attention value of each subspace is concatenated and linearly transformed. a_i represents the value of each subspace. A represents the value of each subspace. W_o is a trainable parameter.

$$a_i = Attention\left(QW_i^Q, KW_i^k, VW_i^V\right) \tag{10}$$

$$A = Concat(a_1, a_2, \ldots, a_8)W_o \tag{11}$$

3.4 Adversarial Transfer Layer

Due to the size of the source and target datasets are imbalance, if such imbalance is not considered, the feature representations extracted from them are incompatible. To better capture shared features, we construct a shared BiLSTM and an adversarial discriminator based on the idea of generative adversarial networks.

Specifically, assumed the output of share BiLSTM is h^{source}. The gradient is changed to the opposite sign, which encourages the shared layer to learn the shared feature representation through adversarial transfer learning. Then through the attention mechanism, the output of the attention layer in the confrontation transfer layer is a_i, and then projected to the scalar $a_i^{'}$ through linear transformation.

$$a_i^{'} = W_s \cdot a_i + b_s \tag{12}$$

Finally, we introduce the adversarial loss l_{AD} to prevent specific information in the source domain from entering the shared space part. The l_{AD} training shared BiLSTM produces shared features, making the adversarial discriminator unable to distinguish the feature representation in the shared feature extractor from the source or the target domain. After training, the adversarial discriminator and shared BiLSTM reach a state of equilibrium.

$$l_{AD} = -\sum_i \left\{ Sent_{i \in D_S} g (1 - a_i^{'})^{\gamma} \log a_i^{'} + Sent_{i \in D_T} (1 - g)(a_i^{'})^{\gamma} \log(1 - a_i^{'}) \right\} \tag{13}$$

where W_s and b_s are all trainable parameters. $Sent_{i \in D_s}$ and $Sent_{i \in D_T}$ are identity functions; γ measures the hard samples and the simple sample loss contribution. $(1 - a_i^{'})^{\gamma}$ (or $(a_i^{'})^{\gamma}$)) controls the loss contribution of each sample. We set a weight g between the source data and the target data to solve the data imbalance problem.

3.5 Decoder Layer

CRF is a feature-flexible, globally optimal labeling framework that learns the constraints from the training data to ensure the validity of the predicted labels. We use the CRF to filter the score for each label output from the neural network model. The loss function of NER is the negative log-likelihood.

$$l_{CRF \epsilon \{source, target\}} = -\sum_{i=1}^{T} \log p(\hat{y}^{(i)} | X^i) \tag{14}$$

The final loss function of our model consists of two parts, the loss for adversarial transfer and the loss for NER in the source domain and target domain, as indicated by the following equation. λ is a super-parameter.

$$L = l_{CRF \epsilon \{source, target\}} + \lambda l_{AD} \tag{15}$$

4 Experiments

We first introduce the datasets, experimental settings. Then, we report the experimental results for the cross-task NER, cross-lingual NER and cross-domain NER and conduct an ablation study.

4.1 Datasets

We perform the experiments on different datasets. The features extracted from the word segmentation task may provide critical information for NER task, thus we augment the features of the NER task by using the features shared between the word segmentation and the NER tasks. We use the MSR dataset for the word segmentation (WS) task, and use the SIGHAN2006 NER dataset (MSRA NER dataset), Weibo NER dataset and Chinese literature dataset for the NER task.

In addition, we also experiment on the CoNLL-2003 English NER, CoNLL-2002 Spanish and Dutch NER, and WNUT-2016 and 2017 twitter NER datasets. We use the CoNLL-2003 English NER dataset as source, the CoNLL-2002 (Spanish) and CoNLL-2002 (Dutch) datasets as target language in the cross-lingual NER task, the WNUT-2016 and WNUT-2017 datasets as target domain in the cross-domain NER task. These statistics are shown in Table 1.

Table 1. The number of sentences for the datasets.

Task		Dataset	Train	Dev	Test
Cross-task	WS	MSR	86924	–	–
	NER	MSRA	46364	5000	4365
		Weibo	1350	270	270
		Chinese literature	24165	1895	2836
Cross-lingual	Source	CoNLL-2003	14018	3249	3249
	Target	CoNLL-2002(Spanish)	7235	1631	1356
		CoNLL-2002(Dutch)	15805	2895	5195
Cross-domain	Source	CoNLL-2003	14018	3249	3249
	Target	WNUT-2016	2394	999	3840
		WNUT-2017	3393	1009	1251

4.2 Experimental Settings

We train the MFAT-NER model on the training and validation datasets, and report the performance of the model on the test dataset. We calculate the precision, recall, F1 scores of main datasets.

Let the dropout rate be 0.5; the learning rate be 0.0005; the attention heads be 8; the weight parameter α be 0.25 and γ be 2.0. We use the Adam optimizer for training with a mini-batch. All experiments are performed on the same machine, namely, Inter(R) Xeon(R) CPU E5–2640 v4 @2.40 GHz and GeForce RTX 2080Ti GPU.

4.3 Experimental Results

MFAT-NER Results. The experimental results on the cross-task NER, cross-lingual NER and cross-domain NER datasets are show in Table 2. The metrics we report include precision, recall and F1 value.

Table 2. The experimental results on the all datasets.

Task	Datasets	P (%)	R (%)	F1(%)
Cross-task	MSRA	92.91	91.04	91.97
	Weibo	62.86	57.00	59.79
	Chinese literature	78.27	84.12	81.09
Cross-lingual	CoNLL-2002(Spanish)	90.57	86.98	88.74
	CoNLL-2002(Dutch)	93.21	90.90	92.06
Cross-domain	WNUT-2016	66.62	45.91	54.36
	WNUT-2017	57.83	46.30	51.30

For the cross-task NER task, the Weibo text is short and flexible, and the public corpus is small and does not have word boundary features, so the Weibo NER dataset has the lowest F1 value compared to the MSRA NER and Chinese literature datasets. For the cross-lingual NER task, the F1 values of the CoNLL-2002 Spanish dataset and the CoNLL-2002 Dutch dataset can achieve 88.74% and 92.06%, respectively. For the cross-domain NER task, the datasets of the WNUT-2016 and the WNUT-2017 are too small so that the F1 value of cross-domain NER is low. The MFAT-NER model still achieves good results on these datasets, which indicates that our model is effective.

Compared with State-of-the-Art Models. We compare the proposed model with the previous models on the Weibo NER and Chinese literature datasets. The results of F1 value are described in Table 3.

For the Chinese literature dataset, the BiLSTM [10] and CRF [11] models are simple and have poor learning ability compared to complex network models. Coupled with the abstract content of Chinese literature, entity boundary recognition is more difficult, so the model performance is not excellent.

For the Weibo dataset, compared with the model proposed by Liu et al. [12], the MFAT-NER model uses the rich word boundary information of word segmentation task to improve the performance of NER task. Compared with the BCAT-NER model [7], the MFAT-NER model uses the word-level and character-level features to generate word vectors with more information. Compared with the CAN-NER [8] model, the MFAT-NER model introduces adversarial transfer learning which can make the boundary information extracted from the word segmentation task and the NER task more compatible. Compared with both DoubADV [13] and WC-GCN + Seq [14] models, the MFAT-NER model shares the character-level features and the final feature representation can be more compatible by adversarial learning. The MECT [15] model outperforms our model, probably because it uses multivariate data embedding and increases the structural information of Chinese radicals, while our model performs slightly worse on a single task in order to achieve model unification.

Table 3. Cross-task comparison with other models.

Model	Weibo	Chinese literature
BiLSTM [10] (1997)	–	66.16
CRF [11] (2001)	–	71.33
BCAT-NER [7] (2018)	53.08	–
WC-LSTM + self-attention [12] (2019)	57.51	–
CAN-NER [8] (2019)	59.31	–
DoubADV [13] (2020)	56.39	–
WC-GCN + Seq [14] (2020)	59.08	–
MECT [15] (2021)	**61.91**	–
Ours	59.79	**81.09**

To evaluate the performance of our proposed model on the cross-lingual NER and the cross-domain NER tasks, we compare the MFAT-NER model with the previous excellent models on the CoNLL-2002(Dutch) and the WNUT-2017 datasets. The results of F1 value are described in Table 4.

Compared with LM-LSTM-CRF [2], BERT-base [16], Flair embedding [17] model, the performance of our model is better than these datasets, which also shows that our method achieves cross-lingual and cross-domain. On the Dutch dataset, our model achieves good results, although it does not have the enhanced data representation like KAWR-FC [1] and CLDG [20]. On the WNUT-2017 dataset, the MFAT-NER model performs better than only using ELMO [4] for NER. Compared with DATNeT [9], the MFAT-NER model uses a multi-head attention mechanism that enables the model to learn more about the internal features of the sequence. Compared to using syntactic, semantic, and visual information (AESI [19], SE-NER [18], InferNER [21]), our model achieves better results without additional information. This also shows that the MFAT-NER model is more general than other models to achieve cross-domain and cross-language unification.

Ablation Study. We conduct ablation experiments on the MSRA NER, Weibo NER, CoNLL-2002(Spanish) and WNUT-2016 datasets. The ablation results of the model are shown in Table 5.

We use the BiLSTM-CRF model as the baseline model which is one of the widely used models in the previous NER tasks. The baseline model adds the multi-head attention mechanism (+MA) to extract different features. Considering the part of shared features contains noisy information, to make the features extracted from the source and target domains more compatible. Adversarial transfer learning (+AT) is introduced to the proposed model. The F1 value is improved on all datasets.

Table 4. Cross-lingual/Cross-domain comparison with other models.

Model	Cross-lingual (Dutch)	Cross-domain (WNUT-2017)
LM-LSTM-CRF [2] (2018)	86.03	39.61
ELMo [4] (2018)	–	42.58
BERT-base [16] (2018)	89.55	46.88
Flair embedding [17] (2018)	90.44	50.24
DATNet [9] (2019)	–	47.91
KAWR-FC [1] (2020)	91.23	–
SE-NER [18] (2020)	–	50.36
AESI [19] (2020)	–	50.68
CLDG [20] (2021)	89.65	–
InferNER [21] (2021)	–	50.52
Ours	**92.06**	**51.30**

We use CNN to extract the character-level features (+CNN+MA+AT), the improvement effect is more significant for the Weibo NER dataset. Because the character-level feature representation will contain deeper semantic information, which allows the model to learn more knowledge. Besides, we use MFAT-NER and the F1 value increase by 1.00%, 1.77%, 1.03% and 1.42% on the four datasets, respectively.

Table 5. Ablation results of the model.

Dataset		Baseline	+MA	+AT	+CNN+MA+AT	Ours
MSRA	P	89.84	90.62	91.73	91.19	92.91
	R	88.42	88.81	89.58	90.05	91.04
	F1	89.13	89.71	90.64	90.97	**91.97**
Weibo	P	58.99	57.81	55.72	55.72	62.86
	R	44.93	47.67	50.68	50.68	57.00
	F1	51.01	52.25	53.08	58.02	**59.79**
CoNLL-2002 (Spanish)	P	81.52	82.09	84.41	85.23	90.57
	R	81.50	82.85	82.77	90.34	86.98
	F1	81.16	82.47	83.58	87.71	**88.74**
WNUT-2016	P	57.20	57.83	61.83	64.16	66.62
	R	41.39	46.30	40.80	45.04	45.91
	F1	46.87	48.04	49.16	52.94	**54.36**

5   Conclusion and Future Work

We propose a unified NER model framework named MFAT-NER for cross-task, cross-language and cross-domain NER. The proposed model integrates the character-level and word-level features and uses the multi-head attention mechanism to further extract semantic information. In addition, to address the problem of difference in the size of datasets, the proposed model introduces an adversarial neural network to set weights between the source and target data to balance their influence. The experimental results show that the proposed model is more transferable, versatile, and has a better comprehensive recognition effect. However, there are still many shortcomings in our work. How to improve the efficiency of the model and better solve the problem of negative transfer is the main work of our next research.

Acknowledgments. Authors sincerely thank the anonymous reviewers for their valuable suggestions that have greatly enhance the quality of the work. The work is supported by the National Natural Science Foundation of China No.U1936109 and No.61876031.

References

1. He, Q., Wu, L., Yin, Y., Cai, H.: Knowledge-graph augmented word representations for named entity recognition. In: Proceedings of the AAAI Conference on Artificial Intelligence, pp. 7919–7926 (2020)
2. Liu, L., et al.: Empower sequence labeling with task-aware neural language model. In: Proceedings of the AAAI Conference on Artificial Intelligence (2018)
3. Peng, D., Wang, Y., Liu, C., Chen, Z.: TL-NER: a transfer learning model for Chinese named entity recognition. Inf. Syst. Front. **22**(6), 1291–1304 (2020)
4. Peters, M., Neumann, M., Iyyer, M., Gardner, M., Zettlemoyer, L.: Deep Contextualized Word Representations (2018)
5. Ni, J., Dinu, G., Florian, R.: Weakly supervised cross-lingual named entity recognition via effective annotation and representation projection. arXiv preprint arXiv:170702483 (2017)
6. Chen, L., Moschitti, A.: Transfer learning for sequence labeling using source model and target data. In: (2019)
7. Cao, P., Chen, Y., Liu, K., Zhao, J., Liu, S.: Adversarial transfer learning for Chinese named entity recognition with self-attention mechanism. In: Proceedings of the 2018 Conference on Empirical Methods in Natural Language Processing (2018)
8. Zhu, Y., Wang, G., Karlsson, B.F.: CAN-NER: convolutional attention network for Chinese named entity recognition. In: (2019)
9. Zhou, J.T., Zhang, H., Jin, D., Peng, X.: Dual adversarial transfer for sequence labeling. IEEE Trans. Pattern Anal. Mach. Intell. **43**, 434–446 (2019)
10. Hochreiter, S., Schmidhuber, J.: Long short-term memory. Neural Comput. **9**(8), 1735–1780 (1997)
11. Lafferty, J., Mccallum, A., Pereira, F.: Conditional random fields: probabilistic models for segmenting and labeling sequence data. Proceedings of ICML (2002)
12. Liu, W., Xu, T., Xu, Q., Song, J, Zu, Y.: An encoding strategy based word-character LSTM for Chinese NER. In: North American Chapter of the Association for Computational Linguistics (2019)
13. Yun, H.U., Zheng, C.: A double adversarial network model for multi-domain and multi-task Chinese named entity recognition. IEICE Trans. Inf. Syst. **103**, 1744–1752 (2020)

14. Tang, Z., Wan, B., Yang, L.: Word-character graph convolution network for Chinese named entity recognition. IEEE/ACM Trans. Audio, Speech, Lang. Process. **28**, 1520–1532 (2020)
15. Wu, S., Song, X., Feng, Z.: MECT: multi-metadata embedding based cross-transformer for Chinese named entity recognition. In: (2021)
16. Devlin, J., Chang, M.W., Lee, K., Toutanova, K.: BERT: pre-training of deep bidirectional transformers for language understanding (2018)
17. Akbik, A., Blythe, D., Vollgraf, R.: Contextual string embeddings for sequence labeling. In: International Conference on Computational Linguistics (2018)
18. Nie, Y., Tian, Y., Song, Y., Ao, X., Wan, X.: Improving named entity recognition with attentive ensemble of syntactic information. In: Findings of the Association for Computational Linguistics: EMNLP 2020 (2020)
19. Nie, Y., Tian, Y., Wan, X., Song, Y., Dai, B.: Named entity recognition for social media texts with semantic augmentation. In: Proceedings of the 2020 Conference on Empirical Methods in Natural Language Processing (EMNLP) (2020)
20. Guo, R., Roth, D.: Constrained labeled data generation for low-resource named entity recognition. In: Findings of the Association for Computational Linguistics: ACL-IJCNLP 2021 (2021)
21. Shahzad, M., Amin, A., Esteves, D., Ngomo, A.C.N.: InferNER: an attentive model leveraging the sentence-level information for named entity recognition in microblogs. In: The 34th International FLAIRS Conference 2021 (2021)

Rethinking the Value of Gazetteer in Chinese Named Entity Recognition

Qianglong Chen[1], Xiangji Zeng[1], Jiangang Zhu[2], Yin Zhang[1(✉)], Bojia Lin[2], Yang Yang[2], and Daxin Jiang[2]

[1] College of Computer Science and Technology, Zhejiang University, Hangzhou, China
{chenqianglong,zengxiangji,zhangyin98}@zju.edu.cn
[2] Microsoft STCA, Beijing, China
{jiangazh,bojial,yayan,djiang}@microsoft.com

Abstract. Gazetteer is widely used in Chinese named entity recognition (NER) to enhance span boundary detection and type classification. However, to further understand the generalizability and effectiveness of gazetteers, the NLP community still lacks a systematic analysis of the gazetteer-enhanced NER model. In this paper, we first re-examine the effectiveness of several common practices of the gazetteer-enhanced NER models and carry out a series of detailed analyses to evaluate the relationship between the model performance and the gazetteer characteristics, which can guide us to build a more suitable gazetteer. The findings of this paper are as follows: (1) the gazetteer has a positive impact on the NER model in most situations. (2) the performance of the NER model greatly benefits from the high-quality pre-trained lexeme embeddings. (3) a good gazetteer should cover more entities that can be matched in both the training set and testing set.

Keywords: Gazetteer · Chinese named entity recognition · Knowledge enhancement

1 Introduction

Gazetteer, also known as the entity dictionary, has been mentioned in various literature about its importance to Chinese NER, such as solving error propagation in Chinese NER [1–4] and integrating rich external knowledge into NER [5,16,17]. Previous studies have proved that compared with the traditional NER model, the gazetteer-enhanced NER model can obtain external boundary and type information from gazetteer knowledge to boost the performance. The typical process of a gazetteer-enhanced NER consists of four stages: (1) Collecting word entries from knowledge bases to construct a gazetteer. The word entries could be named entities or arbitrary phrases. (2) Conducting entry matching on

---

Q. Chen and X. Zeng—Equal contribution.

the target sentence. (3) Encoding sentence and gazetteer knowledge with various encoders. (4) Extracting entities through decoding context-aware representation.

Although several gazetteer-enhanced NER models have been proposed in recent years, there are still several key questions that need to be answered. Firstly, several measures [10] have be developed to analyze the generalization behavior of existing NER models. However, the community is still lacking a detailed and unified evaluation for inspecting the relationship between the gazetteer-enhanced NER model's performance and its three indispensable components (gazetteer, dataset, and model) while now heavily depending on a holistic metric (F1 score). Secondly, the community is growing too fast to lack a comprehensive and systematic empirical study on gazetteer-enhanced NER models for reviewing the promising works in the past years and rethinking the pros and the cons.

To solve the above problems, in this work, we design several experiments which are committed to answering three questions as follows:

- **Q1:** Does gazetteer only have a positive impact on the NER model, or it also has a negative impact?
- **Q2:** Can the gazetteer improve the performance of the NER models based on the pre-trained language model?
- **Q3:** What type of gazetteer is the best gazetteer for improving performance?

To answer **Q1**, we reproduce three promising models and conduct several experiments on five datasets with three gazetteers. While almost all research efforts ignore whether the gazetteer is still helpful to the models enhanced by large scale pre-training language models, to figure out **Q2**, we modify the original static embedding as the pre-trained language model and conduct several new experiments on these new models. Additionally, current research works do not investigate the relationship between the model performance and the gazetteer characteristics, such as gazetteer size, pre-trained lexeme embedding, and lexeme type. To further explore **Q3**, we design experiments to investigate these relationship, which can provide interpretable results for better understanding the causality behind the entity extraction and guide us to build a more suitable gazetteer. Our code is available at this URL[1].

The main contributions of this paper are summarized as follows:

- We first re-examine some promising models with three gazetteers on five datasets with analysis through a fair and comparable environment.
- To further evaluate the effectiveness of gazetteer in pre-trained language models, we modify the gazetteer-enhanced model to adapt the existing pre-trained language models and make detailed analysis.
- Moreover, we conduct a series of explorations to uncover the relationship between the model performance and the gazetteer characteristics, which would bring some new insights for future work.

---

[1] https://github.com/knowledgeresearch/kaner.

Table 1. Models with different architectures. All our models are based on character-level token embeddings.

Model	Token embedding		Gazetteer		
	Gigaword	BERT	Gigaword	SGNS	TEC
BLCRF	✓	✗	✗	✗	✗
PLMTG	✗	✓	✗	✗	✗
SES	✓	✗	✓	✓	✓
SES†	✗	✓	✓	✓	✓
CGN	✓	✗	✓	✓	✓
CGN†	✗	✓	✓	✓	✓
MDGG	✓	✗	✓	✓	✓
MDGG†	✗	✓	✓	✓	✓

2 Task Definition

In general, the gazetteer-enhanced named entity recognition (GENER) task consists of three indispensable components: a gazetteer $G = (l_1, l_2, ..., l_M)$, a dataset $D = \{(X, Y)\}$, and a GENER model M. Here, we denote $X = \{x_1, x_2, ..., x_N\}$ as an input sequence and $Y = \{y_1, y_2, ..., y_N\}$ as the corresponding output tags. To obtain external lexeme information L, we adopt lexeme matching on the input sequence X with the gazetteer G. The goal of the task is to estimate the conditional probability $P(Y|X, L)$ with model M.

3 Model

3.1 GENER Model Selection and Reproduction

For the GENER model selection, we follow some rules as below. Firstly, the results of the model reported by the original paper should be *promising* enough. Secondly, the model's architecture should be *representative* enough. Considering the two points, we divide the existing models into two categories: token embedding modification and context encoder modification. The former integrates extra lexeme information with the token embedding. The latter modifies the context encoder to adapt extra lexeme information. Therefore, we select a model (SES) from the former category and two models (CGN, MDGG) from the latter category to investigate this area's progress. As shown in Table 1, we reproduce three promising GENER models, namely SES, CGN, and MDGG. The SES model [4] integrates external lexeme information into token embeddings. The CGN model [2] and the MDGG model [5] treat the matched lexemes and the original token sequence as a graph, then encode the graph by graph neural networks.

Table 2. Statistics of Gazetteers. *Num.* represents the number of lexeme in a gazetteer. *Dim.* represents the dimension of lexeme embedding. *pre-trained* represents whether the lexeme embeddings are pre-trained, such as Word2vec [20], GloVe [25], etc.

Gazetteer	Num.	Dim.	Pre-trained
TEC	61400	50	✗
Gigaword	704368	50	✓
SGNS	1292607	300	✓

3.2   Model Replacement with Pre-trained Language Model

To assess some components' role, we vary these models in terms of two aspects: different token embeddings or gazetteers. To explore the question **Q2**, we use BERT [8] to replace the original static token embedding. Specifically, we let BERT take the original input and regard BERT's final output as the token embeddings of the GENER model. When training the GENER model, we set the BERT part to have a low learning rate while setting a high learning rate for the remaining part of the GENER model. Additionally, we also implement two baseline NER models: BLCRF and PLMTG. The BLCRF model [21] consists of a bidirectional LSTM and a CRF layer. The PLMTG model consists of a BERT and a MLP layer. All our models are based on character-level token embeddings.

4   Experiments

4.1   Gazetteer and Dataset

Gazetteer. We choose three different gazetteers: Gigaword, SGNS, and TEC, to verify the effectiveness of gazetteer in the NER task. The Gigaword gazetteer [33] contains lots of words from the word segmentator, pre-trained embeddings and character embeddings, which is trained from the Chinese Gigaword corpus[2]. The SGNS gazetteer [14] is trained from Wikipedia and News and contains lots of words from the word segmentator and pre-trained embeddings. The TEC gazetteer [5], collected from the e-commerce domain, contains product and brand names only. The statistics of gazetteers are shown in Table 2.

Dataset. To make the results more convincing, we select five Chinese NER datasets: WeiboNER, ResumeNER, MSRANER, OntoNotes, and ECommerce, which are distributed from a wide range of domains, including social media, financial articles, news, and e-commerce. The WeiboNER dataset [24], annotated from Weibo[3] messages, contains both named and nominal mentions. The ResumeNER dataset [1], collected from Sina Finance[4], consists of senior

---

[2] https://catalog.ldc.upenn.edu/LDC2011T13.

[3] https://weibo.com/.

[4] https://finance.sina.com.cn/stock/.

Table 3. Statistics of selected datasets.

Dataset	Total	Train	Dev	Test
WeiboNER	1890	1350	270	270
ResumeNER	4761	3821	463	477
ECommerce	4987	3989	500	498
OntoNotes	49306	39446	4930	4930
MSRANER	50729	41728	4636	4365

executives' resumes from listed companies in the Chinese stock market. The MSRANER dataset [11] is collected from the news domain. The OntoNotes dataset[5], based on the OntoNotes project, is annotated from a large corpus comprising various text genres, such as news, conversational telephone speech, etc. The ECommerce dataset [5], collected from the e-commerce domain, contains lots of product descriptions. The statistics of datasets are shown in Table 3.

4.2 Fair Model Comparison Setting

Since the hyperparameters in the GENER model are sensitive to different datasets, choosing suitable hyperparameters for each model for fair comparison is one of the most important problem. For each model, we first adjust model hyperparameters on a small dataset (WeiboNER) and then reuse these hyperparameters on the other datasets and gazetteers. We use the micro-average F1 score to evaluate the model performance and we also give the average training speed and the number of parameters to illustrate the model complexity.

4.3 Experimental Results and Analysis

The Effectiveness of Gazetteer in GENER. As shown in the part of the vanilla model of Table 4, the GENER model is outstanding in the scenario where the baseline model BLCRF performs poorly. Specifically, the SES model with the SGNS gazetteer gets the best in most cases. The fly in the ointment is that it has a large amount of parameters (see Table 5), which mainly comes from the word embeddings of SGNS gazetteer. However, compared to the CGN model and the MDGG model, it is still superior in model complexity. The computation time of these two models is mainly restricted by graph neural networks. Additionally, compared to the baseline model, the MDGG model performs relatively poorly on large datasets (MSRANER and OntoNotes) but performs better on small datasets (WeiboNER, ResumeNER, and ECommerce). The results demonstrate that the gazetteer is helpful in most cases. However, an improper gazetteer also brings a negative impact.

---

[5] https://catalog.ldc.upenn.edu/LDC2013T19/.

Table 4. F1 Results on WeiboNER, ResumeNER, ECommerce, MSRANER, Onto-Notes.

Model	Gazeteer	WeiboNER	ResumeNER	ECommerce	MSRANER	OntoNotes
Vanilla Model						
BLCRF	N/A	50.37	92.91	64.99	84.48	90.07
SES	Gigaword	53.04	93.37	69.48	88.05	90.23
	SGNS	**57.22** (+6.85)	93.45	**71.90** (+0.691)	**90.87**(+6.39)	**90.49**(+0.42)
	TEC	52.37	92.94	65.19	85.47	89.96
CGN	Gigaword	51.12	92.72	63.91	86.73	88.23
	SGNS	54.24	92.22	65.89	89.10	88.12
	TEC	49.58	92.82	64.37	85.16	88.15
MDGG	Gigaword	53.16	93.86	70.07	76.16	63.96
	SGNS	56.20	93.83	71.38	76.09	63.48
	TEC	52.88	**93.87**(+0.96)	69.48	84.37	72.26
Revised Model						
PLMTG	N/A	64.35	90.90	76.61	89.58	87.32
SES[†]	Gigaword	67.00	94.91	81.05	**94.18** (+4.6)	**70.66** (-16.66)
	SGNS	67.89	95.76	**81.32**(+4.71)	93.10	57.56
	TEC	41.38	95.74	79.36	93.30	45.90
CGN[†]	Gigaword	45.50	91.53	55.23	81.36	69.65
	SGNS	54.30	92.22	54.94	87.36	54.24
	TEC	27.48	59.67	47.38	37.37	18.89
MDGG[†]	Gigaword	**68.41** (+4.06)	96.11	80.32	90.95	65.46
	SGNS	67.94	95.81	80.73	92.55	44.83
	TEC	67.78	**96.27** (+5.37)	80.11	89.60	66.47

Improvement on Pre-trained Language Models. Although we observe the positive impact of GENER models in most scenarios, almost all existing GENER models ignore to explore whether these gazetteer-enhanced methods can boost the performance of pre-trained language models or not. Driven by **Q2**, we incorporate the pre-trained language model with selected GENER methods. The results are shown in the part of the revised model of Table 4. Surprisingly, compared to the baseline model PLMTG, the BERT-enhanced GENER model is still boosting performance a lot in most scenarios. Furthermore, experimental results demonstrate the effectiveness of gazetteer in improving model performance in most scenarios where the baseline model PLMTG has a relatively higher F1 score. Unfortunately, it seems difficult to learn well on OntoNotes (see Table 4) and CGN model performs poorly in most cases. It may be due to inappropriate hyperparameter selection [13]. Compared with the GENER model without BERT, the BERT-enhanced GENER model can further improve the performance in most cases, which is what we have expected. Compared to the PLMTG model, the gazetteer enhanced model can achieve a better performance, which indicates that *the smaller pre-trained language model is not the NER's ceiling.*

4.4 Proper Gazetteer Exploration

While the GENER model has achieved impressive performance in most scenarios, what kind of gazetteer makes the model perform well still remains to be explored.

Table 5. Model complexity.

Model	Gazeteer	# Params.	# Time
BLCRF	N/A	1.0	1.0
SES	Gigaword	× 27.1	× 1.3
	SGNS	× 287.3	× 1.36
	TEC	× 3.4	× 1.5
CGN	Gigaword	× 27.4	× 8.2
	SGNS	× 286.8	× 8.5
	TEC	× 3.8	× 5.3
MDGG	Gigaword	× 32.5	× 10.0
	SGNS	× 291.9	× 11.1
	TEC	× 11.0	× 6.7

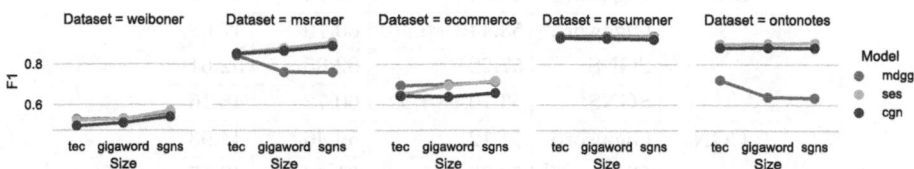

Fig. 1. F1 score changes across different gazetteers. The three gazetteers are on the coordinate axis from left to right according to the gazetteer size (tec → gigaword → sgns).

To answer this question, we design a series of experiments from two aspects: the gazetteer itself, and the interaction between the gazetteer and dataset.

Gazetteer Itself. We begin with characteristics of the gazetteer itself to figure out the relationship between the gazetteer and the model performance. For simplicity, we treat every lexeme in the gazetteer as an indivisible atom in this section. Therefore, the gazetteer's available characteristics are *gazetteer size* and *pre-trained lexeme embedding*.

Gazetteer Size. As shown in Table 2, we list the number of lexeme for each gazetteer. We first plot the relationship between gazetteer size and the model performance across the three gazetteers (see Fig. 1). In most cases, the model performance would increase when the gazetteer size is getting bigger. However, there still exists a few cases that are opposite the former pattern. Then, we re-conduct experiments on WeiboNER with the three GENER models but only select a certain percentage of lexeme for each gazetteer. As shown in Fig. 2, we observe that there is no obvious trend to prove that the larger the gazetteer is, the better the model performance will be. The results show that the model performance is not always positively correlated with the gazetteer size. *A small gazetteer has the ability to play a big role.* It suggests that *the gazetteer quality or suitability may influence the model performance.*

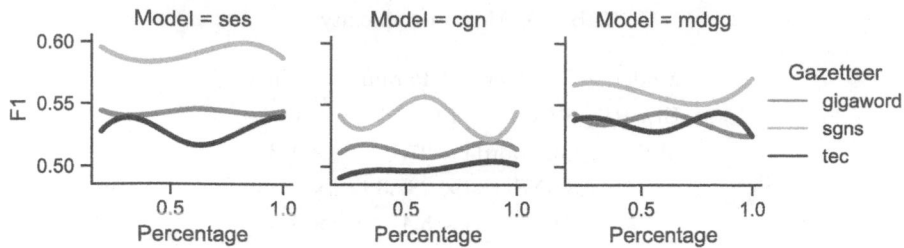

Fig. 2. F1 score changes across the size of the gazetteer itself on WeiboNER.

Table 6. An ablation study of pre-trained lexeme embedding on WeiboNER. ‡ denotes that the gazetteer has no pre-trained lexeme embeddings.

Model	Gazetteer	F1	Precision	Recall
SES	Gigaword	53.04	59.65	47.78
	Gigaword‡	53.44 (+0.40)	60.79	47.68
	SGNS	57.22	62.85	52.61
	SGNS‡	53.70 (−3.52)	60.72	48.16
CGN	Gigaword	51.12	59.46	44.93
	Gigaword‡	50.00 (−1.12)	61.42	42.17
	SGNS	54.24	60.14	49.47
	SGNS‡	50.28 (−3.96)	58.44	44.15
MDGG	Gigaword	53.16	55.92	50.67
	Gigaword‡	53.25 (+0.09)	56.82	50.14
	SGNS	56.20	57.29	55.17
	SGNS‡	54.20 (−2.00)	58.90	50.24

Pre-trained Lexeme Embedding. As shown in Tables 2 and 4, the gazetteer with pre-trained lexeme embedding performs better than the gazetteer without one in most cases. In particular, we have observed that the SGNS gazetteer is almost better than the Gigaword gazetteer. The biggest difference between them is that the former has a better and bigger pre-trained lexeme embedding. We also conduct an experiment on WeiboNER, which is divided into two groups, with pre-trained lexeme embedding or without. As shown in Table 6, we observe that the experiments without pre-trained lexeme embedding, compared to the one with pre-trained lexeme embedding, almost show that the F1 score has dropped significantly. Even for the rest situations, they are only a trivial increase in model performance. The results demonstrate that *a good pre-trained lexeme embedding will bring a positive impact on the model performance.*

Gazetteer × Dataset. In this section, we focus on the matched lexeme in a dataset. Specifically, these matched lexeme will be split into two different interpretable groups, the lexeme set A matched in the training set and the lexeme

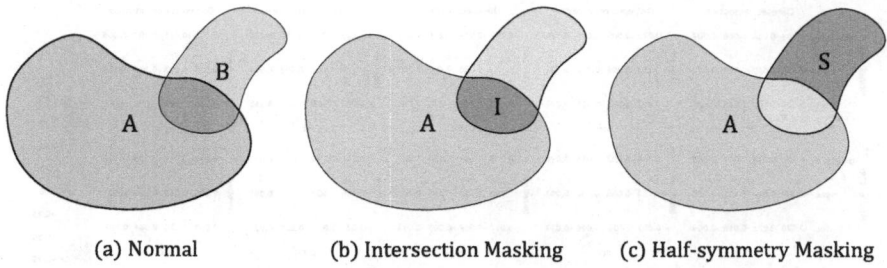

(a) Normal   (b) Intersection Masking   (c) Half-symmetry Masking

Fig. 3. Lexeme set masking in the test set. A denotes the matched lexeme set in the training set. B denotes the matched lexeme set in the test set.

Table 7. Statistics of matched lexeme set between the Dataset and the Gazetteer.

Dataset	Gazetteer	I	S	E	N
WeiboNER	Gigaword	3547	1698	220	5025
	SGNS	3929	2003	278	5654
	TEC	672	191	57	806
ResumeNER	Gigaword	2746	737	157	3326
	SGNS	2715	868	276	3307
	TEC	448	77	11	514
ECommerce	Gigaword	4609	1287	845	5051
	SGNS	5266	1608	1082	5792
	TEC	1513	473	953	1033
MSRANER	Gigaword	20887	4129	1877	23139
	SGNS	21848	4370	2265	23953
	TEC	1902	193	263	1832
OntoNotes	Gigaword	28439	1551	2293	27697
	SGNS	27968	1561	2407	27122
	TEC	2121	81	261	1941

set B matched in the test set (see Fig. 3a). Our goal is to probe what kind of lexeme in the gazetteer would contribute more to the model performance.

Lexeme Generalization. We firstly investigate the lexeme generalization ability: *does the matched lexeme in the test set but unseen in the training set boost the model performance?* Inspired by the concept of casual effects in causality [22], we decide to mask a part of matched lexeme in the test for investigating how the model performance in a trained model will change. We further split B into two small sets. An intersection set between A and B, denoted as

$$I = A \cap B \tag{1}$$

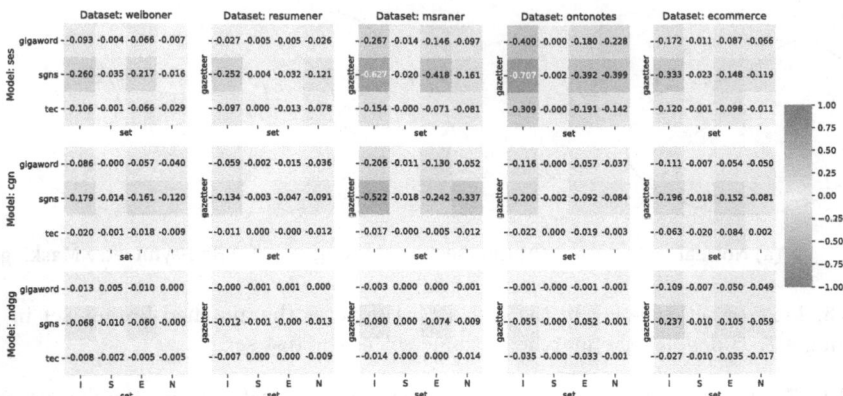

Fig. 4. A heat map of causal effects on masking $I\&S$ and $E\&N$. It demonstrates the performance drop when masking different lexeme sets. The closer the color is to dark purple, the greater the degradation of model performance. This can be regarded as the lexeme set's importance. (Color figure online)

It represents the matched lexeme both shared in the training stage and the test stage (see Fig. 3b). A half-symmetry set in B, denoted as

$$S = (A \cup B) \setminus A \tag{2}$$

It represents the matched lexeme in the test set but unseen in the training set (see Fig. 3c). We mask I and S separately to evaluate the model performance in the test set again. We calculate the causal effects using the difference between the F1 score masked in I and the original F1 score. This index indicates how much the model performance will decrease when masking I. Similarly, we also have another experiment to evaluate the causal effects under the situation of masking S.

Lexeme Type. Secondly, we investigate that what type of lexeme the GENER likes. Here, the type means whether the lexeme is an entity annotated in the whole dataset. We split matched lexeme in the test set into two small sets, the lexeme set E which only includes entities, the lexeme set N which excludes all entities. We also mask the two lexeme sets separately to observe how the model performance will change in the test set. Due to the space limitation, we plot all results of lexeme generalization and lexeme type together in the form of a heat map in Fig. 4. Every column represents a dataset. Every row represents a model. The heat map shows the dropped model performance when masking a specific lexeme set. Table 7 demonstrates the count of four lexeme sets between datasets and gazetteers.

– MASKING $I\&S$: We can see the model performance largely decreases in most scenarios when masking I, while almost unchanged or on reduces a little when masking S. Although the count of S is less than the count of I in all combinations, the former still keeps a larger value. It suggests that it is difficult for the GENER model to generalize to the unmatched lexeme in the training stage.

- MASKING E&N: Contrary to the above experiment, the model performance decreases a lot both in masking E and N, especially on the two big datasets, MSRANER and OntoNotes. However, except for a few limited cases, we can see that the most performance degradation occurs in masking E. We also notice that the count of E is less than the count of N in all combinations. This phenomenon suggests that the entity helps the model to boost performance more.

After the above analysis, we summarized two points: (1) *When building a gazetteer, we should consider more matched lexeme that cover both the training set and the test set. (2) The more entities the gazetteer contains, the larger performance the model may boost.*

5   Related Works

Recent years, lots of methods have been developed for knowledge enhancement in named entity recognition. These methods can be divided into two parts, supervised method and unsupervised method. Most of works follow the supervised fashion. Some works attempt to modify the encoder to adapt the external gazetteer knowledge [1–3,5,6,12,16,17,35]. Although these encoder-based models have achieved surprising results, they perform poorly in encoder transfer-ability and computational complexity. Hence, another group of studies design methods for incorporating gazetteer information with token embedding [4,15,18,19,26,27,29]. The unsupervised method mainly has two works, including PU learning [23] and linked HMMs [30]. It is worth mentioning that [32] introduces lexeme knowledge to slot tagging.

6   Conclusion

In this paper, we first re-examine the effectiveness of several common practices gazetteer-enhanced NER model through a fair and comparable environment. To further evaluate the effectiveness of gazetteer in pre-trained language models, we modify the gazetteer enhanced model to adapt existing pre-trained language models. Moreover, we carry out a series of analysis of the relationship between the performance of model and the gazetteer characteristics, such as what kind of gazetteer can benefit the model well, which can bring new insights for us to build a more suitable gazetteer.

Acknowledgement. This work was supported by the NSFC projects (No. 62072399, No. U19B2042, No. 61402403), Chinese Knowledge Center for Engineering Sciences and Technology, MoE Engineering Research Center of Digital Library, and the Fundamental Research Funds for the Central Universities (No. 226–2022-00070).

References

1. Zhang, Y., Yang, J.: Chinese NER using lattice LSTM. In: ACL (2018)
2. Sui, D., Chen, Y., Liu, K., Zhao, J., Liu, S.: Leverage lexical knowledge for Chinese named entity recognition via collaborative graph network. In: EMNLP (2019)
3. Gui, T., et al.: A lexeme-based graph neural network for Chinese NER. In: EMNLP (2019)
4. Ma, R., Peng, M., Zhang, Q., Wei, Z., Huang, X.: Simplify the usage of lexeme in Chinese NER. In: ACL (2020)
5. Ding, R., Xie, P., Zhang, X., Lu, W., Li, L., Si, L.: A neural multi-digraph model for Chinese NER with gazetteers. In: ACL (2019)
6. Gui, T., Ma, R., Zhang, Q., Zhao, L., Jiang, Y., Huang, X.: CNN-based Chinese NER with lexeme Rethinking. In: IJCAI (2019)
7. Brown, T., et al.: Language models are few-shot learners. In: NeurIPS (2020)
8. Devlin, J., Chang, M., Lee, K., Toutanova, K.: BERT: pre-training of deep bidirectional transformers for language understanding. In: NAACL (2019)
9. Errica, F., Podda, M., Bacciu, D., Micheli, A.: A fair comparison of graph neural networks for graph classification. In: ICLR (2020)
10. Fu, J., Liu, P., Zhang, Q., Huang, X.: Rethinking generalization of neural models: a named entity recognition case study. In: AAAI (2020)
11. Gao, J., Li, M., Wu, A., Huang, C.: Chinese word segmentation and named entity recognition: a pragmatic approach. In: COLING (2005)
12. Jia, S., Ding, L., Chen, X., Xiang, Y.: Incorporating uncertain segmentation information into Chinese NER for social media text. In: ACL (2020)
13. Li G., Müller, M., Thabet, A., Ghanem, B.: DeepGCNs: can GCNs go as deep as CNNs?. In: ICCV (2019)
14. Li, S., Zhao, Z., Hu, R., Li, W., Liu, T., Du, X.: Analogical reasoning on Chinese morphological and semantic relations. In: ACL (2018)
15. Li, X., Yan, H., Qiu, X., Huang, X.: FLAT: Chinese NER using flat-lattice transformer. In: ACL (2020)
16. Lin, H., Lu, Y., Han, X., Sun, L., Dong, B., Jiang, S.: Gazetteer-enhanced attentive neural networks for named entity recognition. In: EMNLP (2019)
17. Liu, T., Yao, J., Lin, C.: Towards improving neural named entity recognition with gazetteers. In: ACL (2019)
18. Liu, W., Xu, T., Xu, Q., Song, J., Zu, Y.: An encoding strategy based word-character LSTM for Chinese NER. In: NAACL (2019)
19. Magnolini, S., Piccioni, V., Balaraman, V., Guerini, M., Magnini, B.: How to use gazetteers for entity recognition with neural models. In: SemDeep-5 (2019)
20. Mikolov, T., Chen, K., Corrado, G., Dean, J.: Efficient estimation of word representations in vector space. In: ICLR (2013)
21. Panchendrarajan, R., Amaresan, A.: Bidirectional LSTM-CRF for named entity recognition. In: PACLIC (2018)
22. Pear, J.: Causality: Cambridge University Press (2009)
23. Peng, M., Xing, X., Zhang, Q., Fu, J., Huang, X.: Distantly supervised named entity recognition using positive-unlabeled learning. In: ACL (2019)
24. Peng, N., Dredze, M.: Named entity recognition for Chinese social media with jointly trained embeddings. In: EMNLP (2015)
25. Pennington, J., Socher, R., Manning, C.: Glove: global vectors for word representation. In: EMNLP (2014)

26. Peshterli, S., Dupuy, C., Kiss, I.: Self-attention gazetteer embeddings for named-entity recognition. In: CoRR, abs/2004.0406 (2020)
27. Chen, Q., Ji, F., Chen, H., Zhang, Y.: Improving commonsense question answering by graph-based iterative retrieval over multiple knowledge sources. In: COLING (2020)
28. Raffel, C., et al.: Exploring the limits of transfer learning with a unified text-to-text transformer. In: JMLR (2020)
29. Rijhwani, S., Zhou, S., Neubig, G., Carbonell, J.: Soft gazetteers for low-resource named entity recognition. In: ACL (2020)
30. Safranchik, E., Luo, S., Bach, S.: Weakly supervised sequence tagging from noisy rules. In: AAAI (2020)
31. Tamborrino, A., Pellicanó, N., Pannier, B., Voitot, P., Naudin, L.: Pre-training is (almost) all you need: an application to commonsense reasoning. In: ACL (2020)
32. Williams, K.: Neural lexemes for slot tagging in spoken language understanding. In: NAACL (2019)
33. Yang, J., Zhang, Y., Dong, F.: Neural word segmentation with rich pretraining. In: ACL (2017)
34. Zeng, X., Li, Y., Zhai, Y., Zhang, Y.: Counterfactual generator: a weakly-supervised method for named entity recognition. In: EMNLP (2020)
35. Zhou, Y., Zheng, X., Huang, X.: Chinese named entity recognition augmented with lexeme memory. In: CoRR, abs/1912.0828 (2020)

Adversarial Transfer for Classical Chinese NER with Translation Word Segmentation

Yongjie Qi, Hongchao Ma[✉], Lulu Shi, Hongying Zan, and Qinglei Zhou

Zhengzhou University, Zhengzhou, China
ma-hc@foxmail.com, {iehyzan,ieqlzhou}@zzu.edu.cn

Abstract. Classical Chinese NER aims to automatically identify named entities in classical texts, which can effectively help people understand the content of classical texts. However, due to the difficulty of annotating classical Chinese texts, the scale of existing datasets seriously restricts the development of classical Chinese NER. To address this challenge, we propose an Adversarial Transfer for Classical Chinese NER (AT-CCNER) model, which transfers features learned from large-scale translation word segmentation to assist recognize classical Chinese named entities. In addition, to reduce the feature differences between modern and classical Chinese texts, AT-CCNER utilizes the adversarial method to better apply to classical Chinese texts. We experimentally demonstrate the effectiveness of our method on the open-source classical Chinese NER dataset C-CLUE. What's more, we compare the effects of translation text of different scales on the experimental results. Our method improves Precision, Recall, and F1 by 3.61%, 3.45%, and 3.54%, respectively, compared to the BiLSTM-CRF model.

Keywords: Classical Chinese NER · Chinese word segmentation · Adversarial learning · Transfer learning

1 Introduction

Named Entity Recognition (NER) is a fundamental task in Natural Language Process (NLP), which aims to identify named entities such as the person, location and organization, etc. in text. NER can help improve the efficiency of NLP downstream tasks, such as relationship extraction [1], knowledge graph construction [24], and knowledge base building [19]. The classical Chinese NER also has enormous research value. Classical Chinese texts are the carriers of more than 5,000 years of Chinese cultural heritage and record the philosophical, humanistic, technological, and social achievements. Moreover, learning classical Chinese is conducive to forming teenagers' values and world outlook, and the digitization of ancient texts can better help teenagers understand and remember them.

Y. Qi and H. Ma—Equal contribution.

W. Lu et al. (Eds.): NLPCC 2022, LNAI 13551, pp. 298–310, 2022.
https://doi.org/10.1007/978-3-031-17120-8_24

Table 1. An example shows that NER and CWS have the same word boundary.

Sentence	太 守 谓 谁? 庐 陵 欧 阳 修 也。							
	tai shou wei shui? lu ling ou yang xiu ye 。							
classical Chinese CWS	太守	谓	谁	?	庐陵	欧阳修	也	。
classical Chinese NER	太 守	谓	谁	?	庐 陵	欧 阳 修	也	。
	JOB JOB	O	O	O	LOC LOC	PER PER PER	O	O
Translation CWS	太守	是	谁	?	庐陵	欧阳修	吧	。

Compared to the NER in modern Chinese and English, a fundamental problem in studying classical Chinese is that classical Chinese is concise, obscure, and challenging to annotate. The relevant datasets are relatively few and small-scale. Some research has been done on the existing classical Chinese NER. For example, Cui et al. [4] used the Jiayan[1] to separate the words of the "SikuQuanshu 四库全书 " as a dictionary, and used automatic annotation plus manual verification to obtain the annotated dataset, then used the Lattice-LSTM model for training. Wang et al. [22] constructed an ALBERT-BiLSTM-CRF model and got better results in the "Febrile Diseases 伤寒论 " NER task.

Dealing with Chinese NER is challenging due to the small number of datasets. In the modern Chinese domain, knowledge transfer can be performed with the help of relevant datasets and tasks. For example, Peng et al. [16] proposed a joint model that integrates Chinese word segmentation and Chinese NER information. Cao et al. [2] proposed an adversarial transfer learning structure that integrates task-sharing information into Chinese NER tasks. Chen et al. [3] proposed a boundary enhancement method to obtain better Chinese NER. We can see that the word segmentation task can help NER. Inspired by the above work, we use the word segmentation information of the translation to help recognize classical Chinese named entities. The Chinese Word Segmentation (CWS) task and the NER task share many domain similarities. As shown in the second and third rows of Table 1, for the sentence "太守谓谁? 庐陵欧阳修也 ", in the NER task, "太守 "、"庐陵 " and "欧阳修 " are named entities, while in the CWS task, they are each a word. But in the classical Chinese CWS domain, there are no large-scale participle annotation datasets. And the research on classical Chinese separation tools is immature.

As shown in the last two rows of Table 1, the named entities in the translation texts are all divided into a single word. In addition, when translating ancient texts, the named entities are often translated straightforwardly, which means they are not changed. Therefore, they have the same word boundaries. Moreover, the research on modern word segmentation tools is more mature than the segmentation of ancient texts. Many Chinese word separation tools, such as jieba[2] and HanLP[3] can achieve outstanding word separation results.

---

[1] https://github.com/jiaeyan/Jiayan .
[2] https://github.com/fxsjy/jieba .
[3] https://github.com/hankcs/HanLP .

The above analysis shows that we can use the word boundary information of translation texts to assist the classical Chinese NER. However, after thousands of years of development, the linguistic difference between translation and classical text is so significant that when using Neural Networks to extract their respective features, they will be distributed in their separate feature spaces. Using adversarial learning, like Domain Adaptation (DA) [18], can make their features distributed in the same feature space.

For the above situation, we propose an Adversarial Transfer for Classical Chinese NER (AT-CCNER) model to improve the recognition effects of classical Chinese NER by using translation word segmentation. Firstly, we use the Chinese word separation tools to separate the translation texts. The obtained word separation data is used as the source domain task data for adversarial learning. Afterward, we transfer the parameters extracted from the adversarial model into the BiLSTM-CRF as its initialization vector and use the word boundary features of the translation to assist in the classical Chinese NER. Finally, we evaluate our approach to the open-source ancient text dataset C-CLUE [10].

The contributions of this paper are as follows:

1) We propose a method for accommodating information about word boundaries in translation to help classical Chinese NER.
2) We use adversarial learning to reduce domain differences and obtain domain-independent features.
3) We evaluate our method on the open-source classical Chinese NER dataset and conduct several comparative experiments to demonstrate the effectiveness of our method.

2   Related Work

Chinese NER. A distinctive feature of Chinese texts, compared to English, is the absence of obvious word boundaries. Therefore, many studies on Chinese NER revolve around models that merge characters and words or use word boundary information. Peng et al. [16] used the LSTM-CRF model to jointly train NER and word separation to improve NER in the Chinese social media domain and achieved good results. Zhang et al. [25] proposed a model Lattice-LSTM, which outperformed character-based and word-based models. Gui et al. [9] introduced a dictionary-based graph neural network with global semantics to alleviate the impact of word ambiguity. Sui et al. [21] presented a Collaborative Graph Network to solve challenges in Chinese NER tasks when it comes to self-matched lexical words as well as the nearest contextual lexical words. Chen et al. [3] proposed a boundary enhancement method, which is equally effective in improving Chinese NER. In addition, Chinese is gradually evolved from pictographs, and the structure also contains the meaning of the characters. Therefore, using character structure is also an important research method. Dong et al. [5] used a BiLSTM-CRF network fusing characters and Chinese radical information to achieve the best performance at that time. Wu et al. [23]

proposed a novel multivariate data embedding-based intersection transformer to improve the performance of Chinese NER by fusing structural information.

Low-Resource NER. There is no annotated corpus or only a small-scale annotated corpus for some languages or fields that are not well researched, and annotating a large-scale corpus is difficult. So it is crucial to use the corpus information in the existing domains to transfer. Mulcaire et al. [14] evaluated the latest methods for multilingual contextual representation and demonstrated that multilingual transfer is an effective method for cross-language transfer. Zhou et al. [26] proposed a dual adversarial transfer network for solving the low-resource NER problem. Simpson et al. [20] proposed a DA method using a combination of Bayesian sequences that achieves robust performance through zero-sample transfer learning.

Adversarial Learning. Adversarial learning research has made significant progress. Goodfellow et al. [8] analyzed the existence of adversarial samples and gave a method to generate adversarial samples. Madry et al. [12] proposed the SOTA adversarial learning method. As for domain adaptation, Saenko et al. [18] first proposed DA in the computer vision field. In the field of NLP, Ruder et al. [17] proposed a novel three-task training method that reduces the time and space complexity of classical three-training. Meftah et al. [13] proposed a method to exploit multi-task learning and single-task fine-tuning by learning a hierarchical model trained across multiple tasks from the source domain and then fine-tuning it on multiple tasks in the target domain and achieving good results.

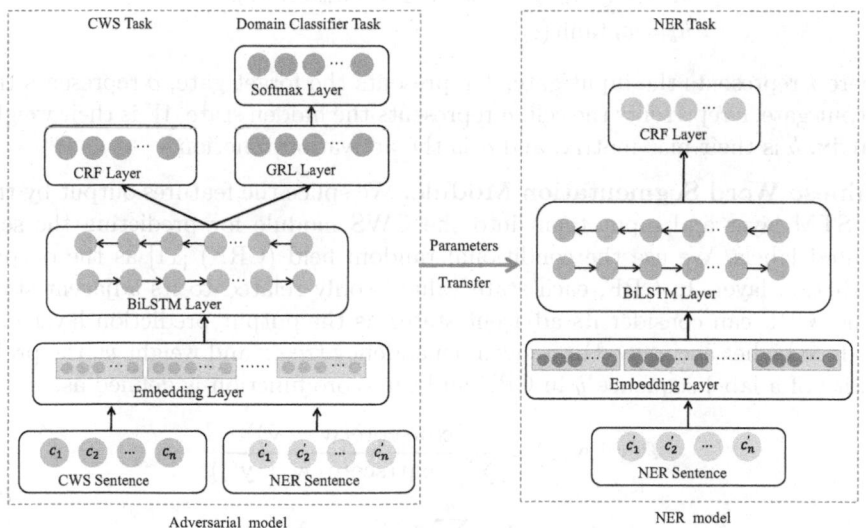

Fig. 1. The architecture of AT-CCNER model.

3   Method

As shown in Fig. 1, the AT-CCNER model mainly includes the adversarial model on the left and the NER model on the right. The adversarial model extracts the word segmentation features of translation and distributes the features in the same space. The NER model is used to predict named entities.

3.1   Adversarial Model

The adversarial model consists of three components: feature extraction module, CWS module, and domain classifier module. The feature extraction module models the input sequence; the CWS module predicts the word separation of the translation texts; the domain classifier module predicts the sentence is the classical Chinese sentence or translation. These components are described below.

Feature Extraction Module. The feature extraction module uses a bidirectional LSTM network. The Recurrent Neural Network (RNN) can flexibly cope with different input sentence lengths. Bidirectional RNN models (BRNN) can better capture sentence-level information. The Long Short-Term Memory Unit (LSTM) effectively solves the gradient vanishing problem of RNNs. The LSTM cell is implemented in the following way:

$$
\begin{aligned}
i_t &= \sigma \left(W_{x_i} x_t + W_{h_i} h_{t-1} + W_{c_i} c_{t-1} + b_i \right) \\
f_t &= \sigma \left(W_{xf} x_t + W_{hf} h_{t-1} + W_{cf} c_{t-1} + b_f \right) \\
c_t &= f_t c_{t-1} + i_t \tanh \left(W_{xc} x_t + W_{hc} h_{t-1} + b_c \right) \\
o_t &= \sigma \left(W_{x_0} x_t + W_{h0} h_{t-1} + W_{c_0} c_t + b_0 \right) \\
h_t &= o_t \tanh \left(c_t \right)
\end{aligned}
\tag{1}
$$

where i represents the input gate, f represents the forget gate, o represents the output gate, c represents the cell, h represents the hidden state, W is their weight matrix, b is their bias matrix, and σ is the activation function.

Chinese Word Segmentation Module. We splice the features output by the BiLSTM layer and input them into the CWS module for predicting the segmented labels. We use the conditional random field (CRF) [11] as the output prediction layer. In CRF, each state value is only related to its adjacent state value. CRF can consider its adjacent states as the output prediction layer and produce higher accuracy. For a given dependency tree τ and weight w, the probability of a label sequence y in CRF and the score function is defined as:

$$
\begin{aligned}
P(\mathbf{y} \mid \mathbf{w}, \tau) &= \frac{\exp(\text{score}(\mathbf{w}, \tau, \mathbf{y}))}{\sum_{\mathbf{y}'} \exp \left(\text{score} \left(\mathbf{w}, \tau, \mathbf{y}' \right) \right)} \\
\text{score}(\mathbf{w}, \tau, \mathbf{y}) &= \sum_{t=0}^{n} T_{y_t, y_{t+1}} + \sum_{t=1}^{n} E_{y_t}
\end{aligned}
\tag{2}
$$

where $T_{y_t, y_{t+1}}$ represents the conversion score from label y_t to y_{t+1}, and E_{y_t} represents the score of label y_t at the t-th position.

Domain Classifier Module. We input the features that the BiLSTM outputs into a Gradient Reversal Layer (GRL) [6] to achieve adversarial effects and make the features of translations and ancient texts distributed in the same feature space. In the back-propagation process, the GRL makes the gradient of the domain classifier loss automatically reversed, thereby achieving an adversarial loss similar to GAN [7]. In contrast, the GRL is an identity transformation in the forward-propagation process. For the input sentence features $X = \{c_1, c_2, ..., c_n\}$, the backward propagation process of GRL can be expressed as:

$$\frac{d_{GRL(X)}}{dx} = -\lambda Loss \tag{3}$$

The parameter λ is not a constant but gradually changes from 0 to 1. The change process of λ is:

$$\lambda = \frac{2}{1 + \exp(-\gamma \cdot p)} - 1 \tag{4}$$

where p is the relative value of the iteration process, and γ is a constant 10 [6].

After that, we use the Softmax layer to predict whether the input sentence is from classical text or translation. For the $Loss_{cws}$ generated in the CWS module and the $Loss_{da}$ generated in this module, we use the weighted average method to obtain the total loss with the weight λ:

$$\text{Loss}(t) = \lambda \cdot \text{Loss}_{cws}(t) + (1 - \lambda) \cdot \text{Loss}_{da}(t) \tag{5}$$

3.2   NER Model

We use the BiLSTM-CRF [15] model. We transfer all parameters of the feature extraction module, including the weights and biases of the forward and backward cells, as the initialization parameters of the BiLSTM layer. Then we use the C-CLUE dataset to train the model and predict the named entities.

4   Experiments

We conduct a series of experiments to demonstrate the performance of our method. The details of the experiments are described below.

Table 2. Statistics of the C-CLUE dataset.

Entities	Train	Dev	Test
Person (PER)	9467	1267	701
Location (LOC)	2962	391	167
Organization (ORG)	1750	242	139
Position (POS)	1698	266	100
Others	110	18	9
Total	15987	2184	1116

4.1 Datasets

We use the classical Chinese NER dataset C-CLUE [10] to evaluate our proposed model. In addition, we also use the classical Chinese-vernacular parallel corpus[4] as our translation data. The description of the two datasets is as follows.

NER Dataset C-CLUE. The publisher used a crowdsourcing system to annotate "Twenty-Four Histories 二十四史 " written by the ancient Chinese dynasties and finally integrated them into the C-CLUE dataset. The dataset contains six categories of entities, including person, location, organization, position, book, and war. The statistics of the dataset are shown in Table 2.

In addition, we find that the dataset does not fully contain all content of "Twenty-Four Histories". It selects some articles in "Records of the Grand Historian 史记 ", "New History of the Five Dynasties 新五代史 ", "History of the Northern Qi 北齐书 " and "Records of the Three Kingdoms 三国志 ".

The Classical Chinese-Vernacular Parallel Corpus. The corpus obtains chapter-level alignment data through crawling, scripting, and manual proofreading. It forms a corpus of about 960,000 sentence pairs, covering most of the classical Chinese books, including "Analects of Confucius 论语 ", "The Words of Mencius 孟子 ", "Records of the Grand Historian", "Records of the Three Kingdoms" and so on.

4.2 Experimental Setup and Evaluation Indicators

Experimental Setup: We strictly use the control variable method in our experiments. In all experiments, the same network layers are set with the same parameters and performed in the same experimental environment.

Evaluation Indicators: In NER, the commonly used evaluation indicators are Precision (P), Recall (R), and F1. Sometimes the R and the P may conflict, and the F1 can comprehensively reflect the model's performance. Therefore, we use the F1 as the main evaluation index, taking the P and R into account.

Table 3. Experimental results on the C-CLUE dataset.

Method	P	R	F1
BERT-base	29.82	35.59	32.12
BERT-wwm	32.98	43.82	35.40
Roberta-zh	28.28	34.93	31.09
ZKY-BERT	33.32	42.71	36.16
BiLSTM-CRF	49.76	54.77	52.15
Lattice-LSTM	51.96	56.92	54.33
AT-CCNER	**53.37**	**58.22**	**55.69**

---

[4] https://github.com/NiuTrans/Classical-Modern.

4.3   Results

The paper [10] conducted a benchmark test, evaluating the performance of the following four pre-trained models: BERT-base, BERT-wwm, and Zhongkeyuan-BERT (ZKY-BERT) on the C-CLUE dataset. In this experiment, we compare our method with the benchmark test. In addition, we also compare the performance of our model with the BiLSTM and Lattice-LSTM models, which are commonly used in Chinese NER.

The experimental results are shown in Table 3. It indicates that, compared with the pre-trained models, our method can better learn the features of ancient texts and achieve the highest P, R, and F1. The main reason is that the training data of the above pre-trained models are not historical books, and the data is quite different from the ancient texts. Using these pre-trained models to predict ancient texts cannot effectively extract historical books' language features. Therefore, the prediction of C-CLUE cannot achieve satisfactory results. And compared with the Lattice-LSTM and BiLSTM-CRF model, our model can effectively use the word segmentation features and achieves better results.

Table 4. Results of ablation experiments.

Method	P	R	F1
AT-CCNER (BiLSTM-CRF+transfer+adversarial)	**53.37**	**58.22**	**55.69**
-adversarial (BiLSTM-CRF+transfer)	52.29	54.58	53.41
-transfer (BiLSTM-CRF+adversarial)	51.79	55.50	53.59
-adversarial-transfer (BiLSTM-CRF)	49.76	54.77	52.15

5   Experimental Analysis and Discussion

We explore the impact of different factors on our method from three perspectives and illustrate the validity of our experiments.

5.1   Ablation Study

In this experiment, we compare the evaluation indicators of the NER model in four cases, as shown in Table 4. The four groups of experiments represent:

-adversarial: We use the BiLSTM-CRF model to learn word segmentation features and transfer the parameters learned by the BiLSTM layer to the NER model BiLSTM-CRF as the initialization parameters.

-transfer: We add a NER task based on the DA model and directly use the features of the domain classifier and translation word segmentation to predict.

-adversarial-transfer: We use the BiLSTM-CRF model to learn the C-CLUE dataset and predict.

Effectiveness of parameter transfer: Compared with the BiLSTM-CRF, the BiLSTM+transfer model transfers the CWS features into the NER model so that the model can use the CWS features for recognition. And it can achieve better performance than using the random initialization model.

Effectiveness of adversarial: Compared with BiLSTM-CRF, BiLSTM-CRF+adversarial can obtain domain-independent features, and features are distributed in the same space to obtain better recognition effects.

However, the CWS features extracted by only parameter transfer and the classical Chinese NER are not in the same feature space. Only using adversarial learning does not effectively utilize the word boundary information of the translation. Therefore, neither method performs as well as our proposed method. Our proposed method of fusing adversarial learning and parameter transfer can make full use of the CWS features of the translation and achieve the best results.

Table 5. Experimental results of three different ranges of translation.

Different translation	Jiayan			HanLP			jieba		
	P	R	F1	P	R	F1	P	R	F1
BiLSTM-CRF	49.76	54.77	52.15	49.76	54.77	52.15	49.76	54.77	52.15
TFTS	51.26	49.93	50.59	51.13	52.32	51.72	49.85	54.24	51.95
SATS	52.88	56.03	54.41	54.03	55.11	54.56	53.49	55.37	54.42
FTS	**54.04**	56.30	55.15	53.27	56.23	54.71	53.37	**58.22**	**55.69**

5.2   Comparison Experiments with Translations of Different Scales

In this experiment, we compare the effects of different translations on the results of classical Chinese NER.

We use jieba (see footnote 2), Jiayan (see footnote 1), and HanLP (see footnote 3) to separate different translation texts. Among them, the first two translations are from the literary-vernacular parallel corpus. The sentence-aligned translations are data from sentence-aligned translations that we crawl, clean, and align based on the training set content of the C-CLUE. The results of the experiments are shown in Table 5.

- **TFTS** represents twenty-four translations of the subtext.
- **SATS** represents sentence alignment translations subtext.
- **FTS** represents Four translations of the subtext.

The results show that the TFTS reduces the recognition effects of NER, while both the SATS and ETS improve the recognition effects of NER.

"Twenty-Four Histories" is the collective name for the twenty-four official histories written by the ancient Chinese dynasties. It spans more than four thousand years. During this period, word usage and sequencing habits changed considerably. Therefore, we can see that using the TFTS, which significantly increases the size of the corpus, but introduces a large amount of noise and reduces the recognition effects. The SATS, on the other hand, has a high degree of utterance similarity, but the data size is small-scale, so the features available for transfer are not as many as others, and the F1 is not as high as the FTS.

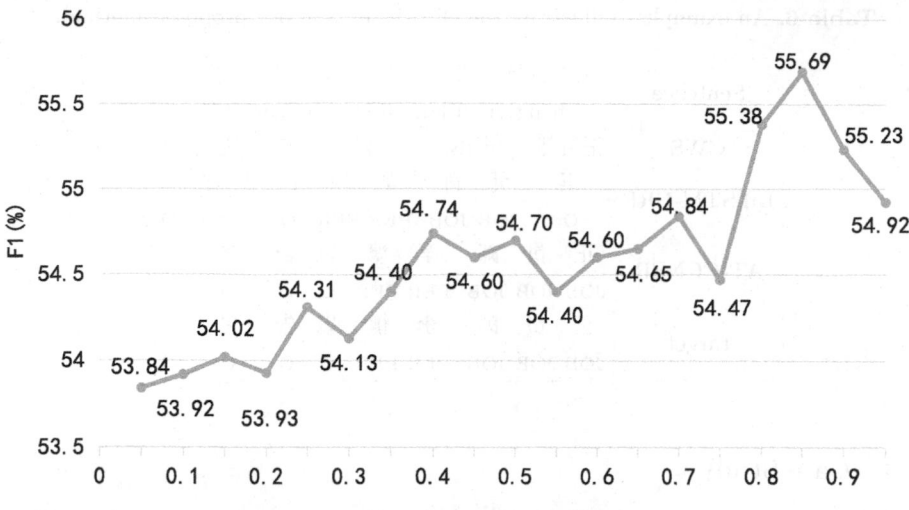

Fig. 2. F1 for different values of λ.

The CWS data with higher similarity to NER data and on a larger scale better affect NER by using the AT-CCNER method. And the data using jieba to disambiguate the translation from four books can reach an F1 of 55.69%, which is a 3.54% improvement over the model using only BiLSTM-CRF. What's more, the results obtained by using different word segmentation tools have certain differences. But using our method to segment the four books can improve the recognition effect, which also shows the effectiveness of our method.

5.3   Selection of λ Values

In this experiment, we compare the effects of different weights in formula (5) on model performance. The results of the experiment are shown in Fig. 2.

The experimental results show that different calculation methods of loss significantly impact the model. As can be seen from the figure, the F1 generally tends to increase as λ increases and achieves the best results at $\lambda = 0.85$, where the F1 reaches 55.69%. After that, the F1 generally tends to decrease. The lowest F1 is 53.84%, an improvement of 1.69% over the BiLSTM-CRF model, which also proves the effectiveness of our method. But different tasks and datasets may have different results, so when the model has more than one task, we should choose the suitable value.

Table 6. An example to illustrate the effectiveness of our proposed method.

Sentence	正 员 郎 李 慎 以 告 之。
	zheng yuan lang li shen yi gao zhi。
CWS	正员郎　李慎　　以　告 之　。
BiLSTM-CRF	正　元 郎　李 慎 以 告 之　。
	O　JOB JOB PER PER O O O O
AT-CCNER	正 员 郎　李 慎 以 告　之　。
	JOB JOB JOB PER PER O O　O　O
target	正 员 郎　李 慎 以 告　之　。
	JOB JOB JOB PER PER O O　O　O

5.4 Case Study

In Table 6, we use a sentence from the C-CLUE test set as an example to illustrate the effectiveness of our method. For the sentence "正员郎李慎以告之", the correct named entity is identified as shown in the target row. For the job name "正员郎", the BiLSTM-CRF incorrectly identifies "元郎" as a word and identifies "正" as a non-entity. In contrast, our method correctly identifies the word boundaries of the word "正员郎" and thus makes the correct prediction.

The AT-CCNER method achieves good results for position, location, and person. However, the results for the book and organization are not satisfactory. The reasons for this phenomenon are 1) Book names belong to a small sample category, and the model cannot learn enough features for correct prediction; 2) The data for transfer are automatically annotated using a word separation tool, which inevitably results in annotation errors.

6 Conclusions

In this paper, we propose an Adversarial Transfer for classical Chinese NER (AT-CCNER) model. Through a series of experiments, we demonstrate that our method can effectively exploit the word segmentation information of translations to improve the recognition effects. And we find that: 1) Both the NER model that transfers into the word segmentation information of translations and the NER model using the adversarial method can improve the performance of the classical Chinese NER and the superposition of the two can obtain the best F1. 2) When using the cross-domain transfer approach, we should expand the size of the source domain dataset based on significant domain similarity. Extensive experimental results show that using the CWS task of translation and adversarial training is feasible to assist classical Chinese NER.

References

1. Bunescu, R.C., Mooney, R.J.: A shortest path dependency kernel for relation extraction. In: Proceedings of the Conference on Human Language Technology and Empirical Methods in Natural Language Processing, pp. 724–731 (2005)
2. Cao, P., Chen, Y., Liu, K., Zhao, J., Liu, S.: Adversarial transfer learning for Chinese named entity recognition with self-attention mechanism. In: Proceedings of the 2018 Conference on Empirical Methods in Natural Language Processing, pp. 182–192 (2018)
3. Chen, C., Kong, F.: Enhancing entity boundary detection for better Chinese named entity recognition. In: Proceedings of the 59th Annual Meeting of the Association for Computational Linguistics and the 11th International Joint Conference on Natural Language Processing (Volume 2: Short Papers), pp. 20–25 (2021)
4. CUI Dan-dan, LIU Xiu-lei, C.R.y.L.X.h.L.Z.Q.L.: Named entity recognition in filed of ancient Chinese based on lattice LSTM. Comput. Sci. **47**(S02), 5 (2020)
5. Dong, C., Zhang, J., Zong, C., Hattori, M., Di, H.: Character-based LSTM-CRF with radical-level features for Chinese named entity recognition. In: Lin, C.-Y., Xue, N., Zhao, D., Huang, X., Feng, Y. (eds.) ICCPOL/NLPCC -2016. LNCS (LNAI), vol. 10102, pp. 239–250. Springer, Cham (2016). https://doi.org/10.1007/978-3-319-50496-4_20
6. Ganin, Y., Lempitsky, V.: Unsupervised domain adaptation by backpropagation. In: International Conference on Machine Learning, pp. 1180–1189. PMLR (2015)
7. Goodfellow, I., et al.: Generative adversarial nets. Advances in neural information processing systems 27 (2014)
8. Goodfellow, I.J., Shlens, J., Szegedy, C.: Explaining and harnessing adversarial examples. Stat **1050**, 20 (2015)
9. Gui, T., Zou, Y., Zhang, Q., Peng, M., Fu, J., Wei, Z., Huang, X.: A lexicon-based graph neural network for Chinese NER. In: Proceedings of the 2019 Conference on Empirical Methods in Natural Language Processing and the 9th International Joint Conference on Natural Language Processing (EMNLP-IJCNLP), pp. 1040–1050. Association for Computational Linguistics, Hong Kong, China, November 2019
10. Ji, Z., Shen, Y., Sun, Y., Yu, T., Wang, X.: C-CLUE: a benchmark of classical Chinese based on a crowdsourcing system for knowledge graph construction. In: Qin, B., Jin, Z., Wang, H., Pan, J., Liu, Y., An, B. (eds.) CCKS 2021. CCIS, vol. 1466, pp. 295–301. Springer, Singapore (2021). https://doi.org/10.1007/978-981-16-6471-7_24
11. Lafferty, J., McCallum, A., Pereira, F.C.: Conditional random fields: Probabilistic models for segmenting and labeling sequence data (2001)
12. Madry, A., Makelov, A., Schmidt, L., Tsipras, D., Vladu, A.: Towards deep learning models resistant to adversarial attacks. arXiv preprint arXiv:1706.06083 (2017)
13. Meftah, S., Semmar, N., Tahiri, M.A., Tamaazousti, Y., Essafi, H., Sadat, F.: Multi-task supervised pretraining for neural domain adaptation. In: Proceedings of the Eighth International Workshop on Natural Language Processing for Social Media, pp. 61–71 (2020)
14. Mulcaire, P., Kasai, J., Smith, N.A.: Low-resource parsing with crosslingual contextualized representations. In: Proceedings of the 23rd Conference on Computational Natural Language Learning (CoNLL), pp. 304–315 (2019)
15. Panchendrarajan, R., Amaresan, A.: Bidirectional lstm-crf for named entity recognition. In: Proceedings of the 32nd Pacific Asia Conference on Language, Information and Computation (2018)

16. Peng, N., Dredze, M.: Improving named entity recognition for Chinese social media with word segmentation representation learning. In: Proceedings of the 54th Annual Meeting of the Association for Computational Linguistics (Volume 2: Short Papers), pp. 149–155 (2016)

17. Ruder, S., Plank, B.: Strong baselines for neural semi-supervised learning under domain shift. In: Proceedings of the 56th Annual Meeting of the Association for Computational Linguistics (Volume 1: Long Papers), pp. 1044–1054 (2018)

18. Saenko, K., Kulis, B., Fritz, M., Darrell, T.: Adapting visual category models to new domains. In: Daniilidis, K., Maragos, P., Paragios, N. (eds.) ECCV 2010. LNCS, vol. 6314, pp. 213–226. Springer, Heidelberg (2010). https://doi.org/10.1007/978-3-642-15561-1_16

19. Shen, W., Wang, J., Luo, P., Wang, M.: Linden: linking named entities with knowledge base via semantic knowledge. In: Proceedings of the 21st international conference on World Wide Web, pp. 449–458 (2012)

20. Simpson, E., Pfeiffer, J., Gurevych, I.: Low resource sequence tagging with weak labels. In: Proceedings of the AAAI Conference on Artificial Intelligence, vol. 34, pp. 8862–8869 (2020)

21. Sui, D., Chen, Y., Liu, K., Zhao, J., Liu, S.: Leverage lexical knowledge for Chinese named entity recognition via collaborative graph network. In: Proceedings of the 2019 Conference on Empirical Methods in Natural Language Processing and the 9th International Joint Conference on Natural Language Processing (EMNLP-IJCNLP), pp. 3830–3840. Association for Computational Linguistics, Hong Kong, China, November 2019

22. Wang, J., Xiao, L., L.J.Y.J.: Research on named entity recognition based on treatise on febrile diseases. Comput. Digit. Eng. **49**(8), 4 (2021)

23. Wu, S., Song, X., Feng, Z.: Mect: Multi-metadata embedding based cross-transformer for Chinese named entity recognition. In: Proceedings of the 59th Annual Meeting of the Association for Computational Linguistics and the 11th International Joint Conference on Natural Language Processing (Volume 1: Long Papers), pp. 1529–1539 (2021)

24. Xie, R., Liu, Z., Jia, J., Luan, H., Sun, M.: Representation learning of knowledge graphs with entity descriptions. In: Proceedings of the AAAI Conference on Artificial Intelligence, vol. 30 (2016)

25. Zhang, Y., Yang, J.: Chinese NER using lattice LSTM. In: Proceedings of the 56th Annual Meeting of the Association for Computational Linguistics (Volume 1: Long Papers), pp. 1554–1564. Association for Computational Linguistics, Melbourne, Australia, July 2018

26. Zhou, J.T., et al.: Dual adversarial neural transfer for low-resource named entity recognition. In: Proceedings of the 57th Annual Meeting of the Association for Computational Linguistics, pp. 3461–3471 (2019)

ArgumentPrompt: Activating Multi-category of Information for Event Argument Extraction with Automatically Generated Prompts

Shenpo Dong[1], Wei Yu[1], Hongkui Tu[1(✉)], Xiaodong Wang[1], Yunyan Zhou[2], Haili Li[1], Jie Zhou[1], and Tao Chang[1]

[1] College of Computer, National University of Defense Technology, Changsha, China
{dsp,yuwei19,xdwang,jiezhou,changtao15}@nudt.edu.cn,
tuhkjet@foxmail.com
[2] State Key Laboratory of Complex Electromagnetic Environment Effects on Electronics and Information System, Luoyang, China
54zyy@sina.com

Abstract. Event Argument Extraction (EAE) task is a critical and challenging subtask for event extraction. The current mainstream approaches are based on manually designed relevant questions for extracting specific argument roles from the text. However, manually crafting templates take time and fail to cover all possible argument roles. To design better and faster questions related to the EAE task, we embrace automatically generated prompts and propose a method called ArgumentPrompt (AMP): activating multi-category of information for event argument extraction with automatically generated prompts. AMP applies automatically generated prompts to eliminate the demand of the time-consuming and labor-intensive question design for the target extraction. To improve the quality of prompts, we mainly apply multi-category information for prompts and a dual-module to augment the guidance of prompts to language models. Experiments demonstrate that AMP can achieve a performance gain of 1.5% and 3.1% on ACE2005 and RAMS, respectively.

1 Introduction

Event argument extraction (EAE) is a critical step for event extraction (EE). Given a sentence and some event triggers, the task of EAE is to 1) identify entities acting as event arguments 2) classify their corresponding roles in the target event. Take this sentence as an example, "In Baghdad, a cameraman died when an American tank fired on the Palestine Hotel." For the *Conflict.Attack* event identified by the trigger word "fired", EAE aims to identify the event arguments (i.e., "Baghdad", "Palestine Hotel", "cameraman", "tank"), and classify the corresponding roles (i.e., "place", "target", "target", "instrument"). This information helps us understand when and where the events occurred. By capturing the critical argument roles in the text, EAE benefits a wide range of downstream natural language processing (NLP) applications, such as document summarization [5], knowledge base augmentation [9], and question answering (QA) [1].

Early works on event argument extraction initially posed the task as a token-level classification problem [3,14,21], and aimed to label each token accordingly. With the

W. Lu et al. (Eds.): NLPCC 2022, LNAI 13551, pp. 311–323, 2022.
https://doi.org/10.1007/978-3-031-17120-8_25

ongoing growth of machine reading comprehension (MRC), Du [7] introduced MRC into EAE, that is, designed enough questions to instruct the model to find the answers (event argument roles). Despite their promising results, existing methods still have some shortcomings. (1) Token-level classification methods only simply capture the internal pattern of input sequences. Most of them treat the argument categories as discrete classifier labels, thus ignoring the similarities of related argument roles across event types. For example, *Conflict.Attack* events and *Justice.Trial-Hearing* events in ACE dataset have *Attacker* and *Adjudicator* argument roles, respectively. Though the role types are different, they refer to their related event's primary "executor". This approach cannot extract well when faced with complex relationships, especially for rare and specialized domain argument roles. (2) For the QA methods (which can also be called MRC methods), their performance is strongly dependent on the quality of questions. Designing questions requires a significant amount of human labor and high-level expertise related to the task background. This problem is pronounced in the cases of specialized field events. For example, it requires a solid understanding of the financial industry to design questions for extracting the event arguments of *Gray rhino*[1] event accurately. Therefore, our research focuses on generating high-quality questions for the EAE task at a low cost.

Inspired by the shortcomings of existing methods, we propose the AMP model. AMP uses automatically generated prompts to activate multi-category information for the EAE task to address the aforementioned issues. To improve the generated prompts quality, we add multi-category information intentionally. The model can better discover the interaction across event types through these prompts. In addition, unlike other QA methods, we also design a decoupled structure to augment the guidance of the prompt information to the language model.

We summarize the main contributions of this paper as follows:

1. To the best of our knowledge, we are the first to apply automatic prompts for the EAE task to avoid the bias of hand-engineered questions and the significant human power consumption. Our methods can acquire suitable prompts without human involvement, even in a completely new field.
2. AMP can generate appropriate prompts. It makes full use of multiple-category of information to assist the language model in the EAE task, including event category information, trigger word information, and entity information. AMP utilizes the similarity of arguments from related events to enhance the performance for less frequent argument categories. We design a decoupled architecture, and it has the advantage that each module focuses on its role and cooperates better.
3. Experimental results demonstrate that AMP outperforms several competitive baselines on both the widely-adopted ACE 2005 dataset and RAMS dataset.

2   Methodology

In this section, we describe the implementation details of AMP, as Fig. 1 illustrates. We encode the input text using a pre-trained BERT [6] encoder. After that, the extraction

---

[1] A professional vocabulary of the financial field, referring to a highly probable, high impact yet neglected threat.

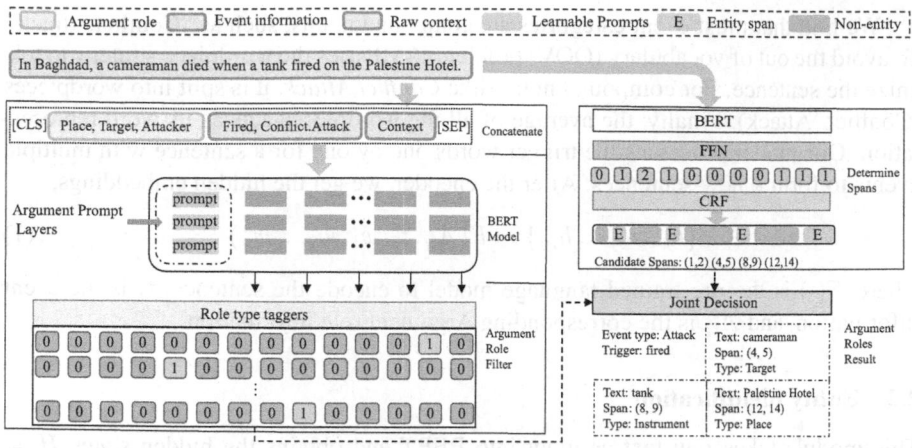

Fig. 1. This diagram illustrates the workflow of AMP. It demonstrates how to extract the relevant arguments of an attack event triggered by the word "fired". Notice that only the Argument Extraction module uses concatenated multiple information and the BERT model with automatic prompts generation. The entity recognition module used original text and BERT model. Take the argument role "Palestine Hotel" as an example. The Argument Extraction module determines the role type (*place*) and rough location (12,13) of the resulting arguments. Then the Entity Identification module further specifies the exact span (12,14) of the arguments.

processing is carried out in two separate modules. An entity identification module determines all entities' start and end positions. Meanwhile, an argument extraction module predicts the categories of the argument roles. Finally, the results of the two models are combined to accomplish the event argument extraction.

2.1 Encoding

Given an input sentence $S = (w_1, w_2, ..., w_n)$ with k triggers $T = \{t_1, t_2, ..., t_k\}$ and corresponding arguments, we use BERT to obtain the contextualized representation. BERT is a bi-directional language representation model based on transformer architecture that could produce more adapted textual representations for many downstream tasks based on token context. Notice that the inputs are not identical between the two modules. The entity identification module uses raw text, while the argument role module uses context with multiple categories of information. Existing methods only treat the argument role types as digital labels and ignore their similarities. Thus, our method applies the argument role types as additional semantic information to help the model understand the events more explicitly. For example, the argument role information consists of mainstream argument role types (e.g., "Instrument, Victim, Place, Target, Attacker") of the event (e.g., Conflict.Attack). Together with the event trigger and event type (e.g., fired, Conflict.Attack), argument role information constitutes additional information that concatenates to the raw text input for the argument role module. This method allows prompts to learn the distribution of argument roles under different event types and how they interact with each other.

We find that most event categories are compound nouns, such as "Conflict.Attack". To avoid the out of vocabulary (OOV) problem, AMP uses the wordpiece strategy to tokenize the sentence. For compound nouns like *Conflict.Attack*, it is split into wordpieces (Conflict, Attack). Finally, the average of all the wordpieces acts as its word representation. Our model processes the trigger words one by one for a sentence with multiple events to form k new sentences. After the encoder, we get the hidden embeddings,

$$\{h_1, h_2, ..., h_m\} = F(A_{t_i}, t_i, w_1, w_2..., w_n) \tag{1}$$

where $F(\cdot)$ is the pre-trained language model to encode the sentence. t_i is the event information, and A_{t_i} is the corresponding Argument role information.

2.2   Entity Identification

This module takes raw text as input into BERT and obtains the hidden states $H = h_1, h_2, ..., h_m$. Then it uses a feedforward network (FFN) to calculate the score vector ($y_i = FFN(h_i)$), where each value in y_i represents the score of the token belonging to the target tag set[2]. After that, to capture the dependencies among predicted tags[3], a linear-chain conditional random field (CRF) layer is used. For this purpose, *<start>* and *<end>* tokens are added in each sentence to assist in training.

The scoring function of a tag path $\hat{\mathcal{L}} = \left\{\hat{l}_i, ..., \hat{l}_n\right\}$ is from [4],

$$S(X, \hat{\mathcal{L}}) = \sum_{i=1}^{n} y_{i,\hat{l}_i} + \sum_{i=0}^{n+1} A_{\hat{l}_i,\hat{l}_{i+1}} \tag{2}$$

where y_{i,l_i} represents the non-normalized probability of the word vector h_i mapping to the label $\hat{l}_i$, and $A_{\hat{l}_i,\hat{l}_{i+1}}$ represents the transition score from $\hat{l}_i$ to $\hat{l}_{i+1}$. The transition matrix A weights are obtained and updated from the CRF training. In order to find an optimal tag sequence, we maximize the log-likelihood of $P(\mathcal{L}|X)$, where $\mathcal{L}$ is the set of all possible tag paths.

$$\log P(\mathcal{L}|X) = S(X, \mathcal{L}) - \log(\sum_{\hat{l} \in \mathcal{L}} e^{s(X,\hat{l})}) \tag{3}$$

This concise yet efficacious module can label the spans of the potential argument roles (all entities).

2.3   Argument Extraction

The module of argument roles extraction consists of three parts.

Optimising Prompts. Our model uses an automatic prompts generation mechanism to avoid the uneven quality of human-designed questions and uses multi-category information to generate higher quality prompts for the argument role category prediction.

---

[2] We use the BIO tag format. The prefixes B-, I-, and O- represent entity start, interior, and non-entity, respectively.

[3] e.g., An entity should not start with an I- tag and end with a B- tag.

Specifically, we add learnable prefix-style prompts [17] to each layer inside BERT. In addition, to exploit the semantic information of argument roles and the similarity between similar event categories, we add event trigger and argument roles information associated with its event type before the original text. **Argument role filter** To maximize the prompts guidance of the semantic aspects for the language model, we want the argument role filter to focus not on the precise location of argument roles but on their semantic categories ($\mathcal{R} = r_1, ..., r_s$). Here we put textual representation h_i in Eq. (1) in a set of multiple classifiers. For each token w_i, we predict whether it corresponds to an argument role $r \in \mathcal{R}$ as:

$$\hat{r}_i = p(r|w_i) = f_{sch}(r, t_j)\sigma(w_r^T h_{ij} + b_r)$$

where σ denotes sigmoid function, and h_{ij} denotes the i-th token representation of the sentence constructed by the event trigger t_j. The indicator function $f_{sch}(r, t_j)$ indicates whether the role r belongs to the type of the event triggered by t_j according to the pre-defined event scheme. The overlapped arguments problem can be addressed by extracting different triggers with the argument role filter separately.

Joint Decision. At last, AMP outputs the event argument roles obtained from the joint decision of the two modules' results. A final event argument role prediction should satisfy two points. 1) Predicted by argument role filter as a non-empty category, that is, a token is predicted to belong to a specific type of argument role. 2) This token is within a specific span of the entity identification module prediction. The token that does not meet either of the conditions will be ignored. Then, the span of the argument role uses the result predicted by the entity identification module, and the category uses the prediction of the argument role filter.

Besides, we adopt an effective strategy for training the Argument Extraction module to make our model more fault-tolerant. Specifically, we randomly select a token (prioritize verbs) as the trigger for a sentence with no event and assign it an event type. The model should learn not to extract arguments when these negative samples appear, and it should predict only an empty list, i.e., [ ]. Such a mechanism makes AMP more robust and alleviates the sparse distribution of event argument roles in the dataset.

3 Experiments

3.1 Datasets and Evaluation Metrics

Following most of the EAE works, we conduct experiments on the widely used Automatic Content Extraction (ACE) 2005[4] dataset, which contains 599 documents that have been annotated with 33 event subtypes and 22 argument roles. We use the same data splitting and preprocessing step as the prior work [21], i.e., the testing set has 40 newswire documents, the validation set has 30 randomly selected documents, and the training set has the remaining 529 documents. In addition, we also conduct experiments on Roles Across Multiple Sentences (RAMS)[5] dataset [8], which is a document-level

---

[4] https://catalog.ldc.upenn.edu/LDC2006T06.

[5] http://nlp.jhu.edu/rams.

cross-sentence argument annotation. It is a new, more difficult dataset containing 9,124 annotated events with 139 event types and 65 argument role types.

As for evaluation, we adopt the same criteria defined in [11]. An event argument is appropriately identified if its spans match any of the reference arguments mentioned in the text. It is successfully classified if its semantic role (22 in ACE total) is likewise correct. To maintain comparability, we use precision (P), recall (R), and F1-score (F1) as evaluation metrics, among which F1 is the most comprehensive metric.

3.2   Baseline Methods

Multiple classic models are selected as the baselines, and these models can be divided into two categories.

- **Classification-based method DMBERT** [22] employs BERT as an encoder and generates representations for each entity mentioned via dynamic multi-pooling. **HMEAE** [23] utilizes the notion of a hierarchy for argument roles and hierarchical modular attention for event argument extraction. **BERD** [25] is a bi-directional entity-level recurrent decoder to generate argument roles by incorporating contextual entities' argument role predictions.
- **QA method EE_QA** [7] formulates the extraction task as a question answering (QA)/machine reading comprehension (MRC) task by designing different questions for each argument role. **GDAP** [20] is a prompt-based method that combines different event and argument types with a prompt template to guide the generation language model (T5-L). **FEAE** [24] uses a curriculum knowledge distillation strategy to train a MRC model. **DocMRC** [16] devises two data augmentation regimes based on MRC. **BART-Gen** [12] formulates the task as conditional generation following event templates.

3.3   Implementation Details

We adopt BERT as the encoder and propose a decoupled architecture as the decoder for the experiment.

BERT. AMP uses $BERT_{Large}$[6] model, and a dropout probability of 0.3 on all layers. The learning rate of BERT is different and is set to $5e-5$.

Training. For other layers, optimising use the AdamW with learning rate of $1e-5$, $\beta_1 = 0.9, \beta_2 = 0.999$. Only the prompt layer has L2 weight decay of 0.001, and the rest are 0. We set the training epochs and batch size to 30 and 12, respectively. Besides, the length of the prompt is set to 64.

3.4   Main Results

Compared with the former state-of-the-art methods on the ACE2005 dataset, the overall performance of our approach is shown on the left of Table 1. Note that the same event detection model (DMBERT) is used for all the models to ensure a fair comparison.

---

[6] https://huggingface.co/models.

Table 1. Argument Extraction Classification on ACE2005 and RAMS. Gold refers to the use of gold triggers instead of predicted triggers. † means replacing the event detection part of EEQA with DMBERT and then performing argument extraction. * means the value from our implementation.

	ACE2005			ACE2005 (Gold)			RAMS (Gold)		
Models	P	R	F1	P	R	F1	P	R	F1
Classification-based									
DMBERT [22]	56.9	57.4	57.2	-	-	-	-	-	-
HMEAE [23]	62.2	56.6	59.3	60.73	56.21	58.38	39.28*	41.86*	40.52*
BERD [25]	59.1	61.5	60.3	-	-	-	-	-	-
QA method									
EEQA [7]	58.1†	56.2†	57.1†	67.88	63.02	65.36	43.98*	40.27*	42.04*
GDAP [20]	48.0	61.6	54.0	69.00	74.20	71.50	-	-	-
FEAE [24]	-	-	-	-	-	-	53.17	42.76	47.40
DocMRC [16]	-	-	-	-	-	-	43.40	48.30	45.70
BART-Gen [12]	-	-	-	-	-	-	41.90	42.50	42.20
AMP freeze BERT	55.2	61.3	58.1	67.81	72.05	69.87	51.51	46.03	48.61
AMP	62.1	61.5	**61.8**	76.26	72.61	**74.91**	53.33	47.96	**50.50**

AMP's advantages can be understood in the following ways. Under the same level of event trigger extraction, AMP's event argument extraction achieves state-of-the-art performance. Compared to the most recent best-performed baseline BERD, AMP obtains an absolute improvement of 1.5 in F1 (60.3 of BERD v.s. 61.8 of AMP). We attribute the solid enhancement to the efficient combination of multi-category information with automatically generated prompts. The AMP model also shows competitiveness for EEQA and GDAP, which also use the QA method. Compared to the hand-designed questions, our auto-generated prompts can guarantee high quality. In addition, unlike these manually designed questions, which can only fetch information from discrete space, our methods can perform well in optimizing continuous language models.

3.5   Performance Analysis

To further explore the performance improvements brought by the AMP model, we discuss and verify the following aspects.

Performance with Gold Triggers. On the RAMS dataset, all Previous work [12, 16, 24] used gold triggers[7] instead of predicted event triggers for the EAE task. Therefore, we conduct an experimental comparison using gold triggers on both ACE2005 and RAMS to explore the potential of the AMP model. As can be seen in Table 1, it obtains absolute 3.4% and 3.1% Arg-C gains on ACE2005 and RAMS, respectively. Based on the experimental results, we can conclude that the AMP model handles the EAE tasks better, whether using the same event detection model or gold triggers.

---
[7] 100% correct event trigger words.

Table 2. Comparison of different prompts. [T] represents the event trigger and event type. [R] represents the category information of the event argument role. Each collection is marked below with its share of the ACE2005. Notice that the prompts in AMP are embedded in each layer of the BERT model. Therefore we only show the approximate text of the last layer's prompts.

Relation	Method	Prompt	F1
Entity	Manual	What is the entity of [T] ?	60.0
(18.3%)	P-tuning	plastic ##quest Whatever ... [T]	61.0
	AMP	##mir ##roid consoles ... [R] [T]	63.2
Place	Manual	Where is the place of [T] ?	46.0
(17.5%)	P-tuning	plastic ##quest Whatever ... [T]	49.5
	AMP	##mir ##roid consoles ... [R] [T]	51.6
Person	Manual	Who is the person of [T] ?	56.0
(9.6%)	P-tuning	plastic ##quest Whatever ... [T]	62.0
	AMP	##mir ##roid consoles ... [R] [T]	62.0
Instrument	Manual	What is the instrument of [T] ?	33.3
(2.3%)	P-tuning	plastic ##quest Whatever ... [T]	0.0
	AMP	##mir ##roid consoles ... [R] [T]	75.0
10 most frequent	Manual	What is the argument of [T] ?	62.1
(84.9%)	P-tuning	abusive slogan article [T]	62.6
	AMP	hushed Libby hardened ... [R] [T]	65.4
5 most uncommon	Manual	What is the argument of [T] ?	40.0
(6.5%)	P-tuning	##aman Board [cls] ...[T]	34.2
	AMP	##rvin denial ##TL ... [R] [T]	51.4

Performance with Different Prompts. To further investigate the quality of our prompt, we conduct a comparison and analysis with three types of prompts, AMP-generated prompts, hand-designed questions, and prefix-tuning prompt [18] on the subsets of ACE2005. We choose hand-crafted questions (99 questions) from EEQA [7] on the ACE2005 dataset. The P-tuning can also automatically produces prompts, which are implemented by a BiLSTM (bidirectional long-short term memory networks) and a two-layer multilayer perceptron (MLP). We sort according to the frequency of occurrence of argument roles and select the collections of "10 most frequently" appear and "5 most uncommon" appear, respectively.

As shown in Table 2, experiments demonstrate that our generated prompts perform better than others in most categories. AMP also eliminates the need for humans to design a vast number (99 in ACE2005) of problems. Compared with the P-tuning prompts, AMP outperforms its performance across the board, especially for the "5 most uncommon" subset. Overall, AMP generates more appropriate prompts for the EAE task and provides excellent help for rare event argument roles extraction.

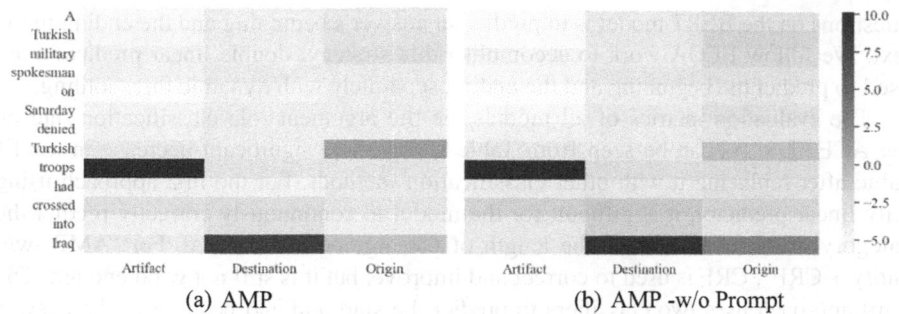

(a) AMP   (b) AMP -w/o Prompt

Fig. 2. Heatmap of sentence vector for the argument roles of "A Turkish military spokesman on Saturday denied Turkish troops had crossed into Iraq".

3.6 Ablation Study

Effect of Prompt and Different Information. To further investigate the contribution of different information to the EAE task, we construct a variety of other inputs, and their performance is shown in Table 3. From the results, we can observe that (1) When only argument role or event type information is taken into account, the F1 performance decreases by 1.6 and 1.3, respectively. (2) When the prompt part is removed, the F1 value drops by 1.1. The results demonstrate the validity of the information used by AMP for EAE. In "AMP -w/o Auto Prompt", the augmented information (argument role and event type information) only appears as discrete text, and the model fails to seek the key of the information. We visualize a heatmap from one wrong case, as shown in Fig. 2. AMP performs better in contexts that require a deeper understanding of the semantics. It points to the critical information of the event and provides a more precise answer to the question "Where is Origin?"

Effect of Different Modules. We further examine the following ablated models to investigate different modules' effectiveness in the decoupled architecture. (i) **AMP -w/o entity + Linear** The model that removes the entity spans module and replaces it with a linear classification layer. This approach labels the sequence directly into BIO format to determine the range of arguments while classifying it. (ii) **AMP -w/o entity + CRF** The model that uses CRF to correct wrongs, CRF is added to the top layer of the first approach. (iii) **AMP -w/o entity + D-Linear** A common way to solve QA

Table 3. The impact of different types of information on AMP.

Model	P	R	F1
DMBERT	56.9	57.4	57.2
AMP	**62.1**	61.5	**61.8**
-w/o Event Type	56.6	**61.3**	58.8
-w/o Argument Role Type	58.3	59.8	59.0
-w/o Auto Prompt	60.2	58.3	59.3

Table 4. Comparison with different modules on ACE2005.

Method	P	R	F1
AMP -w/o entity + Linear	49.7	50.3	50.0
AMP -w/o entity + CRF	58.0	59.4	58.7
AMP -w/o entity + D-Linear	59.6	54.7	57.0
AMP -w/o negative samples	61.9	60.1	61.0
AMP (full)	61.8	60.7	**61.2**

questions on the BERT model is to predict an answer's beginning and the ending in the text. We follow EEQA work to accomplish this strategy: double linear predictors are used to predict the beginning and the ending separately with dynamic thresholding.

The evaluation metrics of all models are the argument role classification rate on the ACE2005. As can be seen from Table 4, there is a significant decrease in the F1 value after replacing it with other classification methods. For the first approach using only linear predictor, it is difficult for the model to continuously correctly predict the category of each token since the length of the argument is unfixed. For "AMP -w/o entity + CRF", CRF is used to correct and improve, but it is still not good enough. The third approach uses two classifiers to predict the start and end position of the answer, respectively, which is a typical method of processing QA tasks on the BERT model. However, it is challenging to locate argument roles and classify them simultaneously. Also, this prediction approach has significant uncertainties, such as ending before the beginning or multiple endings for one beginning, which still need to be investigated and solved. Therefore, we separate the event argument extraction task and make a joint decision last. Tokens (or phrases) are identified as event argument roles only by both the entity extraction model and the argument extraction model confirming, which also reduces the error caused by individual models. Experiments validate that our proposed decoupled architecture and the joint decision can perform better than other classification strategies.

In addition, we observe that AMP performance without the negative samples strategy is slightly degraded. The event trigger detection task will produce some false trigger samples unavoidably, and these samples will affect the model's understanding of the downstream EAE task. The negative samples strategy alleviates this difficulty, making the model more fault-tolerant in reality. In fact, model "AMP -w/o entity + Linear" is one of the separate modules in AMP (i.e., the Argument Extraction module). Another separate module of the AMP, the Entity Identification Module, achieves 91.6 precision, 92.6 recall value and 92.1 F1 on entity identification tasks. Its performance largely helps the accuracy of the joint extraction.

S1: MCI would agree to pay the largest fine imposed so far by the SEC on a company that is not a broker-dealer.
S2: Hunter filed for divorce in LA Superior Court, citing irreconcilable differences with the 58-year-old rock star to whom she has been married for nearly 13 years.

Fig. 3. Case study examples. Arguments and triggers are highlighted by green and purple color, respectively (Color figure online)

3.7 Case Study

To promote understanding of our method, we demonstrate two concrete examples in Fig. 3.

- *Lack background knowledge* There is an event of type Justice.Fine in Fig. 3.S1, and AMP correctly identified MCI and SEC as the event argument. However AMP classifies SEC (which appears uniquely in the full text) as an "entity" rather than an "adjudicator". Without the background knowledge of the full name of the SEC (U.S Securities and Exchange Commission), it is difficult for the model to make judgments about unknown entities.

- *Implicit expression* Extraction of implicit event arguments requires the ability to reason about event roles. In Fig. 3.S2, AMP did not understand that this rock star was alluding to the hunter's marriage partner, so only one person was extracted from this sentence.
- *Lack of sufficient corpus* The distribution of the different categories of arguments in the training data is also highly uneven. Taking the argument role "adjudicator" in S1 as an example, it has only a 0.6% proportion in the ACE2005. However, combined with Table 2, our model alleviates this unbalanced argument role extraction problem.

4   Related Work

Event Argument Extraction. Earlier methods [14,21] apply sequence labeling to accomplish the EAE task, which has made substantial progress. Later on, QA methods [7,10,15,20] demonstrated their effectiveness in extracting argument roles by more semantic information. Yang [26] used a pre-trained model with a state-machine-based span boundary detector. They used multiple binary classifiers on the BERT to overcome the overlapping problem. Our approach addresses this problem by performing multiple extractions of different types. Du [7] took a fresh look at EE by casting it as an MRC problem. They used many specially designed questions about the event argument roles to ask the model. This also brings other problems: How to generate questions? What is the quality of the design questions? Our work introduces an automatic prompts mechanism to solve this problem. It requires no human effort and can be updated during the training procedure to ensure effectiveness.

Prompt Learning. The fine-tuning strategy has improved performance on a diverse variety of natural language tasks. However, these successes come at a price. It is memory-consuming during training because gradients an optimizer states that all parameters must be stored. Inspired by brown [2], the idea of prompt learning has attracted more attention. Prompt refers to leveraging special templates to aid the language model prediction concerning understanding and generation. In terms of EAE, [20] proposes a model called GDAP, which integrates prompts into generative QA to complete the extraction task. However, it still uses manually designed prompts to guide the optimization. This method makes it less general, requiring manual prompt redesign once working on an entirely new dataset. As a result, research into the automatic generation of prompts is also gaining traction. Shin [19] designed an approach (AutoPrompt) to develop automatically-constructed prompts that based on gradient-guided search. Liu [17] has developed P-tuning V2, which is an optimized version for NLU (Natural Language Understanding) tasks based on prefix-tuning [13]. Our work is inspired by P-tuning V2. To better serve the EAE task, we add multi-category information about argument roles after the generated prompt.

5 Conclusion

In this paper, we introduce AMP, a dual-module that combines automatically generated prompts and multiple types of information. AMP addresses how to generate high-quality questions of EAE tasks at a low cost. Experimental results show that AMP achieves state-of-the-art performance in the ACE 2005 dataset. In the future, we will further explore the possibility of incorporating the AMP into a unified model to extract triggers and arguments jointly.

References

1. Berant, J., et al.: Modeling biological processes for reading comprehension. In: EMNLP (2014)
2. Brown, T.B., et al.: Language models are few-shot learners. arXiv preprint arXiv:2005.14165 (2020)
3. Chen, Y., Xu, L., Liu, K., Zeng, D., Zhao, J.: Event extraction via dynamic multi-pooling convolutional neural networks. In: ACL-IJCNLP (2015)
4. Chiu, J.P., Nichols, E.: Named entity recognition with bidirectional lstm-cnns. TACL (2016)
5. Daniel, N., Radev, D., Allison, T.: Sub-event based multi-document summarization. In: Proceedings of the HLT-NAACL 03 Text Summarization Workshop (2003)
6. Devlin, J., Chang, M.W., Lee, K., Toutanova, K.: BERT: pre-training of deep bidirectional transformers for language understanding. In: NAACL (2019)
7. Du, X., Cardie, C.: Event extraction by answering (almost) natural questions. In: EMNLP (2020)
8. Ebner, S., Xia, P., Culkin, R., Rawlins, K., Van Durme, B.: Multi-sentence argument linking. In: ACL (2020)
9. Ji, H., Grishman, R.: Knowledge base population: successful approaches and challenges. In: ACL (2011)
10. Li, F., et al.: Event extraction as multi-turn question answering. In: Findings of EMNLP (2020)
11. Li, Q., Ji, H., Huang, L.: Joint event extraction via structured prediction with global features. In: ACL (2013)
12. Li, S., Ji, H., Han, J.: Document-level event argument extraction by conditional generation. In: NAACL (2021)
13. Li, X.L., Liang, P.: Prefix-tuning: optimizing continuous prompts for generation. arXiv preprint arXiv:2101.00190 (2021)
14. Lin, Y., Ji, H., Huang, F., Wu, L.: A joint neural model for information extraction with global features. In: ACL (2020)
15. Liu, J., Chen, Y., Liu, K., Bi, W., Liu, X.: Event extraction as machine reading comprehension. In: EMNLP (2020)
16. Liu, J., Chen, Y., Xu, J.: Machine reading comprehension as data augmentation: a case study on implicit event argument extraction. In: EMNLP (2021)
17. Liu, X., Ji, K., Fu, Y., Du, Z., Yang, Z., Tang, J.: P-tuning v2: prompt tuning can be comparable to fine-tuning universally across scales and tasks. arXiv preprint arXiv:2110.07602 (2021)
18. Liu, X., et al.: Gpt understands, too. arXiv preprint arXiv:2103.10385 (2021)
19. Shin, T., Razeghi, Y., Logan IV, R.L., Wallace, E., Singh, S.: Autoprompt: Eliciting knowledge from language models with automatically generated prompts. arXiv preprint arXiv:2010.15980 (2020)

20. Si, J., Peng, X., Li, C., Xu, H., Li, J.: Generating disentangled arguments with prompts: A simple event extraction framework that works. arXiv preprint arXiv:2110.04525 (2021)
21. Wadden, D., Wennberg, U., Luan, Y., Hajishirzi, H.: Entity, relation, and event extraction with contextualized span representations. In: EMNLP-IJCNLP (2019)
22. Wang, X., Han, X., Liu, Z., Sun, M., Li, P.: Adversarial training for weakly supervised event detection. In: NAACL (2019)
23. Wang, X., Wang, Z., et al.: Hmeae: hierarchical modular event argument extraction. In: EMNLP-IJCNLP (2019)
24. Wei, K., Sun, X., Zhang, Z., Zhang, J., Zhi, G., Jin, L.: Trigger is not sufficient: Exploiting frame-aware knowledge for implicit event argument extraction. In: ACL-IJCNLP (2021)
25. Xiangyu, X., Ye, W., Zhang, S., Wang, Q., Jiang, H., Wu, W.: Capturing event argument interaction via a bi-directional entity-level recurrent decoder. In: ACL-IJCNLP (2021)
26. Yang, S., Feng, D., Qiao, L., Kan, Z., Li, D.: Exploring pre-trained language models for event extraction and generation. In: ACL, pp. 5284–5294 (2019)

Summarization and Generation (Oral)

Topic-Features for Dialogue Summarization

Zhen Zhang and Junhui Li[✉]

School of Computer Science and Technology, Soochow University, Suzhou, China
lijunhui@suda.edu.cn

Abstract. Texts such as news reports and academic papers come from one single speaker and are well-structured. However, dialogues often come from two or more speakers exchanging information. In this case, the topic or intention may change in a dialogue, and the key information is often scattered in utterances of different speakers, which brings challenges to the abstractive dialogue summarization. It is difficult to apply the traditional topic modeling approaches because of too much noise and the inherent characteristics of dialogue. In order to effectively model the entire dialogue and capture various topic information, this paper proposes a topic-feature approach based on neural topic model, including word-level embedding and dialogue-level representation. Experimental results on the largest dialogue summarization corpus SAMSum show that the proposed approach can significantly improve over competitive baselines. In addition, we also conduct experiments on other datasets from different domains to verify the effectiveness and generality of our proposed approach.

Keywords: Dialogue summarization · Topic features · Seq2Seq model

1 Introduction

Online chatting has become an indispensable component of everyday life. Massive amount of dialogue poses a great challenge to speakers who could be surrounded by lengthy utterances rather than the key information of the dialogue. Therefore, dialogue summarization has been gaining research traction recently.

Dialogue summarization aims to compress a dialogue and distill salient information from it into a shorter message, which could help people effectively capture its highlights without time-consuming dialogue reading and comprehension. Similar as recent studies in this literature [1,2,28], in this paper we focus on abstractive dialogue summarization. Naturally, a simple way for dialogue summarization is to directly apply existing document summarization approaches or models to dialogues. However, different from documents with formal texts, spoken dialogues usually consist of informal texts with multiple topics, in which key information is widely scattered [28]. Moreover, there usually exists too much noise in the context due to irrelevant chats and transcription errors [21]. As a result, informative words are often accompanied by frequent or noisy words, making this task more challenging. In order to better understand the intentions of the speakers, this work focuses on topic-oriented dialogue summarization, which aims to extract semantically consistent topics and generate highly concise summaries to distill the salient information of dialogues.

Recent studies put focus on long and complex oral dialogues, such as meetings and court debates, which usually consist of multiple relevant topics in the whole dialogue flow [9,20,25,27]. Usually, a speaker has a strong and clear motivation to solve problems on a particular topic. To this end, relevant studies recognize topic structure for better modeling dialogue. For example, Chen et al. [1] utilize topic perspective to encode the rich dialogue information structure, and Liu et al. [12] divide a whole dialogue into multiple topic-different segments. Therefore, in these approaches they have to decide on topics in advance, or explicitly split the dialogue into segments with different topics. Since each utterance may contain information of multiple topics, alternatively, in this work we learn both word-level and dialogue-level topic features for better modeling dialogues.

In this paper, we propose a topic-feature approach for dialogue summarization based on neural topic model. Firstly, we introduce the neural topic model (NTM), which consists of two sub-modules: inference module and generation module. The inference module utilizes neural network to infer the topic distribution from each input texts, while the generation module applies it to reconstruct the input. Based on the hypothesis that the topic distribution of the input dialogue should be consistent with the corresponding summary, we restrict the topic distribution information by Kullback-Leibler (KL) divergence. Secondly, in order to obtain topic information and extract semantic topics from different levels, we extract topic-oriented embedding information from both the word-level and dialogue-level, and apply it to the embedding layer of the sequence-to-sequence model. Finally, we conducted experiments on SAMSum [7], Dialog-Sum [3], QMSum [26], CRD3 [16] and Email [4] datasets, which cover mutiple domains: chit-chats, oral English, conference, TV show and Email. Experimental results show that our approach can achieve significant improvement over the baselines of these five datasets.

2   Background

In this section, we will describe the task definition and give a brief introduction to the neural topic model.

2.1   Task Definition

Given an input dialog $\mathcal{D}$, the model aims to generate compressed summary $\mathcal{S}$, where $\mathcal{D}$ consists of $|\mathcal{D}|$ utterances $[u_1, u_2, \cdots, u_{|\mathcal{D}|}]$ and $\mathcal{S}$ consists of $|\mathcal{S}|$ words $[s_1, s_2, \cdots, s_{|\mathcal{S}|}]$. The i-th utterance can be represented as a sequence of words $u_i = [\langle s \rangle, u_{i,1}, \cdots, u_{i,|u_i|}, \langle /s \rangle]$, where $u_{i,j}$ denotes the j-th word in the i-th utterance while $\langle s \rangle$ denotes the beginning of the utterance and $\langle /s \rangle$ denotes the end of the utterance. In addition, each utterance u_i is associated with a speaker p_i. Thus, this task can be formalized as generating the summary S given the dialogue sequence: $\mathcal{D} = [\langle s \rangle, p_1, u_{1,1}, \cdots, \langle /s \rangle, \cdots, \langle s \rangle, p_{|\mathcal{D}|}, u_{|\mathcal{D}|,1}, \cdots, \langle /s \rangle]$.

2.2   Neural Topic Model

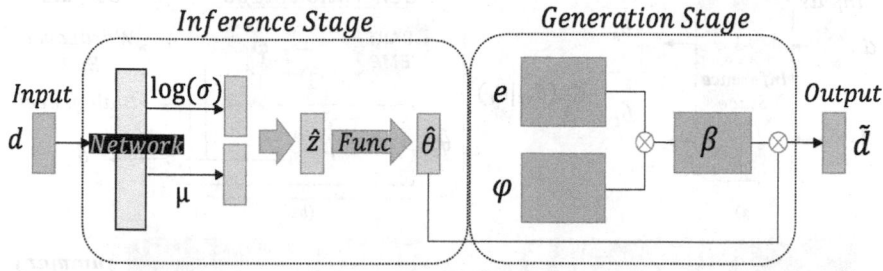

Fig. 1. The architecture of the neural topic model.

The architecture of the neural topic model (NTM) [13] is shown in Fig. 1. It consists of two sub-modules: inference module and generation module. Formally, given the bag-of-words representation of a dialogue $d \in \mathbb{R}^{|V|}$ with stop words removed, we build an inference network $q(\theta|d)$ to approximate the posterior distribution $p(\theta|d)$, where V is the vocabulary. In detail, $q(\theta|d)$ is composed of a function $\theta = f(z)$, where $z \sim N\left(\mu(d), \sigma^2(d)\right)$, and $\mu(d), \sigma^2(d)$ are both the outputs of linear layer. In practical, we use the re-parameterization trick [8] to sample ϵ from $N(0, I^2)$ distribution and calculate $\hat{z} = \mu(d) + \epsilon \cdot \theta(d)$. Then, a sampled $\hat{\theta} \in \mathbb{R}^K$ can be derived as:

$$\hat{\theta} = f(\hat{z}) = softmax(W_\theta \hat{z} + b_\theta), \tag{1}$$

where $W_\theta \in \mathbb{R}^{H \times K}$, $b_\theta \in \mathbb{R}^K$ are trainable parameters and K denotes the number of topics. $\hat{\theta} \in \mathbb{R}^K$ can be viewed as the topic representation of the entire dialogue. Then, we define $\beta \in \mathbb{R}^{K \times |V|}$, $\varphi \in \mathbb{R}^{K \times H}$, $e \in \mathbb{R}^{|V| \times H}$ to represent topic-word distributions, topic vectors and word vectors, respectively, where H is the dimension of vectors, φ is randomly initialized and e is pre-trained word embeddings. Finally, β is computed with φ and e as follows:

$$\beta = softmax(e \cdot \varphi^T). \tag{2}$$

In the generation stage, the reconstructed input $\hat{d}$ is computed with β and θ. We can define the loss function as:

$$L_T = -E_{q(\theta|d)} \left[\log p(d \mid \beta, \theta) \right] \approx - \sum_n \log p\left(w_n \mid \beta, \hat{\theta}\right), \tag{3}$$

where w_n represents the n-th word in d, and the log-likelihood of d can be computed with $\log(\hat{\theta} \cdot \beta)$.

3   Our Approach

In this section, we first obtain topic features based on neural topic model, including word-level and dialogue-level. Then we integrate the two level topic features into BART model for better encoding dialogues (see Fig. 2).

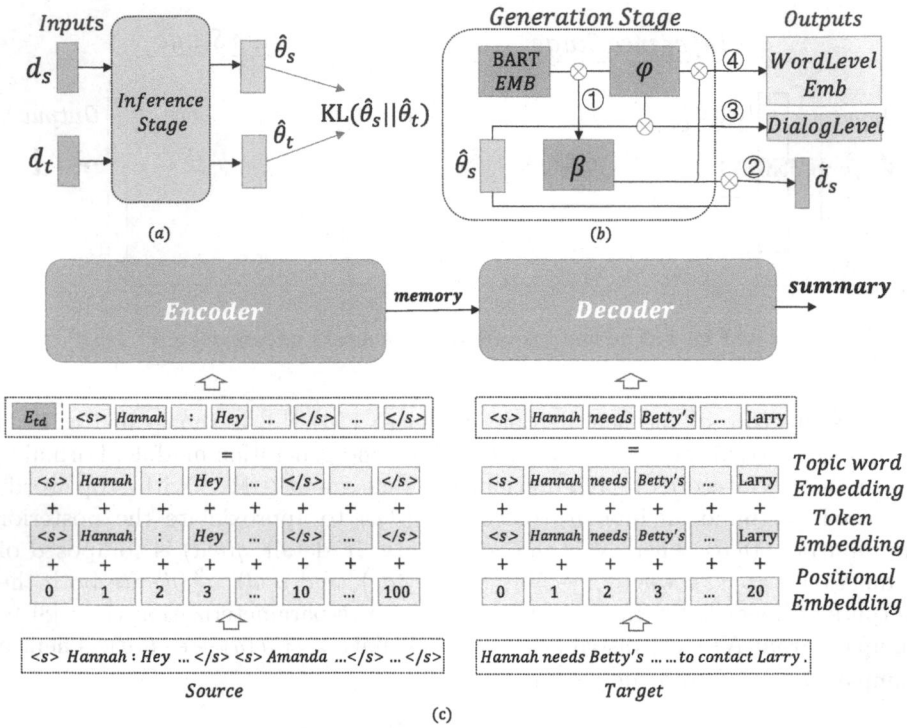

Fig. 2. The architecture of our topic-feature approach based on neural topic model. (a) In the inference stage we obtain the topic distribution of dialogue and corresponding summary and use KL divergence to constrain; (b) In the gengeation stage we obtain word-level topic embedding and dialog-level topic representation; (c) We integrate the two topic features into Seq2Seq Model.

3.1   Topic-Features Based on NTM

The traditional neural topic model generates the topic representation $\hat{\theta}$ of the input dialogue in the inference stage, and generates $\tilde{d}$ in the generation stage in order to restore the input bag-of-words d. We infer that the topic distribution of the input dialogue should be consistent with the corresponding summary. As shown in Fig. 2(a), we input two bag-of-words in the inference stage: d_s represents the bag-of-words of the dialogue, and d_t represents the target sentences (summary). The topic distribution of the two inputs should be consistent, and we use KL divergence to constrain:

$$L_d = KL\left(\widehat{\theta}_s \,\|\, \widehat{\theta}_t\right). \tag{4}$$

In addition, we initialize e by word embedding in BART and utilize β, φ and θ variables to obtain the word-level topic embedding and dialogue-level topic representation in the generation stage as:

$$E_{tw} = \beta^T \cdot \varphi, \tag{5}$$

$$E_{td} = \theta \cdot \varphi, \tag{6}$$

where $E_{tw} \in \mathbb{R}^{|V| \times H}$ denotes word-level topic embedding, and $E_{td} \in \mathbb{R}^H$ denotes topic representation of the entire dialogue. Therefore, the loss function of our neural topic model is L_{tm}:

$$L_{tm} = L_d + L_T. \tag{7}$$

3.2   Integrating Topic Features into Seq2Seq Model

Seq2Seq model with Transformer structure [22] is widely used in the dialogue summarization task. The encoder module is used to encode the input dialogue while the decoder generates the summary. From the NTM, on the one hand we could obtain word-level topic embedding which assigns each word with a topic representation. On the other hand, we could obtain dialogue-level topic representation which summarizes the topic information for the whole dialogue.

Integrating Word-Level Topic Embedding. Following Sennrich and Haddow [19] and Zhang et al. [23], we simply view word-level topic embedding as a feature for both source-side and target-side words. As shown in Fig. 2 (c), we do not change the internal architecture of the encoder and decoder, but modify it at the embedding layer. Taking the source-side input $\mathcal{D}$ as example, we update the input (i.e., X^0) to the encoder as the following:

$$X^0 = \text{TE}\left(\mathcal{D}\right) + \text{PE}\left(\mathcal{D}\right) + \text{TWE}\left(\mathcal{D}\right), \tag{8}$$

where $\text{TE}\left(\cdot\right)$, $\text{PE}\left(\cdot\right)$ and $\text{TWE}\left(\cdot\right)$ return word embedding, positional embedding, and word-level topic embedding, respectively. Similarly, we could update the input to the decoder with word-level topic embedding.

Integrating Dialogue-Level Topic Representation. Dialogue-level topic representation gives an overview of the input dialogue. We, therefore, view the topic representation as an extra input and simply concatenate it with X^0 in Eq. 8, the embedding layer output, i.e.,

$$\hat{X}^0 = [E_{td}; X^0], \tag{9}$$

where $E_{td} \in \mathbb{R}^H$ is the topic representation obtained via Eq. 6. $\hat{X}^0$ then will be used as the embedding layer output, as shown in Fig. 2(c).

3.3 Joint Training

To jointly train the topic model and the summarizer, we design a joint loss which includes the loss function of summarizer L_S and the loss function of topic models L_{tm}. The joint loss function is defined as:

$$L = L_s + \lambda \cdot L_{tm} = L_s + \lambda(L_d + L_T) \tag{10}$$

where λ is a coefficient to balance the losses between the summarizer and topic model.

4 Experiments

4.1 Datasets

Table 1. Details in experimental datasets. # denotes the number of dialogues in the corresponding set.

Dataset	Domain	#Train	#Test	#Valid
SAMSum	Chit-chat	14,732	819	818
DialogSum	Oral English	12,469	500	500
QMSum	Conference	1,257	279	272
CRD3	TV show	13,854	2,485	2,094
Email	Email	215	250	50

We conducted experiments on five dialogue datasets, including SAMSum, DialogSum, QMSum, CRD3 and Email, which are respectively from chats, oral English, conference, TV show and Email domains. Table 1 shows the details of these datasets.

SAMSum [7] contains natural messenger-like dialogues created and written down by linguists fluent in English, reflecting the topics of their real-life dialogues. Language experts are asked to annotate them with short summaries.

DialogSum [3] is a large scale labeled dataset, mostly from real life scenarios. This dataset contains face-to-face spoken dialogues that cover most of daily life, including schooling, work, medication, shops, leisure, and travel.

QMSum [26] collects dialogues from product conferences, academic conferences, and committee meetings. The annotation process consists of three parts: topic segmentation, query generation, and query-based summaries.

CRD3 [16] comes from an unscripted, live TV series in which regular characters play an open-ended role-playing game with dialogue collected from 159 key character episodes. It also includes the corresponding abstract summaries collected from the Fandom Wiki.

Email [4] is from a publicly available W3C corpus, and previous work has also used this dataset for Email summaries, but only provided a small sample of 40 mail communications.

Table 2. Experimental Results on Test Set of SAMSum.

Model	Rouge-1			Rouge-2			Rouge-L		
	F	P	R	F	P	R	F	P	R
PGN [18]	40.08	-	-	15.28	-	-	36.63	-	-
Transformer [22]	37.27	-	-	10.76	-	-	32.73	-	-
D-HGN [5]	42.03	-	-	18.07	-	-	39.56	-	-
TGDGA [24]	43.11	-	-	19.15	-	-	40.49	-	-
MV-BART [1]	45.56	**52.13**	44.68	22.30	**25.58**	22.03	44.70	**50.82**	43.29
S-BART [2]	46.07	51.13	46.24	22.60	25.11	22.81	45.00	49.82	44.47
BART (ours)	45.20	51.92	44.11	21.75	25.13	21.43	44.28	50.40	42.83
TE-BART w/ DR	46.56	51.36	46.92	22.50	24.96	22.70	45.34	49.86	45.04
TE-BART w/ WE	46.31	51.39	46.58	22.53	25.04	22.77	45.17	50.03	44.72
TE-BART w/ both	**46.68**	51.27	**47.25**	**22.77**	25.21	**23.08**	**45.69**	50.21	**45.41**

4.2 Model Settings

Following Chen et al. [2], we use BART-base to initialize our Seq2Seq model in all experiments. For parameters in the original BART encoder/decoder, we follow the default settings and set the learning rate as 3e−5 with 120 warm-up steps. We set the number of hidden dimensions as 768, the number of layers as 6, and the dropout rate as 0.1. The learning rate for parameters in newly added modules is 1e−3 with 60 warm-up steps. We set λ in Eq. 10 as 0.05 and use the same hyperparameters in all datasets. All experiments run on GeForce RTX 1080Ti (11 GB memory).

4.3 Baselines and Metrics

We compare our approach with several other models. For SAMSum [7] dataset, the pointer network [18] uses the pointer mechanism to generate the next word from the vocabulary or from the original sentence. Transformer [22] is a seq2seq model based on the attention mechanism, and D-HGN [5] incorporates common sense to help the model understand dialogue. TGDGA [24] uses topic words and models graph structures for dialogues. Multi-view BART [1] integrates the topic and stage information based on BART. S-BART [2] incorporates discourse relations and action triples in utterances through structured graphs to better encode dialogue.

For evaluation, we report ROUGE [11], which is conventionally adopted as the standard metric for summarization tasks. It mainly involves F1 scores for ROUGE-1, ROUGE-2, and ROUGE-L that measure the word-overlap, bigram-overlap and longest common sequence between the ground truth and the generated summary, respectively.

4.4   Experimental Results on SAMSum

Table 2 shows Rouge scores on SAMSum. It shows that our approach with either word-level topic embedding (i.e., w/ WE) or dialog-level topic representation (i.e., w/ DR) improves the performance on Rouge-1/2/L scores. Moreover, the improvement achieved by the two types of topic features is very close. Finally, our approach achieves the best performance when incorporating the two kinds of features together (i.e., w/ both). Our best model outperforms BART baseline with 1.48 in Rouge-1, 1.02 in Rouge-2, and 1.41 in Rouge-L, respectively.

Compared to previous studies, our approach achieves the best performance on both F1 and Recall over Rouge-1, Rouge-2 and Rouge-L.

4.5   Experimental Results on Other Datasets

Table 3. Experimental Results on datasets of DialogSum, QMSum, CRD3, and Email.

Model	DialogSum			QMSum			CRD3			Email		
	R-1	R-2	R-L	R-1	R-2	R-L	R-1	R-2	R-L	R-1	R-2	R-L
TextRank [4, 26]	-	-	-	16.3	2.7	15.4	-	-	-	19.5	3.9	16.2
Transformer [3]	35.9	8.7	33.5	-	-	-	-	-	-	-	-	-
BERT-ext [4]	-	-	-	-	-	-	-	-	-	25.5	6.2	21.7
BART (ours)	42.3	17.7	40.2	24.1	6.2	22.0	21.2	5.9	19.4	30.3	7.5	31.9
TE-BART w/ WE	43.0	18.1	40.7	24.5	6.2	21.9	22.1	6.4	20.0	**31.6**	8.0	**32.8**
TE-BART w/ DR	43.1	18.1	**41.0**	24.7	6.4	22.0	21.6	6.2	19.7	30.7	7.7	31.8
TE-BART w/ both	**43.3**	**18.5**	41.0	**25.5**	**6.5**	**22.1**	**22.3**	**6.5**	**21.1**	31.4	**8.1**	32.2

Table 3 shows the performance on the other datasets. The results show that some improvements of generating summary have deen achieved. Specifically, for DialogSum dataset, rouge-1 increases by 1.0, rouge-2 by 0.8 and rouge-l by 0.8. For QMSum dataset, rouge-1 increases by 1.4, rouge-2 by 0.3, and rouge-l by 0.1. For CRD3 dataset, rouge-1 increases by 1.1, rouge-2 by 0.6, and rouge-l by 1.7. For the Email dataset, rouge-1 increases by 1.3, rouge-2 by 0.6, and rouge-l by 0.9. This illustrates the robustness and effectiveness of our approach.

4.6   Analysis

Effect of the Number of Topics. Topic number K is an important hyperparameter in neural topic model because it may affect the convergence rate and inference quality of the models. Figure 3 shows the effect of K that ranges from 20 to 100 on the performance of SAMSum. The figure shows that the performance gets higher when K increases from 20 to 50, and then the performance starts to decline when K is over 50. In the experiment, we fix $K = 50$ for the summarization task.

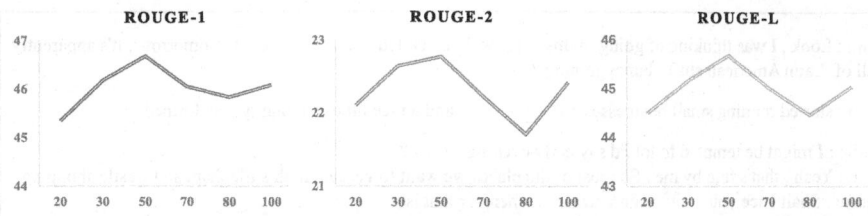

Fig. 3. Effects of the number of topics K on the development set of SAMSum.

Topic Word Distribution. Following Zou et al. [28], we analyse the topic distribution of words. Table 4 shows the word samples in different datasets, where top-10 words with the highest probability in β are listed. We found that words with different topics often contain common semantics that better reflect particular dialogue scenarios. For example, topic T1 in SAMSum dataset is about direction. Topic T2, with words of *official, legal* is an informative topic which relates to legal or political issues. The two topics in DialogSum are similar to those of SAMSum. In QMSum, both topics of T1 and T2 are about conference debate issues while T1 and T2 in CRD3 is about fighting. Moreover, the topics in Email tend to collect words with the same part of speech. Above topics illustrate that topic distribution is usually closely tied to the dataset.

Table 4. Top-10 words of different topics in different datasets.

Dataset	Top-10 Words
SAMSum	T1: between, front, back, next, cross, mid, North, South, central, side
	T2: Official, legal, law, police, criminal, lawyer, tax, illegal, referee, license
DialogSum	T1: back, between, up, front, south, out, mid, North, cross, under
	T2: official, legal, report, man, good, news, law, right, work, police
QMSum	T1: illustrate, view, debate, evaluate, demonstrate, bid, inspection, show, expose, inspect
	T2: ndorse, appalled, warrant, legislature, commission, finance, protocol, province, exhibit, confirms
CRD3	T1: bow, ribbon, knife, pin, attack, ring, basket, scissor, hook, crawl
	T2: head, prosecute, ground, safely, separating, miss, report, catch, handle, address
Email	T1: in, at, to, on, of, over, for, by, with, from
	T2: where, what, there, here, now, then, first, second, almost, most

Finn : **Look**, I was thinking of going to this neighborhood **called** Elephant and Castle **tomorrow**, it's apparently full of Latin American stuff. Fancy joining ? Finn : **started** running small businesses and restaurant , **and a nice little community was formed** Zadie : **I might be tempted to lol I'd say early evening**, 2-ish ? Finn : **Yeah**, **that's fine by me . So most of the places we want to visit are in this Elephant and Castle shopping centre . Shall I see you** at the main entrance , **wherever that is** Zadie : 2 o'clock at unspecified main entrance **then ? Sounds good to mw**
Golden: Finn and Zadie **are going to** Elephant and Castle **tomorrow** at 2. **They will** meet **at the** main entrance.
BART: Zadie and Finn **are going to see a** restaurant **called** Elephant and Castle **tomorrow. They will** meet at 2 pm **at the** main entrance.   ✖ neighborhood
Our model(w/ both): Finn and Zadie **are going to the** Elephant and Castle **tomorrow. They will** meet at 2 pm **at the** main entrance.

Fig. 4. An example of a dialogue in SAMSum and its generation outputs.

Case Study. Figure 4 shows summaries generated by different models for an example dialogue in the SAMSum dataset. In this example, we see that the summary generated by BART includes wrong information since *restaurant* is not consistent with the fact *neighborhood*. By analyzing the topic distribution, we find out that the topic distribution for *restaurant* is quite different from the dialogue-level topic distribution. Specifically, the cosine distance between the topic distributions of *restaurant* and the entire dialogue is 0.27, much lower than the averaged cosine distance 0.72. As a result, by integrating topic information, our model successfully excludes *restaurant* in the output and generates better summary with higher ROUGE scores.

5   Related Work

5.1   Document Summarization

Document summarization aims to condense well-structured documents into short sentences that contain important information, which has received extensive research attention, especially for abstractive summarization. Various approaches have been proposed for abstractive document summarization, such as seq2seq model [17], pointer generator [18] and pre-training model [10]. Since topic modeling could naturally capture topic information in multiple granularities, it is widely used in document summaries to identify the importance and interrelationships of words. More recently, Nguyen et al. [14] utilize the neural topic model to obtain key points and semantic information of the entire document.

5.2   Dialogue Summarization

Different from document Summarization that focus on a single participant, dialogue summarization tends to involve multiple interlocutors. First of all, the key information of dialogue is often scattered in multiple utterances [28], which leads to low information density. Secondly, multiple participants, topic offsets, frequent occurrence of coreferences and domain terminology are inherent in dialogue [6]. The two features make dialogue summarization a challenging task. Recently, with great advances in pre-training models for natural language processing tasks, they have also become main architecture for dialogue summarization, which achieve many advanced results. Previous studies view discourse relations as input features to detect important content in dialogue [15]. The current studies focus on adding ancillary information for better modeling dialogues and utilize various types of keywords to identify core parts of the dialogue, including dialogue entities [27], domain terminology [9], and topic words [24]. In this work, we combine auxiliary information provided by the neural topic model to better model dialogue, including word-level and dialogue-level topic-relevant features.

6   Conclusion

In this paper, we have introduced a topic-feature approach for dialogue summarization by integrating word-level topic embedding and dialogue-level topic representation, which can capture salient information and common semantics. We evaluated our approach with experiments on five datasets covering different domains. Experimental results have showed the robustness and effectiveness of our approach.

Acknowledgments. The authors would like to thank the anonymous reviewers for their constructive feedback. This work was supported by the National Natural Science Foundation of China (Grant No. 61876120).

References

1. Chen, J., Yang, D.: Multi-view sequence-to-. sequence models with conversational structure for abstractive dialogue summarization. In: Proceedings of EMNLP, pp. 4106–4118 (2020)
2. Chen, J., Yang, D.: Structure-aware abstractive conversation summarization via discourse and action graphs. In: Proceedings of ACL, pp. 1380–1391 (2021)
3. Chen, Y., Liu, Y., Chen, L., Zhang, Y.: DialogSum: a real-life scenario dialogue summarization dataset. In: Findings of ACL-IJCNLP, pp. 5062–5074 (2021)
4. Fabbri, A., et al.: ConvoSumm: conversation summarization benchmark and improved abstractive summarization with argument mining. In: Proceedings of ACL, pp. 6866–6880 (2021)
5. Feng, X., Feng, X., Qin, B.: Incorporating commonsense knowledge into abstractive dialogue summarization via heterogeneous graph networks. In: Proceedings of CCL, pp. 964–975 (2021)
6. Feng, X., Feng, X., Qin, B.: A survey on dialogue summarization: recent advances and new frontiers. CoRR abs/2107.03175 (2021)
7. Gliwa, B., Mochol, I., Biesek, M., Wawer, A.: Samsum corpus: a human-annotated dialogue dataset for abstractive summarization. CoRR abs/1911.12237 (2019)

8. Kingma, D.P., Welling, M.: Auto-encoding variational bayes. CoRR abs/1312.6114 (2014)
9. Koay, J.J., Roustai, A., Dai, X., Burns, D., Kerrigan, A., Liu, F.: How domain terminology affects meeting summarization performance. In: Proceedings of COLING, pp. 5689–5695 (2020)
10. Lewis, M., et al.: BART: denoising sequence-to-sequence pre-training for natural language generation, translation, and comprehension. In: Proceedings of ACL, pp. 7871–7880 (2020)
11. Lin, C.Y.: Automatic evaluation of machine translation quality using longest common subsequence and skip-bigram statistics. In: Proceedings of ACL, pp. 74–81 (2004)
12. Liu, J., Zou, Y., Zhang, H., Chen, H., Ding, Z., Yuan, C., Wang, X.: Topic-aware contrastive learning for abstractive dialogue summarization. In: Findings of EMNLP, pp. 1229–1243 (2021)
13. Miao, Y., Grefenstette, E., Blunsom, P.: Discovering discrete latent topics with neural variational inference. In: Proceedings of ICML, pp. 2410–2419 (2017)
14. Nguyen, T., Luu, A.T., Lu, T., Quan, T.: Enriching and controlling global semantics for text summarization. In: Proceedings of EMNLP, pp. 9443–9456 (2021)
15. Qin, K., Wang, L., Kim, J.: Joint modeling of content and discourse relations in dialogues. In: Proceedings of ACL, pp. 974–984 (2017)
16. Rameshkumar, R., Bailey, P.: Storytelling with dialogue: a critical role dungeons and dragons dataset. In: Proceedings of ACL, pp. 5121–5134 (2020)
17. Rush, A.M., Chopra, S., Weston, J.: A neural attention model for abstractive sentence summarization. In: Proceedings of EMNLP, pp. 379–389 (2015)
18. See, A., Liu, P.J., Manning, C.D.: Get to the point: summarization with pointer-generator networks. In: Proceedings of ACL, pp. 1073–1083 (2017)
19. Sennrich, R., Haddow, B.: Linguistic input features improve neural machine translation. In: Proceedings of Conference on Machine Translation, pp. 83–91 (2016)
20. Shang, G., Ding, W., Zhang, Z., Tixier, A., Meladianos, P., Vazirgiannis, M.: Unsupervised abstractive meeting summarization with multi-sentence compression and budgeted submodular maximization. In: Proceedings of ACL, pp. 664–674 (2018)
21. Tixier, A., Meladianos, P., Vazirgiannis, M.: Combining graph degeneracy and submodularity for unsupervised extractive summarization. In: Proceedings of the Workshop on New Frontiers in Summarization, pp. 48–58 (2017)
22. Vaswani, A., et al.: Attention is all you need. In: Proceedings of NIPS, pp. 6000–6010 (2017)
23. Zhang, J., Li, L., Way, A., Liu, Q.: Topic-informed neural machine translation. In: Proceedings of COLING, pp. 1807–1817 (2016)
24. Zhao, L., Xu, W., Guo, J.: Improving abstractive dialogue summarization with graph structures and topic words. In: Proceedings of COLING, pp. 437–449 (2020)
25. Zhao, Z., Pan, H., Fan, C., Liu, Y., Li, L., Yang, M., Cai, D.: Abstractive meeting summarization via hierarchical adaptive segmental network learning. In: Proceedings of WWW, pp. 3455–3461 (2019)
26. Zhong, M., et al.: QMSum: a new benchmark for query-based multi-domain meeting summarization. In: Proceedings of NAACL, pp. 5905–5921 (2021)
27. Zhu, C., Xu, R., Zeng, M., Huang, X.: A hierarchical network for abstractive meeting summarization with cross-domain pretraining. In: Findings of EMNLP, pp. 194–203 (2020)
28. Zou, Y., et al.: Topic-oriented spoken dialogue summarization for customer service with saliency-aware topic modeling. Proceedings of AAAI, pp. 14665–14673 (2021)

Adversarial Fine-Grained Fact Graph for Factuality-Oriented Abstractive Summarization

Zhiguang Gao, Feng Jiang, Xiaomin Chu, and Peifeng Li[✉]

School of Computer Science and Technology, Soochow University, Jiangsu, China
{20204227025,fjiang}@stu.suda.edu.cn, {xmchu,pfli}@suda.edu.cn

Abstract. Although neural abstractive summarization models can generate text with significant fluency and coherence, controlling the correctness of facts in generation remains a challenge. Recent work simply classifies factuality into two categories: factual or non-factual, which is coarse-grained and lacks a deep understanding of the linguistic typology of factual errors. In this paper, we present insights into two main and common factual errors (Semantic Frame Errors and Coreference Error) and propose a LASum model to enhance the factuality of abstractive summarization by adversarial fine-grained fact graph. Specifically, we first construct the fine-grained fact graph for the source document and summary to represent facts, respectively, consisting of a dependency channel and coreference channel to address the above two factual errors. And then we enhance the seq2seq model to grasp the internal facts in the fact graph from an intuitive perspective by adversarial learning (GAN). The experimental results show that our model can substantially improve the factuality compared to several strong baselines.

Keywords: Abstractive summarization · Factuality · Adversarial learning · Fine-grained fact graph

1 Introduction

Although neural abstractive summarization models [8,17] can generate fluent and coherent summaries, the factuality of summaries is still an open question [2,19]: the generated summaries are not consistent with the source document in factuality. Cao et al. [1] and Goyal et al. [5] point out that nearly 30% of the summaries generated by recent neural summarization models have factual errors. The existence of factual errors seriously limits the application of abstractive summarization models.

Recent works [2,19] rely on information extraction (e.g., OpenIE) to enhance the factuality of summarization. Zhu et al. [19] extract relations triples as the fact and integrate the relation representation into the seq2seq model. It is coarse-grained and lacks insight into the linguistic structure of facts because relation triples can only express the relationship between subject, predicate and object.

W. Lu et al. (Eds.): NLPCC 2022, LNAI 13551, pp. 339–351, 2022.
https://doi.org/10.1007/978-3-031-17120-8_27

However, in the generated summary, the components of facts also include adverbials, adjectives, coreference relations, etc.

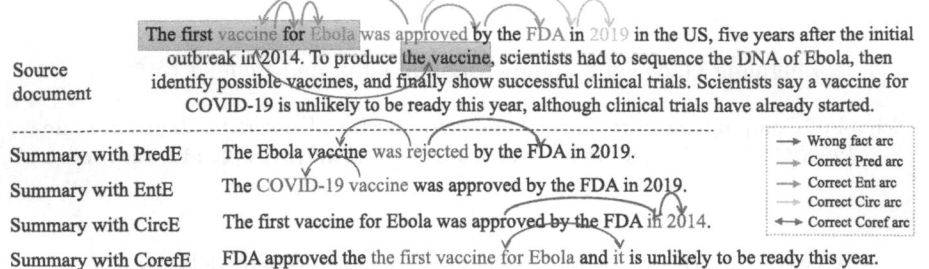

Fig. 1. The example of Semantic Frame errors (PredE, EntE, CircE) and Coreference error. We mark the cause of the corresponding factual error with a red arc. Arcs with other colors show the correct relation.

To deeply understand factual errors from the perspective of linguistics, it is necessary to understand the classification of factual errors and their proportion. Pagnoni et al. [16] devise a typology of factual errors and manually annotate the factuality benchmark FRANK. FRANK consists of human annotations of generated summaries from state-of-the-art summarization systems for the CNN/DM and XSum datasets. In FRANK, 69% of factual errors are Semantic Frame errors (PredE, EntE, CircE) and Coreference error (CorefE), which accounts for the majority. Therefore, in this work, we present insights into these two specific factual errors and propose LASum by modeling adversarial fine-grained fact graph to improve the factuality of summarization.

Semantic Frame errors mean the semantic frame of sentence has factual errors. Semantic framework is composed of predicates and series frame elements (FEs) [16], which can be divided into core and non-core FE. The former is crucial to the meaning of framework, such as subject and object, while the latter provides additional descriptive information, such as location and time. PredE (Predicate Error), EntE (Entity Error) and CircE (Circumstance Error) denote factual errors of predicates, core and non-core FE, respectively. CorefE [16] explains pronouns and other types of references to previously mentioned entities that are either incorrect or have no explicit antecedents, making them disputable.

Figure 1 is the example of Semantic Frame errors and CorefE. It shows that Semantic Frame errors usually occur due to the model's illusion of the dependency relation in the article. For example, the correct dependency arc is $vaccine \rightarrow for, for \rightarrow Ebola$, while model generates summary with dependency arc $COVID-19 \rightarrow vaccine$. Moreover, CorefE is caused by the model doesn't understand the coreference relation, e.g., the pronoun "it" refers to "vaccine for COVID-19" instead of "The first vaccine for Ebola". To enhance the model's perception of semantic framework and coreference relation, we build two fine-grained graphs: the fine-grained dependency graph for Semantic Frame errors and the fine-grained coreference graph for Coreference errors, respectively.

Graph neural network shows effectiveness in lots of areas [9,19] and we have considered using it to encode dependency and coreference graph. However, graph neural network will destroy the structure of the pre-trained model. Many studies [3,16] show that pre-trained seq2seq model, like Bart, can generate summary with high quality. To take advantages of the existing pre-trained seq2seq model, we utilize adversarial learning (GAN) to implicitly model the fine-grained dependency and coreference graph. With the inspiration from image processing, we first transform the fine-grained dependency and coreference graph into a two-channel low-resolution image, denoted as fine-grained fact graph in this work. Then we apply adversarial learning to the fine-grained fact graph, i.e., adversarial fine-grained fact graph to perceive the facts from an intuitive perspective. Particularly, to enhance the perception of facts in the source document and target summary simultaneously, we build the fine-grained fact graphs for both source document and target summary.

We summarize our contributions as follows: (i) to our knowledge, we are the first to enhance factuality from the perspective of linguistics and alleviate the specific factual errors; (ii) we build the fine-grained fact graph to represent the different types of facts; (iii) we apply adversarial learning to the fine-grained fact graph to grasp the internal facts.

2   Related Work

Previous studies on enhancing the factuality of summaires mainly consist of two categories, i.e., encoding relation triples as the fact and using reinforcement learning with the factual evaluation score as the reward.

For the first category, Cao et al. [2] first extract relation triples from the article and concatenate elements in triples as internal facts (subject + predicate + object). And then they use a dual encoder to encode the document and facts simultaneously. Zhu et al. [19] also take relation triples as the fact and build a fact graph according to these triples. Zhu encodes the fact graph with graph neural network and feeds the graph representation into the seq2seq model. The above two studies both take factual errors as a dual-classification problem and ignore the linguistic classification of factual errors.

For the second category, Choubey et al. [3] apply two factual experts (entity overlap and dependency arc entailment) to calculate the factual evaluation score and then take it as a reward for reinforcement learning (RL). Cao et al. [1] focus on external factual error and annotate the external factual dataset XENT. They train a discriminator on XENT and take the score of the discriminator as a reward. In a word, RL is a coarse-grained approach and often not stable enough.

Considering the above problem, we start from the linguistic perspective of factual errors and construct the fine-grained fact graph for the two most common factual errors, and then utilize adversarial fine-grained fact graph to let the model perceive facts from an intuitive perspective. Notably, we transform the dependency and coreference relations into a continuous fine-grained fact graph, and thus our adversarial fine-grained fact graph method will not encounter the problem of "discrete data".

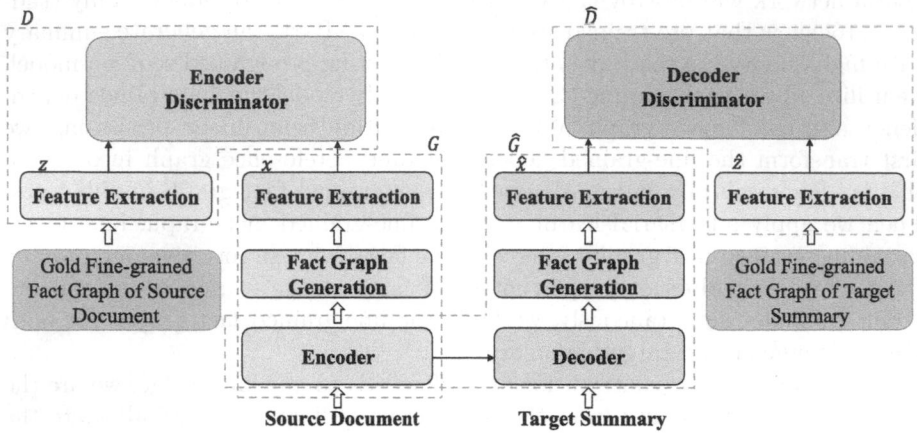

Fig. 2. The Architecture of LASum. LASum consists of two adversarial nets, the encoder-side adversarial net: G, D; and the decoder-side adversarial net: $\hat{G}, \hat{D}$.

3   Methodology

In this section, we first briefly introduce the base system, and then describe how to construct the gold standard and model-generated fine-grained fact graph. Finally we introduce the adversariaL fine-grained fact graph to enhance the fActuality of **Sum**maries (**LASum**). Figure 2 shows the architecture of LASum.

3.1   Basic Seq2seq Architecture

Recent studies show that large transformer-based pre-trained models have made great progress in summary quality, including the factuality [14,16]. Therefore, it is undoubtedly a better choice to improve the factuality on the basis of these pre-trained models. We briefly introduce the seq2seq model used as the base system for adversarial fine-grained fact graph and fix the notation as follows: $x = \{x_1, ..., x_n\}$ denotes the input tokens for the source document; $y = \{y_1, ..., y_m\}$ denotes the sequence tokens for the target summary. Seq2seq model maximizes the log likelihood of the target summary given the input source document (MLE loss)as follows, where $\tilde{x}_n, \tilde{y}_m$ are the token representation with the dimension h.

$$\{\tilde{x}_1, ..., \tilde{x}_n\} = Encoder(\{x_1, ..., x_n\}) \tag{1}$$

$$\{\tilde{y}_1, ..., \tilde{y}_m\} = Decoder(\{y_1, ..., y_m\}, \{\tilde{x}_1, ..., \tilde{x}_n\}) \tag{2}$$

3.2   Graphical Representation of Fine-grained Facts

In this work, our target is to enrich the model's perception of the text's internal facts (Semantic Frame and coreference relations). Usually, model understands facts in two ways: language description for facts [2] or graph representation for relationship between entities [19]. Since the fact graph can more intuitively and comprehensively reflect all kinds of relationships between semantic elements, we explore the graphical representation of fine-grained facts.

For gold standard fine-grained fact graph, we represent the facts of text (source document or target summary) into multi-pattern matrices which is similar to a low resolution image with two color channels (i.e., the coreference (COREF) and dependency (DEP) channels). Gold standard fine-grained fact graph is constructed in a similar way like adjacency matrix in GCN [9]. Specifically, we first get the coreference chains $K = \{k_1, ..., k_m\}$ and the dependency parsing list $D = \{d_1, ..., d_p\}$ of text by Standford Corenlp [12], where k_m is a coreference chain referring to the same object, and d_p is the dependency parsing of the corresponding sentence in the text. And then we construct two matrices, M_{COREF} and M_{DEP}, of size $\eta \times \eta$ corresponding to COREF and DEP graph, where η is the max length of text's tokens. The value in M_{COREF} and M_{DEP} is initialized to 0, and the edges in COREF and DEP graph will be set to 1, e.g., $M_{DEP}[i][j] = 1$, where $i \rightarrow j$ is edge in DEP graph.

(i) **COREF graph.** For each coreference chain $k = \{e^1, ..., e^t\}$ ($k \in K$), e^t is the entity and may consist of more than one word, denoted as $e^t = \{e_1^t, ..., e_p^t\}$. The word e_p^t is tokenized to get the tokens $e_p^t = \{e_{p_1}^t, ..., e_{p_i}^t\}$. We determine the edges for COREF graph at word level, entity level and chain level, respectively. **Word-level connection:** we perform sequential connection for tokens in words. For word $e_p^t = \{e_{p_1}^t, ..., e_{p_i}^t\}$, we connect the tokens in sequence, like $e_{p_i}^t \rightarrow e_{p_{i+1}}^t$. **Entity-level connection:** for words in the entity, we connect the head token of the words in order, such as $e_{p_1}^t \rightarrow e_{p+1_1}^t$. **Chain-level connection:** we do the full connection for the entities in the coreference chain, which is a two-way connection for the first token of the first word of these entities, like $e_{1_1}^t \leftrightarrow e_{1_1}^{t+1}$.

(ii) **DEP graph.** Each sentence dependency paring d ($d \in D$) contains a list of tuples, like (word1, dep_rel, word2), The **Word-level connection** for word1 and word2 is just like constructing COREF graph, and the **Tuple-level connection** is to represent the dependency relation between words. Specifically, we connect the first token of word1 to the first token of word2. After the construction of COREF graph and DEP graph, we merge it as the gold fine-grained fact graph $Q = [M_{COREF}, M_{DEP}]$.

For the model-generated fine-grained fact graph, we transform the model outputs (encoder output or decoder output) into the two-channel image. For COREF and DEP channels, we use two separate graph projection functions to generate COREF graph and DEP graph. Specifically, given the sequence token representation $\tilde{x}_1, ..., \tilde{x}_\eta$ (the output of the encoder or decoder of the seq2seq model), we generate the fact graph by graph projection, as shown in Eq 3.

$$C_{DEP} = f_{dep}(\{\tilde{x}_1, ..., \tilde{x}_\eta\})$$
$$C_{COREF} = f_{coref}(\{\tilde{x}_1, ..., \tilde{x}_\eta\})$$

$$(3)$$

where f_{dep}, f_{coref} are linear regression networks and have dimension $h * \eta$. And then we merge C_{DEP}, C_{COREF} as the model-generated fine-grained fact graph: $W = [C_{COREF}, C_{DEP}]$. In this way, the sequence token representation is abstracted as the fact graph with two channels.

Through the above construction, we obtain the graphical representation for both gold standard and automatically predicted fine-grained fact graph. The graphical representation can provide our model with an intuitive perspective of facts in the text (source document or target summary), which makes the adversarial fine-grained fact graph in Sect. 3.3 possible.

3.3   Adversarial Fine-grained Fact Graph

Pre-trained seq2seq model always generates summaries depending on the prior probability rather than the facts in the source document. To make the seq2seq model generate fact-consistent summary, we propose the LASum model based on adversarial learning to deepen the model's perception of the fine-grained facts in the source document and target summary.

LASum consists of two adversarial nets, the encoder-side adversarial net: G, D, and the decoder-side adversarial net: $\hat{G}, \hat{D}$. The encoder-side adversarial net has the goal that the encoder of seq2seq model perceives the facts in source document and outputs the source document representation with attention to the facts. The decoder-side adversarial net has the goal that while the decoder generates the summary, it also generates the fact graph of the summary, which promotes the decoder to rely on facts in source document rather than prior probability when generating.

The complete structure of LASum is shown in Fig. 2. We give a detailed description of the encoder-side adversarial net for source document's fine-grained fact graph. The decoder-side adversarial net for target summary's fine-grained fact graph has the same structure with the encoder-side. In Sect. 3.2, we get gold fine-grained fact graph Q and the generated fine-grained fact graph W for the source document (target summary for the decoder-side). Considering the source and constructing method of gold and generated fact graph are completely different, we take two isomorphic feature extractors to transform the two kinds of fact graph separately. For feature extraction, in light of our fine-grained fact graph is a 2D image-like matrix, we perform convolution with kernel size 25×25 (5×5 for the decoder-side) to discover the features of the fact graph as follows.

$$Q = Conv2d_{gold}(Q), W = Conv2d_{fake}(W) \tag{4}$$

Max-pooling with window size 20×20 (5×5 for the decoder-side) is used for further feature extraction, and the resulting feature matrices of Q, W are reshaped as $z, x \in R^{1 \times d}$ ($\hat{z}, \hat{x} \in R^{1 \times d}$ for the decoder-side) to serve as the distributed representation of the gold fact graph and fake fact graph.

In this work, we require a discriminator not only experts in classification, but also can continuously give feedback to our seq2seq model even when the generated fact graphs are correctly classified. Based on this, we utilize LSGAN

[13] as our Discriminator which has been proved to be more stable than the original GAN and faces fewer vanishing gradient problem. Formally, our model consists of two adversarial learning nets: (i) **encoder-side adversarial net for source document:** an encoder-side generator G to capture the data distribution P_z over the source document X and a discriminator D to assess the probability that the source document's fact graph comes from X instead of P_z. (ii) **decoder-side adversarial net for target summary:** a decoder-side generator $\hat{G}$ to capture the data distribution $\hat{P}_z$ over the target summary $\hat{X}$ and a discriminator $\hat{D}$ to assess the probability that target summary's fact graph comes from $\hat{X}$ rather than $\hat{P}_z$. Given the distributed representation of the source document's gold fact graph x, the fake fact graph z and the target summary's gold fact graph $\hat{x}$, the fake fact graph $\hat{z}$, we formulate the loss functions as follows.

$$\frac{min}{D} V(D) = \frac{1}{2}\mathbb{E}_{x \sim P_X(x)}[(D(x) - b)^2] + \frac{1}{2}\mathbb{E}_{z \sim P_z(z)}[(D(G(z)) - a)^2] \quad (5)$$

$$\frac{min}{\hat{D}} V(\hat{D}) = \frac{1}{2}\mathbb{E}_{x \sim P_{\hat{X}}(x)}[(\hat{D}(x) - b)^2] + \frac{1}{2}\mathbb{E}_{z \sim \hat{P}_z(z)}[(\hat{D}(\hat{G}(z)) - a)^2] \quad (6)$$

$$\frac{min}{\theta} V(\theta) = \alpha_1 \cdot \frac{1}{2}\mathbb{E}_{z \sim P_z(z)}[(D(G(z)) - c)^2]$$
$$+ \alpha_2 \cdot \frac{1}{2}\mathbb{E}_{z \sim \hat{P}_z(z)}[(\hat{D}(\hat{G}(z)) - c)^2] + \alpha_3 \cdot loss_{MLE} \quad (7)$$

Similar to Zhang [18], we set $a = 0, b = 1, c = 1$ to let G ($\hat{G}$) generate a fact graph as real as the gold one from the source document (target summary). To prevent adversarial loss making seq2seq model deviate too much, we also add the standard language model loss $loss_{MLE}$. θ is the parameter of seq2seq model, $\alpha_1, \alpha_2, \alpha_3$ are the weights of loss. The best combination in our experiment is $\alpha_1 = 0.8, \alpha_2 = 0.8, \alpha_3 = 1.0$.

Technically, G ($\hat{G}$) includes the encoder (encoder and decoder), the graph projection layer for encoder output (decoder output), and the feature extractor for fake fact graph of source document (target summary). Therefore, the back propagation from adversarial loss of D merely updates parameters of the encoder while that of $\hat{D}$ influence the whole seq2seq model. D ($\hat{D}$) consists of the discriminator realized with an MLP (In: feature size d, Hidden: $d/2$, Out: 1), and the feature extractor for gold fact graph of source document (target summary).

4   Experimentation

4.1   Experimental Settings

Datasets. We perform experiments on two datasets: CNN/DM [6] and XSUM [15]. CNN/DM owns three sentences in summary on average and there is a large overlap between the summary and the article, that's why the lead-3 achieves agreeable ROUGE values. XSUM contains articles from BBC and takes the first sentence as the gold summary and the others as the source document. We split the data following BertSum [11]: 287227/13368/11490 (training/validation/test) for CNN/DM, 204045/11332/11334 for XSUM.

Metrics. Following previous works [16,19], we employ ROUGE [10] to evaluate the informativeness of the summary. To evaluate the factuality, we employ the automatic factual evaluation metric: DAE [5], SENT [5] and FactC [7]. DAE relies on whether the dependency arcs in the summary are entailed by the article, which shows a high correlation with human evaluation. In this work, we have set strict standards for DAE: only when all the dependency arcs in the summary are contained in the source document, we think that the summary is factually correct. SENT concatenates source document and the generated summary and feeds it into the pre-trained model, then SENT takes the [CLS] token representation to do a binary (Factual, Non-Factual) classification. FactC is trained on synthetic data that exploits various transformations on the summary. Like SENT, FactC is also a two classification model and takes Bert as the encoder.

Hyper-Parameter Setting. The size of fine-grained fact graph is 2*770*770 (2 is the channels, i.e. COREF and DEP channel) for source document of CNN/DM and XSUM, 2*150*150 (2*60*60) for CNN/DM's (XSUM's) target summary. The learning rate of D ($\hat{D}$) is 5e–4 and that of G ($\hat{G}$) is 2e–6.

4.2 Experimental Results

Table 1 shows the ROUGE and factual evaluation scores on two datasets.

Table 1. ROUGE and factual evaluation scores on CNN/DM and XSUM, R1, R2, RL refer to ROUGE-1, ROUGE-2, ROUGE-L, respectively.

Model	CNN/DM						XSUM					
	R1	R2	RL	DAE	SENT	FactC	R1	R2	RL	DAE	SENT	FactC
BertSum	41.43	19.05	38.55	71.74	87.51	53.93	38.76	16.33	31.15	28.70	61.38	23.56
Unilm	43.33	20.21	40.51	65.21	82.32	36.43	42.14	19.53	34.13	30.54	64.32	22.54
FASum	40.53	17.84	37.40	73.57	79.12	50.14	30.28	10.03	23.76	12.66	65.74	26.20
$FASum_{FC}$	40.38	17.67	37.23	73.80	80.36	51.17	30.20	9.97	23.68	12.03	67.13	26.09
Bart	43.86	20.92	40.64	72.75	84.94	49.60	**45.52**	**22.48**	**37.29**	34.83	65.45	22.98
$LASum_{DE}$	43.13	20.30	39.96	80.52	85.59	51.98	43.93	20.41	35.10	38.16	67.68	23.88
$LASum_{CO}$	42.11	19.55	38.96	74.57	85.54	74.40	44.79	21.26	36.23	37.97	67.88	23.63
$LASum_{E}$	**43.99**	**20.96**	**40.79**	76.61	85.57	46.10	44.65	21.23	35.94	37.55	65.60	24.46
$LASum_{D}$	42.98	20.12	39.46	75.79	86.10	76.51	44.93	21.65	36.29	37.41	66.42	21.90
LASum	43.25	20.21	40.09	**82.51**	**87.61**	**82.40**	44.59	21.48	36.17	**39.02**	**68.10**	**26.33**

Baselines. BertSum [11] takes Bert as the encoder and initialize the parameters of decoder randomly. **Unilm** [4] employs special mask strategies for pretraining and is applicable to both NLU and NLG task. **FASum** [19] builds fact graph by relation triples and feeds the graph representation to the decoder when training. Based on FASum, Zhu et al. [19] propose a corrector FC to modify errors in summary, represented by $FASum_{FC}$ here. **Bart** [8] is a bidirectional and auto-regressive pre-trained model with denoising strategy, we use the fine-tuned model Bart-large-cnn (Bart-large-xsum) from Hugging Face for CNN/DM (XSUM) test set. Notably, when training our LASum, we take Bart-large-cnn (Bart-large-xsum) as the seq2seq model for CNN/DM (XSUM) training set.

Comparison with Previous Studies. LASum has great improvement in factuality while persevering informativeness. For CNN/DM, although the baselines based on pre-trained model (i.e. BertSum, Unilm and Bart) already achieve good results in ROUGE and factuality, their performance is still far from perfect. Compared with the pre-trained baselines, FASum chooses to train from scratch and makes the model focus on relation triples in the source document. It achieves higher DAE value that focuses on the fine-grained facts in the article, with the drops in ROUGE values. Compared with Bart, our LASum improves 9.76% on DAE, 2.67% on SENT and 32.8% on FactC due to its ability in modeling fine-grained facts and the adversarial learning strategy. For XSUM, we can see that the factuality of all models has decreased compared with CNN/DM. XSUM's summary is more abstractive, sometimes the fact in summary may not exist in the source document. Nevertheless, our LASum still achieves the best results on DAE, SENT and FactC. The reason is that LASum not only builds fine-grained fact graph for source document, but also the target summary, which is helpful for the model to infer the fact not appearing in the source document.

4.3   Ablation Study

We do ablation experiment to explore the role of different channels: COREF and DEP, and the role of different adversarial learning nets: encoder-side and decoder-side.

For the role of different channels, $LASum_{DE}$ refers to LASum with only the DEP channel and $LASum_{CO}$ means LASum with only the COREF channel. From Table 1, we can see that on both CNN/DM and XSUM dataset, $LASum_{DE}$ and $LASum_{CO}$ have improved in three factual metrics compared with the SOTA baseline Bart, which proves that the DEP channel and the COREF channel can well model the fine-grained facts in the text. Furthermore, LASum merges DEP channel and COREF channel as a two-channel fine-grained fact graph and achieves the best results in three factual metrics.

For the role of different adversarial learning nets, $LASum_E$ is LASum does adversarial learning only for fine-grained fact graph of the source document and $LASum_D$ is LASum does adversarial learning only for fine-grained fact graph of the target summary. For CNN/DM, $LASum_E$ is 3.5% lower than Bart on FactC, but $LASum_D$ is 26.91% higher than Bart on FactC, with the combination of $LASum_E$ and $LASum_D$, LASum achieves the highest FactC value, which proves that the two adversarial learning nets can complement each other to achieve better results. The same phenomenon also appears on XSUM, where $LASum_D$ is lower and $LASum_E$ is higher on FactC than Bart.

4.4 Human Evaluation on Different Errors

In this paper, we focus on the semantic frame errors (PredE, EntE, CircE) and coreference error (CorefE), so do LASum really alleviates these two errors? To verify this claim, we do the human evaluation according to the data annotation method of FRANK [16].

The human evaluation is carried out by three experts with NLP experience, and we spend two days training them to understand the category of each factual errors defined by Pagnoni [16]. The human evaluation can be divided into two steps: (i) the expert first decides whether the summary is factual, and (ii) if marked not factual, identifies the category of each error. Notably, one summary can have multiple categories of factual errors and we think the summary has this kind of factual error when most of the experts give the same mark.

We randomly select 100 samples from CNN/DM and XSUM test sets respectively and find that in CNN/DM, Bart has 28 samples with factual error while 15 for LASum, and in XSUM, Bart has 51 samples with factual error while 32 for LASum. The number of samples with different categories of factual errors is shown in Fig. 3. From Fig. 3, we can see that LASum significantly alleviates the semantic frame errors and the coreference error. For instance, the number of samples with CorefE drops from 11 (Bart) to 5 (LASum) on CNN/DM. In particular, due to only having one sentence in summary, there are fewer CorefE on XSUM. But we believe our construction of the COREF graph is still helpful to understand the coreference relation in the source document of XSUM.

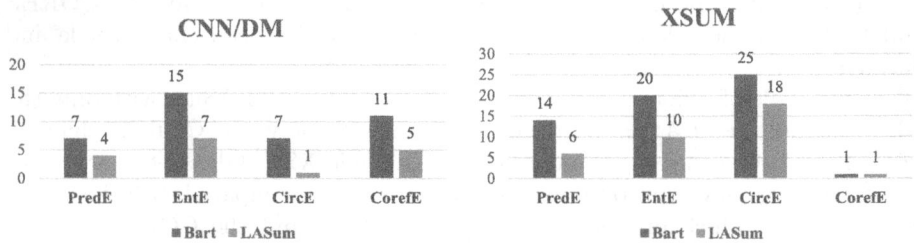

Fig. 3. The number of samples with different categories of factual errors.

4.5 Generality of Adversarial Fine-grained Fact Graph for Promoting Factuality

Bart has a revolutionary improvement over the previous summarization models and our LASum takes Bart as the base system. We have a question that whether the proposed adversarial fine-grained fact graph to promote factuality is general for all seq2seq models or just for Bart?

We choose Pegasus [17] as the base system, i.e., $LASum^P$, and the results are shown in Table 2. For CNN/DM, $LASum^P$ achieves the best results in three factual metrics. For XSUM, $LASum^P_E$ has the highset SENT value, $LASum^P_D$

has the highset DAE value. Despite this, $LASum^P$'s performance of factuality on XSUM is close to the highest one, which proves that our proposed adversarial fine-grained fact graph for promoting factuality is general for the seq2seq models.

Table 2. ROUGE and Factual consistency scores on CNN/DM and XSUM with Pegasus as the base system. $LASum^P$, $LASum_E^P$, $LASum_D^P$ are $LASum$, $LASum_E$, $LASum_D$ with Pegasus as the seq2seq model.

Model	CNN/DM						XSUM					
	R1	R2	RL	DAE	SENT	FactC	R1	R2	RL	DAE	SENT	FactC
Pegasus	**43.90**	**20.99**	**40.77**	66.75	82.28	43.67	47.09	**24.56**	39.32	32.96	64.80	24.44
$LASum_E^P$	43.38	20.59	39.83	74.30	83.25	48.82	46.85	24.04	38.89	37.72	**69.80**	24.75
$LASum_D^P$	43.41	20.58	39.84	73.86	82.85	48.26	**47.35**	24.45	**39.37**	**39.32**	68.89	24.67
$LASum^P$	43.52	20.69	39.91	**78.27**	**85.41**	**49.07**	47.34	24.44	39.35	38.66	69.25	**25.24**

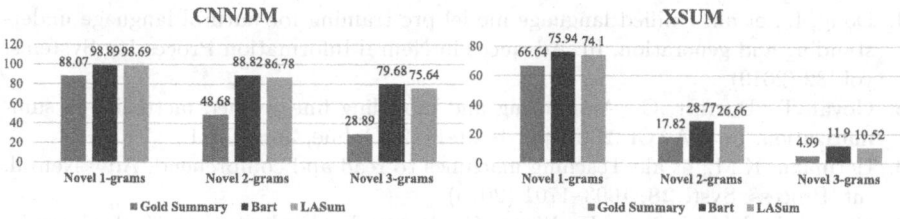

Fig. 4. Percentage of overlapped n-grams in XSUM and CNN/DM summaries, Novel n-grams refers to the ratio of n-grams in summaries that appear in the source document.

4.6 Model Extractiveness

The simple way to increase the factuality is to directly copy sentences from the article when generating. To verify the extractiveness of LASum, we compare the average number of common unigrams (Novel 1-grams), bigrams (Novel 2-grams), and trigrams (Novel 3-grams) between summary and source document for gold summaries, Bart and LASum, as shown in Fig. 4.

We can see that LASum is less extractive than Bart on both CNN/DM and XSUM, which shows LASum improves the factuality not by simply copying sentences. Nevertheless, all Bart and LASum have much more overlap with the article than the gold summary, especially on CNN/DM. The tendency of these seq2seq models to increase the extractiveness is also observed in Choubey [3], which may be the direction of improvement in the future.

5 Conclusion

In this paper, we explore enhancing the model's perception of fine-grained facts based on adversarial learning. Particularly, we propose the transformation of the fine-grained fact graph that has different channels targeted at a specific type of factual error. On this basis, we utilize two LSGAN-based adversarial bots between gold and fake fine-grained fact graph for perceiving facts in source documents and summaries. Experimental results show that our proposed LASum model achieves the best factuality in summaries of CNN/DM and XSUM. Our future work will focus on how to address the other type errors.

References

1. Cao, M., Dong, Y., Cheung, J.C.K.: Inspecting the factuality of hallucinated entities in abstractive summarization. arXiv preprint arXiv:2109.09784 (2021)
2. Cao, Z., Wei, F., Li, W., Li, S.: Faithful to the original: fact aware neural abstractive summarization. In: AAAI, vol. 32 (2018)
3. Choubey, P.K., Vig, J., Liu, W., Rajani, N.F.: Mofe: Mixture of factual experts for controlling hallucinations in abstractive summarization. arXiv preprint arXiv:2110.07166 (2021)
4. Dong, L., et al.: Unified language model pre-training for natural language understanding and generation. In: Advances in Neural Information Processing Systems, vol. 32 (2019)
5. Goyal, T., Durrett, G.: Annotating and modeling fine-grained factuality in summarization. In: NAACL 2021, pp. 1449–1462. Online, June 2021
6. Hermann, K.M., et al.: Teaching machines to read and comprehend. Adv. Neural. Inf. Process. Syst. **28**, 1693–1701 (2015)
7. Kryscinski, W., McCann, B., Xiong, C., Socher, R.: Evaluating the factual consistency of abstractive text summarization. In: EMNLP,D pp. 9332–9346, November 2020
8. Lewis, M., et al.: BART: denoising sequence-to-sequence pre-training for natural language generation, translation, and comprehension. In: ACL, pp. 7871–7880 (2020)
9. Li, Q., Han, Z., Wu, X.M.: Deeper insights into graph convolutional networks for semi-supervised learning. In: AAAI (2018)
10. Lin, C.Y.: Rouge: A package for automatic evaluation of summaries. In: Text Summarization Branches out, pp. 74–81 (2004)
11. Liu, Y., Lapata, M.: Text summarization with pretrained encoders. In: EMNLP, pp. 3730–3740 (2019)
12. Manning, C.D., Surdeanu, M., Bauer, J., Finkel, J.R., Bethard, S., McClosky, D.: The stanford corenlp natural language processing toolkit. In: ACL, pp. 55–60 (2014)
13. Mao, X., Li, Q., Xie, H., Lau, R.Y., Wang, Z., Paul Smolley, S.: Least squares generative adversarial networks. In: IEEE, pp. 2794–2802 (2017)
14. Nan, F., et al.: Improving factual consistency of abstractive summarization via question answering. In: ACL, pp. 6881–6894 (2021)
15. Narayan, S., Cohen, S.B., Lapata, M.: Don't give me the details, just the summary! topic-aware convolutional neural networks for extreme summarization. In: EMNLP, pp. 1797–1807 (2018)
16. Pagnoni, A., Balachandran, V., Tsvetkov, Y.: Understanding factuality in abstractive summarization with FRANK: a benchmark for factuality metrics. In: NAACL 2021, pp. 4812–4829. Online, June 2021

17. Zhang, J., Zhao, Y., Saleh, M., Liu, P.: Pegasus: pre-training with extracted gap-sentences for abstractive summarization. In: ICML, pp. 11328–11339. PMLR (2020)
18. Zhang, L., Kong, F., Zhou, G.: Adversarial learning for discourse rhetorical structure parsing. In: ACL 2021, (Volume 1: Long Papers), pp. 3946–3957 (2021)
19. Zhu, C., et al.: Enhancing factual consistency of abstractive summarization. In: NAACL 2021, pp. 718–733. Online, June 2021

Retrieval, Selection and Writing: A Three-Stage Knowledge Grounded Storytelling Model

Wentao Qin[1,2] and Dongyan Zhao[1,2,3(✉)]

[1] Wangxuan Institute of Computer Technology, Peking University, Beijing, China
{qinwentao,zhaody}@pku.edu.cn
[2] Center for Data Science, AAIS, Peking University, Beijing, China
[3] Institute For Artificial Intelligence, Peking University, Beijing, China

Abstract. Storytelling is a knowledge-driven task, which requires the model to associate relevant information given a context and organize them into a reasonable story. Some knowledge-enhanced storytelling models are proposed. However, there exist certain drawbacks in them, including needing better retrieval and selection strategy. Target on these, we propose a three-stage knowledge grounded storytelling model, which combines semantic knowledge retrieval, a knowledge selection and a story generation module. We build in-domain and open-domain knowledge, which is suitable for story generation. The knowledge selection and story generation modules are built in the readily available transformer-based framework. We devise two approaches to train the knowledge selection module. One is to leverage constructed pseudo labels. Another is to jointly train the knowledge selection and story generation modules, so as to leverage the supervision of the ground-truth story. We conduct experiments on the public ROCStories dataset, and the automatic and human evaluation demonstrates the effectiveness of our method.

Keywords: Text generation · Story generation · Knowledge injection

1 Introduction

A storytelling model aims to create a story given a context. The context can be images [8] or texts [14]. Following [4,20], we target the storytelling task given a short context. A high-quality dataset is the ROCStories proposed by [14]. Table 1 shows two examples of it. The context is one descriptive sentence, and the story to generate is four sentences that should be relevant and consistent with the context. Compared with dialogue generation and summarization tasks, where the context texts are longer than the target texts, the storytelling task here is on the opposite side, i.e., the target texts are longer than the context texts. Sequence-to-sequence (Seq2Seq) model [17] and its variants are prevailing in text generation. However, the task of story generation requires the model to

W. Lu et al. (Eds.): NLPCC 2022, LNAI 13551, pp. 352–363, 2022.
https://doi.org/10.1007/978-3-031-17120-8_28

Table 1. Two examples of the ROCStories. The words in blue are relevant to the words in red in the corresponding row.

Context	Story
anna joined the band .	she was going to play the oboe . her mom was nervous about having to listen to it every day . anna brought the instrument home and started to play . it sounded like a wounded cat !
the girl and her mom went to the pet store .	she heard an animal crying . she walked up to it . she pet the cat . they then decided to buy the cat .

memorize more items in its parameters, which increases the difficulty of learning the mapping from the context to the target.

To tackle this challenge, two types of approaches arise among current work. The first group is to break one-step generation into multi-step generation [2,21,22]. Compared with the one-step generation, multi-step generation leverages human prior knowledge, to make the model imitate human writing procedure, thus decreasing the learning difficulty of the model. Another group treats storytelling as a knowledge-driven generation task [4,20]. For instance, [20] retrieves external knowledge according to the existing or predicted keywords, and uses the retrieved knowledge to feed the generation model as extra input signal.

In this work, we propose a three-stage knowledge grounded storytelling model. We follow the paradigm of retrieval and generation in [20], but our practice differs in several aspects. First, we choose story texts as the knowledge source instead of template-based sentences. Second, they use keyword matching to retrieve relevant knowledge, which might get much unprecise knowledge. For example, for the first sample in Table 1, keyword matching will retrieve all related knowledge that either contains *joined* or *band*. Apparently, we prefer the knowledge which has a similar semantic meaning with *joined the band*. To this end, we leverage semantic similarity to retrieve related knowledge, which has shown its effectiveness in question answering task [11]. Third, the retrieved knowledge needs to be filtered. Aside from using pseudo labels to provide supervision signals for knowledge selection like [20], we further jointly train the selection and generation module according to the signal provided by the golden story.

Specifically, we build story knowledge from two sources: external and internal domain. The external knowledge is built from Children's Book Test [7] and we build internal knowledge from the training part of ROCStories dataset. Each knowledge contains a leading context and several keywords. We use semantic retrieval to obtain Top-N knowledge items with the highest similarity. The corresponding keywords will be sent to the BERT-based selection module to predict their importance. Then the generation module will accept the input together with the selected keywords as input and generate the story. We conduct experiments on ROCStories dataset, and make comparisons with the existing knowledge-driven methods [4,20]. The results demonstrate that our model can generate stories of higher quality on both automatic and human evaluation.

2   Related Work

Storytelling. Storytelling is a challenging task in natural language generation and has attracted much attention from the research field. There are storytelling tasks based on different kinds of context, e.g., visual storytelling [8], story ending generation [5], and story generation given a short text description [4]. Seq2Seq framework, as a mainstream text generation paradigm, was applied to storytelling at first [9]. Unlike short text generation, storytelling needs to generate relatively long text containing multiple sentences, which requires more writing creativity and organization ability. Aimed at this point, a batch of multi-step generation methods are proposed, either by composing a story in one pass with hierarchical structures [1,13,22], or by performing multi-state generation explicit intermediate content creation [2,18,21]. These multi-stage generation approaches first generate some text pieces as a story template, and generate a story based on it. Recently, some knowledge-based methods are proposed for storytelling, including [4] which aimed to train a commonsense-aware model, and [20] which leveraged retrieved knowledge sentences to feed the model.

Knowledge Enhanced Models. In the optimal case, a deep neural model is expected to contain all the necessary knowledge to finish a specific task. However, such an ideal model is impossible to obtain currently. To incorporate knowledge into models, various knowledge enhanced models are put forward in question answering [6,11], dialog generation [3,19] and story generation [4,20]. The similarity among these tasks is they are knowledge-intensive tasks, i.e., the inputs cannot provide the models with enough knowledge to produce reasonable outputs. The methods of introducing knowledge are grouped into implicit and explicit ones. For the implicit methods, the knowledge is stored by the parameters of models, e.g., [4] fine-tuned the pre-trained GPT-2 with template-based sentences, to inject commonsense knowledge. The explicit methods, however, treat knowledge as extra inputs to the models. In detail, they use grounded knowledge [19] or retrieved knowledge [6,11,20] to provide the models with a more informative context. Compared to the implicit ones, explicit methods have several merits, such as better controllability [20], extensibility [11] and interpretability. Our work belongs to the group of explicit methods.

3   Method

3.1   Problem Formalization

Given a context sentence x, and a knowledge source $\mathcal{G}$, our task is to generate the following content $y = \{y_0, y_1, \ldots, y_{l-1}\}$, where l denotes the number of generated tokens. x together y compose a coherent and fluent story. Relevant knowledge texts will be retrieved from $\mathcal{G}$ to assist generation.

3.2   Knowledge Source Construction

The overview of our model is illustrated in Fig. 1. Our model contains three main procedures: *knowledge retrieval* for searching possibly relevant knowledge given a context; *knowledge selection* for conducting precise filtering of knowledge; *story generation* for generating final story. We first introduce how to construct the knowledge source $\mathcal{G}$. In [4,20], they use template-based sentences constructed from some knowledge bases as a knowledge source. In this work, we propose to leverage story texts as the knowledge source. The reason behind this is story texts are more straight for story generation. We construct two knowledge sources $\mathcal{G}_{INT}$ and $\mathcal{G}_{EXT}$. $\mathcal{G}_{INT}$ is built from the training data (as internal in-domain knowledge), and $\mathcal{G}_{EXT}$ is from the public story dataset (as external commonsense knowledge). Each knowledge item in $\mathcal{G}$ (union of $\mathcal{G}_{INT}$ and $\mathcal{G}_{EXT}$) is a short story before post-processing. For $\mathcal{G}_{INT}$, each story in ROCStories dataset acts as a knowledge item. For $\mathcal{G}_{EXT}$, to construct appropriate short stories similar to those in ROCStories dataset, we first choose the narrative articles from Children's Book Test [7]. We then break the articles into small chunks that have a similar number of sentences. In detail, we split each article every five sentences, to match ROCStories dataset. For each knowledge item in $\mathcal{G}$, we treat its first sentence as *index part*, and the rest of sentences as *extended part*. As we named them, the index part will be indexed for knowledge retrieval, and the extended part will be used as external knowledge. For the extended part, we further extract non-stop-word verbs and nouns as keywords. Therefore, each knowledge item in $\mathcal{G}$ contains two components: a sentence s_{index}, and a series of keywords.

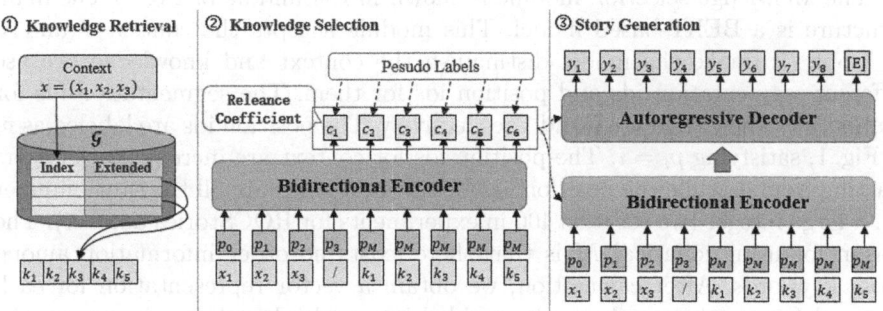

Fig. 1. The overview of our model. It displays three fundamental components from left to right: ① Knowledge Retrieval; ② Knowledge Selection; ③ Story Generation.

3.3   Knowledge Retrieval

With the knowledge source $\mathcal{G}$ in hand, our model can turn to it for inspiration to create a story. Given a context sentence x as input, our model first searches from $\mathcal{G}$ several knowledge items with semantically similar context (i.e., the index part). Following [11], we use a bi-encoder architecture to obtain dense semantic representations of the contexts, mapping them into the same dense embedding space:

$$d(x) = \text{BERT}_1(x), \quad d(z) = \text{BERT}_2(z)$$

where z denotes the sentence s_{index} in a knowledge item, and $d(\cdot)$ represents the representation of $\cdot$, BERT_1 and BERT_2 are both BERT-based encoder. We then compute the inner product $s(x, z)$ between $d(x)$ and $d(z)$ as their similarity. We choose TOP-N knowledge items with highest similarity, and use their extended parts as external knowledge. After removing duplicate keywords in the merged extend parts, we obtain a set of keywords $\mathcal{K} = \{k_1, k_2, ..., k_n\}$.

Due to the massive amount of $\mathcal{G}$, it will consume a lot of time to conduct exact retrieval. Still following [11], we leverage approximate retrieval[1] to decrease the time complexity into sub-linear time. Though this retrieval strategy is approximate, it still yields good empirical search results. In practice, we employ the pre-trained bi-encoder provided by [11] to initialize our bi-encoder.

3.4   Knowledge Selection Module

A direct method to adopt the retrieved knowledge is to concatenate the knowledge with the context and input it to a Seq2Seq model. However, not all parts of the knowledge are equally important. Although the Seq2Seq model is able to learn implicitly to recognize the importance of different parts, the elaborate architecture of model and extra supervision signal for knowledge selection have shown great effectiveness [20]. Here, we design a knowledge selection module, whose objective is to predict the importance of each keyword k_i in $\mathcal{K}$.

The knowledge selection module is shown in the middle of Fig. 1. The main structure is a BERT-based model. This module accepts the context x and $\mathcal{K}$ as input. To make the model distinguish the context and knowledge, we use different segmentation ids and position ids for them. The segmentation ids for context and knowledge are 0 and 1 respectively. The position ids are labeled as p_i in Fig. 1, satisfying $p_i = i$. The position ids for context are incremental integers starting from 0, while the position ids for the knowledge are all the same number M, a large integer (we set it as 400 in experiments for ROCStories dataset). The reason for using identical M is that there exists no order information among those keywords. After calculation, we obtain a vector representation for each keyword (since a keyword may be divided into multiple sub words, we use the mean pooling of representations of these sub words as the initial representation for the keyword. In the story generation module, the processing method is the same). The representation of ith keyword is further applied to a two-layer neural network, and mapped to a scalar c_i, ranging from 0 to 1.

These scalars, which we name as relevance coefficients, will be used in the self-attention operations in the story generation module. Having the relevance coefficients connecting the knowledge selection and story generation module, the knowledge selection module can be trained by the supervision signal of the

---

[1] https://faiss.ai.

ground-truth story. To train a better knowledge selection module, we propose to inject more supervision information. Out of the lack of ground-truth knowledge, we build pseudo labels for each keyword in retrieved knowledge. Given a context sentence x, ground-truth story $y = \{y_0, y_1, \ldots, y_{l-1}\}$, and retrieved keyword set $\mathcal{K}$, we group $\mathcal{K}$ into three categories according to their relevance with y: (a) **Strong**: the keyword that is identical to or synonym of certain y_i. The pseudo label is 1; (b) **Middle**: the keyword that is similar to certain y_i. The definition of similarity is the distance between word a and b in the hypernym-hyponym relation tree is less than 2^2. The pseudo label is 0.5; (c)**None**: other keywords. The pseudo label is 0.

The knowledge of synonym, hypernym, and hyponym is provided by Word-Net[3], and we leverage the interface provided by NLTK[4] to use it. Once we obtain the pseudo labels, denoted as q_i, we compute a mean square loss between all c_i and q_i:

$$\mathcal{L}_{Sel} = u_1 \sum_{i \in R_1} (c_i - q_i)^2 + u_2 \sum_{i \in R_2} (c_i - q_i)^2 + u_3 \sum_{i \in R_3} (c_i - q_i)^2$$

where $R_1 \sim R_3$ represent the indices of keywords of strong, middle and none relevance. We set different weights ($u_1 \sim u_3$) for category imbalance. By training on $\mathcal{L}_{Sel}$, the parameters in the knowledge selection module can be directly updated under the supervision of pseudo labels.

3.5   Story Generation Module

The story generation module is shown in the right part of Fig. 1. We adopt BART as the infrastructure. The input is $\mathcal{K}$ and context x, represented by $w_1, w_2, \ldots, w_m$, where the last n tokens are $k_1, \ldots, k_n$. The input is then encoded with a transformer-based bidirectional encoder. In the decoding phase, when decoding the next token y_i, the decoder will consider the previously decoded tokens and the output of the encoder. Like in the knowledge selection module, the position ids of knowledge are all M. A big difference between our story generation module with the traditional BART lies in that we introduce the relevance coefficients c_i into the encoder and decoder. Recall the self-attention operation in the encoder and attention operation from decoder to encoder, given a query vector v, those attention operations will compute inner product between v and the hidden representation h_i of each w_i. The resulting vector is denoted as $\mathcal{S}$, which will be passed to a scaled softmax operation to obtain attention weights. To introduce the c_i, we construct an relevance coefficient vector $\mathcal{C}$, which satisfies

$$\mathcal{C} = [0, \ldots, 0, \log c_1, \ldots, \log c_n]$$

---

[2] For verbs or nouns, their relation can be organized into a tree, where the parent nodes are more abstract, and the children nodes are more specific.

[3] https://wordnet.princeton.edu/.

[4] http://www.nltk.org.

We then add $\mathcal{S}$ by $\mathcal{C}$ to get an adjusted vector $\mathcal{S}'$: $\mathcal{S}' = \mathcal{S} + \mathcal{C}$, where + represents element-wise addition. $\mathcal{S}'$ will take place of $\mathcal{S}$ in all related attention mechanisms.

The loss for the story generation module is a negative log-likelihood loss

$$\mathcal{L}_{Gen} = -\sum_{i=0}^{l-1} \log p(y_i)$$

where $p(y_i)$ denotes the probability of token y_i in the current output distribution over all tokens in the vocabulary.

3.6   Training and Inference

In training, we first initialize the knowledge selection and story generation model with pre-trained BERT and BART[5]. Then we train the knowledge selection module alone with $\mathcal{L}_{Sel}$ for several epochs, to get better performance on knowledge selection. Last, we train the whole model considering both $\mathcal{L}_{Sel}$ and $\mathcal{L}_{Gen}$. The total loss is a weighted summation of the two losses: $\alpha\mathcal{L}_{Sel} + (1 - \alpha)\mathcal{L}_{Gen}$.

In inference, we first obtain retrieved knowledge according to the context. Then we decide their relevance according to the coefficients c_i predicted by the knowledge selection module. We set c_i to one of $\{0, 0.5, 1\}$ by the nearest principle, and only keep the keywords predicted having strong and middle relevance. Then we input the context, selected keywords and c_i to the story generation module to generate the output story.

4   Experiments

4.1   Data Preparation

We use the public ROCStories Corpus[6] for the experiment. Following [4, 20], we regard the first sentence as the context and left four sentences as the target, and all names in stories are replaced with special placeholders "[MALE]", "[FEMALE]" and "[NEUTRAL]" for male, female and unknown names respectively. We use the training part of ROCStories to construct $\mathcal{G}_{INT}$. For building $\mathcal{G}_{EXT}$, we use the Children's Book Test corpus [7], which contains story texts from children's books. We randomly choose 1 million items as $\mathcal{G}_{EXT}$. We split the data into 18:1:1 for training, validation, and testing.

4.2   Baselines

To evaluate the effectiveness of our proposed model, we compare our method with the following baselines:

- **GPT-2:** It directly fine-tunes the pre-trained GPT-2 on the dataset with the language model objective [16].

---

[5] https://huggingface.co/.
[6] http://www.cs.rochester.edu/nlp/rocstories/.

- **BART:** Like GPT-2, it directly fine-tunes the pre-trained BART on the dataset with the language model objective [10].
- **Knowledge-Enhanced Pre-trained Model (KEPM):** It uses template-based sentences constructed from knowledge bases to fine-tune the pre-trained GPT-2 model, and then further fine-tune the model in story dataset together with a multi-task learning [4].
- **Controllable Generation with External Knowledge (CGEK):** Like KEMP, it uses the same type of knowledge but adopts keyword matching to retrieve knowledge. It trains a knowledge ranker to select relevant knowledge and generate stories in an iterative paradigm [20].

4.3   Implementation Details

We choose the base version of GPT-2, BART, and BERT implemented by *hugginface* for our model and all baselines. For KEPM, we reuse the available public code. For CGEK, we reproduce the code according to the paper. For our model, we train the knowledge selection module and the whole model both until the convergence of loss in the validation set. The α in the total loss $\mathcal{L}$ is set 0.4. The batch size is 8, and AdamW optimizer takes care of parameters updating. We use a warm-up strategy, with the learning rate growing linearly from 0 to 1.5e$-$4 in the first 2,000 steps, and then decreasing linearly to 0 in the remaining steps. We choose Top-5 knowledge items in the knowledge retrieval stage. We calculated the proportion of each category in all the retrieved knowledge. The proportion of keywords of strong, middle and none relevance is about 2%, 18% and 80% respectively. Therefore, we set u_1, u_2, u_3 in $\mathcal{L}_{Sel}$ as 10, 5, 1.

4.4   Evaluation Metrics

For comparing, we employ following evaluation metrics, including three kinds of automatic evaluation metrics and human evaluation:

- **BLEU** measures the similarity of word-level between the generated story and the ground truth, which reflects the fitting ability of models [15].
- **Distinctness** measures the wording diversity by calculating the distinctive n-grams of the generated sentence, used to evaluate the diversity of the story.
- **Embedding-based Metrics** takes account of the semantic level information of the given sources by using different calculation methods [12], including Greedy Matching, Embedding Average, and Vector Extrema. By employing these metrics, we could show how the generated stories are semantically close to the provided ground truth stories.
- **Human Evaluation** is used to evaluate the story from the perspective of human. We first randomly select 100 stories for each model. Then we employed four well-educated humans to score the generated stories. The criteria include readability, consistency, and wording diversity of the story. Each criterion is annotated with three score levels: 1, 2, and 3; the higher, the better.

4.5 Automatic Evaluation

The automatic evaluation result is presented in Table 2. The baselines of GPT-2 and BART have close scores in all metrics. KEPM and CGEK are GPT-2 based models that both leverage knowledge, and their superior performance illustrates the usefulness of external knowledge. Our model uses BART as the main part of the story generation module. Compared with the BART baseline, our method gains a prominent improvement in the BLEU and embedding-based metrics. Meanwhile, our method also performs better in word diversity according to the distinctness value. It can be observed that all knowledge-enhanced models show superior distinctness. This is intuitive that additional knowledge exposed to the model is able to increase the probability of generating stories of richer content. Compared with KEPM and CGEK, our model performs better in all aspects, which demonstrates the effectiveness of our method, including the knowledge source we construct, and the knowledge selection module. The function of these two parts will be discussed in the abalation study.

Table 2. Automatic evaluation result. The table shows BLEU scores (B-i refers BLEU-i), distinctness (D-i refers distinctness of i gram) and embedding based metrics of different models. **w/o** *Sel* represents not using the knowledge selection module, and **only** $\mathcal{G}_{XXX}$ means only using the designative knowledge source.

Model	B-1	B-2	D-1	D-2	Average	Greedy	Extrema
GPT-2	31.48	5.06	2.02	16.21	94.24	75.44	41.76
BART	31.52	5.21	1.98	16.20	94.26	75.49	41.80
KEPM	34.16	6.27	2.30	18.55	94.36	76.27	43.07
CGEK	33.01	5.78	2.45	19.56	94.28	75.78	42.67
Ours	**35.45**	**7.66**	2.49	20.02	**94.63**	**76.65**	**43.54**
w/o *Sel*	33.67	5.97	2.34	18.78	94.32	75.89	42.88
only $\mathcal{G}_{INT}$	34.95	7.01	2.26	18.24	94.54	76.44	43.39
only $\mathcal{G}_{EXT}$	34.78	6.89	**2.87**	**21.45**	94.40	76.32	43.10

4.6 Human Evaluation

The human evaluation results of all models are shown in Table 3. The readability of all models are relatively high compared to other two metrics. The reason is probably that these models all leverage the pre-trained language models, and are able to produce fluent texts. The human evaluation result is consistent with the automatic evaluation result. The knowledge-enhanced models, KEMP, CGEK and our model can produce more fluent, consistent, and diverse stories than the GPT-2 and BART baselines. Especially, our method gains the highest scores among all models, surpasses KEMP and CGEK. Through human evaluation, the validity of our method is further proved.

4.7   Knowledge Prediction Performance

This section tests the effect of knowledge selection module with and without joint training. If the predicted label is the same as the real label, the prediction is correct, otherwise, it is wrong. The accuracy of knowledge prediction is calculated according to the constructed pseudo labels, and the prediction results are shown in Fig. 2. The three parts from left to right are the prediction results of keywords of none relevance, middle relevance and strong relevance. In each part, the three groups from left to right are the proportion of keywords that are predicted to be none relevance, middle relevance and strong relevance respectively. The histogram of correct prediction results is upward, and vice versa. The blue histogram is the result of individual training knowledge selection module (legend of **Part**), and the orange column is the result of joint training after individual training(legend of **Joint**). For keywords of none and middle relevance, the accuracy of model prediction is high, and for keywords of strong relevance, the accuracy of model prediction is low. However, since the keywords of middle and strong relevance are input into the story generation module, if the none relevance is regarded as negative examples and the middle and strong relevance are regarded as positive examples, the accuracy of the model is higher in both categories. In addition, it can be observed that after joint training, the prediction accuracy of knowledge selection model is improved to a certain extent, and the error rate is also decreased, which reflects the effect of joint training.

Table 3. Human evaluation result. Rd., Con., Div. represents readability, consistency, wording diversity.

Model	Rd.	Con.	Div.
GPT-2	2.25	1.90	1.95
BART	2.27	1.89	1.92
KEPM	2.42	2.19	2.15
SGEK	2.40	2.23	2.27
Ours	**2.51**	**2.32**	**2.34**

4.8   Ablation Study

To have a deep insight of the key components of our method, we conduct an ablation study to verify their function. To this end, we experiment a degenerate model without the knowledge selection module and different models with different knowledge sources. The evaluation results are shown in the last three rows of Table 2. **w/o** *Sel* represents the model which does not use the knowledge selection module, which means using the retrieved knowledge and context as input, and the target story, to directly train a BART model. The lower performance of **w/o** *Sel* embodies the necessity of knowledge selection. **only** $\mathcal{G}_{INT}$ is the model that only uses $\mathcal{G}_{INT}$, and **only** $\mathcal{G}_{EXT}$ only uses $\mathcal{G}_{EXT}$. These two models are both inferior to the overall model in BLEU and Embedding-based metrics. The reason may lie in that considering both knowledge sources can bring more relevant knowledge retrieval. It should be noted that the distinctness of **only** $\mathcal{G}_{EXT}$ is higher. This is because $\mathcal{G}_{EXT}$ is quite different from the ROCStories. The retrieved novel knowledge improves the diversity of generated stories.

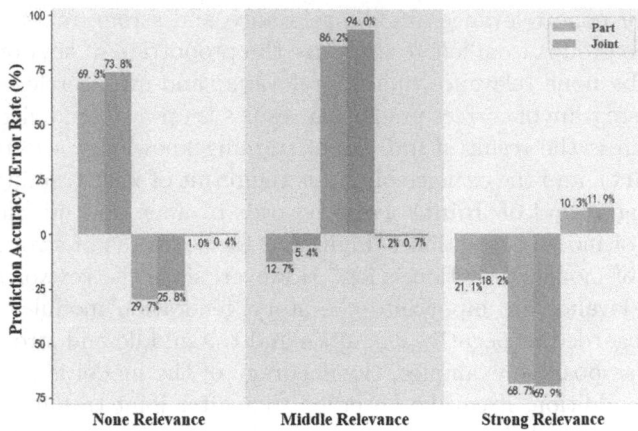

Fig. 2. The performance of knowledge prediction. The three parts from left to right are the prediction results of None, Middle and Strong Relevance respectively. In each part, the three groups from left to right are the proportion predicted to be None, Middle and Strong Relevance. For correctly predicted results, the histogram is upward and vice versa.

5   Conclusion

In this paper, we propose a three-stage knowledge grounded storytelling model, which combines knowledge retrieval, knowledge selection, and story generation. We first construct knowledge source that is suitable for storytelling, including internal knowledge built from ROCStories training dataset, and external knowledge built from open domain stories. Then we adopt semantic retrieval to obtain potential relevant knowledge given the input context. There might exist some irrelevant parts in the retrieved knowledge, therefore we devise a knowledge selection module. The module takes the responsibility of predicting the importance of each part of the retrieved knowledge. The importance scores are further to assist the following story generation. In detail, we use the scores to influence the attention weights in the encoder and decoder of story generation module, which is natural and elegant to the original BART model. We conduct experiments on the short story dataset ROCStories, and compare our method with existing knowledge enhanced storytelling model. The automatic and human evaluation results demonstrate the effectiveness of our proposed method.

Acknowledgments. We thank the reviewers for their valuable comments. This work was supported by the National Key Research and Development Program of China (No. 2020AAA0106602).

References

1. Fan, A., Lewis, M., Dauphin, Y.: Hierarchical neural story generation. In: ACL (2018)
2. Fan, A., Lewis, M., Dauphin, Y.: Strategies for structuring story generation. arXiv (2019)
3. Ghazvininejad, M., et al.: A knowledge-grounded neural conversation model. In: AAAI (2018)
4. Guan, J., Huang, F., Zhao, Z., Zhu, X., Huang, M.: A knowledge-enhanced pre-training model for commonsense story generation. In: TACL (2020)
5. Guan, J., Wang, Y., Huang, M.: Story ending generation with incremental encoding and commonsense knowledge. In: AAAI (2019)
6. Guu, K., Lee, K., Tung, Z., Pasupat, P., Chang, M.W.: Realm: retrieval-augmented language model pre-training. arXiv (2020)
7. Hill, F., Bordes, A., Chopra, S., Weston, J.: The goldilocks principle: reading children's books with explicit memory representations. arXiv (2015)
8. Huang, T.H., et al.: Visual storytelling. In: NAACL (2016)
9. Jain, P., Agrawal, P., Mishra, A., Sukhwani, M., Laha, A., Sankaranarayanan, K.: Story generation from sequence of independent short descriptions (2017)
10. Lewis, M., et al.: Bart: denoising sequence-to-sequence pre-training for natural language generation, translation, and comprehension. arXiv (2019)
11. Lewis, P., et al.: Retrieval-augmented generation for knowledge-intensive NLP tasks. arXiv (2020)
12. Liu, C.W., Lowe, R., Serban, I.V., Noseworthy, M., Charlin, L., Pineau, J.: How not to evaluate your dialogue system: an empirical study of unsupervised evaluation metrics for dialogue response generation. In: EMNLP (2016)
13. Liu, D., et al.: A character-centric neural model for automated story generation. In: AAAI (2020)
14. Mostafazadeh, N., et al.: A corpus and evaluation framework for deeper understanding of commonsense stories. arXiv (2016)
15. Papineni, K., Roukos, S., Ward, T., Zhu, W.J.: Bleu: a method for automatic evaluation of machine translation. In: ACL (2002)
16. Radford, A., et al.: Language models are unsupervised multitask learners. OpenAI blog (2019)
17. Sutskever, I., Vinyals, O., Le, Q.V.: Sequence to sequence learning with neural networks. In: NIPS (2014)
18. Tan, B., Yang, Z., AI-Shedivat, M., Xing, E.P., Hu, Z.: Progressive generation of long text with pretrained language models. arXiv (2020)
19. Wu, Z., et al.: A controllable model of grounded response generation. arXiv (2020)
20. Xu, P., et al.: Megatron-CNTRL: controllable story generation with external knowledge using large-scale language models. arXiv (2020)
21. Yao, L., Peng, N., Weischedel, R., Knight, K., Zhao, D., Yan, R.: Plan-and-write: towards better automatic storytelling. In: AAAI (2019)
22. Yu, M.H., et al.: Draft and edit: automatic storytelling through multi-pass hierarchical conditional variational autoencoder. In: AAAI (2020)

An Adversarial Approach for Unsupervised Syntax-Guided Paraphrase Generation

Tang Xue, Yuran Zhao, Gongshen Liu$^{(\boxtimes)}$, and Xiaoyong Li

School of Electronic Information and Electrical Engineering,
Shanghai Jiao Tong University, Shanghai, China
{jon-snow,zyr527,lgshen,xiaoyongli}@sjtu.edu.cn

Abstract. Paraphrase generation has consistently been a challenging area in the field of NLP. Despite the considerable achievements made by previous research, existing supervised approaches require many annotated paraphrase pairs which are expensive to collect. On the other hand, unsupervised paraphrasing manners usually generate syntactically similar output compared with the source text and lack diversity in grammatical structure. To tangle this challenge, we propose a Transformer-based model applying an Adversarial approach for Unsupervised Syntax-Guided Paraphrase Generation (AUSPG). AUSPG is based on a combination of syntax discriminator and Transformer framework to paraphrase sentences from disentangled semantic and syntactic spaces without the need for annotated pairs. More specifically, we deploy a Transformer encoder without position embedding to obtain semantic representations. The syntax discriminator is utilized to further regularize the semantic space. In addition, the disentanglement enables AUSPG to manipulate the embedding of syntactic space to generate syntax-guided paraphrases. Finally, we conduct extensive experiments to substantiate the validity and effectiveness of our proposal. The results reveal that AUSPG significantly outperforms the existing baselines and generates more diverse paraphrase sentences.

Keywords: Syntax-guided paraphrase · Adversarial approach · Disentanglement

1 Introduction

Paraphrase generation [23] is on the frontier of current neural language processing (NLP) technology. It has benefited a wide range of NLP downstream applications, such as machine translation [36], dialog generation [9] and sentence simplification [39].

In recent years, considerable achievements have been made in NLP tasks based on sequence-to-sequence (Seq2Seq) model [35,40]. Various approaches for paraphrasing are proposed to train on a large number of annotated pairs based

W. Lu et al. (Eds.): NLPCC 2022, LNAI 13551, pp. 364–376, 2022.
https://doi.org/10.1007/978-3-031-17120-8_29

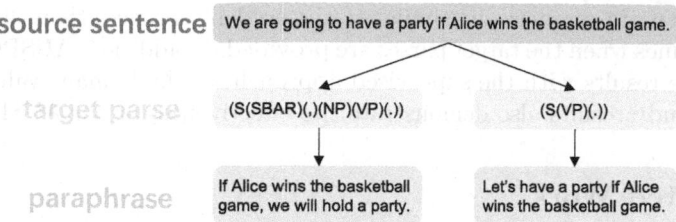

Fig. 1. An example for syntax-guided paraphrase generation. The syntax of output is expected to follow the target parse.

on Seq2Seq structure [7,18,22,25]. Some of them are based on a supervised manner to control the syntax of paraphrase sentences [10,13,15]. Nevertheless, collecting annotated paraphrase pairs is very expensive and causes problems in many languages. To tackle this challenge, various unsupervised methods have been proposed to build a paraphrase model [17,28]. Most of these work are based on vanilla Seq2Seq structure, e.g. variational auto-encoder [4] and back-translation [11]. However, they lack a way to explicitly control the syntax of the output. Sun et al. and Huang et al. [12,30] generate paraphrase from disentangled semantic embedding and syntactic embedding. Without the consideration that syntax and semantics are highly interwoven, their generated paraphrases are often similar to the source sentences and do not follow the target syntax.

In this paper, we aim to disentangle one sentence into a semantic part and a syntactic part. The semantic aspect represents the meaning of the source sentence, while the syntactic one concentrates on the grammatical structure. To paraphrase a sentence, we can keep its semantic aspect and change the syntactic part. Thus, the two sentences are similar in meaning and different in grammatical structure (Fig. 1).

Based on this design, we propose an **A**dversarial approach for **U**nsupervised **S**yntax-guided **P**araphrase **G**eneration (AUSPG). Our AUSPG is based on vanilla Transformer [32] and generates syntactically different paraphrase sentences given various target parses. Our model consists of two encoders, i.e. a semantic encoder and a syntactic one, a syntax discriminator and a decoder. The semantic encoder embeds the unordered input words and focuses on learning the contextualized embedding without syntactic information. The syntax discriminator utilizes an adversarial approach to regularize the semantic spaces. Moreover, the syntactic encoder embeds the linearized target parses and only considers the syntax information. The decoder then takes the combined semantic and syntactic representations as input and gets the generated paraphrases. Our AUSPG learns the connection between the semantics and the grammatical structure by reconstructing the source sentence given its unordered words and the parse sequence. Accordingly, the model can be trained in an unsupervised manner without annotated pairs.

We conduct experiments on four datasets: ParaNMT-50M [33], QQP-Pos [15], PAN [21] and MRPC [6]. The evaluation results indicate that AUSPG generates text that is more syntactically similar to the golden sentences than the unsupervised baselines when the target parses are provided. In addition, AUSPG achieves comparable results with the supervised approaches. The human evaluation and ablation study results also demonstrate the effectiveness of our AUSPG.

2 Related Work

Methods for paraphrase generation can be grouped into two categories: supervised and unsupervised approaches. Traditional supervised methods usually require tailor-made rules, such as rule-based manner [23], thesaurus-based methods [14], and lattice matching approaches [3]. Recently, deep learning models make success in the supervised paraphrase area [7,22,25]. Qian et al. [26] employ semantic style embeddings to enhance the diversity of paraphrase sentences. Iyyer et al. and Goyal et al. [5,10,13] deploy different target syntactic templates to paraphrase sentences. Kumar et al. [15] utilize full exemplar syntactic tree information for paraphrase generation.

Most supervised approaches treated paraphrase generation as a translation task and trained Seq2Seq models utilizing a large amount of parallel pairs [22,37]. To reduce the effort of collecting annotated paraphrase data, unsupervised paraphrase generation has driven lots of attention. Wieting et al. [33] employ back-translation approaches to paraphrase sentences. Zhang et al. [28,38]paraphrase sentences based on variational auto-encoder (VAE). Latent bag-of-words alignment [8] and simulated annealing [19] are also employed for unsupervised paraphrase generation. In addition, large-scale pre-trained language models are induced into unsupervised paraphrase task [24,34]. Other works primarily deploy reinforcement learning(RL) techniques [16,17,27]. RL approaches optimize certain criteria, e.g. BLEU, to reward output that is similar to the source text [17,29].

3 Proposal

3.1 Problem Formulation

Given a sentence $\mathbf{x} = \{x_1, x_2, \ldots, x_n\}$ and a target parse $\mathbf{y} = \{y_1, y_2, \ldots, y_m\}$, we aim to generate a paraphrase sentence $\mathbf{z} = \{z_1, z_2, \ldots, z_l\}$ which has similar semantic meaning of $\mathbf{x}$ while conforming to the syntactic structure of $\mathbf{y}$. Following the previous work [13,38], the target parse $\mathbf{y}$ is a linearized sequence of the constituency parse tree without leaf nodes (i.e., tokens). For instance, the linearized target parse of sentence "*I am fine.*" is "(S (NP (PRP)) (VP (VBP) (ADJP (JJ))) (.)". Consequently, we can consider the parse tree as a special sentence, where its tokens are parentheses and syntactic tags.

3.2 Model Architecture

The main motivation of our syntax-guided paraphrase generation method is to disentangle a source sentence into the semantic space and the syntactic space. Accordingly, after the training process, the model can generate a syntax-specific target sentence by keeping the semantic space of the input sentence unchanged while modifying the syntactic space.

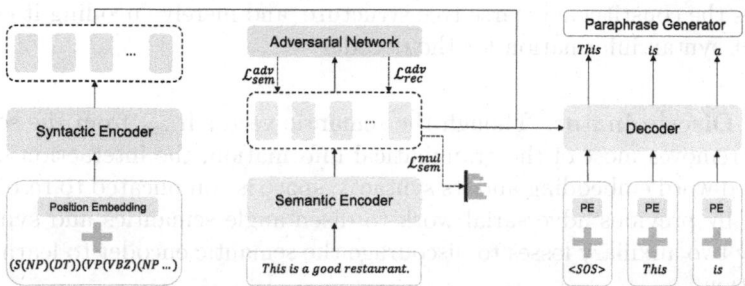

Fig. 2. Architecture of our AUSPG. The semantic encoder and the adversarial network are utilized to get the semantic embedding. The syntactic encoder embeds the syntactic sequence into the syntactic embedding. The decoder takes both semantic and syntactic embeddings to generate paraphrases.

The architecture of our adversarial syntax-guided paraphrase generation model is shown in Fig. 2. Our AUSPG consists of two separate encoders, a syntax discriminator and a decoder. The semantic encoder extracts the semantic knowledge from the source sentence $\mathbf{x} = \{x_1, x_2, \ldots, x_n\}$, while the syntactic encoder obtains the syntactic structure from linearized sequence $\mathbf{y} = \{y_1, y_2, \ldots, y_m\}$. The syntax discriminator is employed to adversarially eliminate the syntactic information from the embedding of semantic encoder. The decoder then deploys the combined semantic and syntactic vectors to generate the target paraphrase sentence $\mathbf{z}$. We present the model details in the following.

Semantic Encoder. The semantic encoder Enc_{sem} is expected to embeds the input sentence $\mathbf{x}$ into semantic vector $\mathbf{h}_{sem}$. We describe the encoding process as:

$$\mathbf{h}_{sem} = \{h_1, h_2, \ldots, h_n\} = Enc_{sem}(\mathbf{x}). \tag{1}$$

To be specific, we adopt a similar idea proposed in [12] that a sentence without order carries most of the semantic information. The evidence is that swapping the object and the subject in a sentence changes its original meaning. Therefore, we require that the semantic encoder removes the position message from the input sentence $\mathbf{x}$. Borrowing from [12], we use a Transformer [32] encoder without position embedding layer to obtain a semantic vector.

Syntactic Encoder. The syntactic encoder is designed to embed the target parse $\mathbf{y}$ into a syntactic vector $\mathbf{h}_{syn}$. The encoding manner is explained as:

$$\mathbf{h}_{syn} = \{h_1, h_2, \ldots, h_m\} = Enc_{syn}(\mathbf{y}). \tag{2}$$

Since we remove the leaf nodes which carry the semantic information of the target sentence, the target parse $\mathbf{y}$ is a sequence that only contains the syntactic tags. Therefore, we can straightforwardly use a Transformer encoder to embed it and get the syntactic vector. In other words, we consider the input sequence preserves the constituency parse tree structure, and merely encoding it captures the exact syntax information for the decoder.

Syntax Discriminator. Though the semantic vector $\mathbf{h}_{sem}$ from the semantic encoder removes most of the grammatical information, the interaction between unordered word embedding and its syntactic space is complicated to resolve [31]. Inspired by previous adversarial work to disentangle semantics and syntax [2], we apply two auxiliary losses to discourage the semantic encoder to learn syntax information.

Intuitively, the model is not expected to predict the syntactic sequence based on the semantic vector $\mathbf{h}_{sem}$. Thus, the first adversarial loss is:

$$\mathcal{L}_{sem}^{adv} = \sum_{i=1}^{m} log p_{adv}(y_i|y_1, y_2, \ldots, y_{i-1}, h_{sem}). \tag{3}$$

Our next intuition is that the model can not generate sentences from a single semantic space. Tao et al. and Ma et al. [20,31] have demonstrated that re-ordering knowledge is indeed learnable. That is, the decoder can reconstruct the source sentence from unordered words by learning to re-order. Accordingly, we introduce the other adversarial loss:

$$\mathcal{L}_{rec}^{adv} = \sum_{i=1}^{n} log p_{rec}(x_i|x_1, \ldots, x_{i-1}, h_{sem}). \tag{4}$$

Moreover, we employ a multi-task loss to ensure that h_{sem} capture the semantic information. To be specific, we predict bag-of-word (BOW) distribution of the source sentence from h_{sem}. The objective is to minimize the following cross-entropy loss against the distribution $\mathbf{t}$ of source sentence:

$$\mathcal{L}_{sem}^{mul} = -\sum\nolimits_{x \in \mathcal{X}} t_x log p(x|h_{sem}). \tag{5}$$

Decoder. The decoder Dec takes the integrated semantic embedding $\mathbf{h}_{sem}$ and syntactic embedding $\mathbf{h}_{syn}$ as the input and gets the target sentence $\mathbf{z}$. That is,

$$\mathbf{z} = \{z_1, z_2, \ldots, z_l\} = Dec([\mathbf{h}_{sem}; \mathbf{h}_{syn}]). \tag{6}$$

We apply Transformer as the decoder of AUSPG to generate the output. Since we disentangle the semantic and syntactic spaces through two separate encoders and a syntax discriminator, the decoder is forced to retrieve semantics from h_{sem} and extract syntactic information from h_{syn}. The attention calculation in AUSPG decoder between h_{sem} and h_{syn} makes the model learn the interaction between semantic and syntactic spaces. As a result, AUSPG has the ability to generate a specific paraphrase given a target parse.

3.3   Training Details

Unsupervised Manner. The design of separate semantic and syntactic encoders makes it possible to learn to paraphrase sentences in an unsupervised manner. To be specific, we disentangle the composition of a sentence into semantic and syntactic spaces and force the decoder to learn the relation between the two spaces. The encoding processes of these two spaces are independent. Thus, the model can learn the ability to paraphrase a sequence from designated semantics and syntax by reconstructing the sequence itself in the training phase without using annotated pairs. It's worth noting that if we don't remove the position embedding in the semantic encoder, the decoder will ignore h_{syn} and copy the source sentence. Consequently, the model doesn't have the ability to paraphrase sentences and always duplicates the input text during the inference time.

Word Dropout. Notice that in the inference time, the golden sentence always includes new words that do not appear in the source sentence. However, if we train the model to reconstruct sentences, it only learns to generate words contained in the source text. To encourage AUSPG to generate more diverse words, we randomly discard some words of the input text during the training phase. More precisely, the probability of word dropout that we adopt is 40% which is proved to be efficient in [12].

3.4   Parse Templates

Considering that the full target parse sequence is not available during inference time, we follow the setting in [12,13] to generate the paraphrase based on parse templates. To be specific, the templates is the top two levels of a full constituency parse tree, e.g. the parse template for "(S (NP (PRP)) (VP (VBP) (ADJP (JJ))) (.))" is "(S (NP) (VP) (.)).

Inspired by [12,13], we train a full parse sequence generator. The architecture of this generator is similar to AUSPG, but does not contain a syntax discriminator. The input of this parse generator consists of two parts: a part-of-speech (POS) tag sequence $\mathbf{tag}_x$ and a target parse template $\mathbf{p}_t$. For instance, the tag sequence for "*I am fine.*" is "<PRP><VBP><JJ><.>". The objective is to predict a full parse sequence $\mathbf{p}_x$ following the given template.

It's worth noting that the training process of the parse generator is in an unsupervised manner as well. This generator can learn to generate a full parse sequence through the reconstruction task. Consequently, we regard our approach as a two-step generation during inference time: First, use the parse generator to encode the template and POS tags of the source text to get a full syntactic sequence. Next, use AUSPG to generate the paraphrase from the full syntactic sequence and source text.

In addition, we notice that not all templates are suitable for some sentences and lead to nonsensical generation. Therefore, the outputs of AUSPG need to be refined with n-gram overlap calculation [13] and sentence similarity computed in [33].

4   Experiments

4.1   Data

We utilize part of ParaNMT-50M [33], a dataset of approximately 50 million paraphrase pairs, to train our AUSPG. To be specific, we select about 8.5 million pairs with high-quality scores as the training set. Since our model is trained in an unsupervised manner, both source and reference sentences can be used for training examples. As a result, our training dataset contains 17 million sentences with their constituency parse sequences. We also sample other 10,000 sentences as testing data.

We evaluate AUSPG on QQP-Pos [15] as well to assess the transferability of AUSPG. The number of QQP-Pos testing sentences is 6,000. In addition, to evaluate the performance of AUSPG on specific datasets, we finetune it on QQS-Pos, PAN [21] containing 5,000 pairs, and MRPC [6] containing 2753 annotated pairs.

4.2   Baselines

To evaluate the effectiveness of our proposal, we compare our methods with several baselines:

Source-O is the method that directly regards source sentences as paraphrase results.

BackTrans is a proposal widely used to paraphrase sentences [11,22,33]. We implement the pretrained EN-DE and DE-EN models[1] to generate paraphrase.

Seq2Seq is a Transformer model we end-to-end trained without disentanglement to analyze the influence of adversaries and separate latent spaces.

SIVAE is a syntax-infused approach [38]. It feeds additional syntactic information into the model without disentangling the semantics and syntax.

SynPG is an unsupervised syntax-guided paraphrase model [12]. It adopts the idea of separating semantic and syntactic spaces.

SGCP is a syntax-guided paraphrase model with two versions SGCP-R and SGCP-F [15]. It prunes the constituency parse tree from height 3 to 10. SGCP-R utilizes the best paraphrase out of many, while SGCP-F uses a full parse tree. To the best of our knowledge, SGCP-R performs better than SGCP-F most time. We choose SGCP-R as our baseline.

---

[1] https://github.com/pytorch/fairseq/tree/main/examples/wmt21.

Table 1. Automatic evaluation and human evaluation results with ground-truth syntactic control. **Val@100** is the validity check of the first 100 test cases, and **Vot** is the percent of received votes for the best paraphrase model among all the baselines. We mark the best results in unsupervised manners, i.e. not including Seq2Seq, SGCP and AESOP, with bold. We also mark the best results of supervised methods with underline.

	Model	BLEU↑	MT↑	R-1↑	R-2↑	R-L↑	S-TED↓	Val@100↑	Vot↑
ParaNMT	Source-O	16.4	29.8	48.5	23.7	50.2	17.4	0	0
	BackTrans	16.2	28.6	46.7	22.5	47.1	18.6	8.2	1.8
	Seq2Seq	23.5	31.9	52.7	28.6	53.7	8.7	18.6	3.8
	SIVAE	12.8	22.5	39.9	20.6	41.7	12.1	26.2	2.4
	SynPG	32.2	35.3	59.7	39.7	62.5	**6.4**	52.6	10.6
	AUSPG*	**38.4**	**41.4**	**60.5**	**46.1**	**65.4**	7.1	**58.0**	**22.8**
	SGCP	35.8	41.2	64.1	41.8	67.5	<u>6.4</u>	62.4	24.2
	AESOP	<u>40.5</u>	<u>43.7</u>	<u>68.9</u>	<u>48.6</u>	<u>71.0</u>	7.6	<u>73.8</u>	<u>34.4</u>
QQP -Pos	Source-O	17.2	31.1	51.9	26.3	52.9	16.2	0	0
	BackTrans	18.9	33.5	54.8	27.6	55.1	14.6	9.6	2.2
	Seq2Seq	15.7	22.4	44.8	21.5	48.2	13.6	6.4	2.6
	SIVAE	13.1	24.3	36.7	15.4	33.9	8.2	30.8	3.2
	SynPG	31.9	38.0	**60.2**	41.3	64.5	**6.6**	45.4	7.8
	AUSPG*	**37.5**	**40.2**	58.3	**43.7**	**65.8**	6.9	**49.6**	**15.4**
	SGCP	38.0	24.8	67.6	45.3	70.0	6.1	65.2	31.8
	AESOP	<u>47.3</u>	<u>49.7</u>	<u>73.3</u>	<u>54.1</u>	<u>75.1</u>	<u>5.6</u>	<u>77.0</u>	<u>37.0</u>

AESOP trains the model with adaptive syntactic control [30]. It first needs an adaptor to select examplers and then adopts a similar idea as [15] do which prunes the parse tree from height 2 to 4. It utilizes source sentences and examplers to train a supervised model. We select AESOP-4 which performs best in the three versions as our baseline.

4.3   Evaluation Metrics

We evaluate the quality of paraphrased sentences on four metrics: (1) BLEU score (2) METEOR score (MT) [1], (3) ROUGE score including ROUGE-1 (R-1), ROUGE-2 (R-2) and ROUGE-L (R-L), (4)and syntax-TED (S-TED) [5] score. Among them, the first three metrics are employed to measure the semantic content that matches between the generated output and golden reference. The syntax-TED score is a matrix used to compute the syntactic tree edit distance between constituency parse trees after removing the word nodes. Accordingly, it can measure the syntactic similarity between the predicted sentence and the reference.

Table 2. Finetuning results on different datasets. Syn-FT and AUS-FT are the finetuning models of SynPG and AUSPG, respectively.

Model	PAN		MRPC	
	BLEU	S-TED	BLEU	S-TED
AUSPG*	27.8	7.1	29.5	7.4
Syn-FT	34.2	6.3	44.6	5.6
AUS-FT*	37.9	**4.8**	**45.3**	5.8
SGCP	**40.1**	**4.8**	42.3	**4.9**

Table 3. Ablation study results of AUSPG on different datasets. Three losses described in Sect. 3.2 are dropped respectively.

Model	ParaNMT		QQP-Pos	
	BLEU	S-TED	BLEU	S-TED
AUSPG	38.4	7.1	37.5	6.9
$-\mathcal{L}_{sem}^{adv}$	34.9	7.5	33.2	6.4
$-\mathcal{L}_{rec}^{adv}$	36.8	6.7	35.4	5.8
$-\mathcal{L}_{sem}^{mul}$	36.5	7.1	37.2	6.1

5 Results

5.1 Automatic Evaluation

We report the automatic evaluation results in Table 1. SynPG and AUSPG perform better than other unsupervised approaches. This demonstrates that the disentanglement of semantics and syntax helps improve the matching accuracy between the predicted output and the golden reference. Furthermore, AUSPG deploys an additional syntax discriminator compared with SynPG. The adversarial approach employed in AUSPG leads to the results that it outperforms SynPG on many evaluation metrics. We notice that with regard to S-TED, SynPG obtain better scores than AUSPG. The reason for this is that some information that helps the semantic and syntactic spaces interact is eliminated due to the adversaries. Moreover, we discover that the AUSPG performs well on QQP-Pos though it is trained just on ParaNMT. This implies that AUSPG indeed has the ability to fuse syntactic structure and semantic knowledge.

On the other hand, AUSPG has competitive or even better results with the supervised approaches in Table 1. Moreover, since our proposal is trained in an unsupervised manner, following [12], we finetune it on the specific dataset for better learning its text features. Table 2 shows the finetuning results. We observe that the performance is much improved and even better than SGCP on some datasets. This demonstrates the potential of the adversarial approach for unsupervised paraphrase generation.

5.2 Human Evaluation

We validate the chosen paraphrases for the first 100 samples in the testing set on Amazon Mturk. The annotations are on a three-grade level: **0** means the predicted text is not a paraphrase of the source sentence.; **1** means the predicted text is a paraphrase but with some grammatical errors; **2** means the source sentence is paraphrased into the predicted text correctly. We binarize the rate **1** and **2** to be valid and the rate **0** to be invalid. We then calculate the ratio of valid cases and report it as Val@100. In addition, we ask five expert labelers to vote for which paraphrase model is best and we report the percentage of

Table 4. An example for case study. AUSPG can generate paraphrases that are more similar to golden references than other unsupervised approaches.

Model	Example from **QQP-Pos**
Source	What is the best way to materialize an idea?
Golden	How can i materialize an idea?
BackTrans	What is the best way to realize an idea?
SIVAE	What is the best way I can realize an idea?
SynPG	How can I materialize on an idea?
AUSPG	How could I materialize an idea?

votes results as Vot in Table 1. We ensure every instance is rated by at least three judges. In result, the paraphrase instances of AUSPG are more valid than unsupervised baselines. AUSPG gets the most votes among these unsupervised methods as well. Consistent with automatic evaluation results, human grading demonstrates the effectiveness of the adversarial approach and disentanglement of semantic and syntactic spaces.

5.3 Ablation Study

In order to further explore the role of syntax discriminator in paraphrase generation, we conduct ablation study on our AUSPG. We report the scores of BLEU and S-TED evaluated on ParaNMT and QQP-Pos corpus in Table 3.

We can see that when removing the adversarial loss $\mathcal{L}_{sem}^{adv}$, the performance drops both on semantic and syntactic evaluation. This implies that $\mathcal{L}_{sem}^{adv}$ helps the model regularize the semantic space and better learn to integrate the semantic and syntactic features. By removing the adversarial loss $\mathcal{L}_{rec}^{adv}$, we observe that the BLEU scores drop, while the S-TED evaluation results rise. The observation indicates that $\mathcal{L}_{rec}^{adv}$ is important for preserving semantics. Furthermore, the embedding of unordered words contains some knowledge about the interaction between semantics and syntax which helps improve the syntax-guided ability. Lastly, we can conclude from the results that $\mathcal{L}_{sem}^{mul}$ plays an essential role in constructing the semantic space.

5.4 Case Study

Table 4 shows the typical examples of the syntax-guided paraphrases from unsupervised baselines and our AUSPG. We observe that without the disentanglement of semantics and syntax, the unsupervised manners intend to copy the source text. The separate latent spaces enable SynPG and AUSPG to generate syntax-guided paraphrases which are more similar to the golden reference. Moreover, adversarial losses deployed in AUSPG construct a regularized semantic space and generate more plausible paraphrases.

6 Conclusion

In this paper, we present an adversarial approach (AUSPG) for unsupervised syntax-guided paraphrase generation. AUSPG is a Transformer-based paraphrase model which targets to control the syntax of paraphrase given syntactic specifications. Specifically, the objective of AUSPG is to disentangle the semantic and syntactic spaces. We adopt two separate encoders to force AUSPG into focusing on encoding semantics and syntax into different spaces. Besides, a syntax discriminator is deployed to regularize the semantic space. The disentanglement enables AUSPG to decouple text features and be trained without annotated pairs. Experimental results on ParaNMT and QQP-Pos corpus show that AUSPG performs better than other unsupervised baselines and achieves competitive results with the supervised manners when the target parses are given. Moreover, our analyses shows that the performance of AUSPG has substantially improved when finetuned on PAN and MRPC datasets. This indicates the potential value of AUSPG in some domains where the annotated sentence pairs are hard to obtain.

Acknowledgment. This work was supported by the Joint Funds of the National Natural Science Foundation of China (Grant No. U21B2020). Gongshen Liu is the corresponding author.

References

1. Banerjee, S., Lavie, A.: Meteor: an automatic metric for MT evaluation with improved correlation with human judgments. In: Proceedings of the ACL Workshop on Intrinsic and Extrinsic Evaluation Measures for Machine Translation and/or Summarization (2005)
2. Bao, Y., et al: Generating sentences from disentangled syntactic and semantic spaces. In: Proceedings of ACL (2019)
3. Barzilay, R., Lee, L.: Learning to paraphrase: an unsupervised approach using multiple-sequence alignment. In: Proceedings of NAACL (2003)
4. Bowman, S., Vilnis, L., Vinyals, O., Dai, A., Jozefowicz, R., Bengio, S.: Generating sentences from a continuous space. In: Proceedings of CoNLL (2016)
5. Chen, M., Tang, Q., Wiseman, S., Gimpel, K.: Controllable paraphrase generation with a syntactic exemplar. In: Proceedings of ACL (2019)
6. Dolan, B., Quirk, C., Brockett, C.: Unsupervised construction of large paraphrase corpora: exploiting massively parallel news sources. In: Proceedings of COLING (2004)
7. Egonmwan, E., Chali, Y.: Transformer and seq2seq model for paraphrase generation. In: Proceedings of the 3rd Workshop on Neural Generation and Translation (2019)
8. Fu, Y., Feng, Y., Cunningham, J.P.: Paraphrase generation with latent bag of words. Proceedings of NeurIPS (2019)
9. Gao, S., Zhang, Y., Ou, Z., Yu, Z.: Paraphrase augmented task-oriented dialog generation. In: Proceedings of ACL (2020)
10. Goyal, T., Durrett, G.: Neural syntactic preordering for controlled paraphrase generation. In: Proceedings of ACL (2020)

11. Hu, J.E., Rudinger, R., Post, M., Van Durme, B.: ParaBank: monolingual bitext generation and sentential paraphrasing via lexically-constrained neural machine translation. In: Proceedings of AAAI (2019)
12. Huang, K.H., Chang, K.W.: Generating syntactically controlled paraphrases without using annotated parallel pairs. In: Proceedings of EACL (2021)
13. Iyyer, M., Wieting, J., Gimpel, K., Zettlemoyer, L.: Adversarial example generation with syntactically controlled paraphrase networks. In: Proceedings of NAACL (2018)
14. Kauchak, D., Barzilay, R.: Paraphrasing for automatic evaluation. In: Proceedings of AACL (2006)
15. Kumar, A., Ahuja, K., Vadapalli, R., Talukdar, P.: Syntax-guided controlled generation of paraphrases. Trans. Assoc. Comput. Linguist. (2020)
16. Li, J., Monroe, W., Ritter, A., Jurafsky, D., Galley, M., Gao, J.: Deep reinforcement learning for dialogue generation. In: EMNLP (2016)
17. Li, Z., Jiang, X., Shang, L., Li, H.: Paraphrase generation with deep reinforcement learning. In: Proceedings of EMNLP (2018)
18. Lin, Z., Wan, X.: Pushing paraphrase away from original sentence: a multi-round paraphrase generation approach. In: Proceedings of ACL Findings (2021)
19. Liu, X., Mou, L., Meng, F., Zhou, H., Zhou, J., Song, S.: Unsupervised paraphrasing by simulated annealing. In: Proceedings of ACL (2020)
20. Ma, S., Sun, X., Wang, Y., Lin, J.: Bag-of-words as target for neural machine translation. In: Proceedings of ACL (2018)
21. Madnani, N., Tetreault, J., Chodorow, M.: Re-examining machine translation metrics for paraphrase identification. In: Proceedings of NAACL (2012)
22. Mallinson, J., Sennrich, R., Lapata, M.: Paraphrasing revisited with neural machine translation. In: Proceedings of EACL (2017)
23. McKeown, K.: Paraphrasing questions using given and new information. Am. J. Comput. Linguist. (1983)
24. Meng, Y., et al.: ConRPG: paraphrase generation using contexts as regularizer. In: Proceedings of EMNLP (2021)
25. Prakash, A., et al.: Neural paraphrase generation with stacked residual LSTM networks. In: Proceedings of COLING (2016)
26. Qian, L., Qiu, L., Zhang, W., Jiang, X., Yu, Y.: Exploring diverse expressions for paraphrase generation. In: Proceedings of EMNLP (2019)
27. Ranzato, M., Chopra, S., Auli, M., Zaremba, W.: Sequence level training with recurrent neural networks. In: Proceedings of ICLR (2016)
28. Roy, A., Grangier, D.: Unsupervised paraphrasing without translation. In: Proceedings of ACL (2019)
29. Siddique, A., Oymak, S., Hristidis, V.: Unsupervised paraphrasing via deep reinforcement learning. In: Proceedings of KDD (2020)
30. Sun, J., Ma, X., Peng, N.: Aesop: Paraphrase generation with adaptive syntactic control. In: Proceedings of EMNLP (2021)
31. Tao, C., Gao, S., Li, J., Feng, Y., Zhao, D., Yan, R.: Learning to organize a bag of words into sentences with neural networks: an empirical study. In: Proceedings of NAACL (2021)
32. Vaswani, A., et al.: Attention is all you need. In: Proceedings of NeurIPS (2017)
33. Wieting, J., Gimpel, K.: Paranmt-50m: pushing the limits of paraphrastic sentence embeddings with millions of machine translations. In: Proceedings of ACL (2018)
34. Witteveen, S., Andrews, M.: Paraphrasing with large language models. In: Proceedings of the 3rd Workshop on Neural Generation and Translation (2019)

35. Wubben, S., Van Den Bosch, A., Krahmer, E.: Paraphrase generation as mono-lingual translation: Data and evaluation. In: Proceedings of the 6th International Natural Language Generation Conference (2010)
36. Yang, X., Liu, Y., Xie, D., Wang, X., Balasubramanian, N.: Latent part-of-speech sequences for neural machine translation. In: Proceedings of EMNLP (2019)
37. Yuan, W., Ding, L., Meng, K., Liu, G.: Text generation with syntax - enhanced variational autoencoder. In: International Joint Conference on Neural Networks, IJCNN 2021, Shenzhen, China, 18–22 July 2021, pp. 1–8. IEEE (2021). https://doi.org/10.1109/IJCNN52387.2021.9533865
38. Zhang, X., Yang, Y., Yuan, S., Shen, D., Carin, L.: Syntax-infused variational autoencoder for text generation. In: Proceedings of ACL (2019)
39. Zhao, S., Meng, R., He, D., Saptono, A., Parmanto, B.: Integrating transformer and paraphrase rules for sentence simplification. In: Proceedings of EMNLP (2018)
40. Zhao, S., Wang, H., Lan, X., Liu, T.: Leveraging multiple MT engines for para-phrase generation. In: Proceedings of COLING (2010)

Online Self-boost Learning for Chinese Grammatical Error Correction

Jiaying Xie, Kai Dang, and Jie Liu[✉]

College of Artificial Intelligence, NanKai University, Tianjin, China
{ying,dangkai}@mail.nankai.edu.cn, jliu@nankai.edu.cn

Abstract. Grammatical error correction (GEC) aims to automatically detect and correct grammatical errors in sentences. With the development of deep learning, neural machine translation-based approach becomes the mainstream approach for this task. Recently, Chinese GEC attracts a certain amount of attention. However, Chinese GEC has two main problems that limit model learning: (1) insufficient data; (2) flexible error forms. In this paper, we attempt to address these limitations by proposing a method called online self-boost learning for Chinese GEC. Online self-boost learning enables the model to generate multiple instances with different errors for model's weaknesses from each original sample within each batch and to learn the new data in time without additional I/O. And taking advantage of the features of the new data, a consistency loss is introduced to drive the model to produce similar distributions for different inputs with the same target. Our method is capable of fully exploiting the potential knowledge of the annotated data. Meanwhile, it allows for the use of unlabeled data to extend to a semi-supervised method. Sufficient experiments and analyses show the effectiveness of our method. Besides, our method achieves a state-of-the-art result on the Chinese benchmark.

Keywords: Chinese grammatical error correction · Self-boost learning · Consistency training

1 Introduction

Grammatical error correction (GEC) is a challenging and meaningful task in natural language processing (NLP), which aims to automatically detect and correct grammatical errors or spelling errors in sentences. It has important applications in text proofreading, foreign language assisted learning, search engine, automatic speech recognition (ASR) and optical character recognition (OCR).

Regarding the incorrect sentence as the source sentence and the correct sentence as the target sentence, GEC can be seen as a machine translation task. With the development of deep learning, neural machine translation (NMT) based on the sequence-to-sequence (seq2seq) architecture is widely applied to this task [4,9,25]. Nevertheless, the NMT-based approach requires a considerable amount

© The Author(s), under exclusive license to Springer Nature Switzerland AG 2022
W. Lu et al. (Eds.): NLPCC 2022, LNAI 13551, pp. 377–389, 2022.
https://doi.org/10.1007/978-3-031-17120-8_30

of annotated data. And data annotation in GEC is costly giving rise to difficulties in obtaining large-scale training data.

Recently, Chinese GEC attracts a certain amount of attention [21,23,26]. With increased interaction between the world's nations, more and more people around the world are learning Chinese and using it. Besides, users are very casual in their text input and voice input in the information age. These lead to more frequent grammatical errors in Chinese. And Chinese expressions are very flexible. Compared to English, it lacks clear word boundaries, verb conjugations and plural suffixes. And different word order may not affect the meaning of the sentence. All those cause it to have a greater variety of error forms. Thus, there are problems here such as sparse data and complex forms leading to poor performance on Chinese GEC.

Moreover, we find that grammatical correction allows multiple incorrect sentences to correspond to the same corrected sentences due to the flexibility of the linguistic expression and the errors made in a real scenario. With a small amount of annotated data and the data given in the form of an incorrect sentence corresponding to a correct answer, it is difficult for the model to constrain different errors to the same corrected answer in practice, we can call this a polymorphism problem. To address these issues, we propose online self-boost learning inspired by previous work of Ge et al. [6] to make full use of the available annotation data and solve the polymorphism problem to some extent.

Our method will enable the model to learn self-generated multiple instances of each original sample within each batch. After the model has been trained on the original data in each batch, we feed the noisy source sentence into the model to make incorrect inferences. The most confident inferences are then combined with the original targets to form new pairs to be input into the model for learning. At this stage, we design a Kullback-Leibler divergence (KL-divergence) consistency loss to drive the output distributions of the same target close to each other, relieving the polymorphism problem. Online self-boost learning has many advantages. First, the data generated by the model itself reflects the weaknesses of the current model and the model can be trained more effectively from it. Second, it can generate different error sentences corresponding to the same target to alleviate the polymorphism problem. Third, self-boost learning is operated within each batch, so the generated data is learned promptly with no additional I/O operations and no changes to the learning rate schedules and the number of update steps. And at last, our method can also be extended to a semi-supervised method by utilizing unlabelled data. We perform experiments and analyses on Chinese GEC and the results give evidence of the effectiveness of our method. And our method achieves a state-of-the-art result.

The contributions of this paper are as follows:

– We propose online self-boost learning to address the problems of Chinese GEC.
– We define the polymorphism problem on GEC and introduce a consistency loss to solve it.

- We demonstrate theoretically and experimentally the clear advantages of online learning, i.e. learning multiple generated data within a batch.
- Our method is proven to be effective and achieves a state-of-the-art result on the Chinese benchmark.

2 Related Work

2.1 Grammatical Error Correction

The early GEC system relies on rules to correct sentences [16], and it could only correct several types of errors. With the advent of statistical machine translation (SMT), researchers begin to treat GEC as a translation task and makes significant progress based on SMT [2,3]. With the rise of deep learning in NLP, NMT with the seq2seq structure make a prominent contribution to text generation. The researchers also adapt end-to-end generation methods based on the seq2seq NMT for GEC [4,25]. And PLM with a seq2seq architecture can naturally be used on GEC. In recent years, some PLMs such as BART [12] are widely adopted on English GEC and show their effectiveness [10].

And researchers present various data augmentation methods to improve the generalization of the model [7,11]. And there are some methods that focus on how to generate more meaningful data. Ge et al. [6] present self-boost learning for GEC. They asked the model to generate multiple inferences from the original data to form new data for the next epoch training after each epoch. In comparison to traditional methods, the data from the model inference does not change in sentence meaning and is better able to reflect the information of the current model, resulting in more effective training. Wang et al. [24] identify weaknesses in the model to generate more valuable training examples inspired by adversarial training.

And there are some studies for Chinese GEC. Zhao et al. [26] add various kinds of random noises to the source sentences dynamically to obtain more abundant error-corrected sentence pairs in the training procedure. Sun et al. [21] propose a synthetic data construction approach through non-autoregressive translation (NAT). These methods greatly improve the performance on GEC.

2.2 Consistency Training

Consistency training can constrain predictions to be invariant to input noise or different models [15,18]. Shen et al. [20] introduce a Jensen-Shannon divergence consistency loss to match the model predictions between different partial views of a given input, maximizing the consensus between multiple views in a stable way. R-Drop [13] makes the two distributions of the same data samples from two sub-models consistent with each other by minimizing the bidirectional KL-divergence between the two distributions. And we apply consistency training to force the model to produce consistent outputs for different incorrect sentences with the same target, enhancing the model's capacity to cope with the polymorphism problem.

3   Method

3.1   Model Architecture

We choose a Chinese BART as our grammatical error correction model and finetune it. Given an input sentence $X = \{x_1, x_2, \ldots, x_m\}$, the model will generate its corresponding corrected sequence $Y = \{y_1, y_2, \ldots, y_n\}$, where m and n are the lengths of sequence X and Y respectively. The model will compute a conditional probability $P(Y \mid X)$ from the error-corrected sentence pair (X, Y):

$$P(Y \mid X) = \prod_{i=1}^{n} P\left(y_i \mid y_1, \ldots, y_{i-1}, X; \theta\right) \tag{1}$$

where θ are model parameters. The goal is to learn model parameters θ to get the probabilistic mapping $P(Y \mid X)$ by maximum likelihood estimation (MLE), that is, minimum negative log likelihood (NLL) loss as follows:

$$l(\theta, X, Y) = -\sum_{i=1}^{n} \log\left(P\left(y_i \mid y_1, \ldots, y_{i-1}, X; \theta\right)\right) \tag{2}$$

Thus, the standard training procedure to update current parameters θ_t for one batch can be described as:

$$\theta_{t+1} = \theta_t - \eta_t \frac{1}{B} \sum_{b \in \mathcal{B}(t)} \nabla_\theta \ell(\theta_t, X_b, Y_b) \tag{3}$$

where t indicates the t-th parameters update, θ_{t+1} are updated parameters, η_t is the current learning rate, B is the size of one batch and $\mathcal{B}(t)$ is the set of samples in the current training batch.

3.2   Online Self-boost Learning

However, since the number of original error-corrected sentence pairs is not sufficient, the conventional model can not get strong correction ability only from these data. Inspired by previous work [6], we propose online self-boost learning to train a GEC model. The process of online self-boost learning is illustrated in Fig. 1. The model will learn self-generated multiple instances of a sample which target its own the weak spots in the same batch.

Instance Generation. In one batch, after the model computes the NLL loss of the original sentence pairs, we add some random noises to each original source sentence X_b in the same batch. For each source sentence, we generate a ratio p from a normal distribution $\mathcal{N}\left(\mu, \sigma^2\right)$ with mean μ and variance σ^2. Then, we select some tokens randomly in the source according to the ratio and do some operations which can be a substitution, deletion or mask. And we can get the corresponding noise sentence $Noise(X_b)$.

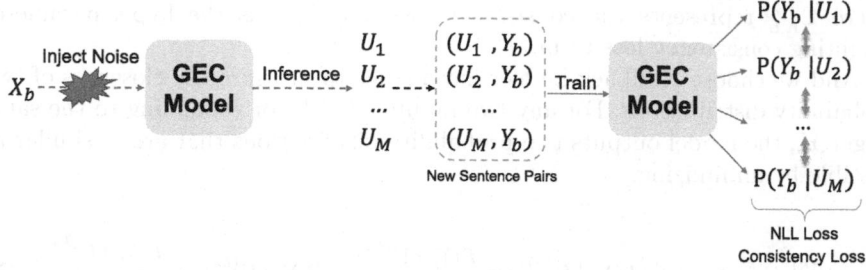

Fig. 1. An illustration of the process of online self-boost learning.

After that, a batch of noise source sentences are input to the model and trick the model to make false predictions. We take the M most confident outputs $(U_1, U_2, ..., U_M)$ by beam search for each noisy input sentence.

$$(U_1, U_2, ..., U_M) = Model_{\theta_t}(Noise(X_b)) \tag{4}$$

Afterwards, the M outputs are formed into M new sentence pairs with the corresponding correct sentence Y_b. The new data captures the weaknesses of the current model. With such data fed back to the model, the model can be corrected more effectively.

Furthermore, we can obtain sentences with more error types in more than one generation. In each generation, we still add random disturbance to the most confident outputs of the last generation. And make the model continue to generate multiple prediction sentences to form new training pairs with the original target sentence. The process can be summarized as follows:

$$U_1^{(0)} = X_b \tag{5}$$

$$(U_1^{(k)}, U_2^{(k)}, ..., U_M^{(k)}) = Model_{\theta_t}(Noise(U_1^{(k-1)})) \tag{6}$$

where k means k-*th* model generation.

Self-boost Learning. For each generation, we sent the new pairs to the model to compute a new loss. In particular, such generation method allows the same target to have multiple inputs with the same meaning but different errors. We take full advantage of the characteristics to design a consistency loss. For different inputs to the same target, the output distributions from the model should be as consistent with each other as possible. Thus, the model is required to calculate a consistency loss of these M output probability distributions in addition to their average NLL loss for the same target sentence. The function of the new loss $\mathcal{L}_S^{(k)}$ of the M pairs with the same target sentence is:

$$\mathcal{L}_S^{(k)} = \frac{1}{M} \sum_{i=1}^{M} \ell\left(\theta_t, U_i^{(k)}, Y_b\right) + \lambda_{KL}\mathcal{L}_{KL}^{(k)} \tag{7}$$

where $\mathcal{L}_{KL}^{(k)}$ represents the consistency loss and λ_{KL} is the hyper-parameter weighting consistency loss term.

And we choose Kullback-Leibler Divergence to measure the closeness of two probability distributions. For any two inputs U_i^k, U_j^k corresponding to the same target Y_b, the model outputs two probability distributions that are as similar as possible by minimizing:

$$\ell_{KL}(U_i^{(k)}, U_j^{(k)}, Y_b) = \frac{1}{2}(P(Y_b \mid U_i^{(k)}) \log \frac{P(Y_b \mid U_i^{(k)})}{P(Y_b \mid U_j^{(k)})} + P(Y_b \mid U_j^{(k)}) \log \frac{P(Y_b \mid U_j^{(k)})}{P(Y_b \mid U_i^{(k)})}) \quad (8)$$

And in one generation, there are M different inputs corresponding to a target, so we define the consistency loss as:

$$\mathcal{L}_{KL}^{(k)} = \frac{M(M-1)}{2} \sum_{i,j \in M \& i \neq j} \ell_{KL}(U_i^{(k)}, U_j^{(k)}, Y_b) \quad (9)$$

Training Process. In summary, the online self-boost learning procedure to update current parameters θ_t for one batch changes to the following:

$$\theta_{t+1} = \theta_t - \eta_t \frac{1}{B} \sum_{b \in \mathcal{B}(t)} (\nabla_\theta \ell(\theta_t, X_b, Y_b) + \nabla_\theta \mathcal{L}_S^{(1)} + \nabla_\theta \mathcal{L}_S^{(2)} + ... + \nabla_\theta \mathcal{L}_S^{(K)}) \quad (10)$$

where K means there are K generations for this batch.

It is worth noting that our approach changes the training strategy within each batch. Compared to the data generated after each epoch, the data generated in each batch is more specific to the current model's weaknesses and can be learned in time without additional I/O operations. This is why we call our method online self-boost learning. Moreover, although our method allows for a larger amount of data to be learned, it only expands the batch in disguise and reduces the variance of the gradient. Hoffer et al. [8] show that such decreased variance reduction enables the model to perform more augmentation training and increase generalization ability with fewer optimization dynamics modifications. Therefore, our method does not need to change the number of update steps performed per epoch and leads to a direct improvement in results over the standard training with a fixed budget for the optimization steps.

3.3 Unlabeled Data Leveraging

At the same time, our method can leverage unlabeled data to extend to a semi-supervised method. For a correct sentence X_r, the model generates incorrect sentences $(U_1', U_2', ..., U_M')$ by inference from the noisy X_r. These incorrect sentences can be composed into new training pairs with the original correct sentences.

4   Experiments

4.1   Datasets

To validate the effectiveness of our method on Chinese GEC, we conduct experiments on the dataset of NLPCC 2018 Task 2 [27]. Following the prior work, We sample 5K sentence pairs as validation data from the train data. And we employ an unlabeled dataset which is obtained by extracting randomly 1M Chinese sentences from the dataset of the WMT20 news translation task [1]. Statistics of the datasets used are shown in Table 1. The official MaxMatch (M^2) scorer[1] is applied to calculate precision, recall and $F_{0.5}$ to evaluate our GEC model.

Table 1. Statistics of the datasets.

Dataset	Split	Sent.	Token src.	Token tgt.
NLPCC-2018	Train	1.15M	24.58M	25.69M
	Valid	5 K	99.3 K	103.3 K
	Test	2 K	58.9 K	–
Unlabeled Data	Train	1.00M	32.00M	32.00M

4.2   Implementation Details

We employ Chinese BART-base[2] [12,19] as our base model and finetune it in the fairseq[3] toolkit. The AdamW optimizer [14] is used to optimize the model and the learning rate increases linearly from 0 to 7×10^{-5} and then decays linearly to 0. The warmup steps are 500 and the total update steps are 20,000. The batch size is set to 5,500 tokens and the accumulation steps are set to 2. And We add label smoothing with an epsilon value of 0.1. The beam size is 10 in the inference phase. To balance the training cost and model performance, we evaluate our method when $M = 2$ and $K = 1$.

4.3   Baselines

We compare our methods to the previous methods on the same annotation data.

- **YouDao** [5] uses five models to correct and a language model to re-rank.
- **AliGM** [27] combines NMT-based, SMT-based and rule-based approaches.
- **BLCU** [17] ensembles four multi-layer convolutional seq2seq models.
- **BERT-encoder** [23] ensembles four Transformer models whose encoders are initialized with BERT.
- **BERT-fuse** [23] acquires representations from BERT and ensembles models.

---

[1] https://github.com/nusnlp/m2scorer.
[2] https://github.com/fastnlp/CPT.
[3] https://github.com/pytorch/fairseq.

- **Dropout-Src** [9] sets the embeddings of source words to 0 randomly in training.
- **Transformer-based** [22] constructs data based on the rule-based destruction method and trains a Transformer-base model.
- **MaskGEC** [26] adds random masks dynamically to the inputs to train.
- **InfoXLM-based** [21] purposes a data construction approach based on NAT, pretrains PLM with generated data and implements MaskGEC to finetune.

4.4   Main Results

Table 2. Performance of methods on the dataset of NLPCC 2018 Task 2.

Model	Type	Unlabeled data	Precision	Recall	$F_{0.5}$
YouDao [5]	Ensemble	–	35.24	18.64	29.91
AliGM [27]	Ensemble	–	41.00	13.75	29.36
BLCU [17]	Ensemble	–	**47.63**	12.56	30.57
BERT-encoder [23]	Ensemble	–	41.94	22.02	35.51
BERT-fuse [23]	Ensemble	–	32.20	23.16	29.87
Dropout-Src [9]	Single	–	39.08	18.80	32.15
Transformer-based [22]	Single	0.74M	39.43	22.80	34.41
MaskGEC [26]	Single	–	44.26	22.18	36.97
InfoXLM-based [21]	Single	10M	45.95	27.94	40.70
BART [12,19]	Single	–	44.23	25.06	38.36
Ours	Single	–	44.67	**28.36**	40.06
Ours	Single	1M	46.45	**28.24**	**41.15**

Table 2 shows the performance of our method and previous methods on the NLPCC 2018 dataset. Our method outperforms other methods. Compared to the traditional fine-tuning on BART, our approach improves the performance on all three metrics, demonstrating the effectiveness of our method. Specifically, the significant increase on recall illustrates that our method can generate a greater variety of incorrect sentences, making the model to correct errors more proactively without reducing the precision of the corrections.

And InfoXLM-based [21] constructs additional 10M data from the rule-based and NAT-based approaches to pretrain PLM and introduces MaskGEC to finetune, achieving a good result. With the aid of 1M unlabeled data from rule-based approach, our method further enhances the correction precision of the model, reaching a state-of-the-art result.

The results show that our method can produce a flexible variety of error sentences with only annotated data, improving the model's ability to detect errors without disrupting the model to the point of losing correction precision. The introduction of unlabelled data can further normalise the model and enhance its correction precision.

4.5   Analysis

Effect of Noising Schemes. We study the effect of various injection noise schemes. The ratio of single noise in a sentence follows a normal distribution $\mathcal{N}(0.1, 0.01)$. The results are shown in Table 3. It can be found that the addition of any type of noise helps to increase the recall of the model correction, i.e. the model can distinguish more errors. And the substitution-based noise works best, as it introduces more perturbations than mask-based noise, but it also facilitates the model to get enough information since most of the meaning and structure of the sentence are preserved compared to deletion-based noise. And we mix the substitution-based noise and mask-based noise, achieving the best result.

Table 3. The effect of various injection noise schemes.

Noise type	Precision	Recall	$F_{0.5}$
Delete	42.61	27.10	38.23
Mask	44.38	26.14	38.95
Substitute	44.00	28.10	39.53
Mix	**44.67**	**28.36**	**40.06**

Effect of Consistency Loss Weight. We perform experiments under different consistency loss weights and the results are presented in Table 4. As the consistency loss weight increases, the precision of the model correction increases. The results prove our idea that the consistency loss can help the model constrain to the same correct answer under diverse error type inputs, improving correction precision and alleviating the polymorphism problem to some extent. When $\lambda_{KL} = 1$, the performance is best.

Table 4. The effect of consistency loss weight.

λ_{KL}	Precision	Recall	$F_{0.5}$
0	44.22	27.92	39.6
0.5	44.69	26.54	39.31
1	44.67	**28.36**	**40.06**
2	**45.09**	27.12	39.82

Effect of Original Data Loss. We explore the necessity of computing the NLL loss of the original data in each batch, as shown in Table 5. The results illustrate that while not calculating the NLL loss of the original data leads the model to be more aggressive in detecting and correcting errors, calculating the loss gives the model a better ability to make the correct corrections. Overall, the original clean data is necessary for the model learning.

Table 5. The effect of the original data loss.

$\ell(od)$	Precision	Recall	$F_{0.5}$
No compute	34.02	**32.98**	33.81
Compute	**44.67**	28.36	**40.06**

Comparison with Offline Self-boost Learning. We compare our online learning approach with the previous offline learning approach. We implement offline learning in such a way that the model infers the original data inputs with noise after one or two epochs, and the model's two best outputs constitute new data to join the training of the subsequent epochs. And because the amount of data increases but the batch size does not change for the offline learning, we raise the total number of update steps to keep the number of epochs learned consistently. As indicated in Table 6 and Fig. 2, the results demonstrate that our online learning approach provides more stable training and make the model more better in all aspects of correction.

Table 6. The comparison with offline self-boost learning.

Self-boost type	Precision	Recall	$F_{0.5}$
Offine(after one epoch)	43.08	25.85	38.01
Offine(after two epoch)	43.26	26.53	38.41
Online	**44.67**	**28.36**	**40.06**

Convergence Analysis. We observe the convergence curves of loss on valid data when applying the standard learning, the offline self-boost learning(after two epoch) and our online self-boost learning, as shown in Fig. 2.(a). It is seen that our method has a clear advantage in that the loss can converge to be smaller for a certain number of update steps. And Fig. 2.(b) displays the performances of the model after each epoch training with the three learning methods and our method has the best performance, proving the effectiveness of our method.

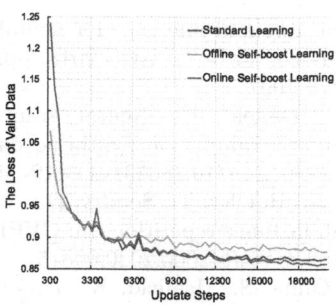

(a) The convergence curve of loss on valid data.

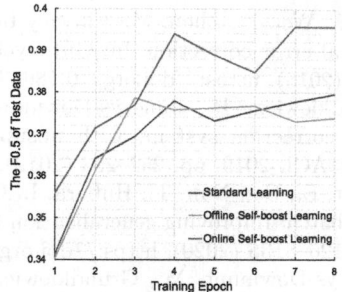

(b) The change curve of $F_{0.5}$ on test data.

Fig. 2. The comparison of standard learning, online self-boost learning and offline self-boost learning.

5 Conclusion

In this paper, we propose an online self-boost learning for training a Chinese GEC model by learning self-generated multiple instances of a sample within each batch. Our method fully exploits existing annotated data to generate more data which targets the current model weaknesses and permits the model to learn new data on time. And a consistency loss is introduced to solve the polymorphism problem. Meanwhile, our method can be expanded to a semi-supervised method by using unlabeled data. Experimental results demonstrate that our method brings a direct improvement with a fixed optimization step. And our method achieves a state-of-the-art result with the introduction of unlabeled data.

Acknowledgement. This research is supported by the National Natural Science Foundation of China under the grant No. 61976119 and the Natural Science Foundation of Tianjin under the grant No. 18ZXZNGX00310.

References

1. Barrault, L., et al.: Findings of the 2020 conference on machine translation (WMT20). In: WMT@EMNLP 2020, pp. 1–55 (2020)
2. Brockett, C., Dolan, W.B., Gamon, M.: Correcting ESL errors using phrasal SMT techniques. In: ACL 2006 (2006). https://doi.org/10.3115/1220175.1220207
3. Chollampatt, S., Ng, H.T.: Connecting the dots: towards human-level grammatical error correction. In: BEA@EMNLP 2017, pp. 327–333 (2017). https://doi.org/10.18653/v1/w17-5037
4. Chollampatt, S., Taghipour, K., Ng, H.T.: Neural network translation models for grammatical error correction. In: IJCAI 2016, pp. 2768–2774 (2016)
5. Fu, K., Huang, J., Duan, Y.: Youdao's winning solution to the NLPCC-2018 task 2 challenge: a neural machine translation approach to Chinese grammatical error correction. In: Zhang, M., Ng, V., Zhao, D., Li, S., Zan, H. (eds.) NLPCC 2018. LNCS (LNAI), vol. 11108, pp. 341–350. Springer, Cham (2018). https://doi.org/10.1007/978-3-319-99495-6_29

6. Ge, T., Wei, F., Zhou, M.: Fluency boost learning and inference for neural grammatical error correction. In: Gurevych, I., Miyao, Y. (eds.) ACL 2018, pp. 1055–1065 (2018). https://doi.org/10.18653/v1/P18-1097

7. Grundkiewicz, R., Junczys-Dowmunt, M., Heafield, K.: Neural grammatical error correction systems with unsupervised pre-training on synthetic data. In: BEA@ACL 2019, pp. 252–263 (2019). https://doi.org/10.18653/v1/w19-4427

8. Hoffer, E., Ben-Nun, T., Hubara, I., Giladi, N., Hoefler, T., Soudry, D.: Augment your batch: Improving generalization through instance repetition. In: CVPR 2020, pp. 8126–8135 (2020). https://doi.org/10.1109/CVPR42600.2020.00815

9. Junczys-Dowmunt, M., Grundkiewicz, R., Guha, S., Heafield, K.: Approaching neural grammatical error correction as a low-resource machine translation task. In: NAACL-HLT 2018, pp. 595–606 (2018). https://doi.org/10.18653/v1/n18-1055

10. Katsumata, S., Komachi, M.: Stronger baselines for grammatical error correction using a pretrained encoder-decoder model. In: AACL/IJCNLP 2020, pp. 827–832 (2020)

11. Kiyono, S., Suzuki, J., Mita, M., Mizumoto, T., Inui, K.: An empirical study of incorporating pseudo data into grammatical error correction. In: EMNLP-IJCNLP 2019, pp. 1236–1242 (2019). https://doi.org/10.18653/v1/D19-1119

12. Lewis, M., et al.: BART: denoising sequence-to-sequence pre-training for natural language generation, translation, and comprehension. In: ACL 2020, pp. 7871–7880 (2020). https://doi.org/10.18653/v1/2020.acl-main.703

13. Liang, X., et al.: R-drop: regularized dropout for neural networks. In: NeurIPS 2021, pp. 10890–10905 (2021)

14. Loshchilov, I., Hutter, F.: Fixing weight decay regularization in Adam. CoRR abs/1711.05101 (2017)

15. Ma, X., Gao, Y., Hu, Z., Yu, Y., Deng, Y., Hovy, E.H.: Dropout with expectation-linear regularization. In: ICLR 2017 (2017)

16. Naber, D.: A rule-based style and grammar checker. University of Bielefeld (2003)

17. Ren, H., Yang, L., Xun, E.: A sequence to sequence learning for Chinese grammatical error correction. In: Zhang, M., Ng, V., Zhao, D., Li, S., Zan, H. (eds.) NLPCC 2018. LNCS (LNAI), vol. 11109, pp. 401–410. Springer, Cham (2018). https://doi.org/10.1007/978-3-319-99501-4_36

18. Sajjadi, M., Javanmardi, M., Tasdizen, T.: Regularization with stochastic transformations and perturbations for deep semi-supervised learning. In: NIPS 2016, pp. 1163–1171 (2016)

19. Shao, Y., et al.: CPT: a pre-trained unbalanced transformer for both Chinese language understanding and generation. CoRR abs/2109.05729 (2021)

20. Shen, D., Zheng, M., Shen, Y., Qu, Y., Chen, W.: A simple but tough-to-beat data augmentation approach for natural language understanding and generation. CoRR abs/2009.13818 (2020)

21. Sun, X., Ge, T., Ma, S., Li, J., Wei, F., Wang, H.: A unified strategy for multilingual grammatical error correction with pre-trained cross-lingual language model. CoRR abs/2201.10707 (2022)

22. Wang, C., Yang, L., Yingying Wang, Y.D., Yang., E.: Chinese grammatical error correction method based on transformer enhanced architecture, no. 6, p. 9 (2020)

23. Wang, H., Kurosawa, M., Katsumata, S., Komachi, M.: Chinese grammatical correction using BERT-based pre-trained model. In: AACL/IJCNLP 2020, pp. 163–168 (2020)

24. Wang, L., Zheng, X.: Improving grammatical error correction models with purpose-built adversarial examples. In: EMNLP 2020, pp. 2858–2869 (2020). https://doi.org/10.18653/v1/2020.emnlp-main.228

25. Yuan, Z., Briscoe, T.: Grammatical error correction using neural machine translation. In: NAACL HLT 2016, pp. 380–386 (2016). https://doi.org/10.18653/v1/n16-1042
26. Zhao, Z., Wang, H.: MaskGEC: improving neural grammatical error correction via dynamic masking. In: AAAI 2020, pp. 1226–1233 (2020)
27. Zhou, J., Li, C., Liu, H., Bao, Z., Xu, G., Li, L.: Chinese grammatical error correction using statistical and neural models. In: Zhang, M., Ng, V., Zhao, D., Li, S., Zan, H. (eds.) NLPCC 2018. LNCS (LNAI), vol. 11109, pp. 117–128. Springer, Cham (2018). https://doi.org/10.1007/978-3-319-99501-4_10

Question Answering (Oral)

Coarse-to-Fine Retriever for Better Open-Domain Question Answering

Xue Liu[1,2] and Fang Kong[1,2(✉)]

[1] Laboratory for Natural Language Processing, Soochow University, Suzhou, China
20205227054@stu.suda.edu.cn, kongfang@suda.edu.cn
[2] School of Computer Science and Technology, Soochow University, Suzhou, China

Abstract. The retriever-reader framework has been widely used in open-domain question answering with great success. Current studies show that better retrieval can greatly improve the performance of final answer extraction and may replace the reader stage. Considering the limited computing resources and the great progress that has been made in reading comprehension, we continue to use the retriever-reader framework and focus on efficient retrieval. In this paper, we propose a new coarse-to-fine retrieval method to take away the semantic noise left by coarse-grained filtering. In particular, we join a fine-grained retriever after the passages generated by the coarse-grained retriever, making all sentences in the passage match more closely with the question. Meanwhile, we use contrastive learning to construct dense vector representation for fine-grained retriever. Experiments on the QA dataset show that our model outperforms the most mainstream model greatly by about 11.7% which importantly gets more out of the operation of retriever.

Keywords: Retriever · Coarse-to-fine · Contrastive learning

1 Introduction

Different from traditional Question Answering (QA) task, which focuses on answering factoid questions, Open-domain Question Answering (ODQA) (Voorhees et al. [16]) is a task that gives answers to questions about nearly everything and answers them based on a collection of texts covering a wide range of topics. So, the inputs of ODQA are one question and an extensive collection of documents. Its output is the possible answer span. For example, given a question like "who wrote the first declaration of human rights", ODQA firstly discovers the most possible documents containing the answer (i.e., candidates) from the massive database and then selects the desired answer span from the candidates and gets the final response "Cyrus".

Previous studies show that the retriever-reader framework is well suited to ODQA tasks, and thus it has become the accepted solution for ODQA. In the stage of retriever, the goal is to efficiently find the most relevant candidate documents to the problem from the mass of texts. While in the stage of reader,

© The Author(s), under exclusive license to Springer Nature Switzerland AG 2022
W. Lu et al. (Eds.): NLPCC 2022, LNAI 13551, pp. 393–404, 2022.
https://doi.org/10.1007/978-3-031-17120-8_31

the goal is to extract answer spans from the obtained candidate documents. Obviously, under this circumstance, the quality of the retriever directly comes to a decision about the content we feed into the reader and indirectly determines whether the answer read by the reader is put right or not.

Recent works in ODQA suggest that "maybe the reader model is not necessary too". Karpukhin et al. [9] divide the document into shorter passages and treats the short units as unique documents. Their study shows that feeding more accurate passages to the reader can actually improve the performance of final answer span extraction. Further, Lee et al. [12] encode all the phrases using dense vectors and only do the nearest neighbor search at inference time. Their study achieves better performance in phrase-level retrieval. But there are 60 billion phrases in Wikipedia, and phrase-level retriever needs more powerful computing resources. In addition, with the development of machine reading comprehension, the reader has made significant progress. In our study, we still employ the retriever-reader framework to do ODQA and mainly focus on the stage of retriever.

Considering the limitation of computing resources, after obtaining candidate passage units, we use contrastive learning and attention mechanism to conduct fine-grained secondary sentence-level retrieval in candidate passages to form candidate sentences (i.e., smaller granularity) and then use the reader to extract answers from new passages composed of candidate sentences. Specifically, we propose a coarse-to-fine passages retriever (CFPR), a novel model with a filtering mechanism that solves the problem of sentences noise bring us. Firstly, we filter out the required passages in the case of coarse granularity, and then we further filter out the highly related sentences to the questions and give up the irrelative ones.

2   Related Works

Since the retriever-reader framework is very intuitive and easy to combine with retrieval tools and machine reading comprehension, many recent studies on open-domain question answering in the last few years have fallen into a two-stage system of reader-retriever. Among them, the retrievers all play a decisive role in the two-stage model. If the retriever finds documents more similar to the question we ask, our reader will have a higher probability of finding the answer.

Search through sparse vector space initiated the beginning of the two-stage retrieval of the retriever-reader. The method was first used widely with BM25 and TF-IDF to represent the relationship between documents and questions (Yang et al. [17], Chen et al. [1], Htut et al. [8], Clark et al. [3]), but sparse vector's shortcomings are soon let be seen. The documents represented by sparse vectors will be limited by the size of the corpus dictionary and is more likely to express the superficial meaning of words. Moreover, their retrievers are at the document level and not trainable.

With the popularity of pre-trained models, researchers have paid attention to dense representations of documents in retriever by degrees following the reader-retriever architecture. Proposed by Das et al. [4], their work opens the prelude of using dense retrieval in ODQA. One of the most critical features of dense representation is that it can enrich the semantic information contained in the vector. Through the training and learning of the pre-trained model, dense representation can also make the retriever more inclined to match vectors at the semantic level. After that, DPR (Karpukhin et al. [9]) is born. It explores splitting original Wikipedia articles into 100-word passages and shows a practical and straightforward way that uses inner product between passages and questions to retrieve.

Lee et al. [13] put forward a passage retrieval method based on scoring the passage in turn by the highest scored phrase in the passage to explore the impact of granularity on search results. Furthermore, Lee et al. [11] use phrase-level granularity for ODQA tasks. They combine the two steps of retriever-reader into one. However, their performance doesn't work best in ODQA. Inspired by their work, we consider that if the granularity is fine to a certain degree, is it necessary to dispense with the reader. At the same time, some work started to use pre-trained language models such as T5 (Roberts et al. [14]) to act as "knowledge storage". However, the performance of the pre-trained model is primarily impacted by the model size. The performance of the T5 with 11B parameters is merely comparable to that of the DPR with only 330M parameters. Computing resources are also a significant measurement factor in real-life applications. Getting better performance with lower resources is the issue we need to consider carefully.

To distinguish the differences between different objects, contrastive learning (He et al. [7], Chen et al. [2]) first sets off an upsurge in CV. Gao et al. [6] took the lead in bringing this technology to NLP and creatively sent one sentence to Bert (Delvin et al. [5]) encoder twice as its positive samples. Since Bert itself has a random dropout function, the two vectors one obtained are different but similar. The challenge of data augmentation which troubles NLP researchers in contrastive learning is solved cleverly by their approach.

3   Model

3.1   Problem Formulation and Notations

Instead of the whole document, we sliced all documents into 100-word passages as our knowledge base. It also served as the document base for our coarse-grained passages retriever. Given questions q and passages p, our coarse-grained passages retriever borrows two different Bert as our encoders to achieve convincing embeddings of questions and passages, respectively. The encoder E_Q is responsible for generating dense embedding of question $q \in R^d$, and E_P is used to map passage to a contiguous embedding, also known as $p \in R^d$. Correspondingly, we can obtain their metrics (similarity) M_k by calculating their inner product of them. Therefore, according to M_k, we can retrieve top-k passages as the results of our coarse-grained passages retriever and thus complete the subsequent tasks.

After splitting the passages above, we can further use our fine-grained sentences retriever to reduce the useless noise in passages. By dividing all passages into sentences and with the help of encoder E_S trained by contrastive learning

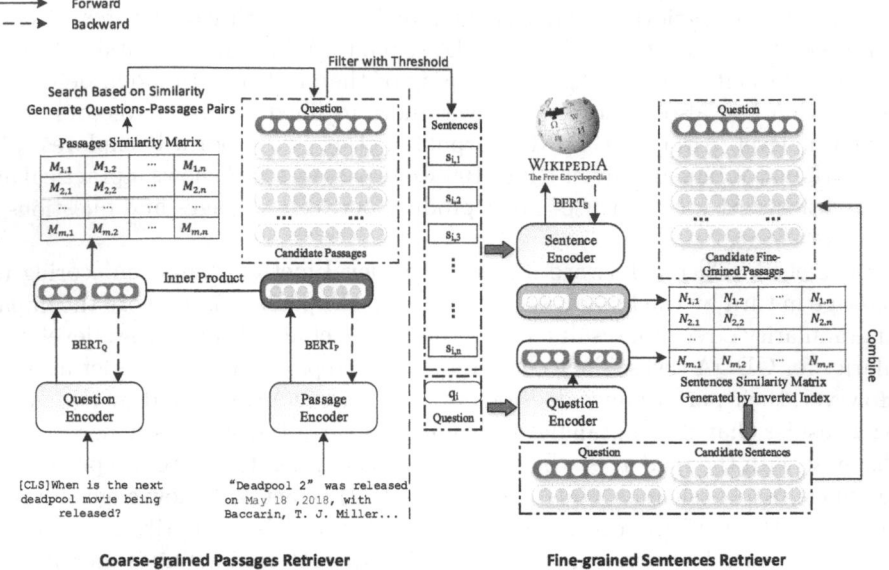

Fig. 1. The architecture of coarse-to-fine passages retriever.

strategy, we can extract candidate sentences $s \in p$ via their metrics (similarity) N_k and complete the selection from coarse-grained to fine-grained. Eventually, we organize the selected sentences into new passages according to the way the original passages are organized and feed them and the question to the reader. All the above processes can be referred to in Fig. 1.

3.2   Coarse-Grained Passages Retriever

Our coarse-grained passages retriever is designed to preferentially filter out the passages relevant to our question at the coarse-grained level. Before encoding passages, we should first ensure the encoders have strong discriminatory performance, i.e., similar passages have a similar presentation and mathematically exhibit smaller metrics. We create the candidate training pairs for each question and several passages $\mathcal{P} = \left\{ q_i, p_{i,1}^{+}, p_{i,2}^{-}, \cdots, p_{i,n}^{-} \right\}_{i=1}^{k}$. In $\mathcal{P}$, we own one question and one corresponding positive passage, and $n-1$ negative passages. During the retriever's training, the method of choosing negative samples determines the retriever's performance in generating highly discriminatory passage embedding. As Karpukhin et al. [9] proposed three different ways to pick up negative passages, we adopt that choosing other questions' golden passages from the same mini-batch as negatives and one highest BM25 passage which doesn't contain answers as hard negative passage. On the contrary, we choose one passage that contains answers with the highest BM25 scores as a positive sample. And BM25 can calculate as:

$$\text{BM25}(q_i, p_i) = \sum_{i=1}^{t} w_i * R(q_{i,j}, p_i) \tag{1}$$

$$w_i = \text{IDF}(q_{i,j}) = \log \frac{N - n(q_{i,j}) + 0.5}{n(q_{i,j}) + 0.5} \tag{2}$$

$$R(q_{i,j}, p_i) = \frac{f_{i,j} * (k + 1)}{f_{i,j} + k * (1 - b + b * \frac{dl}{avdl})} \tag{3}$$

where $q_{i,j}$ is split word in q_i. w_i is the weight of $q_{i,j}$. We use inverse document frequency(IDF) to express w_i in which N shows the size of all passages and $n(q_{i,j})$ denotes the number of passages containing the word $q_{i,j}$. $R(q_{i,j}, p_i)$ is the correlation between $q_{i,j}$ and p_i where $f_{i,j}$ is the frequency of word $q_{i,j}$'s occurrence in the passage p_i. Meanwhile, dl and $avgdl$ are the length of the passage p_i and the average length of all passages in the set $p \in R^d$, respectively. k and b are both hyperparameters.

For example, given question q_i and batch size B, we choose golden $p_{i,j}$ $(i \neq j)$ as negative. Furthermore, we utilize negative log likelihood to act as the loss function:

$$\ell_n = -\log \frac{e^{\text{sim}(q_i, p_i)}}{\sum_{j=1}^{b} e^{\text{sim}(q_i, p_{i,j})}} \tag{4}$$

After training, a mature bi-encoder E_P and E_Q can be used in our subsequent tasks of fine-grained filtering. We encode all passages and questions with the bi-encoder. Then we can calculate the similarity degree by Eq. (5) and organized it accordingly into a similarity matrix M_k. For each distance between question embedding and passage embedding generated by dot product, we regard it as passages' confidence scores corresponding to question and pick up top-k candidate passages for the finer retriever to erase noises irrelevant sentence bring us.

$$\text{Dist}_{\text{coarse}}(\boldsymbol{p}, \boldsymbol{q}) = E_P(\boldsymbol{p})^\top E_Q(\boldsymbol{q}) \tag{5}$$

3.3 Split Passages and Finer Encoder

Get Finer Sentences. When top-k passages are retrieved, we can analyze every passage and locate the sentences irrelevant to the question in the passage by our fine-grained sentences retriever. For the purpose of detecting finer features in the passage, we contribute a sentence-attention system inspired by Vaswani et al. [15].

In the sentence-attention mechanism, we first split the retrieved passage into several sentences according to punctuation like full stop and question marks. Therefore, assuming that a question corresponds to s sentences, then we will get the sentences' sample space $\mathcal{S} = \{q_i, s_{i,1}, s_{i,2}, \cdots, s_{i,n}\}_{i=1}^{s}$.

Contrastive Learning in Training Sentence Encoder. Contrastive learning is recently a popular self-supervised learning paradigm in both NLP and CV. On account of its excellent performance in maintaining the representative and discriminative embeddings, we decide to add it as the cornerstone of our sentence-attention mechanism. We suppose that x^+ are positive samples and x^- are negative samples. The contrastive learning's purpose is to make:

$$\text{score}(f(x), f(x^+)) >> \text{score}(f(x), f(x^-)) \tag{6}$$

The reason why we choose contrastive learning to train our E_S encoder is that our fine-grained sentences retriever should try to expose the sentences that are less relevant to our questions when we set the filtering threshold. If our encoder can distinguish the differences between sentences well in the above cases, it will be very beneficial to our filtering. And the above facts of our model fit the task definition of contrastive learning well.

The difficulty in contrastive learning is how to construct positive and negative pairs better. Following Gao et al. [6], their practices of producing positive examples by feeding input into Bert [5] twice with the help of its dropout function did successively work in building positive samples. In the meantime, we choose negative samples from all the left passages. Due to the large training data size, it is unrealistic to throw all negative samples into memory at one time. Following He et al. [7], we build a queue to store a positive sample and a negative sample as a dictionary for contrastive learning. Encoder E_S dynamically updates the queue so that all negative samples in the sample space can be learned by our encoder. We take InfoNCE which is used for self-supervised learning as our loss function of contrastive learning:

$$\ell_i = -\log \frac{e^{\text{sim}(x_i, x_i^+)/\tau}}{\sum_{j=1}^{N} e^{\text{sim}(x_i, x_j^+)/\tau}} \tag{7}$$

where τ is a temperature hyperparameter and $\text{sim}(x_i, x_i^+)$ is the similarity between x_i and x_i^+ calculated by cosine similarity.

3.4   Index Sentences and Search

With the encoder trained by the contrastive learning strategy, we can better turn the sentences into more discriminative dense representations. Because we split the passages into several pieces that lead to colossal search space, it consumes lots of time to search them. So we demonstrate two search strategies: to search violently, and another is to search via the inverted index and k-means to alleviate the pressure of retrieving.

Violent Search. Our first method of searching sentences is to search embeddings by utilizing violence retrieval. Following Sect. 3.2, we calculate the confidence scores between sentences and questions via inner products, as is shown as follows:

$$\text{Dist}_{\text{fine}}(s, q) = E_s(s)^\top E_Q(q) \tag{8}$$

Table 1. Example of inverted files

Word ID	Word	Inverted List(DocID)
000001	Website	0, 1, 4
000002	World	0, 1, 2, 3
000003	Singer	3, 4
000004	Eat	2, 4

Inverted Index. Our second method is searching through the inverted index. The inverted index is a mechanism which stores large amounts of data for us to search. It is used when the database is large and it saves time on searching. However, the inverted index may lose some accuracy in the search system but we think it's worth otherwise the search time is too long.

In our model, we use a record-level inverted index which contains a list of references to each word in the sentence. To build an inverted file, we should first remove useless stop words. Then we need to chop words and get their root word of them. At last, we should record document IDs and some additional information like word frequency, etc. Table 1 presents an example of inverted files.

Search by K-means. After getting the inverted files, we can use k-means to establish the cluster centers for searching to improve search efficiency. The training step of the k-means algorithm is as follows. First, we need to select the initial k sentences as the initial clustering centers $a_1, a_2, \cdots a_k$. For each sample s_i in the dataset, the distance from it to k cluster centers is calculated. Then we divide s_i into the class corresponding to the cluster center with the smallest distance. For each category a_j, its cluster center (Eq. (9)) is calculated repeatedly until convergence. c_i represents the closest class of sample s_i among the k classes. And the loss function can be designed as Eq. (10) and Eq. (11).

$$a_j = \frac{1}{|c_i|} \sum_{s_i \in c_i} s_i \tag{9}$$

$$\ell_k = \sum_{i=1}^{N} \sum_{j=1}^{K} r_{ij} \cdot \nu(s_i, a_j) \tag{10}$$

$$\nu(s_i, a_j) = \|s_i - a_j\|^2, \quad r_{ij} = \begin{cases} 1 & \text{if } s_i \in j \\ 0 & \text{otherwise} \end{cases} \tag{11}$$

After building the index and searching out our desired sentences, we get the similarity matrix N_k. For our sentence-attention system, we assume that low similarity sentences with question only bring the reader noises. With N_k, we organize these sentences into new passages according to the organization of the original passages and feed them into reader at last.

4 Experiment

4.1 Corpus and Evaluation Metrics

Following Karpukhin et al. [9], we use their English Wikipedia corpus, which contains 21,015,324 passages and each one is a 100-word text block as our source knowledge base. The disk memory occupied by the original Wikipedia dataset can be up to 13.7 GB. Giving thought to calculation speed, we finally decided to reduce the original dataset to remove the content not related to our QA dataset. We create a new Wikipedia subset containing passages paired with questions on the Natural Question dataset. The cropped dataset only takes up 1.06 GB in memory and has 78,050 unique articles, which has 1,642,855 unique passages, significantly reducing the resources we need for calculation. Our Wikipedia subset also keeps the article's title and other information the same as the source dataset. We use the whole Wikipedia as our training dataset of E_S and the Wikipedia subset as our model's knowledge base.

For the QA dataset, we mainly use Natural Questions (NQ) [10] dataset as our train/dev/test corpus. NQ's questions come from the valid questions of google search, and humans annotate answer spans according to real Wikipedia articles. Since the NQ dataset contains more QA pairs and its answers are marked by Wikipedia, our subsequent work is performed on it. We use the simplified version of NQ, which contains 79,168 training samples and only occupies the disk usage of 4 GB.

Researchers typically use F1 measure and Exact Match (EM) as their automatic evaluation Metrics in open-domain question answering. But in our model, compared to F1, EM can accurately evaluate whether our final result is correct or not. So we only take up the strictest evaluation metric Exact Match (EM) as the primary evaluation method. For each question and answer pair, if the model's prediction's answer span exactly matches the true answer, EM equals 1, otherwise equals 0. The description of EM is as follows:

$$\text{EM} = \frac{\text{Number of examples with exact answer match}}{\text{Total number of examples}} \tag{12}$$

4.2 Experimental Settings

During the training period of E_Q and E_P, we train the encoder Bert-base with 30 epochs and the batch size is 8. We also use Adam as our optimizer. The initial learning rate is set to $1e-5$ using linear scheduling with the warm-up.

While training encoder E_S with contrastive learning, we still use Bert-base as our encoder with a batch size of 8 and set the learning rate as $3e-5$. When constructing positive samples with dropout, we set the dropout rate as 0.1 and set the temperature hyperparameter τ to 0.05.

We use a fine-tuned Bert-base trained by our questions and fine-grained passages for the reader. Answer spans are extracted from every passage and get the final answer from one of the answer spans with the highest score. We set the batch size to 8, with the reader's learning rate of $1e-5$. In conclusion, we use two 24 GB NVIDIA GeForce RTX 3090 to train the above model.

Table 2. Performance comparison on the Wikipedia subset database and simplified NQ dataset. DPR_{single} and DPR_{multi} are the same model but pre-trained on single NQ and multi dataset including NQ, TriviaQA and WebQuestions, respectively.

Model	EM
DrQA	26.2
DPR_{single}	33.2
DPR_{multi}	33.7
CFSR	**45.4**

Table 3. Different filtering threshold and top-k in influencing the results of EM.

Top-k	Top-20					Top-100				
Threshold	0	0.2	0.4	0.6	0.8	0	0.2	0.4	0.6	0.8
EM	31.6	39.2	41.8	**42.9**	42.1	33.7	40.1	44.8	45.1	**45.4**

4.3 Experimental Results

In this study, we make a comparison of our CFPR model with the following competitive models:

- **DrQA:** an open domain question answering system proposed by Chen et al. [1]. It first parses the document into a bigram word bag and then converts it into a TF-IDF vector. Then the vectors of all documents are splieced together to be a matrix. After the dot product between the question vector and the sparse matrix of the articles, it finally retrieves the most similar k articles.
- **Baseline:** designed by Karpukhin et al. [9], DPR is the most exceedingly respected one which uses dense embedding for retrieval. DPR follows the retriever-reader framework in ODQA, which uses a simple vector inner product for retrieval but is effective. It has made marvellous achievements whose performance exceeded most models at that time.

The whole Wikipedia dataset could be unsustainable. We all use the Wikipedia subset as our knowledge base and simplified Natural Questions as our QA dataset for fair comparisons. And for encoder E_Q, E_P, E_S, we all use Bert-base as our encoder source. We note that for all experimental results under different conditions, we take the maximum value as the result for the comparative experiments, and the result is shown in Table 2.

4.4 Impact of Threshold

To find out how different fine-grained filtering thresholds influence our performance, for CFPR, we studied the EM predicted by the model according to filtering thresholds and top-k passages we used to feed into the fine-grained sentences retriever.

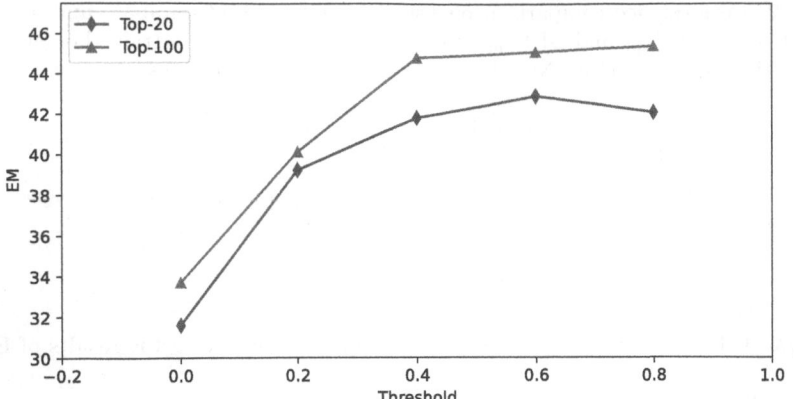

Fig. 2. Line chart that indicates the impact of different thresholds on our final EM with two different top-k passages.

As is shown in Table 3 and Fig. 2, with the same threshold, the more passages we retrieve, the higher EM we will get. For top-20 passages retrieved from the knowledge base, the EM value gradually increased as the threshold gradually increased and reached the vertex when the threshold got 0.6. However, we attempted to increase the threshold to 0.8, the results dropped to 42.1. In the case of top-100 retrieved passages, we can word that our EM value increases with the increase of the threshold. Unlike Top-20 passages, its outcome did not reach a local maximum value when the threshold is at a certain point.

This result suggests that our model is more likely to hit the answer with more passages selected. Performance does not degrade significantly with higher thresholds because the context information is still abundant for the model to detect. Besides, when we retrieve fewer passages, with the threshold of filtering gradually increasing, although a lot of irrelevant noise information is effectively taken away, the model will lose some context information in the circumstance of fewer sentences, resulting in a slight decline in our results after reaching a certain edge.

4.5   Ablation Study

To explore whether the coarse-to-fine filtering plays a decisive role in improving our model, we did ablation experiments on the Wikipedia subset and simplified Natural Questions dataset. Because the embedding learned by contrastive learning can show better uniqueness in the whole sample space, we replace the encoder E_S trained by contrastive learning in CFPR with the encoder of Bert-base without fine-tuning and E_P previously used in coarse-grained passages retriever, respectively. These results are under the same conditions of top-100 passages retrieved by coarse-grained passages retriever and the same datasets.

Table 4. Evaluate different E_s and threshold in influencing our model with the same top-100 passages. Bert$_{base}$ is Bert-base without fine-tune and Bert$_P$ is our E_p trained in coarse-grained passages retriever.

Model	Bert$_{base}$				Bert$_P$				Ours			
Threshold	0.2	0.4	0.6	0.8	0.2	0.4	0.6	0.8	0.2	0.4	0.6	0.8
EM	37.3	39.2	39.9	40.8	**40.6**	42.2	42.7	44.1	40.1	**44.8**	**45.1**	**45.4**

Table 5. A case when the same question is proposed, the difference between predictions in baseline model and our CFPR.

Question	"who won season 13 of hell's kitchen"	
Golden answers	"La Tasha McCutchen"	
Model	Baseline	Ours
Predicted answer	"jean - philippe susilovic"	"la tasha mccutchen"
Passages	"...however, jean - philippe susilovic did not return..."	"kitchen supervisor la tasha mccutchen from..."

The results are summarized in Table 4. We can notice that when the threshold is as low as 0.2, the performance of E_P is better than E_S. Considering why this surprising event may happen, we assume that when the threshold is low, the filtered passages are still close to the original passages, so the effect of contrastive learning is not apparent.

But when we take a look at the complete experimental results, we can discover that even the worst outcome of an untrained Bert-base as our E_S is better than our baseline model. These results also prove the effectiveness of our method, which takes multi-granularity retrieval.

5   Case Study

As is made clear in Table 5, our CFPR successfully predicted the correct answer, but our baseline model predicted the wrong one. After noticing this phenomenon, we check the passages retrieved by the above two models and discover that our model has already filtered out the wrong sentence predicted by the baseline model.

6   Conclusion

In this paper, we propose CFPR, a coarse-to-fine retrieval model. In the design of our model, we have added multi-granular filtering of passages to make the passages we feed into the reader highly relevant to the questions. Our model successfully filters out noise-generating sentences that are counterproductive to our model's predictions and retains sentences with a high probability of containing an answer. Moreover, evaluation results indicate that our model can significantly improve the performance of retriever in open-domain question answering compared to previous works.

Acknowledgments. We would like to thank the reviewers's helpful comments. At the same time, we remain gratitude to Jingren Liu for his valuable comments on our work. This work was supported by Projects 61876118 under the National Natural Science Foundation of China, the National Key R&D Program of China under Grant No. 2020AAA0108600 and the Priority Academic Program Development of Jiangsu Higher Education Institutions.

References

1. Chen, D., Fisch, A., Weston, J., Bordes, A.: Reading Wikipedia to answer open-domain questions. arXiv preprint arXiv:1704.00051 (2017)
2. Chen, T., Kornblith, S., Norouzi, M., Hinton, G.: A simple framework for contrastive learning of visual representations. In: International Conference on Machine Learning, pp. 1597–1607. PMLR (2020)
3. Clark, C., Gardner, M.: Simple and effective multi-paragraph reading comprehension. arXiv preprint arXiv:1710.10723 (2017)
4. Das, R., Dhuliawala, S., Zaheer, M., McCallum, A.: Multi-step retriever-reader interaction for scalable open-domain question answering. arXiv preprint arXiv:1905.05733 (2019)
5. Devlin, J., Chang, M.W., Lee, K., Toutanova, K.: Bert: pre-training of deep bidirectional transformers for language understanding. arXiv preprint arXiv:1810.04805 (2018)
6. Gao, T., Yao, X., Chen, D.: SimCSE: simple contrastive learning of sentence embeddings. In: Empirical Methods in Natural Language Processing (EMNLP) (2021)
7. He, K., Fan, H., Wu, Y., Xie, S., Girshick, R.: Momentum contrast for unsupervised visual representation learning. In: Proceedings of the IEEE/CVF Conference on Computer Vision and Pattern Recognition, pp. 9729–9738 (2020)
8. Htut, P.M., Bowman, S.R., Cho, K.: Training a ranking function for open-domain question answering. arXiv preprint arXiv:1804.04264 (2018)
9. Karpukhin, V., et al.: Dense passage retrieval for open-domain question answering. arXiv preprint arXiv:2004.04906 (2020)
10. Kwiatkowski, T., et al.: Natural questions: a benchmark for question answering research. Trans. Assoc. Comput. Linguist. **7**, 453–466 (2019)
11. Lee, J., Sung, M., Kang, J., Chen, D.: Learning dense representations of phrases at scale. In: Proceedings of the 59th Annual Meeting of the Association for Computational Linguistics and the 11th International Joint Conference on Natural Language Processing (Volume 1: Long Papers) (2021)
12. Lee, J., Sung, M., Kang, J., Chen, D.: Learning dense representations of phrases at scale. arXiv preprint arXiv:2012.12624 (2020)
13. Lee, J., Wettig, A., Chen, D.: Phrase retrieval learns passage retrieval, too. arXiv preprint arXiv:2109.08133 (2021)
14. Roberts, A., Raffel, C., Shazeer, N.: How much knowledge can you pack into the parameters of a language model? arXiv preprint arXiv:2002.08910 (2020)
15. Vaswani, A., et al.: Attention is all you need. In: Advances in Neural Information Processing Systems, vol. 30 (2017)
16. Voorhees, E.M., et al.: The TREC-8 question answering track report. In: TREC, vol. 99, pp. 77–82 (1999)
17. Yang, W., et al.: End-to-end open-domain question answering with Bertserini. arXiv preprint arXiv:1902.01718 (2019)

LoCSGN: Logic-Contrast Semantic Graph Network for Machine Reading Comprehension

Xi Zhao[1], Tingrui Zhang[1], Yuxiao Lu[2], and Guiquan Liu[1(✉)]

[1] School of Computer Science and Technology, University of Science and Technology of China, Hefei, China
{xixilili,zhangtingrui}@mail.ustc.edu.cn, gqliu@ustc.edu.cn
[2] Department of Computer Science, University of California, Los Angeles, USA
legendarybruin@g.ucla.edu

Abstract. Logical reasoning plays a very important role in Natural Language Understanding. In recent years, research on logical reasoning has shown a booming trend. Previous works either construct graphs to perform implicit reasoning or augment labeled training data with consistent symbol logical rules. In this paper, we combine the advantages of both graph based implicit reasoning and symbolic logic based consistent transformation in a deep learning framework. In order to make full use of the semantic and logical structures in text, we exploit Abstract Meaning Representation (AMR) to help logical reasoning, which can explicitly provide core semantic knowledge and logical structures. Based on AMR graph extracted, we design two tasks: 1) Construct joint graph and strengthen the interaction between context and option subgraph to predict right choice. 2) Leverage symbolic rules to construct logical consistent and inconsistent graphs to let model identify and differentiate logical structures in different graphs by contrastive learning. Experiments are conducted on two logical reasoning datasets: Reclor and LogiQA. And our method has a significant improvement over the baselines and most previous methods.

Keywords: Machine reading comprehension · Logic reasoning · Contrastive learning

1 Introduction

In recent years, various datasets and tasks have been proposed in Machine Reading Comprehension (MRC), such as SQuAD [20], HotpotQA [26]. The previous studies in MRC mainly focused on making better use of word meaning, while rarely considered injecting logical information into models. In recent years, research on logical reasoning has shown a booming trend that many tasks and datasets have been proposed, such as LogiQA [16], Reclor [27].

A typical example is shown on Fig. 1. In this example, context describes a flaw logical structure like $(p1 \rightarrow p3) \wedge (p2 \rightarrow p3) \Rightarrow p1 \rightarrow p2$, and the question asks

W. Lu et al. (Eds.): NLPCC 2022, LNAI 13551, pp. 405–417, 2022.
https://doi.org/10.1007/978-3-031-17120-8_32

Context: If (p1) you study history, then (p3) you will appreciate the vast differences among past civilizations, and (p3) you will appreciate these differences provided that (p2) you reflect on your own civilization. Hence , (p1) if you study history (p2) you will reflect on your own civilization.

Question: Which one of the following is most closely parallel in its flawed reasoning to the flawed reasoning in the argument above?

Options:

A. One can become informed about the world provided that one reads the newspaper daily. If one is informed about the world, then one has an appreciation of other cultures. So if one reads the newspaper daily, then one can come to appreciate other cultures.

B. If (q1) you learn Latin, (q3) you can improve your vocabulary, and (q3) you can improve your vocabulary if (q2) you study great works of literature. So (q2) you will study great works of literature if (q1) you learn Latin.

C. Traveling to other countries deepens one's appreciation for their cultures, and this appreciation often encourages one to study the history of those lands. So the study of history increases one's desire to travel.

D. By studying ancient art you begin to appreciate how much was accomplished with limited materials. Appreciation of ancient art leads to a deeper understanding of modem art. Ttherefore, studying ancient art can engender a profound new appreciation for modem art.

Fig. 1. One example in Reclor.

to choose an option with the same flaw logical structure. This requires models to identify multiple logical structures and effectively compare the differences between logical structures.

Some recent works mainly conduct from two directions. Some works [8, 19] construct event-level graph and perform implicit reasoning. Despite their good performance, these methods suffer from several major problems: 1) Due to the constraints of event graph, it is hard to provide a fine-grained view of logical structure which can benefit complex logic reasoning. It also suffers from low accuracy in graph construction. 2) Since only implicit reasoning is performed, it is debatable whether the model can really leverage logical rules to reason. Then, others [23, 24] inject logical rules knowledge into model by leveraging consistent transformation on logical structure to perform data augmentation. These methods can make good use of logical rules, but they can't learn logical structures specifically and are limited to only using contraposition and transitive rules. To take advantage of both rich semantic and logical structure, we explore the usefulness of Abstract Meaning Representation (AMR) [4]. AMR is a semantic formalism that represents meaning of a sentence into a rooted directed graph. Unlike syntactic traits, AMR is a high-level semantic abstraction, that is, different sentences with similar semantics may share the same AMR results. In this paper, we propose LoCSGN, a new approach to solving logical reasoning MRC task which consists of three parts: (1) Parse and align sentences into AMR graphs, then a joint graph of context, question and option is constructed. (2) Leverage a pre-trained models and a Graph Neural Network (GNN) to encode text and graph. (3) Generate logical consistent and inconsistent graphs and let model learn the logical structures by contrastive learning. The main contributions of our work are summarized as follows:

1. We propose an AMR-based joint logical graph which can better integrate semantic and logical structure for Machine Reading Comprehension.
2. We successfully utilize logical rules to construct logical consistent and inconsistent graphs to make model learn the logical structures by contrastive learning.
3. We show the effectiveness of our method by significant improvements on two datasets, Reclor and LogiQA.

2 Related Work

AMR. AMR is a linguistic framework representing the meaning of a sentence as a single-source directed acyclic graph. In recent years, AMR is attracting more attention in academia. Recent advances in AMR parsing [3,5,12,28] and aligning [1,6,17] keep pushing the boundary of performance and have made it possible to benefit downstream tasks. Some works [15,22] leverage the rich semantics of AMR to do transformation from original AMR graphs to target AMR graphs, both translation and summary generation can benefit from such graph transformation. Some works [11,14] integrate AMR graphs with external knowledge source, and leverage entity node of AMR to accurately implement entity linking and graph fusing in commonsense reasoning and question answering. Others [2,25] utilize co-reference and co-occurrence to combine small AMR graphs of multiple short sentences into a large graph, then apply it to do specific tasks like multi-hop question answering and dialogue modeling.

Logical Reasoning in MRC. There have been many works on logical reasoning for MRC recently. DAGN [8] and Focal Reasoner [19] construct graphs where edges are discourse relations and nodes are elementary discourse units. Then they employ GNN to conduct implicit reasoning on such graphs. LReasoner [24] proposes a logical data augmentation framework. It leverages logical rules to transform options and constructs logical consistent data to expand option set. Merit [10] proposes a meta-path guided contrastive learning method to perform self-supervised pre-training. AdaLoGN [13] adaptively infers logical relations to extend event graph and realizes mutual and iterative reinforcement between neural and symbolic reasoning. However, different from previous works, we take advantage of both rich semantic and logical structure of AMR, and compare logical structures on logical consistent and inconsistent graphs.

3 Method

3.1 Joint Graph Construction

AMR Graph. An AMR graph can be denoted as $\mathcal{G} = \langle \mathcal{V}_\mathcal{G}, \mathcal{E}_\mathcal{G} \rangle$. The vertex set $\mathcal{V}_\mathcal{G} \in \mathcal{V}_\mathcal{P} \cup \mathcal{V}_\mathcal{C}$ where $\mathcal{V}_\mathcal{P}$ is a set of propbank predicates and $\mathcal{V}_\mathcal{C}$ is the rest of nodes named as concept. The edge set $\mathcal{E}_\mathcal{G}$ consists of core roles (such as ARG0, ARG1,

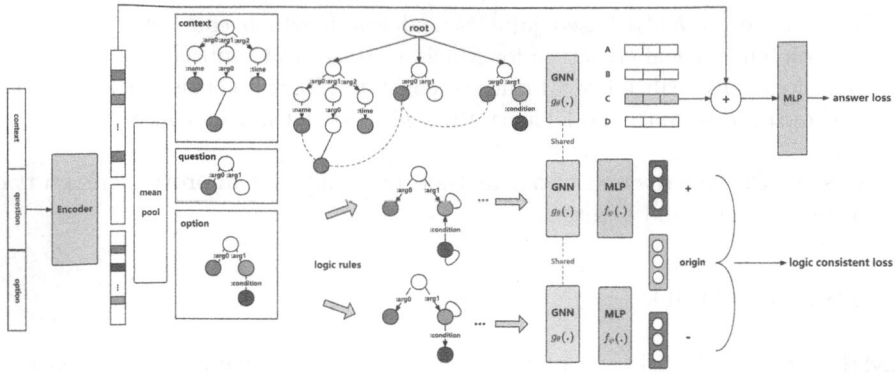

Fig. 2. The overall architecture of LoCSGN.

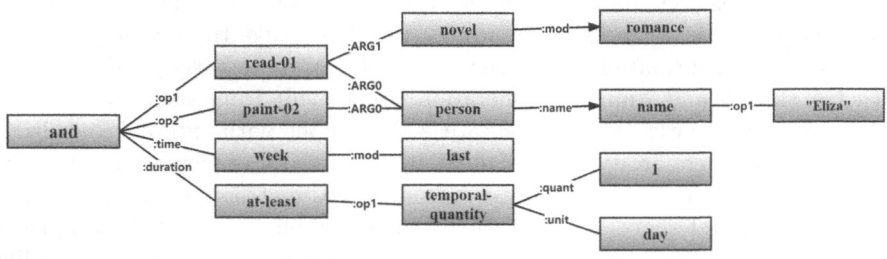

Fig. 3. An AMR graph example.

etc.), non-core roles (such as time, location), logics (such as condition, polarity, etc.), modifiers (mod) and etc. Figure 3 shows an AMR graph example for sentence "There was at least one day last week when Eliza read romance novels and painted". In this graph, person and temporal-quantity are two entity node. Predicates read-01 and paint-02 share the same subject connected by ARG0.

Graph Modifications. To adapt AMR graph to MRC scene, we make some modifications on AMR graph. We first adopt simplification to make model focus on core nodes and connections during graph encoding. We fuse entity nodes into one node, such as person, organization, location, etc. Besides, we recognize and fuse noun phrases subgraph with a part-of-speech parser. For edges, we drop failed identified edges and rarely appeared edges less than 5%. Moreover, since AMR parsing focuses on single sentence. In order to ensure parsing accuracy, we segment context, question and options into sentences and generate AMR graphs for each single sentence. After that, we use the co-occurrences or co-references extracted by neuralcoref[1] to fuse sentence subgraphs.

---

[1] https://github.com/huggingface/neuralcoref.

Graph Interaction. The interactive information among context, question and option plays a key role in MRC. We enhance such interaction during construction of the joint graph. First, a global root node is added as a necessary interaction for some cases without neither the co-occurrence and co-reference among context, question and option. Then, we identify and connect the same entity nodes. Besides, we also add interaction to graph training process, which is detailed in Sect. (3.2).

3.2 Encoder

Context Encoder. Roberta [18] is used as context encoder. Pre-trained model can capture rich contextual semantics of words. We use it to encode input tokens"<s> C </s> Q || O </s>", in which C, Q, O represent context, question and option tokens. We feed the tokens into Roberta to obtain encoded sequence and use it to initialize the node representation of AMR graph.

Graph Encoder. Since the joint AMR graph is a heterogeneous graph containing multiple types of edges, We leverage Graph Convolutional Network (R-GCN) [21] as a mechanism for message passing and aggregating on graphs. R-GCN is proposed to deal with knowledge bases with highly multi-relational data characteristics. At l-th layer, given the hidden state $h_i^l \in \mathbb{R}^d$ of node i in joint AMR graph, the hidden state in the next layer can be calculated via:

$$h_i^{(l+1)} = \sigma \left(\sum_{r \in R} \sum_{j \in N_i^r} \frac{1}{c_{i,r}} W_r^{(l)} h_j^{(l)} + W_0^{(l)} h_i^{(l)} \right) \tag{1}$$

where N_i^r denotes the set of neighbors indices of node i under relation $r \in R$. $W_r^{(l)} \in \mathbb{R}^{d \times d}$ stands a relation-specific weight matrix and $W_0^{(l)} \in \mathbb{R}^{d \times d}$ stands a weight for node i. $c_{i,r}$ stands a normalization constant and is assigned the value $|N_i^r|$. In addition, in order to alleviate insufficient interaction between context and option, we calculated bi-attention interaction between context and option after R-GCN. From human reading's perspective, this design also simulates the process of reading, reasoning and then rereading on refined structure.

$$S_{i,j} = tanh(linear(h_{o_i}, h_{c_j}))$$
$$[\alpha_{i,1}, \alpha_{i,2}..., \alpha_{i,|V_c|}] = softmax(S_{i.})$$
$$A_{h_{o_i}, H_c} = \sum_{h_{c_j} \in H_c} \alpha_{i,j} h_{c_j} \tag{2}$$

where $h_{o_i} \in \mathbb{R}^d$ and $h_{c_j} \in \mathbb{R}^d$ are context and option node representation and $H_c \in \mathbb{R}^{|V_c| \times d}$ is context graph representation. Then we add attended representation $A_{h_{o_i}, H_c}$ to the updated node representation h_{o_i}.

3.3 Logic-Consistency Graph Generation

A well-constructed AMR joint graph can help model make good use of the semantic and logical structures in the text, we then apply constraints to strengthen model's ability to perceive logical structures and reason through logical rules. To achieve this, we define some logical transformations, which can generate logical consistent and inconsistent graphs from original AMR graph according to logical rules. Inspired by [9], we categorize logic transformations into the following categories: categorical reasoning, conditional reasoning, disjunctive reasoning, conjunctive reasoning, transitive reasoning. A complete set of the logic transformations are shown in Table 1.

Table 1. Logical transformations. **Ca** indicates categorical relation while **S** and **N** indicate sufficient and necessary relations. And **All** denotes all the 3 relations.

Reason type		Ori sample	Pos sample	Neg sample
Single logic	Categorical	$\forall A, f(A)$	$\neg \exists A, \neg f(A)$	$\exists A, \neg f(A)$
	Sufficient	$A \xrightarrow{if} B$	$\neg B \to \neg A$	$\neg A \to \neg B$
	Necessary	$A \xrightarrow{only\ if} B$	$\neg A \to \neg B$	$A \to B$
Multi logic	Disjunctive	$(A \vee B) \xrightarrow{S} C$	$A \to C, B \to C$	$\neg A \to \neg C$
	Conjunctive	$(A \wedge B) \xrightarrow{N} C$	$\neg A \to \neg C$	$A \to C, B \to C$
	Transitive	$(A \xrightarrow{All} B) \wedge (B \xrightarrow{All} C)$	$A \to C$	$\neg A \to \neg C$

Categorical Reasoning. First, we use logical consistent transformation in categorical reasoning, and the goal of which is to reason whether a specific concept belongs to a particular category. Due to the complexity of identifying entailment, such as "cat $\subseteq$ animal", we only employ categorical reasoning on quantifiers such as all, both, etc.

$$(\forall A, f(A)) \Leftrightarrow (\neg \exists A, \neg f(A)) \tag{3}$$

Conditional Reasoning. Sufficient and necessary reasoning are based on conditional statements. For example, "if P, then Q" can be expressed as $P \to Q$, "unless P, then Q" can be expressed as $\neg P \to \neg Q$, and "only if P, then Q" can be expressed as $Q \to P$. Based on these relations identified on AMR graph, we adopt contraposition rule to construct logical consistent graph.

$$(A \to B) \Leftrightarrow (\neg A \to \neg C) \tag{4}$$

Multi Logic Reasoning. Based on the extracted categorical and conditional relations, we apply logical rules among multiple logical relations. Due to the complexity of text containing multiple logical relations, we only apply some common rules to ensure the correctness of our logical transformations. For example, in Table 1, when sufficient condition relations are extracted, we will judge whether disjunctive or transitive structures exists among these relations by the former and the latter of each condition relation. And for multiple categorical relations, we will only identify transitive structure such as "all A are B, and all B are C".

Logic Identification. We design a logic extractor to traverse on graph to identify conditional and categorical relations and their multiple logical structures. For logical relations, conditional relations can be identified by condition edge. And sufficient and necessary can be judged according to whether the condition relation contains the modifier "only". For instance, "only if A, then B" can be identified by "node $B \xrightarrow{:condition}$ node $A \xrightarrow{:mod}$ only". For categorical relations, we design a predefined set of quantifiers {all, any, both} to find universal quantifier and identify by "predicate node $f \xrightarrow{:ARG0}$ concept node $A \xrightarrow{:mod}$ universal quantifier". After all logical relations are identified, logic extractor then judges disjunctive, conjunctive and transitive structures among multiple relations of the same type by the former and latter node or subgraph of each relations.

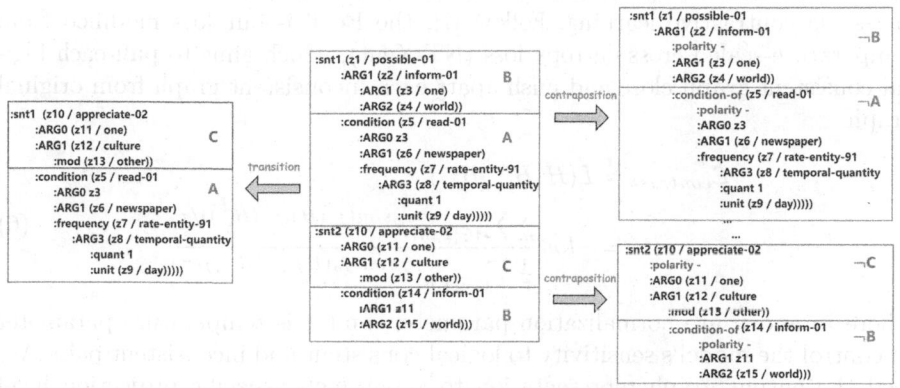

Fig. 4. Logical consistent transformation (shown in PENMAN format) for "One can become informed about the world provided that one reads the newspaper daily. If one is informed about the world, then one has an appreciation of other cultures". ":polarity -" denotes the added negation edge, and ":condition-of" denotes the reversed condition edge.

Logic Transformation. For the identified single logic relations and multi-logic structures, we apply corresponding logic transformations to generate logic consistent and inconsistent graphs. Specifically, there are several operations on graph: adding self-loop edge with relation "negation", adding or modifying other edges, adding or deleting nodes and subgraphs, etc. For example, in Fig. 4, The logical extractor identifies sufficient and transitive structure. For sufficient structure, it adds negation self-loop edge and reverses condition edge. For transitive structure, it deletes subgraph B and adds condition edge between A and C. Notably, for disjunctive and conjunctive structure, we separate their "op" edges that connect each item into "op-and", "op-or" to ensure model can distinguish them. After transformation, we can obtain two sets of graphs : logical consistent graphs $\mathcal{G}_+$ and logical inconsistent graphs $\mathcal{G}_-$. Then, we leverage R-GCN to encode the graphs. In our setting, the transformation graph encoder and joint graph encoder share parameters.

$$[H_{+,1}, H_{+,2}, ..., H_{+,m}] = F_{2-layer}(\mathcal{G}_+)$$
$$[H_{-,1}, H_{-,2}, ..., H_{-,n}] = F_{2-layer}(\mathcal{G}_-)$$
(5)

where $+$ and $-$ are logical consistent and inconsistent label, m and n are the lengths of logical consistent and inconsistent graph set.

Logic Contrastive Learning. In our work, logical comparison is conducted as an auxiliary task only on option graph. Given original option's graph representation H and its logic consistent and inconsistent representation sets H^+, H^- updated by R-GCN, we strengthen the model's ability to learn logical differences via contrastive learning. Follow [7], the Eq. 6 is our loss modified from temperature-scaled cross entropy loss (NT-Xent), which aims to pull each logical consistent graph close and push apart each inconsistent graph from original graph.

$$\mathcal{L}_{contrast} = L(H, H^+, H^-)$$
$$= -log \frac{\frac{1}{m} \sum_{i \in [1,m]} e^{sim(f_o(H), f_+(H_i^+))/\tau}}{\frac{1}{n} \sum_{j \in [1,n]} e^{sim(f_o(H), f_-(H_j^-))/\tau}}$$
(6)

where m and n are normalization parameter, and τ is temperature parameter to control the model's sensitivity to logical consistent and inconsistent pairs. We feed the output graph representation to a parameter-specific projection head $f_{\{o|+|-\}}(\cdot)$, which is a non-linear transformation composed of MLP and maps different graph representation to another latent space. Then, function $sim(\cdot)$ measures the similarity between original graph and logical consistent or inconsistent graphs. We adopt pairwise distance for this similarity function.

3.4   Answer Prediction

The goal of answer prediction module is to output the correct one of the four options. Given four joint graph encodings of four options H_{joint} updated by R-GCN and text encodings H_{text}. We add all graph nodes to the aligned position of their origin text encoding vector. Then, a linear layer is applied for final prediction.

$$\hat{y} = ReLU(linear(H_{joint} + H_{text}))$$
$$\mathcal{L}_{ans} = CrossEntropy(\hat{y}, y)$$
(7)

During training, the overall loss for is:

$$\mathcal{L} = \alpha \mathcal{L}_{ans} + (1 - \alpha)\mathcal{L}_{contrast}$$
(8)

where α is a hyperparameter.

4 Experiments

4.1 Dataset

Our experiments and analysis are carried on two datasets, and both of them are multi-choice MRC requiring logical reasoning ability. Reclor is a dataset from standardized law tests. It contains 6138 questions. The authors divided the test set into easy and hard categories with 24 logical reasoning types. LogiQA is a dataset from National Civil Servants Examinations of China, which is translated into English by experts. It contains 8678 questions.

4.2 Implementation Details

For our model, we adopt advanced AMR parser [5] and aligner [6] to get AMR graph. Then, we adopt Roberta-large and Deberta-xlarge as baselines. We choose Adamw as optimizer with initial learning rate in {1e−5, 2e−5, 3e−5}, warm-up of 0.1 and weight decay of 0.01. The batch size we set is in {16, 24, 32} by setting gradient accumulation, and maximum number of epochs is 10. The hyperparameter α is in {0.3, 0.5, 0.7}. The maximum input length is set to 256 for both Reclor and LogiQA. All the experiments above are conducted on Tesla V100 with 32 GB.

Table 2. Final results on Reclor and LogiQA.

Model/dataset	ReClor				LogiQA	
	Dev	Test	Test-E	Test-H	Dev	Test
RoBERTa	62.6	55.6	75.5	40.0	35.0	35.3
DAGN	65.2	58.2	76.1	44.1	35.5	38.7
LReasoner(Roberta)	66.2	62.4	**81.4**	47.5	38.1	40.6
AdaLoGN(Roberta)	65.2	60.2	79.3	45.1	39.9	40.7
Focal Reasoner	66.8	58.9	77.1	44.6	**41.0**	40.3
MERIT(Roberta)	66.8	59.6	78.1	45.2	40.0	38.9
LoCSGN(Roberta)	**68.2**	**62.6**	78.9	**49.8**	39.8	**42.2**
Deberta	76.2	71.0	82.6	60.2	–	–
MERIT(Deberta)	78.0	73.1	**86.2**	**64.4**	–	–
LoCSGN(Deberta)	**78.6**	**73.2**	84.8	64.1	–	–

4.3 Main Results

Table 2 shows the results of Reclor and LogiQA. The evaluation metric is accuracy. From the results, we can see: 1) Our model outperforms previous models on both Roberta and Deberta. 2) The improvement of our model on hard-type questions is very significant, which indicates that our model can effectively perform logical reasoning. 3) the results on Deberta (DeBERTa-v2-xxlarge) validate our method can benefit stronger pre-trained models with significant improvements.

We also measure the performance on multiple reasoning types. As shown in Fig. 5, our model outperforms baselines on almost all reasoning types except evaluation. By analyzing the data, we guess that it may be a reasoning trap that pre-trained model tends to find answer by semantic matching, which is just shortcut for models. Notably, our model has achieved more than ten points improvement on *Most Strongly Supported*, *Match the Structure*, which can prove the superiority of our method in logical comparison.

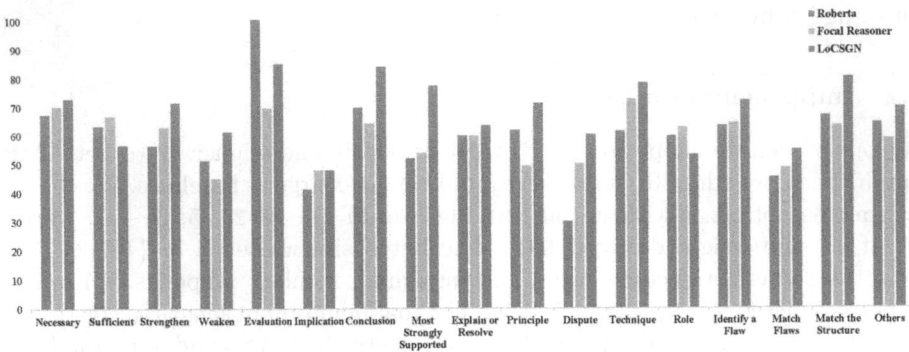

Fig. 5. Results on different reasoning types.

Table 3. Ablation results on Reclor.

Model	Val	Test	Test-E	Test-H
LoCSGN	**68.2**	**62.6**	78.9	**49.8**
Ablation on joint graph				
- coref edge	63.8	60.8	78.9	49.8
- root node	64.2	60.5	77.0	47.5
Ablation on logical contrast				
- logical contrast	65.0	61.0	78.2	47.5
- conditional rule	66.8	61.7	78.9	48.1
- categorical rule	67.1	61.8	**79.1**	48.2
Ablation on graph encoding				
- interaction enhancement	67.3	61.0	78.2	47.5

4.4   Ablation Study

Table 3 shows the results of our ablation studies. We mainly conduct the ablation study to evaluate the effectiveness of the two main technical contributions in our approach: joint AMR construct and logical graph contrast. It can be seen that both of two modules have achieved significant improvements. We can see that the necessary connections in the joint graph and logical contrast are very important. Besides, interaction plays a significant role in our model.

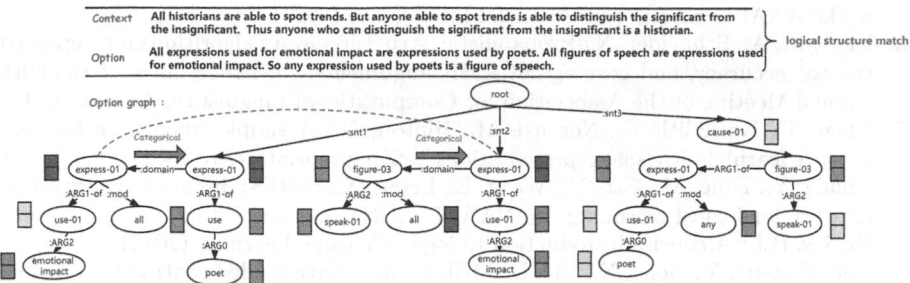

Fig. 6. An case of reasoning process of LoCSGN on option, which contains transitive categorical structure.

4.5 Interpretability: A Case

We apply perturbation-based post hoc techniques to interpret LoCSGN's reasoning process. Specifically, we mask the nodes and connected edges at the input to observe the output's changes, and result is shown in Fig. 6. It can be seen that our model has a high focus on the main logical relations and structures.

5 Conclusion

In this work, we propose a novel method named LoCSGN for logical reasoning in machine reading comprehension. We explore to leverage AMR to uncover semantic and logical structures. Then, we construct logical consistent and inconsistent graphs by logical rules and let model learn the differences of logical graphs structure by contrastive learning. The experimental results verify the effectiveness of our method.

References

1. Anchiêta, R., Pardo, T.: Semantically inspired AMR alignment for the Portuguese language. In: Proceedings of the 2020 Conference on Empirical Methods in Natural Language Processing (EMNLP), pp. 1595–1600 (2020)
2. Bai, X., Chen, Y., Song, L., Zhang, Y.: Semantic representation for dialogue modeling. In: Proceedings of the 59th Annual Meeting of the Association for Computational Linguistics and the 11th International Joint Conference on Natural Language Processing, pp. 4430–4445 (2021)
3. Bai, X., Chen, Y., Zhang, Y.: Graph pre-training for AMR parsing and generation. In: Proceedings of the 60th Annual Meeting of the Association for Computational Linguistics (Volume 1: Long Papers), p. todo, May 2022

4. Banarescu, L., et al.: Abstract meaning representation for sembanking. In: Proceedings of the 7th Linguistic Annotation Workshop and Interoperability with Discourse, pp. 178–186. Association for Computational Linguistics (2013)

5. Bevilacqua, M., Blloshmi, R., Navigli, R.: One spring to rule them both: symmetric AMR semantic parsing and generation without a complex pipeline. In: Proceedings of the AAAI Conference on Artificial Intelligence (2021)

6. Blodgett, A., Schneider, N.: Probabilistic, structure-aware algorithms for improved variety, accuracy, and coverage of AMR alignments. In: Proceedings of the 59th Annual Meeting of the Association for Computational Linguistics, August 2021

7. Chen, T., Kornblith, S., Norouzi, M., Hinton, G.: A simple framework for contrastive learning of visual representations. arXiv preprint arXiv:2002.05709 (2020)

8. Huang, Y., Fang, M., Cao, Y., Wang, L., Liang, X.: DAGN: discourse-aware graph network for logical reasoning. In: NAACL (2021)

9. Hurley, P.J.: A concise introduction to logic. Cengage Learning (2014)

10. Jiao, F., Guo, Y., Song, X., Nie, L.: MERIt: meta-path guided contrastive learning for logical reasoning. In: Findings of ACL. ACL (2022)

11. Kapanipathi, P., et al.: Leveraging abstract meaning representation for knowledge base question answering. In: Findings of the Association for Computational Linguistics: ACL-IJCNLP 2021, pp. 3884–3894 (2021)

12. Lam, H.T., et al.: Ensembling graph predictions for AMR parsing. In: Advances in Neural Information Processing Systems 35: Annual Conference on Neural Information Processing Systems 2021, NeurIPS 2021, 6–14 December 2021, virtual (2021)

13. Li, X., Cheng, G., Chen, Z., Sun, Y., Qu, Y.: AdaLoGN: adaptive logic graph network for reasoning-based machine reading comprehension. In: Proceedings of the 60th Annual Meeting of the Association for Computational Linguistics, pp. 7147–7161 (2022)

14. Lim, J., Oh, D., Jang, Y., Yang, K., Lim, H.S.: I know what you asked: graph path learning using AMR for commonsense reasoning. In: Proceedings of the 28th International Conference on Computational Linguistics, pp. 2459–2471 (2020)

15. Liu, F., Flanigan, J., Thomson, S., Sadeh, N., Smith, N.A.: Toward abstractive summarization using semantic representations. In: Proceedings of the 2015 Conference of the North American Chapter of the Association for Computational Linguistics: Human Language Technologies, pp. 1077–1086 (2015)

16. Liu, J., Cui, L., Liu, H., Huang, D., Wang, Y., Zhang, Y.: LogiQA: a challenge dataset for machine reading comprehension with logical reasoning. In: Proceedings of the Twenty-Ninth International Conference on International Joint Conferences on Artificial Intelligence, pp. 3622–3628 (2021)

17. Liu, Y., Che, W., Zheng, B., Qin, B., Liu, T.: An AMR aligner tuned by transition-based parser. In: EMNLP (2018)

18. Liu, Y., et al.: Roberta: a robustly optimized BERT pretraining approach (2020)

19. Ouyang, S., Zhang, Z., Zhao, H.: Fact-driven logical reasoning. arXiv preprint arXiv:2105.10334 (2021)

20. Rajpurkar, P., Zhang, J., Lopyrev, K., Liang, P.: Squad: 100,000+ questions for machine comprehension of text. In: Proceedings of the 2016 Conference on Empirical Methods in Natural Language Processing, pp. 2383–2392 (2016)

21. Schlichtkrull, M.S., Kipf, T.N., Bloem, P., van den Berg, R., Titov, I., Welling, M.: Modeling relational data with graph convolutional networks. In: ESWC (2018)

22. Song, L., Gildea, D., Zhang, Y., Wang, Z., Su, J.: Semantic neural machine translation using AMR. Trans. Assoc. Comput. Linguist. **7**, 19–31 (2019)

23. Wang, S., et al.: From LSAT: the progress and challenges of complex reasoning. IEEE/ACM Trans. Audio Speech Lang. Process. (2022)

24. Wang, S., et al.: Logic-driven context extension and data augmentation for logical reasoning of text (2021)

25. Xu, W., Zhang, H., Cai, D., Lam, W.: Dynamic semantic graph construction and reasoning for explainable multi-hop science question answering. In: Findings of the Association for Computational Linguistics: ACL-IJCNLP 2021, pp. 1044–1056 (2021)

26. Yang, Z., et al.: HotpotQA: a dataset for diverse, explainable multi-hop question answering. In: Conference on Empirical Methods in Natural Language Processing (EMNLP) (2018)

27. Yu, W., Jiang, Z., Dong, Y., Feng, J.: ReClor: a reading comprehension dataset requiring logical reasoning. In: International Conference on Learning Representations (ICLR), April 2020

28. Zhou, J., Naseem, T., Astudillo, R.F., Florian, R.: AMR parsing with action-pointer transformer. In: Proceedings of the 2021 Conference of the North American Chapter of the Association for Computational Linguistics: Human Language Technologies, pp. 5585–5598 (2021)

Modeling Temporal-Sensitive Information for Complex Question Answering over Knowledge Graphs

Yao Xiao, Guangyou Zhou, and Jin Liu[✉]

School of Computer Science, Wuhan University School of Computer Science,
Central China Normal University, Wuhan, China
{y.xiao,jinliu}@whu.edu.cn, gyzhou@mail.ccnu.edu.cn

Abstract. Question answering over temporal knowledge graphs (TKGQA) has attracted great attentions in natural language processing community. One of the key challenges is how to effectively model the representations of questions and the candidate answers associated with timestamp constraints. Many existing methods attempt to learn temporal knowledge graph embedding for entities, relations and timestamps. However, these existing methods cannot effectively exploiting temporal knowledge graph embeddings to capture time intervals (e.g., "*WWII*" refers to 1939–1945) as well as temporal relation words (e.g., "*first*" and "*last*") appeared in complex questions, resulting in the sub-optimal results. In this paper, we propose a temporal-sensitive information for complex question answering (TSIQA) framework to tackle these problems. We employ two alternative approaches to augment questions embeddings with question-specific time interval information, which consists of specific start and end timestamps. We also present auxiliary contrastive learning to contrast the answer prediction and prior knowledge regarding time approximation for questions that only differ by the temporal relation words. To evaluate the effectiveness of our proposed method, we conduct the experiments on CRONQUESTION. The results show that our proposed model achieves better improvements over the state-of-the-art models that require multiple steps of reasoning.

Keywords: Question answering · Temporal knowledge graphs · Knowledge graph embedding

1 Introduction

Knowledge Graphs (KG) like Freebase [3] and Dbpedia [1] have supported many downstream applications, such as question answering [9, 15, 19, 25, 27] information extraction [2, 20] and sentiment analysis [4, 26]. One big issue is that these existing KGs are usually changed over time since the new entities and new relations will be added in the KGs learning dynamic embeddings for temporal knowledge graphs [8, 22, 24]. We call these KGs with dynamic characteristics as temporal KGs (TKGs). Compared to the traditional static KGs, each fact in TKGs has a timestamp, indicating the fact only occur in a specific time intervals, e.g., *(Bill Clinton, position held, President of USA, 1993, 2001)*.

W. Lu et al. (Eds.): NLPCC 2022, LNAI 13551, pp. 418–430, 2022.
https://doi.org/10.1007/978-3-031-17120-8_33

Considering a query *"What position did Bill Clinton hold between 1993 and 2001"*, the system needs to find the answers from a given TKG with the time constraint. We regard the question answering over a TKG as temporal KGQA.

The dynamic characteristics of KGs present new challenges for temporal KGQA. And the key challenge for temporal KGQA is how to effectively model the representations of questions and the candidate answers associated with timestamp constraints. The early approach aims to decompose questions for temporal reasoning with hand-crafted rules [5,6,11], while some recent works [17,18,21,22] regard temporal KGQA as a link prediction task on the TKGs. The underline idea is that these existing approaches usually employ temporal KG embedding with the one-hop reasoning to predict the answers. Among them, CronKGQA [21] is the representative method, which has achieved promising results for temporal KGQA on simple questions but cannot deal well with the complex questions. Complex question answering over TKGs have the following two challenges: (1) Complex temporal questions usually require information from multiple TKG facts and involve additional time constraints, resulting in unsatisfactory performance for CronKGQA. For instance, to answer the question *"Who held the position of President of USA after WWII"*, it is crucial that we first need to obtain the multiple TKG factual information associated with the annotated entity *"President of USA"* and *"WWII"*, and identify that *"WWII"* occurred between 1939 and 1945. Then we should look for entities linked to the *"President of USA"* in the time interval specified by these times. (2) Existing works usually utilize pre-trained language models for understanding questions without explicitly considering the difference of temporal relation words in questions, resulting in the suboptimal performance. Unlike entity relations, temporal relation words usually involve one or two prepositions (e.g., *"first"*, *"last"*), and each one is presented implicitly in temporal KGs. Thus, any small changes for temporal relation words may lead to different answers.

In this paper, we propose to model temporal-sensitive information for temporal KGQA. First, to enrich the question with additional multiple factual information, we combine the temporal KG embeddings corresponding to the annotated entities involved in the question with their associated temporal facts. Second, we design two complementary methods to capture question-specific time interval information to enhance the question representation. Specifically, for available facts in the temporal KG, we use the annotated entities of the question to search for explicit time intervals from the underlying temporal KG. While for unavailable facts, we propose a new representation mechanism to infer missing temporal information rather than directly recovering timestamps from the temporal KG. Afterwards, we employ a customized encoding layer to fuse these information together into a final question representation. Last, to improve the sensitivity of our model for temporal relations words in the question, we exploit the mutually exclusive answers and prior knowledge regarding time approximation for questions that only differ by the temporal relation words. By distinguish the latent temporal representation between original questions and contrastive questions, we can more effectively solve complex questions (e.g., *"before/after"* or *"first/last"* shown in Table 1) that require a better understanding of the temporal expressions in question.

To verify the effectiveness of the proposed method, we conduct extensive experiments on a recently released temporal KGQA dataset CRONQUESTION [21]. Our results show that the proposed method significantly outperforms varied baselines for

Table 1. Examples for different types of temporal questions. $\{\cdot\}_{head}$, $\{\cdot\}_{tail}$ and $\{\cdot\}_{time}$ correspond to entity/timestamp in the form of fact (s, r, o, t).

Reasoning type	Example question
Simple Entity	What team was $\{Barrie\ Betts\}_{head}$ playing in $\{1960\}_{time}$
Simple Time	When was $\{Manolo\ Pestrin\}_{head}$ playing in $\{AC\ Cesena\}_{tail}$
Before/After	Who was elected the $\{United\ States\ senator\}_{tail}$ after $\{Larry\ Pressler\}_{head}$
First/Last	Which award was last won by $\{Michel\ Bismut\}_{head}$
Time Join	Who were the players playing in $\{German\ National\ Football\ Team\}_{tail}$ with $\{Hans\ Hagen\}_{head}$

complex questions, and achieves absolute increases in various complex reasoning types. Our contributions are as follows: 1) We propose a novel fusion question representation by using two different innovative approaches to obtain temporal interval information about relevant questions. 2) We propose reasonable contrastive learning for improving the sensitivity of the model to temporal relation words in the question, thereby better solving complex question. 3) We conduct extensive experiments on CRONQUESTION dataset. The results show that our TSIQA model outperforms state-of-the-art on various complex questions.

2   Related Work

KGQA methods usually utilize pre-trained KG embeddings to answer questions. Such approaches can perform well on simple questions but cannot handle complex questions well. In order to tackle these limitations, some research studies [9, 19, 25] employ logical reasoning or available auxiliary information in the form of documents. However, the above models cannot well handle temporal constraints.

Recently, additional benchmarks which model temporal information in various domains have drawn much attention. ForecastQA [13] formulates the problem as a multiple-choice QA task and introduces a novel timestamp constraint per question. TempQuestions [10] is a KGQA benchmark for temporal question answering derived by judiciously selecting time-related questions. Based on this dataset, Jia et al. [11] designs TEQUILA to present specific approach to decompose and rewrite the question into non-temporal sub-questions and temporal sub-questions with constraints. However, the KG used here is based on a subset of FreeBase which is a non-temporal KG, it does not have a suitable method to identify temporal facts. Afterwards, Jia et al. [12] proposes EXAQT, an end-to-end system computes question-relevant compact subgraphs in KGs and augments relational graph convolutional networks with time-aware entity embeddings for temporal question answering. But they mostly rely on inflexible hand-crafted rules with limited number of temporal questions to model temporal information.

Subsequently, the largest known temporal KGQA dataset CRONQUESTION [21] is released, which consists of both the temporal questions and the temporal KG where each edge is associated with a time duration. Based on this structural dataset, Saxena et al. [21] proposes CronKGQA that draws on the idea of link prediction task to complete

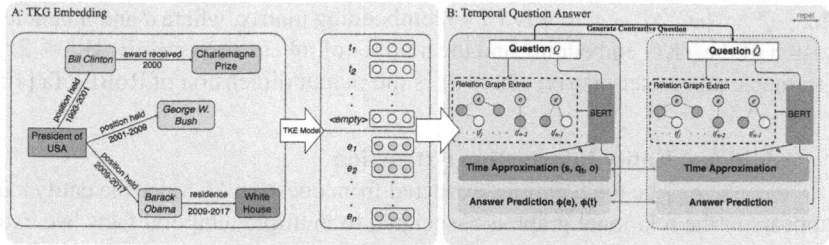

Fig. 1. An illustrative architecture of the proposed model.

reasoning on TKGs with missing entities or timestamps by leveraging TKG embeddings. CronKGQA has demonstrated promising results on simple questions, but cannot deal well with complex questions that consider multiple hops from temporal reasoning. In order to better answer time-order related questions, Shang et al. [23] employs a time-sensitive KG encoder to inject order information into the temporal KG embedding, and proposes a time component to facilitate reasoning over temporal and relational facts of multiple facts.

3 Our Approach

Our proposed method first integrates the question with additional time interval and factual information to enhance question representation, then performs joint training for answer prediction and time-signal contrastive learning to improve the sensitivity of model to temporal signals in questions. Figure 1 shows the general architecture of the model, we will describe the model in details in the following subsections.

3.1 Problem Fromulation

A temporal KG (TKG) is a directed labeled graph which can be described as $\mathcal{G} = (\mathcal{E}, \mathcal{R}, \mathcal{T}, \mathcal{F})$. Each fact in a TKG can be formalized as a quadruple $(s, r, o, t) \in \mathcal{F}$, where the directed label edge indicates that the relation $r \in \mathcal{R}$ occurs between a subject entity $s \in \mathcal{E}$ and an object entity $o \in \mathcal{E}$ at timestamp $t \in \mathcal{T}$. And temporal signals are markers of temporal relations (before, after, first, during, ...).

The representative TKGQA method solves as $\phi(u_{\tilde{s}}, q, u_o, u_t) > \phi(u_{s'}, q, u_o, u_t)$ for each incorrect entities $s' \neq \tilde{s}$, where ϕ is the scoring function and $u_{s'}, u_t, u_{\tilde{s}}$ and $u_{\tilde{o}}$ are pre-trained TKG embeddings [14].

3.2 Information-fusion Question Representation

We use a pre-trained language model to obtain the semantic information of natural language questions. Specifically, the question text q^t is transformed into a semantic matrix Q^b by RoBERTa.

$$Q^b = W^b RoBERTa(q^t) \tag{1}$$

Here $Q^b = \{q_1^b, q_2^b, \cdots, q_n^b\}$ is a $d \times n$ embedding matrix, where d and n denote the dimension of the TKG embedding and the number of tokens respectively. $W^b \in \mathbb{R}^{d \times d_b}$ is an trainable parameter matrix, where d_b is the output dimension of RoBERTa [16].

3.2.1   Additional Entity Information Extraction

Let $\{e_1, e_2, \cdots, e_n\}$ be the n entities extracted from question Q. Since the entity e usually appears in the relational graph is associated to multiple temporal facts, we extract the k-hop neighbor relation sub-graph G_i for each entity e_i. Then by combining these k sub-graphs, we arrange each fact tf in chronological order and feed them into an LSTM network.

$$h_{NRG}^0 = LSTM(h_{tf_1^e}^0, h_{tf_2^e}^0, \cdots, h_{tf_n^e}^0) \tag{2}$$

$$u_{s,o}^l = f\left(\sum_{(s,o)|(s,r,o,t) \in \mathcal{F}} W_t^l u_{s,o}^{l-1} + W^l h_{NRG}^{l-1} \right) \tag{3}$$

After obtaining the final representation, we replace token embeddings of the entities and timestamps in Q^b with these embeddings. As a result, to enrich the question representation, the token embedding matrix incorporating these additional information is expressed as:

$$q_i^e = \begin{cases} W^e u_e & \text{if token } i \text{ linked to an entity } e \\ W^e u_t & \text{if token } i \text{ linked to a timestamp } t \\ q_i^b & others \end{cases} \tag{4}$$

where $Q^e = \{q_1^e, q_2^e, \cdots, q_n^e\}$ and $W^e \in \mathbb{R}^{d \times d}$ is an trainable projectioin.

3.2.2   Time Interval Information Extraction

Complex questions are usually implicit temporal expressions, and the time interval cannot be directly obtained. Consequently, we design two methods to extract these time interval information.

Search Learning. The method utilizes the annotated entities in the question to search relative time intervals from the underlying TKG. In detail, by searching for all the clue facts corresponding to the annotated entities in the relevant questions, we can identify the specific timestamps of these facts. In most cases, we can search for multiple timestamps, so we constrain the time interval between each clue fact and the previous clue fact to no more than m, and only extract the start and end timestamps after sorting in chronologically ascending order. We utilize t_{start} and t_{end} to represent the sorted start and end timestamps.

$$tf^{rel} = \{(s, r, o, t)|(s', r', o', t') \in \mathcal{F} :_{t-1}, t - t' \leq m\} \tag{5}$$

$$t_{start}, t_{end} = sort(tf^{rel}) \tag{6}$$

For the question "*Who was the President of USA after Bill Clinton*", the entities "*President of USA*" and "*Bill Clinton*" appear together in TKG facts with timestamps starting in 1993 and ending in 2001. Accordingly, the time embedding of 1993 and 2001 can be used to further enhance the representation of the question.

Induced Mean Learning. Compared to searching directly from TKG, we provide an alternative approach to obtain time embedding by exploiting the query information and embeddings of the entities to infer missing temporal information.

A *co-sharing* relation r_c is said to be associated with the query entity s_q if s_q appears in any position of the quadruple $(s_q, r_c, \cdot, \cdot)$. And we suppose the set V_{r_c} includes all the entities having the *co-sharing* relation. So the induced mean learning representation of the entities sharing the same r_c can be expressed as:

$$\bar{s}_{im} = \frac{\sum_{s_q \in V_{r_c}} s_q}{|V_{r_c}|} \tag{7}$$

Since entities with the same *co-sharing* relation r_c usually correspond to related timelines, we utilize $\bar{s}_{im}$ to get the representation of t based on the *co-sharing* relation, where $\mathsf{U}(s_q)$ denotes the *co-sharing* relation set of entities s_q and the hyperparameter is $0 \leq \eta \leq 1$.

$$t_{s_q, r_c} = \eta t_{s_q-1, r_c} + (1 - \eta) \frac{\sum_{r_c \in \mathsf{U}(s_q)} \bar{s}_{im}}{\mathsf{U}(s_q)} \tag{8}$$

Subsequently, t_{start} and t_{end} can be generated by exchanging the subject s_q and object o_q respectively.

3.2.3 Information Fusion

After obtaining the required start and end timestamps, we augment the question representation with their corresponding TKG embeddings $u_{t_{start}}$ and $u_{t_{end}}$ as:

$$q_j^h = \begin{cases} q_j^e + u_{t_{start}} + u_{t_{end}} & \text{if token } j \text{ is an entity} \\ q_j^e & \text{if token } j \text{ is the other} \end{cases} \tag{9}$$

where $Q^h = \{q_1^h, \cdots, q_n^h\}$ contains text, entity and time interval information. Finally, we adopt an information fusion layer including a learnable encoder to combine these information together into a single question $Q^t = f(Q^h)$.

3.3 Time-Interact Question Answering

Existing methods usually make time and entity answer prediction independently, which leads to poor performance. Therefore, we add the representation obtained from the time approximation to the answer prediction.

Time Prediction. Based on the embeddings u_s and u_o of annotated entities and the final question embedding q^t, we denote the approximated time function as follows:

$$Re(t) = Re(u_s) \oplus Re(u_{ro}) - Im(u_s) \oplus Im(u_{ro}) \\ Im(t) = Re(u_s) \oplus Im(u_{ro}) + Im(u_s) \oplus Re(u_{ro}) \tag{10}$$

$$t_a = [Re(t_a) \oplus Im(t_a)] \tag{11}$$

where $u_{ro} = u_r \oplus u_o$, $[\oplus]$ is the concatenation function, and $Re(\cdot)$ is the real valued vectors and $Im(\cdot)$ is the imaginary part. After obtaining the time embeddings t_a, we calculate the final score for each time $t \in \mathcal{T}$ as:

$$\phi(t) = Re(<t_a, t>) \tag{12}$$

Entity Prediction. For each entity $e \in \mathcal{E}$, we calculate the final score by:

$$\phi(e) = max(\phi(u_s, q, t_a), \ \phi(u_o, q, t_a)) \tag{13}$$

where $max(\cdot)$ ensures that we ignore the scores when s or o is missing.

Considering the answer of question is either entity or timestamp, we suppose $\phi(x)$ is the answer score $\phi(x) = \phi(t)$ or $\phi(e)$, and then we apply softmax over $\phi(x)$ to calculate answer probability $p_x = softmax(\phi(x))$. Finally, the answer prediction is trained by minimizing the cross-entropy loss as:

$$\mathcal{L}_{original} = -\sum_i^C y_i \log\left(p_x(i)\right) \tag{14}$$

where y_i represents that the i-th candidate element is the true answer and C is the number of all candidate answers.

3.4   Time-signal Contrastive Learning

Since the original loss is not sensitive to the difference of temporal signals implied in the question text, for example, *"What's the first prize Simmons got?"* and *"What's the last prize Simmons got?"* are two distinct questions with totally different answers that can easily lead to mispredictions. We construct a contrastive question to the original question, and then add auxiliary contrastive learning to distinguish the latent temporal representation from the signal pair of contrastive questions.

Given a question $Q = [x_1, \cdots, x_{sig}, \cdots]$, we first build a dictionary for these temporal signal pairs as $D_{sig}=$ {(before, after), (first, last), (after, during), (during, before)}. We use Eq. 11 to get the corresponding time embeddings t_a. Then, for each temporal signal in the question, we replace it with the inverse word in dictionary D_{sig} to generate contrastive question $\hat{Q} = [x_1, \cdots, \hat{x}_{sig}, \cdots]$. And we follow the same way to get corresponding time embeddings t_{ac} of $\hat{Q}$. Subsequently, we distinguish the differences of temporal information implied by the signal pairs as follows where σ denotes the sigmoid function:

$$p_s = \sigma((t_a - t_{ac})^T W) \tag{15}$$

$$\mathcal{L}_{sig} = -\mathbf{1}\left(\hat{x}_{sig} = x_{sig}\right)\log\left(p_s\right) - \mathbf{1}\left(\hat{x}_{sig} \neq x_{sig}\right)\log\left(1 - p_s\right) \tag{16}$$

Afterwards, we obtain each answer scores $\phi = [\varphi_1, \cdots, \varphi_N]$ and $\hat{\phi} = [\hat{\varphi}_1, \cdots, \hat{\varphi}_N]$ where N is total numbers of entities and timestamps. We concatenate them as $\phi_c = [\phi; \hat{\phi}] \in \mathbb{R}^{2 \times N}$. It is obviously that the answer of question Q is definitely

Table 2. Number of different types of reasoning and answer of questions in CRONQUESTION dataset.

	Train	Dev	Test
Simple Entity	90,651	7,745	7,812
Simple Time	61,471	5,197	5,046
Before/After	23,869	1,982	2,151
First/Last	118,556	11,198	11,159
Time Join	55,453	3,878	3,832
Entity Answer	225,672	19,362	19,524
Time Answer	124,328	10,638	10,476
Total	350,000	30,000	30,000

not for question $\hat{Q}$, hence only if the i-th answer is the correct answer for Q we set the answer label y_i as 1 else $y_i = 0$ where $y_c = [y_1, \cdots, y_N]$:

$$\mathcal{L}_{SCL} = -\frac{1}{N} y_i log\left(\frac{exp(\phi_c[0, i])}{exp(\phi_c[0, i]) + \sum_{j=0}^{N} exp(\phi_c(j))}\right) \tag{17}$$

Finally, we joint these three losses together with weighting coefficients γ and β:

$$\mathcal{L} = \mathcal{L}_{original} + \gamma\mathcal{L}_{sig} + \beta\mathcal{L}_{SCL} \tag{18}$$

4 Experiments

4.1 Dataset Description

CRONQUESTION [21] is the largest temporal KGQA dataset. For the KG with temporal annotations, this temporal KG has 328k facts, 125k entities, 203 relations and 1.7k timestamps. Facts with the timestamps in the edge is formalized as (s, r, o, t). For the question required temporal reasoning, CRONQUESTION categorizes questions into simple questions and complex questions. The answer type for the question is divided into the entity answer and the time answer. Moreover, this dataset generates 350k question-answer pairs for training, and 30k for validation and testing respectively. The statistics of the dataset is shown in Table 2.

4.2 Parameter Settings

In our proposed model, we initialize the TKG embedding dimensions d with a dimension of 512 and with a dimension of 768 for pre-trained BERT. We use Adam optimizer with a learning rate of 2×10^{-4}. As for transformer encoding layer, we set $l = 3$ with 4 heads per layer. Hyperparameter values are tuned on the validation dataset, we set the number of GCN layers to 3, LSTM dropout to 0.2 and linear dropout is 0.3. The activation function is $ReLU$. We implement the proposed model using Pytorch.

Table 3. Performance of our approach and baselines on the CRONQUESTION datasets.

Model	Hits@1					Hits@10				
	Overall	Question type		Answer type		Overall	Question type		Answer type	
		Complex	Simple	Entity	Time		Complex	Simple	Entity	Time
BERT	0.071	0.086	0.052	0.077	0.06	0.213	0.205	0.225	0.192	0.253
RoBERTa	0.07	0.086	0.05	0.082	0.048	0.202	0.192	0.215	0.186	0.231
KnowBERT	0.07	0.083	0.051	0.081	0.048	0.201	0.189	0.217	0.185	0.23
EmbedKGQA	0.288	0.286	0.29	0.411	0.057	0.672	0.632	0.725	0.85	0.341
EaE	0.288	0.257	0.329	0.318	0.231	0.678	0.623	0.753	0.668	0.698
CronKGQA	0.647	0.392	0.987	0.699	0.549	0.884	0.802	0.992	0.898	0.857
TempoQR	0.799	0.655	0.990	0.876	0.653	0.957	0.930	0.993	0.972	0.929
TSIQA-Induced	0.759	0.584	0.989	0.856	0.586	0.945	0.906	0.993	0.969	0.900
TSIQA-Search	0.909	0.862	0.989	0.921	0.907	0.975	0.962	0.997	0.979	0.972

Table 4. Hits@1 for different types of complex reasoning.

	Before/After	First/Last	Time join	All
EaE	0.256	0.288	0.168	0.288
CronKGQA	0.288	0.371	0.511	0.647
CronKGQA-Induced	0.348	0.368	0.617	0.674
CronKGQA-Search	0.376	0.431	0.885	0.712
TSIQA-Induced	0.556	0.493	0.85	0.759
TSIQA-Search	0.761	0.862	0.906	0.909

4.3 Baseline Models

We compare our proposed method with various baselines as follows:

BERT: We conduct the experiment on BERT, RoBERTa [16] and KnowBERT which injected information from traditional knowledge bases into BERT. We concatenate their question embedding with the prediction head and do a softmax over all entities and time to predict the answer probabilities.

EaE: EaE [7] is a model that aims to integrate capture declarative entity knowledge in the learned parameters of a language model, which learns entity representations directly from free text. As a baseline on test datasets, we experiment with EaE by replacing BERT embeddings with entity/time embeddings for entity/time mentions.

EmbedKGQA: It exploits the link prediction feature of KG embeddings to alleviate the KG incompleteness problem without using any additional data. To apply it to test datasets, Saxena et al. [21] change the entity embedding matrix to the embeddings corresponding to KG entities, and use random time embeddings during the question answering task.

CronKGQA: CronKGQA [21] is a transformer based solution that takes full advantage of the temporal KG embeddings.

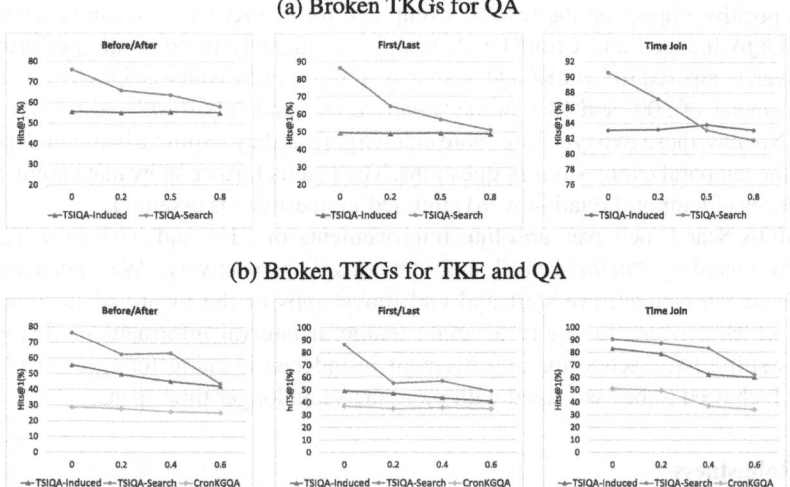

Fig. 2. Model performance vs. different broken types. The x-axis coordinate represents the probability ρ of the fact being broken.

TempoQR: TempoQR [17] introduces a temporal embedding-based scoring function for reasoning complex questions and fuses three specialized information.

4.4   Main Results

Table 3 presents the experimental results. From Table 3, we have the following observations: (1) We see the methods augmented with TComplEx embedding (CronKGQA, TSIQA-Induced, TSIQA-Search) perform significantly better than other methods (BERT, RoBERTa, KnowBERT, EmbedKGQA, EaE). The results demonstrate using specific temporal KG embeddings is helpful for model to focus on the entities and timestamps. (2) Compared to CronKGQA and TempoQR, which do not combine the question representations with temporal interval information and construct the contrastive learning to capture temporal changes, our proposed method achieves the absolute improvement. Taking complex questions at Hits@1 for example, the increase of TSIQA-Search over TempoQR is 19%, while TSIQA-Search achieves absolute increase of 47% over CronKGQA. (3) Comparing TSIQA-Search with TSIQA-Induced, we can see TSIQA-Search achieves absolute increases of 28% and 32% in complex questions and time answer at Hits@1, respectively.

The results show that TSIQA-Search is indeed useful for retrieving the accurate time interval information from the temporal KG, while induced learning is not always able to correctly infer the missing temporal information.

4.5   Ablation Study

To investigate how each component contributes to the final performance, we present the results in Table 4. First, it is obviously that both induced and search learning can have a positive impact on the results. Compared to CronKGQA, we can see that both CronKGQA-Induced and CronKGQA-Search significantly improve the performance. Moreover, compared to CronKGQA-Induced, TSIQA-Induced has achieved substantial improvements of 20% and 13% in the "*before/after*" and "*first/last*" questions, respectively. Notably, these two types are more challenging as they require a better understanding of the temporal expressions in questions. The results further show that capturing the differences of temporal relation words implied in questions is essential.

TSIQA-Search achieves absolute improvements of 21% and 37% over TSIQA-Induced regarding "*before/after*" and "*first/last*", respectively. We speculate that TSIQA-Search can retrieve start and end timestamps of the identified facts at most times, which can provide more accurate temporal interval information. Meanwhile, there is still a large scope for improvement in induced learning for "*first/last*" questions which need to be associated with more facts and longer time spans.

4.6 Robustness

Figure 2a demonstrates the results when the given temporal KG (TKG) is broken in the question answering stage (QA). Since TSIQA-Search needs complete and reliable TKGs for retrieval, the destruction of TKG data in QA stage has a significant impact on it. When a large number of facts are broken ($\rho > 0.5$), its performance is similar to or even worse than TSIQA-Induced. As for TSIQA-Induced, even if the facts are destroyed to varying degrees, its performance has not been greatly affected. Overall, when the given TKG is incomplete or broken, TSIQA-Induced performs more stable than TSIQA-Search despite some slight changes.

Figure 2b shows the results that when the given TKG is broken in both temporal KG embeddings (TKE) and question answering stage. All methods that rely on TKE are obviously affected, but CronKGQA is the least affected due to its low performance. As for TSIQA-Search and TSIQA-Induced, the results of two types have decreased to a large extent. When the probability ρ gradually increases, the performance of two models is finally similar. Regarding "*first/last*" questions, the decline of TSIQA-Search is the largest among all types, which shows that it cannot deal well with this type in this case. Nonetheless, the performance of TSIQA-Search is better than TSIQA-Induced in overall, especially $\rho \leq 0.4$. The result indicates that search learning can provide more valuable information stably and accurately in most cases.

5   Conclusion

In this paper, we introduce temporal-sensitive information question answering (TSIQA) framework that is better able to answer complex temporal questions. We obtain the multiple TKG factual information associated with the annotated entity involved in the question via pre-trained TKG embeddings, while employing two novel methods to identify the time intervals. To further improve the sensitivity of model for temporal relation words in the question and facilitate temporal reasoning, we construct contrastive losses to better distinguish latent temporal representations of contrastive questions. Future research includes improving existing TKG embeddings and addressing unseen question types.

Acknowledgements. This work was supported by the National Natural Science Foundation of China under Grants 61972290 and 61972173, the National Key R&D Program of China under Grant 2018YFC1604000, the Fundamental Research Funds for the Central Universities (No. CCNU22QN015).

References

1. Auer, S., Bizer, C., Kobilarov, G., Lehmann, J., Cyganiak, R., Ives, Z.G.: Dbpedia: a nucleus for a web of open data. In: Proceedings of ISWC (2007)
2. Bastos, A., et al.: RECON: relation extraction using knowledge graph context in a graph neural network. In: Proceedings of WWW (2021)
3. Bollacker, K.D., Evans, C., Paritosh, P.K., Sturge, T., Taylor, J.: Freebase: a collaboratively created graph database for structuring human knowledge. In: Proceedings of SIGMOD (2008)
4. Chen, F., Huang, Y.: Knowledge-enhanced neural networks for sentiment analysis of Chinese reviews. Neurocomputing **368**, 51–58 (2019)
5. Chen, W., Wang, X., Wang, W.Y.: A dataset for answering time-sensitive questions. CoRR (2021)
6. Costa, T.S., Gottschalk, S., Demidova, E.: Event-qa: a dataset for event-centric question answering over knowledge graphs. In: Proceedings of CIKM (2020)
7. Févry, T., Soares, L.B., FitzGerald, N., Choi, E., Kwiatkowski, T.: Entities as experts: sparse memory access with entity supervision. In: Proceedings of EMNLP (2020)
8. García-Durán, A., Dumancic, S., Niepert, M.: Learning sequence encoders for temporal knowledge graph completion. In: Proceedings of EMNLP (2018)
9. He, G., Lan, Y., Jiang, J., Zhao, W.X., Wen, J.: Improving multi-hop knowledge base question answering by learning intermediate supervision signals. In: Proceedings of WSDM (2021)
10. Jia, Z., Abujabal, A., Roy, R.S., Strötgen, J., Weikum, G.: Tempquestions: A benchmark for temporal question answering. In: Proceedings of WWW (2018)
11. Jia, Z., Abujabal, A., Roy, R.S., Strötgen, J., Weikum, G.: TEQUILA: temporal question answering over knowledge bases. In: Proceedings of CIKM (2018)
12. Jia, Z., Pramanik, S., Roy, R.S., Weikum, G.: Complex temporal question answering on knowledge graphs. In: Proceedings of CIKM (2021)
13. Jin, W., et al.: Forecastqa: a question answering challenge for event forecasting with temporal text data. In: Proceedings of ACL (2021)
14. Lacroix, T., Obozinski, G., Usunier, N.: Tensor decompositions for temporal knowledge base completion. In: Proceedings of ICLR (2020)
15. Lan, Y., He, G., Jiang, J., Jiang, J., Zhao, W.X., Wen, J.: A survey on complex knowledge base question answering: Methods, challenges and solutions. In: Proceedings of IJCAI (2021)
16. Liu, Y., Ott, M., Goyal, N.: Roberta: a robustly optimized BERT pretraining approach. CoRR (2019)
17. Mavromatis, C., et al.: Tempoqr: temporal question reasoning over knowledge graphs. In: Proceedings of AAAI (2022)
18. Neelam, S., Sharma, U., Karanam, H.: SYGMA: system for generalizable modular question answering overknowledge bases. CoRR (2021)
19. Qiu, Y., Wang, Y., Jin, X., Zhang, K.: Stepwise reasoning for multi-relation question answering over knowledge graph with weak supervision. In: Proceedings of WSDM (2020)
20. Ren, X., et al.: Cotype: joint extraction of typed entities and relations with knowledge bases. In: Proceedings of WWW (2017)

21. Saxena, A., Chakrabarti, S., Talukdar, P.P.: Question answering over temporal knowledge graphs. In: Proceedings of ACL (2021)
22. Saxena, A., Tripathi, A., Talukdar, P.P.: Improving multi-hop question answering over knowledge graphs using knowledge base embeddings. In: Proceedings of ACL (2020)
23. Shang, C., Wang, G., Qi, P., Huang, J.: Improving time sensitivity for question answering over temporal knowledge graphs. CoRR (2022)
24. Wu, J., Cao, M., Cheung, J.C.K., Hamilton, W.L.: Temp: temporal message passing for temporal knowledge graph completion. In: Proceedings of EMNLP (2020)
25. Xu, K., Lai, Y., Feng, Y., Wang, Z.: Enhancing key-value memory neural networks for knowledge based question answering. In: Proceedings of NAACL (2019)
26. Zhao, A., Yu, Y.: Knowledge-enabled BERT for aspect-based sentiment analysis. Knowl. Based Syst. **221**, 107220 (2021)
27. Zhou, M., Huang, M., Zhu, X.: An interpretable reasoning network for multi-relation question answering. In: Proceedings of COLING (2018)

Knowledge-Enhanced Iterative Instruction Generation and Reasoning for Knowledge Base Question Answering

Haowei Du, Quzhe Huang, Chen Zhang, and Dongyan Zhao[✉]

Peking University, Beijing, China
2001213236@stu.pku.edu.cn, {huangquzhe,zhangch,zhaodongyan}@pku.edu.cn

Abstract. Multi-hop Knowledge Base Question Answering (KBQA) aims to find the answer entity in a knowledge base which is several hops from the topic entity mentioned in the question. Existing Retrieval-based approaches first generate instructions from the question and then use them to guide the multi-hop reasoning on the knowledge graph. As the instructions are fixed during the whole reasoning procedure and the knowledge graph is not considered in instruction generation, the model cannot revise its mistake once it predicts an intermediate entity incorrectly. To handle this, we propose **KBIGER** (**K**nowledge **B**ase **I**terative Instruction **GE**nerating and **R**easoning), a novel and efficient approach to generate the instructions dynamically with the help of reasoning graph. Instead of generating all the instructions before reasoning, we take the $(k-1)$-th reasoning graph into consideration to build the k-th instruction. In this way, the model could check the prediction from the graph and generate new instructions to revise the incorrect prediction of intermediate entities. We do experiments on two multi-hop KBQA benchmarks and outperform the existing approaches, becoming the new-state-of-the-art. Further experiments show our method does detect the incorrect prediction of intermediate entities and has the ability to revise such errors.

Keywords: Knowledge Base Question Answering · Iterative Instruction Generating and Reasoning · Error revision

1 Introduction

Knowledge Base Question Answering(KBQA) is a challenging task that aims to answer the natural language questions with the knowledge graph. With the fast development of deep learning, researchers leverage end-to-end neural networks [8,15] to solve this task by automatically learning entity and relation representations, followed by predicting the intermediate or answer entity. Recently for the KBQA community, there have been more and more interests in solving complicated questions where the answer entities are multiple hops away from the topic

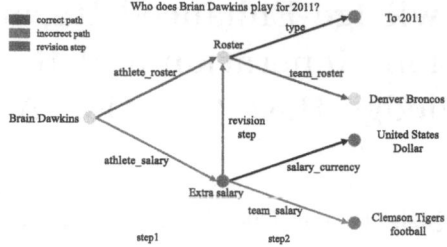

Fig. 1. An example from WebQSP dataset. The red arrows denote the right reasoning path, the blue arrows denote a wrong reasoning path and the purple arrow denotes the revision in our approach. (Color figure online)

entities. One popular way to solve multi-hop KBQA is the information retrieval-based methods, which generate instructions from questions and then retrieve the answer from the Knowledge Graph by using the instructions to guide the reasoning [7,13]. Although achieving good performance on multi-hop KBQA, existing retrieval-based methods treat instruction generation and reasoning as two separate components. Such methods first use the question solely to generate the instructions for all the hops at once and then use them to guide the reasoning. As the instructions are fixed during the whole reasoning procedure and the knowledge graph is not considered in instruction generation, the model cannot revise its mistake once it predicts an intermediate entity incorrectly. When the model reasons to an incorrect intermediate entity, the fixed instruction will guide the reasoning from the wrong prediction, which induces error accumulation.

We take an example in WebQSP, as shown in Fig. 1, to show the importance of knowledge graph on predicting intermediate entity and revising error of incorrect predictions. For the query question "Who does Brian Dawkins play for 2011", its topic entity is the football player "Brian Dawkins". Both "play" and "2011" can be attended to in the instruction generated at the first step. The baseline method NSM [7] reasons to a wrong intermediate entity "extra salary", perhaps because the model mistakes the time constraint "2011" as a regular number and chooses the "extra_salary" entity, which is related with number and currency. At the second step, the instructions by NSM continue to guide the reasoning from the wrong intermediate entity and get the wrong answer "Clemson Tigers football", which does not satisfy the time constraint. However, with the knowledge graph information that the "roster" entity connects to the type entity "to 2011" and the named entity "Denver Broncos (football team)" but the entity "extra_salary" is not linked to another entity by relation "team_roster", the instructions could revise the error by re-selecting the "roster" as the intermediate entity and linking the predicate "play" with the relation "team_roster" to derive the answer entity "Denver Broncos".

To introduce the knowledge graph into generating instructions from the query question, we propose our approach, **K**nowledge **B**ase **I**terative Instruction **GE**nerating and **R**easoning (KBIGER). Our method has two components, the instruction generation component and the reasoning component. At each step, we generate one instruction and reason one hop over the graph under the guidance of the instruction. To generate the k-th instruction, we take both the question and the $(k-1)$-th reasoning graph into consideration. In this way, our model could obtain results of the last reasoning step and will be able to revise the possible mistakes by generating the new instruction. Then we utilize the instruction created to extend the reasoning path. Besides, we also adopt distilling learning to enhance the supervision signal of intermediate entity, following [7]. We do experiments on two benchmark datasets in the field of KBQA and our approach outperforms the existing methods by 1.0 scores Hits@1 and 1.0 scores F1 in WebQSP, 1.4 score and 1.5 score in CWQ, becoming the new state-of-the-art.

Our contributions can be concluded as three folds:

1. We are the first to consider the reasoning graph of previous steps when generating the new instruction, which makes the model be able to revise the errors in reasoning.
2. We create an iterative instruction generation and reasoning framework, instead of treating instruction generation and reasoning as two separate phases as current approaches. This framework could fuse information from question and knowledge graph in a deeper way.
3. Our approach outperforms existing methods in two benchmark datasets in this field, becoming the new state-of-the-art.

2 Related Work

Over the last decade, various methods have been developed for the KBQA task. Early works utilize machine-learned or hand-crafted modules like entity recognition and relation linking to find out the answer entity [1,4,5,17]. With the popularity of neural networks, recent researchers utilize end-to-end neural networks to solve this task. They can be categorized into two groups: semantic parsing based methods [6,8,11,17] and information retrieval based methods [3,10,19,20]. Semantic parsing methods convert natural language questions into logic forms by learning a parser and predicting the query graph step by step. However, the predicted graph is dependent on the prediction of last step and if at one step the model inserts the incorrect intermediate entity into the query graph, the prediction afterward will be unreasonable. Information retrieval-based methods retrieve answers from the knowledge base by learning and comparing representations of the question and the graph. [9] utilize Key-Value Memory Network to encode the questions and facts to retrieve answer entities. To decrease the noise in questions, [18] introduces variance reduction into retrieving answers from the knowledge graph. Under the setting of supplemented corpus and incomplete knowledge graph, [14] proposes PullNet to learn what to retrieve from a corpus. [13] proposes TransferNet to support both label relations and text relations in a unified framework, For purpose of enhancing the supervision of intermediate entity distribution, [7] adopts the teacher-student network in multi-hop KBQA.

However, it ignores the utility of knowledge graph in generating information from questions and the instructions generated are fixed in the whole reasoning process, which undermine the ability to revise incorrect prediction of intermediate entities.

3 Preliminary

In this part, we introduce the concept of knowledge graph and the definition of multi-hop knowledge base question answering task (KBQA).

Knowledge Graph (KG). A knowledge graph contains a series of factual triples and each triple is composed of two entities and one relation. A knowledge graph can be denoted as $G = \{(e, r, e')|e, e' \in E, r \in R\}$, where G denotes the knowledge graph, E denotes the entity set and R denotes the relation set. A triple (e, r, e') means relation r exists between the two entities e and e'. We use N_e to denote the entity neighbourhood of entity e, which includes all the triples including e, i.e., $N_e = \{(e', r, e) \in G\} \cup \{(e, r, e') \in G\}$.

Multi-hop KBQA. Given a natural language question q that is answerable using the knowledge graph, the task aims to find the answer entity. The reasoning path starts from *topic entity* (i.e., entity mentioned in the question) to the answer entity. Other than the topic entity and answer entity, the entities in the reasoning path are called *intermediate entity*. If two entities are connected by one relation, the transition from one entity to another is called one hop. In multi-hop KBQA, the answer entity is connected to the topic entity by several hops.

4 Methodology

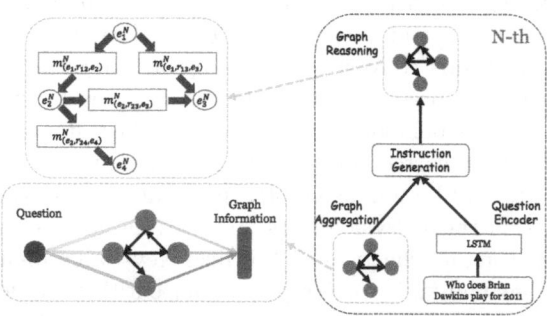

Fig. 2. Method overview

Our approach is made up of two components, Instruction Generation and Graph Reasoning. In the former component, we utilize the query and knowledge graph to generate some instructions for guiding the reasoning. In the graph reasoning component, we adopt GNN to reason over the knowledge graph. We also apply the teacher-student framework, following [7], to enhance the intermediate supervision signal. For each question, a subgraph of the knowledge graph is constructed by reserving the entities that are within n hops away from the topic entity to simplify the reasoning process, where n denotes the maximum hops between the topic entity and the answer (Fig. 2).

4.1   Instruction Generation Component

The objective of this component is to utilize the text of query question and the information of knowledge graph to construct a series of instructions $\{\mathbf{i_k}\}_{k=1}^n \in \mathbb{R}^d$, where $\mathbf{i_k}$ denotes the k-th instruction for guiding the reasoning over the knowledge graph. We use BiLSTM to encode the question to obtain a contextual representation of each word in the question, where the representation of i-th word is denoted as $\mathbf{h_i}$. We utilize the last hidden state $\mathbf{h_l}$ as the semantic representation of the question,i.e.,$\mathbf{q} = \mathbf{h_l}$. Both question and the aggregation result of the previous reasoning graph are used to generate instructions. The instruction generated is adapted to the reasoning graph instead of fixed in the whole reasoning process. We utilize the attention mechanism to attend to different parts of the query at each step. We construct instructions as follows:

$$\mathbf{i}^{(\mathbf{k})} = \sum_{j=1}^{l} \alpha_j^{(k)} \mathbf{h_j} \tag{1}$$

$$\alpha_j^{(k)} = \mathbf{softmax_j}(\mathbf{W}_\alpha(\mathbf{q}^{(\mathbf{k})} \odot \mathbf{h_j})) \tag{2}$$

$$\mathbf{q}^{(\mathbf{k})} = \mathbf{W}^{(\mathbf{k})}[\mathbf{i}^{(\mathbf{k}-1)}; \mathbf{q}; \mathbf{e}_{\mathbf{graph}}^{(k-1)}] + \mathbf{b}^{(\mathbf{k})} \tag{3}$$

where $\mathbf{e}_{\mathbf{graph}}^{(k-1)} \in \mathbb{R}^d$ denotes the representation of $(k-1)$-th reasoning graph which we will explain below and $\mathbf{W}^{(\mathbf{k})} \in \mathbb{R}^{d \times 3d}, \mathbf{W}_\alpha \in \mathbb{R}^{d \times d}, \mathbf{b}^{(\mathbf{k})} \in \mathbb{R}^d$ are learnable parameters.

4.2   Graph Aggregation

In this stage, we combine the query question and KB entity representation to generate the whole graph representation. We adopt the attention mechanism to assign weights to each entity in the reasoning graph and aggregate them into a graph representation. In this way, the model is aware of the graph structure of intermediate entities and has the ability to generate new instructions to revise the incorrect prediction.

$$\mathbf{e}_{\mathbf{graph}}^{(\mathbf{k})} = \sum_{e \in E} \alpha_e^{(k)} \mathbf{e}^{(\mathbf{k})} \tag{4}$$

$$\alpha_e^{(k)} = \frac{\exp(\beta_e^{(k)})}{\sum_{e' \in E} \exp(\beta_{e'}^{(k)})} \tag{5}$$

$$\beta_e^{(k)} = \mathbf{q} \cdot (\mathbf{W_{gate}}\mathbf{e}^{(\mathbf{k})} + \mathbf{b_q}) \tag{6}$$

where $\mathbf{W_{gate}} \in \mathbb{R}^{d \times d}, \mathbf{b_q} \in \mathbb{R}^d$ are parameters to learn and "·" denotes inner product.

4.3 Entity Initialization

We believe the relations involving the entity contain important semantic information of the entity, which can be used to initialize entity. We set the initial entity embedding for each entity in the subgraph by considering the relations involving it:

$$e^{(0)} = \sigma(\sum_{(e',r,e) \in N_e} \mathbf{W_E} \cdot \mathbf{r}) \tag{7}$$

where (e', r, e) denotes a triple in the subgraph, $\mathbf{r} \in \mathbb{R}^d$ denotes the embedding vector of relation r and $\mathbf{W_E}$ is parameter to learn.

4.4 Reasoning Component

The objective of this component is to reason over knowledge graph under the guidance of the instruction obtained by the previous instruction generation component. First, for each triple (e', r, e) in the subgraph, we learn a matching vector between the triple and the current instruction $i^{(k)}$:

$$\mathbf{m}^{(k)}_{(e',r,e)} = \sigma(\mathbf{i}^{(k)} \odot \mathbf{W_R} \mathbf{r}) \tag{8}$$

where $\mathbf{r}$ denotes the embedding of relation r and $\mathbf{W_R}$ are parameters to learn. Then for each entity e in the subgraph, we multiply the activating probability of each neighbour entity e' by the matching vector $\mathbf{m}^{(k)}_{(e',r,e)} \in \mathbb{R}^d$ and aggregate them as the representation of information from its neighbourhood:

$$\hat{\mathbf{e}}^{(k)} = \sum_{(e',r,e)} p^{(k-1)}_{e'} \mathbf{m}^{(k)}_{(e',r,e)} \tag{9}$$

The activating probability of entities is derived from the distribution predicted by the previous reasoning component. We concatenate the previous entity representation with its neighbourhood representation and pass into a MLP network to update the entity representation:

$$\mathbf{e}^{(k)} = \mathbf{MLP}(\mathbf{e}^{(k-1)}; \hat{\mathbf{e}}^{(k)}) \tag{10}$$

Then we compute the distribution of the k-th intermediate entities as follows:

$$\mathbf{p}^{(k)} = \mathbf{softmax}(\mathbf{E}^{(k)} \mathbf{W_E}) \tag{11}$$

where each column of $\mathbf{E}^{(k)}$ is the updated entity embedding $\mathbf{e}^{(k)} \in \mathbb{R}^d$ and $\mathbf{W_E} \in \mathbb{R}^d$ is parameter to learn.

Algorithm 1. Iterative instruction generation and reasoning

1: For each entity in subgraph, initialize entity embedding by Eq. 7. Let n denote the number of hops to reason. Use Glove and LSTM to obtain word embedding $\mathbf{h_j}$ and question embedding $\mathbf{q}$ for the query question.
2: **for** k = 1,2,...,n **do**
3:    Generate instruction based on $\mathbf{i}^{(k-1)}$ and $\mathbf{E}^{(k-1)}$, get $\mathbf{i}^{(k)}$
4:    Reason over knowledge graph based on $\mathbf{i}^{(k)}, \mathbf{P}^{(k-1)}, \mathbf{E}^{(k-1)}$ and get $\mathbf{P}^{(k)}, \mathbf{E}^{(k)}$
5: **end for**
6: Based on the final entity distribution $\mathbf{P}^{(n)}$, take out the entity that has the activating probability over given threshold as answer entities.

4.5   Algorithm

To conclude the above process of iterative instruction generation and reasoning, we organize it as Algorithm 1. We generate the instruction from the question and reason over knowledge graph alternately. The instruction component sends instructions to guide the reasoning and the reasoning component provides the instruction component with knowledge from a related graph. This mechanism allows two components to mutually communicate information with each other.

4.6   Teacher-Student Framework

We adopt a teacher-student framework in our approach to enhance the supervision of intermediate entity distribution following [7]. Both the teacher network and student network have the same architecture where the instruction generation component and reasoning component progress iteratively. The teacher network learns the intermediate entity distribution as the supervision signal to guide the student network. The loss function of the student network is designed as follows:

$$L_1 = \mathbf{D_{KL}}(\mathbf{P_s^{(n)}}, \mathbf{P^*}) \tag{12}$$

$$L_2 = \sum_{k=1}^{n} \mathbf{D_{KL}}(\mathbf{P_s^{(k)}}, \mathbf{P_t^{(k)}}) \tag{13}$$

$$L_s = L_1 + \lambda L_2 \tag{14}$$

$\mathbf{D_{KL}}(\cdot)$ denotes the Kullback-Leibler divergence. $\mathbf{P_s^{(k)}}$ and $\mathbf{P_t^{(k)}}$ denotes the predicted distribution of the k-th intermediate entity by student network and teacher network. $\mathbf{P^*}$ denotes the golden distribution of answer entity. λ is a hyper-parameter to tune.

5 Experiments

Table 1. Statistics about the datasets. The column "**entities**" denotes the average number of entities in the subgraph for each question

Datasets	Train	Dev	Test	Entities
WebQSP	2,848	250	1,639	1,429.8
CWQ	27,639	3,519	3,531	1,305.8

5.1 Datasets, Evaluation Metrics and Implementation Details

We evaluate our method on two widely used datasets, WebQuestionsSP and Complex WebQuestion. Table 1 shows the statistics about the two datasets.

WebQuestionsSP (WebQSP) [17] includes 4,327 natural language questions that are answerable based on Freebase knowledge graph [2], which contains millions of entities and triples. The answer entities of questions in WebQSP are either 1 hop or 2 hops away from the topic entity. Following [12], we prune the knowledge graph to contain the entities within 2 hops away from the mentioned entity. On average, there are 1,430 entities in each subgraph.

Complex WebQuestions (CWQ) [16] is expanded from WebQSP by extending question entities and adding constraints to answers. It has 34,689 natural language questions which are up to 4 hops of reasoning over the graph. Following [14], we retrieve a subgraph for each question using PageRank algorithm. On average, there are 1,306 entities in each subgraph.

Following [7,14,15], we treat the multi-hop KBQA task as a ranking task. For each question, we select a set of answer entities based on the distribution predicted. We utilize two evaluation metrics Hits@1 and F1 that are widely applied in the previous work [12–15]. Hits@1 measures the percent of the questions where the predicted answer entity that has maximum probability is in the set of ground-truth answer entities. F1 is computed by use of the set of predicted answer entities and the set of ground-truth answers. Hits@1 focuses on the entity with the maximum probability in the final distribution predicted and F1 focuses on the complete answer set.

Before training the student network, we pre-train the teacher network on the multi-hop KBQA task. We optimize all models with Adam optimizer, where the batch size is set to 32 and the learning rate is set to 7e−4. The reasoning steps are set to 3 for WebQSP and 4 for CWQ. The coefficient in Eq. 14 is set to 0.05. The hidden size of LSTM and GNN is set to 128.

5.2   Baselines to Compare

KV-Mem [9] takes advantage of Key-Value Memory Networks to encode knowledge graph triples and retrieve the answer entity.

GraftNet [15] uses a variation of graph convolution network to update the entity embedding and predict the answer.

PullNet [14] improves GraftNet by retrieving relevant documents and extracting more entities to expand the entity graph.

EmbedKGQA [12] utilizes pre-trained knowledge embedding to predict answer entities based on the topic entity and the query question.

NSM [7] takes use of the teacher framework to provide the distribution of intermediate entities as supervision signs for the student network. However, NSM fails to consider the utility of the knowledge graph in generating instructions from the question, which constrains the performance.

TransferNet [13] unifies two forms of relations, label form and text form to reason over knowledge graph and predict the distribution of entities.

5.3   Results

Table 2. Results on two benchmark datasets compared with several competitive methods proposed in recent years. The baseline results are from original papers. Our approach significantly outperforms NSM, where p-values of Hits@1 and F1 are 0.01 and 0.0006 on WebQSP, 0.002 and 0.0001 on CWQ.

Models	WebQSP		CWQ	
	Hits@1	F1	Hits@1	F1
KV-Mem	46.7	38.6	21.1	-
GraftNet	67.8	62.8	32.8	-
PullNet	68.1	-	45.9	-
EmbedKGQA	66.6	-	-	-
TransferNet	71.4	-	48.6	-
NSM	74.3	67.4	48.8	44.0
Ours	**75.3**	**68.4**	**50.2**	**45.5**

The results of different approaches are presented in Table 2, by which we can observe the following conclusions: Our approach outperforms all the existing methods on both datasets and evaluation metrics, becoming the new state-of-the-art. It is efficient to introduce the information from knowledge graph into generating instructions from the query question and iteratively proceed the instruction generation component with the reasoning component. Our approach outperforms the previous state-of-the-art NSM by 1.0 Hits@1 score and 1.0 F1 score in WebQSP as well as 1.4 Hits@1 score and 1.5 F1 score in CWQ. CWQ composes more complicated query questions and our model is good at answering complex questions with more hops of reasoning. Compared to the Hits@1 metric, the F1 metric counts on the prediction of the whole set of answer entities instead of the answer that has the maximum probability. The performance of our model in F1 metric shows it can predict the whole answer set instead of just one answer.

6   Analysis

In this part, we do two ablation studies and evaluate the effectiveness of our approach on revising the incorrect prediction of intermediate entities. Furthermore, we give an example from WebQSP to show the revision of incorrect prediction for intermediate entities.

6.1   Ablation Study and Error Revision

To demonstrate the effectiveness of different components of our approach, we do the following ablation study on WebQSP and CWQ datasets:

Ablation Study 1. In this model, we revise the instruction computation by removing the component of graph entity and deriving all the n instructions before the reasoning:

$$\mathbf{q}^{(\mathbf{k})} = \mathbf{W}^{(\mathbf{k})}[\mathbf{i}^{(\mathbf{k}-\mathbf{1})}; \mathbf{q}] + \mathbf{b}^{(\mathbf{k})} \tag{15}$$

$$\alpha_j^{(k)} = \mathbf{softmax_j}(\mathbf{W}_\alpha(\mathbf{q}^{(\mathbf{k})} \odot \mathbf{h_j})) \tag{16}$$

$$\mathbf{i}^{(\mathbf{k})} = \sum_{j=1}^{l} \alpha_j^{(k)} \mathbf{h_j} \tag{17}$$

where n denotes the number of hops between answer and topic entity. We can see in this model, the instruction generated from questions do not consider the information of the knowledge graph, and the instructions are fixed in the whole reasoning process. Regardless of what the structure of knowledge graph is, the instructions sent by questions are the same.

Ablation Study 2. In this model, we remove the teacher network and only use the hard label in datasets for training.

Table 3. Results of ablation models on WebQSP and CWQ.

Models	WebQSP		CWQ	
	Hits@1	F1	Hits@1	F1
-iterative	72.1	66.4	47.7	43.6
-teacher	70.4	64.8	48.2	43.3
KBIGER	**75.3**	**68.4**	**50.2**	**45.5**

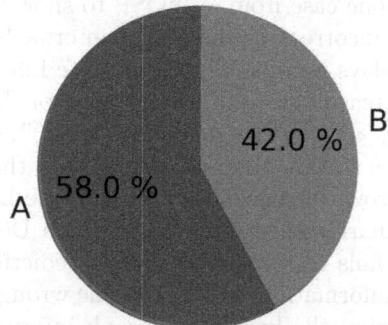

Fig. 3. The proportion of two groups of cases in WebQSP dataset where we get the correct answer but NSM fails. Group A represents the cases where we revise the error and answer correctly; Group B denotes the cases where we predict all the intermediate entities correctly.

As shown in Table 3, we can see if we remove the information of knowledge graph from the instruction generation component, the performance of Hits@1 and F1 on two benchmark datasets will fall down by about 2 points. This reveals that the knowledge graph structure is important for generating flexible instructions from query questions. Without the student network, the evaluation results are lower than our approach. It demonstrates that the supervision signal of intermediate entity distribution can improve the prediction of intermediate entities and answer entities. Though the lack of the student network, ablation model 2 achieves similar results with ablation model 1, which shows the efficiency of utilizing the information of knowledge graph to generate flexible instructions from questions.

To explore whether the introduction of knowledge graph into instruction generation could identify the incorrect prediction of intermediate entities and revise them, we annotated the intermediate entity of the multi-hop data cases where the baseline NSM fails to answer the question correctly but we get the right answer. By checking the reasoning process, we classify the cases into 2 groups and compute the proportion: **1.** the cases where we fail to predict the intermediate entity at first but revise the error in the following steps and answer the question correctly. **2.** the cases where we answer the question correctly by predicting all the intermediate entities correctly.

As shown in Fig. 3, among the cases where our model predicts correctly and baseline NSM fails to answer, 58% are cases where we revise the error of incorrect prediction of an intermediate entity. which shows the efficiency of introducing the knowledge graph into instruction generation in an iterative manner on decreasing the error accumulation along the reasoning path.

6.2 Case Study

In this section, we take one case from WebQSP to show the effectiveness of our method in revising the incorrect prediction of intermediate entities. In Fig. 4, for the question "Who plays London Tipton in Suite Life on Deck?", the purple path denotes the right reasoning path: "Suite Life on Deck (TV series)" $\Longrightarrow$ $series\_cast$ "cast" $\Longrightarrow$ $actor\_starring$ "Brenda Song (actor)", where the entity "cast" satisfies the character constraint "Lonton Tipton". In the first step, our model and NSM predict the wrong intermediate entity "Suite Life of Zack and Cody" because of the high similarity between "Suite Life on Deck" and "Suite Life of Zack and Cody". NSM fails to revise the wrong prediction of the intermediate entity for lack of graph information and derives the wrong answer along the blue path. By contrast, utilizing the knowledge graph information that "Suite Life of Zack and Cody" does not connect to any entity that satisfies the character constraint "Lonton Tipton", our model revises the error of incorrect prediction for intermediate entity and obtain the correct answer "Brenda Song". At the first step, the graph aggregation in our model attends to content-related entities such as "Suite Life of Zack and Cody", which are one hop away from the topic entity. At the second step, the attention weights of "Brenda Song" and "Lonton Tipton" rise from 0.08 to 0.23, indicating the graph structure around the answer entity is focused on by our model. This case shows the effectiveness of introducing knowledge graph into instructions generation on revising the incorrect prediction of an intermediate entity (Fig. 5).

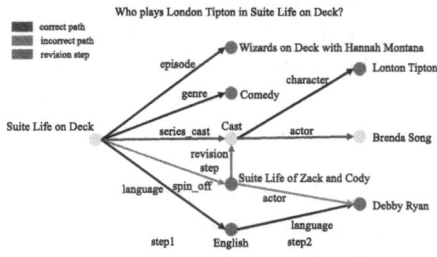

0.20	0.09	Wizards on Deck with Hannah Montana
0.12	0.08	Comedy
0.08	0.23	Brenda Song
0.08	0.15	Cast
0.08	0.23	Lonton Tipton
0.21	0.15	Suite Life of Zack and Cody
0.08	0.09	Debby Ryan
0.12	0.08	English
1st	2nd	

Fig. 4. One Case from WebQSP

Fig. 5. The attention weights of entities in graph aggregation section

7   Conclusion and Future Work

In this paper, we propose a novel and efficient approach KBIGER with the framework of iterative instruction generation and reasoning over the graph. We introduce the knowledge graph structure into instruction generation from the query question and it can revise the error of incorrect prediction for intermediate entities within the reasoning path. We conduct experiments on two benchmark datasets of this field and our approach outperforms all the existing methods. In the future, we will incorporate knowledge graph embedding into our framework to fuse the information from the query question and knowledge graph in a better manner.

References

1. Berant, J., Chou, A., Frostig, R., Liang, P.: Semantic parsing on freebase from question-answer pairs. In: EMNLP, pp. 1533–1544 (2013)
2. Bollacker, K., Evans, C., Paritosh, P., Sturge, T., Taylor, J.: Freebase: a collaboratively created graph database for structuring human knowledge. In: SIGMOD, pp. 1247–1250 (2008)
3. Cohen, W.W., Sun, H., Hofer, R.A., Siegler, M.: Scalable neural methods for reasoning with a symbolic knowledge base. In: ICLR (2020)
4. Dong, L., Wei, F., Zhou, M., Xu, K.: Question answering over freebase with multi-column convolutional neural networks. In: ACL, pp. 260–269 (2015)
5. Ferrucci, D., et al.: Building Watson: an overview of the DeepQA project. AI Mag. **31**(3), 59–79 (2010)
6. Guo, D., Tang, D., Duan, N., Zhou, M., Yin, J.: Dialog-to-action: conversational question answering over a large-scale knowledge base. In: NIPS, pp. 2942–2951 (2018)
7. He, G., Lan, Y., Jiang, J., Zhao, W.X., Wen, J.R.: Improving multi-hop knowledge base question answering by learning intermediate supervision signals. In: WSDM, pp. 553–561 (2021)
8. Liang, C., Berant, J., Le, Q., Forbus, K.D., Lao, N.: Neural symbolic machines: learning semantic parsers on freebase with weak supervision. In: NIPS (2016)
9. Miller, A., Fisch, A., Dodge, J., Karimi, A.H., Bordes, A., Weston, J.: Key-value memory networks for directly reading documents. In: EMNLP (2016)
10. Qiu, Y., Wang, Y., Jin, X., Zhang, K.: Stepwise reasoning for multi-relation question answering over knowledge graph with weak supervision. In: WSDM, pp. 474–482 (2020)
11. Saha, A., Ansari, G.A., Laddha, A., Sankaranarayanan, K., Chakrabarti, S.: Complex program induction for querying knowledge bases in the absence of gold programs. TACL **7**, 185–200 (2019)
12. Saxena, A., Tripathi, A., Talukdar, P.: Improving multi-hop question answering over knowledge graphs using knowledge base embeddings. In: ACL, pp. 4498–4507 (2020)
13. Shi, J., Cao, S., Hou, L., Li, J., Zhang, H.: TransferNet: an effective and transparent framework for multi-hop question answering over relation graph. In: EMNLP (2021)
14. Sun, H., Bedrax-Weiss, T., Cohen, W.W.: PullNet: open domain question answering with iterative retrieval on knowledge bases and text. In: EMNLP (2019)

15. Sun, H., Dhingra, B., Zaheer, M., Mazaitis, K., Salakhutdinov, R., Cohen, W.W.: Open domain question answering using early fusion of knowledge bases and text. In: EMNLP (2018)
16. Talmor, A., Berant, J.: The web as a knowledge-base for answering complex questions. In: NAACL (2018)
17. Yih, S.W.T., Chang, M.W., He, X., Gao, J.: Semantic parsing via staged query graph generation: question answering with knowledge base. In: ACL (2015)
18. Zhang, Y., Dai, H., Kozareva, Z., Smola, A.J., Song, L.: Variational reasoning for question answering with knowledge graph. In: AAAI (2018)
19. Zhao, W., Chung, T., Goyal, A., Metallinou, A.: Simple question answering with subgraph ranking and joint-scoring. In: NAACL (2019)
20. Zhou, M., Huang, M., Zhu, X.: An interpretable reasoning network for multi-relation question answering. In: COLING (2018)

Dialogue Systems (Oral)

MedDG: An Entity-Centric Medical Consultation Dataset for Entity-Aware Medical Dialogue Generation

Wenge Liu[1], Jianheng Tang[2], Yi Cheng[3], Wenjie Li[3], Yefeng Zheng[4],
and Xiaodan Liang[1(✉)]

[1] Sun Yat-sen University, Guangzhou, China
xdliang328@gmail.com
[2] Hong Kong University of Science and Technology, Hong Kong, China
[3] Hong Kong Polytechnic University, Hong Kong, China
alyssa.cheng@connect.polyu.hk, cswjli@comp.polyu.edu.hk
[4] Tencent Jarvis Lab, Shenzhen, China
yefengzheng@tencent.com

Abstract. Medical dialogue systems interact with patients to collect symptoms and provide treatment advice. In this task, medical entities (e.g., diseases, symptoms, and medicines) are the most central part of the dialogues. However, existing datasets either do not provide entity annotation or are too small in scale. In this paper, we present MedDG, an entity-centric medical dialogue dataset, where medical entities are annotated with the help of domain experts. It consists of 17,864 Chinese dialogues, 385,951 utterances, and 217,205 entities, at least one magnitude larger than existing entity-annotated datasets. Based on MedDG, we conduct preliminary research on entity-aware medical dialogue generation by implementing several benchmark models. Extensive experiments show that the entity-aware adaptions on the generation models consistently enhance the response quality but there still remains a large space of improvement for future research. The codes and the dataset are released at https://github.com/lwgkzl/MedDG.

1 Introduction

Online medical consultations have been playing an increasingly important role. According to [1], telemedicine substantially rose from 10% to 75% of general medical consultations before and after the COVID-19 pandemic in UK. However, patients often describe their situations verbosely and communicate with doctors inefficiently online. To address this dilemma, there has been growing research interest in developing automatic medical dialogue systems, which can assist doctors in pre-collecting symptoms and give patients preliminary treatment advice in time.

Different from generic dialogues, medical conversations are characterized by the following features. 1) **Entity-Centric.** Medical entity terms are the most central part of

---

W. Liu, J. Tang, and Y. Cheng—Equal contribution.

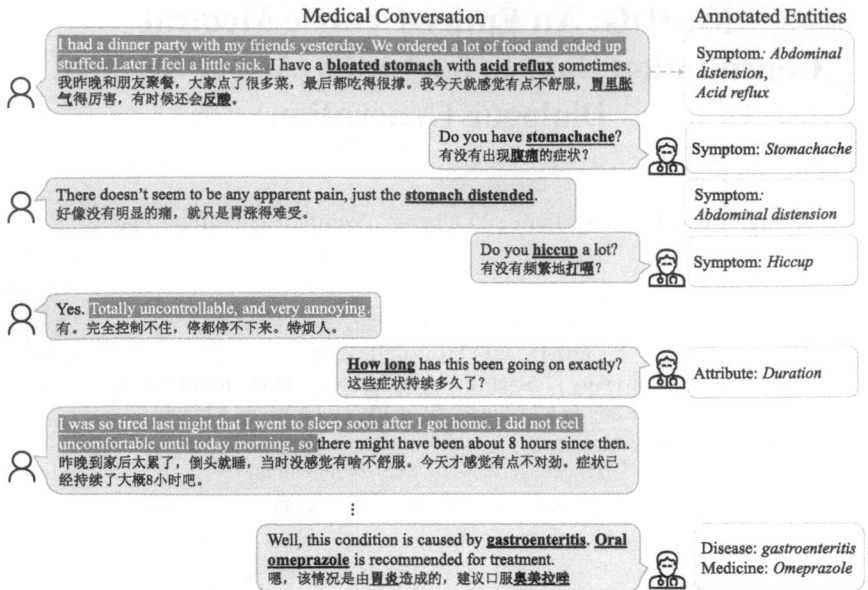

Fig. 1. An example medical consultation dialogue in the MedDG dataset. The entity-related text spans are underlined and their corresponding normalized entities are annotated in the right column. The gray part of the conversation are chit-chat content that barely contributes to medical diagnosis.

medical conversations. They serve as the foundation of accurate diagnosis and therapy. 2) **Redundancy.** Medical conversations usually contain redundant content that barely contributes to the medical diagnosis, as shown in the gray part of Fig. 1. Specifically, we sample 1,000 medical conversations from an online medical consultation platform, *Doctor Chunyu* and manually label the content directly associated with symptom inquiry/description, disease diagnosis, examination, and therapy. We find that 40.1% of the sentences posted by the patients are redundant chit-chat. 3) **Changeable Inquiry Order.** In medical conversations, the doctor's symptom inquiry order is usually changeable. As in Fig. 1, the order of querying "stomachache" and "hiccup" can be exchanged.

Given the above considerations, we argue that it would be beneficial to construct a medical conversation dataset, where the entity-related text spans and the corresponding normalized entities are annotated, as in Fig. 1. On the one hand, the annotation of entities could guide the introduction of external knowledge and help the medical dialogue system learn to focus on the central part of conversations [2], contributing to a better understanding of the dialogue context and a more accurate diagnosis. On the other hand, it could facilitate a more comprehensive evaluation of medical dialogue generation by comparing the generated entity terms with the ones appearing in the following ground-truth responses. Existing datasets, however, either do not provide such entity annotation [3] or are too small in scale [4–7].

Table 1. Comparison of entity-annotated medical dialogue datasets. The two columns below "# Entity Frequency" refer to the average (Avg.) and median (Med.) occurrence time of an entity.

Dataset	# Dialogues	# Utterances	# Entity Labels	# Entity Frequency	
				Avg.	Med.
MZ [7]	710	-	70	67.06	33
DX [6]	527	2,816	46	65.95	12
CMDD [8]	2,067	87,005	**161**	194.39	18
MIE [5]	1,120	18,129	71	93.70	64
MedDG	**17,864**	**385,951**	160	**1357.64**	**428**

Table 2. Occurrence percentage of top four entities in each category.

Disease	%	Symptom	%	Medicine	%	Examination	%	Attribute	%
Entity	%	Entity	%	Entity	%	Entity	%	Entity	%
Gastritis	4.59	Diarrhea	6.00	Omeprazole	2.57	Gastroscope	3.59	Duration	3.77
Enteritis	3.28	Abdominal pain	5.71	Motilium	1.01	Colonoscopy	2.12	Risk factor	1.47
Constipation	2.85	Abdominal ext	4.31	Mosapride	0.95	Stool test	0.46	Pain degree	0.72
Influenza	1.11	Vomit	3.56	Rabeprazole	0.80	Blood test	0.39	Body part	0.48
Total	13.70	**Total**	55.22	**Total**	16.76	**Total**	7.89	**Total**	6.42

In this paper, we present MedDG, an entity-centric Medical Dialogue dataset, with 17,864 Chinese dialogues, 385,951 utterances, and 217,205 entities. As demonstrated in Fig. 1, in MedDG the entity-related text spans are first extracted from the original text and their corresponding normalized entities are then annotated. Specifically, we annotate five catergories of entities, including disease, symptom, medicine, examination, and attribute. Table 2 lists the most frequent entities in each category in MedDG. Compared with existing entity-annotated medical dialogue datasets, MedDG is one (or two) magnitude larger in terms of dialogue and utterance number and the entities covered in MedDG are diverse, as shown in Table 1. Besides, the average and median occurrence times of each entity in MedDG are significantly higher than other corpora, demonstrating that models can learn features of each entity better with MedDG.

Based on MedDG, we conduct preliminary research on entity-aware medical dialogue generation. Several benchmark models are implemented respectively for entity prediction and entity-aware generation. Experimental results show that our entity-aware adaptions of the generation models consistently enhance the response quality, demonstrating that the entity-aware methodology is a worth-exploring direction for this task. In summary, our contributions are three-fold: 1) We collect MedDG, a large-scale entity-centric medical dialogue dataset, at least one magnitude larger than existing entity-annotated datasets; 2) We conduct preliminary research on entity-aware medical dialogue generation by implementing multiple benchmark models and conducting extensive evaluation; 3) We conduct extensive analysis of the benchmark models and demonstrate that the entity-aware methodology consistently achieves better response quality.

2   Related Work

Medical Dialogue Systems. Tasks related to the understanding of medical dialogues have been researched a lot, such as information extraction [5], relation prediction [9], symptom prediction [8] and slot filling [10]. However, the generation part of medical dialogue systems was rarely investigated. Early attempts came from [11–13]. More recently, [6, 14] introduced an end-to-end medical dialogue system based on predefined templates, which suffers from the problem of inflexibility. [3] took an initial step in neural-based medical dialogue generation. They pre-trained several dialogue generation models on large-scale medical corpora and studied the transferability of models to the low-resource COVID-19 dialogue generation task. However, they did not consider medical entities, which are the most central part of medical dialogues.

Medical Dialogue Datasets. [7] first launched a dataset for medical diagnosis, but it only contains some structured data related to the consultation content, rather than dialogues in the form of natural language. The DX dataset [6] contains 527 medical dialogues, but the utterances are automatically generated with templates. [8] collected the CMDD dataset with 2,067 dialogues on four pediatric diseases, and [5] released the MIE dataset with 1,120 dialogues on six cardiovascular diseases. However, both CMDD and MIE were proposed for dialogue understanding tasks, not large enough to build a competitive dialogue system. More recently, [3] collected 3.4 million Chinese medical dialogues from the Internet that make up an extra-large dataset, but the dialogues in it are all unlabeled, so its quality is not guaranteed by human-annotators and it is unable to facilitate research on entity-aware medical dialogue generation. Table 1 summarizes the statistics of public entity-annotated Chinese medical dialogue corpora. Among them, our MedDG dataset is the largest and includes diverse entity types.

3   MedDG Dataset

3.1   Data Collection

The dialogues in MedDG are collected from the gastroenterology department of an online Chinese medical consultation website, *Doctor Chunyu*,[1] where patients can submit posts about their problems and consult qualified doctors for professional advice. In total, more than 100,000 dialogues are collected. Then some low-quality dialogues are filtered out if the number of utterances is not between 10 and 50, or if it contains nontext information, such as graphics or sound. After filtering, there remain 17,864 dialogues, with 385,951 utterances. We select consultations in the gastroenterology department as their related inquiries are common and diverse. In addition, preliminary treatment advice for gastrointestinal problems relies less on medical examinations than the other diseases, and they are thus more suitable for online consultations.

To avoid privacy issues, the *Doctor Chunyu* website has already filtered the sensitive information when releasing consultation content. After collecting the online data,

---

[1] https://www.chunyuyisheng.com/.

we further ensure that there remains no private information by involving two checking approaches. First, we design a set of regular expression rules to extract private information, like ages, telephone numbers, and addresses, and then manually check the extracted results. Second, the annotators are asked to report to us if they observe any privacy issue during entity annotation. Neither of the above approaches find any sensitive information, proving that the source data has a very low risk of privacy issues.

3.2 Entity Annotation

We then conduct entity annotation on the collected dialogues in the form similar to [4]: the entity-related text spans are first extracted from the original text and then normalized into our pre-defined normalized entities, as shown in Fig. 1. To control costs within a reasonable range, we design a semi-automated annotation pipeline. First, we determine the entities to be included in the annotation. Then, domain experts manually annotate 1,000 dialogues in the dataset. Finally, an automatic annotation program is implemented based on the human annotation to label the remaining data.

Entity Determination. After discussing with domain experts, we choose five categories of entities for annotation: disease, symptom, examination and attribute. Then, we further define a total of 160 entities to be included in these categories, referring to the terminology lists in the Chinese medical knowledge graph CMeKG [15] and their frequency in the dataset. There are 12/62/62/20/4 entities, respectively, in the disease/symptom/medicine/examination/attribute category. Table 2 lists the four most frequent entities in each category and their frequency distribution.

Human Annotation. A total of 1,000 dialogues in the dataset are manually annotated. Eight annotators with more than one year of consultation experience are involved in the annotation process. They are asked to spend an average of 5 min on each dialogue, and paid with $50 per hour. To guide the annotators, we write the initial version of annotation manual through discussions with domain experts. The annotators are asked to first conduct trial annotation based on this manual, and report their problems on it. Then we revise the manual based on the found issues, and launch the formal annotation process. Each dialogue is labeled by two annotators independently and the inconsistent part is further judged by a third annotator. The Cohen's kappa coefficient between different pairs of annotators is between 0.948 and 0.976, indicating a strong agreement between annotators (1.0 denotes complete agreement).

Semi-Automatic Annotation. We then develop an automatic annotation program to label the remaining data. As its initial version, a set of regular expression rules are first designed based on the 1,000 human-labeled dialogues. That is, they can accurately cover all the entity annotation in the manually-annotated data. Then, to ensure its annotation quality, we randomly pick 2,000 utterances and invite experts to manually label them again. By comparing the annotation from the experts and the automatic program, we evaluate the annotation quality and further improve the annotation program repeatedly. The above revision procedure is repeated four times. The final version of the annotation program achieves 96.75% annotation accuracy on the 2,000 manually evaluated utterances, which supports the hypothesis that annotation accuracy is greater than 95% on the whole dataset (p-value < 0.01).

3.3 Dataset Statistics

There are 14,864/2,000/1,000 dialogues in the train/dev/test sets. The human-annotated dialogues are put in the test set and the rest are randomly divided into the training and the development sets. Table 3 presents statistics about the number of dialogues, utterances, tokens, and entities in MedDG. Table 2 illustrates the distribution of categories and top four entities in each category. We can see that the proportion of symptoms is the highest, accounting for 55% of the total entity occurences.

Table 3. Statistics about the number of dialogues, utterances, tokens, and entities in MedDG.

# Dialogues	17,864
# Utterances	385,949
# Tokens	6,829,562
# Entities	217,205
Avg. # of utterances in a dialogue	21.64
Avg. # of entities in a dialogue	12.16
Avg. # of tokens in an utterance	17.70
Avg. # of entities in an utterance	0.56

4 Experiments

Based on MedDG, we conduct preliminary research on entity-aware medical dialogue generation. Specifically, we investigate several pipeline methods that first predicts the entities to be mentioned in the upcoming response and then generates the response based on the prediction results. The formal definition of the two tasks involved (*entity prediction* and *entity-based response generation*) are as below. Formally, at each dialogue turn of the consultation system, it has access to the dialogue history consisting of a sequence of utterances from either the patient or the system itself, $X_{1:K} = \{X_1, X_2, ..., X_K\}$. The task of *entity prediction* is to predict the set of entities $E_{K+1} = \{e^1_{K+1}, e^2_{K+1}, ..., e^l_{K+1}\}$ to be mentioned in the upcoming response X_{K+1}. As for *entity-based response generation*, it is to generate the response X_{K+1}, based on the dialogue history $X_{1:K}$ and the entity prediction results E'_{K+1}.

4.1 Baselines

Entity Prediction. Entity prediction is done for each pre-defined entity e_i to decide whether it should be included in the upcoming response. We use first neural encoder to obtain the context vector of the dialogue history, which is then passed to a fully connected layer with a sigmoid function. Formally, the entity prediction process is defined as:

$$h_D = \text{Encoder}(X_{1:K})$$
$$g(e_i) = \text{Sigmoid}(w_p^T h_D) \tag{1}$$

where h_D is the context vector of the dialogue history and w_p is a learnable parameter. We use a binary cross entropy loss computed as:

$$L_e = -y_i \log(g(e_i)) - (1 - y_i)\log(1 - g(e_i)) \tag{2}$$

where $y_i \in \{0, 1\}$ is the ground truth indicating whether e_i will be included in the upcoming response or not. The following baseline models are implemented to encode the dialogue history: **LSTM** [16], **TextCNN** [17], **BERT-wwm** [18], **PCL-MedBERT** [19], **MedDGBERT**. MedDGBERT is a BERT-based model, pretrained on the training set of MedDG with a designed entity-prediction task, which is to predict the masked entities mentioned in the dialogue.

Table 4. Results of the entity prediction task on MedDG, in terms of the precision, recall, F1 scores of all the entities, and the F1 scores of each category. Note that all metrics are presented in percentage (%).

Model	P	R	F1	F1$_D$	F1$_S$	F1$_M$	F1$_E$	F1$_A$
LSTM	25.34	27.75	26.49	31.18	21.72	15.66	25.05	48.95
TextCNN	22.37	30.12	25.67	29.54	20.55	19.01	23.58	50.33
BERT-wwm	26.05	31.09	28.35	31.66	24.27	19.82	26.03	**52.44**
PCL-MedBERT	**26.46**	33.07	29.40	**33.72**	25.62	20.78	27.49	46.85
MedDGBERT	25.34	**36.20**	**29.81**	33.29	**26.39**	**21.35**	**27.60**	49.41

Entity-Based Response Generation. For entity-based response generation, we implement the following two approaches:

Retrieval. Given the predicted entities E'_{K+1}, the retrieval-based method chooses a doctor's utterance U_R in the training set of MedDG as its response. U_R is randomly picked from the utterances which satisfy the condition that their annotated entities E_R are the minimum coverage of all the predicted entities E'_{K+1}.

Entity Concatenation. Given the predicted entities E_{K+1}, we concatenate them with the dialogue history $X_{1:K}$ and then pass them to a generation model. The averaged negative log-likelihood of the target sequence $X_{K+1} = \{w_{K+1}^1, w_{K+1}^2, ..., w_{K+1}^T\}$ is used as the generation loss:

$$\mathcal{L}_g = -\frac{1}{T}\sum_{t=1}^{T} \log P(w_{K+1}^t). \tag{3}$$

We compare the following baseline models to generate responses with entity concatenation: **Seq2Seq** [20], **HRED** [21], **GPT-2** [22], **DialoGPT** [23], **BERT-GPT** [3], and **MedDGBERT-GPT**. BERT-GPT combines the BERT encoder and GPT decoder and is fine-tuned on the MedDialog dataset [3]. MedDGBERT-GPT has the same architecture as BERT-GPT, but its parameter of the BERT encoder are replaced with the weights in MedDGBERT, one of our entity prediction baselines.

4.2 Implementation Details

For the entity prediction methods, prediction is conducted for each predefined entity as a binary classification task, and the final predicted entity set is made up of the ones whose predicted probabilities are greater than 0.5. For the entity-based response generation methods, the entities concatenated in the input of the response generation models are automatically predicted, with the strong entity prediction baseline model MedDG-BERT; and the dialogue history is abbreviated to the last patient's utterance to speed up the experiments. For the three LSTM-based models (LSTM, Seq2seq, HRED), we implement a single-layer LSTM as the encoder or decoder. The dimensions of the word embedding and the hidden states in LSTM are set to 300. We use the Adam optimizer with a mini-batch size of 16 and set the initial learning rate to 0.001. For the other baseline models, we directly follow the implementations in their original papers. The number of training epoch is all bounded at 30, and training will be early-stopped after 5 epochs without improvement.

Table 5. Results of the response generation task on MedDG. "w/o Ent." refers to the entity-ablated version of the above method, which does not perform entity prediction and directly take the dialogue history as input. P_{Ent}, R_{Ent}, $F1_{Ent}$ stand for precision, recall and F1 of the entities mentioned in the generated results. Note that all metrics are normalized to $[0, 100]$.

Model	BLEU-1	BLEU-4	Distinct-1	Distinct-2	P_{Ent}	R_{Ent}	$F1_{Ent}$
Retrieval	23.08	12.58	0.62	9.98	11.44	**36.25**	17.39
Seq2Seq	35.24	19.20	0.75	5.32	12.41	25.65	16.73
w/o Ent.	26.12	14.21	0.88	4.77	14.07	11.45	12.63
HRED	**38.66**	21.19	0.75	7.06	12.01	26.78	16.58
w/o Ent.	31.56	17.28	1.07	8.43	13.29	11.25	12.18
GPT-2	30.87	16.56	0.87	11.20	**14.51**	20.76	17.08
w/o Ent.	29.35	14.47	**1.26**	13.53	7.33	12.22	9.17
DialoGPT	34.90	18.61	0.77	9.87	13.53	21.16	16.51
w/o Ent.	34.57	18.09	0.50	9.92	11.30	9.99	10.61
BERT-GPT	36.54	23.84	0.65	11.25	12.74	28.71	17.65
w/o Ent.	32.69	21.18	0.94	13.80	10.13	11.13	10.61
MedDGBERT-GPT	36.62	**23.99**	0.63	11.04	13.78	28.55	**18.59**
w/o Ent.	32.62	20.95	0.93	**13.88**	10.89	11.59	11.23

Table 6. Human evaluation results of different response generation methods in terms of fluency (Flu.), relevance (Rel.) and expertise (Exp.) on a scale of [1–5].

Model	Flu.	Rel.	Exp.
Retrieval	**4.23**	**4.18**	**4.29**
HRED	3.46	3.16	3.12
w/o Ent	2.84	2.73	2.40
MedDGBERT-GPT	3.93	3.62	3.55
w/o Ent	3.27	2.83	2.69

4.3 Results on Entity Prediction

For the entity prediction task, the evaluation metrics include precision, recall and F1. In addition to the scores evaluated on all the entities, we also calculate the F1 score of the ones in each entity categories, denoted as $F1_D$ (Disease), $F1_S$ (Symptom), $F1_M$ (Medicine), $F1_E$ (Examination), and $F1_A$ (Attribute). The results are shown in Table 4.

Compared with classic RNN and CNN encoders, we can see that the three BERT-based encoders (BERT-wwm, PCL-MedBERT, and MedDGBERT) consistently achieve better performance than LSTM and TextCNN in terms of all metrics. MedDG-BERT outperforms the other two BERT variants in most of the metrics, which demonstrates the effectiveness of including entity prediction in the pretraining process to integrate medical entity knowledge. Comparing the F1 scores of each category, we find that the performance on the attribute category is significantly superior to the one on the others. It is probably because entities in the attribute category follow relatively fixed patterns. For example, after patients' description of their symptoms, doctors would usually further ask about attributes of the symptoms, like duration and pain degree. In comparison, entity prediction on the other four categories are much more challenging, as they contain more types of entities and more heavily rely on domain knowledge. The diversity of different doctors' diagnosis strategies also increases the difficulty.

4.4 Results on Response Generation

Automatic Evaluation. For automatic evaluation, we assess the generated response in two aspects: the text quality and the medical entities it covers. To evaluate text quality, we use the **BLEU-1**, **BLEU-4** [24], **Distinct-1**, and **Distinct-2** [25] metrics. BLEU-1/4 measures lexical similarity, while Distinct-1/2 evaluates text diversity. To evaluate the medical entities covered in the response, we first use the automatic annotation program described in Sec. 3.2 to extract the entities mentioned in the generated responses, and then compare them with the gold entities in terms of precision, recall, and F1, named as P_{Ent}, R_{Ent}, $F1_{Ent}$, respectively. The results are presented in Table 5. The lines begins with "**w/o Ent**" show the ablation results of the corresponding models, which do not perform entity prediction and directly take the dialogue history as input. By analyzing Table 5, we can obtain the following insights.

Entity-Aware Adaptions Consistently Improve the Generation Quality. Comparing the entity-aware methods and their entity-ablated versions (denoted as "w/o Ent." in Table 5), we can see that the entity-aware adaptions significantly enhance both the BLEU and entity-related scores, demontrating the effectiveness of entity-aware methods in improving generation quality. For instance, MedDGBERT-GPT has 14.51% relative improvement on BLEU-4 and 65.54% on $F1_{Ent}$ compared with its entity-ablated version. The entity prediction results utilized by the entity-aware methods are provided by MedDGBERT, whose F1 score is no more than 30%, but the improvement is still significant. More improvement could be expected with stronger entity prediction models in the future. Besides, Distinct-1/2 drop after entity-aware adaptions in some cases, it is mainly because the entity-aware methods tend to generate more specific content, following relatively fixed patterns.

Retrieval vs. Generation. As our retrieval-based method directly respond with utterances in the training set based on the predicted entities without consideration of the contextual information, its BLEU score is lower than generative models, while the entity-related metrics are relatively high. Notably, the entity recall is significantly higher than all the generative methods, because our retrieval strategy ensures that all the predicted entities are covered in the response.

LSTM-Based vs. GPT-Based. Though with much fewer parameters, the BLEU scores of HRED are not lower than those of most GPT-based models. One possible reason is that the GPT models are pre-trained mainly on large-scale chit-chat data, so they tend to generate responses irrelevant to the medical domain. It also explains why GPT-based models have higher distinct scores.

Human Evaluation. We further conduct human evaluation of five selected generation methods, including Retrieval, HRED, MedDGBERT-GPT, and the entity-ablated versions of the latter two. We randomly pick 100 test dialogues, each with an average 9.71 utterances from the doctor. Three annotators involved in our dataset annotation process are asked to rate these models' responses independently between 1 (poor) and 5 (good) in the following three dimensions. 1) **Fluency**: It checks whether the response follows the grammar and semantically correct; 2) **Expertise**: It checks whether the response content is appropriate from a professional medical perspective; 3) **Relevance**: It checks whether the response is relevant to the dialogue history.

The results are shown in Table 6. Surprisingly, the retrieval-based method is significantly superior to other generative models on all metrics, especially in terms of sentence fluency, which is opposite to our automatic evaluation results. This is mainly because the fluency and quality of the retrieved response are guaranteed as they are all doctor-written sentences, while the BLEU metric only measure the similarity between the generation results and the reference utterances in terms of n-grams. Comparison of the four generative models can lead to the same conclusions as in the automatic evaluation that entity-aware methods can improve generation quality. The average Cohen's kappa scores between annotators are 0.41, 0.52, and 0.59 in fluency, relevance, and expertise, respectively.

Table 7. Examples of the generated responses from different methods. The left column lists the patient's utterances, gold responses, predicted and gold entities. The three presented turns belong to the same dialogue. The underlined entities are the ones correctly predicted.

Patient$_1$: I have a dull pain and grunting in the upper right corner of my belly button. (Female, 44 years old) 我肚脐斜右上方隐痛还咕噜噜叫。（女，44岁）	Retrieval	Hello, how long has this situation been? How often do you poop? 您好，这种情况多长时间了？大便一天拉几次。
	HRED	Hello, how long has this been happening? 你好，这种情况多久了？
Gold Response$_1$: Hello, how long has this been going on? 你好，这种情况多久了？	w/o Ent.	Hello, how long has this been happening? 你好，这种情况多久了？
	MedDGBERT-GPT	Hello, how long has this situation been? 您好，请问这个情况多久了？
Predicted Entities: <u>Duration</u> (时长)		
Gold Entities: Duration (时长)	w/o Ent.	Hello, how long has this situation been? 你好，这种情况有长时间了？
Patient$_2$: More than a week. I took a B-ultrasound yesterday and found nothing, but I felt full after eating. 一个多星期。昨天照了B超说没发现什么,但是吃完就觉得饱胀感。	Retrieval	Are there any other discomforts: <u>nausea</u>, heartburn, <u>acid reflux</u>, belching, abdominal distension, abnormal stool, etc? 还有其他不适吗：恶心、烧心、反酸、嗳气,腹胀,大便异常等？
	HRED	Is there any heartburn, <u>acid reflux</u>, bloating, greasy heartburn? 有没有烧心反酸腹胀厌油腻的烧心？
Gold Response$_2$: Are there nausea, vomiting, acid reflux, abdominal pain and diarrhea? 有恶心呕吐反酸，腹痛腹泻吗？	w/o Ent.	Do you have cholecystitis? 有胆囊炎吗？
Predicted Entities: <u>Reflux</u>, Heartburn, Hiccups, <u>Nausea</u>, <u>Abdominal pains</u> (反流，烧心，打嗝，恶心，腹痛)	MedDGBERT-GPT	Do you have <u>acid reflux</u>, heartburn, hiccups, <u>nausea</u> and <u>abdominal pain</u> ? Is your diet normal and regular? 有反酸烧心打嗝恶心腹痛吗？饮食正常规律吗？
Gold Entities: Diarrhea, Abdominal pain, Nausea, Vomiting, Reflux (腹泻,腹痛,恶心,呕吐,反流)	w/o Ent.	Do you usually have heartburn, <u>acid reflux</u>, <u>nausea</u> and bloating? 平常有烧心返酸恶心腹胀吗？

......

Patient$_6$: May I ask what kind of disease I have? 请问您我这个大概是哪里的问题。	Retrieval	This may be caused by <u>gastritis</u>. It is recommended that you have a gastroscope to rule out digestive ulcers. 这个可能是有胃炎,建议您最好做个胃镜,可以排除消化道溃疡。
	HRED	Considering the possibility of <u>gastritis</u>, it is recommended to have a gastroscope exam. 考虑胃炎可能性大，建议做个胃镜看看。
Gold Response$_6$: Your condition may be caused by enteritis, gastritis or gastrointestinal dysfunction. 考虑你这有可能是胃肠炎,胃肠功能紊乱引起的。	w/o Ent.	Consider gastrointestinal? 考虑胃肠？
Predicted Entities: <u>Gastritis</u>, Gastroscope (胃炎,胃镜)	MedDGBERT-GPT	This is a sign of <u>gastritis</u>. An ultrasound of the abdomen is needed to clarify the cause. 这属于胃炎的表现。需要做一下腹部超明确病因。
Gold Entities: Gastrointestinal dysfunction, Gastritis, Enteritis (胃肠功能紊乱,胃炎,肠炎)	w/o Ent.	This position does not exclude gastritis, especially reflux <u>gastritis</u>. 这个位置不能排除胃炎，尤其是反流性胃炎的情况。

Case Study. Table 7 gives three examples of the generated responses from different generaion methods. We can see that with the guidance of these predicted entities, the model responses are more informative and contain more correct entities. For example, in the second turn, HRED accurately includes the entity "acid reflux" under the guidance of predicted entities, while its entity-ablated version generates the wrong entity "cholecystitis". Compared with other methods, MedDGBERT-GPT generates the most number of correct entities in three turns.

5 Conclusion and Future Work

In this paper, we proposed MedDG, a large-scale Chinese medical consultation dataset with annotation of rich medical entities. Based on MedDG, we conducted preliminary research on entity-aware medical dialogue generation, by implementing a pipeline method that first predicts entities to be mentioned and then conducts generation based on these entities. Through extensive experiments, we demonstrated the importance of taking medical entities into consideration. In the future, we will further investigate how to introduce domain knowledge to this task. One possible approach is to model the relationship between different medical entities in MedDG based on medical knowledge graphs like CMeKG [15].

References

1. McCall, B: Could telemedicine solve the cancer backlog? The Lancet Digital Health (2020)
2. Liu, W., Tang, J., Liang, X., Cai, Q.: Heterogeneous graph reasoning for knowledge-grounded medical dialogue system. Neurocomputing **442**, 260–268 (2021)
3. Zeng, G., et al.: MedDialog: large-scale medical dialogue datasets. In Proceedings of EMNLP, pp. 9241–9250 (2020)
4. Lin, X., He, X., Chen, Q., Tou, H., Wei, Z., Chen, T.: Enhancing dialogue symptom diagnosis with global attention and symptom graph. In Proceedings of EMNLP, pp. 5032–5041. Association for Computational Linguistics (2019)
5. Zhang, Y., et al.: MIE: a medical information extractor towards medical dialogues. In Proceedings of ACL, pp. 6460–6469 (2020)
6. Xu, L., Zhou, Q., Gong, K., Liang, X., Tang, J., Lin, L.: End-to-end knowledge-routed relational dialogue system for automatic diagnosis. In Proceedings of AAAI, pp. 7346–7353 (2019)
7. Wei, Z., et al.: Task-oriented dialogue system for automatic diagnosis. In Proceedings of ACL, pp. 201–207 (2018)
8. Lin, X., He, X., Chen, Q., Tou, H., Wei, Z., Chen, T.: Enhancing dialogue symptom diagnosis with global attention and symptom graph. In Proceedings of the 2019 Conference on Empirical Methods in Natural Language Processing and the 9th International Joint Conference on Natural Language Processing (EMNLP-IJCNLP), Hong Kong, China, Nov 2019, pp. 5033–5042. Association for Computational Linguistics (2019)
9. Du, N., Wang, M., Tran, L., Lee, G., Shafran, I.: Learning to infer entities, properties and their relations from clinical conversations. In Proceedings of the 2019 Conference on Empirical Methods in Natural Language Processing and the 9th International Joint Conference on Natural Language Processing (EMNLP-IJCNLP), pp. 4979–4990, Hong Kong, China, Nov 2019. Association for Computational Linguistics (2019)
10. Shi, X., Hu, H., Che, W., Sun, Z., Liu, T., Huang, J.: Understanding medical conversations with scattered keyword attention and weak supervision from responses. In Proceedings of AAAI, pp. 8838–8845 (2020)
11. Ferguson, G., Allen, J., Galescu, L., Quinn, J., Swift, M.: CARDIAC: an intelligent conversational assistant for chronic heart failure patient heath monitoring. In 2009 AAAI Fall Symposium Series (2009)
12. Wong, W., Thangarajah, J., Padgham, L.: Health conversational system based on contextual matching of community-driven question-answer pairs. In: Proceedings of the 20th ACM Conference on Information and Knowledge Management, pp. 2577–2580 (2011)
13. Liu, C., et al.: Augmented LSTM framework to construct medical self-diagnosis android. In ICKM, pp. 251–260. IEEE (2016)
14. Liu, W., et al.: "My nose is running" "are you also coughing": building a medical diagnosis agent with interpretable inquiry logics. arXiv preprint arXiv:2204.13953 (2022)
15. Odmaa, B., et al.: Preliminary study on the construction of Chinese medical knowledge graph. J. Chin. Inf. Process. **33**(10), 1–7 (2019)
16. Hochreiter, S., Schmidhuber, J.: Long short-term memory. Neural Comput. **9**(8), 1735–1780 (1997)

17. Kim, Y.: Convolutional neural networks for sentence classification. In: Proceedings of the 2014 Conference on Empirical Methods in Natural Language Processing (EMNLP), Doha, Qatar, Oct 2014, pp. 1746–1751. Association for Computational Linguistics (2014)
18. Cui, Y., et al.: Pre-training with whole word masking for Chinese BERT. arXiv preprint arXiv:1906.08101 (2019)
19. Ting, L., Bing, Q., Ming, L., Ruifeng, X., Buzhou, T., Qingcai, C.: Pre-training model for Chinese medical text processing-PCL-MedBERT. In: PCL blog (2020)
20. Sutskever, I., Vinyals, O., Le, Q.V.: Sequence to sequence learning with neural networks. In: Advances in Neural Information Processing Systems, pp. 3104–3112 (2014)
21. Serban, I.V., Sordoni, A., Bengio, Y., Courville, A.C., Pineau, J.: Building end-to-end dialogue systems using generative hierarchical neural network models. In: Proceedings of AAAI, pp. 3776–3784 (2016)
22. Radford, A., Wu, J., Child, R., Luan, D., Amodei, D., Sutskever, I.: Language models are unsupervised multitask learners. In: OpenAI Blog (2019)
23. Zhang, Y., et al.: DIALOGPT: large-scale generative pre-training for conversational response generation. In: Proceedings of ACL: System Demonstrations, pp. 270–278. Association for Computational Linguistics (2020)
24. Chen, B., Cherry, C.: A systematic comparison of smoothing techniques for sentence-level BLEU. In: Proceedings of the Ninth Workshop on Statistical Machine Translation, pp. 362–367 (2014)
25. Li, J., Galley, M., Brockett, C., Gao, J., Dolan, B.: A diversity-promoting objective function for neural conversation models. In: Proceedings of NAACL-HLT, pp. 110–119. Association for Computational Linguistics (2016)

DialogueTRGAT: Temporal and Relational Graph Attention Network for Emotion Recognition in Conversations

Junjun Kang[1,2] and Fang Kong[1,2(✉)]

[1] Laboratory for Natural Language Processing, Soochow University, Suzhou, China
20204227051@stu.suda.edu.cn, kongfang@suda.edu.cn
[2] School of Computer Science and Technology, Soochow University, Suzhou, China

Abstract. Emotion Recognition in Conversations (ERC) is the task of identifying the emotions of utterances from speakers in a conversation, which is beneficial to a number of applications, including opinion mining over conversations, developing empathetic dialogue systems, and so on. Many approaches have been proposed to handle this problem in recent years. However, most existing approaches either focus on using RNN-based models to simulate temporal information change in the conversation or graph-based models to take the relationships between the utterances of the speakers into account. In this paper, we propose a temporal and relational graph attention network, named DialogueTRGAT, to combine the strengths of RNN-based models and graph-based models. DialogueTRGAT can better model the intrinsic structure and information flow within a conversation for better emotion recognition. We conduct experiments on two benchmark datasets(IEMOCAP, MELD), and the experimental results demonstrate the great effectiveness of our approach compared with several competitive baselines.

Keywords: Emotion recognition · Graph model · Dialogue modeling

1 Introduction

As a fundamental aspect of human communication, emotions play important roles in our daily lives and are crucial for more natural human-computer interaction. In recent years, with the development of social networks and the construction of large datasets for dialogue, emotion recognition in conversations has become an emerging task for the research community due to its applications in several important tasks such as opinion mining over conversations(Kumar et al. [7]), building an emotional and empathetic dialogue system (Majumder et al.[8], Zhou et al. [16]), and so on.

Emotion recognition in conversations aims to identify the emotion of each utterance in conversations involving two or more speakers. Different from other emotion recognition tasks, conversational emotion recognition is not only for utterances, but also depends on the context and the states of speakers. With the development of deep learning technologies, many approaches have been proposed to handle this problem. They can generally be divided into two categories: RNN-based methods and graph-based methods. But they all have their disadvantages. For the RNN-based methods, they use RNN-based models encoding the utterances temporally, but because RNN has long-term information propagation issues, they tend to aggregate relatively limited information from the nearest utterances for the target utterance, so can't model the long-term dependency within the conversation. For graph-based models, they adopt neighborhood-based graph convolutional networks to model conversational context. In these models, they construct relational edges to directly build the correlation between utterances, thereby alleviating the long-distance dependency issues. But they neglect the sequential characteristic of conversation.

According above discussion, in this paper, we try to combine the advantage of RNN-based models and graph-based models to complement each other. We propose a temporal and relational graph attention network, named DialogueTRGAT to model the conversation as temporal graph structure. In particular, like RNN-based models, we gather historical context information for each target utterance based on the their temporal position in dialogue. For each target utterance, it only receives information from some previous utterances and cannot propagate information backward. In order to model the inter-speaker dependency[1] and self-dependency[2] between utternaces, we follow Ishiwatari et al. [5], use the message aggregation principle of relational graph attention networks(RGAT) to aggregate context information for the target utterance based on the speaker identity between itself and the previous utterances.

Compared with the traditional static graph networks, DialogueTRGAT enables the targe utterance can indirectly attend to the remote context without having to stack too many graphical layers. And it can be seen as an extension of traditional graph neural networks with an additional focus on the temporal dimension. We argue that DialogueTRGAT can better model the flow of information in dialogue and aggregate more meaningful historical contextual information for each target utterance, leading to better emotion recognition.

2   Related Work

We generally classify related works into two categories according to the method of modeling the dialogue context.

RNN-Based Models: Many works capture contextual information in utterance sequences. ICON [3] uses an RNN-based memory network to model contextual information that incorporates inter-speaker and self-dependency. HiGRU [6] propose a hierarchical GRU framework, where lower-level GRU is utterance encoder and the contexts of utterances are captured by the upper-level GRU. Considering the individual speaker state change throughout the conversation, Majumder

---

[1] the speaker's emotions are influenced by others.

[2] emotional inertia of individual speakers.

et al. [9] propose DialogueRNN, which utilizes GRUs to update speakers' states, the global state of the conversation and emotional dynamics. DialogCRN [4] uses LSTM to encode the conversational-level and speaker-level context respectively for each utterance and proposes to apply LSTM-based reasoning modules to extract and integrate clues for emotional reasoning.

Graph-Based Models: Many works model the conversational context by designing a specific graphical structure. For example, DialogueGCN [2] models two relations between speakers: self and inter-speaker dependencies, and utilizes graph network to model the graph constructed by these relations. Base on DialogueGCN, DialogueRGAT [5] uses relational position encoding to combine position information into the graph network structure. ConGCN [15] regards both speakers and utterances as graph nodes, the context-sensitive dependence and the speaker-sensitive dependence are modeled as edges to construct graphical structure. Shen et al. [12] model the dialogue as a directed acyclic graph and use directed acyclic graph neural networks [14] to model the conversation context. Our work is closely related to the graph-based models. But like RNN-based models, our model focuses more on the temporality of information propagation in graphical models than the above-mentioned models.

3   Methodology

3.1   Problem Definition

Given the transcript of a conversation along with speaker information of each constituent utterance, the task is to identify the emotion of each utterance from several pre-defined emotions. Formally, given the input sequence of N number of utterances and corresponding speakers$\{(u_1, s_1), (u_2, s_2), \ldots, (u_N, s_N)\}$, where each utterance $u_i = \{w_{i,1}, w_{i,2}, \ldots, w_{i,T}\}$ consists of T words $u_{i,j}$ and spoken by speaker s_i, $s_i \in S$, where S is the set of the conversation speakers. The task is to predict the emotion label e_i for each target utterance u_i based on its historical context $\{u_1, u_2, ..., u_{i-1}\}$ and the corresponding speaker information.

3.2   Model

Emotion Recognition in Conversations, as a conversational utterance-level understanding task, most of the recent methods consist of three common components including (i) feature extraction for utterances (ii) conversational context encoder, and (iii) the emotion classifier. Our model also follows the paradigm. Figure 1 shows the overall architecture of our model.

Utterance-Level Feature Extraction. Convolutional Neural Networks (CNNs) are effective in learning high-level abstract representations of sentences from constituting words or n-grams. Following (Ghosal et al. [3] Hazarika et al., [9] Majumder et al.[2]), we use a single convolutional layer followed by max-pooling and a fully connected layer to obtain the feature representations for the utterances. We denote $\{h_i\}_{i=1}^{N}$, $h_i \in \mathbb{R}^{d_u}$ as the representation for N utterances.

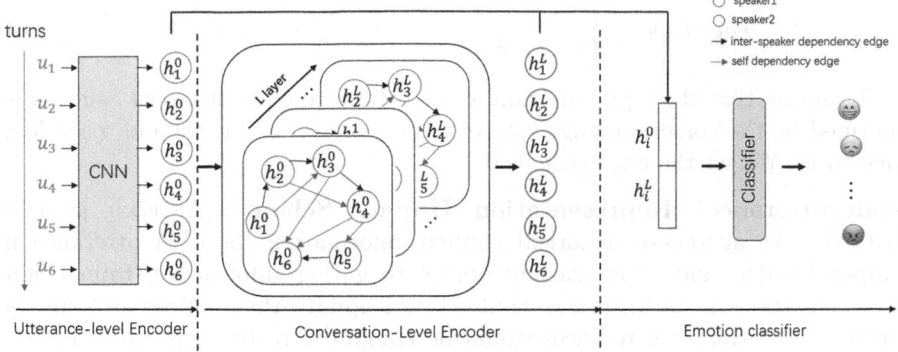

Fig. 1. The overall architecture of our model.

Sequential and Speaker-Level Context Encoder. We model the conversation as a temporal graph structure and propose a temporal and relational graph attention network(TRGAT) to model the controversial context and gather historical context information for target utterance. Our graph structure transmit information in temporal order to imitate the process of dynamic conversation, which can preserve the temporal change information of conversation. The relational graph attention network's message aggregation principle captures both self-dependency and inter-speaker dependency for target utterance.

Graph Structure:Node: Each utterance in a conversation is represented as a node $v_i \in V$. Each node v_i is initialized with the utterance representation h_i. The representation can updated by aggregating the representations of previous utterance within a certain context window through our TRGAT layers. The updated representation is donated as h_i^l, where l denotes the number of TRGAT layers. So we also denoted h_i as h_i^0.

Edges: For each target utterance u_i, its emotion is most likely to be influenced by the utterance between the previous utterance spoken by s_i and the utterance u_{i-1}. We use these utterances as the historical window to aggregate context information for utterance u_i. We argue that it is more reasonable compared to using a fixed-size history window. We regard u_j as the latest utterance spoken by s_i before u_i ($s_j = s_i$). Then for each utterance u_τ in between u_j and u_{i-1}, we make a directed edge from u_τ to u_i. Depending on whether the speaker of u_τ is the same as the speaker of u_i, we divide the edges into two types. Formally, the above process can be expressed by the following formulas:

$$j = \max_j j < i \ \& \ s_j = s_i \tag{1}$$

$$historical \ window = [u_j, u_{j+1}, ..., u_{i-1}] \tag{2}$$

$$edges = \{u_\tau \to u_i\}_{\tau=j}^{i-1} \tag{3}$$

$$edge\ type = \begin{cases} 0 & s_\tau = s_i \\ 1 & s_\tau \neq s_i \end{cases} \quad \tau \in [j, j+1, ..., i-1] \qquad (4)$$

To ensure that the representation of the utterance node at layer l can also be informed by the corresponding representation at layer $l-1$, we add a self-loop edge to u_i. We set the edge type as 0.

Node(utterance) Representation Update Scheme: At each layer of TRGAT, We aggregate historical context information for each utterance in temporal order, and allow each utterance to gather information from neighbors(utterances in its historical window) and update their representations. So the representation of utterances would be computed recurrently from the first utterance to the last one. Follow DialogueRGAT [5], in order to model the self and inter-speaker dependency between utterances, we use the message aggregation principle of relational graph attention networks(RGAT) to aggregate context information for each utterance.

In l-th layer, for each target utterance u_i, the attention weights between u_i and u_τ and the attention weights between u_i and itself are calculated as follows:

$$e_{i,\tau}^l = LeakyReLu\left((a_r^l)^T[W_r^l h_i^{l-1} || W_r^l h_\tau^l]\right) \quad edge\ type(s_\tau, s_i) = r \in \{0,1\} \quad (5)$$

$$e_{i,i}^l = LeakyReLu\left((a_0^l)^T[W_0^l h_i^{l-1} || W_0^l h_i^{l-1}]\right) \qquad (6)$$

$$\alpha_{i,\tau}^l = softmax_i(e_{i,\tau}^l) \qquad (7)$$

$$\alpha_{i,i}^l = softmax_i(e_{i,i}^l) \qquad (8)$$

where $\alpha_{i,\tau}^l$ denotes the edge(attention) weight from u_τ to the target utterance u_i in layer l. $\alpha_{i,i}^l$ denotes self-loop edge weight for u_i in layer l, W_r^l denotes a parameterized weight matrix for edge type r in layer l. a_r^l denotes a parameterized weight vector for edge type r in layer l, W_r and a_r not shared across the layers. T represents transposition. $||$ represents the concatenation operation of vectors. A softmax function is used to obtain the incoming edges whose total weight is 1.

It is worth noting that the attention weights between u_i and u_τ are based on the u_i's hidden state[3] in the $l-1$-th layer (h_i^{l-1})and the u_τ's hidden state in the l-th layer(h_τ^l). The reasons are as follows: we update hidden state for each utterance based on their temporal position and the temporal position of u_τ is in front of u_i. So the hidden state for u_τ has been updated before u_i, donated h_τ^l, when updating the hidden state of u_i, we use the updated hidden state to calculate the attention weight.

Finally, a relational graph attention networks propagation module updates the representation of u_i by aggregating representations of its neighborhood $N(i)$, and an attention mechanism is used to attend to the neighborhood's representations. We define the propagation module as follows:

---

[3] The hidden state of utterance in layer l is equivalent to the representation of utterance in layer l.

$$h_i^l = \left(\sum_r \sum_{\tau \in N^r(i)} \alpha_{i,\tau}^l W_r^l h_\tau^l \right) + \alpha_{i,i}^l W_0^l h_i^{l-1} \tag{9}$$

$$r \in 0,1 \qquad j <= \tau <= u - 1$$

where $N^r(i)$ donates the neighborhood of u_i under the edge type r.

In each layer, TRGAT can adaptively gather context information for target utterance from both the neighboring utterances and the remote utterances because of the following reason: the target utterance can directly interact with the previous utterances in the context window through directed relational edges. And each utterance in context window has gathered context information for itself, so the target utterance can indirectly attend to the remote utterances.

Let's take the conversation in Fig. 1 as an example to illustrate the update process of utterance representation. The dialogue consists of six utterances $\{u_1, u_2, u_3, u_4, u_5, u_6\}$, u_1, u_3, u_6 are spoken by s_1, u_2, u_4, u_5 are spoken by s_2. The historical context for each utterance is shown in Table 1, and the update process of utterance representation in the l-th TRGAT layer is shown in Fig. 2.

Table 1. The utterances and its historical context in conversation.

Utterance	Historical context
u_1	$\{\emptyset\}$
u_2	$\{u_1\}$
u_3	$\{u_1, u_2\}$
u_4	$\{u_2, u_3\}$
u_5	$\{u_4\}$
u_6	$\{u_2, u_3, u_4\}$

Emotion Classification. After obtaining the representations h_i^L of each utterance node through stacking TRGAT layer of L layers, we concatenate the non-contextual representation h_i^0 and the representation h_i^L as the final representation of u_i, and pass it through a feed-forward neural network and a softmax layer to get the emotion distribution:

$$H_i = h_i^0 || h_i^L \tag{10}$$

$$Z_i = ReLu(W_H H_i + b_H) \tag{11}$$

$$P_i = Softmax(W_Z Z_i + b_Z) \tag{12}$$

where W_H and W_Z denote learnable weight matrixes, and b_H and b_Z denote learnable bias vectors.

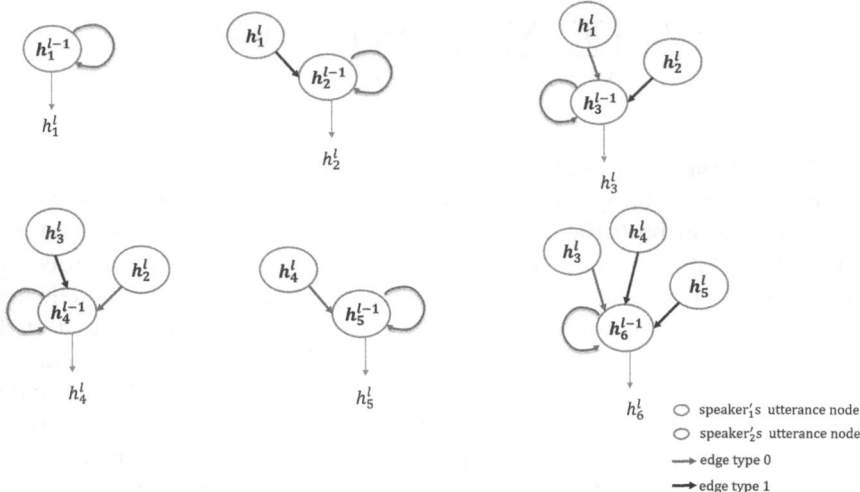

Fig. 2. Each utterance updates the hidden state according to its temporal position in the dialogue. Each subgraph represents the computational graph of the currently updated node(utterance). h_i^{l-1}, h_i^l represents the hidden state of i-th utterance in layer $l-1$ and l respectively. The two speakers' utterances are colored blue and green respectively. The edges represent the direction of the flow of information. The utterance represented by the source node and the tail node of the red arrow is said by the same speaker, which is used to model self-dependency between utterances, and the utterance represented by the source node and the tail node of the black arrow is spoken by different speakers, used to model inter-speaker dependency between utterances. (Color figure online)

4   Experiment

4.1   Datasets and Evaluation Metrics

We evaluate our model on two benchmark datasets: IEMOCAP [1] and MELD [11]. Both datasets are multimodal datasets containing textual, visual, and acoustic information for every utterance of each conversation. In this work, we focus on conversational emotion recognition only from textual information. We leave multimodal dialogue emotion recognition as future work, and when comparing model performance, we also only use the performance of different models in text modalities.

The IEMOCAP dataset contains videos of dyadic conversations where actors perform improvisations or scripted scenarios. Each conversation is segmented into utterances, which are annotated with one of the six emotion labels: happy, sad, neutral, angry, excited, and frustrated.

The MELD dataset comes from the Friends TV series with multiple speakers involved in the conversations. The utterances are annotated with one of seven labels: neutral, happiness, surprise, sadness, anger, disgust, and fear.

The statistics of the two datasets are shown in Table 2. Because IEMOCAP has no validation set, we extract the validation set from the randomly shuffled training set with the ratio of 8:2. Following [2,9], we use the F1-score to evaluate the performance for each emotion class, and use the weighted F1-score to evaluate the overall performance on the two datasets.

Table 2. Statistics of IEMOCAP, MELD

Dataset	# conversations			Avg. conversation len			# utterance		
	Train	Val	Test	Train	Val	Test	Train	Val	est
IEMOCAP	120		31	48		52	5810		1623
MELD	1038	114	280	10	10	9	9989	1109	2610

4.2 Baselines

For a comprehensive performance evaluation, we compared our model with the following baselines:

CNN: As described in Sect. 3.2, it is our utterance representation extractor and trained at the utterance-level without contextual information. **scLSTM** [10]: It captures contextual information from historical utterances by using a unidirectional LSTM. **Memnet** [13]: The current utterance is fed to a memory network, where the memories correspond to historical utterances. The output from the memory network is used as the final utterance representation for emotion classification. **DialogueRNN** [9]: It is a recurrent network that uses two GRUs to track individual speaker's states and global context during the conversation. Further, another GRU is employed to track emotional state through the conversation. **DialogueGCN** [2]: It captures self-dependency and inter-speaker dependency between utterances by using two-layer graph neural networks. For a fair comparison, we remove the directed edges from future utterances to current utterances from the original graph structure to avoid backpropagation of dialogue information. **DialogueRGAT** [5]: Based on DialogueGCN and taking the sequential information of conversation into account, DialogueRGAT propose a kind of relational position encodings that provide RGAT with sequential information. Our handling of graph structures is consistent with DialogueGCN.

4.3 Implementation Settings

We use the following settings to optimize the model parameters during training: the dimension of initial utterance representation is set to 100, 600 for IMEOCAP and MELD respectively. In each TRGAT layer, the size of hidden states is the same as the utterance representation dimension. To prevent our model from overfitting, we adopted drop out after each TRGAT layer and the dropout rate is 0.4. We employed AdamW as the optimizer for model learning and the learning rate is 0.0005. We used the standard cross-entropy loss as the loss function to train the model. On both datasets, we train 100 epochs on the training set and the batch size is 32, saving the model parameters with the best overall performance on the validation set, and finally report the performance on the test set.

For the TRGAT layer size L, we let $L = 3$ for the overall performance comparison by default, but we also carried out experiments with different layer size in Sect. 4.5 to explore how it influence the overall performance.

4.4   Experimental Results

Tabel 3 and Table 4 present the results of IEMOCAP and MELD testing sets, respectively.

Table 3. Performance comparison on the IEMOCAP dataset. The evaluation metrics is F1 for each class. Average(w) = Weighted F1, † denotes results refer to the original paper. * denotes the re-implement results.

Models	Emotion classes						Average (w)
	Happy	Sad	Neutral	Angry	Excited	Frustrated	
CNN	29.9	53.8	40.1	52.4	50.1	55.8	48.2
scLSTM†	34.4	60.9	51.8	56.7	57.9	58.9	54.9
Memnet†	33.5	61.8	52.8	55.4	58.3	59.0	55.1
DialogueRNN†	35.5	69.9	55.3	61.9	62.2	59.4	58.8
DialogueGCN*	36.2	74.1	**56.2**	63.9	62.0	61.7	60.2
DialogueRGAT*	37.1	72.4	56.0	65.8	**62.4**	60.4	60.7
Ours	**39.1**	**75.8**	55.1	**67.2**	61.2	**61.7**	**62.6**

Table 4. Performance comparison on the MELD dataset.

Models	Emotion Classes							Average (w)
	Neutral	Suprise	Fear	Sad	Joy	Disgust	Anger	
CNN	74.9	45.5	3.7	21.1	49.4	8.2	34.5	55.0
scLSTM†	73.8	47.7	5.4	25.1	51.3	5.2	38.4	55.9
Memnet†	72.8	49.4	8.8	24.6	48.3	3.1	42.3	55.6
DialogueRNN†	73.5	49.4	1.2	23.8	50.7	1.7	41.5	55.9
DialogueGCN*	73.1	50.1	8.8	**26.2**	50.3	6.3	39.5	55.7
DialogueRGAT*	74.6	**52.3**	7.2	24.5	**51.5**	7.1	40.9	56.1
Ours	**75.5**	50.2	**10.4**	25.9	51.1	**9.2**	**42.6**	**57.8**

IEMOCAP: In Table 3, our model performs better than all compared models on IMOCAP dataset. Our model attains the best overall performance with improvement over the strongest RNN-based baseline DialogueRNN (+3.8% weight-f1) and the strongest graph-based baseline DialogueRGAT(+1.9% weight-f1).

From the experiment results, the graph-based models(DialogueGCN, DialogueRGAT) perform better than the RNN-based model (DialogueRNN). Perhaps DialogueRNN employs gated recurrent unit (GRUs) to model conversational context, GRUs-based modeling methods can be problematic for many long conversations in IEMOCAP dataset. In contrast, DialogueGCN and DialogueRGAT try to overcome this issue by constructing relational edges to directly model the correlation between utterances. Our model acts like a combination of RNN-based and graph-based models and can better model conversational context.

MELD: For the conversations in MELD dataset, it contains an average of 10 utterances and many conversations containing more than 5 speakers. So this makes the interaction between speakers more difficult than IEMOCAP which only consists of dyadic conversations. So under this circumstance, graph-based models' advantage in encoding context is not that important. So we found that the difference in results between RNN-base models and graph-based models is not as contrasting as it is in the case of IEMOCAP. The overall performance is not significantly different.

But our models still outperform all baseline methods that suggest the efficacy of our context-modeling method. Compared with the best baseline model DialogueRGAT, our model attains +1.7% weight-f1 improvement in overall performance. In addition, our models perform the best on the two minority classes fear and disgust, this demonstrates the capability of our models in recognizing minority emotion classes.

4.5   Model Analysis

Pre-trained Models as Utterance Feature Extractor. With the outstanding performance of pre-trained models in natural language understanding tasks, pre-trained models are often used as utterance feature extractor in recent works. We replace the CNN-based extractor described in Sect. 3.2 with the Roberta-based extractor to demonstrate the effectiveness of our method regardless of what utterance feature extractor is used. The experimental results are shown in Table 5. From the results, all models can gain remarkable improvement by employing the powerful extractor. Our method attains comparable results compared with the state-of-the-art model DAG+Roberta [14] on IEMOCAP dataset. Meanwhile, our model also achieves comparable results with the best baseline models on the MELD dataset.

Number of TRGAT Layers. We further explore the relationship between model performance and number of TRGAT layer, and whether using RGAT's message aggregation principle to aggregate contextual information for each utterance outperforms other graph networks? Here, we use the message aggregation principle used in Graph Attention Network (GAT) [16] and Relational Graph Convolutional Network (RGCN) [13] as a comparative experiment. we denoted the two layers as TGAT and TRGCN. As shown in Fig. 3, we set different

Table 5. Performance comparison of different models using roberta as feature extractor on IEMOCAP and MELD datasets.

Models	IEMOCAP	MELD
Roberta	63.4	62.9
DialogueRNN+Roberta	64.8	**63.6**
DialogueGCN+Roberta	64.9	63.0
DialogueRGAT+Roberta	66.4	62.9
DAG+Roberta	**68.0**	**63.6**
Ours+Roberta	67.9	63.3

TRGAT layers on IEMOCAP and MELD datasets to compare the performance with TGAT and TRGCN.

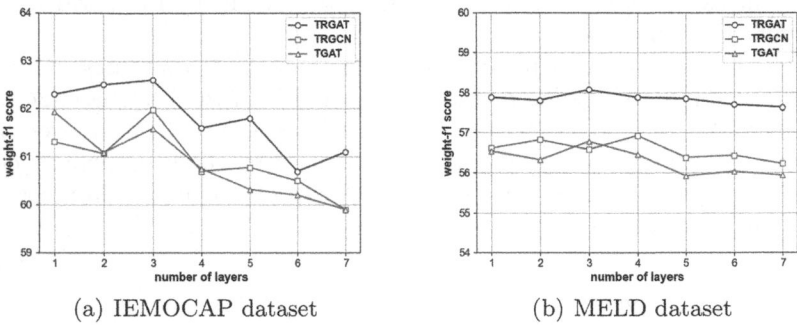

(a) IEMOCAP dataset   (b) MELD dataset

Fig. 3. Test results of TRGAT, TRCN, and TGAT on the IEMOCAP dataset and MELD dataset by different numbers of network layers.

For static graph neural network (GNN) based models such as DialogueGCN and DialogueRGAT, the only way to receive information from remote utterances for an utterance is to stack several GNN layers. However, in our model, at every layer of TRGAT, we can gather remote utterance information indirectly for each utterance by considering the timing of aggregated information. So rather than stacking many TRGAT layers, we can attain competitive performance with few layers on both datasets. Meanwhile, when stacking more TRGAT layers on the IEMOCAP dataset, the model suffers from performance degradation, which is not obvious on the MELD dataset. We believe when the number of TRGAT layers increases, the number of parameters of the model also increases, the IMEOCAP dataset is relatively small and over-fitting occurs. And RGAT's message aggregation principle perform better than GAT and RGCN. Compared with RGAT, GAT's message aggregation principle don't take the relation of the edge into consideration, so it don't model the self-dependency and inter-speaker dependency when gather historical context information for the utterance. Compared with RGCN, RGAT can more flexibly determine the importance of historical utterances to current utterances through an attention mechanism.

5 Conclusion

In this paper, we propose a temporal and relational graph attention network, named DialogueTRGAT, for emotion recognition in conversation. DialogueTR-GAT gathers context information for each utterance based on their temporal position in dialogue and uses the message aggregation principle of relational graph attention networks (RGAT) to aggregate historical context information for each utterance. So it acts like a combination of the RNN-based model and graph-based model. We think it is a more effective way to model the information flow within conversations and can gains more meaningful context cues for each utterance for better emotion recognition. Extensive experiments were conducted and compared with previously proposed methods, our resulting model is more competitive.

Acknowledgments. The authors would like to thank the anonymous reviewers for the helpful comments. This work was supported by Projects 61876118 under the National Natural Science Foundation of China, the National Key RD Program of China under Grant No.2020AAA0108600 and the Priority Academic Program Development of Jiangsu Higher Education Institutions.

References

1. Busso, C., et al.: Iemocap: interactive emotional dyadic motion capture database. Lang. Resour. Eval. **42**(4), 335–359 (2008)
2. Ghosal, D., Majumder, N., Poria, S., Chhaya, N., Gelbukh, A.: Dialoguegcn: a graph convolutional neural network for emotion recognition in conversation. arXiv preprint arXiv:1908.11540 (2019)
3. Hazarika, D., Poria, S., Mihalcea, R., Cambria, E., Zimmermann, R.: ICON: interactive conversational memory network for multimodal emotion detection. In: Proceedings of the 2018 Conference on Empirical Methods in Natural Language Processing, pp. 2594–2604. Association for Computational Linguistics, Brussels, Belgium, Oct-Nov 2018. https://doi.org/10.18653/v1/D18-1280, https://aclanthology.org/D18-1280
4. Hu, D., Wei, L., Huai, X.: Dialoguecrn: contextual reasoning networks for emotion recognition in conversations. arXiv preprint arXiv:2106.01978 (2021)
5. Ishiwatari, T., Yasuda, Y., Miyazaki, T., Goto, J.: Relation-aware graph attention networks with relational position encodings for emotion recognition in conversations. In: Proceedings of the 2020 Conference on Empirical Methods in Natural Language Processing (EMNLP), pp. 7360–7370 (2020)
6. Jiao, W., Yang, H., King, I., Lyu, M.R.: Higru: hierarchical gated recurrent units for utterance-level emotion recognition. arXiv preprint arXiv:1904.04446 (2019)
7. Kumar, A., Dogra, P., Dabas, V.: Emotion analysis of twitter using opinion mining. In: 2015 Eighth International Conference on Contemporary Computing (IC3), pp. 285–290. IEEE (2015)

8. Majumder, N.: Mime: mimicking emotions for empathetic response generation. arXiv preprint arXiv:2010.01454 (2020)
9. Majumder, N., Poria, S., Hazarika, D., Mihalcea, R., Gelbukh, A., Cambria, E.: Dialoguernn: an attentive rnn for emotion detection in conversations. In: Proceedings of the AAAI Conference on Artificial Intelligence, vol. 33, pp. 6818–6825 (2019)
10. Poria, S., Cambria, E., Hazarika, D., Majumder, N., Zadeh, A., Morency, L.P.: Context-dependent sentiment analysis in user-generated videos. In: Proceedings of the 55th annual meeting of the association for computational linguistics (volume 1: Long papers), pp. 873–883 (2017)
11. Poria, S., Hazarika, D., Majumder, N., Naik, G., Cambria, E., Mihalcea, R.: Meld: a multimodal multi-party dataset for emotion recognition in conversations. arXiv preprint arXiv:1810.02508 (2018)
12. Shen, W., Wu, S., Yang, Y., Quan, X.: Directed acyclic graph network for conversational emotion recognition. arXiv preprint arXiv:2105.12907 (2021)
13. Sukhbaatar, S., Weston, J., Fergus, R., et al.: End-to-end memory networks. In: Advances in Neural Information Processing Systems, vol. 28 (2015)
14. Thost, V., Chen, J.: Directed acyclic graph neural networks. arXiv preprint arXiv:2101.07965 (2021)
15. Zhang, D., Wu, L., Sun, C., Li, S., Zhu, Q., Zhou, G.: Modeling both context-and speaker-sensitive dependence for emotion detection in multi-speaker conversations. In: IJCAI, pp. 5415–5421 (2019)
16. Zhou, L., Gao, J., Li, D., Shum, H.Y.: The design and implementation of xiaoice, an empathetic social chatbot. Comput. Linguist. **46**(1), 53–93 (2020)

Training Two-Stage Knowledge-Grounded Dialogues with Attention Feedback

Zhen Li[1], Jiazhan Feng[1], Chongyang Tao[2], and Dongyan Zhao[1,3(✉)]

[1] Wangxuan Institute of Computer Technology, Peking University, Beijing, China
{lizhen63,fengjiazhan,zhaody}@pku.edu.cn
[2] Microsoft Corporation, Beijing, China
[3] State Key Laboratory of Media Convergence Production Technology and Systems, Beijing, China

Abstract. Knowledge-grounded retrieval-based dialogue systems have attracted more and more attention. Among them, the two-stage dialogue models which separate the training stage into knowledge retrieving (via a retriever) and response ranking (via a ranker) are proved powerful. However, these approaches require knowledge-grounded dialogues with corresponding hand-annotated knowledge labels. Therefore, in this paper, we propose training two-stage knowledge-grounded dialogues with knowledge attention feedback from the ranker to the retriever. In each training iteration, the ranker provides knowledge attention scores as pseudo supervised feedback for the optimization of retriever. We conduct experiments on two public data sets. The experimental results demonstrate that our proposed method is superior to the existing baselines.

Keywords: Knowledge-grounded dialogues · Multi-turn context modeling · Retrieval-based dialogues · Knowledge attention feedback

1 Introduction

Building an intelligent dialogue system that can naturally communicate with humans has attracted more and more attention, and many works have focused on open-domain chatbots. Existing research on dialogue systems can be divided into two categories: generation-based methods and retrieval-based ones. The former uses natural language generation technology to directly synthesize a response and the latter selects an appropriate response from a set of candidates with the given context. In this paper, we focus on retrieval-based approaches since they have been adopted in many practical industrial products, such as the social-bot Microsoft Xiaoice [17]. Meanwhile, with the development of information retrieval, natural language representation and pre-training models [1], retrieval-based dialogue system has also gained firm technical support.

Very recently, researchers began to introduce knowledge to dialogue systems since humans can use their background knowledge to communicate with each other, and many impressive works emerge using knowledge and context together

© The Author(s), under exclusive license to Springer Nature Switzerland AG 2022
W. Lu et al. (Eds.): NLPCC 2022, LNAI 13551, pp. 473–484, 2022.
https://doi.org/10.1007/978-3-031-17120-8_37

to select a proper response. In the knowledge-grounded response retrieval task, some researchers directly leverage all knowledge and the dialogue context to predict response, and model knowledge retrieving and response ranking as one stage [4,6,31]. However, these approaches suffer from the inability to handle large numbers of knowledge. In particular, popular pre-trained language models like BERT have input constraints (512 tokens). Therefore, other researchers divide the knowledge-grounded retrieval-based dialogue system into two phases: knowledge retrieving and response ranking [2,19,29] which are implemented by a retriever and a ranker. Firstly, the retriever selects some of the most relevant knowledge according to the dialogue context in the knowledge retrieving phase, and then the ranker retrieves the most matching response according to the retrieved knowledge and the dialogue context. The process of retrieving knowledge can scale down the number of the input knowledge and meet the input constraints like BERT, which is powerful.

As a result, in this paper we propose training two-stage knowledge-grounded dialogues with knowledge attention feedback from the ranker to the retriever. To be specific, inspired by [8], in each iteration the ranker provides knowledge attention scores that reflect the relevance between knowledge and gold responses as pseudo supervised feedback for the optimization of the retriever during training. We conduct experiments on the Wizard of Wikipedia (WoW) [2] and CMU_DoG [32] data sets. The experimental results show that the knowledge attention scores are a good reflection of the relevance of knowledge and our proposed method is better than the existing baselines on both data sets.

Our contributions in this paper are summarized as the following two-fold: (1) we propose training two-stage knowledge-grounded dialogues with knowledge attention feedback from the ranker to the retriever; (2) We evaluate our method on two benchmarks and experiment results show that our model is superior to the existing baselines on both data sets.

2   Related Work

Retrieval-Based Dialogues. In the early stage, researches on retrieval-based dialogue systems mainly focus on single-turn response selection [9,25,26]. Recently, many studies turn to match responses with multi-turn dialogue context [12,21,28,33,34]. Meanwhile, pre-trained language models (PLMs) [1,11] have significantly improved downstream natural language processing tasks, which also attract researchers to adapt them to response selection. [24] employ PLMs to encode each utterance-response pair and aggregate these representations to measure the similarity between context and candidate response. [20] use bi-encoder as the pre-retrieval model and a more complicated architecture such as cross-encoder as the re-ranking model and train them mutually. [5] propose to apply a fine-grained post-training method that reflects the characteristics of the multi-turn dialogue and is highly effective for the response selection task.

Knowledge-Grounded Dialogues. Many recent works demonstrate that the performance of the dialogue models can be further improved with the background knowledge [2,30,31]. [2] collect documents from Wikipedia to build a document-grounded data set with diverse topics; [32] build a document-grounded dialogue data set with topics about movies; [4] propose conducting the interaction between the context and candidate response and between background knowledge and candidate response, which is named as dually interactive matching network (DIM); [3] propose filtering before iteratively referring (FIRE) which employs two filters to filter context and knowledge before response matching; [19] build a knowledge-grounded response selection model by decomposing the training into three tasks.

3   Methodology

As mentioned above, our dialogue model includes two stages: knowledge retrieving and response ranking, which are implemented by the retriever and the ranker respectively. In the first stage, the knowledge sentences set and context are fed to the retriever and the retriever selects some knowledge sentences which are the most relevant to the dialogue scene. Then the ranker processes the selected knowledge sentences and context to calculate the matching score of the candidate response. The candidate response with the highest matching score will be selected as the output of the dialogue model. The retriever and ranker are both initialized by the pre-trained language model BERT [1].

In this section, we first formalize the two-stage knowledge-grounded response retrieval task. Then we introduce training two-stage knowledge-grounded dialogues with knowledge attention feedback from the ranker to the retriever.

3.1   Problem Formalization

Given the knowledge-grounded dialogue data set $D = \{C_i, K_i, r_i, y_i\}_{i=1}^N$, C_i is the context which is a concatenation of multi-turn utterances from the dialogue history. $K_i = \{k_1, k_2, ..., k_{n_k}\}$ is the knowledge set where k_j is the j-th knowledge sentence and n_k is the number of knowledge sentences. r_i is a candidate response for C_i and K_i. y_i is the response label where $y_i = 1$ indicates that r_i is a ground-truth response otherwise $y_i = 0$.

For the two-stage knowledge-grounded response retrieval task, with the dialogue data, the retriever can be formalized as $\phi(k_j, C)$ which calculates the similarity score of the knowledge sentence k_j and selects some knowledge sentences with the highest similarity score as $\bar{K}$. Then the ranker can be formalized as $\theta(\bar{K}, C, r)$ which measures the matching score of the candidate response r. Finally, the goal of the overall two-stage dialogue model is to learn a matching model $g(K, C, r)$ from D. For any new context-knowledge-response triple (K, C, r), $g(K, C, r)$ returns the matching score between r and (K, C) and ranks all candidate responses according to their matching score.

3.2   The Stage of Knowledge Retrieving

During the knowledge retrieving stage, the retriever selects some of the most relevant knowledge about context. For the given dialogue context C and the collection of knowledge sentences $K = \{k_1, k_2, ..., k_{n_k}\}$, the retriever first encodes C and each knowledge sentence $k_i \in K$ to d-dimensional vectors V_{retr}^C and $V_{retr}^{k_i}$ respectively. In this process each token in context or knowledge sentence is fed into the dual-encoder architecture and we take the representation vector of the first token $[CLS]$ as the output vector. Then the similarity score between the dialogue context C and the knowledge sentence k_i can be calculated by the retriever:

$$sim(C, k_i; \phi) = \frac{(V_{retr}^C)^T V_{retr}^{k_i}}{\sqrt{d}} \tag{1}$$

where $\sqrt{d}$ is a relevance score scaling [16], and ϕ is the parameter of the retriever. Then the retriever selects top-m knowledge sentences with the highest similarity score and the $\bar{K}$ can be denoted as $\{\bar{k}_1, \bar{k}_2, ..., \bar{k}_m\}$.

In order to optimize the parameter of the retriever to select more relevant knowledge sentences, we propose to use the knowledge attention scores feedback from the ranker as pseudo labels for optimizing the retriever, which trains the retriever to approximate the knowledge attention scores. Our train process is just like a student-teacher network, where the ranker is the teacher model and produces knowledge attention scores as feedback to train the retriever which is the student model. In this way, our two-stage grounded dialogue model can optimize the retriever without knowledge labels.

As mentioned above, the ranker is initialized by BERT, where with the query, key, and value matrix donated as Q, K, and V, output of the attention layer in BERT can be calculated as [23]:

$$Attention(Q, K, V) = softmax(\frac{QK^T}{\sqrt{d_k}})V \tag{2}$$

where d_k is the dimension of the keys. $softmax(\frac{QK^T}{\sqrt{d_k}})$ is a weight matrix of value matrix, and we donate it as matrix A. If the length of input sequence is l, $A \in R^{l \times l}$. $A_{i,j}$ represents the degree of attention of the i-th word to the j-th word in the input sequence, which we denote as the attention score. We concatenate the m selected knowledge sentences and the ground-truth response r^+ as input to the ranker and compute the attention score for each knowledge. We consider if r^+ has a higher attention score for one knowledge, it means that the gold response pays more attention to this knowledge and this knowledge is more relevant to the current dialogue scene, which is more likely to contain useful information for predicting response.

Therefore, we use the knowledge attention scores feedback from ranker as the knowledge pseudo labels to optimize the retriever. Since there are multiple words in r^+ and t-th selected knowledge $\bar{k}_t$, there are multiple attention scores between r^+ and $\bar{k}_t$. We use the highest score over all the tokens in $\bar{k}_t$ corresponding to r^+ and all attention heads in the last attention layer as the attention score for $\bar{k}_t$, denoted as $G(r^+, \bar{k}_t; \theta)$. For the training objective of the retriever, we use the

KL divergence between the similarity score of knowledge and the attention score as the loss function of the retriever:

$$\mathcal{L}_\phi = \sum_{\bar{k} \in \bar{K}} \widetilde{G}(r^+, \bar{k}; \theta)(\log \widetilde{G}(r^+, \bar{k}; \theta) - \log \widetilde{S}(C, \bar{k}; \phi)) \tag{3}$$

$$\widetilde{G}(r^+, \bar{k}; \theta) = \frac{exp(G(r^+, \bar{k}; \theta)/\tau)}{\sum_{\bar{k}_t \in \bar{K}} exp(G(r^+, \bar{k}_t; \theta)/\tau)} \tag{4}$$

$$\widetilde{S}(C, \bar{k}; \phi) = \frac{exp(sim(C, \bar{k}; \phi)/\tau)}{\sum_{\bar{k}_t \in \bar{K}} exp(sim(C, \bar{k}_t; \phi)/\tau)} \tag{5}$$

In Eq. 4 and Eq. 5, we only use the knowledge in $\bar{K}$ to calculate the loss function and optimize the retriever. We assume that the knowledge sentences which are not selected by the retriever have smaller similarity scores and attention scores, and we introduce a temperature hyper-parameter τ as an alternative.

3.3   The Stage of Response Ranking

With the selected knowledge sentences set $\bar{K}$, dialogue context C and the candidate response r_j, we first concatenate all sequences as the input of the ranker. Then the ranker maps x_j to a d-dimensional vector denoted as $V_{rank}^{x_j}$ (the mapping process will be introduced below) and feeds it into a multi-layer perceptron (MLP) to calculate the matching score between the candidate response and the dialogue context with the selected knowledge sentences:

$$ma(C, \bar{K}, r_j; \theta) = W_2 \cdot f(W_1 \cdot V_{rank}^{x_j} + b_1) + b_2 \tag{6}$$

where W_1, W_2, b_1, b_2 are learnt parameters, θ is the parameter of the ranker and $f(\cdot)$ is a $tanh$ activation function.

Furthermore, inspired by [16], we use knowledge similarity scores in the ranker to assist in response matching. We make the assumption that fusing knowledge similarity scores into calculating the matching score of a candidate response r_j can make the ranker pay more attention to the relevant knowledge sentences. When the ranker maps x_j to $V_{rank}^{x_j}$, each token in x_j is fed into the encoder of the ranker, yielding the embedding sequence $\{v_{[CLS]}, v_1^1, v_1^2, ..., v_t^z, ...\}$ where $v_{[CLS]}$ is the representation vector of $[CLS]$ and v_t^z is the representation vector of z-th token in $\bar{k}_t$ in $\bar{K}$. Then $V_{rank}^{x_j}$ is calculated as:

$$V_{rank}^{x_j} = v_{[CLS]} + \lambda \cdot residual \tag{7}$$

$$residual = \sum_{t=1}^{n_k} avg(\bar{k}_t) \cdot sim(C, \bar{k}_t; \phi) \tag{8}$$

$$avg(\bar{k}_t) = \frac{\sum_{z=1}^{l_t} v_t^z}{l_t} \tag{9}$$

where $residual$ fuses the average representation vector of a knowledge sentence with its similarity score, and the more relevant knowledge sentence which has a

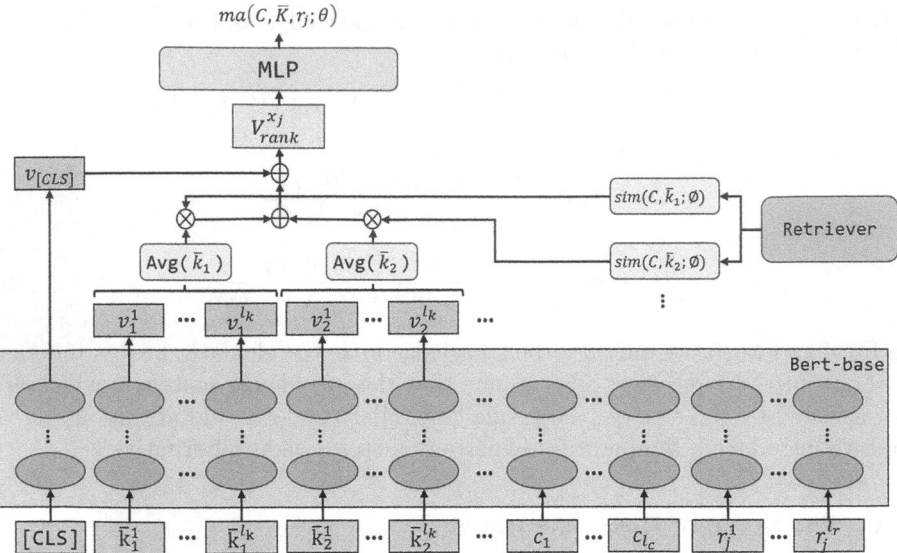

Fig. 1. The architecture of the ranker for response ranking. The retriever is for knowledge retrieving. The similarity scores from the retriever are used to calculate the matching score of the candidate response.

higher similarity score, the greater the proportion of it in *residual*. We add it with $v_{[CLS]}$ to obtain the representation vector $V_{rank}^{x_j}$, which makes the ranker pay more attention to the relevant knowledge. λ is a hyper-parameter. Figure 1 shows the architecture of the ranker.

Then, in order to optimize the ranker, with the ground-truth response labels and the matching scores calculated by Eq. 6, the loss function of the ranker can be defined as the negative log-likelihood loss:

$$\mathcal{L}_\theta = -\log \frac{exp(ma(C, \bar{K}, r^+; \theta))}{\sum_{t=1}^{n_r} exp(ma(C, \bar{K}, r_t; \theta))} \tag{10}$$

where r^+ is the ground-truth response and n_r is the number of candidate response based on context C and knowledge $\bar{K}$.

3.4   Model Learning

In the overall model, we train two-stage knowledge-grounded dialogues with knowledge attention feedback from the ranker to the retriever. The loss function of our model is the sum of $\mathcal{L}_\phi$ and $\mathcal{L}_\theta$:

$$\mathcal{L} = \mathcal{L}_\phi + \mathcal{L}_\theta \tag{11}$$

In each iteration, the training can be described as the following 4-steps:

1) The retriever selects the top-m knowledge sentences with the highest similarity score, denoted as $\bar{K}$.
2) With the $\bar{K}$, context C, candidate response r_j and knowledge similarity score, the ranker calculates the response matching score and optimizes itself.
3) The optimized ranker calculates the knowledge attention scores as feedback to the retriever.
4) Then the retriever uses knowledge attention scores feedback as pseudo labels to optimize itself.

4   Experiment

4.1   Experimental Settings

Benchmarks. One benchmark we use to conduct experiments is the Wizard of Wikipedia (WoW) [2]. In WoW, the knowledge documents are obtained from Wikipedia and cover a variety of topics. WoW contains 1365 topics and 22311 dialogues. The test set is divided into two subsets: Test Seen and Test Unseen. The Test Seen set covers 533 overlapping topics in the training set and the Test Unseen set provides 58 new topics. Another benchmark is the CMU Document Grounded Conversations (CMU_DoG) [32], the knowledge topics in it all focus on popular movies. We select the version released by DGMN [31] which contains 4112 dialogues for a fair comparison. The ratio of positive and negative samples is 1:19 in the validation set and test set.

Baselines. We compare the proposed model with retrieval-based baselines on both data sets individually. For WoW, we use IR Baseline [2], BoW MemNet [18], Transformer MemNet [2], Two-stage Transformer [2] and Two-stage Poly-Encoder [7] as baselines. For CMU_DoG, we use Starspace [27], BoW MemNet [30], KV Profile Memory [14], Transformer [13], Poly-Encoder [7], DGMN [31] and RSM-DCK [6] as baselines. For both data sets, we use PTKGC [19], DIM [4] and FIRE [3] as baselines.

Evaluation Metrics. We measure the performance of the dialogue models using the same evaluation metrics following the previous works. We employ recall $R_{100}@k$ for WoW and $R_{20}@k$ for CMU_DoG as evaluation metrics, where $k = 1$, 2 and 5 for both data sets.

4.2   Implementation Details

During the training procedure, our model is implemented by PyTorch framework [15]. For the balance of performance and efficiency, in our work the retriever is initialized by BERT-small [22] which has fewer parameters while can also have great performance. Meanwhile the ranker is initialized by BERT-base. Both the retriever and the ranker are finetuned using the Adam [10] algorithm. We set the batch size to 4 for training and 2 for evaluating on both data sets. We use the initial learning rate of 3e−5 and 5e−6 for the retriever and the ranker respectively. The max epochs for training are set to 10. The setting of

Table 1. Performance of knowledge retrieving on WoW.

Models	Test seen			Test unseen		
	R@1	R@2	R@5	R@1	R@2	R@5
Random	2.7	–	–	2.3	–	–
IR Baseline	5.8	–	–	7.6	–	–
BoW MemNet	23.0	–	–	8.9	–	–
Transformer	22.5	–	–	12.2	–	–
PTKGC	22.0	31.2	48.8	23.1	32.1	50.7
Ours	**23.8**	**34.5**	**54.5**	21.0	28.6	44.8

Table 2. Performance of response ranking on WoW.

Models	Test seen			Test unseen		
	$R_{100}@1$	$R_{100}@2$	$R_{100}@5$	$R_{100}@1$	$R_{100}@2$	$R_{100}@5$
IR Baseline [2]	17.8	–	–	14.2	–	–
BoW MemNet [18]	71.3	–	–	33.1	–	–
Transformer MemNet [2]	87.4	–	–	69.8	–	–
Two-stage Transformer [2]	84.2	–	–	63.1	–	–
Two-stage Poly-Encoder [7]	87.9	–	–	70.2	–	–
PTKGC [19]	89.5	96.7	98.9	69.6	85.8	96.3
DIM [4]	83.1	91.1	95.7	60.3	77.8	92.3
FIRE [3]	88.3	95.3	97.7	68.3	84.5	95.1
Ours	**91.0**	96.4	98.7	**72.4**	**86.6**	96.2

the utterance input length is different on the two data sets. For WoW data set, the max lengths of knowledge sentence, context and candidate response are set to 40, 80 and 60. For CMU_DoG data set, these parameters are set to 40, 200 and 60. The number of selected knowledge sentences (m) is set to 5. In Eq. 4 and Eq. 5, τ is set to 0.2. In Eq. 7, λ is set to 0.04.

4.3 Evaluation on Knowledge Retrieving

In this section we evaluate the performance of models to retrieve gold knowledge sentences in the WoW data set. The evaluation results are shown in Table 1. Experiment results show that our model is better than all baselines for knowledge retrieving in the Test Seen data set and obtains a comparable performance in Test Unseen data set.

4.4 Evaluation on Response Ranking

In this section, we report the evaluation results of response ranking on WoW and CMU_DoG data sets respectively in Table 2 and Table 3. Our model can

Table 3. Performance of response ranking on CMU_DoG.

Models	$R_{20}@1$	$R_{20}@2$	$R_{20}@5$
Starspace [27]	50.7	64.5	80.3
BoW MemNet [30]	51.6	65.8	81.4
KV Profile Memory [14]	56.1	69.9	82.4
Transformer [13]	60.3	74.4	87.4
Poly-Encoder [7]	72.3	86.1	94.6
PTKGC [19]	66.1	77.8	88.7
DGMN [31]	65.6	78.3	91.2
DIM [4]	78.7	89.0	97.1
RSM-DCK [6]	79.3	88.8	96.7
FIRE [3]	81.8	90.8	97.4
Ours	**83.3**	**91.9**	**98.1**

Table 4. Ablation results on WoW.

Models	Test seen			Test unseen		
	$R_{100}@1$	$R_{100}@2$	$R_{100}@5$	$R_{100}@1$	$R_{100}@2$	$R_{100}@5$
Ours	91.0	96.4	98.7	72.4	86.6	96.2
Ours (w/o. knowledge)	84.1	92.2	96.1	68.4	81.4	92.7
Ours (w/o. attention)	88.2	95.6	98.5	69.1	84.8	94.8
Ours (w/o. residual)	90.2	95.4	98.3	71.1	84.8	94.7

achieve better performance on $R_{100}@1$ than the existing baseline models on WoW, which is the most important metric for response ranking and is better than all the baselines on all the metrics on CMU_DoG. The evaluation results show that the improvement of our model to baselines is statistically significant (t-test, $p < 0.05$).

4.5 Performance Analysis on the Number of Selected Knowledge

As shown in Fig. 2, we also explore the relationship between the number of selected knowledge sentences and the performance of the proposed model. The experiment results demonstrate that on the overall trend, as the number of knowledge increases, the performance of our model improves until the number reaches a certain value, after which the performance stabilizes on Test Seen set and drops on Test Unseen. We think this is because as the number of knowledge increases, so does the relevant information contained in these knowledge sentences which is beneficial to response matching. However when the number of knowledge keeps increasing, the noise carried by irrelevant knowledge would be detrimental to response matching.

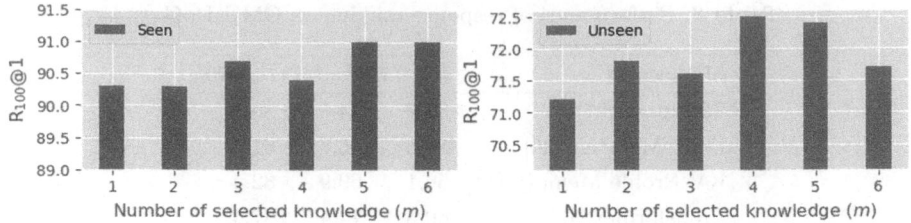

Fig. 2. The performance of our model with the different number of selected knowledge (m) on the Test Seen set and Test Unseen set of WoW.

4.6 Ablation Study

In this section we conduct an ablation study. Table 4 shows the ablation results on WoW. First, we remove the knowledge from the input sequence which is denoted as "*Ours(w/o knowledge)*". We can find that removing knowledge drops the performance which demonstrates the importance of knowledge for response matching. Then, to prove the effectiveness of knowledge attention scores as pseudo feedback, we use the heuristic similarity unigram F1 score between a selected knowledge $\bar{k}_t$ and the ground-truth response r^+ as the pseudo feedback of $\bar{k}_t$ to replace the attention score which can also reflect the relevance of knowledge to the ground-truth response. We denote it as "*Ours(w/o. attention)*" and the evaluation result shows that replacing the attention score as the F1 score leads to a performance drop, which indicates that attention score better reflects the relevance of knowledge. Finally, we remove the $\lambda \cdot residual$ in Eq. 7 and denote it as "*Ours(w/o. residual)*". Performance of "*Ours(w/o. residual)*" is inferior to our model, which indicates that the similarity score of knowledge is beneficial to the response matching.

5 Conclusion

In this paper, we propose training two-stage knowledge-grounded dialogues with knowledge attention feedback from the ranker to the retriever. In each training iteration, the ranker provides knowledge attention scores as pseudo supervised feedback for the optimization of the retriever. Experimental results on WoW and CMU_DoG show that our model is better than the existing baselines and prove the effectiveness of the knowledge attention feedback.

Acknowledgments. This work is supported in part by NSFC (No. 2021YFC 3340304). We would like to thank the anonymous reviewers and action editors for their helpful comments and suggestions.

References

1. Devlin, J., Chang, M.W., Lee, K., Toutanova, K.: BERT: pre-training of deep bidirectional transformers for language understanding. arXiv preprint arXiv:1810.04805 (2018)

2. Dinan, E., Roller, S., Shuster, K., Fan, A., Auli, M., Weston, J.: Wizard of Wikipedia: knowledge-powered conversational agents. arXiv preprint arXiv:1811.01241 (2018)
3. Gu, J.C., Ling, Z.H., Liu, Q., Chen, Z., Zhu, X.: Filtering before iteratively referring for knowledge-grounded response selection in retrieval-based chatbots. arXiv preprint arXiv:2004.14550 (2020)
4. Gu, J.C., Ling, Z.H., Zhu, X., Liu, Q.: Dually interactive matching network for personalized response selection in retrieval-based chatbots. arXiv preprint arXiv:1908.05859 (2019)
5. Han, J., Hong, T., Kim, B., Ko, Y., Seo, J.: Fine-grained post-training for improving retrieval-based dialogue systems. In: Proceedings of the 2021 Conference of the North American Chapter of the Association for Computational Linguistics: Human Language Technologies, pp. 1549–1558 (2021)
6. Hua, K., Feng, Z., Tao, C., Yan, R., Zhang, L.: Learning to detect relevant contexts and knowledge for response selection in retrieval-based dialogue systems. In: Proceedings of the 29th ACM International Conference on Information & Knowledge Management, pp. 525–534 (2020)
7. Humeau, S., Shuster, K., Lachaux, M.A., Weston, J.: Poly-encoders: transformer architectures and pre-training strategies for fast and accurate multi-sentence scoring. arXiv preprint arXiv:1905.01969 (2019)
8. Izacard, G., Grave, E.: Distilling knowledge from reader to retriever for question answering. arXiv preprint arXiv:2012.04584 (2020)
9. Ji, Z., Lu, Z., Li, H.: An information retrieval approach to short text conversation. arXiv preprint arXiv:1408.6988 (2014)
10. Kingma, D.P., Ba, J.: Adam: a method for stochastic optimization. arXiv preprint arXiv:1412.6980 (2014)
11. Liu, Y., et al.: RoBERTa: a robustly optimized BERT pretraining approach. arXiv preprint arXiv:1907.11692 (2019)
12. Lowe, R., Pow, N., Serban, I., Pineau, J.: The ubuntu dialogue corpus: a large dataset for research in unstructured multi-turn dialogue systems. arXiv preprint arXiv:1506.08909 (2015)
13. Mazaré, P.E., Humeau, S., Raison, M., Bordes, A.: Training millions of personalized dialogue agents. arXiv preprint arXiv:1809.01984 (2018)
14. Miller, A., Fisch, A., Dodge, J., Karimi, A.H., Bordes, A., Weston, J.: Key-value memory networks for directly reading documents. arXiv preprint arXiv:1606.03126 (2016)
15. Paszke, A., et al.: PyTorch: an imperative style, high-performance deep learning library. In: Advances in Neural Information Processing Systems, vol. 32 (2019)
16. Sachan, D.S., et al.: End-to-end training of neural retrievers for open-domain question answering. arXiv preprint arXiv:2101.00408 (2021)
17. Shum, H.Y., He, X., Li, D.: From Eliza to Xiaoice: challenges and opportunities with social chatbots. Front. Inf. Technol. Electron. Eng. 19(1), 10–26 (2018)
18. Sukhbaatar, S., Weston, J., Fergus, R., et al.: End-to-end memory networks. In: Advances in Neural Information Processing Systems, vol. 28 (2015)
19. Tao, C., Chen, C., Feng, J., Wen, J.R., Yan, R.: A pre-training strategy for zero-resource response selection in knowledge-grounded conversations. In: Proceedings of the 59th Annual Meeting of the Association for Computational Linguistics and the 11th International Joint Conference on Natural Language Processing (Volume 1: Long Papers), pp. 4446–4457 (2021)

20. Tao, C., Feng, J., Liu, C., Li, J., Geng, X., Jiang, D.: Building an efficient and effective retrieval-based dialogue system via mutual learning. arXiv preprint arXiv:2110.00159 (2021)
21. Tao, C., Wu, W., Xu, C., Hu, W., Zhao, D., Yan, R.: One time of interaction may not be enough: go deep with an interaction-over-interaction network for response selection in dialogues. In: Proceedings of the 57th Annual Meeting of the Association for Computational Linguistics, pp. 1–11 (2019)
22. Turc, I., Chang, M.W., Lee, K., Toutanova, K.: Well-read students learn better: on the importance of pre-training compact models. arXiv preprint arXiv:1908.08962 (2019)
23. Vaswani, A., et al.: Attention is all you need. In: Advances in Neural Information Processing Systems, vol. 30 (2017)
24. Vig, J., Ramea, K.: Comparison of transfer-learning approaches for response selection in multi-turn conversations. In: Workshop on DSTC7 (2019)
25. Wang, H., Lu, Z., Li, H., Chen, E.: A dataset for research on short-text conversations. In: Proceedings of the 2013 Conference on Empirical Methods in Natural Language Processing, pp. 935–945 (2013)
26. Wang, M., Lu, Z., Li, H., Liu, Q.: Syntax-based deep matching of short texts. In: 24th International Joint Conference on Artificial Intelligence (2015)
27. Wu, L., Fisch, A., Chopra, S., Adams, K., Bordes, A., Weston, J.: Starspace: embed all the things! In: Proceedings of the AAAI Conference on Artificial Intelligence, vol. 32 (2018)
28. Wu, Y., Wu, W., Xing, C., Zhou, M., Li, Z.: Sequential matching network: a new architecture for multi-turn response selection in retrieval-based chatbots. arXiv preprint arXiv:1612.01627 (2016)
29. Zhang, C., Wang, H., Jiang, F., Yin, H.: Adapting to context-aware knowledge in natural conversation for multi-turn response selection. In: Proceedings of the Web Conference 2021, pp. 1990–2001 (2021)
30. Zhang, S., Dinan, E., Urbanek, J., Szlam, A., Kiela, D., Weston, J.: Personalizing dialogue agents: i have a dog, do you have pets too? arXiv preprint arXiv:1801.07243 (2018)
31. Zhao, X., Tao, C., Wu, W., Xu, C., Zhao, D., Yan, R.: A document-grounded matching network for response selection in retrieval-based chatbots. arXiv preprint arXiv:1906.04362 (2019)
32. Zhou, K., Prabhumoye, S., Black, A.W.: A dataset for document grounded conversations. arXiv preprint arXiv:1809.07358 (2018)
33. Zhou, X., et al.: Multi-view response selection for human-computer conversation. In: Proceedings of the 2016 Conference on Empirical Methods in Natural Language Processing, pp. 372–381 (2016)
34. Zhou, X., et al.: Multi-turn response selection for chatbots with deep attention matching network. In: Proceedings of the 56th Annual Meeting of the Association for Computational Linguistics (Volume 1: Long Papers), pp. 1118–1127 (2018)

Generating Emotional Responses with DialoGPT-Based Multi-task Learning

Shuai Cao[1,2], Yuxiang Jia[1,3(✉)], Changyong Niu[1], Hongying Zan[1],
Yutuan Ma[1], and Shuo Xu[1]

[1] School of Computer and Artificial Intelligence, Zhengzhou University,
Zhengzhou, China
{ieyxjia,iecyniu,iehyzan}@zzu.edu.cn
[2] vivo AI Lab, Shenzhen, China
[3] Zhengzhou Zoneyet Technology Co., Ltd., Zhengzhou, China

Abstract. Emotion is an essential element for a high quality response, and generating emotional responses is of great significance to a social dialogue system. Traditionally, training an emotional dialogue system needs a large-scale dialogue corpus with emotion labels, which is too expensive for mannual annotation while automatic labeling quality is not guaranteed. Multi-task learning provides a way to learn an emotional response generator through information sharing with emotion recognition tasks. This paper proposes a multi-task learning architecture based on DialoGPT, incorporating response generation with several emotion recognition tasks of different emotion granularities, including both single-label and multi-label classification. Experiments from both automatic evaluation and human evaluation show that the proposed models can generate emotional responses of high quality, outperforming all baseline models in most metrics.

Keywords: Emotion classification · Response generation · Multi-task learning · Generative pre-trained transformer

1 Introduction

Open-domain dialogue system is an important research topic in the field of natural language processing with a wide range of application prospects. Deep learning-based dialogue systems can extract features from dialogue data by neural networks, understand the semantic information of the dialogue, and generate appropriate responses. The performance of text generation has seen a great achievement in virtue of pre-trained language models, such as OpenAI's GPT-2 [15]. Microsoft's DialoGPT [21] focuses on dialog response generation, using large-scale Reddit conversation data to fine-tune GPT-2 to generate near-human level responses.

W. Lu et al. (Eds.): NLPCC 2022, LNAI 13551, pp. 485–496, 2022.
https://doi.org/10.1007/978-3-031-17120-8_38

The DialoGPT model improves the quality of response generation, but does not take into account emotional information. In order to interact naturally with humans, dialogue systems need to be human-like with emotions. Perceiving the emotion of users and generating appropriate responses with emotion is of great significance for open-domain dialogue systems. In fact, several empirical studies have shown that dialogue systems with the ability to communicate emotionally with humans are essential to improve user satisfaction [1]. For this reason, it is valuable to develop a dialogue system that is capable of emotionally interacting with its interlocutors.

Jia et al. [7] build a dialogue system capable of generating responses according to specified emotions on basis of the DialoGPT model. However, there are some problems in practice, such as the need to pre-specify an emotion label when performing response generation, which is not a perfect solution for a well-designed dialogue system. In addition, due to the lack of large-scale dialogue corpora with human-labeled emotion tags, an emotion classifier needs to be trained and then labels the dialogue emotion automatically. In this case, the effect of the emotion classifier will have an impact on the training of the dialogue response generation model. Moreover, Psychological studies [13] have shown that human emotion is quite complex and one sentence may contain multiple types of emotions with different intensities. Therefore, using only a single emotion label is not sufficient to generate emotion-aware responses.

Thus, we propose the MTL-DialoGPT model, an emotional response generation model based on multi-task learning. This model incorporates response generation and emotion recognition into the framework of multi-task learning, so that the model can perceive emotions by information sharing. The number of tasks in multi-task learning can be controlled according to different granularities of emotions. We do not aim at improving the accuracy of emotion recognition. Instead, we focus on generating emotional responses. We build the model based on DialoGPT [21], a state-of-the-art pre-trained language model, for multi-task learning of response generation and emotion recognition.

The contributions of this work include:

- We propose an emotional response generation model based on DialoGPT and multi-task learning, incorporating response generation with emotion recognition tasks.
- We introduce emotion recognition tasks with single-label classification, multi-label classification and different emotion granularities.
- We compare the models from both automatic and human evaluations. Experimental results show that our model outperforms the baseline models in most metrics.

2   Related Work

The Seq2Seq model [17] provides an important foundation for a neural network-based approach to dialogue response generation, which introduces an encoder-decoder architecture to provide a novel solution to the dialogue response generation task. The development of large-scale pre-trained models is greatly facilitated by the introduction of the Transformer model [18]. Radford et al. [14] propose GPT, a large-scale generative pre-trained model based on the Transformer model. Afterwards, Radford et al. [15] train a larger GPT-2 model that could better mimic humans for text generation. Zhang et al. [21] propose a DialoGPT model for dialogue response generation based on GPT-2. The model fine-tunes the GPT-2 model based on 147 million conversations from the Reddit comment chains and achieves a level close to that of humans.

Incorporating emotional information in a dialogue system can improve the quality of response generation to a certain extent. Early dialogue response generation with emotions is implemented based on rules, where templates and rule strategies are formulated in advance for different dialogue scenarios, and then responses are generated based on the input utterances. For example, Parry [2], a chatbot proposed by Stanford University, can simulate human emotions to response according to the formulated rules, but does not really understand the semantic information in the user's utterances.

Zhou et al. [23] propose an Emotional Chat Machine (ECM) model that incorporates discrete emotional information into a Seq2Seq dialogue response generation model, capable of generating responses with specific emotions. Since then, researchers have made different improvements to the ECM model. Zhou et al. [24] utilize emoji based on conditional variational auto-encoder (CVAE) to control emotion response generation. Huang et al. [6] propose three approaches to incorporate emotions for emotion response generation, which differ in how the emotion information is embedded. However, the above models based on the Seq2Seq architecture tend to produce generic but meaningless responses.

Jia et al. [7] propose EmoDialoGPT model, which introduces emotion embedding and emotion prediction loss based on the pre-trained DialoGPT model for specified emotion response generation, and achieves good results. Zandie et al. [20] propose EmpTransfo based on the pre-trained GPT model and multi-task learning with response generation, emotion, action and topic learning, and each learning task corresponds to a Transformer head. Zheng et al. [22] propose a multi-factor hierarchical modeling framework, CoMAE, which hierarchically models three factors: communication mechanism, dialog act and emotion. Experimental results demonstrate that a hierarchical combination of these three factors could better generate responses with appropriate emotions.

3   Methodology

3.1   Model Architecture

We propose the MTL-DialoGPT model based on the pre-trained model DialoGPT and multi-task learning, simultaneously learning response generation, single-label emotion classification and multi-label emotion classification. Through information sharing of the multi-task learning strategy, the response generator becomes emotion-aware.

The architecture of the MTL-DialoGPT model is shown in Fig. 1. It uses DialoGPT as the backbone, and the architecture of DialoGPT is the same as that of GPT-2, which is implemented based on the Transformer decoder. The MTL-DialoGPT model consists of a stack of multiple Transformer decoder base units, each of which consists of two parts, the first consisting of layer normalization, masked multi-head self attention and residual connection, and the second consisting of layer normalization, feed-forward neural network and residual connection. Each basic unit uses masked multi-head self attention to enable the model to perform auto-regressive response generation, and the residual connection and layer normalization make it more stable when training deep models.

Our model contains a response generation task, two single-label emotion recognition tasks and a multi-label emotion recognition task. For the response generation task, the output layer is represented by LM head, while for the single-label and multi-label emotion recognition tasks, the output layers are represented by CLS1 head and CLS2 head, respectively. Finally, the loss weights of the response generation task and each emotion recognition task are computed separately for backpropagation. In addition, we use different granularities of emotions for the three emotion recognition tasks, including 9, 2 and 28 emotions respectively.

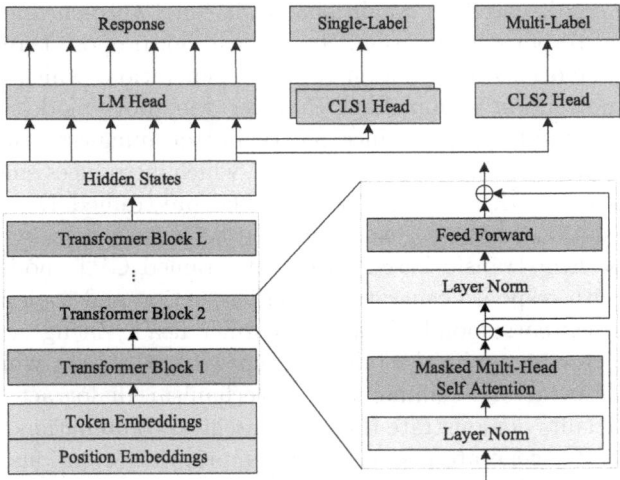

Fig. 1. The architecture of the MTL-DialoGPT model, based on DialoGPT. It contains one LM header, two CLS1 headers and one CLS2 header to solve the response generation, single-label emotion recognition and multi-label emotion recognition tasks, respectively.

3.2   Input Representation

Suppose that the source sentence and target response pairs of a dialogue is denoted by (X, Y), and the emotion text and emotion label in the emotion recognition is denoted by (X, e), where $X = \{x_1, x_2, ..., x_m\}$ and $Y = \{y_1, y_2, ..., y_n\}$

are sentences composed of words. For the response generation task, we splice the source and target utterances as the input, while for the emotion recognition task, the input is the emotion text. Our model uses the same BPE (Byte Pair Encoding) algorithm as the DialoGPT model to encode the sentences. We also introduce positional encoding to compensate for the lack of positional information. Formally, we define the token embedding $T \in \mathbb{R}^{|V| \times d}$ ($|V|$ is the vocabulary size, and d is the size of hidden layer), and the position embedding $P \in \mathbb{R}^{1024 \times d}$ (1024 is the maximum input length of the model). For each token t, its final input embedding is:

$$Emb(t) = T(t) + P(t) \tag{1}$$

3.3   Information Sharing

Multi-task learning usually learns several related tasks together to improve the performance of each task by information sharing [9]. However, the main purpose of our multi-task learning approach is to improve the quality of response generation, and the emotion recognition tasks are only used as auxiliary tasks, which is different from the general multi-task learning.

We also follow the masked multi-head self attention of the DialoGPT model, as this ensures that only information prior to the current position can be attended to when auto-regressive generation is performed. The computation of the masked multi-head self attention is as follows:

$$M_{ij} = \begin{cases} 0, i > j \\ -\infty, i <= j \end{cases} \tag{2}$$

$$MHMA(Q, K, V) = V softmax\left(\frac{K^T Q + M}{\sqrt{d}}\right) \tag{3}$$

where i is the position of the currently generated word, j is the position of the already generated word, Q denotes the query sequence, which is used to retrieve information in the attention mechanism, K, V denotes the sequence of key-value pairs, which is the object of attention for the query sequence, and d is the size of hidden layer.

For a basic unit, the whole computational process can be abstracted as follows:

$$H_{(1)}^l = LayerNorm(MHMA(H^l, H^l, H^l) + H^l) \tag{4}$$

$$H^{l+1} = LayerNorm(FeedForward(H_{(1)}^l) + H_{(1)}^l) \tag{5}$$

where $l \in [1, L]$, and L is the number of basic unit. $H^l \in \mathbb{R}^{d \times N}$ (d is the size of hidden layer and N is the length of the input sequence) is the hidden state matrix of the input sequence at layer l, $H_{(1)}^l \in \mathbb{R}^{d \times N}$ is the calculation result of the first part, $H^{l+1} \in \mathbb{R}^{d \times N}$ is the output of the hidden state matrix after l layer as the input of $l + 1$ layer, and the input of the first layer is the emb in Eq. 1.

3.4   Optimization

The optimization of our model includes three parts: response generation loss, single-label emotion recognition loss, and multi-label emotion recognition loss. For the response generation task, we utilize the negative log-likelihood loss commonly used in language models and described as follows:

$$\mathcal{L}_1 = -\frac{1}{N} \sum_{i=1}^{N} \log P(y_i|X; y_{\leq i-1}) \tag{6}$$

where N is the length of the target response.

For the two single-label emotion recognition tasks, we use cross entropy as the loss function described as follows:

$$\mathcal{L}_2 = \mathcal{L}_3 = -\sum_{i=1}^{C} e_i \log(\widehat{e_i}) \tag{7}$$

where C is the class number, $e = \{e_1, e_2, ..., e_C\}$ is the one-hot representation of the emotion labels, and $\widehat{e_i}$ denotes the probability that the emotion is i-th class.

For the multi-label emotion recognition task, we employ the Binary Cross Entropy with Logits Loss (BCEwithLogitsLoss) function, which is essentially a combination loss of the Sigmoid layer and BCE Loss, described as follows:

$$\mathcal{L}_4 = -\frac{1}{C} \sum_{i=1}^{C} e_i \log\left(\frac{1}{1 + exp(-\widehat{e_i})}\right) + (1 - e_i) \log\left(\frac{exp(-\widehat{e_i})}{1 + exp(-\widehat{e_i})}\right) \tag{8}$$

So the final optimization object is the summation of the above losses:

$$\mathcal{L} = \lambda_1 * \mathcal{L}_1 + \lambda_2 * \mathcal{L}_2 + \lambda_3 * \mathcal{L}_3 + \lambda_4 * \mathcal{L}_4 \tag{9}$$

where λ_1, λ_2, λ_3, λ_4 are the loss weights of each task. We set λ_1 to 1.0 and the sum of λ_2, λ_3 and λ_4 to 1.0 in our experiments.

4   Dataset

We use the DailyDialog dataset [10] for response generation, which is a high-quality multi-round open domain dialogue dataset. It is cleaner but smaller compared to the OpenSubtitles dataset [11]. The DailyDialog contains 13,118 dialogues, with an average of 7.9 rounds per dialogue. Although this dataset is labeled with dialogue emotions, but the emotion category "other" accounts for 83.1%, therefore, we only use the dialogues for the training of the response generation task. We split the multi-round dialogues in the DailyDialog dataset into single-round dialogues, and every two sentences in a round are used as source and target utterances, respectively. Finally, we obtain 89,861 dialogue data. We divide the training, validation and test set in line with to the original data.

Table 1. Distribution of datasets

Dataset	Training	Validation	Test	Total
DailyDialog	76,052	7,069	6,740	89,861
CBET	61,488	7,686	7,686	76,860
SST-2	6,735	872	1,821	9,428
GoEmotions	7,102	878	837	8,817

For the two single-label emotion recognition tasks, we use the CBET dataset collected from Twitter by Shahraki et al. [16] and the SST-2 (The Stanford Sentiment Treebank) dataset, respectively. The CBET dataset contains nine emotion categories, namely *anger, fear, joy, love, sadness, surprise, thankfulness, disgust* and *guilt*. We use this dataset as our core emotion recognition dataset. The dataset contains 81,163 texts, of which 76,860 texts are labeled with one emotion label and the remainders are labeled with two emotion labels. We only use the single-labeled data for the single-label emotion recognition task and divide the dataset into training, validation and test sets with the ratio of 8:1:1. The SST-2 dataset contains 70,042 movie comments with *positive* and *negative* emotion labels. We divide the dataset following previous work, but in order to maintain a balance with the dataset for the multi-label emotion recognition task, we only use 10% of the original training data, and the validation and test sets remain the same.

For the multi-label emotion recognition task, we use the GoEmotions dataset [4]. The dataset contains 58,009 English Reddit comments labeled with some of 27 emotion categories or neutral, which is the largest manually annotated multi-label emotion dataset. The number of comments with two and more labels is 8,817, and we only use the multi-label data for the multi-label emotion recognition task. The detailed distribution of above datasets is shown in Table 1.

5   Experiments

5.1   Experimental Settings

All the models are implemented with PyTorch and Transformers library. To train the MTL-DialoGPT model, we fine-tune on the DialoGPT-Large pre-trained model [19,21] with parameter size of 774 M. The hidden layer size is 1280 and the number of Transformer layers is 36. We fine-tune the model on a NVIDIA RTX 3090 GPU for 64 epochs, with the batch size set to 8 and the learning rate set to 3e−5. The parameters are optimized by Adam [8] with weight decay. We choose the model with the lowest loss on the validation set as the final model for evaluation. We use Beam Search for decoding, where beam size is set to 5. A different loss is calculated for each task and the parameters are updated for each mini-batch.

5.2   Baselines

In order to verify the effectiveness and advantages of our proposed model, we use the same DailyDialog dataset to compare with the previous baseline models. These models are listed as follows:

- *Seq2Seq-dec* [6]. Embedding emotion into the decoder of the Seq2Seq model for generating emotional responses according to the specified emotion labels.
- *EmpTransfo* [20]. Based on the GPT model, multi-task learning is performed on the DailyDialog dataset for response generation, and emotion, action and topic recognition. We compare with EmpTransfo on response generation and emotion recognition tasks.
- *EmoDialoGPT-emb* [7]. A separate emotion embedding layer and an emotion prediction loss are introduced based on the DialoGPT model, and the corresponding emotional responses are generated according to the specified emotion labels.

For the Seq2Seq-dec model and the EmoDialoGPT-emb model, we use the dialogues and emotion labels from the DailyDialog dataset for training. To be fair, we use the DialoGPT-Large model as the pre-trained model for EmoDialoGPT-emb.

5.3   Automatic Evaluation of Response Generation

We evaluate the performance of response generation using automatic evaluation metrics commonly used in dialogue systems [3]. The metrics include word vector based similarity, Distinct, BLEU, NIST, and the average sentence length. Word vector based similarity between the generated response and the target response includes embedding average (AVG), vector extrema (EXT) and greedy matching (GRE). Distinct-1 (d1) and Distinct-2 (d2) evaluate diversity by calculating the proportion of unigram and bigram in the response. BLEU evaluates the consistency by calculating the n-gram between the generated response and the target response, and we use the weighted score of BLEU-$\{1,2,3,4\}$ for evaluation. NIST introduces n-gram of information based on BLEU, and NIST-2 (n2) and NIST-4 (n4) are used. The average sentence length of the responses is denoted by U.

The results of the automatic evaluation of the response generation are shown in Table 2. The response generation is denoted by R, and the emotion recognition with datasets of CBET, SST-2 and GoEmotions are denoted by E9, E2 and E28, respectively. The DialoGPT-FT model is fine-tuned based on the DialoGPT-Large model using only the DailyDialog dataset. From the Table 2, we can find that our proposed models achieve the best results in all metrics except d1 and d2, and overall, R+E9+E2+E28 performs the best. It validates that by leveraging the multi-task learning and introducing more emotion recognition tasks including different emotion granularities, single-label classification and multi-label classification, the quality of the generated responses could get improved.

Table 2. Results of the automatic evaluation of response generation. R stands for response generation, and E* is emotion recognition with * as number of emotion categories. "Human" means that the generated response is the same as the target response.

Model	AVG	EXT	GRE	d1	d2	n2	n4	BLEU	U
Human	100	100	100	7.4	38.24	13.46	16	100	14.45
Seq2Seq-dec	60.18	34.16	43.16	3.03	14.12	0.92	0.93	1.26	12.06
EmpTransfo	60.26	35.25	44.44	5.37	26.5	1.67	1.68	3.84	9.71
EmoDialoGPT-emb	64.24	43.54	51.31	7.37	**33.58**	2.46	2.8	16.94	10.37
DialoGPT	50.73	33.17	40.05	5.17	16.11	0.07	0.07	0.59	6.26
DialoGPT-FT	62.19	41.97	49.57	**7.44**	32.58	1.91	2.16	14.02	9.85
R+E9	71.35	47.81	56.93	6.31	32.66	3.2	3.65	20.27	16.6
R+E9+E2	71.4	47.83	56.94	6.34	32.74	3.27	3.73	20.77	16.39
R+E9+E28	71.61	48.06	57.22	6.21	32.58	3.23	3.69	20.55	**16.81**
R+E9+E2+E28	**71.67**	**48.35**	**57.33**	6.33	32.63	**3.3**	**3.77**	**21.06**	16.28

5.4 Human Evaluation of Response Generation

Following [7,12], we manually evaluate our models and the baseline models in the form of a questionnaire in terms of relevance, fluency, and emotion. We randomly select 100 samples from the test set and then obtain responses from each model. Three evaluators score each response from the above three aspects. The scores range from 1 to 5 (1 meaning not at all, 3 meaning slightly, somewhat, and 5 meaning very much), with higher scores implying better results. The average scores of the human evaluation are shown in Table 3.

Table 3. Results of human evaluation

Model	Relevance	Fluency	Emotion
Seq2Seq-dec	2.77	3.44	2.8
EmpTransfo	2.98	3.47	2.96
EmoDialoGPT-emb	3.13	3.59	3.23
R+E9	3.46	**3.74**	**3.59**
R+E9+E2	3.44	3.63	3.52
R+E9+E28	3.49	3.64	3.53
R+E9+E2+E28	**3.5**	3.67	3.55

We can see that our proposed multi-task learning models outperform the three baseline models in all three human evaluation metrics, which not only make the generated responses more emotional, but also improve relevance and fluency to a certain extent.

5.5   Case Study

An example of the response generation for our models and three baseline models is shown in Table 4. As can be seen, by introducing emotion recognition tasks with different emotion granularities, the generated responses are more empathetic, with emotional signals like "I am afraid", "Oh, dear", "I am sorry", "Don't worry", etc. In addition, it also enriches the content of generated responses to a some extent.

Table 4. Example of response generation

Source	Yesterday I had a runny nose. Now my nose is stuffed up. And I am afraid I have got a temperature
Target	Don't worry, young man. Lat me give you an examination. Open your mouth and say "ah".
Seq2Seq-dec	So what do you do ?
EmpTransfo	Do you have a fever?
EmoDialoGPT-emb	I am not sure. How long have you been like this?
R+E9	I am afraid you have got a cold. Perhaps you should go to a doctor
R+E9+E2	Oh, dear. Maybe you have caught a cold
R+E9+E28	Oh, I am sorry to hear that. You should go to see a doctor
R+E9+E2+E28	Don't worry about it. You have got a cold. I am sure you will be all right soon

5.6   Results of Emotion Recognition

In addition, we show the emotion recognition results on the CBET dataset and the GoEmotions dataset in Table 5. We take precision and macro F1 score as metrics for evaluation. The results show that our proposed multi-task learning models improve the performance on both datasets over the BERT-Large model [5]. R+E9 and R+E9+E2 are trained without the GoEmotions dataset. However, our goal is not to improve emotion recognition but response generation.

Table 5. Results of emotion recognition (%)

Model	CBET		GoEmotions	
	Precision	F1	Precision	F1
BERT-Large	66.16	66.01	58.13	43.88
R+E9	**75.83**	**78.25**	7.44	12.92
R+E9+E2	75.72	77.93	7.38	12.86
R+E9+E28	75.74	78.12	**69.34**	**45.35**
R+E9+E2+E28	75.69	78.11	67.85	45.07

6   Conclusion

In this paper, we focus on generating emotional responses in dialogue systems. We propose a multi-task learning architecture based on DialoGPT, incorporating response generation with several emotion recognition tasks, including both single-label and multi-label classification tasks, and different granularities of emotions. Through information sharing with emotion recognition models in multi-task learning, the response generation model becomes emotion-aware and can generate high quality emotional responses. Experimental results from both automatic evaluation metrics and human evaluation metrics show that the proposed models outperform baseline models in most metrics. Multi-task learning plus generative pre-trained transformer is a promising way for generating emotional responses.

Acknowledgements. We would like to thank the anonymous reviewers for their insightful and valuable comments. This work was supported in part by Major Program of National Social Science Foundation of China (Grant No.17ZDA318, 18ZDA295), National Natural Science Foundation of China (Grant No.62006211), and China Postdoctoral Science Foundation (Grant No.2019TQ0286, 2020M682349).

References

1. Callejas, Z., Griol, D., López-Cózar, R.: Predicting user mental states in spoken dialogue systems. EURASIP J. Adv. Signal Process. **2011**(1), 1–21 (2011)
2. Colby, K.M.: Modeling a paranoid mind. Behav. Brain Sci. 4(4), 515–534 (1981)
3. Csáky, R., Purgai, P., Recski, G.: Improving neural conversational models with entropy-based data filtering. In: Proceedings of the 57th Annual Meeting of the Association for Computational Linguistics, pp. 5650–5669 (2019)
4. Demszky, D., Movshovitz-Attias, D., Ko, J., Cowen, A., Nemade, G., Ravi, S.: Goemotions: a dataset of fine-grained emotions. In: Proceedings of the 58th Annual Meeting of the Association for Computational Linguistics, pp. 4040–4054 (2020)
5. Devlin, J., Chang, M.W., Lee, K., Toutanova, K.: Bert: pre-training of deep bidirectional transformers for language understanding. In: Proceedings of the 2019 Conference of the North American Chapter of the Association for Computational Linguistics: Human Language Technologies, Volume 1 (Long and Short Papers), pp. 4171–4186 (2019)
6. Huang, C., Zaiane, O.R., Trabelsi, A., Dziri, N.: Automatic dialogue generation with expressed emotions. In: Proceedings of the 2018 Conference of the North American Chapter of the Association for Computational Linguistics: Human Language Technologies, Volume 2 (Short Papers), pp. 49–54 (2018)
7. Jia, Y., et al.: EmoDialoGPT: enhancing DialoGPT with emotion. In: Wang, L., Feng, Y., Hong, Y., He, R. (eds.) NLPCC 2021. LNCS (LNAI), vol. 13029, pp. 219–231. Springer, Cham (2021). https://doi.org/10.1007/978-3-030-88483-3_17
8. Kingma, D.P., Ba, J.: Adam: a method for stochastic optimization. arXiv preprint arXiv:1412.6980 (2014)
9. Li, Y., Kazameini, A., Mehta, Y., Cambria, E.: Multitask learning for emotion and personality detection (2021)

10. Li, Y., Su, H., Shen, X., Li, W., Cao, Z., Niu, S.: Dailydialog: a manually labelled multi-turn dialogue dataset. In: Proceedings of the Eighth International Joint Conference on Natural Language Processing (Volume 1: Long Papers), pp. 986–995 (2017)
11. Lison, P., Tiedemann, J.: Opensubtitles 2016: extracting large parallel corpora from movie and tv subtitles (2016)
12. Liu, Y., Du, J., Li, X., Xu, R.: Generating empathetic responses by injecting anticipated emotion. In: ICASSP 2021–2021 IEEE International Conference on Acoustics, Speech and Signal Processing (ICASSP), pp. 7403–7407. IEEE (2021)
13. Plutchik, R.: The nature of emotions: human emotions have deep evolutionary roots, a fact that may explain their complexity and provide tools for clinical practice. Am. Scientist **89**(4), 344–350 (2001)
14. Radford, A., Narasimhan, K., Salimans, T., Sutskever, I.: Improving language understanding by generative pre-training (2018)
15. Radford, A., Wu, J., Child, R., Luan, D., Amodei, D., Sutskever, I.: Language models are unsupervised multitask learners. OpenAI blog **1**(8), 9 (2019)
16. Shahraki, A.G., Zaiane, O.R.: Lexical and learning-based emotion mining from text. In: Proceedings of the International Conference on Computational Linguistics and Intelligent Text Processing, vol. 9, pp. 24–55 (2017)
17. Sutskever, I., Vinyals, O., Le, Q.V.: Sequence to sequence learning with neural networks. Adv. Neural Inf. Process. Syst. **27** (2014)
18. Vaswani, A., et al.: Attention is all you need. In: Proceedings of the 31st International Conference on Neural Information Processing Systems, pp. 6000–6010 (2017)
19. Wolf, T., et al.: Transformers: state-of-the-art natural language processing. In: Proceedings of the 2020 Conference on Empirical Methods in Natural Language Processing: System Demonstrations, pp. 38–45 (2020)
20. Zandie, R., Mahoor, M.H.: Emptransfo: a multi-head transformer architecture for creating empathetic dialog systems. arXiv preprint arXiv:2003.02958 (2020)
21. Zhang, Y., et al.: Dialogpt: large-scale generative pre-training for conversational response generation. In: Proceedings of the 58th Annual Meeting of the Association for Computational Linguistics: System Demonstrations, pp. 270–278 (2020)
22. Zheng, C., Liu, Y., Chen, W., Leng, Y., Huang, M.: Comae: a multi-factor hierarchical framework for empathetic response generation. arXiv preprint arXiv:2105.08316 (2021)
23. Zhou, H., Huang, M., Zhang, T., Zhu, X., Liu, B.: Emotional chatting machine: emotional conversation generation with internal and external memory. In: Proceedings of the AAAI Conference on Artificial Intelligence, vol. 32 (2018)
24. Zhou, X., Wang, W.Y.: Mojitalk: generating emotional responses at scale. In: Proceedings of the 56th Annual Meeting of the Association for Computational Linguistics (Volume 1: Long Papers), pp. 1128–1137 (2018)

Social Media and Sentiment Analysis
(Oral)

A Multibias-Mitigated and Sentiment Knowledge Enriched Transformer for Debiasing in Multimodal Conversational Emotion Recognition

Jinglin Wang[1], Fang Ma[1], Yazhou Zhang[2,3], and Dawei Song[1(✉)]

[1] Beijing Institute of Technology, Beijing, China
{jinglinwang,mfang,dwsong}@bit.edu.cn
[2] Zhengzhou University of Light Industry, Zhengzhou, China
yzzhang@zzuli.edu.cn
[3] State Key Laboratory for Novel Software Technology, Nanjing University, Nanjing, China

Abstract. Multimodal emotion recognition in conversations (mERC) is an active research topic in natural language processing (NLP), which aims to predict human's emotional states in communications of multiple modalities, e,g., natural language and facial gestures. Innumerable implicit prejudices and preconceptions fill human language and conversations, leading to the question of whether the current data-driven mERC approaches produce a biased error. For example, such approaches may offer higher emotional scores on the utterances by females than males. In addition, the existing debias models mainly focus on gender or race, where multibias mitigation is still an unexplored task in mERC. In this work, we take the first step to solve these issues by proposing a series of approaches to mitigate five typical kinds of bias in textual utterances (i.e., gender, age, race, religion and LGBTQ+) and visual representations (i.e., gender and age), followed by a **M**ultibias-**M**itigated and sentiment **K**nowledge **E**nriched bi-modal **T**ransformer (MMKET). Comprehensive experimental results show the effectiveness of the proposed model and prove that the debias operation has a great impact on the classification performance for mERC. We hope our study will benefit the development of bias mitigation in mERC and related emotion studies.

Keywords: Bias mitigation · Multimodal learning · Emotion recognition

1 Introduction

Whether people realize them or not, innumerable implicit prejudices and preconceptions fill human language, and are conveyed in almost all data sources,

---

J. Wang and F. Ma—Contribute equally and share the co-first authorship.

© The Author(s), under exclusive license to Springer Nature Switzerland AG 2022
W. Lu et al. (Eds.): NLPCC 2022, LNAI 13551, pp. 499–512, 2022.
https://doi.org/10.1007/978-3-031-17120-8_39

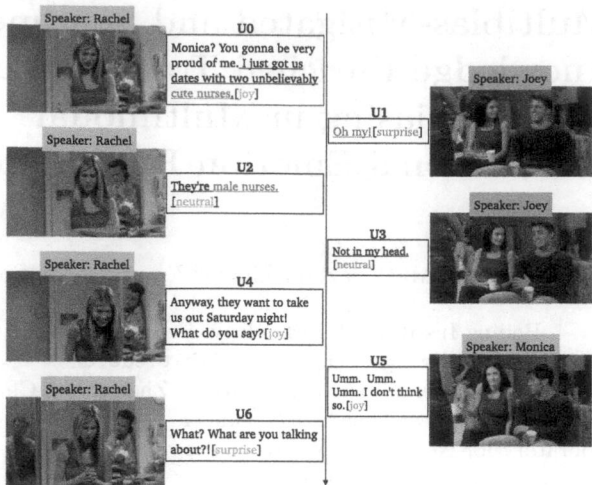

Fig. 1. An illustrative example of gender bias in the multimodal dialogue dataset (MELD). There are three speakers in this conversation: Rachel, Joey, and Monica. In the bracket at the end of each utterance is the emotion type (e.g., joy, surprise, etc.) of it. The underlined sentences and the words highlighted in red express an apparent gender bias, and such bias is further amplified by Joey's facial gestures. (Color figure online)

such as news, reviews and conversations [13,24]. Such prejudices are known to hurt specific groups, and infringe their rights. For example, these two utterances, "older people are not interested in digital technology", or "women are pleasant to look slim", reveal the age and gender biases.

Recent research has shown that pre-trained word representations, e.g., word embeddings (in which each word is represented as a vector in the semantic space), tend to amplify the bias in the data [11,26]. The male names have been proved more likely to be associated with career-related terms than female names, by calculating the similarity between their embeddings [4]. African-American names are also shown to be more likely to be associated with unpleasant terms than European-American names [15]. Unconsciously learning such implicit biases from a dataset that is sampled from all kinds of data sources, leads to the fact that the learned models may further amplify the harmful bias (such as gender or race) when they make decisions [9,21]. In addition, the biased error will propagate to downstream tasks. For example, coreference resolution systems exhibit a gender bias due to the use of biased word embeddings [19]. Facial recognition applications have also been proved to perform worse for the inter-sectional group "darker females" than for either darker individuals or females [2].

In view that human language is multi-modal in nature, human bias also exists in multimodal conversations, e.g., textual and visual utterances. Figure 1 shows an example of the gender bias in a multimodal dialogue dataset[1]. Joey immediately makes an association with a beautiful female nurse and expresses a significant smile when Rachel says "cute nurse", but when Rachel says "they are male nurses", he shows a disappointed-looking facial expression, although his textual response seems neutral.

Therefore, human bias naturally resides in the multimodal expression of emotions in conversations. There has been a great body of literature in debiasing for computer vision [2] and pre-trained language models [25]. However, the existing debias models mainly focus on only one kind of prejudice, e.g., gender or race, where multibias mitigation is still an unexplored task in mERC. This leaves us with a research question: *Whether the current data-driven multi-modal emotion recognition in conversations approaches produce a biased error or not?*

To answer this question, we first propose a series of approaches for debiasing multiple types of bias in multimodal (i.e., textual and visual) conversations. For textual utterances, we propose mitigating five types of bias, including gender, age, race, religion, and LGBTQ+ in word embedding.

For visual utterances, we first propose a subspace-projection-based debiasing approach to mitigate two typical visual biases, i.e., gender and age. It constructs a subspace for each type of visual bias and identifies the type of bias in the visual representation by projecting the representation into the corresponding subspace.

To incorporate the proposed multimodal debiasing methods into the mERC task that involves conversational context modeling, cross-modality interactions capturing and the use of sentiment knowledge, we propose a Muiltibiases Mitigated and sentiment **K**nowledge **E**nriched **T**ransformer (MMKET) as a unified framework. Specifically, it is a bimodal Transformer involving a contextual attention layer to capture the contextual interactions, a bimodal cross-attention layer to capture the cross-modal interactions, and a sentiment attention layer to enrich the debiased representation with sentiment knowledge.

Empirical evaluation has been carried out on two benchmark datasets, and the experimental results shows that the proposed multimodal debiasing methods can effectively mitigate the corresponding biases. We also prove that debiasing the representation of multimodal utterances has a remarkable impact on the performance of mERC models.

2   Generation of Bias

Models and algorithms have never independently created bias. Social bias is exhibited in multiple components of a NLP system, including the training corpus, pre-trained models (e.g., word embeddings), and algorithms themselves [4, 8, 27].

---

[1] Trigger Warning: This paper contains examples of biases and stereotypes seen in society and language representations. These examples may be potentially triggering and offensive. These examples are meant to bring light to and mitigate these biases, and it is not an endorsement.

The bias in the dataset comes from the unbalanced samples and biased labels. In the process of label annotation, the annotators will transfer personal bias to the data, where the algorithm absorbs, thus produces a biased model.

Word embeddings are often trained from large and human-created corpora that contains multifarious biased raw data. Recent literature has demonstrated that gender bias is encoded in word embedding [4,12]. For example, Bolukbasi highlights that "programmer" is more closely associated with "man" while "homemaker" is more closely associated with "woman" in word2vec embeddings trained on the Google News dataset [1].

3　Debiasing Methods

3.1　Mitigating Multiple Biases in GloVe

The recent debiasing models [1,25] have only focused on removing gender bias in word embeddings, particularly GloVe, which has surfaced several social biases [4,20]. In this paper, we propose to mitigate five types of biases in GloVe embeddings, i.e., gender, race, religion, age, and LGBTQ+. Methodologically, we extend the existing Double-Hard Debias method, to multiple types of bias.

Hard Debias is a commonly adopted debiasing strategy in NLP. It projects a pre-trained word embedding vector into a subspace orthogonal to an inferred bias subspace (i.e., direction of a particular type of bias), which is constructed based on a set of pre-defined word pairs (e.g., *young* vs. *old*) characterizing the bias. Wang et al. [25] discovered that word frequency twists the bias direction, and proposed the Double-Hard Debias method [25].

To extend it to multiple types of bias mitigation, we manually define a set of n characterizing word pairs for each type of bias based on typical data biases [20]. Table 1 shows a range of representative examples.

Table 1. The five pre-defined sets of word pairs, where the main difference between each pair of words captures the corresponding bias.

Bias type	Word pairs
Gender	woman-man, girl-boy, she-he, mother-father, daughter-son, gal-guy, female-male
Race	slave-secondary, group-tribe, easy task-cake walk, master-primary
Age	young-old, health-disease, work-retirement, education-pension
Religion	Christian-Muslim, Christianity-Islam, Christ-Allah, Jesus-Muhammad
LGBTQ+	homosexuals-they, husband/wife-spouse, dad/father/mom/mother-parent

The algorithm operates on the five types of bias sequentially, i.e., the debiased word embedding of the first type serves as the input for the second, and so forth. Finally, we get the multibias-mitigated pre-trained word embeddings, which can be used in our proposed MMKET model.

3.2 Mitigating Multiple Biases in Visual Representation

Recent research shows that gender and age bias accounts for a portion of visual bias [6,24]. To mitigate them, we propose two methods: Visual Hard Debias and Projection Debias methods. The Visual Hard Debias method can mitigate the superficial gender and age bias in visual representation. Then we devise the Projection Debias method to further mitigate finer-grained visual bias.

Visual Hard Debias. We assume that, for each type of visual bias, there is a pre-defined set of n image pairs $V_1, V_2, ..., V_n \in S$ (e.g., male-female or young-old), which represent the bias. The images are selected randomly from IMDB-WIKI [18], a publicly available face image dataset with gender and age labels. Let $\vec{v}$ denote an image's visual representation. Let $u_i = \sum_{p \in V_i} \vec{p}/|V_i|$ be the mean of the image representations of V_i in the pre-defined image set. The visual bias subspace VB is spanned by the first $k(\geq 1)$ eigen-vectors of VC), by applying Singular Value Decomposition (SVD) on it.

$$VC := \sum_{i=1}^{m} \sum_{v \in V_i} (\vec{v} - u_i)^T (\vec{v} - u_i)/|V_i| \qquad (1)$$

Here the k is set to 1. As a result, the bias subspace VB becomes a bias direction $\overrightarrow{VB}$. After getting the visual bias subspace, each image representation $\vec{v}$ is debiased through: $\tilde{v} = \vec{v} - (\overrightarrow{VB}^T \cdot \vec{v})\overrightarrow{VB}$.

Projection Debias. In order to further mitigate the finer-grained gender and age bias in the image representation, we propose a new visual debias method, namely Projection Debias. Specifically, it projects the image representation twice into the bias subspaces (e.g., *male* vs. *female*, *young* vs. *old*) respectively.

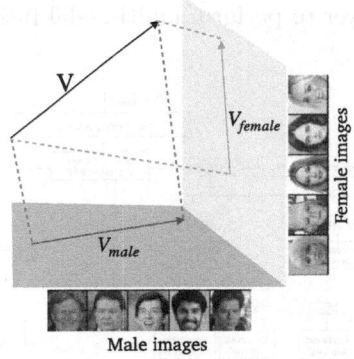

Fig. 2. Projection debias.

By subtracting the two projections from the original visual representation, we get the final debiased representation. Figure 2 shows the Projection Debias method on gender bias.

First we use the IMDB-WIKI [18] to define four sets of images U_i, where $i \in [1, 2, 3, 4]$, corresponding to the female, male, young and old respectively. The we compute the bias subspace as:

$$B_i = \vec{u}_i^{\mathrm{T}} \otimes \vec{u}_i \tag{2}$$

where $i \in [1, 2, 3, 4]$, $\vec{u}_i$ is the first principal component of U_i computed through Principal Component Analysis (PCA). T means the transpose operation, and $\otimes$ means outer product operation. Then we can get the corresponding projection-debiased visual representation through:

$$\hat{v} = \tilde{v} - \sum_{i=1}^{4}(B_i \times \tilde{v}) \tag{3}$$

Then we get the two-step debiased visual representation $\hat{v}$ for an image.

4   The Proposed MMKET Model

We outline the Multibias-mitigated and Sentiment Knowledge Enriched Transformer (MMKET) model (c.f. Fig. 3). In the proposed framework, we apply the Transformer [23] to leverage the debiased contextual and multimodal (text and visual) clues to predict the emotions of the target utterance, due to its ability to capture the context and fast computation. The main ideas are: (1) a multi-modal encoder to create textual and visual representations of contexts and responses, including debiased word embedding (GloVe) and debiased visual representation from the pre-trained EfficientNet Network [22]. (2) The text representation is enriched by sentiment knowledge. (3) The context-aware attention mechanism is proposed to effectively incorporate conversational context. (4) The text representation and non-verbal embedding are forwarded through a self-attention layer and a feed-forward sublayer to perform multimodal fusion.

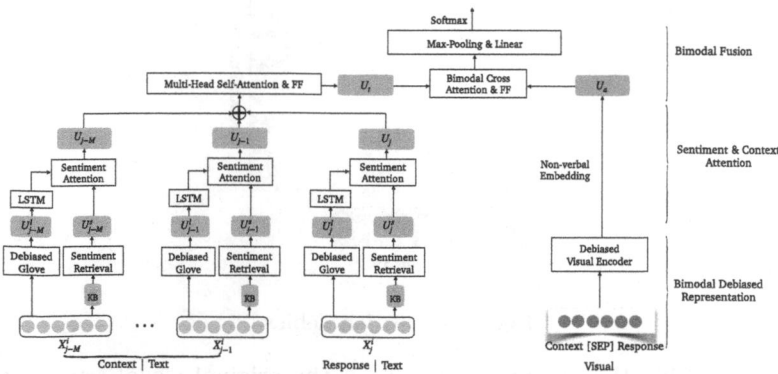

Fig. 3. Overall architecture of the proposed model.

4.1 Task Definition

Suppose our dataset has N data-points, we can represent the i-th data as $\{U_j^i, Y_j^i\}$, $U_j^i = (X_j^i, V_j^i)$, where $i \in \{1, 2, ..., N\}$, $j \in \{1, 2, ..., N_i\}$, which is a collection of $\{utterance, label\}$ pairs, N denotes the number of conversations, and N_i denotes the number of utterances in the i-th conversation. Each utterance consists of two modalities: text (X), video (V). We align the visual features with their corresponding tokens in the text modality. Therefore, both two modalities have the same length. Given an utterance, our task is to predict its emotion label. The objective of the task is to maximize the following function:

$$\Theta = \prod_{i=1}^{N} \prod_{j=1}^{N_i} p(Y_j^i | U_j^i, U_{j-1}^i, ..., U_1^i; \theta) \tag{4}$$

where $U_{j-1}^i, ..., U_1^i$ denote contextual utterances and θ denotes the model parameters set. We denote the number of contextual utterances as M.

4.2 Bimodal Encoder Layer

We extract textual and visual features via the bimodal encoder respectively. For text representation, we use a debiased word embedding layer to convert each token t in X^i into a vector representation $\vec{t} \in \mathbb{R}^d$, where d denotes the size of word embedding. Moreover, the debiased GloVe embeddings (through our debiasing methods presented in Sect. 3.1) are used for initialization in the word embedding layer. Let

$$\vec{t} = \text{Embed}(t) \tag{5}$$

as described in the previous part, we use a sentiment embedding layer to convert each token t in the utterance into a corresponding sentiment features score $\vec{S}_i$ as an additional information source vector. The resulting textual embeddings are fed into the Transformer encoders to further refine textual representation.

For the visual representation, each input video clip is scaled to 480×360, and the pre-trained EfficientNet [22] is used to extract the features. The Transformer encoders are used to learn the visual representations.

4.3 Sentiment Knowledge Attention

In philosophy and psychology, sentiment and emotion are closely related, corresponding to internal and external human affection [7]. Sentiment refers to human's subjective experience and mental attitude, which involves long-term and deep human cognition [5]. Therefore, we hypothesise that the sentiment knowledge will help the task of emotion recognition. Correspondingly, we propose a sentiment knowledge attention mechanism to capture and counterpoise the sentiment representation for each token. Specifically, a gated unit is used to combine the sentiment representation and the original utterance representation.

In our model, we use a commonsense emotion lexicon NRC_VAD [14] as the sentiment knowledge source. The NRC Valence, Arousal, and Dominance (VAD) lexicon include a list of more than 20,000 English words and their valence, arousal, and dominance scores. For a given word and a dimension (V/A/D), the scores range from 0 to 1.

In general, for each word token t in X_j^i, we only retrieve its valence values from the NRC_VAD dictionary, which is the 'positive-negative' dimension. The final sentiment knowledge representation for each text utterance X_j^i is a list of valence scores: $[V(t_1),V(t_2),...V(t_n)]$. The valence scores of tokens that are not included in NRC_VAD are set to 0.5. The sentiment knowledge representation of each text utterance will be used to enrich the text representation and serve the multi-bias mitigation. The gate value g_i for each token x_i is calculated as:

$$g_i = \sigma(W_g h_i + b_g) \tag{6}$$

where h_i is the hidden vector of token x_i from the previous $lstm$ layer, W_g is a learnable linear transformation and b_g is the bias. Then the attention output $\vec{T}$ is calculated as a weighted combination of sentiment enriched and original attention scores:

$$\vec{T_i} = g_i\vec{t_i} + (1 - g_i)\vec{S_i}\vec{t_i} \tag{7}$$

4.4   Bimodal Cross Attention

We use a bimodal cross attention layer [10], which is a multi-head self-attention mechanism, to learn the joint representation of U_l and U_v, $U_l = \vec{T_i}$, where U_l represents sentiment-enriched textual representation and U_v denotes sentiment-enriched visual representation.

Specifically, we create corresponding sets of queries (Q_l, Q_v), keys (K_l, K_v), and values (V_l, V_v) to learn the interaction between textual and visual modalities (U_l, U_v). The modal representation and query set is attached to a multi-head cross attention layer. We also add the normalization layer and residual connections layer after each cross attention layer. Let

$$M_{l,v} = \text{BimodalCrossAttention}(U_l, U_v) \tag{8}$$

4.5   Classification

The bimodal fusion representation is gained from the bimodal cross attention layer, which is shown in Eq. 8. We then add a maxpooling layer to extract the most salient features across the time dimension and yield a one-dimensional vector. Let

$$M_{l,v} = \text{MaxPooling}(M_{l,v}) \tag{9}$$

$$P = \text{softmax}(M_{l,v}W + b) \tag{10}$$

where P represents the output probability, $W \in \mathbb{R}^{d*l}$ and $b \in \mathbb{R}^l$ denote parameters, l denotes the number of classes.

5   Experiments

5.1   Datasets

· **IEMOCAP** [3] A multimodal dataset containing emotional dialogues. Each video contains a single dynamic dialogue, segmented into utterances.
· **MELD** [17] A dataset of TV show scripts collected from `Friends`, which is a multimodal emotion classification dataset.

Both datasets contain textual, visual, and acoustic information for every utterance. We only focus on the textual and visual modalities in this work. Table 2 shows the statistics of the datasets. In all our experiments, 300-dimensional GloVe [16] is leveraged to initialize word embeddings, pre-trained EfficientNet network is used to extract the corresponding feature vectors of images. We use adam as an optimizer with a learning rate of 0.0001 and train. The coefficient of L2 regularization is 10^{-5}, and the batch size is 64.

5.2   Evaluation Metrics

Debiasing. We use k-Means clustering to verify the effectiveness of the debiasing methods. For each type of bias, we take the top 100/500/1000 of the original GloVe embeddings or visual features by calculating their cosine similarity with the specific bias directions. Then, we cluster them into two groups and compute the alignment accuracy for the bias. To visualize the difference, we applied tSNE projection on word embeddings and the image features.

Our Proposed MMKET Model. We evaluate our proposed model on IEMO-CAP and MELD, and adopt F1-score on the test set as our the metric.

Table 2. The data statistics of IEMOCAP and MELD.

Dataset		Dialogues	Utterances
IEMOCAP	Train	100	4810
	Dev	20	1000
	Test	31	1623
MELD	Train	1039	9989
	Dev	114	1109
	Test	280	2610

Table 3. K-Means clustering accuracy (%) of top 100/500/1000 biased words.

Embeddings	Top100	Top500	Top1000
GloVe	100.0	99.9	99.7
Gender-debiased GloVe	86.0	68.7	**55.3**
GloVe	100.0	100.0	99.3
Age-debiased GloVe	100.0	99.2	**98.9**
GloVe	86.5	75.3	54.5
Race-debiased GloVe	86.5	75.1	**54.4**
GloVe	99.5	95.7	96.6
Religion-debiased GloVe	97.0	86.8	**81.6**
GloVe	100.0	99.7	99.3
LGBTQ+-debiased GloVe	94.5	**90.7**	91.1

6   Results and Analysis

6.1   Debiasing Results

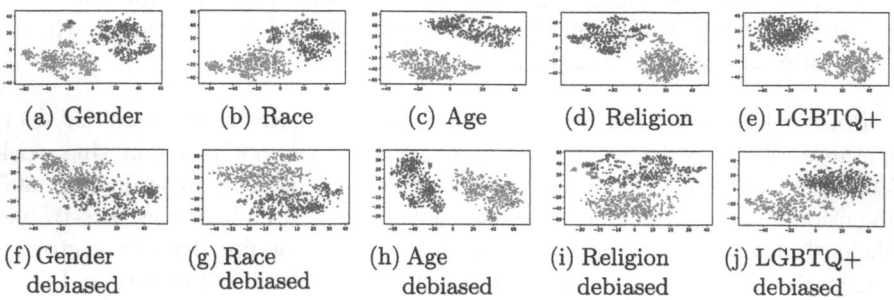

(a) Gender	(b) Race	(c) Age	(d) Religion	(e) LGBTQ+

(f) Gender debiased	(g) Race debiased	(h) Age debiased	(i) Religion debiased	(j) LGBTQ+ debiased

Fig. 4. tSNE visualization of clustering top 500 most biased embeddings (a–e) and their debiased embeddings (f–j).

Mitigating Multiple Biases in GloVe. Table 3 shows the result of K-Means clustering on the original GloVe and the debiased ones. Lower accuracy means fewer bias cues can be learned. The accuracy appears to decrease after the debiasing operation, suggesting the debias method works effectively in embeddings. More intuitively, in the upper row of Fig. 4, word embeddings are divided into two clear parts. In the lower row, the two parts have mixed up, though different biases have varied effects. Among the five proposed biases, gender and religious bias were mitigated most. LGBTQ+ bias also reduced, while racial and age bias did not decrease significantly. We speculate that the racial bias is more implicit in textual data given that the accuracy of the original GloVe is already close to 50. As for the age bias, we consider the bias words like "old" are widely used as unbiased meanings, i.e. "an old tree", "a senven-year-old boy", which decreased the effect of debiasing. Mitigating the racial and age bias will be left to our future work.

Mitigating Multiple Biases in Visual Representation. Table 4 shows the clustering result of biased images. As shown in Fig. 5, the visual representation of images from IMDB-WIKI [18] are projected into a 2D space. Our proposed debiasing methods mix up the images to a noticeable extent, indicating that gender and age bias are mitigated in image representation.

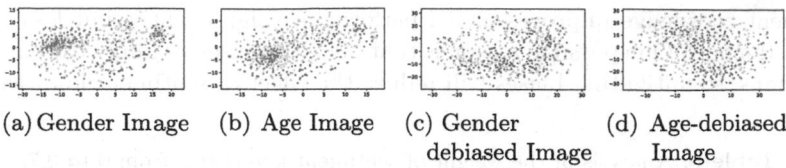

(a) Gender Image   (b) Age Image   (c) Gender
debiased Image

(d) Age-debiased
Image

Fig. 5. tSNE visualization of top 300 most bias image feature (a) and their debiased image feature (b).

Table 4. K-Means clustering accuracy (%) of top 100/300/500 biased images. Lower accuracy means less bias cues.

Visual representation	Top100	Top300	Top500
Gender-biased Images	74.3	70.8	64.5
Gender-debiased Images	61.0	59.3	**53.3**
Age-biased Images	67.2	62.3	59.6
Age-debiased Images	60.7	53.8	**52.5**

6.2   Debiased mERC Results

We make the first step to explore the role of bias plays in mERC tasks. Human emotions contain prejudice, so removing the bias will decrease the emotion classification accuracy, which can explain the results in Table 5 and Table 6. Compared to the single modal results (Table 4), our MMKET model makes full use of the rich information in the Bimodal data and the connection between them, which greatly improves the performance of the algorithm.

Table 5. $T + V$ results (%) on IEMOCAP and MELD dataset, which is mitigating the specific bias.

Mitigated bias	IEMOCAP	MELD
None	57.11	53.93
Gender	56.22	53.22
Race	56.63	53.41
Age	56.76	53.69
Religion	56.09	53.14
LGBTQ+	56.89	53.20
5 Biases	**55.85**	**52.86**

Mitigated bias		IEMOCAP	MELD
Text	Visual		
None	None	58.29	56.35
	Gender&Age	57.61	55.09
5 Biases	None	57.56	55.64
	Gender&Age	56.23	54.25

6.3   Ablation Studies

To further investigate how the sentiment knowledge affects the debias method and mERC, we conduct extensive ablation experiments with the weight of sentiment knowledge of different values, whose results are included in Table 6. The sentiment knowledge improves model performance significantly, but less on the debiased model. One possible reason is that biases themselves imply the emotions of humans, so mitigating biases will reduce the effect of sentiment knowledge.

Table 6. Analysis of the weight of sentiment knowledge from 0 to 0.7.

Dataset	0	0.3	0.5	0.7
MELD	55.93	**56.35**$_{+0.42}$	56.24$_{+0.31}$	56.09$_{+0.16}$
IEMOCAP	57.60	**58.29**$_{+0.69}$	57.96$_{+0.36}$	57.22$_{-0.37}$
Debiased-MELD	54.14	**54.42**$_{+0.28}$	54.31$_{+0.17}$	54.25$_{+0.11}$
Debiased-IEMOCAP	56.37	**56.57**$_{+0.20}$	56.40$_{+0.03}$	56.38$_{+0.01}$

7   Conclusion

In this work, we extend the types of bias in the embedding level (e.g., gender, age, race, religion, and LGBTQ+) and innovatively propose the Projection Debias to mitigate gender and age bias in visual representation. We also present a Multibias-mitigated and Sentiment Knowledge Enriched Transformer (MMKET), taking the first step to explore how the debiasing operation affects the algorithm in multimodal emotion recognition in conversation (mERC). We conduct extensive experiments to show the effectiveness of the proposed model and prove that debias operation and sentiment knowledge has a great impact on the classification performance for the task of mERC. Due to the difference of the biases, the effect of debiasing also varies, which requires further research. Our model also has a few limitations. For example, we only select to mitigate two typical visual biases, while other typles of bias are ignored. Such efforts will be left to our future work. We hope our study will benefit the development of bias mitigation in mERC and other emotion studies.

Acknowledgements. This research was supported in part by Natural Science Foundation of Beijing (grant number: 4222036) and Huawei Technologies (grant number: TC20201228005). This work was supported by National Science Foundation of China under grant No. 62006212, the fund of State Key Lab. for Novel Software Technology in Nanjing University (grant No. KFKT2021B41), and the Industrial Science and Technology Research Project of Henan Province (grant No. 222102210031).

References

1. Bolukbasi, T., Chang, K.W., et al.: Man is to computer programmer as woman is to homemaker? Debiasing word embeddings. In: Proceedings of NeurIPS (2016)
2. Buolamwini, J., Gebru, T.: Gender shades: intersectional accuracy disparities in commercial gender classification. In: Conference on Fairness, Accountability and Transparency (2018)

3. Busso, C., Bulut, M., et al.: IEMOCAP: interactive emotional dyadic motion capture database. Lang. Resour. Eval. (2008). https://doi.org/10.1007/s10579-008-9076-6
4. Caliskan, A., Bryson, J.J., et al.: Semantics derived automatically from language corpora contain human-like biases. Science **356**, 183–186 (2017)
5. Dolan, R.J.: Emotion, cognition, and behavior. Science **298**, 1191–1194(2002)
6. Drozdowski, P., Rathgeb, C., et al.: Demographic bias in biometrics: a survey on an emerging challenge. IEEE Trans. Technol. Soc. **1**, 89–103(2020)
7. Evans, D.: Emotion: The Science of Sentiment. Oxford University Press, USA (2002)
8. Garg, N., Schiebinger, L., Jurafsky, D., Zou, J.: Word embeddings quantify 100 years of gender and ethnic stereotypes. In: Proceedings of the National Academy of Sciences (2018)
9. Goyal, Y., Khot, T., Agrawal, A., et al.: Making the v in VQA matter: elevating the role of image understanding in visual question answering. Int. J. Comput. Vis. (2019)
10. Hasan, M.K., Lee, S., Rahman, W., Zadeh, A., et al.: Humor knowledge enriched transformer for understanding multimodal humor (2021)
11. Kurita, K., Vyas, N., Pareek, A., et al.: Measuring bias in contextualized word representations. In: Proceedings of the First Workshop on Gender Bias in Natural Language Processing (2019)
12. May, C., Wang, A., Bordia, S., et al.: On measuring social biases in sentence encoders. In: Proceedings of ACL (2019)
13. Misra, I., Zitnick, C.L., Mitchell, M., et al.: Seeing through the human reporting bias: visual classifiers from noisy human-centric labels. In: Proceedings of CVPR (2016)
14. Mohammad, S.: Obtaining reliable human ratings of valence, arousal, and dominance for 20,000 English words. In: Proceedings of ACL (2018)
15. Nadeem, M., Bethke, A., Reddy, S.: StereoSet: measuring stereotypical bias in pretrained language models. arXiv preprint arXiv:2004.09456 (2020)
16. Pennington, J., Socher, R., Manning, C.D.: GLOVE: global vectors for word representation. In: Proceedings of EMNLP (2014)
17. Poria, S., Hazarika, D., Majumder, N., et al.: MELD: a multimodal multi-party dataset for emotion recognition in conversations. In: Proceedings of ACL (2019)
18. Rothe, R., Timofte, R., Gool, L.V.: Deep expectation of real and apparent age from a single image without facial landmarks. Int. J. Comput. Vis. (2018). https://doi.org/10.1007/s11263-016-0940-3
19. Rudinger, R., Naradowsky, J., Leonard, B., et al.: Gender bias in coreference resolution. In: Proceedings of ACL (2018)
20. Spliethöver, M., Wachsmuth, H.: Bias silhouette analysis: towards assessing the quality of bias metrics for word embedding models. In: Proceedings of IJCAI (2021)
21. Srinivasan, T., Bisk, Y.: Worst of both worlds: biases compound in pre-trained vision-and-language models. arXiv preprint arXiv:2104.08666 (2021)
22. Tan, M., Le, Q.: EfficientNet: rethinking model scaling for convolutional neural networks. In: Proceedings of ICML (2019)
23. Vaswani, A., Shazeer, N., Parmar, N., et al.: Attention is all you need. In: Proceedings of NeurIPS (2017)
24. Wang, M., Deng, W.: Mitigating bias in face recognition using skewness-aware reinforcement learning. In: Proceedings of CVPR (2020)
25. Wang, T., Lin, X.V., Rajani, N.F., et al.: Double-hard debias: tailoring word embeddings for gender bias mitigation. In: Proceedings of ACL (2020)

26. Webster, K., Wang, X., Tenney, I., et al.: Measuring and reducing gendered corre-
    lations in pre-trained models. arXiv preprint arXiv:2010.06032 (2020)
27. Zhao, J., Wang, T., Yatskar, M., et al.: Gender bias in coreference resolution:
    evaluation and debiasing methods. arXiv preprint arXiv:1804.06876 (2018)

Aspect-Specific Context Modeling
for Aspect-Based Sentiment Analysis

Fang Ma, Chen Zhang, Bo Zhang, and Dawei Song[(✉)]

Beijing Institute of Technology, Beijing, China
{mfang,czhang,bo.zhang,dwsong}@bit.edu.cn

Abstract. Aspect-based sentiment analysis (ABSA) aims at predicting sentiment polarity (SC) or extracting opinion span (OE) expressed towards a given aspect. Previous work in ABSA mostly relies on rather complicated aspect-specific feature induction. Recently, pretrained language models (PLMs), e.g., BERT, have been used as context modeling layers to simplify the feature induction structures and achieve state-of-the-art performance. However, such PLM-based context modeling can be not that aspect-specific. Therefore, a key question is left under-explored: how the aspect-specific context can be better modeled through PLMs? To answer the question, we attempt to enhance aspect-specific context modeling with PLM in a non-intrusive manner. We propose three aspect-specific input transformations, namely aspect companion, aspect prompt, and aspect marker. Informed by these transformations, non-intrusive aspect-specific PLMs can be achieved to promote the PLM to pay more attention to the aspect-specific context in a sentence. Additionally, we craft an adversarial benchmark for ABSA (advABSA) to see how aspect-specific modeling can impact model robustness. Extensive experimental results on standard and adversarial benchmarks for SC and OE demonstrate the effectiveness and robustness of the proposed method, yielding new state-of-the-art performance on OE and competitive performance on SC.

Keywords: Aspect-based sentiment analysis · Context modeling · Pretrained language model

1 Introduction

Aspect-based sentiment analysis (ABSA) aims to infer multiple fine-grained sentiments from the same content, with respect to multiple aspects. A fine-grained sentiment in ABSA can be categorized into two forms, i.e., sentiment and opinion. Accordingly, two sub-tasks of ABSA are aspect-based sentiment classification (SC for short) and aspect-based opinion extraction (OE for short). Given an aspect in a sentence, SC aims to predict its sentiment polarity, while OE aims to extract the corresponding opinion span expressed towards the given aspect. Figure 1 shows an example of SC and OE. In the sentence *"The food is tasty but*

© The Author(s), under exclusive license to Springer Nature Switzerland AG 2022
W. Lu et al. (Eds.): NLPCC 2022, LNAI 13551, pp. 513–526, 2022.
https://doi.org/10.1007/978-3-031-17120-8_40

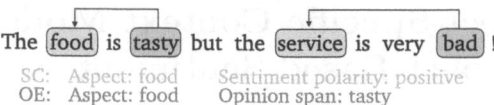

The food is tasty but the service is very bad !

SC: Aspect: food   Sentiment polarity: positive
OE: Aspect: food   Opinion span: tasty

Fig. 1. Example of the SC and OE. The words highlighted in purple represent the given aspects, whereas the words in green represent the corresponding opinion. (Color figure online)

the service is very bad!", if *food* is the given aspect, SC requires a model to give a `positive` sentiment on *food* while OE requires a model to extract *tasty* as the opinion span for the aspect *food.*

An effective ABSA model typically would require either aspect-specific feature induction or context modeling. Prior work in ABSA largely relies on rather complicated aspect-specific feature induction to achieve a good performance. Recently, pretrained language models (PLMs) have been shown to enhance the state-of-the-art ABSA models due to their extraordinary context modeling ability. However, currently the use of PLMs in these ABSA models is aspect-general, but overlooks two key questions: 1) whether the context modeling of a PLM can be aspect-specific; and 2) whether the aspect-specific context modeling within a PLM can further enhance ABSA.

To address the aforementioned key questions, in this paper, we propose to achieve *aspect-specific context modeling* of PLMs with *aspect-specific input transformations*. In addition to the commonly used aspect-specific input transformation that appends an aspect to a sentence, i.e., **aspect companion**, we propose two more aspect-specific input transformations, namely **aspect prompt** and **aspect marker**, to explicitly mark a concerned aspect in a sentence. Aspect prompt shares a similar idea with aspect companion, except that it appends an aspect-oriented prompt instead of sole aspect description to the sentence. Aspect marker distinguishes itself from the above two by introducing two marker tokens, one before and the other after the aspect. As the proposed input transformations are intended to highlight a specific aspect, they in turn can be leveraged to promote the PLM to pay more attention to the context that is relevant to the aspect. Methodologically, this is achieved with a novel aspect-focused PLM fine-tuning model that is guided by the input transformations and essentially performs a joint context modeling and aspect-specific feature induction.

We conduct extensive experiments on both subtasks of ABSA, i.e., SC and OE, with various standard benchmarking datasets for effectiveness test, along with our crafted adversarial ones for robustness test. Since there are only datasets for robustness tests in SC and is currently no dataset for robustness tests in OE, we propose an adversarial benchmark (advABSA) based on [23]'s datasets and methods. That is, the advABSA benchmark can be decomposed to two parts, where the first part is ARTS-SC for SC reused from [23] and the second part is ARTS-OE for OE crafted by us. The results show that models with aspect-specific context modeling achieve the state-of-the-art performance on OE and also outperform various strong SC baseline models without aspect-specific modeling. Overall, these results indicate that aspect-specific context modeling for PLMs can further enhance the performance of ABSA.

To better understand the effectiveness of the three input transformations, we carry out a series of further analyses. After injecting aspect-specific input transformations into a sentence, we observe that the model attends to the correct opinion spans. Hence, we expect that a simple model with aspect-specific context modeling yet without needing complicated aspect-specific feature induction would serve as a sufficiently strong approach for ABSA.

2 Related Work

2.1 Aspect-Based Sentiment Classification (SC)

ABSA falls in the broad scope of fine-grained opinion mining. As a sub-task of ABSA, SC determines the sentiment polarity of a given aspect in a sentence and has recently emerged as an active research area with lots of aspect-specific feature induction approaches. These approaches range from memory networks [18,20], convolutional networks [6,8,28], attentional networks [11,21], to graph-based networks [19,27]. More recently, PLMs such as BERT [3] and RoBERTa [9], have been applied to SC in a context-encoder scheme [17,25] and achieved the state-of-the-art performance. However, PLMs in these models are aspect-general. We aim to achieve aspect-specific context modeling with PLMs so that these models can be further improved.

2.2 Aspect-Based Opinion Extraction (OE)

OE is another sub-task of ABSA, first proposed by [4]. It aims to extract from a sentence the corresponding opinion span describing an aspect. Most work in this area treats OE as a sequence tagging task, for which complex methods are developed to capture the interaction between the aspect and the context [4,5,22]. More recent models such as TSMSA-BERT [5] and ARGCN-BERT [7], adopt PLMs. In TSMSA-BERT, the multi-head self-attention is utilized to enhance the BERT. ARGCN-BERT uses an attention-based relational graph convolutional network with BERT to exploit syntactic information. We will incorporate our aspect-specific context modeling methods into PLMs to see whether the proposed methods can further improve the OE performance.

3 Aspect-Specific Context Modeling

3.1 Task Description

ABSA (Both SC and OE) requires a pre-given aspect. Formally, a sentence is depicted as $S = \{w_1, w_2, \ldots, w_n\}$ that contains n words including the aspect. The aspect $A = \{a_1, a_2, ..., a_m\}$ is composed of m words. The goal of SC is to find

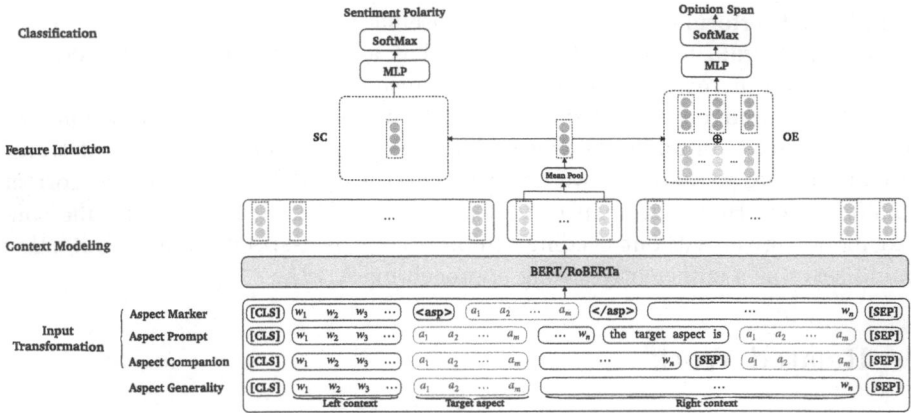

Fig. 2. The architecture of our proposed model based on the three mechanisms.

the sentiment polarity with respect to the given aspect A. OE aims to extract corresponding opinion span based on the given aspect A. Recap the example in Fig. 1 that contains aspect *food*. SC requires a model to give a `positive` sentiment on *food* and OE requires a model to tag the sentence as {0, 0, 0, B, 0, 0, 0, 0, 0, 0, 0,}, indicating the opinion span *tasty* for the aspect *food*.

3.2　Overall Framework

Figure 2 shows the structure of our model. Conventionally, an ABSA model consists of four parts: an input layer, a context modeling layer, a feature induction layer, and a classification layer. For aspect-specific context modeling, we first use an aspect-specific transformation to enrich the input. Next, the PLM is applied to get contextualized representations. Then we apply a mean pool operation on the hidden states of the first and last aspect tokens to induct the aspect-specific feature. For SC, we use the aspect-specific feature as the final representation for sentiment classification. For OE, we concatenate the aspect-specific feature and each token's representation to form the final representation for span tagging.

3.3　Aspect-General Input

The PLM requires a special classification token [CLS] (BERT) or ⟨s⟩ (RoBERTa) be appended to the start of the input sequence, and a separation token [SEP] (BERT) or ⟨/s⟩ (RoBERTa) appended to the end of the input sequence. The original input sentence is converted to the format [CLS] + input sequence + [SEP]. We refer to this format as aspect-general input, termed as **aspect generality**. Most previous work uses it for ABSA tasks, and [CLS] is often used for downstream classification, but there is no clear aspect information and no way of knowing which aspect is the focus.

3.4   Aspect-Specific Input Transformations

We propose three aspect-specific input transformations at the input layer to highlight the aspect in the sentence, namely aspect companion, aspect prompt, and aspect marker. We hypothesize that the three transformations can promote the aspect-awareness of PLM and help PLM achieve an effective aspect-specific context modeling.

Aspect Companion. Inspired by BERT's sentence pair encoding fashion, previous work [24] appends the aspect to the sentence as auxiliary information. Let $\hat{S}$ denote the modified sequence with aspect companion: $\hat{S} = \{\,[\text{CLS}], w_1, \ldots, a_1, \ldots, a_m, \ldots, w_n, [\text{SEP}], a_1, \ldots, a_m, [\text{SEP}]\,\}$. This formatted sequence can help the PLM effectively model the intra-sentence dependencies between every pair of tokens and further enhance the inter-sentence dependencies between the global context and the aspect.

Aspect Prompt. Inspired by recently popular prompt tuning where some natural language prompts can make the PLM complete a task in a cloze-completion style [1,15], we here append to the sentence with an aspect-oriented prompt sentence. Let $\hat{S}$ denote the modified sequence with aspect prompt: $\hat{S} = \{\,[\text{CLS}], w_1, \ldots, a_1, \ldots, a_m, \ldots, w_n, \text{the, target, aspect, is}, a_1, \ldots, a_m, [\text{SEP}]\,\}$. This format sequence prompts the PLM to target at the aimed aspect.

Aspect Marker. Aspect marker inserts markers into the sentence to explicitly mark the boundaries of the concerned aspect. Specifically, we define the markers as two preserved tokens: $\langle\text{asp}\rangle$ and $\langle/\text{asp}\rangle$. We insert them into the input sentence before and after the concerned aspect, to mark the start and end of the given aspect. $\langle\text{asp}\rangle$ indicates the start of the aspect, and $\langle/\text{asp}\rangle$ indicates the end of the aspect. Let $\hat{S}$ denote the modified sequence with aspect marker inserted: $\hat{S} = \{\,[\text{CLS}], w_1, \ldots, \langle\text{asp}\rangle, a_1, \ldots, a_m, \langle/\text{asp}\rangle, \ldots, w_n, [\text{SEP}]\,\}$.

The three *aspect-specific input transformations* gain significant improvement in our experiments (Sect. 5), and this strengthens our hypothesis that injecting the aspect marker at the input layer can help the PLM capture aspect-specific contextual information further.

3.5   Context Modeling

Previous PLM-based ABSA work directly adopts the hidden states of the PLM for downstream classification. However, an empirical observation is that the context words close to the aspect are more semantic-relevant to the aspect [12]. In the case, more sentiment information is possibly contained in the aspect's local context rather than the global context. As a result, the general usage of the hidden states from the PLM loses much local contextual information related to the aspect. With the help of the three input transformations, we obtain the hidden states that incorporate the aspect-oriented local context. Let

$$H = \text{PLM}(\hat{S}) \tag{1}$$

where $H = \{h_1, \ldots, h_1^a, \ldots, h_m^a, \ldots, h_n\}$ represents the sequence of hidden states.

3.6   Feature Induction

As aforementioned, aspect-general feature induction contains the semantic information critical to the whole sentence rather than the given aspect, and the induced aspect-general feature may be aspect-irrelevant when the sentence contains two or more aspects. After getting the global contextual representation H, existing work needs an aspect-specific feature extraction strategy to induce the aspect feature after getting the global contextual representation H. For an enriched aspect-awareness, we adopt the mean pool on the hidden states corresponding to the first and last aspect tokens. Let

$$\hat{H} = \text{MeanPool}([h_1^a, h_m^a]) \tag{2}$$

represent the aspect-specific feature, where h_1^a indicates the hidden state of the first aspect token, and h_m^a indicates the hidden state of the last aspect token. Due to that OE is a token-level classification task, we concatenate the aspect-specific feature $\hat{H}$ and the global contextual representation H as the final aspect-specific contextual representation for tagging.

3.7   Fine-Tuning

After getting the aspect-specific contextual representation $\hat{H}$, an multi-layered Perceptron (MLP) layer is used to fine-tune the proposed BERT or RoBERTa based model. Then we feed the output to a softmax layer to predict the corresponding label. The training objective is to minimize the cross-entropy loss with $\mathcal{L}_2$ regularization. Specifically, the optimal parameters θ are obtained from

$$\mathcal{L}(\theta) = -\sum_{i=1}^{n} \hat{y}_i \log y_i + \lambda \sum_{\theta \in \Theta} \theta^2 \tag{3}$$

where λ is the regularization constant and $\hat{y}_i$ is the predicted label corresponding to ground truth label y_i.

When no input transformation is used, the model is aspect-general and named as PLM-MeanPool and PLM-MeanPool-Concat for SC and OE, respectively. By incorporating the three input transformations, the model becomes more aspect-specific, denoted as +AC (**A**spect **C**ompanion), +AP (**A**spect **P**rompt), and +AM (**A**spect **M**arker) respectively.

4 Experiments

4.1 Datasets

SC Datasets. Following previous work [12], we conduct experiments on two SC benchmarks to evaluate our models' effectiveness and robustness. One is SemEval 2014 [14] (SEMEVAL), which contains data from laptop (SEM-LAP) and restaurant (SEM-REST) domains; the other is the Aspect Robustness Test Set (ARTS-SC) [23], which is derived from the SEMEVAL dataset. Instances in ARTS-SC are generated with three adversarial strategies. Note that each domain from SEMEVAL consists of separate training and test sets, while each domain from ARTS-SC only contains a test set. Since datasets in SEMEVAL do not contain development sets, 150 instances from the training set in each dataset are randomly selected to form the development set. Table 1 shows the statistics of the SC datasets.

OE Datasets. For datasets used in OE [4,22], the original SEMEVAL benchmark annotates the aspects, but not the corresponding opinion spans, for each sentence. To solve the problem, [4] annotates the corresponding opinion spans for each given aspect in a sentence and removes the cases without explicit opinion spans. We use this variant in our OE experiments.

Since there is currently no robustness test set for OE, we follow [23]'s three adversarial strategies to generate an Aspect Robustness Test Set with spans (ARTS-OE) based on SEMEVAL. Specifically, we use these strategies to generate 1002 test instances for the laptop domain (ARTS-OE-LAP) and 2009 test instances for the restaurant domain (ARTS-OE-RES). Each aspect in a sentence is associated with an opinion span for OE. It is worth noting that this adversarial dataset can also be used for other tasks, e.g., aspect sentiment triplet extraction [13]. Table 2 shows the statistics of the OE datasets. Since these OE datasets do not come with a development set, we randomly split 20% of the training set as validation set.

Table 1. Statistics of SC datasets.

Dataset		#pos.	#neu.	#neg.
Sem-Lap	Train	930	433	800
	Test	341	169	128
	Dev	57	27	66
Sem-Rest	Train	2,094	579	779
	Test	728	196	196
	Dev	70	54	26
Arts-SC-Lap	Test	883	407	587
Arts-SC-Rest	Test	1,953	473	1,104

Table 2. Statistics of OE datasets.

Dataset		#sentences	#aspects
Sem-Lap	Train	1,158	1,634
	Test	343	482
Sem-Rest	Train	1,627	2,643
	Test	500	865
ARTS-OE-Lap	Test	1,002	2,404
ARTS-OE-Rest	Test	2,009	5,743

4.2 Comparative Models and Baselines

We carry out an extensive evaluation of the proposed models (with and without transformation), including *PLM-MeanPool* ± *AC/AP/AM* for SC, *PLM-MeanPool-Concat* ± *AC/AP/AM* for OE.

SC Baselines. (a) BERT/RoBERTa-CLS-MLP use the representation of "[CLS]" as a classification feature to fine-tune the BERT/RoBERTa with an MLP layer. (b) AEN-BERT [16] adopts BERT model and attention mechanism to model the relationship between contexts and aspects. (c) LCF-BERT [26] employs Local-Context-Focus design with Semantic-Relative-Distance to discard unrelated sentiment words. (d) BERT/RoBERTa-ASCNN [27] is combined with BERT/RoBERTa and ASCNN model. (e)Roberta-ASGCN [27] use graph convolutional networks to capture the aspect-specific information based on Roberta.

OE Baselines. (a) BERT+Distance-rule [5] is the combination of BERT and Distance-rule. (b) TF-BERT [5] utilizes the average pooling of target word embeddings to represent the target information. (c) SDRN [2] utilizes BERT as the encoder for OE. (d) TSMSA-BERT [5] uses a target-specified sequence labeling method based on multi-head self-attention (TSMSA) to perform OE. (e) ARGCN+BERT [7] adopts the last hidden states of the pretrained BERT as word representations and fine-tune it with the ARGCN model.

4.3 Implementation Details

For fair comparison, we re-produce all baselines based on their open-source codes under the same settings. For experiments with BERT [3] and RoBERTa [9] as the input embeddings, we adopt the BERT-base-uncased model and the RoBERTa-base model as our backbone network, where the learning rate is set to 10^{-5} for SC and $5*10^{-5}$ for OE. During all experiments, AdamW [10] is adopted optimizer in our models. The batch size is 64, and the maximal sequence length is 128. It is worth noting that most previous methods did not use the dev set and may have overfitted the test set. We have made a systematic and comprehensive comparison for the first time under the same settings.

4.4 Evaluation Metrics

For standard performance evaluation, each model is trained, validated and tested on the standard datasets. For SC, we use accuracy and macro-averaged F1-score as performance metrics. Following the previous work [4], we adopt F1-score only as the evaluation metric for OE. An opinion extraction is considered correct only when the opinion span predicted is the same as the ground truth. To evaluate a model's robustness on SC and OE, the model is trained on the standard SEMEVAL datasets and tested on the ARTS-SC and ARTS-OE testsets, respectively. Finally, the experimental results are obtained by averaging five runs with random initialization.

Table 3. Standard and robust experimental results (%) on SC. Our models and better results are bold. The marker † represents that our models outperform the all other models significantly (p < 0.01), and the small number next to each score indicates performance improvement (↑) compared with our aspect-general base model (BERT-MeanPool/RoBERTa-MeanPool).

Models	SEM-LAP				SEM-REST			
	Standard		Robustness		Standard		Robustness	
	Acc.	F1	Acc.	F1	Acc.	F1	Acc.	F1
AEN-BERT	77.37	71.83	71.49	66.37	83.66	75.50	73.24	66.31
LCF-BERT	76.55	71.40	71.19	66.95	81.66	72.24	70.57	62.75
BERT-CLS+MLP	75.42	69.08	54.91	51.21	78.95	67.66	53.86	47.16
RoBERTa-CLS+MLP	79.09	75.36	56.24	54.61	81.93	71.19	60.45	52.02
BERT-ASCNN	76.33	71.09	71.17	66.90	82.66	74.05	75.73	68.17
RoBERTa-ASCNN	81.41	77.22	73.59	70.14	85.93	78.01	78.85	70.69
RoBERTa-ASGCN	81.82	78.28	73.48	69.38	85.66	78.48	79.65	72.56
BERT-MeanPool	76.87	71.71	70.59	66.38	84.27	76.48	77.36	70.64
+AC	75.30	69.62	69.40	64.45	84.12	76.16	76.78	69.86
+AP	76.39	70.91	68.92	63.77	83.89	76.02	76.48	69.34
+AM	76.33	**71.93**↑0.22	**70.78**	**67.06**↑0.68	**84.71**	**78.07** ↑1.59	**78.10**	**72.38** ↑1.74
RoBERTa-MeanPool	81.38	77.68	74.67	71.21	85.41	78.15	79.75	72.73
+AC	**81.54**	77.54	**75.13**	71.02	**86.68**†	**79.69**†↑1.54	**80.63**	**74.03**↑1.30
+AP	**81.85**	**77.91**↑0.23	74.53	70.48	**86.43**	**79.43**↑1.28	**80.72**	**74.09**†↑1.36
+AM	**82.07**†	**78.50**†↑0.82	**75.90**†	**72.59**†↑1.38	**86.41**	**79.58**↑1.43	**80.88**†	**74.04**↑1.31

5 Results and Analysis

5.1 SC Results

Table 3 shows the standard and robustness evaluation results for SC.

Standard Results. Generally, our models with input transformations outperform the baseline models. Before applying the transformations, our base models (BERT/RoBERTa-MeanPool with aspect generality) perform equally good or even better than most baseline models.

Applying the input transformations, especially aspect marker (i.e., +AM), further improves performance significantly. For BERT-based models, the F1-scores of the BERT-MeanPool+AM model are 2.57% and 5.83% higher than AEN-BERT and LCF-BERT respectively on the SEM-REST standard dataset. For RoBERTa-based models, the three transformations are more effective. Specifically, the F1-scores of RoBERTa-MeanPool+AC and RoBERTa-MeanPool+AP improve by up to 1.54% and 1.28% on SEM-REST standard dataset. These results indicate that the proposed input transformations can promote PLMs to achieve effective aspect-specific context modeling.

Among the three transformations, in general AM performs better than AC and AP, indicating that AM is more effective for aspect-specific context modeling in PLMs. While the F1-scores of BERT-MeanPool+AM and

RoBERTa-MeanPool+AM gain improvements by 1.59% and 1.43% on SEM-REST, RoBERTa-MeanPool+AM achieves the terrific results for SC, with F1-score are 78.5% and 79.58% on SEM-LAP and SEM-REST respectively.

Robustness Results. We can see that the performances of the baseline models drop drastically on robustness test sets. In contrast, our models with the transformations are more robust than the baseline models. The most robust model is the RoBERTa-MeanPool+AM, which achieves 72.59% and 74.04% of F1 score on the ARTS-SC-LAP and ARTS-SC-REST robustness test set, representing a 3.21% and 1.48% improvement over the strongest baseline RoBERTa-ASGCN.

The three transformations significantly improve the PLM-MeanPool models' robustness, especially for RoBERTa-MeanPool. Specifically, with AC, AP, and AM, the RoBERTa-MeanPool model's F1-scores are improved by up to 1.30%, 1.36%, and 1.31% on ARTS-SC-REST robustness test set. The model with AM is more robust than the model with AC and AP. These robustness results demonstrate that the transformations can improve our models' robustness.

5.2   OE Results

Tabel 4 shows the standard and robustness results for OE.

Table 4. Standard and robustness evaluation results (F1-score, %) on OE. The first blocks show the results of the BERT-based baseline models (with ∗), which are extracted from the published papers [22] and [5]. Note that there were no robustness results of the baseline models in the original published papers, so that we leave then blank. The results of our models are presented in the second and third blocks.

Models	SEM-LAP		SEM-REST	
	Standard	Robustness	Standard	Robustness
BERT+Distance-rule*	70.54	–	76.23	–
TF-BERT*	72.26	–	78.23	–
SDRN*	80.24	–	83.53	–
TSMSA-BERT*	82.18	–	86.37	–
ARGCN-BERT*	76.36	–	85.42	–
BERT-MeanPool-Concat	68.27	39.68	69.08	44.23
+AC	80.31↑12.04	70.98↑31.30	85.09↑16.01	70.01↑25.78
+AP	79.60↑11.33	68.06↑28.38	85.32↑16.24	70.25↑26.02
+AM	81.06 ↑12.79	71.23↑31.55	85.62↑16.54	69.68↑25.45
RoBERTa-MeanPool-Concat	69.74	38.76	79.03	56.93
+AC	82.78↑13.04	71.26↑32.50	86.03↑7.00	71.42↑14.49
+AP	82.63↑12.89	71.46↑32.30	**86.58**†↑7.55	**71.61**†↑14.68
+AM	**83.83**†↑14.09	**73.69**†↑34.93	86.33↑7.30	71.50↑14.57

Standard Results. Before applying the transformations, our base models (PLM-MeanPool-Concat) perform poorly. On the contrary, with the transformations, our models perform significantly better than baselines. Our BERT-based model with the transformations achieves nearly identical results with the current sota model (TSMSA-BERT). With AC, AP, and AM, the F1-scores of the RoBERTa-MeanPool-Concat model are improved by up to 13.04%, 12.89%, and 14.09% on SEM-LAP, respectively. These results demonstrate that the transformations can promote PLMs to achieve effective aspect-specific context modeling for OE. Our RoBERTa-MeanPool-Concat+AM model achieves the new sota result on OE.

Robustness Results. The performances of our base models (PLM-MeanPool-Concat) drop drastically on robustness test set. Their F1-scores are only 39.68% and 38.76% on ARTS-OE-LAP and 44.23% and 56.93% on ARTS-OE-REST. In contrast, with the transformations, our models are more robust, achieving F1 scores up to 73.69% (RoBERTa-MeanPool-Concat+AM) on ARTS-OE-LAP, and 71.61% (RoBERTa-MeanPool-Concat+AP) on ARTS-OE-REST, demonstrating that the transformations can improve our model's robustness for OE.

Table 5. SC ablation results.

Models	SEM-LAP	SEM-REST
BERT-MeanPool	71.71	76.48
BERT-CLS+MLP	69.08	67.66
+AC	68.82	74.03↑6.37
+AP	70.47↑1.39	76.78↑9.12
+AM	70.24↑1.16	74.19↑6.53
RoBERTa-MeanPool	77.68	78.15
RoBERTa-CLS+MLP	75.36	71.19
+AC	77.62↑2.26	76.04↑4.85
+AP	78.40↑3.04	78.53↑7.34
+AM	78.21↑2.85	79.91↑8.72

Table 6. OE ablation results (F1-score, %).

Models	SEM-LAP	SEM-REST
BERT-MeanPool-Concat	68.27	69.08
BERT-MLP	67.67	61.40
+AC	79.95↑12.28	79.46↑18.06
+AP	80.08↑12.41	81.02↑19.62
+AM	81.50↑13.83	80.02↑18.62
RoBERTa-MeanPool-Concat	69.74	79.03
RoBERTa-MLP	67.92	60.00
+AC	82.18↑14.26	81.59↑21.59
+AP	81.96↑14.04	81.04 ↑21.04
+AM	83.42↑15.50	80.81↑20.81

5.3   Ablation Study

To further investigate the effects of the feature induction and the transformations on aspect-specific context modeling of PLMs, we conduct extensive ablation experiments on standard datasets, whose results are included in Table 5 and 6.

Aspect-Specific Feature Induction. For SC and OE, we start with a simple base model that does not use the aspect feature induction component, but using just a context modeling representation after PLM and append an MLP layer (PLM-CLS-MLP for SC, PLM-MLP for OE). After adding back the aspect feature induction, for SC, our PLM-MeanPool models always give a superior performance than the base model. The F1-scores of BERT-MeanPool are 2.63% higher than BERT-CLS-MLP on Sem-Lap. For OE, our PLM-MeanPool-Concat models perform better than PLM-MLP models. These results demonstrate the effectiveness of the aspect-specific feature induction methods with PLMs.

Aspect-Specific Context Modeling. To investigate the effect of the aspect-specific context modeling with transformations, we add the transformations to the above simple base models. The results show that the transformations bring significant performance improvements, even better than the models with aspect feature induction. Especially the base models with the transformations for OE achieve nearly identical results to BERT/RoBERTa-MeanPool-Concat with transformations. These excellent results demonstrate the effectiveness of the proposed transformations for context modeling, which indirectly explains that context modeling is more critical than aspect feature induction for ABSA.

5.4 Visualization of Attention

To understand the effect of the three transformations, we visualize the attention scores separately offered by our OE model (BERT-MeanPool-Concat) with the transformations, as shown in Fig. 3. The four attention vectors have encoded quite different concerns in the token sequence. We can observe that after applying the transformations, AC, AP, and AM can promote our model to attend to aspect-specific context words and capture the correct opinion spans, thus achieving aspect-specific context modeling in PLM.

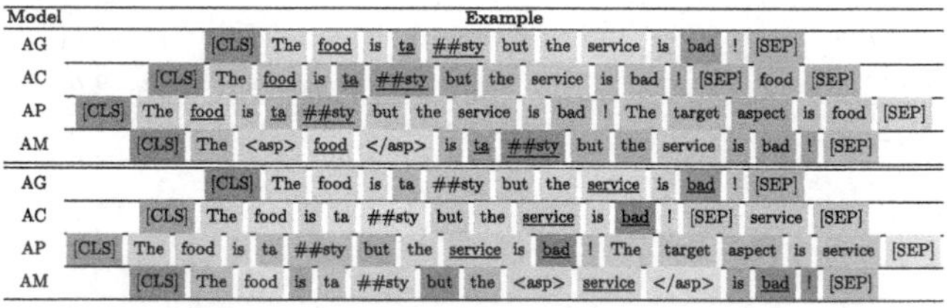

Fig. 3. Attention visualization. Gradient saliency maps for the embedding of each word in the three transformations under BERT architecture. Underlined words are aspects and corresponding opinion spans.

6   Conclusions

In this paper, we propose three aspect-specific input transformations and methods to leverage these transformations to promote the PLM to pay more attention to the aspect-specific context in two aspect-based sentiment analysis (ABSA) tasks (SC and OE). We conduct experiments with standard benchmarks for

SC and OE, along with adversarial ones for robustness tests. Our models with aspect-specific context modeling achieve the state-of-the-art performance for OE and outperform various strong models for SC. The extensive experimental results and further analysis indicated that aspect-specific context modeling can enhance the performance of ABSA.

Acknowledgements. This research was supported in part by Natural Science Foundation of Beijing (grant number: 4222036) and Huawei Technologies (grant number: TC20201228005).

References

1. Brown, T.B., et al.: Language models are few-shot learners. arXiv preprint arXiv:2005.14165 (2020)
2. Chen, S., Liu, J., Wang, Y., Zhang, W., Chi, Z.: Synchronous double-channel recurrent network for aspect-opinion pair extraction. In: Proceedings of ACL (2020)
3. Devlin, J., Chang, M.W., Lee, K., Toutanova, K.: BERT: pre-training of deep bidirectional transformers for language understanding. In: Proceedings of NAACL (2019)
4. Fan, Z., Wu, Z., Dai, X., Huang, S., Chen, J.: Target-oriented opinion words extraction with target-fused neural sequence labeling. In: Proceedings of NAACL (2019)
5. Feng, Y., Rao, Y., Tang, Y., Wang, N., Liu, H.: Target-specified sequence labeling with multi-head self-attention for target-oriented opinion words extraction. In: Proceedings of NAACL (2021)
6. Huang, B., Carley, K.M.: Parameterized convolutional neural networks for aspect level sentiment classification. In: Proceedings of EMNLP (2018)
7. Jiang, J., Wang, A., Aizawa, A.: Attention-based relational graph convolutional network for target-oriented opinion words extraction. In: Proceedings of EACL (2021)
8. Li, X., Bing, L., Lam, W., Shi, B.: Transformation networks for target-oriented sentiment classification. In: Proceedings of ACL (2018)
9. Liu, Y., et al.: RoBERTa: A robustly optimized BERT pretraining approach. arXiv preprint arXiv:1907.11692 (2019)
10. Loshchilov, I., Hutter, F.: Decoupled weight decay regularization. In: International Conference on Learning Representations (2019)
11. Ma, D., Li, S., Zhang, X., Wang, H.: Interactive attention networks for aspect-level sentiment classification. In: Proceedings of IJCAI (2017)
12. Ma, F., Zhang, C., Song, D.: Exploiting position bias for robust aspect sentiment classification. In: Findings of the Association for Computational Linguistics: ACL-IJCNLP 2021. Association for Computational Linguistics, Online, August 2021
13. Peng, H., Xu, L., Bing, L., Huang, F., Lu, W., Si, L.: Knowing what, how and why: a near complete solution for aspect-based sentiment analysis. In: Proceedings of AAAI (2020)
14. Pontiki, M., Papageorgiou, H., Galanis, D., Androutsopoulos, I., Pavlopoulos, J., Manandhar, S.: SemEval-2014 task 4: aspect based sentiment analysis. SemEval 2014 (2014)
15. Schick, T., Schütze, H.: It's not just size that matters: small language models are also few-shot learners. In: Proceedings of NAACL (2021)

16. Song, Y., Wang, J., Jiang, T., Liu, Z., Rao, Y.: Attentional encoder network for targeted sentiment classification. arXiv preprint arXiv:1902.09314 (2019)
17. Song, Y., Wang, J., Liang, Z., Liu, Z., Jiang, T.: Utilizing BERT intermediate layers for aspect based sentiment analysis and natural language inference. arXiv e-prints (2020)
18. Tang, D., Qin, B., Liu, T.: Aspect level sentiment classification with deep memory network. In: Proceedings of EMNLP (2016)
19. Wang, K., Shen, W., Yang, Y., Quan, X., Wang, R.: Relational graph attention network for aspect-based sentiment analysis. In: Proceedings of ACL (2020)
20. Wang, S., Mazumder, S., Liu, B., Zhou, M., Chang, Y.: Target-sensitive memory networks for aspect sentiment classification. In: Proceedings of ACL (2018)
21. Wang, Y., Huang, M., Zhu, X., Zhao, L.: Attention-based LSTM for aspect-level sentiment classification. In: Proceedings of EMNLP (2016)
22. Wu, Z., Zhao, F., Dai, X.Y., Huang, S., Chen, J.: Latent opinions transfer network for target-oriented opinion words extraction. In: Proceedings of AAAI (2020)
23. Xing, X., Jin, Z., Jin, D., Wang, B., Zhang, Q., Huang, X.J.: Tasty burgers, soggy fries: Probing aspect robustness in aspect-based sentiment analysis. In: Proceedings of EMNLP (2020)
24. Xu, H., Liu, B., Shu, L., Philip, S.Y.: Bert post-training for review reading comprehension and aspect-based sentiment analysis. In: Proceedings of NAACL (2019)
25. Yadav, R.K., Jiao, L., Granmo, O.C., Goodwin, M.: Human-level interpretable learning for aspect-based sentiment analysis. In: Proceedings of AAAI (2021)
26. Zeng, B., Yang, H., Xu, R., Zhou, W., Han, X.: LCF: a local context focus mechanism for aspect-based sentiment classification. Appl. Sci. **9**, 3389 (2019)
27. Zhang, C., Li, Q., Song, D.: Aspect-based sentiment classification with aspect-specific graph convolutional networks. In: Proceedings of EMNLP (2019)
28. Zhang, C., Li, Q., Song, D.: Syntax-aware aspect-level sentiment classification with proximity-weighted convolution network. In: Proceedings of SIGIR (2019)

Memeplate: A Chinese Multimodal Dataset for Humor Understanding in Meme Templates

Zefeng Li, Hongfei Lin, Liang Yang$^{(\boxtimes)}$, Bo Xu, and Shaowu Zhang

Dalian University of Technology, Dalian 116024, China
chinese_lzf@mail.dlut.edu.cn, {hflin,liang,xubo,zhangsw}@dlut.edu.cn

Abstract. Humor plays an important role in human communication. Besides language, multimodal information is also of great significance in humor expression and understanding, which promotes the development of multimodal humor research. However, in existing datasets, images and text often have a one-to-one relationship, making it difficult to control image modality variables. It causes the low correlation and low enhancement between the two modalities in humor recognition tasks. Moreover, with the development of Vision Transformers (ViTs), the generalization ability of visual models has been greatly enhanced. Using ViTs alone can achieve impressive performance, but is difficult to explain. In this paper, we introduce Memeplate (Our dataset is available at https://github.com/chineselzf/memeplate.), a novel multimodal humor dataset containing 203 templates, 5,184 memes and manually annotated humor levels. The template transfers images and text into a one-to-many relationship, which can make it easier for researchers to cut through the linguistic lens to multimodal humor. And it provides examples closer to human behavior for generation research. In addition, we provide multiple baseline results on the humor recognition task, which demonstrate the effectiveness of our control over image modality and the importance of introducing multimodal cues.

Keywords: Multimodality · Sentiment analysis · Humor recognition

1 Introduction

As a linguistic phenomenon, humor plays an important role in human communication. Making the AI systems enable to recognize and understand humor will greatly improve the level of linguistic intelligence and bring it closer to human mind. Early research on computational humor is mainly in the NLP community. Mihalcea and Strapparava [18] created a corpus of 16,000 one-liner jokes, and proposed humor-specific features including alliteration, antonymy, and adult slang. After that, they [19] explored several computational models for incongruity resolution and introduced a dataset containing set-ups followed by coherent continuations. In addition, much research [7,24,26] emphasized incongruity in the

© The Author(s), under exclusive license to Springer Nature Switzerland AG 2022
W. Lu et al. (Eds.): NLPCC 2022, LNAI 13551, pp. 527–538, 2022.
https://doi.org/10.1007/978-3-031-17120-8_41

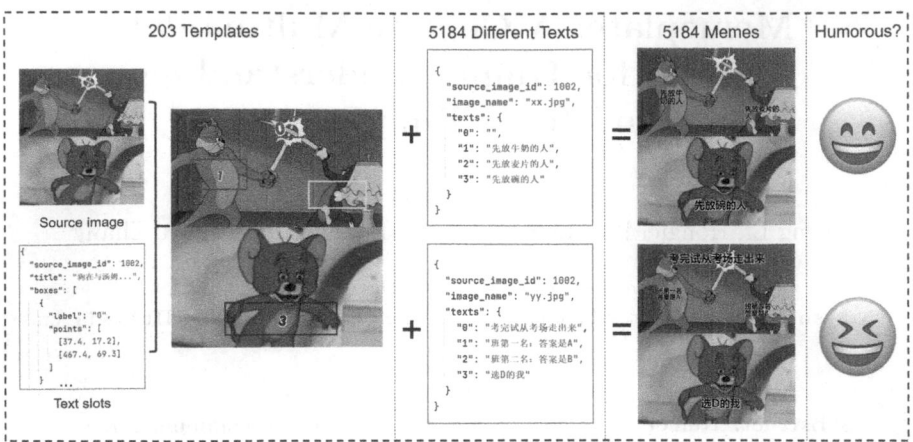

Fig. 1. An example of the Memeplate dataset. A template consists of a source image and several corresponding text slots described by a specific structure. One template can generate memes with different text which may have different humor levels. We offer 5,184 instances with annotated humor levels.

humor. In brief, humor production needs preparation and a sudden twist using a punchline. For example, in the joke "The god promised him a wish, and he said he would become a millionaire. The next day, he became a Zimbabwean.", the first sentence is the context, and the second sentence is the punchline.

However, humor can be expressed not only through language, but visual, acoustic and other modal information as well. As the example shown in Fig. 1, the image provides information not mentioned in the text, i.e., the dog is fighting with Tom, and Jerry is smiling wryly. Each object in the image is associated with a piece of text, which is impossible to obtain the complete logical relationship from the text individually, let alone express humor. After correctly combining the image content with the text (for the second meme), we can get the context "After the exam, the first and second students in the class are arguing over the answer" and the punchline "But I choose a different answer from them".

Therefore, it is important to study humor from a multimodal perspective. Multimodal humor research involves trimodal form (acoustics, vision and text) like videos, and bimodal form (image and text) like memes. For the former, Hasan et al. [9] introduced the UR-FUNNY dataset. And for the latter, Sharma et al. [21] organized SemEval-2020 Task8. Their baseline results show that the combination of two modalities performs better than single modality while Bonheme et al. [5] found that using the single modality led to better results with their models, and the two modalities were uncorrelated. To verify their conclusions, we conducted experiments using the latest models.

Table 1 shows the experimental results. The XCit and BEit show a strong generalization ability, achieving results close to the SOTA. Although image models may learn humorous information, existing research has few conclusions about

Table 1. In the table, the results of SemEval-2020 Task8 show the metrics of four-categories classification for the humorous sub-label of Task C, and the results of CCL-2021 Task4 show the metrics of three-categories classification of Task2.

Modality	Model	SemEval-2020 Task8		CCL-2021 Task4	
		ACC	F1	ACC	F1
Text	BERT [13]	32.20	24.86	45.30	41.15
	RoBERTa [16]	32.96	25.57	44.90	41.52
Image	Swin [17]	30.16	24.59	52.90	48.56
	XCiT [2]	**34.94**	**25.61**	55.90	54.34
	BEiT [3]	30.59	24.90	**63.00**	59.56
Text+Image	RoBERTa+Swin	29.89	24.62	54.30	51.95
	RoBERTa+XCiT	32.10	25.35	49.60	47.17
	RoBERTa+BEiT	30.32	25.43	62.10	**60.80**

humor features in image modality. And we cannot determine whether the patterns learned by image models are relevant to humor. It is more feasible to explain the mechanism of multimodal humor from a textual perspective. Therefore, we intend to create a dataset that constrains image modality but has no effects on multimodal properties.

We are inspired by the meme secondary-creations on the Internet, where a source image is filled with different text to produce different humorous effects. In this case, the information provided by image modality is almost identical for the memes with the same source image, and the humorous effect is mainly determined by the text filled in. The secondary-creation can be considered as using a template approach, by which we create Memeplate, a novel multimodal humor dataset. We aim to make researchers easier to apply the linguistic findings to multimodal humor, and provide examples of meme generation closer to human behavior for humor generation research. Overall, our main contributions are as follows:

- We design a novel annotation scheme to focus on humor in memes from the textual perspective. The main idea is to use templates to constrain the image modality.
- We create a multimodal dataset containing 203 templates and 5,184 memes with manually annotated humor levels based on the scheme. And we offer detailed annotation process and statistical information on the dataset.
- We conduct experiments with multiple baseline models for the humor recognition task on the dataset. The experimental results demonstrate the effectiveness of our control over image modality and the importance of combining multimodal cues.

2   Related Work

The humor dataset is fundamental in computational humor research. Mihalcea and Strapparava [18] created a corpus of 16,000 one-liner jokes. Yang et al. [24] introduced Pun of the Days for pun recognition. Both of them are binary classification tasks. Recently, the humor dataset evolves in a diverse direction, which reflects trends in computational humor.

The first trend is from the classification of humor levels to the research of humor mechanisms. Ahuja et al. [1] collected jokes from Twitter and Reddit, and recognized three major characteristics reflected across all types of jokes including modes, theme and topics. Zhang et al. [25] developed a Chinese humor corpus containing 9,123 jokes with reference to the General Theory of Verbal Humor (GTVH). Their annotations of linguistic humor not only contain the degree of funniness, but contain keywords that trigger humor as well as character relationship, scene, and humor categories as well. Tseng et al. [22] developed a Chinese humor corpus containing 3,365 jokes with five levels of funniness, eight skill sets of humor, and six dimensions of intent.

The second trend is from English to other languages or multi-languages. Castro et al. [7] introduced a humor corpus containing 33,531 Spanish Tweets. The dataset involves binary annotation and humor level annotation with five levels. Then they [6] revised it with crowd notes and presented a 27,000 tweets dataset in total. Instead of using the five-point annotation, they used five different emojis to represent the levels of humor. Blinov et al. [4] constructed a Russian language dataset with over 300,000 short jokes using an automated approach. Khandelwal et al. [14] create a corpus containing English-Hindi code-mixed tweets annotated with humorous or non-humorous tags.

The third trend is from text-based to multimodal. For the trimodal form (acoustics, vision and text), Hasan et al. [9] collected data from TED talks and published the UR-FUNNY multimodal humor dataset with 8,257 humor and 8,257 non-humor instances. Wu et al. [23] used a similar approach to construct the first Chinese multimodal humor dataset, MUMOR. Kayatani et al. [12] study facial expressions in the visual modality and constructed a dataset from The Big Bang Theory. For the bimodal form (image and text), Sharma et al. [21] released approx 10K annotated memes with manually annotated labels, including humorous, sarcasm, offensive, and motivation. Ziser et al. [27] combine humor recognition tasks with the domain of Product Question Answer (PQA). Annotators were presented with a question and the associated product image with caption, and were asked to classify whether the question is humorous or not.

3   Dataset

3.1   Data Collection

To make the dataset objective and comprehensive, data was collected from a range of sources, including social media (Weibo and Tieba) and image recognition websites (Baidu Image and Yandex Image). We searched with keywords, including "迷因图(meme)", "表情包(sticker)", "搞笑图片(funny images)" and "幽默图片(humorous images)" to obtain data from both content and blogger perspectives. For the content results, we directly downloaded them. And for the blogger results, we selected 20 bloggers who were most followed and downloaded the image contents posted by them. To obtain textual information, we extracted the text in memes using PaddleOCR[1] for reference in the data filter and annotation process. In terms of genre, the data we collected included memes, stickers and comics. In general, the language in memes is more standardized and completed, while the language in stickers and comics is more verbalized and fragmented.

3.2 Data Filter

Data filter could be divided into two stages, the first stage was the preliminary filter. Images with unqualified content (e.g. meaningless, politically sensitive, emoji without text, non-Chinese and non-English), text-based content (e.g. a WeChat conversation between two people), and duplicate text were dropped. However, low-resolution images were reserved, as long as the text could be recognized. Because high-quality images could be generated using high-resolution source images and recognized text after template creation. The second stage was the counting filter for further template creation and one-to-many text examples. We counted the memes group by source images manually, and those with less than four repetitions were dropped.

3.3 Image Recognition

Image recognition was conducted with Baidu Image and Yandex Image for two purposes. The first was to obtain high-quality source images, either original images or ones with text boxes but not filled yet (a template in a sense, but requiring manual edit). The second was to expand the existed data using the similar images search function. Since such websites crawl images across the whole Internet, search results can be plentiful. We conducted the similar image search on memes in terms of source images, downloaded the results, and repeated the data filter steps described above.

3.4 Data Annotation

After collection, we obtained **a)** filtered memes, and **b)** source images (one corresponding to several memes without text). Then the dataset was annotated in the following steps:

- **Text slot annotation.** As the example shown in Fig. 1, a template has several text slots labeled with different colors. We specified that the text in memes must be filled in the slots. Each template could have more than

---

[1] https://github.com/PaddlePaddle/PaddleOCR.

one rectangular text slot, but should be able to reasonably accommodate all the text in the filtered memes. One annotator completed this part of the annotation using Labelme[2].

- **Image caption annotation.** As mentioned earlier, humor production requires context and punchlines. Since the text modality rarely contained complete information about context and punchlines, we provided captions to supply image information to text modality from another perspective. We specified that captions needed to describe the objects (required) and actions (optional) in the images. For example, the caption of the image in Fig. 1 is "狗在与汤姆持剑打斗，杰瑞苦笑 (The dog is fighting with Tom with swords and Jerry is smiling wryly)". One annotator completed this part of the annotation.
- **Text extraction and filling.** In the process of data collection, we used OCR tools to extract the text in the memes, however, the quality was poor and manual revision was required. In addition, since we manually annotated text slots in the templates, different paragraphs of text needed to be filled into the corresponding slots manually. The data was split into 40 pieces, and the annotation work was performed by 40 people, each of whom annotated one piece of the data and revised another one.
- **Humor level annotation.** The humor level reflects whether a meme is funny and how funny it is. We classified memes as not funny, slightly funny (tending to be funny), funny (somewhere between slightly and very funny) and very funny (making people laugh) ones. Forty people participated in the annotation and the data was split equally into eight groups, each group was annotated by five people, and each meme was annotated five times.

An important aspect to analyze is the disagreement of the annotation. Different from binary annotation, we annotated no humor and three humor levels, so it is necessary to consider the disagreement between them. For example, a disagreement between strong humor and medium humor should be considered different from a disagreement between strong humor and no humor. We chose Krippendorff's alpha measure [15], which considers this into the formula by using a generic distance function.

We calculated the alpha value for each group (eight in total) and the mean value was 0.348, which was not good enough. After removing the memes with both not funny and very funny annotations, the alpha value went up to 0.399. The results showed the subjectivity of humor, especially when the humor intensity was subdivided. Finally, five annotations of each meme were comprehensively considered.

4   Data Analysis

Our dataset consists of 203 templates (source images) and 5,184 memes (paragraphs of text). According to the characteristics of the dataset, we analyze the data on the meme scale and template scale.

---

[2] https://github.com/wkentaro/labelme.

Table 2. Data Analysis in the meme scale. Here, "#" denotes number, and "avg" denotes average. The train, development and test folds share no template with each other.

Meme	Total	Train	Dev	Test
#instances$_{all}$	5184	3746	700	738
#instances$_{not\ funny}$	402	263	72	67
#instances$_{slightly\ funny}$	1945	1447	244	254
#instances$_{funny}$	2364	1710	313	341
#instances$_{very\ funny}$	473	326	71	76
#characters	105169	76121	14261	14787
#distinct characters	2880	2685	1644	1727
Avg #characters$_{all}$	20.29	20.32	20.37	20.03
Avg #characters$_{not\ funny}$	19.12	19.25	19.14	18.57
Avg #characters$_{slightly\ funny}$	19.27	19.29	19.05	19.35
Avg #characters$_{funny}$	20.83	20.94	21.00	20.13
Avg #characters$_{very\ funny}$	22.77	22.53	23.41	23.21
#distinct templates	203	128	34	41
Avg #text slots used	2.59	2.61	2.52	2.54

Table 2 presents high-level statistics of the dataset on the meme scale. There are 5,184 memes in the whole dataset. In terms of categories, not funny category and very funny category account for a relatively small proportion. It also shows the standard train, development and test folds of the dataset. We try to make the data in each fold have the same distribution. And they share no template with each other, hence standard folds have source image independence which avoids the label leakage.

Figure 2 shows an overview of some important statistics of the dataset. Figure 2(a) shows the distribution of the text length. Figure 2(b) shows the word cloud. The frequent words include "我(I)", "妈妈(mum)", "老师(teacher)", and "朋友(friend)", which shows that we like to tell jokes about our daily life. For example, complaining about mums nagging at home and teachers assigning endless homework at school. Besides, there are some frequent sentences such as "最开始的我(The very beginning of me)" and "时间穿越成功了(Time travel has been successful)", which are the fixed topic sentences in some templates. For the content of the source image, animals are the most frequent, followed by anime characters such as Tom and SpongeBob, indicating that people like to express their humor with cute and funny things. Figure 2(c) demonstrates the distribution of class. Figure 2(d) shows the distribution of the number of corresponding memes for the templates and Fig. 2(e) shows the distribution of the number of text slots for the templates.

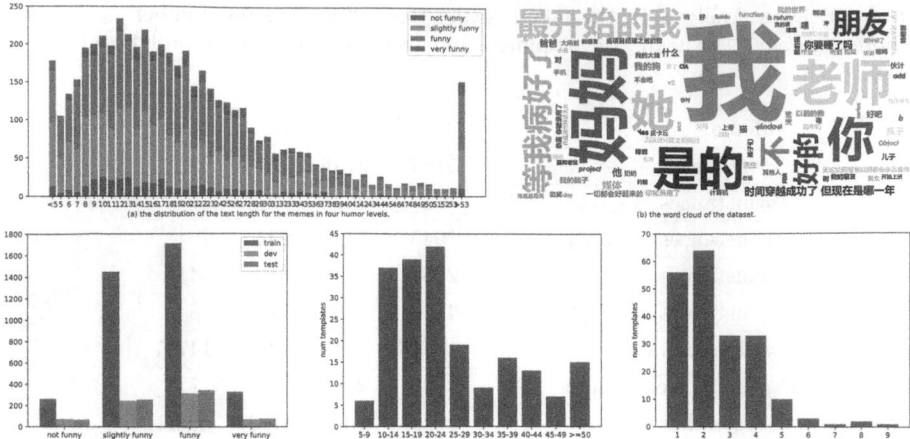

Fig. 2. Overview of the dataset statistics. (a) the distribution of the text length for the memes in four humor levels. (b) the word cloud of the dataset. (c) the distribution of the class of memes in the train, development and test folds. (d) the distribution of the number of corresponding memes for the templates. (e) the distribution of the number of text slots for the templates.

5   Experiments

In this section, our goal is to establish a performance baseline on the humor recognition task for our dataset. We define the task as a four-categories classification task: to classify the given meme as a not funny, slightly funny, funny or very funny one. Accuracy and macro-F1 score are used as evaluation metrics, for the evaluation of overall classes and individual class performance on the models. We also aim to demonstrate the effectiveness of our scheme in dataset construction and figure out the following questions:

- **Q1**: Can baseline models learn some knowledge related to humor from our dataset?
- **Q2**: What is the performance of using single modality, and does our dataset constrain the interference of irrelevant features in image modality?
- **Q3**: Does the information provided by image modality contribute to humor recognition even if many memes have the same source image?
- **Q4**: If the answer to **Q3** is yes, which is the most effective way?
- **Q5**: Is using cross-modal pre-trained models better than using two modal pre-trained models separately?

5.1   Baseline Models

We used the model shown in Fig. 3 to recognize humor. For text input, we encoded the text using Transformers encoder including BERT, RoBERTa and MacBERT [8], while for image input, we extracted both the overall features using image classification models and the ROIs features using object detection models. The image classification models included ResNet-50 [10], XCit and BEit, and the object detection model was Faster-RCNN [20]. We also extracted the features using a Chinese cross-modal pre-trained model namely WenLan [11], in which both modalities interact in the pre-training stage and the cross-modal relationship can be better modeled.

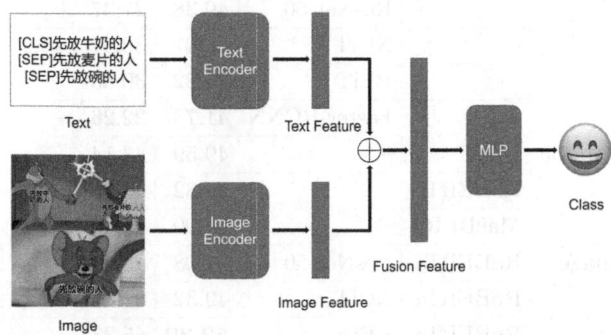

Fig. 3. The structure of our baseline model.

After obtaining both modal feature vectors, we applied the concatenation method as the modality fusion strategy. Subsequently, we added a two-layer MLP after the fusion vector with dropout and ReLU activation function. We used cross-entropy loss function, Adam optimizer and trained models with the early-stop strategy. The train, development and test sets were the standard ones introduced in Sect. 4. We also tested the performance of single modal models by directly connecting the MLP layer with the single modal feature vector. In addition, we introduced image modal information using a different approach, i.e., joining the image caption with the text in memes. This approach only changes the input of the text with caption rather than using the image encoder.

5.2 Results and Analysis

Table 3 shows the experimental results. The results of using normal labels and random labels demonstrate that various models can learn certain knowledge in humor, excluding using image only, which answers **Q1**. Experimental results for using text only show that text modality has a relatively good ability to recognize humor individually. In contrast, the performance of using single image modality is much lower than other models, proving that our annotation scheme, to a large extent, avoids the interference of irrelevant features of image modality, which answers **Q2**. However, it still brings improvement compared to the random cases, indicating that image models have learned some patterns beyond our expectation, which is worth further study.

Table 3. The performance of the baseline models.

Type	Model		Normal		Random	
	Text	Image	ACC	F1	ACC	F1
Text	BERT	–	48.51	40.65	–	–
	RoBERTa	–	50.41	42.91	37.40	24.55
	MacBERT	–	49.45	42.48	–	–
Image	–	ResNet-50	40.38	27.37	–	–
	–	XCiT	46.07	32.61	43.22	19.98
	–	BEiT	43.22	30.80	–	–
	–	Faster-RCNN	41.73	22.26	–	–
Text+Caption	BERT	–	49.59	43.14	–	–
	RoBERTa	–	49.32	43.83	38.48	24.77
	MacBERT	–	50.00	41.46	–	–
Text+Image	RoBERTa	ResNet-50	51.08	45.82	–	–
	RoBERTa	XCiT	49.32	**46.18**	42.82	27.11
	RoBERTa	BEiT	**52.30**	45.33	–	–
	RoBERTa	Faster-RCNN	50.54	43.31	–	–
Text&Image	WenLan	WenLan	50.81	43.02	45.25	16.26

The introduction of image modality brings improvement in most cases, either by introducing image captions in a text form or by introducing image features, which answers **Q3**. In terms of image features, the overall features extracted by CNNs or ViTs work better than the ROIs features extracted by Faster-RCNN, probably because the ROIs features do not interact well with the text features, or the Faster-RCNN weights are frozen in the training process, which answers **Q4**. Furthermore, the improvement of the cross-modal pre-trained model is not significant for our humor recognition task, probably because of its lack of humor-related domain knowledge, which answers **Q5**.

In summary, the baseline models perform not as well as we expected, showing that multimodal humor recognition is a challenging task. Understanding humor needs to match the context to the punchline. However, the context or punchline in a meme may be in the image or text, and combining them correctly can be difficult. In addition, text corresponds to the adjacent object in many memes, but existing methods are difficult to establish this relationship, which brings incoherence to the semantics.

6   Conclusion

This paper presents a novel multimodal humor dataset, Memeplate, which contains 203 templates and 5,184 memes with manually labeled humor levels. It can be used for humor recognition and humor generation research. Unlike previous datasets, we introduce templates that change the relationship between image and text from one-to-one to one-to-many. Since the template controls the variables of image modality, it is more convenient to extend linguistic findings on humor mechanisms to multimodal humor research. And it provides examples closer to human behavior for humor generation tasks. We offer multiple baseline results for the humor recognition task, which confirm the validity of our dataset and the importance of combining multimodal cues. We hope Memeplate will provide future researchers with valuable multimodal training data and contribute to the development of automatic humor understanding systems.

Acknowledgements. This work is supported by National Natural Science Foundation of China (NSFC) Program (No. 62076046). And we would like to thank the anonymous reviewers for their insightful and valuable comments.

References

1. Ahuja, V., Bali, T., Singh, N.: What makes us laugh? Investigations into automatic humor classification. In: Proceedings of the Second Workshop on Computational Modeling of People's Opinions, Personality, and Emotions in Social Media, pp. 1–9 (2018)
2. Ali, A., et al.: XCiT: cross-covariance image transformers. Adv. Neural Inf. Process. Syst. **34**, 20014–20027 (2021)
3. Bao, H., Dong, L., Wei, F.: BEiT: BERT pre-training of image transformers. arXiv preprint arXiv:2106.08254 (2021)
4. Blinov, V., Bolotova-Baranova, V., Braslavski, P.: Large dataset and language model fun-tuning for humor recognition. In: Proceedings of the 57th Annual Meeting of the Association for Computational Linguistics, pp. 4027–4032 (2019)
5. Bonheme, L., Grześ, M.: SESAM at SemEval-2020 task 8: investigating the relationship between image and text in sentiment analysis of memes. In: Proceedings of the Fourteenth Workshop on Semantic Evaluation, pp. 804–816 (2020)
6. Castro, S., Chiruzzo, L., Rosá, A., Garat, D., Moncecchi, G.: A crowd-annotated Spanish corpus for humor analysis. In: Proceedings of the Sixth International Workshop on Natural Language Processing for Social Media, pp. 7–11 (2018)
7. Castro, S., Cubero, M., Garat, D., Moncecchi, G.: Is this a joke? Detecting humor in Spanish tweets. In: Montes-y-Gómez, M., Escalante, H.J., Segura, A., Murillo, J.D. (eds.) IBERAMIA 2016. LNCS (LNAI), vol. 10022, pp. 139–150. Springer, Cham (2016). https://doi.org/10.1007/978-3-319-47955-2_12
8. Cui, Y., Che, W., Liu, T., Qin, B., Wang, S., Hu, G.: Revisiting pre-trained models for Chinese natural language processing. In: Findings of the Association for Computational Linguistics: EMNLP 2020, pp. 657–668 (2020)
9. Hasan, M.K., et al.: Ur-funny: a multimodal language dataset for understanding humor. In: Proceedings of the 2019 Conference on Empirical Methods in Natural Language Processing and the 9th International Joint Conference on Natural Language Processing (EMNLP-IJCNLP), pp. 2046–2056 (2019)
10. He, K., Zhang, X., Ren, S., Sun, J.: Deep residual learning for image recognition. In: Proceedings of the IEEE Conference on Computer Vision and Pattern Recognition, pp. 770–778 (2016)
11. Huo, Y., et al.: WenLan: bridging vision and language by large-scale multi-modal pre-training. arXiv preprint arXiv:2103.06561 (2021)

12. Kayatani, Y., et al.: The laughing machine: predicting humor in video. In: Proceedings of the IEEE/CVF Winter Conference on Applications of Computer Vision, pp. 2073–2082 (2021)
13. Kenton, J.D.M.W.C., Toutanova, L.K.: BERT: pre-training of deep bidirectional transformers for language understanding. In: Proceedings of NAACL-HLT, pp. 4171–4186 (2019)
14. Khandelwal, A., Swami, S., Akhtar, S.S., Shrivastava, M.: Humor detection in English-Hindi code-mixed social media content: Corpus and baseline system. In: Proceedings of the Eleventh International Conference on Language Resources and Evaluation (LREC 2018) (2018)
15. Krippendorff, K.: Computing Krippendorff's alpha-reliability (2011)
16. Liu, Y., et al.: RoBERTa: a robustly optimized BERT pretraining approach. arXiv preprint arXiv:1907.11692 (2019)
17. Liu, Z., et al.: Swin transformer: hierarchical vision transformer using shifted windows. In: Proceedings of the IEEE/CVF International Conference on Computer Vision, pp. 10012–10022 (2021)
18. Mihalcea, R., Strapparava, C.: Making computers laugh: investigations in automatic humor recognition. In: Proceedings of Human Language Technology Conference and Conference on Empirical Methods in Natural Language Processing, pp. 531–538 (2005)
19. Mihalcea, R., Strapparava, C., Pulman, S.: Computational models for incongruity detection in humour. In: Gelbukh, A. (ed.) CICLing 2010. LNCS, vol. 6008, pp. 364–374. Springer, Heidelberg (2010). https://doi.org/10.1007/978-3-642-12116-6_30
20. Ren, S., He, K., Girshick, R., Sun, J.: Faster R-CNN: towards real-time object detection with region proposal networks. Adv. Neural Inf. Process. Syst. **28** (2015)
21. Sharma, C., et al.: Semeval-2020 task 8: Memotion analysis-the visuo-lingual metaphor! In: Proceedings of the Fourteenth Workshop on Semantic Evaluation, pp. 759–773 (2020)
22. Tseng, Y.H., Wu, W.S., Chang, C.Y., Chen, H.C., Hsu, W.L.: Development and validation of a corpus for machine humor comprehension. In: Proceedings of the 12th Language Resources and Evaluation Conference, pp. 1346–1352 (2020)
23. Wu, J., Lin, H., Yang, L., Xu, B.: MUMOR: a multimodal dataset for humor detection in conversations. In: Wang, L., Feng, Y., Hong, Yu., He, R. (eds.) NLPCC 2021. LNCS (LNAI), vol. 13028, pp. 619–627. Springer, Cham (2021). https://doi.org/10.1007/978-3-030-88480-2_49
24. Yang, D., Lavie, A., Dyer, C., Hovy, E.: Humor recognition and humor anchor extraction. In: Proceedings of the 2015 Conference on Empirical Methods in Natural Language Processing, pp. 2367–2376 (2015)
25. Zhang, D., Zhang, H., Liu, X., Lin, H., Xia, F.: Telling the whole story: a manually annotated Chinese dataset for the analysis of humor in jokes. In: Proceedings of the 2019 Conference on Empirical Methods in Natural Language Processing and the 9th International Joint Conference on Natural Language Processing (EMNLP-IJCNLP), pp. 6402–6407 (2019)
26. Zhang, R., Liu, N.: Recognizing humor on twitter. In: Proceedings of the 23rd ACM International Conference on Information and Knowledge Management, pp. 889–898 (2014)
27. Ziser, Y., Kravi, E., Carmel, D.: Humor detection in product question answering systems. In: Proceedings of the 43rd International ACM SIGIR Conference on Research and Development in Information Retrieval, pp. 519–528 (2020)

FuncSA: Function Words-Guided Sentiment-Aware Attention for Chinese Sentiment Analysis

Jiajia Wang[1], Hongying Zan[1,2(✉)], Yingjie Han[1], and Juan Cao[3]

[1] Zhengzhou University, Henan 450001, China
{iehyzan,ieyjhan}@zzu.edu.cn
[2] Peng Cheng Laboratory, Guangdong 518000, China
[3] University of Chinese Academy of Sciences, Beijing 100000, China
caojuan@ict.ac.cn

Abstract. Sentiment analysis is an important natural language processing application that empowers many other technologies, including product review analysis and recommendation systems. Knowledge has been proven crucial for providing supervision information and improving performance. However, Chinese function words' knowledge, especially for degree adverbs, negative adverbs, and conjunctions, which may play an essential role in describing the sentiment polarity, is not well investigated in current Chinese sentiment analysis approaches. In this paper, we propose a **Func**tion words-guided **S**entiment-aware **A**ttention model (FuncSA) for Chinese sentiment analysis to leverage function words' knowledge. Specifically, we integrate discrete sentiment lexical information using degree adverbs, negative adverbs, and conjunctions in the Chinese Function Word Usage Knowledge Base(CFKB), and improve self-attention to integrate function words' knowledge into the model. We implement our approach on several open datasets and show that function words are essential in guiding sentiment identification.

Keywords: Chinese text sentiment analysis · Function words · Attention mechanism

1 Introduction

Sentiment analysis refers to extracting, analyzing, understanding, and generating subjective information in natural language. It has been widely applied in many applications, such as public opinion analysis, recommendation systems, review analysis and generation, and business decision-making. External knowledge is often introduced to help classify the sentiment polarity according to the sentiment words such as happy, sad, and fear. However, sentiment lexicons only construct the relationship between words and sentiments and fail to model the relationship between words and phrases. In particular, Chinese is composed of basic character units, which are influenced by the characteristics of the language

W. Lu et al. (Eds.): NLPCC 2022, LNAI 13551, pp. 539–550, 2022.
https://doi.org/10.1007/978-3-031-17120-8_42

itself with complex grammatical structures, diversified semantics, and diversified expressions. Especially considering that function words, a vital means of expression in Chinese, can help express the semantic relationship between content words. Among them, adverbs and conjunctions significantly influence the sentiment and polarity of sentiment words.

Adverbs, especially degree and negative adverbs, are the influencing factors and judgment conditions considered widely in the existing studies on sentiment classifications [1–8]. When they modify sentiment words, the orientation and intensity of the sentiment polarity will change to a certain extent. For example, "unclean/不干净" is composed of the positive adjective "clean/干净" and the negative adverb "not/不" , so it has a derogatory meaning. The phrase "too clean/过于干净" and "relatively clean/相当干净" under the modification of the degree adverb "too/过于" and "relatively/相当" express different levels of "clean/干净" . Besides, conjunctions are function words with the function of connecting, which can connect words, phrases, clauses, or sentences and indicate causal, inference, hypothesis, conditional, and other linguistic relations [13,14, 16].

Therefore, this paper proposes a framework, **Func**tion words-guided **S**entiment-aware **A**ttention (FuncSA) for Chinese sentiment analysis. FuncSA focuses on the sentiment expressed in the input text and obtains the internal correlated features of sentiment words, adverbs, and conjunctions. In particular, based on calculating the polarity values of emotive words modified by adverbs, different weights are given according to the influence of conjunctions in clauses. The sentiment-aware attention will then adjust the contribution of the sentiment of different clauses. These obtained sentiment semantic representations are effectively utilized to guide the model in conducting Chinese sentiment analysis.

2   Related Work

2.1   Sentiment Analysis

Function Words Irrelevant Methods. Neural networks with attention mechanisms can increase interpretability and sentiment analysis performance [9–12]. Cheng [10] makes the model learn more precise and abundant information by neural network and hierarchical attention network. Li [11] uses the multi-head self-attention to fully extract context representation. Xie [12] uses attention to obtain sentiment information contained in the sentiment words.

Function Words-Relevant Methods. In the early research based on rules or traditional machine learning approaches, adverbs and conjunctions were used to calculate the sentiment [3,4,13] or assist classifiers in predicting the sentiment polarity [5–8]. With the help of deep learning, Qian [1] uses the features of sentiment lexica, negative words, and degree adverbs and achieves good results with LSTM. Liang [14] uses conjunctions to segment phrases to construct graph structures to encode contextual information.

Although these studies have tried to utilize function words in sentiment analysis, their adverbs and conjunctions are mainly based on empirical results. Therefore, combining the existing sentiment lexical resources, this paper introduces the CFKB [15–19] into sentiment analysis. Thereinto, negative adverbs can change the polarity in the modification of sentiment words, degree adverbs can enhance or weaken the tendency, and conjunctions can change or even reverse the sentiment orientation of clauses to varying degrees.

2.2 Chinese Function Word Usage Knowledge Base

Function words are a primary means of expressing grammatical meaning in Chinese [20]. Unlike content words that can act independently as a sentence component, function words have no semantic meaning. They must be attached to content words or phrases to express grammatical meaning, tone, or sentiment. CFKB classifies function words into six categories: adverb, preposition, conjunction, auxiliary word, modality, and locality. It comprehensively describes function words in terms of their attributes, such as POS, definitions, example sentences, and usage descriptions.

CFKB, providing reliable lexical resources for Chinese language processing and semantic understanding, is widely used in the syntactic analysis [21,22], information extraction [23], sentiment analysis [2], and other natural language processing tasks. Li [2]introduced degree adverbs, negative adverbs, and conjunctions in CFKB into sentiment analysis. Experimental results of the rule-based method are better than traditional machine learning methods, showing that function words have essential effects on sentiment word recognition and analysis. However, it still needs to be improved with deep learning methods.

3   Methodology

Based on the context representation obtained by ERNIE, FuncSA uses the sentiment knowledge obtained from lexical resources and CFKB to extract the sentiment-aware semantic information for sentiment analysis. The overall structure is shown in Fig. 1.

3.1   ERNIE Encoder

Pre-trained language models such as BERT [24] have achieved substantial progress in sentiment analysis. Like BERT, ERNIE [25] consists of multiple Transformer encoder layers. In addition, ERNIE is consistent with BERT in training by adding the mask [CLS] and [SEP] before and after the input text. [CLS] is the first token to capture the information representation of the context, which will be used for downstream tasks. [SEP] is at the end of the sentence, indicating the end.

However, ERNIE introduced phrases and entity knowledge in the pre-training stage. Specifically, ERNIE's mask strategy mainly has three ways: First, it adopts

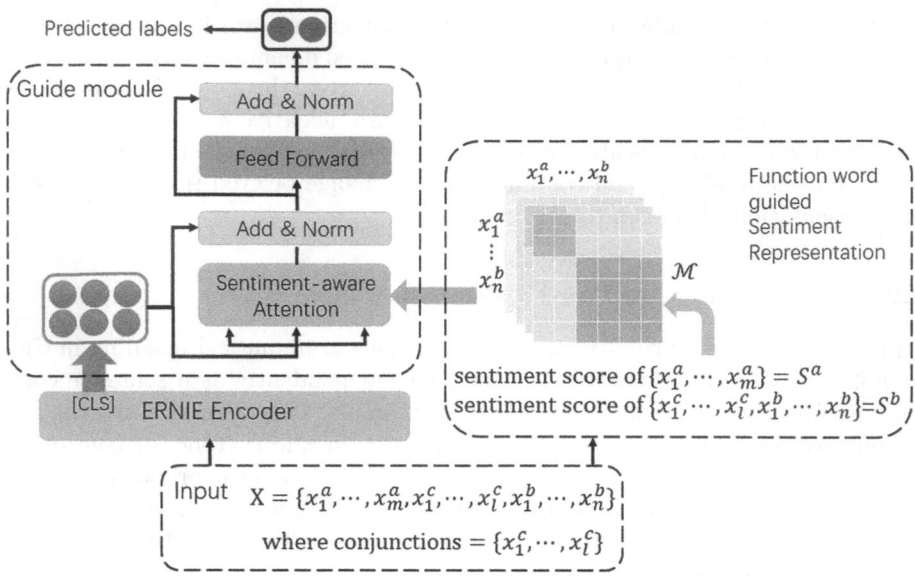

Fig. 1. Overview of FuncSA

the same way as BERT; that is, it masks and learns the expression of each piece in the input. Secondly, it randomly masks phrases to make use of word information. Finally, the entities in the input sentences are masked and predicted in the pre-training stage. ERNIE can learn the entities, phrases, and other external knowledge in the mass corpus to obtain a more reliable language representation through such a mask strategy. Therefore, we utilize ERNIE as the context encoder in Chinese sentiment analysis.

3.2   Function Words-Guided Sentiment Representation

Function words-guided Sentiment Representation is obtained through three steps. 1) Split the input sentence into clauses by conjunction. 2) Calculate the base sentiment score. 3) Weight the sentiment score by conjunctions.

Separate the Input Sentence into Clauses by Conjunctions. Conjunctions have complex and diverse functions and usages and can express various logical relations by connecting phrases, sentences, and texts. This paper selects four kinds of conjunctions in CFKB that express transition, progression, selection, and coordinate. The clauses connected by transition conjunctions usually have opposite sentiment orientations, and the clause after the conjunctions mainly determines the overall sentiment. Selective, progressive, and coordinating conjunctions tend to connect elements with the same polarity of sentiment, while progressive conjunctions tend to be followed by clauses with a more intense sentiment. The input sentence $X = \{x_1^a, ..., x_m^a, x_1^c, ..., x_\ell^c, x_1^b, ..., x_n^b\}$ is divided into

Table 1. Examples of degree adverbs and the weights

Degree level	weight	Samples	number of words
extreme/most	4	beijia/倍加、feichang/非常、jiduan/极端	69
very	3	bushao/不少、fenwai/分外、gewai/格外	42
more	2	geng/更、jiao/较、yu/愈	37
-ish	0.5	lue/略、shao/稍、weimian/未免	29
insufficiently	0.1	buzenme/不怎么、qingdu/轻度、ruo/弱	12
over	5	chaoe/超额、guodu/过度、guofen/过分	30

two clauses $X_a = \{x_1^a, ..., x_m^a\}$ and $X_{c+b} = \{x_1^c, ..., x_\ell^c, x_1^b, ..., x_n^b\}$ by conjunctions $X_c = \{x_1^c, ..., x_\ell^c\}$ with the length of m and $\ell + n$, respectively.

Calculate the Base Sentiment Score. Then, we combine the HowNet, and the National Taiwan University Sentiment Dictionary(NTUSD)[1], and then remove the stop words in the collection and form FuncSA's dictionary for calculating sentiment scores. In addition to sentiment words, the context of sentiment words, especially the degree and negative adverbs, is also essential to sentiment classification.

Degree adverbs significantly influence the strength of the sentiment orientation in sentences. The degree adverbs used in this paper come from HowNet. There are $219\,°C$ words in Chinese, which can be divided into six categories according to degree level: "extreme/most, very, more, -ish, insufficiently, and over". Each category is given a weight to calculate the sentiment score in sentences, and the weight is selected by experience. Examples of degree adverbs and the weights assigned to each category are shown in Table 1.

As for the negative adverbs, we screened all 50 negative adverbs in CFKB. In Chinese, there are double negation and multiple negation cases. When negation occurs even times, the original text logically has an affirmative meaning, and when negation occurs at odd times, the original text indicates a negative meaning. The number of negative adverbs in front of sentiment words is counted, and the sentiment value modified by odd negative adverbs is negative, while the value modified by even negative adverbs remains unchanged.

Based on the above steps, the sentiment scores of clauses X_a and X_{c+b} under the influence of degree adverbs and negative adverbs is S_a and S_{c+b} respectively.

Weight the Sentiment Score by Conjunctions. According to the conjunctions X_c, assign different weights w_1 and w_2 to S_a and S_{c+b} respectively, then the weighted sentiment scores of clauses X_a and X_{c+b} can be expressed as $S_a \times w_1$, $S_b \times w_2$. The weighted scores are assigned to each character in the clauses, and extended to the matrix $A_1 \in \mathbb{R}^{m*m}$, $A_2 \in \mathbb{R}^{(\ell+n)*(\ell+n)}$:

---

[1] http://academiasinicanlplab.github.io/.

$$A_1 = w_1 \times S_a \times \begin{bmatrix} 1 \cdots 1 \\ \vdots \quad \vdots \\ 1 \cdots 1 \end{bmatrix} = \begin{bmatrix} w_1 S_a \cdots w_1 S_a \\ \vdots \quad \vdots \\ w_1 S_a \cdots w_1 S_a \end{bmatrix}$$

$$A_2 = w_2 \times S_b \times \begin{bmatrix} 1 \cdots 1 \\ \vdots \quad \vdots \\ 1 \cdots 1 \end{bmatrix} = \begin{bmatrix} w_2 S_b \cdots w_2 S_b \\ \vdots \quad \vdots \\ w_2 S_b \cdots w_2 S_b \end{bmatrix} \tag{1}$$

Thus, the sentiment-aware representation M guided by function words can be expressed as:

$$M = \begin{bmatrix} A_1 & O \\ O & A_2 \end{bmatrix} \in \mathbb{R}^{(m+\ell+n)*(m+\ell+n)} \tag{2}$$

3.3 Guide Module

FuncSA added one more Transformer encoder layer above ERNIE to integrate function words-guided sentiment representation. A Transformer encoder layer mainly comprises multi-head attention, feed-forward network, and Layer Norm. Self-attention learns the semantic representation of context by calculating the interaction between words. Multi-head self-attention expands feature space by calculating self-attention in different subspaces and improves implementation.

We integrate the sentiment-aware representation M into multi-head self-attention, which constitutes the sentiment-aware attention, to capture the interaction of the sentiment words and the context information. The guide module can learn implicit information in combination with sentiment knowledge in context representation obtained from the pre-trained model.

Specifically, for the context representation H, we apply function words-guided sentiment representation M on the QK^T to obtain self-attention:

$$Attetnion(Q, K, V) = Softmax(\frac{QK^T}{\sqrt{d_K}} + M)V$$

$$where \quad Q = HW^Q, K = HW^K, V = HW^V \tag{3}$$

where QK^T calculates the internal correlation between words in the clause. M is added to the attention score normalized by $\sqrt{d_K}$ and then the weighted attention score is obtained by multiplying $Softmax$ normalization by the V. Therefore, it can exert an influence on self-attention through sentiment information. Then, the attention scores from multiple subspaces are concatenation according to Eq. 4.

$$MultiHead(Q, K, V) = Concat(head_1, ..., head_h)W^O$$

$$where \quad head_i = Attention(Q_i, K_i, V_i) \tag{4}$$

According to Eq. 2, M is the diagonal block matrix so that attention will be limited within each clause. Each character only pays attention to the other in the same clause because the sentiment or polarity has changed with the influence of conjunctions.

Furthermore, layer normalization and a feedforward network are used to accelerate the convergence and enhance the analyses and prediction of the model.

4 Experimental Settings

4.1 Datasets

In this paper, ChnSentiCorp [26], COAE2013[2], and NLPCC2014[3] is selected to verify the performance of FuncSA.

ChnSentiCorp is an online shopping review dataset containing hotels, laptops, and books. To conduct a fair experimental comparison, this article follows the division of datasets in previous studies [25].

COAE2013 is from The Fifth Chinese Opinion Analysis Evaluation. There are 1004 positive reviews among the annotated data and 834 negative reviews. The dataset is divided into train set and test set according to the ratio of 9:1.

NLPCC2014 is from the sentiment classification with deep learning technology task on the 3rd CCF Conference on Natural Language Processing & Chinese Computing, utilizing data from Chinese product review websites, including books, DVDs, and electronic products reviews.

4.2 Baselines

We compare our model with the following baseline methods on both datasets.

1) RNNs or CNNs baselines: BiLSTM [27], BiLSTM+Att [27], TextCNN [28], DPCNN [29].
2) Vallina pre-trained models: BERT, BERT-WWM [30], RoBERTa [31], ERNIE.
3) ERNIE-based models: ERNIE+BiLSTM, ERNIE+BiGRU, and ERNIE+Att.

For the RNNs or CNNs baselines, we used the word vector pre-trained by the Sogou News corpus, running a maximum of 100 epochs with a batch size of 128. Adam optimizer was adopted with a learning rate of 1e-4. For BiLSTM and BiLSTM+Att, the dimension of the hidden layer was set to 128. For TextCNN and DPCNN based on CNN, the number of convolution kernels was 256.

For the pre-trained model baselines, we followed default settings, i.e., 12 layers of multi-head attention with the dimension of the hidden layer set to be 768. The batch size was set as 16, and the learning rate was 5E-5. Adam was used to optimize the cross-entropy loss function.

---

[2] http://www.cipsc.org.cn/hytx/13.html#23.

[3] http://tcci.ccf.org.cn/conference/2014/.

Table 2. Performance comparison of models on four datasets.

Model	ChnSentiCorp-Dev		ChnSentiCorp-Test		COAE2013		NLPCC2014	
	Acc.(%)	F1.(%)	Acc.(%)	F1.(%)	Acc.(%)	F1.(%)	Acc.(%)	F1.(%)
BiLSTM	71.83	71.69	72.25	72.23	85.74	85.39	60.48	60.48
BiLSTM+Att	77.17	77.14	77.50	77.49	86.91	86.76	69.60	69.56
TextCNN	82.75	82.70	82.67	82.67	89.65	89.46	69.04	68.85
DPCNN	83.92	83.92	85.83	85.82	87.30	87.07	62.48	58.88
BERT	93.92	93.91	95.19	95.19	93.57	93.53	79.61	79.61
BERT-WWM	94.17	94.17	94.76	94.76	94.85	94.83	80.21	80.20
RoBERTa	94.00	94.00	94.76	94.76	95.04	95.04	79.57	79.56
ERNIE	94.26	94.25	95.27	95.27	95.77	95.74	80.89	80.88
ERNIE+BiLSTM	93.83	93.83	95.02	95.02	95.59	95.36	80.37	80.36
ERNIE+BiGRU	**94.51**	**94.51**	95.35	95.10	96.32	96.31	80.05	80.02
ERNIE+Att	94.34	94.34	95.44	95.44	96.69	96.67	80.69	80.67
FuncSA	94.43	94.42	**96.20**	**96.20**	**97.43**	**97.41**	**81.37**	**81.35**

5   Experimental Results

5.1   Main Results

The results are shown in Table 2, from which several observations can be obtained. First, the results of vanilla pre-trained models on all datasets are better than the optimal results of the RNNs or CNNs baselines. The pre-trained model can capture long-distance features better than RNNs and CNNs. Second, comparing these vanilla pre-trained models, we found that ERNIE reaches the best accuracy and F1 on both datasets. ERNIE could better adapt to the Chinese language and learn a more appropriate global representation.

Last but not least, comparing the ERNIE-based models, ERNIE+Att has an improvement compared with ERNIE+BiLSTM and ERNIE+BiGRU because attention can adjust the global representation learned by ERNIE to focus on critical areas in the context. FuncSA added sentiment knowledge guided by function words and integrated sentiment knowledge with context information through one more Transformer encoder layer. Compared with ERNIE+Att, FuncSA achieved better results in accuracy and F1, which fully demonstrates the effectiveness of this model.

5.2   Ablation Study

In order to explore the directive role of different classes of function words and lexical information on sentiment-aware attention, we discuss the performance of FuncSA with or without function words-guided sentiment representation M and different function words combination. The results are shown in Table 3.

Results show that although accuracy and F1 of FuncSA are decreased by 0.16% and 0.17% compared with w/o M on the ChnSenticorp-Dev, which may

Table 3. Ablation study.

Model	Lexicon	Adv.	Conj.	ChnSentiCorp-Dev		ChnSentiCorp-Test		COAE2013		NLPCC2014	
				Acc.(%)	F1.(%)	Acc.(%)	F1.(%)	Acc.(%)	F1.(%)	Acc.(%)	F1.(%)
FuncSA	✓	✓	✓	94.43	94.42	**96.20**	**96.20**	**97.43**	**97.41**	**81.37**	**81.35**
w/o M	×	×	×	**94.59**	**94.59**	94.59	94.35	96.88	96.86	81.05	81.04
w/o conj. & adv.	✓	×	×	94.26	94.26	95.52	95.52	97.06	97.05	80.33	80.31
w/o conj.	✓	×	✓	94.09	94.08	95.86	95.86	96.32	96.31	80.73	80.72
w/o adv.	✓	✓	×	94.34	94.34	95.78	95.78	97.06	97.04	80.81	80.80

result from unexpected noise caused by the introduction of the sentiment-aware representation. However, FuncSA is better than others in most datasets, illustrating the function words-guided knowledge can effectively guide the attention to focus on sentiment-specific areas.

Comparing w/o conj. & adv. with w/o conj., it is found that in the ChnSenticorp-Test, and NLPCC2014 datasets, accuracy, and F1 of w/o conj. are all higher than that of W/O conj. & adv., which indicates that adverbs are indispensable.

Comparing w/o conj. & adv. with w/o adv., which both considered sentiment words but did not consider adverbs, the results of w/o adv. were better than the accuracy of w/o conj. & adv. in all datasets, indicating that there is indeed an association between conjunctions and sentiment words in Chinese text sentiment analysis.

Furthermore, by comparing w/o M with the other three variants, it was found that the results of other variants were better than the results of w/o M in the ChnSenticorp-Test, COAE2013, and NLPCC2014. FuncSA makes full use of the sentiment information of lexicons, and the modification of conjunctions and adverbs, thus improving the accuracy of classification.

5.3 Visualization

In order to intuitively compare the semantic expression ability of baseline ERNIE with FuncSA in Chinese text, we use BertViz [32], an open-source attention visualization tool for pre-trained models. For example, the text "房间隔音和餐饮服务都不好(The sound insulation of the room and catering service are not good.)" is the case for the attention view, as shown in Fig. 2. Since different layers have different attention modes, this paper selects the view of all attention subspaces at the last layer, and the color blocks at the top of Fig. 2 distinguish the attention representation of each 12 subspaces. The intensity of the attention distribution in each subspace determines the color saturation of the attention view on the right side of each row.

The leftmost column of the attention head view contains the model input with two identifying masks [CLS] and [SEP] and the comment text. The [CLS] represents the hidden state output of the input, so the attention distribution from the [CLS] to other positions in the sequence was tracked. It can be seen that FuncSA's multiple subspaces pay more attention to the text containing

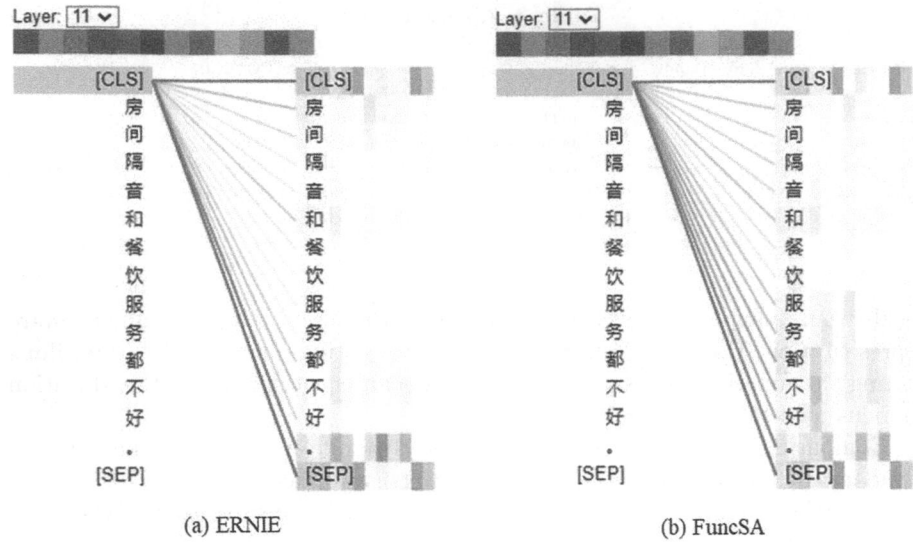

(a) ERNIE   (b) FuncSA

Fig. 2. Attention detail view of ERNIE and FuncSA: (a) ERNIE; (b) FuncSA

negation tendencies "dou buhao/都不好(are not good)" , and it is easier to make correct sentiment polarity classification than ERNIE.

6 Conclusion

This paper mainly introduces FuncSA, a sentiment analysis model which integrates function words-guided sentiment-aware attention. FuncSA integrates discrete sentiment lexical information with degree adverbs, negative adverbs, and conjunctions in CFKB. Sentiment-aware attention is then introduced to assist the pre-trained model in sentiment classification. Experimental results show that the proposed FuncSA can improve the results of Chinese sentiment analysis. This study reveals the validity of sentiment lexical information influenced by function words and verifies the role of adverbs and conjunctions in guiding sentiment changes.

References

1. Qian, Q., Huang, M., Lei, J., Zhu, X.: Linguistically regularized LSTM for sentiment classification. In: ACL 2017–55th Annual Meeting of the Association for Computational Linguistics, Proceedings of the Conference (Long Papers) (2017). https://doi.org/10.18653/v1/P17-1154
2. Li, Y.: Microblog Emotional Dictionary Built and Application on Sentiment Analysis of Microblog. Zhenzhou University (2014)

3. Shi, W., Fu, Y.: Microblog short text mining considering context: a method of sentiment analysis. Jisuanji Kexue/Comput. Sci. **48**(6A), 158–164 (2021). https://doi.org/10.11896/jsjkx.210200089

4. Lipenkova, J.: A system for fine-grained aspect-based sentiment analysis of Chinese. In: ACL-IJCNLP 2015–53rd Annual Meeting of the Association for Computational Linguistics and the 7th International Joint Conference on Natural Language Processing, Proceedings of System Demonstrations (2015). https://doi.org/10.3115/v1/p15-4010

5. Ku, L.W., Huang, T.H., Chen, H.H.: Using morphological and syntactic structures for Chinese opinion analysis. In: EMNLP 2009 - Proceedings of the 2009 Conference on Empirical Methods in Natural Language Processing: A Meeting of SIGDAT, a Special Interest Group of ACL, Held in Conjunction with ACL-IJCNLP 2009 (2009). https://doi.org/10.3115/1699648.1699672

6. Li, C., Wu, H., Jin, Q.: Emotion classification of Chinese microblog text via fusion of BoW and eVector feature representations. In: Communications in Computer and Information Science (2014)

7. He, Y., Zhao, S., He, L.: Micro-text emotional tendentious classification based on combination of emotion knowledge and machine-learning algorithm. J. Intell. **37**(5), 189–194 (2018)

8. Xu, J., Ding, Y., Wang, X.: Sentiment classification for Chinese news using machine learning methods. J. Chin. Inf. Process. **21**(6), 95–100 (2007)

9. Ambartsoumian, A., Popowich, F.: Self-attention: a better building block for sentiment analysis neural network classifiers. In: WASSA 2018–9th Workshop on Computational Approaches to Subjectivity, Sentiment and Social Media Analysis, Proceedings of the Workshop (2018). https://doi.org/10.18653/v1/P17

10. Cheng, Y., Ye, Z., Wang, M., Zhang, Q., Zhang, G.: Chinese text sentiment orientation analysis based on convolution neural network and hierarchical attention network. J. Chin. Inf. Process. **33**(1), 133–142 (2019)

11. Li, Z., Chen, L., Zhang, S.: Chinese text sentiment analysis based on ELMo and Bi-SAN. Appl. Res. Comput. **38**(8), 2303–2307 (2021)

12. Xie, R., Li, Y.: Text sentiment classification model based on BERT and dual channel attention. Shuju Caiji Yu Chuli/J. Data Acquis. Process. **35**(4), 642–652 (2020). https://doi.org/10.16337/j.1004-9037.2020.04.005

13. Liu, Y., Ju, S., Wu, S., Su, C.: Sentiment classification of Chinese texts based on emotion dictionary and conjunction. J. Sichuan Univ. (Nat. Sci. Edn.) **52**(1), 57–62 (2015)

14. Liang, S., Wei, W., Mao, X., Wang, F., He, Z.: BiSyn-GAT+: Bi-Syntax Aware Graph Attention Network for Aspect-based Sentiment Analysis. (2022)

15. Zan, H., Zhang, K., Zhu, X., Yu, S.: Research on the Chinese function word usage knowledge base. Int. J. Asian Lang. Process. **21**(4), 185–198 (2011)

16. Zan, H., Zhang, K., Chai, Y., Yu, S.: Studies on the functional word knowledge base of modern Chinese. J. Chin. Inf. Process. **21**(5), 107–111 (2007)

17. Zhan, H., Zhu, X.: Mianxiang Ziran Yuyan Chuli de Hanyu Xuci Yanjiu yu Guangyi Xuci Zhishiku Goujian [Research on Chinese Function words for Natural Language Processing and Construction of generalized Function words Knowledge Base]. Contemp. Linguist. **11**(2), 124–135 (2009)

18. Zhang, K., Zan, H., Chai, Y., Han, Y., Zhao, D.: Construction and application of the Chinese function word usage knowledge base. Int. J. Knowl. Lang. Process. **4**, 32–42 (2013)

19. Zhang, K., Zan, H., Chai, Y., Han, Y., Zhao, D.: Survey of the Chinese function word usage knowledge base. J. Chin. Inf. Process. **29**(3), 1–8 (2015)

20. Huang, B., Liao, X.: Xiandai Hanyu [Modern Chinese]. Higher Education Press, Beijing (2011)
21. Zan, H., Zhang, J., Lou, X.: Studies on the application of Chinese functional words usages in dependency parsing. J. Chin. Inf. Process. **27**(5), 35–43 (2013)
22. Mu, L., Pang, Y., Zan, H.: Studies on the usage of preposition ZAI in phrase structure syntactic parsing (2014)
23. Zan, H., Zhang, T., Lin, A.: Research on event information extraction based on preposition's usages. Comput. Eng. Design **34**(7), 2570–2574 (2013)
24. Devlin, J., Chang, M.W., Lee, K., Toutanova, K.: BERT: pre-training of deep bidirectional transformers for language understanding. In: NAACL HLT 2019–2019 Conference of the North American Chapter of the Association for Computational Linguistics: Human Language Technologies - Proceedings of the Conference (2019)
25. Sun, Y., et al.: ERNIE: enhanced representation through knowledge integration (2019)
26. Tan, S., Zhang, J.: An empirical study of sentiment analysis for Chinese documents. Exp. Syst. Appl. **34** (2008). https://doi.org/10.1016/j.eswa.2007.05.028
27. Zhang, D., Wang, D.: Relation Classification via Recurrent Neural Network (2015)
28. Kim, Y.: Convolutional neural networks for sentence classification. In: EMNLP 2014–2014 Conference on Empirical Methods in Natural Language Processing, Proceedings of the Conference (2014). https://doi.org/10.3115/v1/d14-1181
29. Johnson, R., Zhang, T.: Deep pyramid convolutional neural networks for text categorization. In: ACL 2017–55th Annual Meeting of the Association for Computational Linguistics, Proceedings of the Conference (Long Papers) (2017). https://doi.org/10.18653/v1/P17-1052
30. Cui, Y., et al.: Pre-training with whole word masking for Chinese bert (2019)
31. Liu, Y., et al.: RoBERTa: a robustly optimized BERT pretraining approach (2019)
32. Vig, J.: A multiscale visualization of attention in the transformer model. In: ACL 2019–57th Annual Meeting of the Association for Computational Linguistics, Proceedings of System Demonstrations (2019). https://doi.org/10.18653/v1/p19-3007

Prompt-Based Generative Multi-label Emotion Prediction with Label Contrastive Learning

Yuyang Chai[1], Chong Teng[1], Hao Fei[2], Shengqiong Wu[1], Jingye Li[1],
Ming Cheng[3], Donghong Ji[1], and Fei Li[1(✉)]

[1] Key Laboratory of Aerospace Information Security and Trusted Computing,
Ministry of Education, School of Cyber Science and Engineering, Wuhan University,
Wuhan, China
{yychai,tengchong,whuwsq,theodorelee,dhji,lifei_csnlp}@whu.edu.cn
[2] School of Computing, National University of Singapore, Singapore, Singapore
haofei37@nus.edu.sg
[3] The first Affiliated Hospital of Zhengzhou University, Zhengzhou, China
fccchengm@zzu.edu.cn

Abstract. Multi-label emotion prediction, which aims to predict emotion labels from text, attracts increasing attention recently. It is ubiquitous that emotion labels are highly correlated in this task. Existing state-of-the-art models solve multi-label emotion prediction in sequence-to-sequence (Seq2Seq) manner, while such label correlations are merely leveraged in decoding side. In this work, we propose an emotion prediction framework to jointly generate emotion labels and template sentences via Seq2Seq language model. On the one hand, our template-based natural language generation method makes better use of generative language model compared with generating label sequences in the prior Seq2Seq-based generative classification model. On the other hand, we introduce the Correlation-based Label Prompts (CLP) through soft prompt learning and contrastive learning, which enables our model to further consider emotion label correlations in encoding side. To demonstrate the effectiveness of our prompt-based generative multi-label emotion prediction model, we perform experiments on the GoEmotions and SemEval 2018 datasets, achieving competitive results, outperforming 7 baselines w.r.t. 3 evaluation metrics. In-depth analyses show the generation manner is much more impressive compared with generating label sequences and our model is particularly effective in label correlation modeling.

Keywords: Emotion prediction · Text generation · Prompt learning · Contrastive learning

1 Introduction

Emotion prediction refers to automatically identify all the possible emotions expressed by individual in a piece of text [1,2], which has been applied to real-world applications, such as stock prediction [3], AI chat robots [4,5], etc. Since

© The Author(s), under exclusive license to Springer Nature Switzerland AG 2022
W. Lu et al. (Eds.): NLPCC 2022, LNAI 13551, pp. 551–563, 2022.
https://doi.org/10.1007/978-3-031-17120-8_43

Sentences	Emotion labels
(S1) I hate the message that's being pushed, and it's even worse that it's being pushed by this guy.	anger, disgust, embarrassment
(S2) Worst advice ever. This would piss me off.	anger, disgust
(S3) Exactly, I remember loving those videos but I was also like 12	love, realization
(S4) Love situations like this...excited to see if he'll make it by tomorrow	love, excitement
(S5) Gods don't die	neutral

Fig. 1. Illustration of the label correlation issue in multi-label emotion prediction.

an instance may often simultaneously involve multiple emotion labels, most relevant works solve this task as multi-label classification problem, a.k.a., multi-label emotion prediction [6,7]. A widely adopted approach in tackling multi-label emotion prediction is the binary relevance (BR) [8], which merely considers each emotion label as an independent binary problem.

Nevertheless, correlations do exist in emotion expressions [9]. Intuitively, emotions in the same polarity own strong correlations. As can be exemplified in Fig. 1, the negative emotion *"disgust"* is more likely to co-exist with *"anger"* rather than the positive emotion *"love"*. However, the correlations between predicted emotions are ignored in BR, which significantly benefits the overall predictions. Thus, the classifier chain (CC) [10] is proposed, which integrates label correlation information along a chain of classifiers. Very recent state-of-the-art works solve multi-label emotion classification in a sequence-to-sequence (Seq2Seq) manner (i.e., one decoding position for one emotion label), achieving considerable improvements [9,11–13]. Nevertheless, clear limitations can still be witnessed in those methods. First, the correlations between emotion labels are merely involved in decoding side and not considered in encoding side. Besides, the Seq2Seq architecture's inherent advantage, i.e., sequential language generation, is not respected in existing label sequence generation work. These hamper Seq2Seq from giving its most for multi-label emotion prediction.

Motivated by the recent progress on language generation together with large pre-trained language models (PLM) [14,15], in this work, we consider modeling the multi-label emotion prediction as a natural sentence generation problem. As shown in Fig. 2, based on a pre-trained Seq2Seq architecture, we generate a template-based natural sentence from which all the possible emotion labels will be yielded. Compared with existing multi-label emotion prediction works, we advance in two aspects. First of all, instead of generating a label sequence in prior Seq2Seq-based method, the text-to-text scheme naturally helps take full advantage of the power of the current generative PLM, e.g., BART [16], T5 [15]. Secondly, inspired by the success of soft prompt tuning [17], we introduce Correlation-based Label Prompts (CLP) to incorporate label correlation in the encoding side of our model.

We firstly introduce label prompts that aim to learn "label-like" representations similar to soft prompts [17], which helps our model better predict emotion labels by taking label information in prompts as references. Then, to involve label correlations in label prompts, we propose an extended contrastive loss to incorporate label correlations during label prompts learning stage and thus obtain CLP. During the contrastive learning, two label representations are forced to be pulled *closer* according to the two label co-exist frequency in corpus-level scope, and two *never* co-existed label's prompts would be pushed *further*. It is noteworthy that the polarity of emotions is not involved in contrastive learning. In this way, we extend the advantages of generative Seq2Seq model and meanwhile enhance the label correlation learning at the encoding side.

We conduct experiments on GoEmotions [1] and SemEval 2018 [2] datasets. Results show that our method achieves competitive performances on both two datasets, in terms of both the settings with and without using PLM. Compared with the current best-performing Seq2Seq models, our model consistently outperforms them on all metrics. Besides, our proposed contrastive loss is proved to be effective in label correlations learning. Our contributions can be summarized as follows:

- We propose transforming the multi-label emotion prediction into a natural language generation paradigm that considers label correlations and make full use of the existing generative PLM.
- We utilize label prompts to capture label information that helps our model better predict emotion labels.
- We propose an extended contrastive loss to obtain Correlation-based Label Prompts, which makes our model be aware of correlations modeling in encoding side.
- Experiments show that our proposed methods are effective and achieve competitive results on two widely-used datasets.[1]

2   Related Work

Emotion Prediction. Emotion prediction is an important branch of sentiment analysis and opinion mining in natural language processing (NLP) community [18–22]. Early works employ emotion lexicons for emotion multi-label classification [7,23]. This method constructs emotion lexicons to tackle emotion classification tasks, while most lexicons cover few domains, which restricts its performances on the short informal text like tweets. Besides, words may convey different emotions in different context [24], which results in mismatch problems with this approach. With the presence of the Transformer-based pre-trained language models, e.g., BERT [25], have been successfully employed in multi-label emotion classification task [1,26].

Similar to our work, Fei et al. (2020) [9] and Huang et al. (2021) [11] tackle multi-label classification problem in Seq2Seq manner. Fei et al. (2020) propose a Latent Memory Network based on the encoder-decoder framework that views multi-label classification as a label sequence generation problem. Huang et al. (2021) propose an LSTM-based Seq2Seq framework Seq2Emo to handle emotion classification and consider emotion correlations implicitly in decoding stage.

---

[1] Code is available at https://github.com/yychai74/Generative-MultiEmo.

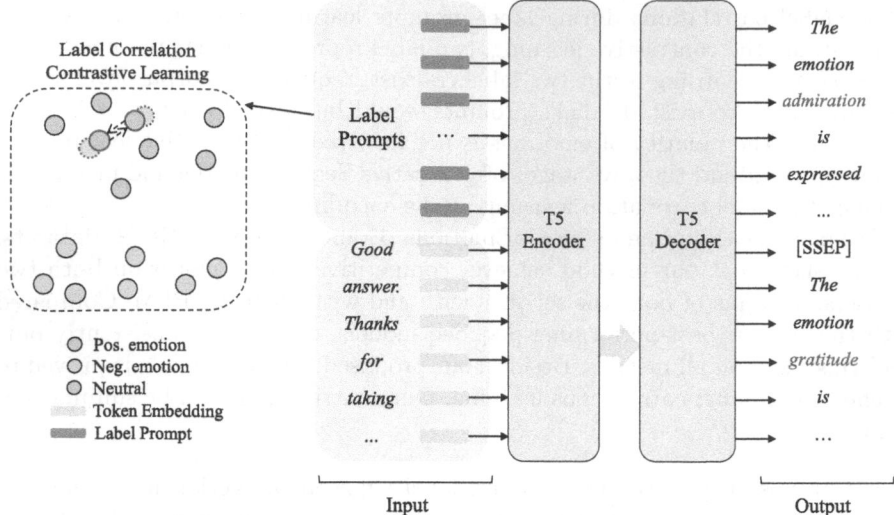

Fig. 2. The overall framework. The hidden representations of CLP are not used in decoder. Particularly, the Label Correlation Contrastive Learning only depends on the co-existence of labels and the distribution of emotions learned by CLP correctly reflects the correlations among emotions with different polarities (cf. Sect. 5.3).

Different from these works, our goal is to generate a natural language sentence rather than a label sequence, which makes full use of generative PLM.

Prompt Learning. Recently, prompt learning has become a new way to make use of the masked language model (MLM) [27,28]. Through designing a discrete prompt for specific downstream work, the MLMs can be fine-tuned to solve various tasks by simply changing prompts, which does not require model reconstructions. Besides, soft prompt (i.e., continuous prompts) [17] is utilized in prompt-tuning where only the prompt parameters need to be trained. Inspired by these works, we introduce label prompts into our framework. The prompts are the same length as the label category size and trained with our model jointly. The prompts would learn label representations during training step, and then our model can take label prompts as references to better predict emotion labels.

Contrastive Learning. Contrastive learning aims to pull "positive" examples together and push "negative" examples apart, which has been widely adopted in the computer vision area [29]. Recently, supervised contrastive learning has been employed to tackle many NLP tasks. Suresh and Ong (2021) [30] introduce a weighted contrastive loss to help model better classify indistinguishable labels in fine-grained classification tasks. In this paper, we propose an extended contrastive loss that aims to incorporate emotion label correlations into the label prompts training stage.

3 Framework

3.1 Task Formulation

In our work, we solve multi-label emotion prediction task in a generative manner. Given a sentence X, we aim to generate a template-based natural sentence Y that contains all predicted emotion labels with our model. If the model generates a sentence with wrong templates or emotions that are beyond the label set, the predictions would be abandoned.

We utilized a template sentence $\mathbf{T}$, *"The emotion a_i is expressed in this sentence."* to construct the target sentences, where a_i is the label the instance X possesses. For multi-labeled instances, we first transfer labels into multiple sentences with template $\mathbf{T}$, then we concatenate them with a pre-defined separation token [SSEP] in the order of labels to obtain the target sequence Y.

3.2 Encoder

Given an input sentence X, we obtain its token embedding matrix $\mathbf{E}_n$ through the internal embedding lookup matrix of PLM, where $\mathbf{E}_n \in \mathbb{R}^{n \times d}$, d denotes the hidden dimension of the encoder and n is the tokenized length of sentence X. Then we concatenate **label prompts $\mathbf{P}_l$** with $\mathbf{E}_n$:

$$\mathbf{E} = \text{Concat}(\mathbf{P}_l, \mathbf{E}_n) \tag{1}$$

where $\mathbf{P}_l \in \mathbb{R}^{l \times d}$ and l denotes the size of emotion categories[2] of the dataset.

The label prompts are trained jointly to learn emotion label representations and the label correlations would be incorporated into label prompts with the usage of our proposed contrastive loss. Then the vectorized word representations are fed into an encoder to obtain the context-sensitive representation:

$$\mathbf{H}^{enc} = \text{Encoder}(\mathbf{E}) \tag{2}$$

where $\mathbf{H}^{enc} \in \mathbb{R}^{(l+n) \times d}$. With the help of self-attention mechanism [31], the correlation-based label information is naturally integrated into the hidden representations of the sentence X.

3.3 Decoder

At the inference stage, the hidden representations obtained from the encoder are fed to the decoder via cross-attention layers. Noteworthily, we do not feed the label prompts to the decoder as in Fig. 2, which will be discussed in Sect. 5.5.

The decoder generates template-based natural sentences in an auto-regressive manner. At the c-th time step, the hidden representations and previous outputs $y_{<c}$ are applied to compute the decoder outputs:

$$\mathbf{H}_c^{dec} = \text{Decoder}(\mathbf{H}_{l:}^{enc}, y_{<c}) \tag{3}$$

---

[2] We do not use the tokenized label token size in this work, so as to ensure that the model focuses label prompts on label level rather than token level.

where l is the size of emotion categories and $\mathbf{H}_{l:}^{enc}$ denotes the hidden representations with label prompts peeled. To obtain the probability for the next token
in the vocabulary set, the softmax function is utilized:

$$P(y_c|y_{<c}, \mathbf{H}_{l:}^{enc}) = \text{Softmax}(\mathbf{W}^T \mathbf{H}_c^{dec} + b) \tag{4}$$

$\mathbf{W} \in \mathbb{R}^{d \times |\mathcal{V}|}$ maps decoder outputs $\mathbf{H}_c^{dec}$ to a logit vector which can be used
to compute probability distribution over vocabulary set, and $|\mathcal{V}|$ represents the
vocabulary set size of PLM. $\mathbf{W}$ and b are all learnable parameters.

3.4 Training

Label Correlation Contrastive Loss. The Supervised Contrastive Loss
(SCL) makes the representations of samples belonging to the same class stay
closer [32,33]. For an instance x_i, the positive set among batch B is given by
$\mathcal{P} = \{p|y_p = y_i, p \neq i\}$, where y_i is the label of x_i. Let I denotes the indexes of
examples in training batch B, then the Supervised Contrastive Loss over batch
B is defined as:

$$\mathcal{L}_B^{SCL} = \sum_{i=1}^{k} \frac{-1}{|\mathcal{P}|} \sum_{p \in \mathcal{P}} \log \frac{\exp(h_i \cdot h_p/\tau)}{\sum_{b \in I, b \neq i} \exp(h_i \cdot h_b/\tau)} \tag{5}$$

where k is batch size, h_i is the representation vector of x_i obtained from an
encoder and τ is temperature hyper-parameter.

However, the SCL brings representations of samples in the same class closer
together, which is inconsistent with our goal of label correlations modeling. In
this case, we extend the aforementioned contrastive loss to enhance label prompts
learning with the awareness of label correlations. We aim to train two label
representations closer if the two label co-exists with a higher probability. Our
proposed supervised Label Correlation Contrastive Loss (LCCL) is defined as:

$$\mathcal{L}_B^{LCCL} = \sum_{i=1}^{l} \frac{-1}{|\mathcal{P}|} \sum_{p \in \mathcal{P}} \log \frac{\exp(e_i \cdot e_p/\tau)}{\sum_{p \in \mathcal{P}} \exp(e_i \cdot e_p/\tau) + \sum_{n \in \mathcal{N}} \exp(e_i \cdot e_n/\tau) + \varepsilon} \tag{6}$$

In Eq. 6, l is the label category size of the dataset, e_i denotes the normalised label
prompt of label a_i[3]. The positive set $\mathcal{P}$ contains the indexes of co-existed labels
with label a_i in training batch B, and the negative set $\mathcal{N}$ contains the indexes of
labels that *never* co-existed with a_i in the overall train set. The hyper-parameter
ε is to ensure label prompts can be correctly trained when $\mathcal{N} = \emptyset$.

Here, unlike Suresh and Ong's work [30] that introduces extra weights, we
model different label correlations in LCCL implicitly since two label embeddings
are pushed closer based on their co-exist frequency. In this case, label correlations
are incorporated into label prompts learning so that our model can better handle
multi-label emotion prediction task with the help of the CLP.

---

[3] The label prompt index are aligned with the emotion label order in corresponding
dataset.

Generative Loss. The cross-entropy loss between the output sentence and the target template sentence is used to optimize the PLM:

$$\mathcal{L}^{CE} = -\sum_{c=1}^{m} \log P(y_c | y_{<c}, \mathbf{H}_c^{enc}) \tag{7}$$

where m denotes the length of target sentence.

Finally, the overall generative framework is optimized using the combination of cross-entropy loss and our proposed LCCL:

$$\mathcal{L} = (1 - \alpha)\mathcal{L}^{CE} + \alpha\mathcal{L}^{LCCL} \tag{8}$$

where α is a hyper-parameter to balance the two parts of the loss function.

Table 1. Data statistics. *Emo.* is the numbers of emotion categories. *Multi.* denotes the percentage of multi-labeled sentences. *Avg.Len.* is the average length of sentences.

Dataset	Train	Dev	Test	Emo.	Multi.	Avg.Len.
GoEmotions	43,410	5,426	5,427	28	16.2%	12.82
SemEval 2018	6,838	886	3,259	11	86.1%	16.04

4 Experiments

Dataset. We conduct our experiments on GoEmotions [1] and Semeval 2018 Task 1 [2] datasets. The details of the two datasets are shown in Table 1. Particularly, we utilize *neutral* to generate template-based sentences for those non-labeled instances in Semeval 2018 dataset, and all predictions that include neutral are restored to original label in the evaluation stage.

Baselines and Metrics. Since GoEmotions is a newly released dataset, we include **Seq2Emo** results reported by Huang et al. (2021) [11] and **BERT** results reported by Demszky et al. (2020) [1]. Seq2Emo is a Seq2Seq model to tackle multi-label classification problem, and label correlations are leveraged in decoding stage. Additionally, Huang et al. report results of **BR** and **CC** with their implementations, which are also included for comparison. For SemEval 2018 dataset, we compare our model with following baselines: **NTUA-SLP** [7] trains a two-layer LSTM network where a large amount of external emotion lexicons are used. **DATN** [6] employs dual attention mechanism to encode tweets into features. Zhou et al. (2020) [26] introduce an emotion network (**EmNet**) that can alleviate the domain mismatch and emotion ambiguity problems of using external lexicons, and we obtain **BERT** and **EmNet+BERT** results from this paper. We include **SGM** results from [11] additionally. Besides, **Seq2Emo** also reports results on SemEval 2018 dataset. We follow former works [2,11,26], using Micro F1 (**MiF**), Macro F1 (**MaF**) scores, and Jaccard Index (**Jacc**) to measure the model performances. The results are averaged over 5 runs.

Experiment Setting. We adopt T5-base [15] from Huggingface Transformers[4] as the backbone framework. Besides, we also employ T5-large for further comparison and all the BERT mentioned in baselines are *base* version. The learning

---

[4] https://huggingface.co/.

rate is set to 4e−5, the batch size is set to 16 and our model is trained for 20 epochs where early stopping strategy is utilized. The hyper-parameter α and ε are set to 0.1 and 0.01 respectively. The temperature parameter of LCCL is found to be 0.3 for GoEmotions and 0.07 for SemEval 2018. Label prompts are randomly initialized and the dimensions are the same as the hidden size of T5. The beam sizes are set to 3 for GoEmotions and 2 for SemEval 2018.

5 Results and Analysis

5.1 Main Results

The results on GoEmotions are shown in Table 2. The first observation we can find is that our proposed model surpasses all baselines on three metrics, and T5$_{large}$ makes further progress. Compared with the state-of-the-art model Seq2Emo with BERT encoder, our model gains 1.03 more scores on Micro F1 and much more consistent improvement on Macro F1 (+4.48 scores), Jaccard Index (+5.11 scores). This proves the significance of our proposed generative multi-label prediction model.

Table 2. Results on GoEmotions dataset. Best results except T5$_{large}$ are shown in bold and the results of T5$_{large}$ are underlined. † and ‡ means the result is significant with $p < 0.01$ and $p < 0.05$ compared with T5$_{base}$ respectively. ∗ denotes results obtained by our implementations.

Model	MiF	MaF	Jacc
BERT	–	46.00	–
BR	58.21	45.38	52.76
CC	58.38	43.92	55.61
Seq2Emo	59.57	47.28	53.79
Seq2Emo+BERT*	59.96	49.04	54.45
T5$_{base}$	60.52	51.43	59.08
T5$_{base}$+CLP	**60.99**‡	**53.52**†	**59.56**‡
T5$_{large}$+CLP	61.32†	53.78†	59.73†

Table 3. Results on SemEval 2018 dataset. The notations are the same with the left table.

Model	MiF	MaF	Jacc
SGM	55.11	–	45.14
NTUA-SLP	70.10	52.80	58.80
DATN	–	54.40	58.30
BERT	70.10	53.00	58.00
Seq2Emo	70.02	51.92	58.67
Seq2Emo+BERT*	70.52	53.48	59.03
EmNet+BERT	**71.60**	**56.50**	59.60
T5$_{base}$	70.95	55.62	60.24
T5$_{base}$+CLP	71.34‡	55.84	**60.80**‡
T5$_{large}$+CLP	71.86†	57.39†	61.41†

Table 4. Generation using different templates on GoEmotions.

Templates	MiF	MaF	Jacc
The emotion a_i is expressed in this sentence	**60.99**	**53.52**	**59.56**
It expressed emotion a_i	60.61	52.75	59.25
It is clear that the emotion a_i is expressed in this sentence.	60.66	52.49	59.16
No template, directly output labels	60.40	52.05	58.81

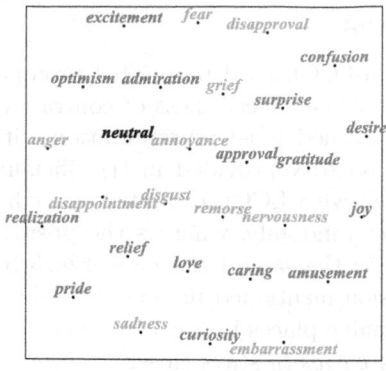

(a) Label prompts.

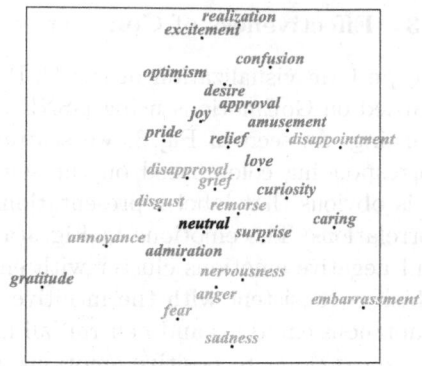

(b) Correlation-based label prompts.

Fig. 3. Visualization of the label prompts on GoEmotions, where orange, green and gray colors correspond with positive, negative and ambiguous emotions respectively. (Color figure online)

As for SemEval 2018 dataset, we show our results in Table 3. Our model achieves state-of-the-art performance on Jaccard Index score and slightly lower but competitive results compared with EmNet. One possible reason is that the SemEval 2018 dataset has fewer training data so that label prompts cannot learn heuristic label representations during training. In this case, CLP does not bring that great improvements as the GoEmotions dataset. Particularly, T5$_{large}$ achieves the state-of-the-art results, verifying the potential of generative multi-label emotion prediction.

We conduct paired t-tests and ablation studies to validate the contributions of CLP to our framework, and the results are shown in Table 2 and Table 3. We can notice that the CLP brings significant performance increases on both datasets, which verifies the effectiveness of CLP in multi-label emotion prediction. Besides, even the T5$_{base}$ outperforms the BERT-based Seq2Emo on two datasets. Further, CLP brings 4.1% Macro F1 score improvement on the more fine-grained GoEmotions dataset, indicating our model can better predict emotion labels that less occur in the dataset with the help of label information contained in the CLP.

5.2 Effect of Natural Language Template

To further analyze the effect of templates to our model, we train our model using different templates, and the results are shown in Table 4. We can observe that different templates make differences in the performance of our model, which is consistent with findings of Liu et al. (2021) [14] and Gao et al. (2021) [28]. Additionally, we also train our model to generate label sequences as SGM and achieve the worst performances on GoEmotions dataset, which verifies the advantage of natural language generation compared with generating label sequences.

5.3 Effectiveness of Contrastive Learning

We perform visualization of the CLP and non-LCCL-used pure label prompts learned on GoEmotions using t-SNE to disclose the effectiveness of contrastive learning. As seen in Fig. 3, we scatter each learned label representation with corresponding color based on the sentiment polarity provided in [1] officially. It is obvious that label representations trained with LCCL own stronger label correlations. The emotions in Fig. 3(a) scatter randomly, whereas the positive and negative emotions cluster with emotions in the same polarity in Fig. 3(b), which is consistent with the intuitive conclusion mentioned in Sect. 1. Besides, ambiguous emotions and neutral fall in reasonable places in Fig. 3(b), e.g., *realization* is closer to positive emotions whereas *curiosity* stays closer to negative emotions.

5.4 Predictions on Different Emotion Label Numbers

We further investigate the predictions of our model for sentences with different numbers of labels, as shown in Table 5. First, the performance on single-labeled sentences is improved, which verifies the helpfulness of the CLP in providing emotion label information during prediction. Then, the CLP enhances the ability of multi-label emotion prediction of our model, indicating that label correlations are highly considered in our model.

Table 5. Jaccard Index score of $T5_{base}$ and $T5_{base}$+CLP on sentences with different numbers of labels.

	GoEmotions			SemEval 2018			
Number of Labels:	1	2	≥ 3	1	2	3	≥ 4
$T5_{base}$	61.84	42.72	34.28	34.70	66.55	66.21	52.33
$T5_{base}$+CLP	62.54	43.68	34.43	35.41	67.26	66.58	53.52

5.5 Should CLP Be Used in Decoder?

After obtaining the hidden representations from encoder, only the encoded token representations are used in decoder via cross-attention layer. One may naturally ask the follow question: *If the CLP are used in decoder, how does the performance become?* We evaluate such hypothesis using the experiment shown in Table 6 and find that the results get hurt for both datasets. Despite the CLP are learning

Table 6. Results with using CLP in decoder.

	MiF	MaF	Jacc
GoEmotions	60.99	53.52	59.56
w. CLP	60.69	51.93	59.11
SemEval 2018	71.34	55.84	60.80
w. CLP	70.75	55.69	60.14

"label-like" representations [17], they are not any true token embeddings in T5 (i.e., not actual tokens in the vocabulary set of T5) and thus do not contain any text meaning. In this case, using CLP that do not own practical text meaning has an adverse effect on text-to-text based generation in T5. Therefore, the CLP should not be used in the decoder.

6 Conclusion

In this work, we propose a generative framework to tackle multi-label emotion prediction, where we introduce Correlation-based Label Prompts (CLP) via prompt learning and contrastive learning. Experimental results on two datasets show that our model outperforms 7 baselines on two datasets significantly and further experiments prove the advantage of template-based language generation compared with generating label sequence. Besides, our model is identified that label correlations are effectively incorporated in the encoding side, which helps our model predict multi-labeled sentences more efficaciously.

Acknowledgment. This work is supported by the National Natural Science Foundation of China (No. 62176187), the National Key Research and Development Program of China (No. 2017YFC1200500), the Research Foundation of Ministry of Education of China (No. 18JZD015), the Youth Fund for Humanities and Social Science Research of Ministry of Education of China (No. 22YJCZH064), the General Project of Natural Science Foundation of Hubei Province (No. 2021CFB385), the Science and Technology Project of Henan Province (No. 222102210112).

References

1. Demszky, D., Movshovitz-Attias, D., Ko, J., Cowen, A., Nemade, G., Ravi, S.: GoEmotions: a dataset of fine-grained emotions. In: Proceedings of the ACL, pp. 4040–4054 (2020)
2. Mohammad, S., Bravo-Marquez, F., Salameh, M., Kiritchenko, S.: Semeval-2018 task 1: affect in tweets. In: Proceedings of the SemEval, pp. 1–17 (2018)
3. Nguyen, T.H., Shirai, K., Velcin, J.: Sentiment analysis on social media for stock movement prediction. Expert Syst. Appl. **42**(24), 9603–9611 (2015)
4. Zhou, H., Huang, M., Zhang, T., Zhu, X., Liu, B.: Emotional chatting machine: Emotional conversation generation with internal and external memory. In: Proceedings of the AAAI, pp. 730–739 (2018)
5. Fei, H., Ren, Y., Zhang, Y., Ji, D.: Nonautoregressive encoder-decoder neural framework for end-to-end aspect-based sentiment triplet extraction. IEEE Trans. Neural Netw. Learn. Syst. 1–13 (2021). https://ieeexplore.ieee.org/abstract/document/9634849
6. Yu, J., Marujo, L., Jiang, J., Karuturi, P., Brendel, W.: Improving multi-label emotion classification via sentiment classification with dual attention transfer network. In: Proceedings of the EMNLP, pp. 1097–1102 (2018)
7. Baziotis, C., et al.: NTUA-SLP at SemEval-2018 task 1: Predicting affective content in tweets with deep attentive RNNs and transfer learning. In: Proceedings of the SemEval, pp. 245–255 (2018)

8. Godbole, S., Sarawagi, S.: Discriminative methods for multi-labeled classification. In: Proceedings of the PAKDD, pp. 22–30 (2004)
9. Fei, H., Zhang, Y., Ren, Y., Ji, D.: Latent emotion memory for multi-label emotion classification. In: Proceedings of the AAAI Conference on Artificial Intelligence, pp. 7692–7699 (2020)
10. Read, J., Pfahringer, B., Holmes, G., Frank, E.: Classifier chains for multi-label classification. Mach. Learn. **85**(3), 333–359 (2011)
11. Huang, C., Trabelsi, A., Qin, X., Farruque, N., Mou, L., Zaiane, O.R.: Seq2Emo: a sequence to multi-label emotion classification model. In: Proceedings of the NAACL, pp. 4717–4724 (2021)
12. Fei, H., Ren, Y., Wu, S., Li, B., Ji, D.: Latent target-opinion as prior for document-level sentiment classification: a variational approach from fine-grained perspective. In: Proceedings of the WWW: the Web Conference 2021, pp. 553–564 (2021)
13. Fei, H., Li, J., Ren, Y., Zhang, M., Ji, D.: Making decision like human: joint aspect category sentiment analysis and rating prediction with fine-to-coarse reasoning. In: Proceedings of the WWW: the Web Conference, pp. 3042–3051 (2022)
14. Liu, J., Teng, Z., Cui, L., Liu, H., Zhang, Y.: Solving aspect category sentiment analysis as a text generation task. In: Proceedings of the EMNLP, pp. 4406–4416 (2021)
15. Raffel, C., et al.: Exploring the limits of transfer learning with a unified text-to-text transformer. J. Mach. Learn. Res. **21**(140), 1–67 (2020)
16. Lewis, M., et al.: BART: denoising sequence-to-sequence pre-training for natural language generation, translation, and comprehension. In: Proceedings of the ACL, pp. 7871–7880 (2020)
17. Lester, B., Al-Rfou, R., Constant, N.: The power of scale for parameter-efficient prompt tuning. In: Proceedings of the EMNLP, pp. 3045–3059 (2021)
18. Fei, H., Zhang, M., Ji, D.: Cross-lingual semantic role labeling with high-quality translated training corpus. In: Proceedings of the 58th Annual Meeting of the Association for Computational Linguistics, pp. 7014–7026 (2020)
19. Fei, H., Wu, S., Ren, Y., Li, F., Ji, D.: Better combine them together! integrating syntactic constituency and dependency representations for semantic role labeling. In: Findings of the Association for Computational Linguistics: ACL/IJCNLP 2021, pp. 549–559 (2021)
20. Fei, H., Li, F., Li, B., Ji, D.: Encoder-decoder based unified semantic role labeling with label-aware syntax. In: Proceedings of the AAAI Conference on Artificial Intelligence, pp. 12794–12802 (2021)
21. Fei, H., Zhang, M., Li, B., Ji, D.: End-to-end semantic role labeling with neural transition-based model. In: Proceedings of the AAAI Conference on Artificial Intelligence, pp. 12803–12811 (2021)
22. Shi, W., Li, F., Li, J., Fei, H., Ji, D.: Effective token graph modeling using a novel labeling strategy for structured sentiment analysis. In: Proceedings of the ACL, pp. 4232–4241 (2022)
23. Wu, S., Fei, H., Ren, Y., Ji, D., Li, J.: Learn from syntax: Improving pair-wise aspect and opinion terms extraction with rich syntactic knowledge. In: Proceedings of the Thirtieth International Joint Conference on Artificial Intelligence, pp. 3957–3963 (2021)
24. Fei, H., Ji, D., Zhang, Y., Ren, Y.: Topic-enhanced capsule network for multi-label emotion classification. IEEE/ACM Trans. Audio Speech Lang. Process. **28**, 1839–1848 (2020)

25. Devlin, J., Chang, M.W., Lee, K., Toutanova, K.: BERT: pre-training of deep bidi-rectional transformers for language understanding. In: Proceedings of the NAACL, pp. 4171–4186 (2019)
26. Zhou, D., Wu, S., Wang, Q., Xie, J., Tu, Z., Li, M.: Emotion classification by jointly learning to lexiconize and classify. In: Proceedings of the COLING, pp. 3235–3245 (2020)
27. Fei, H., Ren, Y., Ji, D.: Retrofitting structure-aware transformer language model for end tasks. In: Proceedings of the 2020 Conference on Empirical Methods in Natural Language Processing, pp. 2151–2161 (2020)
28. Gao, T., Fisch, A., Chen, D.: Making pre-trained language models better few-shot learners. In: Proceedings of the ACL, pp. 3816–3830 (2021)
29. Chen, T., Kornblith, S., Norouzi, M., Hinton, G.: A simple framework for con-trastive learning of visual representations. In: Proceedings of the ICML, pp. 1597–1607 (2020)
30. Suresh, V., Ong, D.: Not all negatives are equal: Label-aware contrastive loss for fine-grained text classification. In: Proceedings of the EMNLP, pp. 4381–4394 (2021)
31. Vaswani, A., et al.: Attention is all you need. In: Advances in Neural Information Processing Systems, pp. 5998–6008 (2017)
32. Khosla, P., et al.: Supervised contrastive learning. In: Advances in Neural Infor-mation Processing Systems, pp. 18661–18673 (2020)
33. Fei, H., Wu, S., Ren, Y., Zhang, M.: Matching structure for dual learning. In: Proceedings of the 39th International Conference on Machine Learning, ICML, pp. 6373–6391 (2022)

Unimodal and Multimodal Integrated Representation Learning via Improved Information Bottleneck for Multimodal Sentiment Analysis

Tonghui Zhang, Changfei Dong, Jinsong Su, Haiying Zhang[✉],
and Yuzheng Li

School of Informatics Xiamen University, Fujian, China
zhang2002@xmu.edu.cn

Abstract. Representation learning is a significant and challenging task in multimodal sentiment analysis (MSA). It aims to improve the performance of model by learning effective unimodal or multimodal representation. To obtain desired characteristics of representation, various constraints are proposed in previous works. However, these constraints are less concerned with the filtering of task-irrelevant information, which is highly correlated with robustness of representation. In this paper, we design a framework based on information bottleneck to filter noise information. By maximizing mutual information between pairwise unimodal representations and minimizing mutual information between unimodal representation and corresponding input, we can promote unimodal representation for including more task-relevant information and filtering out task-irrelevant information. Furthermore, attention bottleneck is embedded into the unimodal encoding process to realize the interaction between different modalities. Then, to improve the discrimination of multimodal representation, we introduce supervised contrastive learning as a constraint of multimodal representation. Last, we conduct extensive experiments on two public multimodal baseline datasets. The experimental results validate the effectiveness of our model.

Keywords: Information bottleneck · Contrastive learning · Representation learning · Multimodal sentiment analysis

1 Introduction

Human can acquire information from different modalities naturally, such as text, visual and audio. Due to the complementary information contained in various modalities, it can assist us to understand the world in a more comprehensive and objective way. And inspired by the advantage of using multiple modalities, researchers would like to build models that can process and relate information

© The Author(s), under exclusive license to Springer Nature Switzerland AG 2022
W. Lu et al. (Eds.): NLPCC 2022, LNAI 13551, pp. 564–576, 2022.
https://doi.org/10.1007/978-3-031-17120-8_44

from multiple modalities, namely multimodal machine learning [2]. As a downstream task, Multimodal Sentiment Analysis (MSA) mainly focuses on extracting sentiment-related information from multimodal data so that to get the union sentiment score by inference. Due to the broad applications in many fields, such as risk assessment, video understanding and fake news detection etc., MSA has become one of the hot topics in multimodal research.

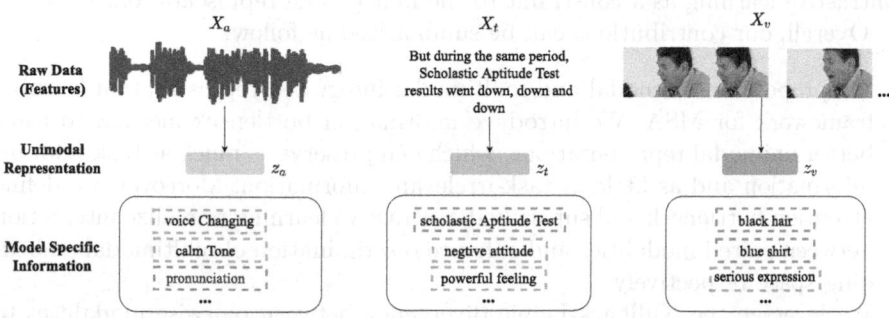

Fig. 1. Example video clip from movie reviews. Task-irrelevant information is marked by red dotted box and task-relevant information is marked by green dotted box. (Color figure online)

The key issues of MSA include multimodal fusion and representation learning. The former focuses on how to extract and integrate information from all input modalities by designing ingenious fusion strategies, such as tensor fusion [30], graph fusion [14], attention based fusion [31], prior knowledge based fusion [26,32] and so on. The later concentrates on optimizing unimodal representations or multimodal one by imposing specific constraints, like reconstruction loss [19,20,27], auxiliary task loss [15,28], measure loss [6,10,11,22,23], etc. Although great progress has been made in MSA during the past, the accuracy is improved slowly now. One possible reason is that the inadequate filtering of task-irrelevant information. For example, the pronunciation included in the audio segment (see Fig. 1) is actually task-irrelevant information that disturb the unimodal representation. However, what to be eliminated is a tough work, so quantitative analysis of information is needed. IB method is proposed to preserve the information needed by decoding and squeeze the bits of encoding for communication coding in [24]. The implementation of IB is based on the maximize and minimize operation of mutual information (MI), where mutual information is a measure of dependences between paired multi-dimensional variables. Inspired by the properties of IB, we hope it can be an effective filter to learn better unimodal representations through the measure of information. Therefore, we propose Unimodal and Multimodal Bottleneck Representation Learning (UMBRL) method. Specially, we maximize MI between pair-wise modalities to preserve task-relevant information, and minimize MI between latent representation and original input for each modality to filter out modality-specific but task-irrelevant information.

Due to the intractability of MI, researchers always boost MI lower bound for MI maximization [3,18,21]. However, minimizing MI in high-dimensional spaces remains a challenging problem [5]. Hence, we give an approximate solution based on Kullback-Leible divergency. To exploit the task-relevant information of unimodal further, we embed attention bottleneck [12,17] to realize message interaction between pairwise modalities. Moreover, to render the learnt embedding space more discriminative with respect to learning task, we take the supervised contrastive learning as a constraint to the multimodal representation.

Overall, our contributions can be summarized as follow:

1. We propose an unimodal and multimodal integrated representation learning framework for MSA. We introduce information bottleneck method to learn better unimodal representations, which can preserve as much as task-relevant information and as little as task-irrelevant information. Moreover, we define attention bottleneck and supervised contrastive learning to realize interaction between paired modalities and enhance discrimination of multimodal embedding space respectively.
2. We leverage the Kullback-Leible divergency between pairwise modalities to approximate implementation the mutual information minimization between unimodal representation and corresponding input. This replacement solves the intractability problem and enhances the robustness of unimodal representation.
3. We conduct comprehensive experiments on CMU-MOSI and CMU-MOSEI datasets and gain superior or comparable results to the state-of-the-art models.

2 Methodology

2.1 Problem Definition

For the MSA task, the input of model includes three unimodal sequential data $X_m^i \in \mathbb{R}^{t \times d}$ from the same video segment $X^i \in \mathcal{X}$, where $m \in v, t, a$ represents visual, text and acoustic modality. And the output of model is sentiment score $\hat{y}_i$, which refers the sentiment polarity and intensity for video segment V_i. Therefore, the final objective of MSA task is to build a well-designed model which can extract useful information from multiple modalities efficiently and make effective inference to predict the true sentiment score y_i based on the extracted information.

2.2 Overall Architecture

The framework of our model is shown in Fig. 2. First, the raw data is converted into numerical sequential vectors X_m. For visual and acoustic modality, following the usual way, we leverage some off-the-shelf methods to extract crucial features, and the details are described in Sect. 4. For text modality, we tokenize the input sequence with a tokenizer. After the digitization operation, we encode unimodal sequential vectors into individual unit-length representations z_m, and during the encoder process, attention bottlenecks are used to convey information between different modalities. In order to improve the robust of encoder, reparameterization trick is used to sample the final unimodal representations $\hat{z}_m$, which later are fused to a single multimodal representation $\hat{z}$ by fusion network. Finally, this multimodal representation will be pass to classification module to predict the corresponding sentiment score $\hat{y}$. At the same time, the model calculates information bottleneck (IB) losses between pairwise modalities and supervised contrastive loss between multimodal representations for each instance.

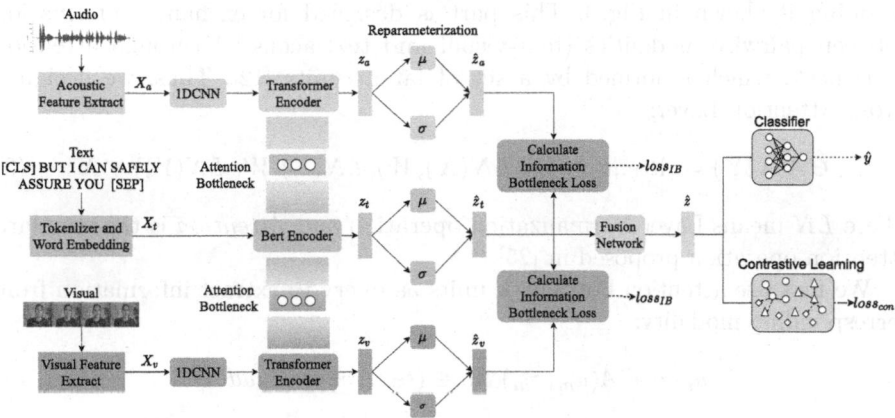

Fig. 2. Overall architecture for UMBRL on modalities text, visual, audio. Triangles, circles and rhombus in contrastive learning stands for instance from different classes and the dotted line means push away whilt solid means pull in close.

2.3 Unimodal Encoding

Unimodal encoding process includes three parts: encoder part, modality interaction part and distribution estimation part. The encoder part is responsible for encode unimodal sequential vectors X_m to individual representations z_m. Specially, we use pre-trained model BERT [8] to encode an input sentence and extract the final results of head embedding ([CLS]) as the text modality representation z_t. Moreover, for visual and acoustic modality, corresponding transformer encoder [25] is used to encode sequential vectors and the last embedding will be extracted as the unimodal representation (z_v, z_a). Considering the limitation of transformer encoder in extracting local information, we add a 1D convolutional layer for visual and acoustic before the formal encoding process:

$$z_t = BERT(X_t) \tag{1}$$

$$z_{v(a)} = Trans(1DCNN(X_{v(a)})) \tag{2}$$

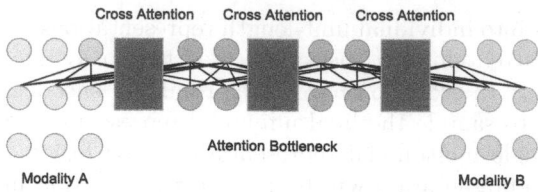

Fig. 3. Example video clip from movie reviews.

The framework of modality interaction part embedded in the process of encoding is shown in Fig. 3. This part is designed for exchange information between pairwise modalities (text-visual and text-acoustic) through attention bottleneck, which is formed by a set of latent units [12]. Thus, we design a Cross-Attention Layer:

$$CA(X, Y) = Attention(W_Q LN(X), W_K LN(Y), W_V LN(Y)) + X \qquad (3)$$

where LN means Layer Normalization operation and $Attention$ is the standard attention operation proposed in [25].

We first use attention bottleneck units as query to extract information from corresponding modality:

$$u_m = CA(u_m, z_m) \quad m \in (text, visual, audio) \qquad (4)$$

And then, we operate cross attention between pairwise attention bottleneck units to exchange information:

$$u_{m_1} = CA(u_{m_1}, u_{m_2}); \quad u_{m_2} = CA(u_{m_2}, u_{m_1}) \qquad (5)$$

Finally, we update the representation of each modality based on these units:

$$z_m = CA(z_m, u_m) \qquad (6)$$

These attention bottleneck units work like a filter, which can squeeze the information that flows through and just retain useful information between modalities. by this way, unimodal representation can supplement itself with the complementary information comes from the other modalities. With this interaction, our model can learn more robust representation to improve the accuracy of sentiment prediction.

Once we complete the encoding and interaction process, during distribution estimation stage, the posterior distribution $p_\theta(z_m^i | X_m^i)$ of each unimodal representation z_m^i is estimated based on the reparameterization trick. It worth noting that θ denotes the parameters of corresponding encoder. Then, we estimate mean μ and variance σ of $p_\theta(z_m^i | X_m^i)$ based on z_m^i. As soon as we obtain μ and σ, we set about to sampling ϵ from $p(z_m^i)$ to generate a group of possible latent representation $\hat{z}_m^i$ of instance X^i. These samples are utilized to enhance the robustness of our encoder and also increase the available data scale potentially.

2.4   Information Bottleneck Loss Function

The unimodal data X_t, X_v and X_a derived from the same video clip are bound to have certain correlation because they share the same multimodal sentiment score. considering the noise information existed in each modality is irrelevant to the downstream task, we maximize the mutual information for modality pairs by maximize the Jensen-Shannon-based estimator $\hat{I}(z_{m_1}^i; z_{m_2}^i)$:

$$I(z_{m_1}^i; z_{m_2}^i) = D_{KL}(p_{\theta_1}(z_{m_1}^i|X_{m_1}^i)||p_{\theta_2}(z_{m_2}^i|X_{m_2}^i))$$
$$\geq E_{X^i \sim \mathcal{X}}[T(z_{m_1}^i, z_{m_2}^i)] - E_{X^i \sim \mathcal{X}, \mathcal{X}^i \sim \mathcal{X}}[T(z_{m_1}^i, z_{m_2}^j)] \qquad (7)$$
$$= \hat{I}(z_{m_1}^i; z_{m_2}^i)$$

$$T(z_{m_1}^i, z_{m_2}^i) = -log(1 + e^{-F(z_{m_1}^i, z_{m_2}^i)}) \qquad (8)$$

where F is a discriminator function that discriminate whether z_{m_1} and z_{m_2} come from the same instance X^i or not.

For the implementation, we optimize the bounds for (text, visual) and (text, acoustic) pairs. We don't maximize the mutual information between visual and acoustic because: 1) visual and acoustic modality are not directly but potentially related through text modality; 2) many previous works [9,23] pointed out that interaction between visual and acoustic may damage the final performance for the task-related information is not evenly distributed between the modalities.

In this section, we minimize the mutual information between latent representation and corresponding original input based on KL divergence by the equation following:

$$I(z_{m_1}; X_{m_1}) + I(z_{m_2}; X_{m_2}) \Rightarrow E_{i \in |\mathcal{X}|}[D_{SKL}(p_{\theta_1}(z_{m_1}^i|X_{m_1}^i)||p_{\theta_2}(z_{m_1}^i|X_{m_2}^i))]$$
$$= \frac{1}{2}E[(D_{KL}(p_{\theta_1}(z_{m_1}^i|X_{m_1}^i)||p_{\theta_2}(z_{m_2}^i|X_{m_2}^i)) + D_{KL}(p_{\theta_2}(z_{m_2}^i|X_{m_2}^i)||p_{\theta_1}(z_{m_1}^i|X_{m_1}^i)))] \qquad (9)$$

The information bottleneck loss function is formulated as:

$$Loss_{IB}(z_{m_1}, z_{m_2}) = -\alpha\hat{I}(z_{m_1}; z_{m_2}) + \beta D_{SKL}(p_{\theta_1}(z_{m_1}|X_{m_1})||p_{\theta_2}(z_{m_2}|X_{m_2})) \qquad (10)$$

2.5   Fusion and Supervised Constrastive Learning

Recently, some existing related work indicate that, when the latent representation holds well properties, overcomplicated fusion method will damage the final performance of model [15]. Alternatively, we concatenate all unimodal latent representation and then pass the result through a fusion network composed of stacked linear-activation layers to obtain the final multimodal representation $\hat{z}$. However, because the multimodal representation $\hat{z}$ is generated by simply non-linear transformation of three unimodal representation, while the unimodal representations are constraint in an unsupervised setting, the learned multimodal representation is hard to be discriminated for classifier. Here, we introduce supervised contrastive learning [13] on $\hat{z}$.

We divide all of the instance into three class-positive, neutral and negative based on the ground truth. Then we hope to pull the representations of the same class to be closer and push the representations of different class further:

$$Loss_{con} = -\gamma \sum_{i \in |\mathcal{X}|} log \frac{exp\hat{z}^i \cdot \hat{z}^{j(i)}/\tau}{\sum_{a \in A(i)} exp\hat{z}^i \cdot \hat{z}^a/\tau} \tag{11}$$

where γ is a hyperparamter that control the impact of supervised contrastive learning, $j(i)$ denotes the instance from the same class of i, $A(i)$ denotes the set of other instances except i and $\tau \in \mathcal{R}^+$ is a scalar temperature parameter [13].

2.6 Training

After obtaining the final prediction of sentiment score $\hat{y}$, we can calculate the main task loss function:

$$Loss_{main} = MAE(\hat{y}, y) \tag{12}$$

The overall loss function includes information bottleneck loss function, supervised contrastive loss function and main task loss function. The equation is formulated as:

$$Loss = Loss_{main} + Loss_{IB}(z_t, z_v) + Loss_{IB}(z_t, z_a) + Loss_{con} \tag{13}$$

3 Experiment

In this section, we present some experiment related details including datasets and evaluation metrics, baselines, experiment results and ablation experiments.

3.1 Datasets and Evaluation Metrics

We conduct experiments on CMU-MOSI [33] and CMU-MOSEI [34], which are two widely used public dataset in MSA research. CMU-MOSI contains 2199 annotated video segments from 89 distinct speakers, and each segment in CMU-MOSI is annotated for sentiment on a $[-3, 3]$ Likert scale. Compared with CMU-MOSI, CMU-MOSEI expands the size of data and contains 23453 video segments from 1000 distinct speakers. CMU-MOSEI also provides emotions of happiness, sadness, anger, fear, disgust, surprise which annotated on a $[0,3]$ Likert scale.

To give a more objective evaluation, we use the same metric set that has been consistently presented and compared before, which include: mean absolute error (MAE), Pearson correlation (Corr), two-class classification accuracy (Acc-2), seven-class classification accuracy (Acc-7) and F1 score. The Acc-2 and F1 score are computed for the positive/negative and non-negative/negative classification results.

3.2   Baselines

In order to inspect the performance of our model, we select the following baselines for comparison:

Tensor fusion network (TFN) [6] encode visual, text and acoustic data separately and fusion these unimodal representations by a 3-fold Cartesian product.

Multimodal Transformer (MULT) [19] learns unimodal representation by translating source modality to target modality using cross-modality attention, and then concatenate each unimodal representation as the multimodal representation.

Interaction Canonical Correlation Network (ICCN) [4] use canonical correlation coefficient between text-visual and text-acoustic pairs to improve the fusion representation of each modality pair, and improve final multimodal representation based on this operation.

Multimodal Adaptation Gate for BERT (MAG-BERT) [30] inspired by the power of BERT, they combine the shift method of text proposed in [13] with BERT to get a better multimodal representation.

Self-supervised Multi-Task Learning (Self-MM) [28] designs a self-supervised unimodal training method based on the relationship between unimodal sentiment value and multimodal sentiment value. By joint training unimodal sentiment analysis task and multimodal sentiment analysis task, it achieves state-of-the-art performance.

MAG-BERT with synergy loss function (MAG-BERT +MMD) [1] inspired by neuroscience ideas about multisensory integration and process, they introduced mutual information and Hilbert-Schmidt criteria (MMD criteria) to measure the dependency between multimodal representation and each unimodal representation. Through maximize mutual information and MMD, they can adjust the training process and get a better performance.

3.3   Experimental Details

In our experiments, we use unaligned raw data. The feature of visual and acoustic modality is extracted by P2FA [29] and COVAREP [7]tools separately. Our model is trained using AdamW optimizer with a linear schedule on a single GeForce GPU. The warmup rate is set to 0.05 based on the total epoch 100. The learning rate is set from $\{1e-5, 2e-5, 5e-5, 1e-4\}$ for parameters of BERT and $\{1e-4, 2e-4, 3e-4, 4e-4, 5e-4,1e-3\}$ for other parameters of our model. The visual transformer and audio transformer are set from $\{3, 4, 5, 6,7\}$ layers. The dimension of representation distribution is set from $\{64, 128,256\}$. The number and dimension of external latent unit are set from $\{1,2,3,4,5\}$ and $\{32, 64, 128, 256\}$ respectively. The number of layers to exchange information with latent unit is set from $\{1,2,3\}$ and the start layer is set from $\{3, 4, 5\}$ for visual(audio) transformers and $\{6,7,8\}$ for Bert.

3.4   Results and Discussion

Table 1 and Table 2 show the results of our experiments. We find that UMBRL yields better or comparable performance for many baselines. Specially, our

Table 1. Results on CMU-MOSI.

Models	CMU-MOSI				
	MAE	Corr	Acc-7	Acc-2	F1
TFN	0.901	0.698	34.9	−/80.8	−/80.7
MULT	0.861	0.711	−	81.5/84.1	80.6/83.9
ICCN	0.862	0.714	39.0	−/83.0	−/83.0
MAG-BERT	0.731	0.789	−	82.5/84.3	82.6/84.3
Self-MM	0.713	0.798	−	**84.00/85.98**	**84.82**/85.95
MAG-BERT+MMD	0.76	0.82	41.9	−/85.6	−
UMBRL	**0.69**	**0.80**	45.7	83.67/**85.98**	83.88/**86.1**

Table 2. Results on CMU-MOSEI.

Models	CMU-MOSEI				
	MAE	Corr	Acc-7	Acc-2	F1
TFN	0.593	0.700	50.2	−/82.5	−/82.1
MULT	0.580	0.703	−	−/82.5	−/82.3
ICCN	0.565	0.713	51.6	−/84.2	−/84.2
MAG-BERT	0.539	0.753	−	83.8/85.2	83.7/85.1
Self-MM	0.530	0.765	−	82.81/85.17	82.53/85.30
MAG-BERT+MMD	0.59	**0.79**	47.9	−/85.4	−
UMBRL	**0.53**	0.768	**53.46**	**83.47/85.64**	**83.22/85.75**

method outperforms the baseline model which also use mutual information to constraint the learning process (MAG-BERT+MMD). This indicates that the operation of mutual information minimization as well as the addition of latent unit and supervised contrastive learning can effectively enhance the quality of unimodal representation and multimodal representation. Compared with the SOTA method (Self-MM), our model performs better in CMU-MOSEI. For the reason, we hypothesis it is because the estimation of mutual information needs more data [16], and in the further work, we would like to verify the correctness of this hypothesis.

3.5   Ablation Study

In order to verify the efficiency of information bottleneck loss function and supervised contrastive learning, we carried a series of ablation study on CMU-MOSEI. The results under different ablation settings are categorized and listed in Table 3. First, we eliminate the MI maximization part of IB. We note a certain degree of decline of the performance, which proves the efficacy of our framework. Moreover, we find that the binary classification performance degradation in the setting of $\hat{I}(z_v; z_a)$, $\hat{I}(z_t; z_v) + \hat{I}(z_v; z_a)$ and $\hat{I}(z_t; z_a) + \hat{I}(z_v; z_a)$ as well as

Table 3. Ablation study on CMU-MOSEI.

Description	MAE	Corr	Acc-7	Acc-2	F1
UMBRL	**0.530**	0.768	53.46	83.47/**85.64**	**83.22/85.75**
IB loss					
$\hat{I}(z_t; z_v)$	0.539	0.766	52.52	83.64/85.2	83.47/85.35
$\hat{I}(z_t; z_a)$	0.535	0.768	53.03	83.43/85.31	83.25/85.48
$\hat{I}(z_v; z_a)$	0.530	0.764	**54.04**	78.86/84.15	78.06/84.04
$\hat{I}(z_t; z_v) + \hat{I}(z_v; z_a)$	0.530	0.766	52.99	80.19/84.48	79.54/84.42
$\hat{I}(z_t; z_a) + \hat{I}(z_v; z_a)$	0.533	**0.769**	52.71	78.36/83.93	77.51/83.79
$\hat{I}(z_t; z_v) + \hat{I}(z_t; z_a) + \hat{I}(z_v; z_a)$	0.5346	0.760	52.75	84.61/85.09	84.51/85.32
SKL loss					
w/o $D_{SKL}(z_t; z_v)$	0.5412	0.764	52.22	84.12/85.25	84.11/85.53
w/o $D_{SKL}(z_t; z_a)$	0.5320	0.763	53.23	79.85/84.53	79.14/84.46
Supervised contrastive loss					
w/o L_{con}	0.5346	0.766	52.97	75.62/82.36	74.53/82.13

the seven-class classification performance degradation in setting of $\hat{I}(z_t; z_v)$ and $\hat{I}(z_t; z_v) + \hat{I}(z_t; z_a) + \hat{I}(z_v; z_a)$. These performance decline provides experimental evidence for the chosen of modality pair for mutual information maximization. Then we eliminate the MI minimization part of IB, and we also note a clear performance drop in all metrics which is more significant for the removement of $D_{SKL}(z_t; z_a)$. Finally, we eliminate the supervised contrastive loss function and we find a significant descend for binary classification performance and slight drop in other metrics, which indicate the effect of contrastive loss for multimodal representation learning.

4   Conclusion

To improve the performance of MSA, in this paper, we present UMBRL to reinforce unimodal and multimodal representations. To promote the learning result, information loss function and supervised contrastive learning are embedded to constrain the unimodal and multimodal representation learning process respectively. Additionally, to address the intractability of mutual information minimization, we give the suboptimal solution to estimate lower bound by the Kullback-Leible divergency between corresponding unimodal representations. Specially, to enhance the robustness of each unimodal representation, attention bottleneck units are introduced to the fusion stage. In experimental section, we conduct comprehensive experiments on two public datasets. The results verify the effectiveness of out model. By conducting comprehensive ablation study further, the importance of IB loss function, attention bottleneck as well as supervised contrastive loss are proved. In future work, we would like to extend our method to semi-supervised setting, which can utilize more unlabeled data and make the model more general.

Acknowledgement. This work is supported by Natural Science Foundation of Fujian Province of China (No. 2020J06001), and Youth Innovation Fund of Xiamen (No. 3502Z20206059). This work is also supported by project S202210384799, S202210384831 supported by XMU Training Program of Innovation and Entrepreneurship for Undergraduates.

References

1. Rahman, W., et al.: Integrating multimodal information in large pretrained transformers. In: Proceedings of the 58th Annual Meeting of the Association for Computational Linguistics, pp. 2359–2369 (2020)
2. Baltrušaitis, T., Ahuja, C., Morency, L.P.: Multimodal machine learning: a survey and taxonomy. IEEE Trans. Pattern Anal. Mach. Intell. **41**(2), 423–443 (2018)
3. Belghazi, M.I., et al.: Mutual information neural estimation. In: International Conference on Machine Learning, pp. 531–540. PMLR (2018)
4. Chen, M., Wang, S., Liang, P.P., Baltrušaitis, T., Zadeh, A., Morency, L.P.: Multimodal sentiment analysis with word-level fusion and reinforcement learning. In: Proceedings of the 19th ACM International Conference on Multimodal Interaction, pp. 163–171 (2017)
5. Cheng, P., Hao, W., Dai, S., Liu, J., Gan, Z., Carin, L.: CLUB: a contrastive log-ratio upper bound of mutual information. In: Proceedings of the 37th International Conference on Machine Learning, pp. 1779–1788 (2020)
6. Colombo, P., Chapuis, E., Labeau, M., Clavel, C.: Improving multimodal fusion via mutual dependency maximisation. In: Proceedings of the 2021 Conference on Empirical Methods in Natural Language Processing, pp. 231–245 (2021)
7. Degottex, G., Kane, J., Drugman, T., Raitio, T., Scherer, S.: COVAREP-a collaborative voice analysis repository for speech technologies. In: 2014 IEEE International Conference on Acoustics, Speech and Signal Processing (ICASSP), pp. 960–964. IEEE (2014)
8. Devlin, J., Chang, M.W., Lee, K., Toutanova, K.: BERT: pre-training of deep bidirectional transformers for language understanding. In: Proceedings of the 2019 Conference of the North American Chapter of the Association for Computational Linguistics: Human Language Technologies, Volume 1 (Long and Short Papers), pp. 4171–4186 (2019)
9. Han, W., Chen, H., Gelbukh, A., Zadeh, A., Morency, L.P., Poria, S.: Bi-bimodal modality fusion for correlation-controlled multimodal sentiment analysis. In: Proceedings of the 2021 International Conference on Multimodal Interaction, pp. 6–15 (2021)
10. Han, W., Chen, H., Poria, S.: Improving multimodal fusion with hierarchical mutual information maximization for multimodal sentiment analysis. In: Proceedings of the 2021 Conference on Empirical Methods in Natural Language Processing, pp. 9180–9192 (2021)
11. Hazarika, D., Zimmermann, R., Poria, S.: MISA: modality-invariant and-specific representations for multimodal sentiment analysis. In: Proceedings of the 28th ACM International Conference on Multimedia, pp. 1122–1131 (2020)

12. Jaegle, A., Gimeno, F., Brock, A., Vinyals, O., Zisserman, A., Carreira, J.: Perceiver: general perception with iterative attention. In: International Conference on Machine Learning, pp. 4651–4664. PMLR (2021)
13. Khosla, P., et al.: Supervised contrastive learning. Adv. Neural. Inf. Process. Syst. **33**, 18661–18673 (2020)
14. Mai, S., Hu, H., Xing, S.: Modality to modality translation: an adversarial representation learning and graph fusion network for multimodal fusion. In: Proceedings of the AAAI Conference on Artificial Intelligence, vol. 34, pp. 164–172 (2020)
15. Mai, S., Zeng, Y., Zheng, S., Hu, H.: Hybrid contrastive learning of tri-modal representation for multimodal sentiment analysis. IEEE Trans. Affective Comput. (2022)
16. McAllester, D., Stratos, K.: Formal limitations on the measurement of mutual information. In: International Conference on Artificial Intelligence and Statistics, pp. 875–884. PMLR (2020)
17. Nagrani, A., Yang, S., Arnab, A., Jansen, A., Schmid, C., Sun, C.: Attention bottlenecks for multimodal fusion. Adv. Neural. Inf. Process. Syst. **34**, 14200–14213 (2021)
18. Oord, A.V.d., Li, Y., Vinyals, O.: Representation learning with contrastive predictive coding. arXiv preprint arXiv:1807.03748 (2018)
19. Pham, H., Liang, P.P., Manzini, T., Morency, L.P., Póczos, B.: Found in translation: learning robust joint representations by cyclic translations between modalities. In: Proceedings of the AAAI Conference on Artificial Intelligence, vol. 33, pp. 6892–6899 (2019)
20. Pham, H., Manzini, T., Liang, P.P., Póczos, B.: Seq2Seq2Sentiment: multimodal sequence to sequence models for sentiment analysis. In: Proceedings of Grand Challenge and Workshop on Human Multimodal Language (Challenge-HML), pp. 53–63 (2018)
21. Poole, B., Ozair, S., van den Oord, A., Alemi, A., Tucker, G.: On variational bounds of mutual information. In: ICML (2019)
22. Shankar, S.: Neural dependency coding inspired multimodal fusion. arXiv preprint arXiv:2110.00385 (2021)
23. Sun, Z., Sarma, P., Sethares, W., Liang, Y.: Learning relationships between text, audio, and video via deep canonical correlation for multimodal language analysis. In: Proceedings of the AAAI Conference on Artificial Intelligence, vol. 34, pp. 8992–8999 (2020)
24. Tishby, N., Pereira, F.C., Bialek, W.: The information bottleneck method. arXiv preprint physics/0004057 (2000)
25. Vaswani, A., et al.: Attention is all you need. Adv. Neural Inf. Process. Syst. **30** (2017)
26. Wang, Y., Shen, Y., Liu, Z., Liang, P.P., Zadeh, A., Morency, L.P.: Words can shift: dynamically adjusting word representations using nonverbal behaviors. In: Proceedings of the AAAI Conference on Artificial Intelligence, vol. 33, pp. 7216–7223 (2019)
27. Wang, Z., Wan, Z., Wan, X.: Transmodality: an end2end fusion method with transformer for multimodal sentiment analysis. In: Proceedings of The Web Conference 2020, pp. 2514–2520 (2020)
28. Yu, W., Xu, H., Yuan, Z., Wu, J.: Learning modality-specific representations with self-supervised multi-task learning for multimodal sentiment analysis. In: Proceedings of the AAAI Conference on Artificial Intelligence, vol. 35, pp. 10790–10797 (2021)

29. Yuan, J., Liberman, M.: Speaker identification on the scotus corpus. J. Acoust. Soc. Am. Impact Factor **123**(5), 3878 (2008)
30. Zadeh, A., Chen, M., Poria, S., Cambria, E., Morency, L.P.: Tensor fusion network for multimodal sentiment analysis. In: Proceedings of the 2017 Conference on Empirical Methods in Natural Language Processing, pp. 1103–1114 (2017)
31. Zadeh, A., Liang, P.P., Mazumder, N., Poria, S., Cambria, E., Morency, L.P.: Memory fusion network for multi-view sequential learning. In: Proceedings of the AAAI Conference on Artificial Intelligence, vol. 32 (2018)
32. Zadeh, A., Liang, P.P., Poria, S., Vij, P., Cambria, E., Morency, L.P.: Multi-attention recurrent network for human communication comprehension. In: Proceedings of the AAAI Conference on Artificial Intelligence, vol. 32 (2018)
33. Zadeh, A., Zellers, R., Pincus, E., Morency, L.P.: MOSI: multimodal corpus of sentiment intensity and subjectivity analysis in online opinion videos. arXiv preprint arXiv:1606.06259 (2016)
34. Zadeh, A.B., Liang, P.P., Poria, S., Cambria, E., Morency, L.P.: Multimodal language analysis in the wild: CMU-MOSEI dataset and interpretable dynamic fusion graph. In: Proceedings of the 56th Annual Meeting of the Association for Computational Linguistics (Volume 1: Long Papers), pp. 2236–2246 (2018)

Learning Emotion-Aware Contextual Representations for Emotion-Cause Pair Extraction

Baopu Qiu[1,2] and Lin Shang[1,2(✉)]

[1] State Key Laboratory for Novel Software Technology, Nanjing University, Nanjing 210023, China
qiubaopu@smail.nju.edu.cn
[2] Department of Computer Science and Technology, Nanjing University, Nanjing 210023, China
shanglin@nju.edu.cn

Abstract. Emotion-Cause Pair Extraction (ECPE) focuses on analyzing emotions and its corresponding causes in a document. Two reasons have made ECPE a more challenging, but more applicable task than the previous Emotion-Cause Extraction (ECE) task: 1) an ECPE model needs to identify both emotions and their corresponding causes without the annotation of emotions. 2) the ECPE task involves finding causes for multiple emotions in a document, while ECE is for one emotion. However, existing ECPE methods fail to meet the second challenge, since they are evaluated on a dataset which exhibits a bias that nearly 90% of documents have only one emotion-cause pair. Thus, we reconstruct the dataset to better meet ECPE settings. We observe that previous SOTA approaches suffer from performance degradation in extracting multiple emotion-cause pairs due to the use of shared context encoder in the joint learning process. In this work, we propose a new pipelined approach that builds on two independent models with unshared context encoders, in which the emotion extraction model only provides input features for the cause extraction model. Experimental results demonstrate that our model can learn distinct contextual representations specific to each emotion, reaching state-of-the-art performance on both datasets and showing robustness in the analysis of more complex document context.

Keywords: Emotion-cause pair extraction · Emotion cause analysis · Representation learning

1 Introduction

Recently, the task about detecting the stimuli of emotions expressed in text has emerged in the area of text emotion analysis. Previous works focus on Emotion Cause Extraction (ECE), which has been proposed by [1] as a word-level

---

Our code and dataset are avaliable at https://github.com/Qbop981001/emotion-aware-eca.

© The Author(s), under exclusive license to Springer Nature Switzerland AG 2022
W. Lu et al. (Eds.): NLPCC 2022, LNAI 13551, pp. 577–590, 2022.
https://doi.org/10.1007/978-3-031-17120-8_45

sequence labeling problem. [2] re-formalized ECE as a clause-level classification problem of finding cause clauses for the given emotion. They released a Chinese dataset collected from SINA city news which has become the benchmark dataset for the ECE task followed by many works [3–7].

Some researchers [8] pointed out that ECE task suffers from two defects: 1) The emotion must be annotated in advance. 2) The goal of ECE neglects the fact that emotions and causes are mutually indicative. They developed the task to emotion-cause pair extraction (ECPE), in which emotion clauses and their corresponding cause clauses are extracted as pairs. To solve the problem, they proposed a two-step pipelined approach, while more recently, the task has been dominated by end-to-end systems that model emotion extraction and cause extraction jointly [9–11].

We re-investigate ECPE's motivation and observe another significant merit of ECPE over ECE, that is, the task involves analysis of more complex document context that contains multiple emotions, multiple causes and multiple semantic roles. As shown in Fig. 1, the example document is divided into *two* different samples in the ECE task since two emotion clauses are annotated. An ECE model takes each annotated emotion clause as input and find its corresponding causes, while an ECPE model takes the whole document as input and extract all possible emotion-cause pairs. Therefore, the model has to process richer, but more complex context information.

Unfortunately, the benchmark ECPE dataset, which previous works are evaluated on, fails to capture this merit. Only 10.23% of documents in this dataset have more than one emotion-cause pair, and only 6.63% of documents have more than one emotion clause. This is due to the fact that the dataset is originally designed for the previous ECE task and many different "documents" are actually excerpts of a same news article. Therefore, we reconstruct the dataset by merging documents with the same context to better meet ECPE settings.

We conduct experiments on the reconstructed dataset and find that current state-of-the-art ECPE methods suffers from severe performance degradation in extracting multiple emotion-cause pairs. We argue that this can be attributed to the shared contextual representations of input document, since these methods jointly perform the emotion extraction and cause extraction process using a shared context encoder. The entangled contextual representation may hinder the model from focusing on the proper part of context when finding causes for a specific emotion. For instance, the clauses c12 and c13 in Fig. 1, "failing to cure the disease while using that much money" is crucial in detecting the causal relationship between c14 and c15, but not relevant for c18 and c17.

To address this problem, we propose a new pipelined approach that builds on two independent context encoders trained separately, one for an emotion extraction model, and another for an emotion-oriented cause extraction model, with the fusion of emotion information merely at its input layer. Based on our experiments, we validate that the cause extraction model can learn emotion-aware contextual representations of the input document. Our approach reaches state-of-the-art in both datasets, and is significantly more effective in extracting multiple emotion-cause pairs, meeting ECPE's motivation to analyze emotion causes in longer and more complex document context.

Our contributions can be summarized as follows:

- We realize another merit of the ECPE task over previous task: it enables the analysis of causes for multiple emotions, which usually occur in longer document context. We argue that current ECPE approaches fail to exploit this merit since the benchmark dataset is biased. We propose a strategy to reconstruct the dataset to better meet ECPE settings.
- We observe that existing models suffer from performance drop in extracting multiple emotion-cause pairs, and attribute this to the use of shared context encoder during the joint learning process. We propose a pipelined approach that learns two independent context encoders, with early fusion of emotion information at the input layer of the cause model to learn contextual representations specific to each extracted emotion.
- Experimental results on both datasets show that our approach achieves state-of-the-art performance in both datasets, and is more effective in extracting multiple emotion-cause pairs.

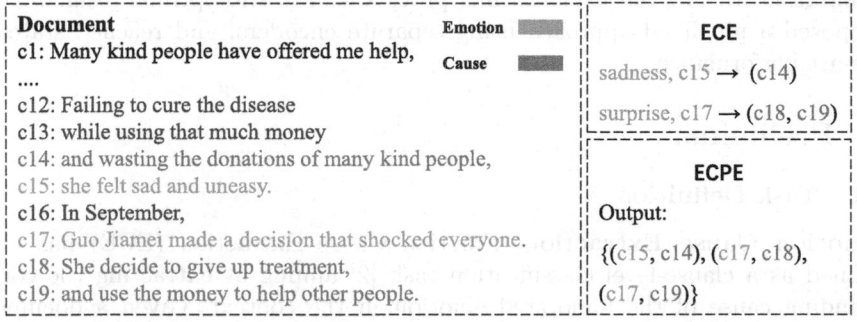

Fig. 1. An Example document from [2]'s dataset, translated from Chinese. Texts in orange and green denote the emotion clauses and cause clauses respectively. (Color figure online)

2   Related Work

Emotion Cause Extraction. [1] first proposed the emotion cause extraction task and released a small scale dataset. Early works adopted rule-based [14], machine-learning-based [15] methods to solve the task. Based on analysis of linguistic features in a Chinese dataset, researchers [16] have suggested that a clause may be the most proper unit for emotion cause analysis in Chinese. [2] re-formalized the task as clause-level binary classification and released a benchmark corpus for the ECE task, followed by many works [3–6].

Emotion Cause Pair Extraction. [8] expanded the task to emotion-cause pair extraction and construct a benchmark ECPE corpus based the [2]'s dataset. [8] proposed a two-step pipeline approach to solve the task, of which the first step uses two component to extract all emotion clauses and cause clauses from the document, and attempts cartesian product to form all possible pairs. In the second step, the candidate pairs are fed into a filter to select emotion-cause pairs. More recently, most following works employ end-to-end models [10,17,20,21] with the belief that joint models capture interactions between subtasks and mitigate error propagation. Some of the models select the result from all possible pairs [9,12,19], and some others regard ECPE as a clause-level sequence labeling problem [13,18]. All these methods focus on the utilization of document context information and have employed various architectures and techniques such as graph convolutional network [19], graph attention network [11] and iterative synchronized multi-task learning [12].

Pipeline Approach vs. Joint Approach. The entity and relation joint extraction task, which involves extracting entities and their relations simultaneously, is a well-known task in information extraction, and is similar to the emotion-cause classifying and pairing process. Many existing works model entity extraction and relation classification jointly while some [22] argued that shared contextual representations during the joint learning process lead to sub-optimal results. They proposed a pipelined approach using separate encoders, and reached state-of-the-art performance.

3   Preliminary

3.1   Task Definition

Emotion Cause Extraction. Emotion Cause Extraction (ECE) has been defined as a clause-level classification task [2] aiming at extracting the corresponding cause of the annotated emotion in the context. Given a document $d = [c_1, ..., c_i, ..., c_{|d|}]$, where c_i is the ith clause in d, and an annotated emotion clause c^e, where $e \in E$,

$$E = \{happiness, sadness, disgust, fear, anger, surprise\} \tag{1}$$

The goal of ECE is to find all the cause clauses of the given emotion clause as $\{c_1^{cau}, c_2^{cau}, ...\}$. Note that only one emotion occur in one sample, while there may be multiple causes corresponding to it.

Emotion-Cause Pair Extraction. [8] developed the ECE task to Emotion-Cause Pair Extraction (ECPE). Given a document $d = [c_1, ..., c_i, ..., c_{|d|}]$, the goal of ECPE is to extract a set of emotion-cause pairs

$$P = \{..., (c^{emo}, c^{cau}), ...\}$$

where c^{emo} is the emotion clause and c^{cau} is its corresponding cause clause. The ECPE task deals with finding multiple causes for multiple emotions in one document.

3.2 Dataset

Bias in the ECPE Benchmark Dataset. Based on SINA city news, [2] released an Chinese emotion cause corpus that has become the benchmark dataset for ECE research, which involves extraction of causes for one annotated emotion. Thus, a large proportion of documents in this dataset contain only one emotion clause, and documents with multiple emotions are split to different samples. Following researchers [8] also use this dataset as the benchmark for ECPE. They merged samples with same text content into one document since in the ECPE task, every document corresponds to one sample.

As Table 1 shows, we can observe that the dataset exhibits a bias that only 10.23% of documents contain multiple emotion-cause pairs, and only 6.63% of documents have more than one emotion. The bias prevents researchers from knowing the performance of their models on multiple emotion-cause pair extraction, which can be regarded as a significant merit of ECPE over previous tasks. We also discover that many different "documents" are actually excerpts from the *same* original news report. During the construction of original ECE dataset, people may only select clauses surrounding the annotated emotion and ignore long-range clauses. This reduces the task's difficulty at the expense of applicability, since in real word, documents such as news article and literary work usually contain multiple emotions, belonging to multiple semantic roles.

Table 1. Statistics of the original dataset and reconstructed dataset

Item	Original dataset	Reconstructed dataset
Doc. total number	1945	1679
Doc. with one emotion cause pair	1746	1348
Doc. with two emotion cause pairs	177	246
Doc. with more than two pairs	22	85
Doc. with more than one emotion	129	295

Dataset Reconstruction Strategy
We manually find all such documents and merge them into one document to rebuild the ECPE benchmark dataset. As Table 1 shows, 17.57% of documents in the reconstructed dataset have multiple emotions while 19.71% of documents have multiple emotion-cause pairs. Our merging strategy reduces the total number of documents and produces longer documents with increased complexity. Figure 2 displays the comparision of the number of clauses in a document between the original and reconstructed dataset. As is shown, the documents in the reconstructed dataset have more clauses and thus more complex document structure. In fact, 37.42% of emotion-cause pairs are located in documents with multiple pairs, indicating that documents in the reconstructed dataset are closer to real-world scenarios.

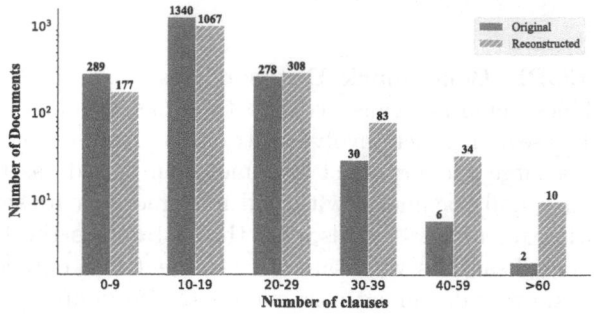

Fig. 2. Statistics of the document length in both datasets.

4   Methodology

As Fig. 3 shows, our approach consists of two independent models, an emotion extraction model and a cause extraction model. We build both of our models on BERT [23] as context encoders, with an multi-label output layer. The emotion extraction model first takes the whole document as input and extract all possible emotion clauses. Then the extracted emotion clauses will be used *one by one* for fusing emotion information at the input layer of the cause extraction model, which we refer to as an emotion-oriented cause extraction model. We will explain the details of both models below and clarify the usage of emotion information as well as document context information in our approach.

4.1   Emotion Extraction Model

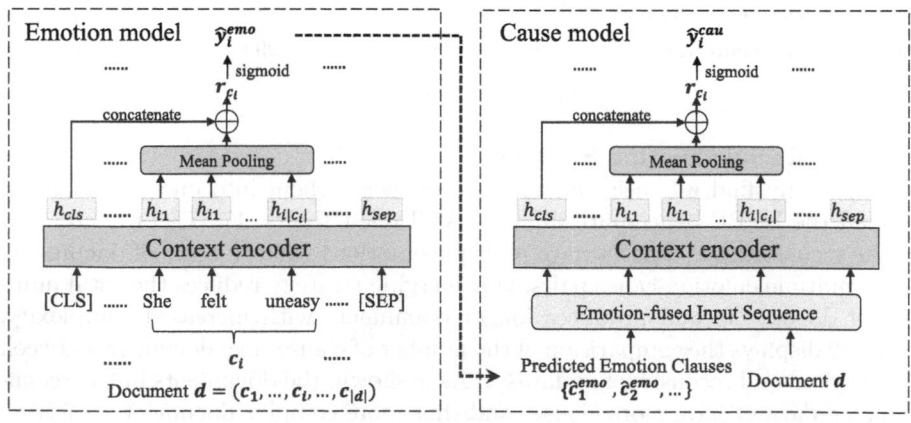

Fig. 3. Model architecture.

Given a document $d = [c_1, ..., c_i, ..., c_{|d|}]$, the model takes it as the input of a pre-trained encoder to obtain a sequence of hidden states denoted by

$$\mathbf{H_D} = (h_{[CLS]}, \mathbf{x_{c_1}}, ..., \mathbf{x_{c_i}}, ..., \mathbf{x_{c_{|d|}}}, h_{[SEP]}) \tag{2}$$

where $\mathbf{x_{c_i}} = (h_{i1}, ..., h_{ij}, ...h_{i|c_i|})$, $h_{ij} \in R^H$ is the output hidden state of jth token in i^{th} clause and $|c_i|$ denotes the number of tokens in i^{th} clause. Then we apply mean pooling to build the representation of each clause, which is defined as:

$$\mathbf{h_{c_i}} = \frac{1}{|c_i|} \sum_{j=1}^{|c_i|} h_{ij} \tag{3}$$

Finally we concatenate the clause representation $\mathbf{h_{c_i}}$ with $[CLS]$ token's output hidden state, $h_{[CLS]}$, as the input of an output layer to predict the probability of the clause being an emotion clause

$$\mathbf{r_{c_i}} = [\mathbf{h_{c_i}}, h_{[CLS]}] \tag{4}$$

$$\hat{y}_i^{emo} = \sigma(w_{emo}^T \mathbf{r_{c_i}} + b_{emo}) \tag{5}$$

where $w_{emo} \in R^{H \times 1}$ and b_{emo} are parameters of the output layer with sigmoid function $\sigma(\cdot)$.

Context Information. In order to examine the impact of context information in the emotion extraction process, we also implement a standard BERT-based sentence classification model in which each single clause is taken as the input without leveraging the context. The details are explained in Sect. 5.3.

4.2 Emotion-Oriented Cause Extraction Model

In the two-step model proposed by [8], there is an cause extraction component that extracts potential cause clauses in a document at first. We found the performance of this component unsatisfying since it ignores the fact that the identification of certain cause clause depends on its corresponding emotion clause. In our approach, we do *not* perform cause extraction *solely*, and instead conduct emotion-oriented cause extraction.

As Fig. 3 shows, the architecture of cause model is very similar to our emotion extraction model, and the only difference lies in the input: we fuse emotion information into the input sequence through three strategies.

Fusing Emotion Information. Previous works have attached importance to the use of emotion information in cause extraction [11,12,21]. However, all of these models use a shared LSTM layer or pre-trained encoder for contextual representations in emotion extraction and cause extraction. We argue that shared context encoders fail to capture proper contextual information for a specific emotion clause, leading to sub-optimal results in extracting multiple emotion-cause pairs in one document. Therefore, we propose strategies to fuse specific emotion information at the input layer of the cause model, as displayed in Fig. 4.

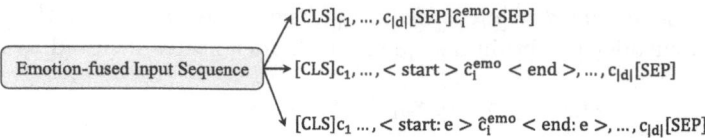

Fig. 4. Emotion-fusing strategies. From top to the bottom, the strategy is denoted by EmotionPrompt, UntypedMarker and TypedMarker in the following expeiments. $e \in E$ is the type of emotion defined in Eq. 1.

The most direct method is to concatenate each predicted emotion clause and its document context as the input. We also attempt to integrate emotion information through extra marker tokens at the start and end position of the predicted emotion clause, and further consider adding the emotion type explicitly. However, since we cannot obtain satisfying results for emotion type classification, we only compare the upper bound of its effectiveness with other emotion-fusing strategies using the ground truth emotion type label. The details of comparative results are elaborated in Sect. 5.3.

4.3   Training and Inference

For both models, we fine-tune the pre-trained encoder using task-specific training objectives. Given a document d, we compute the loss for both models by:

$$L = -\frac{1}{|d|} \sum_{i=1}^{|d|} H(\hat{y}_i, y) \tag{6}$$

where $|d|$ is the number of clauses in the document, $H(\cdot)$ is the binary cross-entropy loss function, $\hat{y}_i$ is $\hat{y}_i^{emo}$ defined by Eq. 5 in the emotion model and $\hat{y}_i^{cau}$ in the cause model, while y is the ground truth label of the clause.

During training, the two models are trained separately, and we use ground truth emotion labels to fuse emotion information in the cause extraction model. During inference, we first use the emotion model to extract emotion clauses in each document and fed each predicted emotion clause into the cause extraction model to generate emotion-aware contextual representations.

5   Experiments

5.1   Evaluation

For evaluation metrics, precison, recall and F1 defined in [8] are used. Most of previous ECPE approaches also evaluate their models on two subtasks: emotion extraction and cause extraction, yet we do this only for emotion extraction since our approach do not perform cause extraction solely.

Table 2. Comparative results of existing models and our approach. For fair comparison, if a model has an implementation based on BERT, we report the BERT-based results, and use †to mark the models that are not BERT-based

Model	Original dataset			Reconstructed dataset			Multiple pairs		
	P(%)	R(%)	F1(%)	P(%)	R(%)	F1(%)	P(%)	R(%)	F1(%)
Indep†[8]	68.32	50.82	58.18	–	–	–	–	–	–
Inter-CE†	69.02	51.35	59.01	–	–	–	–	–	–
Inter-EC†	67.21	57.05	61.28	–	–	–	–	–	–
USL [18]†	71.49	62.79	66.86	–	–	–	–	–	–
SLSN [17]†	68.36	62.91	65.45	–	–	–	–	–	–
LAE-MANN [21]	71.10	60.70	65.50	–	–	–	–	–	–
Tagging [13]	72.43	63.66	67.76	–	–	–	–	–	–
ECPE-2D [9]	72.92	65.44	68.89	–	–	–	–	–	–
RANK-CP [11]	71.19	76.30	73.60	77.89	49.90	60.69	76.88	53.96	63.15
PairGCN [19]	76.92	67.91	72.02	–	–	–	–	–	–
ECPE-MLL [12]	77.00	72.35	74.52	68.46	67.06	67.65	68.84	55.90	61.55
Ours-EmotionPrompt	**77.83**	76.01	**76.81**	71.05	**74.83**	72.85	69.62	61.85	65.19
Ours-UntypedMarker	76.27	75.83	75.96	73.78	73.30	**73.50**	70.94	**62.80**	**66.50**
w/o emotion-fusing	69.70	71.10	70.36	61.95	64.74	59.73	41.06	42.27	41.14

5.2 Experimental Settings

We implement our approach based on `Pytorch` and `Transformers` and use `bert-base-chinese` as the base encoder. For both models, we set the random seed to 42 and use Adam optimizer for training. The learning rate is 2e−5, warmup ratio is 0.1, and threshold of the multi-label output layer is 0.5. In the experiments, we follow previous works [8,9,11,13,17–19,21] to perform 10-fold cross validation and use the same data split of the original dataset.

5.3 Results and Analysis

Comparative Approaches. Most of existing ECPE works are joint models using shared context encoders, except from **Indep**, **Inter-CE** and **Inter-EC**, the three variants of the two-step pipelined models proposed by [8] that serve as the baseline. **Rank-CP** [11] and **ECPE-MLL** [12] are the two previous state-of-the-art approaches and thus we evaluate and compare the performance of these two approaches with ours on the reconstructed dataset as well as on a subset of documents that *only* contain more than one emotion-cause pair, denoted by "Multiple pairs." It should be noted that the pair selection process of the **Rank-CP** model relies on a sentiment lexicon, which may be inflexible in a wider range of application scenarios.

Main Results. Table 2 displays the comparative results. As is shown, our approach achieves state-of-the-art performance in both datasets. Our approach with EmotionPrompt and UnTypedMarker achieves an absolute F1 improvement of

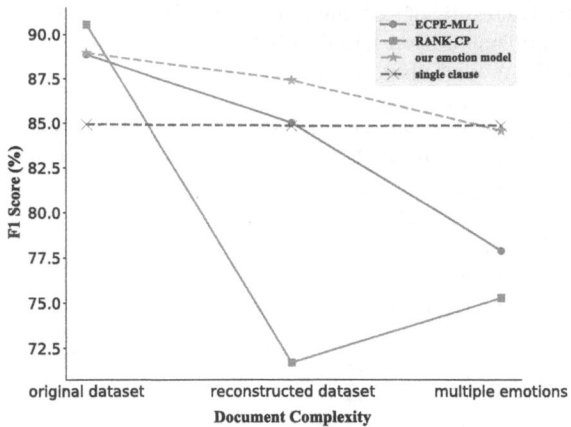

Fig. 5. Results on emotion extraction.

2.29% and 1.44% respectively over the best previous work [12] on the original dataset, and an improvement of 5.20% and 5.85% respectively over [12] on the reconstructed dataset. For the comparison of pipelined approaches, our approach outperform the baseline Inter-EC by 15.53% and 14.68% respectively.

Results on Extracting Multiple Emotion-Cause Pairs. The results show that our approach with UntypedMarker outperforms [11]'s previous work by an absolute F1 of 3.35% on extracting multiple pairs. The performance of [11]'s model increases on multiple pairs mainly because they apply the sentiment lexicon to filter candidate emotion-pairs and tend to select fewer pairs, resulting in high precision rate and low recall rate.

Importance of Emotion-Fusing. In the previous part, we attach importance to contextual representations specific to each emotion clause and fusion of emotion information at the input layer of the cause extraction model. Above results show that both emotion-fusing strategies achieve convincing results, and in order to further validate the impact of emotion-fusing, we conduct ablation experiments by removing emotion information in the cause model.

As shown in Table 2, we can observe a clear gap between our models and the model without fusion of emotion features, especially in the reconstructed dataset and on multiple emotion-cause pairs extraction. Since the classification of an emotion-cause heavily depends on the emotion it corresponds to, it is almost meaningless to perform cause extraction without emotion information, with the decline of 18.59% F1 score in extracting multiple pairs.

Results on Emotion Extraction One motivation of joint approaches in ECPE is that the performance of emotion extraction can also be improved by cause information provided during the joint training process. Indeed, we can observe from Fig. 5 that joint models outperform our model on the original dataset. In

Table 3. Comparative results of the upper bound of emotion-aware cause Extraction

Strategy	P(%)	R(%)	F1(%)
Inter-EC Bound [8]	76.10	70.84	73.28
LAE-ECE [21]	80.80	79.90	80.30
UntypedMarker	84.68	83.54	84.09
TypedMarker	85.44	**84.43**	84.92
EmotionPrompt	**85.99**	83.98	**84.95**

the reconstructed dataset, however, their performance exhibits a clear decline, and even worse in extracting multiple emotions from one document. We assume that cause information obtained via joint training does bring some benefits, but as document complexity grows, shared encoders in joint models fail to capture proper information from entangled context, and the entangled contextual representations provide more noise than benefits for the model. Comparative results between our model and single classification model demonstrate that context information encoded in $h_{[CLS]}$ benefits less as document complexity increases.

Upper Bound of Emotion-Aware Cause Extraction. We consider using emotion type information explicitly. We test the upper bound of emotion-aware cause extraction using ground truth emotion type label for each emotion clause and compare the results between different emotion-fusing strategies and other ECPE methods which also report their upper bound results.

As shown in Table 3, we observe the benefits brought by emotion type between UntypedMarker and TypedMarker, while EmotionPrompt obtains the best F1 score, indicating that it may be better to integrate emotion information through emotional text. Futhermore, there are couple of documents that exceed the max input length of BERT. We split such documents to different parts in the experiments, but text markers cannot be used if the emotion clause is located in another part of an document. Thus, for future works, we suggest the use of EmotionPrompt, which is more flexible, as the emotion-fusing strategy.

5.4   Case Study: Capture Emotion-aware Document Context

In this subsection, we discuss a specific document example in the dataset, which contains 25 clauses, 3 emotion-pairs and 2 different emotion (c7,c10). Part of the document is listed below:

..., c4: the six members of the family live on the two or three thousand Yuan Gong earns from working every month, c5: with so many children, c6: and poor conditions at home, c7: Mr.Gong was very sad. c8: What bothered him more was that, c9: because of over childbirth, c10: his child's registered permanent residence could not be solved.

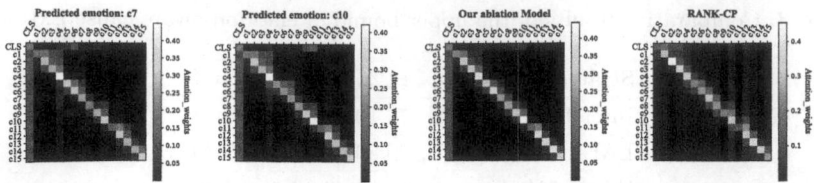

(a) Our EmotionPrompt model fused (b) RANK-CP [11] and our ablation with different emotions c7,c10 at the model without emotion fusing. input layer.

Fig. 6. Document attention heatmap produced by ECPE models for the example in Sect. 5.4. In order to make the figure more intuitive, we only select attention of the first 15 clauses.

As Fig. 6 shows, the fusion of emotion enables our model EmotionPrompt to capture proper document context information. c4 is important in finding causes for both emotions, since it clarifies the background of the document. When finding causes for c7, c5 and c6, which elaborate the concrete condition of Mr.Gong of being poor, are important. For emotion clause c10, c9 and c10 explain why Mr.Gong is "bothered."

As Fig. 6 shows, both of our ablation model and Rank-CP model fail to capture emotion-aware context, either due to the lack of emotion-guided input, or the entangled representation obtained via joint training.

6 Conclusion

In this paper, we realize another significant merit of the ECPE task, which is extracting multiple emotion-cause pairs from longer context, and find that the existing ECPE works fail to capture this merit due to bias in the benchmark dataset they are evaluated on. We reconstruct the dataset and conduct experiments on both datasets, observing that previous SOTA works of ECPE suffer from a performance drop on multiple emotion-cause pair extraction due to the use of shared context encoders. To address the problem, we present a simple but effective approach that builds on two independent context encoders. Experimental results demonstrate that our approach can learn contextual representations specific to each emotion and reaches state-of-the-art performance on both datasets, while showing robustness in extracting multiple emotion-cause pairs among more complex document context.

Acknowledgments. This research is supported by the National Natural Science Foundation of China (No. 51975294). We thank all the anonymous reviewers for their helpful advice, and we thank Weitao Li for help us build the reconstructed ECPE corpus.

References

1. Lee, S.Y., Chen, Y., Huang, C.R.: A text-driven rule-based system for emotion cause detection. In: Proceedings of the NAACL HLT Workshop on Computational Approaches to Analysis and Generation of Emotion in Text, pp. 45–53 (2010)
2. Gui, L., Wu, D., Xu, R., Lu, Q., Zhou, Y.: Event-driven emotion cause extraction with corpus construction. In: EMNLP, pp. 1639–1649 (2016)
3. Gui, L., Hu, J., He, Y., Xu, R., Lu, Q., Du, J.: A question answering approach for emotion cause extraction. In: EMNLP, pp. 1593–1602 (2017)
4. Li, X., Song, K., Feng, S., Wang, D., Zhang, Y.: A co-attention neural network model for emotion cause analysis with emotional context awareness. In: EMNLP, pp. 4752–57 (2018)
5. Xia, R., Zhang, M., Ding, Z.: RTHN: A RNN-transformer hierarchical network for emotion cause extraction. arXiv preprint arXiv:1906.01236 (2019)
6. Fan, C., et al.: A knowledge regularized hierarchical approach for emotion cause analysis. In: EMNLP, pp. 5614–5624 (2019)
7. Yan, H., Gui, L., Pergola, G., He, Y.: Position bias mitigation: a knowledge-aware graph model for emotion cause extraction. In: ACL, pp. 3364–3375 (2021)
8. Xia, R,. Ding, Z.: Emotion-cause pair extraction: a new task to emotion analysis in texts. In: ACL, pp. 1003–1012 (2019)
9. Ding, Z., Xia, R., Yu, J.: ECPE-2D: emotion-cause pair extraction based on joint two-dimensional representation, interaction and prediction. In: ACL, pp. 3161–70(2020)
10. Fan, C., Yuan, C., Du, J., Gui, L., Yang, M., Xu, R.: Transition-based directed graph construction for emotion-cause pair extraction. In: ACL, pp. 3707–3717 (2020)
11. Wei, P., Zhao, J., Mao, W.: Effective inter-clause modeling for end-to-end emotion-cause pair extraction. In: ACL, pp. 3171–3181 (2020)
12. Ding, Z., Xia, R., Yu, J.: End-to-end emotion-cause pair extraction based on sliding window multi-label learning. In: EMNLP, pp. 3574–3583 (2020)
13. Yuan, C., Fan, C., Bao, J., Xu, R.: Emotion-cause pair extraction as sequence labeling based on a novel tagging scheme. In: EMNLP, pp. 3568–3573 (2020)
14. Gao, K., Xu, H., Wang, J.: A rule-based approach to emotion cause detection for Chinese micro-blogs. Expert Syst. Appl. **42**(9), 4517–28 (2015)
15. Ghazi, D., Inkpen, D., Szpakowicz, S.: Detecting emotion stimuli in emotion-bearing sentences. In: Gelbukh, A. (ed.) CICLing 2015. LNCS, vol. 9042, pp. 152–165. Springer, Cham (2015). https://doi.org/10.1007/978-3-319-18117-2_12
16. Chen, Y., Lee, S.Y., Li, S., Huang, C.R.: Emotion cause detection with linguistic constructions. In: COLING, pp. 179–187 (2010)
17. Cheng, Z., Jiang, Z., Yin, Y., Yu, H., Gu, Q.: A symmetric local search network for emotion-cause pair extraction. In: COLING, pp. 139–149 (2020)
18. Chen, X., Li, Q., Wang, J.: A unified sequence labeling model for emotion cause pair extraction. In: COLING, pp. 208–218 (2020)
19. Chen, Y., Hou, W., Li, S., Wu, C., Zhang, X.: End-to-end emotion-cause pair extraction with graph convolutional network. In: COLING, pp. 198–207 (2020)
20. Fan, R., Wang, Y., He, T.: An end-to-end multi-task learning network with scope controller for emotion-cause pair extraction. In: Zhu, X., Zhang, M., Hong, Yu., He, R. (eds.) NLPCC 2020. LNCS (LNAI), vol. 12430, pp. 764–776. Springer, Cham (2020). https://doi.org/10.1007/978-3-030-60450-9_60

21. Tang, H., Ji, D., Zhou, Q.: Joint multi-level attentional model for emotion detection and emotion-cause pair extraction. Neurocomputing **409**, 329–340 (2020)
22. Zhong, Z., Chen, D.: A frustratingly easy approach for entity and relation extraction. In: NAACL, pp. 50–61 (2021)
23. Devlin, J., Chang, M.W., Lee, K., Toutanova, K.: BERT: pre-training of deep bidirectional transformers for language understanding. In: NAACL, pp. 4171–4186 (2019)

NLP Applications and Text Mining
(Oral)

Teaching Text Classification Models Some Common Sense via Q&A Statistics: A Light and Transplantable Approach

Hanqing Tao[1] , Guanqi Zhu[1] , Tong Xu[1,2] , Qi Liu[1,2] , and Enhong Chen[1,2(✉)]

[1] Anhui Province Key Laboratory of Big Data Analysis and Application, University of Science and Technology of China, Hefei, China
{hqtao, zgq}@mail.ustc.edu.cn
{tongxu, qiliuql, cheneh}@ustc.edu.cn
[2] School of Data Science, University of Science and Technology of China, Hefei, China

Abstract. Sociolinguistics believes that common sense is the key factor for people to ensure the robustness of language understanding and text classification in complex social environments. However, commonsense facts are often vague and implicit, and hard to be formalized or combined with current text classification techniques. As an opportunity for us, the Q&A community is a socialized platform for people to communicate knowledge, and implicit common sense can be more easily reflected by the distribution of keywords contained in Q&A data. To this end, our key insight in this paper is to obtain implicit common sense by innovatively exploiting statistical keyword distributions from annotated Q&A corpora to present a **S**tatistics-based **L**abel **I**nteractive **M**odel (SLIM) as an enhancement framework for current deep learning text classification models. Specifically, we first draw inspirations from the sociality shared by Q&A community and commonsense knowledge, and propose a light pre-classification strategy. Then, to exploit the valuable semantics of Q&A domain labels, we devise a commonsense attention module to enhance the textual representation. Afterwards, we design a label interactive attention module to make our methods transplantable to any other deep learning models and text classification datasets. Finally, extensive experiments with several deep learning text classification models on three datasets exactly verify the rationality and effectiveness of our methods.

Keywords: Text classification · Statistical learning · Deep learning · Label learning · Implicit commonsense modeling

1 Introduction

Since the inception of digital documents, automatic text classification has always been regarded as an important method and research topic for information retrieval and natural language processing [2,9]. However, traditional machine learning algorithms are less robust and transplantable in the face of complex language environments due to

---

H. Tao and G. Zhu—Equal contribution.

W. Lu et al. (Eds.): NLPCC 2022, LNAI 13551, pp. 593–605, 2022.
https://doi.org/10.1007/978-3-031-17120-8_46

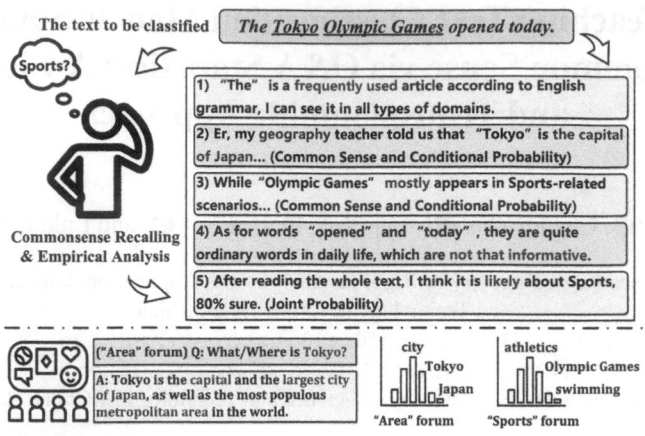

Fig. 1. The subconscious inferences in our mind during text comprehension. Meanwhile, the emergence and distribution of cumulative key words (red ones) in categorized Q&A community forums can implicitly represent human common sense. (Color figure online)

the natural lack of commonsense accumulation and judgment ability. Recently, how to introduce human commonsense knowledge into text modeling has gradually become a research hotspot [3,16].

Generally speaking, when we receive an unfamiliar text, the first reaction in our mind is usually to analyze words one by one via commonsense recalling, and then form a holistic grasp based on accumulated experience and contextual information [6,15]. As shown in Fig. 1, the toy text to be classified contains five segmented words, and each word will prompt us to form a rough empirical analysis. Here, the terms "Tokyo" nd "Olympic Games" are more informative than ordinary words like "the", which correspond to two commonsense domains respectively according to our experience. Additionally, we can also see that the empirical judgment for each word in the upper part of Fig. 1 exhibits a kind of discrete behavior, after which the whole contextual sequence analysis will enable us to further achieve a comprehensive understanding. As a rusult, we might make an oral judgement like "I am 80% sure of this text to be classified as Sports". In fact, looking into the cognitive principles behind the example, we could find *commonsense recalling*, *empirical analysis* and *sequential analysis* are three key issues for text comprehension and classification. Taking *commonsense recalling* first to say, common sense is more like a kind of implicit experience compared with systematically formalized knowledge such as math and physics [7]. It is often hard and even impractical to exactly formalize commonsense facts [12]. Thus using current information extraction techniques to obtain common sense is extremely challenging [21]. Secondly, as for why human beings can gain common sense for intelligent decisions, it is due to the continuous accumulation of conditional experience in daily life [18]. Therefore, as a methodological shift shown in Fig. 2, conditional and joint probabilities play a crucial role in our *empirical analysis*. Thirdly, current deep learning models are known for their

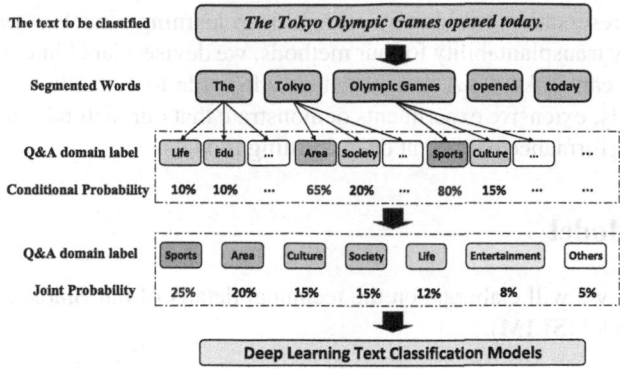

Fig. 2. The idea flow chart of using Q&A data and word frequency statistics to enhance deep learning text classification models.

strong fitting capabilities and excel in contextual characterization and *sequential analysis*, but still have obvious shortcomings in interpretability and transplantability [11]. It might be a good way if we can introduce and characterize common sense from the perspective of probabilistic statistics to conduct an interpretable statistics-based pre-classification strategy before deep learning models.

Fortunately, as an opportunity, relevant sociolinguistic studies on online Q&A communities (Question and Answering community) have proved the sociality and social characteristics of communication and transmission enjoyed by human common sense [1], among which the strict "domain-question" matching form of Q&A data includes abundant words and descriptions highly relevant to commonsense facts [14, 20]. Let's take a look at the lower part of Fig. 1 and imagine how we usually organize the language when we ask questions for help or give answers: 1) Will we include the relevant keywords in the questions and answers as comprehensively as possible? 2) Are these keywords included by questions and answers having a very obvious attribution to their commonsense domain? Without loss of generality, the answer to these two questions is of course "yes". Therefore, it is easy for us to understand that people asking questions tend to use topic-related keywords, and the words in answer are closely related to the question. Thus there is a strong attribution between the words in questions, answers and the corresponding community category labels. If fully annotated Q&A data are exploited with appropriate statistical strategies, deep learning models could be substantially enhanced with human common sense to some extent.

To address the analysis and three issues above, i.e., *commonsense recalling, empirical analysis* and *sequential analysis*, we in this paper present a **S**tatistics-based **L**abel **I**nteractive **M**odel (**SLIM**) as an enhancement framework for current deep learning text classification models, which allows them to be enhanced with improved generalization capabilities and adapted to new data distributions. Specifically, the main contribution of this paper could be summarized as follows: 1) To handle the first two issues of *commonsense recalling* and *empirical analysis*, we innovatively propose a light pre-classification strategy in the perspective of statistical learning and joint probabilistic calculations; 2) Then, to achieve a reasonable introduction of commonsense descriptions for *sequential analysis*, we design a commonsense attention module to enhance the textual representation encoded by current deep learning models; 3) Afterwards, to bring necessary transplantability for our methods, we devise a label interactive attention module which can make Q&A domain labels adaptable to concrete text classification labels. 4) Finally, extensive experiments demonstrate that our methods can substantially enhance the performance of current deep learning models.

2   SLIM Model

In this section, we will elaborate on the technical details of our **Statistics-based Label Interactive Model (SLIM)**.

2.1   Problem Definition

Text Classification. Given an arbitrary unlabeled text $T = \{x_1, x_2, ..., x_m\}$ and a pre-defined label set S containing K different labels, the goal of our task is to train and obtain a classification function $\mathcal{F}$ with the ability to assign a proper label $l \in S$ for T:

$$\mathcal{F}(T) \rightarrow l, \tag{1}$$

where $x_i \in T \ (0 \leq i \leq m)$ stands for the feature vector of the i-th token in T after text preprocessing.

Model Enhancement. Given an arbitrary deep learning model M' with the paradigm of "Encoder-Decoder", the input text T will be transformed into a vector matrix E^M:

$$E^M = M'(T), \tag{2}$$

and the goal of our task is to provide an enhancement framework M for M' so that the classification performance could be improved.

2.2   Overall Architecture of SLIM

As shown in Fig. 3, SLIM comprises two main processes (i.e., *Pre-classification* and *Enhanced Classification*), together with two modules, namely *Commonsense Attention* and *Label Interactive Attention*.

Pre-classification. As illustrated in the example of Fig. 1, whenever we receive new information or see a text, we will instinctively perform discrete analysis for each word of the text based on our experience and commonsense knowledge, thus forming a preliminary classification in mind before thoroughly analyzing the specific sentence structure and contextual information. Specifically, we formalize this *commonsense recalling* and *empirical analysis* as a *Pre-classification* process. And our *Pre-classification* modeling comprises two parts: Q&A Statistical Learning and Bayesian Classification.

1.1) Q&A Statistical Learning. In Sect. 1, we have given a thorough introduction to the sociality of common sense and the characteristics of Q&A community. Additionally,

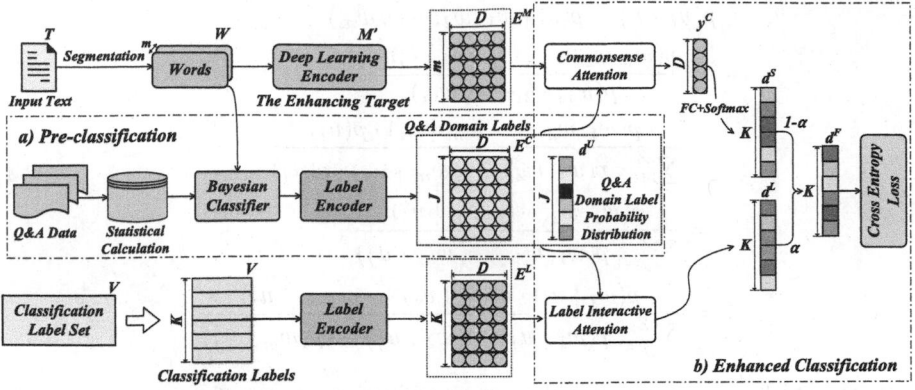

Fig. 3. The overall architecture of our **S**tatistics-based **L**abel **I**nteractive **M**odel (**SLIM**).

as depicted in the lower part of Fig. 1, we can find that Q&A data can be regarded as a subtle bridge between text and common sense, and it would be of great benefit for deep learning models if we can exploit the inherent statistical pattern between text and common sense in Q&A data.

Formally, given a large-scale fully annotated online Q&A corpus, we can obtain many Q&A texts from Z different Q&A domains, where the description text of domains (e.g., "Sports" and "Culture") are called "Domain Label" and the corresponding label set is denoted as $U = \{u_1, u_2, ..., u_Z\}$. In fact, those question texts are actually like mines with abundant keywords closely related to human common sense. Therefore, we choose to segment all questions that belong to it into words discretely, and remove all stopwords to accumulate all the keywords as a domain commonsense word set $C_u = \{c_1, c_2, ..., c_Z\}$ for each Q&A domain $u \in U$. Then, we are able to calculate the conditional probability of any words under each domain.

1.2) Bayesian Classification. Afterwards, given the segmented word sequence $W = \{w_1, w_2, ..., w_m\}$ of input text T, we can conveniently calculate the conditional probability that $w \in W$ belongs to a certain Q&A domain $u \in U$:

$$p(w \mid u) = \frac{\#N(w, u)}{\#N(u)}, \tag{3}$$

where $p(w \mid u)$ could be obtained through the word frequency of w in all the texts labeled with domain u, $\#N(w, u)$ is the number of times that word w appears in the texts labeled with u, and $\#N(u)$ is the total number of occurrences of all words in the texts labeled with u.

Then, we assume that words are conditionally independent of each other, so that each Q&A domain u_i has the same probability $p(u_i) \equiv 1/Z$ ($1 \leq i \leq Z$). Therfore, the joint probability could be calculated in the following Navïe Bayesian way:

$$p(u_i \mid T) = p(u_i \mid w_1, w_2, \cdots, w_m)$$
$$= \frac{p(w_1, w_2, \cdots, w_m \mid u_i) \cdot p(u_i)}{p(w_1, w_2, \cdots, w_m)}$$
$$= \frac{p(w_1, w_2, \cdots, w_m \mid u_i) \cdot p(u_i)}{\sum_{j=1}^{Z} p(w_1, w_2, \cdots, w_m \mid u_j) \cdot p(u_j)} \qquad (4)$$
$$= \frac{p(w_1, w_2, \cdots, w_m \mid u_i)}{\sum_{j=1}^{Z} p(w_1, w_2, \ldots, w_m \mid u_j)}$$
$$= \frac{p(w_1 \mid u_i) \cdot p(w_2 \mid u_i) \cdots p(w_m \mid u_i)}{\sum_{j=1}^{Z} p(w_1 \mid u_j) \cdot p(w_2 \mid u_j) \cdots p(w_m \mid u_j)},$$

through which we can conduct the pre-classification process for any new text by using the Q&A statistics with corresponding label probability distribution $P = \{p_1, p_2, \ldots, p_Z\}$. Then, we select the top J domain labels with the highest probability by denoting their distribution as $P' = \{p'_1, p'_2, \ldots, p'_J\}$, and renormalize their distribution to $d^U = \{d^u_1, d^u_2, \ldots, d^u_J\} \in \mathbb{R}^{1 \times J}$ to tradeoff efficiency:

$$d^u_i = \frac{p'_i}{\sum_{j=1}^{J} p'_J}, where \sum_{j=1}^{J} d^u_j = 1. \qquad (5)$$

To prevent the denominator from being zero and the problem of underflow, we apply Laplace smoothing [22] and take logarithmically for the product results of Eq. 4.

Enhanced Classification. As depicted above, Bayesian analysis can effectively imitate the cognitive process where people transition from prior probability to posterior probability after receiving new information. Meanwhile, since human language embraces important sequence characteristics, the sequence of words can often bring a change of word meaning. Therefore, *sequential analysis* of text can capture context dependencies in line with people's reading thinking process, which is also where deep learning models are good at. Therefore, after *pre-classification*, we need to further combine the advantages of the deep learning model to achieve our goal of model enhancement.

2.1) Commonsense Attention. As for reading comprehension, people usually tend to first read through the whole text to form a preliminary cognition in their minds, and then back to select and match the proper commonsense knowledge based on words of the sentence [17]. Inspired by this cognitive process, we design a *Commonsense Attention* module which can hint our model at relatively important Q&A domain labels in U back with the consideration of deep learning sequential representation E^M. Formally, we regard $E^C = \{e^c_1, e^c_2, \ldots, e^c_J\}$ as *query*, $E^M = \{e^m_1, e^m_2, \ldots, e^m_m\}$ as *key* and *value* at the same time, and the attention mechanism can be obtained as:

$$context\_vec = softmax(\frac{E^C W_C (E^M W_M)^T}{\sqrt{D}}) E^M, \qquad (6)$$

where W_C and W_M are trainable transformation matrices, D is the dimension of the representation, and $context\_vec \in \mathbb{R}^{J \times D}$ are attentive representations corresponding to each Q&A domain label. Besides, since different words of a certain text have different probability distribution $d^U = \{d_1^u, d_2^u, \ldots, d_J^u\}$ over prior Q&A domain labels, intuitively, we can get the final text representation by applying attentive weighted sum on $context\_vec = \{c_1, c_2, \ldots, c_J\}$:

$$y^C = \sum_{j=1}^{J} d_j^u c_j, where \sum_{j=1}^{J} d_j^u = 1. \tag{7}$$

Here, d_j is the j-th dimensional value of $d^U \in \mathbb{R}^{1 \times J}$, and $y^C \in \mathbb{R}^{1 \times D}$ is the commonsense fused text representation.

2.2) Label Interactive Attention. In addition to the text itself, its corresponding classification task label set reflects some real-world collective semantics. If we can semantically interact the commonsense Q&A labels with the labels of classification task, we can reasonably achieve the adaptive alignment and migration of prior information to posterior information. Hence, it is beneficial to explore the semantical correlations between commonsense knowledge and labels of texts, and regard the interactive correlations as a supplement to text sequential classification. To this end, we design a *Label Interactive Attention* module which can act as a revision to sequential classification probabilities. Formally, given a label set $V = \{l_1, l_2, \ldots, l_K\}$ containing K different labels, we manually query the semantics of each label l_i from Oxford English Dictionary [5], then using a Label Encoder to represent the textual descriptions of label set V to achieve label embedding:

$$E^L = LabelEncoder(DescQuery(V)) \\ = \{e_1^l, e_2^l, \ldots, e_K^l\}, \tag{8}$$

where V stands for the label set, K is the number of classes of V, $E^L \in \mathbb{R}^{K \times D}$ is the label embedding. Then, we regard the domain label embedding $E^C = \{e_1^c, e_2^c, \ldots, e_J^c\}$ as querys, $E^L = \{e_1^l, e_2^l, \ldots, e_K^l\}$ as keys, and do the label interactive attention as:

$$A = softmax(\frac{E^C W_C'(E^L W_L)^T}{\sqrt{D}}), \tag{9}$$

where W_C' and W_L are trainable transformation matrices, D is the dimension of the representation, $A \in \mathbb{R}^{J \times K}$ are the interactive attention weights between domain labels and text labels. Further, considering the different weights $d^U = \{d_1^u, d_2^u, \ldots, d_J^u\} \in \mathbb{R}^{1 \times J}$ of domain labels, we adopt an attentive weighted sum on A and get the commonsense supplement distribution d^L over text labels as follows:

$$d^L = d^U A = \{d_1^L, d_2^L, \ldots, d_K^L\}, where \sum_{j=1}^{K} d_j^L = 1. \tag{10}$$

3) Prediction & Loss Function. In order to systematically integrate and balance the *Commonsense Attention* and *Label Interactive Attention*, we raise a controlling parameter α to trade-off the two proposed modules:

$$d^S = softmax(Wy^C + b), \\ d^F = \alpha \times d^L + (1 - \alpha) \times d^S, \tag{11}$$

where W and b respectively denote the weight matrix and bias vector fitted by the fully-connected layer, d^S is the predicted label scores computed through the sequential representation, and d^F is the revised label scores distribution. Then, we adopt the cross-entropy loss function for training:

$$\mathcal{L} = -\sum_{i=1}^{k} y_i \log\left(d_i^F\right), \qquad (12)$$

where y is the ground truth of classification for input text T.

3   Experiments

3.1   Dataset Description

- **TNT**[1] is a public dataset which contains 287,007 texts for training and 95,664 texts for testing categorized into 15 different categories of news. Due to the large-scale of this dataset compared with FCT and CNT below, we mainly apply this dataset to evaluate the comprehensiveness of different methods.
- **FCT**[2] is an official dataset provided by Fudan University with 20 categories covering abundant academic texts for validation. The dataset contains 8,220 texts for training and 8,115 for testing with quite imbalanced samples between different classes. Therefore, we choose it to verify the robustness of different methods.
- **CNT** [24] is another public dataset covering a wide range of 32 different categories of news, which is an ideal choice for evaluating the generalization ability. Specifically, we preprocess and filter the useless text whose length is lower than 2, then get 47,693 texts for training and 15,901 for testing.

3.2   Methods of Comparison

As the aim of our work is to provide a light and transplantable framework for enhancing current deep learning text classification models, we finely select the following four representative models as the backbone of SLIM.

- **TextCNN** [10] is a classic and widely used classification model. It uses a convolutional neural network to extract underlying n-gram features through different contextual window sizes, which is good at capturing the substructure of texts.
- **ELMo** [13] is an embryonic pre-trained model inheriting the advantages of language model, which also embraces the merits of famous LSTM [8] structure. By extracting contextual features of LSTM via word masking and a bidirectional concatenation, it is able to tackle the ambiguous problem of traditional word embeddings.
- **ERNIE** [23] is a quite illuminating pre-trained model which tries to incorporate human prior concepts into pre-training. Through the strategy of unifying the mask of semantic units such as words and specific entities, this model is able to learn a generalized semantic representation of complete concepts.

---

[1] https://www.kesci.com/mw/dataset/5dd645fca0cb22002c94e65d/file.
[2] https://www.kesci.com/home/dataset/5d3a9c86cf76a600360edd04.

Table 1. Experimental results (Accuracy, Precision, Recall and F1-score) (%) of different methods on three datasets.

Methods	TNT				FCT				CNT			
	Acc	Prec	Recall	F1	Acc	Prec	Recall	F1	Acc	Prec	Recall	F1
(1) TextCNN	85.57	**81.63**	79.12	79.29	85.61	67.92	53.04	56.09	73.36	73.91	73.37	73.41
TextCNN+SLIM	**86.34**	79.96	**79.70**	**79.81**	**87.42**	**72.75**	**55.55**	**58.57**	**75.64**	**76.06**	**75.67**	**75.76**
(2) Improvement	0.77%	-1.67%	0.58%	0.52%	1.81%	4.83%	2.51%	2.48%	2.28%	2.15%	2.30%	2.35%
(3) ELMo	73.89	69.10	68.45	68.71	84.71	**79.90**	61.48	66.35	67.76	67.47	67.80	67.36
ELMo+SLIM	**79.83**	**74.28**	**73.92**	**74.07**	**87.37**	77.84	**63.98**	**68.21**	**70.73**	**71.25**	**70.69**	**70.70**
(4) Improvement	5.94%	5.18%	5.47%	5.36%	2.66%	-2.06%	2.50%	1.85%	2.97%	3.78%	2.90%	3.34%
(5) ERNIE	85.64	79.46	79.21	79.32	90.60	85.39	68.85	73.59	79.83	80.41	79.78	79.81
ERNIE+SLIM	**87.13**	**80.72**	**80.69**	**80.69**	**92.46**	**87.06**	**73.79**	**78.20**	**82.04**	**82.16**	**82.04**	**82.04**
(6) Improvement	1.49%	1.25%	1.48%	1.37%	1.86%	1.67%	4.94%	4.61%	2.21%	1.76%	2.26%	2.24%
(7) BERT	86.34	80.24	79.97	80.09	91.49	85.60	74.03	78.26	81.93	82.48	81.88	81.91
BERT+SLIM	**87.46**	**81.04**	**81.09**	**81.05**	**92.96**	**87.20**	**74.78**	**79.13**	**82.74**	**82.90**	**82.74**	**82.75**
(8) Improvement	1.12%	0.80%	1.12%	0.96%	1.48%	1.60%	0.75%	0.87%	0.81%	0.41%	0.86%	0.84%

Table 2. Average improvement of different datasets over all baselines under the enhancement of our SLIM framework.

Dataset	Accuracy	Precision	Recall	F1-score
(1) TNT	2.33%	1.39%	2.16%	2.05%
(2) FCT	1.95%	1.51%	2.68%	2.45%
(3) CNT	2.07%	2.03%	2.08%	2.19%

- **BERT** [4] stands for the current state-of-the-art pre-trained model for natural language processing. It applies a transformer-based framework [19] to replace traditional recurrent neural networks and LSTM units, which is more efficient in capturing long-range textual dependencies.

3.3 Experimental Results

The comparative performance of our proposed framework for enhancing the baseline deep learning predictors are listed in Table 1. As a holistic observation, we can find those deep learning baselines have gained a consistent improvement when equipped with SLIM, demonstrating the macroscopic effectiveness of our method. The reasons why SLIM-enhanced classification models are able to achieve better performance could be concluded into several aspects: 1) In fact, our SLIM framework plays a light auxiliary role which fully absorbs the advantages of statistical learning and deep learning. The ability of SLIM to be aware of informative Q&A data allows deep learning models to form a preliminary statistical cognition of common sense through *pre-classification*; 2) The *commonsense attention* module regards Q&A domain label as a kind of commonsense knowledge, which can filter out low-weight information and enable SLIM to substantially enrich the sequential representation of deep learning models; 3) As the basis for the transplantability of SLIM, the *label interactive attention* module allows prior Q&A domain labels to form a good semantic alignment with any classification dataset labels.

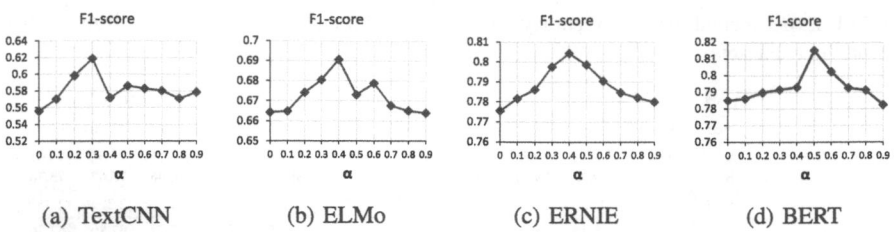

(a) TextCNN   (b) ELMo   (c) ERNIE   (d) BERT

Fig. 4. Performance of different deep learning models under the enhancement of SLIM when hyperparameter α is ranging from 0 to 1 ($\alpha \in [0, 1)$). Thereinto, $\alpha = 0$ means the ablation of label interactive attention module.

For specific models comparison, we notice that the overall performance (F1-score) of ERNIE and BERT is much better than that of TextCNN and ELMo. The main reason is that models other than ERNIE and BERT do not have access to transformer-based structures and the word-word relational information [19], which is very crucial for comprehensive semantic modeling. At the same time, TextCNN gives better performance compared to ELMo on TNT and CNT datasets, but ELMo beats TextCNN by a large margin on the FCT dataset in reverse. For this extraordinary phenomenon, we delve into the characteristics of each dataset and report the average improvement of different datasets over all baselines under the enhancement of SLIM, which is shown in Table 2. As we can see, the improvement over FCT dataset is the most salient (2.68% for Recall and 2.45% for F1-score). Taking the aforementioned *Dataset Description* also into account, we can know that the FCT dataset suffers more from data imbalance and limited scale compared with the other two datasets, therefore TextCNN becomes more vulnerable than ELMo due to its inability of pre-training. Nevertheless, the significant boosting on three datasets brought by SLIM indicates that the ability to be aware of language statistics and human common sense is very beneficial for overcoming the defects of certain datasets. That is to say, under the enhancement of SLIM, baseline deep learning models can effectively maintain robustness when faced with tough datasets.

As a summary, all the results and analysis could substantiate the effectiveness of incorporating statistical information and the proposed attention mechanism in our SLIM framework, where a proper way of formalizing commonsense knowledge can indeed illuminate existing models.

3.4   Hyperparameter Study, Ablation Analysis and Visualization

For the aim of assessing the importance of α in the process of *Enhanced Classification*, we conduct a hyperparameter study in this section. Specifically, we can manipulate the value of α from 0 to 1 to see how it affects the final performance of each deep learning model. Since the primary classification effect of baseline deep learning models will completely disappear when $\alpha = 1$, and $\alpha = 0$ means the ablation of label interactive attention module, therefore we have $\alpha \in [0, 1)$. It should be noted here that the removal of commonsense attention module equals to remove the label interactive attention simultaneously, so that $\alpha = 0$ corresponds to the only ablation variant for SLIM.

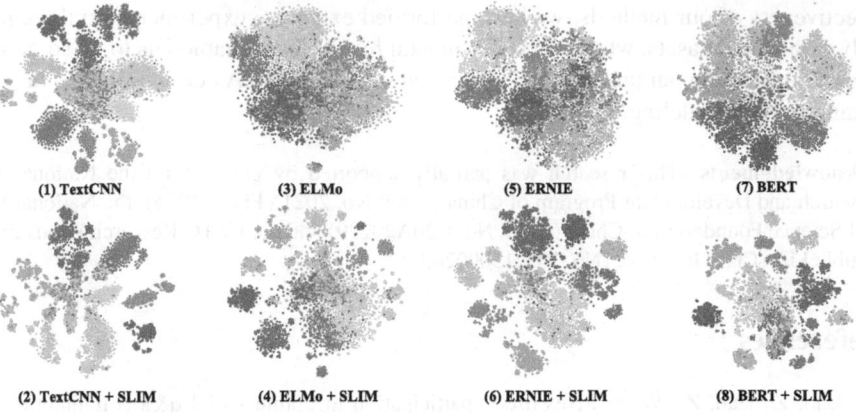

(1) TextCNN   (3) ELMo   (5) ERNIE   (7) BERT

(2) TextCNN + SLIM   (4) ELMo + SLIM   (6) ERNIE + SLIM   (8) BERT + SLIM

Fig. 5. The t-SNE visualization of different methods on testing documents.

Without loss of generality and ensuring the consistency of subsequent case study and visualization, we select a moderate dataset FCT here to examine the effect of hyper-parameter α. And the F1-score results of adjusting α on the FCT dataset are shown in Fig. 4. From the curves of four subfigures, we can draw the following conclusions: First, it is clear that there is a consistent changing trend of performance rising first and then falling, rather than invariant when α increases from 0 to 1. At the same time, the best performance corresponds to a value range of $\alpha \in [0.3, 0.5]$, which indicates that the proposed label interactive attention module can exactly yield positive effects, and a proper combination ratio between two modeling parts (i.e., d^S and d^L) is beneficial for achieving better classification performance. Second, we can find that when the value of α equals 0, the comprehensive performance of each deep learning model (F1-score) becomes either mediocre or the worst. This phenomenon is due to the ablation of the label interactive attention module for the integration of Q&A domain labels and real dataset labels, which proves the necessity and effectiveness of our methods. As a visual analysis of the classification results, we also conduct a t-SNE visualization of different methods in Fig. 5, from which we can find that our SLIM framework can enable baseline models to better distinguish texts between different classes.

4   Conclusion

In this paper, we drew inspirations from people's cognitive principles of text reading comprehension to propose a Statistics-based Label Interactive Model (SLIM) for improved text classification. As a methodological shift compared with other explicit commonsense modeling approaches like knowledge graphs, we provided a novel insight to exploit the label semantics and vocabulary statistics accumulated in the corresponding Q&A community domains. Specifically, SLIM comprises two main processes (i.e., *Pre-classification* and *Enhanced Classification*), together with two modules, namely *Commonsense Attention* and *Label Interactive Attention*. To validate the design and effectiveness of our methods, we have performed extensive experiments on three publicly available datasets, where the experimental results have enabled us to go some way towards enhancing our understanding between socialized Q&A community and implicit commonsense modeling.

Acknowledgments. This research was partially supported by grants from the National Key Research and Development Program of China (Grant No. 2021YFF0901005), the National Natural Science Foundation of China (Grant No. U20A20229) and the USTC Research Funds of the Double First-Class Initiative (No. YD2150002009).

References

1. Bao, Z., Han, Z.: What drives users' participation in online social q&a communities? an empirical study based on social cognitive theory. Aslib J. Inf. Manag. **71**, 637–656 (2019)
2. Cunha, W., et al.: On the cost-effectiveness of neural and non-neural approaches and representations for text classification: a comprehensive comparative study. Inf. Process. Manage. **58**(3), 102481 (2021)
3. Davison, J., Feldman, J., Rush, A.M.: Commonsense knowledge mining from pretrained models. In: Proceedings of the 2019 Conference on Empirical Methods in Natural Language Processing and the 9th International Joint Conference on Natural Language Processing (EMNLP-IJCNLP), pp. 1173–1178 (2019)
4. Devlin, J., Chang, M.W., Lee, K., Toutanova, K.: Bert: pre-training of deep bidirectional transformers for language understanding. In: Proceedings of the 2019 Conference of the North American Chapter of the Association for Computational Linguistics: Human Language Technologies, Volume 1 (Long and Short Papers), pp. 4171–4186 (2019)
5. Weiner, J.A., Simpson, E.S.C.: Oxford English Dictionary (1989)
6. Fischbein, E.: Intuition and proof. Learn. Math. **3**(2), 9–24 (1982)
7. Hammer, D.: Epistemological beliefs in introductory physics. Cogn. Instr. **12**(2), 151–183 (1994)
8. Hochreiter, S., Schmidhuber, J.: Long short-term memory. Neural Comput. **9**(8), 1735–1780 (1997)
9. Hotho, A., Nürnberger, A., Paaß, G.: A brief survey of text mining. In: LDV Forum. vol. 20, pp. 19–62. Citeseer (2005)
10. Kim, Y.: Convolutional neural networks for sentence classification. In: Proceedings of the 2014 Conference on Empirical Methods in Natural Language Processing (EMNLP), pp. 1746–1751. Association for Computational Linguistics (2014)
11. Linardatos, P., Papastefanopoulos, V., Kotsiantis, S.: Explainable AI: a review of machine learning interpretability methods. Entropy **23**(1), 18 (2021)
12. McCarthy, J.: Circumscription-a form of non-monotonic reasoning. Artif. Intell. **13**(1–2), 27–39 (1980)
13. Peters, M., et al.: Deep contextualized word representations. In: Proceedings of the 2018 Conference of the North American Chapter of the Association for Computational Linguistics: Human Language Technologies, Volume 1 (Long Papers), pp. 2227–2237 (2018)
14. Rajagopal, D., Olsher, D., Cambria, E., Kwok, K.: Commonsense-based topic modeling. In: Proceedings of the Second International Workshop on Issues of Sentiment Discovery and Opinion Mining, pp. 1–8 (2013)
15. Sap, M., Horvitz, E., Choi, Y., Smith, N.A., Pennebaker, J.W.: Recollection versus imagination: exploring human memory and cognition via neural language models. In: Association for Computational Linguistics (2020)

16. Singh, P., et al.: The public acquisition of commonsense knowledge. In: Proceedings of AAAI Spring Symposium: Acquiring (and Using) Linguistic (and World) Knowledge for Information Access (2002)

17. Taatgen, N.A., Van Rijn, H., Anderson, J.: An integrated theory of prospective time interval estimation: the role of cognition, attention, and learning. Psychol. Rev. **114**(3), 577 (2007)

18. Tenenbaum, J.B., Kemp, C., Griffiths, T.L., Goodman, N.D.: How to grow a mind: statistics, structure, and abstraction. Science **331**(6022), 1279–1285 (2011)

19. Vaswani, A., et al.: Attention is all you need. In: Advances in Neural Information Processing Systems, pp. 5998–6008 (2017)

20. Xin, Y., Lieberman, H., Chin, P.: Patchcomm: using commonsense knowledge to guide syntactic parsers. In: Proceedings of the International Conference on Principles of Knowledge Representation and Reasoning, vol. 18, pp. 712–716 (2021)

21. Yatskar, M., Ordonez, V., Farhadi, A.: Stating the obvious: extracting visual common sense knowledge. In: Proceedings of the 2016 Conference of the North American Chapter of the Association for Computational Linguistics: Human Language Technologies, pp. 193–198 (2016)

22. Yuan, Q., Cong, G., Thalmann, N.M.: Enhancing Naive Bayes with various smoothing methods for short text classification. In: Proceedings of the 21st International Conference on World Wide Web, pp. 645–646 (2012)

23. Zhang, Z., Han, X., Liu, Z., Jiang, X., Sun, M., Liu, Q.: Ernie: enhanced language representation with informative entities. In: Proceedings of the 57th Annual Meeting of the Association for Computational Linguistics, pp. 1441–1451 (2019)

24. Zhou, Y., Xu, B., Xu, J., Yang, L., Li, C.: Compositional recurrent neural networks for Chinese short text classification. In: 2016 IEEE/WIC/ACM International Conference on Web Intelligence (WI), pp. 137–144. IEEE (2016)

Generative Text Steganography via Multiple Social Network Channels Based on Transformers

Long Yu[1,2], Yuliang Lu[1,2](✉), Xuehu Yan[1,2](✉), and Xianhui Wang[1,2]

[1] National University of Defense Technology, Hefei 230037, China
publicLuYL@126.com, publictiger@126.com
[2] Anhui Province Key Laboratory of Cyberspace Security Situation Awareness and Evaluation, Hefei 230037, China

Abstract. Generative text steganography uses the conditional probability to encode the candidate words when generating tokens by language model, and then selects the corresponding word to output according to the secret message to be embedded, so as to generate stego text. The complex and open characteristics of social network provide a good camouflage environment for the transmission of stego texts, but also bring challenges: transmitting stego text through a single channel is easy to cause the destruction and loss of secret message; the speech of each social account needs to be combined with its background knowledge, so it has different language features. The existing text steganography schemes cannot solve these problems well. This paper proposes a multi-channel generative text steganography scheme in the context of social network, which hides secret message into multiple semantically natural texts, even if only a part of which can reconstruct secret message. Combined with the characteristics of social network, the bag-of-words models are used to control the topics of the stego texts in the process of text generation by language model. Two goal programming models are proposed to optimize the topic relevance and text quality of stego text. The experiment verifies the effectiveness of this scheme.

Keywords: Text steganography · Controllable text generation · Loss tolerance · Robustness · Imperceptibility

1 Introduction

With the wide development and application of the Internet and social network, digital information is easy to obtain, transmit and operate. Therefore, it is essential to protect sensitive information from malicious interference transmitting in public channels. Shannon [13] summarized three basic information security systems, namely, encryption system, privacy system and concealment system. The main purpose of encryption system is to protect the security of confidential message itself and privacy system aims to control access to confidential message.

The concealment system hides confidential message into normal carriers and transmits them through open channels, paying attention to the protection of the existence of confidential message.

Steganography is a key technology of concealment system, which mainly studies how to embed secret information into carrier efficiently and safely. According to the different carrier types, steganography can be divided into image steganography [5], text steganography [7], audio steganography [10] and video steganography [8]. As the primary way of human communication from ancient times to the present, text has a wide range of application scenarios. And the transmission of text in the public channel is robust, because general channel doesn't compress it or interfere with it by noise. These show that texts may be more suitable as carriers for data transmission in social network than images, videos or other carriers.

Generative text steganography uses the language model (LM) to automatically generate stego text. It encodes the text semantic unit in the generation process, and selects the corresponding unit to output according to the secret message to be embedded, so as to realize the embedding of secret message. Therefore, the steganographer has greater freedom in the process of embedding message, so that a high information embedding rate can be expected. Yang et al. [17] proposed fix-length coding (FLC) based on perfect binary tree and variable-length coding (VLC) based on Huffman tree. They encode the Top-K words in the candidate pool predicted by the language model at each moment according to the conditional probability. Xiang et al. [16] modeled natural sentences as letter sequences and used the Char-RNN model to obtain letter-level conditional probability distributions. Zhou et al. [19] adopted an adversarial generative network model for steganographic text generation, and changed the construction method of candidate pool based on Top-K to dynamic candidate pool construction. However, the above schemes only consider the transmission of secret message through a single channel, and cannot effectively control semantic characteristics such as the topic of stego text.

The complex and open characteristics of social network provide a good camouflage environment for the transmission of stego texts, but also bring challenges. Since social networks are public channels, and each social platform is supervised by staff, if they find an account with abnormal behavior, it is likely to take measures to delete or ban the account. The transmission of stegotext through a single channel will result in the loss of secret message if the above situation is encountered. The (k, n) threshold secret sharing (SS) technology satisfies the characteristics of both encryption system and privacy system, which encrypts a secret message into n shares and distributes them. Any k shares can restore the original secret message, while less than k can obtain nothing. The loss-tolerant property of SS creates conditions for multi-channel transmission of secret message. Each social account has its own field of interest, professional direction and other backgrounds, thus possessing different language characteristics. If the semantics of the generated stego text can be effectively controlled in combination with the characteristics of social accounts, the concealment and security of covert communication through social network can be further improved. Controllable text generation (CTG) controls the characteristics of text, such as mood, style, etc., on the premise of ensuring the content [2, 4, 18]. CTG can model

$p(x|\alpha)$, where α is some expected controllable attribute, and x is the generated sample. Combining the characteristics of different social accounts to control the topics of each stego texts in the process of generation, the steganography scheme can be more suitable for application scenarios in the social network environment.

This paper proposes a multi-channel generative text steganography scheme with loss tolerance, robustness and imperceptibility in social network scenarios, which uses secret sharing technology to encrypt secret message into multiple shares, then the candidate words are encoded in the process of generation by a controlled language model, and the corresponding words output are selected according to the shares, so as to generate multiple topic-controlled stegotexts. We summarize the motivations and contributions of this paper as follows:

- Facing the challenge that the existing text steganography scheme only considers covert communication through a single channel, which can easily lead to the destruction or lost of stego text, this paper proposes to use the secret sharing technology to hide the secret message into multiple stego texts, and the original secret message can be recovered by only a part of them.
- In view of the characteristics of social network users' speech based on different backgrounds, this paper proposes to control the topics of the generated stego texts through bag of words (BoW), so that stego texts has stronger concealment.
- This paper proposes two goal programming models, which can optimize the topic relevance and text quality of stego text respectively.

2 Preliminaries and Related Work

2.1 Generative Text Steganography

In the field of natural language processing, text is usually regarded as a word sequence composed of specific words according to semantic association and syntactic rules, and the chain rule is used to describe the language model probability of the joint probability distribution of word sequences [1,9], whose expression is:

$$
\begin{aligned}
P(X) &= P(x_1, x_2, \ldots, x_N) \\
&= P(x_1)P(x_2|x_1) \cdots P(x_N|x_1 x_2 \cdots x_{N-1}) \\
&= \prod_1^N P(x_i|x_1 x_2 \cdots x_{i-1})
\end{aligned}
\tag{1}
$$

where $P(X)$ represents the generation probability of the word sequence $x_1, x_2, \cdots, x_N$, and $P(x_N|x_1 x_2 \cdots x_{N-1})$ denotes the conditional probability of generating word x_N given $x_1 x_2 \cdots x_{N-1}$ above. Due to the diversity of language expressions, for a given $x_1 x_2 \cdots x_{N-1}$, there will usually be more than one candidate x_N, which can make the generated text meet the constraints of semantic and syntactic rules. This provides redundancy for generative information hiding.

Yang et al. [17] proposed to use fixed length coding (FLC) based on a perfect binary tree with height h to encode the words in the candidate pool to achieve the mapping of secret bits to the word space. In the FLC scheme, the prefix text is input into LM to get the candidate words and their probability distribution for the next time step. Then, the candidate pool is truncated to 2^h in descending order of probability, and the candidate words are encoded by perfect binary tree, so that the corresponding words can be selected according to the secret bits to be embedded.

Perplexity (ppl) is usually used as the quality evaluation metric for generated text [6], as shown in Eq. 2.

$$ppl = P(x_1, x_2, \cdots, x_N)^{-\frac{1}{N}}$$
$$= \sqrt[N]{\prod_{i=1}^{N} \frac{1}{P(x_i|x_1, x_2, \cdots, x_{i-1})}} \tag{2}$$

from which we can see that the higher the conditional probability of the word sequence, the lower the perplexity, and the higher the quality.

2.2   Shamir's Polynomial-Based SS

Shamir's polynomial-based SS [12] for (k, n) threshold generates secret data m into n shares based on a $(k-1)$-degree polynomial as Eq. 3, in which $a_0 = m$, and $a_1, a_2, \cdots, a_{k-1}$ are assigned randomly in $[0, p-1]$ and p is a prime number greater than a_0. All modulo operations are performed in a galois field of $GF(p)$.

$$f(x) = (a_0 + a_1 x + \cdots + a_{k-1} x^{k-1}) \bmod p \tag{3}$$

In the sharing phase, given n different random x, we can obtain n shared values by calculating $s_1 = f(x_1), s_2 = f(x_2), \cdots, s_n = f(x_n)$ and take (x_i, s_i) as a secret pair. These n pairs are distributed to n participants. Without loss of generality, x is often taken as $1, 2, \cdots, n$.

In the recovery phase, given any k pairs of $(x_i, s_i)|_{i=1}^{n}$, we can obtain the coefficients of $f(x)$ by Lagrange interpolation as shown in Eq. 4, and then $m = f(0)$.

$$f(x) = \sum_{j=1}^{k} f(i_j) \prod_{\substack{l=1 \\ l \neq j}}^{k} \frac{(x - i_l)}{(i_j - i_l)} \tag{4}$$

In this paper, we put l secret values into $a_i|_{i=0}^{l-1}$, and $a_i|_{i=l}^{k-1}$ are selected in $[0, p-1]$, which can effectively improve the efficiency of information hiding.

2.3   Transformer-Based Controllable Text Generation

Controllable text generation is based on the traditional text generation, adding the control of some attributes, styles, key information of the generated text, so that the generated text can meet our expectations.

Dathathri et al. proposed PPLM to [3] sample from the resulting $P(x|\alpha) \propto P(\alpha|x)P(x)$, and use a transformer [14] to model the distribution of natural language, thus effectively creates a conditional generative model. The following describes the principle of transformer and PPLM. The recurrent interpretation of a transformer [15] can be summarized as Eq. 5.

$$o_{t+1}, H_{t+1} = \text{LM}(x_t, H_t) \tag{5}$$

where H_t is the history matrix consisting of key-value pairs from the past time-steps 0 to t. Then the x_{t+1} is sampled as $x_{t+1} \sim P_{t+1} = \text{Softmax}(To_{t+1})$, where T is a linear transformation that maps the logit vector o_{t+1} to a vector of vocabulary size.

The probability distribution of words in the candidate pool at the next time step can be changed by adjusting H_t so that the probability of more relevant words to the topic is higher. Let ΔH_t be the update to H_t, generation with $(H_t + \Delta H_t)$ shifts the distribution of the generated text such that it is more likely to possess the desired attribute. ΔH_t is initialized at zero and PPLM rewrite the attribute model $P(\alpha|x)$ as $P(\alpha|H_t + \Delta H_t)$ and then make gradient based updates to ΔH_t as follows:

$$\Delta H_t \leftarrow \Delta H_t + \beta \frac{\nabla_{\Delta H_t} \log P(\alpha|H_t + \Delta H_t)}{\|\nabla_{\Delta H_t} \log P(\alpha|H_t + \Delta H_t)\|^{\gamma}} \tag{6}$$

where β is the step size, γ is the scaling coefficient for the normalization term. This update step can be repeated m times; in practice $m = 3$ to 10. Subsequently, a forward pass through the LM is performed to obtain the updated logits $\tilde{o}_{t+1}$ as $\tilde{o}_{t+1}, H_{t+1} = \text{LM}(x_t, \tilde{H}_t)$, where $\tilde{H}_t = H_t + \Delta H_t$. The modified $\tilde{o}_{t+1}$ is then used to generate the new probability distribution $\tilde{P}_{t+1}$ at time step $t + 1$.

3 The Proposed Scheme

3.1 Information Hiding Algorithm

The schematic diagram of the hiding phase is shown in Fig. 1, where we take $h = 2$, $l = 1$ as an example, h is the height of perfect binary tree and l is the number of secret values to hide one time. We choose the smallest prime number greater than 2^h as p. First we slice secret bitstream in several units per h bits and convert these units into secret values in decimal integer form. Then we construct a $(k-1)-$degree polynomial as Eq. 3, and put l secret values in $a_0, a_1, \cdots, a_{l-1}$, the rest $k - l$ coefficients take values in the range $[0, p - 1]$. Then the secret sharing module substitutes $x_i|_{i=1}^n$ into the polynomial to get n shared values $s_i|_{i=1}^n$. The mapping module uses the language model to continuously generate text, and modifies the probability distribution of each time step through BoW corresponding to a specific topic, so that the more topic compatible words in the candidate pool has the greater probability. Then perfect binary tree coding is carried out for the candidate words, corresponding words are selected according to the shared values and put into the stego text. All of the above processes are guided by the goal programming model (GPM).

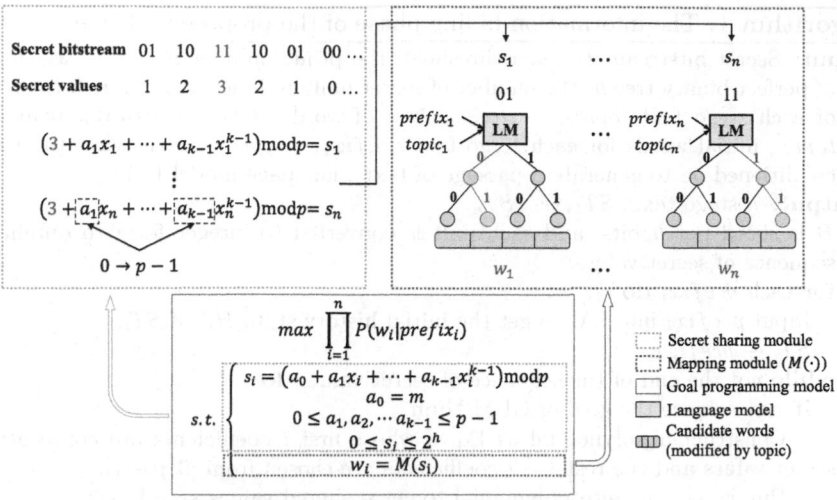

Fig. 1. The schematic diagram of the hiding phase.

The attribute model used in this scheme is the BoWs corresponding to different topics. A BoW is a set of keywords $\{word_1, \cdots, word_z\}$ that specify a topic. $\log P(\alpha|x)$ can be represented as Eq. 7.

$$\log P(\alpha|x) = \log(\sum_i^z P_{t+1}[word_i]) \tag{7}$$

where P_{t+1} is the conditional probability distribution of the output of the language model at moment $t + 1$. We can calculate ΔH_t by Eq. 6 to modify H_t and finally obtain the conditional probability distribution $\tilde{P}_{t+1}$ that satisfies the particular topic.

We propose two goal programming models (GPM-topic and GPM-ppl) to optimize the topic relevance and text quality of the generated stego texts for different applications, respectively. GPM-topic is expressed as Eq. 8.

$$\max \prod_{i=1}^n \tilde{P}(w_i|prefix_i)$$

$$s.t. \begin{cases} s_i = (a_0 + a_1 x_i + \cdots + a_{k-1}x_i^{k-1}) \bmod p \\ a_i = m_i|_{i=0}^{l-1} \\ 0 \leq a_l, a_{l+1}, \cdots, a_{k-1} \leq p - 1 \\ 0 \leq s_i \leq 2^h \\ w_i = M(s_i) \end{cases} \tag{8}$$

where $\tilde{P}(w_i|prefix_i)$ represents the conditional probability of generating the next word w_i when the prior words $prefix_i$ of the i-th stego text is determined, $\tilde{P}$ is modified by BoW_i to make the word probability more relevant to $topic_i$, and

---

Algorithm 1. The information hiding phase of the proposed scheme.

Input: Secret bitstream B; (k, n)threshold; the prime number p; $x_1, \cdots, x_n$; height of perfect binary tree h; the number of secret units to hide at one time l; the topics of each stego text $topic_1, \cdots, topic_n$; bag of words $BoW_1, \cdots, BoW_n$ related to $topic_i$; initial words for each stego text $prefix_1, \cdots, prefix_n$ (is what the LM is conditioned on to generate a passage of text); language model LM.

Output: n stego texts $ST_1, \cdots, ST_n$.

1: B is sliced per h bits, and each unit is converted to integer form to obtain the sequence of secret values;

2: **for** each $prefix_i$ **do**

3:     Input $prefix_i$ into LM to get the initial history state H_t^i of ST_i;

4:     $ST_i \leftarrow prefix_i$;

5: **while** not the end of the sequence of secret values **do**

6:     **if not** achieve the goal of GPM **then**

7:         Construct a polynomial as Eq. 3, whose first l coefficients are consecutive l secret values and the rest $k - l$ coefficients are chosen from $[0, p - 1]$;

8:         Put $x_1, \cdots, x_n$ into polynomial to get n shared values $s_1, \cdots, s_n$;

9:         **for** each s_i **do**

10:             According to BoW_i, using Eq. 6 and Eq. 7 to obtain ΔH_t^i, then we can get the history status $\tilde{H}_t^i \leftarrow H_t^i + \Delta H_t^i$ at this moment modified by $topic_i$;

11:             Input $\tilde{H}_t^i$ and the last word of ST_i into LM to get the modified logits $\tilde{o}_{t+1}$, and softmax $\tilde{o}_{t+1}$ to get the conditional probability distribution $\tilde{P}_{t+1}$ that fits the $topic_i$ at time $t + 1$, then arrange $\tilde{P}_{t+1}$ in descending order, and take the first 2^h words to form the candidate pool;

12:             The words in the candidate pool are encoded by a perfect binary tree, and the corresponding word w_i is selected based on the shared value s_i;

13:     **else**

14:         Add w_i to ST_i;

15: **return** $ST_1, \cdots, ST_n$

$m_i|_{i=0}^{l-1}$ are the consecutive l secret values. $M(\cdot)$ represents the mapping module that maps the shared value s_i through perfect binary tree encoding to the LM-generated word space. Since we choose to put the secret values in the first l coefficients of Eq. 3, the remaining $k - l$ elements are selected from $[0, p - 1]$, which makes the shared values not unique for the same set of secret values. So we can get different combinations of words to output by constantly adjusting the last $k - l$ coefficients of the polynomial. The goal in GPM-topic is to take advantage of this to find the word combination with the largest conditional probability product, i.e., the combination with the strongest relevance to their respective topics, in order to generate more appropriate stego texts. Since the size of the candidate pool is smaller than p, and the operations of SS are all under $GF(p)$, the value range of s_i is $[0, p - 1]$ if no control is applied, so the selection of words will be out of the range of the candidate pool. Therefore, we limit the value of s_i in the constraints of GPM, which can be also achieved by adjusting the $k - l$ coefficients of the polynomial.

Algorithm 2. The information extraction phase of the proposed scheme.

Input: k stego texts $ST_1, \cdots, ST_k$; $x_1, \cdots, x_k$; height of perfect binary tree h; the number of secret units to hide at one time l; the topics of each stego text $topic_1, \cdots, topic_k$; bag of words $BoW_1, \cdots, BoW_k$ related to $topic_i$; language model LM.

Output: Original secret bitstream B.

1: **for** each stego text ST_i **do**
2:      Input the prefix in ST_i into LM to get the original initial history state H_t;
3:      **while** not the end of ST_i **do**
4:          According to BoW_i, using Eq. 6 and Eq. 7 to obtain ΔH_t, then we can get the history status $\tilde{H}_t \leftarrow H_t + \Delta H_t$ at this moment modified by $topic_i$;
5:          Input $\tilde{H}_t$ and the last word of ST_i into LM to get the modified logits $\tilde{o}_{t+1}$, and softmax $\tilde{o}_{t+1}$ to get the conditional probability distribution $\tilde{P}_{t+1}$ that fits the $topic_i$ at time $t+1$, then arrange $\tilde{P}_{t+1}$ in descending order, and take the first 2^h words to form the candidate pool;
6:          Use a perfect binary tree to encode the words in the candidate pool, the codeword corresponding to x_{t+1} is extracted and converted into integer form, then the shared value s_i is obtained, which is then added to $Shares_i$;
7: **for** each s_i in each $Shares_i$ **do**
8:      Put k pairs $(x_i, s_i)|_{i=1}^k$ into Eq. 4, then we can recover a $(k-1)-$degree polynomial, whose first l coefficients are the consecutive l secret values, add them to the secret value sequence;
9: Each integer in the sequence of secret values is converted into the binary form of h bits, then the original secret bitstream B is obtained;
10: **return** B

In the mapping module, we modify the original probability distribution P_{t+1} by using BoW to obtain $\tilde{P}_{t+1}$ with a higher probability of fitting the topic. However, the language model uses a large amount of natural texts for training to fit the natural language distribution, and modifying it will affect the quality of the generated text, which is the cost of enhancing the relevance of the text topic. Inspired by Eq. 2, we propose GPM-ppl to improve the quality of stego text. The form of GPM-ppl is consistent with Eq. 8, except that the modified probability $\tilde{P}$ in the goal is replaced by the original probability distribution P obtained by LM. Therefore, we can find the word combination with the largest original probability product while satisfying the constraints, so that each word and its previous words are closer to the original distribution, thus reducing the perplexity and improving the quality of stego text. But at the same time, this reduces the likelihood of selecting words that match the topic, which inevitably reduces the topic relevance of stego text. Therefore, the choice of GPM should be determined according to the requirements of actual application scenarios.

Algorithm details of the proposed hiding method are shown in Algorithm 1.

3.2 Information Extraction Algorithm

When k or more stego texts are obtained, the extraction of secret message can be performed. The inverse mapping module generates the conditional probability distribution of the next word through the same text generation method as the hiding phase and encodes the candidate pool using a perfect binary tree. Because stego texts are deterministic, there is no need to select candidate words similar to the sampling strategy in the hiding phase, but to find the corresponding codewords to get the shared values. After that, the reconstruct module can recover a polynomial with the shared values using Eq. 4, whose first l coefficients are secret values. Algorithm 2 shows the detailed process of extraction. For the convenience of representation and without loss of generality, we assume that the k stego texts obtained are the first k of the n stego texts.

4   Experiments and Ablation Study

4.1   Experimental Setup

We evaluate the performance of the proposed scheme on a public corpora "A Million News Headlines", which contains 1,226,259 sentences on news headlines published by the Australian news source ABC (Australian Broadcasting Corporation) over an eighteen-year period. We randomly select 100 sentences from the dataset for experiments. We use the 345M parameter GPT-2 model [11] based on the transformer architecture as the text generation model.

To evaluate the quality of stego text we use the perplexity as Eq. 2. For topic relevance, there is no good evaluation index in the current study. Since the purpose of topic control is achieved by BoW adjusting the conditional probability distribution, we decide to use the percentage of words in the stego text belonging to BoW_i to evaluate the topic relevance (TR) with $topic_i$, as shown in Eq. 9.

$$TR_i = \frac{N_{BOW_i}}{N} \times 100\% \tag{9}$$

where TR_i represents the topic relevance of ST_i related to $topic_i$, N is the number of words in ST_i, and N_{BOW_i} represents the number of words in ST_i that appear in BoW_i.

4.2   Effectiveness Demonstration

The hyperparameters of the proposed scheme include (k, n) threshold, the prime number p; the number of secret values to hide at one time l, the topic of each stego text $topic_i$, the height of the perfect binary tree h, and the initial words of each stego text $prefix_i$. Below we show the actual effect of the proposed scheme when these parameters are taken at different values, as shown in Tables 1 and 2. We choose "Secret message" as the secret text. The target topics of stego texts are colored and bracketed (e.g. [military]). The words that appear in BoW are highlighted brightly (e.g., tank). Softer highlighting corresponds to words related to the topic but not in BoW (e.g., turret). The prefix of each sentence is underlined (e.g., More importantly).

Table 1. Stego texts of "Secret message" when $k = 2$, $n = 3$, $l = 1$, $h = 3$, $p = 11$.

ST_1 [military]	More importantly though I can now see what the problem will do to me and I am not a tank and am not getting damage done so far. This will probably cause the enemy team turret tanks tank to get hit and killed
ST_2 [science]	The connection is that we have all become part-time scientists at some of our own research institutions we have our own experiments running, we have a team in residence lab working under contract at another institute laboring in the
ST_3 [legal]	It has been shown in several articles that people do indeed believe the truth when presented a compelling case for why an issue merits a ban for both criminal and national defence laws to include an issue as evidence of their legality and for a

Table 2. Stego texts of "Secret message" when $k = 3$, $n = 4$, $l = 2$, $h = 3$, $p = 11$.

ST_1 [technology]	In brief overview: We're building out new API end point to help with web services in Java 9 (Java 10
ST_2 [politics]	The key aspect of all the arguments that are raised against a state's constitutional power of legislative self governance the authority over
ST_3 [religion]	It has been shown time, that there can always and surely follow in nature a Divine God and God-Man. And God
ST_4 [space]	To review some more details about a project like Spacecraft Launch Mission we'll have some of these satellites orbit our moon

4.3 Ablation Study

We conduct an ablation study with five variants: **B**: the baseline, no topic control, no GPM (that is, the conditional probability distribution is not modified using BoW, and $a_i|_{i=l}^{k-1}$ are chosen randomly); **BP**: no topic control, GPM-ppl; **BT**: topic control, no GPM; **BTP**: topic control, GPM-ppl; **BTT**: topic control, GPM-topic.

We use the 100 sentences selected from Sect. 4.1 as the secret texts and hide them using each of the above five methods, and count the average perplexity and topic relevance of each stego text. The experimental results are shown in Tables 3 and 4.

Through the above experimental results we can draw the following conclusions.

Table 3. Average ppl and TR of stego texts when $k = 2$, $n = 3$, $l = 1$, $h = 3$, $p = 11$

Variants	B	BP	BT	BTP	BTT
Avg. ppl ↓	32.89	13.88	42.21	16.17	18.37
Avg. TR ↑	\	\	7.56 %	4.44 %	13.42 %

Table 4. Average ppl and TR of stego texts when $k = 3$, $n = 4$, $l = 2$, $h = 3$, $p = 11$

Variants	B	BP	BT	BTP	BTT
Avg. ppl ↓	36.00	20.65	53.93	28.46	32.41
Avg. TR ↑	\	\	10.9 %	5.56 %	11.55 %

- In this scheme, the topic control method can effectively increase the probability of the words matching the topic being selected in the process of stego text generation, so that the stego text can meet the specific topic.
- The text quality is affected because the topic control method modifies the probability distribution in the process of text generation, which makes the modified probability distribution inconsistent with the training sample. Therefore, the text quality of the BT method without the optimization of GPM is the worst.
- The BP method optimized by GPM-ppl generates the highest quality stego text, and the perplexity of GPM-ppl optimized BTP method is less than that of BT and BTT, so GPM-ppl can effectively improve the quality of stego text.
- The topic relevance of the BTT method optimized by GPM-topic is the highest, so GPM-topic can effectively improve the topic relevance of stego text.

5   Conclusions

In this paper, we propose a text steganography scheme with loss tolerance, robustness, and imperceptibility, which hides secret message into n fluent and topic-controlled stego texts, where any k or more stego texts can recover the secret message. We first use secret sharing to encrypt secret message into shared values. Then, we use bag-of-words model to modify the conditional probability distribution to make the probability of words that fit the topic larger. Finally, a perfect binary tree is used to map shared values to the word space to generate stego texts. We also propose two goal programming models to optimize topic relevance and text quality of stego texts respectively. In the experimental section, we show some practical examples and perform ablation experiments to illustrate the effectiveness of each module.

References

1. Bengio, Y., Ducharme, R., Vincent, P.: A neural probabilistic language model. In: Advances in Neural Information Processing Systems 13 (2000)

2. Chan, A., Ong, Y.S., Pung, B., Zhang, A., Fu, J.: CoCon: a self-supervised approach for controlled text generation. In: International Conference on Learning Representations (2020)
3. Dathathri, S., et al.: Plug and play language models: a simple approach to controlled text generation. In: International Conference on Learning Representations (2019)
4. Hu, Z., Yang, Z., Liang, X., Salakhutdinov, R., Xing, E.P.: Toward controlled generation of text. In: International conference on machine learning, pp. 1587–1596. PMLR (2017)
5. Hussain, M., Wahab, A.W.A., Idris, Y.I.B., Ho, A.T., Jung, K.H.: Image steganography in spatial domain: a survey. Sig. Process. Image Commun. 65, 46–66 (2018)
6. Jurafsky, D.: Speech & language processing. Pearson Education India (2000)
7. Krishnan, R.B., Thandra, P.K., Baba, M.S.: An overview of text steganography. In: 2017 Fourth International Conference on Signal Processing, Communication and Networking (ICSCN), pp. 1–6. IEEE (2017)
8. Liu, Y., Liu, S., Wang, Y., Zhao, H., Liu, S.: Video steganography: a review. Neurocomputing 335, 238–250 (2019)
9. Manning, C., Schutze, H.: Foundations of statistical natural language processing. MIT press (1999)
10. Mishra, S., Yadav, V.K., Trivedi, M.C., Shrimali, T.: Audio steganography techniques: a survey. In: Bhatia, S.K., Mishra, K.K., Tiwari, S., Singh, V.K. (eds.) Advances in Computer and Computational Sciences. AISC, vol. 554, pp. 581–589. Springer, Singapore (2018). https://doi.org/10.1007/978-981-10-3773-3_56
11. Radford, A., et al.: Language models are unsupervised multitask learners. OpenAI blog 1(8), 9 (2019)
12. Shamir, A.: How to share a secret. Commun. ACM 22(11), 612–613 (1979)
13. Shannon, C.E.: Communication theory of secrecy systems. Bell Syst. Tech. J. 28(4), 656–715 (1949)
14. Vaswani, A., et al.: Attention is all you need. In: Advances in Neural Information Processing Systems 30 (2017)
15. Wolf, T., et al.: Transformers: state-of-the-art natural language processing. In: Proceedings of the 2020 Conference on Empirical Methods in Natural Language Processing: System Demonstrations, pp. 38–45 (2020)
16. Xiang, L., Yang, S., Liu, Y., Li, Q., Zhu, C.: Novel linguistic steganography based on character-level text generation. Mathematics 8(9), 1558 (2020)
17. Yang, Z.L., Guo, X.Q., Chen, Z.M., Huang, Y.F., Zhang, Y.J.: Rnn-stega: linguistic steganography based on recurrent neural networks. IEEE Trans. Inf. Forensics Secur. 14(5), 1280–1295 (2018)
18. Zellers, R., et al.: Defending against neural fake news. In: Advances in Neural Information Processing Systems 32 (2019)
19. Zhou, X., Peng, W., Yang, B., Wen, J., Xue, Y., Zhong, P.: Linguistic steganography based on adaptive probability distribution. In: IEEE Transactions on Dependable and Secure Computing (2021)

MGCN: A Novel Multi-Graph Collaborative Network for Chinese NER

Yingqi Zhang[1], Wenjun Ma[1], and Yuncheng Jiang[1,2(✉)]

[1] School of Computer Science, South China Normal University,
Guangzhou 510631, China
{zhangyingqi,jiangyuncheng}@m.scnu.edu.cn, phoenixsam@sina.com
[2] School of Artificial Intelligence, South China Normal University,
Foshan 528225, China

Abstract. Named Entity Recognition (NER), one of the most important directions in Natural Language Processing (NLP), is an essential pre-processing step in many downstream NLP tasks. In recent years, most of the existing methods solve Chinese NER tasks by leveraging word lexicons, which has been empirically proven to be useful. Unfortunately, not all word lexicons can improve the performance of the NER. Some self-matched lexical words will either disturb the prediction of character tag, or bring the problem of entity boundaries confusion. Thus, the performance of the NER model will be lowered by such irrelevant lexical words. However, to the best of our knowledge, none of the existing methods can solve these challenges. To address these issues, we present a novel Multi-Graph Collaborative Network (MGCN) for Chinese NER. More specifically, we propose two innovative modules for our methods. Firstly, we build connections among characters to eliminate interferential influences of the noisiness in lexical knowledge. Secondly, by constructing relationship between contextual lexical words, we solve the problem of boundaries confusion. Finally, experimental results on the benchmark Chinese NER datasets show that our methods are not only effective, but also outperform the state-of-the-art (SOTA) results.

Keywords: Chinese NER · Lexical knowledge · Graph neural network

1 Introduction

NER is mainly dedicated to identifying and classifying unstructured texts into predefined semantic categories such as person names, locations, etc. [12,23]. NER not only acts as a standalone tool for information extraction (IE) [1], but also plays an essential role in a variety of NLP applications such as text understanding [25], information retrieval [8], recommendation system [5], etc.

In contrast with NER in English, Chinese NER is relatively difficult because sentences in Chinese are not naturally segmented. Therefore, it is common for Chinese NER to first perform word segmentation by using an existing Chinese Word Segmentation (CWS) system and then use a sequence labeling model based

© The Author(s), under exclusive license to Springer Nature Switzerland AG 2022
W. Lu et al. (Eds.): NLPCC 2022, LNAI 13551, pp. 618–630, 2022.
https://doi.org/10.1007/978-3-031-17120-8_48

on word-level to separate sentence [6]. However, it is difficult for the CWS system to correctly segment query sentences, which will result in error propagation. In order to solve this problem, there are some methods resorting to performing Chinese NER directly at the character-level, which has been empirically proven to be effective [14]. However, such methods cannot exploit the lexical knowledge. With this consideration, Zhang et al. [24] proposed the Lattice-LSTM model to exploit explicit word and word sequence information. However, the architecture of this model is too complicated, which causes relatively poor training and inference speeds. Besides the Lattice-LSTM model, Sui et al. [19] proposed a Collaborative Graph Network to use word information by integrating lexical knowledge. Their models use lexical word information to obtain great experimental results, but they neglect the interferential influences of the noisiness in lexical matched words. Therefore, there are still two challenges.

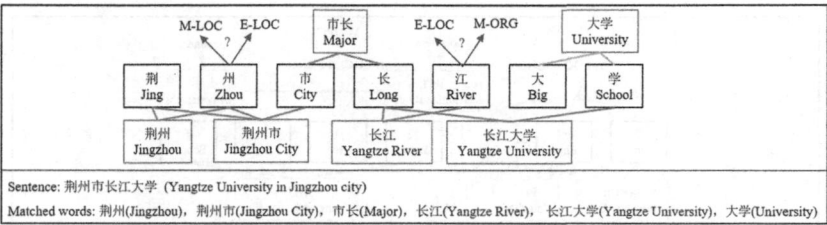

Fig. 1. An example sentence influenced by the noisiness in lexical knowledge

The first challenge is how to eliminate the interferential influences of the noisiness in lexical matched words. As shown in Fig. 1, for the sentence "荆州市长江大学" (there is Yangtze University in Jingzhou city), the words "荆州市" (Jingzhou City) and "荆州" (Jingzhou) are the self-matched words of the character "荆" (Jing) in this sentence. If the word "荆州" (Jingzhou) is recognized as an entity in the sentence, it influences the prediction of the characters "州" (Zhou) and "市" (City), which will influence the meaning of this sentence. In details, the character "州" (Zhou) may be predicted as an "E-LOC" tag, and the character "市" (City) may be incorrectly predicted as a "B-PER" tag. Worst of all, the model may recognize the words "荆州" (Jingzhou), "市长" (Major), and "江大学" (Daxue Jiang) as three entities in this sentence, respectively. But in fact, the meaning of this sentence presents that there is Yangtze University in Jingzhou city. It is not that Daxue Jiang is a major in Jingzhou city. As we can know from above, the matched word "荆州" (Jingzhou) is noisiness for the sentence, which interferes the prediction of the NER models.

The second challenge is how to solve the problem of entity boundaries confusion. For the same example of "荆州市长江大学" (there is Yangtze University in Jingzhou city), the matched words "长江大学" (Yangtze University) and "长江" (Yangtze River) are the self-matched words of the character "长" (Long). The matched words "长江大学" (Yangtze University) and "大学" (University) are the self-matched words of the character "大" (Big).

Due to the influences of the matched words "长江" (Yangtze River) and "大学" (University), the model cannot define the boundary of sub-sentence "长江大学" (Yangtze University). That is, the character "江" (River) may be predicted as an "E-LOC" tag, and the character "大" (Big) may be predicted as a "B-ORG" tag. Hence, based on such tags, the model may recognize the words "长江" (Yangtze River) and "大学" (University) as two entities, which is caused by the confusion of entity boundaries. In fact, the word "长江" (Yangtze River) is just a part of the true entity "长江大学" (Yangtze University) in this sentence, as well as the word "大学" (University), and it does not indicate the longest river in China. However, to the best of our knowledge, none of the existing methods can solve this problem. For example, these methods cannot incorporate the words "长江" (Yangtze River) and "大学" (University) into the word "长江大学" (Yangtze University).

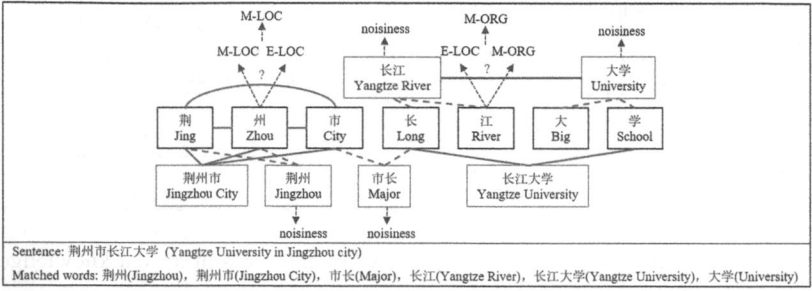

Fig. 2. An example sentence fully exploiting lexical knowledge

In order to solve the above challenges, we think that the connections among characters should be built, and the relationships between the nearest contextual matched words should be fully considered. As shown in Fig. 2, the connections among characters can solve the first challenge. If the character "州" (Zhou) has a connection with its predecessor (the character "荆" (Jing)) or successor (the character "市" (City)), at the same time, the character "荆" (Jing) has a connection with the character "市" (City). Based on graph neural network, these characters are more likely recognized as an entity. In this way, we can eliminate the interferential influences of the matched word "荆州" (Jingzhou). For the second challenge, the relationships among contextual lexical words can overcome the obstacle of boundaries confusion. Specifically, if the word "长江" (Yangtze River) has been seen as an entirety, as well as the word "大学" (University), there is not any connection between the words "长江" (Yangtze River) and "大学" (University), which may cause incorrect prediction. Therefore, we can use the matched word "长江大学" (Yangtze University) to construct a relationship between the matched words "长江" (Yangtze River) and "大学" (University). In this way, the words "长江" (Yangtze River) and "大学" (University) are incorporated into the word "长江大学" (Yangtze University), and the model just recognizes the word "长江大学" (Yangtze University) as an entity. The more detailed explanation is introduced in Sect. 3.

In this vein, we propose a novel multi-graph collaborative network model. Specifically, we construct three word-character interactive graphs in the graph layer for achieving our methods. The first graph is the Constructing graph, which not only builds connections among characters, but also constructs the most decisive self-matched words in a sentence. The second graph is the Associating graph, which exploits the enhanced relationships among characters to build relationships between the contextual words, and connections between the character and its nearest words. The third graph is the Boundary graph, which is designed for confirming the boundaries of named entities, in order to solve the confusion of entity boundaries. Since different graphs have different functions, they will cooperate with each other via a fusion layer.

In summary, our main contributions are as follows: 1) we propose a novel multi-graph collaborative network for Chinese NER tasks; 2) we eliminate the interferential influences of the noisiness in matched words by constructing connections among characters; 3) we solve the problem of entity boundary confusion by building relationships between contextual words; 4) experimental results show that our methods outperform the SOTA results.

2   Related Work

Some previous Chinese NER studies have shown that character-based methods [11], can outperform word-based counterparts [7], due to the error propagation caused by CWS. Recently, some lexical knowledge methods have been widely used to augment character information for Chines NER, which has been empirically proven to be effective [18]. Especially, the Lattice-LSTM model proposed by Zhang et al. [24] not only avoids error propagation, but also models characters and potential words simultaneously.

Transformer-based methods have also been used with lexical enhancement [13]. Especially, Flat-Lattice Transformer proposed by Li et al. [13] can convert the lattice structure into a flat structure consisting of spans. This method not only has an excellent parallelization ability, but also leverages the lattice information. Besides, graph neural networks have been successfully applied to Chinese NER tasks [4,19,26]. Gui et al. [4] has proposed a lexicon-based graph network for Chinese NER. This method treats the named entities as a node classification task, which can avoid error propagation and leverage lexical knowledge.

In this work, we adopt a novel multi-graph collaborative network method that builds three word-character interactive graphs with different functions. This method not only leverages lexical knowledge, but also solves problems caused by noisiness in lexicon words.

3   Methodology

In this section, we first introduce the construction of three word-character interactive graphs. Then, we introduce the structure of our training model for solving Chinese NER tasks.

3.1   The Construction of Graphs

We construct three word-character interactive graphs to achieve our methods. For any graph, the vertices of the graph consist of characters and the lexical words matched by the corresponding characters in the sentence. For example, an input sentence can be represented as $s = \{荆, 州, 市, 长, 江, 大, 学\}$. In order to utilize potential words in the sentence, we match all lexical words of every character. All lexical words matched by the corresponding characters can be represented as $l = \{荆州市, 荆州, 市长, 长江大学, 长江, 大学\}$. Thus, the vertices of three interactive graphs are denoted as $V = \{荆, \ldots, 长江大学, \ldots\}$.

The vertices of three interactive graphs are the same, but the edges of each graph are different. For this, we introduce adjacency matrix to represent the edges of each graph. The values in the adjacency matrix indicate whether there are relations between vertices or not in a graph. Since the functions of different graphs are different, their adjacency matrices are also different.

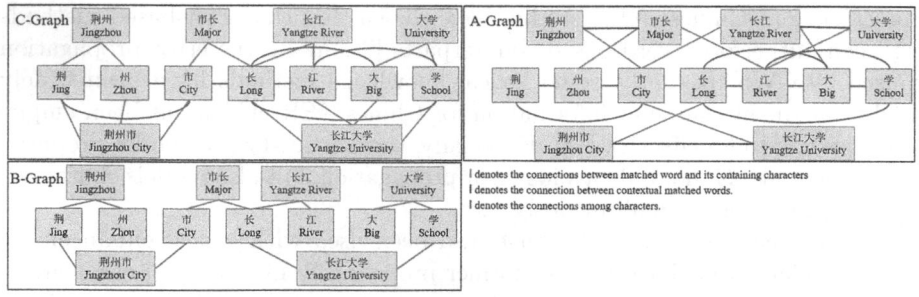

Fig. 3. Three word-character interactive graphs

Associating Graph. Inspired by Sui et al. [19], we build the Associating graph (A-graph). With this graph, we not only build relationships among contextual words, but also connections between character and its nearest words, by using the enhanced relationships among characters. Firstly, we should augment relationships among characters. As shown in Fig. 3, if a lexical word l_i contains character set $C = \{c_1, c_2, \ldots, c_p\}, c_n, c_m \in C$, the (c_n, c_m)-entry of the A-graph corresponding adjacency matrix A^A is assigned a value of 1. To capture the semantic information between the character and its nearest contextual words, if a lexical word l_i matches the nearest character c, $A^A_{l_i c}$ will be assigned a value of 1. Moreover, in order to build relationship between lexical words, if a lexical word l_i is the previous or next context of another lexical word l_j, the (l_i, l_j)-entry of the A-graph corresponding adjacency matrix A^A is assigned a value of 1.

Boundary Graph. The Boundary graph (B-graph) is constructed to use self-matched lexical words to determine the boundaries of entities, in order to eliminate the confusion of entity boundaries. As shown in Fig. 3, if a lexical word l_i contains many characters, we need to leverage its contained first character or last character c. Therefore, the (l_i, c)-entry of the B-graph corresponding adjacency matrix A^B is assigned a value of 1.

Constructing Graph. With this Constructing graph (C-graph), we not only build connections among characters, but also construct the most decisive self-matched words in a sentence. As shown in Fig. 3, if a lexical word l_i contains character set $C = \{c_1, c_2, \dots, c_p\}, c_n, c_m \in C$, we will assign the (l_i, c_n)-entry of the C-graph corresponding adjacency matrix A^C a value of 1, as well as the (c_n, c_m)-entry.

3.2   The Whole Architecture of Our Model

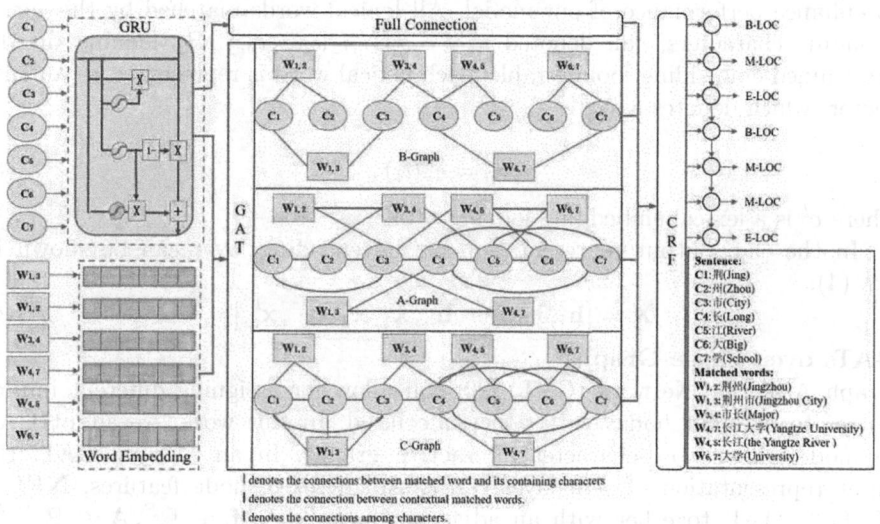

Fig. 4. The architecture of our model

As shown in Fig. 4, the whole architecture of our training model is as follows. First of all, every character in the input sequence is converted into a dense vector. Secondly, we utilize a bidirectional Gated Recurrent Unit to capture contextual information of input sequence, and then fuse it with three word-character interactive graphs, respectively. In the end, the results of the final predictions are obtained through Conditional Random Field (CRF).

Encoding Layer
The input of the training model based on characters is a sentence. The sentence can be denoted as $s = \{c_1, c_2, \cdots, c_n\}$, where c_i is the i-th character in a sentence. By looking up the embedding vector, each character c_i can be represented as a dense vector, which denotes as $\mathbf{x}_i^c$:

$$\mathbf{x}_i^c = e^c(c_i),\tag{1}$$

where e^c is a character embedding lookup table.

Recurrent Neural Network (RNN) is beneficial to capturing contextual information of Chinese sentences. In this paper, we adopt a bidirectional Gated Recurrent Unit (GRU) network. Compared with other RNNs, GRU has a merit in training speed. As shown in Eq. (2), the bidirectional GRU can be applied to the input sentence $\mathbf{x}^c = \{\mathbf{x}_1^c, \mathbf{x}_2^c, \cdots, \mathbf{x}_n^c\}$, and then we can obtain the contextual representation $\mathbf{H} = \{\mathbf{h}_1, \mathbf{h}_2, \cdots, \mathbf{h}_n\}$.

$$\mathbf{h}_i = \overrightarrow{GRU}\left(\mathbf{x}_i^c, \overrightarrow{\mathbf{h}}_{i-1}\right) \oplus \overleftarrow{GRU}\left(\mathbf{x}_i^c, \overleftarrow{\mathbf{h}}_{i+1}\right).\tag{2}$$

We utilize lexical knowledge to augment the character representation, in order to enhance performance of our model. All lexical words matched by the corresponding characters, can denoted as $l = \{l_1, l_2, \cdots, l_m\}$. By looking up the pre-trained embedding lookup table, each lexical word is represented as a dense vector, which denotes as $\mathbf{x}_i^l$:

$$\mathbf{x}_i^l = e^l(l_i),\tag{3}$$

where e^l is a lexical embedding looking table.

In the end, output representation of the encoding layer can be shown in Eq. (4).

$$\mathbf{X} = \left[\mathbf{h}_1, \mathbf{h}_2, \cdots, \mathbf{h}_n, \mathbf{x}_1^l, \mathbf{x}_2^l, \cdots, \mathbf{x}_m^l\right].\tag{4}$$

GATs over These Graphs
Graph Attention Network (GAT) [20] can allow for assigning different importances to different nodes with a neighborhood. In this work, we adopt GAT to model three word-character interactive graphs. In an M-layer GAT, the input representation of j-th layer consists of a set of node features, $\mathbf{NF}^j = \{\mathbf{f}_1, \mathbf{f}_2, \ldots, \mathbf{f}_N\}$, together with an adjacency matrix $\mathbf{A}$, $\mathbf{f}_i \in \mathbb{R}^F, \mathbf{A} \in \mathbb{R}^{N \times N}$, where F denotes the dimension of features at j-th layer and N is the number of nodes. The output representation of j-th layer is a new set of node features differing with others $\mathbf{NF}^{(j+1)} = \{\mathbf{f}_1', \mathbf{f}_2', \ldots, \mathbf{f}_N'\}$. Every GAT operation with K different and independent attention heads is shown in Eqs. (5) and (6):

$$\mathbf{f}_i' = \overset{K}{\underset{k=1}{\|}} \sigma\left(\sum_{j \in \mathcal{N}_i} \alpha_{ij}^k \mathbf{W}^k \mathbf{f}_j\right),\tag{5}$$

$$\alpha_{ij}^k = \frac{\exp\left(\text{LeakyReLU}\left(\mathbf{a}^{\mathrm{T}}\left[\mathbf{W}^k\mathbf{f}_i\|\mathbf{W}^K\mathbf{f}_j\right]\right)\right)}{\Sigma_{k\in\mathscr{N}_i}\exp\left(\text{LeakyReLU}\left(\mathbf{a}^{\mathrm{T}}\left[\mathbf{W}^k\mathbf{f}_i\|\mathbf{W}^K\mathbf{f}_k\right]\right)\right)}, \tag{6}$$

where concatenation operation is denoted as $\|$. The nonlinear activation function is denoted as σ. The adjacent nodes of node i in a graph are denoted as $\mathscr{N}_i$. The attention coefficients are denoted as α_{ij}^k, $\mathbf{W}^k \in \mathbb{R}^{F'\times F}$ and $\mathbf{a} \in \mathbb{R}^{2F'}$. The single-layer feed-forward neural network is denoted as $\mathbf{a} \in \mathbb{R}^{2F'}$. Note that, KF' is the dimension of the output $\mathbf{f}_i'$, and F' is the dimension of the final output features. Finally, the averaging in the last layer will be kept.

$$\mathbf{f}_i^{final} = \sigma\left(\frac{1}{K}\sum_{k=1}^{K}\sum_{j\in\mathscr{N}_i}\alpha_{ij}^k\mathbf{W}^k\mathbf{f}_j\right). \tag{7}$$

In detail, three independent graph attention networks are built for modeling three different word-character interactive graphs. Three independent graph attention networks can be denoted as $GAT1$, $GAT2$, and $GAT3$, respectively. The same vertex set is shared by three word-character interactive graphs. The input node features of all GAT models are the input representation X, which is shown in Eq. (4). These three GAT models denote different output node features, as shown in Eq. (8):

$$G_K = GAT_K\left(X, A^p\right), \tag{8}$$

where $\mathbf{G}_k \in \mathbb{R}^{F'\times(n+m)}$, $k \in \{1, 2, 3\}$, $p \in \{C, A, B\}$, n is the number of characters in the sentence, and m is the number of the lexical words matched by characters in the sentence. We do not need all columns of these matrices, because some columns are interferential for our model. Therefore, the front n columns of these matrices are kept to decode labels.

$$\mathbf{Q}_k = \mathbf{G}_k[:, 0 : n], k \in \{1, 2, 3\}. \tag{9}$$

Fusion Layer

In our model, three graphs have different functions. To utilize the merits of different interactive graphs, we use a fusion layer to fuse three $GATs$. In addition, the input representation of original characters is also needed. Therefore, the input representation of the fusion layer is the contextual representation $\mathbf{H}$ and the output of the $GATs$ $\mathbf{Q}_i, i \in \{1, 2, 3\}$. The fusion equation is as follows:

$$\mathbf{R} = \mathbf{W}_1\mathbf{H} + \mathbf{W}_2\mathbf{Q}_1 + \mathbf{W}_3\mathbf{Q}_2 + \mathbf{W}_4\mathbf{Q}_3, \tag{10}$$

where $\mathbf{W}_y, y \in \{1, 2, 3, 4\}$, is a trainable matrix. We can obtain a collaborative matrix $\mathbf{R}$ from a fusion layer, which can integrate these different matrices. The matrix $\mathbf{R}$ includes contextual information, the relations among characters and the relationship between nearest words.

Decoding

A standard CRF [9] layer is adopted to capture the dependencies between successive labels. For any input sentence $s = \{c_1, c_2, \cdots, c_n\}$, the input representation of this layer is $\mathbf{R} = \{\mathbf{r}_1, \mathbf{r}_2, \cdots, \mathbf{r}_n\}$ and the probability of a label sequence $y = \{y_1, y_2, \cdots, y_n\}$ is as follows:

$$p(y \mid s) = \frac{\exp\left(\sum_i \left(\mathbf{W}^{y_i} \mathbf{r}_i + \mathbf{T}_{(y_{i-1}, y_i)}\right)\right)}{\sum_{y'} \exp\left(\sum_i \left(\mathbf{W}^{y_i'} r_i + \mathbf{T}_{(y_{i-1}', y_i')}\right)\right)}, \tag{11}$$

where an arbitrary label sequence is denoted as y_i'. A model parameter specific to the i_{th} character in the sentence is denoted as $\mathbf{W}^{y_i}$ and the associating matrix is denoted as $\mathbf{T}$. The first-order Viterbi algorithm [21] is used to find the highest scored label sequence over a character-based input representation. Given a manually labeled training data $\{(s_i, y_i)\}|_{i=1}^N$, the optimized model is obtained by using sentence-level log-likelihood loss with L_2 regularization.

$$L = -\sum_{i=1}^N \log\left(P\left(y_i \mid s_i\right)\right) + \frac{\lambda}{2} \|\Theta\|^2. \tag{12}$$

As shown in Eq. 12, the L_2 regularization parameter is represented as λ, and the training parameters set is denoted as Θ.

4   Experiment

In this section, we show experimental processes, including tested datasets, evaluation metric (F1) and so on. We test our methods with three datasets. Specifically, our datasets include MSRA [10], Weibo NER [17] and E-commerce [2].

4.1   Overall Performance

Table 1. Main results on all datasets.

Models	MSRA	E-commerce	Weibo-ALL	Weibo-NM
Lattice-LSTM [24]	93.18	-	58.79	62.25
CAN-NER [26]	92.97	-	59.31	62.98
LR-CNN [3]	93.71	-	59.92	66.67
LGN [4]	93.46	-	60.21	64.98
SoftLexicon(LSTM) [15]	93.66	73.59	61.42	62.22
+bichar [15]	94.06	73.88	59.81	64.20
MECT [22]	94.32	72.27	63.30	62.51
LGCN [16]	94.08	-	61.10	65.30
Ours	**94.34**	**76.42**	**64.31**	**71.46**

Evaluation metric is F1 value.

MSRA. There is a larger amount of data in MSRA dataset, compared with other datasets. There is an important task to evaluate the robustness and effectiveness of training model besides the problem about quality and consistency of the annotation. Our methods can keep stronger robustness in front of these problems because we consider the relationships among characters well. The C-graph bridges the gap between characters with some relationships. In addition, the A-graph builds connections between self-matched lexical words. Moreover, the B-graph solves the problem of confusion in entity boundaries. The results in Table 1 show that our methods are effective and useful. Compared with the MECT model [22], our methods not only obtain the slightly better performance, but also do not depend on the quality of structure decomposition dictionary of Chinese character.

Weibo and E-commerce. NER datasets on informal text are more challenging than on formal text because of the shortness and noisiness. Compared with other datasets, there is more shortness and noisiness in Weibo and E-commerce datasets, which may cause poor performance of the neural model. In addition, the connections among entities are not close together. With this consideration, we construct the C-graph. The C-graph can build the close relationships among characters by using lexicon knowledge. Those close relationships are beneficial to the recognition of entities. The results on these two datasets show that our methods are useful, as shown in Table 1. Compared with the MECT model [22], our model can outperform it by 4.15%, 1.01%, 8.95% in F1 score on E-commerce, Weibo-All, and Weibo-NM datasets, respectively.

4.2   Effectiveness

The ablation experiments show the effectiveness of three interactive graphs based on word-character.

Comparison Settings. The specific details of the ablation studies are as follows: 1) GRU+CRF: baseline model. 2) GRU + A: just keep the A-graph. 3) GRU + A + B: without the C-graph.

Table 2. Ablation study

Models	MSRA	E-commerce	Weibo-ALL	Weibo-NM
GRU+CRF	87.80	61.89	48.02	51.87
GRU+A	91.14	68.15	60.43	67.41
GRU+C	90.5	67.04	60.99	66.66
GRU+B	92.41	68.32	62.41	65.34
GRU+A+C	93.85	74.18	63.24	68.63
GRU+A+B	93.64	73.45	63.48	69.37
GRU+C+B	94.07	74.97	64.17	69.89
Complete model	**94.34**	**76.42**	**64.31**	**71.46**

Comparison Results. The results of the ablation study are shown in Table 2. We can know that removing any graph can cause badly poor performance of the model in different datasets. In addition, we see that "GRU+CRF" obtains worse results than others from any dataset, which obviously shows that our methods are effective and useful. Moreover, we know that the relationship between nearest words is beneficial to Chinese NER from "GRU+C+B" model. In conclusion, the statistics of ablation experiments show that each graph is indispensable, but the best performance can be obtained by them together.

5   Conclusion

In this paper, we present a novel multi-graph collaborative network to solve the problem caused by noisiness in lexical knowledge. Specifically, we build connections among characters to eliminate the interferential influences of the noisiness in matched words. Secondly, by constructing relationship between contextual lexical words, we solve the problem of boundaries confusion. In the end, we construct three word-character interactive graphs with different functions. The various experiments show that our methods are effective and useful.

Acknowledgements. The works described in this paper are supported by The National Natural Science Foundation of China under Grant Nos. 61772210 and U1911201; The Project of Science and Technology in Guangzhou in China under Grant No. 202007040006.

References

1. Dai, W., Hua, X., Lv, R., Bo, R., Chen, S.: The solution of Xiaomi AI lab to the 2021 language and intelligence challenge: multi-format information extraction task. In: Natural Language Processing and Chinese Computing, pp. 496–508 (2021)
2. Ding, R., Xie, P., Zhang, X., Lu, W., Li, L., Si, L.: A neural multi-digraph model for Chinese NER with gazetteers. In: Proceedings of the 57th Annual Meeting of the Association for Computational Linguistics, pp. 1462–1467 (2019)
3. Gui, T., Ma, R., Zhang, Q., Zhao, L., Jiang, Y.G., Huang, X.: CNN-based Chinese NER with lexicon rethinking. In: IJCAI, pp. 4982–4988 (2019)
4. Gui, T., et al.: A lexicon-based graph neural network for chinese NER. In: Empirical Methods in Natural Language Processing, pp. 1039–1049 (2019)
5. Hao, B., et al.: Negative feedback aware hybrid sequential neural recommendation model. In: Zhu, X., Zhang, M., Hong, Yu., He, R. (eds.) NLPCC 2020. LNCS (LNAI), vol. 12431, pp. 279–291. Springer, Cham (2020). https://doi.org/10.1007/978-3-030-60457-8_23
6. He, H., Sun, X.: F-score driven max margin neural network for named entity recognition in Chinese social media. In: European Chapter of the Association for Computational Linguistics, pp. 713–718 (2017)
7. He, J., Wang, H.: Chinese named entity recognition and word segmentation based on character. In: Third International Joint Conference on Natural Language Processing, IJCNLP, pp. 128–132 (2008)

8. Hersh, W.: Information retrieval. In: Shortliffe, E.H., Cimino, J.J. (eds.) Biomedical Informatics. LGTS, pp. 755–794. Springer, Cham (2021). https://doi.org/10.1007/978-3-030-58721-5_23

9. Lafferty, J.D., McCallum, A., Pereira, F.C.N.: Conditional random fields: Probabilistic models for segmenting and labeling sequence data. In: Proceedings of the Eighteenth International Conference on Machine Learning, pp. 282–289 (2001)

10. Levow, G.A.: The third international Chinese language processing bakeoff: Word segmentation and named entity recognition. In: SIGHAN Workshop on Chinese Language Processing, pp. 108–117 (2006)

11. Li, H., Hagiwara, M., Li, Q., Ji, H.: Comparison of the impact of word segmentation on name tagging for Chinese and Japanese. In: Proceedings of the Ninth International Conference on Language Resources and Evaluation.,pp. 2532–2536 (2014)

12. Li, H., Xu, H., Qian, L., Zhou, G.: Multi-layer joint learning of Chinese nested named entity recognition based on self-attention mechanism. In: Zhu, X., Zhang, M., Hong, Yu., He, R. (eds.) NLPCC 2020. LNCS (LNAI), vol. 12431, pp. 144–155. Springer, Cham (2020). https://doi.org/10.1007/978-3-030-60457-8_12

13. Li, X., Yan, H., Qiu, X., Huang, X.: FLAT: Chinese NER using flat-lattice transformer. In: Proceedings of the 58th Annual Meeting of the Association for Computational Linguistics, pp. 6836–6842 (Jul 2020)

14. Liu, Z., Zhu, C., Zhao, T.: Chinese named entity recognition with a sequence labeling approach: Based on characters, or based on words? In: Advanced Intelligent Computing Theories and Applications, With Aspects of Artificial Intelligence, pp. 634–640 (2010)

15. Ma, R., Peng, M., Zhang, Q., Wei, Z., Huang, X.: Simplify the usage of lexicon in Chinese NER. In: Proceedings of the 58th Annual Meeting of the Association for Computational Linguistics, pp. 5951–5960 (2020)

16. Nie, Y., Zhang, Y., Peng, Y., Yang, L.: Borrowing wisdom from world: modeling rich external knowledge for Chinese named entity recognition. Neural Comput. Appl. **34**(6), 4905–4922 (2022)

17. Peng, N., Dredze, M.: Named entity recognition for Chinese social media with jointly trained embeddings. In: Proceedings of the 2015 Conference on Empirical Methods in Natural Language Processing, pp. 548–554 (2015)

18. Song, B., Bao, Z., Wang, Y.Z., Zhang, W., Sun, C.: Incorporating lexicon for named entity recognition of traditional Chinese medicine books. In: Zhu, X., Zhang, M., Hong, Yu., He, R. (eds.) NLPCC 2020. LNCS (LNAI), vol. 12431, pp. 481–489. Springer, Cham (2020). https://doi.org/10.1007/978-3-030-60457-8_39

19. Sui, D., Chen, Y., Liu, K., Zhao, J., Liu, S.: Leverage lexical knowledge for Chinese named entity recognition via collaborative graph network. In: EMNLP-IJCNLP, pp. 3830–3840 (2019)

20. Velickovic, P., Cucurull, G., Casanova, A., Romero, A., Liò, P., Bengio, Y.: Graph attention networks. In: International Conference on Learning Representations (2018)

21. Viterbi, A.J.: Error bounds for convolutional codes and an asymptotically optimum decoding algorithm. IEEE Trans. Inf. Theory **13**(2), 260–269 (1967)

22. Wu, S., Song, X., Feng, Z.: MECT: Multi-metadata embedding based cross-transformer for Chinese named entity recognition. In: ACL-IJCNLP, pp. 1529–1539 (2021)

23. Yan, T., Huang, H., Mao, X.-L.: SciNER: a novel scientific named entity recognizing framework. In: Zhu, X., Zhang, M., Hong, Yu., He, R. (eds.) NLPCC 2020. LNCS (LNAI), vol. 12430, pp. 828–839. Springer, Cham (2020). https://doi.org/10.1007/978-3-030-60450-9_65
24. Zhang, Y., Yang, J.: Chinese NER using lattice LSTM. In: Gurevych, I., Miyao, Y. (eds.) Association for Computational Linguistics, pp. 1554–1564 (2018)
25. Zhang, Z., Han, X., Liu, Z., Jiang, X., Sun, M., Liu, Q.: Ernie: enhanced language representation with informative entities. arXiv preprint arXiv:1905.07129 (2019)
26. Zhu, Y., Wang, G.: CAN-NER: convolutional attention network for Chinese named entity recognition. In: NAACL, pp. 3384–3393 (2019)

Joint Optimization of Multi-vector Representation with Product Quantization

Yan Fang[1], Jingtao Zhan[1], Yiqun Liu[1(✉)], Jiaxin Mao[2], Min Zhang[1],
and Shaoping Ma[1]

[1] Department of Computer Science and Technology, Institute for Artificial
Intelligence, Beijing National Research Center for Information Science
and Technology, Tsinghua University, Beijing 100084, China
fangy21@mails.tsinghua.edu.cn, {yiqunliu,z-m,msp}@tsinghua.edu.cn
[2] Beijing Key Laboratory of Big Data Management and Analysis Methods, Gaoling
School of Artificial Intelligence, Renmin University of China, Beijing 100872, China

Abstract. Dense retrieval models represent queries and documents with
one or multiple fixed-width vectors and retrieve relevant documents via
nearest neighbor search. Recently these models have shown improvement
in retrieval performance and have drawn increasing attention from the IR
community. Among a variety of dense retrieval models, the models that
employ multiple vectors to represent texts achieve the state-of-the-art
ranking performance. However, the multi-vector representation schema
imposes tremendous storage overhead compared with single-vector representation, which may hinder its application in practical scenarios. We
therefore intend to apply vector compression methods such as Product
Quantization (PQ) to reduce the storage cost and improve retrieval efficiency. However, the gap between the original embeddings and the quantized vectors may degenerate retrieval performance. Recently, improved
dense retrieval models such as JPQ have been proposed to reduce storage space while maintaining ranking effectiveness by jointly training the
encoder and PQ index. They have achieved promising improvement in
the single-vector dense retrieval scenario. We therefore try to introduce
this joint optimization framework to tackle the storage overhead of the
multi-vector models. The key idea is to Jointly optimize Multi-vector
representations with Product Quantization (JMPQ). JMPQ prevents
effectiveness degeneration by leveraging a joint optimization framework
for the query encoding and index compressing processes. We evaluate
the performance of JMPQ on publicly available ad-hoc retrieval benchmarks. Extensive experimental results show that JMPQ substantially
reduces the memory footprint while achieving ranking effectiveness on
par with or even better than its uncompressed counterpart.

Keywords: Dense retrieval · Index compression · Neural ranking

W. Lu et al. (Eds.): NLPCC 2022, LNAI 13551, pp. 631–642, 2022.
https://doi.org/10.1007/978-3-031-17120-8_49

1   Introduction

Dense Retrieval [7,13] has become increasingly popular in recent years and has achieved the state-of-the-art ranking effectiveness. It effectively leverages the pre-trained language models [4,15,20] to abstract the text and uses nearest neighbor search for retrieval. Experimental results show that dense retrieval substantially outperforms the traditional lexical retrieval methods like BM25 [18].

Dense retrieval models can be classified into two categories, namely single-vector representation models [14,22,25] and multi-vector representation models [5,12,16]. The single-vector models encode text to one dense vector, while the multi-vector models utilize multiple vectors to represent the text. The multi-vector models facilitate more fine-grained interactions compared with the single-vector models and thus lead to better ranking effectiveness. One of the most popular multi-vector models is ColBERT [12], which utilizes token-level multi-vector representations for queries and documents and establishes the state-of-the-art ranking effectiveness. However, multi-vector models require multiple vectors for each document, leading to a huge embedding index, which is usually tens of times larger than that of the single-vector models. The large embedding index questions its application ability in practical use.

To compress the embedding index of multi-vector models, we propose JMPQ, which stands for **J**ointly optimizing **M**ulti-vector representations with **P**roduct **Q**uanti-zation. JMPQ is inspired by JPQ [23], which is used to compress the embedding index of single-vector dense retrieval models. However, the large number of vectors in the multi-vector scenario brings more pressure on search efficiency, and multi-vector models require a more detailed aggregation method compared to single-vector models. Following JPQ, JMPQ utilizes PQ to com-press the embedding index of multi-vector models to reduce storage cost. It fur-ther employs Inverted File System (IVF) to accelerate the search and introduces vector reconstruction for aggregation. JMPQ also leverages a joint optimization method to prevent effectiveness degeneration caused by the PQ compression. During training, JMPQ end-to-end retrieves top-ranked documents and com-putes ranking loss based on the retrieval results. It then back-propagates the gradients to the query encoder and PQ index. With PQ and the joint optimiza-tion strategy, JMPQ can improve ranking effectiveness in an storage-efficient way.

To verify the effectiveness and efficiency of JMPQ, we base on ColBERT to conduct extensive experiments on publicly available ad-hoc retrieval benchmarks and compare JMPQ against a wide range of existing dense retrieval models and compression methods. Experimental results show that: 1) JMPQ significantly compresses the embedding index of multi-vector models (e.g. ColBERT) by over 10 times and still achieves comparable ranking effectiveness. 2) JMPQ substan-tially outperforms other compression methods, including unsupervised methods and supervised methods. 3) JMPQ substantially outperforms the competitive single-vector dense retrieval baselines.

2   Related Works

In this section, we recap related work in dense retrieval and index compression.

2.1   Dense Retrieval

Dense retrieval models encode the query and the document into dense vectors and use nearest neighbor search to retrieve documents. Based on the number of representations per text, dense retrieval models can be classified as single-vector models, such as ANCE [22] and ADORE [25], and multi-vector models, such as COIL [5], MEBERT [16], and ColBERT [12,19]. The single-vector models encode text to one dense vector and thus may result in a limited capacity to abstract sufficient semantic information [16]. On the contrary, the multi-vector models encode text to multiple dense vectors and are capable of modeling token-level interactions. One of the most famous multi-vector retrieval models is ColBERT [12], which represents text with token-level embeddings. Given a query $q = q_0 q_1 ... q_l$ and a document $d = d_0 d_1 ... d_n$, ColBERT computes the token-level term embeddings q and d:

$$q = \{q_0, q_1, ..., q_l\} = \text{Encoder}(q_0 q_1 ... q_l) \tag{1}$$

$$d = \{d_0, d_1, ..., d_n\} = \text{Encoder}(d_0 d_1 ... d_n) \tag{2}$$

During retrieval, ColBERT employs the MaxSim function to aggregate token-level relevance scores as the document relevance scores:

$$s(q, d) := \sum_{i \in [|q|]} \max_{j \in [|d|]} q_i \cdot d_j^T \tag{3}$$

Although multi-vector models perform better on ranking effectiveness, they also increase the storage overhead by a large margin.

2.2   Index Compression

Vector compression methods have been widely applied. According to the training process, they can be categorized as unsupervised and supervised methods.

Unsupervised Methods. Popular unsupervised compression methods include Product Quantization (PQ) [6,10] and Locality Sensitive Hashing (LSH) [9]. There are several variants of PQ, such as OPQ [6] and RQ [1]. OPQ adds a linear transformation before quantization. RQ utilizes residual for compression. Most unsupervised methods optimize the task-independent reconstruction error and thus cannot benefit from the supervised signals.

Supervised Methods. Several studies have explored supervised methods for compression. MoPQ [21] proposes a novel objective MCL and a sample augmentation strategy DCS, which together can effectively contribute to the optimal retrieval accuracy. JPQ [23] jointly trains the encoder and PQ index with hard negative sampling, which is specifically designed for dense retrieval and directly optimizes the ranking effectiveness. RepCONC [24] models quantization as a constrained clustering process and further supports optimization of the dual-encoders and the quantization index in an end-to-end manner.

JMPQ is inspired by JPQ, but has the following two main distinctions from JPQ. Firstly, JMPQ introduces IVF to improve retrieval efficiency in the case of huge number of vectors in the multi-vector scenario. Note that RepCONC also utilizes IVF in the inference stage for efficiency, while JMPQ involves it in both training and inference stages. Secondly, both JPQ and RepCONC directly rely on the PQ index to calculate the vector inner-product as the relevance score. However, multi-vector models require a more detailed aggregation of the inner product. Thus, JMPQ has an additional vector reconstruction process for aggregation and re-ranking.

3   JMPQ Model

We propose JMPQ, Jointly optimize Multi-vector representations with Product Quantization. In this section, we will outline the overall architecture of JMPQ, describe the training strategy and analyze its efficiency.

3.1   Overall Architecture

Figure 1 illustrates the overall architecture of JMPQ. Following the procedure of ColBERT, JMPQ pre-computes token-level document embeddings and builds the IVFPQ index. It performs a two-stage retrieval. At the first stage, top-K document term embeddings are retrieved by the compressed index. At the second stage, JMPQ reconstructs the candidate document embeddings and then uses the scoring function Eq. (3) for re-ranking.

3.2   The IVFPQ Index

The IVFPQ index supports compressed index storage and efficient retrieval. It consists of the Inverted File System (IVF) and the Product Quantization (PQ).

Inverted File System. JMPQ employs IVF to accelerate the search. IVF first uses K-means [8] to generate P clusters and assigns each document embedding to its nearest cluster. For a given query embedding, only the nearest n clusters are searched. IVF stores the center embeddings of each cluster:

$$\mathcal{C}_i \in R^D (1 \leq i \leq P) \tag{4}$$

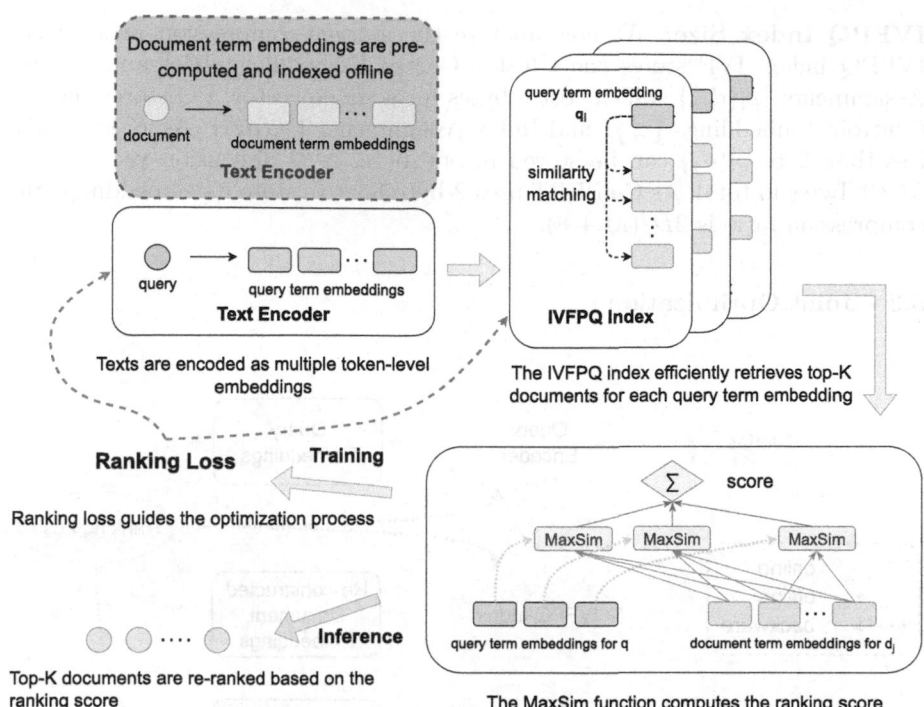

Fig. 1. Overall Architecture of JMPQ. Token-level document term embeddings are pre-computed offline for indexing. Given a query, JMPQ encodes it as multiple query term embeddings. The IVFPQ index performs efficient retrieval to get top-K documents for each query term embedding. The irrelevant documents are treated as hard negatives during training. At inference time, JMPQ uses the MaxSim function to re-rank the retrieved documents.

JMPQ then uses PQ to quantize the residual of the document term embedding to its cluster center. Let $\rho(\boldsymbol{d}_j)$ denote the cluster $\boldsymbol{d}_j$ is assigned to, the residual embedding equals to:

$$\boldsymbol{r}_{\boldsymbol{d}_j} = \boldsymbol{d}_j - \mathcal{C}_{\rho(\boldsymbol{d}_j)} \tag{5}$$

Product Quantization. PQ defines M sets of embeddings, each including K embeddings of dimension D/M, where D denotes the embedding dimension:

$$\boldsymbol{c}_{i,j} \in R^{\frac{D}{M}} \quad (1 \le i \le M, 1 \le j \le K) \tag{6}$$

For a given residual embedding $\boldsymbol{r}_{\boldsymbol{d}_j}$, PQ picks one centroid embedding from each set and concatenates them as $\boldsymbol{r}_{\boldsymbol{d}_j}^{\dagger}$:

$$\boldsymbol{r}_{\boldsymbol{d}_j} \rightarrow \boldsymbol{r}_{\boldsymbol{d}_j}^{\dagger} = \boldsymbol{c}_{1,\phi_1(\boldsymbol{d}_j)}, \boldsymbol{c}_{2,\phi_2(\boldsymbol{d}_j)} \cdots, \boldsymbol{c}_{M,\phi_M(\boldsymbol{d}_j)} \in R^D \tag{7}$$

where $\phi_i(\boldsymbol{d}_j)$ denotes the picked centroid embedding for the ith set.

IVFPQ Index Size. We now analyze the storage compression ratio of the IVFPQ index. IVF stores the Cluster Center Embeddings $\{C_i\}$ and Cluster Assignments $\{\rho_i(d_j)\}$, which cost 8 bytes for a single vector. PQ stores the PQ Centroid Embeddings $\{c_{i,j}\}$ and Index Assignments $\{\phi_i(d_j)\}$. As K is usually less than 256, $\phi_i(d_j)$ can be stored in one byte. A D dimension vector takes $M + 8$ bytes in total. As ColBERT uses 2-byte float to store its embeddings, the compression ratio is $2D/(M + 8)$.

3.3   Joint Optimization

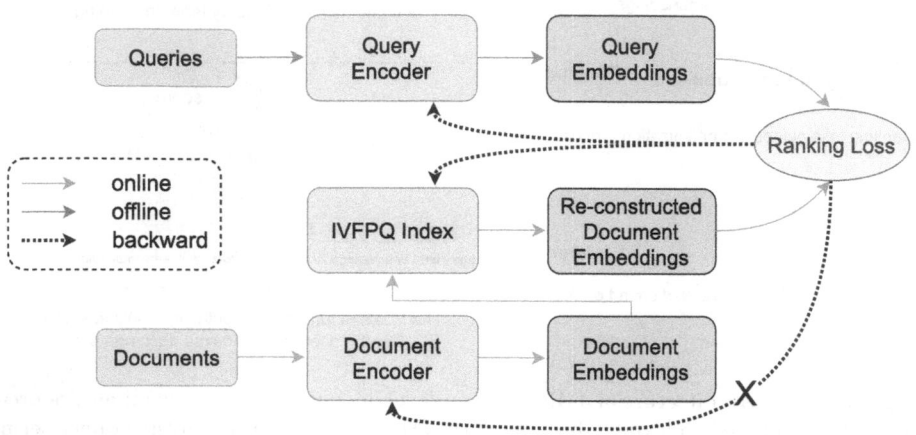

Fig. 2. The training workflow of JMPQ

Figure 2 illustrates the training workflow of JMPQ. Firstly, JMPQ generates the document term embeddings using the document encoder initialized with the well-trained ColBERT and unsupervisely builds the IVFPQ index in the offline stage. Secondly, JMPQ reconstructs the quantized term embeddings from the IVFPQ index by:

$$d_j^\dagger = c_{1,\phi_1(d_j)}, c_{2,\phi_2(d_j)} \cdots, c_{M,\phi_M(d_j)} + C_{\rho(d_j)} \tag{8}$$

Thirdly, the query term embeddings generated by the query encoder are used to compute the relevance scores with the reconstructed document term embeddings:

$$s(q, d^\dagger) := \sum_{i \in [|q|]} \max_{j \in [|d^\dagger|]} q_i \cdot d_j^{\dagger T} \tag{9}$$

Finally, the relevance scores are used to compute the ranking loss and then update the query encoder and PQ centroid embeddings with gradient descent:

$$\text{loss} = \mathcal{L}(s(q, d^{\dagger+}), s(q, d^{\dagger-})) \tag{10}$$

Since the loss is computed based on the end-to-end retrieval results, the parameters are updated to directly improve the ranking effectiveness. Note that document encoder is fixed during the training procedure for the following two reasons. Firstly, JMPQ uses the reconstructed embeddings to compute the relevance scores and the computation cost of the document encoder can be saved. Secondly, such approach eliminates the need to rebuild the IVFPQ index after each parameter update, thus enables JMPQ to utilize dynamic hard negatives [26] for better ranking effectiveness.

4   Experiment Setup

In this section, we present our experimental settings, including datasets, baselines, and implementation details.

4.1   Dataset and Metrics

We conduct experiments with popular ad-hoc retrieval benchmarks from the TREC 2019 Deep Learning Track and the TREC 2020 Deep Learning Track [2, 3, 17]. MS MARCO Passage Retrieval has a corpus of 8.8M passages, 0.5M training queries, 7k development queries (**MARCO Passage**), 43 test queries from the TREC 2019 (**DL2019**), and 43 test queries from the TREC 2020 (**DL2020**). We report MRR@10, Recall@100 for MARCO Passage, and nDCG@10, Recall@100 for both the TREC test sets. All the metrics are based on the full-corpus retrieval results.

4.2   Baselines

We consider both the uncompressed and compressed retrieval models as our baselines. For uncompressed retrieval models, we compare our JMPQ with traditional Bag-of-Words models such as BM25 [18] and single-vector neural models such as ANCE [22], ADORE [25], and TCT-ColBERT [14]. We also include ColBERT [12] as the multi-vector retrieval model baseline. For the compressed retrieval models, we select JPQ [23] and RepCONC [24] as single-vector supervised baselines. They share the same model architecture and initialization. We include unsupervised PQ [10] and PQ+RQ [19] as compression baselines for ColBERT. Notice that we also report ColBERTv2 [19] (which is further trained with hard negatives based on v1) in our results.

4.3   Implementation Details

We build our models based on ColBERTv1 [12] and Faiss ANNS Library [11]. The embedding dimension is 128. When implementing JMPQ, K is set to 256, and M is set to 16. We train the unsupervised IVFPQ index as initialization with 30% of the corpus embeddings. As for the training settings of JMPQ, we use AdamW optimizer, batch, size of 32, and cross-entropy loss. For the query encoder, the learning rate is set to 5e−6, and for PQ parameters, the learning rate is set to 1e−5. The number of clusters P is set to 32,768, and the multi-probing parameter n is set to 32. At the first stage, the top 1,024 matches are retrieved for each query term embedding. Considering the computation cost during training, we do not re-rank the retrieved documents to get the top-irrelevant documents, but we randomly sample 255 irrelevant documents from the candidates as hard negatives. At inference time, we re-rank the candidates to get the top 1,000 documents.

5   Experiments

Now we empirically evaluate the proposed JMPQ and compare it with different types of baselines. We summarize the ranking effectiveness, index size and query latency in Table 1. Note that the multi-vector models are initialized with ColBERTv1 [12]. We also report the performance of the multi-vector models initialized with ColBERTv2 [19] in Table 2. We next compare the overall performance of JMPQ and baseline models, and then analyze the details from the following three aspects.

5.1   Overall Comparison with Retrieval Models

Table 1. Overall Comparison with Retrieval Models on MARCO Passage, DL2019 and DL2020. */** denotes the difference between JMPQ and the baselines at $p < 0.05/0.01$ level using the two-tailed pairwise t-test.

Model	Index	MARCO		DL2019		DL2020		Latency
	GB	M@10	R@100	N@10	R@100	N@10	R@100	ms
BM25 [18]	0.59	0.187**	0.670**	0.497**	0.497**	0.488**	0.567**	60
ANCE [25]	25	0.330**	0.852**	0.645**	0.548**	0.646*	0.640**	7600
ADORE [25]	25	0.347*	0.876	0.683	0.582**	0.665	0.673*	7600
JPQ [23]	0.83	0.341**	0.868**	0.677	0.575**	0.671	0.670*	720
RepCONC [24]	0.47	0.340**	0.864**	0.668*	0.569**	0.666	0.640**	346
ColBERT [12]	147	**0.361**	0.873**	0.706	0.587**	0.676	0.683*	423
PQ+RQ [19]	23	0.360	0.866**	0.704	0.588**	0.681	0.669*	230
PQ [10]	14	0.344**	0.860**	0.684	0.564**	0.650**	0.656**	522
JMPQ	14	0.356	**0.881**	**0.717**	**0.636**	**0.693**	**0.715**	522

According to the results in Table 1, JMPQ achieves competitive ranking effectiveness compared with the uncompressed ColBERT [12] with a 10x smaller index. Meanwhile, JMPQ significantly outperforms ColBERT on DL2019 and DL2020. As for the query latency, the encoding and re-ranking stages of ColBERT, PQ+RQ [19], PQ [10] and JMPQ are done with one GeForce 2080Ti

GPU, and the index searching stage is measured with one Intel Xeon E5-2630 V4 CPU (single thread). JMPQ is slightly slower than the original ColBERT. The reason is that JMPQ introduces extra time cost in the reconstruction process, while ColBERT simply loads the embeddings from disk. We also notice that PQ+RQ has a larger reduction in latency. We contribute this to its Index Inversion technique. Table 2 shows a similar result that the proposed JMPQ is able to achieve comparable results with a compressed index. Note that the R@100 we report on DL2019 are different from the results in JPQ paper because different thresholds are used to calculate the metrics.

Table 2. Comparison with Multi-vector Retrieval Models with ColBERTv2 as initialization. PQ+RQ denotes the compression method used in ColBERTv2

Model	Index	MARCO		DL2019		DL2020	
	GB	M@10	R@100	N@10	R@100	N@10	R@100
ColBERT v2 [19]	147	**0.399**	**0.911**	0.744	0.638	**0.754**	0.755
PQ+RQ (ColBERT v2)	23	0.396	0.907	0.747	0.643	0.750	**0.761**
PQ (ColBERT v2)	14	0.386	0.904	0.744	0.636	0.735	0.741
JMPQ (ColBERT v2)	14	0.390	**0.911**	**0.752**	**0.646**	0.742	0.748

5.2 Comparison with Multi-vector Retrieval Models

This section compares JMPQ with the uncompressed multi-vector retrieval models. Since the index compression process of JMPQ introduces information loss, it is reasonable that its ranking effectiveness is inferior to the uncompressed ColBERT [12]. However, according to the results, the ranking effectiveness of JMPQ is competitive with or even outperforms the uncompressed ColBERT, which indicates that joint optimization can lead to significant effectiveness improvement without extra supervised signals.

From Table 2, we can see that JMPQ has only marginal improvement compared to the uncompressed ColBERTv2, which is less than the improvement of ColBERTv1 in Table 1. We believe the primary reason is that ColBERTv2 introduces hard negative sampling during training, which is consistent with the training strategy of JMPQ, and thus the improvement is not as large as expected.

5.3 Comparison with Other Compression Methods

This section compares JMPQ with other compression methods.

According to Table 1 and Table 2, the unsupervised PQ [10] severely hurts the ranking effectiveness compared with the uncompressed ColBERT [12], while JMPQ can significantly outperform the PQ baseline by leveraging a joint optimization framework. Compared with PQ+RQ [19], which is similar to JMPQ and quantizes the residual embeddings with PQ and RQ, JMPQ still substantially outperforms it with a relatively smaller index at most of the metrics for both the ColBERTv1 and v2 initialization. It further demonstrates the benefits of the supervised signals and the joint optimization framework.

As for the supervised compression methods, which also utilize joint optimization, RepCONC [24] and JPQ [23] achieve notable ranking effectiveness among the single-vector models while significantly reducing the index size. JMPQ outperforms them by a large margin. We attribute this to the powerful representation capabilities of the multi-vector models over the single-vector ones. It is worth noticing that the compressed index of single-vector models, such as 0.83G for JPQ, is much smaller and is about 1/17 of the index size of JMPQ. This is because, in the multi-vector scenario, the number of embedding vectors of the corpus could be hundreds of times greater than the single-vector scenario. In our experiments, the corpus has 8.8M embeddings for JPQ and RepCONC, while it has over 590M embeddings for JMPQ, which is over 60x than the single-vector models. Additionally, according to Sect. 3.2, a single vector takes an extra 8 bytes in the IVF for just storing the embedding ids, which in total occupies 4.7G storage space.

5.4 Comparison with Single-vector Retrieval Models

We now compare JMPQ with competitive single-vector dense retrieval baselines. According to the results, JMPQ substantially outperforms all the single-vector baselines. Compared with ANCE [22], ADORE [25], and TCT-ColBERT [14], which are uncompressed dense retrieval models, JMPQ achieves impressive effectiveness improvement while the compressed index size is almost halved, as JMPQ enables modeling token-level interactions with multi-vector representations.

6   Conclusions

This paper presents JMPQ based on JPQ. It jointly optimizes the encoding and the compression processes in an end-to-end manner in the multi-vector representation scenario. We conduct experiments on popular ad-hoc retrieval benchmarks, where JMPQ achieves competitive or better ranking effectiveness than the uncompressed dense retrieval models, with over 10x compression on index size. JMPQ also substantially improves the ranking performance compared with JPQ and RepCONC due to the strong representation capabilities of the multi-vector models. The results demonstrate the effectiveness of JMPQ and highlight that a compressed embedding index can benefit from supervised signals and be effective in the first-stage retrieval. It is worth noticing that although we only conduct experiments based on ColBERT and the MaxSim aggregation method, we believe that JMPQ can be applied to any multi-vector models as well as to any inner-product-based aggregation methods.

Acknowledgment. This work is supported by the Natural Science Foundation of China (Grant No. 61732008) and Tsinghua University Guoqiang Research Institute.

References

1. Barnes, C.F., Rizvi, S.A., Nasrabadi, N.M.: Advances in residual vector quantization: a review. IEEE Trans. Image Process. **5**(2), 226–262 (1996)
2. Craswell, N., Mitra, B., Yilmaz, E., Campos, D.: Overview of the TREC 2020 deep learning track (2021)
3. Craswell, N., Mitra, B., Yilmaz, E., Campos, D., Voorhees, E.M.: Overview of the TREC 2019 deep learning track. arXiv preprint arXiv:2003.07820 (2020)
4. Devlin, J., Chang, M.W., Lee, K., Toutanova, K.: BERT: pre-training of deep bidirectional transformers for language understanding. arXiv preprint arXiv:1810.04805 (2018)
5. Gao, L., Dai, Z., Callan, J.: COIL: revisit exact lexical match in information retrieval with contextualized inverted list. arXiv preprint arXiv:2104.07186 (2021)
6. Ge, T., He, K., Ke, Q., Sun, J.: Optimized product quantization. IEEE Trans. Pattern Anal. Mach. Intell. **36**(4), 744–755 (2013)
7. Guo, J., Cai, Y., Fan, Y., Sun, F., Zhang, R., Cheng, X.: Semantic models for the first-stage retrieval: a comprehensive review. arXiv preprint arXiv:2103.04831 (2021)
8. Hartigan, J.A., Wong, M.A.: Algorithm as 136: a k-means clustering algorithm. J. Royal Stat. Soc. Ser. c (applied statistics) **28**(1), 100–108 (1979)
9. Indyk, P., Motwani, R.: Approximate nearest neighbors: towards removing the curse of dimensionality. In: Proceedings of the Thirtieth Annual ACM Symposium on Theory of Computing, pp. 604–613 (1998)
10. Jegou, H., Douze, M., Schmid, C.: Product quantization for nearest neighbor search. IEEE Trans. Pattern Anal. Mach. Intell. **33**(1), 117–128 (2010)
11. Johnson, J., Douze, M., Jégou, H.: Billion-scale similarity search with GPUs. IEEE Trans. Big Data **7**(3), 535–547 (2019)
12. Khattab, O., Zaharia, M.: ColBERT: efficient and effective passage search via contextualized late interaction over BERT. In: Proceedings of the 43rd International ACM SIGIR Conference on Research and Development in Information Retrieval, pp. 39–48 (2020)
13. Lin, J., Nogueira, R., Yates, A.: Pretrained transformers for text ranking: BERT and beyond. Synth. Lect. Hum. Lang. Technol. **14**(4), 1–325 (2021)
14. Lin, S.C., Yang, J.H., Lin, J.: Distilling dense representations for ranking using tightly-coupled teachers. arXiv preprint arXiv:2010.11386 (2020)
15. Liu, Y., et al.: RoBERTa: a robustly optimized BERT pretraining approach. arXiv preprint arXiv:1907.11692 (2019)
16. Luan, Y., Eisenstein, J., Toutanova, K., Collins, M.: Sparse, dense, and attentional representations for text retrieval. Trans. Assoc. Comput. Linguist. **9**, 329–345 (2021)
17. Nguyen, T., et al.: MS MARCO: a human generated machine reading comprehension dataset. In: CoCo@ NIPS (2016)
18. Robertson, S.E., Walker, S.: Some simple effective approximations to the 2-Poisson model for probabilistic weighted retrieval. In: SIGIR 1994, pp. 232–241. Springer (1994). https://doi.org/10.1007/978-1-4471-2099-5_24
19. Santhanam, K., Khattab, O., Saad-Falcon, J., Potts, C., Zaharia, M.: ColBERTv2: effective and efficient retrieval via lightweight late interaction (2021)
20. Vaswani, A., et al.: Attention is all you need. Adv. Neural Inf. Process. Syst. **30** (2017)

21. Xiao, S., Liu, Z., Shao, Y., Lian, D., Xie, X.: Matching-oriented product quantization for ad-hoc retrieval. arXiv preprint arXiv:2104.07858 (2021)
22. Xiong, L., et al.: Approximate nearest neighbor negative contrastive learning for dense text retrieval. arXiv preprint arXiv:2007.00808 (2020)
23. Zhan, J., Mao, J., Liu, Y., Guo, J., Zhang, M., Ma, S.: Jointly optimizing query encoder and product quantization to improve retrieval performance. In: Proceedings of the 30th ACM International Conference on Information and Knowledge Management, pp. 2487–2496 (2021)
24. Zhan, J., Mao, J., Liu, Y., Guo, J., Zhang, M., Ma, S.: Learning discrete representations via constrained clustering for effective and efficient dense retrieval (2021)
25. Zhan, J., Mao, J., Liu, Y., Guo, J., Zhang, M., Ma, S.: Optimizing dense retrieval model training with hard negatives. In: Proceedings of the 44th International ACM SIGIR Conference on Research and Development in Information Retrieval, pp. 1503–1512 (2021)
26. Zhan, J., Mao, J., Liu, Y., Guo, J., Zhang, M., Ma, S.: Optimizing dense retrieval model training with hard negatives. In: Proceedings of the 44th International ACM SIGIR Conference on Research and Development in Information Retrieval, pp. 1503–1512 (2021)

Distill-AER: Fine-Grained Address Entity Recognition from Spoken Dialogue via Knowledge Distillation

Yitong Wang[1,2], Xue Han[2(✉)], Feng Zhou[1], Yiting Wang[2], Chao Deng[2], and Junlan Feng[2]

[1] Beijing University of Posts and Telecommunication, Beijing, China
{devil817,zfeng}@bupt.edu.cn
[2] JiuTian Team, China Mobile Research Institute, Beijing, China
{hanxueai,wangyiting,dengchao,fengjunlan}@chinamobile.com

Abstract. Fine-grained address entity recognition from spoken dialogue is an important but challenging task because there are multiple types of address entities distributed across the multi-round dialogue context. Existing work typically formulates this problem as a fine-grained named entity recognition task, which in our scenario suffers from a high cost of training data annotation. On the other hand, large-scale full standard addresses could be easily crawled from the web pages like Google Maps and annotated with fine-grained address tags with limited human effort. Leveraging this, we propose a distillation approach (Distill-AER) for transferring knowledge from the large-scale labeled full standard address dataset to the fine-grained address entity recognition task in a spoken dialogue context scenario. We further construct a labeled spoken dialogue dataset with address entities using the data augmentation paradigm we proposed, which could benefit future research. Experimental results show that Distill-AER significantly outperforms other competitive baselines.

Keywords: Entity recognition · Address extraction · Knowledge distillation

1 Introduction

Fine-grained address entity recognition from spoken dialogue is an important task in many applications, such as E-commerce assistant, post-sale service or restaurant booking agent [1]. In this paper, we consider Chinese address entity recognition without loss of generality. The scenario considered in this paper is the extraction of fine-grained address entities distributed through the multi-round spoken dialogue contexts. Figure 1 depicts an example of such a dialogue between a customer and an after-service call center. The call-center asks the customer's address for completing customer information files, so as to facilitate the subsequent maintenance service. Address entities have multiple tags or labels,

© The Author(s), under exclusive license to Springer Nature Switzerland AG 2022
W. Lu et al. (Eds.): NLPCC 2022, LNAI 13551, pp. 643–655, 2022.
https://doi.org/10.1007/978-3-031-17120-8_50

such as province (Zhejiang province), city (Hangzhou), and so on. These fine-grained address entities are recognized and then typically combined to form a full standard address (FS-addr) for a wide range of location-based applications. We focus on the fine-grained address entity recognition task (FG-AER) in this paper, leaving the full standard address combination task for future research.

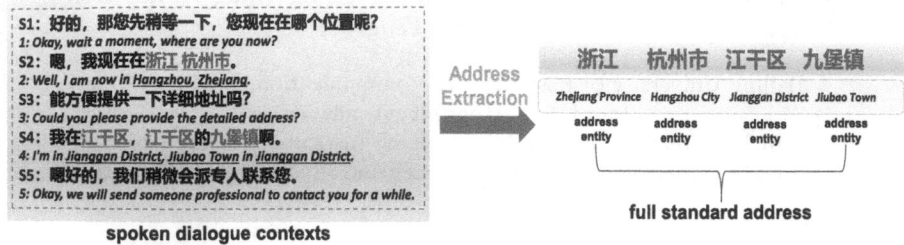

spoken dialogue contexts

Fig. 1. An example of Chinese address entity recognition from spoken dialogue.

Most similar to our work is [2]. They formulate the address extraction as a name entity recognition (NER) problem and propose an algorithm to label U.S. addresses with an appropriate label which falls within the predefined 8 label classes (e.g., state, house number). However, their NER task input is pre-processed to be in the form of a full standard address, which is not the case with our problem. Other researches [3–5] consider extracting address entities to be a task of fine-grained named entity recognition (FG-NER), usually adopting BiLSTM (Bidirectional Long Short-Term Memory) [6] and CRF (Conditional Random Fields) [7] as the model architecture. However, these FG-NER models suffer from a high cost of training data annotation because humans must annotate more categories than coarse-grained NER [8]. Furthermore, the increasing NER categories make human annotators more likely to make errors, affecting model's performance.

The lack of labeled data is even worse in our scenario due to the diversity and complexity of multi-round dialogue scenario. Firstly, it is difficult to obtain sufficient dialogue data containing fine-grained labeled address entities. Second, different types of address entities are always scattering across multi-round sentences, making annotation laborious and time-consuming [9]. On the other hand, large-scale FS-addr (e.g., 杭州市江干区九堡镇航海路电子商务园- *Ecommerce park, Hanghai Road, Jiubao Town, Jianggan District, Hangzhou City*) could be easily crawled from web pages such as Google Maps[1]. We could annotate such FS-addr data with fine-grained address tags using well-studied address segmentation methods [10] with limited human efforts.

Leveraging this, we propose Distill-AER, a distillation approach for transferring knowledge learned from the large-scale labeled FS-addr dataset to the

---

[1] https://www.google.com/maps.

FG-AER task in a dialogue context scenario. To be more specific, 1) Based on the innovative data augmentation paradigm put forward by us, we generate a labeled dialogue dataset called Dialogue-AER. Dialogue-AER contains multiple types of address entities scattered throughout the spoken dialogue, leveraging the publicly available labeled FS-addr data. 2) The labeled FS-addr dataset is used to pre-train the BiLSTM-CRF-based Teacher first. The trained Teacher model is then fixed, and the knowledge is distilled by by calculating the emission distillation loss between the Teacher and Student models. The distilled knowledge helps the Student model mitigate the effect of noises in the dialogue context, improving FG-AER task's performance. 3) Experimental results on both our dataset and real-world downstream dialogue data show the improvement of Distill-AER, respectively, when compared to strong baselines.

2 Related Work

Named Entity Recognition. A large and growing body of literature has investigated named entity recognition which is an important topic in natural language processing [11–13]. Recently, there have been plenty of researches focused on coarse-grained NER [14–16], but most existing studies mainly recognize a relatively small number of named entity categories such as person, organization, location, etc. [17], which is different from our situation. In this paper, our system adopts a creative knowledge distillation method for the fine-grained address entity recognition task in the spoken dialogue scenario.

Chinese Address Element Segmentation. With the rapid development of deep learning and natural language processing technologies, Chinese word segmentation based on neural networks has also achieved satisfactory results. [10] brings up a gated recursive neural network (GRNN) for Chinese word segmentation, which contains reset and update gates to incorporate the complicated combinations of the context character. [18] presents a method of Chinese address element segmentation based on a Bi-GRU neural network. [19] uses the dictionary to segment the address and BERT-CRF to tag each token. [20] proposes a local spatial context-based framework to extract local toponyms and segment Chinese textual addresses.

Knowledge Distillation. The Knowledge Distillation (KD) method [21] employs a teacher model and tries to minimize the KL divergence between the teacher distribution and the student model distribution. Previous work has shown that KD can significantly boost prediction accuracy in natural language processing [22–24]. In the recent years, KD has been applied for the sequence labeling tasks [25–27], which can be regarded as a way to deal with the dialogue contextual Chinese address extraction problem. These works inspire the innovation of our work, which will be discussed in the next section.

3   Methodology

Because of the difficulty of FG-AER task, we apply the idea of knowledge distillation to develop our model: a well-trained Teacher model leverages its knowledge to assist the training process of a Student model for FG-AER in dialogue contexts. Figure 2 depicts the overall architecture of our method, which will be introduced next.

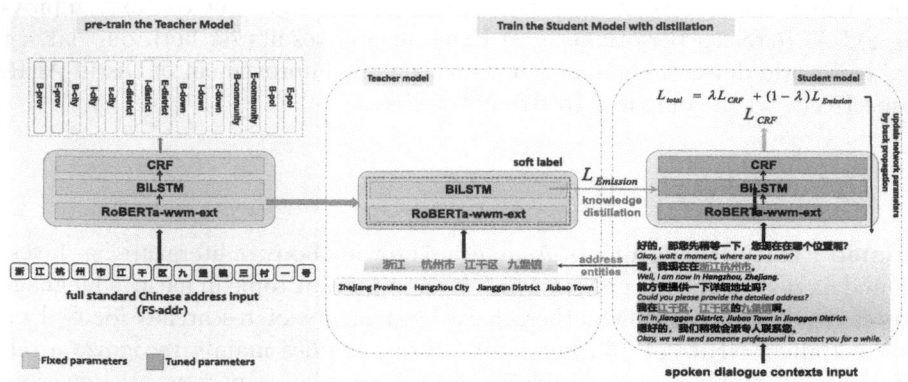

Fig. 2. The architecture of our proposed Distill-AER. The Teacher Model employs its knowledge to aid in the calculation of the Student Model's loss function.

3.1   Problem Formulation

The problem of address entity recognition from dialogue is formulated as a sequence labeling task. Given a student model input, $X = \{x_1, x_2, ..., x_M\}$, x_i denotes the i-th character in a spoken dialogue containing address entities with length M. The output is a tag sequence $Y = \{y_1, y_2, ..., y_M\}$, where $y_i \in \gamma$, $1 \leq i \leq M$ and γ is the set of predefined tags following the BIOE tagging scheme. Each tag in γ is indicated by B-(begin), I-(inside), E-(end) of an entity with its category (e.g., B-City, I-City and E-City). For a character which is not inside of any entity, its tag is O-(outside).

The FG-AER task aims at discovering a list of address entities $EList_{category} = \{E^1, E^2, ..., E^n\}$. Each address entity E^i is scattered across different sentences in a dialogue context according to the predicted tags. $E^i = \{x_{start}, x_{start+1}, ..., x_{end-1}, x_{end}\}$ is a substring of X satisfying $start \leq end$. We call the character-level set of these address entities collectively X_{addr}. Let $X_{nonaddr} = X - X_{addr}$, as $X_{nonaddr}$ is a set of characters which are not inside of any entity. Each character in $X_{nonaddr}$ is labeled as tag O.

The model training procedure is separated into two stages: the teacher model training stage and the student model distillation stage.

3.2   The Teacher Model Training Stage

The teacher model consists of a context encoder and a tag decoder. We use pre-trained Chinese RoBERTa-wwm-ext[2] [28] as the deep bidirectional representations for input to generate character-level embeddings. BiLSTM [6] is adopted for the context encoder to capture the context dependencies. CRF [7] is deemed as the tag decoder to predict tags for characters in the input sequences. To pre-train the teacher model for the address entity recognition task, we initially use full standard address data (See footnote 4), which is defined as a character-level input sequence $L = \{l_1, l_2, ..., l_N\}$ of length N. Then we assign a label $y \in \gamma$ to each $l \in L$ where γ is the address tag set specified earlier.

3.3   The Student Model Distillation Stage

In this stage, we bring up a approach which encourages the student model to improve its generalization performance by the teacher model's knowledge of address entities. Similar to the teacher model, the student model is built with a BiLSTM-CRF model structure and the input representation is generated from RoBERTa-wwm-ext. As for the trained teacher model, we fix the parameters of RoBERTa-wwm-ext and BiLSTM layer. The knowledge from the teacher model is distilled for the student's FG-AER task by calculating the emission distillation loss between these two models' BiLSTM layers. The following describes the process of training a student model.

The character-level set X_{addr} of all address entities contained in the student model input X is used as the input of the teacher model in the distillation stage, generating the emission scores Z^T_{addr} after the teacher's BiLSTM layer. Then we simply feed the emission scores into Eq. 1 to calculate the emission probabilities P^T_{addr} of the teacher model as the soft label:

$$P^T_{addr} = softmax(Z^T_{addr}) \tag{1}$$

In the same way, we can also get the emission probabilities P^S_{addr} of the student model. The distillation loss function is defined as the cross entropy between P^T_{addr} and P^S_{addr}:

$$L_{Emission} = CE(P^T_{addr}, P^S_{addr})$$
$$= -\sum_{i=1}^{t} \sum_{j=1}^{|\gamma|} p^T(y_t = \gamma_j | X_{addr}) \log(p^S(y_t = \gamma_j | X_{addr})) \tag{2}$$

where t is the length of X_{addr}, and γ is the predefined tag space.

The final joint loss of the student model is defined as below:

$$L_{total} = \lambda L_{CRF} + (1 - \lambda)L_{Emission} \tag{3}$$

---

[2] https://github.com/ymcui/Chinese-BERT-wwm.

where L_{CRF} is calculated from the student model's CRF loss function feeding the whole spoken dialogue X as input. λ is a hyper-parameter employed to control the weight of the distillation loss.

The overall knowledge distillation process of Distill-AER is illustrated in Algorithm 1.

Algorithm 1. Distillation process

Input: Multi-turn spoken dialogue context
Output: A list of address entities
 1: Train the Teacher model with full standard address data for address entity recognition task.
 2: Initialize parameters of the Student model and fix the parameters of the trained teacher model.
 3: **repeat**
 4:    For each mini-batch, given the dialogue as input X, get L_{CRF} of the Student model.
 5:    Do forward propagation to calculate P_{addr}^{T} and P_{addr}^{S} of Teacher and Student models using X_{addr} contained in the input X.
 6:    Calculate the $L_{Emission}$ by Eq.2, L_{total} by Eq.3 and then do back propagation for the Student model.
 7: **until** Convergence of Student model

---

4   Data Augmentation

Due to the lack of labeled dialogues containing address entities, we propose a data augmentation paradigm to construct the labeled dialogue dataset, for our FG-AER task on dialogue contexts. In general, the paradigm is made up of two parts: Dialogue Enrichment to expand dialogue datasets and ASR Simulator to imitate the spoken dialogue contexts in real downstream scenarios.

4.1   Dialogue Enrichment

There exist a few open source datasets of high quality. For example, the CUCC dialogue dataset(See footnote 3) and CMCC downstream dialogue data which include address entities scattered in the sentences, and some labeled full standard address datasets for address element segmentation tasks. Benefitting from the above datasets, we expand the dialogue data by replacing each entity in the origin dialogue with another new entity which is collected from full standard address datasets. This effective strategy preserves the structure of the high-quality dialogues. In addition, we adopt some conventional data enrichment methods, such as lexical substitution, back translation and so on [29].

4.2   ASR Simulator

In spoken dialogues, automatic speech recognition (ASR) makes a range of mistakes. We present ASR Simulator which can capture spoken language characteristics from numerous perspectives, to bridge the gap between real spoken dialogues and dialogues we generated previously. Following the prior works [30,31], we implement five strategies to simulate the phenomena occurred in downstream dialogues: 1) **Pause**: randomly insert some filler words, like "呃 (uh)", "嗯 (well)", and so on. 2) **Repeat**: repeat the previous characters or phrases as is customary when people talk. 3) **Repair**: provide an incorrect pronunciation at first and then rectify it, to imitate the slip of the tongue. 4) **Restart**: add some frequent prefixes in the start of a sentence. 5) **Insert**: put a random entity from the same FS-addr anywhere in the sentence. The examples of ASR Simulator are shown in Table 1.

Table 1. Examples of our ASR Simulator.

Original sentence		我 在 九堡镇 的 九环路 上 O O *Town* O *Road* O
ASR Simulator strategies	Pause	我 在 嗯，九堡镇 的 九环路 上 O O O O *Town* O *Road* O
	Repeat	我 在 在 在九堡镇 的 九环路 上 O O O O *Town* O *Road* O
	Repair	我 在 旧，不，九堡镇 的 九环路 上 O O O O O O *Town* O *Road* O
	Restart	我 在，我 在九堡镇 的 九环路上 O O O O O *Town* O *Road* O
	Insert	我 在 江干区 九堡镇 的 九环路 上 O O *District* *Town* O *Road* O

5   Experiments

5.1   Datasets

FS-addr Dataset. For the teacher model pre-training, we leverage a labeled full standard Chinese address dataset provided by Tianchi Competitions(See footnote 4), which contains 8.8K full standard addresses with 16 categories. More FS-addr data can be crawled from websites like BaiDu Maps and labeled with limited efforts following [10].

CUCC-AER. The CUCC call-center dialogue dataset provided by DataFountain Competition[3] is transcribed by a real-world downstream speech recognition system, including plenty of transcription errors. We filter out inapplicable dialogues and finally select 200 dialogues which contain address entities and manually label the filtered data with 16 different categories of address entities, to evaluate the Distill-AER's performance on the spoken dialogues from real-life service environment.

---

[3] https://www.datafountain.cn/competitions/536/datasets.

Dialogue-AER. We create a labeled spoken dialogue context dataset called Dialogue-AER, which is constructed according to the paradigm in Sect. 4. Specifically, about 328 groups of dialogue templates we used to create dialogues are extracted from CUCC-AER(See footnote 3) and CMCC downstream dialogue data, while optional entities are constructed based on the FS-addr dataset(See footnote 4). Finally, a labeled dialogue dataset of 8.8K groups of dialogue contexts with 16 categories of fine-grained address entities has been created. The generated dialogue's average length is 133 and the maximum length is 255 in Dialogue-AER. As is shown in Fig. 3, the entity categories distribution is similar for both the training and validation sets. Our sample code and dataset are openly available[4].

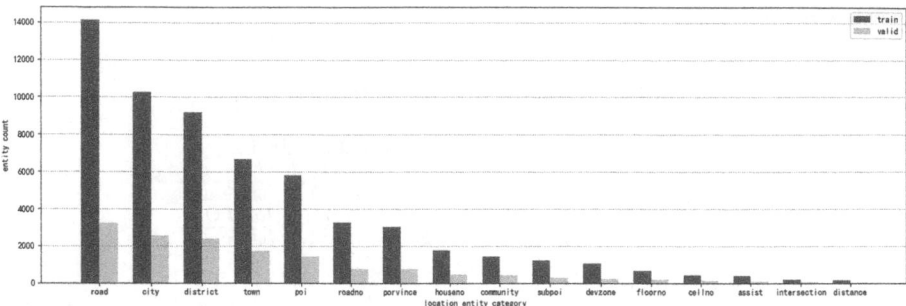

Fig. 3. Entities distribution for train and valid sets.

The details of fine-grained address entities contained in all these three datasets are shown in Table 2. All datasets have tag O-(outside) to define the characters which are not inside of any entity.

5.2   Experimental Details

Baseline Models We evaluate the performance of the proposed Distill-AER model by comparing it with several strong baseline methods. Baseline-1 uses the structure of Bert-base-Chinese[5]-CRF, while Baseline-2 adopts Bert-base-Chinese-BiLSTM-CRF as the architecture. Baseline-3 employs RoBERTa-wwm-ext-CRF as the structure. Baseline-4 is the trained teacher model of Distill-AER. Baseline-5 is based on the student model without using the knowledge distillation method.

Implementation Details. For hyperparameter settings, the max sequence length of RoBERTa-wwm-ext is 256. The hidden state size of BiLSTM is 128 and the dropout rate is set as 0.1 for BiLSTM output. We use the AdamW optimizer

---

[4] https://github.com/Devil0817/Dataset-Addr-NER-generation.
[5] https://huggingface.co/bert-base-chinese.

Table 2. Interpretations and examples for each entity type used in our datasets, according to the address hierarchical order from top to bottom.

Label	Interpretation	Example
PROVINCE	name of a province	浙江 Zhejiang Province
CITY	name of a city	杭州市 Hangzhou City
DISTRICT	name of a district in a city	西湖区 Xihu District
TOWN	name of a town or a boulevard	九堡镇 Jiubao Town
ROAD	name of a road	航海路 Hanghai Road
INTERSECTION	road junction	交叉口 Intersection
ROADNO	road number	5号 #5
DEVZONE	a economic development zone	开发区 Development Zone
COMMUNITY	name of a community or a village	宁安社区 Ningan Community
POI	name of the point of interest	衢州人民医院 Quzhou Hospital
SUBPOI	name of the second point of interest	放射科 Radiology Department
ASSIST	a phrase indicating relative position	对面 Opposite
DISTANCE	amount of space between two points	100米 100m
HOUSENO	house number	3幢 Block #3
CELLNO	cell number	2单元 Unit #2
FLOORNO	floor number	6层 Level 60

in a mini-batch size of 64 with learning rate $\gamma = 2 \times 10^{-5}$. λ is set to 0.8 during the experiments. The split of 80% for train, 10% for validation and 10% for test is used. In each experiment, the models are trained for 5 epochs. Finally, the models with the best validation loss are saved and utilized for testing.

5.3   Result and Analysis

As shown in Table 3, we present the performance of our Distill-AER model and other compared baselines on Dialogue-AER dataset. We can draw the following insights from the results: In all cases, our model outperforms all baselines. When using the same corpus to train models, the result indicates that Baseline-3 model consistently outperforms Baseline-1 by 0.91% F1 improvement on average with the same structures, demonstrating the success of the pre-trained RoBERTa-based model in learning deep bidirectional representations in dialogue contexts. The Baseline-2's result reveals the advantage of the architecture of BiLSTM-CRF dealing with fine-grained NER task. Depending on the above results, we choose RoBERTa-BiLSTM-CRF (Baseline-5) as the base architecture of our model.

Table 3. Experiment results of all methods on Dialogue-AER, and the best performance is highlighted in boldface.

Methods	P	R	F1
Baseline-1 (BERT-CRF)	87.54	85.64	86.52
Baseline-2 (BERT-BiLSTM-CRF)	82.52	91.40	86.94
Baseline-3 (RoBERTa-CRF)	87.93	87.05	87.43
Baseline-4 (Teacher)	73.83	80.53	74.98
Baseline-5 (Student without KD)	90.39	89.32	89.84
Distill-AER model	**94.20**	**91.91**	**92.94**

Compared to Baseline-5 without knowledge distillation, our Distill-AER model improves F1 by 3.1% on average.

Figure 4 shows the learning curves of address entity recognition F1 score on the validation sets of Dialogue-AER over training epochs. This figure demonstrates that our model learns quickly and converges early, proving the robustness of Distill-AER model and the effectiveness of applying the idea of knowledge distillation.

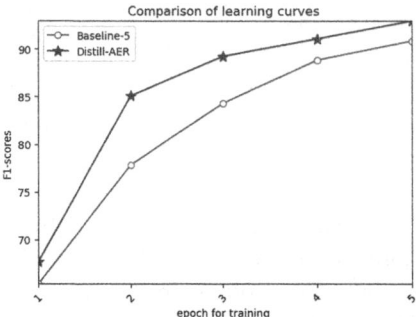

Fig. 4. Comparison of learning curves: Distill-AER model and Baseline-5 (same structure but without distillation) on Dialogue-AER.

Table 4 reveals that Distill-AER outperforms baseline models on real-world downstream data. In particular, the F1 score for our method is nearly 3.2% higher than the Baseline-5 when applying knowledge distillation. Compared to Dialogue-AER, the reason why the metrics of CUCC-AER dropped may be that the data in CUCC-AER is more irregular and contains more noises. In summary, Distill-AER has a much greater advantage than the other models in dealing with FG-AER task on spoken dialogue contexts. The results of the downstream data prove the feasibility of our method for real-world applications.

Table 4. Performance of baselines and Distill-AER on CUCC-AER.

Methods	P	R	F1
Baseline-1 (BERT-CRF)	65.72	61.72	61.75
Baseline-2 (BERT-BiLSTM-CRF)	65.43	67.74	66.56
Baseline-3 (RoBERTa-CRF)	64.66	64.64	63.35
Baseline-5 (Student without KD)	67.74	67.72	67.34
Distill-AER	**69.77**	**73.37**	**70.54**

6 Conclusion

We propose an effective method called Distill-AER to extract address entities from dialogue contexts. Experiments on the spoken dialogue context data show the effectiveness of Distill-AER model. In the future, we would study the combination of full standard address by their hierarchical constraint relationships. In addition, the context information will be considered and fully utilized to improve the performance of our model.

References

1. Eligüzel, N., Çetinkaya, C., Dereli, T.: Comparison of different machine learning techniques on location extraction by utilizing geo-tagged tweets: a case study. Adv. Eng. Inform. **46**, 101151 (2020)
2. Yaman, E., Krdžalic-Koric, K.: Address entities extraction using named entity recognition. In: 2019 7th International Conference on Future Internet of Things and Cloud Workshops (FiCloudW), pp. 13–17. IEEE (2019)
3. Xu C, Li J, Luo X, et al. Dlocrl: A deep learning pipeline for fine-grained location recognition and linking in tweets. The World Wide Web Conference, pp. 3391–3397 (2019)
4. Zhang, H., Liu, L., Jiang, H., et al.: Texsmart: a text understanding system for fine-grained NER and enhanced semantic analysis. arXiv preprint arXiv:2012.15639 (2020)
5. Wu, G., Tang, G., Wang, Z., et al.: An attention-based BiLSTM-CRF model for Chinese clinic named entity recognition. IEEE Access **7**, 113942–113949 (2019)
6. Schuster, M., Paliwal, K.K.: Bidirectional recurrent neural networks. IEEE Trans. Signal Process. **45**(11), 2673–2681 (1997)
7. Lafferty J, McCallum, A., Pereira, F.C.N.: Conditional random fields: probabilistic models for segmenting and labeling sequence data (2001)
8. Mai, K., Pham, T.H., Nguyen, M.T., et al.: An empirical study on fine-grained named entity recognition. In: Proceedings of the 27th International Conference on Computational Linguistics, pp. 711–722 (2018)
9. Shan, S., Li, Z., Yang, Q., et al.: Geographical address representation learning for address matching. World Wide Web **23**(3), 2005–2022 (2020)

10. Chen, X., Qiu, X., Zhu, C., et al.: Gated recursive neural network for Chinese word segmentation. In: Proceedings of the 53rd Annual Meeting of the Association for Computational Linguistics and the 7th International Joint Conference on Natural Language Processing (Volume 1: Long Papers), pp. 1744–1753 (2015)

11. Xu Y, Huang H, Feng C, et al.: A supervised multi-head self-attention network for nested named entity recognition. In: Proceedings of the AAAI Conference on Artificial Intelligence, vol. 35, no. 16, pp. 14185–14193 (2021)

12. Misawa, S., Taniguchi, M., Miura, Y., et al.: Character-based bidirectional LSTM-CRF with words and characters for Japanese named entity recognition. In: Proceedings of the First Workshop on Subword and Character Level Models in NLP, pp. 97–102 (2017)

13. Xue, M., Yu, B., Zhang, Z., et al.: Coarse-to-fine pre-training for named entity recognition. arXiv preprint arXiv:2010.08210 (2020)

14. Lin, H., Lu, Y., Tang, J., et al.: A rigorous study on named entity recognition: can fine-tuning pretrained model lead to the promised land? arXiv preprint arXiv:2004.12126 (2020)

15. Ju, M., Miwa, M., Ananiadou, S.: A neural layered model for nested named entity recognition. In: Proceedings of the 2018 Conference of the North American Chapter of the Association for Computational Linguistics: Human Language Technologies, Volume 1 (Long Papers), pp. 1446–1459 (2018)

16. Monaikul, N., Castellucci, G., Filice, S., et al.: Continual learning for named entity recognition. In: Proceedings of the Thirty-Fifth AAAI Conference on Artificial Intelligence, pp. 13570–13577 (2021)

17. Zhu, H., He, C., Fang, Y., et al.: Fine grained named entity recognition via seq2seq framework. IEEE Access 8, 53953–53961 (2020)

18. Li, P., Luo, A., Liu, J., et al.: Bidirectional gated recurrent unit neural network for Chinese address element segmentation. ISPRS Int. J. Geo Inf. 9(11), 635 (2020)

19. Zhang, H., Ren, F., Li, H., et al.: Recognition method of new address elements in Chinese address matching based on deep learning. ISPRS Int. J. Geo Inf. 9(12), 745 (2020)

20. Kuai, X., Guo, R., Zhang, Z., et al.: Spatial context-based local toponym extraction and Chinese textual address segmentation from urban POI data. ISPRS Int. J. Geo Inf. 9(3), 147 (2020)

21. Hinton, G., Vinyals, O., Dean, J.: Distilling the knowledge in a neural network. arXiv preprint arXiv:1503.02531 2(7) (2015)

22. Sanh, V., Debut, L., Chaumond, J., et al.: DistilBERT, a distilled version of BERT: smaller, faster, cheaper and lighter. arXiv preprint arXiv:1910.01108 (2019)

23. Jiao, X., Yin, Y., Shang, L., et al.: TinyBERT: distilling BERT for natural language understanding. In: Findings of the Association for Computational Linguistics: EMNLP 2020, pp. 4163–4174 (2020)

24. Sun, Z., Yu, H., Song, X., et al.: Mobilebert: a compact task-agnostic Bert for resource-limited devices. arXiv preprint arXiv:2004.02984 (2020)

25. Tsai, H., Riesa, J., Johnson, M., et al.: Small and practical BERT models for sequence labeling. arXiv preprint arXiv:1909.00100 (2019)

26. Yang, H., Huang, S., Dai, X., et al.: Fine-grained knowledge fusion for sequence labeling domain adaptation. arXiv preprint arXiv:1909.04315 (2019)

27. Orihashi, S., Yamazaki, Y., Makishima, N., et al.: Hierarchical knowledge distillation for dialogue sequence labeling. arXiv preprint arXiv:2111.10957 (2021)

28. Cui, Y., Che, W., Liu, T., et al.: Pre-training with whole word masking for Chinese Bert. IEEE/ACM Trans. Audio Speech Lang. Process. 29, 3504–3514 (2021)

29. Chaudhary, A.: A visual survey of data augmentation in NLP (2020)
30. Tian, X., Huang, X., He, D., et al.: TOD-DA: towards boosting the robustness of task-oriented dialogue modeling on spoken conversations. arXiv preprint arXiv:2112.12441 (2021)
31. Feng, S.Y., Gangal, V., Wei, J., et al.: A survey of data augmentation approaches for NLP. arXiv preprint arXiv:2105.03075 (2021)

KGAT: An Enhanced Graph-Based Model for Text Classification

Xin Wang[1] , Chao Wang[1(✉)], Haiyang Yang[1], Xingpeng Zhang[1], Qi Shen[2],
Kan Ji[1], Yuhong Wu[1], and Huayi Zhan[3]

[1] Southwest Petroleum University, Chengdu, China
{xinwang,xpzhang,jikan}@swpu.edu.cn
{202021000484,202021000482,202121000494}@stu.swpu.edu.cn
[2] Chang'an University, Xi'an, China
2018900932@chd.edu.cn
[3] Sichuan Changhong Electric Co. Ltd, Mianyang, China
huayi.zhan@changhong.com

Abstract. As a fundamental task in natural language processing, text classification, which is to predict the class label of a given text, has been intensively studied. Consequently, a host of techniques have been developed, among which techniques that are based on graph neural network and its variant *e.g.,* graph attention network (GAT) achieved impressive performances, as they show superiority in dealing with complex graph-structured data. Despite effectiveness, most of these techniques suffer from several limitations, *e.g.,* incapability in well-capturing correlation among words in a text. In light of these, we propose a comprehensive approach KGAT which incorporates multi-head GAT with enhanced attention and customized ReadOut operation for text classification. (1) Our approach constructs a *text graph* G_T with edge weights from a text such that both semantic and structural information (with correlation degree) can be well captured. (2) On text graph G_T, a novel attention mechanism is incorporated in a multi-head GAT for representation learning. (3) Our approach customizes ReadOut operation such that the representation of a text is refined by using a set of influential nodes of G_T. Intensive experimental studies on both typical benchmark datasets and a newly created one (**Sensitive**) show that our approach substantially outperforms other baseline methods and yields a promising technique for text classification.

Keywords: Graph attention network · Multi-head attention mechanism · Text classification

1 Introduction

Text classification is a classic problem in the field of natural language processing (NLP) and provides fundamental methodologies for other NLP tasks, such as topic labeling, sentiment analysis, intent detection, cyberspace security, and so

W. Lu et al. (Eds.): NLPCC 2022, LNAI 13551, pp. 656–668, 2022.
https://doi.org/10.1007/978-3-031-17120-8_51

on. The problem has been investigated from the perspective of machine learning and was settled by techniques based on Naive Bayes [6], k-Nearest Neighbors [18], Support Vector Machines [3] and so on. However, these traditional techniques rely heavily on feature engineering for text representation, which leads to high labor costs and low efficiency. In recent year, with the rapid development of deep learning, neural-network-based techniques were involved to address the problem, e.g., TextCNN [7], TextRNN [11], TextRCNN [8], etc. In particular, Graph Neural Network [17] (GNN), a special kind of neural network, is leveraged for the task and achieves excellent performances.

Deep learning based techniques rely on text representation heavily. In light of this, various unsupervised methods are proposed to learn word or document representations. The emergence of word vector models such as GloVe [16] and Word2Vec [13] provide solutions to transform text data from high-dimensional, high-sparse forms into continuous dense data, similar to the transformation on images and speeches. However, the transformation on a sentence is often processed sequentially with the embedding of each word, which ignores (potentially important) structural information among words/phrases within a text. To tackle the issue, investigators advocate expressing sentences with graph structures, which can well express relationship among objects. While, this task is nontrivial for classic deep learning based techniques. Fortunately, graph neural network (GNN) is proposed shortly and showed strong capability in dealing with graph data. GNN is first proposed by [17]. Then [15] proposed a graph-CNN model for text classification and achieved better performance than classical models, e.g., CNN, LSTM. Essentially, GNN-based models transform a serialized text into a graph, thus node-level representation can be refined by referencing the underlying topological structure. Moreover, graph embedding, which expresses graph nodes or subgraphs in the form of vectors, provides a new type of representation for the task of classification. Following this way, [25] proposed TextGCN that builds a graph to capture the relationship of words that appeared in the entire corpus for text classification, while different meanings of the same word were not considered. Text-level-GNN [4] and Texting [26] are extensions of TextGCN, still, they did not consider the weight of each edge when constructing the graph. However, different neighbor nodes have different effects on word nodes, which should not be simply omitted.

In response to the above problems, we propose a novel text classification approach based on GAT. Instead of building a single corpus level graph, we produce a sentence level graph, referred to as *text graph*, for each input text. The *text graph* can well capture correlation relationship among words, which facilitates the calculation of attention coefficients. We improve multi-head GAT with enhanced attention mechanism for node-level feature learning. We also develop a new ReadOut function for finalizing structure-level representation, in particular, a wise strategy is incorporated for influential nodes identification. Via experimental studies, the method we proposed shows superiority in various datasets. To sum up, our contributions are as follows:

- We propose to construct an undirected weighted graph to better capture the correlation strength of the words within a text.
- We develop a multi-head GAT with enhanced attention mechanism. This new model substantially improves representation learning at node-level.
- We customize the ReadOut operation to finalize graph-level representations. In particular, an effective heuristic method for independent set searching is employed to identify influential nodes.
- We produce a labeled dataset Sensitive. As far as we know, the dataset is the first Chinese dataset in cyberspace security and fills a critical void in the area.
- We conduct intensive experiments on both benchmark datasets and Sensitive. The performance of our approach illustrates its superiority compared to other competitive baseline models.

2   Related Work

We now review text classification techniques that are based on deep learning and graph neural networks.

Methods Based on Deep Learning. For the characteristic of automatically learning high-dimensional features, deep learning models, such as CNN [7], RNN [14], are also applied to text classification tasks, which avoid tedious manual feature engineering and perform better than traditional machine learning methods. And the attention mechanism is introduced to strengthen the expressive ability of the models. Hierarchical attention networks (HAN) [24] and Attention-based LSTM [1,20,29] attention to networks. However, it is usually difficult for the local sliding window in the sequential learning model to capture the dependencies between words far apart in long sentences.

Methods Based on GNNs. Graph Neural Networks (GNNs) have attracted much attention [23,27,28] for their powerful representation capability in dealing with unstructured data. In GNNs, the text classification problem is abstracted as a graph node classification problem. To enable the GNN-based model to support online testing and reduce memory consumption, Text-level-GNN [4] builds graphs for each input text to obtain global information. And TextING [26] builds individual graphs for each document and learns text-level word interactions by GNN to effectively produce embeddings for obscure words in the new text. Graph theory is also combined with convolution to solve the task of text classification. TextGCN [25] builds a heterogeneous graph model and extracts co-occurrence information between overall words. And SGC [22] reduces unnecessary complexity and redundant calculations by iteratively eliminating nonlinearities and collapsing weight matrices between consecutive layers. Attention mechanism can enhance the feature learning ability of networks and is also introduced into GNNs. Graph attention network (GATs) calculates the attention weight of the neighbors of the source node. Deep attention diffusion graph neural network (DADGNN) [12] captures the connection between a word and its distant neighbors at the node-level attention layer to obtain a more accurate document-level representation. HyperGAT proposes to learn text embeddings by applying hyper-graphs over documents. However, the aforementioned models pay less attention to polysemy and edge weight.

3   Method

The working flow of our approach is shown in Fig. 1a. As can be seen, the model, denoted by KGAT, consists of three parts, *i.e.,* Text Graph Construction, Message Passing, and ReadOut. We next illustrate them in details.

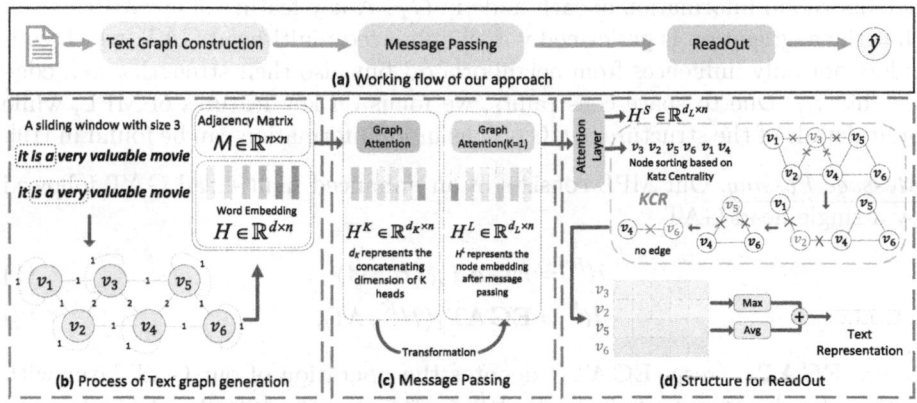

Fig. 1. The working flow and structure of KGAT

3.1   Text Graph Construction

Let $\mathbf{T} = [t_1, t_2, \cdots, t_n]$ denote a text, where each t_i refers to the i-th word of $\mathbf{T}$. Given such a text $\mathbf{T}$ to be classified, our approach converts it into a *text graph*, that incorporates both semantic and structural information of $\mathbf{T}$.

Text Graph. The construction process of a text graph works as follows.

(I) A sliding window with size l ($l < |\mathbf{T}|$) is initialized and then moved word by word on $\mathbf{T}$ until reaching the rightmost side. During the period, if a pair of words are *covered* by the window, their co-occurrence frequency will be increased by one. After the above process, the co-occurrence frequency of each pair of words is obtained.

(II) The *text graph* $G_T = (V, E, f_v, f_w)$ is generated by including a set of nodes in V such that each node v_i in V corresponds to a word t_i in $\mathbf{T}$ and a set of edges (v_i, v_j) in E if the co-occurrence frequency $\tau(v_i, v_j)$ (or τ_{ij} for short when it is clear from context) of v_i and v_j is above zero. Moreover, each node v_i in V carries a tuple $f_v(v_i)$ consisting of the node id of v_i and a d-dimensional vector $\boldsymbol{h}_i \in \mathbb{R}^d$ corresponding to the embedding of t_i. Each edge $e = (v_i, v_j)$ in E takes an integer $f_w(e)$ as the weight of e, where $f_w(e) = \tau_{ij}$.

From graph G_T, one can immediately obtain two matrices $\mathcal{H}$ and $\mathcal{M}$. The matrix $\mathcal{H}$ is defined as $[h_1, h_2, \cdots, h_n] \in \mathbb{R}^{d \times n}$, where h_i ($i \in [1, n]$) indicates the word embedding of i-th word in $\mathbf{T}$. For the (adjacency) matrix $\mathcal{M}$, its entry $a_{i,j}$ indicates the edge weight $f_w(v_i, v_j)$ of (v_i, v_j). Taking the sentence "*it is a very valuable movie*" from a benchmark dataset as an example, by using a sliding window with $l = 3$, one can obtain a *text graph* along with its adjacency matrix as shown in Fig. 1b.

3.2 Message Passing with Enhanced GAT

Given a text graph G_T, a message passing layer (MPL) is developed to aggregate neighborhood information of each node in G_T. A key feature of our MPL lies in that the aggregation is performed via an enhanced multi-head GAT, which considers not only influences from neighborhood but also their strengths, *i.e.*, edge weights τ_{ij}. Due to space constraints, we focus on key features of MPL, while omit details of the structure of a GAT, as more information can be found in [19].

Message Passing. Our MPL consists of an enhanced multi-head GAT followed by a single head GAT.

$$\mathcal{H}^K = \mathbf{EGAT}_K(\mathcal{H}, \mathcal{M}), \tag{1}$$

$$\mathcal{H}^L = \mathbf{EGAT}_1(\mathcal{H}^K, \mathcal{M}), \tag{2}$$

where $\mathbf{EGAT}_K$ (resp. $\mathbf{EGAT}_1$) denotes the operation of our GAT layer with with K heads (resp. a single head), $\mathcal{H}^K \in \mathbb{R}^{d_K \times n}$ is the output of $\mathbf{EGAT}_K$ and $\mathcal{H}^L \in \mathbb{R}^{d_L \times n}$ as the output of $\mathbf{EGAT}_1$ is the the final result of our MPL. In fact, $\mathbf{EGAT}_K$ concatenates different features from multiple heads, by following Eq. 3, that is defined as follows.

$$h_i' = \left\|_{\kappa=1}^{K} \sigma \left(\sum_{j \in \mathcal{N}_i} \alpha_{ij}^\kappa \mathbf{W}^\kappa h_j \right), \tag{3}$$

where $\|$ represents concatenation, K is the number of heads, σ represents the nonlinear function, $\mathcal{N}_i$ represents all direct neighbors of v_i, $\mathbf{W}^\kappa$ is a learnable weight matrix, which is shared by all nodes in the κ-th head. Note that $\alpha_{ij}^\kappa = \text{Softmax}(\beta_{ij}^\kappa)$ is the normalized enhanced attention coefficient of v_j to v_i computed by the κ-th head, and β_{ij}^κ is the enhanced attention coefficient, which indicates the importance of v_j to v_i.

$$\beta_{ij}^\kappa = \text{LeakyReLU}(\boldsymbol{a}^\kappa[\mathbf{W}^\kappa h_i \| \mathbf{W}^\kappa h_j]) \tau_{ij}, \tag{4}$$

For a pair of embedding h_i and h_j at κ-th head ($\kappa \in [1, K]$), a matrix $\mathbf{W}^\kappa \in \mathbb{R}^{d' \times d}$ is used for linear transformation. Two embedding are then concatenated through the operation $\|$ in Eq. (3), and transformed via a learnable vector $\boldsymbol{a}^\kappa \in \mathbb{R}^{1 \times 2d'}$. Afterwards, LeakyReLU is applied as the activation function, followed by a transformation imposed by τ_{ij}. Note that by involving τ_{ij} in the attention mechanism, our MPL is able to incorporate the correlation degree of words t_i and t_j in a text, and hence can capture attention coefficients more accurately.

After operation via MPL, each node v in G_T aggregates feature information of all its direct neighbors, indicating that the representation of v is refined by referencing its context information.

3.3   ReadOut for Prediction

After process through MPL, a customized ReadOut operation (shown in Fig. 1d) is developed for text classification.

Attention Layer. The node representation $\mathcal{H}^L$ of a G_T is updated via an attention layer. We then obtain a new representation $\mathcal{H}^S \in \mathbb{R}^{d_L \times n}$, which is defined as:

$$\mathcal{H}^S = \sigma(\mathbf{W}_1 \mathcal{H}^L + \mathbf{b}_1) \odot \tanh(\mathbf{W}_2 \mathcal{H}^L + \mathbf{b}_2), \qquad (5)$$

where parameters $\mathbf{W}_1 \in \mathbb{R}^{1 \times d_L}$, $\mathbf{W}_2 \in \mathbb{R}^{d_L \times d_L}$, $\mathbf{b}_1, \mathbf{b}_2 \in \mathbb{R}^n$ are learned during training; σ and $\tanh$ are typical non-linear functions; $\odot$ represents the dot product of matrices. Indeed, the former part works as an attention mechanism, while the latter part is for non-linear transformation.

Identifying Influential Nodes. To predict the class label of a text, some of its words *e.g.*, stop words, are often not helpful. To downplay the influences from those useless words, it is necessary to identify *influential* nodes in G_T and obtain a representation from them for classification. To this end, we compute *Katz Centrality Ranking* (KCR) of the nodes in G_T and picks influential ones via KCR. Briefly, katz centrality [21] is a variant of eigenvector centrality that not only considers influences *e.g.*, centrality, from direct neighbors, but also leverages a coefficient to adjust centrality of the central node itself. The operation to obtain the katz centrality is defined as follows:

$$C_{Katz} = (I - \gamma \cdot \mathcal{M})^{-1}\delta, \qquad (6)$$

where $C_{Katz} \in \mathbb{R}^n$ is a n dimensional vector with each entry corresponding to the katz centrality of a node, and n is the numbers of nodes in G_T; constant γ is a damping factor and usually set to be less than the largest eigenvalue λ, *i.e.*, $\gamma < \frac{1}{\lambda}$; and constant δ serves as a bias; I and $\mathcal{M}$ represent the identity matrix and adjacency matrix, respectively.

Given C_{Katz}, influential nodes can be identified as follows. (a) Nodes in G_T are sorted according to their centrality specified in C_{Katz}. (b) Nodes with higher centrality are picked repeatedly, until each edge of G_T has at least one end point in a set $\mathcal{Z}$, that is used for maintaining influence nodes. Essentially, above process simulates the progress of identifying an independent set from a graph. As shown in Fig. 1d, a sorted list $\{v_3, v_2, v_5\ v_6, v_1, v_4\}$ is obtained according to C_{Katz} of G_T; then v_3, v_2, v_5 and v_6 are selected as influential nodes as they form an independent set of G_T. Now, we are ready to generate a representation for G_T.

Graph Representations. Based on the set $\mathcal{Z}$ of influential nodes and their representations $\mathcal{H}^S$, a pooling operation, specified in Eq. 7 is performed to obtain a new representation $\mathcal{H}_\eta \in \mathbb{R}^{d_L}$, that is used for classification. Intuitively, the pooling with avg averages the features of all the influential words, while the other operation max is to highlight the role of the most influential word.

$$\mathcal{H}_\eta = \mathsf{avg}(\boldsymbol{h}_1^S, \cdots, \boldsymbol{h}_{|\mathcal{Z}|}^S) + \mathsf{max}(\boldsymbol{h}_1^S, \cdots, \boldsymbol{h}_{|\mathcal{Z}|}^S), \tag{7}$$

where $\boldsymbol{h}_i^S$ $(i \in [1, |\mathcal{Z}|])$ represents the feature of the i-th node in $\mathcal{Z}$.

Prediction. Given the text representation $\mathcal{H}_\eta$, it is fed into the multi-layer perceptron with a single layer for prediction. In particular, the Softmax and cross-entropy functions are used for loss evaluation:

$$\mathcal{L}\mathsf{oss} = -\sum_i y_i \log(\hat{y}_i), \tag{8}$$

where $\hat{y} = \mathsf{Softmax}(\mathbf{W}_c\mathcal{H}_\eta + \mathbf{b}_c)$ is the predicted label, and weight $\mathbf{W}_c$, bias $\mathbf{b}_c$ are trainable parameters.

4   Experiments

In this section, we conduct comprehensive experimental studies to show the performance of our model.

4.1   Experimental Setup

Datasets. For fair comparison, we used a set of typical benchmark datasets for text classification. Table 1 shows the summary of the datasets we used. In a nutshell, the datasets can be categorized into two types, one for long corpus and the other one for short corpus. Specifically, _R8_ and _R52_ are subsets of Reuters 21578 datasets. _MR_ is a movie review dataset for binary sentiment classification. _SST-1_ and _SST-2_ are extension of _MR_. _TREC_ [9] is a question dataset. Sensitive[1] is a dataset manually labeled by us. It contains 15035 short texts in Chinese and is classified into six types: drugs, violence, accidents, gambles, covid-19, and others.

Table 1. Summary statistics of the datasets.

Dataset	Long Corpus			Short Corpus				
	R8	R52	Ohsumed	MR	SST-1	SST-2	TREC	Sensitive
#Docs	7,674	9,100	7,400	10,662	11,855	9,613	5,952	15,035
#Train	5,485	6,532	3,357	7,108	9,645	7,792	5,452	12,028
#Test	2,189	2,568	4,043	3,554	2,210	1,821	500	3,007
Avg.Length	41.90	44.37	79.57	18.46	16.80	16.92	10.63	10.73
Max.Length	247	248	192	46	46	46	31	52
#Class	8	52	23	2	5	2	6	6

---

[1] https://github.com/do-Hines/textGAT-MI.git.

Table 2. Accuracy (%) on benchmark datasets. We report results as mean ± standard deviation after 10 runs. The bold font and underline are the champion and runner-up respectively.

Model	R8	R52	Ohsumed	MR	SST-1	SST-2	TREC
TF-IDF+LR	93.74±0.00	86.95±0.00	54.66±0.00	74.59±0.00	41.18±0.00	79.63±0.00	96.81±0.00
CNN	95.71±0.52	87.59±0.48	58.44±1.06	77.75±0.72	42.30±0.41	80.27±0.42	93.62±0.55
Bi-LSTM	96.31±0.33	90.54±0.91	49.27±1.07	77.68±0.86	42.63±0.66	80.11±0.49	93.32±0.72
CNN-BiLSTM	96.66±0.61	92.62±0.49	52.21±0.23	76.62±0.39	43.12±0.40	81.93±0.46	94.12±0.51
fastText	96.13±0.21	92.81±0.09	57.70±0.49	75.14±0.20	36.08±0.81	81.45±0.16	91.29±0.69
Text-GCN	97.07±0.10	93.56±0.18	68.36±0.56	76.74±0.20	40.65±0.06	81.25±0.09	91.40±0.39
SGC	97.20±0.10	94.00±0.20	68.50±0.30	75.90±0.30	41.63±0.41	76.22 ±0.13	92.29±1.26
Text-level GNN	97.80±0.20	94.60±0.30	69.40±0.60	75.47±0.60	43.02±0.65	81.75±0.36	94.09±0.36
HyperGAT	<u>97.97±0.23</u>	94.98±0.27	69.90±0.34	78.32±0.27	41.96±0.35	81.26±0.72	93.55±1.79
DADGNN	**98.15±0.16**	**95.16±0.22**	-	78.64±0.29	45.15±0.26	**84.32±0.15**	97.99±0.52
w/o edge weights	97.34±0.15	94.70±0.33	<u>70.16±0.43</u>	<u>78.75±0.34</u>	<u>45.71±0.53</u>	83.42±0.23	<u>98.16 ±0.25</u>
w/o KCR	97.30±0.21	94.61±0.29	69.88±0.52	78.64±0.53	45.45±0.50	83.31±0.35	97.98±0.38
KGAT(ours)	97.41±0.16	<u>95.00±0.33</u>	**70.24±0.32**	**79.03±0.30**	**45.83±0.35**	<u>83.71±0.43</u>	**98.18±0.27**

Baselines. We consider three types of models as baseline methods.

- Traditional machine learning method TF-IDF+LR.
- Traditional deep learning methods, _e.g.,_ CNN [7], Bi-LSTM [11], CNN-BiLSTM [10], and fastText [5].
- Graph-based methods, _e.g.,_ Text-GCN [25], SGC [22], Text-level GNN [4], HyperGAT [2], and DADGNN [12].

Parameter Settings. In our test, we used the following settings: batch size of 512, initial learning rate of 0.001, sliding window of size 5. To avoid over-fitting, we also adopt the dropout operation with a rate of 0.5. To calculate KCR, γ , δ are fixed as 0.01 and 1, respectively. We implemented an 8-head KGAT (by default) and used the Adam optimizer to train KGAT for 200 epochs with early-stopping strategy. The length of the text we intercept varies according to different datasets. For typical benchmark datasets, their original split for training and testing is followed; for Sensitive, we randomly pick 80% as training and use the remaining for testing (see Table 1 for details). We used pre-trained GloVe word vectors [16] with $d = 300$ as the default input features while out-of-vocabulary words are randomly sampled from a uniform distribution [-0.01, 0.01].

Evaluation Metrics. On benchmark datasets, Accuracy is used as the evaluation metric. While on Sensitive, Precision, Recall, F1-Score, and Accuracy are used.

4.2   Prediction Accuracy

We show the prediction accuracy of our approach vs. baseline models on both benchmark datasets and Sensitive.

Comparison on Benchmark Datasets. Table 2 shows the accuracy of various models on benchmark datasets. We find the following. (1) KGAT performs better than baseline models, as it ranks top 1 *w.r.t.* accuracy on 4 datasets and top 2 on *R52* and *SST2*. (2) On 4 datasets with short text, our KGAT achieve the best performance on three and reached second place on the *SST2*. This shows that our approach works well on short texts. (3) On *R8* with long text, all models achieve high accuracy. Though KGAT performs slightly worse than some GNN models, it still beats other counterparts, showing that it can effectively capture long-distance semantic relations.

Table 3. The performance of different models On Sensitive.

Model	Precision	Recall	F1-Score	Accuracy
CNN	92.58±0.60	91.83±0.40	92.17±0.43	94.01±0.27
Bi-LSTM	91.20±0.75	91.02±0.67	91.02±0.69	93.25±0.52
CNN-BiLSTM	92.63±0.53	92.16±0.74	92.36±0.53	94.25±0.39
fastText	89.15±0.08	87.17±0.09	88.12±0.08	91.15±0.09
Text-GCN	89.59±0.23	90.36±0.30	89.93±0.25	92.32±0.17
SGC	86.18±0.21	89.49±0.13	87.71±0.17	89.69±0.18
Text-level GNN	93.64±0.21	93.80±0.11	93.70±0.18	94.21±0.17
w/o edge weights	95.57±0.23	95.53±0.21	95.54±0.18	96.48±0.15
w/o KCR	96.12±0.30	95.56±0.30	95.82±0.19	96.68±0.15
KGAT(ours)	**96.23±0.30**	**95.60±0.32**	**95.90±0.27**	**96.78±0.22**

Comparison on Sensitive. Results on Sensitive are shown in Table 3. Our KGAT exhibits the best performance on all metrics, increasing more than 2% points. It demonstrates that KGAT works quite well on Chinese dataset. Since Sensitive is a dataset regarding cyberspace security, the excellent performance of KGAT on Sensitive also shows that our method is of great practical significance in the field of cybersecurity.

Ablation Study. To investigate the contribution of each module in KGAT, we conduct a series of ablation studies on all evaluation datasets. Concretely, *w/o edge weight* is a variant that calculates attention coefficient without edge weight, and *w/o* KCR is a variant that Readout without Katz Centrality Ranking. The results are shown in the last three rows of Tables 2 and 3, respectively. We find that including edge weights when calculating attention improves accuracy. This observation verifies that a text graph with edge weight can better capture the contextual relationship between words, which is beneficial for calculating more accurate attention coefficients. Moreover, the performance gap between *w/o* KCR and KGAT shows the effectiveness of choosing key nodes for graph-level representation.

Inductive Capability. To examine the inductive capability of KGAT, we vary the proportion of training data from 1% to 80% on *MR* and *Ohsumed.* Two baseline models Text-GCN and SGC are used for comparison. Figure 2 shows that (1) KGAT achieves the best accuracy, showing a better capability to summarize new words; and (2) all models perform better with larger training data, as expected.

4.3   Supplementary Studies

We conduct three supplementary experiments to reveal influences caused by hyper-parameters.

Number of Heads. To see how model performance is influenced by the change of head numbers, we conduct a supplementary study *w.r.t.* varied heads. Figure 3 shows the accuracy changes under varied head numbers on *MR*, Sensitive and *Ohsumed*, respectively. As can be seen, starting from $K = 1$, the accuracy increases when the number of attention heads increases. While the accuracy decreases in both datasets when $K > 8$. It shows that multi-head attention with appropriate head numbers can improve model performance.

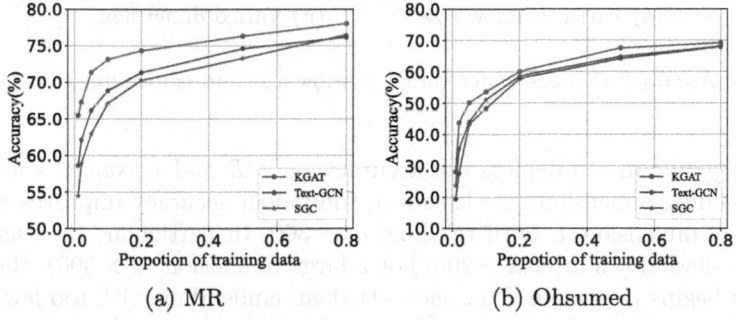

(a) MR   (b) Ohsumed

Fig. 2. Test with varied training data (1%, 2%, 5%, 10%, 20%, 50%, 80%) on MR and Ohsumed. The less training data is, the more new words are in the test.

Size of Sliding Window. The construction of a text graph is influenced by the size l of the sliding window. Therefore, the parameter l will inevitably affect the performance of KGAT. Figure 4a shows the accuracy of KGAT under different window sizes on *Ohsumed* and *TREC* respectively. The x-axis represents the window size, and the y-axis represents accuracy. It can be seen that the accuracy reaches top when $l = 5$ (resp. $l = 5$) on *Ohsumed* (resp. *TREC*), hence the optimal window size of texts is $l = 5$ in our method.

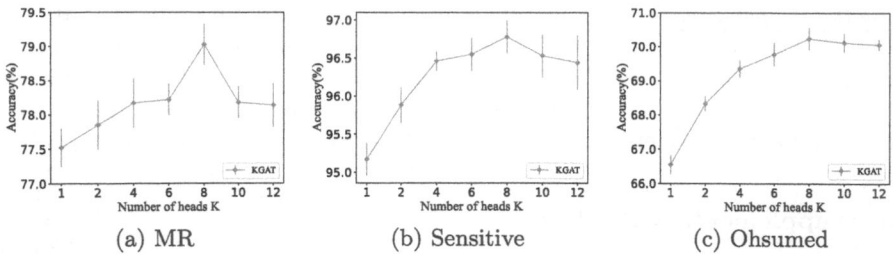

(a) MR   (b) Sensitive   (c) Ohsumed

Fig. 3. Tests on three datasets with different number of heads. Other datasets show the same trend, omitted for space.

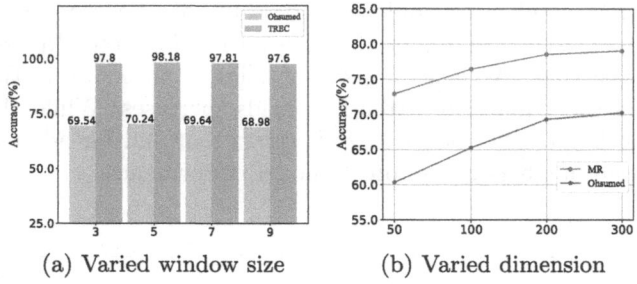

(a) Varied window size   (b) Varied dimension

Fig. 4. Accuracy changes under varied window size and embedding dimension.

Dimensions. Figure 4b depicts the accuracy on *MR* and *Ohsumed* with different embedding dimensions. As is shown, the model accuracy improves with the increase of dimension d, until reaching $d = 300$. In particular, the increase of accuracy slows down after $d > 200$. For a large dimension ($d > 300$), the model accuracy begins to decline. This shows that an embedding with too low dimension cannot propagate label information to neighbor nodes well, while a too high dimensional embedding still can not improve model performance, and may cost extra training time.

5   Conclusion and Future Work

In the paper, we propose a comprehensive approach for text classification. We have introduced techniques to construct *text graphs*, that captures correlation degrees among words. We have also developed a GAT-based model with multi-head and enhanced attention mechanism for representation learning. We have proposed a customized ReadOut operation to finalize the representation for a text. Via intensive experimental studies, our approach shows promising results on multiple benchmark datasets and Sensitive, a newly published dataset.

We have utilized Stanford Dependency-Parser and conducted tests by using dependency trees instead. The results show that incorporating dependency trees does not significantly improves performances. While, we will keep working on this direction. Another direction worth exploring is multi-label classification. Extending the model to incorporate edge features (rather than occurrence frequency) would be another interesting topic.

Acknowledgement. This work is supported by Sichuan Scientific Innovation Fund (No. 2022JDRC0009) and the National Key Research and Development Program of China (No. 2017YFA0700800).

References

1. Cheng, J., Dong, L., Lapata, M.: Long short-term memory-networks for machine reading. In: EMNLP, pp. 551–561 (2016)
2. Ding, K., Wang, J., Li, J., Li, D., Liu, H.: Be more with less: hypergraph attention networks for inductive text classification. In: EMNLP, pp. 4927–4936 (2020)
3. Forman, G.: BNS feature scaling: an improved representation over TF-IDF for SVM text classification. In: CIKM, pp. 263–270 (2008)
4. Huang, L., Ma, D., Li, S., Zhang, X., Wang, H.: Text level graph neural network for text classification. In: EMNLP-IJCNLP, pp. 3442–3448 (2019)
5. Joulin, A., Grave, E., Bojanowski, P., Mikolov, T.: Bag of tricks for efficient text classification. In: EACL, pp. 427–431 (2017)
6. Kim, S.B., Han, K.S., Rim, H.C., Myaeng, S.H.: Some effective techniques for Naive Bayes text classification. IEEE TKDE **18**(11), 1457–1466 (2006)
7. Kim, Y.: Convolutional neural networks for sentence classification. In: EMNLP, pp. 1746–1751 (2014)
8. Lai, S., Xu, L., Liu, K., Zhao, J.: Recurrent convolutional neural networks for text classification. In: AAAI, pp. 2267–2273 (2015)
9. Li, X., Roth, D.: Learning question classifiers. In: COLING (2002)
10. Lin, Y., Xu, G., Xu, G., Chen, Y., Sun, D.: Sensitive information detection based on convolution neural network and bi-directional LSTM. In: TrustCom, pp. 1614–1621 (2020)
11. Liu, P., Qiu, X., Huang, X.: Recurrent neural network for text classification with multi-task learning. In: IJCAI, pp. 2873–2879 (2016)
12. Liu, Y., Guan, R., Giunchiglia, F., Liang, Y., Feng, X.: Deep attention diffusion graph neural networks for text classification. In: EMNLP, pp. 8142–8152 (2021)
13. Mikolov, T., Chen, K., Corrado, G., Dean, J.: Efficient estimation of word representations in vector space. In: ICLR (2013)
14. Mikolov, T., Karafiát, M., Burget, L., Cernocký, J., Khudanpur, S.: Recurrent neural network based language model. In: ISCA, pp. 1045–1048 (2010)
15. Peng, H., et al.: Large-scale hierarchical text classification with recursively regularized deep graph-CNN. In: Proceedings of the 2018 World Wide Web Conference, pp. 1063–1072 (2018)
16. Pennington, J., Socher, R., Manning, C.D.: GloVe: global vectors for word representation. In: EMNLP, pp. 1532–1543 (2014)
17. Scarselli, F., Gori, M., Tsoi, A.C., Hagenbuchner, M., Monfardini, G.: The graph neural network model. IEEE Trans. Neural Netw. **20**(1), 61–80 (2009)
18. Tan, S.: An effective refinement strategy for KNN text classifier. Elsevier ESWA **30**(2), 290–298 (2006)
19. Velickovic, P., Cucurull, G., Casanova, A., Romero, A., Liò, P., Bengio, Y.: Graph attention networks. In: ICLR (2018)

20. Wang, Y., Huang, M., Zhu, X., Zhao, L.: Attention-based LSTM for aspect-level sentiment classification. In: EMNLP, pp. 606–615 (2016)
21. Was, T., Skibski, O.: An axiomatization of the eigenvector and Katz centralities. In: AAAI, pp. 1258–1265 (2018)
22. Wu, F., de Souza, A.H., Zhang, T., Fifty, C., Yu, T., Weinberger, K.Q.: Simplifying graph convolutional networks. In: ICML, pp. 6861–6871 (2019)
23. Wu, Z., Pan, S., Chen, F., Long, G., Zhang, C., Yu, P.S.: A comprehensive survey on graph neural networks. IEEE TNNLS **32**(1), 4–24 (2021)
24. Yang, Z., Yang, D., Dyer, C., He, X., Smola, A.J., Hovy, E.H.: Hierarchical attention networks for document classification. In: NAACL-HLT, pp. 1480–1489 (2016)
25. Yao, L., Mao, C., Luo, Y.: Graph convolutional networks for text classification. In: AAAI, pp. 7370–7377 (2019)
26. Zhang, Y., Yu, X., Cui, Z., Wu, S., Wen, Z., Wang, L.: Every document owns its structure: inductive text classification via graph neural networks. In: ACL, pp. 334–339 (2020)
27. Zhang, Z., Cui, P., Zhu, W.: Deep learning on graphs: a survey. IEEE TKDE **34**(1), 249–270 (2022)
28. Zhou, J., et al.: Graph neural networks: a review of methods and applications. AI Open **1**, 57–81 (2020)
29. Zhou, X., Wan, X., Xiao, J.: Attention-based LSTM network for cross-lingual sentiment classification. In: EMNLP, pp. 247–256 (2016)

Automatic Academic Paper Rating Based on Modularized Hierarchical Attention Network

Kai Kang[1], Huaping Zhang[1(✉)], Yugang Li[1], Xi Luo[2],
and Silamu Wushour[3]

[1] Beijing Institute of Technology, Beijing 100081, China
{3120210985,Kevinzhang,lyg}@bit.edu.cn
[2] Beijing Union University, Beijing 100101, China
xxtluoxi@buu.edu.com
[3] Xinjiang University, Xinjiang 830046, China
wushour@xju.edu.cn

Abstract. Automatic academic paper rating (AAPR) remains a difficult but useful task to automatically predict whether to accept or reject a paper. Having found more task-specific structure features of academic papers, we present a modularized hierarchical attention network (MHAN) to predict paper quality. MHAN uses a three-level hierarchical attention network to shorten the sequence for each level. In the network, the modularized parameter distinguishes the semantics of functional chapters. And a label-smoothing mechanism is used as a loss function to avoid inappropriate labeling. Compared with MHCNN and plain HAN on an AAPR dataset, MHAN achieves a state-of-the-art accuracy of 65.33%. Ablation experiments show that the proposed methods are effective.

Keywords: Automatic academic paper rating · Modularized · Hierarchical

1 Introduction

The number of academic papers is increasing enormously with the development of scientific researches. Whether a paper is accepted is usually decided through peer review, which is exhausting, time-consuming, laborious, biased, and prejudiced. An automatic rating method would help to determine whether to accept a paper efficiently and objectively.

With the growth of annotated data and the development of natural language processing technology, automatic academic paper rating (AAPR) becomes feasible. Kang [1] published a widely-cited dataset for peer-reviewing, which collected 10.7K conferences in NLP fields while Yang [2] provided the Arxiv Academic Paper Dataset with 50.0K source papers. In recent years, researchers formulate AAPR as a binary prediction task, and solve it with feature-engineering [3–6] or

© The Author(s), under exclusive license to Springer Nature Switzerland AG 2022
W. Lu et al. (Eds.): NLPCC 2022, LNAI 13551, pp. 669–681, 2022.
https://doi.org/10.1007/978-3-031-17120-8_52

end-to-end neural networks [2,7]. Having learned from human reviewers, models evaluate papers in a multi-dimensional way, and provide a reference for reviewers to make accept/reject decisions.

According to the features of academic papers, we found three methods to modify the network and to achieve better performance at predicting acceptance or rejection, with the following motivation.

Academic Papers Are Much Longer Than Regular Documents. To tackle the long-text problem, recurrent neural networks (RNNs) use gating mechanisms [8,9] to avoid the vanishing gradient problem, and convolutional neural networks (CNNs) use deeper networks to expand the receptive field [10]. Nevertheless, they do not fit well with extremely long documents like academic papers. Transformers (BERT [11]) is inefficient at long documents due to its self-attention module being highly complex. Apart from these basic networks, modified networks such as MHCNN, HAN, and transformer variants are proposed. MHCNN uses only two-level attention-based CNN and another attention layer, which can not guarantee sufficient receptive field for each level. HAN [12] only uses only two-level attention-based RNN, which is not deep enough for academic papers. Last but not least, transformer variants [13,14] are unsuitable to introduce task-specific attention with a flattened input. Thus, we provides **a three-level hierarchical structure** in which each RNN only needs to deal with one short sentence, which reduces the semantic loss in computation. The three-level attention mechanism enables the model to more effectively judge the importance of texts, and to facilitate the allocation of attention weights more effectively.

Academic Papers Convey Different Meanings in Different Sections. On other tasks, researchers use the same parameters for pattern recognition (parameter sharing), assuming that the location of the pattern does not affect its meaning. Yet, in the AAPR task, the structure of a paper breaks the assumption of parameter sharing. An idea in related work represents the work of other researchers, while in the method section, it is more likely the author's theory, therefore the design of **modularized parameters** is able to effectively use structural information effectively.

Academic Papers Can Be Evaluated Inconsistently in Peer review. For example, NIPS 2014 observed that two committees disagreed on accept/reject decisions on more than a quarter of papers [15]. Thus, we introduce **label-smoothing** to improve the robustness of false labels, which reduces overfitting on inappropriate labels and improves the generalization ability of a model.

In summary, we make the following contributions:

- A modularized hierarchical attention network model with a three-level HAN and modularized parameters is proposed for the AAPR task;

– A label-smoothing mechanism is introduced to the loss function to avoid overfitting due to noise in the training dataset;
– Preprocessed by our method, our model outperformed baselines in the Arxiv Academic Paper Dataset [2].

2 Related Work

Automatic academic paper rating is a hard but important sub-task of the automated scholarly paper review (ASPR), which aims to help editors and reviewers in peer-reviewing with computational support.

ASPR. ASPR is highly integrated, including parsing, screening, reviewing, commenting, and evaluating [16]. Among them, reviewing has a long history of feature-engineering work, including originality [17], quality [18], clarity [19], and significance [20]. Commenting includes summarization [21] and comment generation [22,23], which aims to generate reviews automatically. Evaluating includes scoring and accept/reject decision making, which is a classification task. ASPR tasks offer help and references for peer-reviewing thereby improving its efficiency and reducing its subjectivity.

AAPR. AAPR task is to make an accept/reject prediction based on a paper. Recent studies use feature engineering and end-to-end model to evaluate papers. Kang [1] defined 22 coarse-grained features and 4 lexical features, and applied machine learning to evaluate papers. Following this work, researchers introduced more fine-grained features [3,4] and algorithms [5]. Yang [2] proposed an end-to-end model called MHCNN; they used ACNN on the chapters' content and executed attentive pooling at the chapter level to achieve accept/reject prediction. Noticing the importance of structural text information, Wenniger [24] introduced HAN to the model and improved the accuracy of academic paper quality prediction by adding structure tags. Apart from that, vision information has also been taken into consideration [7,25].

3 Method

Considering the long-text problem, the structural information, and the inconsistent labels, we propose the following method.

3.1 Preprocessing

To fit the hierarchical network, it is significant to divide the paper into segments of specific formats.
Paper-Level-Truncation. A scholarly document usually consists of a title, abstract, introduction, and sections on methods, conclusion, and related work. Considering that sections are named differently, we use regular expressions to match sections.

Module-Level-Truncation. For each module, *sentence_tokenize* from the
NLTK package is used to get the module-level segment. Because the abstract is
preprocessed beforehand, we do not treat this part.

Sentence-Level-Truncation. For each sentence, we use the word_tokenize
function to get a truncated sequence, limiting the length of sentences to 16
words according to our statistics.

3.2 Modularized Hierarchical Attention Network

A paper usually includes a title, abstract, introduction, and sections on related
work, methods, and conclusions. Each chapter contains sentences, which contain
different words. Such tertiary structural information may facilitate more accurate
predictions. Our proposed model is shown in Fig. 1.

The figure shows a sentence in the introduction. The model encodes embeddings of each word of the sentence by sentence-level BiGRU, and gives the sentence embeddings based on the sentence-level attention layer. Sentence embedding in the introduction is transformed into embedding of the introduction.
Paper-level attention gives the embedding of the paper based on each module's
embedding, and gives the logits of accept/reject.

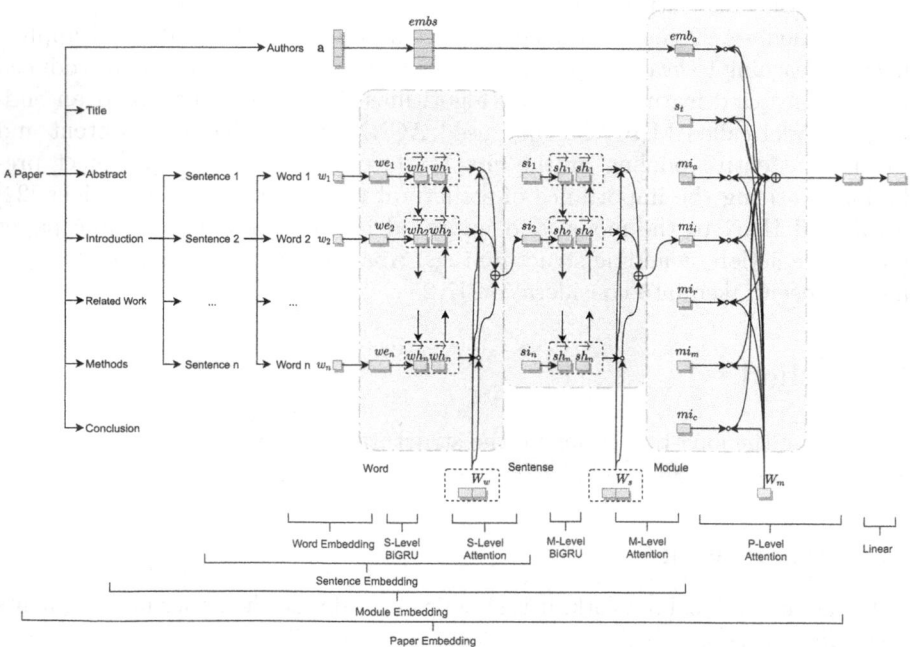

Fig. 1. Modularized hierarchical attention network

Embedding Layer. For texts, we use GloVe to encode and freeze word vec-
tor embedding parameters. Given the token sequence $x = x_1, x_2, \ldots, x_{|x|}$ as

input, embedding layer first computes the hidden vector representation $\mathbf{E_{word}} = \mathbf{e_{w1}}, \mathbf{e_{w2}}, \dots, \mathbf{e_{w|x|}}$.

$$\mathbf{E_{word}} = W_w(x_1, x_2, \dots, x_{|x|}) \tag{1}$$

where $W_w(\cdot)$ is a function map that map tokens to GloVe embeddings.

For authors appearing in the train set, we use a randomly initialized set of parameters to embed encodings, which are then trained along with the other parts.

$$\mathbf{E_{author}} = W_a(a_1, a_2, \dots, a_{|a|}) \tag{2}$$

where a_i means an author of an academic paper, $|a|$ is the number of authors, and W_a is the learnable weight to encode authors.

Encoding Layer. We use the gated recurrent unit (GRU) [9] for encoding at each level. For input token embedding in a sentence, the new encoding representation $\mathbf{O_s} = \mathbf{o_{s1}}, \mathbf{o_{s2}}, \cdots, \mathbf{o_{s|s|}}$ and hidden states $\mathbf{H_s} = \mathbf{h_{s1}}, \mathbf{h_{s2}}, \cdots, \mathbf{h_{s|s|}}$ at the sentence level is provided by S(entence)-Level Bi(direction)-GRU.

$$\mathbf{O_s}, \mathbf{H_s} = Bi\_GRU_{S_{Level}}(\mathbf{e_{w1}}, \mathbf{e_{w2}}, \dots, \mathbf{e_{w|s|}}) \tag{3}$$

where $|s|$ is the length of the sentence.

For hidden representation of sentence $\mathbf{O_s}$, module-level encoding representation $\mathbf{O_m} = \mathbf{o_{m1}}, \mathbf{o_{m2}}, \cdots, \mathbf{o_{m|m|}}$ and hidden states $\mathbf{H_m} = \mathbf{h_{m1}}, \mathbf{h_{m2}}, \cdots, \mathbf{h_{m|m|}}$ at the module level is provided by M(odule)-Level Bi(direction)-GRU.

$$\mathbf{O_m}, \mathbf{H_m} = Bi\_GRU_{M_{Level}}(\mathbf{e_{s1}}, \mathbf{e_{s2}}, \dots, \mathbf{c_{s|m|}}) \tag{4}$$

where $|m|$ is the number of the sentences in a module, and e_{si} is being computed in attentive pooling layer from h_{si} and o_{si}.

Attentive Pooling Layer. The encoding representation $\mathbf{O}, \mathbf{H}$ for the previous level is compressed by attention pooling into a new encoding representation $\boldsymbol{E}$ with length 1 and dimension d.

$$\begin{cases} \mathbf{E_s} = AP_s(\mathbf{O_s}, \mathbf{H_s}, \mathbf{W_w}) \\ \mathbf{E_m} = AP_m(\mathbf{O_m}, \mathbf{H_m}, \mathbf{W_s}) \end{cases} \tag{5}$$

where $AP_s(\cdot)$ and $AP_m(\cdot)$ are attentive pooling functions, which take $\mathbf{O_s}$ or $\mathbf{O_m}$ as $\mathbf{K}$, and take $\mathbf{H_s}$ or $\mathbf{H_m}$ as $\mathbf{V}$. A randomly initialized vector $\mathbf{W_w}$ or $\mathbf{W_s}$ is being taken as $\mathbf{Q}$, whose parameters are learnable.

$$a_i = softmax(f(Q, K_i)) = \frac{exp(f(Q, K_i))}{\sum_j exp(f(QK_j))} \tag{6}$$

$$E = AP(Q, K, V) = \sum_j a_{ij} V_j \tag{7}$$

where f is a dot product function.

For P(assage)-Level Attention, authors' embedding $\mathbf{E_a}$ should also be computed as $\mathbf{O}$ and $\mathbf{H}$.

$$\mathbf{E_p} = AP_p(O_p, H_p, W_m) \tag{8}$$

where AP_p is the attentive pooling function in paper-level.

Projecting Layer. For author representation after embedding, multiple author-embedded representations of the same paper are projected onto an encoding, and aggregated with other modules to produce a module-level encoding.

$$\mathbf{E_a} = MLP(E_{author}) \tag{9}$$

The final paper-level representation E_p obtained must be mapped to a tensor of length 2 for accept/reject prediction by a softmax function.

$$\mathbf{P} = softmax(MLP(E_p)) \tag{10}$$

A cross-entropy loss function introducing a label-smoothing mechanism is computed as the training objective function.

3.3 Modularized Parameters

Considering that views are expressed by different modules, we use modularized parameters in sentence- and module-level Bi-GRU. By using different parameters, capacity of the neural network is increased, and models can encode each module more specifically.

3.4 Label-Smoothing

Since biases and prejudices exist in labels, we use label-smoothing in the loss function to improve the robustness of the model and reduce the impact of improper labels. Specifically, when parameters are updating, we set an error rate ϵ. For each prediction, it is substituted for other predictions with a probability ϵ, and retains the prediction with a probability $1 - \epsilon$.

4 Experiments and Results

We present our experimental setup and baselines as follows. A comparative experiment was carried out to highlight our performance on an academic document.

4.1 Experimental Setup

The public dataset used in this experiment was created by Yang [2] by collecting data on academic papers in the field of artificial intelligence. The origin dataset consisted of 50K academic papers in LaTeX format. Following Yang's setting [2], we sampled 20K papers as our dataset.

Papers were divided into title, author, abstract, text, category, and venue, which marks whether the paper was accepted. The dataset was divided into training, validation, and test sets at an 8:1:1 ratio. The details are shown in Table 1.

Table 1. Distribution of dataset

Label	Train	Valid	Test	Total
Accept	8203	1032	1013	8192
Reject	8181	1016	1035	8192
Total	16384	2048	2048	20480

Table 2. Hyperparameters of experiment

	Name	Details	Detail-parameters
Trainer	–	batch_size	32
		max-num-epoch	50
Model	Embedding	author_vocab_size	20000
		author_embed_dim	64
		text_vocac_size	40000
		text_embed_dim	300
	Bi-GRU	hidden_size	32, 32, 64
		dropout-rate	0.2, 0.2, 0.1
	Attention	Q_dim	32, 32, 64
Optimizer	AdamW	max-lr	0.004
		weight-decay	0.05
	One-Circle	warmup-epoch	20
Criterion	LabelSmoothCE	Epsilon	0.05

We used PyTorch for our code, and a single GeForce RTX 1080 Ti GPU for our experiments. Table 2 gives an overview of the hyperparameters for this task. Considering that the number of positive and negative samples of the dataset are basically balanced, the performance of the model can be reflected by accuracy, so we only use this metric for evaluation.

4.2 Baseline

After preprocessing through the use of our method, we compare our model against the following baselines:

- **Random Prediction.** Because the positive and negative examples in our dataset are well balanced, we can randomly predict whether a paper can be accepted with a probability of nearly 50%.

- **Traditional Neural Network.** LSTM, CNN, and GRU were used in this task. Concatenating all the texts of the paper into a long sequence as input, these three representative neural network models extract features and give predictions. HAN has also been tested, and it can be seen as a two-level attention network with shared parameters.
- **Modularized Hierarchical CNN.** With a paper divided into sections, we put each part into an attention-based CNN, then used attentive pooling to get its representation. Since we did not obtain the dataset-splitting information and hyper-parameters from the paper [2], we redid the experiment in our setting, and used GloVe as embedding for fairness.

4.3 Comparative Experiment

After preprocessing by our method, we compared it with other baselines with results shown in Table 3, from which we can see that the proposed model is able to obtain higher accuracy than traditional neural networks and other advanced models.

Table 3. Results of comparative experiment

Model	Acc
Random	50.54
LSTM [8]	58.67
GRU [9]	60.13
CNN [26]	62.18
MHCNN [2]	62.97
HAN [12]	63.95
MHAN (ours)	**65.33**

4.4 Comparative Experiment with Pretrained Language Model

Longformer, Big Bird, and BERT were tested as baselines. Without structural information, we set global attention to [CLS] only in Longformer and Big Bird. The maximum sequence length was set to 3072. Since BERT can only deal with 512 tokens, we put the abstract of the paper into the models and predicted the label. Furthermore, we replaced the GloVe by BERT(medium)[1] as the embedding layer.

---

[1] Models can be found at https://huggingface.co/prajjwal1/bert-medium..

Table 4. Comparative experiment on pretrained language models

Model	Acc
BERT [11] (abstract)	63.57
Big Bird [14]	62.01
Longformer [13]	63.67
MHAN (ours) [1]	64.26

[1]We replaced GloVe by BERT(medium) as the embedding layer.

As shown in Table 4, the results of the pretrained language model were unanticipated.

To reduce the computation and memory complexity, transformer variants use global, band, dilated, random, and block local attention, which could not fit well with three-level hierarchical structure of academic papers, and have to share parameters in each module. With **modularized hierarchical** attention, the task-specific model reached comparable (better) performance (compared with Big Bird and Longformer).

As for GloVe, which contains more word embedding (1.9M vocabulary) than BERT (30K sub-tokens), can reduce parameters for GRU with a smaller embedding dimension. It is likely the reason why MHAN with Glove outperforms MHAN with BERT-medium.

5   Ablation Experiments

To demonstrate the effectiveness of the proposed model, we conducted three experiments on our modified module, especially on its hierarchical structure and module information.

Table 5. Ablation experiment for hierarchical attention [1]

Attention	Acc	Attention	Acc
None (AGRU)	62.13	Word level	62.97
Sentence level	63.03	word+sentense level (HAN)	63.95
Module level	62.26	word+module level	63.52
Sentence+module level	63.27	**All (ours)**	**65.33**

[1]We used label-smoothing in these experiments for fairness.

We attempted to combine each level with another level of MHAN, and obtained eight model structures. HAN uses word- and sentence-level attention simultaneously, while our methods use three-level attention. Experiments were conducted to visualize the influence of the hierarchal structure on the model (Table 5). To effectively compare the performance of the hierarchical and traditional models, the author coding part that did not get embedded into the text module information structure was removed. From the results of the ablation experiments, we can see the influence of the hierarchical structure on the model: the model utilizing GRU and an attention mechanism without a hierarchical structure performed carried out the worst performance, with an accuracy of only 62.13%. We suggest the following reasons:

1. The RNN is unable to cope with long-term dependency, and excessively long sequences cause additional semantic loss;
2. A single attention mechanism layer has a limited model expression ability, which is insufficient to allocate attention on a long sequence. The performance of the attention mechanism is enhanced through the three-level HAN.

We have also found that the sentence-level attention mechanism can produce greater gains, likely because many sentences are converted by tables, pictures, and other information. The model cannot extract enough effective information from them, and the attention mechanism helps to remove the encoding of these sentences.

Table 6. Ablation experiment for modularized parameters

Parameters	Accuracy
Shared	62.77
Modularized	**65.33**

We conducted ablation experiments on the modularized weights of MHAN to explore whether the shared weights within each chapter bring performance gains to the model. Although the shared weights reduce the number of parameters, at that time the semantics of different chapters vary widely, and the semantic features cannot be extracted effectively by using the same weights. The results are shown in Table 6.

A scholarly paper includes six sections, i.e., the title, authors, abstract, related work, methods, and conclusion. Each was removed from MHAN to form six control groups, which were compared with the original model.

Table 7. Ablation experiment for sections

Module	Accuracy	Change
w/o title	63.92	−1.15
w/o author	**65.33**	**+0.26**
w/o abstract	62.71	−2.36
w/o related work	65.02	−0.05
w/o method	64.96	−0.11
w/o conclusion	64.20	−0.87
Full data	65.07	−

The comparison results are shown in Table 7, from which we can see that the abstract, title, and conclusion have a greater impact on model performance, and the accuracy of the model decreases by 2.36%, 1.15%, and 0.87% respectively after removing each of them. However, related work and methods have little impact on model accuracy. Having virtualized the attention score and conducted error analysis, we found that attention scores tend to polarize in sections with natural language. However, attention scores are similar in the methods section, which contains many notations.

We find that accuracy improves after removing the author's coding information, which is different from the experiment of AAPR [2], where the author's information increased the accuracy by 3.1%. After analysis, we suggest these possible reasons:

1. The author embedding dimension should be appropriately reduced, and the learning rate of the author embedding layer should be lower than that of the rest of the text module to prevent overfitting;
2. Authors appearing in many test sets do not appear in the training set, and the high proportion of unregistered words reduces the performance of the model.

Table 8. Parameter experiment for label-smoothing

ϵ	0.0	0.025	**0.05**	0.10	0.20
Acc	63.94	64.50	**65.33**	63.27	64.10

Table 8 shows the effect of the parameter ϵ of label-smoothing on both models' performance, from which it can be seen that the model has the highest accuracy when ϵ is around 0.05. Analyzing the experimental results, we can conclude that label-smoothing can improve the generalization ability of the model when ϵ is in the interval from 0 to 0.05, while when ϵ continues to rise from 0.05, the neural network cannot effectively distinguish between positive and negative samples, and the performance appears to fall back.

6 Conclusion

We applied MHAN to the automatic academic paper rating task; using the Arxiv Academic Paper Dataset, we compared the proposed method with baselines and carried out ablation experiments to explore its impact on each method, as well as on each part of the paper. Experimental results showed that hierarchical network, modularized parameters, and label-smoothing worked effectively, and our method outperformed the baselines.

In the future, we will introduce structural information and create hierarical attention to Longformer for the AAPR task.

Acknowledgments. This work is partly supported by the Beijing Natural Science Foundation (No. 4212026) and the Fundamental Strengthening Program Technology Field Fund (No. 2021-JCJQ-JJ-0059).

References

1. Kang, D., et al.: A dataset of peer reviews (PeerRead): collection, insights and NLP applications. In: Proceedings of the 2018 Conference of the North American Chapter of the Association for Computational Linguistics: Human Language Technologies, Volume 1 (Long Papers), pp. 1647–1661 (2018)
2. Yang, P., Sun, X., Li, W., Ma, S.: Automatic academic paper rating based on modularized hierarchical convolutional neural network. In: Proceedings of the 56th Annual Meeting of the Association for Computational Linguistics (Volume 2: Short Papers), pp. 496–502 (2018)
3. Qiao, Feng, Xu, Lizhen, Han, Xiaowei: Modularized and attention-based recurrent convolutional neural network for automatic academic paper aspect scoring. In: Meng, Xiaofeng, Li, Ruixuan, Wang, Kanliang, Niu, Baoning, Wang, Xin, Zhao, Gansen (eds.) WISA 2018. LNCS, vol. 11242, pp. 68–76. Springer, Cham (2018). https://doi.org/10.1007/978-3-030-02934-0_7
4. Leng, Y., Yu, L., Xiong, J.: DeepReviewer: collaborative grammar and innovation neural network for automatic paper review. In: 2019 International Conference on Multimodal Interaction, pp. 395–403 (2019)
5. Skorikov, M., Momen, S.: Machine learning approach to predicting the acceptance of academic papers. In: 2020 IEEE International Conference on Industry 4.0, Artificial Intelligence, and Communications Technology (IAICT). IEEE (2020)
6. Vincent-Lamarre, P., Larivière, V.: Textual analysis of artificial intelligence manuscripts reveals features associated with peer review outcome. Quant. Sci. Stud. **2**(2), 662–677 (2021)
7. Shen, A., Salehi, B., Baldwin, T., Qi, J.: A joint model for multimodal document quality assessment. In: 2019 ACM/IEEE Joint Conference on Digital Libraries (JCDL), pp. 107–110. IEEE (2019)
8. Hochreiter, S., Schmidhuber, J.: Long short-term memory. Neural Comput. **9**(8), 1735–1780 (1997)
9. Cho, K., et al.: Learning phrase representations using RNN encoder-decoder for statistical machine translation (2014)
10. He, K., Zhang, X., Ren, S., Sun, J.: Deep residual learning for image recognition. In: Proceedings of the IEEE Conference on Computer Vision and Pattern Recognition, pp. 770–778 (2016)

11. Kenton, J.D.M.W.C., Toutanova, L.K.: BERT: pre-training of deep bidirectional transformers for language understanding. In: Proceedings of NAACL-HLT, pp. 4171–4186 (2019)

12. Yang, Z., Yang, D., Dyer, C., He, X., Smola, A., Hovy, E.: Hierarchical attention networks for document classification. In: Proceedings of the 2016 Conference of the North American Chapter of the Association for Computational Linguistics: Human Language Technologies, pp. 1480–1489 (2016)

13. Beltagy, I., Peters, M.E., Cohan, A.: Longformer: the long-document transformer. arXiv preprint arXiv:2004.05150 (2020)

14. Zaheer, M., et al.: Big bird: transformers for longer sequences. Adv. Neural Inf. Process. Syst. **33**, 17283–17297 (2020)

15. Langford, J., Guzdial, M.: The arbitrariness of reviews, and advice for school administrators. Commun. ACM **58**(4), 12–13 (2015)

16. Lin, J., Song, J., Zhou, Z., Shi, X.: Automated scholarly paper review: possibility and challenges. arXiv preprint arXiv:2111.07533 (2021)

17. Shibayama, S., Yin, D., Matsumoto, K.: Measuring novelty in science with word embedding. PLoS ONE **16**(7), e0254034 (2021)

18. Daudaravicius, V.: Automated evaluation of scientific writing: AESW shared task proposal. In: Proceedings of the Tenth Workshop on Innovative Use of NLP for Building Educational Applications, pp. 56–63 (2015)

19. Springstein, M., Müller-Budack, E., Ewerth, R.: QuTI! quantifying text-image consistency in multimodal documents. In: Proceedings of the 44th International ACM SIGIR Conference on Research and Development in Information Retrieval, pp. 2575–2579 (2021)

20. Hou, Y., Jochim, C., Gleize, M., Bonin, F., Ganguly, D.: TDMSci: a specialized corpus for scientific literature entity tagging of tasks datasets and metrics. In: Proceedings of the 16th Conference of the European Chapter of the Association for Computational Linguistics: Main Volume, pp. 707–714 (2021)

21. Gupta, Y., et al.: The effect of pretraining on extractive summarization for scientific documents. In: Proceedings of the Second Workshop on Scholarly Document Processing, pp. 73–82 (2021)

22. Wang, Q., Zeng, Q., Huang, L., Knight, K., Ji, H., Rajani, N.F.: ReviewRobot: explainable paper review generation based on knowledge synthesis. In: Proceedings of the 13th International Conference on Natural Language Generation, pp. 384–397 (2020)

23. Yuan, W., Liu, P., Neubig, G.: Can we automate scientific reviewing? arXiv preprint arXiv:2102.00176 (2021)

24. de Buy Wenniger, G.M., van Dongen, T., Aedmaa, E., Kruitbosch, H.T., Valentijn, E.A., Schomaker, L.: Structure-tags improve text classification for scholarly document quality prediction. In: Proceedings of the First Workshop on Scholarly Document Processing, pp. 158–167 (2020)

25. Huang, J.B.: Deep paper gestalt. arXiv preprint arXiv:1812.08775 (2018)

26. Kim, Y.: Convolutional neural networks for sentence classification. In: Proceedings of the 2014 Conference on Empirical Methods in Natural Language Processing (EMNLP), pp. 1746–1751. Association for Computational Linguistics, Doha, Qatar (2014)

PromptAttack: Prompt-Based Attack for Language Models via Gradient Search

Yundi Shi, Piji Li$^{(\boxtimes)}$, Changchun Yin, Zhaoyang Han, Lu Zhou, and Zhe Liu

Nanjing University of Aeronautics and Astronautics, Nanjing, Jiangsu, China
{shiyundi,pjli,ycc0801,sunrisehan,lu.zhou,zhe.liu}@nuaa.edu.cn

Abstract. As the pre-trained language models (PLMs) continue to grow, so do the hardware and data requirements for fine-tuning PLMs. Therefore, the researchers have come up with a lighter method called *Prompt Learning*. However, during the investigations, we observe that the prompt learning methods are vulnerable and can easily be attacked by some illegally constructed prompts, resulting in classification errors, and serious security problems for PLMs. Most of the current research ignores the security issue of prompt-based methods. Therefore, in this paper, we propose a malicious prompt template construction method (**PromptAttack**) to probe the security performance of PLMs. Several unfriendly template construction approaches are investigated to guide the model to misclassify the task. Extensive experiments on three datasets and three PLMs prove the effectiveness of our proposed approach PromptAttack. We also conduct experiments to verify that our method is applicable in few-shot scenarios.

Keywords: Prompt learning · Gradient search attack method · Sentiment classification

1 Introduction

The emergence of pre-trained language models (PLMs) has facilitated the development of Natural Language Processing (NLP) [3]. The research approach based on PLMs is usually in a "pre-train → fine-tune" paradigm. In the pre-training stage, the models are trained using a large amount of data. In the fine-tuning stage, the PLMs are tuned by small datasets (compared with the data size in the pre-training stage) collected for different downstream tasks. The method achieves good results on many NLP tasks.

However, as the size of the pre-trained models continues to increase, the hardware and data requirements for fine-tuning PLMs are also increasing [7]. At the same time, diverse downstream tasks also lead to complex model design. The researchers propose a method for setting fill-in-the-blank templates for downstream tasks. The purpose is to make the downstream tasks use the model as

This research is supported by the National Natural Science Foundation of China (No. 62106105) and the National Key R&D Program of China (No. 2021YFB3100700).

W. Lu et al. (Eds.): NLPCC 2022, LNAI 13551, pp. 682–693, 2022.
https://doi.org/10.1007/978-3-031-17120-8_53

Method	Template	Examples
Manual	{sentence}The movie is [P].	I like this movie. The movie is [MASK]
Autoprompt	{sentence} [T] [T] [T] [T] [T] [P].	I like this movie. Atmosphere alot dialogue Clone totally [MASK].
P-tuning	e([CLS]),e(TOKEN), e(TOKEN),h_0 , h_1, ... h_i, e([P]).	e([CLS]),e(Amazing), e(Movie), e(!),h_0 , h_1, ... h_i, e([MASK]).
PromptAttack	{sentence} [T] [T] [T] [T] [T] [P].	I like this movie. GCue Gimperfect Gpackets Gperfume GNer [MASK].

Fig. 1. Prompts of different approaches.

consistently as possible with the tasks in the pre-training phase without fine-tuning all the parameters. It has gradually evolved into prompt learning [7], a lighter approach to solve NLP tasks.

The prompt-based model consists of three steps: First, we need a PLM with the masked pre-training task. Second, we need to construct a template in cloze form. For example, in the sentiment classification task, for the sentence "This is the best movie I've ever watched.", we can create the template like "The movie is [MASK]", and then use PLMs to predict which emotional word (e.g. "great", "bad") should be filled into the masked position. At last, the answer predicted by PLMs is converted into the real label. Words such as "great" and "wonderful" should correspond to positive, and words such as "terrible" and "bad" should correspond to negative. We call this map a verbalizer. Initially, the templates are set manually. However, if we want to design an efficient template, we require numerous experiments, much relevant knowledge, and high cost. So researchers begin to explore how to build templates automatically. In the first three rows in Fig. 1, we show the examples of the manual template (Manual), the automatic discrete template (Autoprompt [11]), and the automatic continuous template (P-tuning [8]).

In recent years, text analysis and understanding based on deep learning have become the core technology of various NLP applications. Despite its popularity and excellent performance, studies have shown that the models are **vulnerable to malicious attacks**. Considering its increasing application in many real-world security-sensitive tasks, the vulnerability has caused great concern and high attention to the models' security. Therefore, safety has gradually become a new research hotspot, and more and more researchers focus on attack and defense. Although the prompt has shown excellent performance in various tasks, including text understanding and text generation, its **vulnerability and security** has not been comprehensively and deeply evaluated. Deploying such models in real systems may have large security risks, and using these models without sufficient awareness of potential security risks may lead to serious consequences. Therefore, it is very necessary to conduct in-depth research on the security issues of the prompt-based model. Recently, adversarial attacks and backdoor attacks have become the primary threat in the field of AI security. We believe that the two attack methods are also applicable to the prompt-based model. Besides, we think that the attack can also target the template which is the unique part of the prompt. Many papers have verified the choice of the template has a significant impact on the model prediction results. Therefore, in theory, if the template we build is malicious, the accuracy of the model prediction can be greatly reduced.

According to the above analysis, we propose an attack method **PromptAttack** to construct malicious templates by automatically searching for discrete tokens. First, our label map is automatically selected. We use the logical classifier to find the relationship between the word and the label, and select the *top-k* words with the highest correlation value as the corresponding words of the label. Second, we find tokens according to a variant of the gradient search strategy and select the *top-k* tokens, which meet our requirements, as candidate words. Then, we replace the token of the existing templates on the principle of random replacement or beam search. We calculate the prediction accuracy of each template on the train dataset and select the one that minimizes the prediction accuracy as the final template. Finally, we consider the stealth of the attack, i.e. the readability of the constructed template, so we choose to utilize GPT-2 to generate the template with lower perplexity. In the last row of Fig. 1, we depict an example of templates created by our proposed attack method. The contributions of our paper are as follows:

(1) We consider that the prompt still has the risk of being attacked, and almost no other papers have considered this problem.
(2) Our attack method PromptAttack is to attack the prompt-specific template.
(3) We evaluate the attack method on three datasets and three pre-trained models, and the experimental results prove the effectiveness of PromptAttack.
(4) Our attack method is still effective in few-shot cases.

2   Related Work

2.1   Prompt Learning

In the recent two years, prompt learning has made great progress, from discrete prompts to continuous prompts, from text-only prompts to multimodal prompts, and from white-box prompts to black-box prompts. Schick et al. [12] proposed the Pattern-Exploiting Training (PET) method. The template and verbalizer for this method are manually defined. Schick [11] also proposed the method of using the Likelihood Ratio to automatically search verbalizer. Shin et al. [13] designed a discrete prompt named Autoprompt, and in their method, both the template and the verbalizer are automatically constructed. The *prefix-tuning* proposed by Li et al. [6], and the *P-tuning* proposed by Liu et al. [8] are typical methods for constructing continuous prompts. *CPT* by Yao et al. [18], *CLIP* by Radford et al. [10], and *CoOp* by Zhou et al. [19] are all representative methods of multimodal prompt.

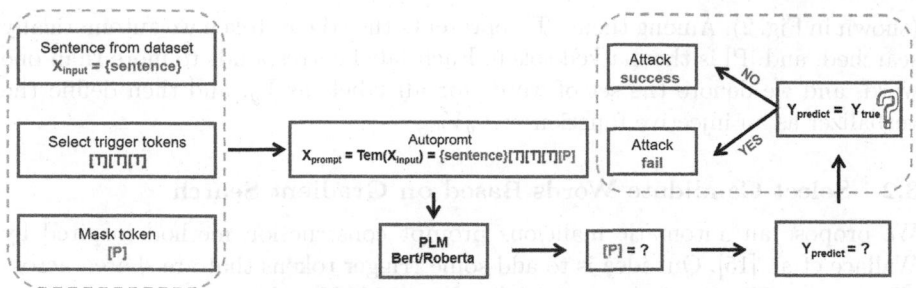

Fig. 2. The overview of PromptAttack. Firstly, we use the three parts in the virtual box on the left to form a template. Then, we use the template as the input of PLMs, and the output is the predicted token on the mask position. Finally, the model maps the results to the labels and compares the predicted label with the real label

2.2 Attack Methods

Attack methods are mainly divided into two forms: adversarial attack and backdoor attack. The adversarial attack occurs in the model testing phase. Papernot et al. [9] first pointed out that attackers can generate adversarial examples by adding noise to the text, which may make the classifier misclassify. Ebrahimi et al. [1] proposed an attack method *HotFlip*, which can generate adversarial examples in a white-box situation. Li et al. [5] proposed the *TEXTBUGGER* method, which can generate adversarial examples in both white-box and black-box situations. The backdoor attack occurs in the model training phase. The attacker injects poisoned samples into the train dataset, thereby embedding backdoor triggers in the trained deep learning model. Backdoor attacks were first proposed by Gu et al. [2] and further exploited on NLP models (Kurita et al. [4]). For the attack of the prompt method, there are only the *AToP* and *BToP* methods proposed by Xu et al. [17].

3 Methodology

3.1 Overview

On basis of Shin's [13] Autoprompt method, we propose our attack method PromptAttack. The main idea is to select the tokens that can make the final prediction result drop to form our template. So how to select the final tokens become the most critical problem. Initially, we find trigger tokens as candidate words by using the gradient search method. And then we choose the token sequence with the best attack result as the final template by random replacement or beam search algorithm. The whole process of PromptAttack is shown in Fig. 2.

For the convenience of distinction, the sentences obtained from the dataset are denoted by X_{input}. The prompts that are input to the PLMs are denoted by X_{prompt}. The template defines the format of the prompt: X_{input} [T] [T] [T] [P]

(shown in Fig. 2). Among them, [T] represents the trigger token we automatically searched, and [P] is the masked token. Each label corresponds to more than one word, and we denote the set of words for all labels as V_y, and then define the verbalizer as an injective function v: $L_y V_y$.

3.2   Select Candidate Words Based on Gradient Search

We propose an automatic malicious prompt construction method inspired by Wallace et al. [15]. Our idea is to add some trigger tokens that are shared across all prompts. These tokens are initialized as [MASK] tokens, and our goal is to minimize the predicted probability $\mathcal{P}(y|X_{prompt})$ in Eq. (1) of the true label by iterative updating.

$$\mathcal{P}(y|X_{prompt}) = \sum_{w \in V_y} \mathcal{P}([MASK] = w|X_{prompt}) \tag{1}$$

Use each token (represented by w) in the vocabulary V to replace the j-th token in the trigger token sequence in turn and then calculate the loss of w on the true label y. The first-order approximation of the loss change of this replacement process is expressed as Eq. (2):

$$Approximation(w) = \boldsymbol{w}_{in}^T \nabla log \mathcal{P}(y|X_{prompt}) \tag{2}$$

where $\boldsymbol{w}_{in}$ is the input embedding of token w. We backpropagate to get the gradient of token w, which is $\nabla log \mathcal{P}(y|X_{prompt})$ in Eq. (2).

Since we calculate Eq. (2) based on the real label, the larger the value, the more likely that the token will cause the final prediction to be correct, and vice versa. To achieve the desired effect of eventually causing the prediction result to be wrong, we choose the k words with the smallest *Approximation* value as the candidate set V_{cand} of the trigger token, as shown in Eq. (3):

$$V_{cand} = \underset{w \in V}{top\text{-}k}(-Approximation(w)) \tag{3}$$

3.3   Selection of Token Sequences

In the previous section, we introduce how to choose candidate words for trigger tokens, so the next step is how to reasonably choose the token sequences that meet our requirements. The selected sequence will be used as the final template to participate in training and testing. In this part, we propose three methods for selecting token sequences: random replacement, beam search, and GPT-2.

Random Replacement Strategy. In each iteration, we randomly select a position in the token sequence and traverse the tokens in the candidate set to replace the word at that position. Each replacement will form a new prompt to interact with the PLMs. We choose the least accurate sequence on the train dataset as the final template of the current iteration and evaluate its accuracy on the test dataset. After multiple rounds of iterations, we select the one with the lowest accuracy in the testing phase as the ultimate template. The specific algorithm is shown in Algorithm 1.

Algorithm 1. Random replacement

Input: Trigger token candidates: candidates;
          Trigger token number: N
          Iteration number: K
Output: The token sequence: $final\_sequence$
1: $Tem = [``[MASK]", ``[MASK]", ``[MASK]", ``[MASK]", ``[MASK]"]$
2: $M = len(candidates)$
3: $accuracy[M] = 0$
4: $best\_metric = accuracy(test\_file, Tem)$ ▷ accuracy on test dataset
5: $final\_sequence = Tem$
6: **for** $i = 0; i < K; i + +$ **do**
7:     $pos = random.randrange(N)$ ▷ Random select one position
          ▷ Each word in cnadiates replaces the word at the specified position in turn
8:     **for** m in $enumerate(candidates)$ **do**
9:         $Tem[pos] = m$
10:         $accuracy[i] = train\_accuracy(train, Tem)$ ▷ accuracy on train dataset
11:     **end for**
          ▷ Select the sequence with the best result in this iteration
12:     $best\_candidate\_score = accuracy.min()$
13:     $best\_sequence = accuracy.argmin()$
14:     $test\_metric = accuracy(test\_file, best\_sequence)$ ▷ accuracy on test dataset
15: **end for**
16: **if** $test\_metric < best\_metric$ **then**   ▷ select the best sequence and best metric
17:     $final\_sequence = best\_sequence$
18:     $best\_metric = test\_metric$
19: **end if**

Beam Search Method. During the experiment, we find that the random replacement method may not replace the [MASK] token in all positions, especially in the case of few-shot. Therefore, we consider using the beam search strategy, which has better stability.

All trigger tokens are initialized to [MASK] and are selected from left to right. Beam search has a hyperparameter beam size, set to k. In the first time step, all candidate words replace the <mask> in the first position in turn and are evaluated on the training set. We select the *top-k* sequences, which have the best result on the train dataset, as the candidates at the first step. In the i-th time step, based on the sequences of the previous step, all candidate words replace the token in the i-th position in turn, and select the *top-k* sequences with the best attack effect as candidate sequences in this step. At last, we select the optimal trigger token. The method is shown in Fig. 3.

Generate Token Sequences Using GPT-2. Both the random replacement strategy and the beam search strategy simply focus on how to improve the attack success rate and don't consider the **fluency of the generated token sequences**. Therefore, we consider using GPT-2 to generate the token sequence.

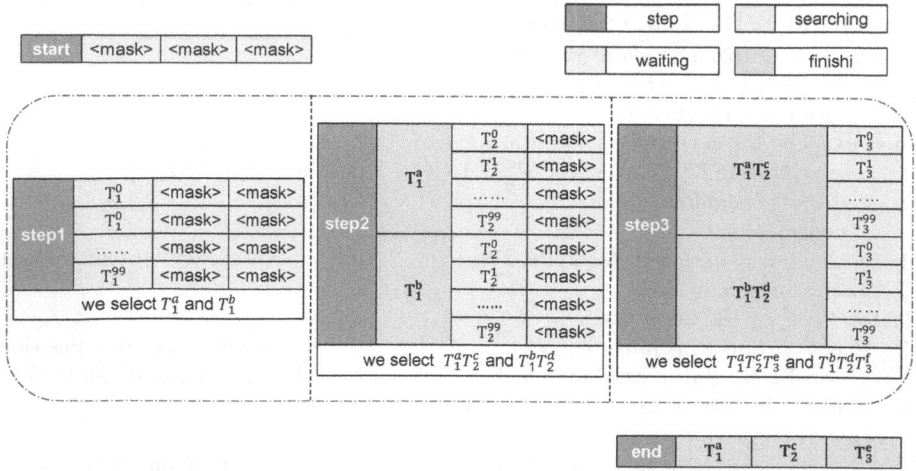

Fig. 3. The example of token selection for beam search method. In this example, candidate number = 100, beamwidth = 2, token number = 3. After each step, we choose the two templates with the lowest model accuracy as the basis for the next step.

Further, the readability of the template is enhanced, and the approach also increases the concealment of the generated malicious template.

Initially, we train GPT-2 model with all the text in the train dataset. Each token in the candidate set is used as the first token in turn and we use the trained GPT-2 model to generate sequences based on the first word. The sequence with the worst result on the training set has been selected as the final sequence, and its performance on the test dataset and perplexity (PPL) were assessed.

3.4   Automatic Selection of Label Mapping

We adopt the automatic label selection method proposed by Shin et al. [13]. We select the set of tokens V_y by an automatic method with two steps.

In the first step, we train a logistic classifier to predict labels using the context containing [MASK] token at i-th position. The encoding result by transformers of the context is devoted by $h^{(i)}$. This output $\mathcal{P}(y|h^{(i)})$ (in Eq. (4)) can express the relationship of the input and the label.

$$\mathcal{P}(y|h^{(i)}) \propto exp(h^{(i)}\boldsymbol{y} + \beta_y), \tag{4}$$

where $\boldsymbol{y}$ and β_y are the learned weights and bias terms for label y, and i denotes the index of the [MASK] token.

In the second step, we replace $h^{(i)}$ with the output word embedding $\boldsymbol{w}_{out}$ of the PLMs to obtain the score $s(y, w)$. It is known that the greater the correlation between $h^{(i)}$ and y, the larger the $\mathcal{P}(y|h^{(i)})$. So the larger the s, the more relation between the word and label. So we choose the k highest scoring words to construct the label set V_y.

4   Experiments

Sentiment analysis is a fundamental task in NLP, which refers to classifying texts into two or more types according to the meaning and emotional information expressed in the text. Our experiments are mainly for the sentiment classification task, and we use the PyTorch implementation and pre-trained weights provided by the transformer Python library [16].

4.1   Datasets

We use three sentiment classification datasets, namely **SST-2** [14], **IMDB**, and **Amazon Video_Games**.

SST-2 Dataset. SST-2 (The Stanford Sentiment Treebank), a single-sentence classification dataset, contains sentences from movie reviews and human comments on their sentiments. The dataset is divided into two categories based on emotion: positive mood (label corresponds to 1) and negative mood (label corresponds to 0). The SST-2 dataset is from https://github.com/ucinlp/autoprompt.

IMDB Dataset. IMDB (Internet Movie Database) is an online database of movie actors, movies, TV stars, and movie productions. Labels are represented by 0 and 1, with 0 representing negative and 1 representing positive. The IMDB dataset is from https://www.kaggle.com/datasets/uttam94/imdb-mastercsv.

Amazon Video_Game Dataset. The dataset we use is the sub-dataset of the Amazon dataset about Video_Games. We select the summary of users' reviewers as the inputs of the sentiment classification task. In our experiments, we consider reviews rated 1.0 and 2.0 as negative (the label is 0), and reviews rated 4.0 and 5.0 as positive (the label is 1). We get the Amazon review dataset from https://nijianmo.github.io/amazon/index.html.

4.2   Setup

In the following sections, we use the Bert_base model, Roberta_base model, and Roberta_large model as pre-trained models respectively.

Dataset Processing. On each kind of dataset, we select 24,000 pieces of data as the train dataset, including the same account of data for each category. We choose approximately 1000 pieces of data to form the test dataset, and the data in each category is also equal.

Baseline. We choose the Autoprompt method proposed by Shin et al. [13] as the baseline. And we evaluate the attack performance of PromptAttack by calculating the drop in the model accuracy under the same conditions.

Parameter Settings. The number of tokens constituting the template is 5, in other words, the template's format is "{sentence} [T] [T] [T] [T] [T] [P]." The number of words corresponding to the label is 3. The batch size is 24 in the train process and 48 in the test process. The candidate set includes 100 trigger tokens.

Table 1. Results of label mapping.

	Labe: 0	Label: 1
Bert_base	{coward, ##cket, Ordnance}	{extraordinary, wealth, natural}
Roberta_base	{worst, ĠWorse, Ġblames}	{illance, ĠLens, shine}
Roberta_large	{Ġworse, Ġincompetence, ĠWorse}	{ĠCris, Ġmarvelous, Ġphilanthrop}

4.3   Result and Analysis

Selection Results of Words Corresponding to Labels. In this process, we perform 50 iterations, and each iteration outputs 50 words that can be mapped with the label. We choose top-3 among them as our final results. Table 1 shows the label corresponding words on the **SST-2** dataset under the three pretrained models.

It can be seen from Table 1 that the label words found by different models are completely not the same. Because the word segmentation rules of Bert and Roberta are different, the corresponding words cannot be identical. From the above results, most of the words corresponding to label 0 are derogatory words, and most of the words corresponding to label 1 are commendatory words, which is in line with our cognition of manually selecting label words.

Experimental Results of the SST-2 Dataset on Three Pre-trained Models. The data outside the parentheses is the model prediction accuracy(Accuracy). The part in parentheses is the percentage of accuracy drop, that is, the difference(Diff) between PromptAtatck's accuracy and the Autoprompt's accuracy; the bolded part represents the best attack effect of the **SST-2** dataset under each model.

It can be seen from the data in Table 2 that our two methods can effectively reduce the accuracy no matter which pre-trained model is based on. Among them, the beam search method based on the Roberta_large model achieves the best attack effect. The attack success rates of the two strategies on Robrta_large can respectively reach 47.36% and 56.77%. In addition, we can see that the attack effect based on the Roberta model is better than the result based on the Bert model.

Table 2. Results of the SST-2 dataset on three pre-trained models. Metric: Accuracy (Diff)

	Autoprompt	Random		Beamsearch	
Bert	82.30%	44.61%	**(37.69%)**	49.08%	(33.22%)
Roberta_base	85.44%	46.90%	(38.54%)	44.03%	**(41.41%)**
Roberta_large	89.79%	42.43%	(47.36%)	33.02%	**(56.77%)**

Table 3. Results of **SST-2/IMDB/Amazon** dataset on Roberta_large. Metric: Accuracy (Diff)

	Autoprompt	Random		Beamsearch	
SST-2	89.79%	42.43%	(47.36%)	33.02%	**(56.77%)**
IMDB	84.45%	43.23%	**(41.22%)**	49.69%	(34.76%)
Amazon	87.23%	42.00%	**(45.23%)**	46.9%	(40.33%)

Results of SST-2/IMDB/Amazon Dataset on Roberta_large. From Table 2 we can see that the **SST-2** dataset performs best on Roberta_large model, so we evaluate the **IMDB** dataset and the **Amazon** dataset on Roberta_large model. The experimental results are shown in Table 3.

The data in Table 3 shows that based on the Roberta_large model, PromptAttack is effective on all three datasets, and the attack success rate can reach more than 40%. The results also verify the general applicability of our method.

Validation of the Method of GPT-2. Considering the invisibility of automatically constructing templates, we propose the method of using GPT-2 to generate smoother templates. The readability of the template is evaluated using PPL (perplexity), and the experimental results based on the Roberta_large model are shown in Table 4.

The table shows three indicators: perplexity (PPL), model prediction accuracy, and the generated token sequences. From Table 4, we can first see that the token sequence generated by the GPT-2 method can reduce the accuracy of the model, that is, the attack can be successful. It also can be seen that the token sequence generated by the GPT-2 method has the lowest perplexity, which proves the effectiveness of the GPT-2 method. At the same time, we can find that the beam search method has the lowest accuracy and the highest perplexity, while the GPT-2 method has the highest accuracy and the lowest perplexity. That is to say, while the perplexity of the generated token sequence is reduced, it will also lead to the deterioration of the experimental attack performance.

Table 4. The perplexity of the template in different ways.

	PPL	Accuracy	Token sequence
Beamsearch	1506.17	33.02%	Ġwhereas ĠHammer '' Ġeffectiveness Ctrl
Random	144.94	42.43%	ĠCue Ġimperfect Ġpackets Ġperfume ĠNer
GPT-2	76.68	49.08%	Ġconvenience, Ġseries Ġdisgusting Ġunfortunate Ġdisable

Table 5. Results under few-shot conditions. Metric: Accuracy (Diff)

Dataset	Model	Autoprompt	Random		Beamsearch	
SST-2	Roberta_base	80.16%	49.08%	(31.08%)	40.48%	**(39.68%)**
	Roberta_large	73.97%	46.69%	(27.28%)	46.22%	**(27.75%)**
Amazon	Roberta_base	74.70%	47.01%	**(27.69%)**	48.05%	(26.65%)
	Roberta_large	70.69%	43.47%	**(27.22%)**	45.70%	(24.99%)
IMDB	Roberta_base	66.46%	49.27%	(17.19%)	44.79%	**(21.67%)**
	Roberta_large	69.98%	46.67%	**(23.31%)**	48.85%	(21.13%)

Experimental Results in the Case of Few-Shot. The fact that the prompt is also valid in few-shot situations is an important advantage of the method. The baseline method has verified in their paper that the Autoprompt method is effective in the few-shot case. Therefore we try to explore whether PromptAttack is useful in the few-shot case.

We randomly select 100 pieces from each category of data in each dataset to form a few-shot dataset and conduct attack experiments on Roberta_base and Roberta_large models. And we obtain the following experimental results, as shown in Table 5.

We can see that all three datasets can be successfully attacked in the few-shot case on the two pre-trained models. It is worth noting that on the **SST-2** dataset and **Amazon** dataset, the attack success rate of Roberta_base is higher than that of Roberta_large. In our analysis, the reason for this may be that most of the texts in these two datasets are short sentences. When the train data is small and the text length is short, the larger-scale model will overfit in classification. The text of the **IMDB** dataset is mostly long sentences, which is not easy to overfit, so the attack success rate on the Roberta_large model is still higher.

5   Conclusion and Future Work

Most current researches ignore the security issues of the prompt model, and especially its unique template part is vulnerable to attack. Therefore, we propose an attack method PromptAttack based on the template innovatively. The method is evaluated by three datasets for sentiment classification and three pre-trained language models. The experiment results verify the effectiveness of our attack way and show that our method is also applicable to the few-shot case.

In the future, we can continue to research prompt security issues. On the one hand, PromptAttack only targets discrete prompts, and the follow-up study can focus on attacking continuous prompts. On the other hand, our method is a white-box attack that needs to know all the parameters of the model, and we can try to design a black-box attack method.

References

1. Ebrahimi, J., Rao, A., Lowd, D., Dou, D.: Hotflip: White-box adversarial examples for text classification. arXiv preprint arXiv:1712.06751 (2017)
2. Gu, T., Liu, K., Dolan-Gavitt, B., Garg, S.: Badnets: evaluating backdooring attacks on deep neural networks. IEEE Access **7**, 47230–47244 (2019)
3. Han, X., et al.: Pre-trained models: past, present and future. AI Open **2**, 225–250 (2021)
4. Kurita, K., Michel, P., Neubig, G.: Weight poisoning attacks on pre-trained models. arXiv preprint arXiv:2004.06660 (2020)
5. Li, J., Ji, S., Du, T., Li, B., Wang, T.: Textbugger: generating adversarial text against real-world applications. arXiv preprint arXiv:1812.05271 (2018)
6. Li, X.L., Liang, P.: Prefix-tuning: optimizing continuous prompts for generation. arXiv preprint arXiv:2101.00190 (2021)
7. Liu, P., Yuan, W., Fu, J., Jiang, Z., Hayashi, H., Neubig, G.: Pre-train, prompt, and predict: a systematic survey of prompting methods in natural language processing. arXiv preprint arXiv:2107.13586 (2021)
8. Liu, X., et al.: Gpt understands, too. arXiv preprint arXiv:2103.10385 (2021)
9. Papernot, N., McDaniel, P., Swami, A., Harang, R.: Crafting adversarial input sequences for recurrent neural networks. In: MILCOM 2016–2016 IEEE Military Communications Conference, pp. 49–54. IEEE (2016)
10. Radford, A., et al.: Learning transferable visual models from natural language supervision. In: International Conference on Machine Learning, pp. 8748–8763. PMLR (2021)
11. Schick, T., Schmid, H., Schütze, H.: Automatically identifying words that can serve as labels for few-shot text classification. arXiv preprint arXiv:2010.13641 (2020)
12. Schick, T., Schütze, H.: Exploiting cloze questions for few shot text classification and natural language inference. arXiv preprint arXiv:2001.07676 (2020)
13. Shin, T., Razeghi, Y., Logan IV, R.L., Wallace, E., Singh, S.: Autoprompt: Eliciting knowledge from language models with automatically generated prompts. arXiv preprint arXiv:2010.15980 (2020)
14. Socher, R., Perelygin, A., Wu, J., Chuang, J., Manning, C.D., Ng, A.Y., Potts, C.: Recursive deep models for semantic compositionality over a sentiment treebank. In: Proceedings of the 2013 Conference on Empirical Methods in Natural Language Processing. pp. 1631–1642 (2013)
15. Wallace, E., Feng, S., Kandpal, N., Gardner, M., Singh, S.: Universal adversarial triggers for attacking and analyzing nlp. arXiv preprint arXiv:1908.07125 (2019)
16. Wolf, T., et al.: Huggingface's transformers: State-of-the-art natural language processing. arXiv preprint arXiv:1910.03771 (2019)
17. Xu, L., Chen, Y., Cui, G., Gao, H., Liu, Z.: Exploring the universal vulnerability of prompt-based learning paradigm. arXiv preprint arXiv:2204.05239 (2022)
18. Yao, Y., Zhang, A., Zhang, Z., Liu, Z., Chua, T.S., Sun, M.: Cpt: colorful prompt tuning for pre-trained vision-language models. arXiv preprint arXiv:2109.11797 (2021)
19. Zhou, K., Yang, J., Loy, C.C., Liu, Z.: Learning to prompt for vision-language models. arXiv preprint arXiv:2109.01134 (2021)

A Joint Label-Enhanced Representation Based on Pre-trained Model for Charge Prediction

Jingpei Dan[✉], Xiaoshuang Liao, Lanlin Xu, Weixuan Hu, and Tianyuan Zhang

Computer Science and Technology, Chongqing University, Chongqing, China
danjingpei@cqu.edu.cn

Abstract. As one of the important subtasks of legal judgment prediction, charge prediction aims to predict the final charge according to the fact description of a legal case. It can help make legal judgments or provide legal professional guidance for non-professionals. Most existing works focus on predicting charges only based on the fact description of a legal case while ignoring the semantic information of charge labels. Moreover, suffering from data imbalance in real applications, they are not applicable to predict few-shot charges by lack of training data. To address these issues, we propose a novel legal text presentation based on pre-trained model for charge prediction, named joint label-enhanced representation (JLER), which provides abundant information of charge labels as additional legal knowledge for pre-trained model to improve the charge prediction performance. JLER can improve predicting accuracy and interpretability by combining the charge label information enhanced by double-layer attention with legal text information, along with relieving the impact of data imbalance by fine-tuning pre-trained model from both text features side and charge label one. Experimental results on two real-world datasets demonstrate that our proposed model achieves significant and consistent improvements compared to the state-of-the-art baselines. Specifically, our model outperforms the baselines by about 13.9% accuracy on few-shot charge prediction. It is indicated that the proposed JLER model has good performance for charge prediction and is prospected to be applied to other subtasks of legal judgement prediction.

Keywords: Charge prediction · Text representation · Pre-trained models · Few-shot

1 Introduction

With the rapid development of artificial intelligence (AI) and the increasing demand for legal intelligence, legal judgments have been predicted by applying AI methods in recent years. Charge prediction that aims to automatically predict charge by a given fact description of legal case plays an important role for legal intelligence as one of subtasks in legal judgment prediction. It can not only improve the work efficiency of legal practitioners and give more professional legal guidance, but also provide corresponding legal guidance and assistance for people without any legal background knowledge.

© The Author(s), under exclusive license to Springer Nature Switzerland AG 2022
W. Lu et al. (Eds.): NLPCC 2022, LNAI 13551, pp. 694–705, 2022.
https://doi.org/10.1007/978-3-031-17120-8_54

Automatic charge prediction has been studied for decades, and researchers have proposed varieties of methods. At the early stage, mathematical or quantitative [1–3] methods were widely applied, but they were mostly restricted to small datasets with few labels. Some researchers spent a lot of time to design shallow textual features manually, and then predicted charges by utilizing machine learning algorithms. For example, Katz et al. [4] predicted the judgment of the US Supreme Court by leveraging unique feature engineering. However, the features artificially extracted were not able to well capture the semantic information of legal documents. With the development of deep learning, some researchers have proposed to employ deep neural networks [5–7] to predict charges. For instance, Hu et al. [5] integrated ten criminal-related attributes proposed by legal professionals into the neural network model as additional information, so as to effectively improve the interpretability of the prediction results and prediction accuracy of few-shot charges in legal cases. However, these prediction models are usually too complex to achieve satisfactory performances.

Pre-trained models have been recently applied on large-scale universal corpus and fine-tuned in combination with specific downstream tasks. Great success has been achieved by employing pre-trained models that can significantly improve performances of deep learning models in various NLP tasks. Some researchers have constructed pre-trained models on legal corpus [8, 9], and many scholars have directly applied pre-trained models [10, 11] to solve legal judgment prediction tasks. Chalkidis et al. [12] has proposed the Hier-bert model based on *bert* [13], of which the experimental results on the data set of the European Court of Human Rights verified its better performance than other deep learning models (such as BiGRU, HAN, etc.). However, most models are directly used as basic encoders without further exploration.

In order to improve accuracy and interpretability, there are two major challenges applying pre-trained models to charge prediction. First, since the legal text data involving professional knowledge and terms are different from the common text data, which result in unsatisfactory performance when directly employing pre-trained models to legal judgement tasks, it might be helpful for improving the reasoning ability between legal concepts by integrating legal knowledge into pre-trained models. Second, the number of cases on various charges are highly imbalanced. For example, according to our statistics on the CAIL2018 [14] dataset, the amount of data samples of the ten most common crimes in the task of charge prediction, such as theft, traffic accident, and intentional injury, etc., is nearly 80% of the whole dataset, while the sample coverage ratio of some few-shot charges is only less than 1%. Although most previous works have good performances on common charge predictions, they cannot deal with few-shot charge predictions well due to the lack of sufficient training data. Therefore, it is crucial to deal with the data imbalance in legal documents.

To address these issues, we propose a Joint Label-Enhanced Representation (JLER) based on pre-trained model for charge prediction. The proposed model can improve accuracy and stability of charge prediction by providing abundant semantic label information as additional knowledge for the pre-trained model, and it can also improve the interpretability of prediction results and extremely relieve the impact of data imbalance. More specifically, we first utilize a double-layer attention mechanism, named as label-enhancer, to get label-enhanced representations. In the first layer, the self-attention is used to increase the interaction among charge label representations to capture syntactic or semantic features among labels. The cross-attention in the second layer is used to get the label feature-enhanced representations by inducing label-specific features from case description representation. Then, we employ the label-enhanced representations to calculate the attention score for the whole case representation to get the final joint label-attentive representations. This makes it possible for the pre-trained model to be tuned by the features of both case description and labels. Finally, a classifier is used to predict charge based on the obtained JLER.

To summarize, the main contributions of this paper are as follows:

1. Based on the abundant semantic information contained in the charge labels of legal judgments, we propose a novel legal text representation, named Joint Label-Enhanced Representation (JLER), which provide abundant information of charge labels as additional legal knowledge for pre-trained model to improve the charge prediction performance. Experimental results demonstrate that our proposed model achieves significant and consistent improvements compared to the state-of-the-art baselines. Besides, our model also can be more robust and stable by remaining available and effective charge label information.
2. Different from the traditional fine-tuning pre-trained models, we utilize the enhanced label representations to fine-tune the pretrained model so that the parameters of the pre-trained model can be further adjusted and optimized to boost the performance on charge prediction.
3. Our proposal is verified by comparative experiments on two public real-world datasets from Chinese AI and Law challenge (CAIL2018). The experimental results show that our model significantly outperforms the state-of-the-art baselines by more than 13.9% improvements in accuracy for few-shot charge prediction, which indicate its capacity of relieving the problem of data imbalance.

2   Charge Prediction Based on JLER Model

In this section, we will introduce our model in details. First, we give the basic definition of charge prediction task. Then, we describe the components of our model framework and introduce the details of implementation of each module.

2.1 Problem Definition

The fact description of legal case is seen as a word sequence $S^d = \{w_1, w_2, \ldots, w_n\}$, where $w_i \in V$ denotes a word and n is the length of sequence. V is the fixed vocabulary. Similarly, let the set of charge labels $S^c = \{c_1, c_2, \ldots, c_k\}$, where $c_i = \{w_{i1}, w_{i2}, \ldots, w_{im}\}$ represents a word sequence of length m. Our goal is to utilize these abundant semantic labels information and the fact description of legal case as input, then we learn a classifier to predict final charge $y_i \in Y$ for each c_i in S^c as output.

2.2 Overview of Charge Prediction Based on JLER Model

In charge prediction task, there are usually abundant semantic information involved in labels of charge. In order to adequately exploit the information of labels, we propose the JLER based on pre-trained model for charge prediction. As shown in Fig. 1, we proposed model mainly consists of three modules, including Encoder Layer, Label Enhancer, and Classifier. For a legal case, its JLER is first obtained by combining the contextual representation of legal case and labels generated in encoder layer and the feature-enhanced label representation generated by the label enhancer. Based on the JLER, a classifier consisting of CNN and MLP is adopted to predict the final charge.

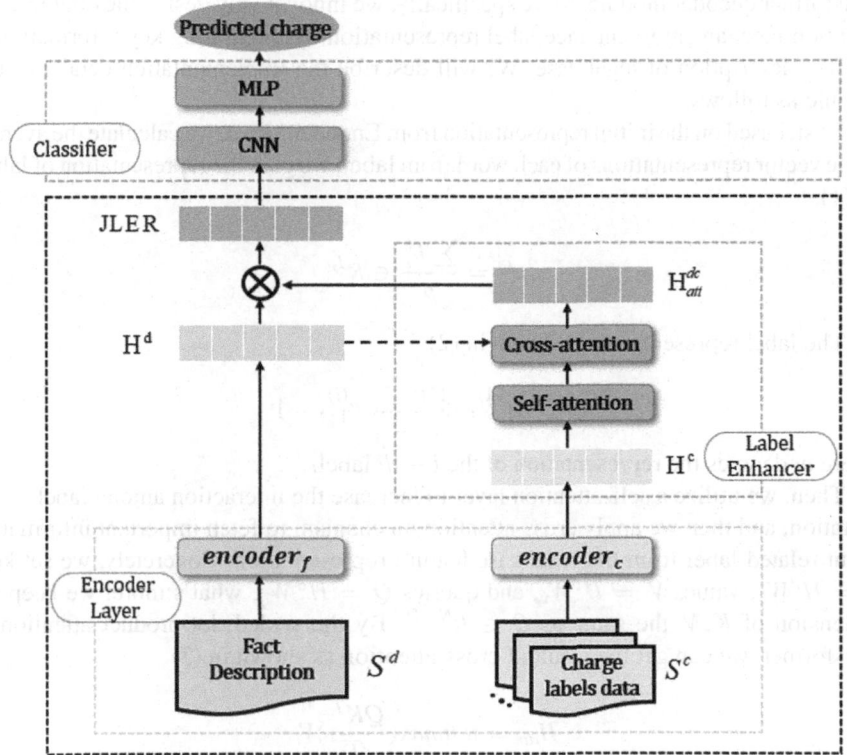

Fig. 1. JLER based on pre-trained model for charge prediction.

2.3 JLER Model

Encoder Layer. We design the encoders (including $encoder_f$ and $encoder_c$) to generate the contextual representation of the legal case and charge labels. *Bert*, as a general pre-training model, has widely applied to many natural language processing tasks. To fairly compare with other methods, we set *bert* as our basic encoder to get the contextual representations. *Bert* employs a bidirectional transformer, which enables the model to learn bidirectional contextual information during the training process.

For a given fact descriptions of legal case, throughout the multi-layer self-attention encoding of $encoder_f$, the contextual representation for legal case can be obtained, representing as $H^d = (h_1^d, h_2^d, ..., h_m^d) \in R^{m \times d_s}$, where d_s denotes the dimension of the last hidden layer of *bert*. Similarly, given arbitrary charge descriptions S^c, we can obtain their output of the hidden states $H^c = (h_1^c, h_2^c, ..., h_p^c) \in R^{m \times d_s}$ as the contextual representation of labels.

Label Enhancer. To further integrate the label representation, we input the legal case representation and the label initial representation to the Label Enhancer which based on transformer decoder module. More specifically, we innovatively design the double-layer attention mechanism to enhance label representation by integrating key information of the fact description of legal case. We will describe the implementation details of this module as follows.

Frist, based on the initial representation from Encoder Layer, we calculate the average of the vector representations of each word from label, we gain the representation of labels by (1).

$$e^{c_i} = \frac{\sum h_i^c}{p} \in R^{d_s} \tag{1}$$

The label representation is shown in (2)

$$E = [e_1^{(1)}, e_1^{(2)}, ..., e_1^{(i)}, ...] \tag{2}$$

where e_i denotes the representation of the $i - th$ label.

Then, we utilize a self-attention layer to increase the interaction among label representation, and then we apply cross-attention mechanism to fetch important information about related label from the legal case feature representation. Concretely, we set keys $K = H^c W_k$, values $V = H^c W_v$, and queries $Q = H^d W_q$, what's more, we keep the dimension of K, V the same as $Q \in R^{N \times D}$. By the scaled dot-product attention of transformer, we can get the result of cross-attention as shown in (3).

$$H_{att} = softmax(\frac{QK^T}{\sqrt{D_k}})V \tag{3}$$

After cross-attention we connect feedforward neural network with fully layers. In order to prevent gradient disappearance and network degradation in the case of network deepening, residual connection is carried out simultaneously.

$$H_{att}^{dc} = max(0, H_{att}W_1 + b_1)W_2 + b_2 \tag{4}$$

where W_1, W_2 denote the parameter matrix, b_1, b_2 denote the bias vectors. Such structure is stacked up n times, we can calculate the final label-attentive legal case representation H_{att}^{dc} by (4).

JLER. We propose a novel text representation based on pre-trained model. Specifically, we concatenate the representation of legal case H^d and the final label-attentive document representation H^{dc}_{att} to get the final text representation by (5). It can improve accuracy and stability of charge prediction by integrating case information and abundant labels information simultaneously.

$$JLER = [H^d; H^{dc}_{att}] \tag{5}$$

2.4 Classifier

We design the Classifier to predict the final charge. Since CNN [15] is one of the commonly used effective methods for modeling text sequential data, we employ CNN to extract the fusion feature of legal case representation and label-enhanced representation, and then adopt a fully connected network (MLP) and *Relu* function to generate the most possible charge.

CNN contains convolution operations for n-gram feature extraction and the max-pooling operations to obtain final representation. In this process, we can detect and select the most abundant n-gram features.

First, we put JLER into the CNN. The final feature representation Z is obtained by convolution operations and max-pooling operation of CNN. With the final representation Z, we apply a transformation followed by *relu* function (6) and obtain the final prediction as

$$y^c_i = ReLu(W^i_3 Z + b^i_3) \tag{6}$$

Here, W^i_3, b^i_3 are parameters specific to $i - th$ task, y^c_i denote the prediction result of $i - th$ task.

We use the cross-entropy loss function (7) for each task and sum up losses to train our model.

$$L = - \sum_i^c y_i log(y^c_i) \tag{7}$$

where y_i is the ground-truth label, and c is the number of charges.

3 Experiments

To verify the effectiveness of the proposed model, we conduct a series of experiments on several real-world datasets. In this section, we will first introduce the datasets and provide the important settings of model in experiment, and then compare the performance of our model with the baselines and analyze the effect of each module in our model.

3.1 Dataset Construction

We use CAIL2018 [14] dataset to evaluate the performance of our model. It consists of two public datasets from Chinese AI and Law challenge (CAIL2018), CAIL-small (the exercise stage data) and CAIL-big (the first stage data). Each sample in these datasets is a legal case, and each case has the same organization structure, including the following parts, the factual description of the case, and the results of relevant laws, charges and the terms of penalty. Both datasets have 196 charges but different scales of case number. The detailed statistics of the CAIL2018 are shown in Table 1.

Table 1. The description of datasets.

	Training set	Testing set
Call-small	154592	32508
Call-big	1710856	217016

In CAIL-small dataset, additional 17,131 samples are provided as the validation set. In the CAIL-big dataset, there are some cases with multiple charges, i.e., multi-label samples. As our model aims to explore the effectiveness of the charge labels information. we filter out these multi-label samples due to our model only study the single charge label sample. Our model infers the charge in terms of the factual description that will be combined with all the label semantics information.

3.2 Baselines for Comparative Experiments

As described below, the first four typical text classification models and the other two advance charge prediction models are compared with the proposed model as baselines.

TFIDF + SVM: Term-frequency inverse document frequency (TFIDF) [16] is used to extract features of inputs, and SVM [17] is adopted as the classifier.

CNN: The CNN [15] with multiple filter widths is implemented as text classifier.

BiLSTM + ATT [18]: A bidirectional LSTM with an attention mechanism is used to capture contextual semantics and automatically select important features by attention during training, which is a variant of neural network based on attention mechanism.

Bert + fine-tuning: Combining pre-trained models with downstream task models and fine-tuning the parameters of the pre-trained models.

Fact-Law Att: Fact-Law Attention Model [7] is an attention-based neural network method for criminal charge prediction task.

Attribute-Att: Hu et al. [5] propose Attribute attentive Charge Prediction Model which can predict the attributes and charges simultaneously.

3.3 Experiment Settings and Evaluating Metrics

For TFIDF + SVM, the experiments are conducted by extracting feature sizes up to 2000 and training SVM using linear kernels. In addition, for comparison, we establish a set of neural models. Before the experiments, we use word2vec [19] for word embedding with a size of 100. For CNN, the filter width was set to {2, 3, 4, 5}, each filter size is 25 and the hidden state size is 100. The other two models are more advanced which are proposed by Hu et al. [5] and Luo et al. [7] respectively. We set the LSTM hidden size of Hu's model to 100, and for the other parameters of these two models we remain the same as the original models.

Table 2. Charge prediction results on CAIL-small and CALL-big.

	CALL-small				CALL-big			
	Acc	MP	MR	F1	Acc	MP	MR	F1
TFIDF + SVM	0.758	0.487	0.423	0.425	0.918	0.671	0.535	0.570
CNN	0.792	0.512	0.443	0.465	0.934	0.669	0.504	0.548
BiLSTM + Att	0.824	0.589	0.597	0.588	0.941	0.727	0.669	0.675
Bert + Fine Tune	0.839	0.573	0.535	0.540	0.948	0.724	0.665	0.664
Fact-Law Att	0.847	0.656	0.626	0.624	0.955	0.702	0.714	0.701
Attribute-Att	0.848	0.663	0.692	0.673	0.959	0.751	0.723	0.723
Our model	**0.862**	**0.768**	**0.796**	**0.767**	**0.977**	**0.841**	**0.824**	**0.831**

Our JLER model use *bert* as basic encoder and set the maximum length of document to 500 tokens. The dimension of word embedding is 128, and the numbers of multiple attention is 8. Label-Enhanced Representation is assigned for each class on downstream tasks. In the training process, we use Adam optimizer [20] and set the learning rate to 0.001. For each of the above models, we train 16 epochs on CAIL-small and CAIL-big and complete the charge prediction task on the corresponding testing set. We employ accuracy (Acc.), macro-precision (MP), macro-recall (MR) and macro-F1 (F1) as the evaluating metrics.

3.4 Experimental Results and Analysis

Table 2 shows the comparative experimental results of our model with baselines on two datasets. According to the results, JLER model outperforms all previous baselines in all evaluating metrics with a significant margin on two datasets. More specifically, compared to the previous state-of-the-art in charge prediction [5, 7], our model achieves 1.4% and 1.8% absolutely improvements under Acc on two datasets respectively, which demonstrates the effectiveness of our JLRE model for charge prediction. It indicates that our model can be capable of capturing the abundant semantic information of charge labels that are crucial for charge prediction.

In JLER model, the proposed Label Enhancer part, combine case information with abundant semantic information of charge labels, which significantly improve performance of charge prediction. Specifically, a double attention mechanism consisting of self-attention and cross-attention is applied to capture significant information of charge labels can be more effective. Consequently, our model achieves state-of-the-art performance on two datasets without any additional tedious work as other charge prediction models do.

3.5 Comparative Experiments of Few-Shot Charge Prediction

As shown in Table 2, almost all existing methods have unsatisfactory performances in term of macro-F1, which indicates that they cannot well deal with few-shot charge prediction. On the contrary, our model achieves promising improvements of 9.4% and 10.8% in macro-F1on two datasets, respectively, which demonstrates the robustness and effectiveness of our model.

In order to further illustrate the effectiveness of the JLER model in handling few-shot charge prediction, we run a set of experiments on charges with few-shot. We select some charges less than 100 in the CAIL-small and Table 3 shows the performance of our JLER model and other baselines. According to accuracy, our model achieves about 29.3% improvement compared to TFIDF + SVM model and a considerable improvement by 13.9% over the state-of-the-art baseline [5]. This indicates that the semantic information of few-shot charges can be captured by our model and plays an important role in the charge prediction task. The main reason for the capacity of relieving the problem of data imbalance is that we utilize the enhanced label representations with a label enhancer to fine-tune the pre-trained models. This operation can complement for the shortage of few-shot data.

Table 3. Charge prediction results on few-shot charges.

	Acc.	F1
TFIDF + SVM	0.205	0.152
CNN	0.304	0.241
BiLSTM + ATT	0.212	0.150
Bert + Fine Tuning	0.371	0.290
Fact-Law Att	0.355	0.211
Attribute-att	0.359	0.223
Our model	0.498	0.375

As shown in the Fig. 2, we plot the Error Rate by employ different models on the six few-shot charges. Specifically, we randomly select six kinds of few-shot charges from CALL-small. we define the charges between 10 cases and 100 cases are few-shot samples. The numbers on the x-axis represent different charges. we can clearly find that our model obtains the start-of-the-art performance on different few-shot charges.

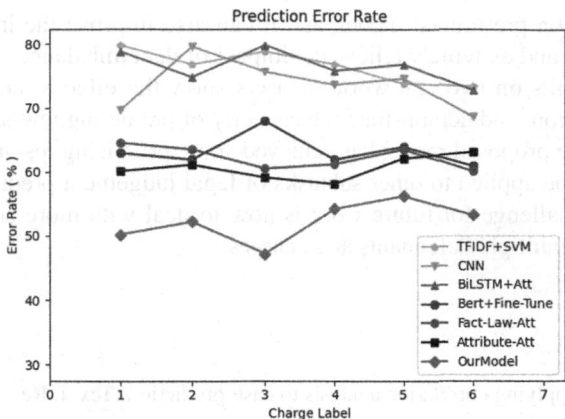

Fig. 2. Prediction error rate of all models.

3.6 Ablation Test

Our model is characterized by the Label Enhancer, which consists of a self-attention mechanism module and a cross-attention module. Thus, we design ablation tests respectively to investigate the effectiveness of these modules. As shown in Table 4, JLER w/o Cross indicate the model without the use of a cross-attention mechanism. JLER w/o Self indicate the model without the self-attention mechanism.

Table 4. Experimental results of ablation test on CAIL-small.

Metrics	Acc.	MP	MR	F1
Our model	**0.859**	**0.768**	**0.796**	**0.767**
JLER w/o Cross	0.845	0.742	0.754	0.731
JLER w/o Self	0.840	0.731	0.734	0.723

As shown in Table 4, we can observe that the performance degrades obviously after removing the cross-attention layer or self-attention layer. The result of macro-F1 decreases at least 3.6%. Therefore, it can be seen that the cross-attention mechanism and the self-attention play irreplaceable roles in our model.

4 Conclusion

In this paper, we focus on the task of charge prediction by given fact descriptions of legal cases. We propose a Joint Labels-Enhanced Representation model that can integrate case description and abundant labels information simultaneously. Specifically, our model gained the enhanced label representation by utilizing a double-layer mechanism of self-attention and cross-attention. It can improve accuracy and stability of charge prediction based on pre-trained model, and it can also improve the interpretability of prediction results and extremely relieve the impact of data imbalance. The comparative experimental results on two real-world datasets show the effectiveness of our model on charge prediction, and demonstrate the capacity of predicting few-shot charges with limited cases. The proposed model has achieved some promising results on charge prediction and may be applied to other subtasks of legal judgement prediction in the next work. Another challenge for future work is how to deal with more complicated legal cases containing multiple defendants and charges.

References

1. Nagel, S.S.: Applying correlation analysis to case prediction. Tex. l. Rev. **42**(7), 1006–1017 (1964)
2. Segal, J.A.: Predicting supreme court cases probabilistically: the search and seizure cases, 1962–1981. Am. Political Sci. Rev. **78**(4), 891–900 (1984)
3. Lauderdale, B.E., Clark, T.S.: The supreme court's many median justices. Am. Political Sci. Rev. **106**(4), 847–866 (2012)
4. Katz, D.M., Bommarito, M.J., Blackman, J.: A general approach for predicting the behavior of the supreme court of the United States. PLoS ONE **12**(4), e0174698 (2017)
5. Hu, Z., Li, X., Tu, C., Liu, Z., Sun., M.: Few-shot charge prediction with discriminative legal attributes. In: Proceedings of the COLING (2018)
6. Zhong, H., Guo, Z., Tu, C.: Legal judgment prediction via topological learning. In: Proceedings of the 2018 Conference on Empirical Methods in Natural Language Processing, pp. 3540–3549. Association for Computational Linguistics, Brussels, Belgium (2018)
7. Luo, B., Feng, Y., Xu, J., Zhang, X., Zhao, D.: Learning to predict charges for criminal cases with legal basis, pp. 2727–2736 (2017)
8. Shaghaghian, S., Feng, L.Y., Jafarpour, B., Pogrebnyakov, N.: Customizing contextualized language models for legal document reviews. In: Proceedings of the IEEE International Conference on Big Data (Big Data), pp. 2139–2148 (2020)
9. Shao, Y., et al.: BERT-PLI: modeling paragraph-level interactions for legal case retrieval. In: Proceedings of IJCAI, pp. 3501–3507 (2020)
10. Liu, Y., et al.: Roberta: a robustly optimized bert pretraining approach. ArXiv abs/1907.11692 (2019)
11. Zhong, H., Zhang, Z., Liu, Z., Sun, M.: Open Chinese Language Pre-trained Model Zoo. Technical Report (2019)
12. Chalkidis, I., Fergadiotis, M., Malakasiotis, P., Aletras, N., Androutsopoulos, I.: LEGAL-BERT: "preparing the muppets for court". In: Proceedings of EMNLP: Findings, pp. 2898–2904 (2020)
13. Devlin, J., Chang, M.-W., Lee, K., Toutanova, K.: Bert: pre-training of deep bidirectional transformers for language understanding. In: Proceedings of NAACL HLT, pp. 4171–4186 (2019)
14. Xiao, C., et al.: CAIL2018: a large-scale legal dataset for judgment prediction. ArXiv abs/1807.02478 (2018)
15. Kim, Y.: Convolutional neural networks for sentence classification. EMNLP (2014)
16. Salton, G., Buckley, C.: Term-weighting approaches in automatic text retrieval. Inf. Process. Manage. **24**(5), 513–523 (1988)
17. Suykens, J.A., Vandewalle, J.: Least squares support vector machine classifiers. Neural Process. Lett. **9**(3), 293–300 (1999)

18. Xu, K., et al.: Show, attend and tell: neural image caption generation with visual attention. In: Proceedings of the International Conference on Machine Learning (ICML), pp. 2048–2057 (2015)
19. Mikolov, T., Sutskever, I., Chen, K., Corrado, G.S., Dean, J.: Distributed representations of words and phrases and their compositionality. In: Advances in Neural Information Processing Systems, pp. 3111–3119 (2013)
20. Kingma, D.P., Ba, J.: Adam: A method for stochastic optimization. arXiv preprint arXiv: 1412.6980 (2014)

Multi-view Document Clustering with Joint Contrastive Learning

Ruina Bai, Ruizhang Huang[⊠], Yongbin Qin, and Yanping Chen

State Key Laboratory of Public Big Data, College of Computer Science
and Technology, Guizhou University, Guiyang 550025,
Guizhou, People's Republic of China
rzhuang@gzu.edu.cn

Abstract. Multi-view document clustering, which learns common representations from multiple views to achieve consistent partition, has emerged lots of increasing work. Though promising performance has been demonstrated in various applications, their view representations are learned with no consideration of achieving a consistent clustering partition. In this paper, we propose a Multi-view document Clustering model with Joint Contrastive learning (MCJC) to address the aforementioned issue. Our model learns the view representations with a joint contrastive learning module by introducing a task-specific objective so that it can effectively achieve consistency both in cluster-wise and feature-wise hidden spaces. Meanwhile, in the clustering module, we collect the view-level cluster agreement and document-level clustering partition to refine the contrastive learning and obtain document assignments. As a result, the proposed model can use a joint contrastive module to learn clustering-friendly representation and through multi-level clustering to achieve better clustering performance. Extensive experiments on real datasets demonstrate that our model achieves state-of-the-art clustering effectiveness.

Keywords: Multi-view document clustering · Contrastive learning · Deep clustering

1 Introduction

Multi-view documents become widespread in application scenarios due to the diversity of text representation. For example, news articles can be expressed not only by the features from the traditional content view but also by a set of propagation behavior features, such as the readers and the forwarders of the news articles. A research paper can be described by the set of discriminative content features or by the views of researchers, including paper authors, reference authors, and citation authors. Multi-view document clustering, which aims to discover a consistent clustering partition based on multiple document views, has received increasing research interest. Recently, many proposed multi-view clustering methods are consisted of representation learning and clustering

© The Author(s), under exclusive license to Springer Nature Switzerland AG 2022
W. Lu et al. (Eds.): NLPCC 2022, LNAI 13551, pp. 706–719, 2022.
https://doi.org/10.1007/978-3-031-17120-8_55

refinement, and the clustering loss is used to optimize the view learning network and cluster centers simultaneously.

Despite its success, one limitation of existing models is that the view representations are learned with no consideration of achieving a consistent clustering partition. Specifically, each view representation focuses on its own features guided by within-view reconstruction. It is hard to ensure that all view representations have a consistent opinion on clustering assignment. As a result, views do not agree on document partition results, thus it leads to degraded multi-view document clustering performance. Therefore, it is useful for learning meaningful view representations for document clustering, which not only contain high-order view features, but also consider the agreement of the partition decision among multiple views. Recently, contrastive learning has become popular and can be applied to achieve the consistent objective for representation learning. Standard contrastive methods seek to embed consistent samples nearby in the latent space while embedding inconsistent ones far apart by maximizing the mutual information between correlated samples [8]. Based on this characteristic, contrastive learning is very suitable for multi-view clustering tasks. However, there is little existing work applying contrastive learning on multi-view documents clustering.

In reality, there is a crucial issue that needs to be considered when introducing contrastive learning to multi-view document clustering. Traditional contrastive learning is used for different descriptions of data to learn a general representation for various downstream tasks. It does not achieve mutual guidance and promotion with multi-view document clustering. From the viewpoint of representation learning, contrastive learning for feature-wise information is trained without a task-specific objective. It cannot guarantee that the obtained representation is suitable for multi-view document clustering. How to capture task-specific/cluster-wise information while learning view representations is important. From the viewpoint of clustering refinement, contrastive learning can not be optimized by the multi-view clustering loss. The view-consistency objective is neglected in clustering refinement, which cannot be used to optimize the contrastive learning process. The multi-view clustering loss focuses on the consistent document partitions in a fused space, instead, contrastive learning should be optimized through multiple view opinions. In this case, the existing multi-view clustering objective may not refine the contrastive learning well, even mislead the final document clustering. Therefore, it is needed to utilize multi-level clustering optimization to refine the representations of contrastive learning.

In this paper, we address the aforementioned issue by proposing a novel Multi-view document Clustering model with Joint Contrastive learning (MCJC). To train contrastive learning with a task-specific objective, we construct a cluster-wise contrastive loss on feature matrix to capture the consistency of cluster distribution between view pairs. Specifically, a joint contrastive module with cluster-wise and feature-wise losses is designed for discovering the consistency of view pairs. In clustering refinement, we introduce a multi-level clustering module, which captures view-level cluster agreement and document-level clustering partition, to refine consistent representations of contrastive learning and obtain cluster assignments simultaneously. The proposed MCJC effectively combines the strengths of both the autoencoder-based view representation pretraining module and contrastive learning module with a joint objective, and a multi-level clustering module. And MCJC only needs batch-wise optimization and thus can be easily applied to large-scale multi-view document datasets. Extensive experiments on real datasets demonstrate that our model achieves state-of-the-art clustering effectiveness.

2   Related Work

Multi-view Clustering. Existing multi-view clustering taxonomy involves two categories: traditional methods and deep learning methods. NMF-based multi-view clustering methods [12,19,34,36] employ nonnegative matrix factorization (NMF) to seek common latent factors which are low-dimensional representations among multiple views. Some multi-view clustering models based on subspace clustering have also been proposed [2,20,26,31]. A series of multi-view subspace clustering models (MLRSSC) [2] are investigated to learn a joint subspace representation by constructing an affinity matrix shared among all views; MSC_IAS [26] learns an intact space by integrating encoded complementary information. These traditional and statistical models have a common drawback, as they cannot extract complex structures within the data. Since DEC [28] provided an optimization target for deep clustering, deep multi-view clustering has received increasing attention. [17] extends the DEC model to multi-view data. A joint framework of deep multi-view clustering (DMJC) is proposed which learns the multiple deep embedded features, multi-view fusion mechanism, and clustering assignment simultaneously. DAMC [16] adopts auto-encoders to learn latent representations shared by multiple views, and meanwhile leverages adversarial training to further capture the data distribution and disentangle the latent space. DEMVC [29] learns feature representation and clustering assignment through collaborative training. Deep multi-view subspace clustering models are investigated, at last, DMVSSC [23] and MvDSCN [35] extract multi-view deep features by convolutional auto-encoders, then learn a joint self-expressive representation across all views. The S2DMVSC [22] model integrates spectral clustering and affinity learning into a deep learning framework.

Contrastive Learning. Contrastive learning [8] is to map the input data into a feature space, which divides the samples into positive and negative pairs according to whether the samples are the same class or not. It is one of the unsupervised methods that have developed rapidly in recent years [3,9,10,27]. There are some works to study the relevance between contrastive learning and multi-view learning. The contrastive multi-view coding [24](CMC), obtains robust representations by the multiple views augmentation of an image. And [6,13,25] found that it can help extract consistent information by applying contrastive methods on multiple views. However, most of these works are for image data and cannot be extended to more than two views, such as COMPLETER [18] and SURE [30].

3 Model

Problem Statement. Given a multi-view document dataset $\{x_i^1, x_i^2, \cdots, x_i^V\}_{i=1}^N$, each sample has V views that contain different information and N is the data size. Multi-view clustering aims to group them into K clusters.

As illustrated in Fig. 1, we consider the dataset with two views for simplicity of description. Our model consists of three components, namely the View Representations pretraining Module(VRM), the Joint Contrastive learning Module(JCM), and the Multi-level Clustering Module(MCM). In brief, the VRM extracts view-specific features by reconstructing each view individually. After that, the JCM applies contrastive learning in the hidden matrix H^v, to capture the view consistency. Finally, the MCM discovers view-level and document-level partitions. It uses the view-level cluster agreement and document-level clustering confidence to refine contrastive learning and cluster learning simultaneously. In the following, we will describe the three components in detail and introduce the learning with more than two views at the end.

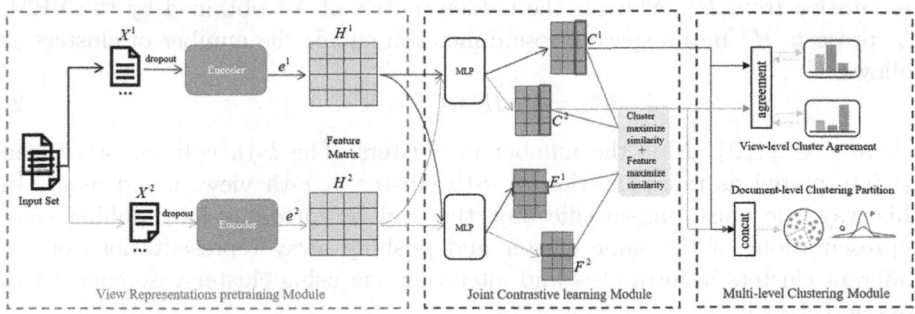

Fig. 1. The framework of the proposed MCJC with two views.

3.1 View Representation Pretraining Module (VRM)

Given a multi-view document dataset $X = \{X^v\}_{v=1}^V$, each view is represented by X^v. Each document x_i in X is represented by $\{x_i^1, x_i^2\}$, $i \in \{1, \cdots, N\}$. In which V is the number of views, N is the number of documents of dataset. The view representation pretraining module aims to learn view-specific features from each view. To preserve high-order features, the VRM is initialized with V denoising autoencoders, and is trained to reconstruct the inputs after corruption. The VRM network of each view v is designed as follows:

$$\tilde{X}^v = Dropout(X^v)$$
$$H^v = e^v(\tilde{X}^v; \Theta_e^v) \qquad (1)$$
$$\hat{X}^v = d^v(H^v; \Theta_d^v)$$

where $Dropout(\cdot)$ is a stochastic mapping that randomly sets a portion of its input dimensions to 0. The portion is determined according to the characteristics of the dataset. Θ_e^v and Θ_d^v are the parameters of encoder e^v and decoder d^v. X^v is the document matrix for inputting, H^v is the hidden feature and $\hat{X}$ is the reconstruction of X^v. Training is performed by minimizing the reconstruction loss $||X^v - \hat{X}^v||_2^2$. We use the encoder as our initial mapping from the original view space to the view-specific feature space. After the process of VRM, we can get a set of view-specific feature matrices $\{H^v\}_{v=1}^V$.

3.2   Joint Contrastive Learning Module (JCM)

The idea behind the JCM is to employ contrastive learning to get view representations with a cluster-wise objective, to encourage accurate cluster-wise and feature-wise discrimination during the contrastive learning process.

Inspired by [4,15] about the idea of "label as representation", we regard the cluster-wise information as the different cluster distribution on each sample. Specifically, we apply a two-layer nonlinear MLP ϕ_C to extract cluster-wise representation from H^v, which is the hidden matrix of X^v obtained by the VRM. ϕ_C projects H^v into a space whose dimension equals the number of clusters as follows:

$$C^v = \phi_C(H^v), C^v \in \mathbb{R}^{N \times K} \tag{2}$$

where $v \in \{1,2\}$, K is the number of clusters. The k-th column of C^v can be interpreted as representation of k-th cluster in v-th view, noted as c_k^v. In this way, the clustering-specific objective can be introduced by pulling close representations of the same cluster and pushing away representations of the different clusters in intra-view and inter-view via using cluster-wise contrastive loss on C^v.

The same as ϕ_C, we also stack a two-layer nonlinear MLP ϕ_F to map the H^v to a subspace where the feature-wise contrastive loss is applied, namely

$$F^v = \phi_F(H^v), F^v \in \mathbb{R}^{N \times M} \tag{3}$$

where M is the output dimensions of ϕ_F.

Cluster-wise Contrastive Loss. The aim of cluster-wise contrastive learning is to distinguish cluster c_k^v from all other clusters except $c_k^{\bar{v}}$, no matter the clusters are in view v or other views. In which $v, \bar{v} \in \{1,2\}$, and $\bar{v}$ is another view except view v. Without loss of generality, the following loss function for c_k^v is adopted to learn maximize the cluster-wise view consistency:

$$l_c(k,v) = -\log \frac{exp(sim(c_k^v, c_k^{\bar{v}})/\tau_C)}{\sum_{l=1}^K [exp(sim(c_k^v, c_l^v)/\tau_C) + exp(sim(c_k^v, c_l^{\bar{v}})/\tau_C)]} \tag{4}$$

where $sim(c_k^v, c_k^{\bar{v}})$ is the cosine similarity of positive pair which is formed by representations of the same cluster from different views. $sim(c_k^v, c_l^v)$ is the cosine similarity of intra-view negative pairs, and $sim(c_k^v, c_l^{\overline{v}})$ represents the cosine similarity of inter-view negative pairs. τ_C is the cluster-wise temperature parameter to control the softness, and we fix it as 1.0.

To avoid the trivial solution that most instances are assigned to the same cluster [11,33], the entropy $H(C^v, C^{\overline{v}}) = -\sum_{k=1}^{K}[P(c_k^v)log(P(c_k^v) + P(c_k^{\overline{v}})log(P(c_k^{\overline{v}}))]$ of cluster assignment probabilities is token into consideration, where $P(c_k^v) = \sum_{j'=1}^{N}\frac{c_{j'k}^v}{||c^v||_1}, v \in \{1,2\}$. The cluster-wise contrastive loss can be computed by

$$\mathscr{L}_C(X^1, X^2) = \frac{1}{2K}\sum_{k=1}^{K}\sum_{v=1}^{V}l_c(k,v) - \frac{1}{2}\sum_{v=1}^{V}H(C^v, C^{\overline{v}}) \tag{5}$$

Feature-wise Contrastive Loss. Different from C^v, the $f_i^v \in F^v$ is learned for conducting contrastive learning on the feature-wise space. To maximize the feature-wise consistency, without generality, the loss for f_i^v is in the form of

$$l_f(i,v) = -log\frac{exp(sim(f_i^v, f_i^{\overline{v}})/\tau_F)}{\sum_{j=1}^{N}[exp(sim(f_i^v, f_j^v)/\tau_F) + exp(sim(f_i^v, f_j^{\overline{v}})/\tau_F)]} \tag{6}$$

where $i \in [1, N]$, N is the number of documents. $sim(\cdot)$ is the cosine similarity. τ_F is the feature-wise temperature parameter to control the softness. Since we hope to identify all positive pairs across the dataset, the feature-wise contrastive loss is computed over every document, namely,

$$\mathscr{L}_F(X^1, X^2) = \frac{1}{2N}\sum_{i=1}^{N}\sum_{v=1}^{V}l_f(i,v) \tag{7}$$

Joint Contrastive Learning Loss. To capture the consistency via two contrastive learning processes simultaneously, we define the joint objective function as follows:

$$\mathscr{L}_{JCL} = \mathscr{L}_C + \mathscr{L}_F \tag{8}$$

By performing the above joint contrastive learning loss, the view-specific information is converted as much as possible into consistent information shared by all views. The obtained representations not only contain high-order view features, but also consider the task-specific objective in the contrastive learning process.

3.3   Multi-level Clustering Module (MCM)

In this part, a multi-level clustering module, which contains the view-level cluster agreement and document-level clustering partition, is designed to refine contrastive learning and clustering via view-level agreement and document-level confidence. After the joint contrastive learning process, the cluster-wise representations as part of clustering loss continuously optimize the clustering results.

According to the design of cluster-wise contrastive learning, the c_i^v is a K-dimensional vector i-th row of C^v, K is the number of clusters. Here, we construct a multi-view cluster agreement matrix A via the assigned cluster of each document with different views, and each element of A is defined as:

$$a_{ij} := \begin{cases} 1, & if \ \sum_v^V o_{ik}^v \geq \frac{V}{2} \\ 0, & otherwise \end{cases} \tag{9}$$

where O^v is the binary matrix corresponding to C^v, i-th row of O^v is a one-hot representation of $argmax(c_i^v)$, o_{ik}^v is the element of O^v, and $i \in [1, \cdots, N]$, $k \in [1, \cdots, K]$. For document x_i, if there are more than one 1 in soft label $A_{i\cdot}$, we will randomly select a view result. $A_{i\cdot}$ is the i-th row vector of matrix A. Then the view-level cluster agreement loss is calculated as follows:

$$\mathscr{L}_A = -\frac{1}{N} \sum_v \sum_i log(A_{i\cdot} \cdot (C_{i\cdot}^v)^T) \tag{10}$$

Here we treat the multi-view agreement cluster as a constraint shared by all views and use it to refine the contrastive learning. Furthermore, we introduce a document-level clustering partition to get the final clustering assignment. The document-level clustering loss is defined as the KL divergence proposed by [28]:

$$\mathscr{L}_{KL} = KL(P\|Q) \tag{11}$$

where Q is the probability of assigning document, and P is the auxiliary target distribution. Cluster centers are initialized by standard k-means clustering on concatenating feature space $[C^1, \cdots, C^V]$. The details can be found in [28].

Finally, the whole model is constantly optimized by continuously minimizing the following loss:

$$\mathscr{L}_{CLU} = \mathscr{L}_A + \mathscr{L}_{KL} \tag{12}$$

3.4   The JCM Training with More Than Two Views

We present more general formulations of the JCM that can handle any number of views, instead, other modules do not need to change. Inspired by [5,24], we introduce two strategies for multi-view contrastive learning, "main view" and "full view" respectively.

Suppose there is a collection of V views $\{X^1, \cdots, X^V\}$. The "main view" formulation sets apart one view that we want to optimize over, for X^1, and builds pair-wise representations between X^1 and each other view $X^v, v \neq 1$, by optimizing the sum of a set of pair-wise objectives:

$$\mathscr{L}_{JCL} = \sum_{v \neq 1}^V [\mathscr{L}_C(X^1, X^v) + \mathscr{L}_F(X^1, X^v)] \tag{13}$$

More general formulation is the "full view" where we consider all view pairs $(v, \omega), v \neq \omega$, and generate $\binom{n}{2}$ pairs in total. By involving all pairs, the objective function that we optimize is:

$$\mathscr{L}_{JCL} = \sum_{1 \leq v < \omega \leq V} [\mathscr{L}_C(X^v, X^\omega) + \mathscr{L}_F(X^v, X^\omega)] \tag{14}$$

The computational cost of the full view formulation is combinatorial in the number of views. However, this enables the full view formulation to capture more information between different views, which may prove useful for downstream tasks. This was also confirmed in our experiments.

4 Experiments

4.1 Datasets

Four real-world text corpora were used to generate 5 datasets to conduct extensive experiments.

(1) **3-sources**[1] is a news articles corpus collected from 3 online news sources: BBC, Reuters, and Guardian. There are 948 news articles of 6 topic classes in 3-sources corpus. We chose those topics that are available in all 3 data sources to derive the *3-sources* dataset. (2) **Reuters** was introduced in [1]. Documents in the *Reuters corpus* are organized in 6 classes written in 5 different languages. Each language as a document view. The *Reuters* dataset is derived by randomly sampling 100 documents from each class. (3) **Aminer corpus**[2] is a research paper dataset that is mainly used to study the research social network. Each paper is associated with its abstract, authors, year, venue, and title. We derived two text datasets from Aminer corpus the same as [1]. Specifically, *Aminer* which contains 4,306 samples and its subset *Aminer(700)*. (4) **HUFFPOST2018 corpus** is news from HUFFPOST news.[3]. Each news contains a headline, short description, news content, related pictures, video, and so on. We derived HUFF-POST2018 news with the headline and short description (*HUFF news* for short), which contains 22,756 randomly selected news from 10 topical areas.

4.2 Experimental Setting

In the proposed model, the encoders and decoders of VRM are all the fully-connected architectures. Specifically, the encoders have the same structure of d^v-600-200-2000-ω, where d^v denotes the dimension of v-th view inputs, ω is the dimension of H^v. The independent decoders are with a dimensionality of ω-2000-200-600-d^v. The output dimensions of ϕ_F and ϕ_C in JCM are decided by different datasets. Our model was optimized using the Adam algorithm with the learning rate 1e−3 for JCM and 3e−3 for MCM. We conducted our experiments on a Ubuntu server with NVIDIA Tesla T4 GPU with a 16 GB memory size. The initial weights and bias used the default settings of PyTorch.

---

[1] http://mlg.ucd.ie/datasets/3sources.html.

[2] https://www.aminer.cn/data.

[3] https://www.huffpost.com.

We compared our proposed model with a wide range of benchmark multi-view clustering algorithms including traditional multi-view subspace clustering (a series of MLRSSC models) [2], flexible multi-view representation (FMR) for clustering [14], MSC_IAS [26], and anchor-based APMC [7]. Besides, AE^2-Nets [32], MvDSCN [35], MDCE [1], DEMVC [29], COMPLETER [18] and SURE [30] were investigated for comparison since they are state-of-the-art deep clustering models for multi-view clustering, where the last two are multi-view contrastive clustering. Noted that, the setting of above methods are same as [1].

We evaluated clustering performance using two metrics: normalized mutual information (NMI) and unsupervised clustering accuracy (CA). Both of these metrics scale from 0 to 1 and higher values indicate better performance.

4.3   Comparisons with State of the Arts

Table 1 depicts the experimental results for the proposed models and 15 representative state-of-the-art multi-view clustering models on all real-world datasets. MCJC_M and MCJC_F are the proposed model with different strategies.

Table 1. Clustering results on all real datasets.

	3-sources		Reuters		Aminer		Aminer(700)		HUFF news	
	NMI	CA	NMI	CA	NMI	CA	NMI	CA	NMI	CA
P-MLRSSC	53.60	55.74	37.51	51.82	84.97	96.70	84.26	96.00	–	–
C-MLRSSC	53.44	56.33	37.83	53.27	85.05	96.73	84.26	96.00	–	–
P-KMLRSSC	46.67	50.80	37.19	56.50	85.45	96.70	82.50	95.50	–	–
C-KMLRSSC	46.12	50.98	36.52	56.41	87.37	97.21	82.50	95.50	–	–
MSC_IAS	55.13	66.86	36.50	50.22	85.47	96.80	82.37	95.50	34.06	39.76
APMC	63.44	70.41	39.32	40.00	86.26	96.96	85.60	96.50	26.01	42.14
FMR	51.11	59.59	34.90	48.57	84.63	96.24	82.42	95.67	–	–
AE^2-Nets	54.44	59.82	34.68	53.11	86.08	96.88	83.19	95.63	–	–
MvDSCN	52.25	63.91	36.09	55.33	84.54	96.59	78.33	94.57	26.70	40.01
DEMVC	49.97	44.24	32.61	51.67	87.12	97.26	83.15	95.71	26.85	42.95
MDCE-AE	50.10	52.75	36.63	56.88	85.18	96.61	83.64	96.00	23.74	39.25
MDCE-NAE	53.39	59.88	43.56	59.25	87.05	97.16	85.56	96.50	31.13	41.85
MDCE-CAE	65.04	73.43	42.06	59.08	**88.37**	97.44	86.63	97.00	24.99	36.03
COMPLETER	×	×	×	×	85.02	96.42	78.00	94.37	2.66	22.38
SURE	×	×	×	×	82.27	95.52	79.77	95.00	0.76	21.49
MCJC_M	70.64	79.88	43.95	59.50	88.28	97.47	87.83	97.14	41.93	56.54
MCJC_F	**73.92**	**84.20**	**45.76**	**60.50**	88.28	**97.47**	**87.83**	**97.14**	**41.93**	**56.54**

The "–" means we cannot get clustering results on the dataset because the large-scale or high-dimensionality dataset occupies many computation resources. The "×" means the model can only apply to two views dataset.

According to the results, MCJC_F significantly outperforms these state-of-the-art baselines by a large margin on *3-sources*, *Reuters* and *HUFF news*. In particular, the proposed model surpasses the closest competitor MDCE-related model by 8.88% on *3-sources*, 3.70% on *Reuters* and 10.70% on *HUFF news* in terms of NMI. With Aminer corpus, various models perform consistently, which indicates that the quality of this data is good. Nevertheless, our model still achieves the highest performance on many metrics. We paid more attention to COMPLETER and SURE that contain the contrastive learning module, the poor results on *HUFF news* may be because of the sparsity of the text. In the proposed model, we not only focus on this issue in each component but can handle data with more than two views. The remarkable results demonstrate the powerful clustering ability of our model, which benefits from the incorporation of all the components.

Apart from that, a multi-view contrastive learning strategy is a crucial part of our model to extend to more than two views. In this paper, we apply the "main view" and "full view" strategies to all datasets to understand the importance of each view, the results reported as MCJC_M and MCJC_F. Notably, (1) MCJC_M implies the best result obtained using the "main view" strategy, and (2) for the dataset of two views, MCJC_M and MCJC_F are the same. The results illustrate that making full use of the complementarities among multiple views will have a positive impact on the downstream tasks.

4.4   Ablation Studies

This part contains the ablation experiments of the joint contrastive learning module and the multi-view clustering module.

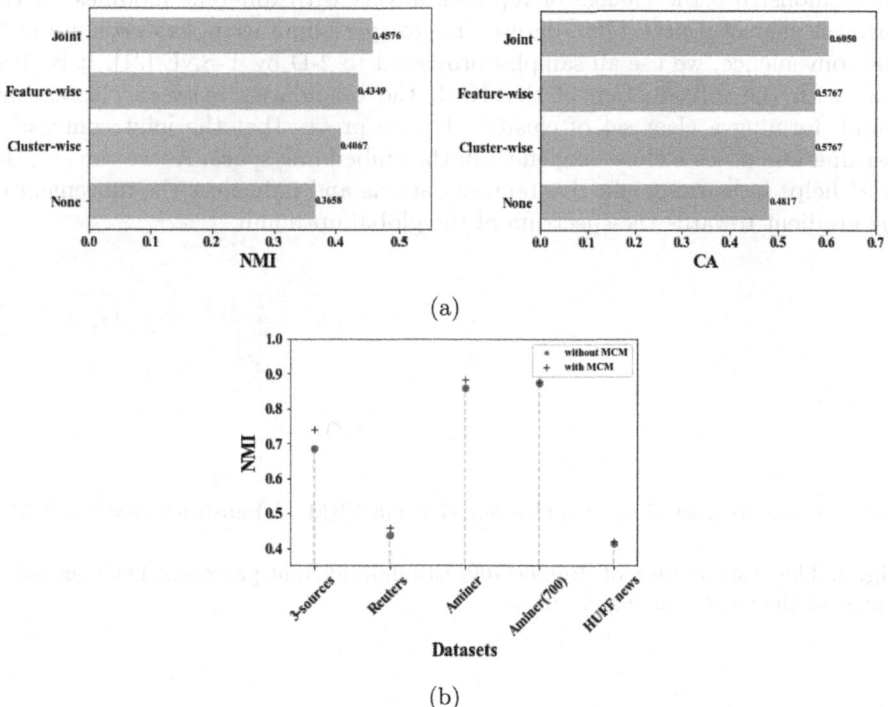

(a)

(b)

Fig. 2. (a) is the impact of the joint contrastive learning module on Reuters. (b) is the comparison with or without multi-level clustering module on all datasets.

The Impact of Joint Contrastive Learning. We apply the different learning processes on the *Reuters* dataset in order to illustrate the importance of the joint contrastive learning module, the results as reported in Fig. 2a. We found that it would be a normal result due to the view-specific features of the view representations pretraining module, thus avoiding degenerating into a random model and better than CONAN [13]. The results of the joint contrastive learning module illustrate that cluster-wise and feature-wise contrastive learning processes are crucial to learn view consistency and can promote clustering.

The Impact of the Clustering Module. In this part, we mainly explain the role of the multi-level clustering module in the proposed model. As shown in Fig. 2b, the module shows different effects on different datasets. The effect is more obvious on datasets with a small sample size, i.e. *3-sources* and *Reuters*. Various works have shown that large quantities of data pairs are crucial to the performance of contrastive models [9], therefore, the joint contrastive learning module does not mine enough on small-scale datasets. And for document with two views, the construct of A_{ij} in Eq. (9) will introduce randomness, which is also not friendly to clustering assignments, shown as *HUFF news*.

4.5   Visualization

We demonstrate the change of representations with different modules on the abstract view of *Aminer(700)* dataset due to space limitation, as shown in Fig. 3. For convenience, we use all samples projected to 2-D by T-SNE [21]. It is clear that with the introduction of the JCM, the boundaries between clusters are found, forming a clear set of clusters. It also proves that the joint contrastive learning loss poses a clustering effect in the embedding space. As we can see, the JCM helps in learning effective representations and influences the movement of the gradient towards the spectrum of the global optimum.

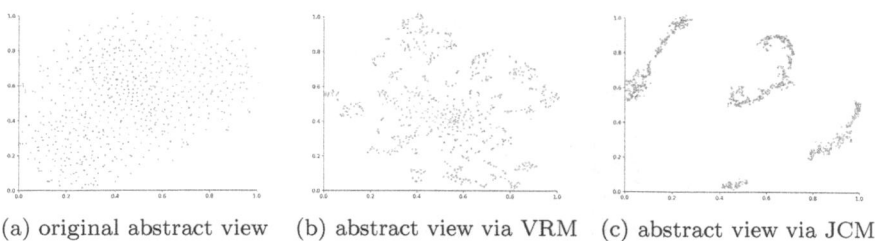

(a) original abstract view   (b) abstract view via VRM   (c) abstract view via JCM

Fig. 3. The abstract view of *Aminer(700)* through different processes. Different colors represent the corresponding clusters.

5   Conclusion

In this paper, we propose a novel multi-view document clustering model named MCJC, which can capture view-consistency objectives and achieve consistent document clustering by joint contrastive learning and multi-level clustering module, respectively. Through the proposed model, not only the cluster-wise and feature-wise information are used for learning common representation, but also view-level and document-level clustering losses are introduced to refine the final result. Extensive experiments demonstrate that the proposed model outperforms the state-of-the-art counterparts on multiple real multi-view document datasets.

Although the effectiveness that showed by our model, the utilization of the feature-wise contrastive learning in the clustering module is not sufficient, thus how to fuse the representation learned by feature-wise contrastive loss into the clustering process to improve final performance reasonably will be the focus of our future work.

Acknowledgement. This work is supported by the Joint Funds of the National Natural Science Foundation of China under Grant No. U1836205 and the National Natural Science Foundation of China under Grant No. 62066007.

References

1. Bai, R., Huang, R., Chen, Y., Qin, Y.: Deep multi-view document clustering with enhanced semantic embedding. Inf. Sci. **564**, 273–287 (2021)
2. Brbić, M., Kopriva, I.: Multi-view low-rank sparse subspace clustering. Pattern Recogn. **73**, 247–258 (2018)
3. Chen, T., Kornblith, S., Norouzi, M., Hinton, G.: A simple framework for contrastive learning of visual representations. In: International Conference on Machine Learning, pp. 1597–1607. PMLR (2020)
4. Dang, Z., Deng, C., Yang, X., Huang, H.: Doubly contrastive deep clustering. arXiv preprint arXiv:2103.05484 (2021)
5. Fan, S., Wang, X., Shi, C., Lu, E., Lin, K., Wang, B.: One2multi graph autoencoder for multi-view graph clustering. In: Proceedings of The Web Conference 2020, pp. 3070–3076 (2020)
6. Federici, M., Dutta, A., Forré, P., Kushman, N., Akata, Z.: Learning robust representations via multi-view information bottleneck. arXiv preprint arXiv:2002.07017 (2020)
7. Guo, J., Ye, J.: Anchors bring ease: an embarrassingly simple approach to partial multi-view clustering. In: Proceedings of the AAAI Conference on Artificial Intelligence, vol. 33, pp. 118–125 (2019)
8. Hadsell, R., Chopra, S., LeCun, Y.: Dimensionality reduction by learning an invariant mapping. In: 2006 IEEE Computer Society Conference on Computer Vision and Pattern Recognition (CVPR 2006), vol. 2, pp. 1735–1742. IEEE (2006)
9. He, K., Fan, H., Wu, Y., Xie, S., Girshick, R.: Momentum contrast for unsupervised visual representation learning. In: Proceedings of the IEEE/CVF Conference on Computer Vision and Pattern Recognition, pp. 9729–9738 (2020)
10. Henaff, O.: Data-efficient image recognition with contrastive predictive coding. In: International Conference on Machine Learning, pp. 4182–4192. PMLR (2020)

11. Hu, W., Miyato, T., Tokui, S., Matsumoto, E., Sugiyama, M.: Learning discrete representations via information maximizing self-augmented training. In: International Conference on Machine Learning, pp. 1558–1567. PMLR (2017)
12. Huang, S., Kang, Z., Xu, Z.: Auto-weighted multi-view clustering via deep matrix decomposition. Pattern Recogn. **97**, 107015 (2020)
13. Ke, G., Hong, Z., Zeng, Z., Liu, Z., Sun, Y., Xie, Y.: Conan: contrastive fusion networks for multi-view clustering. In: 2021 IEEE International Conference on Big Data (Big Data), pp. 653–660. IEEE (2021)
14. Li, R., Zhang, C., Hu, Q., Zhu, P., Wang, Z.: Flexible multi-view representation learning for subspace clustering. In: Proceedings of the 28th International Joint Conference on Artificial Intelligence, pp. 2916–2922. AAAI Press (2019)
15. Li, Y., Hu, P., Liu, Z., Peng, D., Zhou, J.T., Peng, X.: Contrastive clustering. In: 2021 AAAI Conference on Artificial Intelligence (AAAI) (2021)
16. Li, Z., Wang, Q., Tao, Z., Gao, Q., Yang, Z., et al.: Deep adversarial multi-view clustering network. In: IJCAI, pp. 2952–2958 (2019)
17. Lin, B., Xie, Y., Qu, Y., Li, C., Liang, X.: Jointly deep multi-view learning for clustering analysis. arXiv preprint arXiv:1808.06220 (2018)
18. Lin, Y., Gou, Y., Liu, Z., Li, B., Lv, J., Peng, X.: Completer: incomplete multi-view clustering via contrastive prediction. In: Proceedings of the IEEE/CVF Conference on Computer Vision and Pattern Recognition, pp. 11174–11183 (2021)
19. Liu, J., Wang, C., Gao, J., Han, J.: Multi-view clustering via joint nonnegative matrix factorization. In: Proceedings of the 2013 SIAM International Conference on Data Mining, pp. 252–260. SIAM (2013)
20. Luo, S., Zhang, C., Zhang, W., Cao, X.: Consistent and specific multi-view subspace clustering. In: Thirty-Second AAAI Conference on Artificial Intelligence (2018)
21. Van der Maaten, L., Hinton, G.: Visualizing data using t-sne. J. Mach. Learn. Res. **9**(11), 2579–2605 (2008)
22. Sun, X., Cheng, M., Min, C., Jing, L.: Self-supervised deep multi-view subspace clustering. In: Asian Conference on Machine Learning, pp. 1001–1016. PMLR (2019)
23. Tang, X., Tang, X., Wang, W., Fang, L., Wei, X.: Deep multi-view sparse subspace clustering. In: Proceedings of the 2018 VII International Conference on Network, Communication and Computing, pp. 115–119 (2018)
24. Tian, Y., Krishnan, D., Isola, P.: Contrastive multiview coding. In: Vedaldi, A., Bischof, H., Brox, T., Frahm, J.-M. (eds.) ECCV 2020. LNCS, vol. 12356, pp. 776–794. Springer, Cham (2020). https://doi.org/10.1007/978-3-030-58621-8_45
25. Tsai, Y.H.H., Wu, Y., Salakhutdinov, R., Morency, L.P.: Self-supervised learning from a multi-view perspective. arXiv preprint arXiv:2006.05576 (2020)
26. Wang, X., Lei, Z., Guo, X., Zhang, C., Shi, H., Li, S.Z.: Multi-view subspace clustering with intactness-aware similarity. Pattern Recogn. **88**, 50–63 (2019)
27. Wu, Z., Xiong, Y., Yu, S.X., Lin, D.: Unsupervised feature learning via non-parametric instance discrimination. In: Proceedings of the IEEE Conference on Computer Vision and Pattern Recognition, pp. 3733–3742 (2018)
28. Xie, J., Girshick, R., Farhadi, A.: Unsupervised deep embedding for clustering analysis. In: Proceedings of the 33rd International Conference on International Conference on Machine Learning-Volume 48, pp. 478–487 (2016)
29. Xu, J., Ren, Y., Li, G., Pan, L., Zhu, C., Xu, Z.: Deep embedded multi-view clustering with collaborative training. Inf. Sci. **573**, 279–290 (2021)
30. Yang, M., Li, Y., Hu, P., Bai, J., Lv, J.C., Peng, X.: Robust multi-view clustering with incomplete information. IEEE Trans. Pattern Anal. Mach. Intell. (2022)

31. Zhang, C., et al.: Generalized latent multi-view subspace clustering. IEEE Trans. Pattern Anal. Mach. Intell. **42**(1), 86–99 (2018)
32. Zhang, C., Liu, Y., Fu, H.: Ae2-nets: autoencoder in autoencoder networks. In: Proceedings of the IEEE/CVF Conference on Computer Vision and Pattern Recognition, pp. 2577–2585 (2019)
33. Zhang, X., Wang, S., Wu, Z., Tan, X.: Unsupervised image clustering algorithm based on contrastive learning and k-nearest neighbors. Int. J. Mach. Learn. Cybern. **13**, 2415–2423 (2022). https://doi.org/10.1007/s13042-022-01533-7
34. Zhao, H., Ding, Z., Fu, Y.: Multi-view clustering via deep matrix factorization. In: Thirty-First AAAI Conference on Artificial Intelligence (2017)
35. Zhu, P., Hui, B., Zhang, C., Du, D., Wen, L., Hu, Q.: Multi-view deep subspace clustering networks. arXiv preprint arXiv:1908.01978 (2019)
36. Zong, L., Zhang, X., Zhao, L., Yu, H., Zhao, Q.: Multi-view clustering via multi-manifold regularized non-negative matrix factorization. Neural Netw. **88**, 74–89 (2017)

Multimodality and Explainability (Oral)

A Multi-step Attention and Multi-level Structure Network for Multimodal Sentiment Analysis

Chuanlei Zhang[1], Hongwei Zhao[1], Bo Wang[2(✉)], Wei Wang[2], Ting Ke[1], and Jianrong Li[1]

[1] School of Artificial Intelligence, Tianjin University of Science and Technology, Tianjin, China
{97313114,keting,lisa_ljr}@tust.edu.cn, zhaohongwei@mail.tust.edu.cn
[2] Sitonholy(Tianjin) Technology Co., Ltd., Tianjin, China
{wangbo,wangwei}@aiserver.cn

Abstract. Multimodal sentiment analysis aims to predict sentiment polarity from several modalities, which is an essential task for widespread applications. The core part of this task is to design a suitable fusion schema to integrate the heterogeneous information from different modalities. However, previous methods usually adopted simple interaction strategies, such as gate or attention mechanisms, which may lead to extracted features containing redundant information. In addition, most of them only focus on the interaction information between single modality, ignoring the modality pair's interaction information. In this paper, we propose a Multi-step Attention and Multi-level Structure network (MAMS) to address the above problems. Specifically, the multi-step attention mechanism extracts the critical information multiple times during the fusion process, which can reduce the interference of redundant information. Furthermore, the multi-level structure can capture both single modality's and modality pair's interaction information. Experimental results on two datasets (CMU-MOSI and CMU-MOSEI) demonstrate the superiority and effectiveness of our proposed MAMS model.

Keywords: Multimodal fusion · Sentiment analysis · Multi-step attention mechanism

1 Introduction

Sentiment analysis has boomed in recent NLP research, which aims at getting machines to predict sentiment polarity (positive or negative) based on a given sentence [2]. Multimodal sentiment analysis (MSA) is a branch of sentiment analysis, which usually fuses textual (spoken words), visual (facial gestures and expressions), and acoustic (vocal expressions) modalities information to predict the overall sentiment polarity of the video clips [19]. However, these multimodal

© The Author(s), under exclusive license to Springer Nature Switzerland AG 2022
W. Lu et al. (Eds.): NLPCC 2022, LNAI 13551, pp. 723–735, 2022.
https://doi.org/10.1007/978-3-031-17120-8_56

signals are heterogeneous and in different feature spaces. Meanwhile, they possess consistent and independent information leading to various expressions of sentiment tendencies for the same video clips. Accordingly, it is necessary to design a fusion strategy that can combine multimodal information.

Previous approaches have made some contributions in multimodal sentiment analysis to fuse these signals. Rahman et al. [11] introduced a multimodal adaptation gate to capture interaction information. Yang et al. [18] presented mask multimodal attention to combine the information of text and audio modalities. However, these methods have two weaknesses. Firstly, they only use a single-step approach to fuse information from multiple modalities, susceptible to noise fragments. Generally, videos are often spoken expressions and contain repetitive words and pauses that interfere with information fusion. As shown in Fig. 1, the man states that the film is not as charming as the previous Robin Hood series. For the text modality, we observe that the lacked the charm fragment in the green square contains more sentiment information, which is more critical for the sentiment analysis task. Similarly, only a tiny portion contains sentiment information for the image and audio modalities. Secondly, most of them only consider the fusion between single modality, ignoring the information of modality pair, which leads to incomplete use of information.

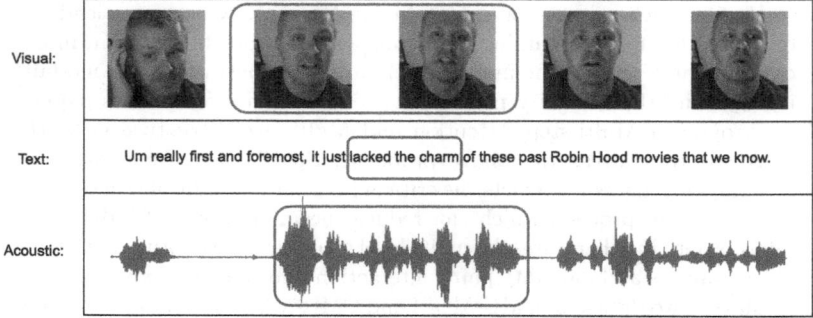

Fig. 1. An example of multimodal signals, including text, acoustic and visual modalities in the MOSI dataset. The green circle contains sentiment information. (Color figure online)

To address these two points, we propose a novel deep neural network, called the Multi-step Attention and Multi-level Structure network (MAMS), aiming to extract essential interaction information during the fusion process and focus on modality pair information. It can be divided into three modules. Firstly, the sequence encoders use the original modality signals to learn the contextual information representation of each modality. Secondly, the modality interactor is designed to effectively integrate the multimodal features. Meanwhile, the multi-step attention allows for repeated extraction of valuable pieces, which will reduce the interference of redundant and repetitive information during the fusion process. The underlying motivation is that if an interaction can extract mutual knowledge in a single step, the model can gradually accumulate useful information by stacking several such steps and eventually capture the semantic relationships between modalities [13]. In addition, the multi-level structure is a hierarchical architecture that can extract interaction information of the single modality and modality pair. Thirdly, the predictor uses a fully connected network to predict the sentiment polarity (positive or negative) based on the multimodal features. The overall framework of our model is demonstrated in Fig. 2, which will be introduced in detail in Sect. 3.

The contributions in this paper can be summarized as follows:

- We design a Multi-step Attention and Multi-level Structure network (MAMS) to predict multimodal sentiment polarity.
- The multi-step attention mechanism is introduced to reduce the redundant and duplicate information during the fusion process.
- The multi-level structure can focus on both single modality's and modality pair interaction information.
- Experimental results on two publicly available datasets (CMU-MOSI and CMU-MOSEI) show that our model achieves comparable performance and proves the effectiveness of the proposed multi-step attention mechanism and multi-level structure.

2   Related Work

Multimodal sentiment analysis (MSA) combines information from several sources, such as text, visual and acoustic signals, to predict the overall sentiment polarity of video clips. Early fusion and late fusion are the original methods for fusing multimodal signals. Early fusion methods [16] concatenate the features of each modality at the input layer and feed them together into a classifier. Late fusion methods [23] model each modality separately and weight the decision results at the inference layer.

Deep neural networks have been widely applied in multimodal sentiment analysis with satisfactory results. Poria et al. [10] adopted CNNs and RNNs to extract multimodal information with multiple kernels learning. Zadeh et al. [19] proposed a tensor fusion network to model intra-modal and inter-modal information in an end-to-end way. Motivated by encoder-decoder structure in neural machine translation, some studies modeled the utterances by translating one modality to another modality. Pham et al. [9] proposed the Multimodal Cyclic Translation Network model (MCTN) to learn robust joint multimodal representations by translating between modalities. Mai et al. [8] proposed an Adversarial Representation Graph Fusion framework (ARGF), which can translate the distributions of source modality to that of target modality. Tang et al. [12] used Coupled-translation to explore bi-directional interaction of modalities which can ensure the robustness of missing modalities.

Recently, the attention mechanism has become increasingly popular. Rahman et al. [11] presented a multimodal attention gate to adjust the position of the words to a new position based on nonverbal cues. Gu et al. [5] selected the informative features in the text and audio modalities with the attention mechanism. Yang et al. presented mask multimodal attention to extract the interaction information between modalities. However, these approaches only adopted a vanilla attention mechanism, leading to extracted features containing redundant information. Our proposed approach can further mitigate the interference of redundant information through the multi-step attention mechanism.

3   Methodology

In this section, the architecture of our model is illustrated in Fig. 2. It is mainly composed of three modules. Firstly, three sequence encoders can encode the original signals into features containing intra-modal information. Secondly, a modality interactor fuses the features of three modalities. Finally, a predictor uses the feature containing interaction information to predict the sentiment labels.

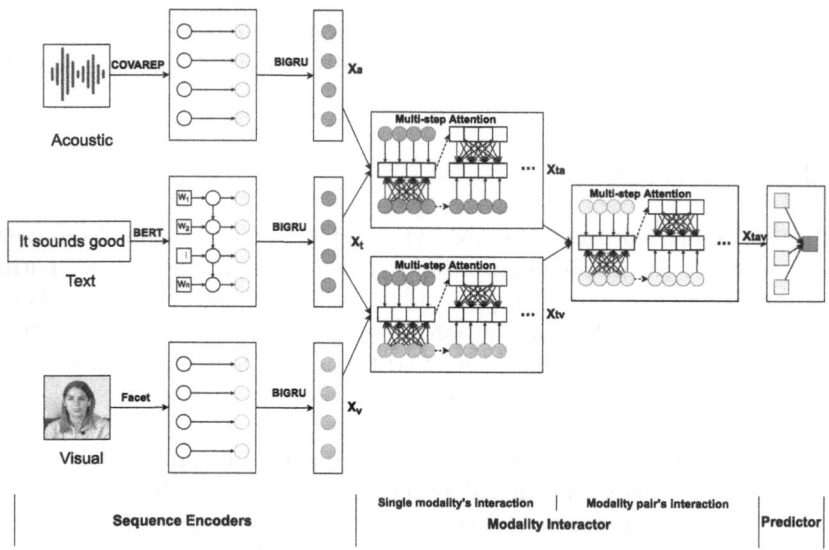

Fig. 2. The network architecture of MAMS. It consists of three components: Sequence Encoders for extracting respective intra-modal features; Modality Interactor for fusing multimodal features, which includes multi-level structure and multi-step attention; Predictor for sentiment prediction.

3.1   Sequence Encoders

The Sequence Encoders are responsible for encoding raw modality signals to obtain respective contextual features.

Text Modality. The pre-trained language model, BERT [4], is used as a text encoder. The sentences are filled or truncated to the same length, $T = (\omega_1, \omega_2..., \omega_n)$, where ω_i is the token. Following the convention of BERT, we add two particular tokens, [CLS] and [SEP], at the head and tail of the sentences, $T = (\omega_0, \omega_1..., \omega_{n+1})$. And then, they are passed into BERT to obtain the word embeddings M_t, as:

$$M_t = \text{BERT}(\omega_i), i \in [1, ..., n] \tag{1}$$

where $M_t \in \mathbb{R}^{T_t \times d_t}$. T_t is the text sequence length and d_t is the size of text features.

Since the input modality sequences are time series, they are temporal dependent. We use a Bi-directional Gated Recurrent Unit (BIGRU) to capture the internal dependencies and project them to a consistent sequence length by connecting a linear layer. There are the obtained features, as:

$$X_t = \text{BiGRU}(M_t) \tag{2}$$

where $X_t \in \mathbb{R}^{T_t \times d_k}$. d_k is the feature size common to all modalities.

Acoustic and Visual Modality. For acoustic modality, we use COVAREP [3] to extract its features. These features include 12 Mel-frequency cepstral coefficients, pitch tracking and voiced/unvoiced segmenting features, glottal source parameters, peak slope parameters, and maxima dispersion quotients. For the visual modality, the Facet library [1] is used to extract a set of visual features including facial action units, facial landmarks, head pose, gaze tracking, and HOG features. There are the obtained features, as:

$$M_a = \text{COVAREP}(A) \tag{3}$$

$$M_v = \text{Facet}(V) \tag{4}$$

where $M_a \in \mathbb{R}^{T_a \times d_a}$, $M_v \in \mathbb{R}^{T_v \times d_v}$. T_a and T_v are the sequence length of acoustic and visual sequences. d_a and d_v are the sizes of acoustic and visual features.

Following the previous works [11,14], P2FA is used to get them aligned with the text at the word level. And then, we fill the acoustic and visual sequences with the zero vector to be consistent with the length of the text modality sequence.

Similar to text modality, BiGRUs extract intra-modal information in the acoustic and visual modality, as:

$$X_a = \text{BiGRU}(M_a) \tag{5}$$

$$X_v = \text{BiGRU}(M_v) \tag{6}$$

where $X_a \in \mathbb{R}^{T_t \times d_k}$, $X_v \in \mathbb{R}^{T_v \times d_k}$. d_k is the feature size common to all modalities.

3.2 Modality Interactor

The modality interactor is the core module of this model, which utilizes multi-step attention and multi-level structure to obtain comprehensive multimodal features. We first introduce the multi-step attention mechanism and then use it in a multi-level structure.

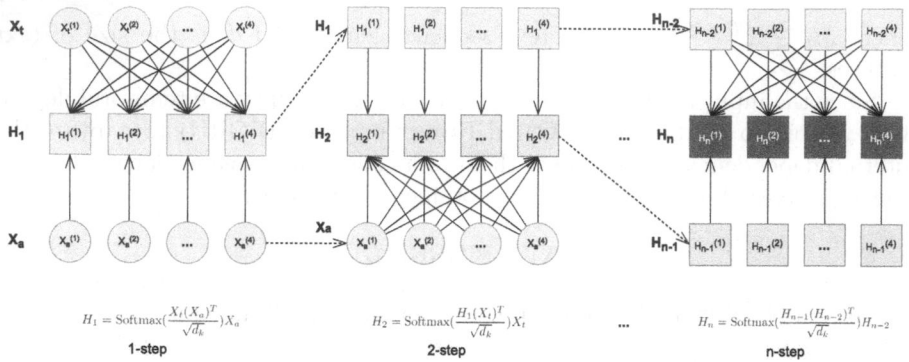

$$H_1 = \text{Softmax}(\frac{X_t(X_a)^T}{\sqrt{d_k}})X_a$$ $$H_2 = \text{Softmax}(\frac{H_1(X_t)^T}{\sqrt{d_k}})X_t$$ ... $$H_n = \text{Softmax}(\frac{H_{n-1}(H_{n-2})^T}{\sqrt{d_k}})H_{n-2}$$

1-step   **2-step**   **n-step**

Fig. 3. Illustration of multi-step attention mechanism. Take the fusion of text and acoustic modalities as an example.

Multi-step Attention. During the fusion process, redundant and repetitive information interferes with the extraction of key information. It is well known that attention mechanisms [5] have been widely applied to various areas of deep learning, which can focus on critical information. If a one-step interaction can extract knowledge between modalities, the model can gradually accumulate useful information by stacking several such steps and eventually capture the semantic relationships between modalities [13]. Multi-step attention mechanism is capable of learning the importance of different modalities and thus extracts the key information during the fusion process.

As shown in Fig. 2, Multi-step attention is used in three places: text and audio, text and visual, and text-audio pair and text-visual pair. We take the example of text and audio fusion, also known as Eq. 10. The other two are also treated in the same way.

X_t and X_a are the representation of text and audio. First, as shown in Fig. 3, we apply the multiplicative attention mechanism [15] to the process of text and audio fusion. Specifically, we treat the text as query and treat the audio as key and value, which can screen out the useful audio parts based on the text information. H_1 is the new hidden representation of audio considering the text. We denote this result H_1 as the 1-step attention.

$$H_1 = \text{Softmax}(\frac{X_t(X_a)^T}{\sqrt{d_k}})X_a \qquad (7)$$

And then, we treat H_1 as query and treat text as key and value using audio information to screen out helpful text parts. H_2 is the new hidden feature considering audio which is called 2-step attention.

$$H_2 = \text{Softmax}(\frac{H_1(X_t)^T}{\sqrt{d_k}})X_t \tag{8}$$

In the same way, H_{n-1} is used as query and H_{n-2} is used as key and value, which will further screen out the helpful audio/text parts. H_n is the n-step attention.

$$H_n = \text{Softmax}(\frac{H_{n-1}(H_{n-2})^T}{\sqrt{d_k}})H_{n-2} \tag{9}$$

Multi-level Structure. The multi-level structure, as shown in Fig. 2, aims to obtain unimodal interaction information and bimodal interaction information. Specifically, the single modality features are fused into modality pair's information at the first level through attention mechanism mentioned above. The text is the central modality to form text-acoustic and text-visual modality pairs, since the text is the primary source of information [14].

$$X_{ta} = \text{Multi} - \text{step}(X_t, X_a) \tag{10}$$

$$X_{tv} = \text{Multi} - \text{step}(X_t, X_v) \tag{11}$$

Then, in the same manner, the two modality pairs are fused to generate features containing all modalities information at the second level. The structure can explicitly capture interaction information of single modality and modality pair.

$$X_{tav} = \text{Multi} - \text{step}(X_{ta}, X_{tv}) \tag{12}$$

3.3 Predictor

The predictor is a fully connected linear network that can predict sentiment labels. Loss function includes task loss and L2 regularization. The mean square error is used as the task loss function, and the regularization is used to prevent overfitting.

$$Y = \text{DNN}(X_{tav}) \tag{13}$$

$$L = \frac{1}{m}\sum_{i=1}^{m}(y^{(i)} - \hat{y}^{(i)})^2 + \lambda\sum_{i=1}^{n}\omega_i^2 \tag{14}$$

4   Experiment

4.1   Experimental Setting

Datasets. To demonstrate the effectiveness of our work, CMU-MOSI and CMU-MOSEI benchmark datasets are chosen.

CMU Multimodal Opinion-level Sentiment Intensity (CMU-MOSI) [23] is a popular dataset for multimodal sentiment analysis, including 93 opinion videos from YouTube movie reviews narrated by 89 different speakers. Each video is divided into several segments, and the whole dataset contains 2199 segments. Online workers annotate the sentiment intensity of these segments on the Amazon Mechanical Turk website. The sentiment intensity ranges from −3 to 3, which means highly negative to highly positive with a linear scale.

CMU Multimodal Opinion Sentiment and Emotion Intensity (CMU-MOSEI) dataset [22] is an improved version of CMU-MOSI. MOSEI has more samples, more topics, more speakers, and more accurate annotation, which contains 23,453 annotated video segments from 1,000 distinct speakers and 250 topics. The dataset, like MOSI, is annotated for the sentiment on [−3, 3].

Evaluation Metric. There are four different metrics we use to evaluate performance of model. As in that literature [14,21], we recorded the experimental results in two categories: classification and regression. For regression, we adopt mean absolute error (MAE), which computes the error between the predicted value and the actual number label directly and Pearson correlation (Corr), measuring the standard deviation. For classification, we evaluate the performance with binary classification accuracy (Acc-2) and F1 score in two forms: negative/non-negative (with zero) [21], negative/positive (without zero) [14].

Implementation Details. We use the AdamW optimizer [7] to optimize all parameters during the training process. The learning rate is set to 1e−5, the dropout is set to 0.2, the maximum sequence length is 50, the feature vector size is 74 for audio, 47 for video, 768 for text, and 60 training epochs. We use an NVIDIA TESLA T4 16 GB GPU and PyTorch to complete our experiments.

4.2   Baseline Model

We pick a few baselines to verify the validity of our model in both CMU-MOSI and CMU-MOSEI datasets.

TFN [19] Tensor Fusion Network (TFN) uses three sub-networks to encode text, acoustic, and visual respectively, and then performs an outer product operation on the three vectors to obtain multimodal features.

MFN [20] Memory Fusion Network (MFN) [22] uses LSTMs and attention mechanism to capture the intra-modal and inter-modal interaction information.

MulT [14] The Multimodal Transformer (MulT) extends the Transformer encoder to multimodal tasks to achieve modal alignment and fusion.

M-BERT [11] M-BERT incorporates multimodal adaptation gates on the pre-trained language model BERT to change the semantic space representation of words to express multimodal sentiment.

MISA [6] Modality-Invariant and -Specific Representations (MISA) accomplishes multimodal information fusion by extracting modality-consistent and modality-specific representations through LSTMs and self-attention mechanisms.

BIMHA [17] Bimodal Information-augmented Multi-Head Attention (BIMHA) uses a multi-head attention mechanism to focus on bimodal information for multimodal information fusion.

Table 1. Experimental results on CMU-MOSI dataset. For Acc and F1, the number on the left of "/" is based on [22], and the number on the right of "/" is based on [14]. ^{h} means the higher score is better. ^{l} means the lower score is better.

	$Acc^h(\%)$	$F1^h(\%)$	MAE^l	$Corr^h$
TFN	77.99/79.08	77.95/79.11	0.947	0.673
MFN	77.67/78.87	77.63/78.90	0.927	0.670
MulT	79.71/80.98	79.63/80.95	0.880	0.702
M-Bert	82.54/84.30	82.59/84.30	**0.731**	0.789
MISA	81.84/83.54	81.82/83.58	0.777	0.778
BIMHA	78.57/80.18	78.55/80.23	0.929	0.663
MAMS	**83.65/85.19**	**83.46/85.21**	0.754	**0.798**

4.3   Comparative Analysis

We evaluate our model on the CMU-MOSI and CMU-MOSEI datasets by four metrics. Table 1 shows the results on MOSI, where the accuracy and F1 values achieve 1.00% and 0.89% improvement (average of the left and right side of "/"). For the regression task, the Pearson correlation coefficient achieves an improvement of 0.009. The mean absolute error is lower than the best result of 0.023. Since the MOSI dataset is relatively small, M-Bert is more capable of achieving better results using a simple multimodal adaptation gate mechanism. Table 2 shows the results on MOSEI, where the accuracy and F1 values achieved an improvement of 0.10% and 0.85%, respectively. In the regression task, an improvement of 0.026 is achieved on the Pearson correlation coefficient metric, and an improvement of 0.011 is achieved on the mean absolute error. This indicates that the multi-level structure improves the effectiveness of modality fusion by exploiting the modality pair's interaction information. Also, it implies that the multi-step attention mechanism automatically learns the importance of the information and thus extracts the key information during the fusion process.

Table 2. Experimental results on CMU-MOSEI dataset. For Acc and F1, the number on the left of "/" is based on [22], and the number on the right of "/" is based on [14]. ^{h} means the higher score is better. ^{l} means the lower score is better.

	$Acc^h(\%)$	$F1^h(\%)$	MAE^l	$Corr^h$
TFN	78.50/81.89	78.96/81.74	0.573	0.714
MFN	78.94/82.86	79.55/82.85	0.573	0.718
MulT	81.15/84.63	81.56/84.52	0.559	0.733
M-Bert	83.79/85.23	83.74/85.08	0.539	0.753
MISA	80.67/84.67	81.12/84.66	0.558	0.752
BIMHA	83.19/83.93	83.21/83.64	0.562	0.729
MAMS	**83.98/85.34**	**85.42/85.14**	**0.528**	**0.779**

4.4   Ablatioin Study

To verify the validity of each component in this paper, we conduct three sets of ablation experiments on the CMU-MOSI dataset. The results are shown in Table 3, Table 4, and Table 5.

First, we explore the effectiveness of attention steps. In Table 3, we observe that 2-step attention achieves the best results. However, three and more steps weaken the performance of the model. The reason is that excessive steps may filter out some valuable information.

Table 3. Experimental results of different step numbers. ^{h} means the higher score is better. ^{l} means the lower score is better.

	$Acc^h(\%)$	$F1^h(\%)$	MAE^l	$Corr^h$
1-step	81.61/83.82	78.50/83.78	0.780	0.770
2-step	**83.65/85.19**	**83.46/85.21**	**0.754**	**0.798**
3-step	82.77/84.73	80.78/84.79	0.881	0.736
4-step	81.31/83.66	77.93/83.61	0.777	0.769

Second, we explore the importance of the multi-level structure, where level numbers affect the degree of modal combination. Specifically, the first level structure only contains the fusion of information between single modality. The second level structure can focus on the fused information of modality pairs. In Table 4, the experimental results illustrate that the inclusion of fused modality pair information can improve the performance of multimodal sentiment analysis.

Table 4. Experimental results of different level numbers. ^{h} means the higher score is better. ^{l} means the lower score is better.

	$Acc^h(\%)$	$F1^h(\%)$	MAE^l	$Corr^h$
One level	82.77/84.43	80.00/84.39	0.776	0.776
Two levels	**83.65/85.19**	**83.46/85.21**	**0.754**	**0.798**

Table 5. Experimental results of different modality pairs. ^{h} means the higher score is better. ^{l} means the lower score is better. T: text, A: acoustic, V: visual.

	$Acc^h(\%)$	$F1^h(\%)$	MAE^l	$Corr^h$
TA+TV (Ours)	**83.65/85.19**	**83.46/85.21**	**0.754**	**0.798**
VA+VT	82.63/84.58	79.59/84.53	0.788	0.775
AV+AT	81.17/82.44	79.29/82.52	0.834	0.767
AT+VT+AT	82.34/84.43	78.73/84.30	0.767	0.789

Third, the model is based on modality pair's fusion. Therefore, it is necessary to explore which modality is used as the central modality. We conduct four experiments for text-related, visual-related, audio-related, and full modal pairs respectively. In Table 5, the experimental results show that text-related modality pair gain the best result. Text modality contains richer semantic information than other modalities [14]. However, when all modality pairs participate in modal fusion, we do not get better results. The reason may be that redundant information participation may cause harmful effects and bring about malicious noise that can corrupt the collected information.

5 Conclusion

We propose a Multi-step Attention and Multi-level Structure network (MAMS), which extracts essential information during the fusion process and focuses on the interaction information of modality pair. Experimental results on MOSI and MOSEI datasets show that our approach outperforms previous methods. The ablation experiments show the importance of each component of our model.

In future work, we plan to design more effective integration strategies in multimodal sentiment analysis. Besides, we consider incorporating more external information into the model, such as the speaker's age, gender, and education level.

References

1. Baltrušaitis, T., Robinson, P., Morency, L.P.: Openface: an open source facial behavior analysis toolkit. In: 2016 IEEE Winter Conference on Applications of Computer Vision (WACV), pp. 1–10. IEEE (2016)

2. Birjali, M., Kasri, M., Beni-Hssane, A.: A comprehensive survey on sentiment analysis: approaches, challenges and trends. Knowl.-Based Syst. **226**, 107134 (2021)
3. Degottex, G., Kane, J., Drugman, T., Raitio, T., Scherer, S.: Covarep—a collaborative voice analysis repository for speech technologies. In: 2014 IEEE International Conference on Acoustics, Speech and Signal Processing (ICASSP), pp. 960–964. IEEE (2014)
4. Devlin, J., Chang, M.W., Lee, K., Toutanova, K.: Bert: pre-training of deep bidirectional transformers for language understanding. arXiv preprint arXiv:1810.04805 (2018)
5. Gu, Y., Yang, K., Fu, S., Chen, S., Li, X., Marsic, I.: Multimodal affective analysis using hierarchical attention strategy with word-level alignment. In: Proceedings of the Conference. Association for Computational Linguistics. Meeting, vol. 2018, p. 2225. NIH Public Access (2018)
6. Hazarika, D., Zimmermann, R., Poria, S.: Misa: modality-invariant and-specific representations for multimodal sentiment analysis. In: Proceedings of the 28th ACM International Conference on Multimedia, pp. 1122–1131 (2020)
7. Loshchilov, I., Hutter, F.: Decoupled weight decay regularization. arXiv preprint arXiv:1711.05101 (2017)
8. Mai, S., Hu, H., Xing, S.: Modality to modality translation: an adversarial representation learning and graph fusion network for multimodal fusion. In: Proceedings of the AAAI Conference on Artificial Intelligence, vol. 34, pp. 164–172 (2020)
9. Pham, H., Liang, P.P., Manzini, T., Morency, L.P., Póczos, B.: Found in translation: learning robust joint representations by cyclic translations between modalities. In: Proceedings of the AAAI Conference on Artificial Intelligence, vol. 33, pp. 6892–6899 (2019)
10. Poria, S., Chaturvedi, I., Cambria, E., Hussain, A.: Convolutional MKL based multimodal emotion recognition and sentiment analysis. In: 2016 IEEE 16th International Conference on Data Mining (ICDM), pp. 439–448. IEEE (2016)
11. Rahman, W., et al.: Integrating multimodal information in large pretrained transformers. In: Proceedings of the Conference. Association for Computational Linguistics. Meeting, vol. 2020, p. 2359. NIH Public Access (2020)
12. Tang, J., Li, K., Jin, X., Cichocki, A., Zhao, Q., Kong, W.: Ctfn: Hierarchical learning for multimodal sentiment analysis using coupled-translation fusion network. In: Proceedings of the 59th Annual Meeting of the Association for Computational Linguistics and the 11th International Joint Conference on Natural Language Processing (Volume 1: Long Papers), pp. 5301–5311 (2021)
13. Tao, C., Wu, W., Xu, C., Hu, W., Zhao, D., Yan, R.: One time of interaction may not be enough: Go deep with an interaction-over-interaction network for response selection in dialogues. In: Proceedings of the 57th Annual Meeting of the Association for Computational Linguistics, pp. 1–11 (2019)
14. Tsai, Y.H.H., Bai, S., Liang, P.P., Kolter, J.Z., Morency, L.P., Salakhutdinov, R.: Multimodal transformer for unaligned multimodal language sequences. In: Proceedings of the Conference. Association for Computational Linguistics. Meeting, vol. 2019, p. 6558. NIH Public Access (2019)
15. Vaswani, A., et al.: Attention is all you need. In: Advances in Neural Information Processing Systems, vol. 30 (2017)
16. Williams, J., Kleinegesse, S., Comanescu, R., Radu, O.: Recognizing emotions in video using multimodal DNN feature fusion. In: Proceedings of Grand Challenge and Workshop on Human Multimodal Language (Challenge-HML), pp. 11–19 (2018)

17. Wu, T., et al.: Video sentiment analysis with bimodal information-augmented multi-head attention. Knowl.-Based Syst. **235**, 107676 (2022)
18. Yang, K., Xu, H., Gao, K.: CM-Bert: cross-modal Bert for text-audio sentiment analysis. In: Proceedings of the 28th ACM International Conference on Multimedia, pp. 521–528 (2020)
19. Zadeh, A., Chen, M., Poria, S., Cambria, E., Morency, L.P.: Tensor fusion network for multimodal sentiment analysis. arXiv preprint arXiv:1707.07250 (2017)
20. Zadeh, A., Liang, P.P., Mazumder, N., Poria, S., Cambria, E., Morency, L.P.: Memory fusion network for multi-view sequential learning. In: Proceedings of the AAAI Conference on Artificial Intelligence, vol. 32 (2018)
21. Zadeh, A., Liang, P.P., Poria, S., Vij, P., Cambria, E., Morency, L.P.: Multi-attention recurrent network for human communication comprehension. In: Thirty-Second AAAI Conference on Artificial Intelligence (2018)
22. Zadeh, A., Pu, P.: Multimodal language analysis in the wild: CMU-MOSEI dataset and interpretable dynamic fusion graph. In: Proceedings of the 56th Annual Meeting of the Association for Computational Linguistics (Long Papers) (2018)
23. Zadeh, A., Zellers, R., Pincus, E., Morency, L.P.: Mosi: multimodal corpus of sentiment intensity and subjectivity analysis in online opinion videos. arXiv preprint arXiv:1606.06259 (2016)

ADS-Cap: A Framework for Accurate and Diverse Stylized Captioning with Unpaired Stylistic Corpora

Kanzhi Cheng, Zheng Ma, Shi Zong, Jianbing Zhang$^{(\boxtimes)}$, Xinyu Dai, and Jiajun Chen

National Key Laboratory for Novel Software Technology, Nanjing University, Nanjing, China
{chengkz,maz}@smail.nju.edu.cn, {szong,zjb,daixinyu,chenjj}@nju.edu.cn

Abstract. Generating visually grounded image captions with specific linguistic styles using unpaired stylistic corpora is a challenging task, especially since we expect stylized captions with a wide variety of stylistic patterns. In this paper, we propose a novel framework to generate **A**ccurate and **D**iverse **S**tylized **Cap**tions (ADS-Cap). Our ADS-Cap first uses a contrastive learning module to align the image and text features, which unifies paired factual and unpaired stylistic corpora during the training process. A conditional variational auto-encoder is then used to automatically memorize diverse stylistic patterns in latent space and enhance diversity through sampling. We also design a simple but effective recheck module to boost style accuracy by filtering style-specific captions. Experimental results on two widely used stylized image captioning datasets show that regarding consistency with the image, style accuracy and diversity, ADS-Cap achieves outstanding performances compared to various baselines. We finally conduct extensive analyses to understand the effectiveness of our method. (Our code is available at https://github.com/njucckevin/ADS-Cap.)

Keywords: Stylized image captioning · Contrastive learning · Conditional variational auto-encoder

1 Introduction

Automatic image captioning has attracted extensive attention in computer vision and natural language processing community [1,16,26]. Most existing image captioning models focus on generating factual captions without any emotions or styles. To get descriptions that are more similar to those from humans, stylized image captioning task has been proposed to not only focus on the visual content but also incorporate specific linguistic styles into captions [7,17]. It has a variety of downstream applications, such as generating captions that are engaging for users in chatbots, or inspiring people with attractive descriptions when photo captioning on social media.

© The Author(s), under exclusive license to Springer Nature Switzerland AG 2022
W. Lu et al. (Eds.): NLPCC 2022, LNAI 13551, pp. 736–748, 2022.
https://doi.org/10.1007/978-3-031-17120-8_57

| Baseline | a brown dog is running through the grass <u>to meet his lover.</u> | a black dog is running through the water <u>to meet his lover.</u> | a black and white dog is playing with a frisbee <u>to meet his lover.</u> |
| ADS-Cap | a brown dog is running in the grass <u>towards his loving owner.</u> | a black dog runs through the water <u>with full of joy.</u> | a black and white dog is playing with a frisbee on the grass , <u>dreaming of olympic glory.</u> |

Fig. 1. Sample outputs of ADS-Cap compared to the baseline approach, in a typical image scene (dog) with romantic style.

There have been many recent advances regarding stylized image captioning task. Most prior works follow the traditional methodology of first pretraining models on large-scale factual image-caption pairs, such that they are able to describe the visual content accurately. These models are then fine-tuned on small monolingual textual corpora to fuse the specific linguistic styles [9,29]. However, two key challenges still remain to be addressed. First, fine-tuning on unpaired stylistic corpora makes the model focus more on linguistic styles and thus cause inconsistency with images [7,9]. Some efforts attempt to find a medium between vision and text for unpaired stylistic corpora, i.e., semantic terms [18] or scene graph [29], but it reduces performance caused by the conversion error. Second, the diversity of stylistic patterns is largely overlooked by previous efforts. To illustrate the importance of diversity, in Fig. 1 we provide captions generated by a compelling baseline model (details in Sect. 4.2). We observe it tends to generate the same normal style phrase "to meet his lover" for different images of the similar scene. It significantly deviates from the purpose of stylized image captioning task. Moreover, stylistic corpora are usually in small-scale, making it difficult for existing methods to generate a wide variety of stylistic patterns.

In this work, we propose an end-to-end framework for accurate and diverse stylized image captions generation, using contrastive learning and conditional variational auto-encoder. To solve the challenge that the model is trained on unpaired stylistic corpora, we unify the training process into a conditional generation pattern: for factual image-caption pairs, captions are generated based on image; for unpaired stylized captions, captions are generated based on the object words extracted from the original captions using an object vocabulary. Then, contrastive learning is used for aligning image features and object words features together, thus fine-tuning on unpaired stylistic corpora does not reduce the consistency with images. We also adopt a conditional variational auto-encoder framework to alleviate the lack of diversity in the second challenge. It can automatically memorize diverse stylistic patterns in training stage. During inference, sampling different latent variables leads to different style phrases, thus enhancing the diversity of generation. Furthermore, we design a simple but effective recheck module that can boost style accuracy by filtering out style-specific captions from a set of candidates. Experiments on several datasets demonstrate that our framework outperforms the state-of-the-art methods, in terms of consistency with the image, consistency with the linguistic style and diversity.

2   Proposed Method

Given an input image x and a specific style label s, our multi-style image captioning task aims at generating a caption y^s that is semantically related to the given image x and consistent with the linguistic style s. To train such multi-style image captioning models, two types of datasets are normally used: (1) a large-scale paired factual dataset $D_f = \{(x_i, y_i^f)|_i\}$, with the i-th image x along with its corresponding factual caption y_i^f; and (2) a set of unpaired stylized datasets $D_s = \{y_i^s|_i\}$, where y_i^s denotes the i-th stylized sentence with style s, $s \in \{s_1, s_2, ..., s_K\}$ represents K different styles.

Overview. The overall framework of ADS-Cap is presented in Fig. 2. It consists of three components: (1) a contrastive learning module that aims at unifying the training process for paired factual and unpaired stylistic corpora (in Sect. 2.1); (2) a conditional variational auto-encoder that memorizes style knowledge and improve diversity (in Sect. 2.2); and (3) a recheck module that further boosts style accuracy by filtering style-specific captions (in Sect. 2.4).

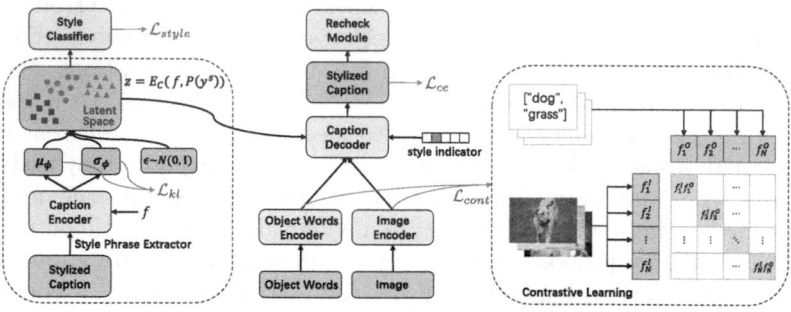

Fig. 2. Overview of our ADS-Cap framework. Blue parts indicate input and output. Yellow parts indicate modules with learnable parameters. Red parts are the latent space constructed by our framework. (Color figure online)

2.1   Training with Unpaired Stylistic Corpora

Our first goal is to find an intermediate for unpaired stylistic corpora D_s, so that it can be used in the same way as the factual image-caption pairs D_f for model training. Here we take the approach of extracting object words from original captions. These object words are then aligned by contrastive learning. During training, the model is learned to generate captions from image features for paired data and from object words features for unpaired data. Since these images features and object words features have been semantically aligned in the shared multi-modal embedding space, the inconsistency between generated captions from object words and original images is considerably eliminated.[1]

Specifically, we first filter object words o from the original caption y using an object vocabulary $V_{objects}$ of 1,600 words from VG dataset [13].[2] Then datasets can be extended to $D'_f = \{((x_i, o_i), y_i^f)|_i\}, D'_s = \{o_i, y_i^s|_i\}$, respectively. For paired samples $\{(x_i, o_i)|_i\}$ in dataset D'_f, we obtain image feature f_i^I and object words feature f_i^O through a deep CNN image encoder E_I and an object words embedding encoder E_O. We then use contrastive learning to align image features and object words features, by maximizing the cosine similarity of matched features while minimizing the cosine similarity of unmatched features (illustrated in Fig. 2). Formally, for a mini-batch with N pairs, the training objective for a given pair (x_i, o_i) is:

$$\mathcal{L}_{cont} = -\log \frac{e^{sim(f_i^I, f_i^O)/\tau}}{e^{sim(f_i^I, f_i^O)/\tau} + \sum_{j=1, j \neq i}^{N} e^{sim(f_i, f_j)/\tau}}, \quad (1)$$

where $sim(\cdot, \cdot)$ is the cosine similarity and τ is a temperature hyperparameter.

2.2 Conditional Variational Auto-Encoder (CVAE)

We also aim at improving the diversity of stylistic patterns in generated captions. We thus use the CVAE framework, which can automatically encode diverse style knowledge into latent space and enhance diversity through sampling.

Our CVAE works as follows. We first use a style phrase extractor P to extract the style phrase from the original caption, and the caption encoder E_C encodes the style phrase as latent variable z . Then the caption decoder D_C reconstructs the input caption with the aid of latent variable z, i.e., $\hat{y}^s = D_C(x, s, z)$. During training, the encoder E_C and decoder D_C are optimized by maximizing the lower bound on the contidional data-log-likelihood $p(y^s|x, s)$, i.e.,

$$\log p_\theta(y^s|x, s) \geq \mathbb{E}_{q_\phi(z|y^s, x, s)} [\log p_\theta(y^s|z, x, s)] - D_{KL}(q_\phi(z|y^s, x, s), p(z|x, s)), \quad (2)$$

where θ and ϕ are parameters for D_C and E_C respectively.

In practice, we adopt a variant of CVAE by assuming z is independent with style s, then the training objective for CVAE is $\mathcal{L}_{CVAE} = \mathcal{L}_{ce} + \mathcal{L}_{kl}$, with:

$$\mathcal{L}_{ce} = -\log p_\theta(y^s|z, x, s), \quad \mathcal{L}_{kl} = D_{KL}(q_\phi(z|y^s, x), p(z|x)). \quad (3)$$

In addition, a style classifier C_S is adopted to divide the latent space by style.

Style Phrase Extractor. Since we focus on the diversity of stylistic pattern rather than the whole sentence, we need a style phrase extractor P to extract style phrase from original caption to ensure that the latent variable $z = E_C(f, P(y^s))$ contain only knowledge of style-related part. We adopt the style phrase extraction algorithm developed by [14], which first measure the style intensity of each word in a caption through the attention output of a well-trained style classifier, and then extract the top-intensity words as style phrase.

---

[1] We generate descriptions based on images rather than object words during inference.
[2] We do not use VG for training, but use the object categories as a generic vocabulary.

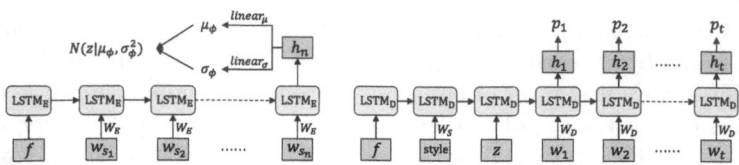

Fig. 3. Architecture of our caption encoder (left) and decoder (right). W_S, W_E and W_D are embeddings for style labels, style phrases and captions, respectively.

Prior Distribution. Existing works have shown that the choice of prior distribution has crucial influences on CVAE behavior [2,27]. In this work, we design a conditional prior distribution to ensure that the sampled latent variables are suitable for the image to be described. Specifically, we model prior $p(z|x)$ as a Gaussian distribution $\mathcal{N}(z|\mu_k, I)$, whose mean μ_k is calculated by image feature or object words feature, and the standard deviation is an identity matrix.

The KL-divergence between two Gaussian prior and posterior is derived as:

$$D_{\mathrm{KL}}\left(q_\phi(z|y^s, x), p(z|x)\right) = -\log(\sigma_\phi) + \frac{1}{2}\left(\sigma_\phi^2 + \|\mu_\phi - \mu_k\|_2^2\right) - \frac{1}{2}, \qquad (4)$$

where μ_ϕ and σ_ϕ are mean and standard deviation of posterior distribution calculated by encoder (discussed in next section).

Encoder and Decoder Architecture. Our architecture for the encoder and decoder are shown in Fig. 3. Caption encoder E_C uses LSTM to encode the input style phrase sequence as LSTM hidden state h_n at the last step, and then h_n is transformed to mean vector μ_ϕ and log variances vector $\log \sigma_\phi^2$ by two linear layers. Caption decoder D_C uses a different LSTM to generate stylized caption. It receives the image feature f^I or object words feature f^O as the first input, then the style embedding vector $W_S(s)$, then the latent variable z sampling in posterior or prior when training or testing. After that, the decoder predicts word probability distribution p_t using hidden state h_t sequentially.

Style Classifier. We build a style classifier C_S on the latent space that predicts the style label s corresponding to latent variable z. It has two advantages: (1) After training, the classifier actually divides the latent space into several regions by style. It allows us to efficiently obtain latent variables with specific style using reject sampling method when testing. (2) Such classification task implicitly ensures discriminative style knowledge is contained in latent space. Specifically, a softmax regression classifier C_S is applied to the latent variable z for style classification, i.e., $p(s) = C_S(z)$, with a cross-entropy loss:

$$\mathcal{L}_{style} = -\log p(s). \qquad (5)$$

2.3 Training Objective

Our overall objective function is as follows:

$$\mathcal{L}_{all} = \lambda_{cont}\mathcal{L}_{cont} + \lambda_{ce}\mathcal{L}_{ce} + \lambda_{kl}\mathcal{L}_{kl} + \lambda_{style}\mathcal{L}_{style}, \qquad (6)$$

where λ_{cont}, λ_{ce}, λ_{kl} and λ_{style} are hyperparameters that balance the losses.

2.4 Recheck Module

Since the size of factual data we use is much larger than stylized data, we observe that the generated captions sometimes can not express linguistic style adequately. To tackle this challenge, we design an effective recheck module that filters captions with specified style from candidates. During testing, for a set of generated candidate captions $c = \{\hat{y}_1, \hat{y}_2, ..., \hat{y}_n\}$, we first score each caption using a well-trained style discriminator $I(\hat{y}_n) = D(\hat{y}_n)$, where $I(\hat{y}_n) \in [0, 1]$ denotes the style strength of caption $\hat{y}_n$. Then we filter out captions from c whose style strength $I(\hat{y}_n)$ exceeds the set threshold (set as 0.9 in practice) from forward to backward to determine the final generated captions. This recheck approach is different from previous re-ranking methods [22,23], which reduce diversity because common style phrases tend to have higher style strength.

3 Experimental Settings

Datasets. We conduct our experiments on two benchmark stylized image captioning datasets: FlickrStyle10K [7] and SentiCap [17]. FlickrStyle10K contains 10,000 images, each image having one romantic caption and one humorous caption. However, only the training set with 7,000 images is publicly available. Following [9], we randomly select 6,000 for training (400 samples from the training set are for validation), and 1,000 for testing. SentiCap contains 2,360 images with 5,013 positive captions and 4,500 negative captions. The positive and negative subsets contain 998/673 and 997/503 images for training/testing respectively, and we split 100 samples from the training set for validation.

In all experiments, the training partition of MSCOCO [15] is used as factual dataset D_f, which contains 82,783 images and 5 factual captions for each image. For stylized data, only captions are used during training, while both images and captions are used for evaluation.

Implementation Details. We use ResNet-152 [11] to extract 2,048-dimensional features from images. The dimensions of hidden states for caption encoder E_C, caption decoder D_C, and several embeddings are set to 1,024. The image features and object words features are aligned in a 1,024-dimensional multi-modal embedding space. For contrastive learning, the temperature τ is 0.1. For CVAE framework, we use a dimension of 100 for the latent space. The values of hyper-parameters λ_{cont}, λ_{ce}, λ_{kl} and λ_{style} are set to 0.1, 1.0, 0.02 and 2.0, respectively. We use the Adam optimizer [12] with a learning rate of 5e-5 for training.

4 Experimental Results

4.1 Quality of Generated Captions

Metrics and Baselines. Following [9,29], we first evaluate the quality of the generated stylized captions from two aspects: content accuracy and style accuracy. Content accuracy captures the relevancy between caption and image. It

Table 1. Results of content and style accuracy in romantic, humorous, positive and negative styles. B1, B3, M, C, ppl and cls are abbreviations for Bleu-1, Bleu-3, METEOR, CIDEr, perplexity and style classification accuracy, respectively.

FlickStyle								SentiCap							
Style	Model	B1	B3	M	C	ppl	cls	Style	Model	B1	B3	M	C	ppl	cls
Roman	StyleNet	13.3	1.5	4.5	7.2	52.9	37.8	Pos	StyleNet	45.3	12.1	12.1	36.3	24.8	45.2
	MSCap	17.0	2.0	5.4	10.1	20.4	88.7		MSCap	46.9	16.2	16.8	55.3	19.6	92.5
	MemCap	19.7	4.0	7.7	19.7	19.7	91.7		MemCap	51.1	17.0	16.6	52.8	18.1	96.1
	ADS-Cap	**25.6**	**6.7**	**10.9**	**33.1**	10.6	**95.9**		ADS-Cap	**52.5**	**18.9**	**18.5**	**64.8**	**13.1**	**99.7**
Humor	StyleNet	13.4	0.9	4.3	11.3	48.1	41.9	Neg	StyleNet	43.7	10.6	10.9	36.6	25.0	56.6
	MSCap	16.3	1.9	5.3	15.2	22.7	91.3		MSCap	45.5	15.4	16.2	51.6	19.2	93.4
	MemCap	19.8	4.0	7.2	18.5	17.0	97.1		MemCap	49.2	18.1	15.7	59.4	18.9	**98.9**
	ADS-Cap	**23.7**	**6.3**	**10.3**	**31.6**	**12.8**	**97.3**		ADS-Cap	**52.3**	**21.0**	**18.0**	**65.1**	**12.4**	98.2

includes Bleu-n [20], METEOR [3] and CIDEr [25]. Such metrics calculate relevancy by n-gram overlap between candidates and ground truth captions. Style accuracy measures whether a caption conforms to a specific linguistic style. For this purpose, the style classification accuracy (cls) and the average perplexity (ppl) are adopted. The cls is calculated by the proportion of generated captions that correctly reflects the desired style. In practice, we use logistic regression style classifiers trained for each of four styles, using stylized datasets D_s and factual dataset D_f. The trained classifiers achieve an average accuracy of 96%. The ppl is calculated by a tri-gram statistical language model toolkit SRILM [24]. A lower ppl indicates more fluent and appropriately stylized captions.

We compare ADS-Cap with the following state-of-the-art baselines for stylized image captioning task with unpaired stylistic corpora: *StyleNet* [7] devises a novel factored LSTM component with matrix decomposition, which automatically distills the style knowledge in the monolingual text corpora. *MSCap* [9] proposes an adversarial learning network and a back-translation module to generate visually grounded and style-controllable captions. *MemCap* [29] develops a sentence decomposing algorithm to extract style-related part, then explicitly encodes the knowledge about linguistic styles with memory mechanism. We do not compare with [14], since they use additional Flickr30K dataset as factual data, which is in-domain with FlickrStyle10K.

Results. Table 1 summarizes the results of content accuracy and style accuracy in four styles. We observe that ADS-Cap achieves the state-of-the-art results compared with previous works. It shows that ADS-Cap can describe visual content appropriately while controlling the linguistic style.

4.2 Diversity of Generated Captions

We evaluate the diversity of generated captions across images and within one image (see sample results in Fig. 4 for differences between these two diversities). Specifically, we focus on the diversity of style phrases in generated stylized captions rather than the entire sentences. Results of ADS-Cap are compared to a baseline model that replaces CVAE with a standard encoder-decoder framework.

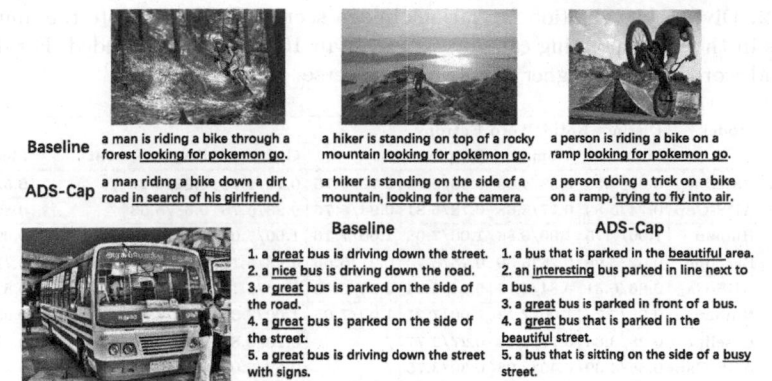

Fig. 4. Captions generated by baseline and ADS-Cap for two types of diversity (in Sect. 4.2), with humorous and positive styles.

Diversity Across Images. To compare the capabilities of generating diverse stylistic patterns across images with similar scenes, we first select seven high-frequency image scenes in testing splits, i.e., man, woman, people, boy, girl, dog and cat. We then adopt two metrics to calculate the diversity of style phrases in the generated captions under each scene.

(1) *Uniqueness.* Uniqueness measures the quantity of different style phrases in generated stylized captions. Specifically, we calculate the ratio of distinct style phrases to all style phrases in each scene [2].

(2) *Uniformity.* We evaluate uniformity by the entropy of word frequency distribution [19]. Formally, entropy is defined as $-\sum_{1 \leq i \leq V} \log_2 [p(w_i)] \times p(w_i)$, where $p(w_i)$ is the frequency of word w_i in a style phrases vocabulary of size V. Higher entropy means more diverse stylistic patterns.

The results of diversity across images are shown in Table 2. We observe ADS-Cap substantially outperforms the baseline model in terms of uniqueness and uniformity across all styles, but still exists deficiency compared to human performance. It suggests our proposed CVAE approach can memorize the low-frequency style phrases in latent space, which are often ignored by encoder-decoder baseline, thus finally improving the diversity by sampling in latent space.

Diversity for One Image. Our CVAE-based approach has natural advantages in generating multiple various stylized captions for one image, because CVAE can efficiently obtain different results by sampling different latent variables. In contrast, the previous encoder-decoder model can only generate multiple captions by beam search, which is known to be less diverse [27]. For quantitative comparison, we employ several automatic diversity metrics that are widely used in image captioning [2]: Distinct calculates the number of distinct style phrases; Div-n computes the ratio of distinct n-grams in style phrases. As shown in Table 3, our ADS-Cap achieves better results than the baseline model on all three metrics. It

Table 2. Diversity evaluation for various image scenes. Slashes denote the number of samples in the corresponding category is less than 10, thus it is excluded. For distinct ratio and word entropy, higher means more diverse.

Style	Model	Distinct Ratio/Word Entropy							
		Man	Woman	People	Boy	Girl	Dog	Cat	Mean
Roman	Baseline	0.31/4.35	0.57/4.39	0.58/5.26	0.72/4.75	0.71/5.10	0.22/3.27	/	0.52/4.53
	ADS-Cap	0.74/5.89	0.77/5.68	0.78/5.81	0.94/5.76	0.93/5.76	0.66/5.53	/	0.80/5.74
	Human	1.00/7.75	1.00/6.86	1.00/7.08	1.00/7.16	1.00/7.08	0.97/7.28	/	0.99/7.20
Humor	Baseline	0.62/5.98	0.75/5.56	0.75/5.73	0.91/5.56	0.93/5.72	0.33/4.21	/	0.71/5.46
	ADS-Cap	0.86/6.31	0.84/6.19	0.84/6.24	0.95/6.00	0.96/6.16	0.77/5.68	/	0.87/6.10
	Human	0.98/7.76	1.00/7.13	1.00/7.21	1.00/7.05	1.00/7.38	0.96/7.20	/	0.99/7.29
Pos	Baseline	0.28/3.84	0.29/2.58	0.27/2.77	/	0.20/0.88	0.40/2.04	0.23/1.60	0.27/2.28
	ADS-Cap	0.35/4.39	0.40/3.96	0.30/3.75	/	0.67/2.05	0.83/3.14	0.39/2.55	0.49/3.31
	Human	0.55/5.48	0.44/3.75	0.58/5.22	/	0.76/2.85	0.84/3.38	0.53/3.62	0.62/4.05
Neg	Baseline	0.08/0.88	0.22/1.39	0.16/1.76	/	0.83/2.04	0.50/2.38	0.66/3.70	0.41/2.03
	ADS-Cap	0.33/2.94	0.38/3.04	0.22/2.55	/	1.0/2.16	0.71/3.37	0.87/4.31	0.58/3.06
	Human	0.69/4.65	0.53/3.96	0.57/4.60	/	0.93/4.22	1.00/4.53	0.87/5.08	0.76/4.51

Table 3. Result of diversity for one image

FlickrStyle					SentiCap				
Style	Model	Distinct	Div-1	Div-2	Style	Model	Distinct	Div-1	Div-2
Roman	Baseline	**87.0%**	0.44	0.59	Pos	Baseline	50.5%	0.38	0.37
	ADS-Cap	**87.0%**	**0.65**	**0.79**		ADS-Cap	**65.2%**	**0.53**	**0.49**
Humor	Baseline	82.1%	0.49	0.65	Neg	Baseline	44.4%	0.35	0.36
	ADS-Cap	**90.8%**	**0.67**	**0.82**		ADS-Cap	**52.0%**	**0.41**	**0.40**

demonstrates that our model is able to generate captions with diverse stylistic patterns for an image.

4.3 Analysis

Ablation Study. We conduct ablation experiments to study the effects of the proposed contrastive learning method and recheck module. We evaluate the following methods for training with unpaired data: *StyleNet* [7] which train unpaired stylistic corpora as a pure language model; *MSCap* [9] which design a "merging" mode to infuse visual features. Results are shown in Table 4. We observe that replacing contrastive learning with these methods makes content accuracy and style accuracy drop significantly. It validates the importance of unifying the two types of data by contrastive learning. We also observe that the model without recheck module performs worse in style accuracy, which shows that the recheck module contributes to ensuring specified linguistic styles.

Latent Space Visualization. We visualize the learned latent space in our model in Fig. 5. We observe it is divided by the style classifier C_S into multiple regions, each corresponding to a style. Meanwhile, a variety of style phrases are

Table 4. Ablation study result. The values of each metric are the average of four styles (i.e., Roman, Humor, Pos and Neg).

Model	B1	B3	M	C	ppl	cls
ADS-Cap	**38.7**	**13.5**	**14.2**	**49.2**	11.7	**97.6**
ADS-Cap (StyleNet)	30.9	9.6	13.5	28.4	**10.4**	86.7
ADS-Cap (MSCap)	35.6	11.2	12.6	40.7	13.0	86.6
ADS-Cap w/o recheck	**38.7**	13.2	13.9	47.8	12.0	76.0

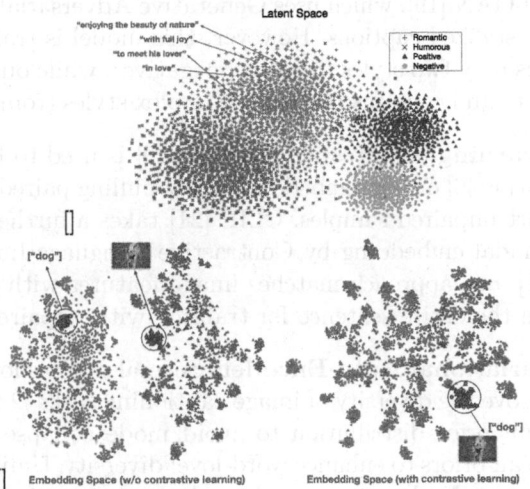

Fig. 5. (a) Latent space visualized by t-SNE. Each color corresponds to latent variables with a specific style. (b) Comparison of multi-modal embedding space (t-SNE plots) with and without contrastive learning. Green and red represent object words features and image features respectively.

encoded into latent variables, thus sampling in latent space can generate captions with diverse stylistic patterns.

Multi-modal Embedding Space. We also visualize the multi-modal embedding space in Fig. 5 to demonstrate the effectiveness of contrastive learning. We observe that two types of features have been semantically aligned in the shared embedding space, which mitigates the inconsistency between generating captions from two types of features.

5 Related Work

Stylized Image Captioning. Earlier methods in stylized image captioning task use parallel stylized image-caption data [5,17,28]. Lately, [14] proposed a novel data augmentation framework to extend parallel stylized data for training.

Recent works most focused on using unpaired data to reduce reliance on paired data [4,7,9,18,29]. Some methods trained pure language model [7,9] or auto-encoder [4] on unpaired stylistic corpora to incorporate styles, which ignoring the consistency with image. Some efforts search an explicit medium between vision and text, i.e., semantic terms [18] and scene graph [29]. However, conversion error between generating caption from images and mediums lead to the decline of model performance. In contrast, our method solves this problem by implicitly aligning image and text features through contrastive learning.

We note all above works ignore the diversity of generated stylized captions except ATTEND-GAN [19], which uses Generative Adversarial Networks to generate human-like stylized captions. However, this model is trained with parallel data and contains only two styles (positive, negative), while our model is trained with unpaired data and contains two other complex styles (romantic, humorous).

Contrastive Learning. Contrastive learning [10] is used to learn high-quality image representation [6] or text embedding [8] by pulling paired samples together and pushing apart unpaired samples. CLIP [21] takes a further step of learning effective multi-modal embedding by Contrastive Language-Image Pre-training. Compared to [21], our approach matches image features with object words features rather than the entire sentence for training with unpaired corpora.

Conditional Variational Auto-Encoder. Several works show that CVAE can significantly improve the diversity of image captioning tasks [2,27]. [27] proposed Additive Gaussian prior distribution to avoid mode collapse and [2] designed sequential Gaussian priors to enhance word-level diversity. Unlike these methods, our model encodes style phrase rather than the entire caption into latent space and uses a style classifier to divide the latent space by linguistic styles.

6   Conclusion

In this paper, we proposed a novel framework ADS-Cap for stylized image captioning task using contrastive learning and conditional variational auto-encoder. Our model can be efficiently trained with unpaired stylistic corpora. Our learned model can generate visually grounded, style-controllable and diverse image descriptions by sampling in latent space. Extensive experiments on two stylized image captioning datasets demonstrate the effectiveness of our method.

References

1. Anderson, P., et al.: Bottom-up and top-down attention for image captioning and visual question answering. In: CVPR (2018)
2. Aneja, J., Agrawal, H., Batra, D., Schwing, A.: Sequential latent spaces for modeling the intention during diverse image captioning. In: ICCV (2019)
3. Banerjee, S., Lavie, A.: Meteor: An automatic metric for mt evaluation with improved correlation with human judgments. In: ACL workshop (2005)

4. Chen, C.K., Pan, Z., Liu, M.Y., Sun, M.: Unsupervised stylish image description generation via domain layer norm. In: AAAI (2019)
5. Chen, T., et al.: "factual" or "emotional": Stylized image captioning with adaptive learning and attention. In: ECCV (2018)
6. Chen, T., Kornblith, S., Norouzi, M., Hinton, G.: A simple framework for contrastive learning of visual representations. In: ICML (2020)
7. Gan, C., Gan, Z., He, X., Gao, J., Deng, L.: Stylenet: generating attractive visual captions with styles. In: CVPR (2017)
8. Gao, T., Yao, X., Chen, D.: Simcse: Simple contrastive learning of sentence embeddings. arXiv preprint arXiv:2104.08821 (2021)
9. Guo, L., Liu, J., Yao, P., Li, J., Lu, H.: Mscap: multi-style image captioning with unpaired stylized text. In: CVPR (2019)
10. Hadsell, R., Chopra, S., LeCun, Y.: Dimensionality reduction by learning an invariant mapping. In: CVPR (2006)
11. He, K., Zhang, X., Ren, S., Sun, J.: Deep residual learning for image recognition. In: CVPR (2016)
12. Kingma, D.P., Ba, J.: Adam: a method for stochastic optimization. arXiv preprint arXiv:1412.6980 (2014)
13. Krishna, R., et al.: Visual genome: connecting language and vision using crowdsourced dense image annotations. IJCV (2017)
14. Li, G., Zhai, Y., Lin, Z., Zhang, Y.: Similar scenes arouse similar emotions: parallel data augmentation for stylized image captioning. In: ACM Multimedia (2021)
15. Lin, T.Y., et al.: Microsoft coco: common objects in context. In: ECCV (2014)
16. Lu, J., Xiong, C., Parikh, D., Socher, R.: Knowing when to look: adaptive attention via a visual sentinel for image captioning. In: CVPR (2017)
17. Mathews, A., Xie, L., He, X.: Senticap: generating image descriptions with sentiments. In: AAAI (2016)
18. Mathews, A., Xie, L., He, X.: Semstyle: learning to generate stylised image captions using unaligned text. In: CVPR (2018)
19. Nezami, O.M., Dras, M., Wan, S., Paris, C., Hamey, L.: Towards generating stylized image captions via adversarial training. In: PRICAI (2019)
20. Papineni, K., Roukos, S., Ward, T., Zhu, W.J.: Bleu: a method for automatic evaluation of machine translation. In: ACL (2002)
21. Radford, A., Kim, J.W., Hallacy, C., Ramesh, A., Goh, G., Agarwal, S., Sastry, G., Askell, A., Mishkin, P., Clark, J., et al.: Learning transferable visual models from natural language supervision. arXiv preprint arXiv:2103.00020 (2021)
22. Ramesh, A., et al.: Zero-shot text-to-image generation. ICML (2021)
23. Shen, L., Sarkar, A., Och, F.J.: Discriminative reranking for machine translation. In: NAACL (2004)
24. Stolcke, A.: Srilm-an extensible language modeling toolkit. In: Seventh international conference on spoken language processing (2002)
25. Vedantam, R., Lawrence Zitnick, C., Parikh, D.: Cider: consensus-based image description evaluation. In: CVPR (2015)
26. Vinyals, O., Toshev, A., Bengio, S., Erhan, D.: Show and tell: a neural image caption generator. In: CVPR (2015)
27. Wang, L., Schwing, A.G., Lazebnik, S.: Diverse and accurate image description using a variational auto-encoder with an additive gaussian encoding space. NIPS (2017)

28. You, Q., Jin, H., Luo, J.: Image captioning at will: a versatile scheme for effectively injecting sentiments into image descriptions. arXiv preprint arXiv:1801.10121 (2018)
29. Zhao, W., Wu, X., Zhang, X.: Memcap: memorizing style knowledge for image captioning. In: AAAI (2020)

MCIC: Multimodal Conversational Intent Classification for E-commerce Customer Service

Shaozu Yuan[1], Xin Shen[1,2], Yuming Zhao[1], Hang Liu[1], Zhiling Yan[1], Ruixue Liu[1], and Meng Chen[1(✉)]

[1] JD AI, Beijing, China
{yuanshaozu,zhaoyuming3,liuhang55,yanzhiling,liuruixue,
chenmeng20}@jd.com
[2] Australian National University, Canberra, Australia
u6498962@anu.edu.au

Abstract. Conversational intent classification (CIC) plays a significant role in dialogue understanding, and most previous works only focus on the text modality. Nevertheless, in real conversations of E-commerce customer service, users often send images (screenshots and photos) among the text, which makes multimodal CIC a challenging task for customer service systems. To understand the intent of a multimodal conversation, it is essential to understand the content of both text and images. In this paper, we construct a large-scale dataset for multimodal CIC in the Chinese E-commerce scenario, named MCIC, which contains more than 30,000 multimodal dialogues with image categories, OCR text (the text contained in images), and intent labels. To fuse visual and textual information effectively, we design two vision-language baselines to integrate either images or OCR text with the dialogue utterances. Experimental results verify that both the text and images are important for CIC in E-commerce customer service.

Keywords: Conversational intent classification · Multimodal dataset

1 Introduction

Conversational customer service has been widely deployed and achieved great success in recent years, which facilitates the development of dialogues that help users to achieve their goals. To better understand dialogues and serve for some downstream tasks, conversational intent classification (CIC) that aims at identifying the user intents behind their utterances has become increasingly important.

Previous works of CIC mainly based on the text modality [16–19], but E-commerce customer service naturally contains lots of multimodal conversations. Users usually leverage images to help illustrate their goals or supplement more information of the conversation background. As shown in Fig. 1(a), it is difficult to infer the intent of *delivery delay* from the utterance *"Still no update, why?"* without the image that shows the customer paid for a coat and was waiting for delivery. Therefore, images are ubiquitous in such conversations and crucial to intent classification. Despite the importance, less attention has been devoted to multimodal CIC in real scenarios. One challenge for this task is the lack of a large-scale annotated dataset, since collecting multimodal dialogues and labelling intents for them are much more time-consuming and labor-intensive.

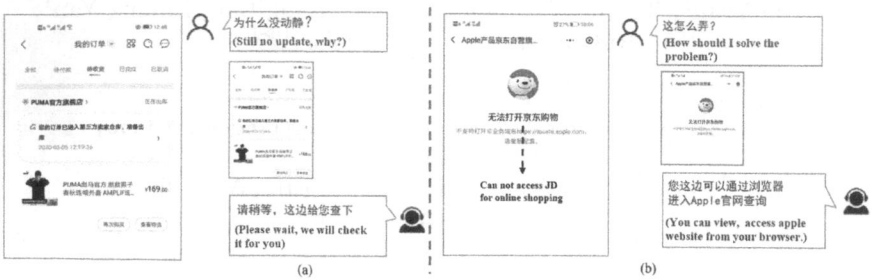

Fig. 1. Examples of multimodal conversations in E-commerce customer service. User utterances are in orange and staff utterances are in green. (Color figure online)

In this paper, we collect a large-scale dataset for **M**ultimodal **C**onversational **I**ntent **C**lassification, named MCIC. MCIC consists of more than 30,000 dialogues that focus on after-sales topics between users and customer service staff and contain at least one image per session. Moreover, there are more than 200 intents in the dataset, which cover most user intents in the E-commerce scenario. Specifically, over 50% images are screenshots and 80% images has some text. We observe that text in images carries essential information for image understanding. As shown in Fig. 1(b), the text extracted from the image "*can not access JD for online shopping*" reveals the situation in which the user meets difficulty when accessing JD online. To better assist intent classification with such images, we also apply an Optical Character Recognition (OCR) model to extract the text from images.

Moreover, we design two models based on the BERT architecture [28], VisualBERT and OCRBERT, to capture the interaction between user utterances and visual signals, i.e., images and OCR text. VisualBERT integrates the text and visual features extracted from ResNet [13] model to infer the intent, while OCR-BERT captures the interaction between OCR text and dialogue utterances via BERT to obtain the intents. Since there is no pre-trained vision-language model released to the public in Chinese version, we use the single modality model BERT [28] as our baseline. Compared with BERT, both models achieve improvement under the automatic evaluation.

In short, our contribution is twofold: (1) We construct a large-scale dataset for multimodal conversational intent classification, with various annotated labels, including image categories, OCR text, and intents. (2) We design two BERT-based baselines to utilize multimodal information and conduct experiments to prove that it is necessary to integrate both visual and textual features into models for MCIC.

2   Related Work

For conversational intent classification (CIC), most datasets are constructed for task-oriented dialogues. MultiWOZ [16] is a large-scale multi-domain dataset that consists of around 10K crowd-sourced human-to-human dialogues with 13 intent types. MDC [17] consists of human-annotated conversational data in three domains (movie-ticket booking, restaurant reservation, and taxi booking) with 11 intents. SGD [18] dataset contains over 16K multi-domain conversations spanning 16 domains and 86 intents. CrossWOZ [19] is the first large-scale Chinese multi-domain Wizard-of-Oz dataset proposed recently, and has 6,012 dialogues covering 6 intents. E-IntentConv [1] contains real online E-commerce conversations between users and staff with diverse and complex intents. The above datasets are text-based, and their intents are labelled only grounded on pure-text conversations.

Table 1. The overview of related datasets for intent classification.

Dataset	Dialogue	Image	Intent	# Dialogues	# Average Turns	# Images	# Intents
MultiWOZ [16]	✓	✗	✓	8,438	13.7	0	13
MDC [17]	✓	✗	✓	10,087	7.5	0	11
SGD [18]	✓	✗	✓	16,142	20.4	0	86
CrossWOZ [19]	✓	✗	✓	5,012	16.9	0	6
E-IntentConv [1]	✓	✗	✓	1,134,487	20	0	289
Portraits of Politicians [20]	✗	✓	✓	0	0	1,124	9
Motivations [21]	✗	✓	✓	0	0	10,191	256
MDID [22]	✗	✓	✓	0	0	1,299	8
Intentonomy [23]	✗	✓	✓	0	0	14,455	28
SIMMC 2.0 [15]	✓	✓	✓	11,244	10.4	1,566	10
MCIC	✓	✓	✓	**30,716**	**8.4**	**30,716**	**212**

Some works also focus on intent recognition from images, which is called image intent classification. [20] defined 9 dimensions of persuasive intents of a politician implied through a photo. [21] collected a new dataset of people performing actions annotated with likely motivations. Intentonomy [23] comprises 14K images covering a wide range of everyday scenes. These images were manually annotated with 28 intent categories derived from a social psychology taxonomy. Image content may not enough to explain its meanings, then some researchers added the text (e.g., captions) to assist the image understanding. For example, [22] tried to extract intents from multimodal data like Instagram posts and proposed MDID dataset that consists of 1299 public Instagram posts with 8 intents.

Different from all the datasets above, our dataset combines conversations and images to fulfill multimodal CIC. The most similar work to ours is SIMMC 2.0 [15] that labels task-oriented dialogues with 10 intents, while our dataset consists of large-scale dialogues with 200+ intents in E-commerce scenario, and the annotation of intents fully takes visual information into consideration. We summarize these mentioned datasets in Table 1.

3   Dataset Construction

3.1   Data Collection and Pre-Processing

We sample 500,000 conversations between users and customer service staff from **JD.com**[1], which is a leading online shopping platform that sells over tens of thousands of brands and over 40.2 million items. To protect the users' privacy and remove the invalid textual conversation, the data is processed by following three steps: (1) To guarantee each conversation session contains at least one image, we first remove pure-text conversations. (2) For the purpose of protecting an individual's privacy while maintaining the integrity of the conversation, we replace sensitive text, like user name, user ID, address and telephone number, with special tokens <NAME>, <ID>, <ADDRESS> and <TEL> respectively. (3) To filter user-sensitive images, such as some screenshots with personal name, telephone number and home address, we extract textual information from the image and detect if it contains sensitive information with regular expression. Then the conversations with the detected image will be removed from the dataset.

3.2   Data Annotation

After pre-processing, we obtain 30,716 valid conversations. To promote relevant research and make the dataset more valuable, we exploit both automatic and manual methods to annotate the dataset with different labels, including intents, image categories, and OCR text from images.

Intent Annotation. In the context of E-commerce, the communications between users and customer service staff are involved in a multimodal setting, where users tend to apply both images and text to express their intents and goals. These intents, which covers 212 types, are indirect and diverse. Ten crowd-sourcing annotators are hired to not only understand the meaning of the text and image in a session but also select the right intent from intent candidates. We observe that the image intent is usually consistent with the intent of its surrounding text. To reduce the workload of annotators, we train a text-based intent classifier with 700,000 labelled context to provide intent candidates for each user utterance. The annotator could choose a proper intent from the candidates, or

---

[1] https://www.jd.com/.

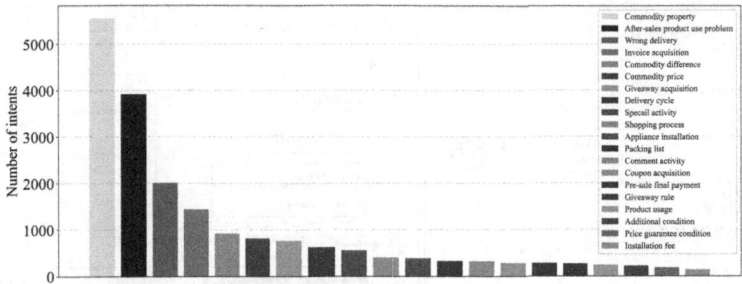

Fig. 2. The intent distribution of MCIC dataset.

infer the intent from the image and text if the actual one is not included in those candidates. The intent selected the most is regarded as the final result.

Image Category Identification. Considering that the image categories may be beneficial for MCIC and a reliable CNN feature extractor requires images with category labels for training, we also provide image categories in our dataset. We divide all the images into 26 types, such as app screenshots and commodity pictures, and invite three professional customer service staff to annotate the image categories.

Optical Character Recognition. OCR is a well-studied task in the literature, thus we choose two open-source models that have been utilized in many scenarios to extract the text information from images. Specifically, we first use EAST [8] model to detect the text blocks, and then the identified blocks are fed into RCNN [10] to obtain text in images. To ensure the quality of extracted text, the output texts under the threshold of 0.5 are dropped.

3.3 Data Statistics and Demonstration

Table 2. Statistics of conversations.

Total dialogue sessions	30,716
Total utterances	844,661
Average utterances per session	27.5
Total turns	257,024
Average turns per session	8.4
Max turns	218
Min turns	1

Table 3. Statistics of visual information.

Total images	30,716
Total OCR texts	678,503
Average OCR texts	26.0
Max OCR texts	275
Min OCR texts	0
Images with OCR texts	26,123
Ratio of images with OCR texts	85.05%

In Table 2, it can been seen that MCIC dataset includes 30,716 multi-turn conversation sessions and 844,661 utterances[2]. The number of turns[3] for a session

---

[2] An image in a session is regarded as an utterance in our multimodal dataset.

[3] A "turn" in a conversation is marked by one back-and-forth interaction: the user speaks and the staff follows, or vice-versa.

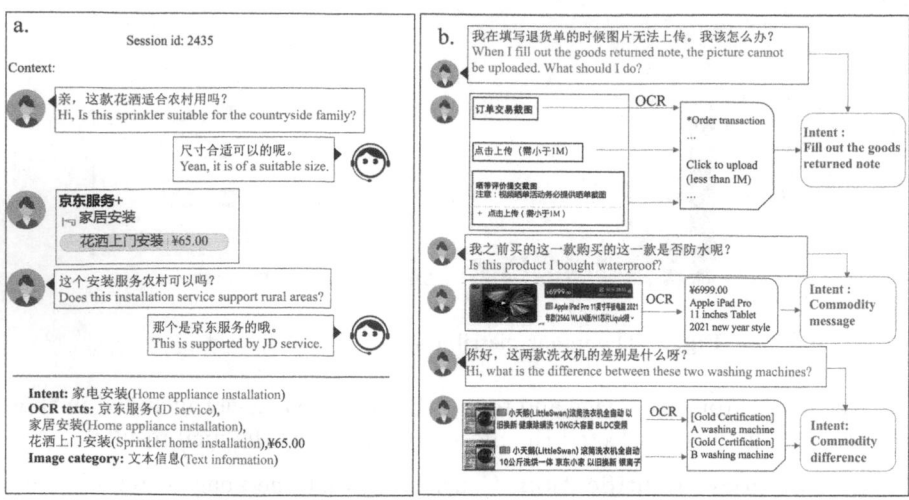

Fig. 3. Overview of MCIC Dataset. (a) A sample from MCIC dataset with intent, OCR text, and image category. (b) Three summarised samples with different user intents. (color figure online)

ranges from 1 to 218, and the average number of turns per session is 8.4. In Table 3, the number of extracted OCR texts ranges from 0 (no extracted Chinese characters from the image) to 275, and 85.05% images have extracted text. The OCR text is provided as auxiliary information to facilitate the performance of MCIC.

Figure 2 illustrates the distribution of Top-20 intents with the most occurrences. It can be seen that the Top-5 intents are: commodity property, after-sales product use problem, wrong delivery, invoice acquisition, and commodity difference. For online shopping, people often ask about the attributes of a commodity in the form of text and images. Compared with simply using text to ask, the usage of images can not only reduce the communication time but also make it easier for the customer service staff to understand user intents.

We further show a sample of MCIC dataset in Fig. 3(a), which has five items including session id, context, intent, OCR text, and image category. The context is multimodal dialogue (the image is saved as URL link) between the user and customer service staff[4]. Each session id is unique to distinguish different examples. The other three items are annotations. The intent, annotated by annotators according to the whole context, is the target of MCIC task. The OCR text and image category are auxiliary information of the image.

In Fig. 3(b), we present three typical samples whose intents are "fill out the goods", "commodity message" and "commodity difference", respectively. As shown in these samples, it is challenging to understand user intents with textual information solely, which indicates the necessity of combining both textual

---

[4] Because of the space limitation, we only show part of context in the figure.

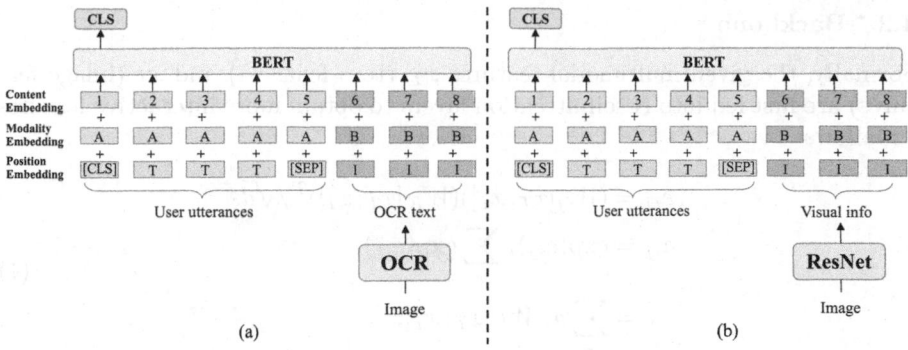

Fig. 4. Overview of our two proposed baselines, (a) OCRBERT and (b) VisualBERT. We utilize different colors to denote multimodal inputs in the embedding layer.

and visual information for conversation understanding. Moreover, we also highlight the important OCR text from the images, and it shows that these texts contribute to the MCIC task.

4 Framework

Since existing open-source vision-language pretrained models are in English version, there is no suitable model for our Chinese MCIC task. Previous work [27] has shown that BERT [28] can not only be beneficial for NLP-related tasks but also facilitate the model performance in multimodal applications. Therefore, we propose two BERT-based baselines to accommodate multimodal inputs and evaluate their performance of intent classification on MCIC dataset. Figure 4 illustrates the architecture of our proposed models and we introduce model details in the following parts. **Note that** the user utterances in model input are 2 surrounding user utterances of the input image, one before and one after the image (marked with red boxes in Fig. 3(a)).

4.1 Input Embedding

The original BERT model is designed for language modeling, to adopt it multimodal inputs, we modify the embedding layer before feeding them to the model. There are three kinds of embeddings involved in our model: **Position Embedding** is the index of the token in the flattened multimodal sequence (user utterances are followed by the visual information), which is the same as that of BERT. **Modality Embedding**, used to distinguish different modalities, takes two possible values: "A" for the user utterances, and "B" for the input image. **Content Embedding** is composed of utterance tokens and image features.

4.2 Backbone

Formally, the given multimodal features x_T (text features) and x_I (image features) are first fed into N self-attention layers to obtain more interactive features as follows:

$$e_{ij} = (W_Q[x_T; x_I])(W_K[x_T; x_I])^T / \sqrt{d},$$
$$a_{ij} = \exp(e_{ij}) / \sum_r \exp(e_{ir}),$$
$$c = \sum_j a_{ij} W_V[x_T; x_I], \tag{1}$$

where W_Q, W_K, W_V are learnable parameters, a_{ij} represents the attention weight, c is attentive feature, and d is the dimension of W_Q.

To classify the intent, we experimentally adopt the representation z of the special token "[CLS]", and feed it into a fully-connected layer with a softmax activation function:

$$\sigma(z_i) = \frac{e^{z_i}}{\sum_{j=1}^{K} e^{z_j}} \quad for \ i = 1, 2, \dots, K, \tag{2}$$

where K is the number of intents and $\sigma(z_i)$ represents the predicted score of each intent.

4.3 OCRBERT

OCRBERT explicitly incorporates OCR text from the images to promote the multimodal intent classification. We adopt pretrained BERT that has been already pretrained on a large-scale Chinese corpus to help obtain contextualized character representations. For model input, we directly concatenate "[CLS]" with the characters T in user utterances and the OCR text I extracted from the image, where the text characters and the OCR characters are split by a special token "[SEP]" and different OCR texts are distinguished with "|". Finally, the final hidden state of the "[CLS]" token is used for intent classification.

4.4 VisualBERT

VisualBERT is designed to capture the interaction between textual and visual information. VisualBERT is also based on BERT whose self-attention layers can automatically learn different levels of alignment between two modalities. The visual features of an image are extracted from a pretrained ResNet [13] model. Here, we design two variants by exploiting different visual features. VisualBERT(*) utilizes the original 882048 visual features, while VisualBERT adopts the pooling feature with 2048 dimensions. To learn a cross-modality relationship between the image features and linguistic tokens, their embeddings are fed into a multi-layer bidirectional transformer encoder. Similarly, the final hidden state of the special token "[CLS]" is used for intent classification.

5   Experiments

In this section, we introduce experimental settings, experimental results, and the results of case study and attention visualization.

5.1   Experimental Settings

We split the MCIC dataset with 27,000 samples for training, 2,000 for validation, and 1,716 for test in our experiments. In order to assess the performance of different models, we use "Accuracy" as the quantitative metric for automatic evaluation.

Images in MCIC dataset are first resized to 256256 pixels. Then we extract visual representations with ResNet [13] pretrained with image category labels. Specifically, we extract two kinds of visual features: the local feature and the global feature. For the former, we split the original image into 64 regions, and the local feature is extracted from the last convolution layer. The global feature, as the global representation of the whole image, is extracted from the pooling layer. The local feature is of 882048 dimensions, while the global feature is of 2048 dimensions. To avoid the model being interfered by the noise contained in the OCR text, the OCR text with low predicted score and that in relatively small regions are discarded.

During training stage, the number of attention heads in BERT is 12, and the batch size is set to 16 for both VisualBERT and OCRBERT. Besides, Dropout is employed with the rate of 0.1, and the maximum length of the multimodal inputs for VisualBERT and OCRBERT is set to 512. All models are fine-tuned for 10 epochs by the Adam Optimizer [11] with an initial learning rate of 5e-5, and are implemented based on PyTorch with 4 T P40 GPUs.

Table 4. The performance of our proposed models and BERT. Note that Visual-BERT(*) utilizes the $8 \times 8 \times 2048$ visual features, while VisualBERT adopts the pooling feature with 2048 dimensions.

Model	BERT	VisualBERT	VisualBERT(*)	OCRBERT
Accuracy	85.66%	85.87%	86.03%	87.41%

5.2   Experimental Results

We choose textual BERT as the baseline to evaluate the effectiveness of the multimodal input and our proposed models. Table 4 reports the accuracy results on MCIC dataset.

Both OCRBERT and VisualBERT outperform the BERT, which reveals the necessity of fusing multimodal information. The VisualBERT(*) that exploits local features shows superiority compared with VisualBERT that utilize global features. We argue that the reason for this is that VisualBERT(*) takes better advantage of visual features, and it selectively focuses on important regions of an image by deep interaction of multiple self-attention layers.

Interestingly, OCRBERT achieves the best result with 87.41% accuracy score. OCRBERT improves the accuracy by 1.75% compared with BERT, and 1.38% compared with VisualBERT(*). This indicates that the OCR text is more effective for multimodal conversational intent classification in E-commerce customer service.

5.3   Case Study

INPUT	OCR	BERT	OBERT	VBERT	GT
这样了,我需要新建一个地图吗? (It shows this message, should I create a new map?)	暂停清洗拖布 (stop clean the mop) 地图学习中,暂不 支持使用此功能	其他 (Other)	售后商品 使用问题 (use of after-sale goods)	物流无更新 (Logistics information not updated)	售后商品 使用问题 (use of after-sale goods)
收到这样了 (It is like this when I receive the express.)	None	货已收到 (goods received)	属性咨询 (Property consulting)	损坏 (Broken)	损坏 (Broken)

Fig. 5. The results of case study. OBERT, VBERT, and GT denote OCRBERT, VisualBERT, and the ground-truth label, respectively. We translate the most remarkable OCR text due to space limitation.

The upper case in Fig. 5 shows a typical example in which the OCR text can boost the model performance of intent classification. The OCR text *"stop cleaning the map"* in the image, which reveals that the cleaning robot does not work, is beneficial for OCRBERT to identify the intent *"use of after-sale goods"*. Conversely, without the assistance of OCR text, BERT and VisualBERT fail to capture the real intent.

The lower case shows that visual information also plays an essential role in the multimodal intent classification task. Since there is no OCR text information provided in the image, it is challenging to understand *"the goods is broken"* only from the text *"It is like this when I receive the express"*. The visual information benefits VisualBERT to infer the right intent compared with OCRBERT and BERT.

5.4   Visualization

In order to study why OCRBERT shows more competitive performance, we visualize the self-attention weights of OCRBERT. We find that the OCR text is directly associated with the intent, which can help the model understand user utterances better. As shown in Fig. 6, the attention weights imply that the OCR texts *"coupon"* and *"not available"* are more important to infer the intent *"coupon is not available"*, which are implicit cues that are not contained in the input text.

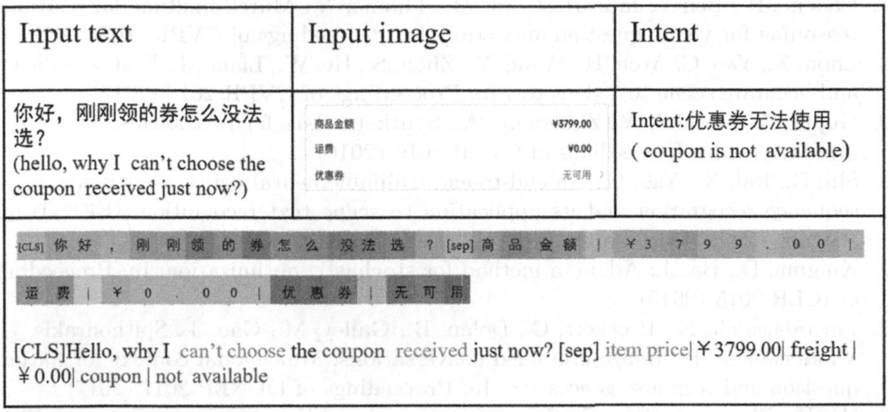

Input text	Input image	Intent
你好，刚刚领的券怎么没法选？ (hello, why I can't choose the coupon received just now?)	商品金额　¥3799.00 运费　¥0.00 优惠券　无可用	Intent:优惠券无法使用 (coupon is not available)

[CLS] 你 好 ， 刚 刚 领 的 券 怎 么 没 法 选 ？ [sep] 商 品 金 额 | ￥ 3 7 9 9 . 0 0 |

运 费 | ￥ 0 . 0 0 | 优 惠 券 | 无 可 用

[CLS]Hello, why I can't choose the coupon received just now? [sep] item price| ￥ 3799.00| freight | ￥ 0.00| coupon | not available

Fig. 6. The visualization result of attention weights from OCRBERT to infer the intent "coupon is not available". The darker color denotes that the character is more important for intent classification.

6   Conclusions

In this paper, we construct a large-scale dataset for multimodal conversational intent classification (MCIC), with different annotated labels, including image categories, OCR text, and intents. To promote relevant research, we design two BERT-based baselines to integrate multimodal input with deep interaction and verify the effectiveness of these models on our dataset. Users of this dataset are encouraged to explore more complicated architectures and learn a joint representation of dialogue text, images, and OCR text. And the dataset will be further enriched, including increasing the numbers of dialogues and variety of image categories, in the future.

References

1. Liu, R., Chen, M., Liu, H., Shen, L., Song, Y., He, X.: Enhancing multi-turn dialogue modeling with intent information for E-commerce customer service. In: Zhu, X., Zhang, M., Hong, Yu., He, R. (eds.) NLPCC 2020. LNCS (LNAI), vol. 12430, pp. 65–77. Springer, Cham (2020). https://doi.org/10.1007/978-3-030-60450-9_6
2. Chen, M., et al.: The jddc corpus: a large-scale multi-turn Chinese dialogue dataset for e-commerce customer service. In: Proceedings of LREC 2022 (2020)

3. Liao, L., Ma, Y., He, X., Hong, R., Chua, T.: Knowledge-aware multimodal dialogue systems. In: Proceedings of ACM MM 2018 (2018)
4. Das, A., et al.: Visual dialog. In: Proceedings of CVPR 2017 (2017)
5. Cai, Y., Cai, H., Wan, X.: Multi-modal sarcasm detection in twitter with hierarchical fusion model. In: Proceedings of ACL 2019 (2019)
6. Antol, S., et al.: Vqa: visual question answering. In: Proceedings of ICCV 2015 (2015)
7. Cadene, R., Ben-Younes, H., Cord, M., Thome, N.: Murel: multimodal relational reasoning for visual question answering. In: Proceedings of CVPR 2019 (2019)
8. Zhou, X., Yao, C., Wen, H., Wang, Y., Zhou, S., He, W., Liang, J.: East: an efficient and accurate scene text detector. In: Proceedings of CVPR 2017 (2017)
9. Gupta, A., Vedaldi, A., Zisserman, A.: Synthetic data for text localisation in natural images. In: Proceedings of CVPR 2016 (2016)
10. Shi, B., Bai, X., Yao, C.: An end-to-end trainable neural network for image-based sequence recognition and its application to scene text recognition. IEEE Trans. Pattern Anal. Mach. Intell. **39**(11), 2298–2304 (2016)
11. Kingma, D., Ba, J.: Adam: a method for stochastic optimization. In: Proceedings of ICLR 2015 (2015)
12. Mostafazadeh, N., Brockett, C., Dolan, B., Galley, M., Gao, J., Spithourakis, G., Vanderwende, L.: Image-grounded conversations: Multimodal context for natural question and response generation. In: Proceedings of IJCNLP 2017 (2017)
13. He, K., Zhang, X., Ren, S., Sun, J.: Deep residual learning for image recognition. In: Proceedings of CVPR 2016 (2016)
14. Shuster, K., Humeau, S., Bordes, A., Weston, J.: Image chat: engaging grounded conversations. In: Proceedings of ACL 2020 (2020)
15. Kottur, S., Moon, S., Geramifard, A., Damavandi, B.: SIMMC 2.0: a task-oriented dialog dataset for immersive multimodal conversations. In: Proceedings of EMNLP 2021 (2021)
16. Budzianowski, P., et al.: MultiWOZ-a large-scale multi-domain wizard-of-Oz dataset for task-oriented dialogue modelling. In: Proceedings of EMNLP 2018 (2018)
17. Li, X., Wang, Y., Sun, S., Panda, S., Liu, J., Gao, J.: Microsoft dialogue challenge: building end-to-end task-completion dialogue systems. Journal: arXiv preprint arXiv:1807.11125 (2018)
18. Rastogi, A., Zang, X., Sunkara, S., Gupta, R., Khaitan, P.: Towards scalable multi-domain conversational agents: The schema-guided dialogue dataset. In: Proceedings of the AAAI Conference on Artificial Intelligence, vol. 34(05), pp. 8689–8696 (2020)
19. Zhu, Q., Huang, K., Zhang, Z., Zhu, X., Huang, M.: Crosswoz: a large-scale Chinese cross-domain task-oriented dialogue dataset. TACL. **8**, 281–295 (2020)
20. Joo, J., Li, W., Steen, F., Zhu, S.: Visual persuasion: inferring communicative intents of images. In: Proceedings of CVPR 2014 (2014)
21. Vondrick, C., Oktay, D., Pirsiavash, H., Torralba, A.: Predicting motivations of actions by leveraging text. In: Proceedings of CVPR 2016 (2016)
22. Kruk, J., Lubin, J., Sikka, K., Lin, X., Jurafsky, D., Divakaran, A.: Integrating text and image: determining multimodal document intent in instagram posts. In: Proceedings of IJCNLP 2019 (2019)
23. Jia, M., Wu, Z., Reiter, A., Cardie, C., Belongie, S., Lim, S.: Intentonomy: a Dataset and Study towards Human Intent Understanding. In: Proceedings of CVPR 2021 (2021)

24. Saha, A., Khapra, M., Sankaranarayanan, K.: Towards building large scale multi-modal domain-aware conversation systems. In: Proceedings of ACL 2018 (2018)
25. Farhadi, A., et al.: Every picture tells a story: generating sentences from images. In: Daniilidis, K., Maragos, P., Paragios, N. (eds.) ECCV 2010. LNCS, vol. 6314, pp. 15–29. Springer, Heidelberg (2010). https://doi.org/10.1007/978-3-642-15561-1_2
26. Zhao, N., Li, H., Wu, Y., He, X., Zhou, B.: The JDDC 2.0 Corpus: A Large-Scale Multimodal Multi-Turn Chinese Dialogue Dataset for E-commerce Customer Service. Journal: arXiv preprint arXiv:2109.12913 (2021)
27. Rahman, W., Hasan, M., Zadeh, A., Morency, L., Hoque, Mohammed E.: M-bert: Injecting multimodal information in the bert structure. Journal: arXiv preprint arXiv:1908.05787 (2019)
28. Devlin, J., Chang, M.-W., Lee, K., Toutanova, K.: BERT: pre-training of deep bidirectional transformers for language understanding. In: Proceedings of NAACL-HLT 2019 (2019)

Fundamentals of NLP (Poster)

KBRTE: A Deep Learning Model for Chinese Textual Entailment Recognition Based on Synonym Expansion and Sememe Enhancement

Yalei Liu, Lingling Mu$^{(\boxtimes)}$, and Hongying Zan

Zhengzhou University, Henan 450001, China
{iellmu,iehyzan}@zzu.edu.cn

Abstract. The mainstream textual entailment recognition models ignore the existing language knowledge, so the inference knowledge from the training data is limited, and the generalization ability is not strong. Therefore, this paper proposes a model KBRTE (fusing Knowledge Base in RTE) that combines an attention mechanism and a pre-trained model and uses word vectors based on sememe representation in the HowNet. We use the enhanced CNLI and XNLI datasets as the model's training set. On the basis of these datasets, monosemous and polysemous in the CiLin are integrated to further enhance the knowledge. Experimental results show that this method could bring significant gains.

Keywords: Textual entailment · Attention mechanism · Pre-trained model · CiLin · HowNet

1 Introduction

Recognizing Textual Entailment (RTE) is important in natural language processing. It can assist the research of other natural language processing tasks, such as reading comprehension, question answering systems and information retrieval [1]. The purpose of RTE is to infer the semantic relationship between a given premise (P) and a hypothesis sentence (H). Table 1 shows the data examples.

With the development of deep learning, more and more people have used this method to recognize the RTE and have achieved good results in the English corpus, but the progress in the Chinese datasets is relatively slow. There are two main reasons: on the one hand, the scale of the English RTE corpus is larger than the Chinese one; on the other hand, the difference between Chinese and English leads to the poor effect of model recognition. At the same time, the inference knowledge learned from the training data based on the deep learning method is limited, so the model's generalization ability is not strong [2]. However, incorporating external knowledge can effectively enhance the learning and generalization ability of the model. The commonly used English knowledge base is the WordNet [3]. The commonly used Chinese knowledge bases are the HowNet [4] and the CiLin [5].

This paper uses the CiLin extended by Harbin Institute of Technology researchers[1]. By fusing the synonyms of monosemous in the CiLin, the datasets CNLI-m and XNLI-m are generated. On this basis, the appropriate word senses of polysemous are fused, and the expanded datasets CNLI-m-p and XNLI-m-p are generated [6]. Then, the encoding of sentences is further optimized by using vector representations based on sememes in HowNet. Therefore, integrating an external knowledge base based on deep learning can enhance the model's generalization ability.

Table 1. Examples of RTE data.

Premise	Hypothesis	Label
It's just a hunch	It's just a guess	Entailment
It takes too much planning	It doesn't require much planning	Contradiction
Women in a circle	The women started dancing	Neutral

This paper proposes a model KBRTE (fusing Knowledge Base in RTE), which mainly uses the synonym-expanded dataset of the CiLin, and uses the sememe information in the HowNet to improve the representation of words. The accuracy of this method is 81.33% on the CNLI dataset and 80.61% on the XNLI dataset. The innovations of this paper are as follows:

(1) The model uses the datasets CNLI-m and XNLI-m of monosemous expansion from the CiLin, and the datasets CNLI-m-p and XNLI-m-p of monosemous and polysemous expansions.
(2) The model uses the co-attention mechanism and the RoBERTa model to capture the semantic relationship between sentences.
(3) The model encodes the sentences by using the sememe vector representation based on the HowNet.

2   Related Work

Currently, the mainstream RTE methods include deep learning methods based on the attention mechanism, pre-trained model, deep learning method integrating knowledge and so on.

The deep learning model based on the attention mechanism used the attention mechanism to capture the semantic relationship between sentences. For example, the decomposable attention model used the alignment method and attention mechanism to calculate word's weight vectors. The best result was

---

[1] http://www.ltp-cloud.com/download.

86.8% on the SNLI dataset [7]. The ESIM (Enhanced LSTM) model [8] not only used the sequence model and tree model to obtain the semantic information of sentences but also used the attention mechanism to calculate the sentence matching and achieved the best accuracy of 88% on the SNLI dataset. An RTE model based on the co-attention mechanism used the BiLSTM and CNN network to identify the textual entailment relationship in combination with the attention mechanism and achieved an accuracy of 80.38% on the CNLI dataset [10].

The method based on the pre-trained model used the pre-training model to provide more semantic information for the sentence encoding. For example, the word vector representation pre-trained language model BERT is based on the two-way self-attention mechanism, which refreshed the records of multiple natural language processing tasks [11]. The Chinese pre-trained model RoBERTa [12] is an improvement of the BERT model. The model has reached the state-of-the-art level on multiple GLUE tasks. A large-scale multilingual pre-trained model [14] improved the performance of cross-language migration tasks and achieved an average accuracy of 82.4% on the XNLI dataset. A method to transfer a monolingual language model to another new language in an unsupervised way at the lexical level proved that zero sample transfer could achieve good results without relying on a word dictionary and multilingual joint training. It achieved an average accuracy of 69.5% on the XNLI dataset, and 70.3% on the Chinese dataset of XNLI [15].

The deep learning method fused with knowledge can make the model learn more inference knowledge and enhance the learning and generalization ability of the model. For example, the KIM model [16] fused with external knowledge, which integrated the word relationship of the WordNet into the enhanced attention model. The optimal results were 88.6% in the SNLI dataset and 77.9% in the MultiNLI related fields, and 77.4% in the MultiNLI cross fields dataset. The SAC model [17] integrated sememe knowledge, which mainly used the sememe of words to accurately capture the exact meaning of words in a specific context, and verified that the fused sememe information could effectively improve the performance of word vectors in two tasks: word similarity calculation and analogy inference. A fine-tuning method based on the CiLin and pre-trained word vector used the synonym information in the CiLin to enhance the semantic representation [18].

3   Model

The KBRTE model mainly consists of two parts, namely the RoBERTa module and the Co-Attention module. The Co-Attention module is composed of three parts: the encoding layer, the interaction layer and the aggregation layer. The input of the Co-Attention module is the premise and hypothesis sentences which fuse the synonyms of monosemous and the appropriate sense of polysemous in the CiLin [6]. The encoding layer uses the word and sense vector to encode the sentence [17]. The sense vector is generated by the SAC model which is based on the sememe information in the HowNet and context. The purpose of the interaction layer is to obtain the semantic relationship by calculating the attention weight of the words. The aggregation layer concatenates the feature vectors of the encoding layer and the attention weights of the interaction layer. The KBRTE model structure is shown in Fig. 1.

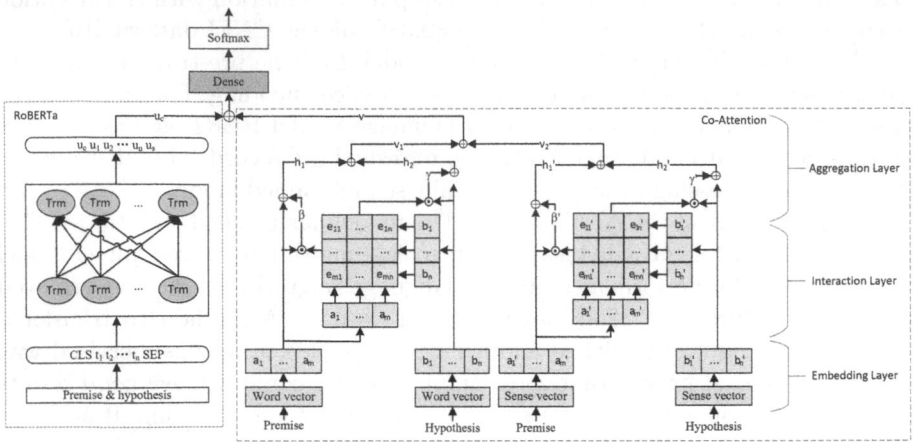

Fig. 1. The KBRTE model structure.

3.1   RoBERTa Module

The text vectorization of the RoBERTa model is realized through the encoder part of the transformer. The specific structure is shown in the left part of Fig. 1. The output of the RoBERTa model has two forms: one is the character level vector, which is the vector representation corresponding to each character of the input text; the other is the sentence level vector, that is, the vector of the leftmost [CLS] special symbol output. This paper uses the sentence level vector as the final output and records it as μ.

3.2   Co-Attention Module

Encoding Layer. Since word vectors are very important for text entailment tasks, word vectors and sense vectors generated by the SAT model [17] based on sememe information and context in the HowNet are used.

Assuming that the target word w has n different senses, S_j^w represents the j-th sense of w. Assuming that the j-th sense of w has m semes, $x_i^{(S_j)}$ represents the i-th sememe corresponding to the j-th sense of w. And w_c is the average of the word vectors of the context of word w. Use the original word vector to initialize the sememe vector and the word vector of the context word. The sense vector of the word is obtained by directly adding and averaging its corresponding sememe vectors, as shown in formula (1). The attention calculation based on the word sense vector of the context word is shown in Eq. (2). The word-sense-based word vector representation of w is shown in Eq. (3).

$$S_j^w = \frac{1}{m} \sum_{i=1}^{m} x_i^{(S_j)} \tag{1}$$

$$att(S_j^{(w)}) = \frac{exp(w_c \cdot S_j^{(w)})}{\sum_{i=1}^{n} exp(w_c \cdot S_j^{(w)})} \tag{2}$$

$$w = \sum_{j=1}^{n} att(S_j^{(w)}) \cdot S_j^{(w)} \tag{3}$$

For example, the sense vector of "convenience" in Fig. 2 is obtained by averaging its sememe vectors. Then the word vector is obtained by calculating the attention weight of each sense vector and it's context word vector.

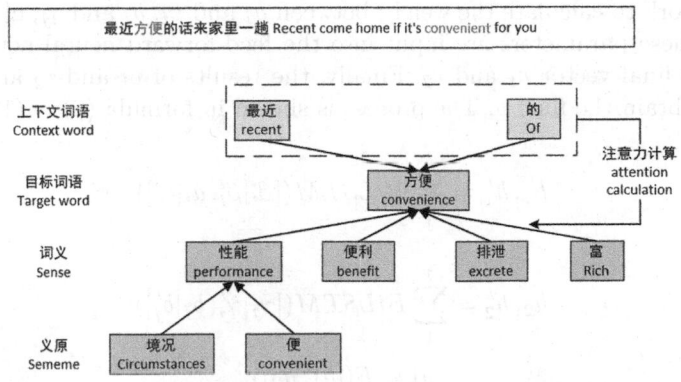

Fig. 2. Example of vector calculation process.

The words of the premise and the hypothesis sentence are encoded using the generated word vectors based on sememe information and context, and the word vector sequences $a = (a_1...a_m)$ and $b = (b_1...b_n)$ are obtained, respectively. We use the sense vector corresponding to each word to initialize the words of the premise and the hypothesis sentence, and obtain the sense vector sequence $a' = (a'_1,...a'_m)$ and $b' = (b'_1...b'_n)$, respectively. Where m and n represent the lengths of the vector sequences of premise sentences and hypotheses, respectively.

Interaction Layer. Firstly, use a, a' respectively as the rows, and use b, b' respectively as columns to build matrix $E_{mn} = a^T b$, $E'_{mn} = a'^T b'$ .Then align the element e_{ij} in E_{mn} and the element e'_{ij} in E'_{mn} respectively, and calculate the attention weight β_i, γ_j and the attention weight β_i', γ_j'. The process is shown shown in formulas (4) $\sim$ (7).

$$\beta_i = \sum_n^1 \frac{exp(e_{ij})}{\sum_{k=1}^j exp(e_{ik})} b_j \tag{4}$$

$$\gamma_j = \sum_m^1 \frac{exp(e_{ij})}{\sum_{k=1}^i exp(e_{jk})} a_i \tag{5}$$

$$\beta_i' = \sum_n^1 \frac{exp(e_{ij}')}{\sum_{k=1}^j exp(e_{ik}')} b_j' \tag{6}$$

$$\gamma_j' = \sum_m^1 \frac{exp(e_{ij}')}{\sum_{k=1}^i exp(e_{jk}')} a_i' \tag{7}$$

Aggregation Layer. The parameter h_1,h_2,h_1',h_2' is obtained by using the BiL-STM network to calculate the weight between a_i and β_i, b_j and γ_j, a_i' and β_i', b_j' and γ_j'. These parameters are input into the feed-forward neural network F to obtain the final vector v_1 and v_2. Finally, the results of v_1 and v_2 are concatenated to obtain the final v. The process is shown in formula (8) $\sim$ (12).

$$h_1, h_1' = \sum_1^i BiLSTM([\beta_i|\beta_i', a_i|a_i']) \tag{8}$$

$$h_2, h_2' = \sum_1^j BiLSTM([\gamma_j|\gamma_j', b_j|b_j']) \tag{9}$$

$$v1 = F([h_1, h_2]) \tag{10}$$

$$v2 = F([h_1', h_2']) \tag{11}$$

$$v = F([v_1, v_2]) \tag{12}$$

The output result in μ of the RoBERTa model, and the result v of the aggregation layer are concatenated. The vector $\tau \in R^3$ is extracted through the feed-forward neural network H. Finally, we use the softmax function to obtain the final classification label l. The process is shown in formulas (13) $\sim$ (14).

$$\tau = H([v, \mu]) \tag{13}$$

$$l = softmax(\tau) \tag{14}$$

4 Experiment

4.1 Data Set

In order to verify the effectiveness of the method, the CNLI[2] and XNLI-ZH[3] dataset are selected for experimental evaluation. The scale of the CNLI and XNLI-ZH datasets is shown in Table 2.

Table 2. Category statistics of the CNLI and XNLI dataset.

		E	C	N	Total
CNLI	Train	29,738	28,937	31,325	90,000
	Dev	3,485	3,417	3,098	10,000
	Test	3,475	3,343	3,182	10,000
XNLI-ZH	Train	130,899	130,903	130,900	392,702
	Dev	830	830	830	2,490
	Test	1,670	1,670	1,670	5010

By fusing the synonyms in the CiLin from the CNLI and XNLI-ZH datasets, the CNLI-m and XNLI-m datasets enhanced by monosemous words, and the CNLI-m-p and XNLI-m-p datasets enhanced by monosemous and polysemous words [6].

4.2 Experimental Setup

The experimental environment used is Python 3.6 and Tensorflow-GPU-1.13.0. Then we use the open source Chinese word segmentation tool jieba-0.39 to segment words. The dimension of the word vector is 300. See Table 3 for main parameters.

Table 3. Main Hyper-parameters settings.

Parameter	Value
learning_rate	2E-5
hidden_size	1024
max_seq_len	64
dropout	0.5
batch size	32

---

[2] http://www.cips-cl.org/static/CCL2018/call-evaluation.html#task3.
[3] https://cims.nyu.edu/~sbowman/xnli/.

The activation function in the experiment uses Relu, the optimization method uses the AdamOptimizer algorithm, and the loss function uses quadratic cross-entropy function.

The accuracy rate ACC is used as the judgment standard in the experiment. During calculation, average micro statistics are carried out for each label, as shown in equation (15).

$$ACC = \frac{l_{correct}}{l} \tag{15}$$

where $l_{correct}$ represents all labels with correct classification and l is the original label of the dataset.

4.3   Baseline Model

To verify the effectiveness of the KBRTE model, the following models are selected for comparison:

(1) The Co-Att model is the attention mechanism module in the KBRTE model. It draws on the Decomposable Attention [31] method and uses the attention mechanism to capture the interaction information between sentences.
(2) The S-LSTM-Att model [9] first used the S-LSTM neural network to learn the encode representation of the sentence, and then the local semantic representation of the sentence is learned using a bidirectional attention mechanism.
(3) The DAM+Antonym vector model [20] integrated an antonym knowledge vector based on the Decomposable Attention model.
(4) The MT-DNN model [13] used a pre-trained model and multi-task learning to train the language model.
(5) The RoBERTa model [12] is an improvement of the BERT model, mainly used a transformer encoder, which has reached state-of-the-art on many glue tasks.
(6) The SRL attention+BERT model [19] is characterized by combining the deep semantic information in the sentence with the encoding part of the transformer model to enhance the self-attention mechanism to capture sentence semantic information.

4.4   Experimental Result

In this paper, two sets of experiments are designed to verify the effectiveness of the representation based on the sememe vector and the effect of using different vector representations on the synonym expansion dataset.

(1) Verify the validity of vector representation based on sememe information. The accuracy of the above model on the test set of the CNLI and XNLI-ZH datasets is shown in Table 4.

Table 4. The accuracy of different models on the CNLI and XNLI dataset.

Model	CNLI Test(%)	XNLI Test(%)
Co-Att	64.85	61.76
S-LSTM-Att	70.62	65.55
DAM	76.00	—
MT-DNN	78.57	77.76
RoBERTa	79.45	78.90
SRL-Attention+BERT	80.28	—
KBRTE	81.33	80.61

It can be seen that the results of the KBRTE model on the CNLI and XNLI datasets are better than other comparable models. The accuracy of the KBRTE model on the CNLI test set is 0.92% higher than that of the SRL attention+BERT model, 5.20% higher than that of the DAM+Antonym vector, and 15% higher than that of the Co-Att model. The accuracy of the KBRTE model on the test set of XNLI is 1.5% higher than that of the RoBERTa model, 15% higher than that of the S-LSTM-Att model and 18% higher than that of the Co-Att model. Therefore, the results show that the method of integrating knowledge bases is effective and improves the accuracy of textual entailment recognition.

(2) Verify the effectiveness of using different vector representations on the different datasets

The KBRTE-SV model uses only sense vector representations based on sememe information and context. The KBRTE-WV model uses only word vector representations. The KBRTE model uses a combination of sense vector and word vector representations. The accuracy of the different models on both datasets is shown in Table 5.

Table 5. Using different vectors to represent the accuracy of different models.

Model	CNLI(%)	XNLI(%)	CNLI-m(%)	XNLI-m(%)	CNLI-m-p(%)	XNLI-m-p(%)
KBRTE-SV	80.34	79.73	80.42	79.95	80.51	79.85
KBRTE-WV	80.41	79.96	80.54	80.01	80.77	80.74
KBRTE	80.52	80.10	80.61	80.25	81.33	80.61

It can be seen from the above experimental results that the KBRTE model performs well on all datasets. Improving the encoding layer by sense vectors and word vectors is effective. Compared with the KBRTE-SV model, the accuracy of the KBRTE model is improved by 0.18%, 0.2%, 0.6% on the CNLI, CNLI-m, CNLI-m-p datasets, respectively. And the accuracy of the KBRTE model is improved by 0.1%, 0.1%, and 0.4% than the KBRTE-WV model. Therefore, it can be seen that the KBRTE model can improve the effect of textual entailment recognition to a certain extent by using sense vector and word vector on the CNLI-m-p dataset and achieves an accuracy of 81.33%.

For the XNLI dataset, the accuracy of the KBRTE model is 0.2% higher than that of the KBRTE-WV model on the XNLI and XNLI-m datasets. Furthermore, the KBRTE-WV model outperforms the KBRTE model and achieves a 0.15% improvement in accuracy on the XNLI-m-p dataset. Therefore, the KBRTE-WV model performs better on the XNLI-m-p dataset and achieves an accuracy of 80.74%.

4.5   Category Analysis

This paper analyzes the number of correct recognition of each category of different models KBRTE-WV, KBRTE-SV, and KBRTE on the CNLI-m-p dataset. The results are shown in Table 6.

Table 6. The correct number of recognitions by different models on each labels.

Model	Neutral(%)	Entailment(%)	Contradicition(%)	Total(%)
KBRTE-SV	29.18	36.10	34.72	80.51
KBRTE-WV	29.57	35.69	34.74	80.77
KBRTE	29.47	35.78	34.95	81.33

It can be seen from Table 6 that for neutral categories, the KBRTE-WV model is better, and the KBRTE-SV model is less effective; for the entailed categories, using the KBRTE-SV model is better; for the contradiction category, the effect of using the KBRTE model is better, and the effect of using the KBRTE-SV and KBRTE-WV models is poor. Compared with other models, the KBRTE-SV model is the most effective for identifying entailment relationships; the KBRTE-WV model is better for identifying neutral relationships; the KBRTE model is the most effective for identifying contradiction relationships. Therefore, the classification effect of the model on each category is different using different vector representations.

4.6   Samples Analysis

This paper selects a data sample from the CNLI dataset, in which the premise is "two people are sitting at the table.", the hypothetical sentence is "men are eating at the table.", and the label is "neutral". The classification results of the KBRTE-SV, KBRTE-WV and KBRTE models in this example are given in Table 7.

It can be seen from the table that the KBRTE-SV and KBRTE-WV models have incorrect recognition results and are determined to be a contradiction, while the KBRTE models have correct recognition results and are determined to be

Table 7. Sample error analysis text.

Model	Result
KBRTE-SV	Contradiction
KBRTE-WV	Contradiction
KBRTE	Neutral

neutral. Therefore, it can be seen that the classification effect of the model is better when the KBRTE model has used the sense vector and word vector, which is conducive to the recognition of the model.

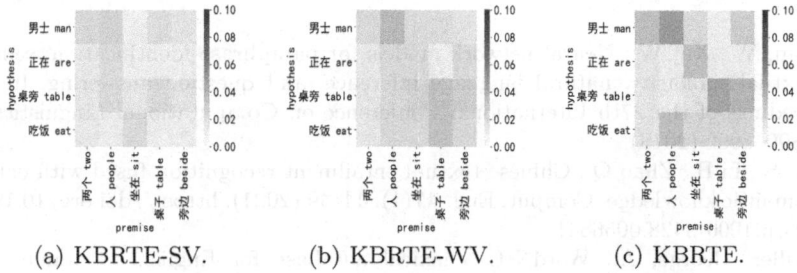

    (a) KBRTE-SV.   (b) KBRTE-WV.   (c) KBRTE.

Fig. 3. Attention weight matrix of the sentence.

Figure 3 shows the weight matrix of the KBRTE-SV model using sense vector, the KBRTE-WV model using word vector, and the KBRTE model using sense vector and word vector for attention calculation. Compared with the KBRTE-SV and KBRTE-WV models, the KBRTE model is more conducive to calculating the attention weights between sentences to capture the relationship between sentences. For example, the attention weights between the words "men" and "people", "table" and "table", the darker colour indicates the greater the attention weight. Therefore, when the KBRTE model is used, the semantic information between sentences can be better captured, and the difference between the same and different parts of sentences can be obtained.

5 Conclusion

This paper proposes a KBRTE model. The main contribution is to fuse the synonyms in the CiLin during data pre-processing and use the sememe information in the HowNet to generate the representation of sense and word vector. The model achieves 81.33% accuracy on the CNLI-m-p test set and 80.61% accuracy on the XNLI-m-p test set. The experimental results show that the model can effectively enhance knowledge, and the fusion of the information in the HowNet can improve the representation of words. Then, using the RoBERTa model and co-attention mechanism can further enhance the ability of the model to capture sentence semantics to further improve the model's recognition performance. On the other hand, due to the lack of computing ability of the model, the recognition effect of some sentences with complex semantics is not very good. In the future, we will consider how to strengthen the model's ability to understand sentences with deep meaning to improve the effect of model recognition.

Acknowledgment. We are very grateful to the anonymous reviewers for their constructive opinions, the Science and Technique Program of Henan Province under Grant No. 192102210260, and the Teaching Reform Program of Zhengzhou University under Grant No. 2021ZZUJGLX131.

References

1. Lan, W., Xu, W.: Neural network models for paraphrase identification, semantic textual similarity, natural language inference, and question answering. In: Proceedings of the 27th International Conference on Computational Linguistics, pp. 3890–3902 (2018)
2. Li, S., Li H., Zhao Q.: Chinese textual entailment recognition fused with external semantic knowledge. Comput. Eng. **47**(1), 44–49 (2021). https://doi.org/10.19678/j.issn.1000-3428.0056841
3. Miller, George, A.: WordNet: a lexical database for English. Commun. ACM **38**(11), 39–41 (1995)
4. Dong, Z., Dong, Q.: HowNet - a hybrid language and knowledge resource. In: International Conference on Natural Language Processing and Knowledge Engineering, pp. 820–824 (2003)
5. Mei, J., Zhu, Y., Gao, Y.: TongYiCi CiLin.: Shanghai Lexicographical Publishing House (1983)
6. Liu, Y., Mu, L., Zan, H.: A deep learning model fused with word sense knowledge for textual entailment recognition. In: International Conference on Asian Language Processing (IALP), pp. 189–194. IEEE (2021)
7. Parikh, A., Tckstrm, O., Uszkoreit, J.: A decomposable attention model for natural language inference. arXiv preprint arXiv:1606.01933 (2016)
8. Chen, Q., Zhu, X., Ling, Z.: Enhanced LSTM for natural language inference. arXiv preprint arXiv:1609.06038 (2016)
9. Hu, C., Wu, C., Yang, Y.: Extended S-LSTM based textual entailment recognition. J. Comput. Res. Develop. **57**(7), 1481–1489 (2020)
10. Huang, S., Xiao, S., Du, Y.: Chinese textual entailment recognition method based on hybrid attention. J. Beijing Univ. Inf. Technol. **35**(3), 89–93.98 (2020). https://doi.org/10.16508/j.cnki.11-5866/n.2020.03.017
11. Devlin, J., Chang, M., Lee, K.: BERT: pre-training of deep bidirectional transformers for language understanding. arXiv preprint arXiv:1810.04805 (2018)
12. Cui, Y., Che, W., Liu, T.: Pre-training with whole word masking for Chinese BERT. IEEE/ACM Trans. Audio Speech Lang. Process, **29**, 3504–3514 (2021)
13. Liu, X., He, P., Chen, W.: Multi-task deep neural networks for natural language understanding. arXiv preprint arXiv:1901.11504 (2019)
14. Conneau, A., Khandelwal, K., Goyal, N.: Unsupervised cross-lingual representation learning at scale. arXiv preprint arXiv:1911.02116 (2019)

15. Artetxe, M., Ruder, S., Yogatama, D.: On the cross-lingual transferability of mono-lingual representations. arXiv preprint arXiv:1911.02116 (2019)

16. Qian, C., Zhu, X., Ling, Z.: Neural natural language inference models enhanced with external knowledge. arXiv preprint arXiv:1711.04289 (2017)

17. Niu, Y., Xie, R., Liu, Z.: IMproved word representation learning with sememes. In: Proceedings of the 55th Annual Meeting of the Association for Computational Linguistics, pp. 2049–2058 (2017)

18. Yu, Q., Wang, B., Liu, M.: A fine-tuning method based on Tongyi CiLin and pre-trained word embedding. Chinese J. Inf. **34**(10), 27–32 (2020)

19. Zhang, Z., Zeng, Y., Pang, Y.: A Chinese textual entailment recognition method incorporating semantic role and self-attention. J. Electron. **48**(11), 2162–2169 (2020)

20. Wang, H.: Text entailment recognition based on integration of language knowledge and deep learning and its application. Harbin Institute of Technology (2019)

Information Extraction and Knowledge Graph (Poster)

Emotion-Cause Pair Extraction via Transformer-Based Interaction Model with Text Capsule Network

Cheng Yang[✉] and Jie Ding

School of Computer and Information Engineering, Zhejiang Gongshang University, Hangzhou, China
yangyangyang3701@gmail.com

Abstract. The goal of Emotion-Cause Pair Extraction is to extract the emotion clause and the corresponding cause clause from the unmarked document level text. The two steps solution has the disadvantage of error propagation and fails to make full use of context information. In this paper, we propose an end to end neural network. The model uses Transformer with different granularity to extract hierarchical text features, and uses the text capsule network to model the relationship between the local text features of emotion cause pair and the overall causal relationship. We also utilize a filter mechanism to alleviate the problem of sample imbalance of ECPE task. The experimental results show that our model has achieved great performance improvement, which is higher than most baseline methods on F1 score.

Keywords: Emotion-cause pair extraction · Transformer · Capsule network · Sentiment analysis

1 Introduction

Text sentiment analysis [11,24,25] aims at identifying the emotion tendency, attitudes and opinions from texts. Most previous work focused on the sentiment classification task [12,13] and determining the sentiment polarities of the person subject. The causes that trigger the subject's emotion expression are equally important. Therefore, emotion cause extraction (ECE) has become a popular topic, with the goal of extracting the cause explanation corresponding to the emotion expression in the text.

Previous methods of emotion cause extraction rely on rules [8,12,13,23] or feature engineering [6,14,23], and such methods are time-consuming and labor-intensive. Recently, related works have attempted to solve this problem using neural network models based on the Attention mechanism [7,22]. [7] proposed a CNN-based Attention mechanism to better obtain the word-level features of the input sequence. The Transformer-based approach [21] achieved superior performance by using a Multi-head Self-Attention mechanism based on Multi-head and a multi-layer stacking architecture.

© The Author(s), under exclusive license to Springer Nature Switzerland AG 2022
W. Lu et al. (Eds.): NLPCC 2022, LNAI 13551, pp. 781–793, 2022.
https://doi.org/10.1007/978-3-031-17120-8_60

Example

"[It's a vulnerable feeling]¹,[thinking that someone is going to judge you and your ability to do a job or task based on your health or an impairment]²",[says Rachael Mole]³,[a non-profit organization that helps disabled and chronically ill people to find accessible and inclusive employers]⁴. "[Having to justify yourself]⁵.[feeling like you have to do even more to make up for a perceived weakness]⁶,[over-explaining your health in order to take sick-leave --- it makes you exhausted]⁷.

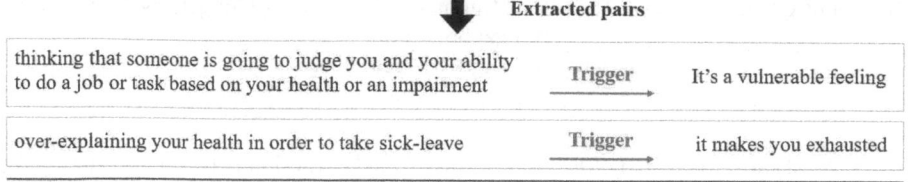

Extracted pairs

---

thinking that someone is going to judge you and your ability to do a job or task based on your health or an impairment	Trigger →	It's a vulnerable feeling
over-explaining your health in order to take sick-leave	Trigger →	it makes you exhausted

---

Fig. 1. An example containing two emotion-cause pairs for the ECPE task. We use different shades of color to visualize them. Where (1,2) is the first emotion-cause pair, clause 1 is the emotion clause and clause 2 is the corresponding cause clause; (8,7) is the second emotion-cause pair, clause 8 is the emotion clause and clause 7 is the corresponding cause clause.

Although emotion cause extraction has made some theoretical and methodological progress, the task of emotion cause extraction has inherent drawbacks: the need to first annotate the emotion before extracting the cause, i.e., to extract the cause using the given emotion. The need to annotate in advance The premise of emotion limits its application in realistic scenarios on the one hand, and fails to exploit the mutual benefits of the emotion-cause structure on the other. To this end, [21] proposed a new ECE framework for text sentiment analysis, i.e. emotion-cause pair extraction (ECPE), which aims to extract all potential pairs of emotion clauses and corresponding cause clauses in the unannotated text. Figure 1 shows an example. Even in the same emotion text, there may be multiple opposite emotion polarities expressed by different emotion words and associated with different cause clauses. This suggests that we need to have a comprehensive understanding of the content and structure of the text in order to reason causally and finally extract the emotion-cause pair.

Overall, the emotion-cause pair extraction task is a more challenging task due to the implicit nature of emotion expressions and the diversity of cause explanations. The existing 2-steps solution [20] has shown its effectiveness on ECPE. However, this pipeline framework has an inherent drawback that error propagation may occur. In addition, the reciprocity of related tasks cannot be fully exploited. Considering the strong correlation between ECE and ECPE tasks, a corresponding solution is to use ECE tasks to complement ECPE tasks, and [3,4,20] investigated the use of multi-task learning to model their relationship. Although previous work has achieved satisfactory results, we believe that relying solely on parameter sharing of multi-task learning to mine ECE task and ECPE task correlations is insufficient. More importantly, how to utilize the information between different clause pairs in order to guide each other for emotion-cause pair extraction has not been fully explored. In addition, there is a lack of favorable methods to capture the underlying characteristics of the emotion cause pair, as a more fine-grained representation is needed to capture information between them.

The main contributions of our work are summarized as follows:

1. We propose an Transformer-based interaction model with text capsule network (TITCN), by integrating different levels of text information for the ECPE task. The proposed method takes the entire document as input and calculates the probability of each clause pair as a potential emotion-cause pair.
2. We firstly introduce the capsule neural network for the relation extraction task ECPE. Different from the original capsule network on the image classification task, we design a text capsule network which is proved to be effective by the ablation study.
3. The proposed model considers integrating hierarchical features by modeling the token-sentence-document structure.

2   Related Work

Emotion is a subject's specific response to an important event. In order to obtain the key points related to emotion, some studies have tried to extract the key elements that trigger emotion, such as uncovering the cause explanation behind the emotion expression. [9] firstly proposed the Emotion Cause Extraction (ECE) task and defined it as a word-level extraction task. They constructed a dataset from Academia Sinica Balanced Chinese Corpus, labeled the cause explanation and extracted the corresponding cause explanation from the given emotion expression. Machine learning methods such as SVM and CRF are used to detect emotion and cause explanation. [19] transformed the ECE task from word-level to sentence-level. [21] followed this approach to construct a Chinese corpus from SINA City News. Existing methods of ECE rely on emotion annotation, which is extremely time-consuming and costly, limiting the application of emotion cause extraction in real-life scenarios. To address this problem, [20] proposed a novel task based on ECE, namely Emotion-Cause Pair Extraction (ECPE), with the goal of extracting both emotions and corresponding causes from unlabeled text.

Recent research has attempted to define unified frameworks to handle ECPE tasks. [1] considered this task as a link prediction problem and learn the links from emotions to causes by using a multi-task framework. [10] explored the using of multi-level attention mechanism to capture the relationship between two clauses in emotion-cause structure. [2] integrated the representation, interaction and prediction of emotion-cause pairs by using an unified framework. Most of the previous methods focus on the direct prediction of clause pair, but do not pay attention to the relationship between the local text features of emotion cause pair and the overall causality.

Therefore, this paper proposes an emotion-cause pair extraction model (TITCN) based on capsule network. The model uses Transformer to extract hierarchical text features, combined with the superior spatial information extraction ability of capsule network, to explore the relationship between the local fine-grained features of emotion cause pair and the overall causality.

3   Preliminaries

3.1   Capsule Network

The Capsule Network [15], as a method sensitive to spatial information, can utilize rich text structure information, such as word location information and semantic information. It can effectively encode text and have powerful text expression ability. Therefore, Capsule Network meets the need of determining whether a clause pair has an emotional reason relationship. Figure 2 shows the structure of the capsule neural network.

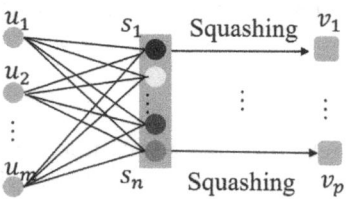

Fig. 2. The architecture of the capsule neural network.

As shown in Fig. 2, u_i represents the output vector of capsule i of the current layer, while the output vector v_j of Capsule j of the next layer is determined as follows:

$$v_j = squash(s_j) = \frac{\|s_j\|^2}{1 + \|s_j\|^2} \cdot \frac{s_j}{\|s_j\|} \tag{1}$$

$$s_j = \sum_i c_{ij} * \hat{u}_{j|i}, \hat{u}_{j|i} = w_{ij} u_i \tag{2}$$

where w_{ij} is the weight matrix between capsule i of the current layer and capsule j of the next layer, and c_{ij} is the coupling coefficient calculated by *softmax* function as follows:

$$c_{ij} = \frac{\exp(b_{ij})}{\sum_k \exp(b_{ik})} \tag{3}$$

where each b_{ij} represents the strength coefficient between capsule i and capsule j, which can be determined by the Dynamic Routing algorithm.

4 Methodology

As shown in Fig. 3, we propose a new end-to-end neural framework for the ECPE task, called Transformer-based interaction model with text capsule network (TITCN). The proposed model takes the whole document as inputs, and calculates the probability of potential emotion-cause pair of each clause pair.

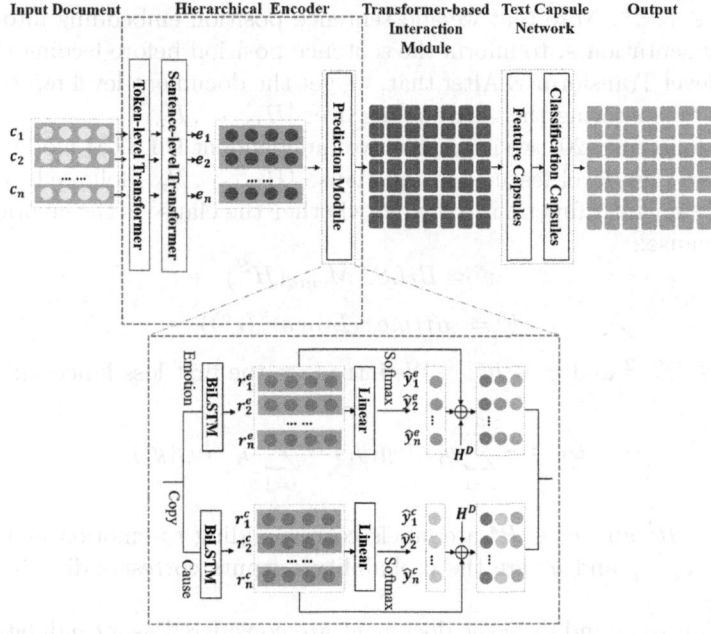

Fig. 3. The network architecture of the proposed model.

4.1 Hierarchical Encoder

Given a document with n clauses as $D = [c_1, c_2, ..., c_n]$, where c_i corresponds to the ith clause in the document and $c_i = [w_{1i}, w_{2i}, \cdots, w_{li}]$, w_{mi} is the ith token for clause c_i. The goal of the ECPE task is to extract all emotion-cause pairs with potential causality:

$$P = \{\cdots, (c_i^e, c_j^c), \cdots\}(1 \leq i, j \leq n) \tag{4}$$

where c_i^e is one emotion clause, c_j^c is the corresponding cause clause.

In the hierarchical encoder module, a Transformer is used to capture the hierarchical structure of D. Firstly, we utilize a word-level Transformer to gain token-level feature representation:

$$h_i = Transformer(c_i) \tag{5}$$

where $h_i \in R^{l \times d}$ means the new feature representation through Transformer. For a sentence embedding h_i, we conduct a max-pooling operation over the token-level feature representation to get the embedding $s_i \in R^d$ for it. Next, a sentence-level Transformer module is utilized to capture the interaction among all sentences. Then we can get the document-aware representations.

$$[H_1, \cdots, H_n] = Transformer(s_1, \cdots, s_n) \tag{6}$$

where $H_i \in R^{1 \times d}$. Note that we add sentence position embedding into the sentence representation s_i to inform the sentence position before feeding them into sentence-level Transformer. After that, we get the document-level representation $H^D \in R^d$ by operating the max-pooling over $[H_1, \cdots, H_n]$.

Then, following [20], we introduce two independent BiLSTM modules to further extract high-level features for all clause $[H_1, \cdots, H_n]$, followed by a linear layer and a softmax function to predict whether the clause is the emotion clause or cause clause::

$$r^e = BiLSTM_{emo}(H^S) \tag{7}$$

$$\hat{y}^e = softmax(Linear_e(r^e)) \tag{8}$$

where $\hat{y}^e \in R^{n \times 2}$ and $\hat{y}^c \in R^{n \times 2}$. We introduce the first loss function:

$$L_1 = - \sum_{i=1}^{n} y_i^e \cdot log(\hat{y}_i^e) - \sum_{i=1}^{n} y_i^c \cdot log(\hat{y}_i^c) \tag{9}$$

where $y_i^e \in R^2$ and $y_i^c \in R^2$ are labels corresponding to emotion and cause of the clause c_i. $\hat{y}_i^e$ and $\hat{y}_i^c$ are the probability outputs corresponding to emotion and cause.

Any clauses c_i and c_j in the document are considered as a candidate pair by both concatenating the clause representations and document representation H^D as follows:

$$M = (M_{i,j}), \quad i, j = 1, 2, \cdots, n \tag{10}$$

where $M_{(i,j)} = [r_i^e; H^D; r_j^c; H^D] \in R^{(4h+2d)}$.

4.2   Transformer-Based Interaction Module

To reduce the computational complexity, following [2] and [19], we construct the emotion-cause pairs by constraining the computing on the clause pairs of c_i^e and c_j^c with the condition $|i - j| \leq dis$, where dis is a positive integer. We use Transformer [18] to model the relationship of these pairs.

More importantly, by excluding a large number of negative samples (not the emotion-cause pairs), the sample imbalance issue can be overcome to a great extent and the model bias may be avoided. In the experiment, we also used all clause pairs for comparison.

4.3   Text Capsule Network

Transformer concentrates on the extraction of global text information via the multi-head self-attention computation. However, its representation and transformation ability for local information is insufficient. To further enhance the local feature representation, we introduce the text capsule network module into the proposed model by using two layers, i.e. the feature capsule layer and the target capsule layer, as shown in Fig. 4.

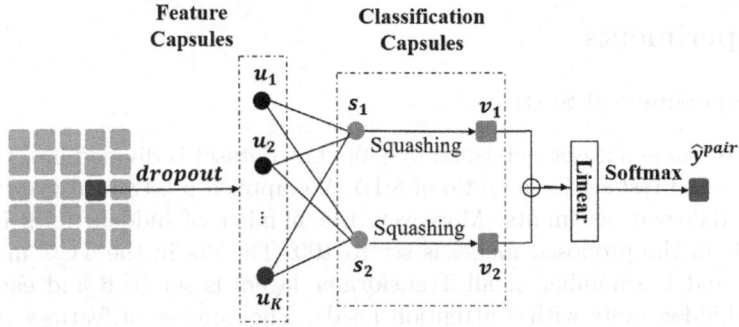

Fig. 4. The network architecture of the text capsule network module.

The raw input of capsule network is a single vector u that is the output o_{ij} from previous module. The feature capsule layer, composed of some feature capsules, aims at extracting local feature information for each clause pair to fit with the input of the next capsule layer. In this layer, two mechanisms were designed for the input of capsule network. In the first way, two vectors $u_1 \in R^{2h+d}$ and $u_2 \in R^{2h+d}$ are the input of two feature capsules, split from the output u of the TCC module. In the other way, in order to extract enough information from the clause pair, we dropout the clause pair representation several times to greatly increase the number of low-level capsules of feature capsule layer:

$$u_i = dropout(u) \tag{11}$$

where $i = 1, 2, \cdots, k$, and k indicates the number of dropout operations.

Moreover, the target capsule layer contains two high-level capsules that the number of them represents the categories of this classification task.

Then, two 1-dimensional capsules v_1 and v_2 are operated by concatenation to obtain a 1-dimensional vector. The dimension is then reduced to R^2 through the Linear layer, and the effective features are integrated. The length 2 represents the number of relationships for a clause-pair. Finally, the probability of occurrence of each category is obtained by the softmax activation function:

$$\hat{y}_{i,j} = Softmax(Linear(v_1; v_2)) \tag{12}$$

where $\hat{y}_{(i,j)} \in R^2$. Then, the second cross entropy loss function is used for training L_2:

$$L_2 = L_{\text{isPair}} + \lambda L_{\text{notPair}} \tag{13}$$

where L_{isPair} and $L_{notPair}$ are the loss of positive pairs and negative pairs, respectively. The λ is a hyperparameter to scale the effect of negative pairs. The final loss function is composed of two parts:

$$L = L_1 + L_2 \tag{14}$$

where L_1 is the loss function that extracts the emotion clause and cause clause phases. L_1 and L_2 work together to optimize the TITCN model.

5   Experiments

5.1   Experimental Settings

We use the same dataset published by [20]. The dataset is divided into training, validation and test set in the ratio of 8:1:1. We applied pre-trained word vectors from BERT-wwm as inputs. Moreover, the number of hidden units from all BiLSTMs in the proposed model is set to 100. The dis in the TCC module is set to 3 and the number of all Transformer layers is set to 6 and each layer has 768 hidden units with 8 attention heads. The number of features capsules is set to k = 10. The number of routings for the capsule network is set to 6. We use grid search for λ from [0.2, 0.4, 0.6, 0.8]. We utilize Adam to update the learnable parameters. The batch size and the learning rate are set to 64 and 0.005, respectively. The hyperparameter λ is 0.6.

5.2   Results and Analysis

We compare the proposed TITCN model with other existing approaches, which are listed as: ECPE-2Steps [20], E2EECPE [16], LAE-MANN [17], RANKCP [19], ECPE-2D [2], TransECPE [4] and MTST [5].

Table 1 shows the performance comparison of the proposed model and the baseline models in ECPE task and two sub-task.

TITCN is the framework proposed in this paper. It has three variants, which $TITCN^{\spadesuit}$ represents the interaction of the feature representation of all clause pairs in the TCC, and the first setting is used in the capsule network. $TITCN^{\heartsuit}$ indicates that only part of the claim pairs are modeled in the TCC module, and the first setting of the capture network is used. $TITCN^{\dagger}$ indicates that the TCC module also performs feature interaction on part clause pairs, but uses the second setting of the capsule network.

Firstly, the experimental results shown in Table 1. Compared with the seven baseline models, the F1 score of the three TITCN models in the emotion cause pair extraction task increased by 1.60%, 2.50% and 3.80% respectively.

Secondly, in the two subtasks of emotion clause extraction and cause clause extraction, our TITCN method is better than ECPE-2Steps in both subtasks. In this regard, we attribute the improvement to multi task learning. Compared with ECPE-2Steps model, TITCN trains three tasks: emotion clause extraction, cause clause extraction and emotion-cause pair extraction in a unified framework. Compared with the baseline models such as E2EECPE, TITCN is second only

Table 1. Performance comparison of the proposed model with other baseline methods. We implemented RANKCP and MTST according to the released code.

Model	Emotion extraction			Cause extraction			Emotion-cause pair extraction		
	P	R	F1	P	R	F1	P	R	F1
Indep	0.838	0.807	0.821	0.690	0.567	0.621	0.683	0.508	0.582
Inter-CE	0.849	0.812	0.830	0.681	0.563	0.615	0.690	0.514	0.590
Inter-EC	0.836	0.811	0.823	0.704	0.608	0.651	0.672	0.571	0.613
E2EECPE	0.860	0.792	0.824	0.706	0.603	0.650	0.648	0.611	0.628
LAE-MANN	0.899	0.800	0.847	-	-	-	0.711	0.607	0.655
RANKCP	0.870	0.841	0.855	0.693	0.674	0.682	0.670	0.655	0.661
ECPE-2D	0.864	**0.922**	**0.891**	0.734	**0.693**	0.712	0.729	0.654	0.689
TransECPE	0.872	0.824	0.847	0.756	0.647	0.697	0.737	0.631	0.688
MTST	0.848	0.712	0.773	0.760	0.633	0.691	0.731	0.607	0.663
$TITCN^{\spadesuit}$	0.878	0.787	0.822	0.778	0.673	**0.716**	0.822	**0.658**	0.714
$TITCN^{\heartsuit}$	0.896	0.770	0.857	0.779	0.685	0.713	0.833	0.645	0.723
$TITCN^{\dagger}$	**0.899**	0.775	0.854	**0.783**	0.676	0.715	**0.837**	0.654	**0.727**

to ECPE2D model in the extraction task of emotion clause, and is about 0.4% better than the best model in the extraction task of cause clause. Most baseline models such as ECPE-2Step use LSTM and Attention mechanism as encoders to obtain the feature representation of clauses. Different from this method, we use the sequence modeling method based on Transformer, and further design the hierarchical document feature extraction model of token-sentence-document. The excellent feature extraction ability of Transformer, combined with hierarchical document representation method, directly affects the extraction effect of the model in the two sub tasks of emotion clause extraction and cause clause extraction.

Moreover, ECPE-2Step, E2EECPE, TransECPE and MTST extract the emotion cause pair by calculating all candidate clause pairs, which will cause serious bias problems in the trained classification model and reduce the performance. TITCN filters out a large number of negative samples through the Transformer with Constrained Computation mechanism, which greatly alleviates the sample imbalance of ECPE tasks, thus improving the performance of the model. Although RANKCP and ECPE2D also use the method of calculating some candidate pairs, they either do not interactively model many candidate sentence pairs, or do not extract the fine-grained features of a single sentence pair. TITCN models the relationship between local text features and overall causality of emotion-cause pair through text capsule network, and the spatial information of local features and overall causality is transmitted between feature capsules and target capsules, so as to achieve better classification effect of emotion-cause pair.

5.3 Ablation Study

Table 2. Experimental results of the ablation study.

Model	Emotion extraction			Cause extraction			Emotion-cause pair extraction		
	P	R	F1	P	R	F1	P	R	F1
TITCN	**0.890**	**0.775**	**0.849**	**0.783**	**0.676**	**0.715**	**0.837**	0.624	**0.727**
-TF	0.870	0.768	0.848	0.772	0.668	0.701	0.802	0.610	0.703
-TCC	0.875	0.758	0.836	0.768	0.640	0.706	0.814	0.619	0.706
-CapNet	0.873	0.735	0.846	0.777	0.667	0.704	0.682	**0.638**	0.664

In order to further evaluate the role and contribution of each sub module in the TITCNmodel, we used the $TITCN^\dagger$ model which performed well in the comprehensive task to conduct ablation experiments to study the effects of different parts. As shown in Table 2, "-TF" means to remove the Transformer module and use the BiLSTM+Attention mechanism as the sense encoder as usual. "-TCC" means to remove the Transformer with Constrained Computation sub module. "-CapNet" means to remove the Text Capsule Network sub module.

When the Transformer is removed and the BiLSTM+Attention mechanism is used as the encoder, the overall performance of the model decreases slightly, which shows that BiLSTM+Attention has certain advantages in sequence modeling and has the functions of long-term memory and strengthening features, but there are still some deficiencies in text feature extraction.

When TCC is removed, the F1 score of the three subtasks decreased, which shows that using Transformer model to obtain the text information contained in all candidate emotion-cause pairs has a positive effect on the performance of the model, and TCC can alleviate the problem of sample imbalance.

By removing the text capsule network sub module, F1 score decreased significantly, reducing by 0.3%, 1.1% and 6.3% respectively on the three tasks, which shows that although transformer has strong feature extraction ability and can extract the features of candidate sentence pairs, it does not consider the relationship between the local text features of emotion-cause pair and the overall causality. From the results, using Text Capsule Network to classify candidate pairs of emotional reasons can greatly improve the accuracy of classification.

5.4 Qualitative Analysis

We select some texts from the test data for case study, which contain a certain number of emotion-cause pairs. The results are shown in Fig. 5. For the case where the motion clause and cause clause are closely distributed in the document, such as example 1, the relative distances between their motion clause and cause clause is 1. In this case, our model can get the correct prediction results.

Example 2 shows a document with much emotion-cause pairs. In general, it often needs multiple sub sentences to fully describe the reasons for the subject's emotional expression. Different clauses have different emphases, but they

Id	Content	Predictions	Ground Truth
1	[据白金跃介绍][1],[1988年至今][2],[他向国家各部委提出合理化建议1000多条][3].[并多次被各部委采纳][4].[曾荣获国家十二五建言献策个人一等奖河北省建言献策三等奖][5].[当日][6].[跟中新网记者谈起建言献策的初衷][7],[白跃陷入回忆][8],[并略显激动][9].	[(9,8)]	[(9,8)]
2	[为尽快将女子救下][1], [指挥员立即制订了救援方案][2]. [第一组在楼下铺设救生气垫][3]. [并对周围无关人员进行疏散][4]. [另一组队员快速爬上6楼][5], [在楼内对女子进行劝说][6]. [劝说过程中][7], [消防官兵了解到][8],[该女子是由于对方拖欠工程款][9]. [家中又急需用钱][10]. [生活压力大][11], [无奈才选择跳楼轻生][12].	[(12,9), (12,10), (12,11)]	[(12,9), (12,10), (12,11)]
3	[男子不远千里会网友][1], [发现女子长相与照片判若两人体形也相差甚远][2]. [女子辩称][3], [自己就是照片中的人][4], [不过是化了妆][5], [用了美图工具][6]. [大失所望之余][7], [男子认为受到欺骗][8], [怒火之下大打出手][9]. [最终][10], [经永嘉桥头派出所调解][11], [双方达成和解][12]. [男子当天乘飞机回家][13].	[(7,8)]	[(7,2)]

Fig. 5. We selected several texts from the test dataset and visualize the emotion-cause pair with different shades of color, where Ground Turth represents the real annotation result of each emotion-cause pair; Predictions represents the prediction results of titcn model. Each text contains a different number of emotion cause pairs.

describe an event together. Therefore, it is difficult to completely extract all the reasons corresponding to emotion claim. Our model can extract all emotion cause pairs without omission.

Example 3 shows the situation where emotional reasons are far apart in the document. Among them, the relative distance between emotion and cause clause is 5. Our model cannot capture too far away emotion cause pairs, which is due to the limitation of TCC mechanism. This way omits some emotion cause pairs, which may reduce the accuracy of the model.

6   Conclusion

In this paper, we propose an end-to-end framework to extract the emotion cause pair in documents. This method emphasizes the relationship between the local features of modeling sentence pairs and the overall emotion cause relation-ship. TITCN model uses the excellent feature extraction ability of Transformer to extract token-sentence-document hierarchical features. In addition, TITCN filters out a large number of negative samples from the characteristics of the data set, which alleviates the category imbalance of this task. Further, the each clause pair is modeled by using the capsule neural network to extract more rich text information. Using the advantages of capsule network, the overall classification accuracy can be improved. Further ablation experiments explored the role of each component of the model. For future research, we can try to optimize the dynamic routing algorithm of capsule neural network and analyze it in text data sets in other fields.

References

1. Chen, Y., Lee, S.Y.M., Li, S., Huang, C.R.: Emotion cause detection with linguistic constructions. In: Proceedings of the 23rd International Conference on Computational Linguistics (Colling 2010), pp. 179–187 (2010)
2. Ding, Z., Xia, R., Yu, J.: Ecpe-2d: emotion-cause pair extraction based on joint two-dimensional representation, interaction and prediction. In: Proceedings of the 58th Annual Meeting of the Association for Computational Linguistics, pp. 3161–3170 (2020)
3. Fan, C., et al.: A knowledge regularized hierarchical approach for emotion cause analysis. In: Proceedings of the 2019 Conference on Empirical Methods in Natural Language Processing and the 9th International Joint Conference on Natural Language Processing (EMNLP-IJCNLP), pp. 5614–5624 (2019)
4. Fan, C., Yuan, C., Du, J., Gui, L., Yang, M., Xu, R.: Transition-based directed graph construction for emotion-cause pair extraction. In: Proceedings of the 58th Annual Meeting of the Association for Computational Linguistics, pp. 3707–3717 (2020)
5. Fan, C., Yuan, C., Gui, L., Zhang, Y., Xu, R.: Multi-task sequence tagging for emotion-cause pair extraction via tag distribution refinement. IEEE/ACM Trans. Audio Speech Lang. Process. **29**, 2339–2350 (2021)
6. Gao, K., Xu, H., Wang, J.: A rule-based approach to emotion cause detection for Chinese micro-blogs. Expert Syst. Appl. **42**(9), 4517–4528 (2015)
7. Gui, L., Xu, R., Wu, D., Lu, Q., Zhou, Y.: Event-driven emotion cause extraction with corpus construction. In: Social Media Content Analysis: Natural Language Processing and Beyond, pp. 145–160. World Scientific (2018)
8. Gui, L., Yuan, L., Xu, R., Liu, B., Lu, Q., Zhou, Yu.: Emotion cause detection with linguistic construction in Chinese Weibo text. In: Zong, C., Nie, J.-Y., Zhao, D., Feng, Y. (eds.) NLPCC 2014. CCIS, vol. 496, pp. 457–464. Springer, Heidelberg (2014). https://doi.org/10.1007/978-3-662-45924-9_42
9. Lee, S.Y.M., Chen, Y., Huang, C.R.: A text-driven rule-based system for emotion cause detection. In: Proceedings of the NAACL HLT 2010 Workshop on Computational Approaches to Analysis and Generation of Emotion in Text, pp. 45–53 (2010)
10. Li, X., Feng, S., Wang, D., Zhang, Y.: Context-aware emotion cause analysis with multi-attention-based neural network. Knowl.-Based Syst. **174**, 205–218 (2019)
11. Mohammad, S.M.: Sentiment analysis: detecting valence, emotions, and other affectual states from text. In: Emotion Measurement, pp. 201–237. Elsevier, Amsterdam (2016)
12. Ou, G., et al.: Exploiting community emotion for microblog event detection. In: Social Media Content Analysis: Natural Language Processing and Beyond, pp. 439–456. World Scientific (2018)
13. Qadir, A., Riloff, E.: Learning emotion indicators from tweets: hashtags, hashtag patterns, and phrases. In: Proceedings of the 2014 Conference on Empirical Methods in Natural Language Processing (EMNLP), pp. 1203–1209 (2014)
14. Russo, I., Caselli, T., Rubino, F., Boldrini, E., Martínez-Barco, P., et al.: Emo-Cause: an easy-adaptable approach to emotion cause contexts. In: Association for Computational Linguistics (ACL) (2011)

15. Sabour, S., Frosst, N., Hinton, G.E.: Dynamic routing between capsules. In: Advances in Neural Information Processing Systems, vol. 30 (2017)
16. Song, H., Zhang, C., Li, Q., Song, D.: End-to-end emotion-cause pair extraction via learning to link. arXiv preprint arXiv:2002.10710 (2020)
17. Tang, H., Ji, D., Zhou, Q.: Joint multi-level attentional model for emotion detection and emotion-cause pair extraction. Neurocomputing **409**, 329–340 (2020)
18. Vaswani, A., et al.: Attention is all you need. In: Advances in Neural Information Processing Systems, vol. 30 (2017)
19. Wei, P., Zhao, J., Mao, W.: Effective inter-clause modeling for end-to-end emotion-cause pair extraction. In: Proceedings of the 58th Annual Meeting of the Association for Computational Linguistics, pp. 3171–3181 (2020)
20. Xia, R., Ding, Z.: Emotion-cause pair extraction: a new task to emotion analysis in texts. arXiv preprint arXiv:1906.01267 (2019)
21. Xia, R., Zhang, M., Ding, Z.: RTHN: a RNN-transformer hierarchical network for emotion cause extraction. arXiv preprint arXiv:1906.01236 (2019)
22. Xu, B., Lin, H., Lin, Y., Diao, Y., Yang, L., Xu, K.: Extracting emotion causes using learning to rank methods from an information retrieval perspective. IEEE Access **7**, 15573–15583 (2019)
23. Yada, S., Ikeda, K., Hoashi, K., Kageura, K.: A bootstrap method for automatic rule acquisition on emotion cause extraction. In: 2017 IEEE International Conference on Data Mining Workshops (ICDMW), pp. 414–421. IEEE (2017)
24. Yadollahi, A., Shahraki, A.G., Zaiane, O.R.: Current state of text sentiment analysis from opinion to emotion mining. ACM Comput. Surv. (CSUR) **50**(2), 1–33 (2017)
25. Zhang, S., Wei, Z., Wang, Y., Liao, T.: Sentiment analysis of Chinese micro-blog text based on extended sentiment dictionary. Futur. Gener. Comput. Syst. **81**, 395–403 (2018)

Summarization and Generation (Poster)

Employing Internal and External Knowledge to Factuality-Oriented Abstractive Summarization

Zhiguang Gao, Feng Jiang, Xiaomin Chu, and Peifeng Li[✉]

School of Computer Science and Technology, Soochow University,
Suzhou, Jiangsu, China
{20204227025,fjiang}@stu.suda.edu.cn, {xmchu,pfli}@suda.edu.cn

Abstract. Abstractive summarization models based on neural network have successfully generated human-readable and fluent summaries. However, the generated summary often has factual errors: it is inconsistent with the facts included in the source document (internal factual error) or commonsense knowledge (external factual error). To alleviate these two factual errors, we propose a novel **K**nowledge **A**ware **Sum**marization model (KASum) that enhances the factuality of the summary by integrating internal and external knowledge simultaneously. First, KASum obtains external knowledge by utilizing the pre-trained model ERNIE combined with Knowledge Graph (KG) to reduce external factual errors. Besides, KASum obtains internal knowledge by extracting the source document's Semantic Role Information (SRI) to improve internal factuality. Finally, KASum captures the interaction of internal and external knowledge by an interactive attention module to avoid internal and external factual errors further. Experimental results on CNN/DM and XSUM show that KASum significantly improves the factuality of the generated summary compared with strong baseline models.

Keywords: Abstractive summarization · Factuality · Internal knowledge · External knowledge

1 Introduction

Neural abstractive summarization methods based on the seq2seq architecture [7,16] have made advances in fluency and coherence. By leveraging the pre-trained language model, the previous researches [12,14] further make excellent progress in informativeness that is usually evaluated by the ROUGE [13] score. Nevertheless, how to correct the factual errors in the summaries generated by these abstractive summarization models is still a challenging task.

Wojciech et al. [11] and Goyal et al. [8] point out that nearly 30% of the summaries generated by these abstractive summarization models have factual errors. By analyzing the generated summaries, we define two kinds of factual errors: 1) **Internal factual error.** The hallucination phenomenon that the

© The Author(s), under exclusive license to Springer Nature Switzerland AG 2022
W. Lu et al. (Eds.): NLPCC 2022, LNAI 13551, pp. 797–809, 2022.
https://doi.org/10.1007/978-3-031-17120-8_61

Table 1. Example of the internal and external factual error.

Example of the internal factual error:
SourceText: ··· Readers were curious about the effects of medical marijuana in easing symptoms of various ailments, asking how it could help with everything from life-threatening illnesses and neurological conditions to chronic pain and post-traumatic stress disorder. ···
Generated summary: ··· Users asked how it could help with life-threatening illnesses and neurological conditions
Example of the external factual error:
Source Text: ··· Shamima Begum and Amira Abase, both 15, and Kadiza Sultana, 16, crossed over the Turkish-Syrian border last February and are believed to be living in the Syrian city of Raqqa ···
Generated summary: ··· They are believed to be living in the Raqqa of UK, where they could beunder the control of female insurgents. ···

summary sometimes distorts or fabricates the facts in the source document. 2) **External factual error.** The summary does not accord with commonsense knowledge and objective facts. Table 1 shows the examples of the internal and external factual error in the summaries generated by BertSum [14], respectively. For the example of internal factual error, the summary is inconsistent with the facts in the source document, i.e., BertSum mistakenly confuses the subject "readers" with "users". The summary generated by BertSum also has external factual error because it does not conform to objective facts: "Raqqa" is a city of Syrian, while the generated summary believes that "Raqqa" is a city of UK.

Previous studies mainly only consider internal factual error [3,19] or external factual error [2,9] for enhancing the factuality of summaries and do not consider two as a whole. Therefore, we propose the **K**nowledge **A**ware **Sum**marization model (KASum) to address these two kinds of factual errors simultaneously.

To alleviate the external factual error, we leverage the ERNIE model [18] that fuses the knowledge in the KG during pre-training for introducing external knowledge. Specifically, we first use the entity linking tool Tagme [5] to extract the entities in the source document and link these entities to Knowledge Graph (KG). Finally, we utilize TransE [1] to get the entity representation and feed them into ERNIE to obtain external knowledge.

To alleviate the internal factual error, we regard the SRI (Semantic Role Information) of source document as internal facts and encode it as internal knowledge. Specifically, we define a list of rules to filter the semantic role candidate tuples extracted from the source document and obtain the SRI with core semantics. Compared with the encoding relation triples [19] that often have high redundancy and poor generalization, the extracted SRI is more coherent and captured by the model easier.

Moreover, we design an interactive attention module to capture the interaction between external knowledge and internal knowledge, which simultaneously deals with those internal and external factual errors. Thus, our model further reduces these two types of errors by mutually supplementing the information of external and internal knowledge.

Our contributions are summarized as follows: (1) we analyze the summaries generated by previous abstractive summarization models and define two kinds of factual errors: internal factual error and external factual error; (2) we propose the KASum model that addresses internal and external factual error simultaneously; (3) both the automatic factual metric evaluation and human evaluation show that our KASum significantly improves the factuality of the summaries in comparison with the strong baselines on the datasets CNN/DM and XSUM.

2   Related Work

The work of enhancing the factuality of generated summaries can be divided into two categories: the studies on internal and external factual error.

Internal Factual Error. Most previous studies use the triples extracted from the source document as internal fact. Cao et al. [3] extract relational triples from source documents as supplementary to enhance internal factuality. Zhu et al. [19] first extract the triples from source documents and connect the entities in the triples to build a graph. And then the graph is encoded by graph neural network and fed into Transformer-based decoder layer to generate fact-consistent summaries. However, the extracted triples often contain redundant information, which is inconsistent with the essence of the summary compressing the information. Therefore, we define a list of rules to get SRI that only retains core semantics as internal fact.

External Factual Error. Previous work often obtains the external knowledge from KG. To alleviate those external factual errors, Meng et al. [2] manually annotate the external factuality discriminated dataset at the entity level and train the factuality discriminator on this basis. They take the score of the factuality discriminator as a reward to enhance the external factuality through reinforcement learning. Gunel et al. [9] take the external knowledge graph information into account. They get the representation of entities in KG by TransE [1] which is an efficient entity representation method of KG, and then inject entity information into abstractive summarization model. However, they ignore the difference between the entity representation and the source document representation in vector space when adding external knowledge. Therefore, we use the pre-trained model ERNIE [18] to encode the entity representation obtained by TransE and the source document representation in the same vector space. ERNIE assimilates the external entity representation in the pre-training stage, which helps integrate the external knowledge into the source document representation.

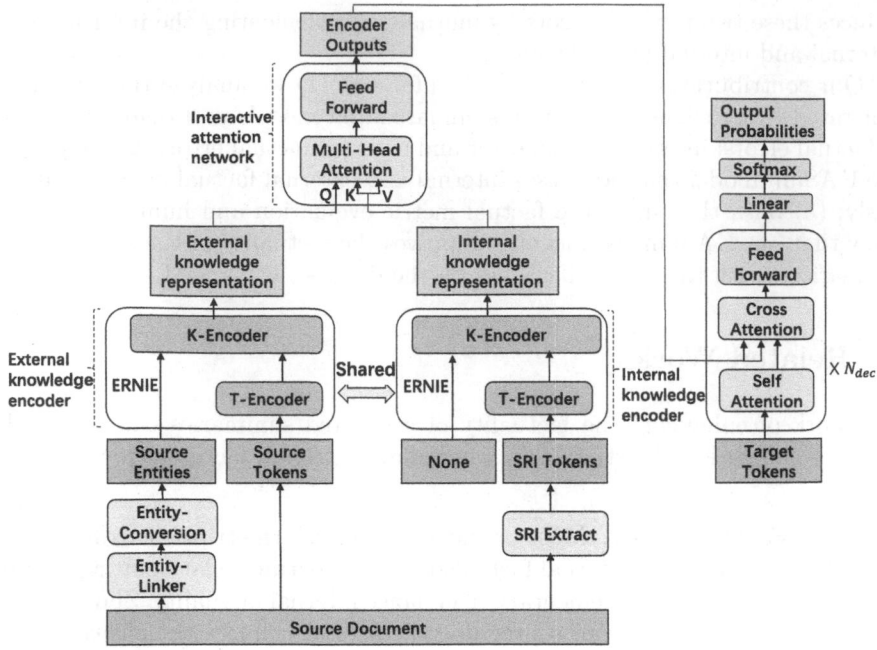

Fig. 1. The architecture of KASum.

3 KASum

Figure 1 shows the overall framework and implementation details of our model KASum. Consisted with the standard abstractive summarization models, KASum follows the seq2seq architecture and is composed of the Encoder and Decoder. The Encoder includes an external knowledge encoder, an internal knowledge encoder, and an interactive attention network, while the Decoder is composed of the decoder layers of the Transformer [17].

3.1 External Knowledge Encoder on ERNIE

Since external knowledge can be represented by the relation among entities in KG, we obtain the vector representation of entities by the effective TransE [1]. Previous work [9] injects the entity vector to the abstractive summarization model directly, which ignore the spatial difference between the entity vector and the representation of the source document. To address this issue, we integrate the entity vectors by ERNIE that integrates the entities in the pre-training stage and is trained on large-scale corpora. Therefore, ERNIE can better fuse the entity information with the source document in the same vector space.

As shown in Fig. 1, ERNIE is composed of the lower textual encoder (T-Encoder) and the upper knowledgeable encoder (K-Encoder) [18]. Thus, the input of the external knowledge encoder is divided into two parts. One part is the tokens of the source document $X_{token} = \{w_1, w_2, \ldots, w_m\}$, where w_i is the i-th token in the source document and m is the number of tokens. The other part is entities with rich information in the source document.

T-Encoder is composed of multi transformer encoder layers and computes lexical and syntactic features $\tilde{w}_1, \ldots, \tilde{w}_m$ as follows.

$$\{\tilde{w}_1, \tilde{w}_2, \ldots, \tilde{w}_m\} = \text{T-Encoder}(\{w_1, w_2, \ldots, w_m\}) \tag{1}$$

We obtain external knowledge through entity link, which contains two steps as follows. (1) Entity link. We use the entity linking tool Tagme [5] to extract the entities from the source document and link them to the entity objects in the corresponding Wikipedia. (2) Entity conversion. We transform these entity objects into the corresponding entity embeddings (In experiment, we use the trained entity embeddings provided by ERNIE). Specifically, we use the entity vector trained by TransE algorithm to initialize these entity objects and obtain the source entities with external knowledge. The mathematical signs of source entities is $\{e_1, e_2, \ldots, e_j\}$, where e_i is a vector with dimension D=100.

After all this, ERNIE adopts the knowledgeable encoder (K-Encoder) to inject the knowledge information into language representation. To be specific, both $\{e_1, e_2, \ldots, e_j\}$ and $\{\tilde{w}_1, \tilde{w}_2, \ldots, \tilde{w}_m\}$ are fed into K-Encoder for fusing heterogeneous information and computing final output embeddings as follows.

$$\{w_1^o, w_2^o, \ldots, w_m^o\} = \text{K-Encoder}(\{\tilde{w}_1, \tilde{w}_2, \ldots, \tilde{w}_m\}, \{e_1, e_2, \ldots, e_j\}) \tag{2}$$

where $\{w_1^o, \ldots, w_m^o\}$ is the representation of external knowledge, and w_m^o is a vector whose dimension is 768. By introducing external knowledge, KASum can understand the commonsense knowledge.

3.2   Internal Knowledge Encoder on SRI

We adopt SRI instead of triples to highlight internal knowledge because SRI mainly has two advantages as follows: (1) SRI contains the core semantics of the sentences in the source document, which can assist in generating summaries with key information; (2) SRI can better represent the facts in the source document because SRI describes the relation between each component.

Firstly, we extract the candidate tuples of the semantic roles in each sentence by AllenNLP [6]. And then we filter these redundant candidate tuples according to the following three rules to obtain SRI.

(1) **Concise Core Semantics.** For each candidate tuple, only ARG 0–1 and predicate (V) are retained, and all other unimportant elements are discarded.

(2) **Semantic Integrity.** We remove the candidate tuples with incomplete semantics (for example, the candidate tuples that do not contain ARG-0 or ARG-1).

(3) **Reducing Semantic Overlap.** We delete those small candidate tuples contained in large tuples.

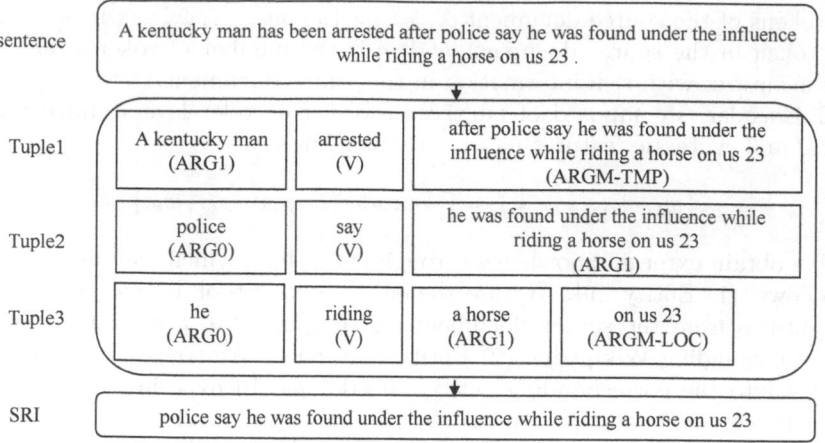

Fig. 2. The example of extracting SRI for the sentence.

Finally, if a sentence has multiple candidate tuples after filtering, these candidate tuples are spliced with commas. If a sentence does not have any candidate tuples, we use None to represent it.

As shown in Fig. 2, Tuple 1–3 is the candidate tuples extracted from the source document, and SRI represents the semantic role information filtered by rules. Tuple 1 does not contain ARG 0 and is discarded according to the rule 2. According to the rule 3, Tuple 3 is discarded because it is included in Tuple 2.

After extracting the SRI of each sentence in the source document, we splice them together and tokenize it into sequence tokens $S_{token} = \{v_1, v_2, \ldots, v_t\}$, where v_i is the i-th token in SRI and t is the number of tokens. To reduce the parameters of the KASum model, the internal knowledge encoder shares ERNIE with the external knowledge encoder, which also implicitly interacts information between the two encoders. Notably, We do not link entities here because SRI only retains arguments and predicates which contain fewer entities. The input of the internal knowledge encoder is only the SRI of the source document as follows.

$$\{\tilde{v}_1, \tilde{v}_2, \ldots, \tilde{v}_t\} = \text{T-Encoder}(\{v_1, v_2, \ldots, v_t\})$$
$$\{v_1^o, v_2^o, \ldots, v_t^o\} = \text{K-Encoder}(\{\tilde{v}_1, \tilde{v}_2, \ldots, \tilde{v}_t\}, \{0, 0, \ldots, 0\}) \tag{3}$$

where $\{\tilde{v}_1, \tilde{v}_2, \ldots, \tilde{v}_t\}$ is the intermediate representation of SRI after T-Encoder, $\{v_1^o, v_2^o, \ldots, v_t^o\}$ is the internal knowledge representation of the source document obtained after K-Encoder, while $\tilde{v}_t$, v_t^o is a vector whose dimension is 768. By encoding the SRI, the model can enhance the perception of the internal facts in source document.

3.3   Fusing Internal and External Knowledge

Our goal is to mitigate the internal and external factual errors simultaneously, therefore, a knowledge fusion module integrating internal and external knowledge is more important.

We design the knowledge fusion module inspired by the cross attention module in Transformer [17]. The cross attention has two inputs. One is the target summary representation encoded by self-attention, and the other is the representation of the source document. Cross attention realizes the information fusion between them through an interactive attention mechanism. We have tried to adopt a similar approach to realize internal and external knowledge integration: take the external knowledge representation as the query vector (Q) and the internal knowledge representation as the key, value pair vector (K and V). Notably, we directly concatenate external and internal knowledge representation as the encoder output, however, the ROUGE value drops a lot due to this integration method is excessively shallow. What's more, we also tried to take internal knowledge representation as the query vector (Q), however, the factuality score is a little lower than above strategy we adopted, because external knowledge representation has all the information of the source document. Hence, it is more suitable as a query vector.

Specifically, we obtain Q, K, and V as shown in Eq. (4), and the interactive attention is shown in Eq. (5), where W^Q, W^K, W^V are the parameters that the model needs to learn, and their dimensions are $h*h$. The dimension of H is $m*h$, m is the sequence length of the source document, h is the hidden size (768) of ERNIE, d is the scaling coefficient, and FFH is a two-layer fully connected network.

$$Q = \{w_1^o, w_2^o, \ldots, w_m^o\}W^Q, K = \{v_1^o, v_2^o, \ldots, v_t^o\}W^K, V = \{v_1^o, v_2^o, \ldots, v_t^o\}W^V \tag{4}$$

$$H = Softmax(\frac{QK^T}{\sqrt{d}})V, Encoder\_Outputs = FFH(H) \tag{5}$$

3.4   Decoder

In this section, we analyze the mismatch between KASum's Encoder and Decoder and put forward a solution. Decoder consists of six decoder layers of Transformer [17] initialized randomly. Encoder and Decoder mismatch in the training stage, because the former is pre-trained while the latter has to be trained from scratch. It will cause the training phase to be unstable since Encoder may be overfitting while Decoder is underfitting. Following Liu [14], we design a specific fine-tuning schedule for Encoder and Decoder and use two Adam optimizers for them, respectively. Each of them with different warmup-steps and learning rates. We assume that the pre-trained encoder should be fine-tuned with a smaller learning rate declining slowly and the untrained decoder is just the opposite, as shown in Eqs. 6 and 7.

$$lr_E = \tilde{lr}_E \cdot min(step^{-0.5}, step \cdot warmup_E^{-1.5}) \qquad (6)$$

$$lr_D = \tilde{lr}_D \cdot min(step^{-0.5}, step \cdot warmup_D^{-1.5}) \qquad (7)$$

where $\tilde{lr}_E = 2e^{-3}$, and $warmup_E = 20,000$ for Encoder and $\tilde{lr}_D = 0.1$, and $warmup_D = 10,000$ for Decoder.

Following previous studies [4,12,14], we use the standard MLE loss to train our model.

4   Experimentation

In this section, we conduct experiments to verify the effectiveness of our model KASum.

4.1   Experimental Settings

We evaluate our models on two datasets, **CNN/DM** [10] and **XSUM** [15]. The gold summary of CNN/DM has a lot of overlap with the source document so that the extractive summarization models perform well. XSUM takes the first sentence as the gold summary and the others as the source document. XSUM is more abstractive and abstractive summarization models trained on it sometimes can't recover the information in the gold summary according to the source document. Following Liu et al. [14], the training, validation and test sets are 287227, 13368 and 11490 samples for CNN/DM, and 204045, 11332 and 11334 samples for XSUM.

We use ROUGE to evaluate the informativeness of the summary and use three factual evaluation metrics (DAE, SENT, FactC) to evaluate the factuality. ROUGE is a traditional summary evaluation metric and ROUGE-1, ROUGE-2, and ROUGE-L are applied to measure the overlap between generated summary and gold summary. Although ROUGE can reflect the informativeness of the summary [19], it can not evaluate the factuality [8,11]. Considering this, we use three factual evaluation metrics DAE [8], SENT [8], and FactC [11] to evaluate the factuality of the generated summary. DAE is a dependency-level factual evaluation metric that judges the generated summary as factual if and only if all the dependency arcs in the generated summary are predicted to be factually correct. SENT is a sentence-level factual evaluation metric. Specifically, the input of the SENT model is the generated summary and the source document, and the output is the binary label that is consistent or inconsistent with the facts. Like SENT, FactC is also sentence-level and does a binary classification for factuality. The difference is that FactC is trained on the synthetic dataset while SENT is trained on the human-annotated dataset.

We train KASum on two V100 GPUs and update the parameters every 5 steps. The total number of training steps is 200000. Label smoothing is used to prevent over-fitting, and the smoothing coefficient is set to 0.1.

4.2   Experimental Results

Table 2 shows the ROUGE and factual scores of different models on CNN/DM and XSUM datasets.

Table 2. ROUGE and factual consistency scores on CNN/DM and XSUM, where R1, R2, RL refer to ROUGE-1, ROUGE-2, ROUGE-L, respectively.

| Model | CNN/DM | | | | | | XSUM | | | | | |
	R1	R2	RL	DAE	SENT	FactC	R1	R2	RL	DAE	SENT	FactC
BottomUP	41.22	18.68	38.34	71.43	74.60	44.29	26.91	7.66	20.01	1.49	39.26	6.67
BertSum	41.43	19.05	38.55	71.74	87.51	53.93	38.76	16.33	31.15	28.70	61.38	23.56
Unilm	43.33	20.21	40.51	65.21	82.32	36.43	42.14	19.53	34.13	30.54	64.32	22.54
FASum	40.53	17.84	37.40	73.57	79.12	50.14	30.28	10.03	23.76	12.66	65.74	26.20
$FASum_{FC}$	40.38	17.67	37.23	73.80	80.36	51.17	30.20	9.97	23.68	12.03	**67.13**	26.09
Bart	43.86	20.92	40.64	72.75	84.94	49.60	45.52	22.48	37.29	34.83	65.45	22.98
$KASum_{ext}$	41.27	18.96	38.32	76.93	88.91	53.03	38.65	16.54	31.20	28.92	61.67	22.74
$KASum_{int}$	41.37	19.00	38.41	76.33	89.69	55.75	37.69	15.85	30.38	33.32	63.05	23.65
KASum	41.44	19.19	38.50	**78.11**	**90.09**	**59.70**	39.33	17.11	31.71	**35.03**	65.27	**27.10**

Baselines. BottomUP [7] uses a bottom-up approach to generate summaries. **BertSum** [14] introduces the pre-trained model BERT to generate the summary. **Unilm** [4] utilizes large-scale text corpora for pre-training and special masking strategy for generative tasks. **FASum** [19] enhances the factuality of the generated summary by encoding the triples extracted from the source document through the graph neural network. **FC** is a fact corrector introduced in FASum, which aims at correcting the generated summary through the replacement of nouns. $FASum_{FC}$ is the result of FASum corrected the factual errors by FC. **Bart** [12] is a seq2seq pre-trained model and achieves the highest ROUGE scores.

Compared with the Baselines. Our model KASum outperforms all baseline models on three factual evaluation metrics except for SENT in XSUM. For CNN/DM, KASum achieves the best performance on DAE, SENT and FactC. For example, it is 5.36%, 4.54% higher than Bart, FASum on DAE. For XSUM, we can see that the factual metric scores drop a lot compared with CNN/DM because the XSUM dataset is more abstractive. However, due to introducing external knowledge and enhancing attention to internal facts, KASum still achieves the best performance on DAE and FactC and has comparable performance on SENT that is a coarse-grained metric with a larger unit of measurement. Overall, KASum performs best in terms of factuality by introducing external knowledge and enhancing the perception of internal knowledge. In addition, we have noticed that KASum's ROUGE values are a little lower than Bart and Unilm. Notably, ROUGE values do not always reflect the factual consistency, sometimes even showing an inverse relationship [2,19]. We can also draw such a conclusion from Table 2. KASum's ROUGE value is a little lower than Unilm, but its factuality scores outperform Unilm substantially. What's more, the parameter of KASum is 191 M, much smaller than those of Bart, Unilm, and FASum, which are about 400 M. Therefore, the KASum's reasoning speed is faster and is easier to deploy in practical applications.

Ablation Experiment. We do ablation experiment to explore the role of internal knowledge and external knowledge. $KASum_{ext}$ refers to KASum with only external knowledge encoder, while $KASum_{int}$ refers to KASum with only internal knowledge encoder. As shown in Table 2, for CNN/DM, both $KASum_{ext}$ and $KASum_{int}$ outperform baselines on the factual evaluation, which proves that our proposed internal knowledge encoder and external knowledge encoder are helpful in promoting factuality. When integrating them together, our KASum achieves the best grades on three factual metrics. For XSUM, although $KASum_{ext}$ or $KASum_{int}$ alone is lower than Bart on factual metrics, KASum complements internal and external knowledge through interactive attention network and has the best performance on factuality overall.

Table 3. Human evaluation results of summaries for 100 randomly sampled articles in CNN/DM and XSUM test set. Fact, Abs, Infor refer to Factuality, Abstractness, Informativeness respectively.

Model	CNN/DM			XSUM		
	Fact	Abs	Infor	Fact	Abs	Infor
BertSum	0.72	0.35	0.70	0.36	0.61	0.42
FASum	0.68	0.46	0.69	0.40	0.67	0.28
KASum	**0.77**	**0.47**	**0.72**	**0.45**	**0.69**	**0.47**

5   Analysis

5.1   Human Evaluation

In addition to automatic factual evaluation metric, we also perform the human evaluation for the generated summary from three perspectives: abstractness, factuality, and informativeness. (i) **Abstractness** measures the degree of abstraction of the summary and can be divided into three levels: (1) the generated summary is exactly the same as sentences in the source document (0 point), (2) new words are generated (1 point), and (3) new sentences are generated (2 point). (ii) **Factuality** is divided into two levels: (1) the generated summary is consistent with the facts in the source document and conforms to common sense (1 point),

(2) otherwise (0 point). (iii) **Informativeness** indicates whether the generated summary contains the main content of the source document. It is highly subjective and can be divided into three levels: (1) the generated summary summarizes the main content of the article (2 point), (2) it only summarizes some important content (1 point), and (3) it is irrelevant to the source document (0 point).

We randomly select 100 samples from the respective test sets of CNN/DM and XSUM and ask three experts with NLP experience to evaluate the generated summary. We ensure that the three evaluators complete the evaluation independently, and they don't know which model the current summary belongs to when evaluating. The final score of each sample is the average of the scores given by the three evaluators. Table 3 shows the results of human evaluation. For both CNN/DM and XSUM, KASum outperforms FASum and BertSum significantly on factuality, abstractness, and informativeness.

For factuality, KASum outperforms FASum, BertSum on both XSUM and CNN/DM datasets, which is consistent with the three automatic factual evaluation metrics. It proves that the summary of the KASum model is more factual in human's view. Also, KASum surpasses FASum, BertSum over informativeness on two datasets, which shows that our KASum model not only achieves the best results in factuality, but also refines the core information of the source document. For abstractness, KASum is 1%, 12% higher than FASum, BertSum in CNN/DM and 2%, 8% higher than FASum, BertSum in XSUM, this reveals that our KASum model gets good grades in factuality is not by simply copying sentences from the source document.

5.2   Case Study

Table 4 shows examples of CNN/DM and summaries generated by KASum and several baselines. Due to integrating internal and external knowledge, KASum generates summaries that are more consistent with source documents and objective facts. For article1, BertSum believes that ogle county is Louis's third largest city, which is inconsistent with objective facts, while KASum introduces the external knowledge and generates the correct relation even though the phrase "in ogle county, Illinois" is not appearing in the article. For article2, BertSum generates summary inconsistent with article, while our KASum focuses on internal facts and generates "Andrew Getty is the grandson of J. Paul Getty", which is the true relationship in KG and consistent with the article.

Table 4. Examples of CNN/DM articles and summaries generated by different models.

Article1: ··· Eight tornadoes were reported Wednesday in Oklahoma, Kansas and Mis-souri, the storm prediction center said. ··· It could have been worse as severe tornado damage dotted a path not far from the dense populations of Chicago and Rockford – the state's third largest city ···

BertSum: ··· The tornado cut a 22-mile path through ogle county, the state's third largest city.

FASum: ··· The journalist says there were eight tornadoes wednesday in Oklahoma, Kansas and Mis-souri

KASum: A tornado ripped through a 22-mile path in ogle county, Illinois. A large and dangerous twister touched down 70 mi outside of St. louis

Article2: Andrew Getty, the 47-year-old grandson of J. Paul Getty, died Tuesday afternoon in his home in Los Angeles, according to a statement from his mother and father. ··· Where the Getty family fortune came from Gordon Getty is one of three sons of J. Paul Getty, the oil tycoon who was thought to be the richest man in the world at the time of his death in 1976. ···

BertSum: Andrew Getty's death appears to be an accident, coroner 's office says. He is one of three sons of J. Paul Getty, the richest man in 1976. ···

FASum: The 47-year-old grandson of J. Paul Getty died Tuesday afternoon in his home in Los Angeles, police say. ···

KASum: Andrew Getty is the grandson of J. Paul Getty. Getty's death appears to be natural or an accident, a coroner's official says. A female friend is at the home where Getty died and is cooperating with investigators

---

6   Conclusion

Considering the two common factual errors in abstractive summarization: internal and external factual errors, we propose the KASum model to enhance the factuality of the summaries. KASum introduces external knowledge by KG, enhances internal fact attention by SRI, and integrates them further by cross attention mechanism. The experimental results show that KASum significantly improves the factuality compared with the benchmark models. Our future work will focus on how to integrate more common knowledge to summarization.

References

1. Bordes, A., Usunier, N., Garcia-Duran, A., Weston, J., Yakhnenko, O.: Translating embeddings for modeling multi-relational data. In: Advances in Neural Information Processing Systems 26 (2013)
2. Cao, M., Dong, Y., Cheung, J.C.K.: Inspecting the factuality of hallucinated entities in abstractive summarization. arXiv preprint arXiv:2109.09784 (2021)
3. Cao, Z., Wei, F., Li, W., Li, S.: Faithful to the original: fact aware neural abstractive summarization. In: Proceedings of the AAAI Conference on Artificial Intelligence, vol. 32 (2018)
4. Dong, L., et al.: Unified language model pre-training for natural language understanding and generation. In: Advances in Neural Information Processing Systems, vol. 32 (2019)

5. Ferragina, P., Scaiella, U.: TAGME: on-the-fly annotation of short text fragments (by wikipedia entities). In: Proceedings of the 19th ACM international conference on Information and knowledge management, pp. 1625–1628 (2010)
6. Gardner, M., et al.: AllenNLP: a deep semantic natural language processing platform. arXiv preprint arXiv:1803.07640 (2018)
7. Gehrmann, S., Deng, Y., Rush, A.: Bottom-up abstractive summarization. In: EMNLP, pp. 4098–4109 (2018)
8. Goyal, T., Durrett, G.: Annotating and modeling fine-grained factuality in summarization. In: NAACL, pp. 1449–1462 (2021)
9. Gunel, B., Zhu, C., Zeng, M., Huang, X.: Mind the facts: knowledge-boosted coherent abstractive text summarization. arXiv preprint arXiv:2006.15435 (2020)
10. Hermann, K.M., et al.: Teaching machines to read and comprehend. Adv. Neural. Inf. Process. Syst. **28**, 1693–1701 (2015)
11. Kryscinski, W., McCann, B., Xiong, C., Socher, R.: Evaluating the factual consistency of abstractive text summarization. In: EMNLP, pp. 9332–9346 (2020)
12. Lewis, M., et al.: BART: denoising sequence-to-sequence pre-training for natural language generation, translation, and comprehension. In: ACL, pp. 7871–7880 (2020)
13. Lin, C.Y.: Rouge: a package for automatic evaluation of summaries. In: Text Summarization Branches Out, pp. 74–81 (2004)
14. Liu, Y., Lapata, M.: Text summarization with pretrained encoders. In: EMNLP, pp. 3730–3740 (2019)
15. Narayan, S., Cohen, S.B., Lapata, M.: Don't give me the details, just the summary! topic-aware convolutional neural networks for extreme summarization. In: EMNLP, pp. 1797–1807 (2018)
16. See, A., Liu, P.J., Manning, C.D.: Get to the point: summarization with pointer-generator networks. In: ACL, pp. 1073–1083 (2017)
17. Vaswani, A., et al.: Attention is all you need. In: Advances in Neural Information Processing Systems, pp. 5998–6008 (2017)
18. Zhang, Z., Han, X., Liu, Z., Jiang, X., Sun, M., Liu, Q.: ERNIE: enhanced language representation with informative entities. In: ACL, pp. 1441–1451 (2019)
19. Zhu, C., et al.: Enhancing factual consistency of abstractive summarization. In: NAACL, pp. 718–733 (2021)

Abstractive Summarization Model with Adaptive Sparsemax

Shiqi Guo[1], Yumeng Si[1], and Jing Zhao[2,3]([✉])

[1] School of Computer Science and Technology, East China Normal University,
Shanghai 200241, China
{71194506014,51215901107}@stu.ecnu.edu.cn
[2] School of Computer Science and Technology,
East China Normal University, Shanghai 200062, China
[3] Shanghai Key Laboratory of Multidimensional Information Processing,
East China Normal University, Shanghai 200241, China
jzhao@cs.ecnu.edu.cn

Abstract. Abstractive summarization models mostly rely on Sequence-to-Sequence architectures, in which the softmax function is widely used to transform the model output to simplex. However, softmax's output probability distribution often has the long-tail effect especially when the vocabulary size is large. Many unrelated tokens occupy too many probabilities so they will reduce the training efficiency and effect. More recently, some work has begun to design mapping functions to gain sparse output probabilities to ignore these irrelevant tokens. In this paper, we propose Adaptive Sparsemax which can self-adaptively control the sparsity of the model's output. Our method combines sparsemax and temperature mechanism, and the temperature value can be learned by the neural network. One of the advantages of our method is that it doesn't need any hyperparameter. The experimental result on CNN-Daily Mail and LCSTS dataset shows that our method has better performance on the abstractive summarization task than baseline models.

Keywords: Abstractive summarization · Seq2Seq · Adaptive sparsemax

1 Introduction

Abstractive summarization task is benefited from Sequence-to-Sequence architectures [22] for its flexibility to generate text [8,9,20,23]. In natural language tasks based on Sequence-to-Sequence models, the target tokens are usually encoded to One Hot vector, so it is necessary to restrict the output of the model to a normalized probability distribution. Softmax [2] is the most commonly used method to regularize the output of the model because it is differentiable and simple to evaluate. However, the output of softmax is dense, all candidate tokens have non-zero probabilities. This will lead to a long-tail effect especially when the dictionary of the training model is large [24]. Even though the probabilities of many words are extremely low, they still occupy certain probabilities, which make the outputs less likely to be the correct words.

Due to this drawback of Softmax, many recent works are focusing on generating sparse output such as Sparsemax [17], α-entmax [19], Sparsegen-lin [14] and so on. Researches show that models with appropriate sparsity have better performance and interpretability [5,16]. Some of the papers also attempts to reduce the computational complexity of the model by applying sparse method [3,25]. However, little work was done to study how to adaptively adjust the degree of sparsity of the model's output probability distribution.

In this paper, we propose the Adaptive Sparsemax method. The method can change the sparsity of the model output probability adaptively. We introduce Sparsemax [17] into our method to obtain sparse output. Specifically, by adding a network structure to the Sequence-to-Sequence model and using the Temperature [1] method, we give the model the ability to adaptively adjust the sparsity of the output. The experimental results show that our method obtains better performance than the baseline.

Our contributions are as follows:

- We propose the Adaptive Sparsemax method. The introduction of the Temperature method and Sparsemax function allows the model to adaptively change the sparsity of the output probabilities.
- The experiments on CNN/Daily Mail (CNN-DM) dataset show that our approach has improved the performance of the Pointer-Generator model, where the ROUGE-1, ROUGE-2 scores are increased by 0.40 and 0.28 respectively.
- The experiments on LCSTS dataset show that our approach has improved the performance of the Transformer model, where the ROUGE-1, ROUGE-2 scores are increased by 2.25 and 1.16 respectively.
- Based on the analysis of the entropy of the output probabilities, we give an insight into how our method affects the output probability distribution of the summarization model.

The rest of the paper is structured as follows: Sect. 2 introduces the related work in the area of abstractive summarization. Section 3 describes our proposed Adaptive Sparsemax, and we will also give a brief introduction to Sparsemax. Section 4 presents the detailed experimental process and the analysis of the results. At last, we conclude this paper in Sect. 5.

2   Related Work

Recently, many methods which intend to change the output probability distribution of Softmax have been proposed. One kind of these methods is sampling, where a portion of the overall probability distribution is selected heuristically and the remaining probabilities of the distribution are trimmed. Top-k [7] and Top-p [12] are typical sampling approaches. The Top-k method is to select top k words with the highest probabilities in each step. The problem with Top-k is that the choice of the value of k is difficult because the entropy of the probability distribution of the model output is different at different steps in the summary generation process. In those steps with a flat probability distribution, the probability gap between possible tokens is not large. Using a small k may cause the model to sloppily eliminate a large number of possible tokens, which will increase the risk that the model will converge in the wrong direction. To solve this problem, Top-p is proposed in which a certain portion of the probabilities are kept. In Top-p method, all possible tokens are first sorted by the probability from large to small. Then it will only keep those tokens whose accumulated probability is exactly greater than the threshold p.

In addition to sampling methods, other methods achieve similar results. [4] classifies the distribution according to the frequencies of words occurrence before the model output passes through Softmax so that the frequencies of words in the same category are close. This allows the size of the vocabulary for a single category to be reduced, thus balancing the probabilities of words in each category. [6] introduces another network in the Transformer model, as opposed to the Attention mechanism to learn the least relevant words and set the output value of the irrelevant words to negative infinity, so that the probability after calculation by the Softmax calculation gives a probability close to zero.

All of these methods have the same feature, which is to artificially make the probability distribution steep. From the perspective of uncertainty, these methods reduce the entropy of the probability distribution. This idea works because it increases the gap between correct words and incorrect words, allowing the model to distinguish correct words from incorrect words more effectively. In the training process, the loss of correct words is reduced, and the loss of wrong words is increased, which leads to increase training efficiency.

3   The Proposed Adaptive Sparsemax Method

In this section, we introduce our proposed method in detail. Specifically, we first describe the Sparsemax function, including the calculation method and the reason why we introduce this function. Then we introduce our proposed Adaptive Sparsemax Method. Finally, we introduce how we apply the Adaptive Sparsemax method to abstractive summarization models, such as Pointer-Generator Networks [21] and Transformer [23].

3.1   Sparsemax

In Sequence-to-Sequence based model, we usually transform the model's output to a simplex. The most common way to accomplish this goal is to use the Softmax function, which is given by:

$$\text{softmax}_i(\mathbf{z}) = \frac{exp\ z_i}{\sum_j exp\ z_j}. \tag{1}$$

From the Eq. (1), it can be seen that Softmax is dense and all components of its output distribution are larger than zero. This means that even very small values of probability can affect the results of the model to some extent.

In order to enable the model to output sparse results, [17] proposed Sparse-max. It can be understood intuitively as shown in Fig. 1. Assuming the input vector is $\mathbf{X}$, draw a histogram of each component of $\mathbf{X}$ and imagine taking a ruler parallel to the x-axis of the image and moving it down from the top of the image until the probabilities above the ruler are summed to 1. The value of $\mathbf{X}$ above the ruler is the result of Sparsemax. This function sets part of the components of vector $\mathbf{X}$ to 0, so the result becomes sparse.

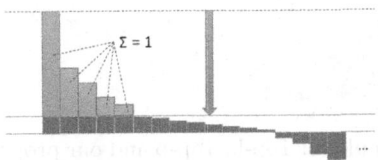

Fig. 1. Schematic diagram of Sparsemax calculation.

Define $\Delta^{K-1} = \{\mathbf{p} \in \mathbb{R}|\mathbf{1}^T\mathbf{p} = 1, \mathbf{p} \geq 0\}$ as normalized probability distribution in K-1 dimensions. Formally, sparsemax is defined as :

$$\text{sparsemax}_i(\mathbf{z}) = \arg\min_{p \in \Delta^{K-1}} \| \mathbf{p} - \mathbf{z} \|^2. \tag{2}$$

One of the closed-form solutions of Sparsemax is as follows:

$$\text{sparsemax}_i(\mathbf{z}) = [z_i - \tau(\mathbf{z})]_+, \tag{3}$$

where $\tau : \mathbb{R}^K \to \mathbb{R}$ is a function that satisfies $\sum_j [z_j - \tau(\mathbf{z})]_+ = 1$. τ can be expressed as follows: Let $\mathbf{z}$ be the sorted set that $z_{(1)} \geqslant z_{(2)} \geqslant \cdots \geqslant z_{(K)}$ and let $k(\mathbf{z}) = max\{k \in [K]|1 + kz_{(k)} > \sum_{j \leqslant k} z_{(j)}\}$. Then,

$$\tau(\mathbf{z}) = \frac{(\sum_{j \leqslant k(\mathbf{z})} z(j)) - 1}{k(\mathbf{z})} = \frac{(\sum_{j \in S(\mathbf{z})} z_j) - 1}{|S(\mathbf{z})|}, \tag{4}$$

where $S(\mathbf{z}) = \{j \in [K]|sparsemax_j(\mathbf{z}) > 0\}$ is the support of sparsemax($\mathbf{z}$).

3.2 Adaptive Sparsemax

In this section, we propose our Adaptive Sparsemax method. Suppose the output probability distribution of the original model is D and the probability distribution of the new output is D' and the value of Temperature is T, then the equation describing the adaptive sparsemax method is given by:

$$D' = \text{sparsemax}(D/T), \tag{5}$$

where T is limited between 0 and 1.

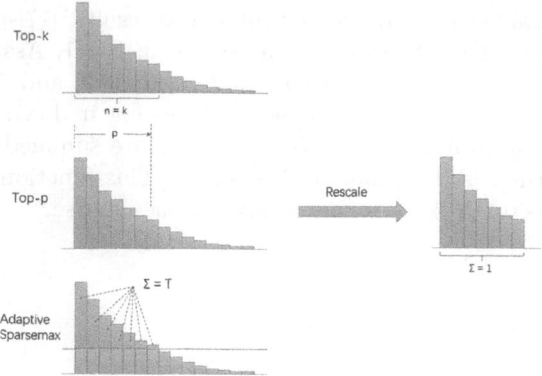

Fig. 2. Visual comparison plot of Top-k, Top-p and our proposed Adaptive Sparsemax.

Refer to Fig. 2, using the Temperature method on Sparsemax is equivalent to summing the probability of the area above the ruler to the value of T, and rescale the new probability so that the sum equals 1.

As the sum of the components of the original probability distribution is 1, when the value of T equals 1, the output of the original model is fed into Sparsemax without scaling, so there is no effect of Sparsemax at this point. When the value of T is between 0 and 1, it is equivalent to moving the ruler down until the components above the ruler sum up to T, and the probability distribution under the ruler is cut. The sparsity of the output increases as the value of T approaches zero. When the T value is less than the difference between the maximum value and the next largest value in the original probability distribution, the output distribution becomes One hot distribution. This method is equivalent to Hardmax, and the distribution reaches the sparsest state. Since the original probability distribution is kept as it is when the Temperature value is greater than or equals 1, we can limit the range of the Temperature value between 0 and 1.

The design intends to adjust the sparsity of the model's output during training. We found that the entropy of each step in the summary generation process is different. Besides, in different stages of training, the entropy of the model output distribution is also different. In the early stage of training, the entropy of the output distribution of the model is relatively large due to the low fitting degree of the model to the data. As the number of training steps increases, the fit of the model to the data increases, and the entropy of the distribution output by the model decreases.

In addition, we mentioned that the Top-p was proposed to solve the difficulty of the Top-k method in dealing with the distribution of different entropy. According to the defect of Top-k on flat distribution pointed out in the literature [12], Top-p will perform better than Top-k method on high-entropy distribution. However, Top-p still needs to set hyperparameters, and the appropriate value of p is different for different models and datasets. Finding a suitable p value remains a problem.

Through the above analysis, we think that the sparsity of the model's output can be dynamically adjusted by our method to adapt to the changes in the output distribution entropy of different stages of decoding, different stages of training, and different datasets of different models in a summary generation. And our method is not just a replacement for Softmax, but can deal with the probability distribution of all kinds of function outputs.

3.3   Application of Adaptive Sparsemax on Abstractive Summarziation Models

The main issue of the application of our proposed Adaptive Sparsemax is to calculate the Temperature value. Our solution to this issue is that we use a neural network module to calculate the value of T.

Firstly, we apply our method on Pointer-Generator Networks [21]. The modified model after applying our method is shown in Fig. 3.

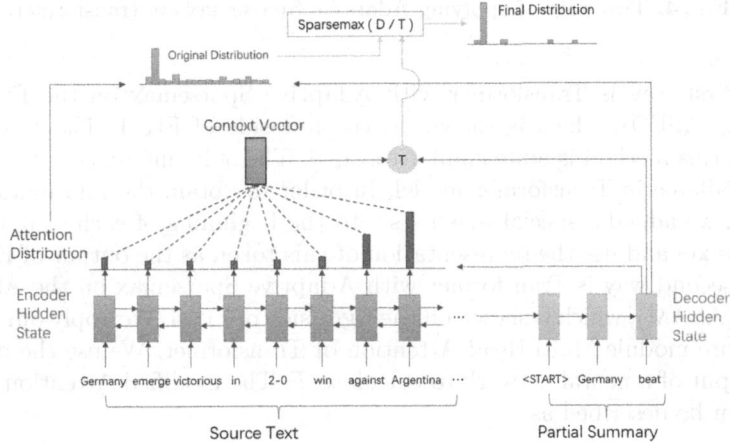

Fig. 3. Schematic diagram of the model structure after applying the adaptive sparseness method on the PGN model.

The calculation of the output probability distribution can be described as,

$$T = (1 - \epsilon) * \text{sigmod}(W_c c_t + W_s s_t + W_x x_t),$$
$$D' = \text{sparsemax}(D/(T + \epsilon)), \tag{6}$$

where ϵ is a very small positive number and we take $1e - 12$, c_t is the context vector of Attention outputs, s_t is the hidden state of Decoder and x_t is the input of Decoder. W_c, W_s, W_x are the weights learned by the neural network. We used the context vector output by the Attention method in the Encoder of the model and the output of the current step of the Decoder as the input of the network.

We also apply our method on Transformer [23] in two different ways, which can be displayed graphically in Fig. 4.

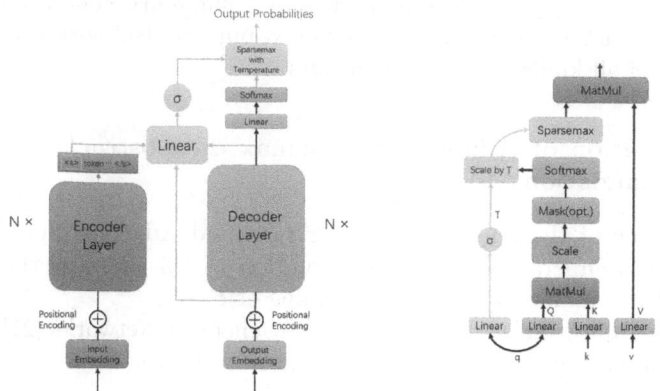

Fig. 4. Two ways of applying Adaptive Sparsemax on Transformer.

The first way is Transformer with Adaptive Sparsemax on the Final Distribution (ASFD), which is shown on the left side of Fig. 4. The formula for applying this method is quite similar to Eq. 6. The only difference is that c_t in 6 is not available in Transformer model. In order to obtain the information from Encoder, we added a special token <s> to the beginning of each sample of the original texts and use the representation of this token as the output of Encoder.

The second way is Transformer with Adaptive Sparsemax on the Attention Module (ASAM), which is shown on the right side of Fig. 4. We apply our method on the core module Multi-Head Attention of Transformer. We use the matrix q as the input of a neural network to calculate T. The modified Attention module which can be described as,

$$T = \text{sigmoid}(W_t q),$$

$$\text{Attention}(q, k, v) = \text{sparsemax}(\text{softmax}(\frac{W_q q (W_k k)^T}{\sqrt{d_k}})\frac{1}{T})W_v v, \qquad (7)$$

where q, k, v are the inputs of the Attention module, W_q, W_k, W_v, W_t are the transformation matrices of the inputs. d_k is the embedding dimension.

4   Experiment

4.1   Datasets

For PGN model, we conduct experiments on CNN-DM [11,18] dataset to evaluate our proposed method. The CNN-DM dataset contains online news articles and their summaries, which is widely used for abstractive summarization tasks. Following [21], we use the non-anonymized version of the CNN-DM dataset, which has 287,226 training pairs, 13,368 validation pairs, and 11,490 test pairs. During the experiment, we set the maximum length of the original text and the reference summary to 400 and 100 respectively.

For the Transformer model, we conduct experiments on LCSTS [13] which is a Chinese short text summarization dataset. It contains more than 2.4 million training pairs, which are crawled from Weibo.

4.2 Experiment Setup

For the experiments on PGN model, we followed the setup in [21]. We turn off the Coverage mechanism in the first 230,000 steps and then turn on it in the next 5000 steps.

To compare the effectiveness of our method with other methods on PGN model and CNN-DM, we completed experiments based on the same code, including direct replacement of Softmax with Sparsemax, 1.5-Entmax, sampling the final output distribution using the top-p algorithm, etc. For Sparsemax and 1.5-Entmax, we borrow the code from [19][1].

For the experiments on Transformer model, we followed the setup in [6] and [23]. We trained for 70 epochs.

4.3 Result Analysis

We used ROUGE score [15] to evaluate the comparison methods, which is the most popular evaluation metric in the field of text summarization. ROUGE scores can be divided into ROUGE-N and ROUGE-L. ROUGE-N represents the degree of coincidence of the N consecutive word segmentations between the reference summary and the generated summary. ROUGE-1 and ROUGE-2 are the two most commonly used metrics, and ROUGE-L indicates the degree of overlap between the longest subsequence between the reference and the generated summaries. All ROUGE scores contain both accuracy and recall values, and the general reference is the F1 value of both. The results can be found in Table 1.

As we can see from Table 1, Sparsemax and 1.5-Entmax methods do not perform very well on PGN models using the CNN-DM datasets. The Top-p method works better than the baseline with a p-value of 0.99. Compared with the baseline method, the adaptive sparse distribution method improves the ROUGE-1 score by 0.4 points, the ROUGE-2 score by 0.28 points, and the ROUGE-L score by 0.24 points, which is the highest score among all methods.

As we can see from Table 2, our methods significantly improved the performance of Transformer Model on summarization task. The ROUGE-1 score was improved by 2.25 points on ASFD and 1.36 points on ASAM.

We mentioned earlier that we use Temperature to control the sparsity of the Sparsemax output, and the Temperature value is learned by an additional neural

---

[1] https://github.com/deep-spin/entmax.

Table 1. Experimental results of the proposed Adaptive Sparsemax method and comparison methods on the PGN model

Method	ROUGE-1	ROUGE-2	ROUGE-L
Pointer-Generator+Sparsemax (2017) [17]	39.37	17.23	36.07
Pointer-Generator (2018) [8]	39.53	17.28	36.38
Pointer-Generator+1.5-Entmax (2019) [19]	38.23	16.53	35.27
Pointer-Generator+Top-p (0.98) (2019) [12]	39.04	17.04	35.74
Pointer-Generator+Top-p (0.99) (2019) [12]	39.61	17.44	36.25
Pointer-Generator (2021) [10]	39.39	17.34	36.16
Pointer-Generator+Adaptive Sparsemax (Ours)	**39.79**	**17.62**	**36.40**

Table 2. Experimental results of the proposed Adaptive Sparsemax method on the Transformer model

Method	ROUGE-1	ROUGE-2	ROUGE-L
Transformer [6]	41.93	28.28	38.32
Transformer (2021) [10]	41.73	28.44	39.58
Transformer + ASFD	**43.98**	**29.6**	**40.81**
Transformer + ASAM	43.09	29.16	39.8

network. Figure 5 shows the relationship between the Temperature value of the trained model and the entropy of the output of the entire model. On the left of Fig. 5 is a scatter plot of the relationship between Temperature and entropy.

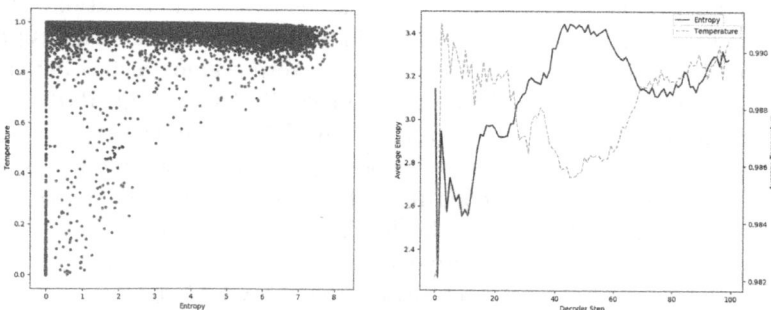

Fig. 5. The relationship between the temperature value generated by the adaptive sparse distribution method and the output entropy.

The Temperature value indicates how many probabilities we keep from the original probability distribution. The lower the temperature value is, the sparser the probability distribution would be. We can see that most of the Temperature values are concentrated above 0.9. There is hardly a single point on the lower right half of the graph, which means that our method does not give lower Temperature values when the entropy output by the model is high. This means that our method takes a more conservative strategy for high-entropy distributions without creating the problem as Top-k methods truncate too much on flat distributions. In contrast, in the low entropy region, our method sometimes gives a lower Temperature, which implies a more aggressive sampling strategy, and the Top-p method cannot dynamically adjust the sampling ratio as such.

On the right side of Fig. 5 is an analysis of the output entropy at different positions of the sentence and the trend of Temperature values. As we can see, at the beginning of a sentence, the output entropy has a rapid decline, and because the PGN model overlays a proportion of the final distribution with the Attention distribution, the entropy of the sentence is not very high at the beginning, and then the entropy trend starts to increase, and only after the average length of the generated summary reaches 58 does the entropy start to decrease (The overall uncertainty is reduced as part of the sentence ends). The interesting thing is that the change in Temperature value is almost the opposite of the trend of entropy. At the beginning of the sentence, the Temperature value is at its lowest, followed by a rapid rise and then a slow fall. For higher entropy, our method adopts a lower Temperature value, that is, adds more sparsity. For locations with lower entropy, our method takes the opposite strategy. This phenomenon can also be reflected in the left image of Fig. 5. The scatter in the upper left corner of the plot is more compact and has a higher average Temperature value. This effect is more obvious when the Temperature value is greater than 0.9. Since the mean Temperature is between 0.98 and 0.99, we set the p-values to be 0.98 and 0.99 when conducting top-p comparison experiments.

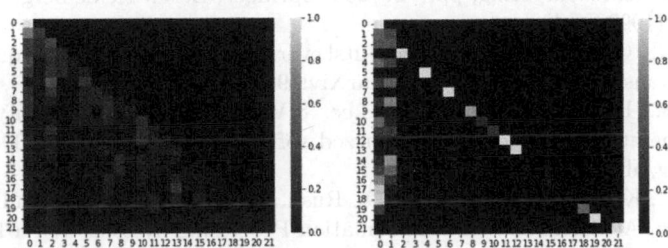

Fig. 6. The attention matrix of Attention Module in Transformer before and after applying Adaptive Sparsemax Method.

Besides, we also record a random sample's attention matrix of the Transformer model. As we can see from Fig. 6, the attention matrix becomes sparser after applying the Adaptive Sparsemax method, which shows that our method can also affect the attention weights of Transformer and leads to better performance and interpretability.

From the above analysis, we can see that our method has different adjustment strategies for different samples. Since the outputs of both Encoder and Decoder are introduced into the module of our method, the method can use the information of both for learning. Due to the introduction of adaptive learning neural networks, compared with other methods, our method has the advantage of not needing to set hyperparameters, which also means that our method can adjust the distribution in a finer way.

5   Conclusion

In this paper, we present the Adaptive Sparsemax method and apply it to the abstractive summarization task. Our approach adaptively adjusts the sparsity of the output distribution. The experimental results we give demonstrate that our method effectively improves the performance of the model. The analysis shows how our method impact the output distribution of the model. In the future study, we want to apply our method to other models and bring new insights into the sparsity in those models.

Acknowledgements. This work was supported by the NSFC Project 62006078 and STCSM Project 22ZR1421700.

References

1. Ackley, D.H.: A learning algorithm for boltzmann machines. Cognitive Science 9 (1985)
2. Bridle, J.S.: Probabilistic interpretation of feedforward classification network outputs, with relationships to statistical pattern recognition. In: Soulié, F.F., Hérault, J. (eds.) Neurocomputing, pp. 227–236. Springer, Berlin Heidelberg, Berlin, Heidelberg (1990)
3. Child, R., Gray, S., Radford, A., Sutskever, I.: Generating long sequences with sparse transformers. arXiv preprint arXiv:1904.10509 (2019)
4. Choi, B., Hong, J., Park, D.K., Lee, S.W.: F2-softmax: Diversifying neural text generation via frequency factorized softmax. CoRR abs/2009.09417 (2020), arxiv.org/abs/2009.09417
5. Deng, Y., Kim, Y., Chiu, J., Guo, D., Rush, A.: Latent alignment and variational attention. Advances in Neural Information Processing Systems 31 (2018)
6. Duan, X., Yu, H., Yin, M., Zhang, M., Luo, W., Zhang, Y.: Contrastive attention mechanism for abstractive sentence summarization. In: Proceedings of the 2019 Conference on Empirical Methods in Natural Language Processing and the 9th International Joint Conference on Natural Language Processing (EMNLP-IJCNLP), pp. 3035–3044 (2019)
7. Fan, A., Lewis, M., Dauphin, Y.: Hierarchical neural story generation. In: Proceedings of the 56th Annual Meeting of the Association for Computational Linguistics (Volume 1: Long Papers), pp. 889–898 (2018)
8. Gehrmann, S., Deng, Y., Rush, A.M.: Bottom-up abstractive summarization. In: Proceedings of the 2018 Conference on Empirical Methods in Natural Language Processing, pp. 4098–4109 (2018)
9. Gu, J., Lu, Z., Li, H., Li, V.O.: Incorporating copying mechanism in sequence-to-sequence learning. In: Proceedings of the 54th Annual Meeting of the Association for Computational Linguistics (Volume 1: Long Papers), pp. 1631–1640 (2016)

10. Guo, S., Zhao, J., Sun, S.: Resilient abstractive summarization model with adaptively weighted training loss. In: International Joint Conference on Neural Networks, IJCNN 2021, Shenzhen, China, pp. 1–8. IEEE (2021)
11. Hermann, K.M., et al.: Teaching machines to read and comprehend. Adv. Neural. Inf. Process. Syst. **28**, 1693–1701 (2015)
12. Holtzman, A., Buys, J., Du, L., Forbes, M., Choi, Y.: The curious case of neural text degeneration. In: International Conference on Learning Representations (2019)
13. Hu, B., Chen, Q., Zhu, F.: Lcsts: a large scale Chinese short text summarization dataset. In: Proceedings of the 2015 Conference on Empirical Methods in Natural Language Processing, pp. 1967–1972 (2015)
14. Laha, A., Chemmengath, S.A., Agrawal, P., Khapra, M., Sankaranarayanan, K., Ramaswamy, H.G.: On controllable sparse alternatives to softmax. Advances in neural information processing systems 31 (2018)
15. Lin, C.Y.: Rouge: a package for automatic evaluation of summaries. In: Text summarization branches out, pp. 74–81 (2004)
16. Malaviya, C., Ferreira, P., Martins, A.F.: Sparse and constrained attention for neural machine translation. arXiv preprint arXiv:1805.08241 (2018)
17. Martins, A.F.T., Astudillo, R.F.: From softmax to sparsemax: A sparse model of attention and multi-label classification. CoRR abs/1602.02068 (2016), arxiv.org/abs/1602.02068
18. Nallapati, R., Zhou, B., dos Santos, C.N., Gülçehre, Ç., Xiang, B.: Abstractive text summarization using sequence-to-sequence RNNs and beyond. In: Goldberg, Y., Riezler, S. (eds.) Proceedings of the 20th SIGNLL Conference on Computational Natural Language Learning, CoNLL 2016, Berlin, Germany, 11–12 August, 2016, pp. 280–290. ACL (2016)
19. Peters, B., Niculae, V., Martins, A.F.T.: Sparse sequence-to-sequence models. CoRR abs/1905.05702 (2019). arxiv.org/abs/1905.05702
20. Rush, A.M., Chopra, S., Weston, J.: A neural attention model for abstractive sentence summarization. In: Proceedings of the 2015 Conference on Empirical Methods in Natural Language Processing, pp. 379–389 (2015)
21. See, A., Liu, P.J., Manning, C.D.: Get to the point: Summarization with pointer-generator networks. In: Proceedings of the 55th Annual Meeting of the Association for Computational Linguistics (Volume 1: Long Papers), pp. 1073–1083 (2017)
22. Sutskever, I., Vinyals, O., Le, Q.V.: Sequence to sequence learning with neural networks. Adv. Neural. Inf. Process. Syst. **27**, 3104–3112 (2014)
23. Vaswani, A., et al.: Attention is all you need. In: Advances in neural information processing systems, pp. 5998–6008 (2017)
24. Xu, J., Desai, S., Durrett, G.: Understanding neural abstractive summarization models via uncertainty. arXiv preprint arXiv:2010.07882 (2020)
25. Zhao, G., Lin, J., Zhang, Z., Ren, X., Su, Q., Sun, X.: Explicit sparse transformer: Concentrated attention through explicit selection. arXiv preprint arXiv:1912.11637 (2019)

Hierarchical Planning of Topic-Comment Structure for Paper Abstract Writing

Mingyue Han[1], Ruifang He[1,2(✉)], and Huijie Wang[2]

[1] State Key Laboratory of Communication Content Cognition,
People's Daily Online China, Beijing, China
[2] Tianjin Key Laboratory of Cognitive Computing and Application,
College of Intelligence and Computing, Tianjin University, Tianjin, China
{rfhe,wanghj_s}@tju.edu.cn

Abstract. Paper abstract writing aims to generate medium-long content with the given paper title. It is challenging to generate coherent and accurate paper abstract. Previous work utilize graph data for assistance, while they cannot perform well in long-term coherence due to the lack of efficient text planning, or simply utilize the knowledge graph without distinguishing, thus introducing redundant information which may impair the quality of generated abstract. To this end, we propose a hierarchical planning model based on topic-comment structure for paper abstract writing. Specifically, first we acquire a sequence of topics from graph data in discourse-level planning about what each sentence to do, and then plan comments in sentence-level planning about how to do with the corresponding topic. Topic and comment are the core of abstract. Furthermore, in the second-stage planning, we propose a novel planning mechanism that can separate the knowledge graph into comment subgraphs. It only preserves useful vertices that reduces the candidate set. Experiments prove our model's effectiveness in generating coherent and accurate paper abstracts, and its overall performance is better than the baseline models in both automatic and human evaluation.

Keywords: Natural language generation · Text planning · Knowledge graph · Hierarchical structure

1 Introduction

Paper abstract writing is the first crucial step to express the scientific paper, which aims to generate the coherent and accurate abstract with the given paper title. A paper abstract has multiple sentences, and it focuses more on the overall coherence. Furthermore, we expect each sentence in abstract has its own meaning to describe an aspect of paper accurately, for example, what the paper is about.

However, there are at least two challenges in paper abstract writing. First, previous work [19,24] mainly make extensions based on sequential neural networks that cannot obtain long-term coherence. The limited paper title aggravates

© The Author(s), under exclusive license to Springer Nature Switzerland AG 2022
W. Lu et al. (Eds.): NLPCC 2022, LNAI 13551, pp. 822–834, 2022.
https://doi.org/10.1007/978-3-031-17120-8_63

Table 1. An excerpt of abstract of paper "A trainable...challenge". The red are topics and the bold are comments. The abstract consists of sentence (a–c). The sentences follow the topic-comment structure, topic about what the sentence do and comment about how to do.

A trainable trajectory formation model TD-HMM parameterized for the LIPS 2008 challenge [1]
(a) trainable trajectory formation model predicts **articulatory trajectories** of a talking face from **phonetic input.**
(b) trainable trajectory formation model basically uses **hmm-based synthesis** but asynchrony between acoustic and gestural boundaries
(c) the hmm triphones and the phasing model are trained simultaneously using an **iterative analysis-synthesis loop**

this issue [5, 26]. Second, recent researches prove that injecting knowledge graphs can improve the quality of generated text [2, 4, 9, 13, 26] in other NLG (natural language generation) tasks. While, most of them inject the representation of knowledge graphs into the generator without distinguishing (utilizing knowledge graph without planning when generates different sentence). It is not the best solution for paper abstract writing to obtain the long-term coherence. Moreover, there is redundant information in knowledge graph, and utilizing them without distinguishing can impair the quality of generated abstract.

We present the human-written paper abstract in Table 1. Human-written abstract prefers valuable and informative words and avoids safe but meaningless content. We deem the sentence in abstract follows the topic-comment structure [6], the topic is about what the sentence do, and the comment is about how to do. For example, the "hmm triphones" is the topic of what the sentence(c) talks about, and the "iterative analysis-synthesis loop" is about how to talk about the topic. Each sentence has its own topic that expresses what the sentence to do. The comment provides the detail information about the corresponding topic how to do, it can further avoid sentences meaning repetitiveness even they have same topic as sentence (a–b) show.

To this end, we propose hierarchical planning of topic-comment structure for paper abstract writing (short as the T-C model). As Fig. 1 shows, there are two-stage planning. 1) Topic planning is the discourse-level planning that plans a sequence of topics about what each sentence is to do. 2) Comment planning is the sentence-level planning that plans a comment sub-graph through planning mechanism for the corresponding topic. There are distinctive sub-graphs for different topics. We define the combination of k_{th} topic and k_{th} comment sub-graph as the sentence role for k_{th} sentence.

Furthermore, to obtain the corresponding comment sub-graph for each sentence and reduce the candidate set, we design a planning mechanism that can score vertex in the knowledge graph with the given topic. Comment sub-graph only preserves relevant vertices whose score over hyperparameter β and masks irrelevant vertices.

We evaluate the model on AGENDA dataset [10]. Our model shows its advantage in both automatic and human evaluations. Extensive analysis and case studies are provided to investigate the reason causing the advantage. Our contribution can be summarized as follows:

- We propose a hierarchical planning of topic-comment structure for paper abstract writing. To the best of our knowledge, we are the first to utilize the topic-comment structure in paper abstract writing. It also can be applied to other NLG task.
- We design a planning mechanism that can separate the knowledge graph into sub-graph with the given topic. The sub-graph only contains related information to corresponding topic, it can reduce the candidate set and improve the quality of generated abstract.
- Extensive experiments show our model is effective.

2   Related Work

2.1   Text Generation Model

It is difficult for neural models to obtain long-term coherence. In short text generation, [2,5,9,21], the knowledge graph can improve the quality of the short text. However, the main reason that existing models cannot obtain long-term coherence is most of them lack overall consideration and arrangement of text structure. Moreover, most of them learn the representation of knowledge graph and input them into the decoder without distinguishing, that bring the redundant information.

Text planning is a feasible method to solve the above issues. Recent neural models [11,16,18,21] learn a plan from the input data, and then generate text relying on the plan. These methods try to generate short text, and they cannot take their superior performance into paper abstract writing [7,15,16]. What's more, most of them are only concerned about the discourse-level planning. Thus, we propose a model architecture that can apply to paper abstract writing. It reduces the knowledge graph and models the text structure from discourse and sentence level.

2.2   Paper Abstract Writing

Paper abstract writing [10,24] aims to generate coherent and accurate abstracts with the given paper title. Different from the text summarization that compresses long text into short text, our task generates a long abstract from a short input. There are multiple sentences in an abstract, in human-written abstract, each sentence has its own role to describe the different aspects of the paper. Thus, the sentence role should be considered. Sentence role is about what information is to be presented in a single sentence. We deem the sentence role follows the topic-comment structure [6]. It splits the sentence into two parts: topic and comment. The topic is what the sentence does, and the comment is about how to do it. Following this theory, we propose a hierarchical planning model, which can plan the topic and the corresponding comment for each sentence.

3 Basic Notations

Our model is trained on AGENDA dataset to learn paper abstract writing. The paper title $X = \{x_1, x_2, \ldots, x_m, <sum>\}$ has m tokens, where x_i is the i_{th} token in title, the special token $<sum>$ is the average sum of representation of all tokens . Knowledge graph $\mathcal{G} = \{V, E\}$, the set of vertices $V = \{v_1, v_2, \ldots, v_{|V|}\}$, where $|V|$ is the size of the vertices set. $E = \{e_{ij}\}$ is the edge set, e_{ij} is the edge between v_i and v_j. The abstract $Y = \{Y_1, Y_2, \ldots, Y_n\}$, where Y_i is the i_{th} sentence that consists of $Y_i = \{w_{i1}, w_{i2}, \ldots, w_{ij}, <sum>\}$ where w_{ij} is the j_{th} word in i_{th} sentence, the special token $<sum>$ is the average sum of all tokens in Y_i. We define the topic as $T = \{t_1, t_2, \ldots, t_n\}$ and comment sub-graph as $g = \{g_1, g_2, \ldots, g_n\}$, and there are n topics and comment sub-graph.

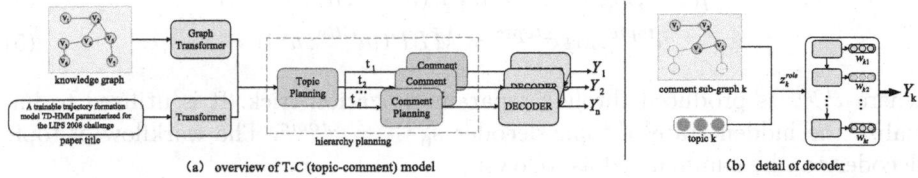

(a) overview of T-C (topic-comment) model   (b) detail of decoder

Fig. 1. The left is the overview of T-C (topic-comment) model. The right is the detail information of decoder when generate k_{th} sentence. v_4 is the topic for k_{th} sentence. The blue is copied from comment sub-graph. (Color figure online)

4 Model

4.1 Encoder

Transformer [22] encoder and Graph Transformer [3] encoder are utilized to encode paper title and knowledge graph respectively.

The Transformer encoder [22] takes paper title as input. We can get the title representation H_l^{title} at l layer in Transformer encoder as follow:

$$H_l^{title} = FFN(MHA(H_{l-1}^{title}, H_{l-1}^{title}, H_{l-1}^{title})) \quad (1)$$

where FFN is the fully-connected feed-forward network and the MHA is multi head attention. We define the H^{title} as the hidden state at final layer, where $H^{title} = \{h^{x_1}, h^{x_2}, \ldots, h^{x_m}, h^{<sum>}\}$, h^{x_i} is the hidden state of x_i, and define the $h^{title} = h^{<sum>}$ as the hidden state of title.

The graph Transformer encoder [3] replaces sinusoidal positional embedding which can help encoder distance-aware information. The representations of vertex and edge at l layer H_l^V and H_l^E can be formulated as follows:

$$H_l^V = FFN(MHA(H_{l-1}^V, H_{l-1}^V, H_{l-1}^V)) \quad (2)$$

$$H_l^E = FFN(MHA(H_{l-1}^E, H_{l-1}^E, H_{l-1}^E)) \quad (3)$$

We define the final layer outputs as $H^{\mathcal{G}} = \{h^{v_1}, h^{v_2}, \ldots, h^{v_{|V|}}\}$, where h^{v_i} is the output of v_i at final layer. We process $H^{\mathcal{G}}$ by LSTM layer to obtain the overall hidden state of knowledge graph $h^{\mathcal{G}}$.

4.2   Topic Planning

Topic planning module studies how to generate a sequence of topics to discern sentences functional differences. We utilize the latent variable z^{topic} that carries implicit information from input data to initialize the topic decoder. Topic decoder can pick out a sequence of related vertices from knowledge graph [14, 17, 21] as the topic plan.

In training phase, z^{topic} is sampled from posterior distribution that has mean μ and variance $\log \sigma$, and in testing phase, it is sampled from prior distribution.

$$\mu^{topic}, \log \sigma^{topic} = MLP([h^{title}; h^{\mathcal{G}}; h^{topic}]) \tag{4}$$

$$\hat{\mu}^{topic}, \log \hat{\sigma}^{topic} = MLP([h^{title}; h^{\mathcal{G}}]) \tag{5}$$

where z^{topic} is produced through reparameterization trick. It is utilized to initialize the hidden state of topic decoder $s_0^{topic} = z^{topic}$. The workflow of topic decoder can be summarized as follows:

$$s_k^{topic} = Dec([idx_{k-1}; z^{topic}], s_{k-1}^{topic}) \tag{6}$$

$$idx_k = Softmax(Tanh(W^{topic}([s_k^{topic}; H^{\mathcal{G}}]) + b^{topic}) \tag{7}$$

$$\hat{t}_k = v_{idx_k} \tag{8}$$

where W^{topic} and b^{topic} are trainable parameters in topic decoder, s_k^{topic} is the hidden state of topic decoder at k_{th} step. We do not plan topic directly, instead generate the vertex index in $\mathcal{G}$ which can better train the model. idx_k is the probability distribution of index over knowledge graph, and the idx_k means topic decoder picks the v_{idx_k} as the generated topic $\hat{t}_k$.

Finally, we can get the set of generated index $idx = \{idx_1, idx_2, \ldots, idx_n\}$ and obtained topic set $\hat{T}$.

Topic Planning Loss: we short prior distribution and posterior distribution as $p(z^{topic})$ and $q(z^{topic})$ respectively. Thus the loss function $logP(\hat{T}|X, \mathcal{G})$ (L_1) is:

$$L_1 = E_{q(z^{topic})}[logP(idx|X, \mathcal{G}, z^{topic})] - D_{kl}(q(z^{topic})||p(z^{topic})) \tag{9}$$

4.3   Comment Planning

Each sentence has its own topic and comment, in this section we present how to plan the comment sub-graph for k_{th} sentence with t_k. The comment is about what being said about the topic, thus the vertex in comment sub-graph should be close with t_k and coherent with previous sentences in abstract. We devise a segment mechanism to achieve this goal.

Plan mechanism separates the knowledge graph into sub-graph through scoring each vertex, whose score below β will be masked. While, the scoring process is not only rely on the relevance of topic t_k, but also takes the coherent with previous roles into account.

The workflow of comment decoder can be seen as follows:

$$s_k^{com} = Dec\left(h^{t_k}, s_{k-1}^{com}\right) \tag{10}$$

$$sc\hat{o}re_{1:|V|} = Sigmoid(Tanh(W^{com}([s_k^{com}; H^{\mathcal{G}}]) + b^{com})) \tag{11}$$

$$g_k = \{v_i \mid sc\hat{o}re_i > \beta\} \tag{12}$$

W^{com} and b^{com} are trainable parameters in planning mechanism, s_k^{com} is the hidden state of comment decoder at k_{th}, the $sc\hat{o}re_{1:|V|}$ is the vertex score under the hidden state s_k^{com}, $sc\hat{o}re_i$ reveals the necessity of v_i in k_{th} sentence, and g_k is the comment sub-graph of topic t_k that only contains vertex whose score over β.

Comment Planning Loss: L_2^k is the binary cross entropy loss of comment module at k_{th} time.

$$L_2^k = -\sum_{v<|V|} score_i log(sc\hat{o}re_i) - (1 - score_i)log(1 - sc\hat{o}re_i) \tag{13}$$

in which $sc\hat{o}re_i$ is the score from planning mechanism, the $score_i$ is the vertex score for g_k in dataset obtained by heuristics.

4.4   Generation Module

We employ a latent variable z_k^{role} to model the role of sentence Y_k. Throw the topic planning and comment planning, we have the topic information and comment sub-graph. To ensure the context coherent, we force the role of sentence not only learn the topic and comment, but also learn the previous sentence roles.

Sentence role z_k^{role} is effected by previous role, we set s_k^{role} as the hidden state of sentence role. Thus, the sampling of z_k^{role} is same as the z^{topic}, we set μ_k^{role} and σ_k^{role} as the mean and variance of posterior distribution and $\hat{\mu}_k^{role}, \log \hat{\sigma}_k^{role}$ is for prior distribution.

$$s_k^{role} = LSTM(z_{k-1}^{role}, s_{k-1}^{role}) \tag{14}$$

$$\mu_k^{role}, \log \sigma_k^{role} = MLP([h^{t_k}; h^{g_k}; s_k^{role}; h^{Y_k}]) \tag{15}$$

$$\hat{\mu}_k^{role}, \log \hat{\sigma}_k^{role} = MLP([h^{t_k}; h^{g_k}; s_k^{role}]) \tag{16}$$

The sentence role z_k^{role} can be utilized to instruct sentence generation, and h^{Y_k} is the hidden state of Y_k. It is obtained similar to h^{title}, and only used in training phase. Y_k is processed by Transformer encoder and set the hidden state of token $<sum>$ as h^{Y_k}.

Sentence Generation: Sentence decoder is initialized by sentence role: $s_{k0}^{word} = z_k^{role}$.

$$s_{kt}^{word} = Dec([emb(w_{kt}); \tilde{H}^{t_k}; \tilde{H}^{g_k}; z_k^{role}], s_{kt-1}^{word})$$

s_{kt}^{word} is the t_{th} hidden state for k_{th} sentence generation. $\tilde{H}^{t_k}$ is the variant of H^{t_k} after attention mechanism, $\tilde{H}_k^g$ is the same.

The predictive probability of a word can be decomposed into two parts [17], either generation from the vocabulary or copying from the comment sub-graph.

$$w_{kt} = p_{kt} * \alpha_{kt}^{vocab} + (1 - p_{kt}) * \alpha_{kt}^{copy} \tag{17}$$

$$\alpha_{kt}^{copy} = Softmax(Tanh(W^{copy}([s_{kt}^{word}; H^{g_k}]) + b^{copy})) \tag{18}$$

w_{kt} is the t_{th} token of k_{th} sentence, α_{kt}^{vocab} is the probability distribution from the decoder, and α_{kt}^{copy} is the probability of coping from comment sub-graph. We use p_{kt} to control the combination of topic and comment.

$$p_{kt} = Softmax(Tanh(W^{word}([s_{kt}^{word}, H_k^{tp}; H_k^g]) + b^{word})) \tag{19}$$

where the W^{word} and b^{word} are trainable parameters.

Generation Module Loss. L_3^k is the loss of generation in k_{th} sentence. To avoid the copy vertex continuously, we employ a supervised signal to control $\tilde{p}_{kt}$ whether copy.

$$L_3^k = \sum_{t<n} E_{q(z_k^{role})}[logP(w_{kt}|t_k, g_k, z_k^{role})] - D_{kl}(q(z_k^{role})||p(z_k^{role}))$$

$$- \sum_{t<n} p_{kt}log(\tilde{p}_{kt}) - (1 - p_{kt})log(1 - \tilde{p}_{kt}) \tag{20}$$

4.5 Model Training

The loss consists of three parts: (1) topic planning loss L_1, (2) comment loss L_2 is the sum of all inner blocks, (3) generation loss L_3.

$$L = L_1 + \sum_{k<n} (L_2^k + L_3^k)$$

5 Experiments

5.1 Datasets and Implementation Details

We evaluate T-C model on AGENDA dataset [10], which Fig. 2 is from Semantic Scholar Corpus that contains 40k AI paper title and its abstract, and provides paired knowledge graph with title. The detailed information of the dataset are presented as Fig. 2 shows. The average length of abstract is 141.2. There are 5.56 sentences in abstract, and each sentence has 20.49 words on average. The knowledge graph contains 12.42 vertices on average that the average length of vertex is 2.5.

We adopt a 6 layers Transformer and 6 layers Graph Transformer as encoder in inter block. Transformer and Graph Transformer encoder have 8 heads, and set the size of embedding is 512. We also set the size of hidden state size as 512, the size of latent variable is 30. We adopt best performance $\beta = 0.4$. All decoders in our T-C model are based on bidirectional GRU model with 2 layers. We set max decoding sentence length as 15. We train model with Adam optimizer with batch size 16, and learning rate 0.0005. We multiply 0.1 to the KL divergence terms to prevent posterior collapse.

	Title	Abstract	KG
vocab	29k	77k	54k
tokens	413K	5.8M	1.2M
entities	-	-	518k
avg length	9.9	141.2	2.5
avg sentences	1	5.56	-
avg words	9.8	20.49	-
avg edges	-	-	4.43
avg vertices	-	-	12.42

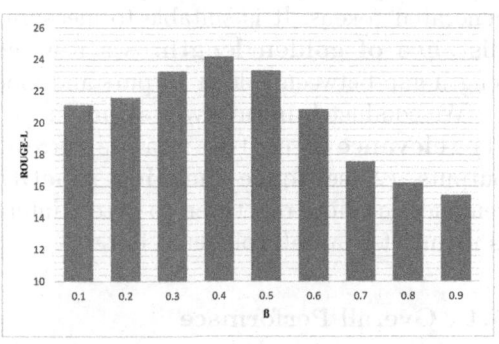

Fig. 2. Detailed information of AGENDA dataset.

Fig. 3. The effect of β in comment module

5.2 Baselines

We compare our model with the following baselines:

(1) **Seq2Seq** [20]: a basic and representative encoder-decoder structure that can adapt to most text generation task.
(2) **Rewriter** [24]: multi-pass decoding model based on seq2seq, can iteratively examine, improve and polish the abstract with inputs guidance.
(3) **CVAE** [27]: proposed in dialogue generation task. It also has strong capacity in long text generation.
(4) **ml-cvae** [19]: has multi-level encoder and multi-level decoder based on latent variable model, takes sentence structure into consideration.
(5) **GAT** [23]: is a knowledge enhanced model. It takes knowledge graph as input to generate long text.
(6) **Graphwriter** [10]: a data-to-text model. It has Graph Transformer as encoder and copy mechanism in decoder and converts disconnected labeled graph to connect unlabeled graph for Graph Transformer encoder.
(7) **BART** [12]: a pre-trained model, has been fine-tuned on the downstream datasets with language model objective.
(8) **Stylized** [11]: a planning model based on BART. With leading topics, it can generate distinctive sentence.

5.3 Metric

The **automatic evaluation** metrics are as follows: (1) **BLEU** can measure n-gram overlapping proportion, which is the similarity between the generation outputs and golden outputs in terms of n-gram. (2) **ROUGE** is a kind of recall-based metric, we adopt ROUGE-L that measures the longest common subsequence. (3) **DISTINCT** is enable to measure the ratio of distinct n-grams in generated tokens. It is suitable to measure the inner-sentence incoherence. (4) **distance of golden length**: is a new metric that can measure the average length gap between golden outputs and model outputs.

We conduct **human evaluation** on the generated text using three metrics: (1) **relevance** is used to measure correlation between inputs and generated outputs. (2) **sentence meaning repetition** is used to measure the rate of sentence meaning repetition to detect inter-sentence coherence. (3) **coherence** is mainly for overall coherence in text.

5.4 Overall Performace

5.4.1 Automatic Evaluation

Table 2 shows the experimental results of all baselines and our model.

Table 2. The automatic evaluation of baselines. The up-arrow means the higher the score, the better the performance. Down-arrow means the lower the score, the better the performance. The best scores are bolded, and the second best scores are underlined.

Models	BLEU-1↑	BLEU-2 ↑	BLEU-4↑	ROUGE-L↑	Dist-4↑	distance↓
seq2seq	18.184	7.92	1.525	16.642	82.62	62.61
rewriter	22.492	9.091	1.773	15.908	86.95	31.19
CVAE	20.462	11.988	2.543	14.681	52.83	5.20
ml-cvae	27.013	16.694	5.360	18.380	61.83	_4.92_
GAT	36.042	22.093	_12.741_	24.375	70.13	10.48
graphwriter	_38.495_	_25.690_	**13.023**	_27.640_	73.72	27.33
BART	24.728	10.571	2.136	16.742	88.71	34.41
Stylized	25.961	18.076	4.554	19.203	**92.72**	52.02
Ours	**39.823**	**25.932**	10.511	**29.253**	_91.51_	**4.14**

We can observe that: (1) Compared with rewriter and ml-cvae, seq2seq and CVAE have worse score because they have flat structure. They ignore the sentence role that model sentence structure explicitly, proving the effectiveness of the sentence role. Our model has better performance as we consider structure information and adopt external knowledge graph.

(2) The comparison between T-C model and graph model (GAT, graphwirter) demonstrates that just inject external knowledge cannot solve long text generation thoroughly. Although graphwriter reach the best score in BLEU-4, because

the average length of vertex is 2.5, it copy vertex continuously can obtained the higher BLEU-4 score without the coherent. While, our model get a slightly inferior score in BLEU-4, it has a better performance in overall evaluation and avoid the sentence meaning repetitiveness.

(3) Stylized has the highest distinct score. With numerous data pre-trained, stylized has strong ability to generate diversity text. But it cannot obtain the consistency. It tends to generate long text that is irrelevant to the input because the understanding ability of pre-trained model in new task is not enough [8,25]. Incomplete modeling of sentence roles can not reach the overall performance. Instead, T-C model has a balance between consistent and diversity.

5.4.2 Human Evaluation

We first randomly sample 100 examples from rewriter, ml-cvae, stylized and graphwriter, and then require participants mark sampled examples in the range of 1–10. In human metrics, relevance and coherence expect higher score, and sentence meaning repetition expects lower score that means less repetitiveness.

Table 3. Human evaluation

Models	relev	repeti	coher
rewriter	3.58	5.78	4.59
ml-cvae	3.24	7.96	5.54
stylized	5.68	6.21	6.89
graphwriter	7.58	7.98	6.23
Ours	7.94	4.84	7.04

Table 4. Ablation study

Models	BLEU-1	Rouge-L	Dist-1
Ours	39.82	29.25	63.95
-graph	19.58	13.23	22.47
-role	29.74	17.85	28.18
-comment	35.05	20.13	23.92

As the Table 3 shows, We unexpectedly find that rewriter model has better performance in sentence meaning repetition than other models, it can be owing to the multi-pass decoding. Another surprise is graphwriter model. It receives the worst score in sentence meaning repetition, proving that the simply coping vertex from knowledge graph leads to incoherence. Our model avoids the shortage and improve its performance in overall human evaluation.

What's more, there are divergence in Stylized. Most of participants think Stylized has better performance in shorter text (less than 100 words) and has worse performance in longer text (more than 100 words). It is a typical case for most language models because longer text means complicated relationship. The dreadful performance in sentence meaning repetition also proving our model with inner-sentence structure is better than model who only consider topic planning.

5.5 Ablation Study

To further explore the impact of different components in our model. We express ablation study by training ablated versions of our model: without knowledge graph, without sentence role, and without comment planning. Our model cannot only take topic planning away and preserve comment planning, because the comment planning relies on the topic result. We present in Table 4.

As the absence of external knowledge, T-C model cannot utilize knowledge graphs to mitigate the gap of length between inputs and outputs. Therefore the result of -w/o graph obviously has the worst performance, explaining the importance of sufficient inputs. In T-C model without sentence role abbreviated as -w/o role. It leverages external knowledge graph, but not plans sentence role also without topic and comment planning. Thus, the flat graph model cannot capture structure information and has worse performance. We test effectiveness of model without comment, the -w/o comment cannot catch up with T-C model at all metric, because only considering topic planning is incomplete to model sentence structure.

The ablated experiments support our assumption: (1) external knowledge graph can help long text generation. (2) structure information covers some important semantic information. (3) inter- and inner-sentence structures also favorable to long text generation.

5.6 Parameter Analysis

In comment planning and generation module, we set a hyperparameter β to control the comment sub-graph construction. We validate the impact of different β in metric ROUGE-L.

We find two rules from the Fig. 3. Firstly, the highest score is at $\beta = 0.4$. In AGENDA dataset, there are only 20% vertices in knowledge graph can be used in a single sentence. Ideally we should set $\beta = 0.8$ as the Fig. 3 shows, however, considering the impact of relationship between different vertices, it is reasonable to set $\beta = 0.4$. Secondly, although the ROUGE-L score declines overall, the score at $\beta = 0.1, 0.2$ still higher than $\beta = 0.8, 0.9$. Because larger β means stricter entry. With a relax β that most of vertices have chance to be hold up, the comment graph can carry much more information than stricter β. With the strictest $\beta = 1.0$, T-C model degrades to a model that only consider topic, and has a terrible score.

6 Conclusion

We propose a novel hierarchical planning model of topic-comment structure for paper abstract writing. It adopts the topic-comment structure as theory basis to support the hierarchical planning. We first plan a sequence of topics that about what each sentence to do, and then plan the comment sub-graph related to the topic that about how to do. The combination of topic and comment can decide the sentence role and better model the sentence generation. Experiments prove our model's effectiveness in generating paper abstract.

Acknowledgments. Our work is supported by the National Natural Science Foundation of China (61976154), the National Key R&D Program of China

(2019YFC1521200), the State Key Laboratory of Communication Content Cognition, People's Daily Online (No. A32003)

References

1. Bailly, G., Govokhina, O., Breton, G., Elisei, F., Savariaux, C.: The trainable trajectory formation model td-hmm parameterized for the lips 2008 challenge. In: Interspeech 2008–9th Annual Conference of the International Speech Communication Association, p. 561 (2008)
2. Cheng, L., et al.: Ent-desc: entity description generation by exploring knowledge graph. In: Proceedings of the 2020 Conference on Empirical Methods in Natural Language Processing (EMNLP), pp. 1187–1197 (2020)
3. Dwivedi, V.P., Bresson, X.: A generalization of transformer networks to graphs. In: Methods and Applications, AAAI Workshop on Deep Learning on Graphs (2021)
4. Guan, J., Huang, F., Zhao, Z., Zhu, X., Huang, M.: A knowledge-enhanced pretraining model for commonsense story generation. Trans. Assoc. Comput. Linguist. 8, 93–108 (2020). https://doi.org/10.1162/tacl-a-00302. https://aclanthology.org/2020.tacl-1.7
5. Guan, J., Mao, X., Fan, C., Liu, Z., Ding, W., Huang, M.: Long text generation by modeling sentence-level and discourse-level coherence. In: Proceedings of the 59th Annual Meeting of the Association for Computational Linguistics and the 11th International Joint Conference on Natural Language Processing (Volume 1: Long Papers), pp. 6379–6393. Association for Computational Linguistics, Online, August 2021. https://doi.org/10.18653/v1/2021.acl-long.499, https://aclanthology.org/2021.acl-long.499
6. Halliday, M.A.K., Matthiessen, C.M., Halliday, M., Matthiessen, C.: An Introduction to Functional Grammar. Routledge, London (2014)
7. Junyi Li, W.X.Z., Wei, Z., Yuan, N.J., Wen, J.R.: Knowledge-based review generation by coherence enhanced text planning. In: SIGIR (2021)
8. Kassner, N., Schütze, H.: Negated and misprimed probes for pretrained language models: birds can talk, but cannot fly. In: Proceedings of the 58th Annual Meeting of the Association for Computational Linguistics, pp. 7811–7818. Association for Computational Linguistics, Online, July 2020. https://doi.org/10.18653/v1/2020.acl-main.698, https://aclanthology.org/2020.acl-main.698
9. Ke, P., et al.: JointGT: graph-text joint representation learning for text generation from knowledge graphs. In: Findings of the Association for Computational Linguistics: ACL-IJCNLP 2021, pp. 2526–2538, August 2021
10. Koncel-Kedziorski, R., Bekal, D., Luan, Y., Lapata, M., Hajishirzi, H.: Text generation from knowledge graphs with graph transformers. In: Proceedings of the 2019 Conference of the North American Chapter of the Association for Computational Linguistics: Human Language Technologies, Volume 1 (Long and Short Papers), pp. 2284–2293, June 2019
11. Kong, X., Huang, J., Tung, Z., Guan, J., Huang, M.: Stylized story generation with style-guided planning. In: Findings of the Association for Computational Linguistics: ACL-IJCNLP 2021, pp. 2430–2436 (2021)
12. Lewis, M., et al.: Bart: denoising sequence-to-sequence pre-training for natural language generation, translation, and comprehension. In: Proceedings of the 58th Annual Meeting of the Association for Computational Linguistics, pp. 7871–7880 (2020)

13. Liang, Y., Meng, F., Zhang, Y., Chen, Y., Xu, J., Zhou, J.: Infusing multi-source knowledge with heterogeneous graph neural network for emotional conversation generation. In: Proceedings of the AAAI Conference on Artificial Intelligence, vol. 35, pp. 13343–13352 (2021)
14. Puduppully, R., Dong, L., Lapata, M.: Data-to-text generation with content selection and planning. In: Proceedings of the AAAI Conference on Artificial Intelligence, vol. 33, pp. 6908–6915 (2019)
15. Puduppully, R., Lapata, M.: Data-to-text generation with macro planning. Trans. Assoc. Comput. Linguist. **9**, 510–527 (2021)
16. Qiao, L., Yan, J., Meng, F., Yang, Z., Zhou, J.: A sentiment-controllable topic-to-essay generator with topic knowledge graph. In: Proceedings of the 2020 Conference on Empirical Methods in Natural Language Processing: Findings, pp. 3336–3344 (2020)
17. See, A., Liu, P.J., Manning, C.D.: Get to the point: summarization with pointer-generator networks. In: Proceedings of the 55th Annual Meeting of the Association for Computational Linguistics (Volume 1: Long Papers), pp. 1073–1083 (2017)
18. Shao, Z., Huang, M., Wen, J., Xu, W., Zhu, X.: Long and diverse text generation with planning-based hierarchical variational model. In: Proceedings of the 2019 Conference on Empirical Methods in Natural Language Processing and the 9th International Joint Conference on Natural Language Processing (EMNLP-IJCNLP), pp. 3257–3268 (2019)
19. Shen, D., et al.: Towards generating long and coherent text with multi-level latent variable models. In: Proceedings of the 57th Annual Meeting of the Association for Computational Linguistics, pp. 2079–2089, July 2019
20. Sutskever, I., Vinyals, O., Le, Q.V.: Sequence to sequence learning with neural networks, vol. 27 (2014)
21. Trisedya, B., Qi, J., Zhang, R.: Sentence generation for entity description with content-plan attention. In: Proceedings of the AAAI Conference on Artificial Intelligence, vol. 34, pp. 9057–9064 (2020)
22. Vaswani, A., et al.: Attention is all you need. In: Advances in Neural Information Processing Systems, pp. 5998–6008 (2017)
23. Veličković, P., Cucurull, G., Casanova, A., Romero, A., Liò, P., Bengio, Y.: Graph attention networks. In: International Conference on Learning Representations (2018)
24. Wang, Q., et al.: Paper abstract writing through editing mechanism. In: Proceedings of the 56th Annual Meeting of the Association for Computational Linguistics (Volume 2: Short Papers), pp. 260–265, July 2018
25. Wang, S., Khabsa, M., Ma, H.: To pretrain or not to pretrain: examining the benefits of pretrainng on resource rich tasks. In: Proceedings of the 58th Annual Meeting of the Association for Computational Linguistics, pp. 2209–2213. Association for Computational Linguistics, Online, July 2020. https://doi.org/10.18653/v1/2020.acl-main.200,https://aclanthology.org/2020.acl-main.200
26. Yang, P., Li, L., Luo, F., Liu, T., Sun, X.: Enhancing topic-to-essay generation with external commonsense knowledge. In: Proceedings of the 57th Annual Meeting of the Association for Computational Linguistics, pp. 2002–2012 (2019)
27. Zhao, T., Zhao, R., Eskenazi, M.: Learning discourse-level diversity for neural dialog models using conditional variational autoencoders. In: Proceedings of the 55th Annual Meeting of the Association for Computational Linguistics (Volume 1: Long Papers), pp. 654–664 (2017)

Question Answering (Poster)

Deep Structure-Aware Approach for QA Over Incomplete Knowledge Bases

Qian Chen[1,2], Xiaoying Gao[1(✉)], Xin Guo[1], and Suge Wang[1,2]

[1] School of Computer and Information Technology, Shanxi University, Taiyuan
030006, Shanxi, China
870733176@qq.com
[2] Key Laboratory Computational Intelligence and Chinese Information Processing
of Ministry of Education, Shanxi University, Taiyuan 030006, Shanxi, China

Abstract. The incompleteness of Knowledge Base (KB) greatly limits
the performance of Question Answering (QA) system. Combining documents and incomplete KBs to develop QA system has become a hot
spot in the research of Knowledge Base Question Answering (KBQA).
Recent work ignores the relevance of KB and documents, and hinder
the fusion of structured knowledge and unstructured text. This paper
firstly builds a question-related subgraph entity encoder (QRS-Encoder)
to gain nodes embedding; secondly, a structure-aware document reader
(SAD-Reader) with deep structure information and related question is
constructed, which can capture the Meta Dependency Path (MDP) nodes
in the dependency graph constructed from question related documents.
The MDP nodes are fused into node embedding representation in SAD-
Reader, which effectively increases the node's attention to the non-local
dependencies in the document. Empirical results on WebQSP dataset
show that our model outperforms state-of-the-art (SOTA) model in terms
of both F1 and Hit@1 under incomplete KBs setting, which proves the
effectiveness of our model.

Keywords: KBQA · Knowledge-aware reader · MDP nodes

1 Introduction

Knowledge Base (KB) is an essential resource for answering factoid questions in
QA system. Knowledge Base Question Answering (KBQA) [2,14,15] has applied
widely in many applications such as chat robots, intelligent customer service,
and machine reading comprehension. However, KB with a well-designed and
complicated schema is hard to construct, since it requires lots of human efforts,
and this inevitably limits the coverage of KB [1]. In fact, KB is often incomplete
and insufficient to cover full evidence required by open-domain questions [16]. A
large amount of documents are available on the Internet, and these unstructured
textual data potentially contain correct answers to user questions. Thus how to
effectively use textual evidence to improve the performance of QA system over
incomplete KBs has become a hot spot in the research of KBQA.

© The Author(s), under exclusive license to Springer Nature Switzerland AG 2022
W. Lu et al. (Eds.): NLPCC 2022, LNAI 13551, pp. 837–849, 2022.
https://doi.org/10.1007/978-3-031-17120-8_64

The task of KBQA is to answer simple or multi-constrained complex types of questions on the KB [19]. To answer simple questions requires only one triple in KB, while to answer multi-constrained complex type of question requires reasoning on multiple triples in KB. However they all ignore the fact that QA system can not answer questions correctly based on incomplete KB, and whether the schema in the KB can represent all related knowledge is unknown. That is to say both the schema and the triple may be incomplete. Textual information is generally used to make up for incomplete KB for automatic QA research. UNISCHEMA [12] uses a universal schema to map the KB and the knowledge extracted from the document to the same embedding space, and a Key-Value Memory Network is used to store knowledge for questions answering, but the interaction between KB and document is ignored. Some researches [4,17] have achieved great performance in one single document that contain the right answer. However, the effect is not obvious when dealing with multiple documents. SGReader [16] can distinguish relevant information from irrelevant ones when read multiple documents combined with KB. Text-Enhanced KBQA [6] enriches entity representation by text semantic information and complements the relations in KB through structured information of the text. However, the extraction of KB-enhanced document information is insufficient, in which the attention between the question and KB is lacked, and the interaction between the text information and the question is also ignored.

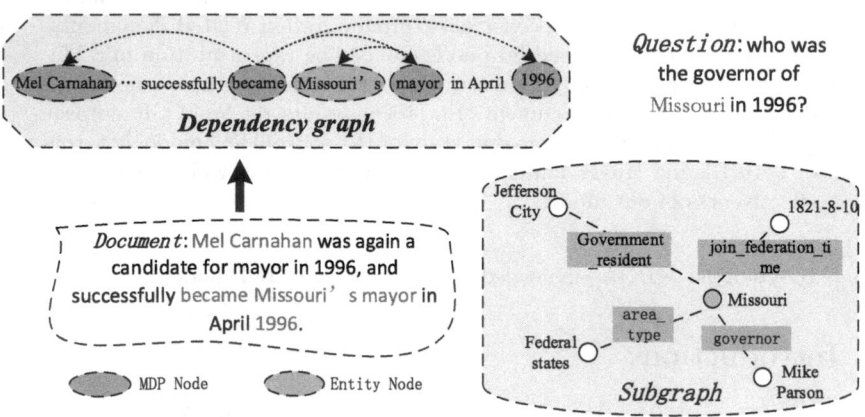

Fig. 1. A real case extracted from WebQSP

A real case from WebQSP dataset is shown in Fig. 1 in which the answer to the question cannot be obtained directly from incomplete KB. Fortunately the text segment in the document contained the answer, *e.g.*, *Mel Carnahan became Missouri's mayor in 1996*, which can effectively supplement the KB. That means QA system can flexibly obtain answers to questions from either KB or text, and this will greatly make up low coverage of the KB. However existed model cannot jointly model the text and KB well. The interactive behavior between textual data and triple data has not been deeply investigated.

The main contributions of this paper can be summarized as follows: (1) We propose to build MDP nodes based on dependency graph in order to effectively capture non-local dependencies related to documents entities; (2) We propose a joint model composed of QRS-Encoder and SAD-Reader that can deeply aggregate background knowledge and the text documents to enhance the ability of KBQA system; (3) Compared with SOTA models, our model has achieved significantly improvements in terms of both F1 and Hit@1 on the WebQSP dataset especially under incomplete KB settings.

2 Related Work

Generally, KBQA methods are divided into information-retrieval based approaches and semantic-parsing based approaches. Specifically, the former obtains answer by ranking candidate entities from textual data using information retrieval models, while the latter maps the question into a logical expression and execute query over KB through this logical expression to get final answers.

The construction of a KB with good design and complex patterns requires huge human power and material resources with continuous updating. Therefore, existing KB cannot probably cover all related information to answer the question in QA system. Early KBQA methods only use one triplet in KB to answer some simple questions, which is less affected by the incompleteness of KB. Thus researchers began to conduct research on Question Answering (QA) over incomplete KB [1]. However, it is difficult to answer complex question with multiple constraints in QA system over incomplete KB, which requires multi-hop reasoning. Due to the large-scaled and easily-accessed textual data, researchers gradually apply external text as the information supplement of incomplete KB in KBQA system. UNISCHEMA [12] proposes to encode the effective information extracted from both KB and text in one space, and stored in a key-value memory network; However, good performance can be achieved in single document scenario, and the interaction between KB and text information is also ignored. SGReader [16] selects candidate information related to question from either document sets and KB with irrelevant information ignored automatically. Text-Enhanced KBQA [6] uses textual information to enrich the entity representation in Knowledge Graph, and missing relationships in KB is made up by enriched entity and text information in this model. However, these models only consider the interaction between KB and text information, ignoring the interaction between question and text information or KB.

3 Model

3.1 Task Description

The concerned task in this paper is QA over incomplete KB and related documents, the goal of which is to answer questions from a given subgraph and related documents, where KB are often incomplete to cover sufficient evidence required by questions. Specifically, given a KB subgraph $G = \{ (e_s, r, e_o)\}$, a document set $D = \{d_1, d_2, \cdots, d_{|D|}\}$ and a question $q = \{t_1^q, t_2^q, \cdots, t_{|Q|}^q\}$, in which e_s is the subject entity, e_o is the object entity, and r is the relationship from e_s to e_o. The answer entity e^A is obtained from either subgraph entity sets or entities in documents.

We adopt the same setting as [13] for consistency and fairness, where the KB are downsampled to different extents. The KB subgraph is retrieved by Personalized PageRank [8], the document set is obtained from the Wiki by existing document retriever [2], and the entities that are marked in the documents and connected to the entities in KB subgraph.

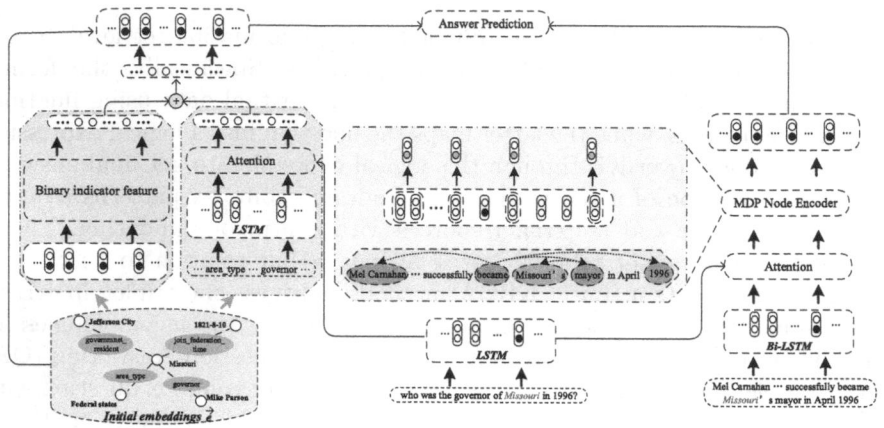

Fig. 2. The structure of the model

The main frame of our proposed model is demonstrated in Fig. 2. The model is composed of two parts, i.e. a question-related subgraph entity encoder (QRS-Encoder) (3.2) and a structure-aware document reader (SAD-Reader) with deep structure information and related question (3.3).

3.2   QRS-Encoder

QRS-Encoder mainly consists of relation attention over question, a neighbor entities attention and an aggregator from neighbors. The main idea is to employ graph attention mechanism to accumulate message of each subgraph entity from its linked neighbors. The graph attention considers two important aspects, i.e. whether the neighbor relation is relevant to the question and whether the neighbor entity is a entity mentioned by the question. QRS-Encoder finally outputs a semantic representation for each entity [16]. Unlike the hard matching mechanism in extra attention over topic entity neighbors [16], we use a soft matching score instead.

Relation Attention over Question. In order to obtain relation attention over question, we first apply LSTM to encode both the question $q = \{t_1^q, t_2^q, \cdots, t_Q^q\}$ and the relation $r = \{t_1^r, t_2^r, \cdots, t_M^r\}$, the hidden context embedding for question and relation are $H_q \in \mathbb{R}^{Q \times n}$ and $h_r \in \mathbb{R}^{M \times n}$ respectively, where Q denotes the number of tokens in question q and M represent the number of tokens in relation r. n is the dimension of the hidden state of both question and relation; then the representation of relation h_r with self-attention is computed using following equations:

$$H_q = LSTM(t_1^q, t_2^q, \cdots, t_Q^q), \tag{1}$$

$$h_r = LSTM(t_1^r, t_2^r, \cdots, t_M^r), \tag{2}$$

$$h_r = h_r \odot softmax(W_r \cdot h_r), \tag{3}$$

where $\odot$ denotes element-wise multiplication, t_i^q and t_j^r represent question token and relation token respectively, $softmax(\cdot)$ executes softmax operation by row when performed over matrix and $W_r \in \mathbb{R}^{M \times M}$ is a trainable parameter. H_r can be obtained by summarizing on the second dimension of $\mathbb{H}_r$, i.e. $H_r = \sum_{j=1}^{M} \mathbb{H}_{r_{[:j:]}} \in \mathbb{R}^{K \times n}$. $\mathbb{H}_r = [h_{r_1}, h_{r_2}, \cdots, h_{r_K}] \in \mathbb{R}^{K \times M \times n}$ is a three-order tensor, in which h_{r_K} is the K-th relation.

Since different neighbor relation have different impact on the target entity, and only related entity in the question can interact with each realtion, we consider making H_r pay attention to each of the question token by attention mechanism, and the neighbor relation attention score $S_r \in \mathbb{R}^{K \times 1}$ is obtained as follows:

$$S_r = H_r \cdot (H_q^T \cdot \sum_{k=1}^{K} softmax(H_q \cdot H_{r_k}^T)). \tag{4}$$

Node-neighbore Attention. Since the neighbor entities appeared in the question can provide more effective information for answering the question, we use soft matching mechanism to measure how much the neighbor entity is relevant to an entity mentioned by the question.

$$sm[E_o] = softmax(E_o \cdot H_q^T) \cdot H_q, \tag{5}$$

where $E_o = [e_{o_1}, e_{o_2}, \cdots, e_{o_K}] \in \mathbb{R}^{K \times n}$ denotes the representation of K neighbor entity node. e_{o_K} is the K-th entity node representation.

Aggregator from Neighbors. According to the results obtained by the relation attention over question and the node-neighbor attention, the final attention score $\tilde{S}_{(r_j, e_{o_j})}$ for each neighbor (r_j, e_{o_j}) is obtained by

$$\tilde{S}_{(r_j, e_{o_j})} = sm[E_o]_j + S_{r_j}. \tag{6}$$

The updated representation of each entity in subgraph e^u is calculated as follows:

$$e^u = g^k e + (1 - g^k) \sum_{(r_j, e_{o_j}) \in N_e} S_{(r_j, e_{o_j})} sigmoid(W_k[r_j; e_{o_j}]), \tag{7}$$

where g^k is a conditional gate mechanism [16] used to determine how much information comes from neighbors and how much information needs to be retained. N_e is a set of neighbor node of entity e.

3.3   SAD-Reader

SAD-Reader mainly consists of document representation over question, MDP nodes and an entity-document aggregator. Specifically, document representation over question is obtained by fusing question information and the entity appeared in the question using BiLSTM [7]; MDP nodes are constructed through dependency graph; Entity-document aggregator learns the updated representation by combining the background knowledge from subgraph, dependency structure information from MDP nodes and document representation over question from the first component of SAD-Reader.

Document Representation over Question. First, from the respective of question, H_q^e is used to collect the entities' information that appeared in the subgraph. H_q^d is denoted as a hybrid question representation that integrate H_q and H_q^e. H_q^d is used as a question-aware information and will be fed into document embeddings. The computation detail for H_q^e and H_q^d is described as follows:

$$H_q^e = \sum_{e \in \varepsilon} e^u / |\varepsilon|, \tag{8}$$

where $|\varepsilon|$ is the number of elements in the entity set that mentioned in the question.

$$H_q^d = g^h H_q + (1 - g^h) \tanh(W_q[H_q; H_q^e; H_q - H_q^e; H_q \odot H_q^e]), \tag{9}$$

where g^h is linear gate mechanism based on H_q^e and H_q, and W_q is a trainable parameter.

Then, Bi-LSTM networks is applied to encode each document $d = \{t_1^d, \cdots, t_{l_d}^d\}$, and we get the hidden state H_d'. $O_d \in \mathbb{R}^{l_d \times n}$ is a document embedding that fusing the question-document attention by H_q^d and n is the hidden dimension:

$$H_d' = BiLSTM(t_1^d, \cdots, t_{l_d}^d), \tag{10}$$

$$O_d = H_d' \odot softmax(H_d' \cdot (H_q^d)^T) \cdot H_q^d, \tag{11}$$

where l_d is the length of document d.

MDP Nodes Construction. Meta Dependency Paths (MDP) was first introduced in the field of Document-Level Relation Extraction [10], in which the MDP nodes are essentially a token set where the token element comes from the shortest dependency path. Unlike other sentence-level structure information, MDP nodes can capture rich non-local interaction information. MDP nodes can perform inference across sentences thus global semantic information can be propagated along dependency paths over the whole document. In our task, the motivation is obvious that the answer to the question cannot be obtained directly from incomplete KB, but may be hidden in any position of a document.

According to the syntax dependency relationship, we construct a dependency graph for each entity in the document, and the path $p = \{p_1^w, \cdots, p_{l_p}^w\}$ is essentially the word sets that embody the meta dependency structure along the dependency path excluding the entity tokens, where l_p represents the number of words appearing in the path. An example of MDP nodes can be shown in Fig. 1. The word-level MDP node is denoted as $H_p \in \mathbb{R}^{l_p \times n}$, which can be obtained from document embedding O_d. Unlike [10], MDP nodes in this paper is used to enhance document representation in deep aggregation.

Entity-document Aggregator. Answer prediction requires knowledge, retrieved document, and question. Knowledge comes from each entity in subgraph e^u in Sect. 3.2. Retrieved document originates from document embedding O_d that fusing the question-document attention in Sect. 3.3. MDP nodes information H_p, document embedding O^d and entities in subgraph e^u are related to the question. Thus, we use entity-document aggregator to aggregate these three factors in one manner, and experimental results show that this approach can improve the performance of QA system.

Specifically, we first compute the updated document representation $H^d \in \mathbb{R}^{l_d \times n}$ with a gate function g^d:

$$H_{w_i}^d = g^d[e_{w_i^u}; f_p(H_p^{w_i})] + (1 - g^d)O_d^{w_i}, \tag{12}$$

where $f_p(\cdot)$ is a linear transformation over MDP nodes embedding. g^d dynamically controls the input proportion between entities information $[e_{w_i^u}; f_p(H_p^{w_i})]$ and the document embedding $O_d^{w_i}$.

After applying LSTM to encode updated the document representation H^d, we then obtain representation of document d.

$$d = LSTM(H_{w_1}^d, \cdots, H_{w_i}^d, \cdots, H_{w_{l_d}}^d) \tag{13}$$

Finally, the representation of each entity e can be calculated by aggregating all documents containing entity e.

$$e^d = \frac{1}{|D^e|} \sum_{d \in D^e} d, \tag{14}$$

where D^e represents document set in which each element of document contains entity e.

3.4 Answer Prediction

The goal of this paper is to give the answer according to incomplete KB, related documents and a question. We regard this task as a similarity matching between the question and the entity set, in which there are two parts, i.e. updated entity representation e^u from subgraph and updated document embeddings e^d from Sect. 3.3. The probability of each entity from $[e^u; e^d]$ be the right answer can be inferred as follows:

$$e^A = sigmoid(H_q^d W_s[e^u; e^d]), \tag{15}$$

where $W_s \in \mathbb{R}^{n \times 2n}$ is a trainable parameter. Naturally, the entity with the highest probability is regarded as the right answer.

4 Experiment Setup

4.1 Dateset and Metrics

We use WebQSP [18] dataset to evaluate our model. Table 1 describes the statistic information about WebQSP dataset.

Table 1. Statistics of the WebQSP dataset

Dataset	Questions train / dev / test	#entity	Avg entities in documents	Avg linked documents	Coverage
WebQSP	2848 / 250 / 1639	1429.8	4.6	43.6	94.9%

WebQSP contains 4737 questions in total, in which 2848 is used for training, 250 for validation, and 1639 for testing. #entity is the average number of entities in each subgraph. avg linked documents means the average number of documents retrieved by each question. coverage represents the proportion of the subgraphs that contain at least one entity for the answer.

$F1$ and $Hit@1$ is used to evaluate the performance of our model. $Hit@1$ is an index to measure the recall rate, which represents the accuracy rate of the best answer predicted by the model.

4.2 Baselines

We compare our methods with the following models:

① **GraftNet (GN)** [13] uses graph convolution neural network to aggregate information in KB. Specifically, GN-EF (early fusion) directly regards KB and documents as a heterogeneous graph, which obtains the answer score of each entity by aggregating information on the graph; GN-LF (late fusion) first regards KB and document as two separate graphs, and then it aggregates the answer scores;

② **Key-Value Memory Network (KVMN)** [9] uses KB and document set as storage units to answer questions;

③ **SG+KAT** [16] uses SGReader and KATReader to obtain KB and documents information respectively;

④ **TEKG** [6] uses text information to enrich the entity representation, and supplements the relationships in KB with the latent structural information of text.

⑤ **Retriever-Transducer-Checker (ReTraCK)** [3] contains three parts: a retriever can retrieve relevant KB information, a transducer is used to generate correctly logical form in syntax and a checker is applied to guarantee transducer programs that are consistent with KB.

4.3 Training Details

For input layer, we use 300-dimension GloVe embeddings [11] as word representaion, and adopt the same pre-trained entity embeddings as used in [13]. The dimension of both entity embeddings and the hidden state of LSTM is set to 100. In QRS-Encoder, we set the max word length in question and relation to 10 and 8 respectively, and the maximum number of neighbor entities is set to 50. In SAD-Reader, the word number of documents is limited to 50, the dimension of the hidden state of BiLSTM is set to 100, and the maximum number of MDP nodes is 30. The batch size and the max number of epochs are 8 and 100, respectively. We apply Adam optimizer [5] to minimize the binary cross-entropy loss, in which learning rate is set to 0.003.

4.4 Experimental Results

We conduct experiments over WebQSP following the settings of [16], which includes 10%KB, 30%KB and 50%KB. Experimental results in terms of F1 and Hit@1 are shown in Table 2.

Table 2. Experimental results on WebQSP

Model		KVMN	GN-LF	GN-EF	SG+KAT	TEKG	ReTrack	ours
KB-only	F1	38.1	60.9	62.5	58.1	60.3	**74.7**	61.5
	Hit@1	46.5	64.7	66.3	66.2	66.8	**74.6**	67.1
10%KB+Text	F1	14.4	17.0	17.7	18.9	19.9	–	**28.3**
	Hit@1	24.6	29.8	31.5	33.6	33.7	–	**44.8**
30%KB+Text	F1	17.7	25.9	25.2	27.1	27.5	–	**28.5**
	Hit@1	27.0	39.1	40.7	42.6	42.8	–	**46.0**
50%KB+Text	F1	23.6	35.6	34.7	36.1	37.1	–	**39.7**
	Hit@1	32.5	46.2	49.9	52.7	52.8	–	**54.4**
100%KB+Text	F1	30.9	56.8	60.4	57.3	**60.6**	–	59.9
	Hit@1	40.5	65.4	67.8	67.2	**68.4**	–	67.5

From Table 2, we see that (1) ReTrack model gets better performance under KB-only settings, and (2) TEKG model achieves competitive results under 100%KB+Text setting. However, this paper focuses on QA over incomplete KB and the performance of our model outperforms TEKG model when KB is complete. Although our model cannot achieve the best performance in 100%KB+Text setting, it is very close to the result of TEKG model. Meanwhile, ReTrack model is proposed to solve large scale KBQA rather than considering the completeness of KB setting, which cannot deal with QA task with the absence of supporting evidence in KB. Since the SG+KAT model uses knowledge-aware KAReader to obtain text information which contains the prior knowledge from incomplete KB, its performance is better than Graft-Net and KV Memory Network. Table 2 shows that our model achieves significant performance on WebQSP dataset over incomplete KB setting, i.e. 10%KB+Text, 30%KB+Text, 50%KB+Text, which illustrates the effectiveness of our model over incomplete KB. Particularly, our model in 10%KB + text setting gets competitive results and improves F1 and His@1 by 8.4 and 11.1 respectively. The reason can be analyzed as: (1) We fully consider the deep semantic structural information that enable model precisely locate the target answer entity through dependency path hidden in the documents, regardless of the answer existence in the subgraph; (2) our model can enhance document representation by combining MDP nodes, subgraph knowledge and document semantic information; (3) soft matching mechanism alleviates the problem that different entity mentioned with the same entity be ignored in the hard matching scenario.

4.5   Ablation Study

SAD-Reader aggregates entities in subgraph e^u and MDP nodes information H_p in the document embedding with quetions-aware information. In order to evaluate the effectiveness of each factor in SAD-Reader, we conduct ablation experiments under 50% KB setting. Specifically, we design three variant models:

- **Question Info** removes question-document attention H_q^d, which is a hybrid question representation integrating H_q and H_q^e in Sect. 3.3, that means document embedding only uses BiLSTM networks.

- **Subgraph Info** removes the knowledge from each entity in subgraph e^u in entity-document aggregator (3.3). Updated document representation H^d is obtained by MDP nodes information H^p and document embedding O^d. This variant model lacks information from incomplete KB.

- **MDP Nodes** removes the MDP nodes information in entity document aggregator (3.3), which lacks global semantic information along dependency paths over the whole document.

Experiment results are shown in Table 3. We observed that: 1) by removing the question-document attention H_q^d, the performance of model drops by 1.2% and 1.4% in terms of both Hit@1 and F1, which indicates the importance of document representation concerning question information and is sufficient only using BiLSTM to obtain document embedding; 2) the validity of variant model

-Subgraph Info drops, which implies that the knowledge from subgraph can provide effective background information that can affect the performance of the model; 3) the results of *-MDP Nodes* also show that MDP Nodes can highlight the non-local dependencies related to document entities and is beneficial for updated document representation H^d in entity-document aggregator; 4) we note that the performance of our full model achieves significant improvement, which proves the validity of MDP nodes, the question-aware information and the entity subgraph embedding from KB.

Table 3. Experimental results of model analysis

Model		Full Model	-Question Info	-Subgraph Info	-MDP Nodes
50%KB+Text	F1	39.7	38.3	37.9	36.1
	Hit@1	54.4	53.2	53.1	52.7

4.6 Case Study

We select 3 cases on 50%KB setting, as shown in Table 4, we discover that:

Table 4. Case analysis in the 50%KB setting

1)	Question: Where is Danish located?
	Groundtruth: **Europe (fb:m.02j9z)**
	QRS-Encoder(only): **Europe (fb:m.02j9z)**
	QRS-Encoder + SAD-Reader: Hedeby (fb:m.03nv9)
2)	Question: Who plays Kenneth on 30 Rock?
	Groundtruth: **Jack McBrayer (fb:m.0h27vc)**
	QRS-Encoder(only):Maria Thayer (fb:m.0gxr55)
	QRS-Encoder + SAD-Reader: **Jack McBrayer (fb:m.0h27vc)**
3)	Question: Where did Robert Boyle study?
	Groundtruth: **University College (fb:m.0ymf1), Eton College (fb:m.0dzbl)**
	QRS-Encoder(only): Anglo-Irish people (fb:m.0152s7)
	QRS-Encoder + SAD-Reader: **Eton College (fb:m.0dzbl)**

① In sample 1), the subgraph contains the answer entity. Regardless of answer evidence availability in related document, our full model can extract the right answer correctly. *SG+KAT* failed to give the right answer under this scenario since document introduce noise to the top rank candidate answer list, while our model can promote the ranking of answer entity in related subgraph using soft matching which proves the advantage of soft matching mechanism in the extraction of node neighbor information (3.2).

② In sample 2), the answer entity is not contained in incomplete KB, background knowledge from the KB can provide the answer entity-related information to answer question and used to the updated document representation H^d in entity-document aggregator (3.3). Sample 2) shows that QRSEncoder (only) can predict the type of answer entity, *e.g.*, person, but fail to obtain right answer entity *e.g.*, Jack McBrayer.

③ Sample 3) shows that the path from entity mentioned in question to answer entity is lost in incomplete KB, while the answer given by QRSEncoder (only) is not related to the question. We note that the answer from full model is consistent with groundtruth, which demonstrates that SAD-Reader can capture deep structure information by entity-document aggregator (3.3).

5   Conclusion

We propose a new QA model over incomplete KB and related documents, which is composed of QRS-Encoder and SAD-Reader. Specifically, our model obtains nodes embedding from incomplete KB by QRS-Encoder, in which we use soft matching mechanism to alleviate the problem that different entity mentioned with the same entity be ignored in the hard matching scenario. MDP nodes information are integrated into updated document representation in SAD-Reader, which effectively increases the node's attention to the non-local dependencies in documents. Experiments show that our model outperforms SOTA models by 8.4% and 11.1% in terms of F1 and Hit@1 respectively, which proves that soft matching mechanism can improve the performance of model, and MDP nodes can enhance the connection between the incomplete KB and unstructured text through dependency path.

Question answer over incomplete KB task still faces lots of challenges. In the future, we will conduct further research from the following two aspects: How to enable QA model understand the intention of the question correctly; Is there other strategies to tackle with knowledge incompleteness when the answer entity is not contained in incomplete KB. We will apply table-type knowledge to provide the background information for incomplete KB.

Acknowledgments. This work was supported by the National Science Foundation under Grant No. 62076158, National Science Foundation of Shanxi Province under Grant No. 201901D111032.

References

1. Min, B., Ralph G., Li W., Chang W., David G.: Distant supervision for relation extraction with an incomplete knowledge base. In: NAACL (2013)
2. Chen, D., Adam F., Jason W., Antoine B.: Reading wikipedia to answer open-domain questions. In: ACL (2017)

3. Chen, S., Liu, Q., Yu, Z., Lin, C., Lou, J., Jiang, F.: ReTraCk: a flexible and efficient framework for knowledge base question answering. In: Proceedings of the 59th Annual Meeting of the Association for Computational Linguistics and the 11th International Joint Conference on Natural Language Processing: System Demonstrations (2021)

4. Xiong, C., Zhong, V., Socher, R.: DCN+: Mixed objective and deep residual coattention for question answering. arXiv abs/1711.00106 (2018)

5. Kingma, D., Ba, J.: Adam: a method for stochastic optimization. CoRR abs/1412.6980 (2015)

6. Han, J., Cheng, B., Wang, X.: Open domain question answering based on text enhanced knowledge graph with hyperedge infusion. In: EMNLP (2020)

7. Hochreiter, S., Schmidhuber, J.: Long short-term memory. Neural Comput. **9**, 1735–1780 (1997)

8. Haveliwala, T.: Topic-sensitive pagerank. In: WWW 2002 (2002)

9. Miller, A., Fisch, A., Dodge, J., Karimi, A., Bordes, A., Weston, J.: Key-value memory networks for directly reading documents. arXiv abs/1606.03126 (2016)

10. Nan, G., Guo, Z., Sekulic, I., Lu, W.: Reasoning with latent structure refinement for document-level relation extraction. In: ACL (2020)

11. Pennington, J., Socher, R., Manning, C.: GloVe: global vectors for word representation. In: EMNLP (2014)

12. Das, R., Zaheer, M., Reddy, S., McCallum, A.: Question answering on knowledge bases and text using universal schema and memory networks. arXiv abs/1704.08384 (2017)

13. Sun, H., Dhingra, B., Zaheer, M., Mazaitis, K., Salakhutdinov, R., Cohen, W.: Open domain question answering using early fusion of knowledge bases and text. In: EMNLP (2018)

14. Song, J., Qu, X., Hu, Z., Li, Z., Gao, J., Zhang, J.: A subgraph-based knowledge reasoning method for collective fraud detection in E-commerce. Neurocomputing **461**, 587–597 (2021)

15. Wang, S., et al.: R3: reinforced reader-ranker for open-domain question answering. arXiv abs/1709.00023 (2017)

16. Xiong, W., Yu, M., Chang, S., Guo, X., Wang, W.: Improving question answering over incomplete KBs with knowledge-aware reader. In: ACL (2019)

17. Yu, A.W., et al.: QANet: combining local convolution with global self-attention for reading comprehension. arXiv abs/1804.09541 (2018)

18. Yih, W., Richardson, M., Meek, C., Chang, M., Suh, J.: The value of semantic parse labeling for knowledge base question answering. In: ACL (2016)

19. Zia, T., Windridge, D.: A generative adversarial network for single and multi-hop distributional knowledge base completion. Neurocomputing **461**, 543–551 (2021)

An On-Device Machine Reading Comprehension Model with Adaptive Fast Inference

Fulai Nan, Jin Wang[✉], and Xuejie Zhang

School of Information Science and Engineering, Yunnan University, Kunming, China
wangjin@ynu.edu.cn

Abstract. Pretrained language models (PrLMs) have been widely used in machine reading comprehension (MRC) tasks. Although PrLMs can learn powerful representations from large-scale corpora, it introduces the problem of model redundancy, which severely restricts the application of mobile devices. Recent studies have suggested the use of early exit (EE) methods for the fast inference of PrLMs. However, there are two limitations to the application of existing EE methods. First, different Transformer layers have different capabilities for learning semantic features. Thus, the lower layers may behave differently from the higher layers. As a result, the earlier the exit from the model, the lower its performance. Second, a greedy search is applied to the classifiers exiting either the start or the end position. However, the start and end positions may also be related. Choosing only one best candidate might be suitable for the current step, but it may be a suboptimal choice in global inference. To address these issues, this study proposes an on-device MRC model with fast inference based on an EE strategy. To ensure that the lower layers have similar abilities as the higher layers, we propose the use of self-distillation to transfer knowledge from the higher layers to the lower ones. Furthermore, a dynamic programming strategy was applied to choose the optimal confidence combination of both the start and end classifiers to better select the exit layers in the inference stage. Experimental results on both SQuAD 1.1 and 2.0 show that the inference of the proposed model is accelerated at the minimum cost of performance loss, thereby outperforming previous EE models.

Keywords: Machine reading comprehension · Dynamic early exit · Self-distillation · Adaptive inference

1 Introduction

Machine reading comprehension (MRC) aims to teach machines to understand and answer questions using unstructured texts. It has a wide range of potential applications in smartphones, such as voice assistants, intelligent customer service, voice chat robots, and web search.

© The Author(s), under exclusive license to Springer Nature Switzerland AG 2022
W. Lu et al. (Eds.): NLPCC 2022, LNAI 13551, pp. 850–862, 2022.
https://doi.org/10.1007/978-3-031-17120-8_65

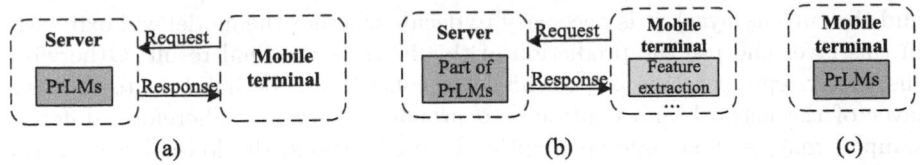

Fig. 1. Schematic diagrams of three architectures for mobile deployment applications.

Early MRC studies explored the Stanford question answering dataset (SQuAD) [11], which consisted of over 100,000 question answer pairs formulated from Wikipedia articles. The challenge was to train a machine learning model to answer questions based on a contextual document. When provided with a contextual document (free-form text) and a question, the model returns the subset of the text most likely to answer the question. AI practitioners worldwide try to address this problem in a variety of ways. Unfortunately, no model outperformed the human benchmark until bidirectional encoder representations from Transformers (BERT) [1] were introduced. Based on the Transformer encoder-decoder architecture in BERT, other pretrained language models (PrLMs), such as RoBERTa [7], ALBERT [6], XLNet [18], ERNIE [12] and GPT [4], have been widely used in various NLP fields. These models were pretrained on a large-scale corpus without annotations to learn universal language representations. This was beneficial for downstream NLP tasks, which can avoid training a new model from scratch. Owing to the rapid growth of intelligent internet applications in mobile devices, potential applications such as voice assistants, search engines, and voice navigation require the deployment of more powerful MRC models.

There are three main architectures for deploying PrLMs for MRC, as shown in Fig. 1. First, PrLMs can be deployed on the server to provide access to users through the network. On the other hand, some modules, such as feature extraction, can be transferred to the smartphone, so that the application can post the intermediate results to the server for subsequent calculations. It should be noted that both the architectures rely heavily on the network. Once the device is offline, all PrLM services are inaccessible. The third architecture completely deploys PrLMs on the device. With innovations in device hardware, some recent mobile processor chips have begun to introduce neural computing engines [14]. Although mobile devices already have a certain ability to accelerate the inference of neural models, Gasmi et al. [3] propose the large number of parameters in PrLMs will incur huge computational costs on resource and battery power to mobile devices, which may hinder their deployment on devices.

To accomplish this goal, existing studies have suggested the use of model compression, such as pruning [9], quantization [19], and knowledge distillation [8]. However, these methods reduce the number of layers, and the parameters cause the accuracy of inference to drop accordingly [5]. Another viable solution is to use the technique of conditional computation, for example, the early exit (EE) strategy. Specifically, an EE classifier was inserted into every pair of Transformer encoder. Given the currently obtained prediction results (from the previous layer and the current layer), it is necessary to decide whether the model will exit early in this layer and use the prediction of this layer as the final result. Otherwise, the vector representation [21] of this layer continues to be inputted to the next layer of the network and continues to propagate forward. Therefore, different samples may exist at different depths. In other words, the lower layers of the model can handle simple samples, whereas the harder samples use the output of the deeper network to make better predictions.

Furthermore, there are two more limitations of applying existing EE methods for MRC. First, the EE models were trained in two stages. Namely, the backbone network of PrLM is first trained and then frozen to train the EE classifiers. This separate training process freezes the PrLM backbone network, resulting in weak knowledge transfer classifiers between multiple EE. Also, a previous study [11] indicated that surface features are expressed in the lower layers, syntactic features are expressed more in the middle layers, and semantic features are expressed in higher layers of PrLMs. This brings up a contradiction: the earlier the model exits, the fewer semantic features are learned for the task; thus, the lower the performance of the model. Second, the span-extraction MRC task requires the model to predict both start and end positions [10]. Using DeeBERT [15] and BranchyNet [13], a greedy search is applied to select the best candidate with a confidence beyond the threshold for either the start or end classifier. However, the start and end positions are potentially related. Choosing only one best candidate might be suitable for the current step, but it may be a suboptimal choice in global inference.

To this end, this study proposes a fast-inference MRC model based on the EE strategy (MRC-EE), which can be deployed in resource-constrained devices. Instead of separately training the backbone and EE classifiers, the proposed MRC-EE simultaneously trained both components in each training step. To ensure that the lower layers can obtain the same powerful representation ability as the higher layers, we propose using self-distillation [20] to transfer knowledge from the latter to the former. That is, the start and end classifiers in the last layer were applied as the teachers to guide the training of the previous layers, which were regarded as the students. By minimizing the KL-divergence [17], the EE classifier of the students were trained as equally effective as the start and end classifiers in the last layer. Additionally, we provide a dynamic programming strategy to choose the optimal confidence combination of both the start and end classifiers to better select the exit layers in the inference stage. To prevent the model from obtaining the highest confidence in the last layer, thus losing the desire to exit early, we introduce a penalty on the increment of the layers. Once the search for the optimal combination becomes deeper, the confidence will receive a greater penalty, forcing the model to choose the optimal solution combination at a lower layer.

Extensive experiments were conducted on the SQuAD dataset, including both 1.1 and 2.0 versions. The results show that the proposed MRC-EE model achieves a good balance between the model performance and inference time. The dynamic EE algorithm with self-distillation and penalty mechanisms significantly reduced the inference time but preserved the performance of the model.

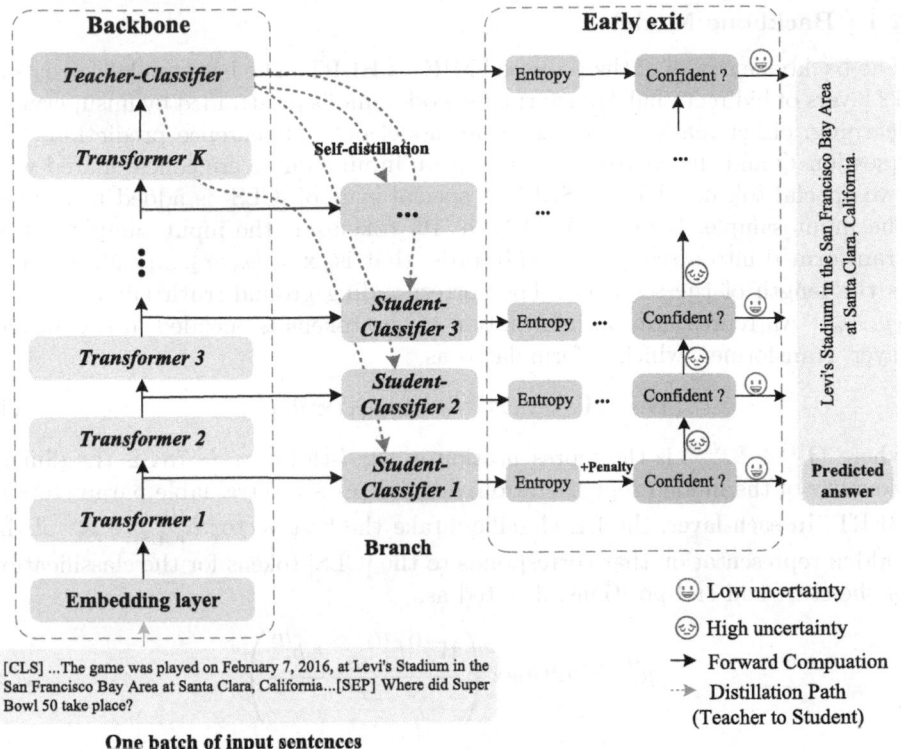

Fig. 2. Self-distillation and dynamic early exit mechanism model structure diagram.

Compared to EE methods with greedy search, the proposed method can search for the optimal combination of exit layers for both the start and end classifiers in the lower layers. Meanwhile, the proposed MRC-EE not only suppresses unnecessary computations for simple samples but also provides a dynamic EE strategy for different samples.

The remainder of this paper is organized as follows. Section 2 describes the proposed MRC-EE model in details. Section 3 summarizes the experimental results of several previous models. The conclusions are presented in Sect. 4.

2 Machine Reading Comprehension Model with Early Exiting

This section presents the proposed MRC-EE model in detail. Figure 2 shows the overall architecture of the proposed EE strategy for MRC, where the performance of the teacher model is transferred to the student model through self-distillation. Thus, when the student model exits from the lower layer, the teacher model is able to perform well. Subsequently, a dynamic EE strategy is adopted to achieve a comprehensive trade-off between performance and inference speed. The code is available at: https://github.com/nanfulai/MRC-EE.

2.1   Backbone Model

The backbone model of the proposed MRC is BERT. The base model consists of 12 layers of bidirectional Transformer encoder and is pre-trained by unsupervised learning, either masking the language model or next-sentence prediction. The question Q and the context C of the given input sample are concatenated with two special tokens, that is, [SEP]. A special symbol [CLS] is added in front of the input sample. Using a WordPiece [16] tokenizer, the input sample is first transformed into a sequence of subwords, that is, $\mathbf{x} = [x_1, x_2, ..., x_N]$, where N is the length of the sequence. The corresponding ground-truth label was $y = \{y_s, y_e\}$. All representation information of the tokens is encoded in a multiple-layer Transformer, which is formulated as,

$$\mathbf{H}^{(1)}, \mathbf{H}^{(2)}, ..., \mathbf{H}^{(L)} = f_{\text{BERT}}(\mathbf{x}; \theta_{\text{BERT}}) \tag{1}$$

where $\mathbf{H}^{(l)} \in \mathbb{R}^{N \times d}$ is the representation in the l-th layer, $d=784$ is the dimensionality of the hidden representation, and θ_{BERT} is the trainable parameters in BERT. In each layer, the EE classifiers take the first vector $h_{[\text{CLS}]}^{(l)} \in \mathbb{R}^d$ of the hidden representation that corresponds to the [CLS] tokens for the classification of the start and end positions, denoted as,

$$\hat{y}_s^{(l)} = \text{softmax}\left(\frac{W_s^{(l)} h_{[\text{CLS}]}^{(l)} + b_s^{(l)}}{\tau}\right) \tag{2}$$

$$\hat{y}_e^{(l)} = \text{softmax}\left(\frac{W_e^{(l)} h_{[\text{CLS}]}^{(l)} + b_e^{(l)}}{\tau}\right) \tag{3}$$

where $\hat{y}_s^{(l)} \in \mathbb{R}^N$ and $\hat{y}_e^{(l)} \in \mathbb{R}^N$ are the predicted probability distributions for the start and end positions, respectively; $W_s^{(l)} \in \mathbb{R}^{N \times d}$, $W_e^{(l)} \in \mathbb{R}^{N \times d}$, $b_s^{(l)} \in \mathbb{R}^N$ and $b_e^{(l)} \in \mathbb{R}^N$ are trainable weights and biases for the classifiers, and τ is the temperature that is used to control the smoothness of the output distribution. The larger the temperature τ, the smoother are the probability distributions. Based on this, the task-specific training objective is to minimize the categorical cross-entropy:

$$\mathcal{L}_{CE} = -\frac{1}{M} \sum_M \left[\mathbb{I}(y_s) \circ \log \hat{y}_s^{(L)} + \mathbb{I}(y_e) \circ \log \hat{y}_e^{(L)}\right] \tag{4}$$

where M is the number of training samples, $\mathbb{I}(y)$ denotes a one-hot vector with the y-th component being one, and $\circ$ represents the element-wise multiplication operation.

2.2   Self-distillation

To ensure that the EE classifiers in the lower layers perform competitively with the classifiers in the final layer, we performed self-distillation to transfer knowledge from the final layer as the teacher, to the previous layers as students.

Algorithm 1. Early-Exiting Inference

Input: Training sample $\mathbf{x}$, the penalty $\rho^{(l)}$
Output: Predicted probability distribution $\hat{y}_s^{(i)}, \hat{y}_e^{(j)}$
1: **for** $l = 1$ to N **do**
2:     **for** $i = 1, j = 1$ to l **do**
3:         $\hat{y}_s^{(i)} = f_s^{(i)}(\mathbf{x}; \theta_{\text{BERT}})$, $\hat{y}_e^{(j)} = f_e^{(j)}(\mathbf{x}; \theta_{\text{BERT}})$
4:         $\mathbb{E}_s^{(i)} = Ent(\hat{y}_s^{(i)})$, $\mathbb{E}_e^{(j)} = Ent(\hat{y}_e^{(j)})$
5:         **if** $\mathbb{E}_s^{(i)} + \mathbb{E}_e^{(j)}$ **is minimum of all possible combinations and** $\mathbb{E}_s^{(l)} +$
$\mathbb{E}_e^{(l)} + \rho^{(l)} < S$ **then**
6:         **break**
7: **return** $\hat{y}_s^{(i)}, \hat{y}_e^{(j)}$

The loss function of self-distillation measures the Kullback-Leibler divergence between the teacher and student, which can be denoted as:

$$\mathcal{L}_s = \tau^2 \frac{1}{M} \sum_M \sum_{l=1}^{L-1} \text{KL}(\hat{y}_s^{(L)} \| \hat{y}_s^{(l)}) \tag{5}$$

$$\mathcal{L}_e = \tau^2 \frac{1}{M} \sum_M \sum_{l=1}^{L-1} \text{KL}(\hat{y}_e^{(L)} \| \hat{y}_e^{(l)}) \tag{6}$$

$$\mathcal{L}_{SD} = (\mathcal{L}_s + \mathcal{L}_e)/2 \tag{7}$$

The final training objective is a weighted sum over both cross-entropy and KL-divergence for self-distillation:

$$\mathcal{L} = \alpha \mathcal{L}_{CE} + (1 - \alpha)\mathcal{L}_{SD} \tag{8}$$

where α is a weight coefficient used to balance both losses, the default of which is set to 0.5.

2.3 Adaptive Inference

Using self-distillation, the representation of BERT in the lower layers could be sufficient to support the classifier in making correct classification decisions. If all samples pass through all layers, redundant computation and excessive inference occur. Therefore, this study proposes an adaptive-inference strategy. As shown in Fig. 2, the entropy values of the probability distribution of the EE classifiers in each layer are defined as the confidence of the early exit. These entropy values were calculated as follows:

$$\mathbb{E}_s^{(l)} = -\sum_d p_s^{(l)} \log p_s^{(l)} = \ln(\sum_d \exp(p_s^{(l)})) - \frac{\sum_{d_r} p_s^{(l)} \exp(p_s^{(l)})}{\sum_d \exp(p_s^{(l)})} \tag{9}$$

$$\mathbb{E}_e^{(l)} = -\sum_d p_e^{(l)} \log p_e^{(l)} = \ln(\sum_d \exp(p_e^{(l)})) - \frac{\sum_d p_e^{(l)} \exp(p_e^{(l)})}{\sum_d \exp(p_e^{(l)})} \qquad (10)$$

where l represents the number of layers of the EE and d is the dimensional representation of the hidden layer of the EE classifier. First, a threshold S was set for EE. When the input sample reached a layer, its entropy value for the start and end positions was calculated using Eq. (9) and Eq. (10). Algorithm 1 presents the adaptive inference algorithm.

Because the extraction of the MRC answer is a process of determining both the start and end positions of the answer, there should be a relationship between them. When a sample reached the l-th layer, we independently predict the start and end positions. Here, $\hat{y}_s^{(i)}$ and $\hat{y}_e^{(j)}$ are the output probability distributions for the start and end positions in the i-th and j-th layers, respectively. To explore this relationship, we use the combination in which the sum of $\mathbb{E}_s^{(l)}$ and $\mathbb{E}_e^{(l)}$ is the smallest as the optimal solution. Once the combination of the entropy value of the start and end below the threshold S, i.e., $\mathbb{E}_s^{(l)} + \mathbb{E}_e^{(l)} + \rho^{(l)} < S$, the corresponding results $\hat{y}_s^{(i)}$ and $\hat{y}_e^{(j)}$ are returned.

To prevent the model from obtaining the lowest entropy in the last layer, thus losing the desire to exit early, a penalty $\rho^{(l)}$ was introduced on the increment of the layers, defined as,

$$\rho^{(l)} = \rho^{(0)} * l \qquad (11)$$

where $\rho^{(0)}$ is the initialized penalty value set to 0.05, and l is the number of layers in the model. Once the search for the optimal combination becomes deeper, the confidence will receive a greater penalty, forcing the model to choose the optimal solution combination at a lower layer. Otherwise, the model continues with the next layer of inference when it is greater than the threshold value, i.e., $\mathbb{E}_s^{(l)} + \mathbb{E}_e^{(l)} + \rho^{(l)} > S$. Intuitively, a larger S leads to faster but less accurate prediction, whereas a smaller S leads to a more accurate but slower prediction.

3 Experiments

This section summarizes the experimental results against several previous baselines to demonstrate the effectiveness of the proposed MRC-EE model.

3.1 Datasets and Evaluation Metrics

Empirical experiments were conducted using the SQuAD 1.1 and SQuAD 2.0 English extraction reading comprehension datasets released by Stanford University. The official metrics, including both the match result (EM) and F1-score, were used to evaluate the performance of the model. The EM is defined as the score when the predicted answer given by the model is exactly the same as the standard answer.

Table 1. Comparison between baseline (BERT), MRC-EE, and other compression methods.

Methods	SQuAD 1.1			SQuAD 2.0		
	F1 %	EM %	Time %	F1 %	EM %	Time%
BERT-base	87.8	80.5	100	74.4	71.7	100
DistilBERT	85.0	78.2	50	68.8	65.2	50
LayerDrop	84.9	77.7	50	67.2	64.9	50
DeeBERT	85.2	78.0	53.6	69.7	65.8	57.3
MRC-EE	**85.7**	**78.6**	**45.2**	**70.5**	**66.7**	**50.8**

Table 2. Experimental results of ablation experiments.

Methods	SQuAD 1.1			SQuAD 2.0		
	F1 %	EM %	Time %	F1 %	EM %	Time %
BERT-base	87.8	80.5	100	74.4	71.7	100
MRC-EE w/o EE	88.1	80.9	100	74.6	72.1	100
MRC-EE w/o self-distillation	84.2	76.6	63.6	68.1	64.8	69.8
MRC-EE	**85.7**	**78.6**	**45.2**	**70.5**	**66.7**	**50.8**

When calculating the acceleration ratio of the dynamic EE of the model, the ratio of the number of sample exit layers to the total number of layers in the model was used as the acceleration ratio. For example, the comparison baseline model is a 12-layer Transformer structure, φ samples exit at the m-th layer of the model, and δ samples exit at the n-th layer. The acceleration ratio is calculated as follows:

$$A_r = \frac{\varphi * m + \delta * n}{12(\varphi + \delta)} \tag{12}$$

3.2 Implementation Details

The backbone of the experiment was a 12-layer BERT-based model with a hidden size of 768. During training, the output of the final layer was applied to guide the training of the EE classifiers on each layer. By comparing the sum of the entropy value and the penalty value of the sample output by the classifier and the preset confidence threshold, it is determined whether the sample exits. When the entropy value of the input sample is less than the confidence threshold, the input sample is directly exited from this layer; otherwise, it is sent to the next layer to improve model inference efficiency. By using a grid search strategy, the threshold is set to 1.2 to achieve a better balance between performance and acceleration ratio. The distillation temperature τ was set to 2 and the learning rate was 3e−5. The maximum length of the input samples after tokenization was 384, the batch size was 16, the epoch was 12, and the distillation loss linear weight defaults to 0.5.

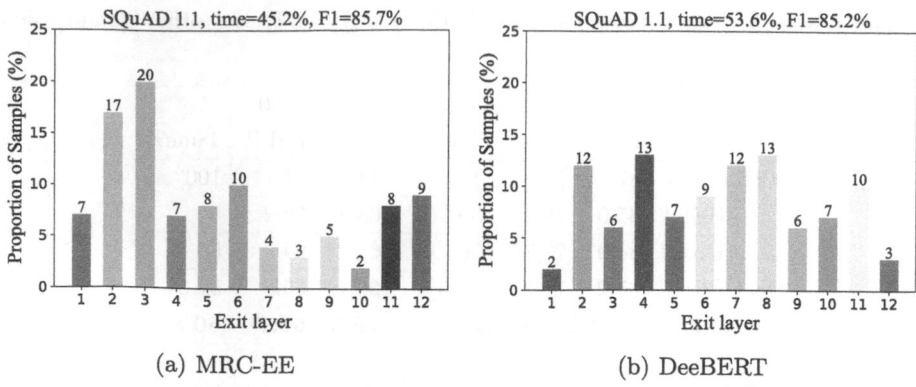

Fig. 3. Distribution of different performances of early exiting classifier on SQuAD 1.1.

3.3   Experimental Results and Analysis

Table 1 lists the experimental results of the different models for the two datasets. Several baselines were also implemented on a 12-layer BERT-base, such as Distil-BERT, LayerDrop [2], and DeeBERT. DistilBERT is a 6-layer knowledge distillation model. LayerDrop adopts interval clipping to preserve the 6-layer structure of the model, and DeeBERT performs dynamic EE on the 12-layer BERT model.

In SQuAD 1.1, MRC-EE achieves an F1-score of 85.7%. Compared to the BERT-base, the performance dropped by approximately 2.1%, but the inference time was only 45.2% of the baseline. Meanwhile, compared with several other methods, we have a small lead in F1-score indicators and a 5% to 8% improvement in the acceleration ratio. In SQuAD 2.0, MRC-EE still maintains a stable performance, with an F1-score reaching 70.5%, which is a 3.9% loss in F1-score compared to BERT-base while keeping the inference time compressed by approximately half. Compared with DeeBERT, MRC-EE leads to improved performance and inference time, especially in the acceleration ratio. Compared with DistilBERT and LayerDrop, the acceleration ratio was slightly lower, but we improve the F1-score by 1.7% to 3.3%. In summary, the superiority of the proposed method is demonstrated.

Figure 3 shows the different performance distributions of the EE classifier for SQuAD 1.1. The figure shows the distribution of the sample exit layers for MRC-EE and DeeBERT. The introduction of exits and penalties can increase the concentration of the samples in the lower layer exit. The distribution of the DeeBERT sample exit layers was relatively uniform. In contrast, most of the MRC-EE exited from the lower layers. As shown in Fig. 4, for the top seven EE classifiers, the proposed MRC-EE classifier is much higher than the DeeBERT classifier for both F1-score and EM metrics on both datasets. In SQuAD 1.1, the F1-score of the first EE classifier of MRC-EE was nearly 13% higher than that of DeeBERT, and the EM was approximately 17% higher. In SQuAD 2.0, the EE classifiers of MRC-EE had more obvious performance advantages than those of DeeBERT. This is because DeeBERT's EE classifier lacks the higher layer

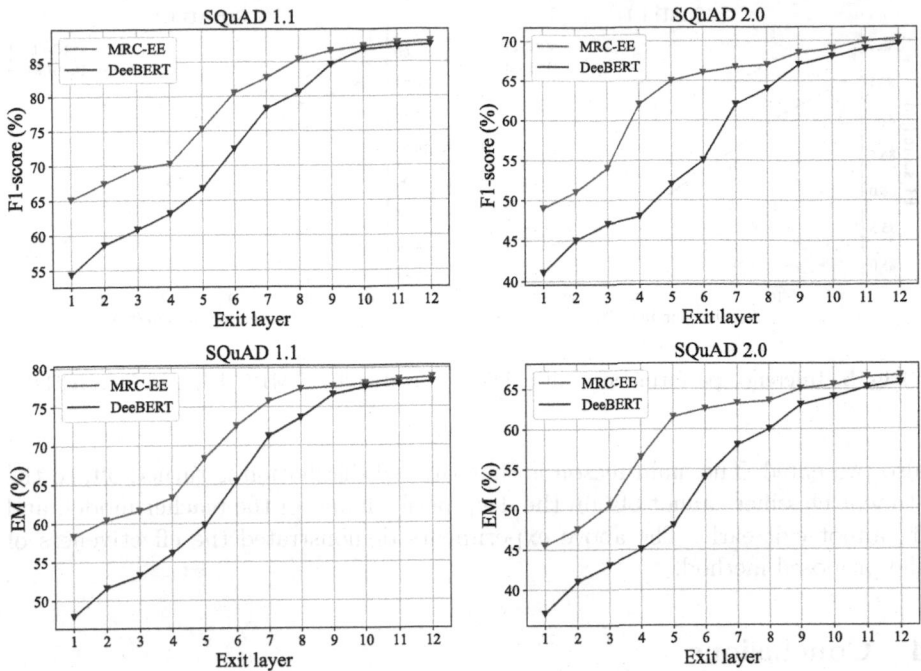

Fig. 4. The performance comparison of MRC-EE and DeeBERT for EE classifiers on SQuAD 1.1 and SQuAD 2.0.

semantic information, resulting in weaker expressiveness and incorrect decision-making of the EE classifier. This shows the effectiveness of self-distillation in the MRC-EE model, making lower classifiers also have strong performance. In SQuAD 1.1 dataset, adjusting the thresholds of MRC-EE and DeeBERT, with the same acceleration ratio, the F1-score and EM of MRC-EE are significantly higher than those of DeeBERT, as shown in Fig. 5.

3.4 Ablation Experiments

As shown in Table 2, the experiments for removing the EE module and self-distillation were performed on the MRC-EE. By removing the EE, the performance of the model is significantly improved; however, the inference time is increased because every sample tends to exit at the final layer. Compared with BERT-base, self-distillation showed a slight improvement in model performance, with an F1-score of 88.1%. The purpose of self-distillation is to increase the generalization and layer performance of student classifiers. The performance and acceleration ratio of the model were significantly reduced by removing the self-distillation and retaining the dynamic EE module. However, the F1-score was 1.5% lower than that of MRC-EE, the EM was 2% lower, and the acceleration ratio was approximately 18% lower. In SQuAD 2.0, a similar phenomenon is

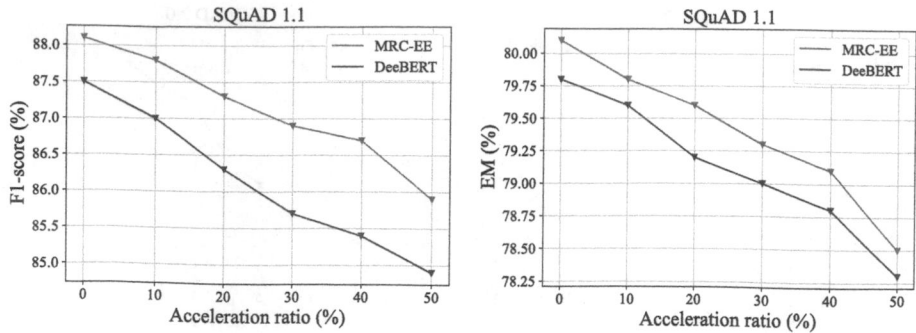

Fig. 5. Inference performance and efficiency trade-offs of MRC-EE and DeeBERT.

also presented. The main reason is that the self-distillation is turned off, so the student classifier cannot obtain the deep performance of the teacher model, and it cannot exit early. The above experiments demonstrated the effectiveness of the proposed method.

4   Conclusions

This study proposes a fast-inference MRC model with a dynamic EE mechanism to facilitate the deployment of MRC applications in resource-constrained devices. First, the self-distillation method was used to enable the student model to obtain a deep performance of the teacher model. Furthermore, we provide a dynamic programming strategy to choose the optimal confidence combination of both the start and end classifiers to better select the exit layers in the inference stage. To prevent the model from obtaining the highest confidence in the last layer, thus losing the desire to exit early, we introduce a penalty on the increment of the layers. Once the search for the optimal combination becomes deeper, the confidence will receive a greater penalty, forcing the model to choose the optimal solution combination at a lower layer. Extensive experiments have shown that this method performs well in MRC tasks. Compared with other methods, this method can achieve a better trade-off between performance and inference speed.

Future work will attempt to introduce heterogeneous attention graph networks and EE of different layers to further improve the performance and inference speed of the model.

Acknowledgment. This work was supported by the National Natural Science Foundation of China (NSFC) under Grants Nos. 61702443, 61966038, and 61762091, in part by the Graduate Research and Innovation Foundation of Yunnan University (No.2021Y173). The authors would like to thank the anonymous reviewers for their construction comments.

References

1. Devlin, J., Chang, M.W., Lee, K., Toutanova, K.: BERT: pre-training of deep bidirectional transformers for language understanding. In: Proceedings of the 2019 Conference of the North American Chapter of the Association for Computational Linguistics: Human Language Technologies (NAACL-HLT 2019), pp. 4171–4186 (2019)
2. Fan, A., Grave, E., Joulin, A.: Reducing transformer depth on demand with structured dropout. arXiv preprint arXiv:1909.11556 (2019)
3. Gasmi, K., Dilek, S., Tosun, S., Ozdemir, S.: A survey on computation offloading and service placement in fog computing-based IoT. J. Supercomput. **78**(2), 1983–2014 (2021). https://doi.org/10.1007/s11227-021-03941-y
4. Hu, Z., Dong, Y., Wang, K., Chang, K.W., Sun, Y.: GPT-GNN: generative pre-training of graph neural networks. In: Proceedings of the 26th ACM SIGKDD International Conference on Knowledge Discovery and Data Mining, pp. 1857–1867 (2020)
5. Kong, J., Wang, J., Zhang, X.: Accelerating pretrained language model inference using weighted ensemble self-distillation. In: Proceedings of the CCF International Conference on Natural Language Processing and Chinese Computing (NLPCC), pp. 224–235 (2021)
6. Lan, Z., Chen, M., Goodman, S., Gimpel, K., Sharma, P., Soricut, R.: ALBERT: a lite BERT for self-supervised learning of language representations. arXiv preprint arXiv:1909.11942 (2019)
7. Liu, Y., et al.: RoBERTa: a robustly optimized BERT pretraining approach. arXiv preprint arXiv:1907.11692 (2019)
8. Mirzadeh, S.I., Farajtabar, M., Li, A., Levine, N., Matsukawa, A., Ghasemzadeh, H.: Improved knowledge distillation via teacher assistant. In: Proceedings of the AAAI Conference on Artificial Intelligence, vol. 34, pp. 5191–5198 (2020)
9. Molchanov, P., Mallya, A., Tyree, S., Frosio, I., Kautz, J.: Importance estimation for neural network pruning. In: Proceedings of the IEEE/CVF Conference on Computer Vision and Pattern Recognition, pp. 11264–11272 (2019)
10. Nan, F., Wang, J., Zhang, X.: Mirror distillation model with focal loss for Chinese machine reading comprehension. In: Proceedings of the 2021 International Conference on Asian Language Processing (IALP), pp. 7–12 (2021)
11. Rajpurkar, P., Zhang, J., Lopyrev, K., Liang, P.: SQuAD: 100,000+ questions for machine comprehension of text. In: Proceedings of the 2016 Conference on Empirical Methods in Natural Language Processing, pp. 2383–2392 (2016)
12. Sun, Y., et al.: ERNIE: enhanced representation through knowledge integration. arXiv preprint arXiv:1904.09223 (2019)
13. Teerapittayanon, S., McDanel, B., Kung, H.T.: BranchyNet: fast inference via early exiting from deep neural networks. In: Proceedings of the 23rd International Conference on Pattern Recognition (ICPR), pp. 2464–2469 (2016)
14. Wolowiec-Korecka, E., Kula, P., Paweta, S., Pietrasik, R., Sawicki, J., Rzepkowski, A.: Neural computing for a low-frictional coatings manufacturing of aircraft engines' piston rings. Neural Comput. Appl. **31**(9), 4891–4901 (2019)
15. Xin, J., Tang, R., Lee, J., Yu, Y., Lin, J.: DeeBERT: dynamic early exiting for accelerating BERT inference. In: Proceedings of the 58th Annual Meeting of the Association for Computational Linguistics, pp. 2246–2251 (2020)

16. Xu, H., Huang, Y., Zhu, Y., Audhkhasi, K., Ramabhadran, B.: Convolutional dropout and wordpiece augmentation for end-to-end speech recognition. In: ICASSP 2021–2021 IEEE International Conference on Acoustics, Speech and Signal Processing (ICASSP), pp. 5984–5988 (2021)

17. Xu, X.B., Zhao, X.L., Wang, G.Q.: Kl divergence adaptive weight combination multi-classifier emotion recognition method fused with bimodality. In: 2022 3rd Asia Service Sciences and Software Engineering Conference, pp. 95–101 (2022)

18. Yang, Z., Dai, Z., Yang, Y., Carbonell, J., Salakhutdinov, R.R., Le, Q.V.: XLNet: generalized autoregressive pretraining for language understanding. In: Advances in Neural Information Processing Systems, vol. 32 (2019)

19. Zhai, P., Zhu, Z., Zhou, X., Cai, Y., Zhang, F., Li, Q.: An on-chip power-supply noise analyzer with compressed sensing and enhanced quantization. IEEE J. Solid-State Circuits 57(1), 302–311 (2021)

20. Zhang, L., Song, J., Gao, A., Chen, J., Bao, C., Ma, K.: Be your own teacher: improve the performance of convolutional neural networks via self distillation. In: Proceedings of the IEEE/CVF International Conference on Computer Vision, pp. 3713–3722 (2019)

21. Zhang, Y., Wang, J., Yu, L.C., Zhang, X.: MA-BERT: learning representation by incorporating multi-attribute knowledge in transformers. In: Findings of the Association for Computational Linguistics: ACL-IJCNLP 2021, pp. 2338–2343 (2021)

Author Index

Printed in the United States
by Baker & Taylor Publisher Services

Printed in the United States
by Baker & Taylor Publisher Services